THE COMPLETE
KCHRONICLES

FOR JASPER OWEN KNIGHT

Über-thanks to Shawna Gore and the lovely folks at Dark Horse for their righteous skills and patience; to Shannon Wheeler for all the invaluable advice and for turning me on to them; to Kyle Baker for the intro; to Dave Eggers and Eric Drooker for the fine blurbs; to Jennifer and Jon at Manic D and Brett and Chris at Top Shelf for publishing the original books; gracias to Aaron MacGruder, Harvey Pekar, Garry Trudeau, Carol Lay, Pete, Jeff, Lisa, and everyone else who contributed to the original editions; to Steve Notley, Tom Beland, Garrett Izumi, Nina Paley, Jaime Crespo, Sergio Aragones, Ted Rall, Mikhaela Reid, and the rest of the Cartoonists With Attitude, Andrew & Shaenon, Rod and Summerlea at the Cartoon Art Museum, and Jeannie and the Schulz Museum for your friendship and support. To all the editors and publications who've run the strip over the years; and to the incredibly loyal and faithful readers who've read, written, and rallied around the strip for close to two decades.

But most of all, thanks to my family, especially my fantastically phenomenal wife Kerstin, for their undying support, understanding, and love (even though I make fun of them).

Other books by Keith Knight

I LEFT MY ARSE IN SAN FRANCISCO

RED, WHITE, BLACK & BLUE

ARE WE FEELING SAFER YET?

BEGINNER'S GUIDE TO COMMUNITY-BASED ARTS

. . . and the four books collected here!

THE COMPLETE KCHRONICLES

by Keith Knight

Foreword by Kyle Baker

Dark Horse Books®

Publisher **MIKE RICHARDSON**

Editor **SHAWNA GORE**

Assistant Editor **JEMIAH JEFFERSON**

Cover Designer **STEPHEN REICHERT**

Production Designer **JOSH ELLIOTT**

Published by Dark Horse Books

A division of Dark Horse Comics, Inc.

10956 SE Main Street

Milwaukie, OR 97222

First edition July 2008

ISBN 978-1-59307-943-7

1 3 5 7 9 10 8 6 4 2

Printed in Hong Kong

TABLE OF CONTENTS

FOREWORD!

"Mr. Baker, I'm calling on behalf of Keith Knight."
"We already have a black cartoonist," I answered, hanging up the phone.

A moment later I received an e-mail, which explained that although Keith gets that response a lot, I was actually being solicited for an introduction to his book. So here it is.

HOW TO MAKE KEITH KNIGHT LIKE YOU.

As a Keef fan, you'll want him to become your friend if ever you meet. First thing you should do is enthusiastically inform him that he looks just like the drawings he does of himself. Cartoonists love that.

Then tell him you're surprised he's not as funny in real life. Ask him to say something funny, and then stare at him expectantly. If his wife is there, tell her that she's a good sport for letting her husband make fun of her in such a public forum as a cartoon. Now, she'll probably try to change the subject, but don't let up! Mention how most women wouldn't stand for being drawn all googly-eyed and big-nosed, and ask her how she stands it, especially since she's so much prettier in real life.

Ask Keith where he gets his ideas. Tell him that something happened to you recently that was just like something out of his comic strips, then tell him the story. Tell him he can use it. He'll say something like, "maybe," but don't let up. Keep asking him if he really thinks it's funny and if he's really going to use it.

I urge everyone who buys this book to follow the instructions above.

There is no need to thank me.

—Kyle Baker

Chapter One

Dances with Sheep

Cartoons from 1993-1996   *Boston/San Francisco/London*   *The Gay Gene*

The Trip from Hell   *Stepping in Hippie*

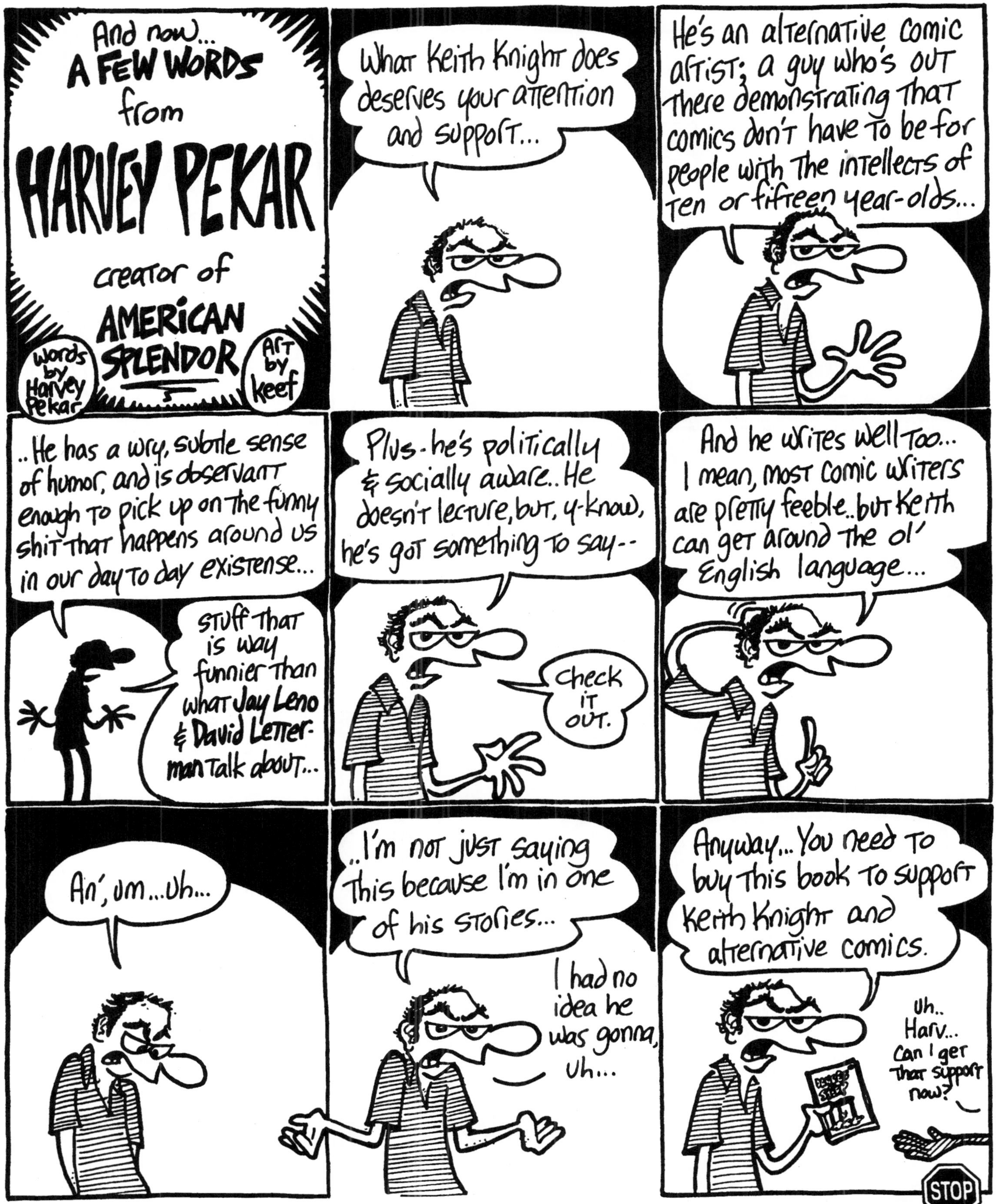

And now... A FEW WORDS from HARVEY PEKAR creator of AMERICAN SPLENDOR
Words by Harvey Pekar
Art by keef
What Keith Knight does deserves your attention and support...
He's an alternative comic artist; a guy who's out there demonstrating that comics don't have to be for people with the intellects of ten or fifteen year-olds...
..He has a wry, subtle sense of humor, and is observant enough to pick up on the funny shit that happens around us in our day to day existense...
Stuff that is way funnier than what Jay Leno & David Letterman talk about...
Plus-he's politically & socially aware.. He doesn't lecture, but, y-know, he's got something to say--
Check it out.
And he writes well too... I mean, most comic writers are pretty feeble..but Keith can get around the ol' English language...
An', um...uh...
..I'm not just saying this because I'm in one of his stories...
I had no idea he was gonna, uh...
Anyway... You need to buy this book to support Keith Knight and alternative comics.
Uh.. Harv... Can I get that support now?
STOP

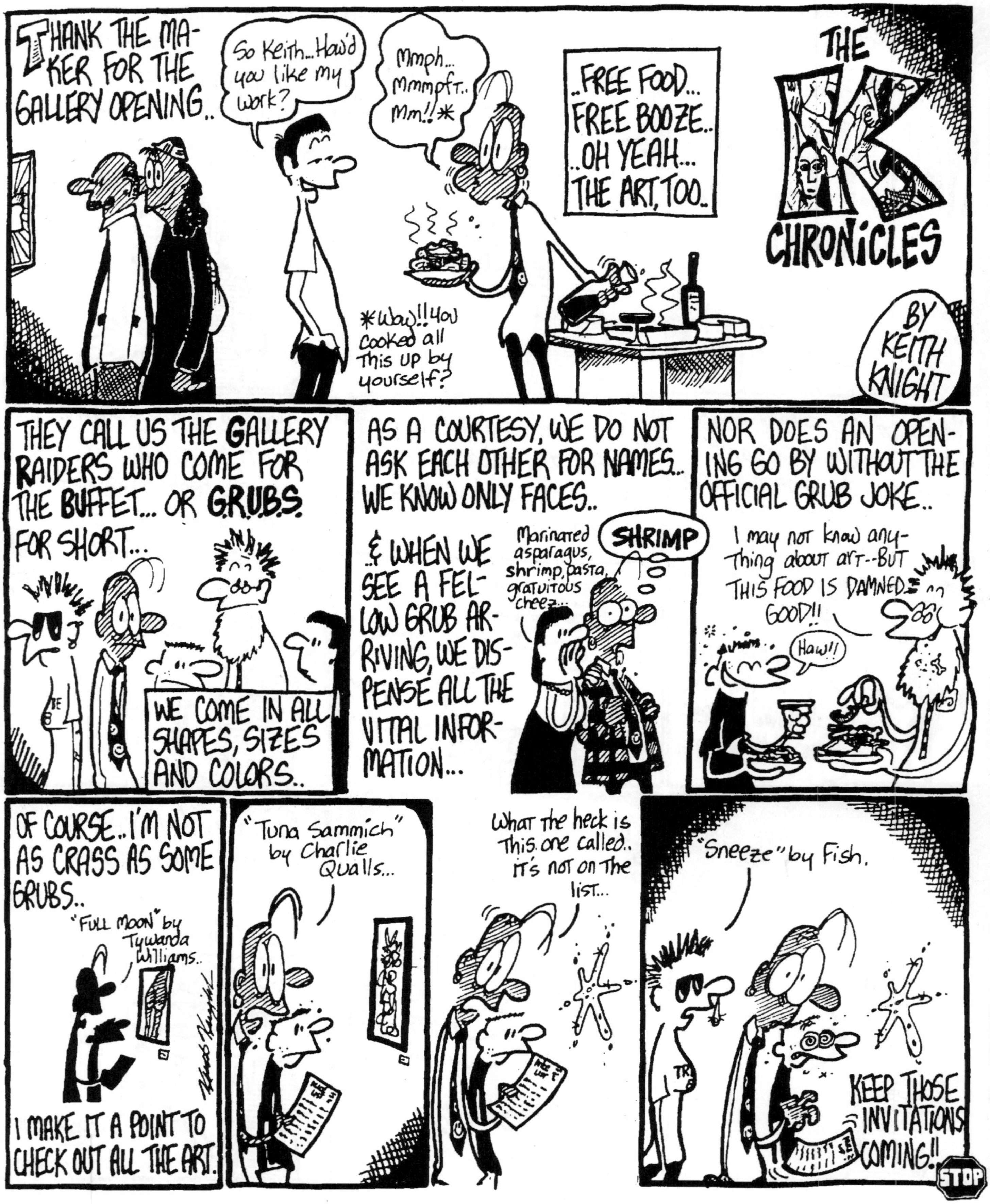
THANK THE MAKER FOR THE GALLERY OPENING..
So Keith...How'd you like my work?
Mmph... Mmmpft.. Mm!!*
*Wow!! You cooked all This up by yourself?
..FREE FOOD... FREE BOOZE.. ..OH YEAH... THE ART, TOO..
THE K CHRONICLES
BY KEITH KNIGHT
THEY CALL US THE GALLERY RAIDERS WHO COME FOR THE BUFFET... OR G.R.U.B.S. FOR SHORT...
WE COME IN ALL SHAPES, SIZES AND COLORS..
AS A COURTESY, WE DO NOT ASK EACH OTHER FOR NAMES.. WE KNOW ONLY FACES..
..& WHEN WE SEE A FELLOW GRUB ARRIVING, WE DISPENSE ALL THE VITAL INFORMATION...
Marinated asparagus, shrimp, pasta, gratuitous cheez...
SHRIMP
NOR DOES AN OPENING GO BY WITHOUT THE OFFICIAL GRUB JOKE..
I may not know anything about art--BUT THIS FOOD IS DAMNED GOOD!!
Haw!!
OF COURSE..I'M NOT AS CRASS AS SOME GRUBS..
"FULL MOON" by Tywanda Williams..
I MAKE IT A POINT TO CHECK OUT ALL THE ART.
"Tuna Sammich" by Charlie Qualls...
What the heck is This one called.. it's not on The list...
"Sneeze" by Fish.
KEEP THOSE INVITATIONS COMING!!
STOP

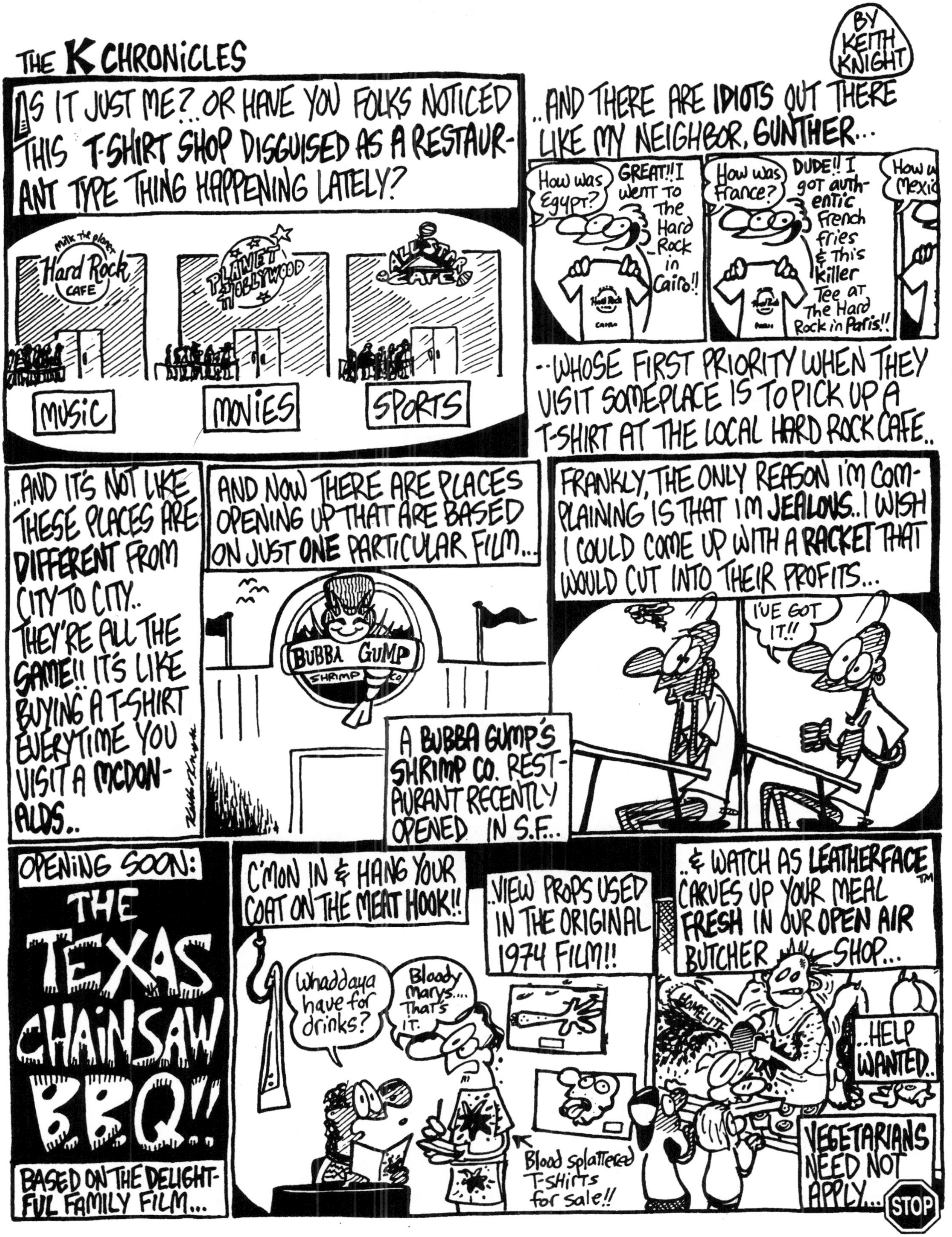
THE K CHRONICLES
BY KEITH KNIGHT
IS IT JUST ME?... OR HAVE YOU FOLKS NOTICED THIS T-SHIRT SHOP DISGUISED AS A RESTAURANT TYPE THING HAPPENING LATELY?
Hard Rock CAFE
PLANET HOLLYWOOD
ALL STAR CAFE
MUSIC
MOVIES
SPORTS
..AND THERE ARE IDIOTS OUT THERE LIKE MY NEIGHBOR, GUNTHER...
How was Egypt?
GREAT!! I went to the Hard Rock in Cairo!!
How was France?
DUDE!! I got authentic French fries & this killer Tee at the Hard Rock in Paris!!
How w Mexic
--WHOSE FIRST PRIORITY WHEN THEY VISIT SOMEPLACE IS TO PICK UP A T-SHIRT AT THE LOCAL HARD ROCK CAFE..
..AND IT'S NOT LIKE THESE PLACES ARE DIFFERENT FROM CITY TO CITY.. THEY'RE ALL THE SAME!! IT'S LIKE BUYING A T-SHIRT EVERYTIME YOU VISIT A MCDONALDS..
AND NOW THERE ARE PLACES OPENING UP THAT ARE BASED ON JUST ONE PARTICULAR FILM...
BUBBA GUMP SHRIMP CO
A BUBBA GUMP'S SHRIMP CO. RESTAURANT RECENTLY OPENED IN S.F..
FRANKLY, THE ONLY REASON I'M COMPLAINING IS THAT I'M JEALOUS.. I WISH I COULD COME UP WITH A RACKET THAT WOULD CUT INTO THEIR PROFITS...
I'VE GOT IT!!
OPENING SOON:
THE TEXAS CHAINSAW B.B.Q!!
BASED ON THE DELIGHTFUL FAMILY FILM...
C'MON IN & HANG YOUR COAT ON THE MEAT HOOK!!
..VIEW PROPS USED IN THE ORIGINAL 1974 FILM!!
Whaddaya have for drinks?
Bloody marys.... That's it.
Blood splattered T-shirts for sale!!
..& WATCH AS LEATHERFACE™ CARVES UP YOUR MEAL FRESH IN OUR OPEN AIR BUTCHER SHOP...
HOMELITE
..HELP WANTED..
VEGETARIANS NEED NOT APPLY...
STOP

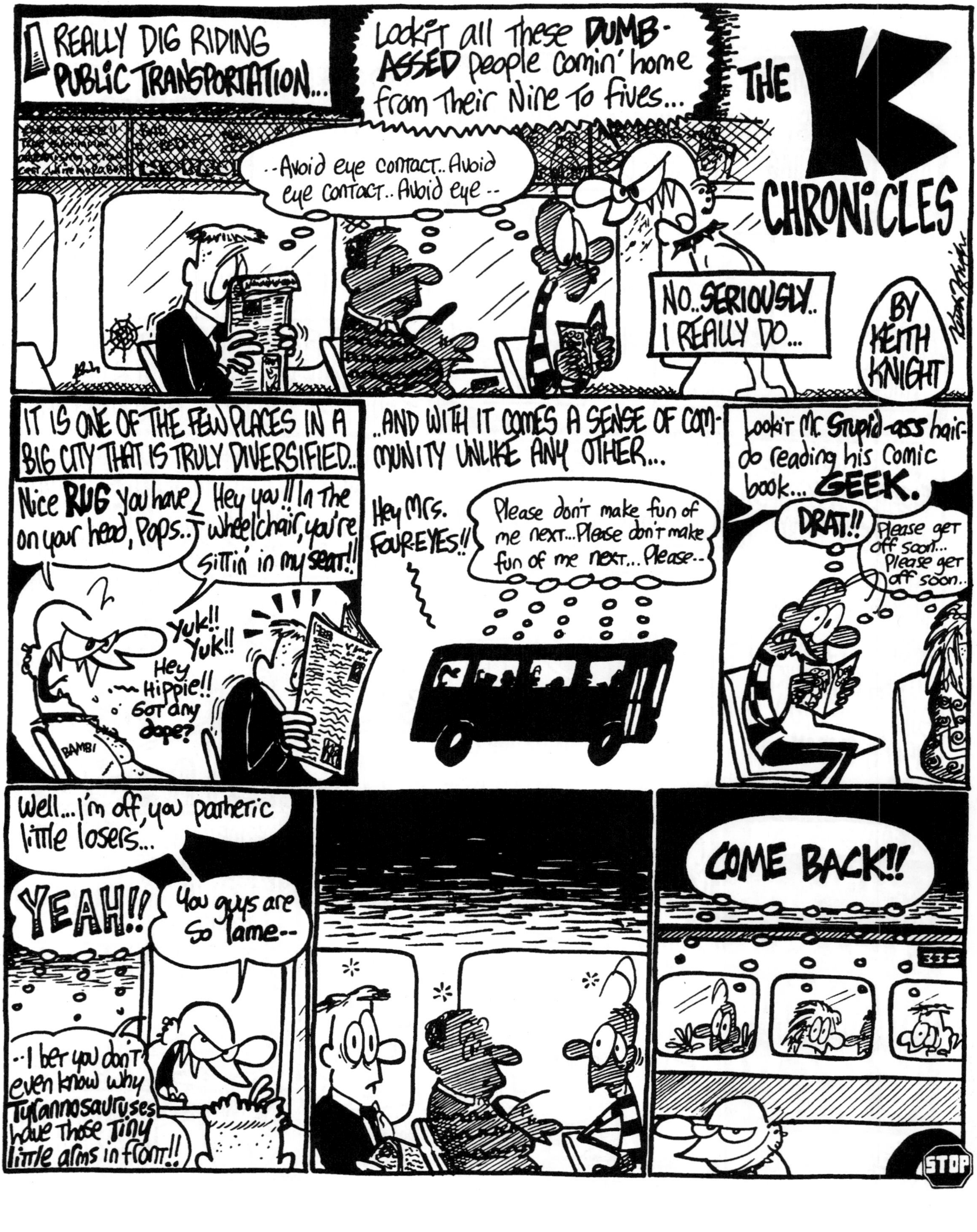

I REALLY DIG RIDING PUBLIC TRANSPORTATION...
Lookit all these DUMB-ASSED people comin' home from Their Nine To fives...
THE K CHRONICLES
..Avoid eye contact.. Avoid eye contact.. Avoid eye ..
NO..SERIOUSLY.. I REALLY DO...
BY KEITH KNIGHT
IT IS ONE OF THE FEW PLACES IN A BIG CITY THAT IS TRULY DIVERSIFIED..
Nice RUG you have on your head, Pops..
Hey you!! In the wheelchair, you're sittin' in my seat!!
YUK!! YUK!!
Hey Hippie!! Got any dope?
BAMBI
..AND WITH IT COMES A SENSE OF COMMUNITY UNLIKE ANY OTHER...
Hey Mrs. FOUR-EYES!!
Please don't make fun of me next...Please don't make fun of me next... Please..
Lookit Mr. Stupid-ass hair-do reading his comic book... GEEK.
DRAT!!
Please get off soon... Please get off soon..
Well...I'm off, you pathetic little losers...
YEAH!!
You guys are so lame--
..I bet you don't even know why Tyrannosauruses have those Tiny little arms in front!!
COME BACK!!
STOP

THE **K** CHRONICLES "BOOGIE KNIGHTS" BY KEITH KNIGHT

SO THERE I WAS...GETTING MY ROUTINE CHECKUP AT THE DENTIST...

...WHEN SUDDENLY...

OH NO.

All done... Here...Take a look..

...IT WAS MY WORST NIGHTMARE--

...I HAD A **HUGE** SNOT SITTING IN MY RIGHT NOSTRIL...

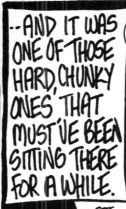

--AND IT WAS ONE OF THOSE HARD, CHUNKY ONES, THAT MUST'VE BEEN SITTING THERE FOR A WHILE.

zit

cat scratches

-?

IT'S HARSH ENOUGH THAT DENTISTS HAVE TO STARE DOWN YOUR THROAT FOR SUCH A LONG TIME... BUT WITH THAT OVER-HEAD LAMP THAT LIGHTS UP YOUR WHOLE FACE AND UP YOUR NOSE...≡BLEAH≡

WHAT REALLY PISSES ME OFF ARE THE SO-CALLED "FRIENDS" I RAN INTO BEFORE MY APPOINTMENT WHO MADE NO MENTION OF IT...

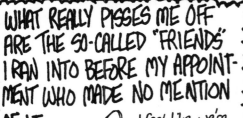

I feel like we're friends enough for me to say this--

...Your comic **SUCKED** last week.

Anything else?

Nope.

I PICKED MY NOSE AFTER SHE LEFT THE ROOM & MADE MY WAY TOWARDS THE EXIT FEELING MIGHTY SMALL...

See you in 6 months...

HEY!!

EXIT

OH SH--!!

WHAT'S WORSE IS SOME LITTLE SNOT BAGGED ME TRYING TO SWIPE THE "HIGHLIGHTS" FROM THE WAITING ROOM

STOP

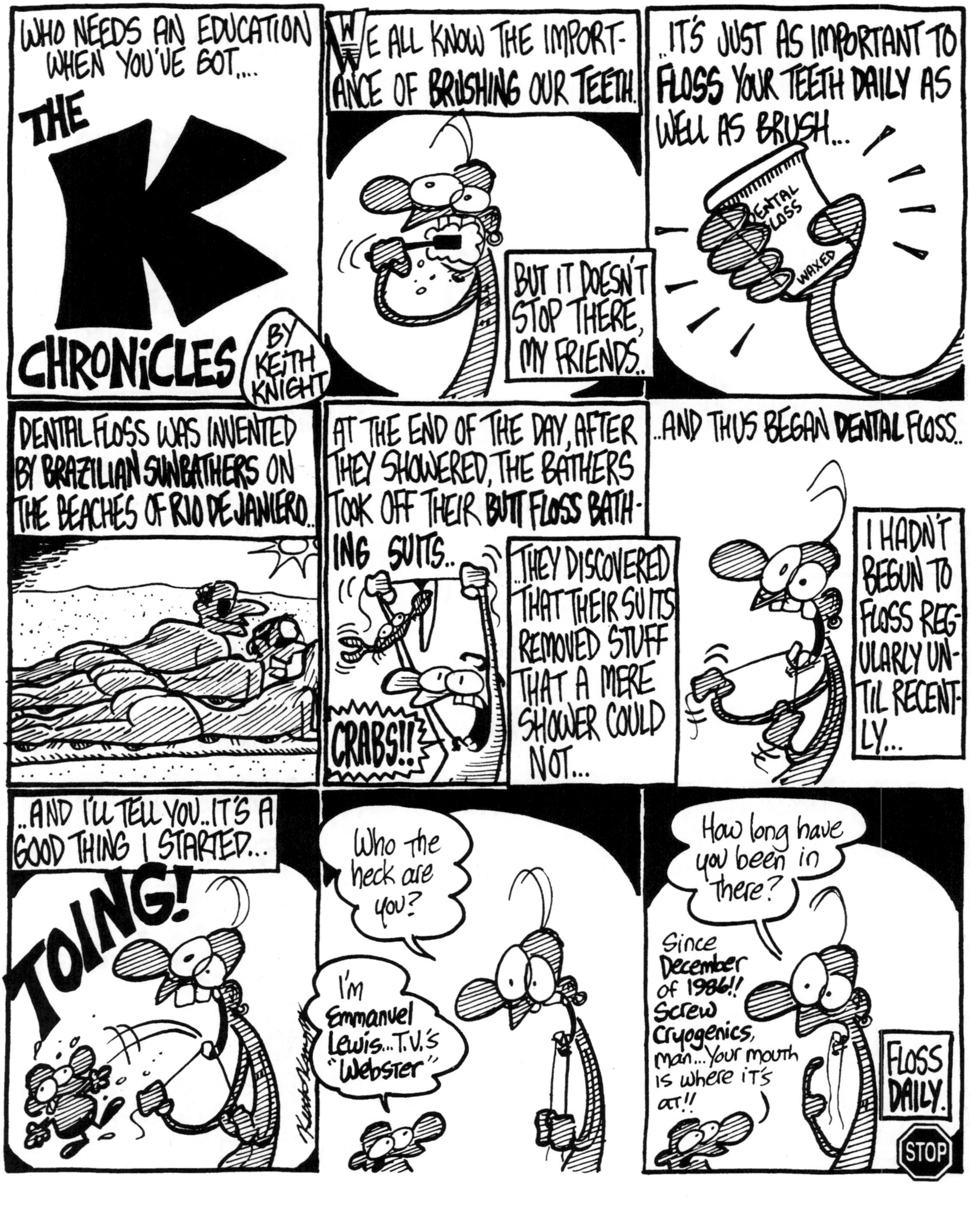
WHO NEEDS AN EDUCATION WHEN YOU'VE GOT....
THE K CHRONICLES
BY KEITH KNIGHT
WE ALL KNOW THE IMPORTANCE OF BRUSHING OUR TEETH.
BUT IT DOESN'T STOP THERE, MY FRIENDS..
..IT'S JUST AS IMPORTANT TO FLOSS YOUR TEETH DAILY AS WELL AS BRUSH...
DENTAL FLOSS
WAXED
DENTAL FLOSS WAS INVENTED BY BRAZILIAN SUNBATHERS ON THE BEACHES OF RIO DE JANIERO..
AT THE END OF THE DAY, AFTER THEY SHOWERED, THE BATHERS TOOK OFF THEIR BUTT FLOSS BATHING SUITS..
..THEY DISCOVERED THAT THEIR SUITS REMOVED STUFF THAT A MERE SHOWER COULD NOT...
CRABS!!
..AND THUS BEGAN DENTAL FLOSS..
I HADN'T BEGUN TO FLOSS REGULARLY UNTIL RECENTLY...
..AND I'LL TELL YOU..IT'S A GOOD THING I STARTED...
TOING!
Who the heck are you?
I'm Emmanuel Lewis...T.V.'s "Webster"
How long have you been in there?
Since December of 1986!! Screw Cryogenics, man...Your mouth is where it's at!!
FLOSS DAILY.
STOP

 My dentist framed a print of this strip and hung it in her office.

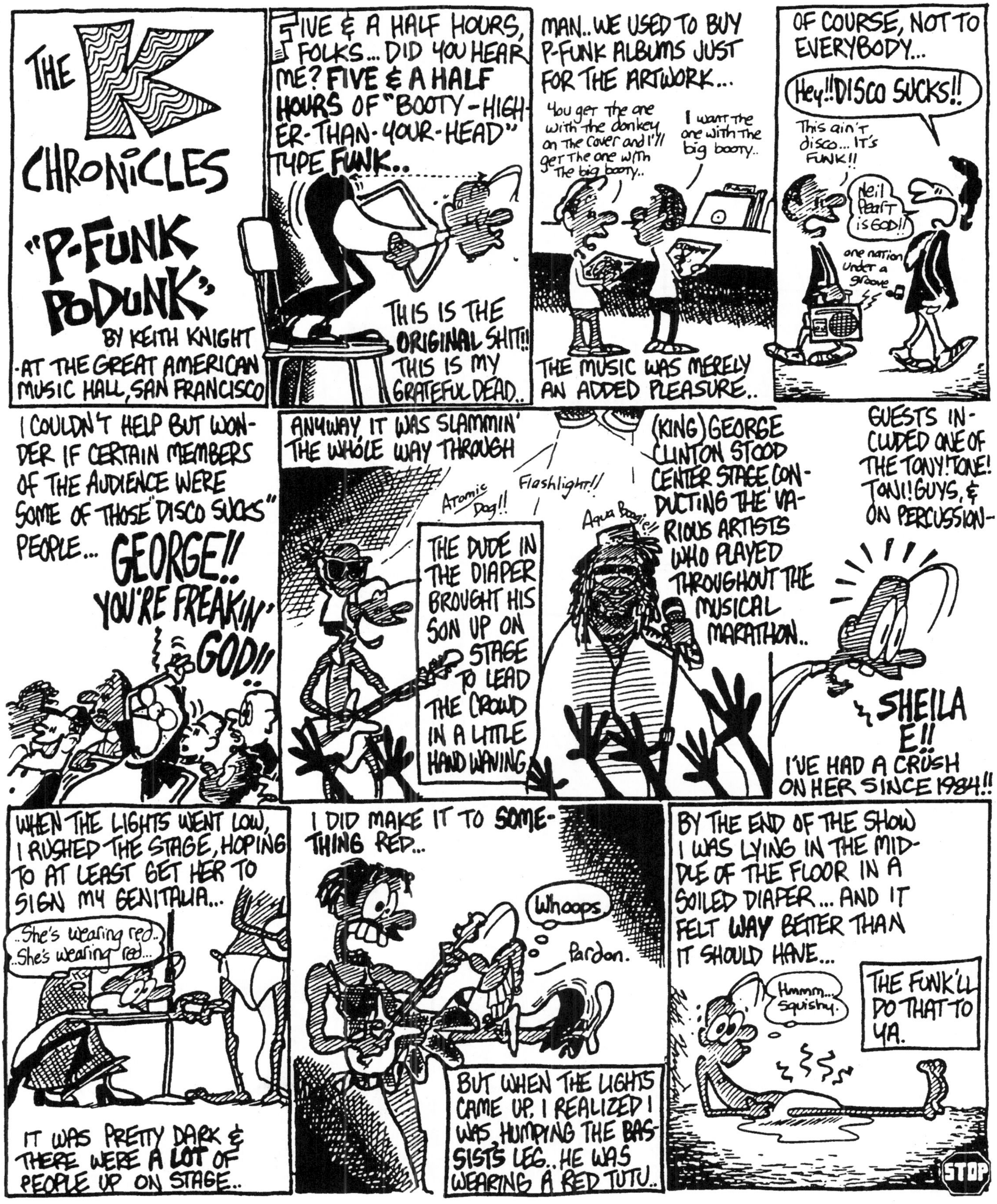
THE K CHRONICLES
"P-FUNK PODUNK"
BY KEITH KNIGHT
-AT THE GREAT AMERICAN MUSIC HALL, SAN FRANCISCO
FIVE & A HALF HOURS, FOLKS... DID YOU HEAR ME? FIVE & A HALF HOURS OF "BOOTY-HIGHER-THAN-YOUR-HEAD" TYPE FUNK..
THIS IS THE ORIGINAL SHIT!! THIS IS MY GRATEFUL DEAD..
MAN.. WE USED TO BUY P-FUNK ALBUMS JUST FOR THE ARTWORK...
You get the one with the donkey on the cover and I'll get the one with the big booty..
I want the one with the big booty..
THE MUSIC WAS MERELY AN ADDED PLEASURE..
OF COURSE, NOT TO EVERYBODY...
Hey!! DISCO SUCKS!!
This ain't disco... It's FUNK!!
Neil Peart is GOD!!
one nation under a groove
I COULDN'T HELP BUT WONDER IF CERTAIN MEMBERS OF THE AUDIENCE WERE SOME OF THOSE "DISCO SUCKS" PEOPLE...
GEORGE!! YOU'RE FREAKIN' GOD!!
ANYWAY, IT WAS SLAMMIN' THE WHOLE WAY THROUGH
Atomic Dog!!
Flashlight!!
Aqua Boogie!!
THE DUDE IN THE DIAPER BROUGHT HIS SON UP ON STAGE TO LEAD THE CROWD IN A LITTLE HAND WAVING
(KING) GEORGE CLINTON STOOD CENTER STAGE CONDUCTING THE VARIOUS ARTISTS WHO PLAYED THROUGHOUT THE MUSICAL MARATHON..
GUESTS INCLUDED ONE OF THE TONY! TONI! TONÉ! GUYS, & ON PERCUSSION-
SHEILA E!!
I'VE HAD A CRUSH ON HER SINCE 1984!!
WHEN THE LIGHTS WENT LOW, I RUSHED THE STAGE, HOPING TO AT LEAST GET HER TO SIGN MY GENITALIA...
..She's wearing red.. ..She's wearing red...
IT WAS PRETTY DARK & THERE WERE A LOT OF PEOPLE UP ON STAGE..
I DID MAKE IT TO SOMETHING RED...
Whoops.
Pardon.
BUT WHEN THE LIGHTS CAME UP, I REALIZED I WAS HUMPING THE BASSIST'S LEG.. HE WAS WEARING A RED TUTU..
BY THE END OF THE SHOW I WAS LYING IN THE MIDDLE OF THE FLOOR IN A SOILED DIAPER... AND IT FELT WAY BETTER THAN IT SHOULD HAVE...
Hmmm... Squishy.
THE FUNK'LL DO THAT TO YA.
STOP

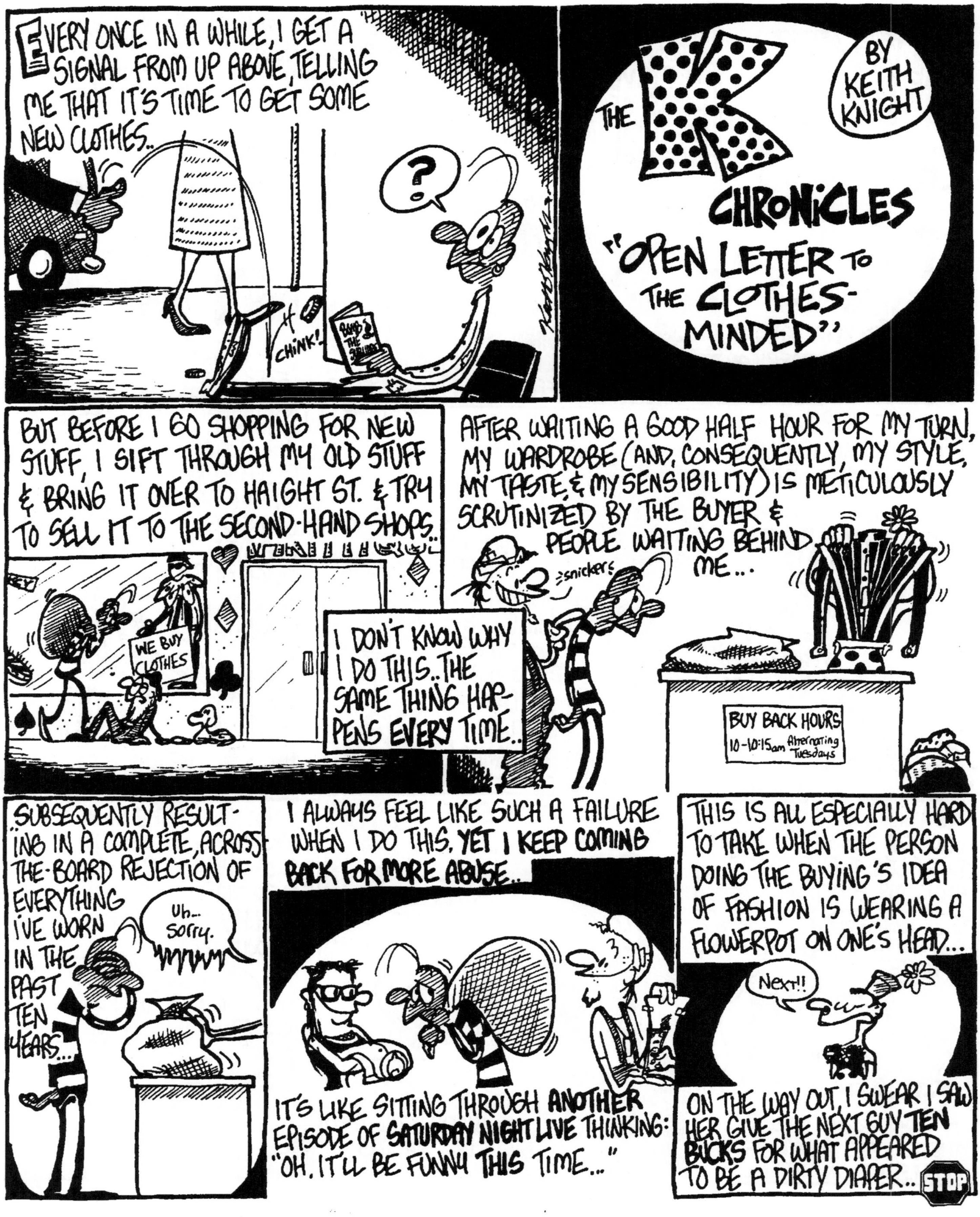
EVERY ONCE IN A WHILE, I GET A SIGNAL FROM UP ABOVE, TELLING ME THAT IT'S TIME TO GET SOME NEW CLOTHES..
?
CHINK!
THE K CHRONICLES
BY KEITH KNIGHT
"OPEN LETTER TO THE CLOTHES-MINDED"
BUT BEFORE I GO SHOPPING FOR NEW STUFF, I SIFT THROUGH MY OLD STUFF & BRING IT OVER TO HAIGHT ST. & TRY TO SELL IT TO THE SECOND-HAND SHOPS..
WE BUY CLOTHES
I DON'T KNOW WHY I DO THIS.. THE SAME THING HAPPENS EVERY TIME..
AFTER WAITING A GOOD HALF HOUR FOR MY TURN, MY WARDROBE (AND, CONSEQUENTLY, MY STYLE, MY TASTE, & MY SENSIBILITY) IS METICULOUSLY SCRUTINIZED BY THE BUYER & PEOPLE WAITING BEHIND ME...
snicker
BUY BACK HOURS 10-10:15am Alternating Tuesdays
SUBSEQUENTLY RESULTING IN A COMPLETE, ACROSS-THE-BOARD REJECTION OF EVERYTHING I'VE WORN IN THE PAST TEN YEARS...
Uh.. sorry.
I ALWAYS FEEL LIKE SUCH A FAILURE WHEN I DO THIS. YET I KEEP COMING BACK FOR MORE ABUSE..
IT'S LIKE SITTING THROUGH ANOTHER EPISODE OF SATURDAY NIGHT LIVE THINKING: "OH, IT'LL BE FUNNY THIS TIME..."
THIS IS ALL ESPECIALLY HARD TO TAKE WHEN THE PERSON DOING THE BUYING'S IDEA OF FASHION IS WEARING A FLOWERPOT ON ONE'S HEAD...
Next!!
ON THE WAY OUT, I SWEAR I SAW HER GIVE THE NEXT GUY TEN BUCKS FOR WHAT APPEARED TO BE A DIRTY DIAPER..
STOP

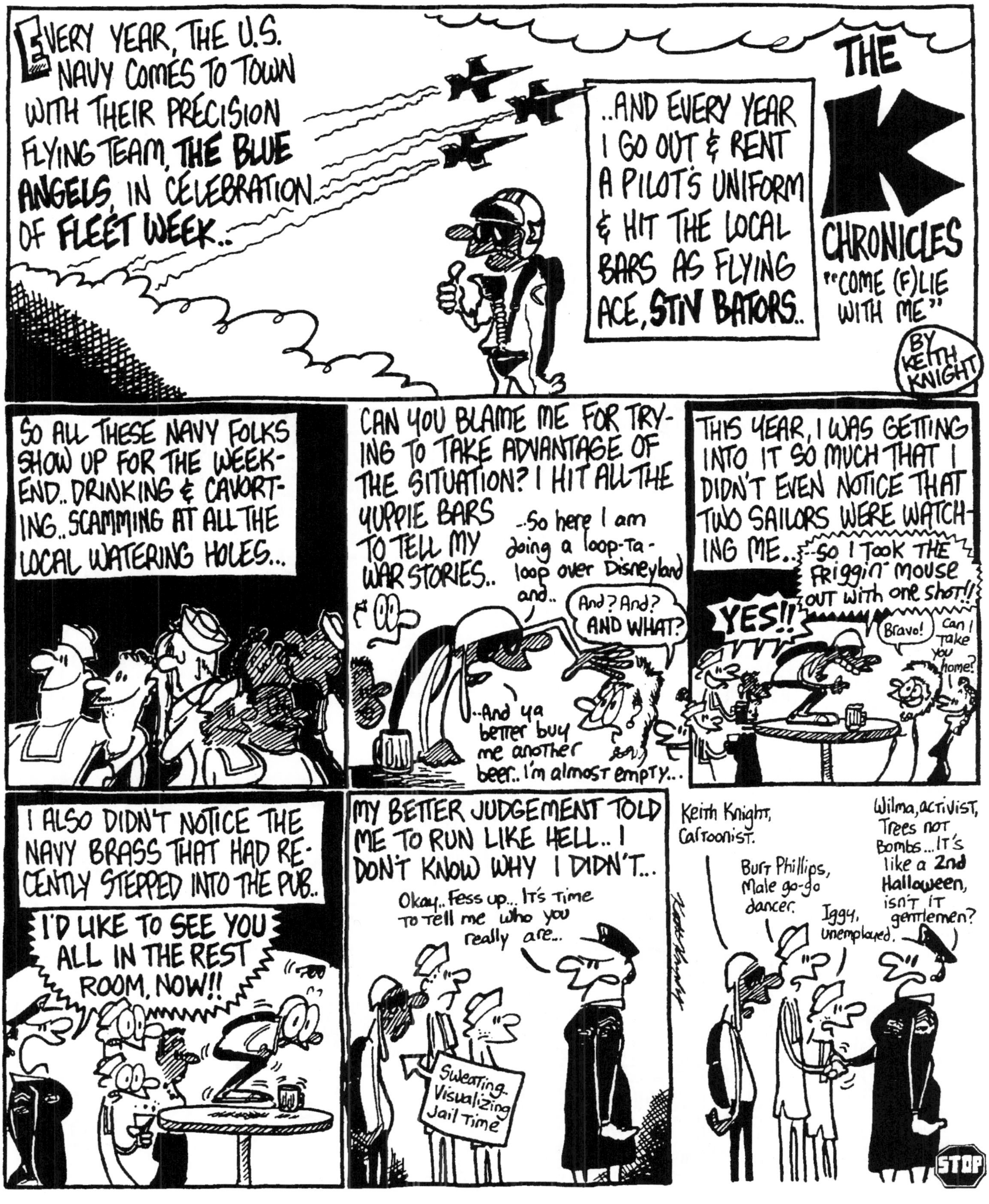
EVERY YEAR, THE U.S. NAVY COMES TO TOWN WITH THEIR PRECISION FLYING TEAM, THE BLUE ANGELS, IN CELEBRATION OF FLEET WEEK..
..AND EVERY YEAR I GO OUT & RENT A PILOT'S UNIFORM & HIT THE LOCAL BARS AS FLYING ACE, STIV BATORS..
THE K CHRONICLES
"COME (F)LIE WITH ME"
BY KEITH KNIGHT
SO ALL THESE NAVY FOLKS SHOW UP FOR THE WEEK-END.. DRINKING & CAVORT-ING.. SCAMMING AT ALL THE LOCAL WATERING HOLES...
CAN YOU BLAME ME FOR TRY-ING TO TAKE ADVANTAGE OF THE SITUATION? I HIT ALL THE YUPPIE BARS TO TELL MY WAR STORIES..
..So here I am doing a loop-ta-loop over Disneyland and..
And? And? AND WHAT?
..And ya better buy me another beer.. I'm almost empty...
THIS YEAR, I WAS GETTING INTO IT SO MUCH THAT I DIDN'T EVEN NOTICE THAT TWO SAILORS WERE WATCH-ING ME..
..So I Took THE Friggin' mouse out with one shot!!
YES!!
Bravo!
Can I Take you home?
I ALSO DIDN'T NOTICE THE NAVY BRASS THAT HAD RE-CENTLY STEPPED INTO THE PUB..
I'D LIKE TO SEE YOU ALL IN THE REST ROOM, NOW!!
MY BETTER JUDGEMENT TOLD ME TO RUN LIKE HELL.. I DON'T KNOW WHY I DIDN'T..
Okay.. Fess up... It's Time To Tell me who you really are..
Sweating.. Visualizing Jail Time
Keith Knight, Cartoonist.
Burt Phillips, Male go-go dancer.
Iggy, unemployed.
Wilma, activist, Trees not Bombs... It's like a 2nd Halloween, isn't it gentlemen?
STOP

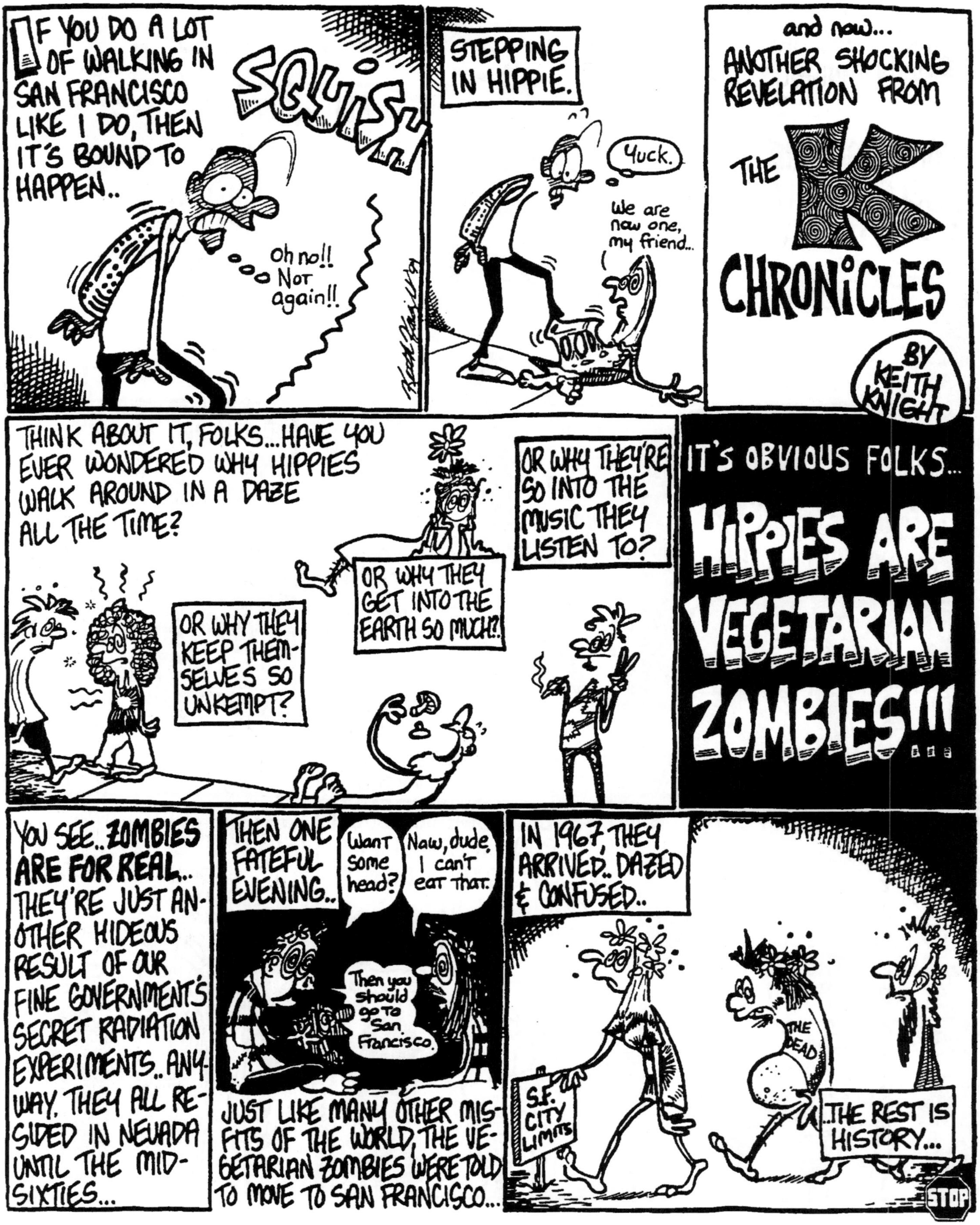
IF YOU DO A LOT OF WALKING IN SAN FRANCISCO LIKE I DO, THEN IT'S BOUND TO HAPPEN..
SQUISH
Oh no!! Not again!!
STEPPING IN HIPPIE.
Yuck.
We are now one, my friend...
and now... ANOTHER SHOCKING REVELATION FROM
THE K CHRONICLES
BY KEITH KNIGHT
THINK ABOUT IT, FOLKS...HAVE YOU EVER WONDERED WHY HIPPIES WALK AROUND IN A DAZE ALL THE TIME?
OR WHY THEY KEEP THEMSELVES SO UNKEMPT?
OR WHY THEY GET INTO THE EARTH SO MUCH?!
OR WHY THEY'RE SO INTO THE MUSIC THEY LISTEN TO?
IT'S OBVIOUS FOLKS...
HIPPIES ARE VEGETARIAN ZOMBIES!!!
YOU SEE.. ZOMBIES ARE FOR REAL... THEY'RE JUST ANOTHER HIDEOUS RESULT OF OUR FINE GOVERNMENT'S SECRET RADIATION EXPERIMENTS.. ANYWAY, THEY ALL RESIDED IN NEVADA UNTIL THE MID-SIXTIES...
THEN ONE FATEFUL EVENING..
Want some head?
Naw, dude, I can't eat that.
Then you should go to San Francisco.
JUST LIKE MANY OTHER MISFITS OF THE WORLD, THE VEGETARIAN ZOMBIES WERE TOLD TO MOVE TO SAN FRANCISCO...
IN 1967, THEY ARRIVED.. DAZED & CONFUSED..
S.F. CITY LIMITS
THE DEAD
..THE REST IS HISTORY...
STOP

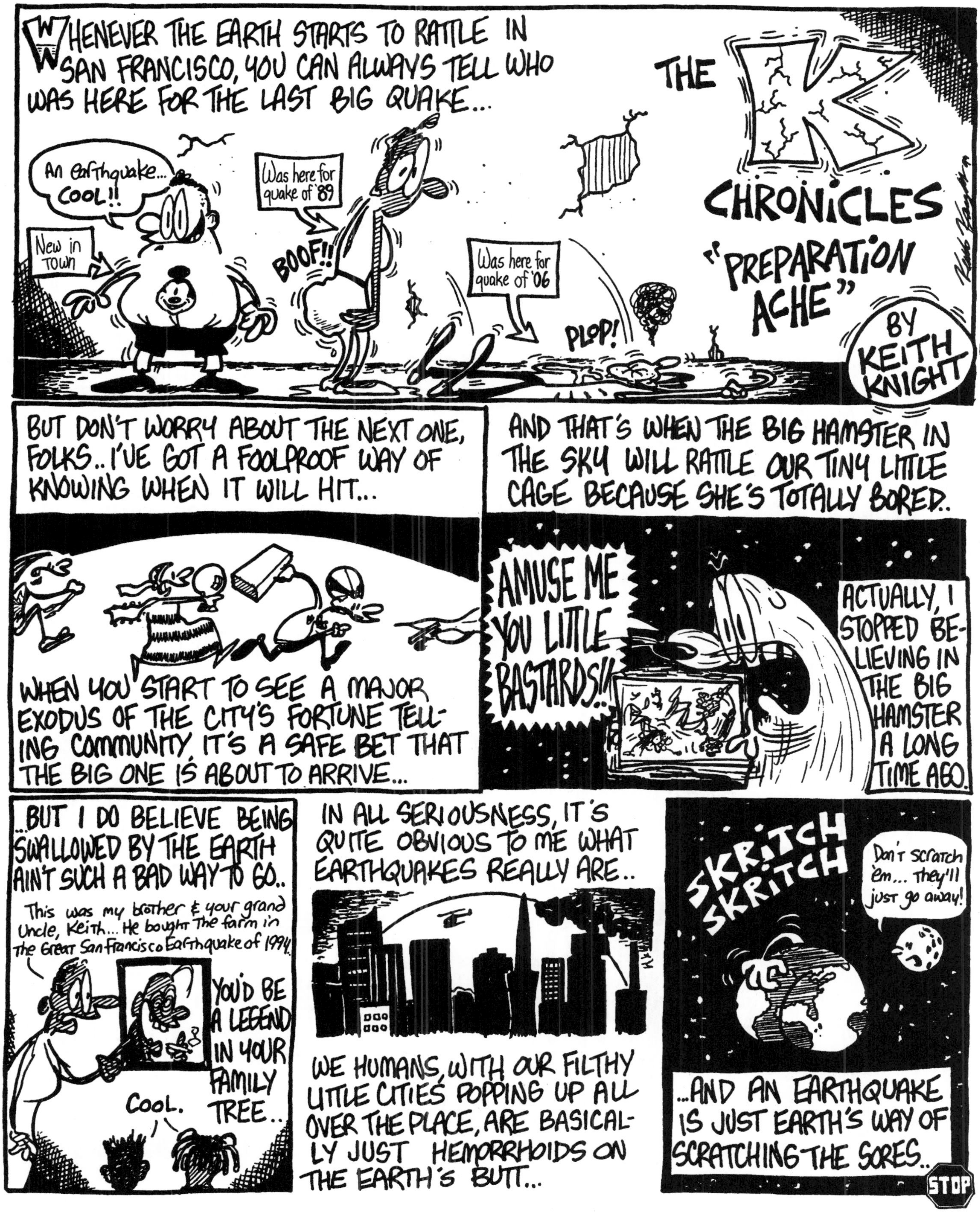
THE K CHRONICLES
"PREPARATION ACHE"
BY KEITH KNIGHT
WHENEVER THE EARTH STARTS TO RATTLE IN SAN FRANCISCO, YOU CAN ALWAYS TELL WHO WAS HERE FOR THE LAST BIG QUAKE...
An Earthquake... COOL!!
New in Town
Was here for quake of '89
BOOF!!
Was here for quake of '06
PLOP!
BUT DON'T WORRY ABOUT THE NEXT ONE, FOLKS.. I'VE GOT A FOOLPROOF WAY OF KNOWING WHEN IT WILL HIT...
WHEN YOU START TO SEE A MAJOR EXODUS OF THE CITY'S FORTUNE TELLING COMMUNITY, IT'S A SAFE BET THAT THE BIG ONE IS ABOUT TO ARRIVE...
AND THAT'S WHEN THE BIG HAMSTER IN THE SKY WILL RATTLE OUR TINY LITTLE CAGE BECAUSE SHE'S TOTALLY BORED..
AMUSE ME YOU LITTLE BASTARDS!!
ACTUALLY, I STOPPED BELIEVING IN THE BIG HAMSTER A LONG TIME AGO.
..BUT I DO BELIEVE BEING SWALLOWED BY THE EARTH AIN'T SUCH A BAD WAY TO GO..
This was my brother & your grand Uncle, Keith... He bought the farm in the Great San Francisco Earthquake of 1994.
YOU'D BE A LEGEND IN YOUR FAMILY TREE..
COOL.
IN ALL SERIOUSNESS, IT'S QUITE OBVIOUS TO ME WHAT EARTHQUAKES REALLY ARE..
WE HUMANS, WITH OUR FILTHY LITTLE CITIES POPPING UP ALL OVER THE PLACE, ARE BASICALLY JUST HEMORRHOIDS ON THE EARTH'S BUTT...
SKRITCH SKRITCH
Don't scratch 'em... they'll just go away!
..AND AN EARTHQUAKE IS JUST EARTH'S WAY OF SCRATCHING THE SORES..
STOP

This is the first of many times where God makes an appearance in the strip as a hamster.

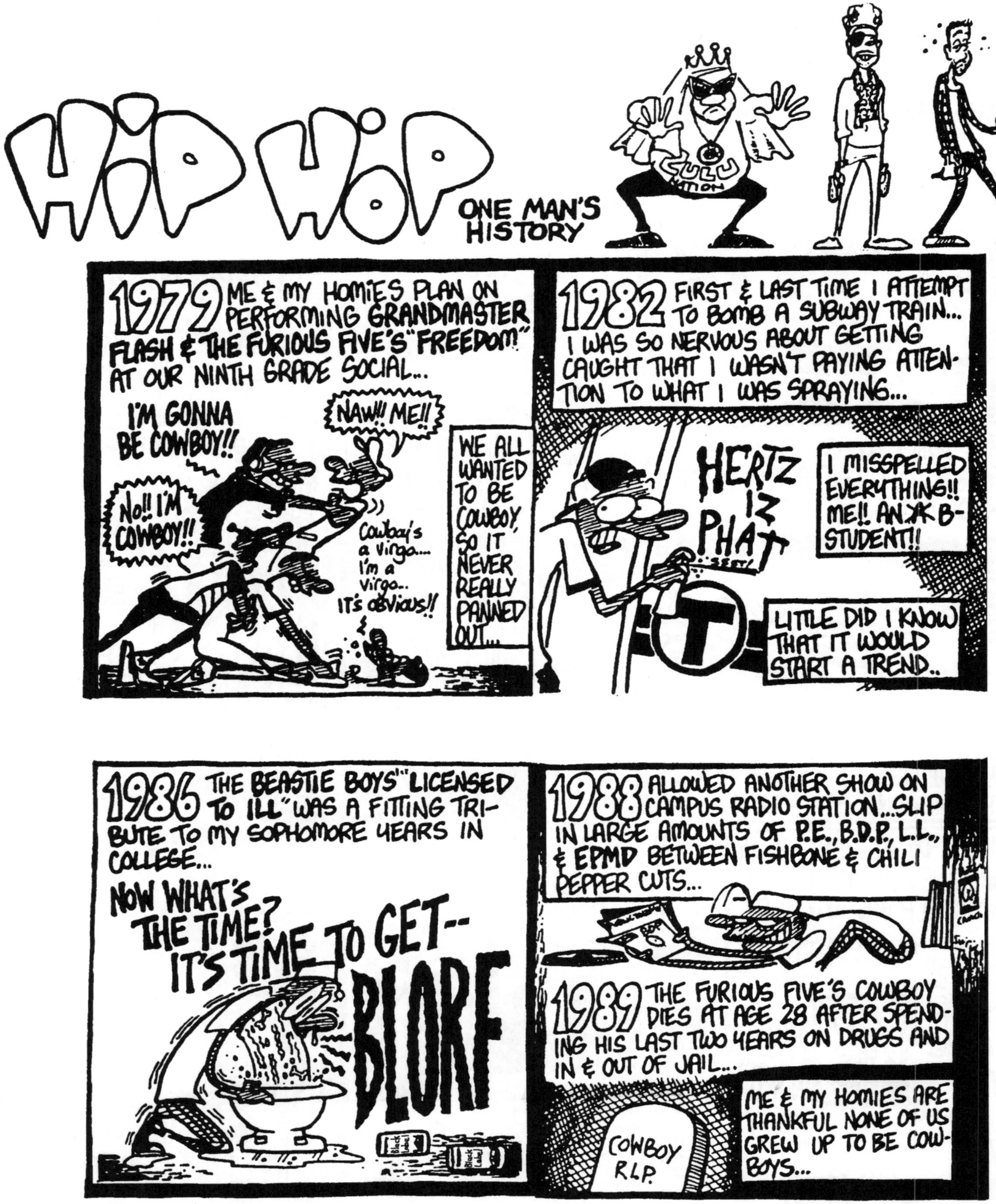
HIP HOP
ONE MAN'S HISTORY
CULU NATION
1979 ME & MY HOMIES PLAN ON PERFORMING GRANDMASTER FLASH & THE FURIOUS FIVE'S "FREEDOM" AT OUR NINTH GRADE SOCIAL...
I'M GONNA BE COWBOY!!
NAW!! ME!!
No!! I'M COWBOY!!
Cowboy's a Virgo... I'm a Virgo... IT'S obvious!!
WE ALL WANTED TO BE COWBOY, SO IT NEVER REALLY PANNED OUT...
1982 FIRST & LAST TIME I ATTEMPT TO BOMB A SUBWAY TRAIN... I WAS SO NERVOUS ABOUT GETTING CAUGHT THAT I WASN'T PAYING ATTENTION TO WHAT I WAS SPRAYING...
HERTZ IZ PHAT
I MISSPELLED EVERYTHING!! ME!! AN A B-STUDENT!!
LITTLE DID I KNOW THAT IT WOULD START A TREND..
1986 THE BEASTIE BOYS' "LICENSED TO ILL" WAS A FITTING TRIBUTE TO MY SOPHOMORE YEARS IN COLLEGE...
NOW WHAT'S THE TIME? IT'S TIME TO GET--
BLORF
Black Label
1988 ALLOWED ANOTHER SHOW ON CAMPUS RADIO STATION...SLIP IN LARGE AMOUNTS OF P.E., B.D.P., L.L., & EPMD BETWEEN FISHBONE & CHILI PEPPER CUTS...
1989 THE FURIOUS FIVE'S COWBOY DIES AT AGE 28 AFTER SPENDING HIS LAST TWO YEARS ON DRUGS AND IN & OUT OF JAIL...
COWBOY R.I.P.
ME & MY HOMIES ARE THANKFUL NONE OF US GREW UP TO BE COWBOYS...

Hip-hop stars from top l to r: Afrika Bambaata, Slick Rick, MCA of the Beastie Boys, Kid from Kid'n'Play. Bottom l to r: Flava Flav, Ice-T, Ice Cube, B-Real from Cypress Hill.

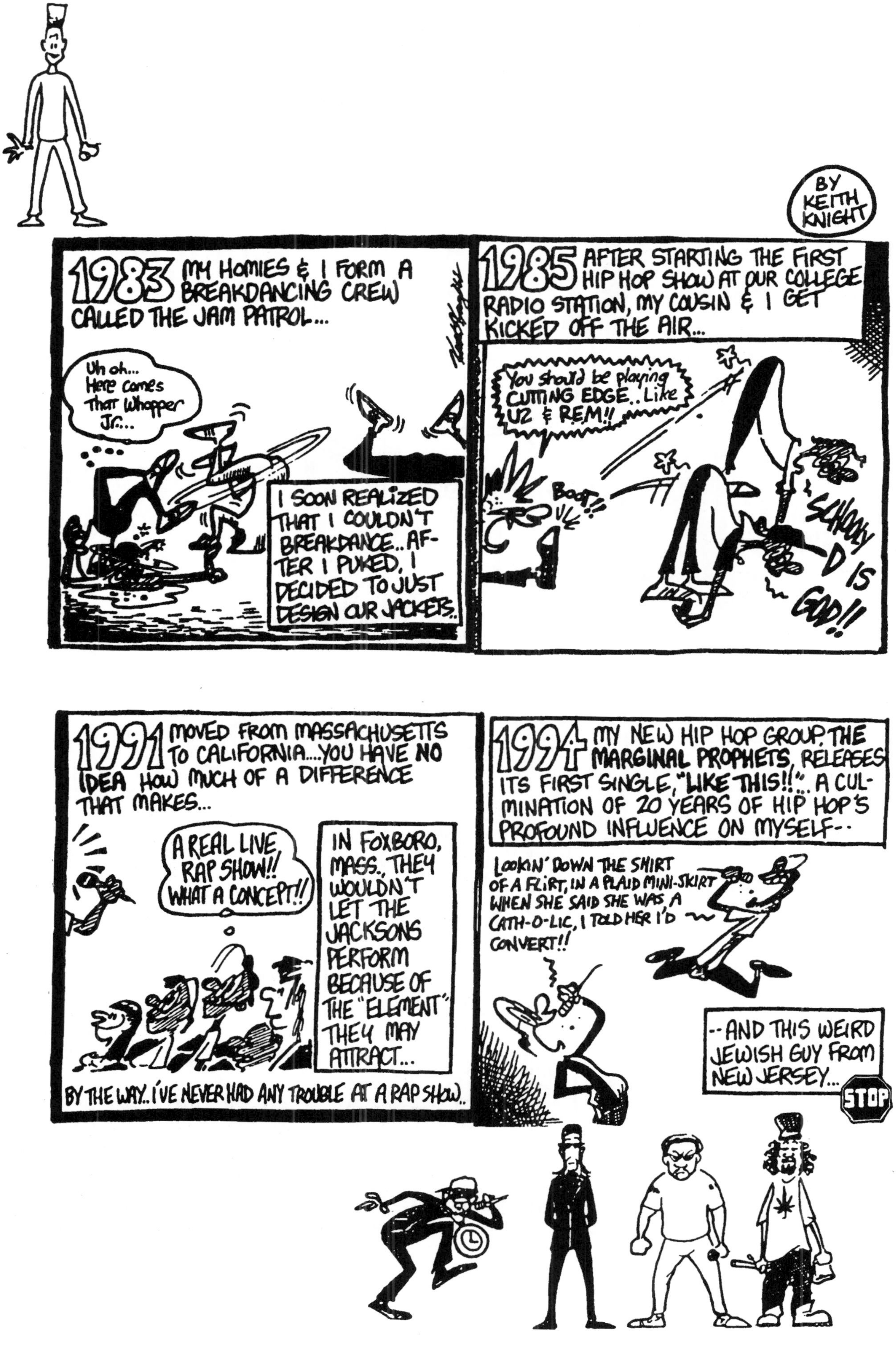

BY KEITH KNIGHT
1983 MY HOMIES & I FORM A BREAKDANCING CREW CALLED THE JAM PATROL...
Uh oh... Here comes that Whopper Jr...
I SOON REALIZED THAT I COULDN'T BREAKDANCE...AFTER I PUKED, I DECIDED TO JUST DESIGN OUR JACKETS..
1985 AFTER STARTING THE FIRST HIP HOP SHOW AT OUR COLLEGE RADIO STATION, MY COUSIN & I GET KICKED OFF THE AIR...
You should be playing CUTTING EDGE.. Like U2 & R.E.M!!
Boot!!
SCHOOLLY D IS GOD!!
1991 MOVED FROM MASSACHUSETTS TO CALIFORNIA....YOU HAVE NO IDEA HOW MUCH OF A DIFFERENCE THAT MAKES...
A REAL LIVE RAP SHOW!! WHAT A CONCEPT!!
IN FOXBORO, MASS., THEY WOULDN'T LET THE JACKSONS PERFORM BECAUSE OF THE "ELEMENT" THEY MAY ATTRACT...
BY THE WAY.. I'VE NEVER HAD ANY TROUBLE AT A RAP SHOW..
1994 MY NEW HIP HOP GROUP, THE MARGINAL PROPHETS, RELEASES ITS FIRST SINGLE, "LIKE THIS!!"... A CULMINATION OF 20 YEARS OF HIP HOP'S PROFOUND INFLUENCE ON MYSELF--
LOOKIN' DOWN THE SHIRT OF A FLIRT, IN A PLAID MINI-SKIRT WHEN SHE SAID SHE WAS A CATH-O-LIC, I TOLD HER I'D CONVERT!!
--AND THIS WEIRD JEWISH GUY FROM NEW JERSEY...
STOP

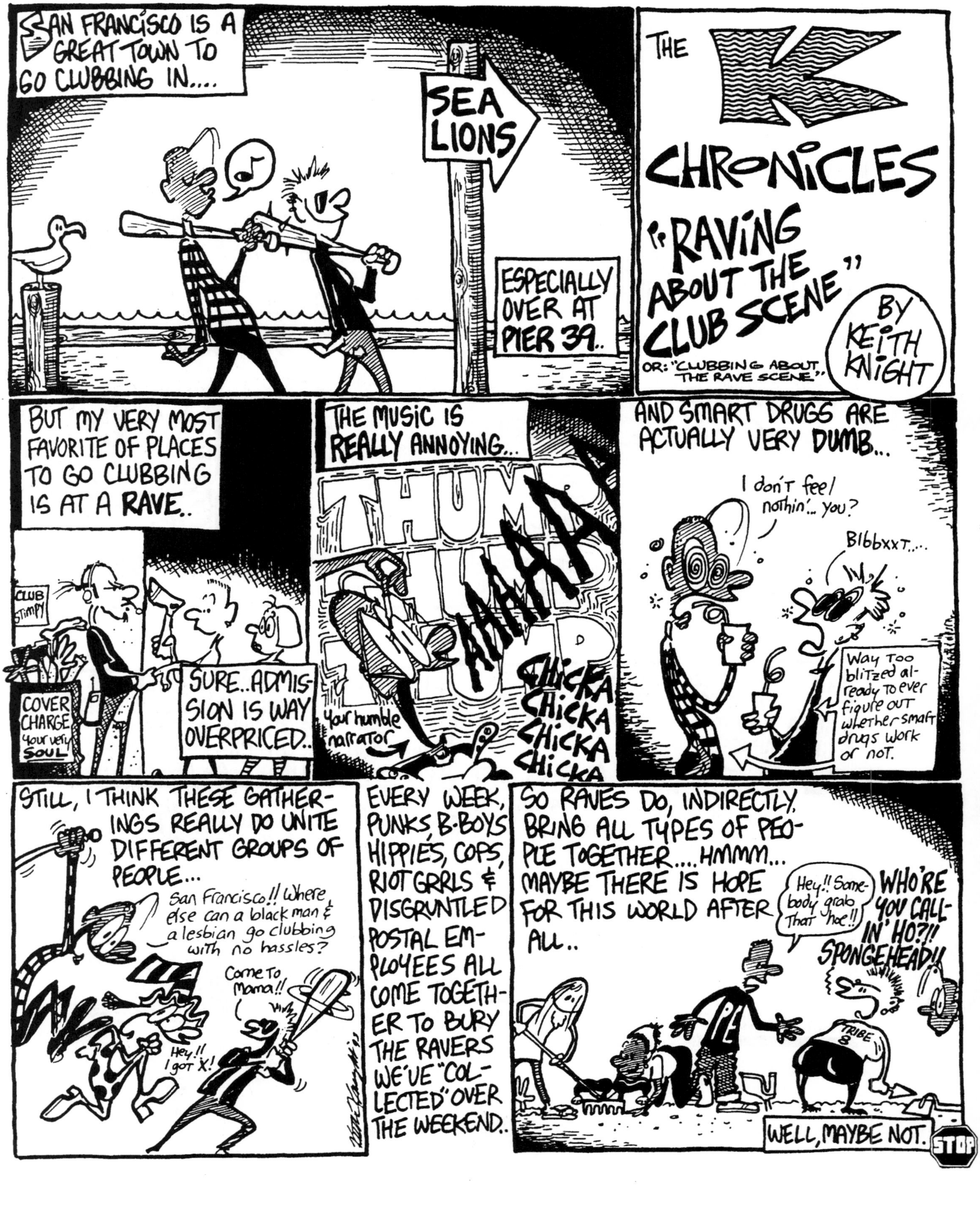
SAN FRANCISCO IS A GREAT TOWN TO GO CLUBBING IN....
SEA LIONS
ESPECIALLY OVER AT PIER 39..
THE K CHRONICLES
"RAVING ABOUT THE CLUB SCENE"
OR: "CLUBBING ABOUT THE RAVE SCENE"
BY KEITH KNIGHT
BUT MY VERY MOST FAVORITE OF PLACES TO GO CLUBBING IS AT A RAVE..
CLUB STIMPY
COVER CHARGE your very SOUL
SURE..ADMISSION IS WAY OVERPRICED..
THE MUSIC IS REALLY ANNOYING..
THUMP THUMP THUMP
AAAAAA
CHICKA CHICKA CHICKA CHICKA
Your humble narrator
AND SMART DRUGS ARE ACTUALLY VERY DUMB...
I don't feel nothin'.. you?
Blbbxxt.....
Way Too blitzed already to ever figure out whether smart drugs work or not.
STILL, I THINK THESE GATHERINGS REALLY DO UNITE DIFFERENT GROUPS OF PEOPLE...
San Francisco!! Where else can a black man & a lesbian go clubbing with no hassles?
Come To Mama!!
Hey!! I got X!
EVERY WEEK, PUNKS, B-BOYS HIPPIES, COPS, RIOT GRRLS & DISGRUNTLED POSTAL EMPLOYEES ALL COME TOGETHER TO BURY THE RAVERS WE'VE "COLLECTED" OVER THE WEEKEND..
SO RAVES DO, INDIRECTLY, BRING ALL TYPES OF PEOPLE TOGETHER....HMMM... MAYBE THERE IS HOPE FOR THIS WORLD AFTER ALL..
Hey!! Somebody grab That 'hoe!!
WHO'RE YOU CALLIN' HO?!! SPONGEHEAD!!
TRIBE 8
WELL, MAYBE NOT.
STOP

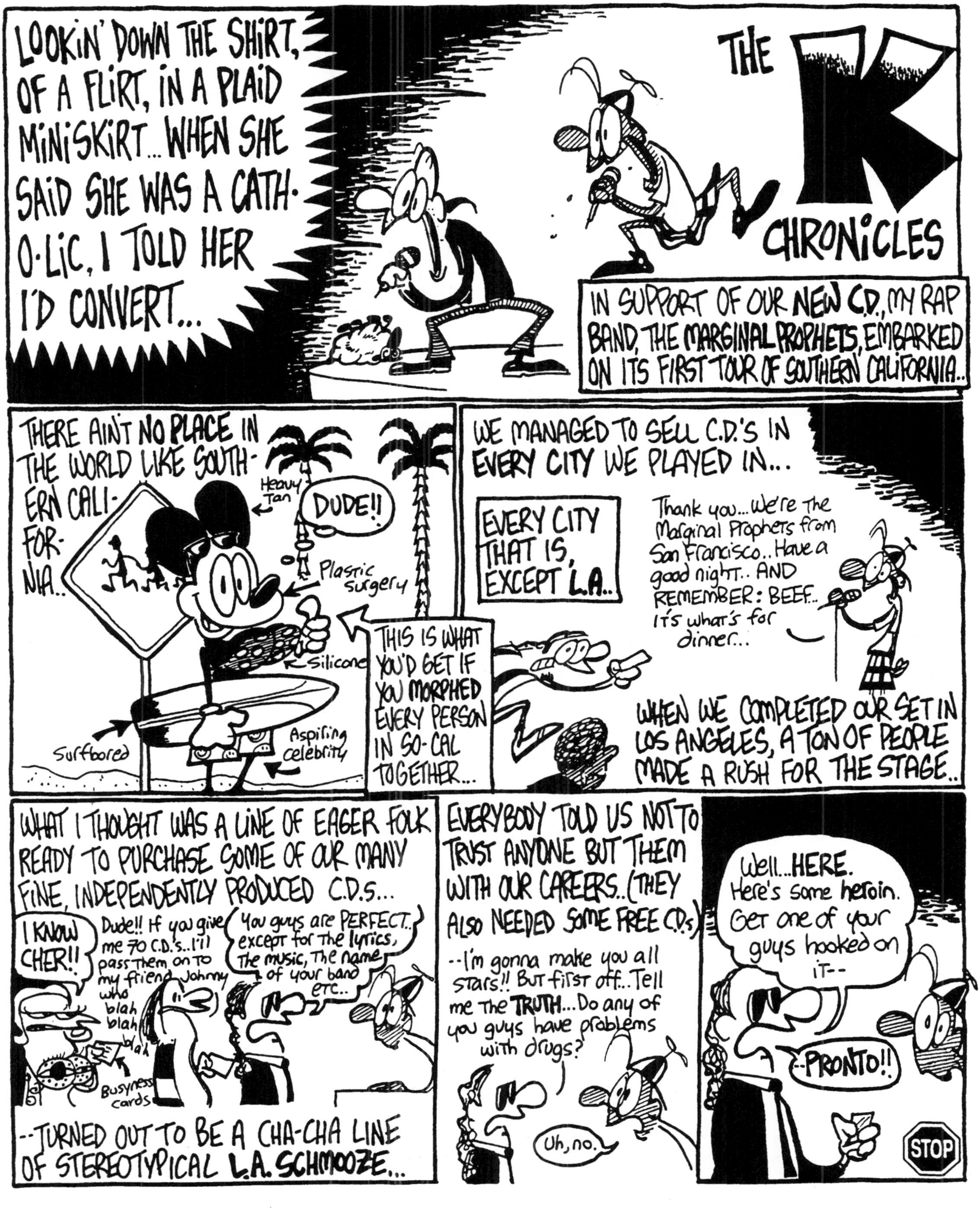

LOOKIN' DOWN THE SHIRT, OF A FLIRT, IN A PLAID MINISKIRT... WHEN SHE SAID SHE WAS A CATH-O-LIC, I TOLD HER I'D CONVERT...
THE K CHRONICLES
IN SUPPORT OF OUR NEW C.D., MY RAP BAND, THE MARGINAL PROPHETS, EMBARKED ON ITS FIRST TOUR OF SOUTHERN CALIFORNIA..
THERE AIN'T NO PLACE IN THE WORLD LIKE SOUTH-ERN CALI-FOR-NIA..
Heavy Tan
DUDE!!
Plastic surgery
Silicone
Surfbored
Aspiring celebrity
THIS IS WHAT YOU'D GET IF YOU MORPHED EVERY PERSON IN SO-CAL TOGETHER...
WE MANAGED TO SELL C.D.'S IN EVERY CITY WE PLAYED IN...
EVERY CITY THAT IS, EXCEPT L.A..
Thank you... We're the Marginal Prophets from San Francisco.. Have a good night.. AND REMEMBER: BEEF.. It's what's for dinner..
WHEN WE COMPLETED OUR SET IN LOS ANGELES, A TON OF PEOPLE MADE A RUSH FOR THE STAGE..
WHAT I THOUGHT WAS A LINE OF EAGER FOLK READY TO PURCHASE SOME OF OUR MANY FINE, INDEPENDENTLY PRODUCED C.D.S...
I KNOW CHER!!
Dude!! If you give me 70 C.D.'s..I'll pass them on to my friend Johnny who blah blah blah
You guys are PERFECT.. except for the lyrics, the music, the name of your band etc...
Busyness cards
--TURNED OUT TO BE A CHA-CHA LINE OF STEREOTYPICAL L.A. SCHMOOZE...
EVERYBODY TOLD US NOT TO TRUST ANYONE BUT THEM WITH OUR CAREERS..(THEY ALSO NEEDED SOME FREE C.D.s)
--I'm gonna make you all stars!! But first off... Tell me the TRUTH... Do any of you guys have problems with drugs?
Uh, no.
Well... HERE. Here's some heroin. Get one of your guys hooked on it--
--PRONTO!!
STOP

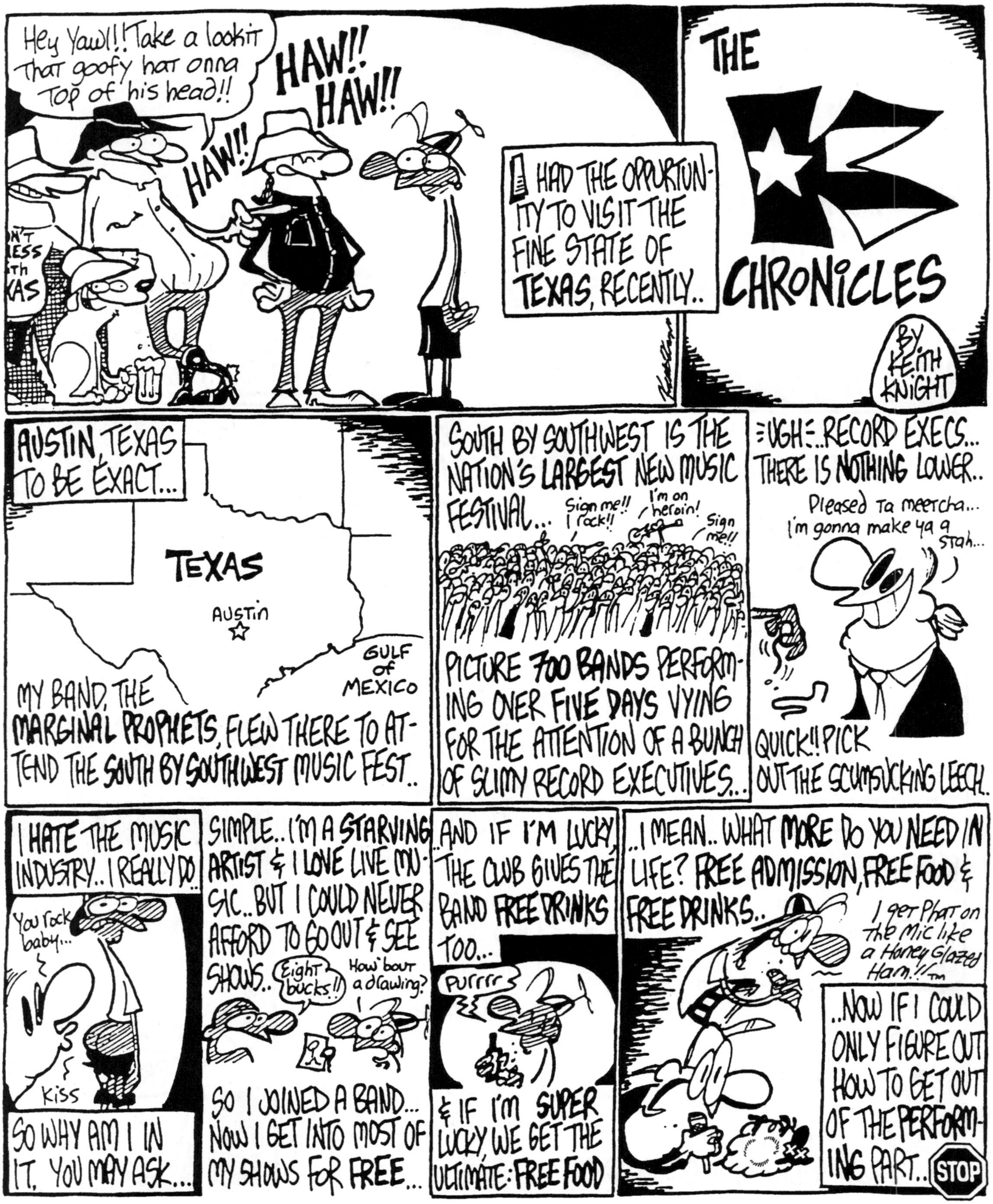

Hey Yawl!! Take a lookit that goofy hat onna Top of his head!!
HAW!! HAW!!
HAW!!
DON'T MESS with TEXAS
I HAD THE OPPURTUNITY TO VISIT THE FINE STATE OF TEXAS, RECENTLY..
THE
CHRONICLES
BY KEITH KNIGHT
AUSTIN, TEXAS TO BE EXACT...
TEXAS
AUSTIN
GULF OF MEXICO
MY BAND, THE MARGINAL PROPHETS, FLEW THERE TO ATTEND THE SOUTH BY SOUTHWEST MUSIC FEST..
SOUTH BY SOUTHWEST IS THE NATION'S LARGEST NEW MUSIC FESTIVAL...
Sign me!! I rock!!
I'm on heroin!
Sign me!!
PICTURE 700 BANDS PERFORMING OVER FIVE DAYS VYING FOR THE ATTENTION OF A BUNCH OF SLIMY RECORD EXECUTIVES...
UGH... RECORD EXECS... THERE IS NOTHING LOWER..
Pleased ta meetcha... I'm gonna make ya a stah...
QUICK!! PICK OUT THE SCUMSUCKING LEECH..
I HATE THE MUSIC INDUSTRY.. I REALLY DO..
You rock baby...
Kiss
SO WHY AM I IN IT, YOU MAY ASK...
SIMPLE.. I'M A STARVING ARTIST & I LOVE LIVE MUSIC.. BUT I COULD NEVER AFFORD TO GO OUT & SEE SHOWS..
Eight bucks!!
How 'bout a drawing?
SO I JOINED A BAND... NOW I GET INTO MOST OF MY SHOWS FOR FREE...
..AND IF I'M LUCKY, THE CLUB GIVES THE BAND FREE DRINKS TOO...
Purrrr
& IF I'M SUPER LUCKY, WE GET THE ULTIMATE: FREE FOOD
..I MEAN.. WHAT MORE DO YOU NEED IN LIFE? FREE ADMISSION, FREE FOOD & FREE DRINKS..
I get Phat on the Mic like a Honey Glazed Ham!!™
..NOW IF I COULD ONLY FIGURE OUT HOW TO GET OUT OF THE PERFORMING PART..
STOP

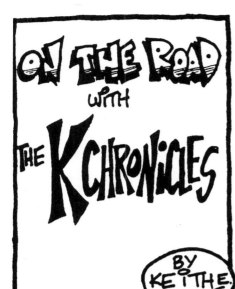

ON THE ROAD with THE K CHRONICLES

BY KEITH KNIGHT

WHEN I MADE MY BIG MOVE ACROSS THE COUNTRY.. I DID ONE OF THOSE AUTO DRIVEAWAY GIGS...

YOU GIVE THEM A DEPOSIT, THEY GIVE YOU A KEY TO A CAR THAT NEEDS TO BE DRIVEN CROSS COUNTRY!

THEY TOLD ME I'D PROBABLY GET SOME LITTLE SUB-COMPACT, SO IMAGINE MY SURPRISE WHEN IT TURNED OUT TO BE A* BRAND NEW MERCURY COUGAR!!

You're drooling on the hood, son..

*IT'S fun to read it like you're a game show announcer.

ME & MY COLLEGE PAL HAD 10 DAYS WITH HER..AND A WHOLE COUNTRY TO COVER...

UNFORTUNATELY, THE COMPANY BROUGHT US BACK TO REALITY...

OUR PLAN

Start THEIR PLAN

Finish

THEY ALLOT ONLY A CERTAIN AMOUNT OF MILES SO YOU CAN'T DRIVE THE CAR INTO OBLIVION..

THAT MAKES SENSE.. IT WAS COOL ANYWAY..IT'S INCREDIBLE TO SEE THE COUNTRY FOR REAL, NOT FROM SOME DUMB BOOK...

STUCKEYS

KANSAS

STUCKEYS

UTAH

SANDS   STUCKEYS   CAESA

I THINK LAS VEGAS IS GONNA TURN OUT TO BE A LOT LIKE BLACK OLIVES.. I DON'T LIKE IT NOW, BUT I'LL ENJOY IT WHEN I GET OLD...

ANYWAY.. I THINK CARS REALLY ARE SOME WEIRD PSYCHOLOGICAL EXTENSION OF MEN'S PENISES...

FIRST CAR, 1986 Chevelle Malibu '74 Classic (4 door) PENIS SIZE: 1¼ inch

2ND (and last) CAR, 1988 Plymouth Volare '78 PENIS SIZE: ½ inch

WITH THIS CAR, I WAS A CHANGED MAN...

MEN'S ROOM

JUST HOLD IT OVER THE BOWL... AND DON'T FORGET TO SHAKE IT THIS TIME!!!

ALAS..SOON ENOUGH WE REACHED L.A. & IT WAS TIME TO GIVE UP THE KEYS...

NO!!NO!!SHE'S MINE, GAWDAMMIT!!

AUTO DRIVEAWAY IS A LOT LIKE BEING A SURROGATE MOTHER...IT WAS AN UGLY SCENE...

| 25

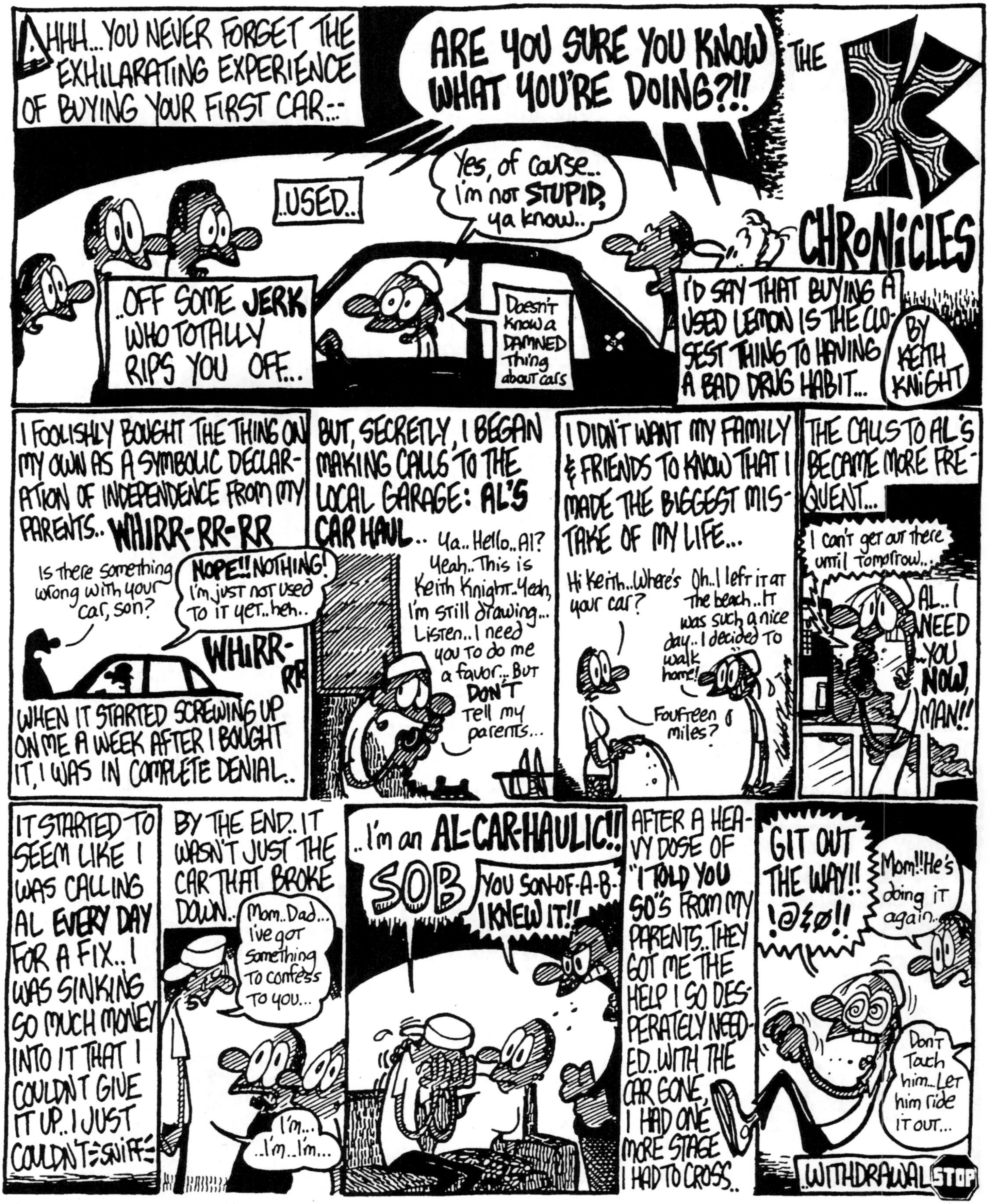

AHHH... YOU NEVER FORGET THE EXHILARATING EXPERIENCE OF BUYING YOUR FIRST CAR...
ARE YOU SURE YOU KNOW WHAT YOU'RE DOING?!!
THE K CHRONICLES
..USED..
Yes, of course.. I'm not STUPID, ya know..
..OFF SOME JERK WHO TOTALLY RIPS YOU OFF...
Doesn't know a DAMNED Thing about cars
I'D SAY THAT BUYING A USED LEMON IS THE CLOSEST THING TO HAVING A BAD DRUG HABIT...
BY KEITH KNIGHT
I FOOLISHLY BOUGHT THE THING ON MY OWN AS A SYMBOLIC DECLARATION OF INDEPENDENCE FROM MY PARENTS..
WHIRR-RR-RR
Is there something wrong with your car, son?
NOPE!! NOTHING! I'm just not used to it yet..heh..
WHIRR-RR
WHEN IT STARTED SCREWING UP ON ME A WEEK AFTER I BOUGHT IT, I WAS IN COMPLETE DENIAL..
BUT, SECRETLY, I BEGAN MAKING CALLS TO THE LOCAL GARAGE: AL'S CAR HAUL..
Ya.. Hello.. Al? Yeah.. This is Keith Knight.. Yeah, I'm still drawing... Listen.. I need you to do me a favor... But DON'T Tell my parents...
I DIDN'T WANT MY FAMILY & FRIENDS TO KNOW THAT I MADE THE BIGGEST MISTAKE OF MY LIFE...
Hi Keith.. Where's your car?
Oh.. I left it at the beach.. It was such a nice day.. I decided to walk home!
Fourteen miles?
THE CALLS TO AL'S BECAME MORE FREQUENT...
I can't get out there until tomorrow...
AL.. I NEED YOU NOW, MAN!!
IT STARTED TO SEEM LIKE I WAS CALLING AL EVERY DAY FOR A FIX.. I WAS SINKING SO MUCH MONEY INTO IT THAT I COULDN'T GIVE IT UP.. I JUST COULDN'T =SNIFF=
BY THE END.. IT WASN'T JUST THE CAR THAT BROKE DOWN..
Mom..Dad... I've got something to confess to you...
I'm... ..I'm..I'm...
.. I'm an AL-CAR-HAULIC!!
SOB
YOU SON-OF-A-B- I KNEW IT!!
AFTER A HEAVY DOSE OF "I TOLD YOU SO'S FROM MY PARENTS.. THEY GOT ME THE HELP I SO DESPERATELY NEEDED.. WITH THE CAR GONE, I HAD ONE MORE STAGE I HAD TO CROSS..
GIT OUT THE WAY!! !@&Ø!!
Mom!! He's doing it again..
Don't Touch him... Let him ride it out...
..WITHDRAWAL
STOP

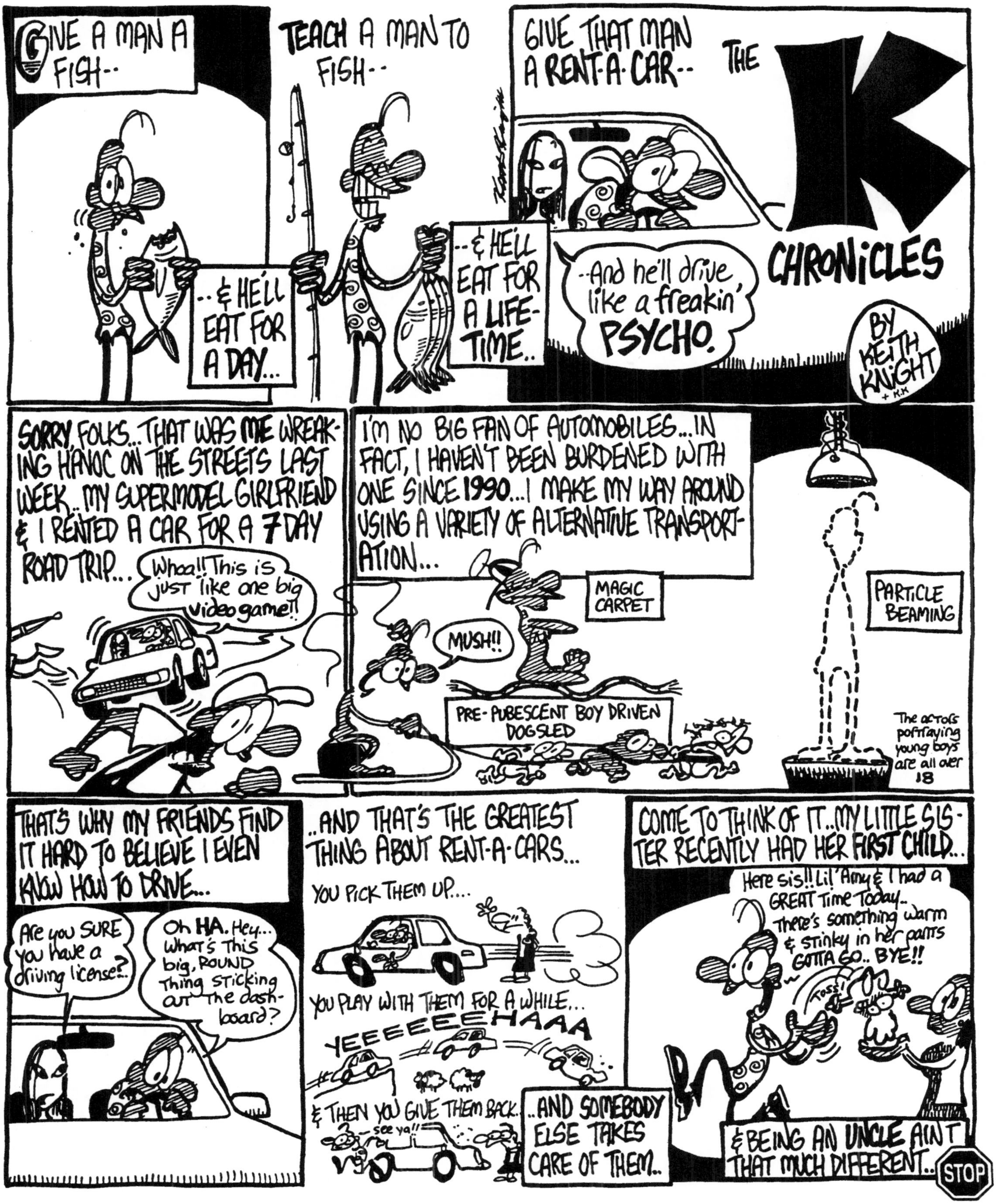
GIVE A MAN A FISH--
..& HE'LL EAT FOR A DAY...
TEACH A MAN TO FISH--
--& HE'LL EAT FOR A LIFE-TIME..
GIVE THAT MAN A RENT-A-CAR--
--And he'll drive like a freakin' PSYCHO.
THE K CHRONICLES
BY KEITH KNIGHT
SORRY, FOLKS...THAT WAS ME WREAKING HAVOC ON THE STREETS LAST WEEK.. MY SUPERMODEL GIRLFRIEND & I RENTED A CAR FOR A 7 DAY ROAD TRIP...
Whoa!! This is just like one big videogame!!
I'M NO BIG FAN OF AUTOMOBILES...IN FACT, I HAVEN'T BEEN BURDENED WITH ONE SINCE 1990...I MAKE MY WAY AROUND USING A VARIETY OF ALTERNATIVE TRANSPORTATION...
MAGIC CARPET
MUSH!!
PRE-PUBESCENT BOY DRIVEN DOGSLED
PARTICLE BEAMING
The actors portraying young boys are all over 18
THAT'S WHY MY FRIENDS FIND IT HARD TO BELIEVE I EVEN KNOW HOW TO DRIVE...
Are you SURE you have a driving license?..
Oh HA. Hey... What's This big, ROUND Thing sticking out the dash-board?
..AND THAT'S THE GREATEST THING ABOUT RENT-A-CARS...
YOU PICK THEM UP....
YOU PLAY WITH THEM FOR A WHILE...
YEEEEEEEHAAAA
& THEN YOU GIVE THEM BACK..
see ya!!
..AND SOMEBODY ELSE TAKES CARE OF THEM..
COME TO THINK OF IT..MY LITTLE SISTER RECENTLY HAD HER FIRST CHILD...
Here sis!! Lil' Amy & I had a GREAT Time Today.. There's something warm & stinky in her pants GOTTA GO.. BYE!!
TOSS!
& BEING AN UNCLE AIN'T THAT MUCH DIFFERENT..
STOP

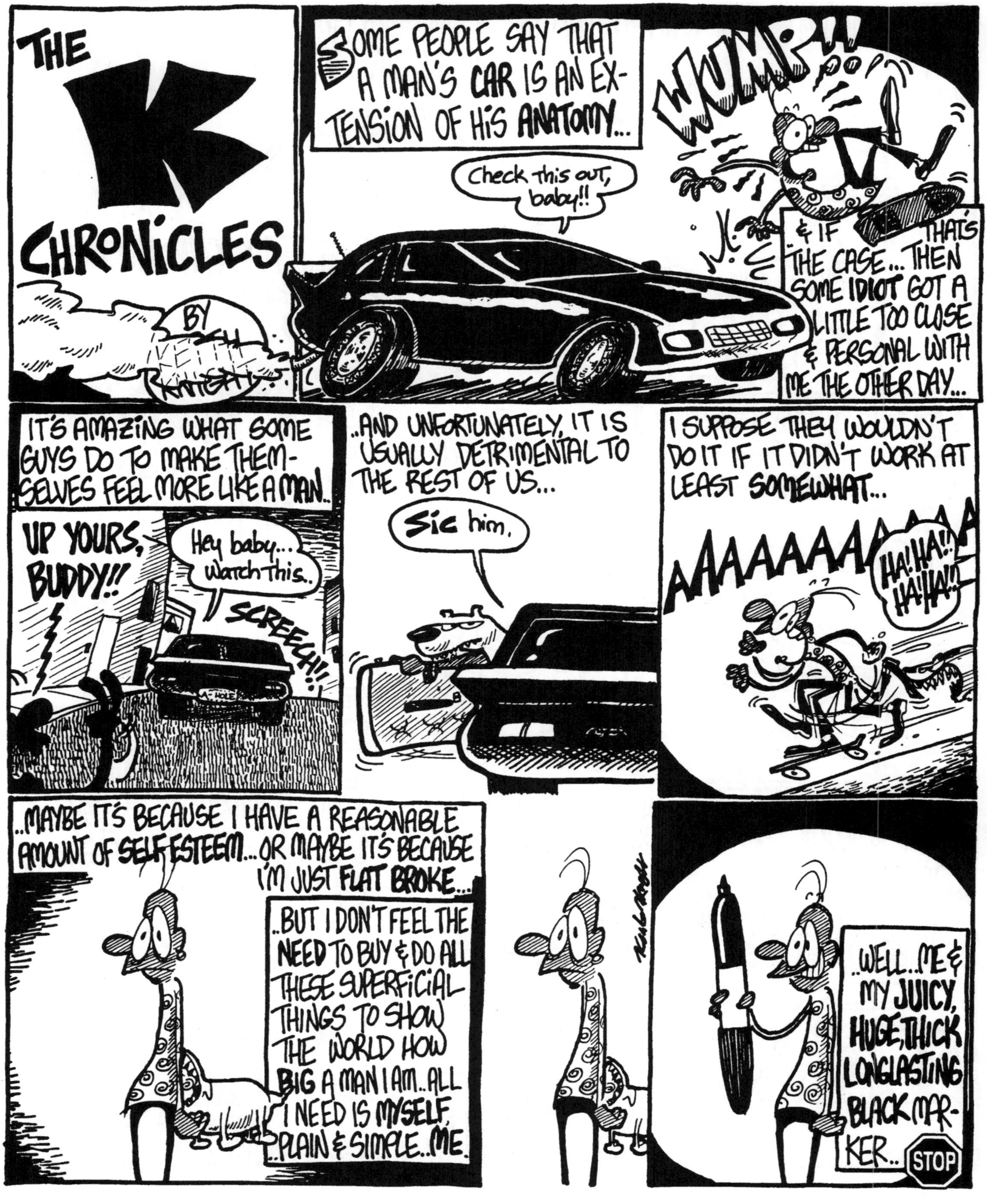
THE K CHRONICLES
BY KEITH KNIGHT
SOME PEOPLE SAY THAT A MAN'S CAR IS AN EXTENSION OF HIS ANATOMY...
Check this out, baby!!
WUMP!!
...& IF THAT'S THE CASE... THEN SOME IDIOT GOT A LITTLE TOO CLOSE & PERSONAL WITH ME THE OTHER DAY...
IT'S AMAZING WHAT SOME GUYS DO TO MAKE THEMSELVES FEEL MORE LIKE A MAN...
UP YOURS, BUDDY!!
Hey baby... Watch this..
SCREEECH!!!
..AND UNFORTUNATELY, IT IS USUALLY DETRIMENTAL TO THE REST OF US...
Sic him.
I SUPPOSE THEY WOULDN'T DO IT IF IT DIDN'T WORK AT LEAST SOMEWHAT...
AAAAAAAAAAAA
HA! HA!! HA! HA!!
..MAYBE IT'S BECAUSE I HAVE A REASONABLE AMOUNT OF SELF ESTEEM... OR MAYBE IT'S BECAUSE I'M JUST FLAT BROKE...
..BUT I DON'T FEEL THE NEED TO BUY & DO ALL THESE SUPERFICIAL THINGS TO SHOW THE WORLD HOW BIG A MAN I AM.. ALL I NEED IS MYSELF, PLAIN & SIMPLE.. ME.
..WELL.. ME & MY JUICY, HUGE, THICK LONGLASTING BLACK MARKER...
STOP

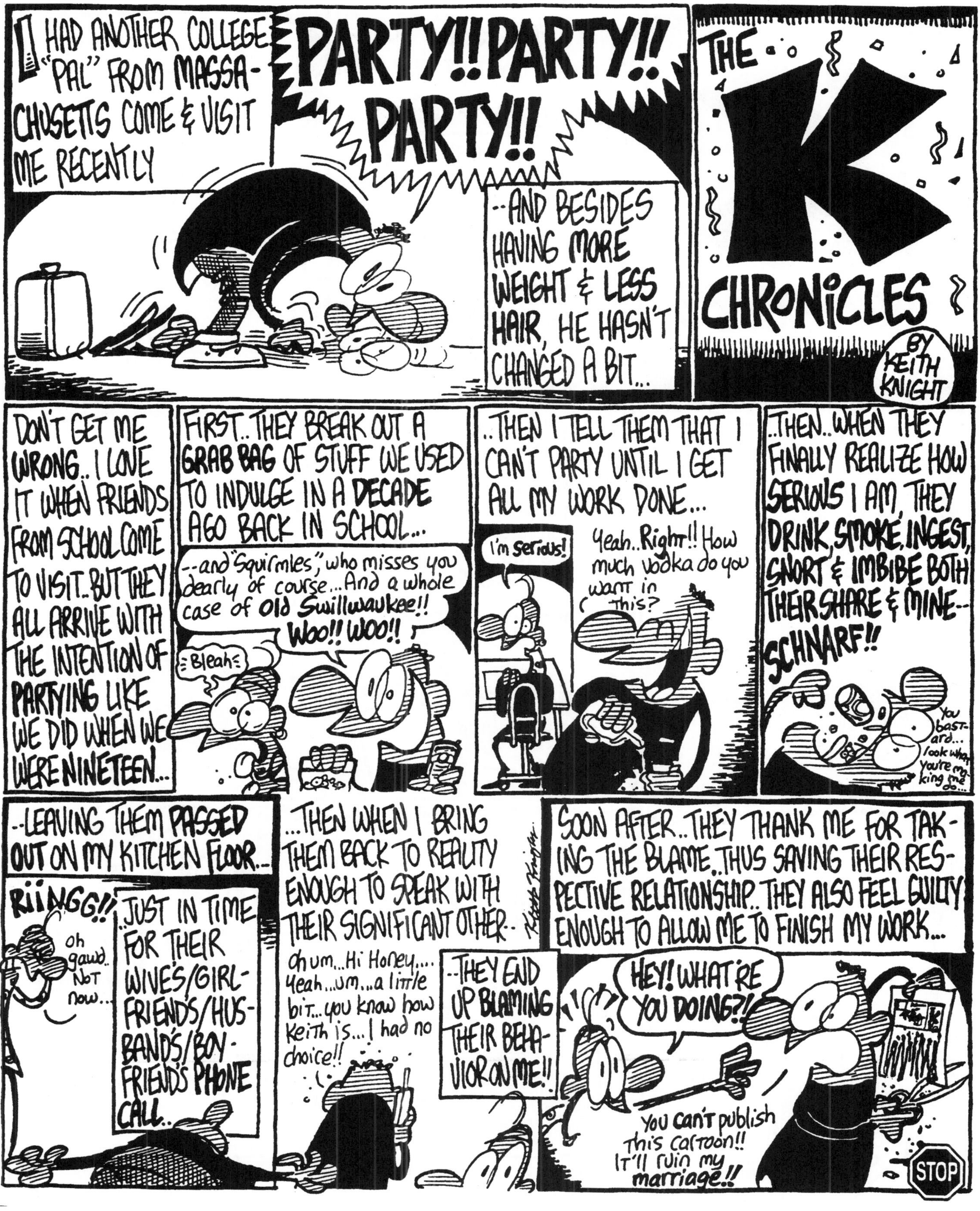

I HAD ANOTHER COLLEGE "PAL" FROM MASSACHUSETTS COME & VISIT ME RECENTLY
PARTY!! PARTY!! PARTY!!
--AND BESIDES HAVING MORE WEIGHT & LESS HAIR, HE HASN'T CHANGED A BIT...
THE K CHRONICLES
BY KEITH KNIGHT
DON'T GET ME WRONG.. I LOVE IT WHEN FRIENDS FROM SCHOOL COME TO VISIT.. BUT THEY ALL ARRIVE WITH THE INTENTION OF PARTYING LIKE WE DID WHEN WE WERE NINETEEN...
FIRST.. THEY BREAK OUT A GRAB BAG OF STUFF WE USED TO INDULGE IN A DECADE AGO BACK IN SCHOOL...
--and "Squirmles," who misses you dearly of course... And a whole case of Old Swillwaukee!!
Woo!! Woo!!
Bleah
..THEN I TELL THEM THAT I CAN'T PARTY UNTIL I GET ALL MY WORK DONE...
I'm serious!
Yeah.. Right!! How much vodka do you want in this?
..THEN.. WHEN THEY FINALLY REALIZE HOW SERIOUS I AM, THEY DRINK, SMOKE, INGEST, SNORT & IMBIBE BOTH THEIR SHARE & MINE--
SCHNARF!!
You bastard... look what you're making me do...
--LEAVING THEM PASSED OUT ON MY KITCHEN FLOOR...
RIINGG!!
oh gawd.. NOT now...
..JUST IN TIME FOR THEIR WIVES/GIRLFRIENDS/HUSBANDS/BOYFRIENDS PHONE CALL..
...THEN WHEN I BRING THEM BACK TO REALITY ENOUGH TO SPEAK WITH THEIR SIGNIFICANT OTHER..
oh um... Hi Honey.... yeah... um... a little bit... you know how Keith is... I had no choice!!
--THEY END UP BLAMING THEIR BEHAVIOR ON ME!!
SOON AFTER.. THEY THANK ME FOR TAKING THE BLAME.. THUS SAVING THEIR RESPECTIVE RELATIONSHIP.. THEY ALSO FEEL GUILTY ENOUGH TO ALLOW ME TO FINISH MY WORK...
HEY! WHAT'RE YOU DOING?!
You can't publish this cartoon!! It'll ruin my marriage!!
STOP

Now that I'm married, I use all my friends the same way.

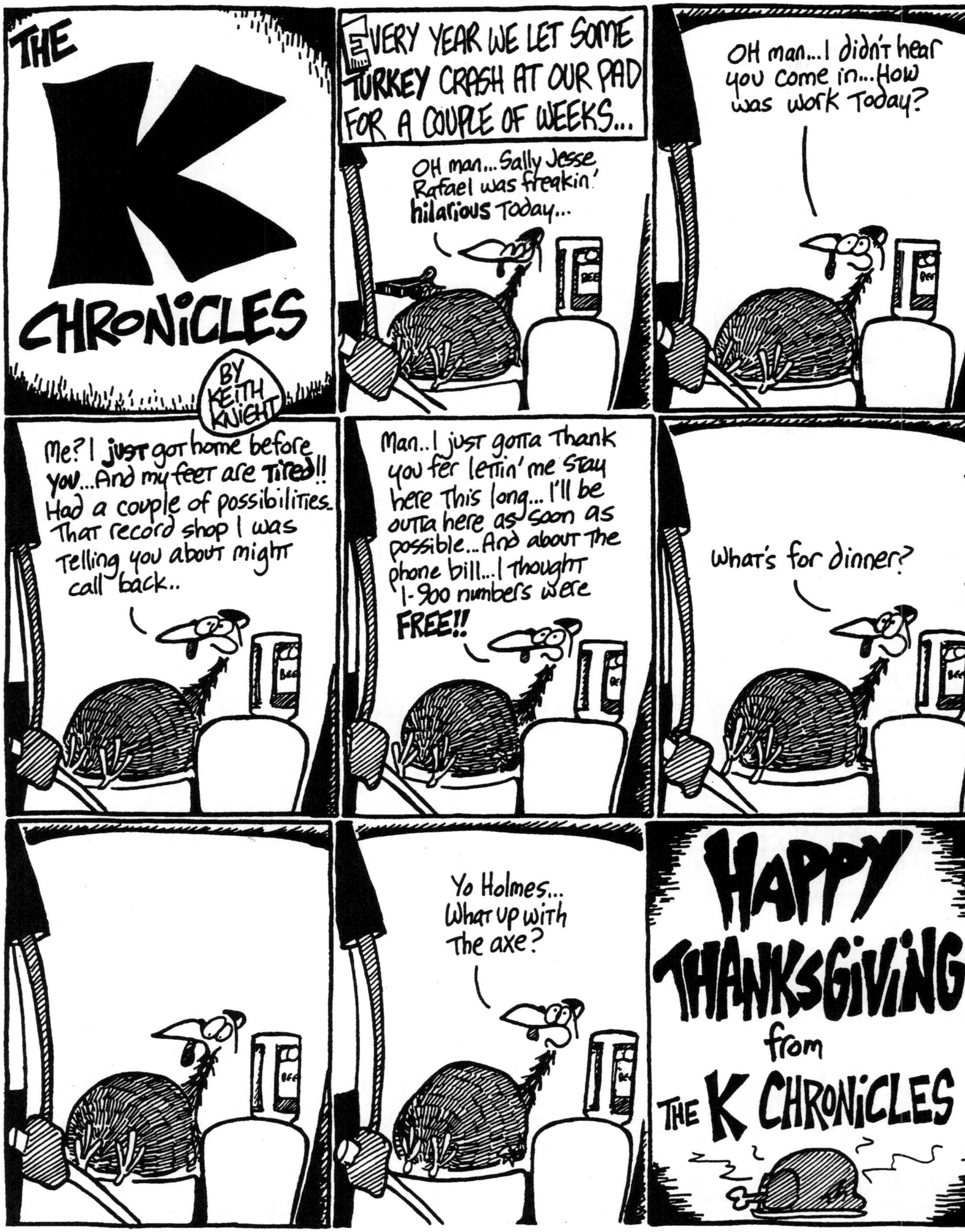
THE K CHRONICLES
BY KEITH KNIGHT
EVERY YEAR WE LET SOME TURKEY CRASH AT OUR PAD FOR A COUPLE OF WEEKS...
OH man... Sally Jesse Rafael was freakin' hilarious Today...
OH man... I didn't hear you come in... How was work Today?
Me? I just got home before you... And my feet are Tired!! Had a couple of possibilities. That record shop I was Telling you about might call back..
Man.. I just gotta Thank you fer lettin' me stay here This long... I'll be outta here as soon as possible... And about the phone bill... I thought 1-900 numbers were FREE!!
What's for dinner?
Yo Holmes... What up with The axe?
HAPPY THANKSGIVING from THE K CHRONICLES

The first comic to feature the recurring Turkey character.
I developed an animated show around this character for Nickelodeon that never went past the early stages.

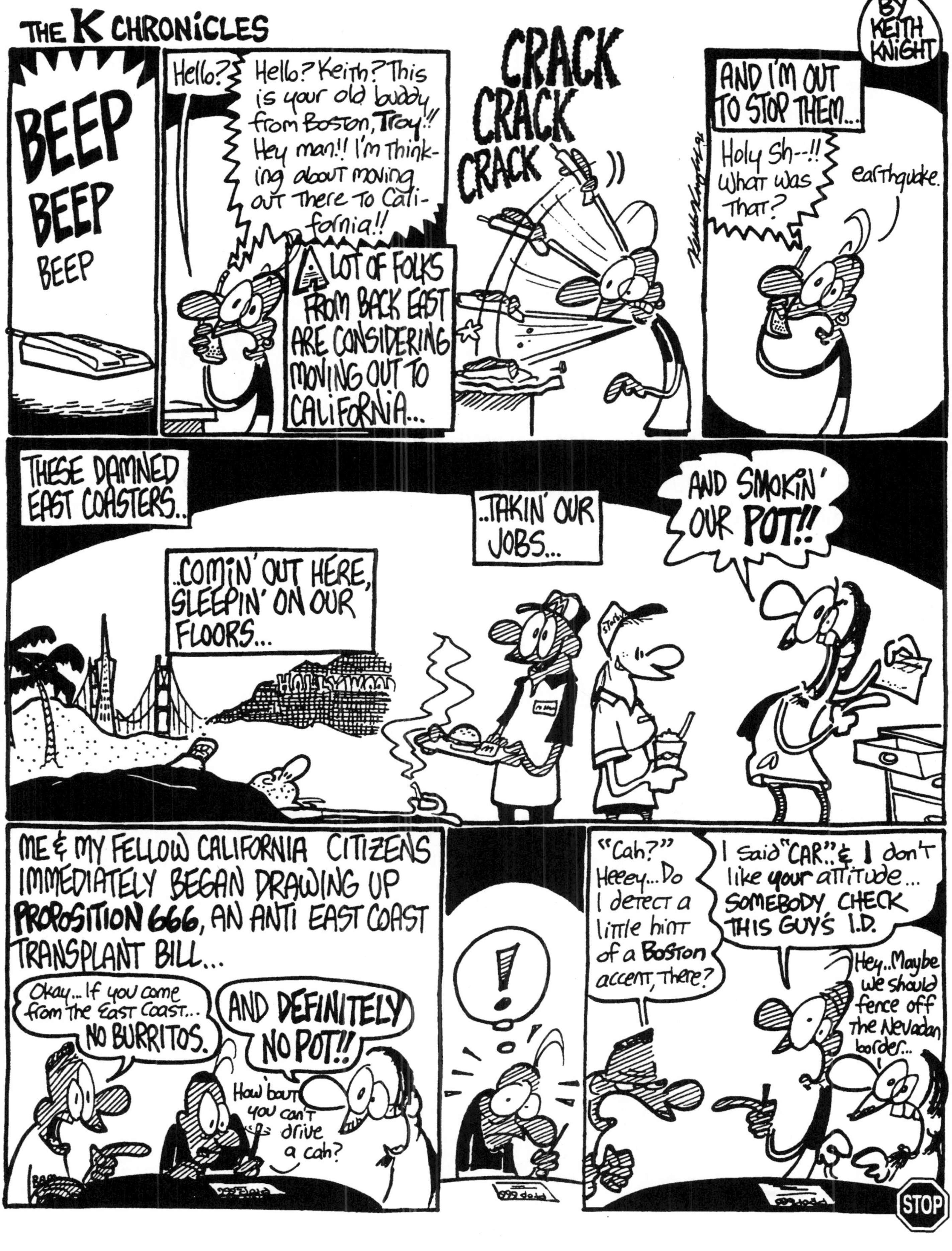

THE K CHRONICLES
BY KEITH KNIGHT
BEEP
BEEP
BEEP
Hello?
Hello? Keith? This is your old buddy from Boston, Troy!! Hey man!! I'm thinking about moving out there to California!!
A LOT OF FOLKS FROM BACK EAST ARE CONSIDERING MOVING OUT TO CALIFORNIA...
CRACK
CRACK
CRACK
AND I'M OUT TO STOP THEM...
Holy Sh--!! What was that?
earthquake.
THESE DAMNED EAST COASTERS..
..COMIN' OUT HERE, SLEEPIN' ON OUR FLOORS...
..TAKIN' OUR JOBS...
AND SMOKIN' OUR POT!!
ME & MY FELLOW CALIFORNIA CITIZENS IMMEDIATELY BEGAN DRAWING UP PROPOSITION 666, AN ANTI EAST COAST TRANSPLANT BILL...
Okay... If you come from the East Coast... NO BURRITOS.
AND DEFINITELY NO POT!!
How 'bout you can't drive a cah?
!
"Cah?" Heeey... Do I detect a little hint of a Boston accent, there?
I said "CAR"..& I don't like your attitude... SOMEBODY CHECK THIS GUY'S I.D.
Hey..Maybe we should fence off the Nevadan border...
STOP

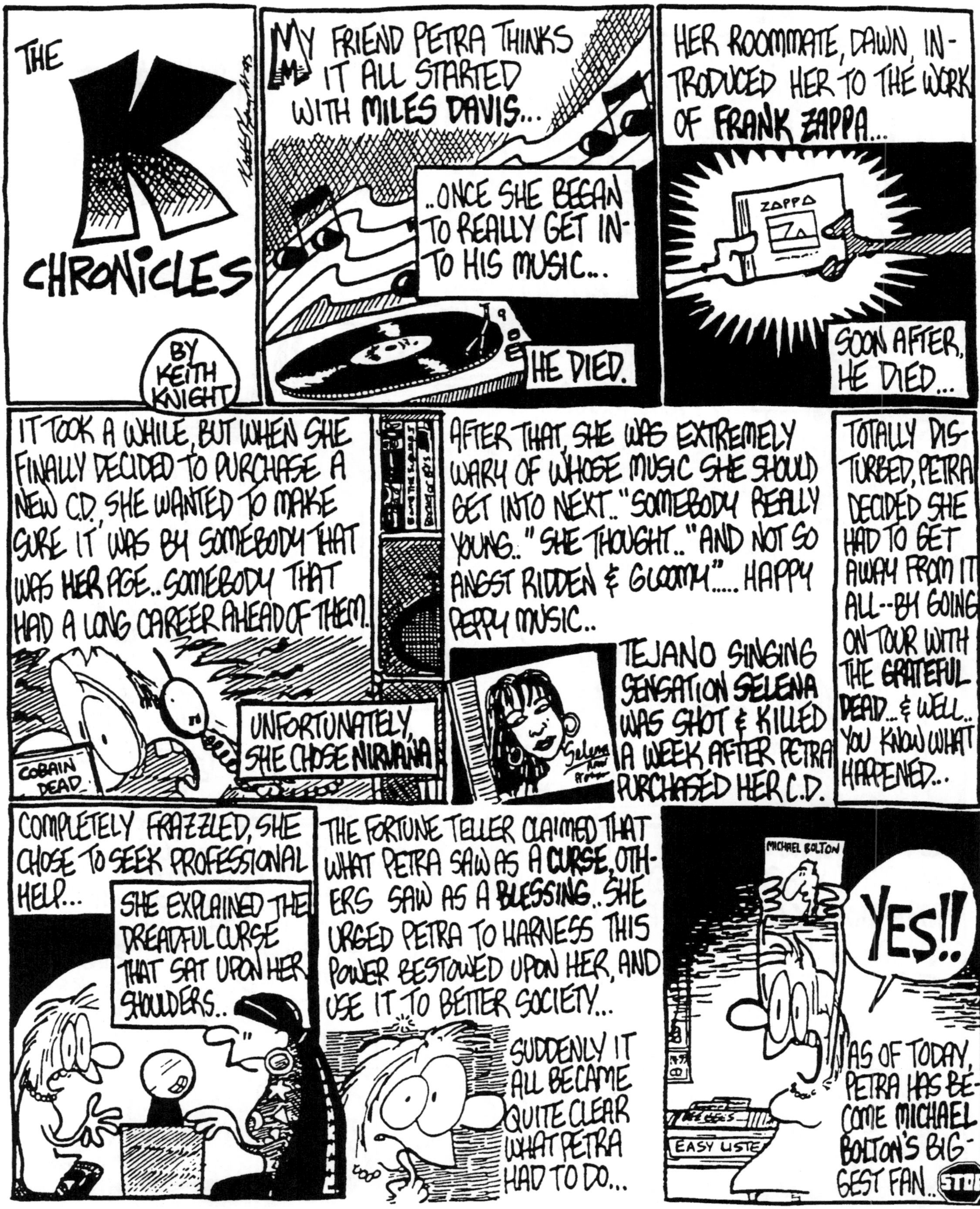
THE K CHRONICLES
BY KEITH KNIGHT
MY FRIEND PETRA THINKS IT ALL STARTED WITH MILES DAVIS...
..ONCE SHE BEGAN TO REALLY GET INTO HIS MUSIC...
HE DIED.
HER ROOMMATE, DAWN, INTRODUCED HER TO THE WORK OF FRANK ZAPPA...
ZAPPA
SOON AFTER, HE DIED...
IT TOOK A WHILE, BUT WHEN SHE FINALLY DECIDED TO PURCHASE A NEW C.D., SHE WANTED TO MAKE SURE IT WAS BY SOMEBODY THAT WAS HER AGE.. SOMEBODY THAT HAD A LONG CAREER AHEAD OF THEM.
UNFORTUNATELY, SHE CHOSE NIRVANA
COBAIN DEAD
AFTER THAT, SHE WAS EXTREMELY WARY OF WHOSE MUSIC SHE SHOULD GET INTO NEXT.. "SOMEBODY REALLY YOUNG.." SHE THOUGHT.. "AND NOT SO ANGST RIDDEN & GLOOMY"..... HAPPY PEPPY MUSIC..
TEJANO SINGING SENSATION SELENA WAS SHOT & KILLED A WEEK AFTER PETRA PURCHASED HER C.D.
TOTALLY DISTURBED, PETRA DECIDED SHE HAD TO GET AWAY FROM IT ALL--BY GOING ON TOUR WITH THE GRATEFUL DEAD... & WELL.. YOU KNOW WHAT HAPPENED...
COMPLETELY FRAZZLED, SHE CHOSE TO SEEK PROFESSIONAL HELP...
SHE EXPLAINED THE DREADFUL CURSE THAT SAT UPON HER SHOULDERS..
THE FORTUNE TELLER CLAIMED THAT WHAT PETRA SAW AS A CURSE, OTHERS SAW AS A BLESSING.. SHE URGED PETRA TO HARNESS THIS POWER BESTOWED UPON HER, AND USE IT TO BETTER SOCIETY...
SUDDENLY IT ALL BECAME QUITE CLEAR WHAT PETRA HAD TO DO...
MICHAEL BOLTON
YES!!
EASY LISTE
AS OF TODAY, PETRA HAS BECOME MICHAEL BOLTON'S BIGGEST FAN..
STOP

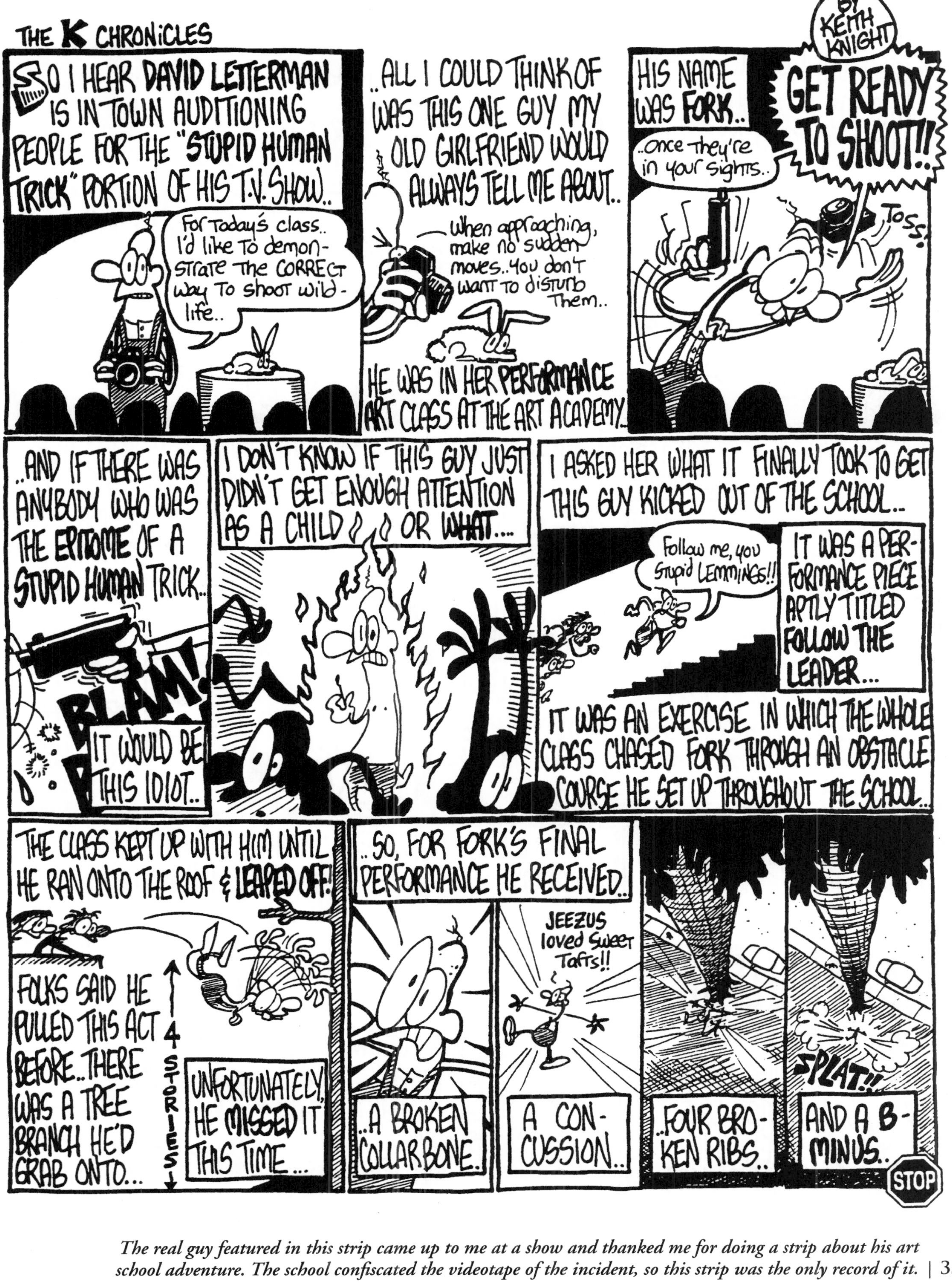
THE K CHRONICLES
BY KEITH KNIGHT
SO I HEAR DAVID LETTERMAN IS IN TOWN AUDITIONING PEOPLE FOR THE "STUPID HUMAN TRICK" PORTION OF HIS T.V. SHOW..
For Today's class.. I'd like to demonstrate The CORRECT way To shoot wildlife..
..ALL I COULD THINK OF WAS THIS ONE GUY MY OLD GIRLFRIEND WOULD ALWAYS TELL ME ABOUT..
When approaching, make no sudden moves..You don't want to disturb Them..
HE WAS IN HER PERFORMANCE ART CLASS AT THE ART ACADEMY..
HIS NAME WAS FORK..
..once they're in your sights..
GET READY TO SHOOT!!
TOSS
..AND IF THERE WAS ANYBODY WHO WAS THE EPITOME OF A STUPID HUMAN TRICK..
BLAM!
IT WOULD BE THIS IDIOT..
I DON'T KNOW IF THIS GUY JUST DIDN'T GET ENOUGH ATTENTION AS A CHILD OR WHAT....
I ASKED HER WHAT IT FINALLY TOOK TO GET THIS GUY KICKED OUT OF THE SCHOOL...
Follow me, you Stupid LEMMINGS!!
IT WAS A PERFORMANCE PIECE APTLY TITLED FOLLOW THE LEADER...
IT WAS AN EXERCISE IN WHICH THE WHOLE CLASS CHASED FORK THROUGH AN OBSTACLE COURSE HE SET UP THROUGHOUT THE SCHOOL..
THE CLASS KEPT UP WITH HIM UNTIL HE RAN ONTO THE ROOF & LEAPED OFF!
FOLKS SAID HE PULLED THIS ACT BEFORE..THERE WAS A TREE BRANCH HE'D GRAB ONTO...
4 STORIES
UNFORTUNATELY, HE MISSED IT THIS TIME...
..SO, FOR FORK'S FINAL PERFORMANCE HE RECEIVED..
..A BROKEN COLLARBONE.
JEEZUS loved Sweet Tarts!!
A CONCUSSION..
..FOUR BROKEN RIBS..
SPLAT!!
AND A B-MINUS..
STOP

The real guy featured in this strip came up to me at a show and thanked me for doing a strip about his art school adventure. The school confiscated the videotape of the incident, so this strip was the only record of it.

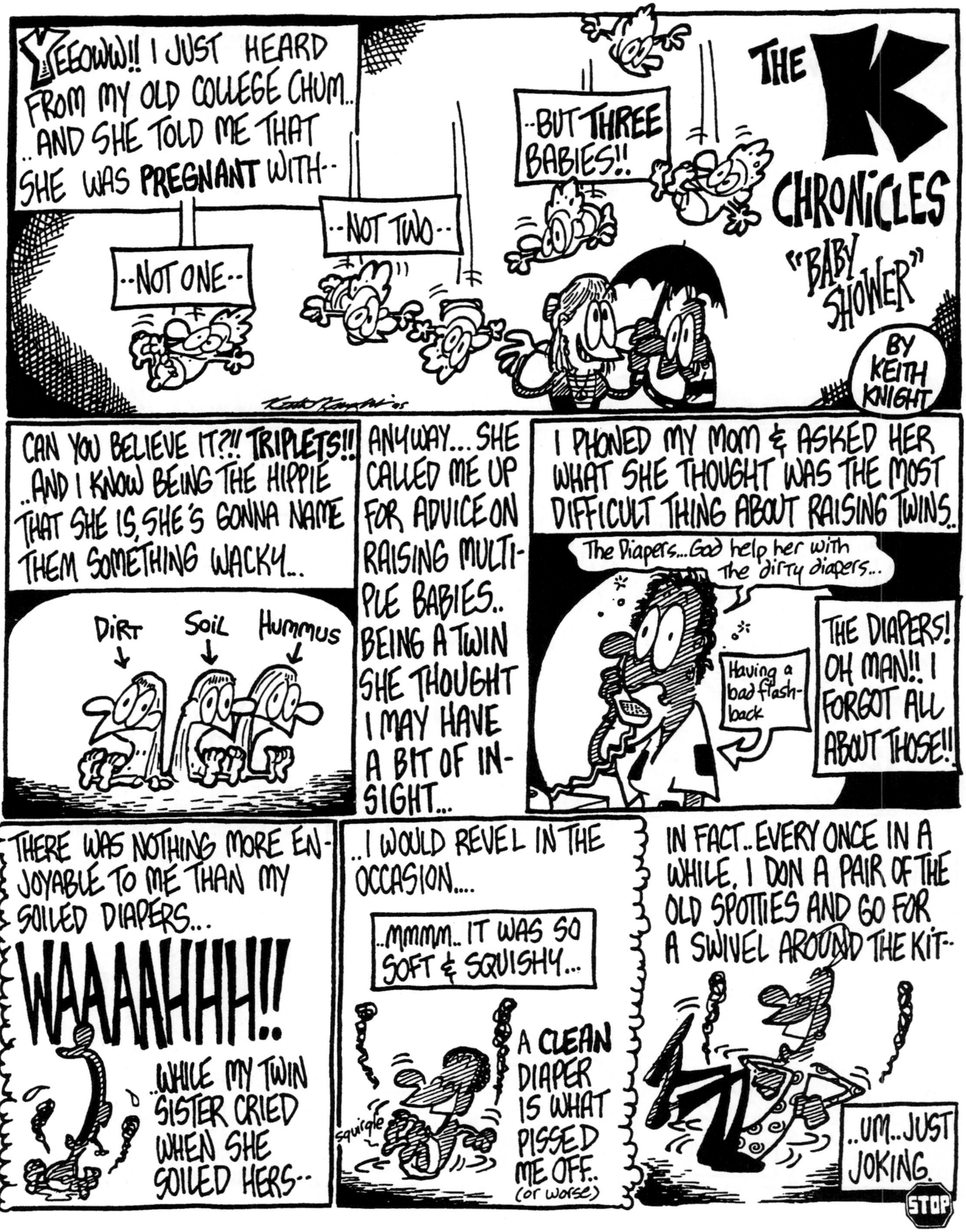
YEEOWW!! I JUST HEARD FROM MY OLD COLLEGE CHUM.. ..AND SHE TOLD ME THAT SHE WAS PREGNANT WITH-
..NOT ONE..
..NOT TWO..
..BUT THREE BABIES!!
THE K CHRONICLES
"BABY SHOWER"
BY KEITH KNIGHT
CAN YOU BELIEVE IT?!! TRIPLETS!! ..AND I KNOW BEING THE HIPPIE THAT SHE IS, SHE'S GONNA NAME THEM SOMETHING WACKY..
DIRT
SOIL
HUMMUS
ANYWAY.... SHE CALLED ME UP FOR ADVICE ON RAISING MULTIPLE BABIES.. BEING A TWIN SHE THOUGHT I MAY HAVE A BIT OF INSIGHT...
I PHONED MY MOM & ASKED HER WHAT SHE THOUGHT WAS THE MOST DIFFICULT THING ABOUT RAISING TWINS..
The Diapers...God help her with the dirty diapers...
Having a bad flash-back
THE DIAPERS! OH MAN!! I FORGOT ALL ABOUT THOSE!!
THERE WAS NOTHING MORE ENJOYABLE TO ME THAN MY SOILED DIAPERS...
WAAAAHHH!!
..WHILE MY TWIN SISTER CRIED WHEN SHE SOILED HERS-
..I WOULD REVEL IN THE OCCASION....
..MMMM.. IT WAS SO SOFT & SQUISHY...
squigle
A CLEAN DIAPER IS WHAT PISSED ME OFF.. (or worse)
IN FACT..EVERY ONCE IN A WHILE, I DON A PAIR OF THE OLD SPOTTIES AND GO FOR A SWIVEL AROUND THE KIT-
..UM..JUST JOKING.
STOP

 Dirt, Soil and Hummus are now teenagers. They also have two more brothers: Tofu and Soybean.

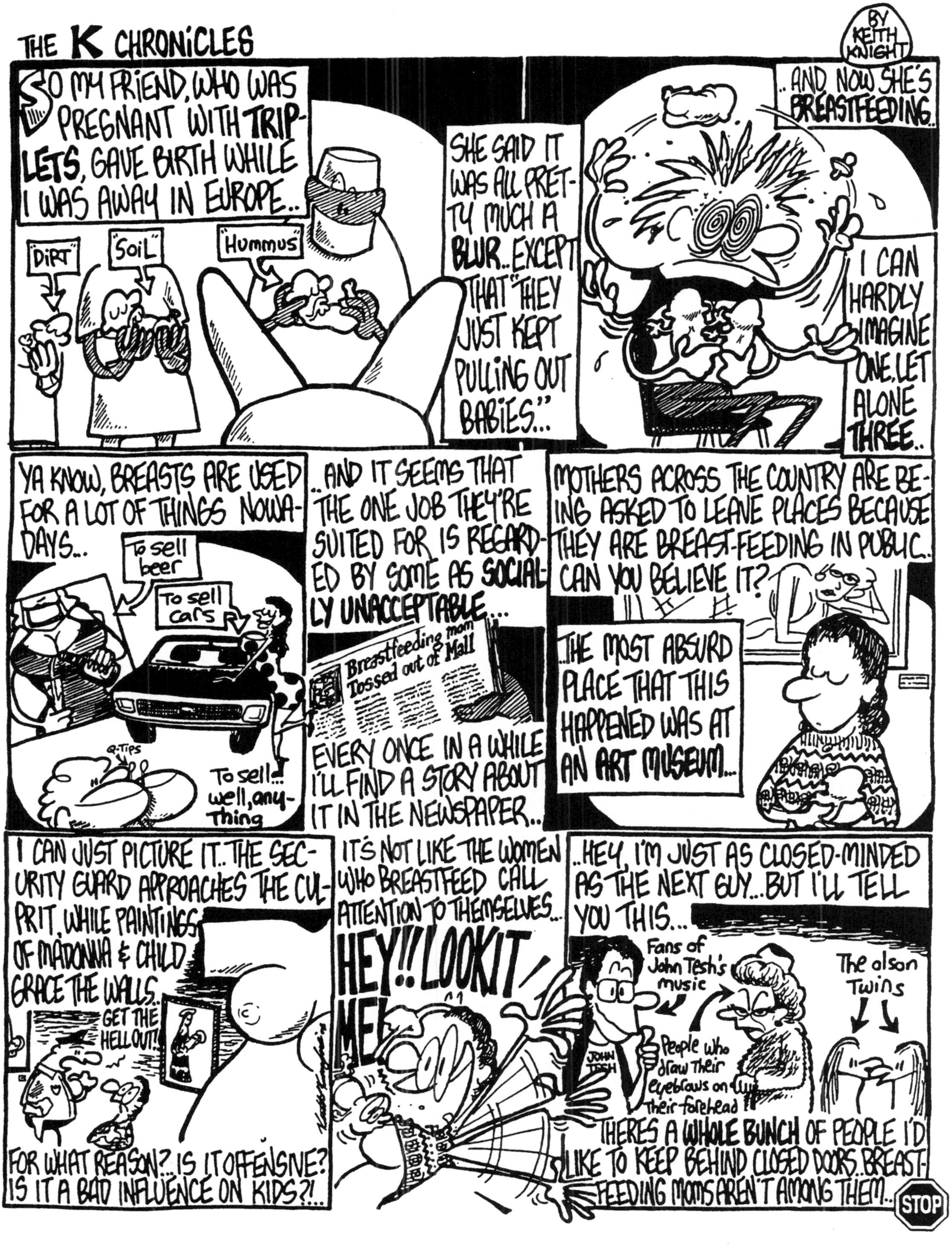
THE K CHRONICLES
BY KEITH KNIGHT
SO MY FRIEND, WHO WAS PREGNANT WITH TRIPLETS, GAVE BIRTH WHILE I WAS AWAY IN EUROPE..
"DIRT"
"SOIL"
"HUMMUS"
SHE SAID IT WAS ALL PRETTY MUCH A BLUR.. EXCEPT THAT "THEY JUST KEPT PULLING OUT BABIES"...
..AND NOW SHE'S BREASTFEEDING..
I CAN HARDLY IMAGINE ONE, LET ALONE THREE..
YA KNOW, BREASTS ARE USED FOR A LOT OF THINGS NOWADAYS..
To sell beer
To sell cars
Q-Tips
To sell... well, any-thing
..AND IT SEEMS THAT THE ONE JOB THEY'RE SUITED FOR IS REGARDED BY SOME AS SOCIALLY UNACCEPTABLE...
Breastfeeding mom Tossed out of Mall
EVERY ONCE IN A WHILE I'LL FIND A STORY ABOUT IT IN THE NEWSPAPER..
MOTHERS ACROSS THE COUNTRY ARE BEING ASKED TO LEAVE PLACES BECAUSE THEY ARE BREAST-FEEDING IN PUBLIC.. CAN YOU BELIEVE IT?
..THE MOST ABSURD PLACE THAT THIS HAPPENED WAS AT AN ART MUSEUM...
I CAN JUST PICTURE IT.. THE SECURITY GUARD APPROACHES THE CULPRIT, WHILE PAINTINGS OF MADONNA & CHILD GRACE THE WALLS..
GET THE HELL OUT!!
FOR WHAT REASON?.. IS IT OFFENSIVE? IS IT A BAD INFLUENCE ON KIDS?!..
IT'S NOT LIKE THE WOMEN WHO BREASTFEED CALL ATTENTION TO THEMSELVES...
HEY!! LOOKIT ME!
..HEY, I'M JUST AS CLOSED-MINDED AS THE NEXT GUY... BUT I'LL TELL YOU THIS...
Fans of John Tesh's music
JOHN TESH
People who draw their eyebrows on their forehead
The olson Twins
THERES A WHOLE BUNCH OF PEOPLE I'D LIKE TO KEEP BEHIND CLOSED DOORS.. BREAST-FEEDING MOMS AREN'T AMONG THEM...
STOP

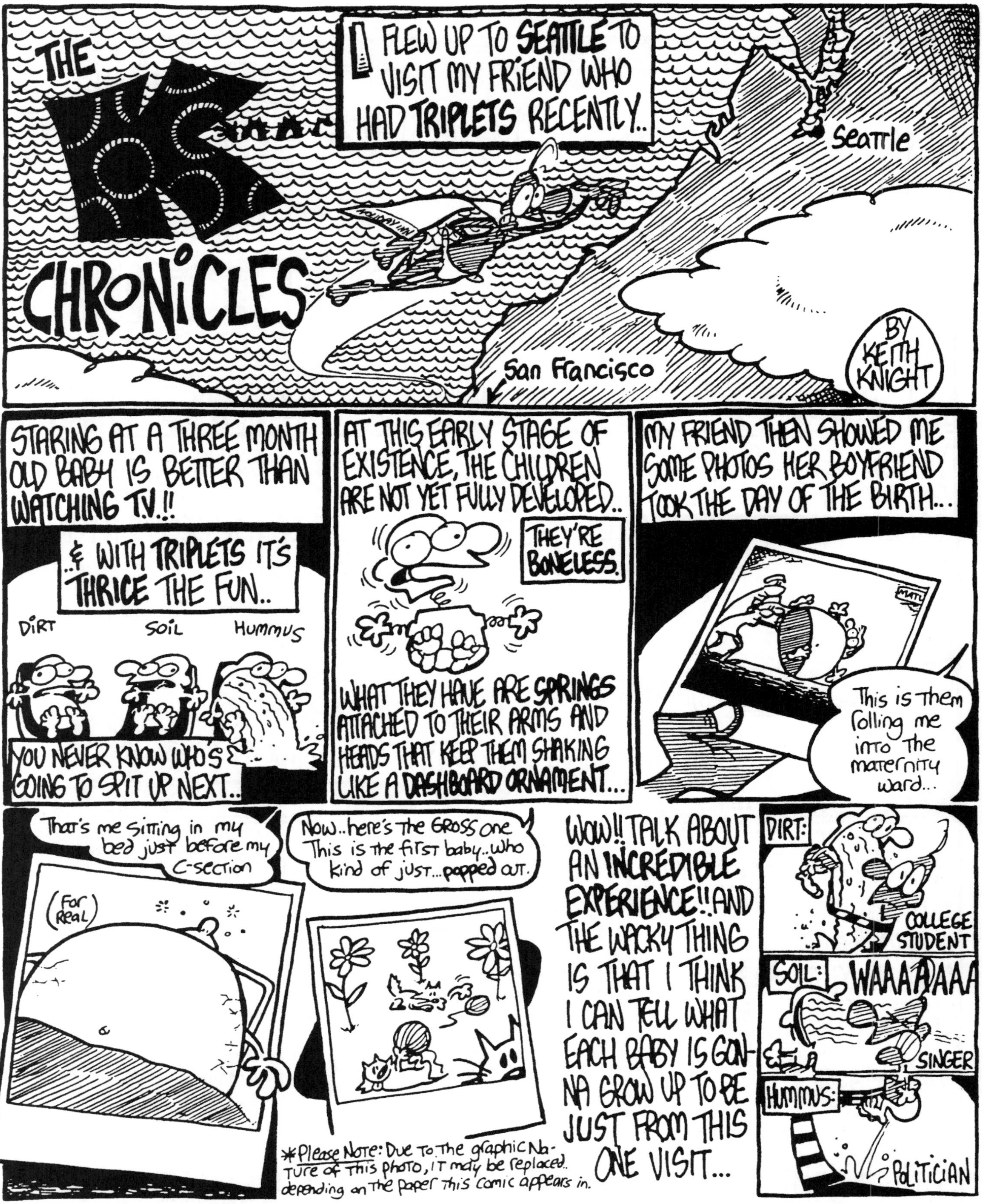

THE K CHRONICLES
I FLEW UP TO SEATTLE TO VISIT MY FRIEND WHO HAD TRIPLETS RECENTLY..
HOLIDAY INN
Seattle
San Francisco
BY KEITH KNIGHT
STARING AT A THREE MONTH OLD BABY IS BETTER THAN WATCHING T.V.!!
..& WITH TRIPLETS IT'S THRICE THE FUN..
DIRT
SOIL
HUMMUS
YOU NEVER KNOW WHO'S GOING TO SPIT UP NEXT..
AT THIS EARLY STAGE OF EXISTENCE, THE CHILDREN ARE NOT YET FULLY DEVELOPED..
THEY'RE BONELESS.
WHAT THEY HAVE ARE SPRINGS ATTACHED TO THEIR ARMS AND HEADS THAT KEEP THEM SHAKING LIKE A DASHBOARD ORNAMENT...
MY FRIEND THEN SHOWED ME SOME PHOTOS HER BOYFRIEND TOOK THE DAY OF THE BIRTH...
This is them rolling me into the maternity ward...
That's me sitting in my bed just before my C-section
(For Real)
Now..here's the GROSS one This is the first baby..who kind of just...popped out.
WOW!! TALK ABOUT AN INCREDIBLE EXPERIENCE!! AND THE WACKY THING IS THAT I THINK I CAN TELL WHAT EACH BABY IS GONNA GROW UP TO BE JUST FROM THIS ONE VISIT...
DIRT:
COLLEGE STUDENT
SOIL:
WAAAAAAA
SINGER
HUMMUS:
POLITICIAN
*Please Note: Due to the graphic nature of this photo, it may be replaced depending on the paper this comic appears in.

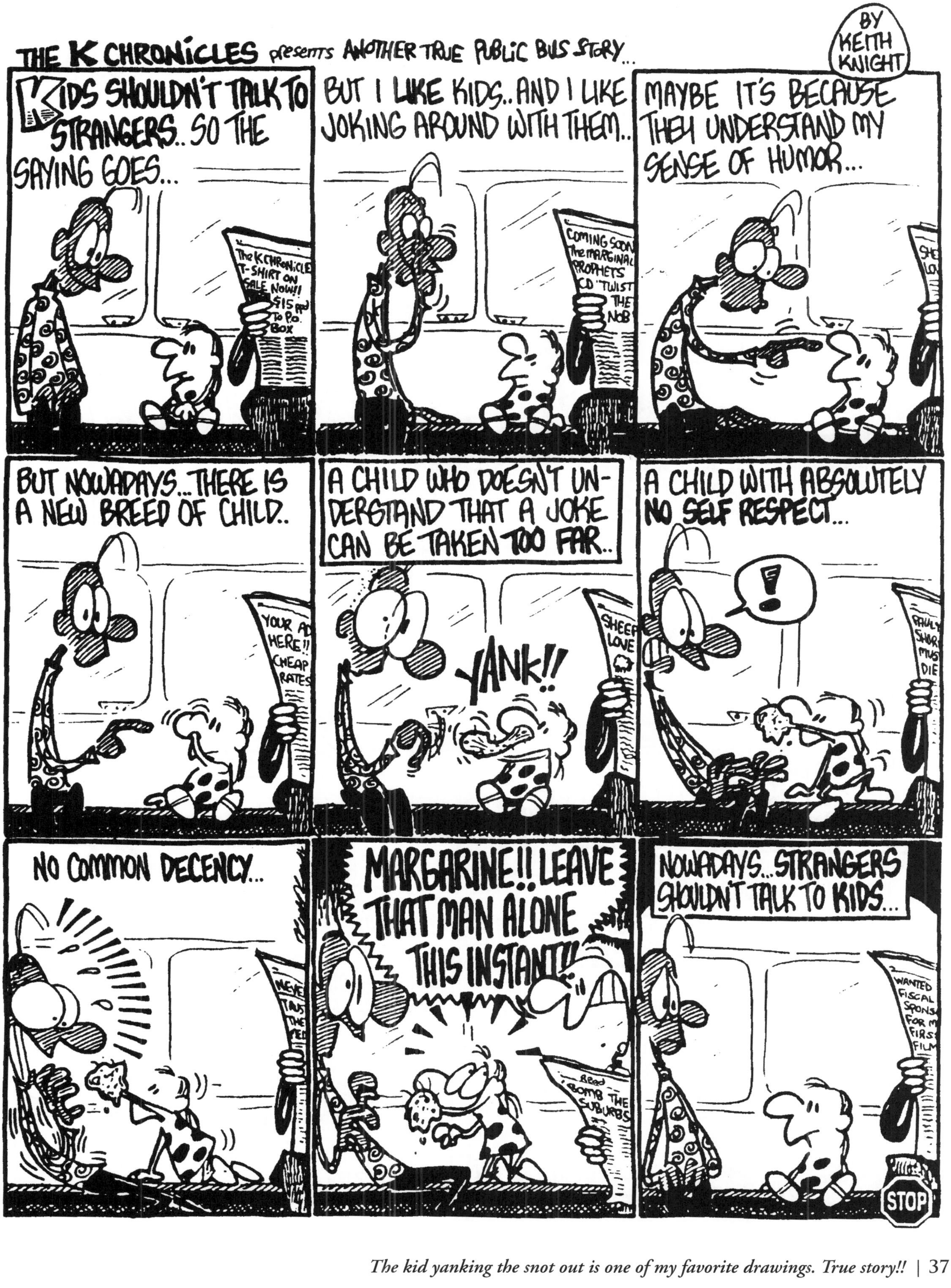
THE K CHRONICLES presents ANOTHER TRUE PUBLIC BUS STORY...
BY KEITH KNIGHT
KIDS SHOULDN'T TALK TO STRANGERS.. SO THE SAYING GOES...
The K CHRONICLE T-SHIRT ON SALE NOW!! $15 ppd To P.O. BOX
BUT I LIKE KIDS.. AND I LIKE JOKING AROUND WITH THEM..
COMING SOON The MARGINAL PROPHETS CD "TWIST THE NOB"
MAYBE IT'S BECAUSE THEY UNDERSTAND MY SENSE OF HUMOR...
BUT NOWADAYS... THERE IS A NEW BREED OF CHILD..
HERE!! CHEAP RATES
A CHILD WHO DOESN'T UNDERSTAND THAT A JOKE CAN BE TAKEN TOO FAR..
YANK!!
SHEEP LOVE
A CHILD WITH ABSOLUTELY NO SELF RESPECT...
!
NO COMMON DECENCY...
MARGARINE!! LEAVE THAT MAN ALONE THIS INSTANT!!
BOMB THE SUBURBS
NOWADAYS... STRANGERS SHOULDN'T TALK TO KIDS...
STOP

The kid yanking the snot out is one of my favorite drawings. True story!!

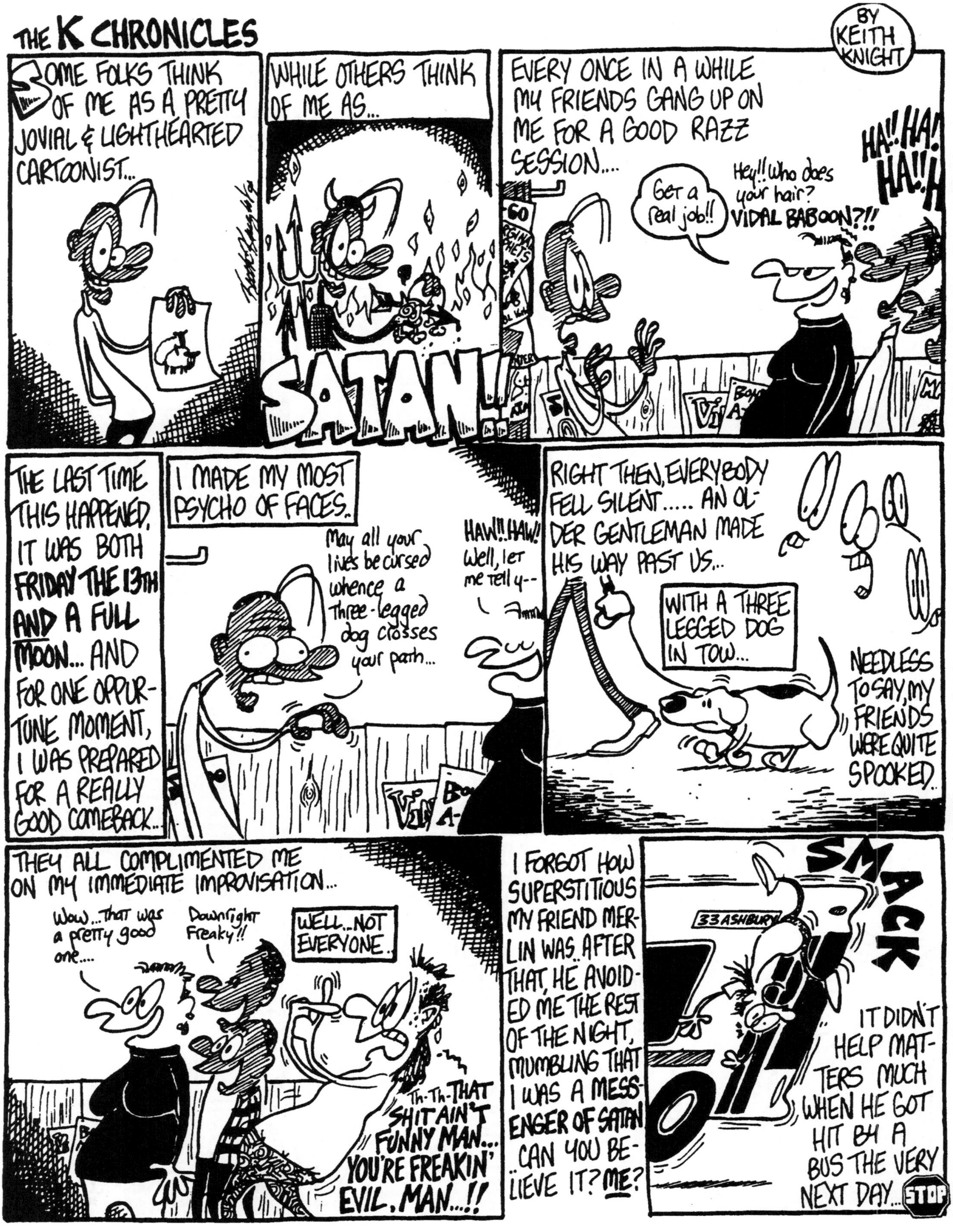
THE K CHRONICLES
BY KEITH KNIGHT
SOME FOLKS THINK OF ME AS A PRETTY JOVIAL & LIGHTHEARTED CARTOONIST...
WHILE OTHERS THINK OF ME AS...
SATAN!!..
EVERY ONCE IN A WHILE MY FRIENDS GANG UP ON ME FOR A GOOD RAZZ SESSION....
Get a real job!!
Hey!! Who does your hair? VIDAL BABOON?!!
HA!! HA!! HA!!
THE LAST TIME THIS HAPPENED, IT WAS BOTH FRIDAY THE 13TH AND A FULL MOON... AND FOR ONE OPPURTUNE MOMENT, I WAS PREPARED FOR A REALLY GOOD COMEBACK...
I MADE MY MOST PSYCHO OF FACES..
May all your lives be cursed whence a three-legged dog crosses your path...
HAW!! HAW! Well, let me tell y--
RIGHT THEN, EVERYBODY FELL SILENT...... AN OLDER GENTLEMAN MADE HIS WAY PAST US...
WITH A THREE LEGGED DOG IN TOW...
NEEDLESS TO SAY, MY FRIENDS WERE QUITE SPOOKED..
THEY ALL COMPLIMENTED ME ON MY IMMEDIATE IMPROVISATION...
Wow... That was a pretty good one....
Downright Freaky!!
WELL... NOT EVERYONE..
Th-Th-THAT SHIT AIN'T FUNNY MAN... YOU'RE FREAKIN' EVIL, MAN...!!
I FORGOT HOW SUPERSTITIOUS MY FRIEND MERLIN WAS.. AFTER THAT, HE AVOIDED ME THE REST OF THE NIGHT, MUMBLING THAT I WAS A MESSENGER OF SATAN. CAN YOU BELIEVE IT? ME?
SMACK
33 ASHBURY
IT DIDN'T HELP MATTERS MUCH WHEN HE GOT HIT BY A BUS THE VERY NEXT DAY...
STOP

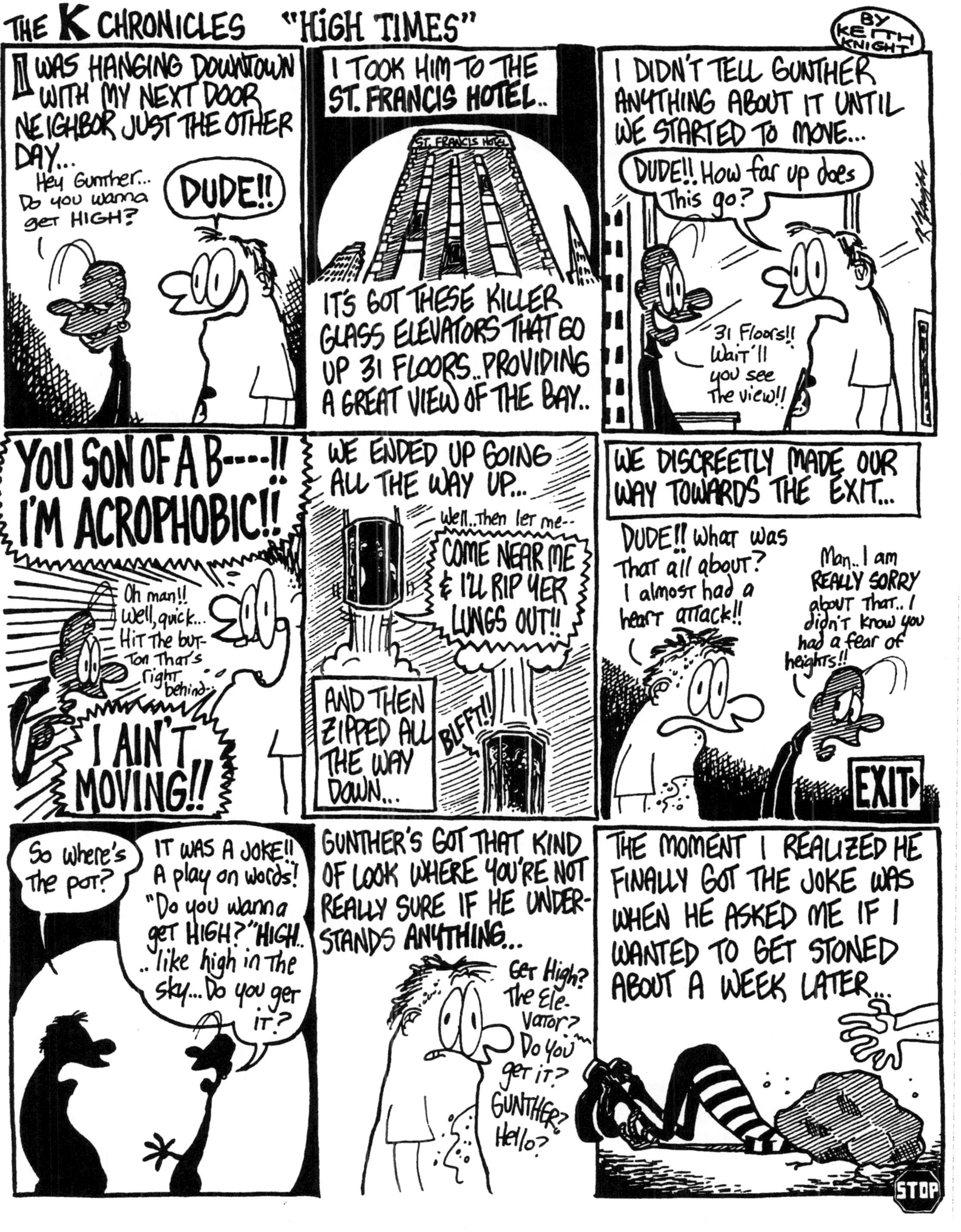

THE K CHRONICLES "HIGH TIMES"
BY KEITH KNIGHT
I WAS HANGING DOWNTOWN WITH MY NEXT DOOR NEIGHBOR JUST THE OTHER DAY...
Hey Gunther... Do you wanna get HIGH?
DUDE!!
I TOOK HIM TO THE ST. FRANCIS HOTEL..
ST. FRANCIS HOTEL
IT'S GOT THESE KILLER GLASS ELEVATORS THAT GO UP 31 FLOORS..PROVIDING A GREAT VIEW OF THE BAY..
I DIDN'T TELL GUNTHER ANYTHING ABOUT IT UNTIL WE STARTED TO MOVE...
DUDE!! How far up does This go?
31 Floors!! Wait'll you see The view!!
YOU SON OF A B----!! I'M ACROPHOBIC!!
Oh man!! Well, quick... Hit The button That's right behind--
I AIN'T MOVING!!
WE ENDED UP GOING ALL THE WAY UP...
Well..Then let me--
COME NEAR ME & I'LL RIP YER LUNGS OUT!!
AND THEN ZIPPED ALL THE WAY DOWN...
BLFFT!!
WE DISCREETLY MADE OUR WAY TOWARDS THE EXIT...
DUDE!! What was That all about? I almost had a heart attack!!
Man.. I am REALLY SORRY about that.. I didn't know you had a fear of heights!!
EXIT
So where's The pot?
IT WAS A JOKE!! A play on words! "Do you wanna get HIGH?" HIGH.. ..like high in The sky...Do you get it?
GUNTHER'S GOT THAT KIND OF LOOK WHERE YOU'RE NOT REALLY SURE IF HE UNDERSTANDS ANYTHING...
Get High? The Elevator? Do You get it? GUNTHER? Hello?
THE MOMENT I REALIZED HE FINALLY GOT THE JOKE WAS WHEN HE ASKED ME IF I WANTED TO GET STONED ABOUT A WEEK LATER...
STOP

This was the first strip to feature Gunther, who is based on a So-Cal stoner I met at the youth hostel I worked at. |

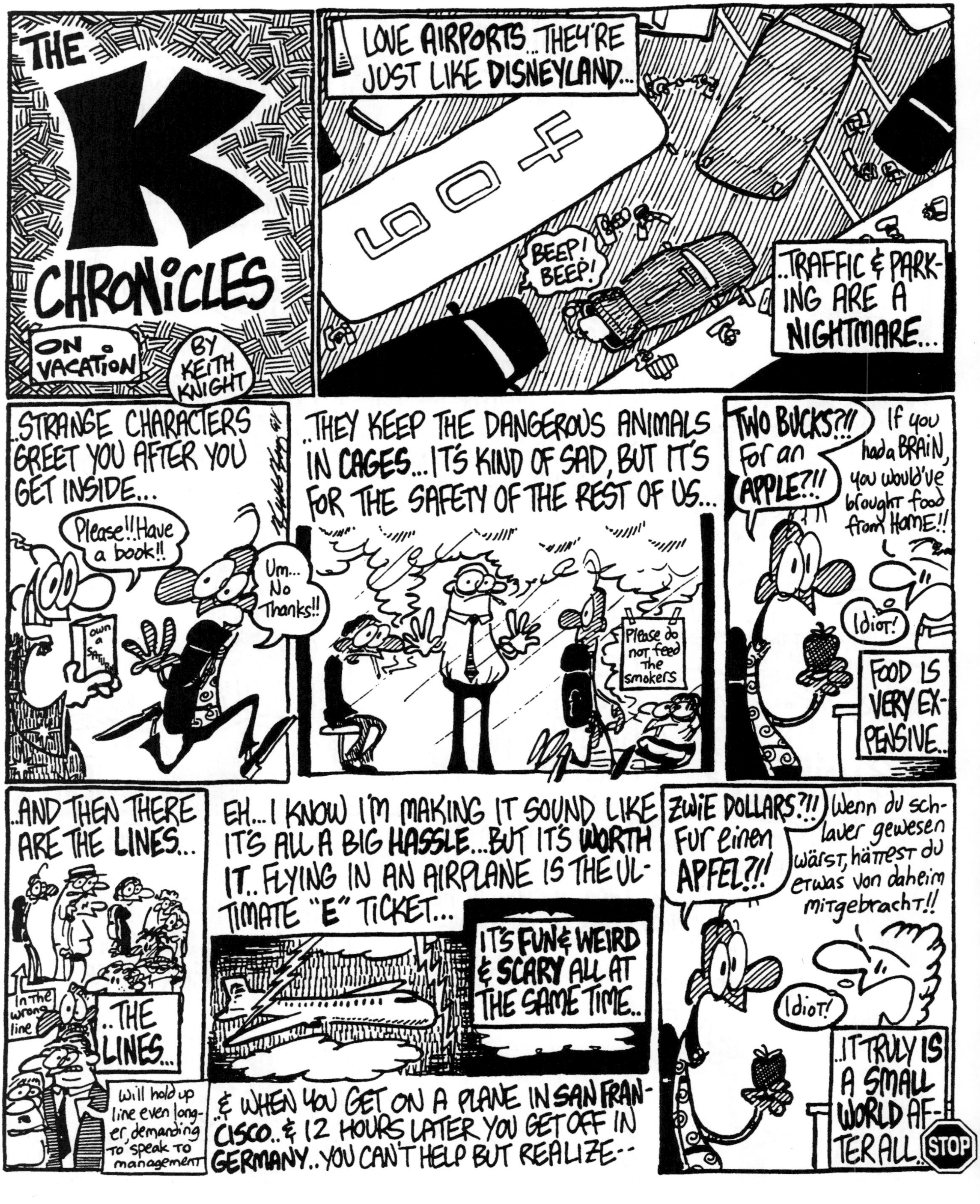
THE K CHRONICLES
ON VACATION
BY KEITH KNIGHT
I LOVE AIRPORTS... THEY'RE JUST LIKE DISNEYLAND...
BEEP! BEEP!
..TRAFFIC & PARKING ARE A NIGHTMARE...
..STRANGE CHARACTERS GREET YOU AFTER YOU GET INSIDE...
Please!! Have a book!!
Um... No Thanks!!
..THEY KEEP THE DANGEROUS ANIMALS IN CAGES... IT'S KIND OF SAD, BUT IT'S FOR THE SAFETY OF THE REST OF US...
Please do not feed the smokers
TWO BUCKS?!! For an APPLE?!!
If you had a BRAIN, you would've brought food from HOME!!
Idiot!
FOOD IS VERY EXPENSIVE..
..AND THEN THERE ARE THE LINES...
In the wrong line
..THE LINES...
Will hold up line even longer, demanding to speak to management
EH... I KNOW I'M MAKING IT SOUND LIKE IT'S ALL A BIG HASSLE...BUT IT'S WORTH IT.. FLYING IN AN AIRPLANE IS THE ULTIMATE "E" TICKET...
IT'S FUN & WEIRD & SCARY ALL AT THE SAME TIME..
..& WHEN YOU GET ON A PLANE IN SAN FRANCISCO.. & 12 HOURS LATER YOU GET OFF IN GERMANY.. YOU CAN'T HELP BUT REALIZE--
ZWIE DOLLARS?!! Fur einen APFEL?!!
Wenn du schlaver gewesen wärst, hättest du etwas von daheim mitgebracht!!
Idiot!
..IT TRULY IS A SMALL WORLD AFTER ALL.
STOP

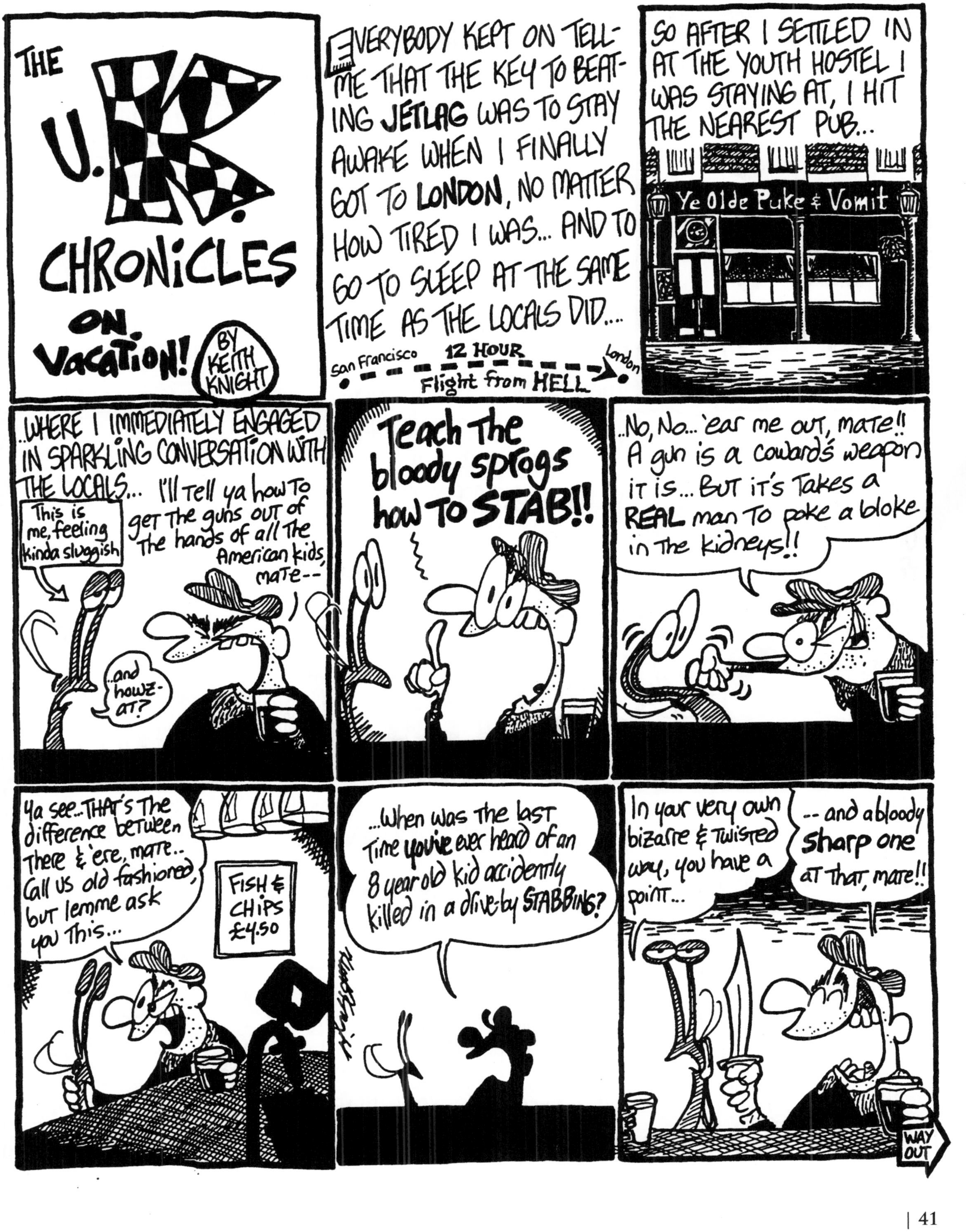
THE U.K. CHRONICLES ON VACATION!
BY KEITH KNIGHT
EVERYBODY KEPT ON TELL-ME THAT THE KEY TO BEAT-ING JETLAG WAS TO STAY AWAKE WHEN I FINALLY GOT TO LONDON, NO MATTER HOW TIRED I WAS... AND TO GO TO SLEEP AT THE SAME TIME AS THE LOCALS DID....
San Francisco 12 HOUR Flight from HELL London
SO AFTER I SETTLED IN AT THE YOUTH HOSTEL I WAS STAYING AT, I HIT THE NEAREST PUB...
Ye Olde Puke & Vomit
..WHERE I IMMEDIATELY ENGAGED IN SPARKLING CONVERSATION WITH THE LOCALS...
This is me, feeling kinda sluggish
I'll Tell ya how To get The guns out of The hands of all The American kids, mate--
..and howz-at?
Teach The bloody sprogs how To STAB!!
..No, No... 'ear me out, mate!! A gun is a coward's weapon it is... But it's Takes a REAL man To poke a bloke in The kidneys!!
Ya see...THAT's The difference between There & 'ere, mate.. Call us old fashioned, but lemme ask you This...
FISH & CHIPS £4.50
...When was The last Time you've ever heard of an 8 year old kid accidently killed in a drive-by STABBING?
In your very own bizarre & Twisted way, you have a point...
-- and a bloody sharp one at That, mate!!
WAY OUT

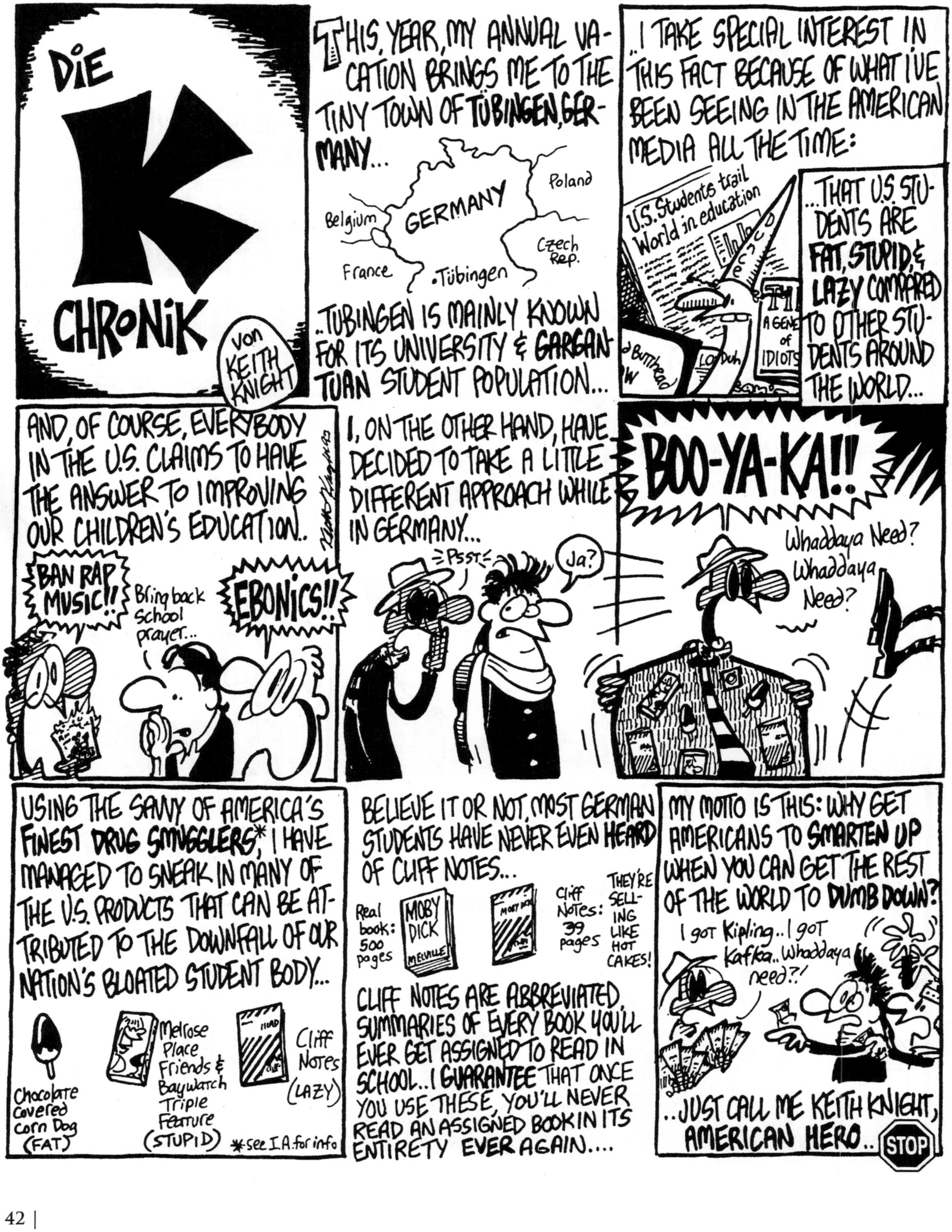

DIE K CHRONIK
von KEITH KNIGHT
THIS YEAR, MY ANNUAL VACATION BRINGS ME TO THE TINY TOWN OF TÜBINGEN, GERMANY...
GERMANY
Belgium
France
Poland
Czech Rep.
•Tübingen
..TUBINGEN IS MAINLY KNOWN FOR ITS UNIVERSITY & GARGANTUAN STUDENT POPULATION...
..I TAKE SPECIAL INTEREST IN THIS FACT BECAUSE OF WHAT I'VE BEEN SEEING IN THE AMERICAN MEDIA ALL THE TIME:
U.S. Students trail World in education
A GENE of IDIOTS
...THAT U.S. STUDENTS ARE FAT, STUPID, & LAZY COMPARED TO OTHER STUDENTS AROUND THE WORLD...
AND, OF COURSE, EVERYBODY IN THE U.S. CLAIMS TO HAVE THE ANSWER TO IMPROVING OUR CHILDREN'S EDUCATION..
BAN RAP MUSIC!!
Bring back school prayer...
EBONICS!!
I, ON THE OTHER HAND, HAVE DECIDED TO TAKE A LITTLE DIFFERENT APPROACH WHILE IN GERMANY...
PSST
Ja?
BOO-YA-KA!!
Whaddaya Need? Whaddaya Need?
USING THE SAVVY OF AMERICA'S FINEST DRUG SMUGGLERS*, I HAVE MANAGED TO SNEAK IN MANY OF THE U.S. PRODUCTS THAT CAN BE ATTRIBUTED TO THE DOWNFALL OF OUR NATION'S BLOATED STUDENT BODY...
Chocolate Covered Corn Dog (FAT)
Melrose Place Friends & Baywatch Triple Feature (STUPID)
Cliff Notes (LAZY)
*see I.A. for info
BELIEVE IT OR NOT, MOST GERMAN STUDENTS HAVE NEVER EVEN HEARD OF CLIFF NOTES...
Real book: 500 pages
MOBY DICK MELVILLE
Cliff Notes: 39 pages
THEY'RE SELLING LIKE HOT CAKES!
CLIFF NOTES ARE ABBREVIATED SUMMARIES OF EVERY BOOK YOU'LL EVER GET ASSIGNED TO READ IN SCHOOL...I GUARANTEE THAT ONCE YOU USE THESE, YOU'LL NEVER READ AN ASSIGNED BOOK IN ITS ENTIRETY EVER AGAIN....
MY MOTTO IS THIS: WHY GET AMERICANS TO SMARTEN UP WHEN YOU CAN GET THE REST OF THE WORLD TO DUMB DOWN?
I got Kipling..I got Kafka..Whaddaya need?!
..JUST CALL ME KEITH KNIGHT, AMERICAN HERO..
STOP

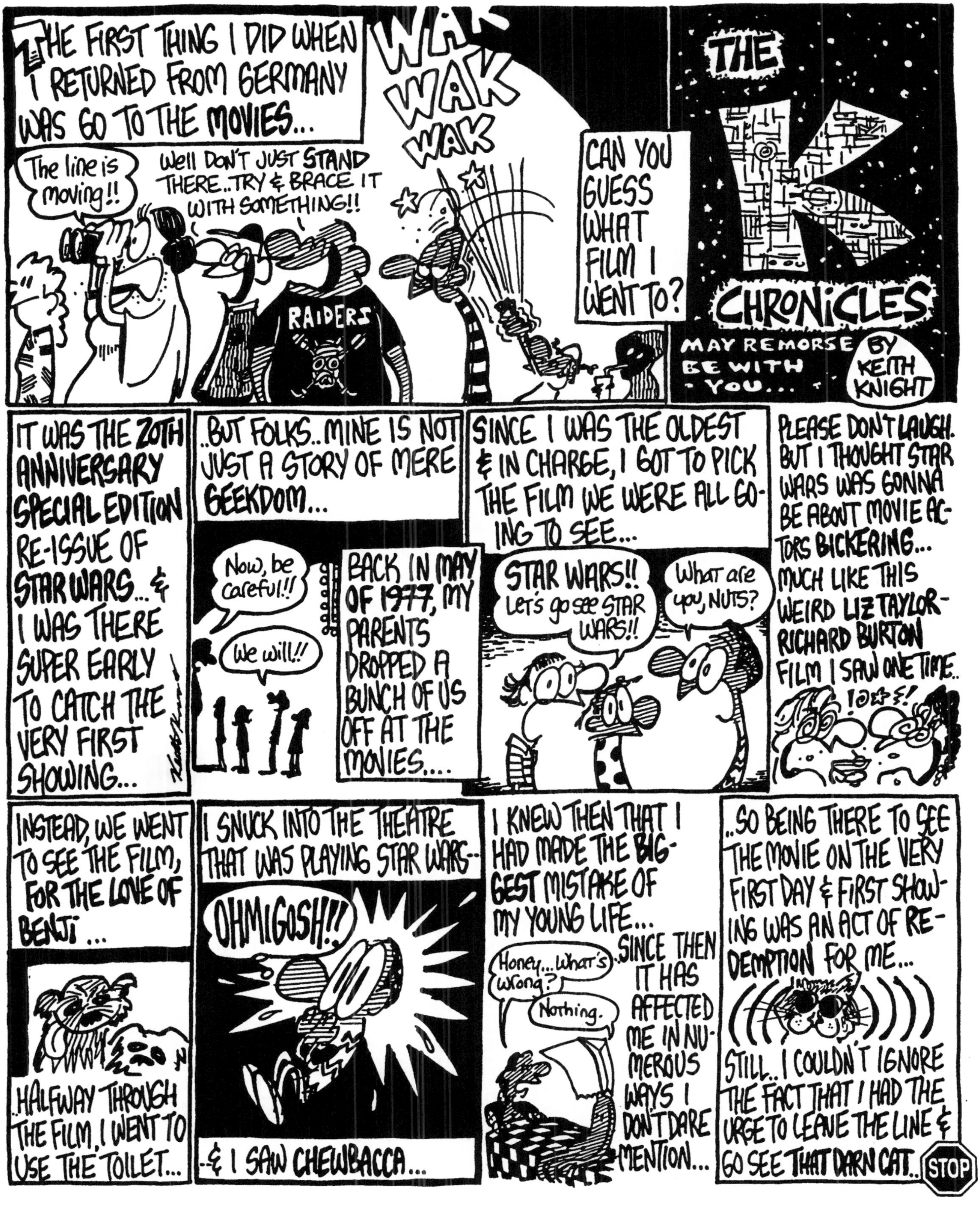
THE FIRST THING I DID WHEN I RETURNED FROM GERMANY WAS GO TO THE MOVIES...
The line is moving!!
WELL DON'T JUST STAND THERE.. TRY & BRACE IT WITH SOMETHING!!
RAIDERS
WAK WAK WAK
CAN YOU GUESS WHAT FILM I WENT TO?
THE K CHRONICLES
MAY REMORSE BE WITH YOU...
BY KEITH KNIGHT
IT WAS THE 20TH ANNIVERSARY SPECIAL EDITION RE-ISSUE OF STAR WARS... & I WAS THERE SUPER EARLY TO CATCH THE VERY FIRST SHOWING...
..BUT FOLKS.. MINE IS NOT JUST A STORY OF MERE GEEKDOM...
Now, be careful!!
We will!!
BACK IN MAY OF 1977, MY PARENTS DROPPED A BUNCH OF US OFF AT THE MOVIES....
SINCE I WAS THE OLDEST & IN CHARGE, I GOT TO PICK THE FILM WE WERE ALL GOING TO SEE...
STAR WARS!! Let's go see STAR WARS!!
What are you, NUTS?
PLEASE DON'T LAUGH. BUT I THOUGHT STAR WARS WAS GONNA BE ABOUT MOVIE ACTORS BICKERING... MUCH LIKE THIS WEIRD LIZ TAYLOR-RICHARD BURTON FILM I SAW ONE TIME..
INSTEAD, WE WENT TO SEE THE FILM, FOR THE LOVE OF BENJI...
..HALFWAY THROUGH THE FILM, I WENT TO USE THE TOILET...
I SNUCK INTO THE THEATRE THAT WAS PLAYING STAR WARS--
OHMIGOSH!!
-& I SAW CHEWBACCA...
I KNEW THEN THAT I HAD MADE THE BIGGEST MISTAKE OF MY YOUNG LIFE...
Honey... What's wrong?
Nothing.
..SINCE THEN IT HAS AFFECTED ME IN NUMEROUS WAYS I DON'T DARE MENTION...
..SO BEING THERE TO SEE THE MOVIE ON THE VERY FIRST DAY & FIRST SHOWING WAS AN ACT OF REDEMPTION FOR ME...
STILL.. I COULDN'T IGNORE THE FACT THAT I HAD THE URGE TO LEAVE THE LINE & GO SEE THAT DARN CAT..
STOP

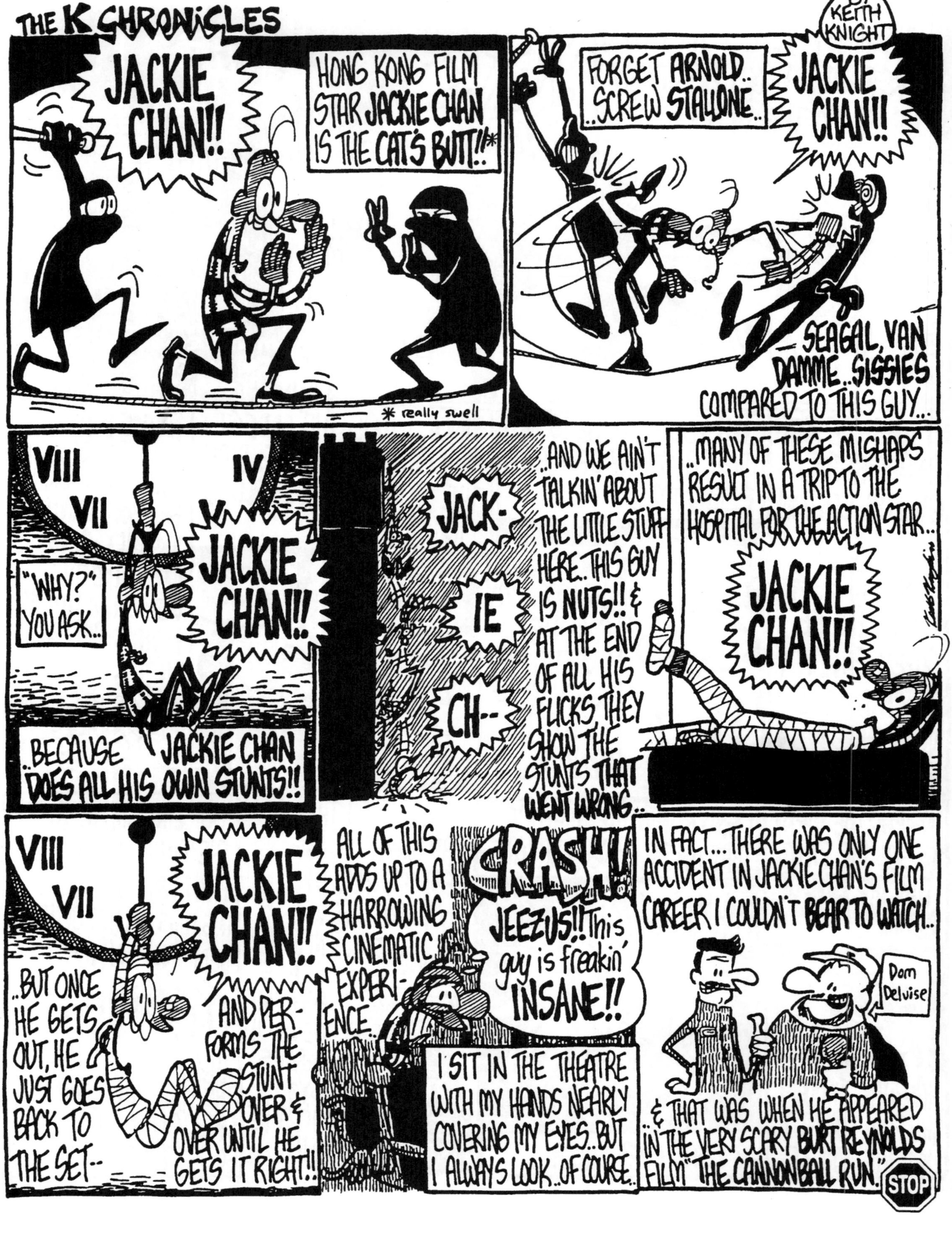
THE K CHRONICLES
BY KEITH KNIGHT
JACKIE CHAN!!
HONG KONG FILM STAR JACKIE CHAN IS THE CAT'S BUTT!!*
* really swell
FORGET ARNOLD.. ..SCREW STALLONE..
JACKIE CHAN!!
SEAGAL, VAN DAMME..SISSIES COMPARED TO THIS GUY..
VIII IV VII V
"WHY?" YOU ASK..
JACKIE CHAN!!
..BECAUSE JACKIE CHAN DOES ALL HIS OWN STUNTS!!
JACK-
IE
CH--
..AND WE AIN'T TALKIN' ABOUT THE LITTLE STUFF HERE..THIS GUY IS NUTS!! & AT THE END OF ALL HIS FLICKS THEY SHOW THE STUNTS THAT WENT WRONG..
..MANY OF THESE MISHAPS RESULT IN A TRIP TO THE HOSPITAL FOR THE ACTION STAR..
JACKIE CHAN!!
VIII VII
JACKIE CHAN!!..
..BUT ONCE HE GETS OUT, HE JUST GOES BACK TO THE SET--
AND PER-FORMS THE STUNT OVER & OVER UNTIL HE GETS IT RIGHT!!
ALL OF THIS ADDS UP TO A HARROWING CINEMATIC EXPERI-ENCE..
CRASH!
JEEZUS!! This guy is freakin' INSANE!!
I SIT IN THE THEATRE WITH MY HANDS NEARLY COVERING MY EYES..BUT I ALWAYS LOOK..OF COURSE..
IN FACT...THERE WAS ONLY ONE ACCIDENT IN JACKIE CHAN'S FILM CAREER I COULDN'T BEAR TO WATCH..
Dom Deluise
..& THAT WAS WHEN HE APPEARED IN THE VERY SCARY BURT REYNOLDS FILM "THE CANNONBALL RUN."
STOP

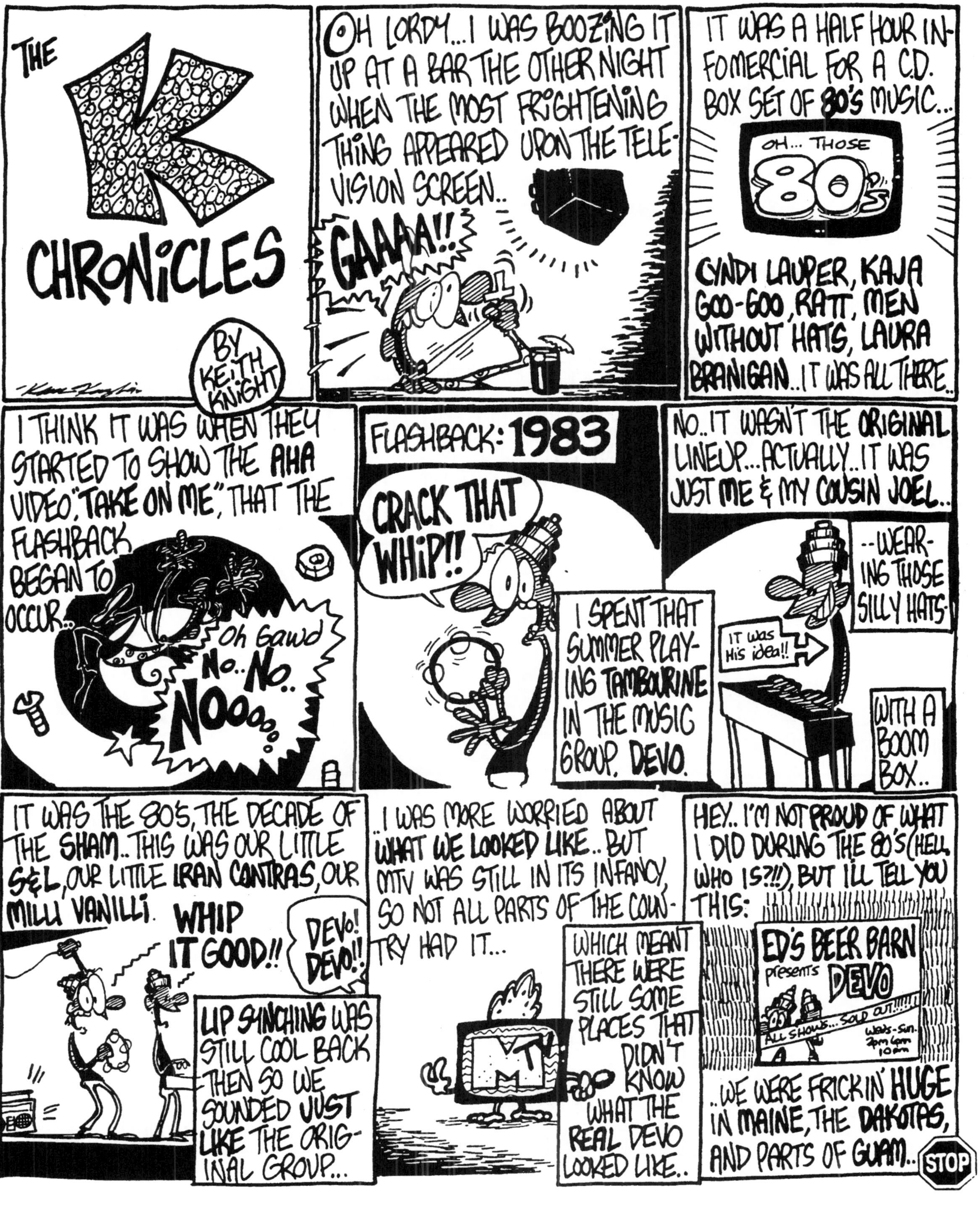

THE K CHRONICLES
BY KEITH KNIGHT
OH LORDY... I WAS BOOZING IT UP AT A BAR THE OTHER NIGHT WHEN THE MOST FRIGHTENING THING APPEARED UPON THE TELEVISION SCREEN..
GAAAA!!
IT WAS A HALF HOUR INFOMERCIAL FOR A C.D. BOX SET OF 80'S MUSIC...
OH... THOSE 80's
CYNDI LAUPER, KAJA GOO-GOO, RATT, MEN WITHOUT HATS, LAURA BRANIGAN.. IT WAS ALL THERE..
I THINK IT WAS WHEN THEY STARTED TO SHOW THE AHA VIDEO "TAKE ON ME", THAT THE FLASHBACK BEGAN TO OCCUR..
Oh Gawd
No.. No.. NOooooo
FLASHBACK: 1983
CRACK THAT WHIP!!
I SPENT THAT SUMMER PLAYING TAMBOURINE IN THE MUSIC GROUP, DEVO.
NO.. IT WASN'T THE ORIGINAL LINEUP... ACTUALLY.. IT WAS JUST ME & MY COUSIN JOEL..
--WEARING THOSE SILLY HATS-
IT was His idea!!
WITH A BOOM BOX..
IT WAS THE 80'S, THE DECADE OF THE SHAM.. THIS WAS OUR LITTLE S&L, OUR LITTLE IRAN CONTRAS, OUR MILLI VANILLI.
WHIP IT GOOD!!
DEVO! DEVO!!
LIP SYNCHING WAS STILL COOL BACK THEN SO WE SOUNDED JUST LIKE THE ORIGINAL GROUP...
..I WAS MORE WORRIED ABOUT WHAT WE LOOKED LIKE.. BUT MTV WAS STILL IN ITS INFANCY, SO NOT ALL PARTS OF THE COUNTRY HAD IT...
WHICH MEANT THERE WERE STILL SOME PLACES THAT DIDN'T KNOW WHAT THE REAL DEVO LOOKED LIKE..
HEY.. I'M NOT PROUD OF WHAT I DID DURING THE 80'S (HELL, WHO IS?!!), BUT I'LL TELL YOU THIS:
ED'S BEER BARN presents DEVO
ALL SHOWS... SOLD OUT!!!
..WE WERE FRICKIN' HUGE IN MAINE, THE DAKOTAS, AND PARTS OF GUAM..
STOP

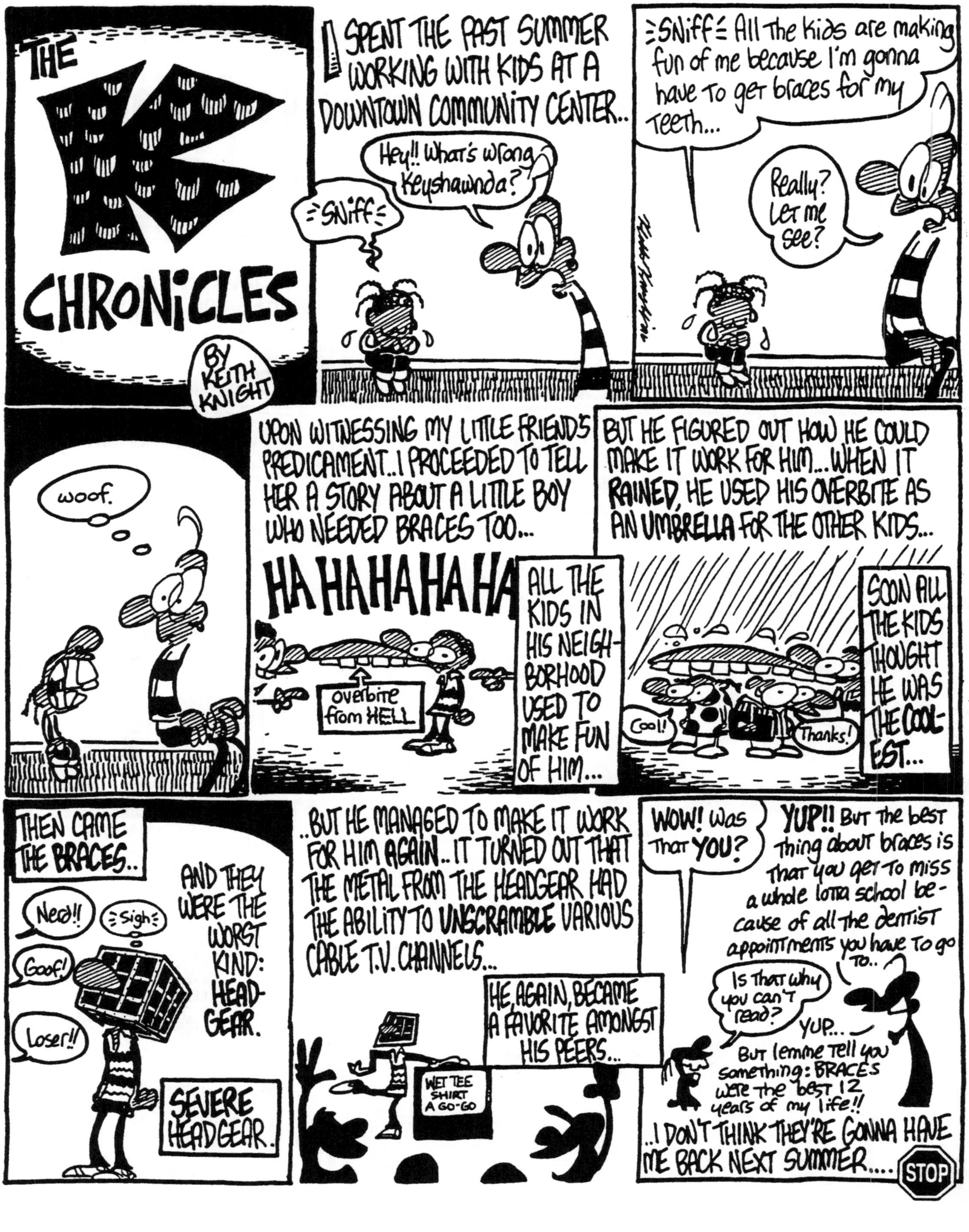
THE K CHRONICLES
BY KEITH KNIGHT
I SPENT THE PAST SUMMER WORKING WITH KIDS AT A DOWNTOWN COMMUNITY CENTER..
Hey!! What's wrong Keyshawnda?
SNIFF
SNIFF All the kids are making fun of me because I'm gonna have to get braces for my teeth...
Really? Let me see?
woof.
UPON WITNESSING MY LITTLE FRIEND'S PREDICAMENT..I PROCEEDED TO TELL HER A STORY ABOUT A LITTLE BOY WHO NEEDED BRACES TOO...
HA HA HA HA HA
ALL THE KIDS IN HIS NEIGHBORHOOD USED TO MAKE FUN OF HIM...
overbite from HELL
BUT HE FIGURED OUT HOW HE COULD MAKE IT WORK FOR HIM...WHEN IT RAINED, HE USED HIS OVERBITE AS AN UMBRELLA FOR THE OTHER KIDS...
Cool!
Thanks!
SOON ALL THE KIDS THOUGHT HE WAS THE COOLEST...
THEN CAME THE BRACES..
AND THEY WERE THE WORST KIND: HEADGEAR.
Nerd!!
Sigh
Goof!
Loser!!
SEVERE HEADGEAR.
..BUT HE MANAGED TO MAKE IT WORK FOR HIM AGAIN..IT TURNED OUT THAT THE METAL FROM THE HEADGEAR HAD THE ABILITY TO UNSCRAMBLE VARIOUS CABLE T.V. CHANNELS...
HE, AGAIN, BECAME A FAVORITE AMONGST HIS PEERS...
WET TEE SHIRT A GO-GO
WOW! Was That YOU?
YUP!! But the best thing about braces is that you get to miss a whole lotta school because of all the dentist appointments you have to go to..
Is that why you can't read?
YUP...
But lemme tell you something: BRACES were the best 12 years of my life!!
..I DON'T THINK THEY'RE GONNA HAVE ME BACK NEXT SUMMER....
STOP

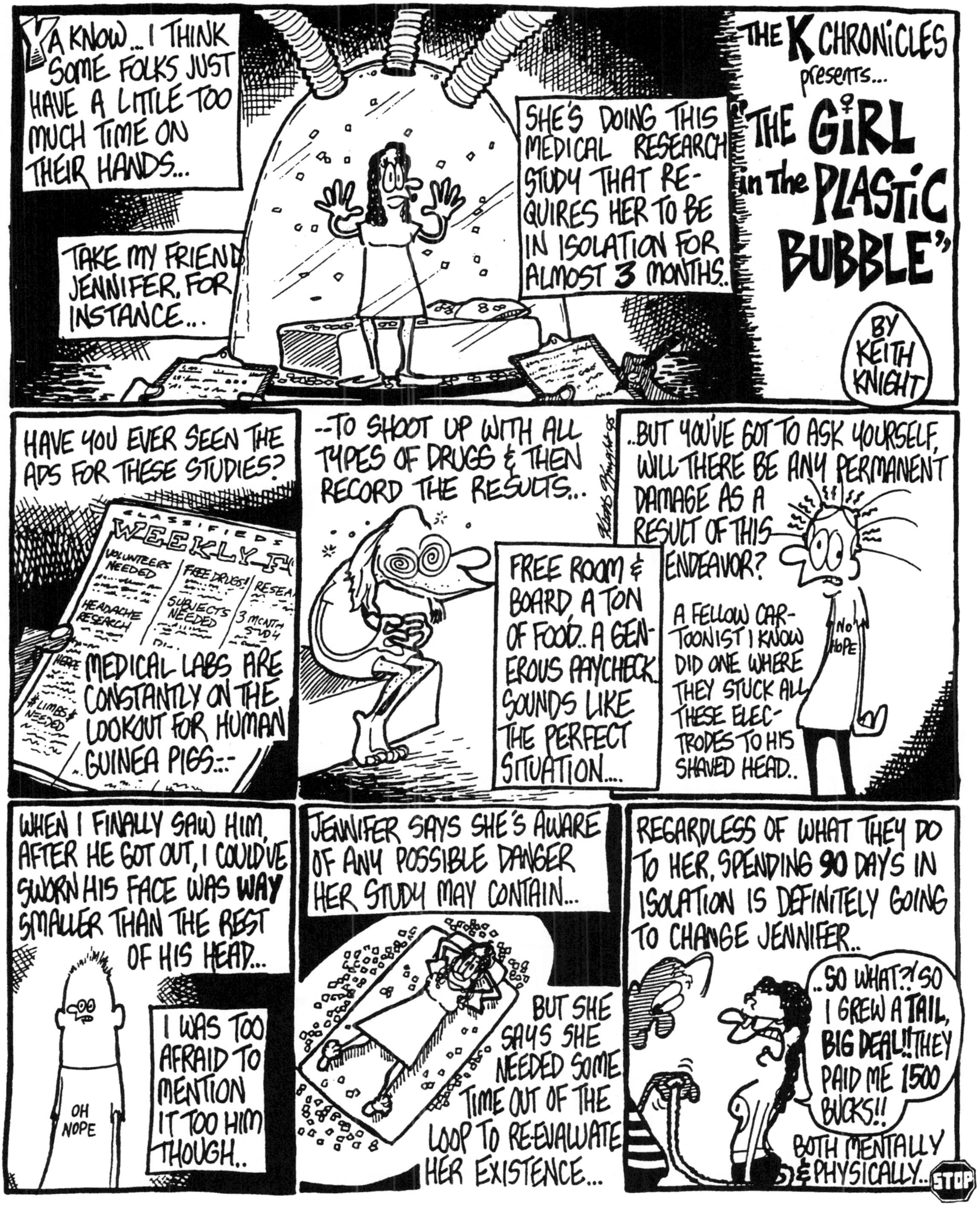

YA KNOW... I THINK SOME FOLKS JUST HAVE A LITTLE TOO MUCH TIME ON THEIR HANDS...
TAKE MY FRIEND JENNIFER, FOR INSTANCE...
SHE'S DOING THIS MEDICAL RESEARCH STUDY THAT REQUIRES HER TO BE IN ISOLATION FOR ALMOST 3 MONTHS..
THE K CHRONICLES presents...
"THE GIRL in the PLASTIC BUBBLE"
BY KEITH KNIGHT
HAVE YOU EVER SEEN THE ADS FOR THESE STUDIES?
CLASSIFIEDS
WEEKLY
VOLUNTEERS NEEDED
FREE DRUGS!
HEADACHE RESEARCH
SUBJECTS NEEDED
3 MONTH STUDY
#LIMBS NEEDED
MEDICAL LABS ARE CONSTANTLY ON THE LOOKOUT FOR HUMAN GUINEA PIGS..-
--TO SHOOT UP WITH ALL TYPES OF DRUGS & THEN RECORD THE RESULTS...
FREE ROOM & BOARD, A TON OF FOOD.. A GENEROUS PAYCHECK.. SOUNDS LIKE THE PERFECT SITUATION....
..BUT YOU'VE GOT TO ASK YOURSELF, WILL THERE BE ANY PERMANENT DAMAGE AS A RESULT OF THIS ENDEAVOR?
A FELLOW CARTOONIST I KNOW DID ONE WHERE THEY STUCK ALL THESE ELECTRODES TO HIS SHAVED HEAD..
NO HOPE
WHEN I FINALLY SAW HIM, AFTER HE GOT OUT, I COULD'VE SWORN HIS FACE WAS WAY SMALLER THAN THE REST OF HIS HEAD...
OH NOPE
I WAS TOO AFRAID TO MENTION IT TOO HIM THOUGH..
JENNIFER SAYS SHE'S AWARE OF ANY POSSIBLE DANGER HER STUDY MAY CONTAIN...
BUT SHE SAYS SHE NEEDED SOME TIME OUT OF THE LOOP TO RE-EVALUATE HER EXISTENCE...
REGARDLESS OF WHAT THEY DO TO HER, SPENDING 90 DAYS IN ISOLATION IS DEFINITELY GOING TO CHANGE JENNIFER..
..SO WHAT?! SO I GREW A TAIL, BIG DEAL!! THEY PAID ME 1500 BUCKS!!
BOTH MENTALLY & PHYSICALLY..
STOP

The fellow cartoonist is Jeff Levine, who put out No Hope *and* Destroy All Comics *during the zine wars of the early '90s.* |

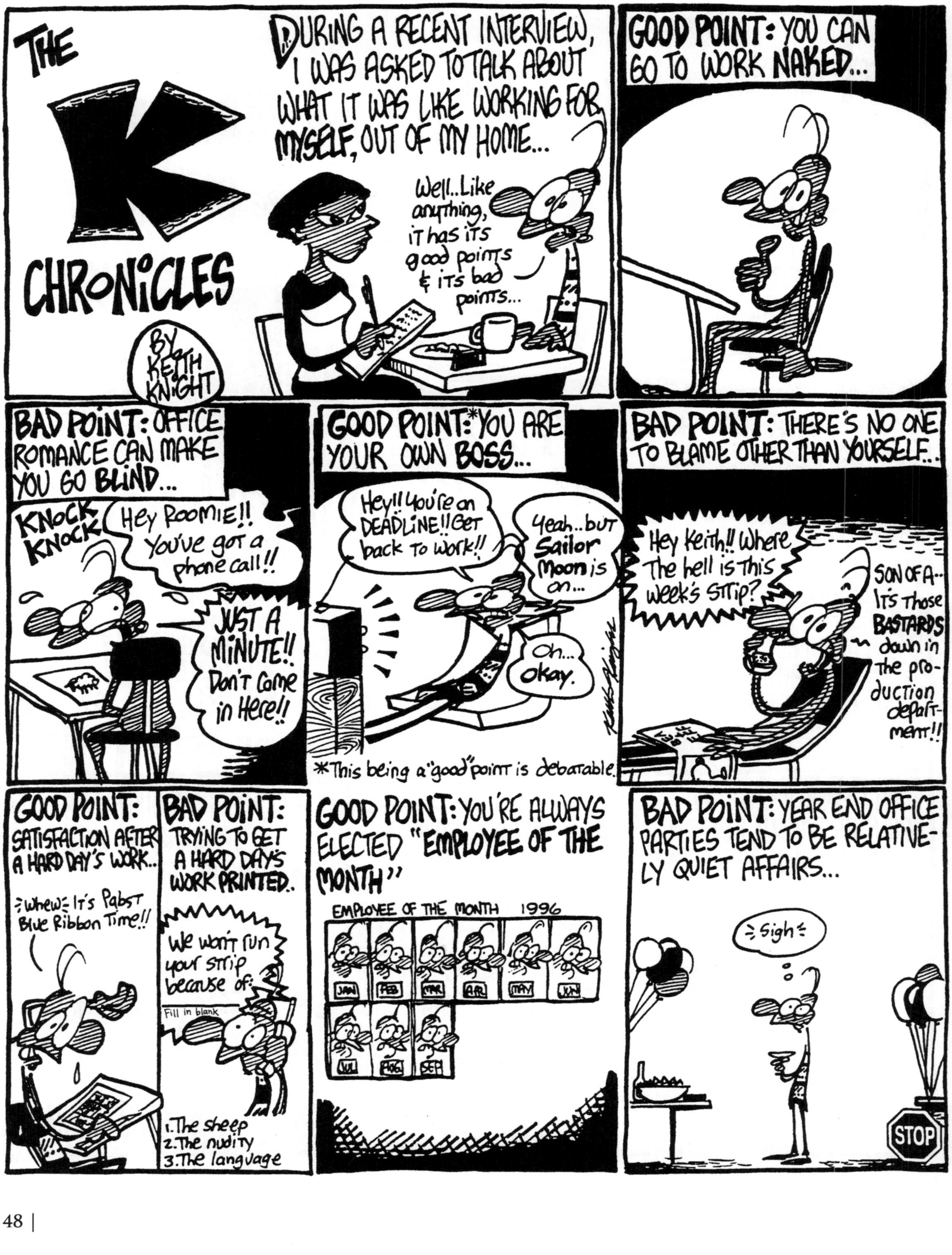
THE K CHRONICLES
BY KEITH KNIGHT
DURING A RECENT INTERVIEW, I WAS ASKED TO TALK ABOUT WHAT IT WAS LIKE WORKING FOR MYSELF, OUT OF MY HOME...
Well..Like anything, it has its good points & its bad points...
GOOD POINT: YOU CAN GO TO WORK NAKED...
BAD POINT: OFFICE ROMANCE CAN MAKE YOU GO BLIND...
KNOCK KNOCK
Hey Roomie!! You've got a phone call!!
JUST A MINUTE!! Don't come in Here!!
GOOD POINT:* YOU ARE YOUR OWN BOSS...
Hey!! You're on DEADLINE!! Get back to work!!
Yeah..but Sailor Moon is on...
Oh... okay.
*This being a "good" point is debatable.
BAD POINT: THERE'S NO ONE TO BLAME OTHER THAN YOURSELF...
Hey Keith!! Where the hell is this week's strip?
SON OF A-- It's those BASTARDS down in the production department!!
GOOD POINT: SATISFACTION AFTER A HARD DAY'S WORK...
Whew! It's Pabst Blue Ribbon Time!!
BAD POINT: TRYING TO GET A HARD DAY'S WORK PRINTED..
We won't run your strip because of:
Fill in blank
1. The sheep
2. The nudity
3. The language
GOOD POINT: YOU'RE ALWAYS ELECTED "EMPLOYEE OF THE MONTH"
EMPLOYEE OF THE MONTH 1996
JAN FEB MAR APR MAY JUN
JUL AUG SEP
BAD POINT: YEAR END OFFICE PARTIES TEND TO BE RELATIVELY QUIET AFFAIRS...
Sigh
STOP

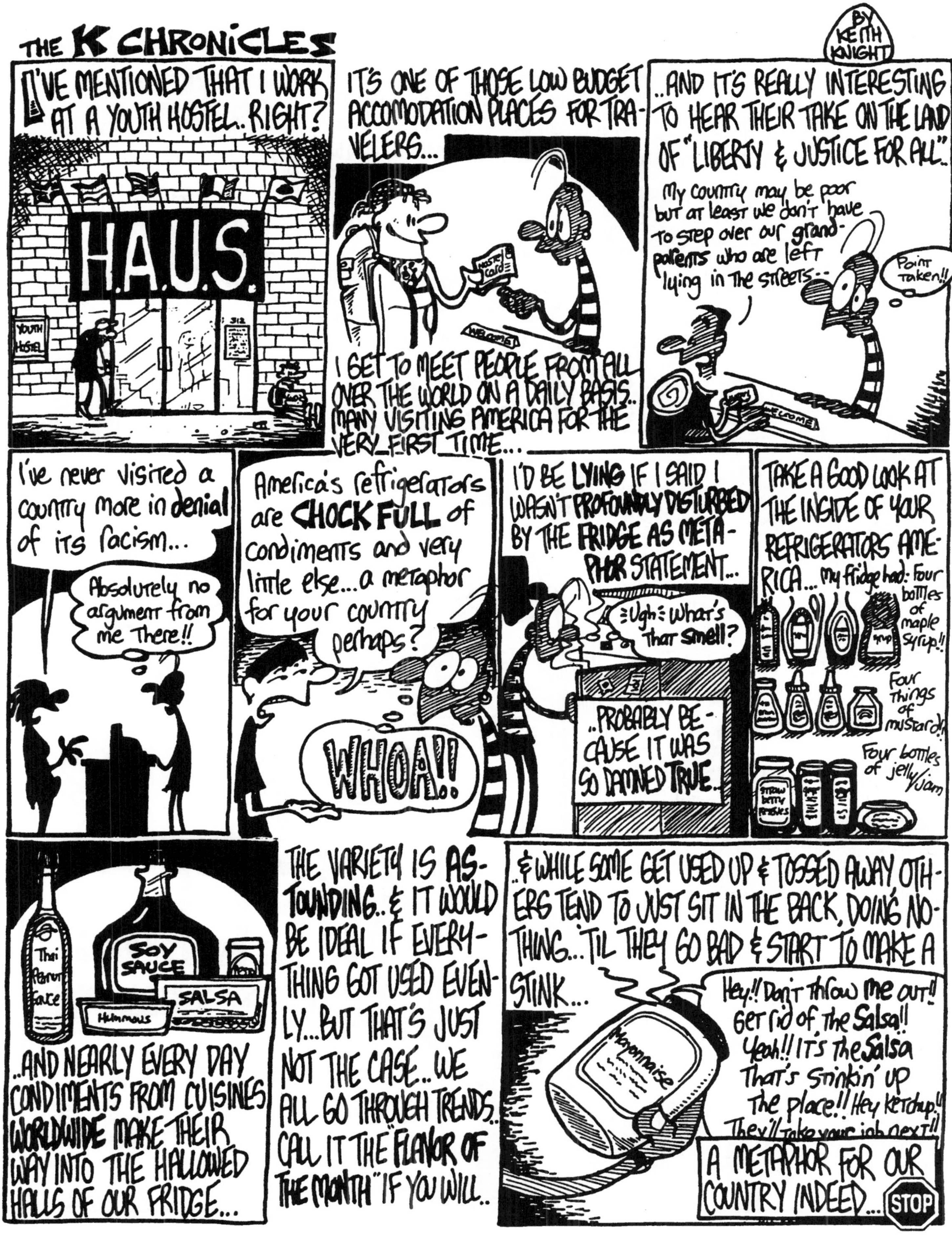
THE K CHRONICLES
BY KEITH KNIGHT
I'VE MENTIONED THAT I WORK AT A YOUTH HOSTEL.. RIGHT?
H.A.U.S.
YOUTH HOSTEL
IT'S ONE OF THOSE LOW BUDGET ACCOMODATION PLACES FOR TRAVELERS...
I GET TO MEET PEOPLE FROM ALL OVER THE WORLD ON A DAILY BASIS.. MANY VISITING AMERICA FOR THE VERY FIRST TIME...
..AND IT'S REALLY INTERESTING TO HEAR THEIR TAKE ON THE LAND OF "LIBERTY & JUSTICE FOR ALL"..
My country may be poor but at least we don't have to step over our grandparents who are left lying in the streets..
Point taken!!
I've never visited a country more in denial of its racism...
Absolutely no argument from me there!!
America's refrigerators are CHOCK FULL of condiments and very little else... a metaphor for your country perhaps?
WHOA!!
I'D BE LYING IF I SAID I WASN'T PROFOUNDLY DISTURBED BY THE FRIDGE AS METAPHOR STATEMENT...
Ugh! What's that smell?
..PROBABLY BECAUSE IT WAS SO DAMNED TRUE..
TAKE A GOOD LOOK AT THE INSIDE OF YOUR REFRIGERATORS AMERICA... My fridge had: Four bottles of maple syrup!!
Four things of mustard!!
Four bottles of jelly/jam
Thai Peanut Sauce
SOY SAUCE
SALSA
Hummous
..AND NEARLY EVERY DAY CONDIMENTS FROM CUISINES WORLDWIDE MAKE THEIR WAY INTO THE HALLOWED HALLS OF OUR FRIDGE...
THE VARIETY IS ASTOUNDING.. & IT WOULD BE IDEAL IF EVERYTHING GOT USED EVENLY...BUT THAT'S JUST NOT THE CASE.. WE ALL GO THROUGH TRENDS.. CALL IT THE "FLAVOR OF THE MONTH" IF YOU WILL..
..& WHILE SOME GET USED UP & TOSSED AWAY OTHERS TEND TO JUST SIT IN THE BACK, DOING NOTHING.. 'TIL THEY GO BAD & START TO MAKE A STINK...
Hey!! Don't throw me out!! Get rid of the Salsa!! Yeah!! It's the Salsa that's stinkin' up the place!! Hey ketchup!! They'll take your job next!!
Mayonnaise
A METAPHOR FOR OUR COUNTRY INDEED...
STOP

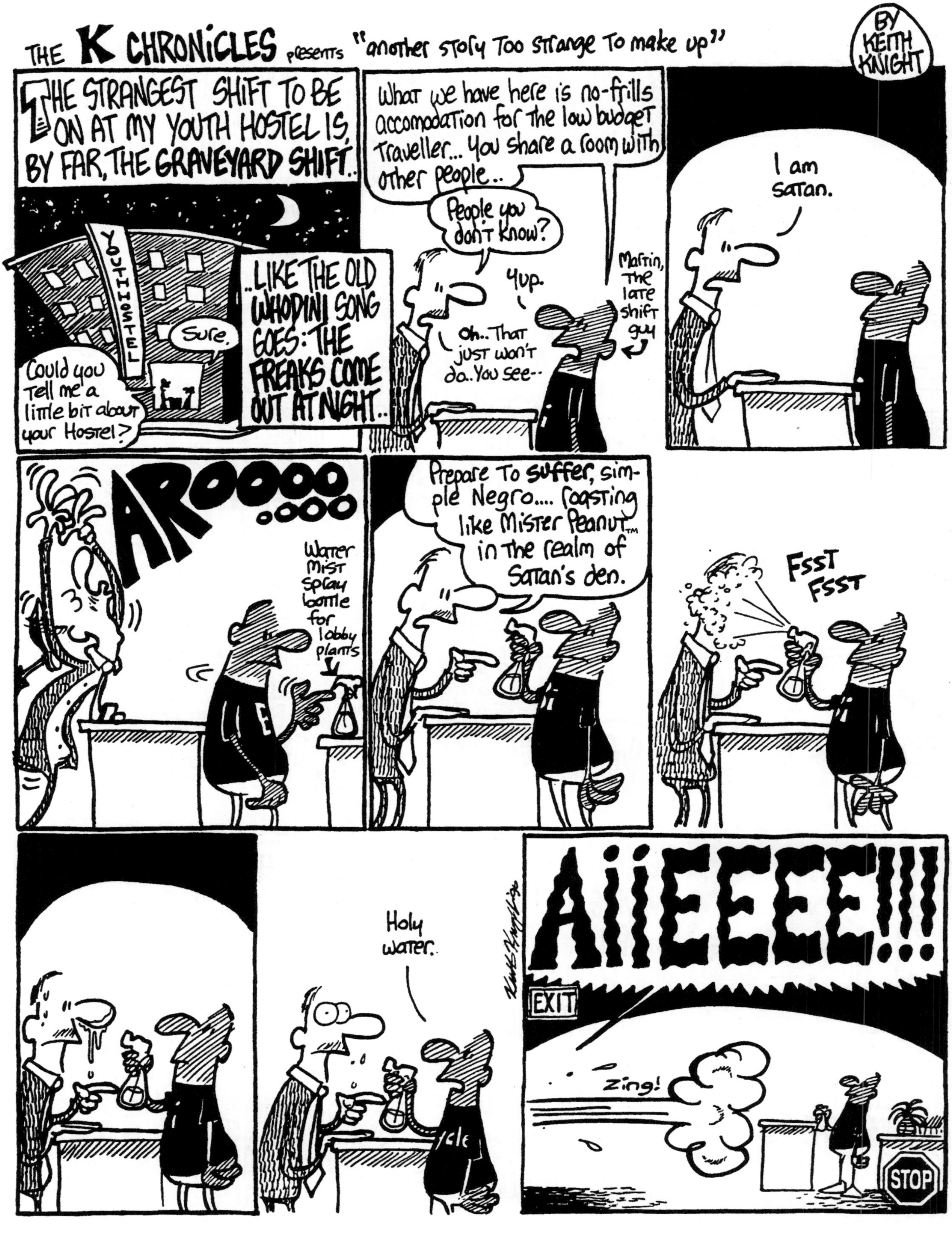
THE K CHRONICLES presents "another story too strange to make up"
BY KEITH KNIGHT
THE STRANGEST SHIFT TO BE ON AT MY YOUTH HOSTEL IS, BY FAR, THE GRAVEYARD SHIFT..
YOUTH HOSTEL
Could you tell me a little bit about your Hostel?
Sure.
..LIKE THE OLD WHODINI SONG GOES: THE FREAKS COME OUT AT NIGHT..
What we have here is no-frills accomodation for the low budget Traveller... You share a room with other people..
People you don't know?
Yup.
Oh.. That just won't do.. You see--
Martin, the late shift guy
I am Satan.
AROOOO.OOOO
Water mist spray bottle for lobby plants
Prepare to suffer, simple Negro.... roasting like Mister Peanut™ in the realm of Satan's den.
FSST FSST
Holy water.
AiiEEEE!!!
EXIT
Zing!
STOP

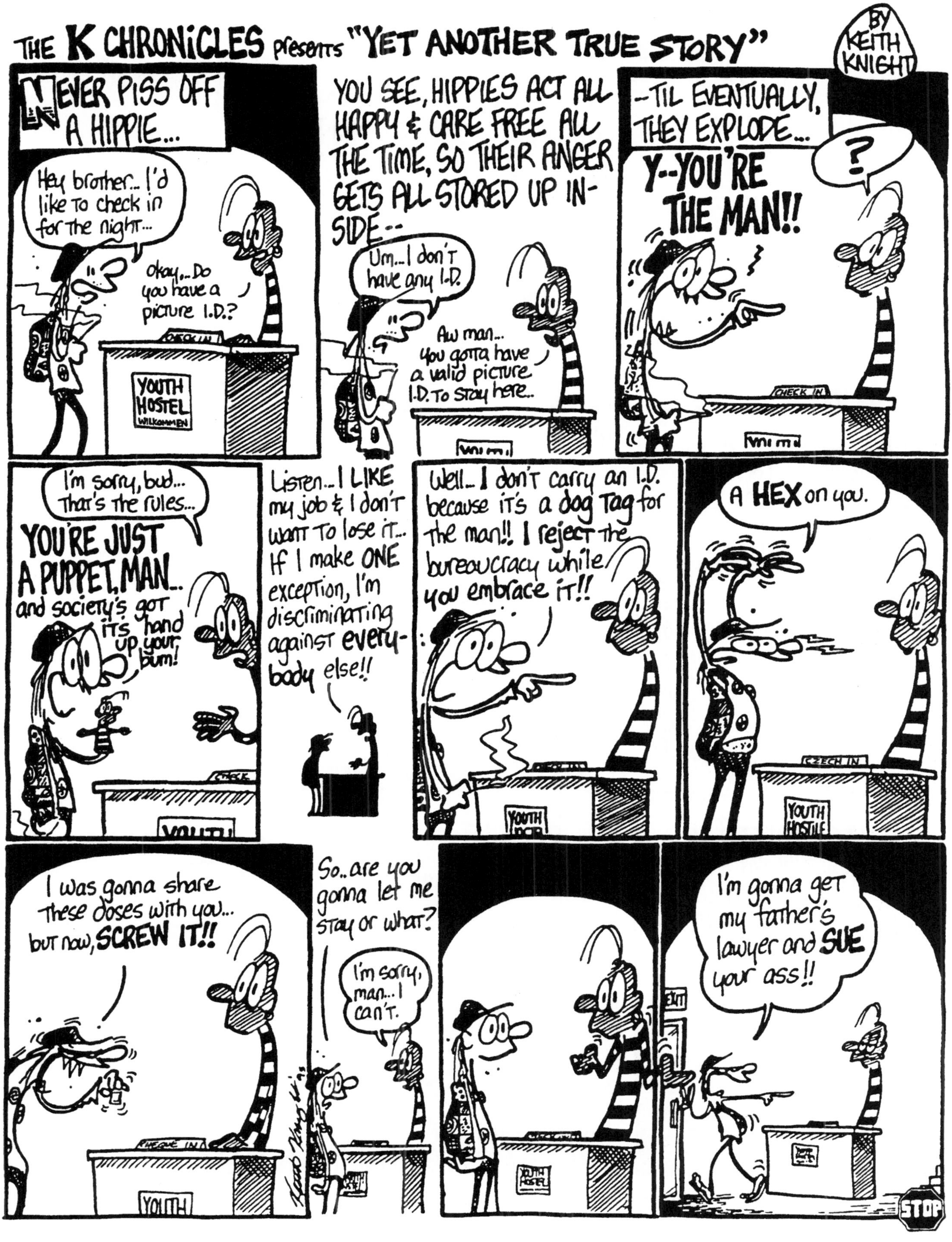

THE K CHRONICLES presents "YET ANOTHER TRUE STORY"
BY KEITH KNIGHT
NEVER PISS OFF A HIPPIE...
Hey brother... I'd like to check in for the night...
okay... Do you have a picture I.D.?
YOUTH HOSTEL WILKOMMEN
YOU SEE, HIPPIES ACT ALL HAPPY & CARE FREE ALL THE TIME, SO THEIR ANGER GETS ALL STORED UP IN-SIDE--
Um... I don't have any I.D.
Aw man... you gotta have a valid picture I.D. to stay here..
--TIL EVENTUALLY, THEY EXPLODE...
Y--YOU'RE THE MAN!!
?
CHECK IN
I'm sorry, bud... That's the rules...
YOU'RE JUST A PUPPET, MAN... and society's got its hand up your bum!
Listen... I LIKE my job & I don't want to lose it... If I make ONE exception, I'm discriminating against every-body else!!
Well... I don't carry an I.D. because it's a dog tag for the man!! I reject the bureaucracy while you embrace it!!
A HEX on you.
CZECH IN
YOUTH HOSTILE
I was gonna share these doses with you... but now, SCREW IT!!
CHEQUE IN
YOUTH
So.. are you gonna let me stay or what?
I'm sorry, man... I can't.
YOUTH HOSTEL
I'm gonna get my father's lawyer and SUE your ass!!
EXIT
STOP

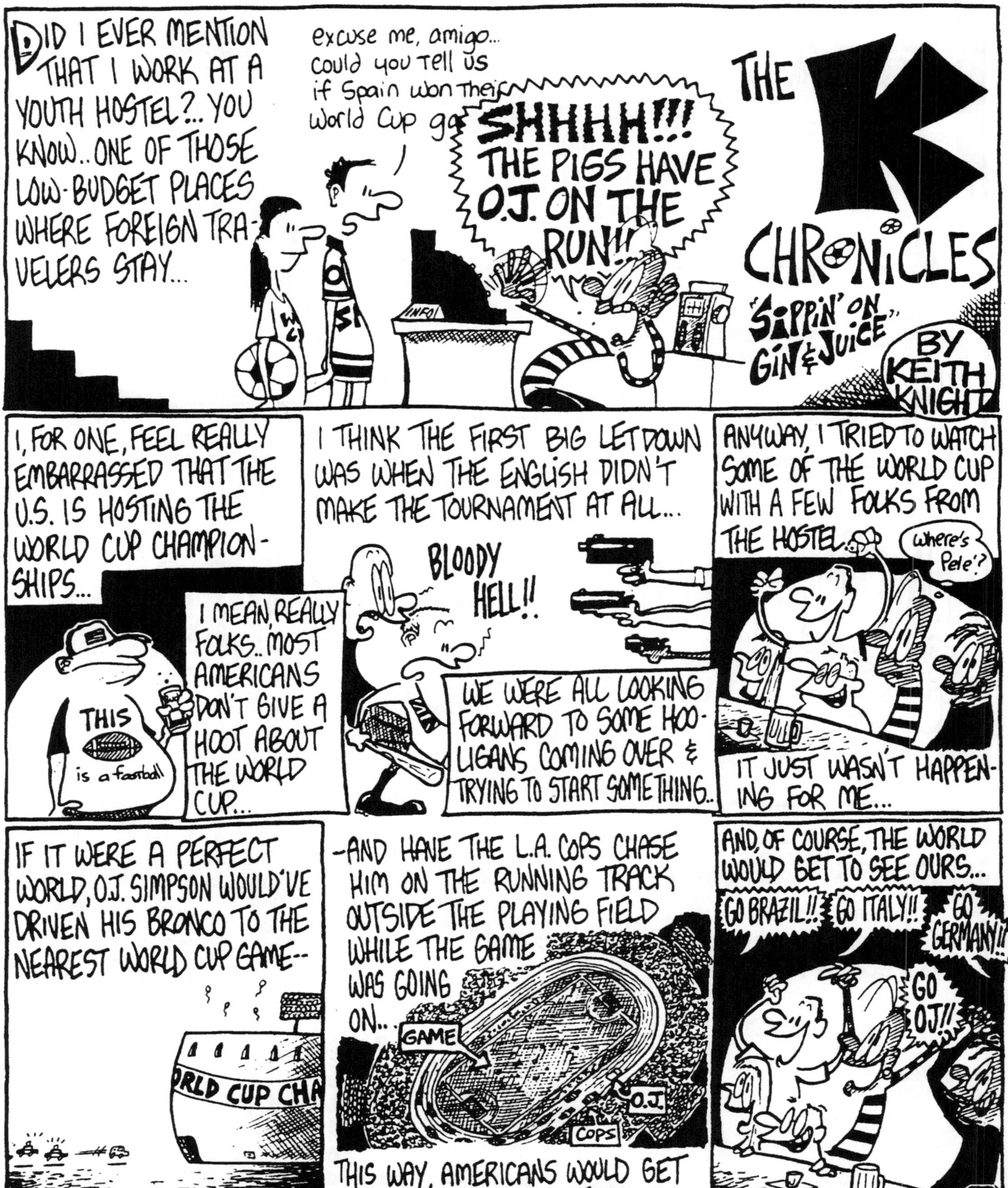
DID I EVER MENTION THAT I WORK AT A YOUTH HOSTEL?.. YOU KNOW.. ONE OF THOSE LOW-BUDGET PLACES WHERE FOREIGN TRAVELERS STAY...
excuse me, amigo... could you tell us if Spain won their World Cup ga
SHHHH!!! THE PIGS HAVE O.J. ON THE RUN!!
INFO
THE K CHRONICLES
"SIPPIN' ON GIN & JUICE"
BY KEITH KNIGHT
I, FOR ONE, FEEL REALLY EMBARRASSED THAT THE U.S. IS HOSTING THE WORLD CUP CHAMPIONSHIPS...
THIS is a football
I MEAN, REALLY FOLKS.. MOST AMERICANS DON'T GIVE A HOOT ABOUT THE WORLD CUP...
I THINK THE FIRST BIG LETDOWN WAS WHEN THE ENGLISH DIDN'T MAKE THE TOURNAMENT AT ALL...
BLOODY HELL!!
WE WERE ALL LOOKING FORWARD TO SOME HOOLIGANS COMING OVER & TRYING TO START SOMETHING..
ANYWAY, I TRIED TO WATCH SOME OF THE WORLD CUP WITH A FEW FOLKS FROM THE HOSTEL..
Where's Pele'?
IT JUST WASN'T HAPPENING FOR ME...
IF IT WERE A PERFECT WORLD, O.J. SIMPSON WOULD'VE DRIVEN HIS BRONCO TO THE NEAREST WORLD CUP GAME--
RLD CUP CHA
-AND HAVE THE L.A. COPS CHASE HIM ON THE RUNNING TRACK OUTSIDE THE PLAYING FIELD WHILE THE GAME WAS GOING ON..
GAME
O.J.
COPS
THIS WAY, AMERICANS WOULD GET TO SEE THE WORLD'S GREATEST PASSION..
AND, OF COURSE, THE WORLD WOULD GET TO SEE OURS...
GO BRAZIL!!
GO ITALY!!
GO GERMANY!!
GO OJ!!
STOP

 One of my favorite early strips.

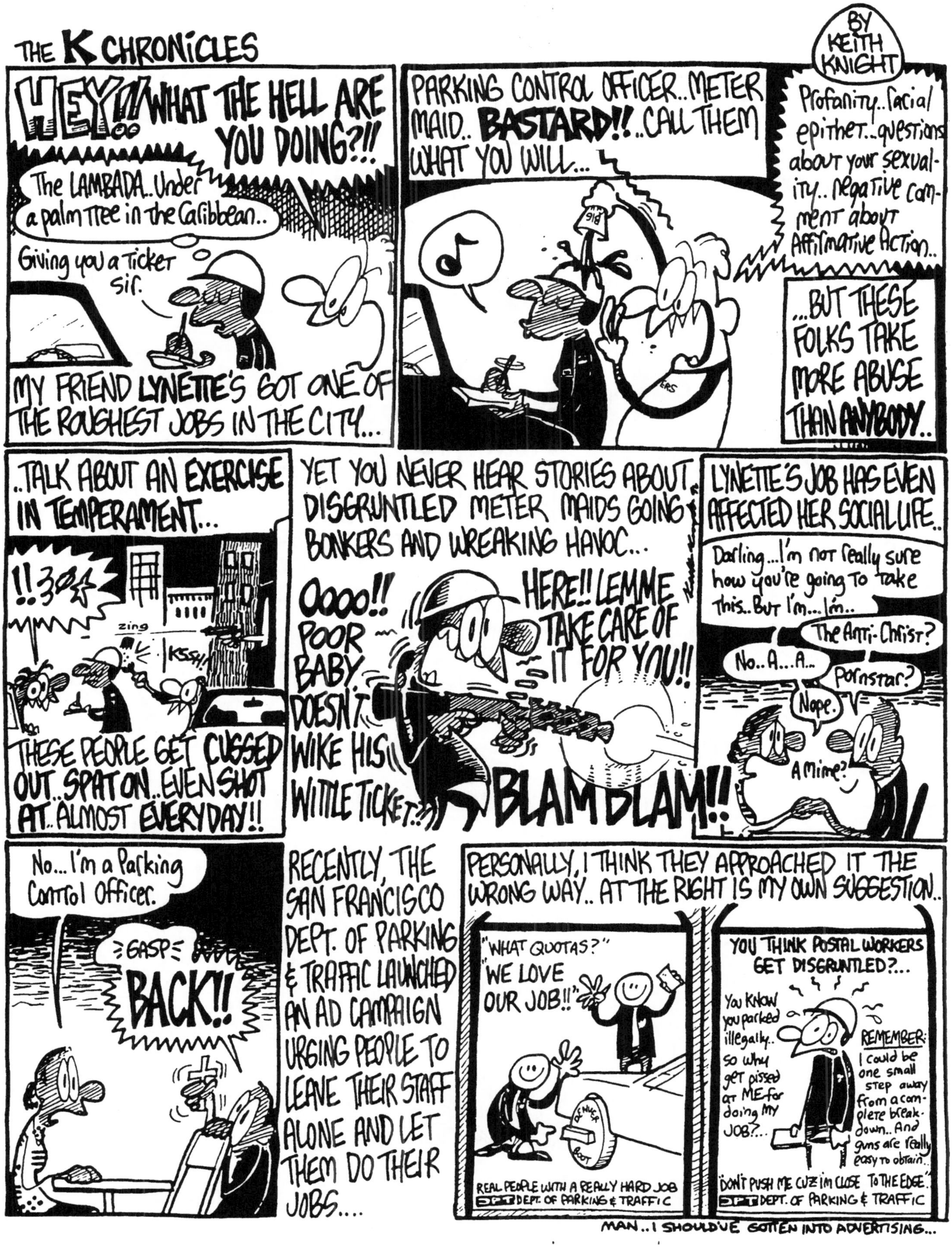
THE K CHRONICLES
BY KEITH KNIGHT
HEY!! WHAT THE HELL ARE YOU DOING?!!
The LAMBADA.. Under a palm tree in the Caribbean..
Giving you a Ticket sir.
MY FRIEND LYNETTE'S GOT ONE OF THE ROUGHEST JOBS IN THE CITY...
PARKING CONTROL OFFICER.. METER MAID.. BASTARD!!.. CALL THEM WHAT YOU WILL...
Profanity.. racial epithet... questions about your sexuality.. negative comment about Affirmative Action..
...BUT THESE FOLKS TAKE MORE ABUSE THAN ANYBODY..
..TALK ABOUT AN EXERCISE IN TEMPERAMENT...
zing
KSSH
THESE PEOPLE GET CUSSED OUT.. SPAT ON.. EVEN SHOT AT.. ALMOST EVERY DAY!!
YET YOU NEVER HEAR STORIES ABOUT DISGRUNTLED METER MAIDS GOING BONKERS AND WREAKING HAVOC...
OOOO!! POOR BABY DOESN'T WIKE HIS WITTLE TICKET?!
HERE!! LEMME TAKE CARE OF IT FOR YOU!!
BLAM BLAM!!
LYNETTE'S JOB HAS EVEN AFFECTED HER SOCIAL LIFE..
Darling... I'm not really sure how you're going to take this.. But I'm... I'm...
The Anti-Christ?
No.. A... A..
Pornstar?
Nope.
A Mime?
No... I'm a Parking Control Officer.
GASP
BACK!!
RECENTLY, THE SAN FRANCISCO DEPT. OF PARKING & TRAFFIC LAUNCHED AN AD CAMPAIGN URGING PEOPLE TO LEAVE THEIR STAFF ALONE AND LET THEM DO THEIR JOBS....
PERSONALLY, I THINK THEY APPROACHED IT THE WRONG WAY.. AT THE RIGHT IS MY OWN SUGGESTION..
"WHAT QUOTAS?"
"WE LOVE OUR JOB!!"
BOOT
REAL PEOPLE WITH A REALLY HARD JOB
DPT DEPT. OF PARKING & TRAFFIC
YOU THINK POSTAL WORKERS GET DISGRUNTLED?...
You KNOW you parked illegally.. so why get pissed at ME for doing MY JOB?...
REMEMBER: I could be one small step away from a complete breakdown.. And guns are really easy to obtain.
"DON'T PUSH ME CUZ I'M CLOSE TO THE EDGE."
DPT DEPT. OF PARKING & TRAFFIC
MAN.. I SHOULD'VE GOTTEN INTO ADVERTISING...

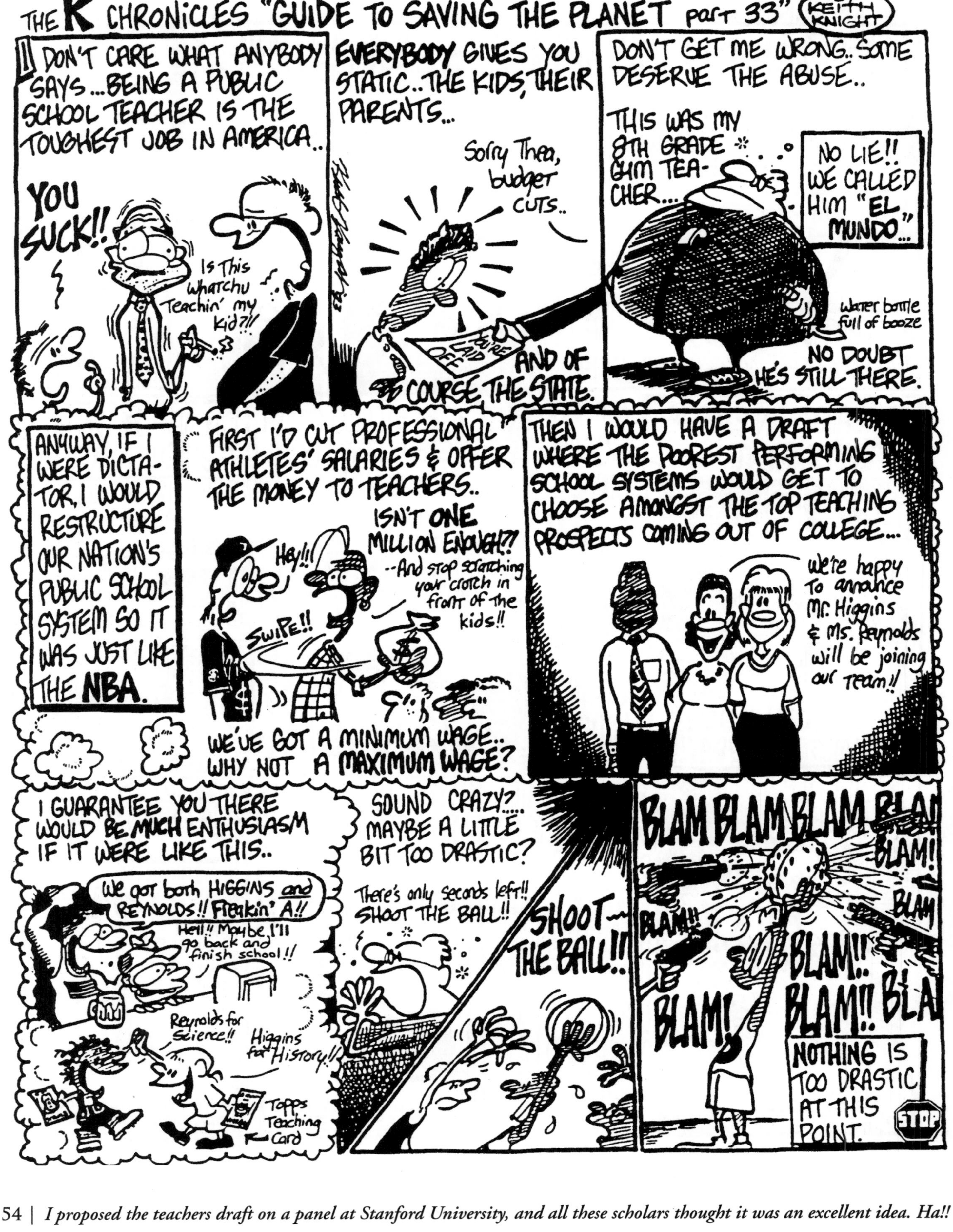
THE K CHRONICLES "GUIDE TO SAVING THE PLANET part 33"
BY KEITH KNIGHT
I DON'T CARE WHAT ANYBODY SAYS...BEING A PUBLIC SCHOOL TEACHER IS THE TOUGHEST JOB IN AMERICA..
YOU SUCK!!
Is This whatchu Teachin' my kid?!!
EVERYBODY GIVES YOU STATIC..THE KIDS, THEIR PARENTS...
Sorry Thea, budget cuts..
YOU'RE LAID OFF
AND OF COURSE THE STATE.
DON'T GET ME WRONG..SOME DESERVE THE ABUSE..
THIS WAS MY 8TH GRADE GYM TEACHER....
NO LIE!! WE CALLED HIM "EL MUNDO"...
Water bottle full of booze
NO DOUBT HE'S STILL THERE.
ANYWAY, IF I WERE DICTATOR, I WOULD RESTRUCTURE OUR NATION'S PUBLIC SCHOOL SYSTEM SO IT WAS JUST LIKE THE NBA.
FIRST I'D CUT PROFESSIONAL ATHLETES' SALARIES & OFFER THE MONEY TO TEACHERS..
Hey!!
ISN'T ONE MILLION ENOUGH??
--And stop scratching your crotch in front of the kids!!
SWIPE!!
WE'VE GOT A MINIMUM WAGE.. WHY NOT A MAXIMUM WAGE?
THEN I WOULD HAVE A DRAFT WHERE THE POOREST PERFORMING SCHOOL SYSTEMS WOULD GET TO CHOOSE AMONGST THE TOP TEACHING PROSPECTS COMING OUT OF COLLEGE...
We're happy to announce Mr. Higgins & Ms. Reynolds will be joining our Team!!
I GUARANTEE YOU THERE WOULD BE MUCH ENTHUSIASM IF IT WERE LIKE THIS..
We got both HIGGINS and REYNOLDS!! Freakin' A!!
Hell!! Maybe I'll go back and finish school!!
Reynolds for Science!!
Higgins for History!!
Topps Teaching Card
SOUND CRAZY?.... MAYBE A LITTLE BIT TOO DRASTIC?
There's only seconds left!! SHOOT THE BALL!!
SHOOT THE BALL!!
BLAM BLAM BLAM BLAM
BLAM!
BLAM!!
BLAM
BLAM!!
BLAM!! BLAM!! BLA
BLAM!
NOTHING IS TOO DRASTIC AT THIS POINT.
STOP

 I proposed the teachers draft on a panel at Stanford University, and all these scholars thought it was an excellent idea. Ha!!

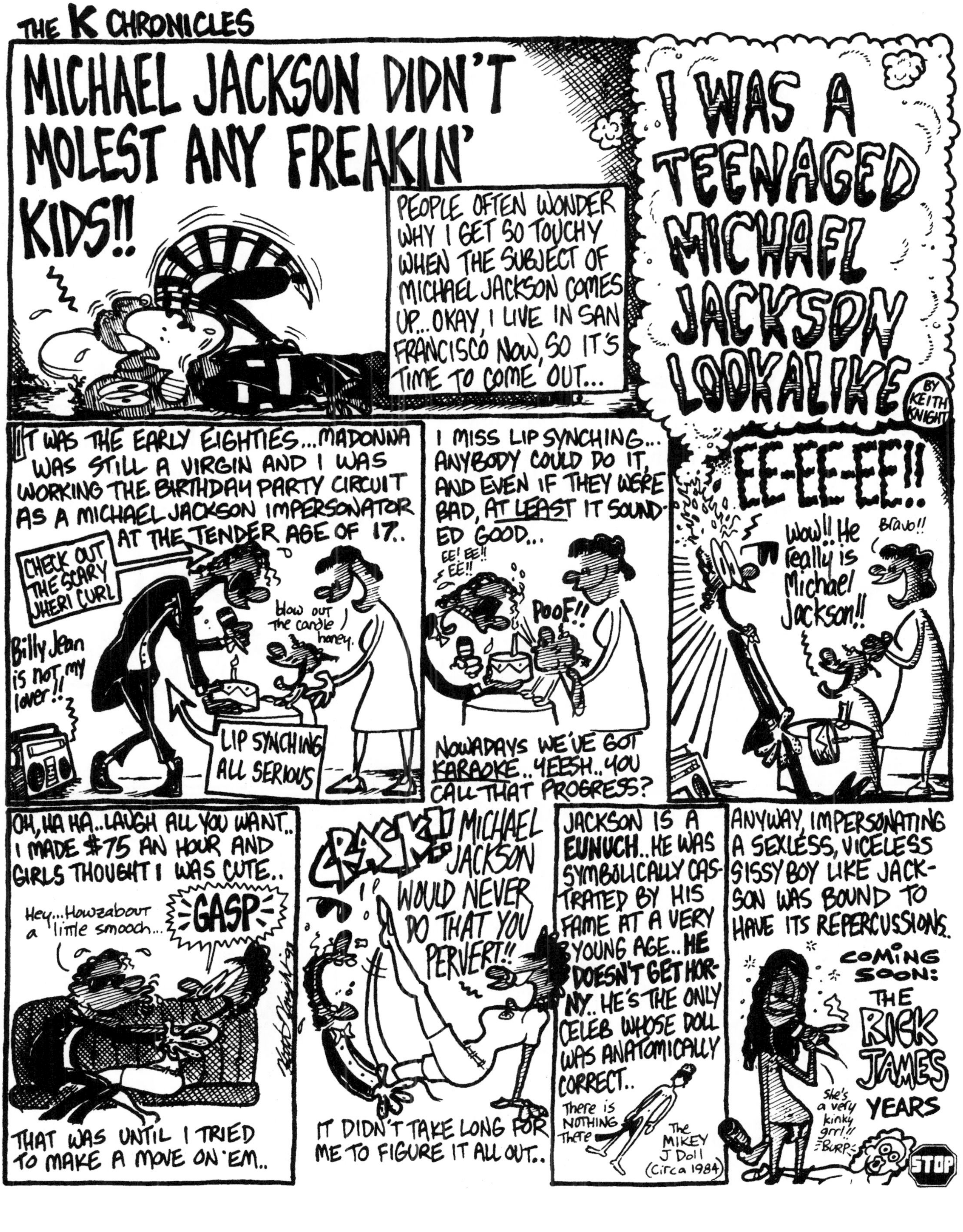
THE K CHRONICLES
MICHAEL JACKSON DIDN'T MOLEST ANY FREAKIN' KIDS!!
PEOPLE OFTEN WONDER WHY I GET SO TOUCHY WHEN THE SUBJECT OF MICHAEL JACKSON COMES UP... OKAY, I LIVE IN SAN FRANCISCO NOW, SO IT'S TIME TO COME OUT...
I WAS A TEENAGED MICHAEL JACKSON LOOKALIKE
BY KEITH KNIGHT
IT WAS THE EARLY EIGHTIES... MADONNA WAS STILL A VIRGIN AND I WAS WORKING THE BIRTHDAY PARTY CIRCUIT AS A MICHAEL JACKSON IMPERSONATOR AT THE TENDER AGE OF 17..
CHECK OUT THE SCARY JHERI CURL
Billy Jean is not my lover!!
blow out the candle honey.
LIP SYNCHING ALL SERIOUS
I MISS LIP SYNCHING... ANYBODY COULD DO IT, AND EVEN IF THEY WERE BAD, AT LEAST IT SOUNDED GOOD...
EE! EE!! EE!!
POOF!!
NOWADAYS WE'VE GOT KARAOKE.. YEESH.. YOU CALL THAT PROGRESS?
EE-EE-EE!!
Wow!! He really is Michael Jackson!!
Bravo!!
OH, HA HA.. LAUGH ALL YOU WANT.. I MADE $75 AN HOUR AND GIRLS THOUGHT I WAS CUTE..
Hey... Howzabout a little smooch...
GASP
THAT WAS UNTIL I TRIED TO MAKE A MOVE ON 'EM..
CRACK!
MICHAEL JACKSON WOULD NEVER DO THAT YOU PERVERT!!
IT DIDN'T TAKE LONG FOR ME TO FIGURE IT ALL OUT..
JACKSON IS A EUNUCH.. HE WAS SYMBOLICALLY CASTRATED BY HIS FAME AT A VERY YOUNG AGE.. HE DOESN'T GET HORNY.. HE'S THE ONLY CELEB WHOSE DOLL WAS ANATOMICALLY CORRECT..
There is NOTHING there
The MIKEY J Doll (Circa 1984)
ANYWAY, IMPERSONATING A SEXLESS, VICELESS SISSY BOY LIKE JACKSON WAS BOUND TO HAVE ITS REPERCUSSIONS.
COMING SOON: THE RICK JAMES YEARS
She's a very kinky grrl!!
BURP
STOP

I'm working on developing this strip into a graphic novel. |

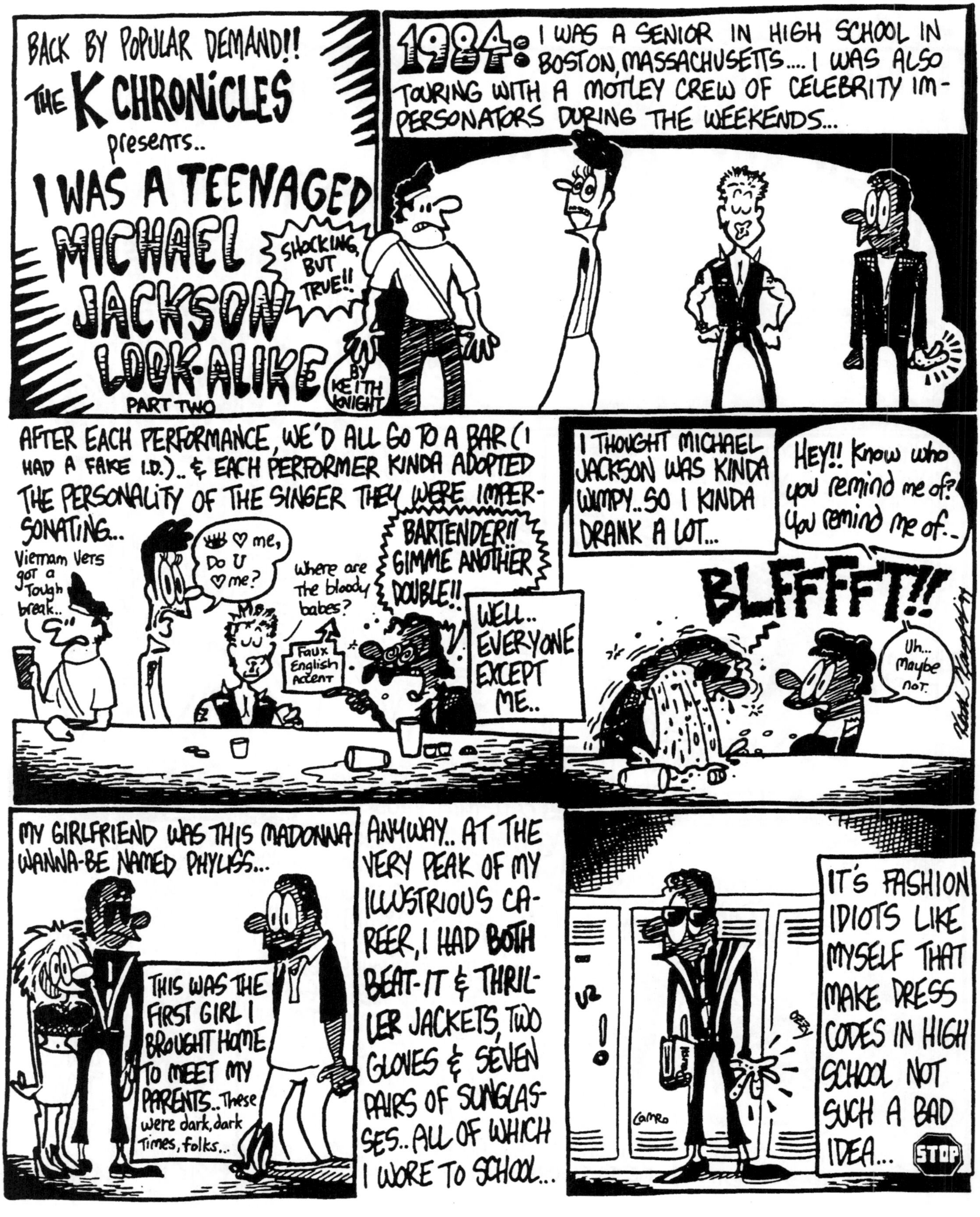
BACK BY POPULAR DEMAND!!
THE K CHRONICLES
presents..
I WAS A TEENAGED MICHAEL JACKSON LOOK-ALIKE
SHOCKING, BUT TRUE!!
BY KEITH KNIGHT
PART TWO
1984: I WAS A SENIOR IN HIGH SCHOOL IN BOSTON, MASSACHUSETTS.... I WAS ALSO TOURING WITH A MOTLEY CREW OF CELEBRITY IMPERSONATORS DURING THE WEEKENDS...
AFTER EACH PERFORMANCE, WE'D ALL GO TO A BAR (I HAD A FAKE I.D.).. & EACH PERFORMER KINDA ADOPTED THE PERSONALITY OF THE SINGER THEY WERE IMPERSONATING...
Vietnam Vets got a Tough break..
I ♡ me, Do U ♡ me?
Where are the bloody babes?
Faux English Accent
BARTENDER!! GIMME ANOTHER DOUBLE!!
WELL.. EVERYONE EXCEPT ME..
I THOUGHT MICHAEL JACKSON WAS KINDA WIMPY.. SO I KINDA DRANK A LOT...
HEY!! Know who you remind me of? You remind me of..
BLFFFT!!
Uh... Maybe not.
MY GIRLFRIEND WAS THIS MADONNA WANNA-BE NAMED PHYLISS...
THIS WAS THE FIRST GIRL I BROUGHT HOME TO MEET MY PARENTS.. These were dark, dark Times, folks...
ANYWAY.. AT THE VERY PEAK OF MY ILLUSTRIOUS CAREER, I HAD BOTH BEAT-IT & THRILLER JACKETS, TWO GLOVES & SEVEN PAIRS OF SUNGLASSES.. ALL OF WHICH I WORE TO SCHOOL...
IT'S FASHION IDIOTS LIKE MYSELF THAT MAKE DRESS CODES IN HIGH SCHOOL NOT SUCH A BAD IDEA...
STOP

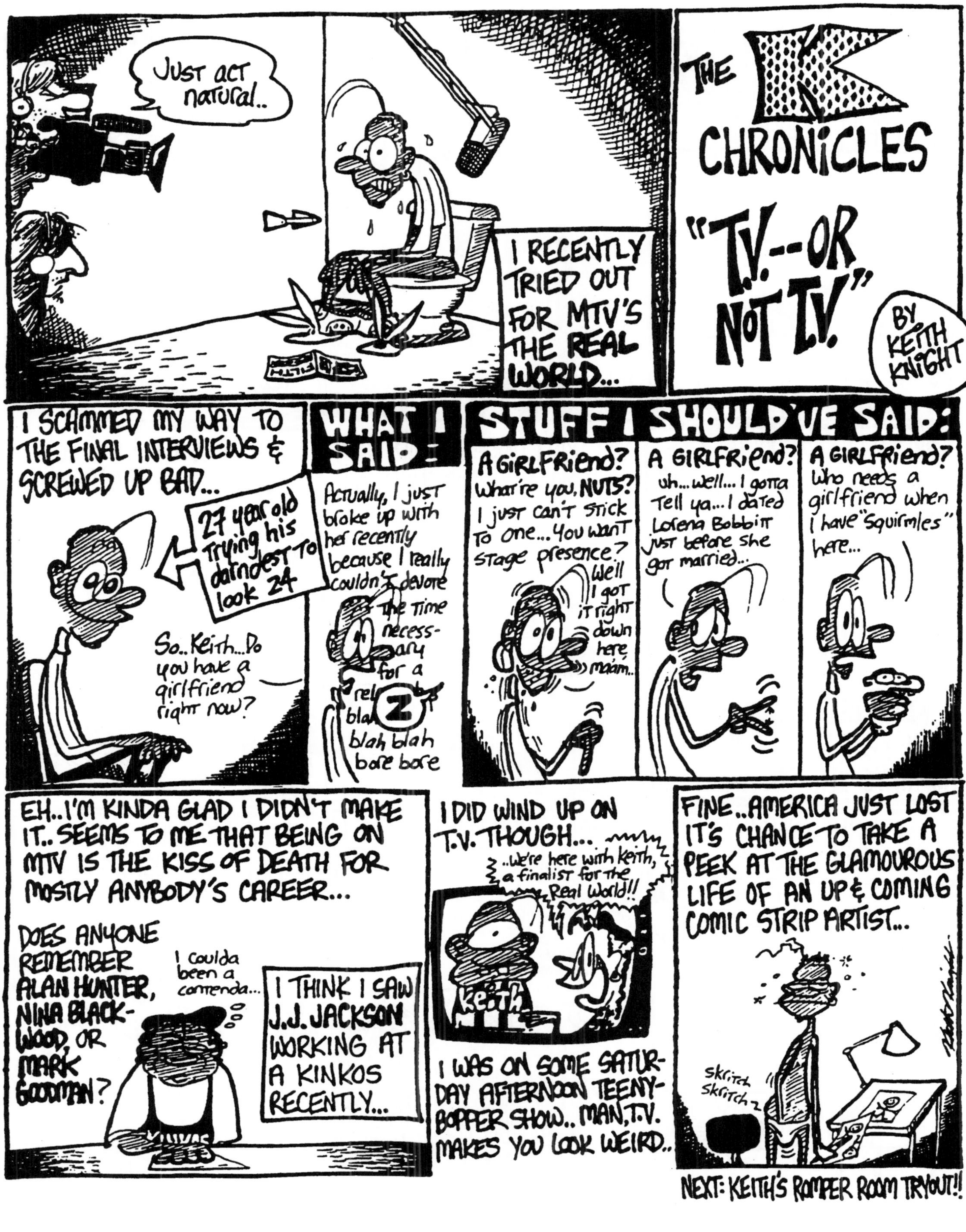

JUST ACT natural..
I RECENTLY TRIED OUT FOR MTV'S THE REAL WORLD...
THE K CHRONICLES
"T.V.--OR NOT T.V."
BY KEITH KNIGHT
I SCAMMED MY WAY TO THE FINAL INTERVIEWS & SCREWED UP BAD...
27 year old trying his darndest to look 24
So.. Keith...Do you have a girlfriend right now?
WHAT I SAID:
Actually, I just broke up with her recently because I really couldn't devote the time necessary for a rel... blah blah blah bore bore
STUFF I SHOULD'VE SAID:
A GIRLFRIEND? What're you, NUTS? I just can't stick to one... You want stage presence? Well I got it right down here, ma'am..
A GIRLFRIEND? uh... well... I gotta Tell ya... I dated Lorena Bobbitt just before she got married...
A GIRLFRIEND? Who needs a girlfriend when I have "Squirmles" here...
EH.. I'M KINDA GLAD I DIDN'T MAKE IT.. SEEMS TO ME THAT BEING ON MTV IS THE KISS OF DEATH FOR MOSTLY ANYBODY'S CAREER...
DOES ANYONE REMEMBER ALAN HUNTER, NINA BLACKWOOD, OR MARK GOODMAN?
I coulda been a contenda...
I THINK I SAW J.J. JACKSON WORKING AT A KINKOS RECENTLY...
I DID WIND UP ON T.V. THOUGH...
..We're here with Keith, a finalist for the Real World!!
KEITH
I WAS ON SOME SATURDAY AFTERNOON TEENYBOPPER SHOW.. MAN, T.V. MAKES YOU LOOK WEIRD..
FINE.. AMERICA JUST LOST IT'S CHANCE TO TAKE A PEEK AT THE GLAMOUROUS LIFE OF AN UP & COMING COMIC STRIP ARTIST...
Skritch Skritch
NEXT: KEITH'S ROMPER ROOM TRYOUT!!

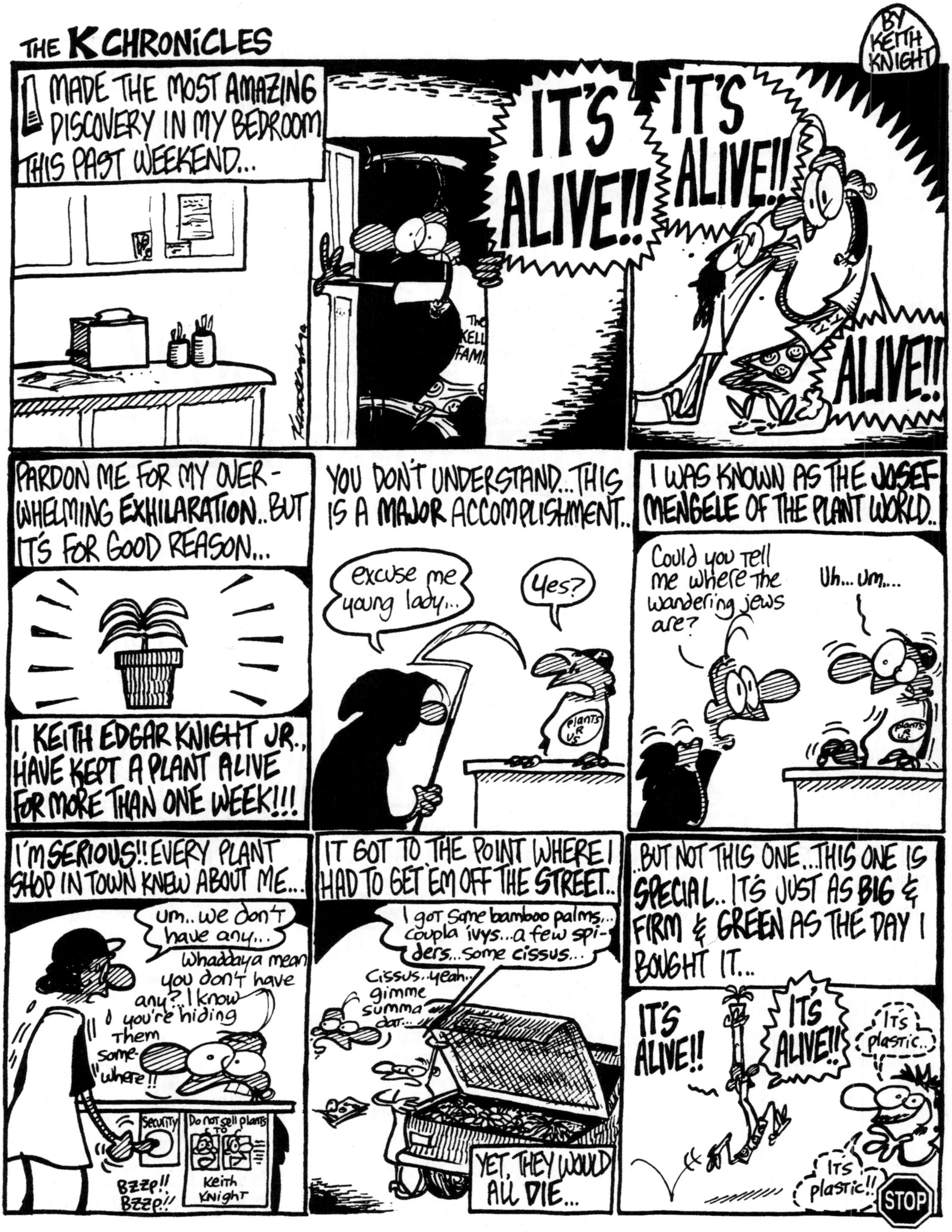
THE K CHRONICLES
BY KEITH KNIGHT
I MADE THE MOST AMAZING DISCOVERY IN MY BEDROOM THIS PAST WEEKEND...
IT'S ALIVE!!
IT'S ALIVE!!
ALIVE!!
PARDON ME FOR MY OVER-WHELMING EXHILARATION.. BUT IT'S FOR GOOD REASON...
I, KEITH EDGAR KNIGHT JR., HAVE KEPT A PLANT ALIVE FOR MORE THAN ONE WEEK!!!
YOU DON'T UNDERSTAND... THIS IS A MAJOR ACCOMPLISHMENT..
excuse me young lady...
Yes?
Plants R Us
I WAS KNOWN AS THE JOSEF MENGELE OF THE PLANT WORLD..
Could you tell me where the wandering jews are?
Uh... um....
Plants R Us
I'M SERIOUS!! EVERY PLANT SHOP IN TOWN KNEW ABOUT ME...
um.. we don't have any...
Whaddaya mean you don't have any? I know you're hiding them some-where!!
Security
Do not sell plants to
Keith Knight
Bzzp!! Bzzp!!
IT GOT TO THE POINT WHERE I HAD TO GET 'EM OFF THE STREET..
I got some bamboo palms... coupla ivys...a few spi-ders...some cissus...
Cissus..yeah.. gimme summa dat...
YET, THEY WOULD ALL DIE...
..BUT NOT THIS ONE...THIS ONE IS SPECIAL.. IT'S JUST AS BIG & FIRM & GREEN AS THE DAY I BOUGHT IT...
IT'S ALIVE!!
IT'S ALIVE!!
It's plastic..
It's plastic!!
STOP

To research this strip, I called the Holocaust Museum, and then a local plant shop. When they said "Wandering Jew" was a kind of plant, I nearly pooped my pants.

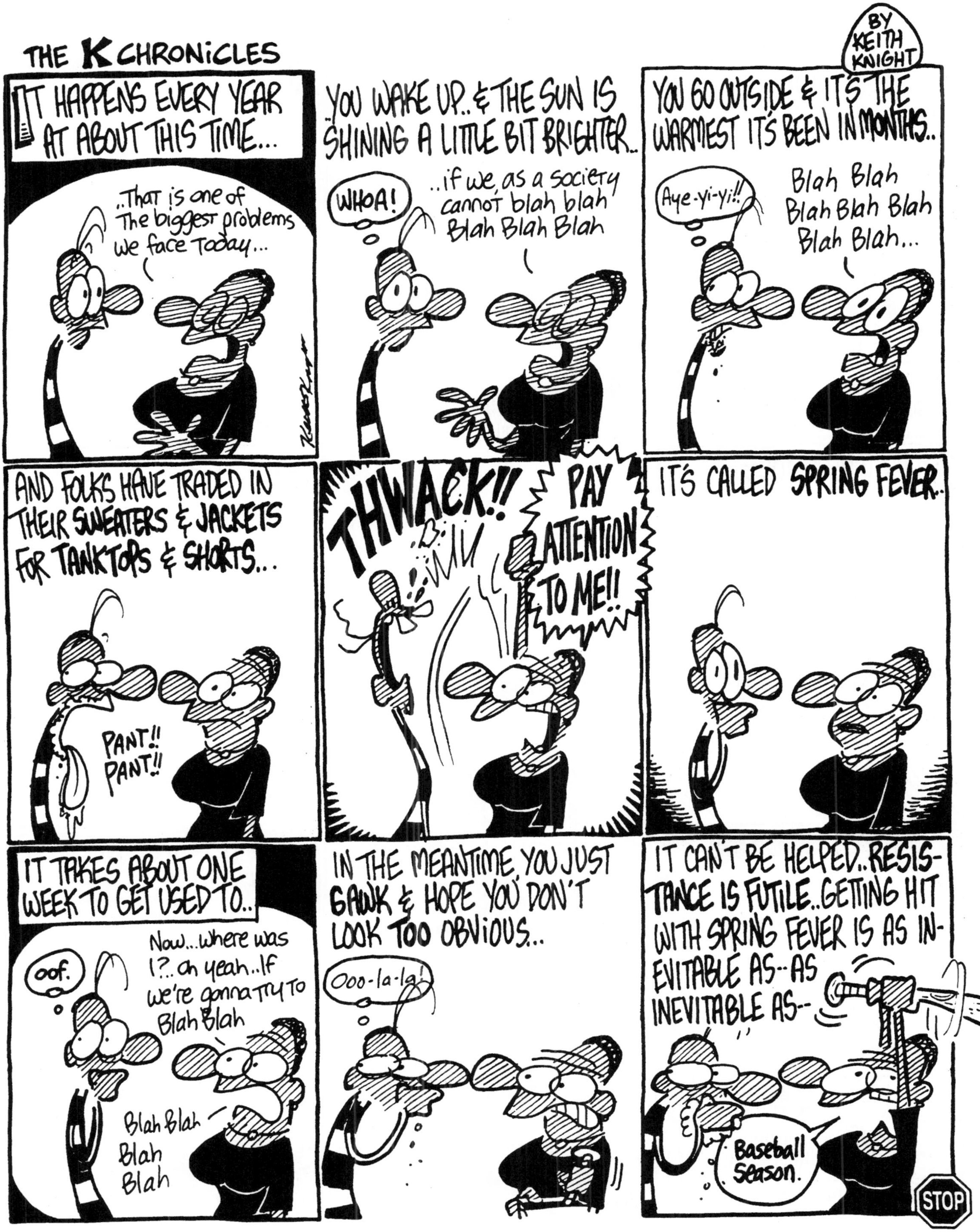
THE K CHRONICLES
BY KEITH KNIGHT
IT HAPPENS EVERY YEAR AT ABOUT THIS TIME...
..That is one of The biggest problems we face Today...
..YOU WAKE UP.. & THE SUN IS SHINING A LITTLE BIT BRIGHTER..
WHOA!
..if we, as a society cannot blah blah Blah Blah Blah
YOU GO OUTSIDE & IT'S THE WARMEST IT'S BEEN IN MONTHS..
Aye-yi-yi!!
Blah Blah Blah Blah Blah Blah Blah...
AND FOLKS HAVE TRADED IN THEIR SWEATERS & JACKETS FOR TANKTOPS & SHORTS...
PANT!! PANT!!
THWACK!!
PAY ATTENTION TO ME!!
IT'S CALLED SPRING FEVER..
IT TAKES ABOUT ONE WEEK TO GET USED TO..
oof.
Now...where was I?..oh yeah..If we're gonna try to Blah Blah
Blah Blah Blah Blah
IN THE MEANTIME, YOU JUST GAWK & HOPE YOU DON'T LOOK TOO OBVIOUS..
Ooo-la-la!
IT CAN'T BE HELPED..RESISTANCE IS FUTILE..GETTING HIT WITH SPRING FEVER IS AS INEVITABLE AS--AS INEVITABLE AS--
Baseball Season.
STOP

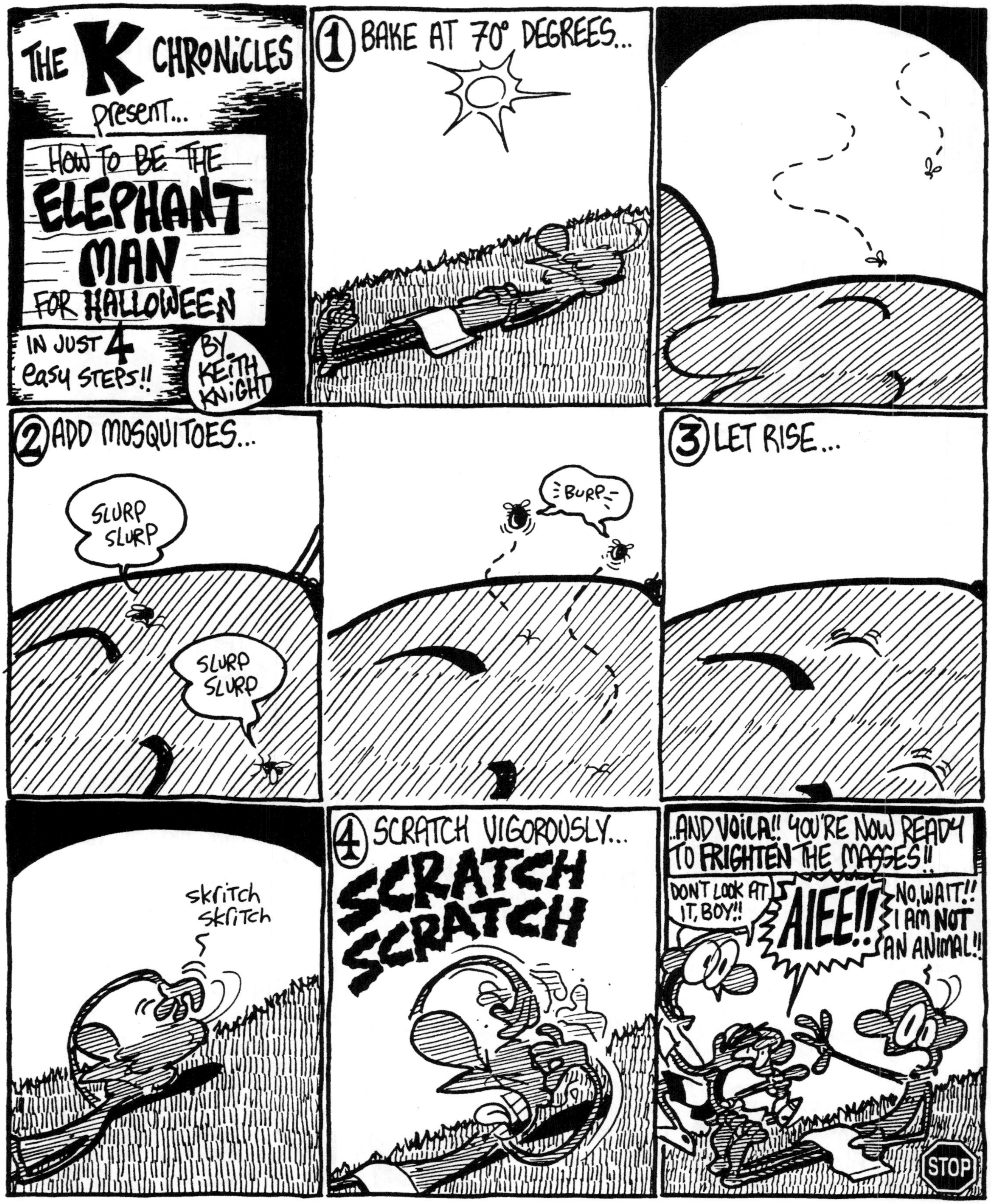
THE K CHRONICLES
present...
HOW TO BE THE
ELEPHANT MAN
FOR HALLOWEEN
IN JUST 4 easy STEPS!!
BY KEITH KNIGHT
1 BAKE AT 70° DEGREES...
2 ADD MOSQUITOES...
SLURP SLURP
SLURP SLURP
BURP
3 LET RISE...
skritch skritch
4 SCRATCH VIGOROUSLY...
SCRATCH SCRATCH
..AND VOILA!! YOU'RE NOW READY TO FRIGHTEN THE MASSES!!
DON'T LOOK AT IT, BOY!!
AIEE!!
NO, WAIT!! I AM NOT AN ANIMAL!!
STOP

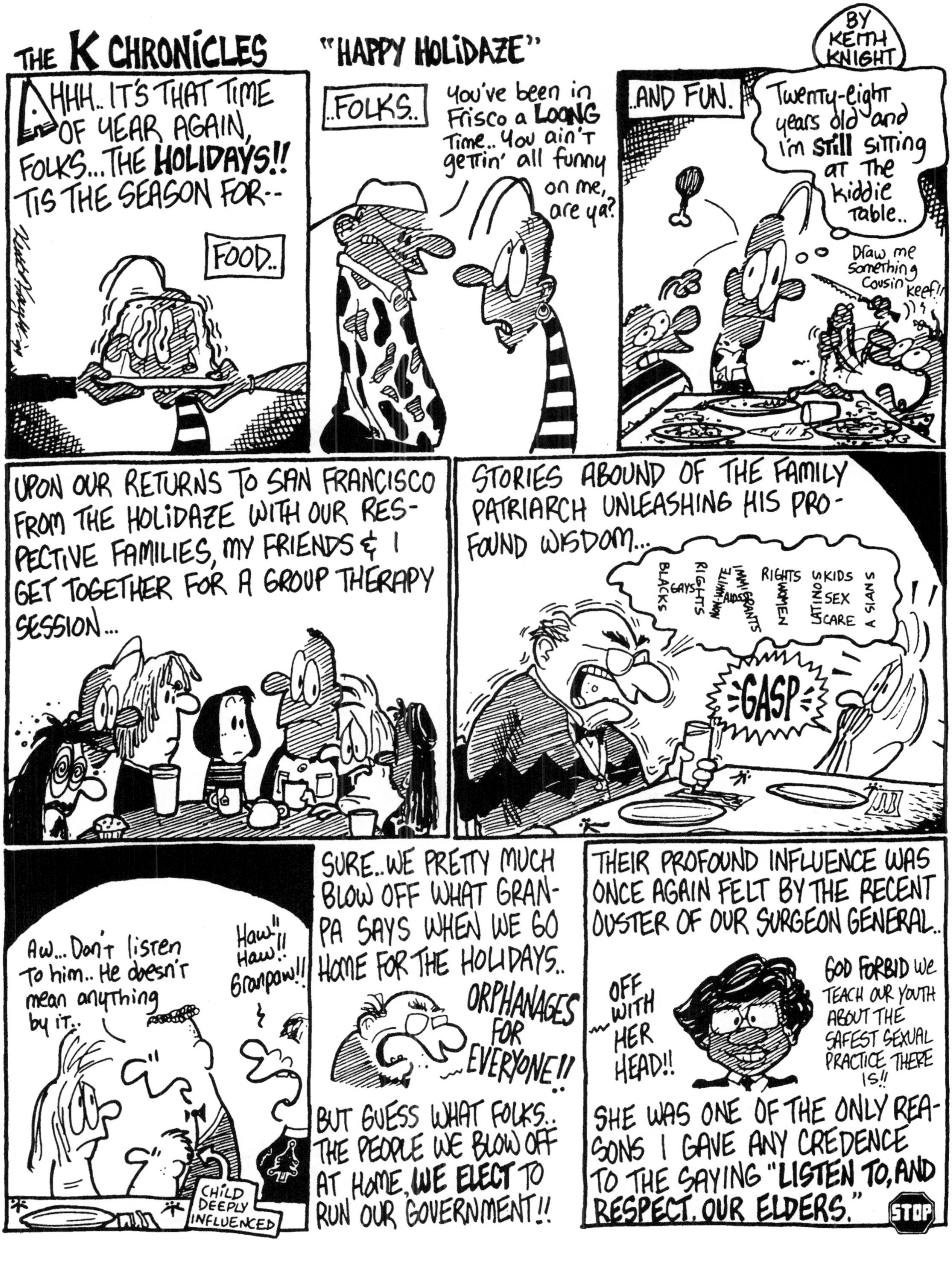
THE K CHRONICLES
"HAPPY HOLIDAZE"
BY KEITH KNIGHT
AHHH.. IT'S THAT TIME OF YEAR AGAIN, FOLKS... THE HOLIDAYS!! TIS THE SEASON FOR--
FOOD..
..FOLKS..
You've been in Frisco a LOOONG Time.. You ain't gettin' all funny on me, are ya?
..AND FUN.
Twenty-eight years old and I'm STILL sitting at the kiddie table..
Draw me something Cousin Keef!!
UPON OUR RETURNS TO SAN FRANCISCO FROM THE HOLIDAZE WITH OUR RESPECTIVE FAMILIES, MY FRIENDS & I GET TOGETHER FOR A GROUP THERAPY SESSION...
STORIES ABOUND OF THE FAMILY PATRIARCH UNLEASHING HIS PROFOUND WISDOM...
BLACKS GAYS RIGHTS NON-WHITE AIDS IMMIGRANTS RIGHTS WOMEN LATINOS KIDS SEX CARE ASIANS
GASP
Aw... Don't listen to him.. He doesn't mean anything by it..
Haw!! Haw!! Granpaw!!
CHILD DEEPLY INFLUENCED
SURE..WE PRETTY MUCH BLOW OFF WHAT GRANPA SAYS WHEN WE GO HOME FOR THE HOLIDAYS..
ORPHANAGES FOR EVERYONE!!
BUT GUESS WHAT FOLKS.. THE PEOPLE WE BLOW OFF AT HOME, WE ELECT TO RUN OUR GOVERNMENT!!
THEIR PROFOUND INFLUENCE WAS ONCE AGAIN FELT BY THE RECENT OUSTER OF OUR SURGEON GENERAL..
OFF WITH HER HEAD!!
GOD FORBID WE TEACH OUR YOUTH ABOUT THE SAFEST SEXUAL PRACTICE THERE IS!!
SHE WAS ONE OF THE ONLY REASONS I GAVE ANY CREDENCE TO THE SAYING "LISTEN TO, AND RESPECT, OUR ELDERS."
STOP

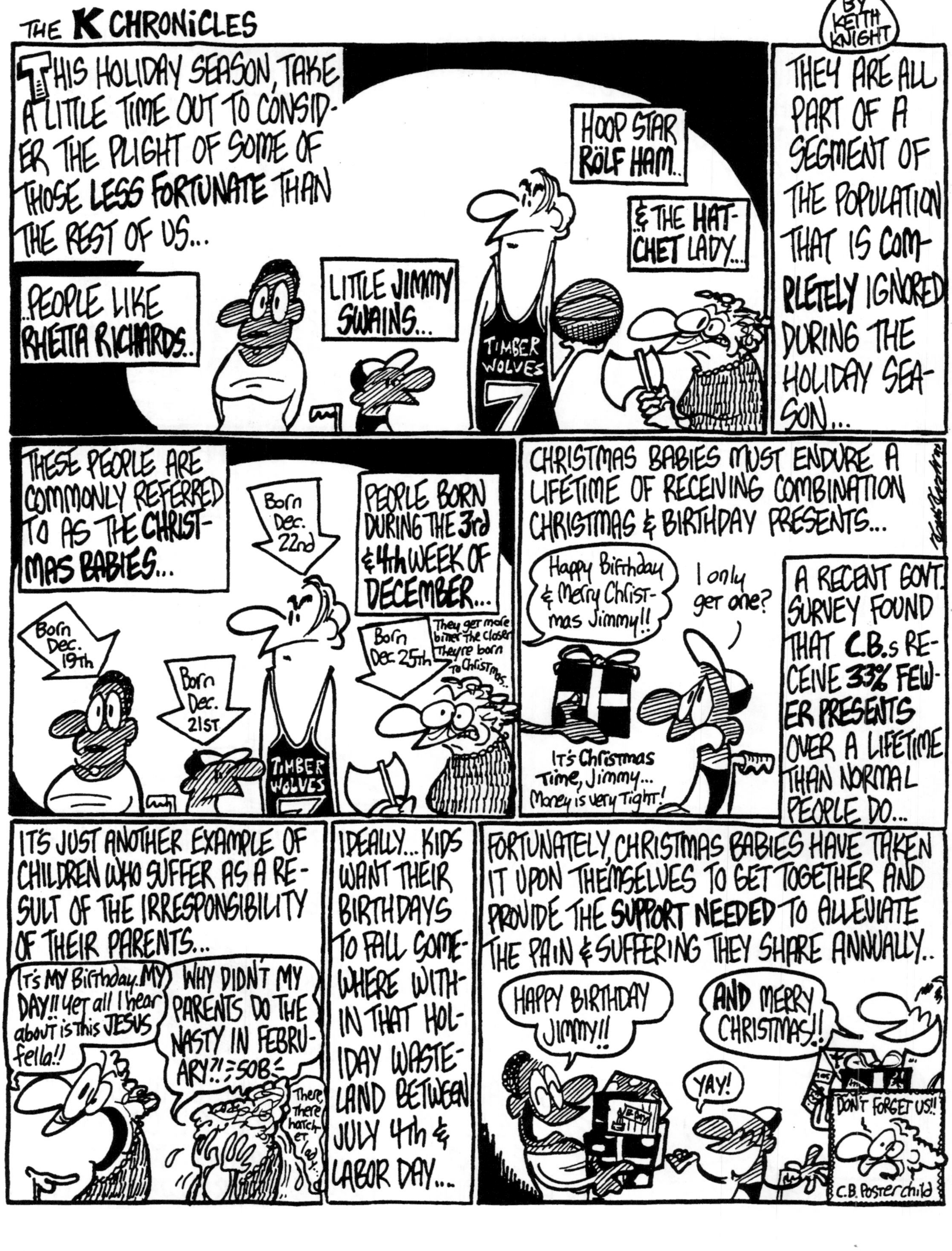
THE K CHRONICLES
BY KEITH KNIGHT
THIS HOLIDAY SEASON, TAKE A LITTLE TIME OUT TO CONSIDER THE PLIGHT OF SOME OF THOSE LESS FORTUNATE THAN THE REST OF US...
..PEOPLE LIKE RHETTA RICHARDS..
LITTLE JIMMY SWAINS...
HOOP STAR RÖLF HAM..
& THE HATCHET LADY...
TIMBER WOLVES 7
THEY ARE ALL PART OF A SEGMENT OF THE POPULATION THAT IS COMPLETELY IGNORED DURING THE HOLIDAY SEASON...
THESE PEOPLE ARE COMMONLY REFERRED TO AS THE CHRISTMAS BABIES...
Born Dec. 19th
Born Dec. 21st
Born Dec. 22nd
PEOPLE BORN DURING THE 3rd & 4th WEEK OF DECEMBER...
Born Dec. 25th
They get more bitter the closer they're born to Christmas..
TIMBER WOLVES 7
CHRISTMAS BABIES MUST ENDURE A LIFETIME OF RECEIVING COMBINATION CHRISTMAS & BIRTHDAY PRESENTS...
Happy Birthday & Merry Christmas Jimmy!!
I only get one?
It's Christmas Time, Jimmy... Money is very Tight!
A RECENT GOVT. SURVEY FOUND THAT C.B.s RECEIVE 33% FEWER PRESENTS OVER A LIFETIME THAN NORMAL PEOPLE DO...
IT'S JUST ANOTHER EXAMPLE OF CHILDREN WHO SUFFER AS A RESULT OF THE IRRESPONSIBILITY OF THEIR PARENTS...
It's MY Birthday. MY DAY!! yet all I hear about is this JESUS fella!!
WHY DIDN'T MY PARENTS DO THE NASTY IN FEBRUARY?!! SOB
There, there hatchet lady...
IDEALLY... KIDS WANT THEIR BIRTHDAYS TO FALL SOMEWHERE WITHIN THAT HOLIDAY WASTELAND BETWEEN JULY 4th & LABOR DAY...
FORTUNATELY, CHRISTMAS BABIES HAVE TAKEN IT UPON THEMSELVES TO GET TOGETHER AND PROVIDE THE SUPPORT NEEDED TO ALLEVIATE THE PAIN & SUFFERING THEY SHARE ANNUALLY..
HAPPY BIRTHDAY JIMMY!!
AND MERRY CHRISTMAS!!
YAY!
DON'T FORGET US!!
C.B. Poster child

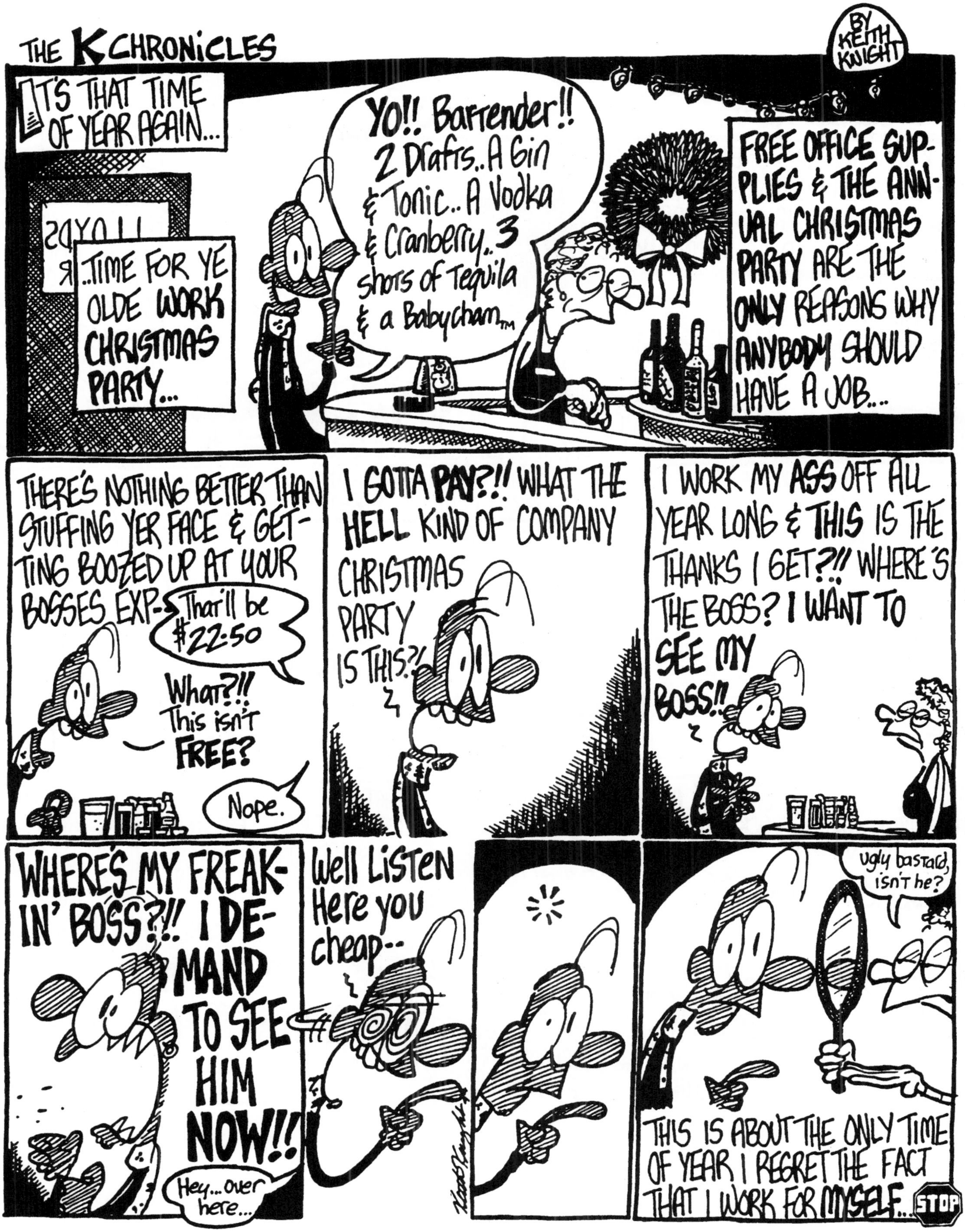
THE K CHRONICLES
BY KEITH KNIGHT
IT'S THAT TIME OF YEAR AGAIN...
...TIME FOR YE OLDE WORK CHRISTMAS PARTY...
YO!! Bartender!! 2 Drafts.. A Gin & Tonic.. A Vodka & Cranberry.. 3 shots of Tequila & a Babycham™
FREE OFFICE SUPPLIES & THE ANNUAL CHRISTMAS PARTY ARE THE ONLY REASONS WHY ANYBODY SHOULD HAVE A JOB...
THERE'S NOTHING BETTER THAN STUFFING YER FACE & GETTING BOOZED UP AT YOUR BOSSES EXP-
That'll be $22.50
What?!! This isn't FREE?
Nope.
I GOTTA PAY?!! WHAT THE HELL KIND OF COMPANY CHRISTMAS PARTY IS THIS?!
I WORK MY ASS OFF ALL YEAR LONG & THIS IS THE THANKS I GET?!! WHERE'S THE BOSS? I WANT TO SEE MY BOSS!!
WHERE'S MY FREAKIN' BOSS?!! I DEMAND TO SEE HIM NOW!!
Hey... over here...
Well Listen Here you cheap--
ugly bastard, isn't he?
THIS IS ABOUT THE ONLY TIME OF YEAR I REGRET THE FACT THAT I WORK FOR MYSELF...
STOP

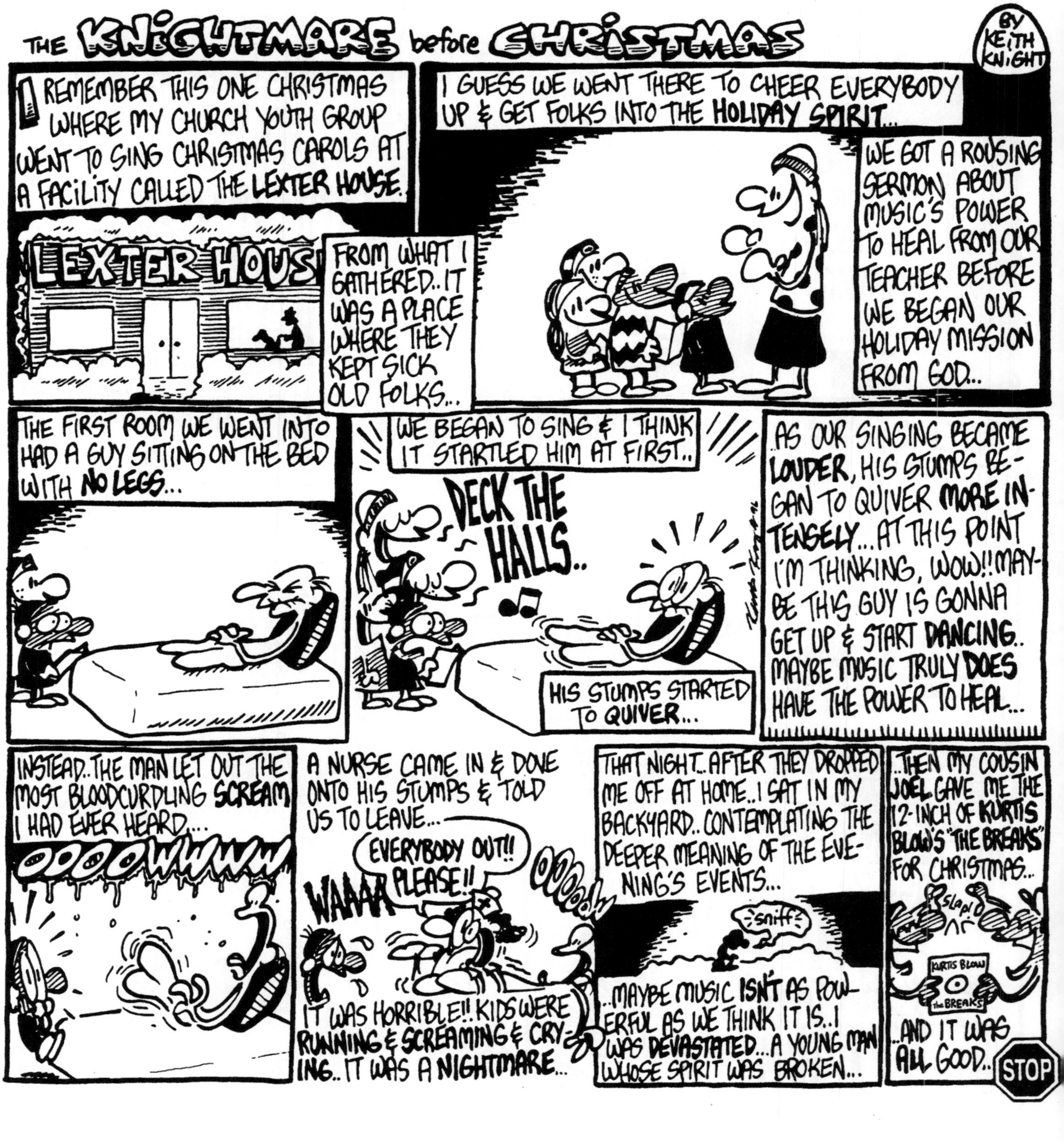
THE KNIGHTMARE before CHRISTMAS
BY KEITH KNIGHT
I REMEMBER THIS ONE CHRISTMAS WHERE MY CHURCH YOUTH GROUP WENT TO SING CHRISTMAS CAROLS AT A FACILITY CALLED THE LEXTER HOUSE.
LEXTER HOUS
FROM WHAT I GATHERED.. IT WAS A PLACE WHERE THEY KEPT SICK OLD FOLKS...
I GUESS WE WENT THERE TO CHEER EVERYBODY UP & GET FOLKS INTO THE HOLIDAY SPIRIT...
WE GOT A ROUSING SERMON ABOUT MUSIC'S POWER TO HEAL FROM OUR TEACHER BEFORE WE BEGAN OUR HOLIDAY MISSION FROM GOD..
THE FIRST ROOM WE WENT INTO HAD A GUY SITTING ON THE BED WITH NO LEGS...
WE BEGAN TO SING & I THINK IT STARTLED HIM AT FIRST..
DECK THE HALLS..
HIS STUMPS STARTED TO QUIVER...
..AS OUR SINGING BECAME LOUDER, HIS STUMPS BEGAN TO QUIVER MORE INTENSELY... AT THIS POINT I'M THINKING, WOW!! MAYBE THIS GUY IS GONNA GET UP & START DANCING.. MAYBE MUSIC TRULY DOES HAVE THE POWER TO HEAL...
INSTEAD.. THE MAN LET OUT THE MOST BLOODCURDLING SCREAM I HAD EVER HEARD...
OOOOWWWW
A NURSE CAME IN & DOVE ONTO HIS STUMPS & TOLD US TO LEAVE...
EVERYBODY OUT!! PLEASE!!
WAAAA
IT WAS HORRIBLE!! KIDS WERE RUNNING & SCREAMING & CRYING.. IT WAS A NIGHTMARE...
THAT NIGHT.. AFTER THEY DROPPED ME OFF AT HOME.. I SAT IN MY BACKYARD.. CONTEMPLATING THE DEEPER MEANING OF THE EVENING'S EVENTS...
sniff
..MAYBE MUSIC ISN'T AS POWERFUL AS WE THINK IT IS.. I WAS DEVASTATED... A YOUNG MAN WHOSE SPIRIT WAS BROKEN...
..THEN MY COUSIN JOEL GAVE ME THE 12-INCH OF KURTIS BLOW'S "THE BREAKS" FOR CHRISTMAS...
SLAP!
KURTIS BLOW
THE BREAKS
..AND IT WAS ALL GOOD..
STOP

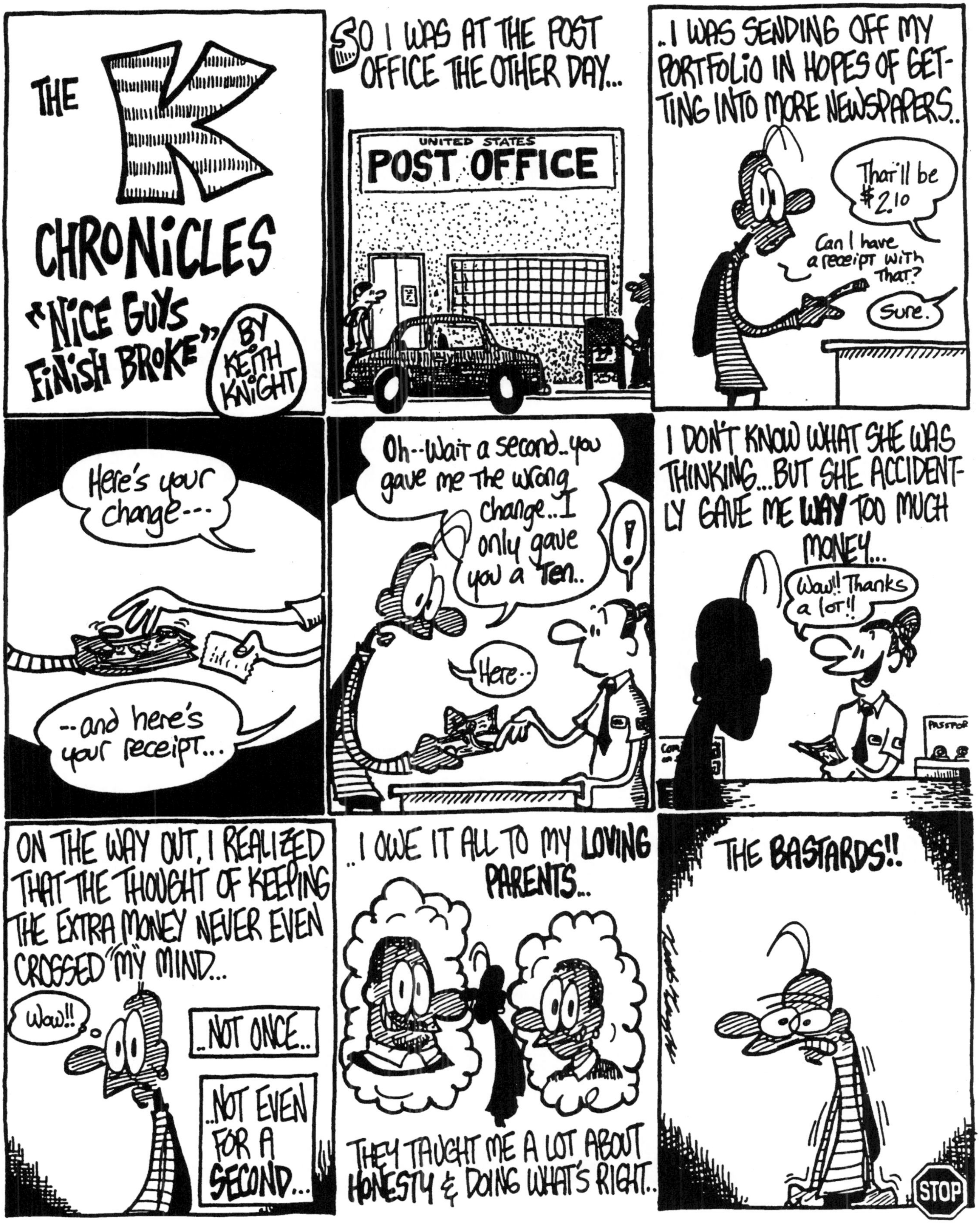
THE K CHRONICLES
"NICE GUYS FINISH BROKE"
BY KEITH KNIGHT
SO I WAS AT THE POST OFFICE THE OTHER DAY...
UNITED STATES POST OFFICE
..I WAS SENDING OFF MY PORTFOLIO IN HOPES OF GETTING INTO MORE NEWSPAPERS..
That'll be $2.10
Can I have a receipt with that?
Sure.
Here's your change---
--and here's your receipt...
Oh--Wait a second..you gave me the wrong change..I only gave you a Ten..
!
Here..
I DON'T KNOW WHAT SHE WAS THINKING...BUT SHE ACCIDENTLY GAVE ME WAY TOO MUCH MONEY...
Wow!! Thanks a lot!!
ON THE WAY OUT, I REALIZED THAT THE THOUGHT OF KEEPING THE EXTRA MONEY NEVER EVEN CROSSED MY MIND...
Wow!!
..NOT ONCE..
..NOT EVEN FOR A SECOND...
..I OWE IT ALL TO MY LOVING PARENTS..
THEY TAUGHT ME A LOT ABOUT HONESTY & DOING WHAT'S RIGHT..
THE BASTARDS!!
STOP

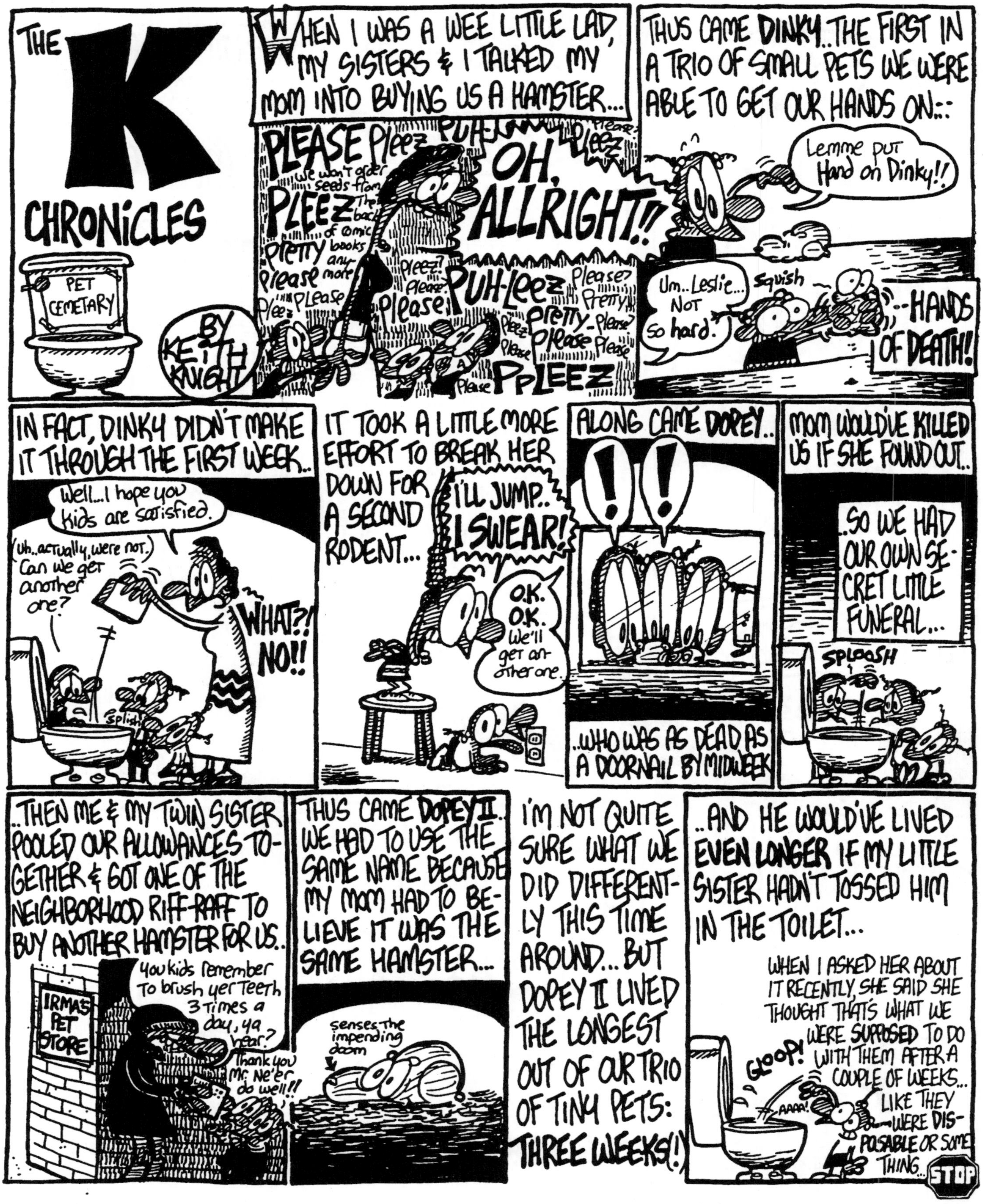
THE K CHRONICLES
PET CEMETARY
BY KEITH KNIGHT
WHEN I WAS A WEE LITTLE LAD, MY SISTERS & I TALKED MY MOM INTO BUYING US A HAMSTER...
PLEASE Pleez PUH-Leez Please? Pleez
We won't order seeds from the back of comic books anymore
PLEEZ
Pretty please
Please Pleez Please?
Please
PUH-Leez Please? Pretty
Pleez Pretty-Please? Please Please Please
Please PPLEEZ
OH, ALLRIGHT!!
THUS CAME DINKY.. THE FIRST IN A TRIO OF SMALL PETS WE WERE ABLE TO GET OUR HANDS ON:..
Lemme put Hand on Dinky!!
Um.. Leslie... Not so hard.
Squish
..HANDS OF DEATH!
IN FACT, DINKY DIDN'T MAKE IT THROUGH THE FIRST WEEK..
Well...I hope you kids are satisfied.
(uh..actually, were not.) Can we get another one?
WHAT?! NO!!
splish
IT TOOK A LITTLE MORE EFFORT TO BREAK HER DOWN FOR A SECOND RODENT...
I'LL JUMP.. I SWEAR!
O.K. O.K. We'll get another one.
ALONG CAME DOPEY..
! !
..WHO WAS AS DEAD AS A DOORNAIL BY MIDWEEK
MOM WOULD'VE KILLED US IF SHE FOUND OUT..
..SO WE HAD OUR OWN SECRET LITTLE FUNERAL...
SPLOOSH
..THEN ME & MY TWIN SISTER POOLED OUR ALLOWANCES TOGETHER & GOT ONE OF THE NEIGHBORHOOD RIFF-RAFF TO BUY ANOTHER HAMSTER FOR US..
IRMA'S PET STORE
You kids remember to brush yer teeth 3 times a day, ya hear?
Thank you Mr. Ne'er do well!!
THUS CAME DOPEY II. WE HAD TO USE THE SAME NAME BECAUSE MY MOM HAD TO BELIEVE IT WAS THE SAME HAMSTER...
senses the impending doom
I'M NOT QUITE SURE WHAT WE DID DIFFERENTLY THIS TIME AROUND... BUT DOPEY II LIVED THE LONGEST OUT OF OUR TRIO OF TINY PETS: THREE WEEKS(!)
..AND HE WOULD'VE LIVED EVEN LONGER IF MY LITTLE SISTER HADN'T TOSSED HIM IN THE TOILET...
WHEN I ASKED HER ABOUT IT RECENTLY, SHE SAID SHE THOUGHT THAT'S WHAT WE WERE SUPPOSED TO DO WITH THEM AFTER A COUPLE OF WEEKS... LIKE THEY WERE DISPOSABLE OR SOMETHING...
GLOOP!
AAAA!
STOP

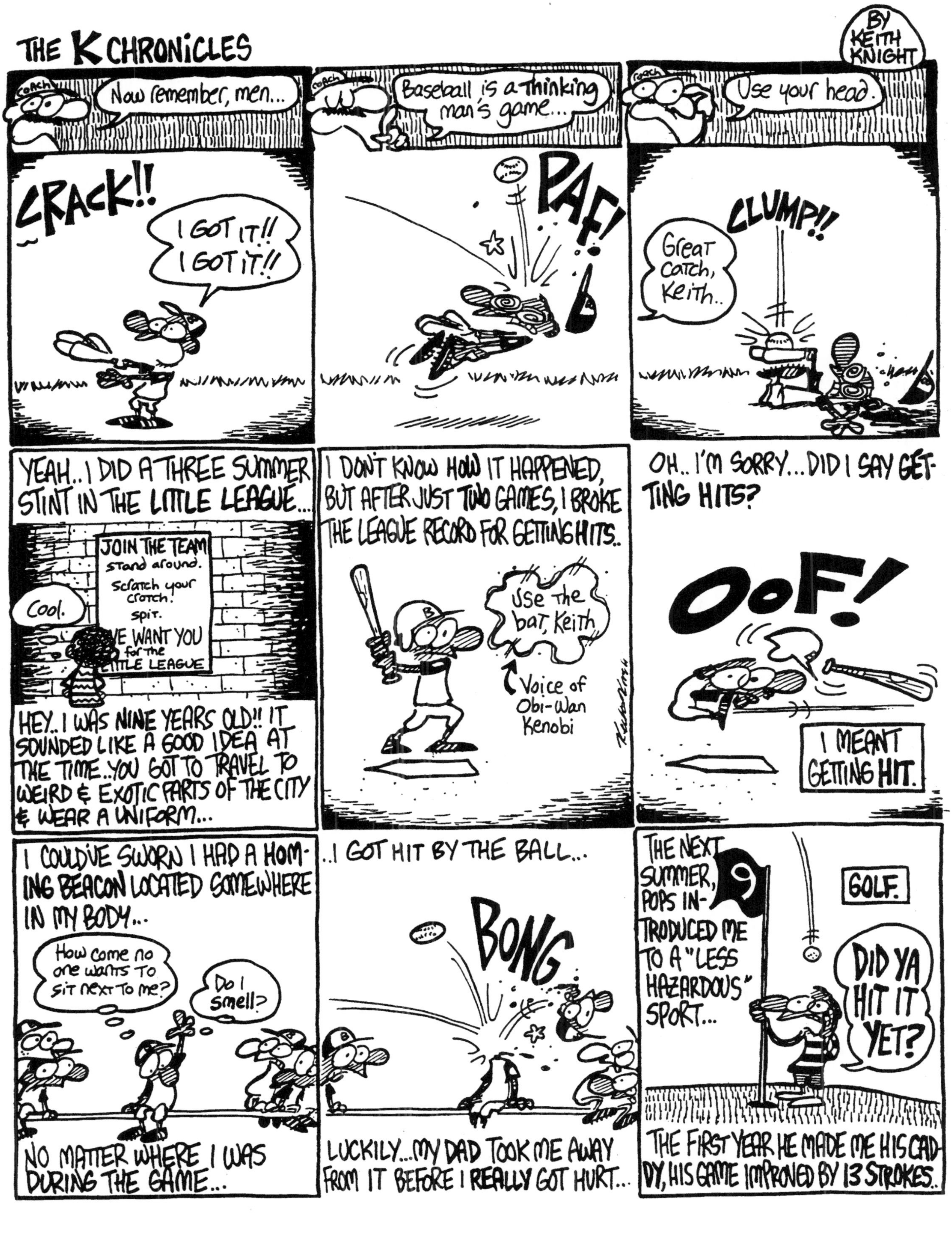
THE K CHRONICLES
BY KEITH KNIGHT
COACH
Now remember, men...
Baseball is a thinking man's game...
Use your head.
CRACK!!
I GOT IT!! I GOT IT!!
PAF!
CLUMP!!
Great catch, Keith..
YEAH.. I DID A THREE SUMMER STINT IN THE LITTLE LEAGUE...
JOIN THE TEAM
Stand around.
Scratch your crotch.
Spit.
WE WANT YOU for the LITTLE LEAGUE
Cool.
HEY.. I WAS NINE YEARS OLD!! IT SOUNDED LIKE A GOOD IDEA AT THE TIME.. YOU GOT TO TRAVEL TO WEIRD & EXOTIC PARTS OF THE CITY & WEAR A UNIFORM...
I DON'T KNOW HOW IT HAPPENED, BUT AFTER JUST TWO GAMES, I BROKE THE LEAGUE RECORD FOR GETTING HITS..
Use the bat, Keith..
Voice of Obi-Wan Kenobi
OH.. I'M SORRY... DID I SAY GETTING HITS?
OOF!
I MEANT GETTING HIT.
I COULD'VE SWORN I HAD A HOMING BEACON LOCATED SOMEWHERE IN MY BODY...
How come no one wants to sit next to me?
Do I smell?
NO MATTER WHERE I WAS DURING THE GAME...
..I GOT HIT BY THE BALL...
BONG
LUCKILY... MY DAD TOOK ME AWAY FROM IT BEFORE I REALLY GOT HURT...
THE NEXT SUMMER, POPS INTRODUCED ME TO A "LESS HAZARDOUS" SPORT...
9
GOLF.
DID YA HIT IT YET?
THE FIRST YEAR HE MADE ME HIS CADDY, HIS GAME IMPROVED BY 13 STROKES.

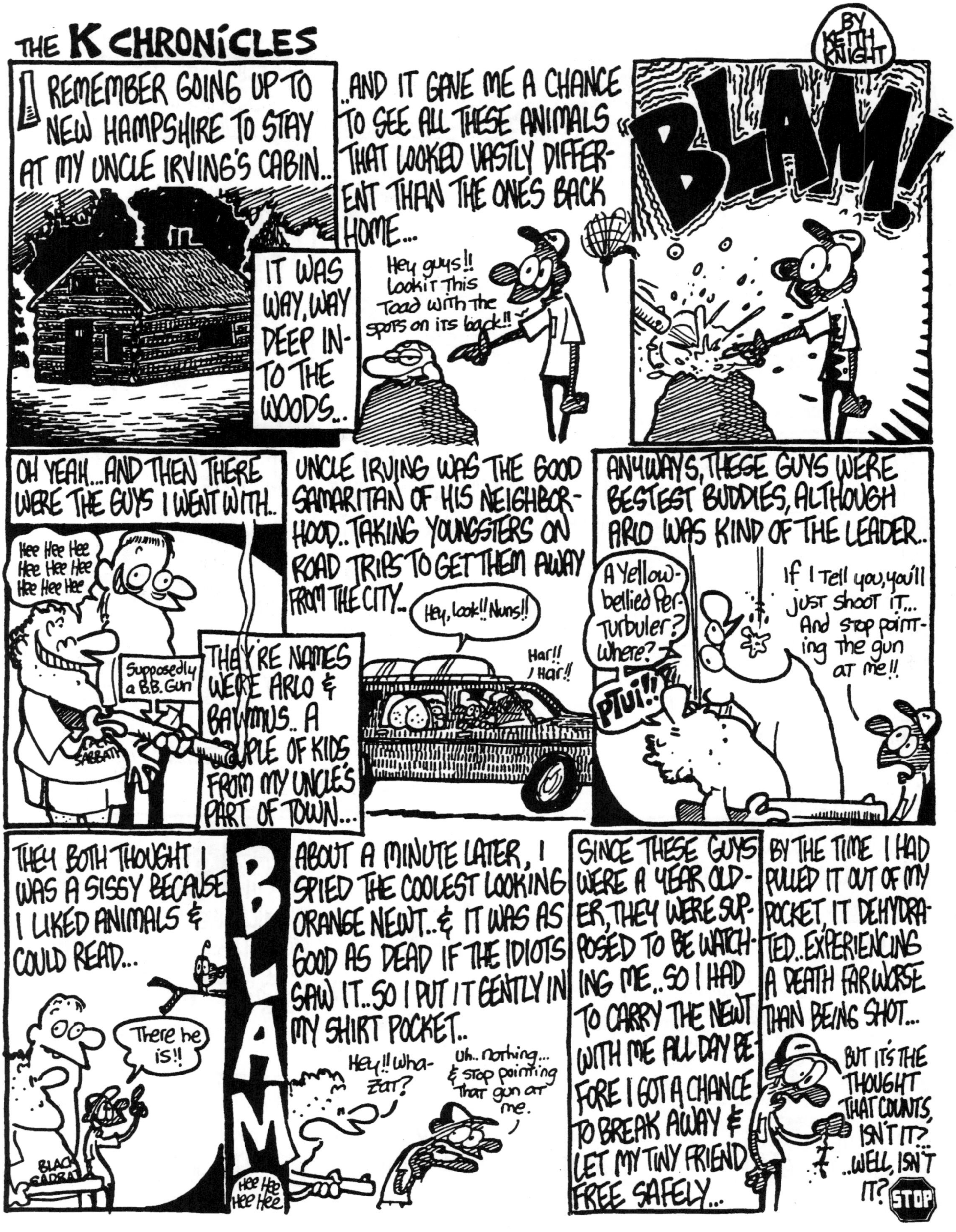
THE K CHRONICLES
BY KEITH KNIGHT
I REMEMBER GOING UP TO NEW HAMPSHIRE TO STAY AT MY UNCLE IRVING'S CABIN..
IT WAS WAY, WAY DEEP INTO THE WOODS..
..AND IT GAVE ME A CHANCE TO SEE ALL THESE ANIMALS THAT LOOKED VASTLY DIFFERENT THAN THE ONES BACK HOME...
Hey guys!! Lookit This Toad with the spots on its back!!
BLAM!
OH YEAH...AND THEN THERE WERE THE GUYS I WENT WITH..
Hee Hee Hee Hee Hee Hee Hee Hee Hee
Supposedly a B.B. Gun
THEY'RE NAMES WERE ARLO & BAWMUS.. A COUPLE OF KIDS FROM MY UNCLE'S PART OF TOWN...
UNCLE IRVING WAS THE GOOD SAMARITAN OF HIS NEIGHBORHOOD.. TAKING YOUNGSTERS ON ROAD TRIPS TO GET THEM AWAY FROM THE CITY..
Hey, Look!! Nuns!!
Har!! Har!!
ANYWAYS, THESE GUYS WERE BESTEST BUDDIES, ALTHOUGH ARLO WAS KIND OF THE LEADER..
A Yellow-bellied Perturbuler? Where?
PTUI!!
If I Tell you, you'll just shoot it... And stop pointing the gun at me!!
THEY BOTH THOUGHT I WAS A SISSY BECAUSE I LIKED ANIMALS & COULD READ...
There he is!!
BLAM
Hee Hee Hee Hee
ABOUT A MINUTE LATER, I SPIED THE COOLEST LOOKING ORANGE NEWT..& IT WAS AS GOOD AS DEAD IF THE IDIOTS SAW IT..SO I PUT IT GENTLY IN MY SHIRT POCKET..
Hey!! Wha-Zat?
Uh.. nothing... & stop pointing that gun at me.
SINCE THESE GUYS WERE A YEAR OLDER, THEY WERE SUPPOSED TO BE WATCHING ME..SO I HAD TO CARRY THE NEWT WITH ME ALL DAY BEFORE I GOT A CHANCE TO BREAK AWAY & LET MY TINY FRIEND FREE SAFELY...
BY THE TIME I HAD PULLED IT OUT OF MY POCKET, IT DEHYDRATED..EXPERIENCING A DEATH FAR WORSE THAN BEING SHOT...
BUT IT'S THE THOUGHT THAT COUNTS, ISN'T IT?... ..WELL, ISN'T IT?
STOP

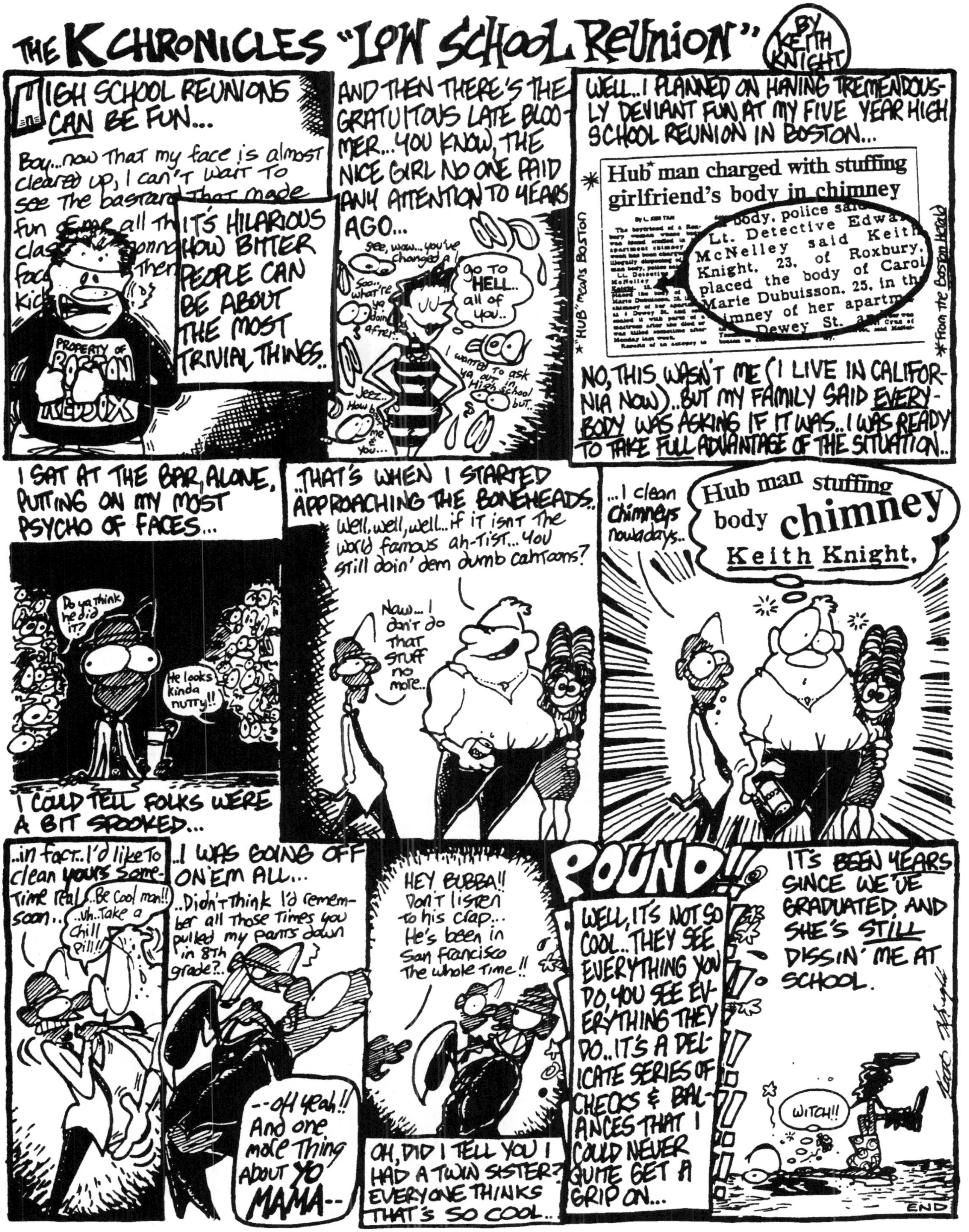
THE K CHRONICLES "LOW SCHOOL REUNION"
BY KEITH KNIGHT
HIGH SCHOOL REUNIONS CAN BE FUN...
Boy...now That my face is almost cleared up, I can't wait To see The bastard That made
IT'S HILARIOUS HOW BITTER PEOPLE CAN BE ABOUT THE MOST TRIVIAL THINGS..
PROPERTY OF
AND THEN THERE'S THE GRATUITOUS LATE BLOOMER... YOU KNOW, THE NICE GIRL NO ONE PAID ANY ATTENTION TO YEARS AGO...
gee, wow...you've changed a l
Sooo.. what're ya doin after..
go to HELL.. all of you..
I wanted To ask ya out in High school but..
Jeez.. How bout me & you...
WELL.. I PLANNED ON HAVING TREMENDOUSLY DEVIANT FUN AT MY FIVE YEAR HIGH SCHOOL REUNION IN BOSTON...
Hub* man charged with stuffing girlfriend's body in chimney
body, police said. Lt. Detective Edwa McNelley said Keith Knight, 23, of Roxbury, placed the body of Carol Marie Dubuisson, 25, in the chimney of her apartm Dewey St.
* "HUB" means BOSTON
* from the Boston Herald
NO, THIS WASN'T ME (I LIVE IN CALIFORNIA NOW).. BUT MY FAMILY SAID EVERYBODY WAS ASKING IF IT WAS.. I WAS READY TO TAKE FULL ADVANTAGE OF THE SITUATION..
I SAT AT THE BAR, ALONE, PUTTING ON MY MOST PSYCHO OF FACES...
Do ya think he did it?
He looks kinda nutty!!
I COULD TELL FOLKS WERE A BIT SPOOKED...
..THAT'S WHEN I STARTED APPROACHING THE BONEHEADS..
Well, well, well... if it isn't The world famous ah-tist... You still doin' dem dumb cahtoons?
Naw... I don't do that stuff no more..
...I clean chimneys nowadays..
Hub man stuffing body chimney Keith Knight,
..in fact.. I'd like To clean yours some-Time real soon..
..Be cool man!!
..uh.. Take a chill pill!!
..I WAS GOING OFF ON'EM ALL...
..Didn't Think I'd remember all Those Times you pulled my pants down in 8th grade?..
--oH yeah!! And one more Thing about YO MAMA--
HEY BUBBA!! Don't listen to his crap... He's been in San Francisco The whole Time!!
OH, DID I TELL YOU I HAD A TWIN SISTER? EVERYONE THINKS THAT'S SO COOL..
POUND!!
WELL, IT'S NOT SO COOL.. THEY SEE EVERYTHING YOU DO, YOU SEE EVERYTHING THEY DO.. IT'S A DELICATE SERIES OF CHECKS & BALANCES THAT I COULD NEVER QUITE GET A GRIP ON...
IT'S BEEN YEARS SINCE WE'VE GRADUATED, AND SHE'S STILL DISSIN' ME AT SCHOOL.
WITCH!!
END

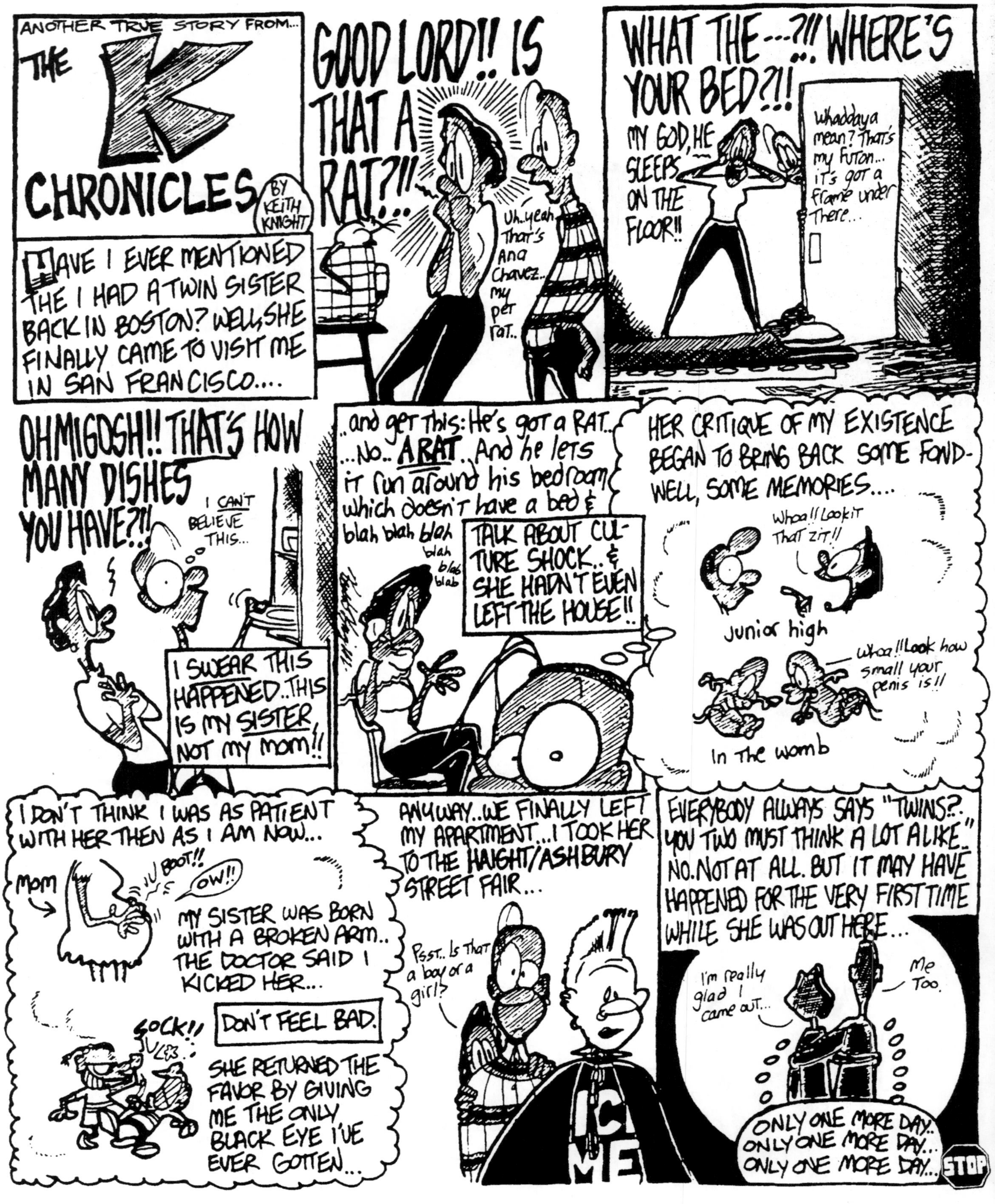

ANOTHER TRUE STORY FROM...
THE K CHRONICLES
BY KEITH KNIGHT
HAVE I EVER MENTIONED THE I HAD A TWIN SISTER BACK IN BOSTON? WELL, SHE FINALLY CAME TO VISIT ME IN SAN FRANCISCO....
GOOD LORD!! IS THAT A RAT?!!...
Uh..yeah That's Ana Chavez.. my pet rat..
WHAT THE ---?!! WHERE'S YOUR BED?!!
MY GOD, HE SLEEPS ON THE FLOOR!!
Whaddaya mean? That's my Futon... it's got a frame under There...
OHMIGOSH!! THAT'S HOW MANY DISHES YOU HAVE?!!
I CAN'T BELIEVE THIS...
I SWEAR THIS HAPPENED..THIS IS MY SISTER, NOT MY MOM!!
..and get this: He's got a RAT.. ...No.. A RAT.. And he lets it run around his bedroom which doesn't have a bed & blah blah blah blah blab blab
TALK ABOUT CULTURE SHOCK..& SHE HADN'T EVEN LEFT THE HOUSE!!
HER CRITIQUE OF MY EXISTENCE BEGAN TO BRING BACK SOME FOND- WELL, SOME MEMORIES....
Whoa!! Lookit That zit!!
Junior high
Whoa!! Look how small your penis is!!
In The womb
I DON'T THINK I WAS AS PATIENT WITH HER THEN AS I AM NOW...
Mom
BOOT!!
OW!!
MY SISTER WAS BORN WITH A BROKEN ARM.. THE DOCTOR SAID I KICKED HER...
DON'T FEEL BAD.
SOCK!!
SHE RETURNED THE FAVOR BY GIVING ME THE ONLY BLACK EYE I'VE EVER GOTTEN...
ANYWAY..WE FINALLY LEFT MY APARTMENT...I TOOK HER TO THE HAIGHT/ASHBURY STREET FAIR...
Psst.. Is That a boy or a girl?
EVERYBODY ALWAYS SAYS "TWINS?.. YOU TWO MUST THINK A LOT ALIKE." NO. NOT AT ALL. BUT IT MAY HAVE HAPPENED FOR THE VERY FIRST TIME WHILE SHE WAS OUT HERE...
I'm really glad I came out...
Me Too.
ONLY ONE MORE DAY.. ONLY ONE MORE DAY... ONLY ONE MORE DAY...
STOP

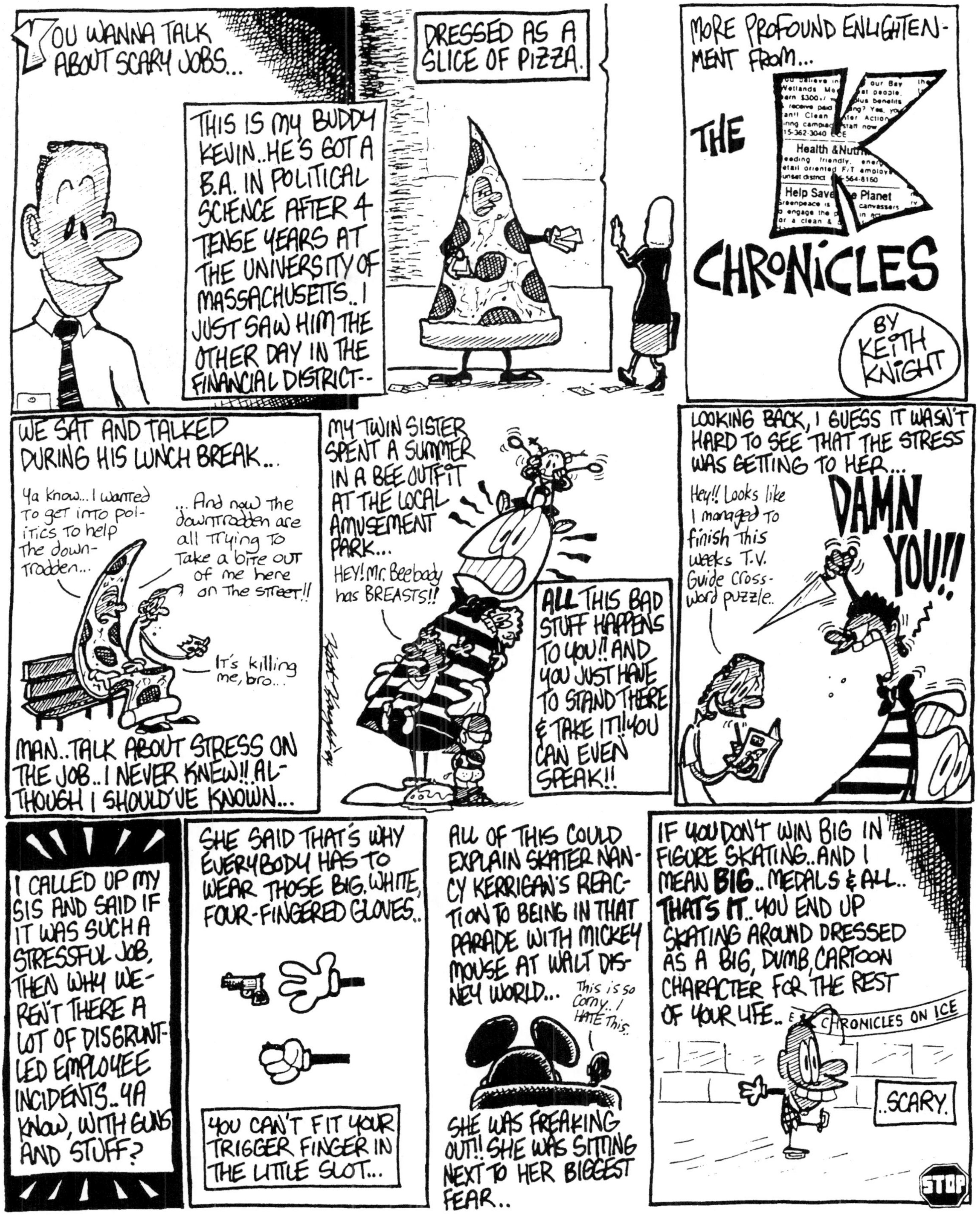

YOU WANNA TALK ABOUT SCARY JOBS...
THIS IS MY BUDDY KEVIN..HE'S GOT A B.A. IN POLITICAL SCIENCE AFTER 4 TENSE YEARS AT THE UNIVERSITY OF MASSACHUSETTS..I JUST SAW HIM THE OTHER DAY IN THE FINANCIAL DISTRICT--
DRESSED AS A SLICE OF PIZZA.
MORE PROFOUND ENLIGHTENMENT FROM...
THE K CHRONICLES
BY KEITH KNIGHT
WE SAT AND TALKED DURING HIS LUNCH BREAK...
Ya know... I wanted to get into politics to help the downtrodden...
...And now the downtrodden are all trying to take a bite out of me here on the street!!
It's killing me, bro...
MAN..TALK ABOUT STRESS ON THE JOB..I NEVER KNEW!! ALTHOUGH I SHOULD'VE KNOWN...
MY TWIN SISTER SPENT A SUMMER IN A BEE OUTFIT AT THE LOCAL AMUSEMENT PARK...
HEY! Mr. Beebody has BREASTS!!
ALL THIS BAD STUFF HAPPENS TO YOU!! AND YOU JUST HAVE TO STAND THERE & TAKE IT!! YOU CAN EVEN SPEAK!!
LOOKING BACK, I GUESS IT WASN'T HARD TO SEE THAT THE STRESS WAS GETTING TO HER...
Hey!! Looks like I managed to finish this weeks T.V. Guide crossword puzzle..
DAMN YOU!!
I CALLED UP MY SIS AND SAID IF IT WAS SUCH A STRESSFUL JOB, THEN WHY WEREN'T THERE A LOT OF DISGRUNTLED EMPLOYEE INCIDENTS..YA KNOW, WITH GUNS AND STUFF?
SHE SAID THAT'S WHY EVERYBODY HAS TO WEAR THOSE BIG, WHITE, FOUR-FINGERED GLOVES..
YOU CAN'T FIT YOUR TRIGGER FINGER IN THE LITTLE SLOT...
ALL OF THIS COULD EXPLAIN SKATER NANCY KERRIGAN'S REACTION TO BEING IN THAT PARADE WITH MICKEY MOUSE AT WALT DISNEY WORLD...
This is so corny..I HATE This.
SHE WAS FREAKING OUT!! SHE WAS SITTING NEXT TO HER BIGGEST FEAR..
IF YOU DON'T WIN BIG IN FIGURE SKATING..AND I MEAN BIG..MEDALS & ALL.. THAT'S IT..YOU END UP SKATING AROUND DRESSED AS A BIG, DUMB, CARTOON CHARACTER FOR THE REST OF YOUR LIFE..
CHRONICLES ON ICE
..SCARY.
STOP

This is one of three strips that were adapted into the award-winning live action German short Jetzt Kommt ein Karton.

BY KEITH KNIGHT

"..your humor is sharp, witty, and gently self deprecating... blah, blah.. the usual drivel...

Okay... Here's a letter from **Jim Brawski** of Abalone, New Mexico..

Jim writes: "Hey Keith, How come you have that stupid piece of hair sticking out of your head?"

I'M GLAD YOU ASKED, JIM.. AS MANY OF YOU ALREADY KNOW, I HAVE A **TWIN** SISTER, **TRACY!** WHAT VERY FEW PEOPLE KNOW IS THAT WE WERE BORN **SIAMESE** TWINS...

(photo courtesy of Jet magazine)

..CONNECTED BY THE VERY PIECE OF HAIR YOU ASK ABOUT..

THE MEDICAL UNIT WE WERE BORN IN SAID THEY WOULD BE ABLE TO SEPARATE US.. BUT IT WOULD BE A VERY RISKY OPERATION.. AFTER ALL, THIS WAS 1966...

YOU SEE..ALTHOUGH THE STRANDS OF HAIR CONTAINED NO VITAL ORGANS.. THEY DID CONTAIN STUFF THAT WAS JUST AS IMPORTANT...

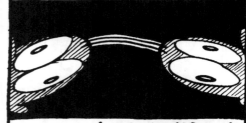

INIMITABLE **STYLE, CHARM, CHARISMA** & A VERY HEAVY **LIBIDO**..

..IT WAS FAR TOO DANGEROUS TO CUT IT DOWN THE MIDDLE.. SO ONLY ONE OF US WAS ABLE TO KEEP THE HAIR ...WHILE THE OTHER WAS DESTINED TO WALLOW IN MEDIOC-

THAT's IT!! HOLD IT RIGHT THERE!!

signed from

Hey...Whaddaya know... It's my sist--

I'M GETTING PRETTY SICK OF YOU MAKING FUN OF ME IN YOUR COMIC STRIPS!!

Aw..C'mon Trace.. It's all just a joke.. No one really believes anything I write...

BOLLOCKS!! I HAVEN'T GOTTEN A DATE SINCE THAT FARM ANIMAL STRIP YOU DID ABOUT ME..JUST BECAUSE YOU LACK SELF CONFIDENCE, DON'T TAKE IT OUT ON ME!! Self Deprecating my ass!!

OW

BOOT

..This guy has ego for days!!

..NOW..LET ME TELL YOU A LITTLE SOMETHING ABOUT MY **BROTHER'S** RECURRING

This comic is lovingly dedicated to my twin sister, **Tracy**, whose 29th birthday is this week.

CURSES.. Foiled again...

Next Time... more gently, self-deprecating comics featuring ME, ME, ME!!

Kiss Kiss

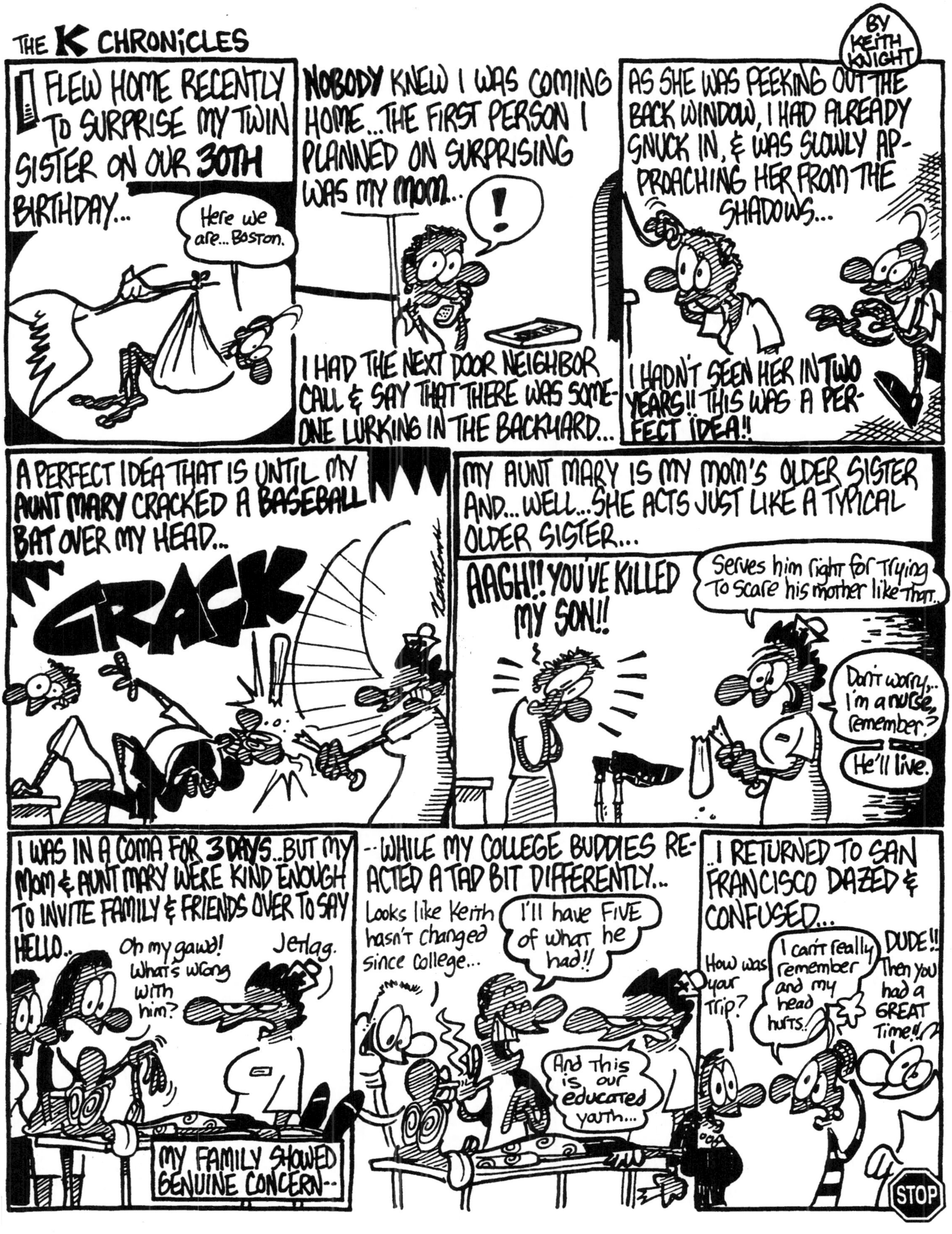
THE K CHRONICLES
BY KEITH KNIGHT
I FLEW HOME RECENTLY TO SURPRISE MY TWIN SISTER ON OUR 30TH BIRTHDAY...
Here we are... Boston.
NOBODY KNEW I WAS COMING HOME... THE FIRST PERSON I PLANNED ON SURPRISING WAS MY MOM...
!
I HAD THE NEXT DOOR NEIGHBOR CALL & SAY THAT THERE WAS SOMEONE LURKING IN THE BACKYARD...
AS SHE WAS PEEKING OUT THE BACK WINDOW, I HAD ALREADY SNUCK IN, & WAS SLOWLY APPROACHING HER FROM THE SHADOWS...
I HADN'T SEEN HER IN TWO YEARS!! THIS WAS A PERFECT IDEA!!
A PERFECT IDEA THAT IS UNTIL MY AUNT MARY CRACKED A BASEBALL BAT OVER MY HEAD...
CRACK
MY AUNT MARY IS MY MOM'S OLDER SISTER AND... WELL... SHE ACTS JUST LIKE A TYPICAL OLDER SISTER...
AAGH!! YOU'VE KILLED MY SON!!
Serves him right for trying to scare his mother like that..
Don't worry,.. I'm a nurse, remember?
He'll live.
I WAS IN A COMA FOR 3 DAYS..BUT MY MOM & AUNT MARY WERE KIND ENOUGH TO INVITE FAMILY & FRIENDS OVER TO SAY HELLO..
Oh my gawd! What's wrong with him?
Jetlag.
MY FAMILY SHOWED GENUINE CONCERN--
--WHILE MY COLLEGE BUDDIES REACTED A TAD BIT DIFFERENTLY...
Looks like Keith hasn't changed since college...
I'll have FIVE of what he had!!
And this is our educated youth...
..I RETURNED TO SAN FRANCISCO DAZED & CONFUSED...
How was your trip?
I can't really remember and my head hurts.
DUDE!! Then you had a GREAT Time!!
STOP

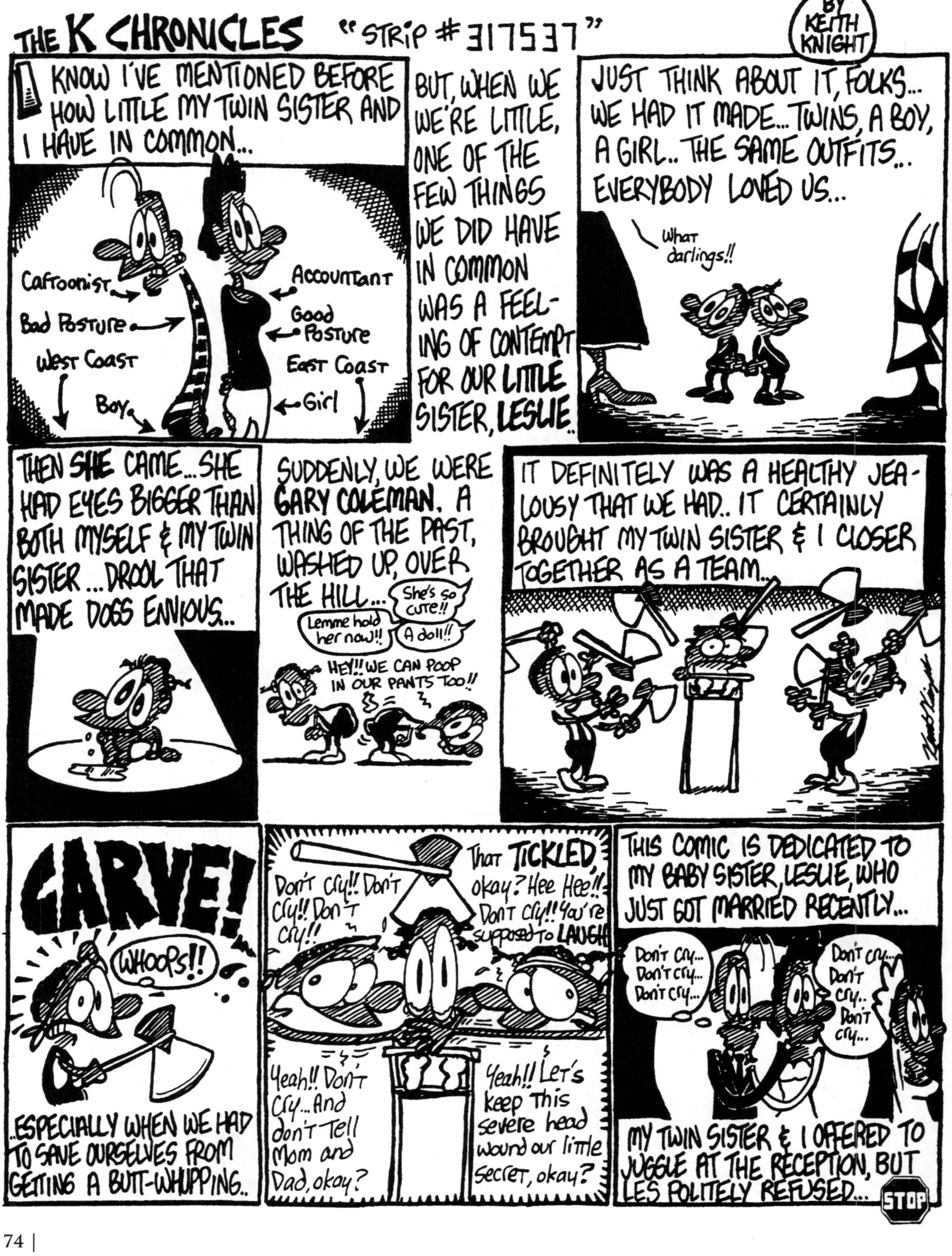
THE K CHRONICLES "STRIP #317537"
BY KEITH KNIGHT
I KNOW I'VE MENTIONED BEFORE HOW LITTLE MY TWIN SISTER AND I HAVE IN COMMON...
Cartoonist
Bad Posture
West Coast
Boy
Accountant
Good Posture
East Coast
Girl
BUT, WHEN WE WE'RE LITTLE, ONE OF THE FEW THINGS WE DID HAVE IN COMMON WAS A FEELING OF CONTEMPT FOR OUR LITTLE SISTER, LESLIE..
JUST THINK ABOUT IT, FOLKS... WE HAD IT MADE... TWINS, A BOY, A GIRL.. THE SAME OUTFITS... EVERYBODY LOVED US...
What darlings!!
THEN SHE CAME... SHE HAD EYES BIGGER THAN BOTH MYSELF & MY TWIN SISTER ...DROOL THAT MADE DOGS ENVIOUS...
SUDDENLY, WE WERE GARY COLEMAN. A THING OF THE PAST, WASHED UP, OVER THE HILL...
She's so cute!!
Lemme hold her now!!
A doll!!
HEY!! WE CAN POOP IN OUR PANTS TOO!!
IT DEFINITELY WAS A HEALTHY JEALOUSY THAT WE HAD.. IT CERTAINLY BROUGHT MY TWIN SISTER & I CLOSER TOGETHER AS A TEAM...
CARVE!
WHOOPS!!
..ESPECIALLY WHEN WE HAD TO SAVE OURSELVES FROM GETTING A BUTT-WHUPPING..
Don't cry!! Don't cry!! Don't cry!!
That TICKLED, okay? Hee Hee!! Don't cry!! You're supposed to LAUGH!
Yeah!! Don't cry... And don't tell Mom and Dad, okay?
Yeah!! Let's keep this severe head wound our little secret, okay?
THIS COMIC IS DEDICATED TO MY BABY SISTER, LESLIE, WHO JUST GOT MARRIED RECENTLY...
Don't cry... Don't cry... Don't cry...
Don't cry... Don't cry.. Don't cry...
MY TWIN SISTER & I OFFERED TO JUGGLE AT THE RECEPTION, BUT LES POLITELY REFUSED...
STOP

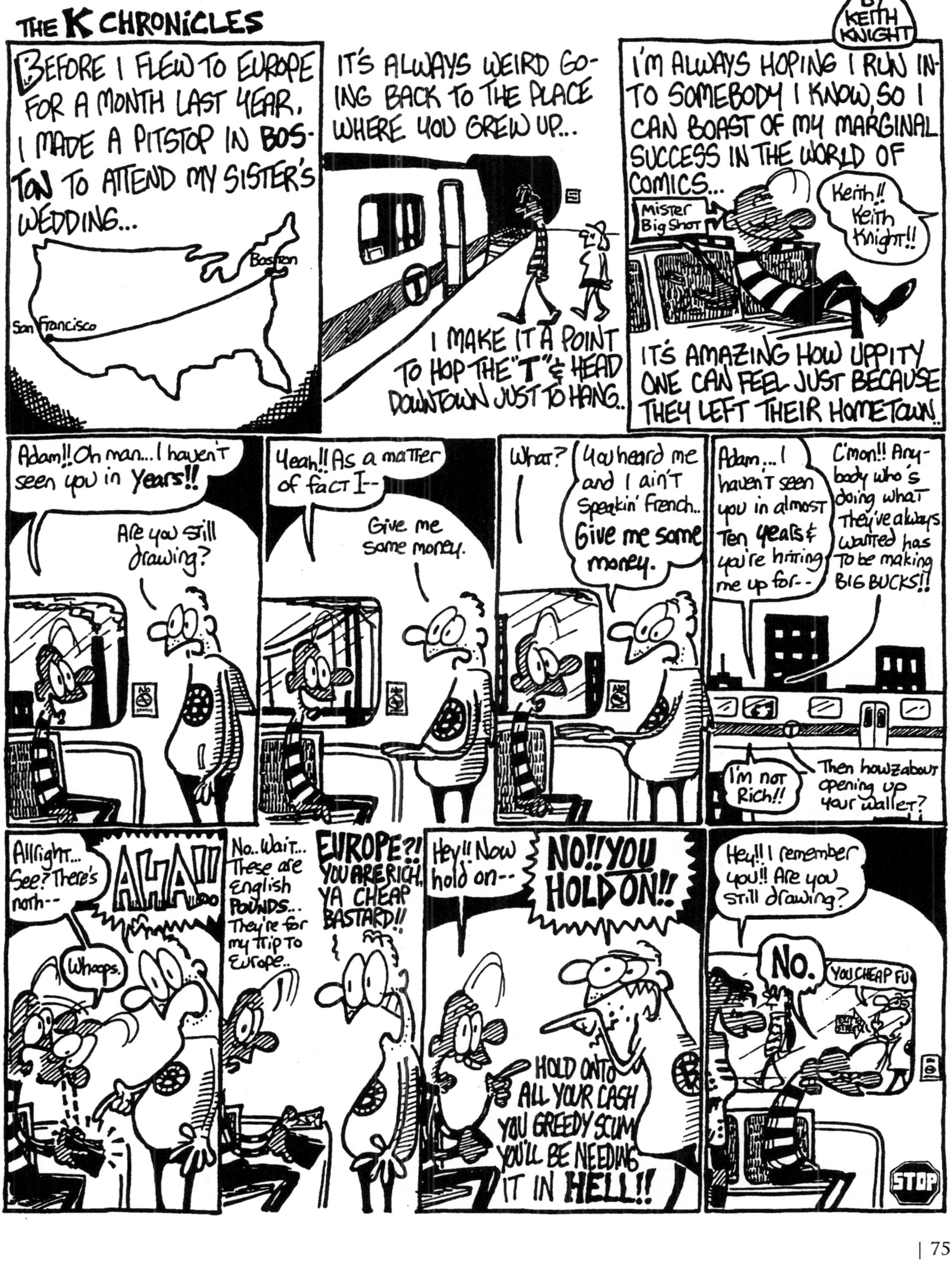
THE K CHRONICLES
BY KEITH KNIGHT
BEFORE I FLEW TO EUROPE FOR A MONTH LAST YEAR, I MADE A PITSTOP IN BOSTON TO ATTEND MY SISTER'S WEDDING...
Boston
San Francisco
IT'S ALWAYS WEIRD GOING BACK TO THE PLACE WHERE YOU GREW UP...
I MAKE IT A POINT TO HOP THE "T" & HEAD DOWNTOWN JUST TO HANG..
I'M ALWAYS HOPING I RUN INTO SOMEBODY I KNOW, SO I CAN BOAST OF MY MARGINAL SUCCESS IN THE WORLD OF COMICS...
Mister Big Shot
Keith!! Keith Knight!!
IT'S AMAZING HOW UPPITY ONE CAN FEEL JUST BECAUSE THEY LEFT THEIR HOMETOWN..
Adam!! Oh man... I haven't seen you in Years!!
Are you still drawing?
Yeah!! As a matter of fact I--
Give me some money.
What?
You heard me and I ain't Speakin' French.. Give me some money.
Adam... I haven't seen you in almost Ten years & you're hitting me up for--
C'mon!! Anybody who's doing what They've always wanted has To be making BIG BUCKS!!
I'm not Rich!!
Then howzabout opening up your wallet?
Allright... See? There's noth--
AHA!!
Whoops.
No.. Wait... These are English POUNDS... They're for my trip to Europe..
EUROPE?! YOU ARE RICH, YA CHEAP BASTARD!!
Hey!! Now hold on--
NO!! YOU HOLD ON!!
HOLD ONTO ALL YOUR CASH YOU GREEDY SCUM YOU'LL BE NEEDING IT IN HELL!!
Hey!! I remember you!! Are you still drawing?
No.
YOU CHEAP FU
STOP

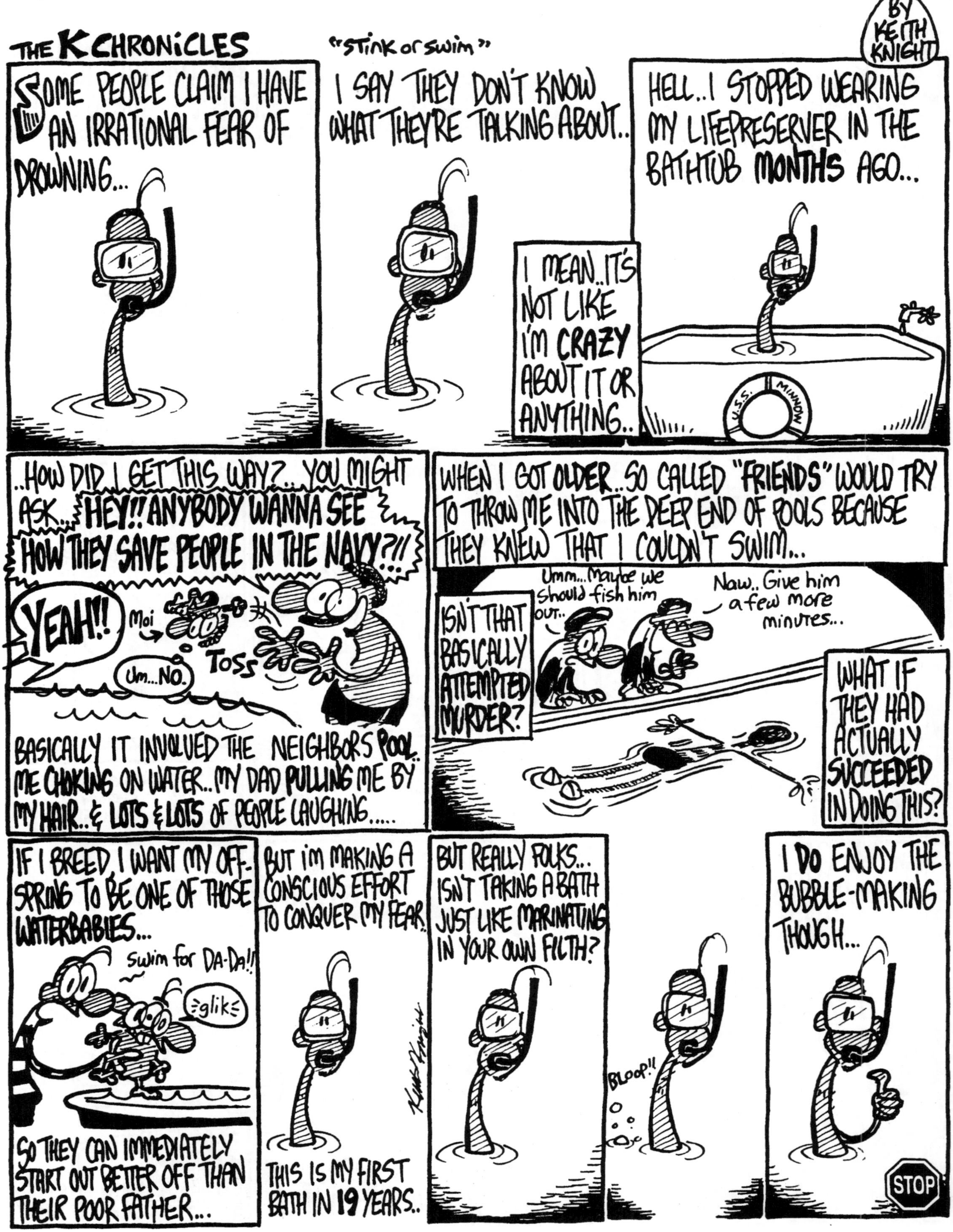
THE K CHRONICLES
"STINK OR SWIM"
BY KEITH KNIGHT
SOME PEOPLE CLAIM I HAVE AN IRRATIONAL FEAR OF DROWNING...
I SAY THEY DON'T KNOW WHAT THEY'RE TALKING ABOUT..
HELL..I STOPPED WEARING MY LIFEPRESERVER IN THE BATHTUB MONTHS AGO...
I MEAN..IT'S NOT LIKE I'M CRAZY ABOUT IT OR ANYTHING..
U.S.S. MINNOW
..HOW DID I GET THIS WAY?.. YOU MIGHT ASK...
HEY!! ANYBODY WANNA SEE HOW THEY SAVE PEOPLE IN THE NAVY?!!
YEAH!!
Moi
TOSS
Um...NO.
BASICALLY IT INVOLVED THE NEIGHBOR'S POOL.. ME CHOKING ON WATER.. MY DAD PULLING ME BY MY HAIR..& LOTS & LOTS OF PEOPLE LAUGHING.....
WHEN I GOT OLDER..SO CALLED "FRIENDS" WOULD TRY TO THROW ME INTO THE DEEP END OF POOLS BECAUSE THEY KNEW THAT I COULDN'T SWIM...
ISN'T THAT BASICALLY ATTEMPTED MURDER?
Umm...Maybe we should fish him out..
Naw.. Give him a few more minutes...
WHAT IF THEY HAD ACTUALLY SUCCEEDED IN DOING THIS?
IF I BREED, I WANT MY OFF-SPRING TO BE ONE OF THOSE WATERBABIES...
Swim for DA-DA!!
glik
SO THEY CAN IMMEDIATELY START OUT BETTER OFF THAN THEIR POOR FATHER...
BUT I'M MAKING A CONSCIOUS EFFORT TO CONQUER MY FEAR..
THIS IS MY FIRST BATH IN 19 YEARS..
BUT REALLY FOLKS... ISN'T TAKING A BATH JUST LIKE MARINATING IN YOUR OWN FILTH?
BLOOP!!
I DO ENJOY THE BUBBLE-MAKING THOUGH...
STOP

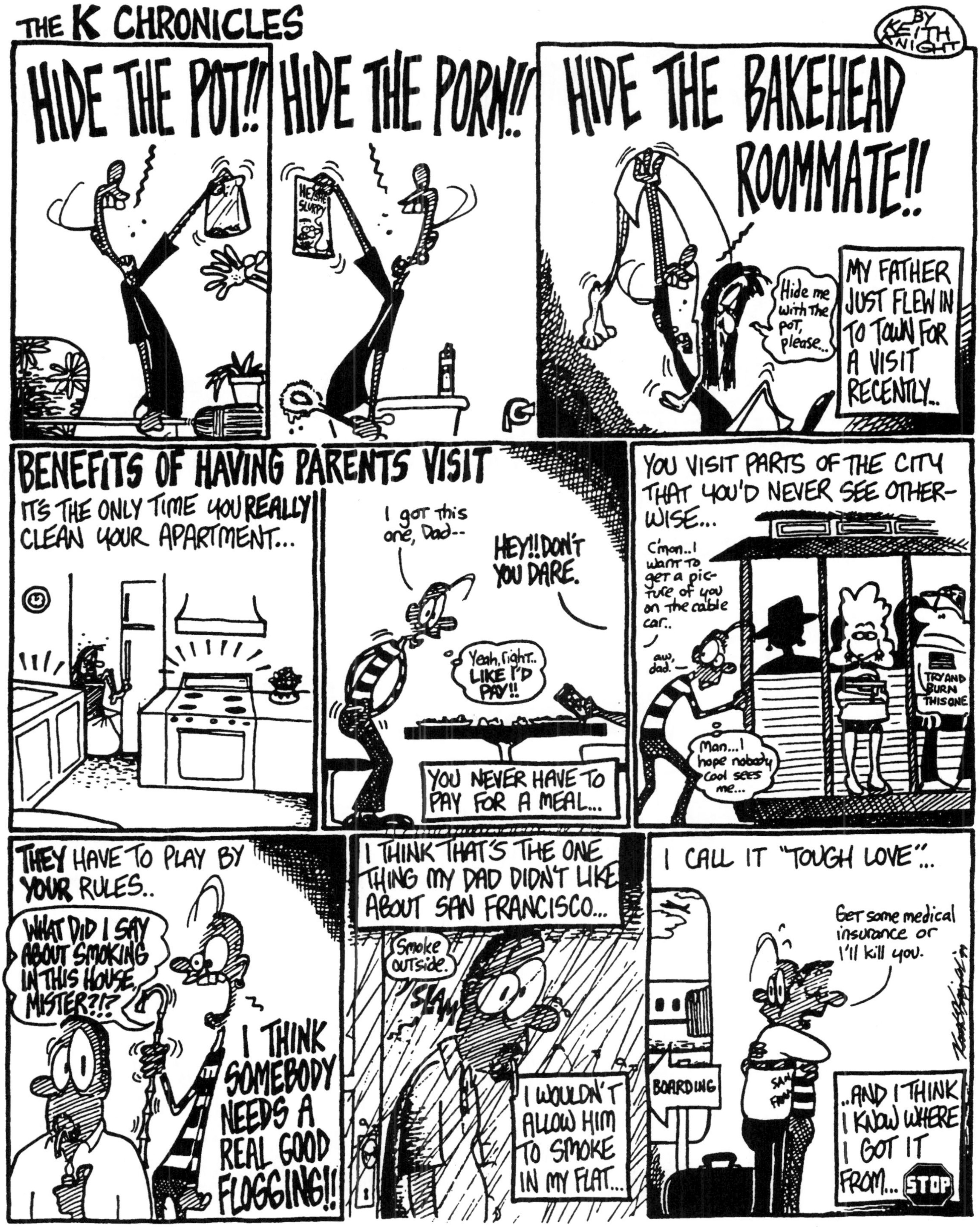

THE K CHRONICLES
BY KEITH KNIGHT
HIDE THE POT!!..
HIDE THE PORN!!..
HE/SHE SLURPY
HIDE THE BAKEHEAD ROOMMATE!!..
Hide me with the pot, please...
MY FATHER JUST FLEW IN TO TOWN FOR A VISIT RECENTLY..
BENEFITS OF HAVING PARENTS VISIT
IT'S THE ONLY TIME YOU REALLY CLEAN YOUR APARTMENT...
I got this one, Dad--
HEY!! DON'T YOU DARE.
Yeah, right.. LIKE I'D PAY!!
YOU NEVER HAVE TO PAY FOR A MEAL...
YOU VISIT PARTS OF THE CITY THAT YOU'D NEVER SEE OTHERWISE...
C'mon..I want to get a picture of you on the cable car..
aw, dad..
TRY AND BURN THIS ONE
Man...I hope nobody cool sees me...
THEY HAVE TO PLAY BY YOUR RULES..
WHAT DID I SAY ABOUT SMOKING IN THIS HOUSE, MISTER?!?
I THINK SOMEBODY NEEDS A REAL GOOD FLOGGING!!
I THINK THAT'S THE ONE THING MY DAD DIDN'T LIKE ABOUT SAN FRANCISCO...
Smoke outside.
SLAM
I WOULDN'T ALLOW HIM TO SMOKE IN MY FLAT...
I CALL IT "TOUGH LOVE"...
Get some medical insurance or I'll kill you.
BOARDING
SAN FRAN
..AND I THINK I KNOW WHERE I GOT IT FROM...
STOP

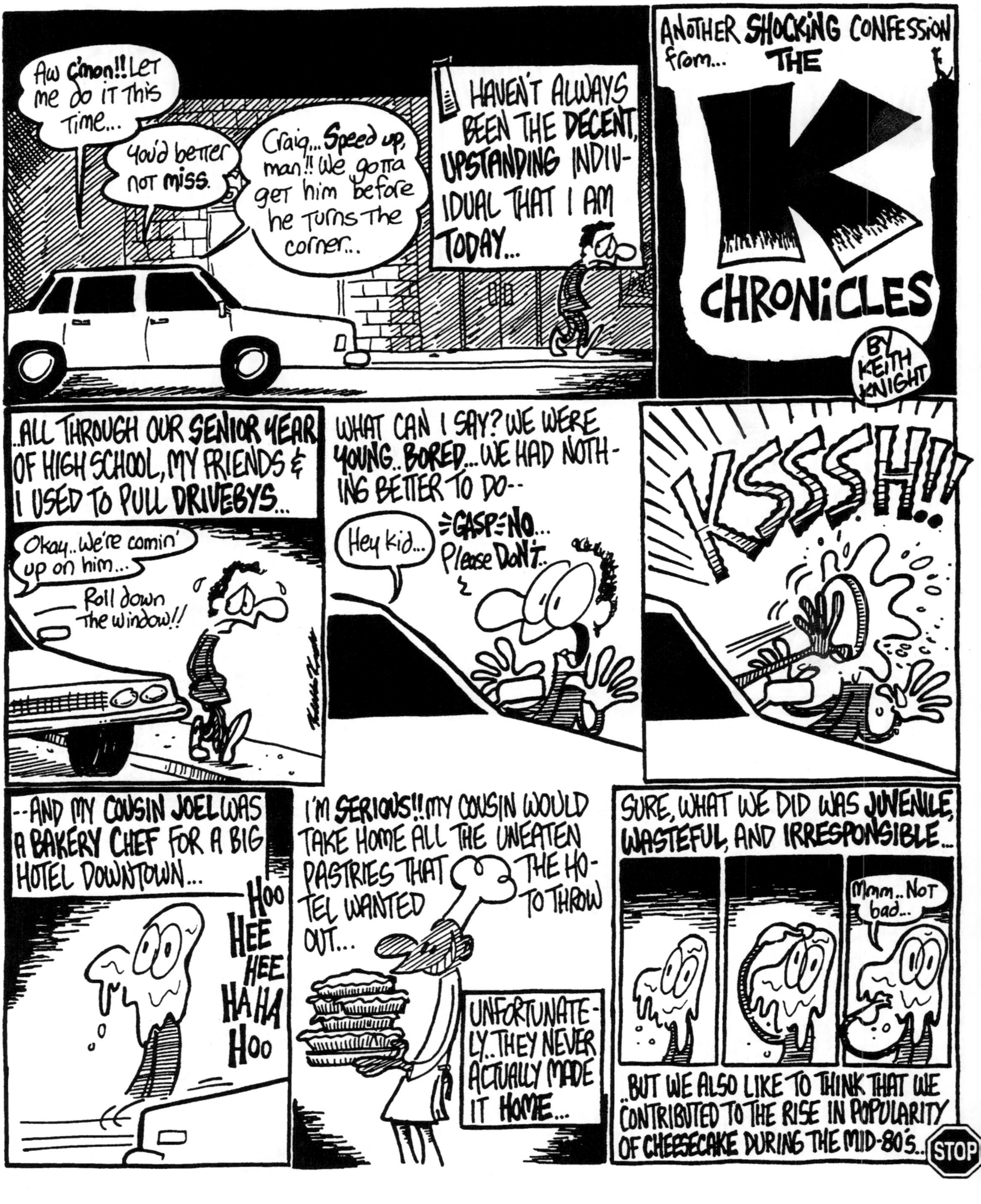

Aw c'mon!! Let me do it this time...
You'd better not miss.
Craig... Speed up, man!! We gotta get him before he turns the corner...
I haven't always been the decent, upstanding individual that I am today...
ANOTHER SHOCKING CONFESSION from... THE K CHRONICLES
BY KEITH KNIGHT
...ALL THROUGH OUR SENIOR YEAR OF HIGH SCHOOL, MY FRIENDS & I USED TO PULL DRIVEBYS...
Okay.. We're comin' up on him...
Roll down the window!!
WHAT CAN I SAY? WE WERE YOUNG.. BORED... WE HAD NOTHING BETTER TO DO--
Hey kid...
=GASP= NO... Please DON'T..
KSSSSH!!!
--AND MY COUSIN JOEL WAS A BAKERY CHEF FOR A BIG HOTEL DOWNTOWN...
HOO HEE HEE HA HA HOO
I'M SERIOUS!! MY COUSIN WOULD TAKE HOME ALL THE UNEATEN PASTRIES THAT THE HOTEL WANTED TO THROW OUT...
UNFORTUNATELY.. THEY NEVER ACTUALLY MADE IT HOME...
SURE, WHAT WE DID WAS JUVENILE, WASTEFUL, AND IRRESPONSIBLE...
Mmm.. Not bad...
..BUT WE ALSO LIKE TO THINK THAT WE CONTRIBUTED TO THE RISE IN POPULARITY OF CHEESECAKE DURING THE MID-80's..
STOP

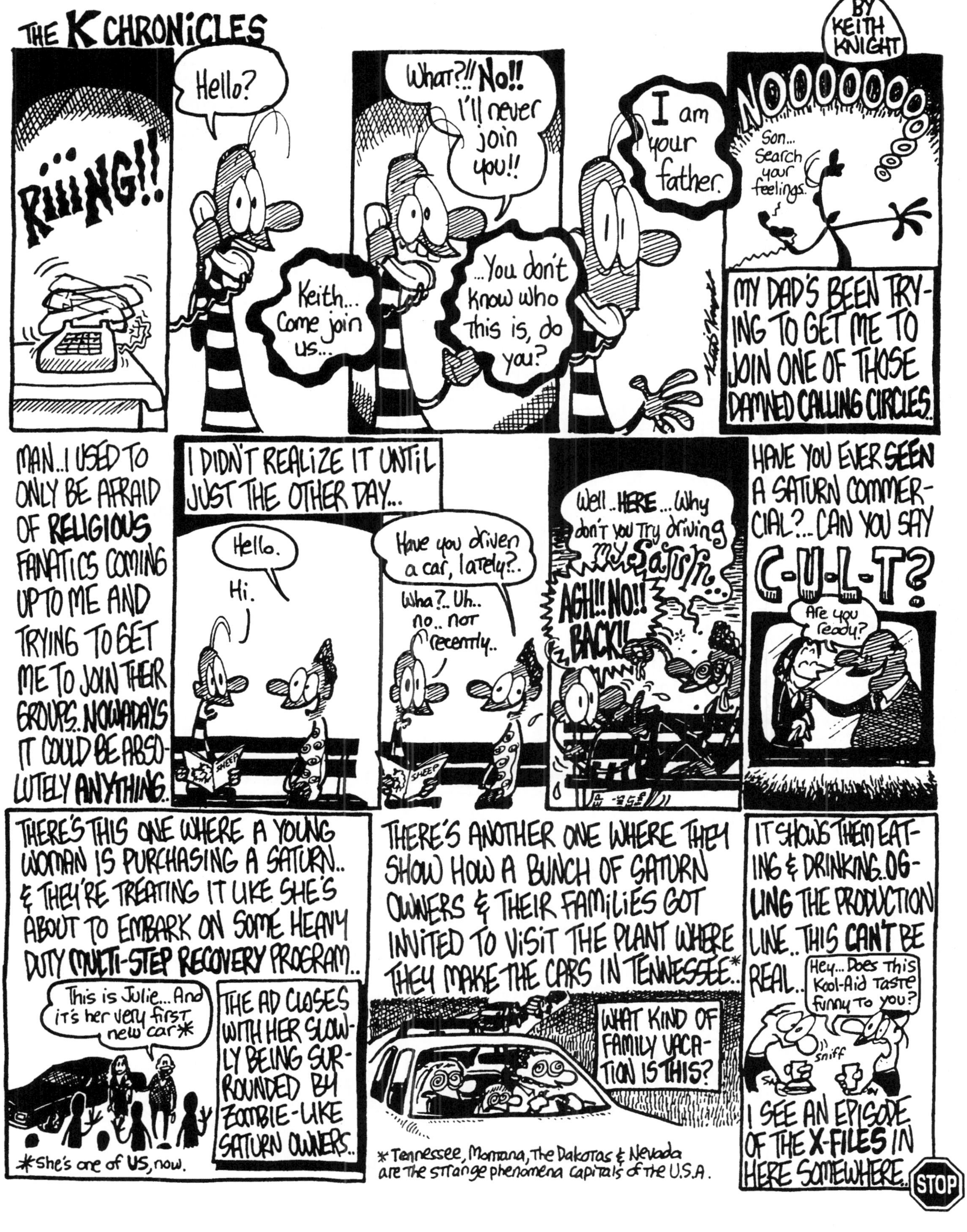

THE K CHRONICLES
BY KEITH KNIGHT
...RIIING!!
Hello?
Keith... Come join us...
What?!! No!! I'll never join you!!
...You don't know who this is, do you?
I am your father.
NOOOOOOOOOOOO
Son... Search your feelings.
MY DAD'S BEEN TRYING TO GET ME TO JOIN ONE OF THOSE DAMNED CALLING CIRCLES..
MAN..I USED TO ONLY BE AFRAID OF RELIGIOUS FANATICS COMING UP TO ME AND TRYING TO GET ME TO JOIN THEIR GROUPS..NOWADAYS IT COULD BE ABSOLUTELY ANYTHING..
I DIDN'T REALIZE IT UNTIL JUST THE OTHER DAY...
Hello.
Hi.
SHEEP
Have you driven a car, lately?..
Wha?..Uh.. no.. not recently..
SHEEP
Well..HERE...Why don't you try driving my Saturn...
AGH!! NO!! BACK!!
HAVE YOU EVER SEEN A SATURN COMMERCIAL?...CAN YOU SAY C-U-L-T?
Are you ready?
THERE'S THIS ONE WHERE A YOUNG WOMAN IS PURCHASING A SATURN.. & THEY'RE TREATING IT LIKE SHE'S ABOUT TO EMBARK ON SOME HEAVY DUTY MULTI-STEP RECOVERY PROGRAM..
This is Julie...And it's her very first new car*
THE AD CLOSES WITH HER SLOWLY BEING SURROUNDED BY ZOMBIE-LIKE SATURN OWNERS..
*She's one of US, now.
THERE'S ANOTHER ONE WHERE THEY SHOW HOW A BUNCH OF SATURN OWNERS & THEIR FAMILIES GOT INVITED TO VISIT THE PLANT WHERE THEY MAKE THE CARS IN TENNESSEE*..
WHAT KIND OF FAMILY VACATION IS THIS?
*Tennessee, Montana, The Dakotas & Nevada are the strange phenomena capitals of the U.S.A.
IT SHOWS THEM EATING & DRINKING..OGLING THE PRODUCTION LINE..THIS CAN'T BE REAL..
Hey...Does This Kool-Aid Taste funny To you?
sniff
I SEE AN EPISODE OF THE X-FILES IN HERE SOMEWHERE..
STOP

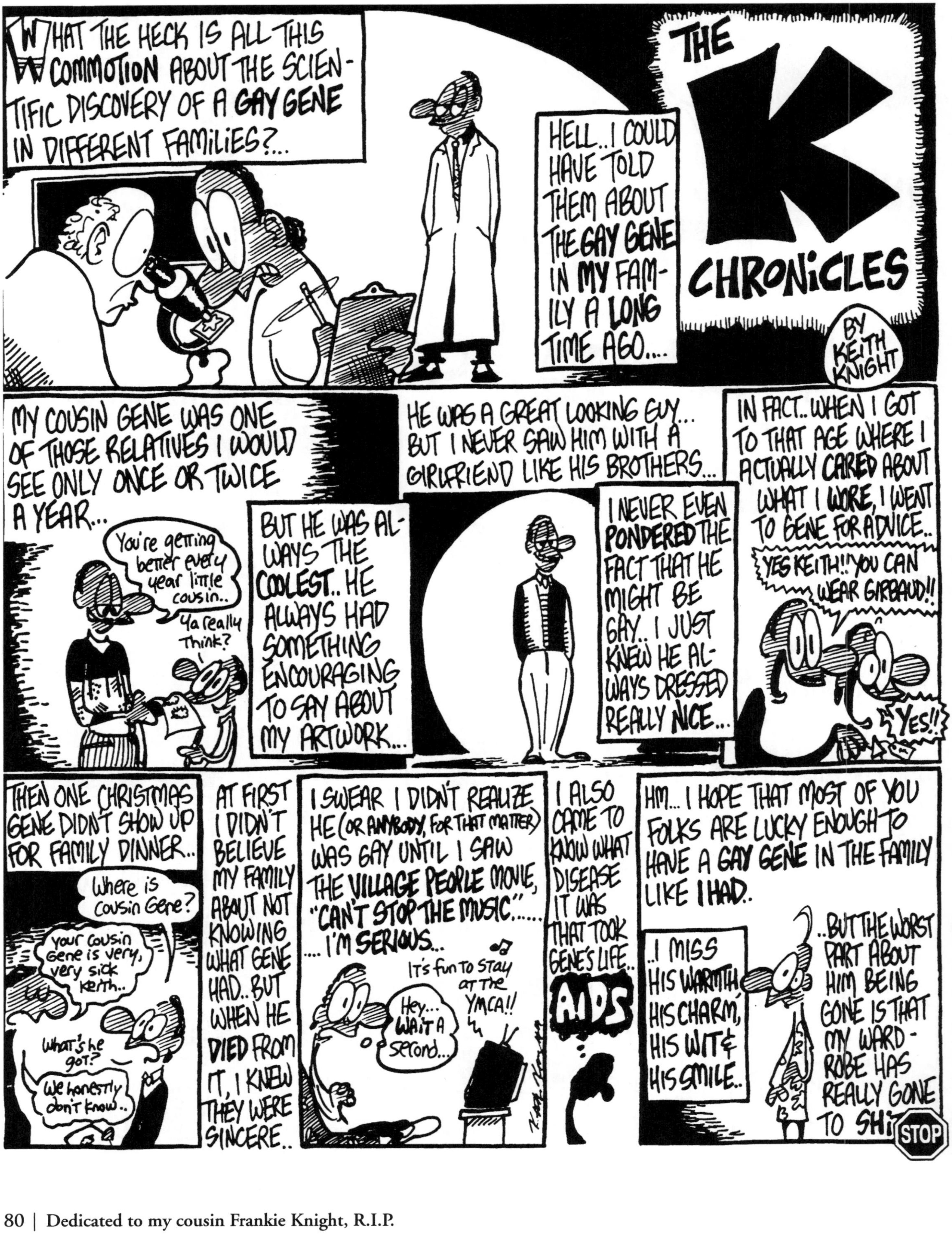
THE K CHRONICLES
BY KEITH KNIGHT
WHAT THE HECK IS ALL THIS COMMOTION ABOUT THE SCIENTIFIC DISCOVERY OF A GAY GENE IN DIFFERENT FAMILIES?...
HELL.. I COULD HAVE TOLD THEM ABOUT THE GAY GENE IN MY FAMILY A LONG TIME AGO....
MY COUSIN GENE WAS ONE OF THOSE RELATIVES I WOULD SEE ONLY ONCE OR TWICE A YEAR...
You're getting better every year little cousin..
Ya really Think?
BUT HE WAS ALWAYS THE COOLEST.. HE ALWAYS HAD SOMETHING ENCOURAGING TO SAY ABOUT MY ARTWORK...
HE WAS A GREAT LOOKING GUY... BUT I NEVER SAW HIM WITH A GIRLFRIEND LIKE HIS BROTHERS...
I NEVER EVEN PONDERED THE FACT THAT HE MIGHT BE GAY.. I JUST KNEW HE ALWAYS DRESSED REALLY NICE...
IN FACT.. WHEN I GOT TO THAT AGE WHERE I ACTUALLY CARED ABOUT WHAT I WORE, I WENT TO GENE FOR ADVICE..
YES KEITH!! YOU CAN WEAR GIRBAUD!!
YES!!
THEN ONE CHRISTMAS GENE DIDN'T SHOW UP FOR FAMILY DINNER..
Where is cousin Gene?
Your cousin Gene is very, very sick keith..
What's he got?
We honestly don't know..
AT FIRST I DIDN'T BELIEVE MY FAMILY ABOUT NOT KNOWING WHAT GENE HAD.. BUT WHEN HE DIED FROM IT, I KNEW THEY WERE SINCERE..
I SWEAR I DIDN'T REALIZE HE (OR ANYBODY, FOR THAT MATTER) WAS GAY UNTIL I SAW THE VILLAGE PEOPLE MOVIE, "CAN'T STOP THE MUSIC"...... I'M SERIOUS...
It's fun to stay at the YMCA!!
Hey... WAIT A Second...
I ALSO CAME TO KNOW WHAT DISEASE IT WAS THAT TOOK GENE'S LIFE..
AIDS
HM... I HOPE THAT MOST OF YOU FOLKS ARE LUCKY ENOUGH TO HAVE A GAY GENE IN THE FAMILY LIKE I HAD..
..I MISS HIS WARMTH, HIS CHARM, HIS WIT & HIS SMILE..
..BUT THE WORST PART ABOUT HIM BEING GONE IS THAT MY WARDROBE HAS REALLY GONE TO SHI
STOP

 Dedicated to my cousin Frankie Knight, R.I.P.

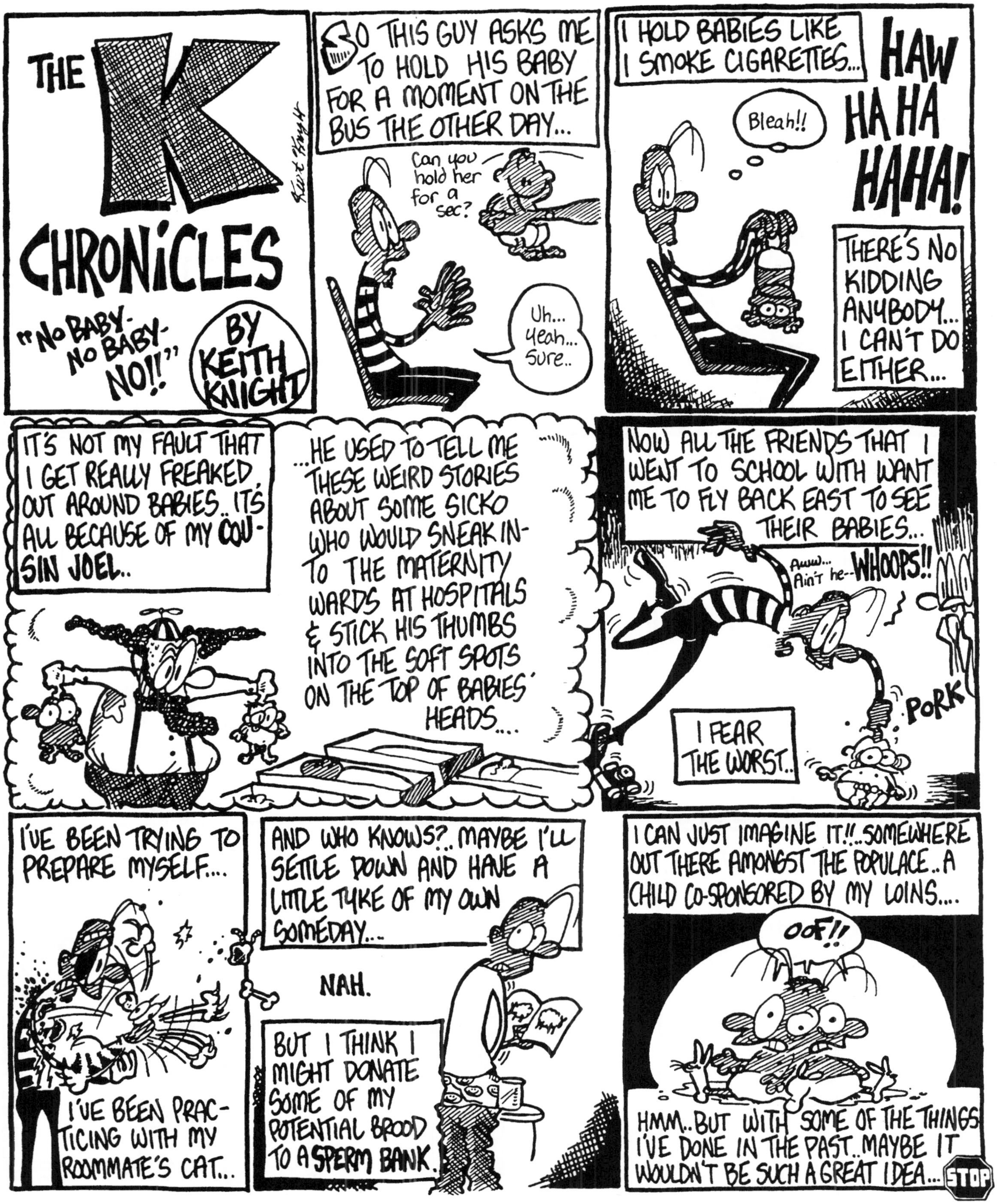
THE K CHRONICLES
"No Baby-No Baby-NO!!"
BY KEITH KNIGHT
SO THIS GUY ASKS ME TO HOLD HIS BABY FOR A MOMENT ON THE BUS THE OTHER DAY...
Can you hold her for a sec?
Uh... yeah... sure..
I HOLD BABIES LIKE I SMOKE CIGARETTES...
Bleah!!
HAW HA HA HAHA!
THERE'S NO KIDDING ANYBODY... I CAN'T DO EITHER...
IT'S NOT MY FAULT THAT I GET REALLY FREAKED OUT AROUND BABIES.. IT'S ALL BECAUSE OF MY COUSIN JOEL..
...HE USED TO TELL ME THESE WEIRD STORIES ABOUT SOME SICKO WHO WOULD SNEAK INTO THE MATERNITY WARDS AT HOSPITALS & STICK HIS THUMBS INTO THE SOFT SPOTS ON THE TOP OF BABIES' HEADS....
NOW ALL THE FRIENDS THAT I WENT TO SCHOOL WITH WANT ME TO FLY BACK EAST TO SEE THEIR BABIES...
Aww... Ain't he--WHOOPS!!
PORK
I FEAR THE WORST..
I'VE BEEN TRYING TO PREPARE MYSELF....
I'VE BEEN PRACTICING WITH MY ROOMMATE'S CAT...
AND WHO KNOWS?..MAYBE I'LL SETTLE DOWN AND HAVE A LITTLE TYKE OF MY OWN SOMEDAY...
NAH.
BUT I THINK I MIGHT DONATE SOME OF MY POTENTIAL BROOD TO A SPERM BANK.
I CAN JUST IMAGINE IT!!..SOMEWHERE OUT THERE AMONGST THE POPULACE..A CHILD CO-SPONSORED BY MY LOINS....
OOF!!
HMM..BUT WITH SOME OF THE THINGS I'VE DONE IN THE PAST..MAYBE IT WOULDN'T BE SUCH A GREAT IDEA...
STOP

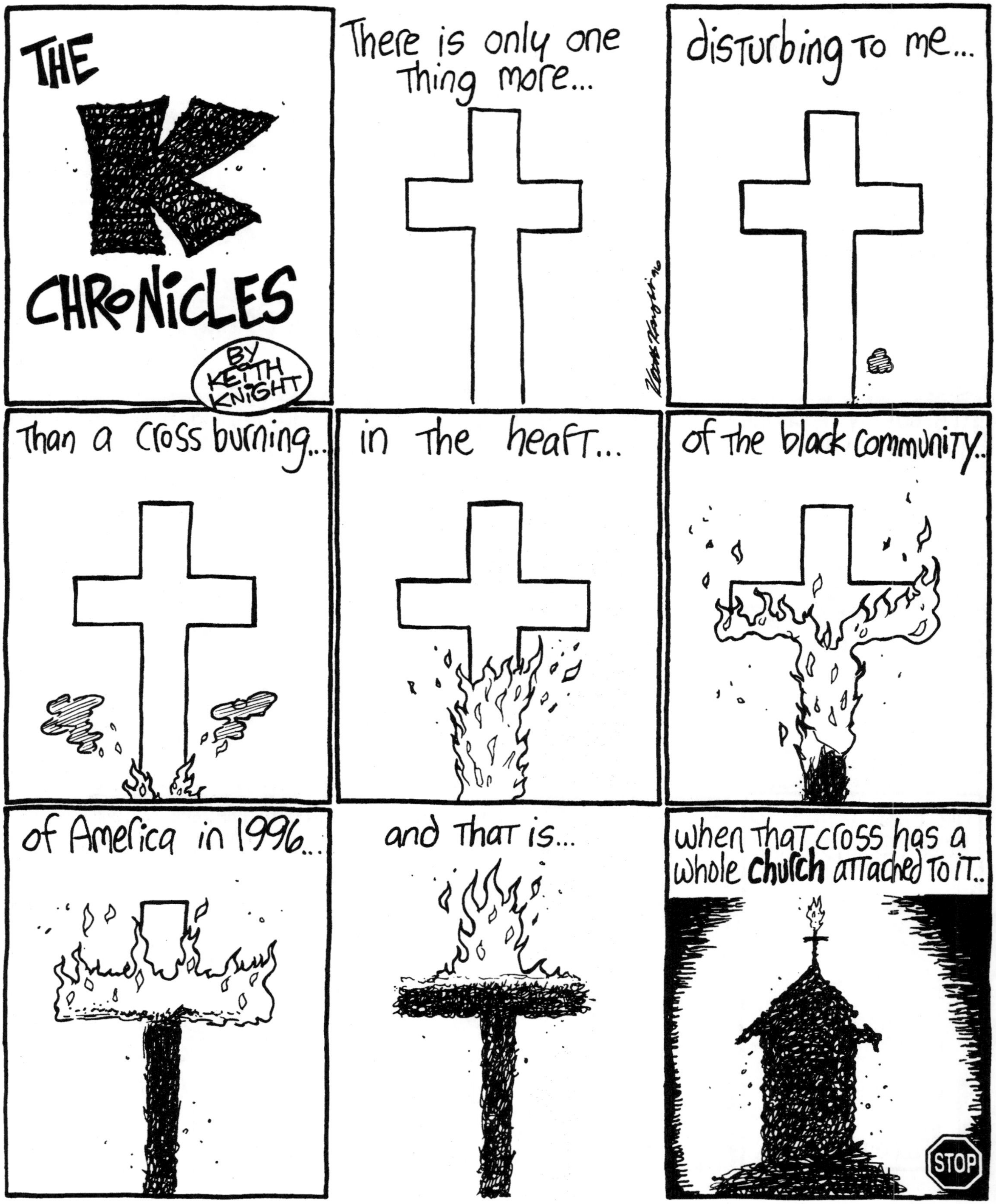

THE K CHRONICLES
BY KEITH KNIGHT
There is only one thing more...
disturbing to me...
than a cross burning...
in the heart...
of the black community...
of America in 1996...
and that is...
when that cross has a whole church attached to it...
STOP

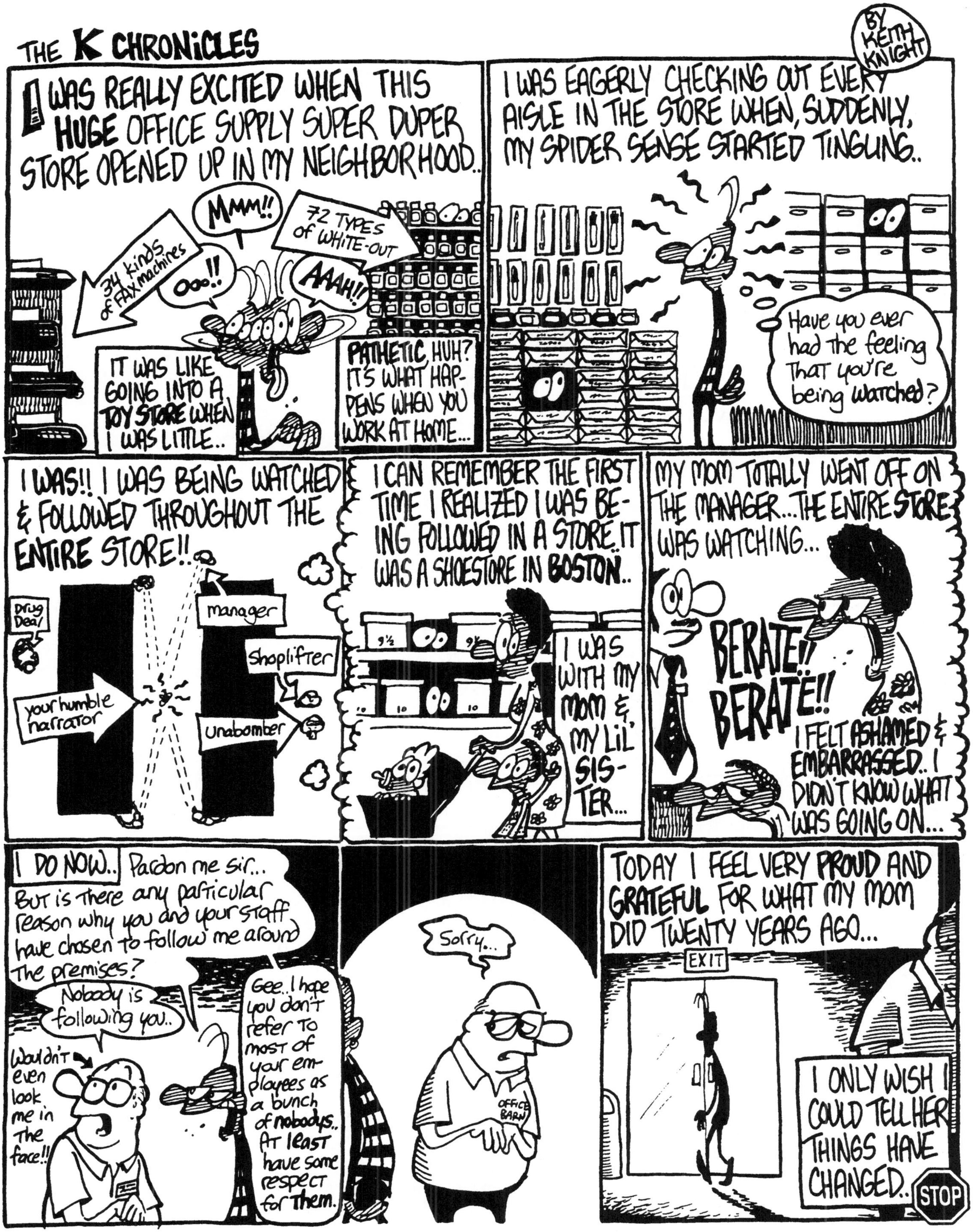
THE K CHRONICLES
BY KEITH KNIGHT
I WAS REALLY EXCITED WHEN THIS HUGE OFFICE SUPPLY SUPER DUPER STORE OPENED UP IN MY NEIGHBORHOOD..
MMM!!
72 TYPES OF WHITE-OUT
34 kinds of FAX machines
Ooo!!
AAAH!!
IT WAS LIKE GOING INTO A TOY STORE WHEN I WAS LITTLE..
PATHETIC, HUH? IT'S WHAT HAPPENS WHEN YOU WORK AT HOME...
I WAS EAGERLY CHECKING OUT EVERY AISLE IN THE STORE WHEN, SUDDENLY, MY SPIDER SENSE STARTED TINGLING..
Have you ever had the feeling That you're being watched?
I WAS!! I WAS BEING WATCHED & FOLLOWED THROUGHOUT THE ENTIRE STORE!!..
Drug Deal
manager
shoplifter
your humble narrator
unabomber
I CAN REMEMBER THE FIRST TIME I REALIZED I WAS BEING FOLLOWED IN A STORE..IT WAS A SHOESTORE IN BOSTON..
I WAS WITH MY MOM & MY LIL' SISTER...
MY MOM TOTALLY WENT OFF ON THE MANAGER...THE ENTIRE STORE WAS WATCHING...
BERATE!! BERATE!!
I FELT ASHAMED & EMBARRASSED.. I DIDN'T KNOW WHAT WAS GOING ON...
I DO NOW..
Pardon me sir... But is there any particular reason why you and your staff have chosen to follow me around the premises?
Nobody is following you..
Wouldn't even look me in the face!!
Gee.. I hope you don't refer to most of your employees as a bunch of nobodys.. At least have some respect for them.
Sorry...
OFFICE BARN
TODAY I FEEL VERY PROUD AND GRATEFUL FOR WHAT MY MOM DID TWENTY YEARS AGO...
EXIT
I ONLY WISH I COULD TELL HER THINGS HAVE CHANGED..
STOP

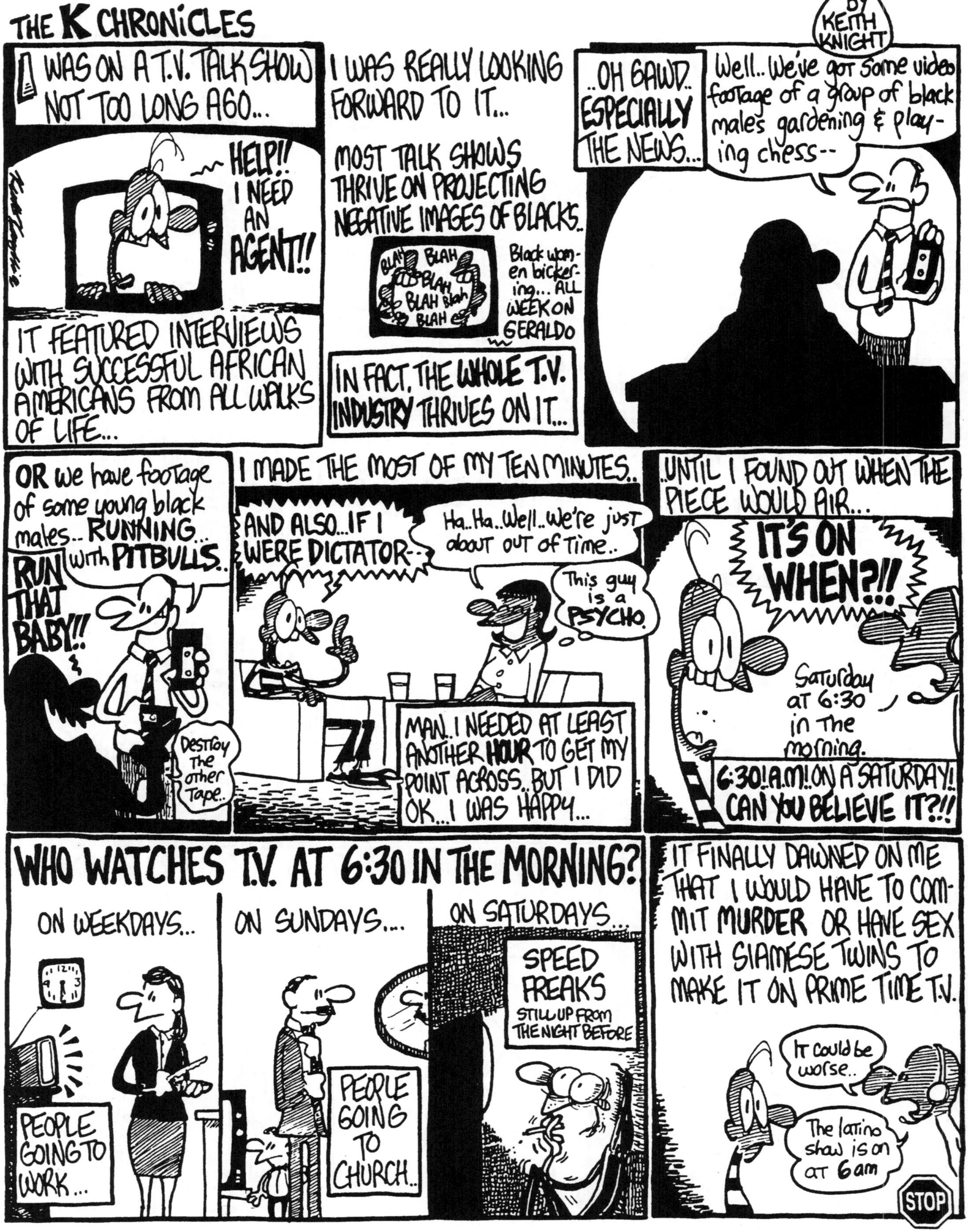
THE K CHRONICLES
BY KEITH KNIGHT
I WAS ON A T.V. TALK SHOW NOT TOO LONG AGO...
HELP!! I NEED AN AGENT!!
IT FEATURED INTERVIEWS WITH SUCCESSFUL AFRICAN AMERICANS FROM ALL WALKS OF LIFE...
I WAS REALLY LOOKING FORWARD TO IT...
MOST TALK SHOWS THRIVE ON PROJECTING NEGATIVE IMAGES OF BLACKS..
BLAH BLAH BLAH BLAH BLAH Blah BLAH
Black women bickering... ALL WEEK ON GERALDO
IN FACT, THE WHOLE T.V. INDUSTRY THRIVES ON IT...
..OH GAWD.. ESPECIALLY THE NEWS...
Well.. We've got some video footage of a group of black males gardening & playing chess--
OR we have footage of some young black males.. RUNNING... with PITBULLS..
RUN THAT BABY!!
Destroy The other Tape..
I MADE THE MOST OF MY TEN MINUTES..
AND ALSO...IF I WERE DICTATOR--
Ha..Ha..Well..We're just about out of Time..
This guy is a PSYCHO.
MAN..I NEEDED AT LEAST ANOTHER HOUR TO GET MY POINT ACROSS..BUT I DID OK...I WAS HAPPY...
..UNTIL I FOUND OUT WHEN THE PIECE WOULD AIR...
IT'S ON WHEN?!!
Saturday at 6:30 in the morning.
6:30!A.M!ON A SATURDAY!! CAN YOU BELIEVE IT?!!
WHO WATCHES T.V. AT 6:30 IN THE MORNING?
ON WEEKDAYS...
PEOPLE GOING TO WORK...
ON SUNDAYS....
PEOPLE GOING TO CHURCH..
ON SATURDAYS...
SPEED FREAKS STILL UP FROM THE NIGHT BEFORE
IT FINALLY DAWNED ON ME THAT I WOULD HAVE TO COMMIT MURDER OR HAVE SEX WITH SIAMESE TWINS TO MAKE IT ON PRIME TIME T.V.
It could be worse..
The latino show is on at 6am
STOP

I was being interviewed on the San Francisco Main Library's front steps when a guy walked up and yelled "I AM NOT A SPEED FREAK!!"

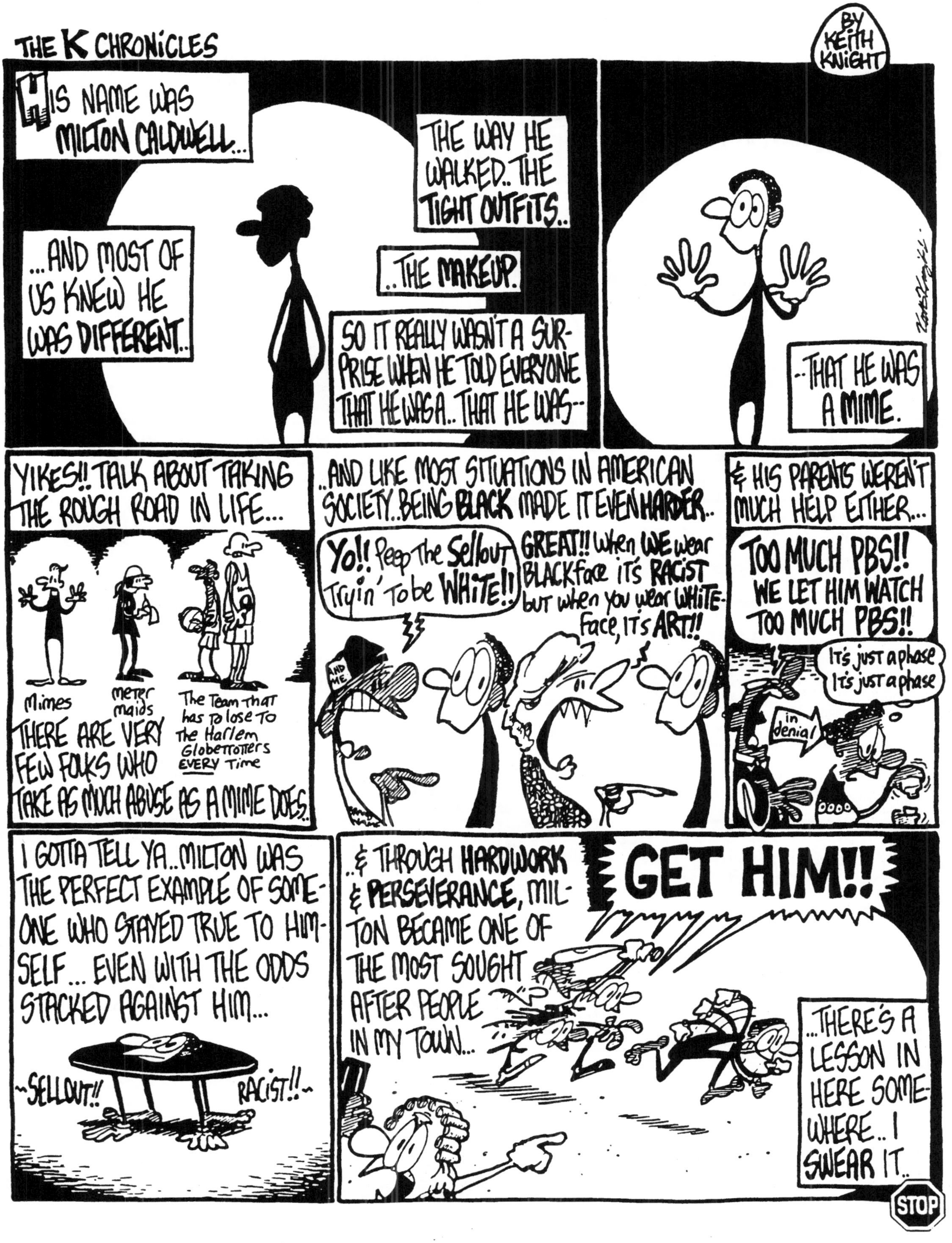
THE K CHRONICLES
BY KEITH KNIGHT
HIS NAME WAS MILTON CALDWELL...
THE WAY HE WALKED.. THE TIGHT OUTFITS..
...AND MOST OF US KNEW HE WAS DIFFERENT..
..THE MAKEUP.
SO IT REALLY WASN'T A SUR-PRISE WHEN HE TOLD EVERYONE THAT HE WAS A.. THAT HE WAS--
--THAT HE WAS A MIME.
YIKES!!. TALK ABOUT TAKING THE ROUGH ROAD IN LIFE...
Mimes
meter maids
The Team that has to lose to the Harlem Globetrotters EVERY Time
THERE ARE VERY FEW FOLKS WHO TAKE AS MUCH ABUSE AS A MIME DOES..
..AND LIKE MOST SITUATIONS IN AMERICAN SOCIETY..BEING BLACK MADE IT EVEN HARDER..
Yo!! Peep the Sellout Tryin' To be WHITE!!
GREAT!! When WE wear BLACKface it's RACIST but when you wear WHITE-Face, it's ART!!
& HIS PARENTS WEREN'T MUCH HELP EITHER...
TOO MUCH PBS!! WE LET HIM WATCH TOO MUCH PBS!!
It's just a phase It's just a phase
in denial
I GOTTA TELL YA..MILTON WAS THE PERFECT EXAMPLE OF SOME-ONE WHO STAYED TRUE TO HIM-SELF... EVEN WITH THE ODDS STACKED AGAINST HIM...
~SELLOUT!!
RACIST!!~
..& THROUGH HARDWORK & PERSEVERANCE, MIL-TON BECAME ONE OF THE MOST SOUGHT AFTER PEOPLE IN MY TOWN...
GET HIM!!
...THERE'S A LESSON IN HERE SOME-WHERE.. I SWEAR IT..
STOP

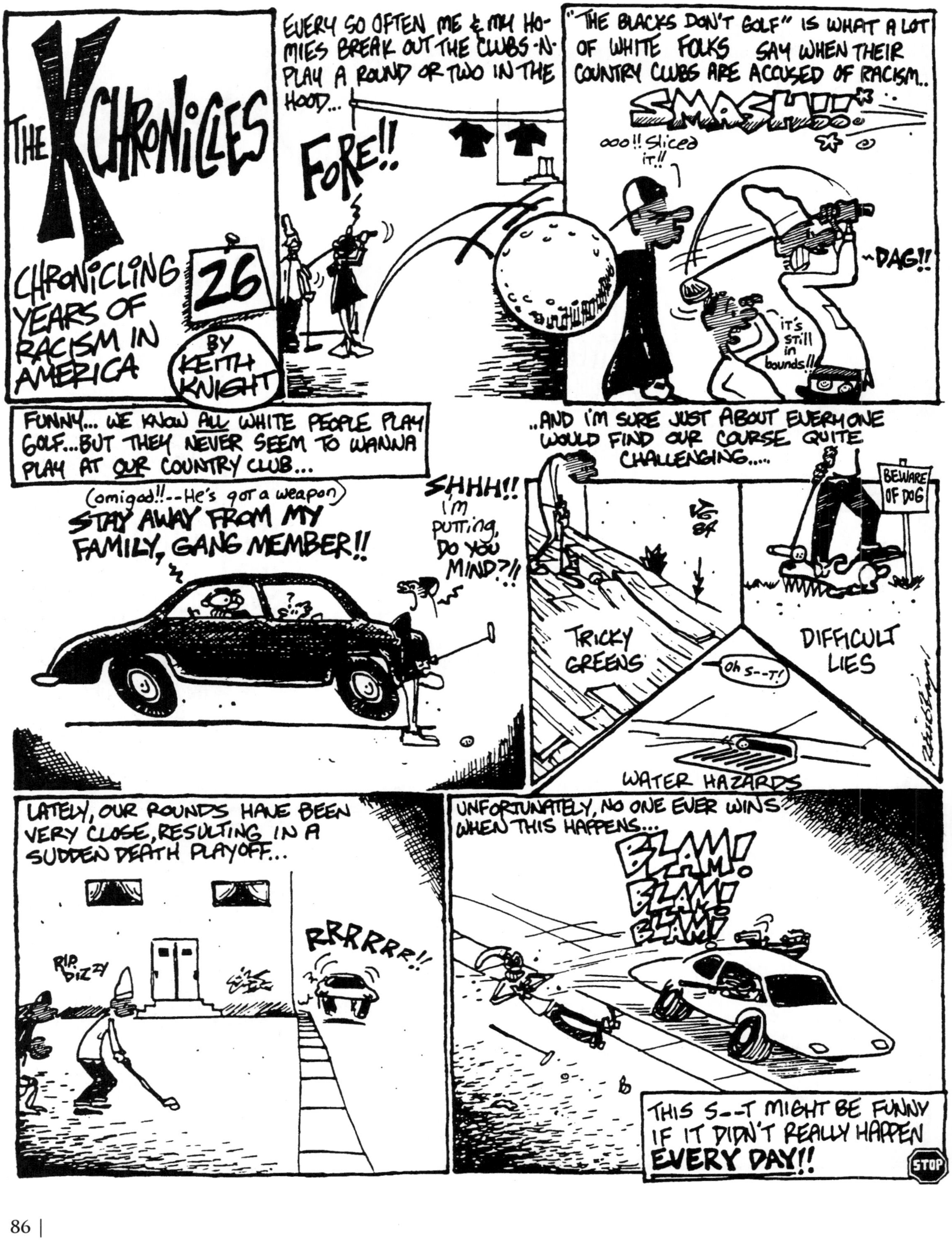

THE K CHRONICLES
CHRONICLING 26 YEARS OF RACISM IN AMERICA
BY KEITH KNIGHT
EVERY SO OFTEN ME & MY HOMIES BREAK OUT THE CLUBS-N-PLAY A ROUND OR TWO IN THE HOOD...
FORE!!
"THE BLACKS DON'T GOLF" IS WHAT A LOT OF WHITE FOLKS SAY WHEN THEIR COUNTRY CLUBS ARE ACCUSED OF RACISM..
SMASH!!
ooo!! Sliced it!!
~DAG!!
it's still in bounds!!
FUNNY... WE KNOW ALL WHITE PEOPLE PLAY GOLF...BUT THEY NEVER SEEM TO WANNA PLAY AT OUR COUNTRY CLUB...
(omigod!!--He's got a weapon)
STAY AWAY FROM MY FAMILY, GANG MEMBER!!
SHHH!! I'm putting, DO YOU MIND?!!
..AND I'M SURE JUST ABOUT EVERYONE WOULD FIND OUR COURSE QUITE CHALLENGING.....
BEWARE OF DOG
TRICKY GREENS
DIFFICULT LIES
Oh S--T!
WATER HAZARDS
LATELY, OUR ROUNDS HAVE BEEN VERY CLOSE, RESULTING IN A SUDDEN DEATH PLAYOFF...
R.I.P. DIZZY
RRRRRR!!
UNFORTUNATELY, NO ONE EVER WINS WHEN THIS HAPPENS...
BLAM! BLAM! BLAM!
THIS S--T MIGHT BE FUNNY IF IT DIDN'T REALLY HAPPEN EVERY DAY!!
STOP

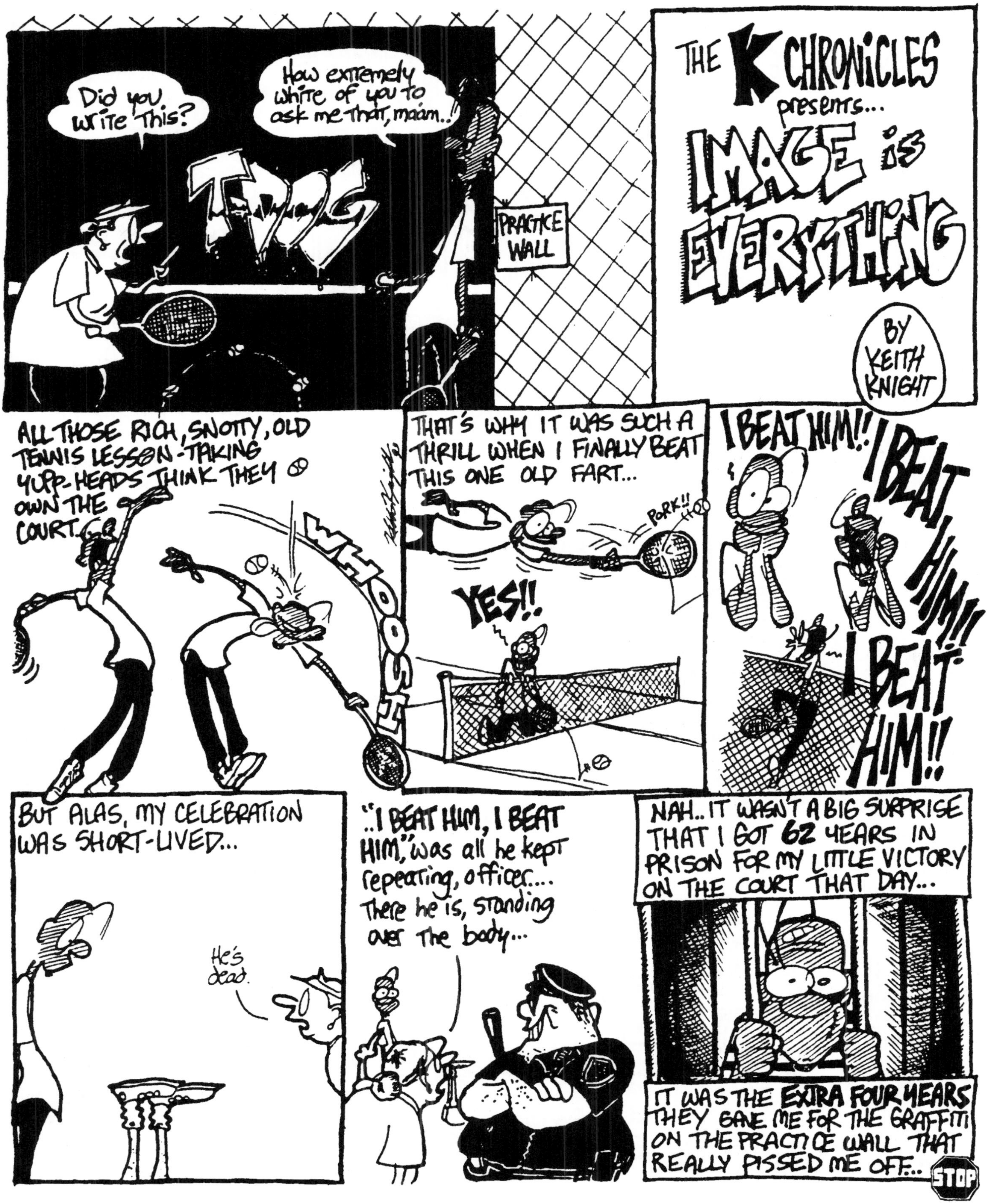
THE K CHRONICLES presents...
IMAGE is EVERYTHING
BY KEITH KNIGHT
Did you write this?
How extremely white of you to ask me that, ma'am..!
T-DOG
PRACTICE WALL
ALL THOSE RICH, SNOTTY, OLD TENNIS LESSON-TAKING YUPP-HEADS THINK THEY OWN THE COURT...
WHOOSH
THAT'S WHY IT WAS SUCH A THRILL WHEN I FINALLY BEAT THIS ONE OLD FART...
PORK!!
YES!!
I BEAT HIM!!
I BEAT HIM!!
I BEAT HIM!!
BUT ALAS, MY CELEBRATION WAS SHORT-LIVED...
He's dead.
"I BEAT HIM, I BEAT HIM," was all he kept repeating, officer.... There he is, standing over the body...
NAH.. IT WASN'T A BIG SURPRISE THAT I GOT 62 YEARS IN PRISON FOR MY LITTLE VICTORY ON THE COURT THAT DAY...
IT WAS THE EXTRA FOUR YEARS THEY GAVE ME FOR THE GRAFFITI ON THE PRACTICE WALL THAT REALLY PISSED ME OFF...
STOP

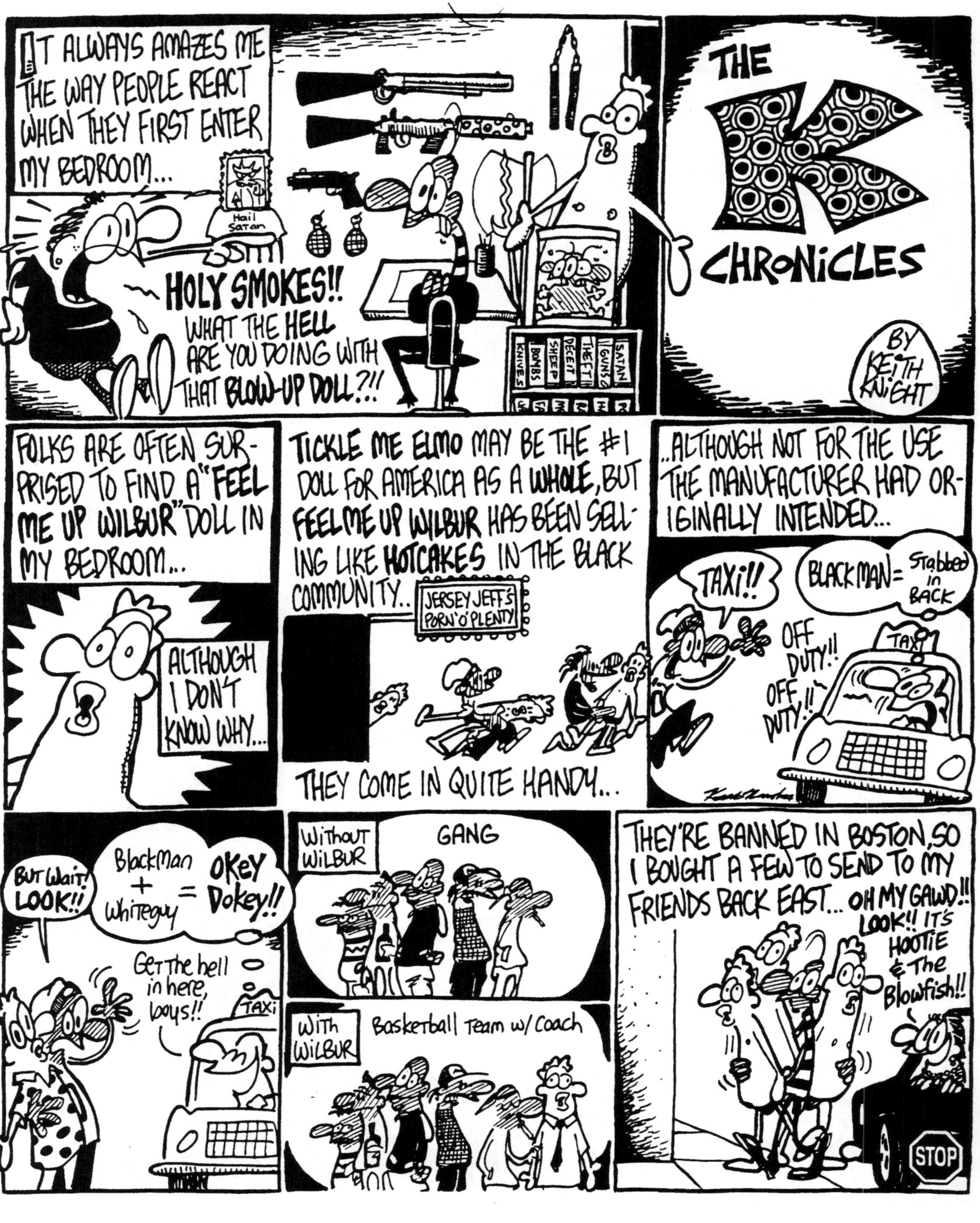
IT ALWAYS AMAZES ME THE WAY PEOPLE REACT WHEN THEY FIRST ENTER MY BEDROOM...
Hail Satan
HOLY SMOKES!! WHAT THE HELL ARE YOU DOING WITH THAT BLOW-UP DOLL?!!
KNIVES
BOMBS
SHEEP
DECEIT
THEFT
GUNS
SATAN
THE K CHRONICLES
BY KEITH KNIGHT
FOLKS ARE OFTEN SURPRISED TO FIND A "FEEL ME UP WILBUR" DOLL IN MY BEDROOM...
ALTHOUGH I DON'T KNOW WHY...
TICKLE ME ELMO MAY BE THE #1 DOLL FOR AMERICA AS A WHOLE, BUT FEEL ME UP WILBUR HAS BEEN SELLING LIKE HOTCAKES IN THE BLACK COMMUNITY...
JERSEY JEFF'S PORN 'O' PLENTY
THEY COME IN QUITE HANDY...
...ALTHOUGH NOT FOR THE USE THE MANUFACTURER HAD ORIGINALLY INTENDED...
TAXI!!
BLACK MAN = Stabbed in BACK
OFF DUTY!!
OFF DUTY!!
TAXI
BUT WAIT! LOOK!!
BlackMan + Whiteguy = OKEY DOKEY!!
Get the hell in here, boys!!
TAXI
Without WILBUR
GANG
With WILBUR
Basketball Team w/ Coach
THEY'RE BANNED IN BOSTON, SO I BOUGHT A FEW TO SEND TO MY FRIENDS BACK EAST... OH MY GAWD!! LOOK!! IT'S HOOTIE & The Blowfish!!
STOP

 One of my top three favorite comics that I've done.

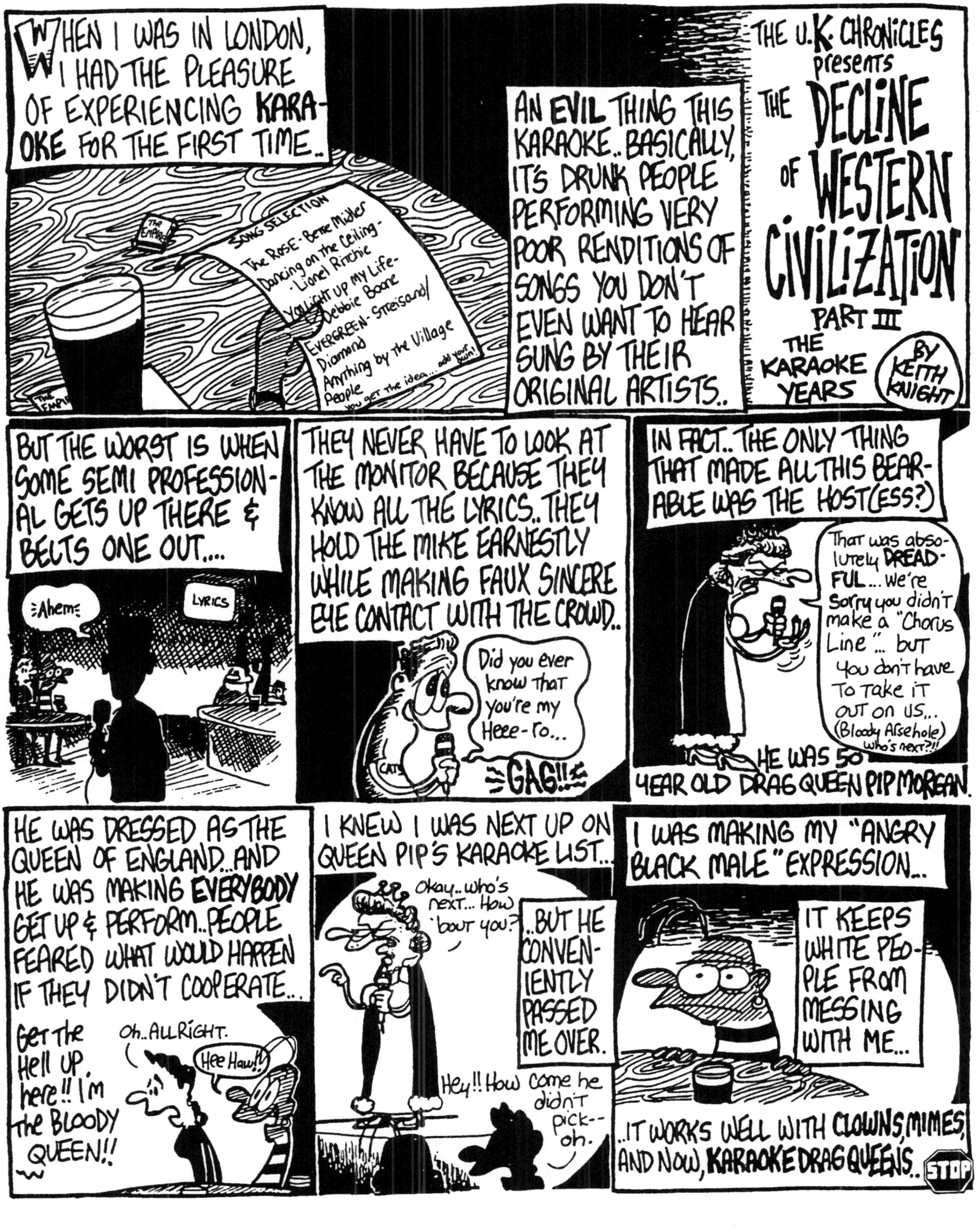

WHEN I WAS IN LONDON, I HAD THE PLEASURE OF EXPERIENCING **KARAOKE** FOR THE FIRST TIME..
SONG SELECTION
The Rose - Bette Midler
Dancing on the Ceiling - Lionel Ritchie
You Light Up My Life - Debbie Boone
Evergreen - Streisand/Diamond
Anything by the Village People
you get the idea... add your own!
AN **EVIL** THING THIS KARAOKE.. BASICALLY, IT'S DRUNK PEOPLE PERFORMING VERY POOR RENDITIONS OF SONGS YOU DON'T EVEN WANT TO HEAR SUNG BY THEIR ORIGINAL ARTISTS..
THE U.K. CHRONICLES presents
THE DECLINE OF WESTERN CIVILIZATION
PART III
THE KARAOKE YEARS
BY KEITH KNIGHT
BUT THE WORST IS WHEN SOME SEMI PROFESSIONAL GETS UP THERE & BELTS ONE OUT....
Ahem
LYRICS
THEY NEVER HAVE TO LOOK AT THE MONITOR BECAUSE THEY KNOW ALL THE LYRICS.. THEY HOLD THE MIKE EARNESTLY WHILE MAKING FAUX SINCERE EYE CONTACT WITH THE CROWD..
Did you ever know that you're my Heee-ro...
GAG!!
IN FACT.. THE ONLY THING THAT MADE ALL THIS BEARABLE WAS THE HOST(ESS?)
That was absolutely **DREADFUL**... We're sorry you didn't make a "Chorus Line"... but you don't have to take it out on us... (Bloody Arsehole) who's next?!!
HE WAS 50 YEAR OLD DRAG QUEEN **PIP MORGAN**.
HE WAS DRESSED AS THE QUEEN OF ENGLAND.. AND HE WAS MAKING **EVERYBODY** GET UP & PERFORM.. PEOPLE FEARED WHAT WOULD HAPPEN IF THEY DIDN'T COOPERATE...
Get the Hell up here!! I'm the Bloody QUEEN!!
Oh.. ALLRIGHT.
Hee Haw!!
I KNEW I WAS NEXT UP ON QUEEN PIP'S KARAOKE LIST...
Okay.. who's next... How 'bout you?
..BUT HE CONVENIENTLY PASSED ME OVER.
Hey!! How come he didn't pick-- oh.
I WAS MAKING MY "ANGRY BLACK MALE" EXPRESSION...
IT KEEPS WHITE PEOPLE FROM MESSING WITH ME...
..IT WORKS WELL WITH **CLOWNS, MIMES,** AND NOW, **KARAOKE DRAG QUEENS**..
STOP

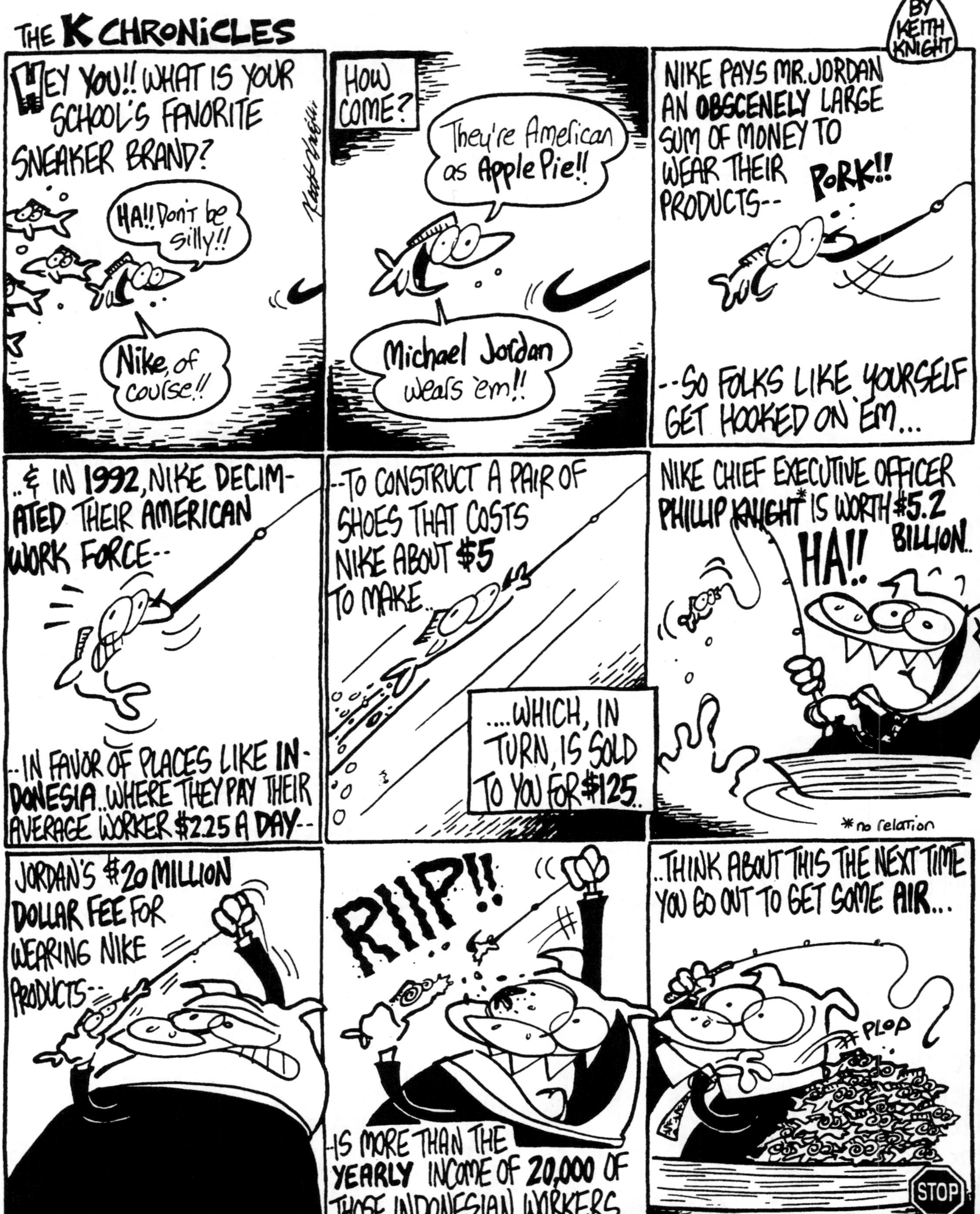
THE K CHRONICLES
BY KEITH KNIGHT
HEY YOU!! WHAT IS YOUR SCHOOL'S FAVORITE SNEAKER BRAND?
Nike, of course!!
HA!! Don't be silly!!
HOW COME?
Michael Jordan wears 'em!!
They're American as Apple Pie!!
NIKE PAYS MR. JORDAN AN OBSCENELY LARGE SUM OF MONEY TO WEAR THEIR PRODUCTS--
PORK!!
--SO FOLKS LIKE YOURSELF GET HOOKED ON 'EM...
...& IN 1992, NIKE DECIMATED THEIR AMERICAN WORK FORCE--
--IN FAVOR OF PLACES LIKE INDONESIA.. WHERE THEY PAY THEIR AVERAGE WORKER $2.25 A DAY--
--TO CONSTRUCT A PAIR OF SHOES THAT COSTS NIKE ABOUT $5 TO MAKE...
....WHICH, IN TURN, IS SOLD TO YOU FOR $125..
NIKE CHIEF EXECUTIVE OFFICER PHILLIP KNIGHT* IS WORTH $5.2 BILLION..
HA!!
*no relation
JORDAN'S $20 MILLION DOLLAR FEE FOR WEARING NIKE PRODUCTS--
RIIIP!!
--IS MORE THAN THE YEARLY INCOME OF 20,000 OF THOSE INDONESIAN WORKERS...
..THINK ABOUT THIS THE NEXT TIME YOU GO OUT TO GET SOME AIR...
PLOP
STOP

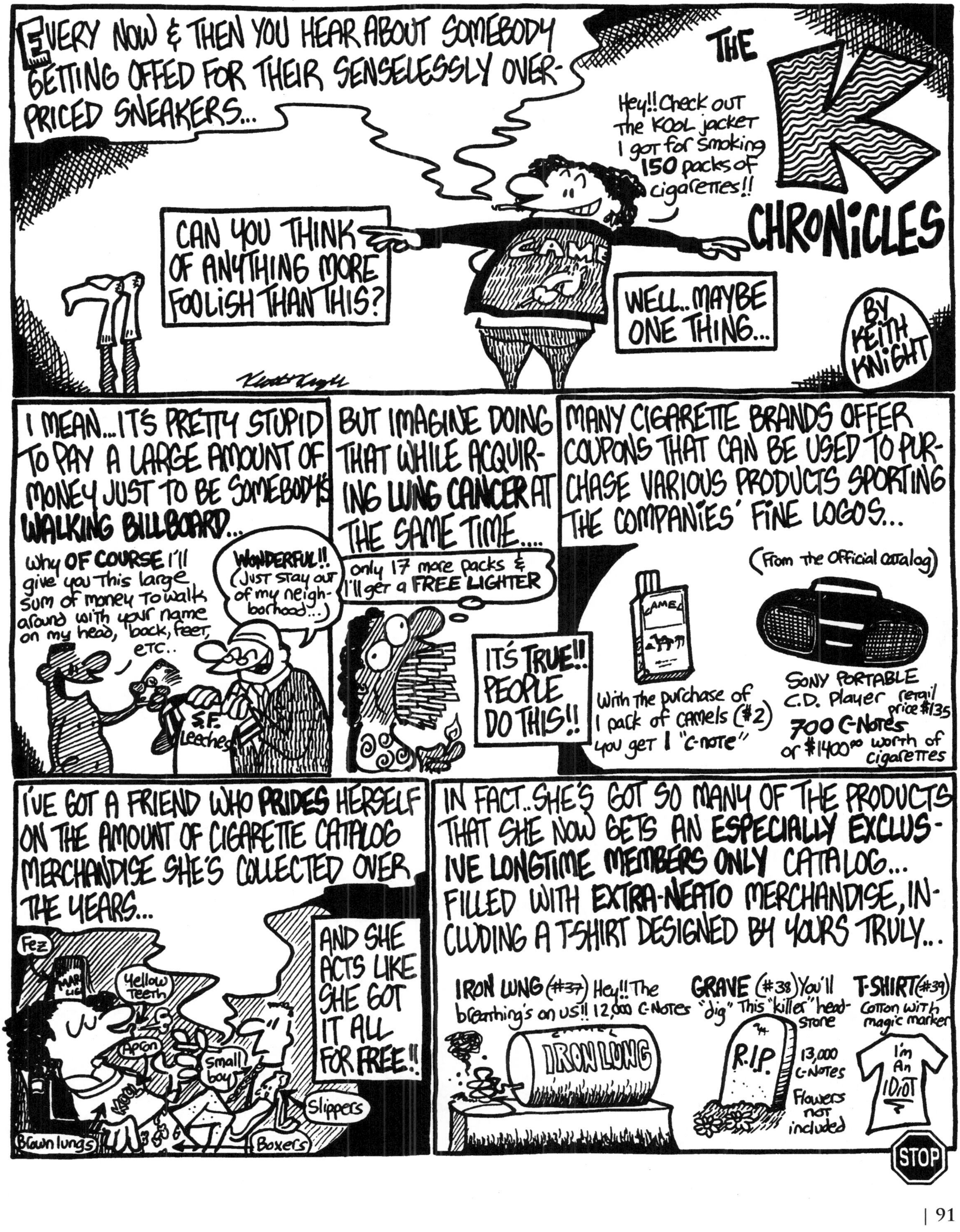

EVERY NOW & THEN YOU HEAR ABOUT SOMEBODY GETTING OFFED FOR THEIR SENSELESSLY OVER-PRICED SNEAKERS...
THE K CHRONICLES
Hey!! Check out the KOOL jacket I got for smoking 150 packs of cigarettes!!
CAN YOU THINK OF ANYTHING MORE FOOLISH THAN THIS?
WELL.. MAYBE ONE THING...
BY KEITH KNIGHT
Keith Knight
I MEAN... IT'S PRETTY STUPID TO PAY A LARGE AMOUNT OF MONEY JUST TO BE SOMEBODY'S WALKING BILLBOARD...
Why OF COURSE I'll give you this large sum of money to walk around with your name on my head, back, feet, etc..
WONDERFUL!! (JUST STAY OUT OF MY NEIGH-BORHOOD...)
S.F. Leeches
BUT IMAGINE DOING THAT WHILE ACQUIR-ING LUNG CANCER AT THE SAME TIME....
only 17 more packs & I'll get a FREE LIGHTER
IT'S TRUE!! PEOPLE DO THIS!!
MANY CIGARETTE BRANDS OFFER COUPONS THAT CAN BE USED TO PUR-CHASE VARIOUS PRODUCTS SPORTING THE COMPANIES' FINE LOGOS...
(From the Official catalog)
CAMEL
With the purchase of 1 pack of camels (#2) you get 1 "C-note"
SONY PORTABLE C.D. Player retail price $135
700 C-Notes or $1400.00 worth of cigarettes
I'VE GOT A FRIEND WHO PRIDES HERSELF ON THE AMOUNT OF CIGARETTE CATALOG MERCHANDISE SHE'S COLLECTED OVER THE YEARS...
Fez
Yellow Teeth
Apron
Small boy
Slippers
Brown lungs
Boxers
AND SHE ACTS LIKE SHE GOT IT ALL FOR FREE!!
IN FACT.. SHE'S GOT SO MANY OF THE PRODUCTS THAT SHE NOW GETS AN ESPECIALLY EXCLUS-IVE LONGTIME MEMBERS ONLY CATALOG... FILLED WITH EXTRA-NEATO MERCHANDISE, IN-CLUDING A T-SHIRT DESIGNED BY YOURS TRULY...
IRON LUNG (#37) Hey!! The breathing's on us!! 12,000 C-Notes
IRON LUNG
GRAVE (#38) You'll "dig" This "killer" head-stone
R.I.P.
13,000 C-Notes
Flowers not included
T-SHIRT (#39) Cotton with magic marker
I'm An IDIOT
STOP

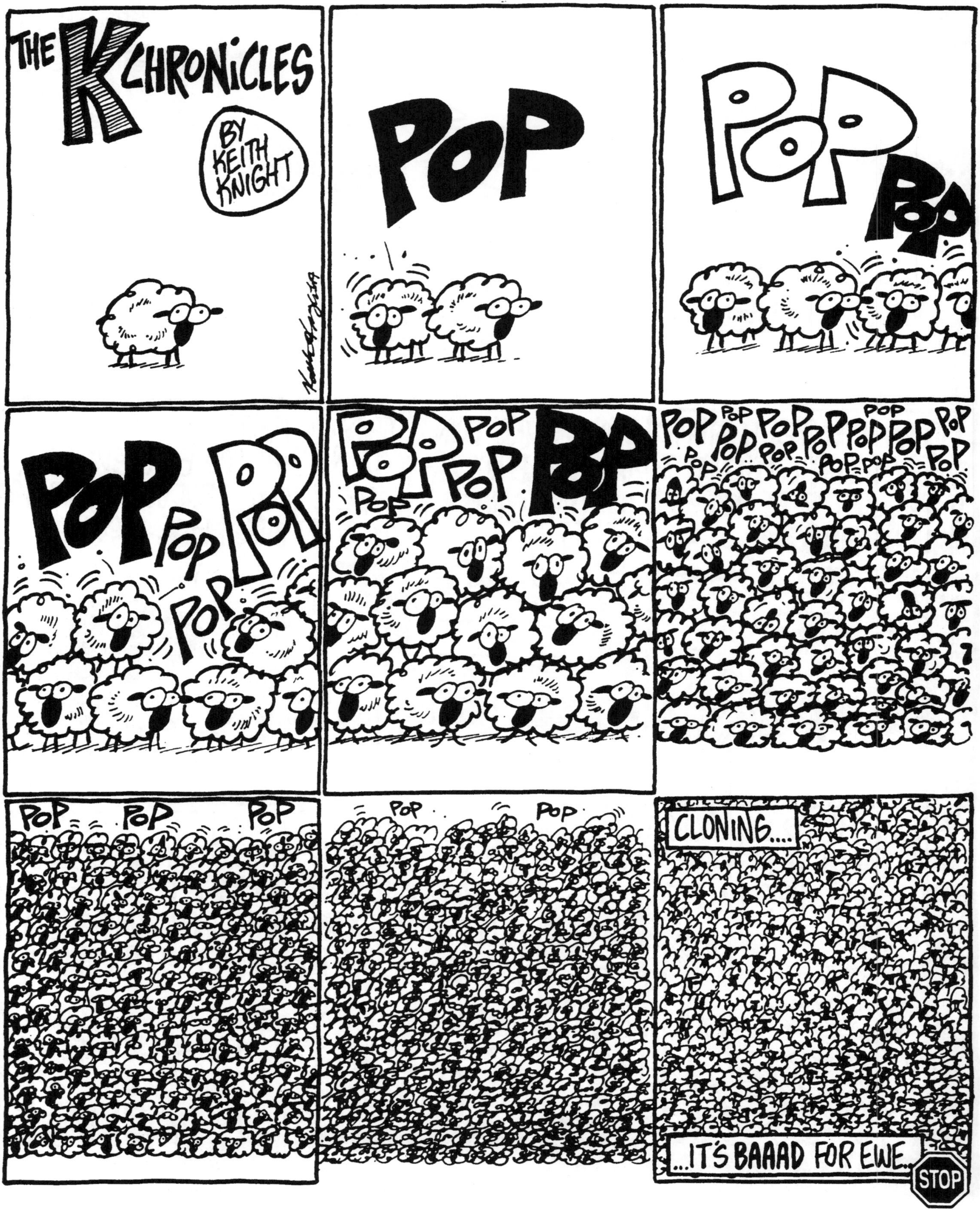
THE K CHRONICLES
BY KEITH KNIGHT
POP
POP POP
POP POP POP POP POP
POP POP POP POP POP POP
POP POP POP
POP POP
CLONING....
...IT'S BAAAD FOR EWE...
STOP

THE K CHRONICLES

BY KEITH KNIGHT

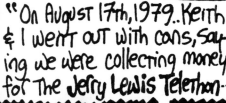

SCREW COMICS!! I think I'll run for State Governor!!

CAN YOU IMAGINE WHAT IT WOULD BE LIKE TO RUN FOR POLITICAL OFFICE NOWADAYS?

"On August 17th, 1979.. Keith & I went out with cans, saying we were collecting money for The Jerry Lewis Telethon--

..BUT WE KEPT THE MONEY!!"

SPLAT!!

I MEAN... THERE IS SO MUCH MUD-SLINGING IT'S INCREDIBLE..

"Um...Yeah.. I was his girlfriend,, during his 5th year at college..

POLITICIANS ARE SPENDING MILLIONS OF DOLLARS SEARCHING THEIR OPPONENTS PASTS FOR DIRTY LITTLE SECRETS...

"Did he inhale? HA!! INHALED, SNORTED, SUPPOSITED... Let's just say he was still a sophomore when we were together..."

SPLORF!!

FORGET ABOUT THE ISSUES... JUST PREPARE TO HAVE YOU, YOUR FAMILY & YOUR FRIENDS' LIVES EXPOSED FOR ALL TO JUDGE.

"I met Keith at a party when I first moved to San Francisco.... And what he did with an inflatable sheep, a small paint brush, 3 egg yolks, and a large ham was the most disturbing thing I've ever seen...."

SPLOOSH!!

THERE'S ONLY SO MUCH ABUSE THE AVERAGE JOE CAN TAKE... IT'S NO SURPRISE THAT A LOT OF DECENT, QUALIFIED PEOPLE NEVER RUN FOR POLITICAL OFFICE..

BLUB!

IT'S ALSO NO SURPRISE TO SEE THE TYPE OF PEOPLE THAT DO RUN...

WOO-HAA!!

VOTE

STOP

| 93

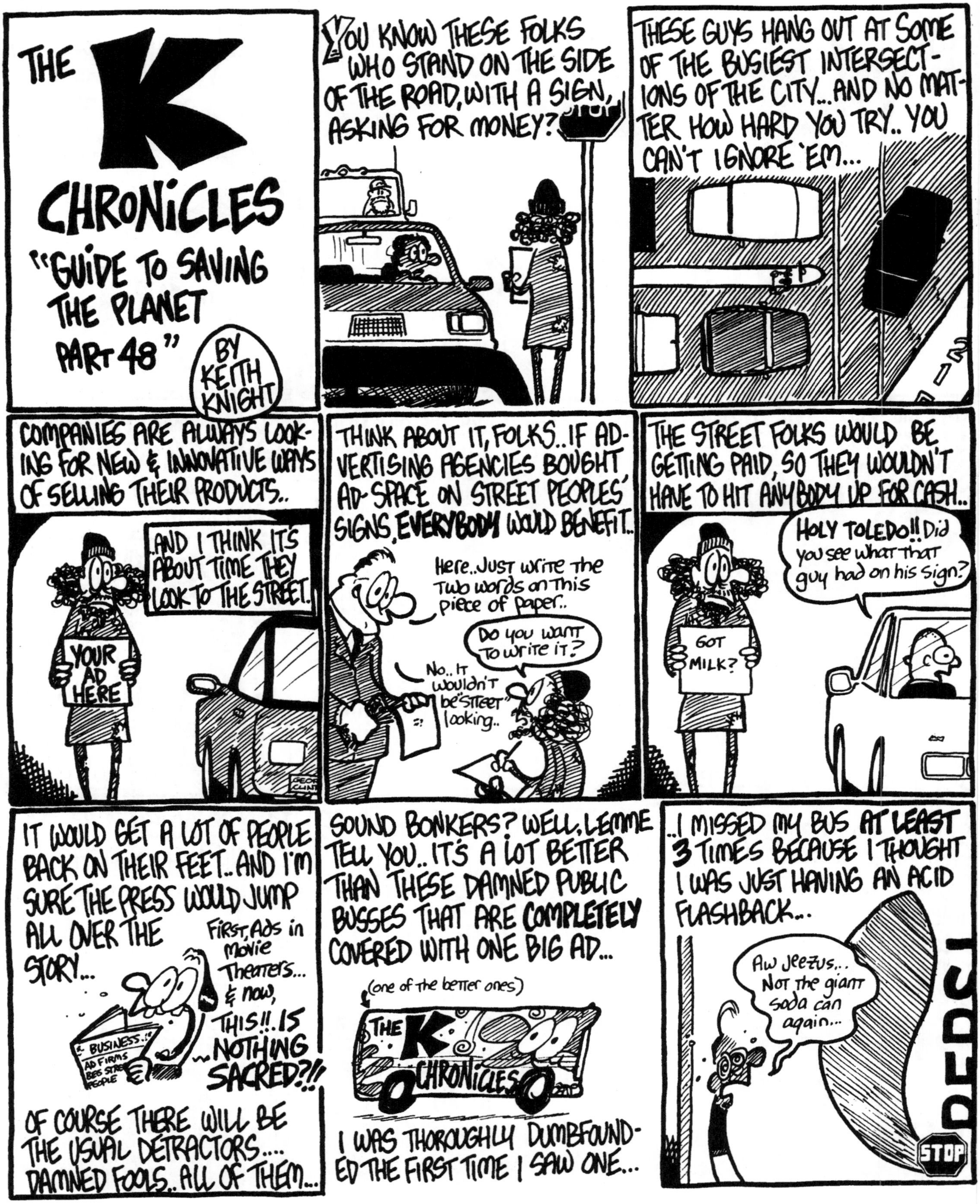

THE K CHRONICLES
"GUIDE TO SAVING THE PLANET PART 48"
BY KEITH KNIGHT
YOU KNOW THESE FOLKS WHO STAND ON THE SIDE OF THE ROAD, WITH A SIGN, ASKING FOR MONEY?
THESE GUYS HANG OUT AT SOME OF THE BUSIEST INTERSECTIONS OF THE CITY... AND NO MATTER HOW HARD YOU TRY.. YOU CAN'T IGNORE 'EM...
COMPANIES ARE ALWAYS LOOKING FOR NEW & INNOVATIVE WAYS OF SELLING THEIR PRODUCTS..
AND I THINK IT'S ABOUT TIME THEY LOOK TO THE STREET.
YOUR AD HERE
THINK ABOUT IT, FOLKS.. IF ADVERTISING AGENCIES BOUGHT AD-SPACE ON STREET PEOPLES' SIGNS, EVERYBODY WOULD BENEFIT..
Here.. Just write the Two words on This piece of paper..
Do you want To write it?
No.. It wouldn't be "street" looking..
THE STREET FOLKS WOULD BE GETTING PAID, SO THEY WOULDN'T HAVE TO HIT ANYBODY UP FOR CASH..
HOLY TOLEDO!! Did you see what that guy had on his sign?
GOT MILK?
IT WOULD GET A LOT OF PEOPLE BACK ON THEIR FEET.. AND I'M SURE THE PRESS WOULD JUMP ALL OVER THE STORY...
First, Ads in movie Theaters... & now, THIS!!.. IS NOTHING SACRED?!!
BUSINESS
AD FIRMS BEG STREET PEOPLE
OF COURSE THERE WILL BE THE USUAL DETRACTORS.... DAMNED FOOLS.. ALL OF THEM...
SOUND BONKERS? WELL, LEMME TELL YOU.. IT'S A LOT BETTER THAN THESE DAMNED PUBLIC BUSSES THAT ARE COMPLETELY COVERED WITH ONE BIG AD...
(one of the better ones)
THE K CHRONICLES
I WAS THOROUGHLY DUMBFOUNDED THE FIRST TIME I SAW ONE...
..I MISSED MY BUS AT LEAST 3 TIMES BECAUSE I THOUGHT I WAS JUST HAVING AN ACID FLASHBACK...
Aw Jeezus... Not the giant soda can again...
PEPSI
STOP

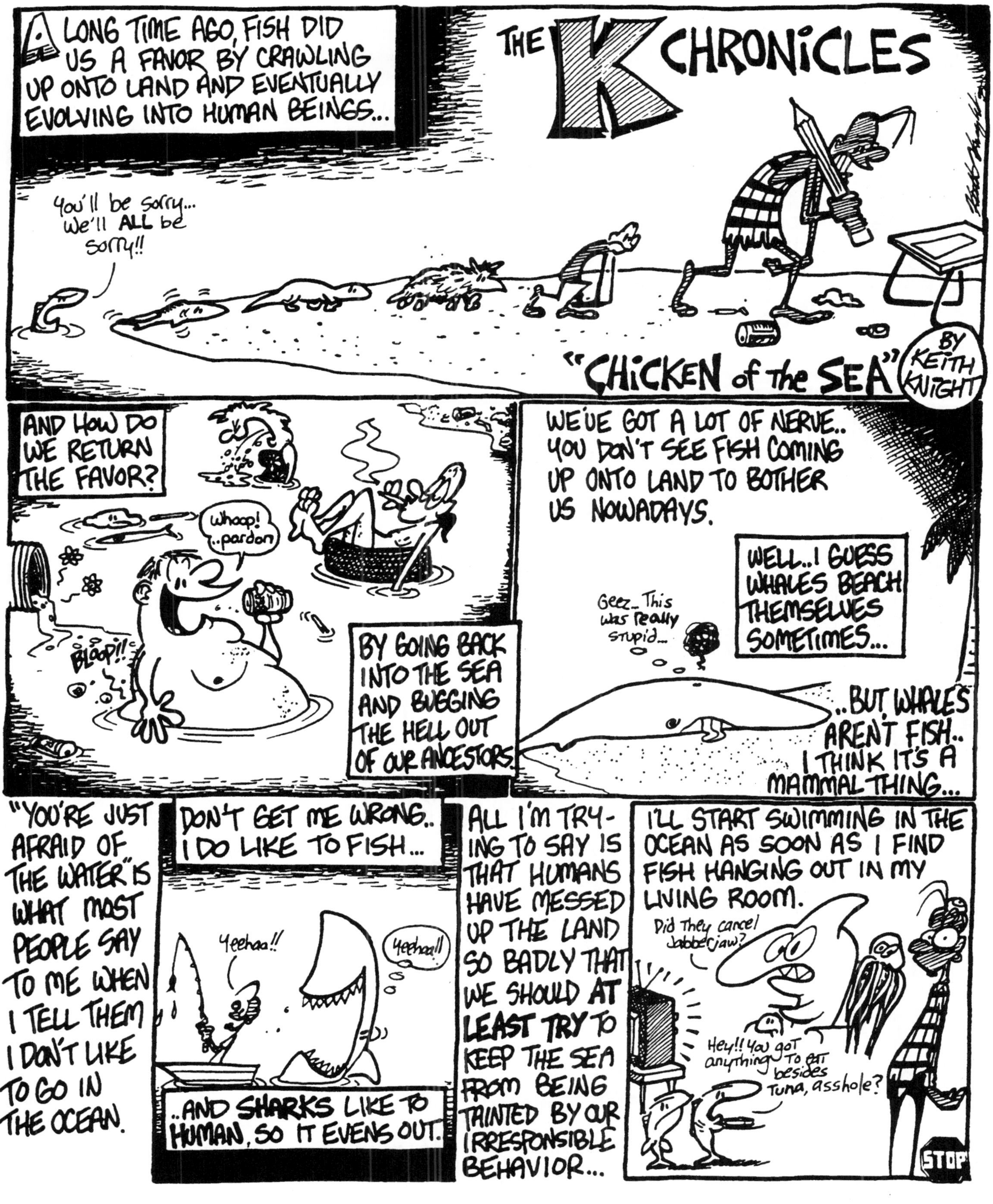

A LONG TIME AGO, FISH DID US A FAVOR BY CRAWLING UP ONTO LAND AND EVENTUALLY EVOLVING INTO HUMAN BEINGS...
THE K CHRONICLES
You'll be sorry... We'll ALL be sorry!!
"CHICKEN of the SEA"
BY KEITH KNIGHT
AND HOW DO WE RETURN THE FAVOR?
Whoop! ..pardon
BLOOP!!
BY GOING BACK INTO THE SEA AND BUGGING THE HELL OUT OF OUR ANCESTORS.
WE'VE GOT A LOT OF NERVE.. YOU DON'T SEE FISH COMING UP ONTO LAND TO BOTHER US NOWADAYS.
WELL..I GUESS WHALES BEACH THEMSELVES SOMETIMES...
Geez.. This was really stupid...
..BUT, WHALES AREN'T FISH.. I THINK IT'S A MAMMAL THING...
"YOU'RE JUST AFRAID OF THE WATER" IS WHAT MOST PEOPLE SAY TO ME WHEN I TELL THEM I DON'T LIKE TO GO IN THE OCEAN.
DON'T GET ME WRONG.. I DO LIKE TO FISH...
Yeehaa!!
Yeehaa!!
..AND SHARKS LIKE TO HUMAN, SO IT EVENS OUT.
ALL I'M TRYING TO SAY IS THAT HUMANS HAVE MESSED UP THE LAND SO BADLY THAT WE SHOULD AT LEAST TRY TO KEEP THE SEA FROM BEING TAINTED BY OUR IRRESPONSIBLE BEHAVIOR...
I'LL START SWIMMING IN THE OCEAN AS SOON AS I FIND FISH HANGING OUT IN MY LIVING ROOM.
Did They cancel Jabberjaw?
Hey!! You got anything to eat besides Tuna, asshole?
STOP

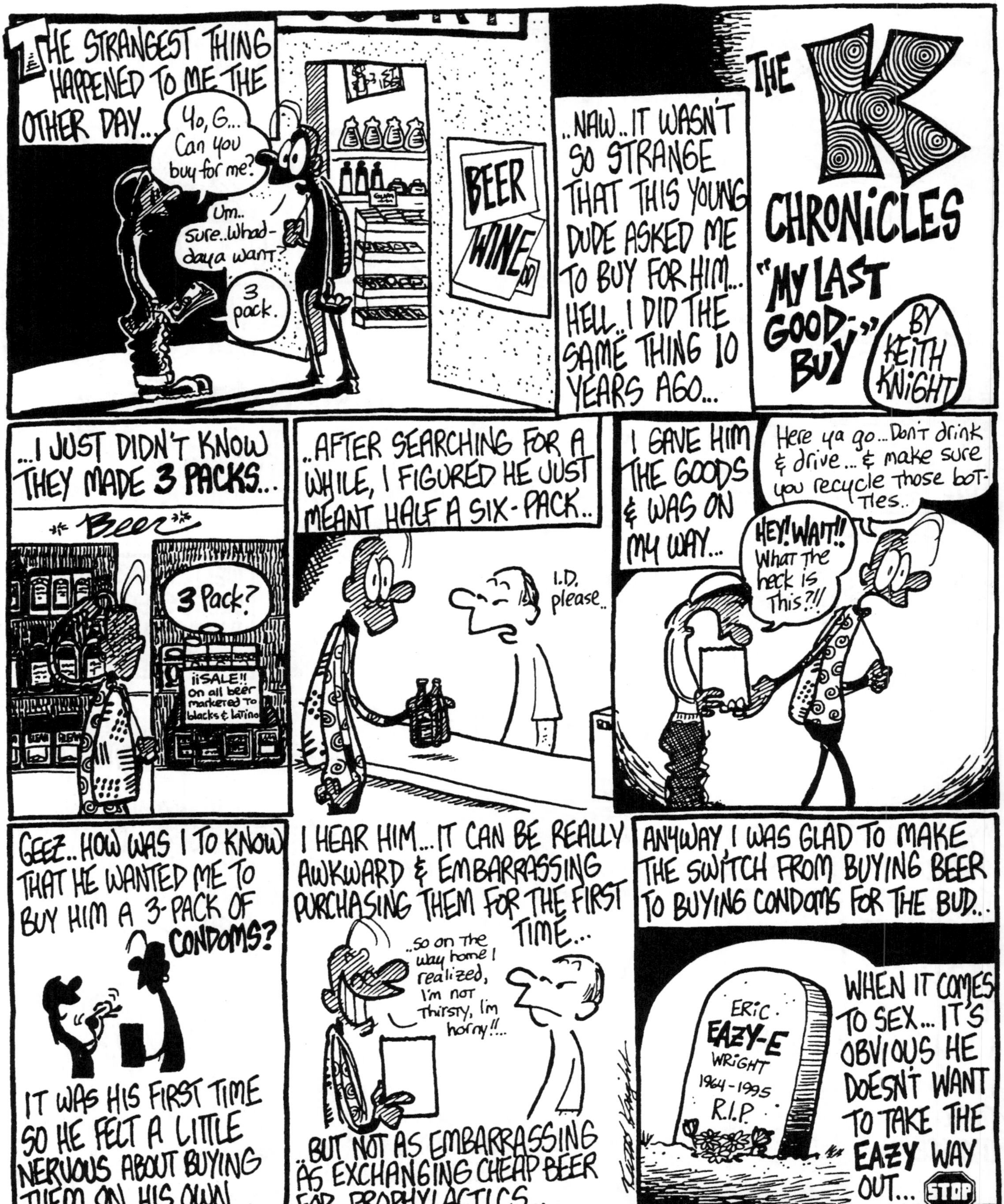
The K Chronicles
"My Last Good-Buy" By Keith Knight
The strangest thing happened to me the other day...
Yo, G... Can you buy for me?
Um.. Sure..Whad-daya want?
3 pack.
BEER
WINE
..Naw..it wasn't so strange that this young dude asked me to buy for him... Hell..I did the same thing 10 years ago...
...I just didn't know they made 3 packs...
Beer
3 Pack?
¡¡SALE!! on all beer marketed to blacks & latinos
..After searching for a while, I figured he just meant half a six-pack..
I.D. please..
I gave him the goods & was on my way...
Here ya go... Don't drink & drive... & make sure you recycle those bot-tles..
HEY! WAIT!! What the heck is this?!!
Geez.. How was I to know that he wanted me to buy him a 3-pack of condoms?
It was his first time so he felt a little nervous about buying them on his own...
I hear him... It can be really awkward & embarrassing purchasing them for the first time...
..so on the way home I realized, I'm not thirsty, I'm horny!!...
..But not as embarrassing as exchanging cheap beer for prophylactics...
Anyway, I was glad to make the switch from buying beer to buying condoms for the bud..
Eric Eazy-E Wright 1964-1995 R.I.P.
When it comes to sex... it's obvious he doesn't want to take the Eazy way out...
STOP

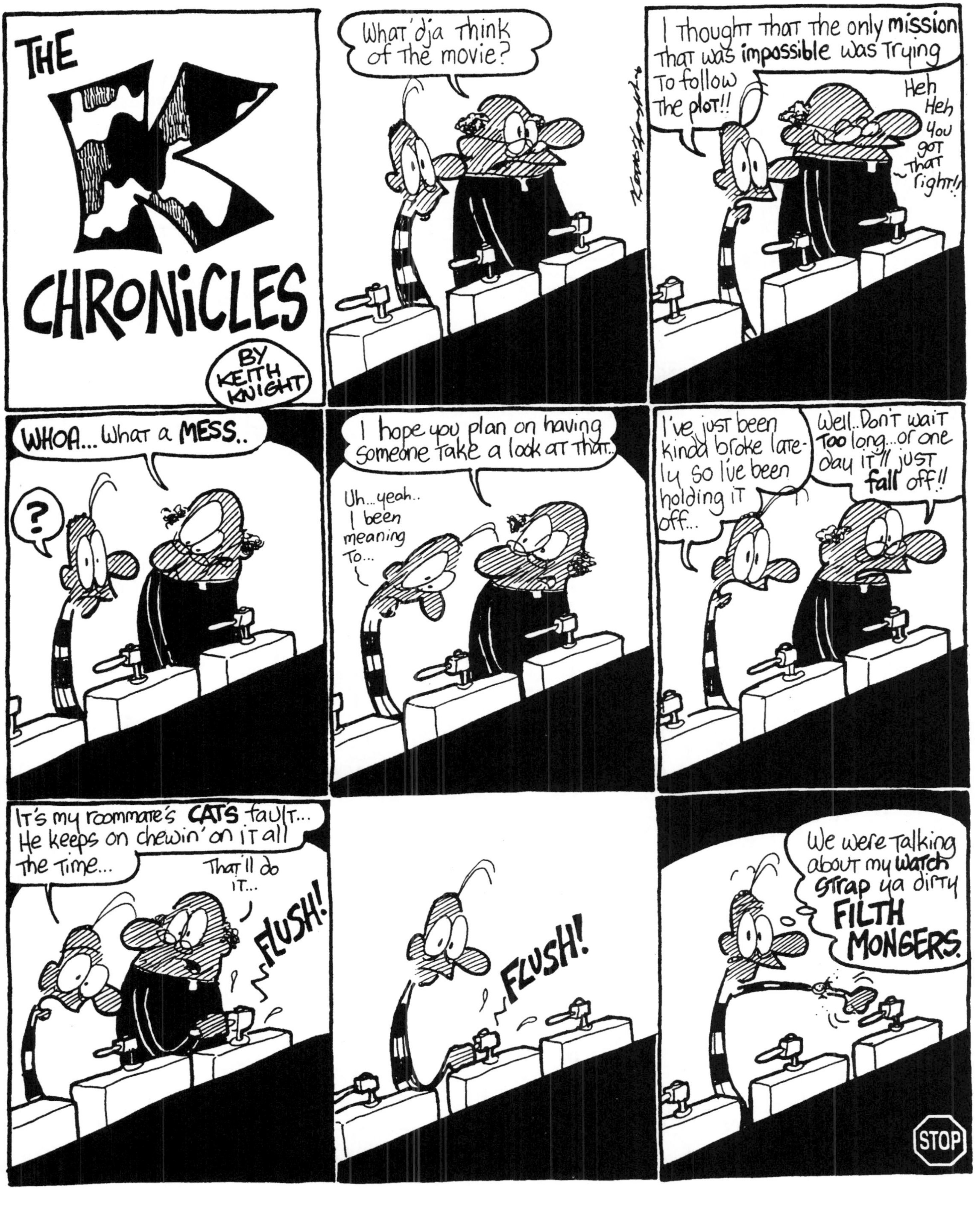
THE K CHRONICLES
BY KEITH KNIGHT
What'dja think of the movie?
I thought that the only mission that was impossible was trying to follow the plot!!
Heh Heh You got that right!!
WHOA... What a MESS..
?
I hope you plan on having someone take a look at that..
Uh...yeah.. I been meaning to...
I've just been kinda broke lately so I've been holding it off...
Well..Don't wait too long...or one day it'll just fall off!!
It's my roommate's CAT'S fault... He keeps on chewin' on it all the time...
That'll do it...
FLUSH!
FLUSH!
We were talking about my watch strap ya dirty FILTH MONGERS.
STOP

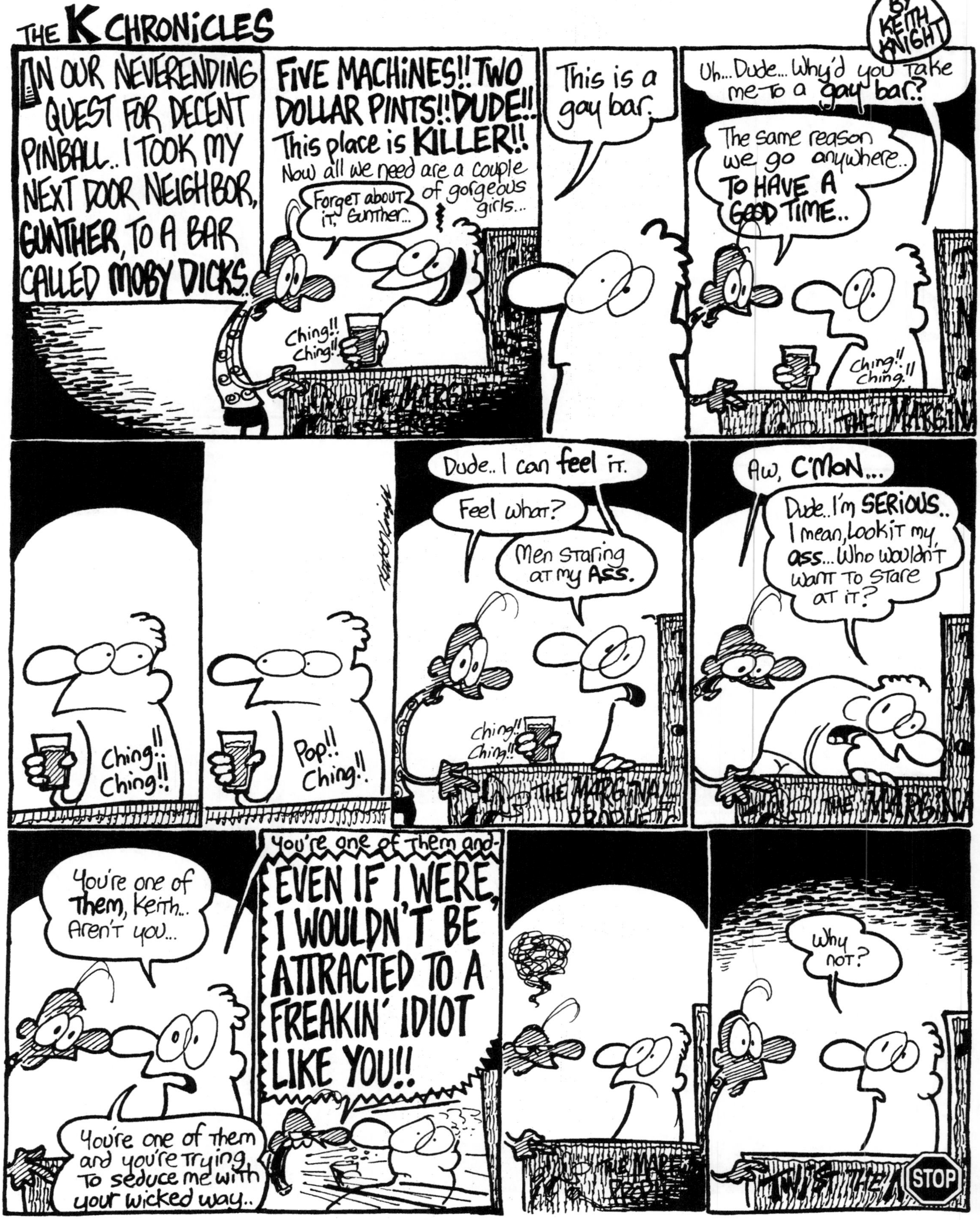
THE K CHRONICLES
BY KEITH KNIGHT
IN OUR NEVERENDING QUEST FOR DECENT PINBALL.. I TOOK MY NEXT DOOR NEIGHBOR, GUNTHER, TO A BAR CALLED MOBY DICKS..
FIVE MACHINES!! TWO DOLLAR PINTS!! DUDE!! This place is KILLER!! Now all we need are a couple of gorgeous girls...
Forget about it, Gunther...
Ching!! Ching!!
This is a gay bar.
Uh... Dude... Why'd you take me to a gay bar?
The same reason we go anywhere.. TO HAVE A GOOD TIME..
Ching!! Ching!!
Ching!! Ching!!
Pop!! Ching!!
Dude.. I can feel it.
Feel what?
Men staring at my ASS.
Ching!! Ching!!
Aw, C'MON...
Dude.. I'm SERIOUS.. I mean, lookit my ass... Who wouldn't want to stare at it?
You're one of them, Keith... Aren't you...
You're one of them and you're trying to seduce me with your wicked way..
You're one of them and-
EVEN IF I WERE, I WOULDN'T BE ATTRACTED TO A FREAKIN' IDIOT LIKE YOU!!
Why not?
STOP

 Moby Dicks. The last great pinball spot in San Francisco.

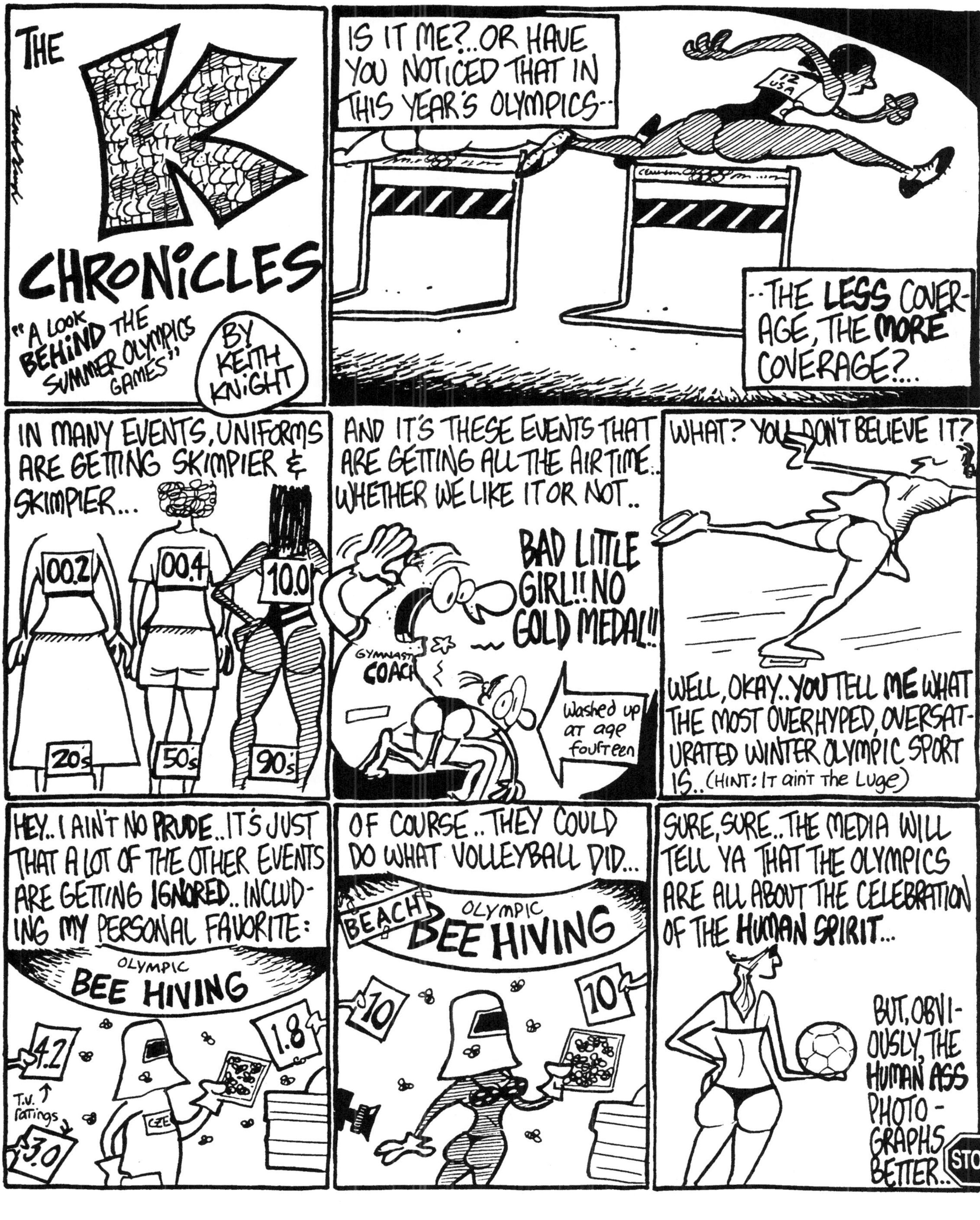
THE K CHRONICLES
"A LOOK BEHIND THE SUMMER OLYMPICS GAMES"
BY KEITH KNIGHT
IS IT ME?...OR HAVE YOU NOTICED THAT IN THIS YEAR'S OLYMPICS--
12 USA
--THE LESS COVERAGE, THE MORE COVERAGE?...
IN MANY EVENTS, UNIFORMS ARE GETTING SKIMPIER & SKIMPIER...
00.2
00.4
10.0
20's
50's
90's
AND IT'S THESE EVENTS THAT ARE GETTING ALL THE AIR TIME.. WHETHER WE LIKE IT OR NOT..
BAD LITTLE GIRL!! NO GOLD MEDAL!!
GYMNASTIC COACH
Washed up at age fourteen
WHAT? YOU DON'T BELIEVE IT?
WELL, OKAY.. YOU TELL ME WHAT THE MOST OVERHYPED, OVERSATURATED WINTER OLYMPIC SPORT IS.. (HINT: It ain't the Luge)
HEY.. I AIN'T NO PRUDE.. IT'S JUST THAT A LOT OF THE OTHER EVENTS ARE GETTING IGNORED.. INCLUDING MY PERSONAL FAVORITE:
OLYMPIC BEE HIVING
4.2
1.8
T.V. ratings
3.0
CZE
OF COURSE.. THEY COULD DO WHAT VOLLEYBALL DID...
BEACH OLYMPIC BEE HIVING
10
10
SURE, SURE.. THE MEDIA WILL TELL YA THAT THE OLYMPICS ARE ALL ABOUT THE CELEBRATION OF THE HUMAN SPIRIT...
BUT, OBVIOUSLY, THE HUMAN ASS PHOTOGRAPHS BETTER...
STOP

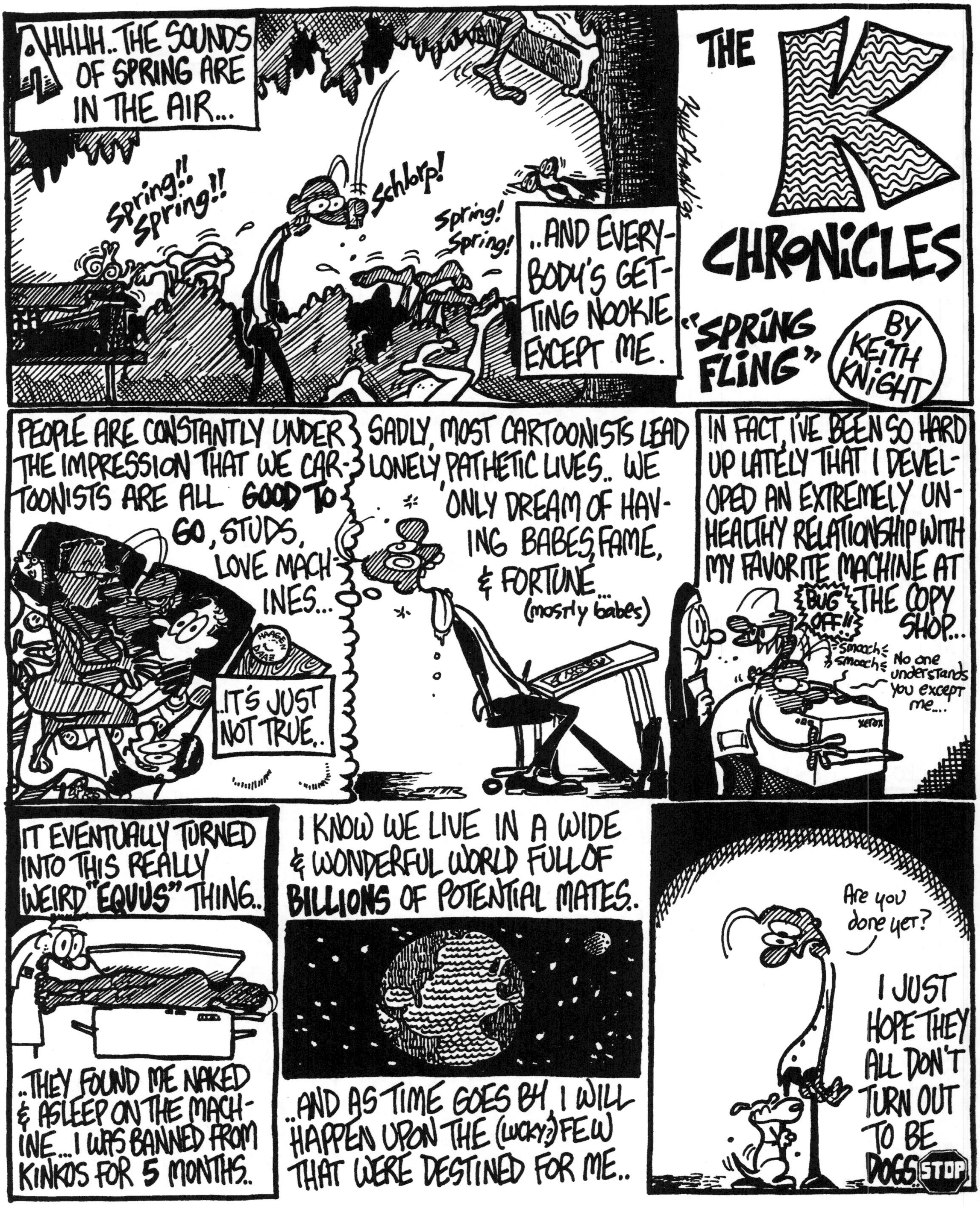
AHHHH.. THE SOUNDS OF SPRING ARE IN THE AIR...
Spring!! Spring!!
Schlorp!
Spring! Spring!
..AND EVERYBODY'S GETTING NOOKIE EXCEPT ME.
THE K CHRONICLES
"SPRING FLING"
BY KEITH KNIGHT
PEOPLE ARE CONSTANTLY UNDER THE IMPRESSION THAT WE CARTOONISTS ARE ALL GOOD TO GO, STUDS, LOVE MACHINES...
HAAGEN DAAZ
..IT'S JUST NOT TRUE..
SADLY, MOST CARTOONISTS LEAD LONELY, PATHETIC LIVES.. WE ONLY DREAM OF HAVING BABES, FAME, & FORTUNE...
(mostly babes)
IN FACT, I'VE BEEN SO HARD UP LATELY THAT I DEVELOPED AN EXTREMELY UNHEALTHY RELATIONSHIP WITH MY FAVORITE MACHINE AT THE COPY SHOP...
BUG OFF!!
smooch smooch
No one understands you except me...
xerox
IT EVENTUALLY TURNED INTO THIS REALLY WEIRD "EQUUS" THING..
..THEY FOUND ME NAKED & ASLEEP ON THE MACHINE... I WAS BANNED FROM KINKOS FOR 5 MONTHS..
I KNOW WE LIVE IN A WIDE & WONDERFUL WORLD FULL OF BILLIONS OF POTENTIAL MATES..
..AND AS TIME GOES BY, I WILL HAPPEN UPON THE (LUCKY?) FEW THAT WERE DESTINED FOR ME..
Are you done yet?
I JUST HOPE THEY ALL DON'T TURN OUT TO BE DOGS..
STOP

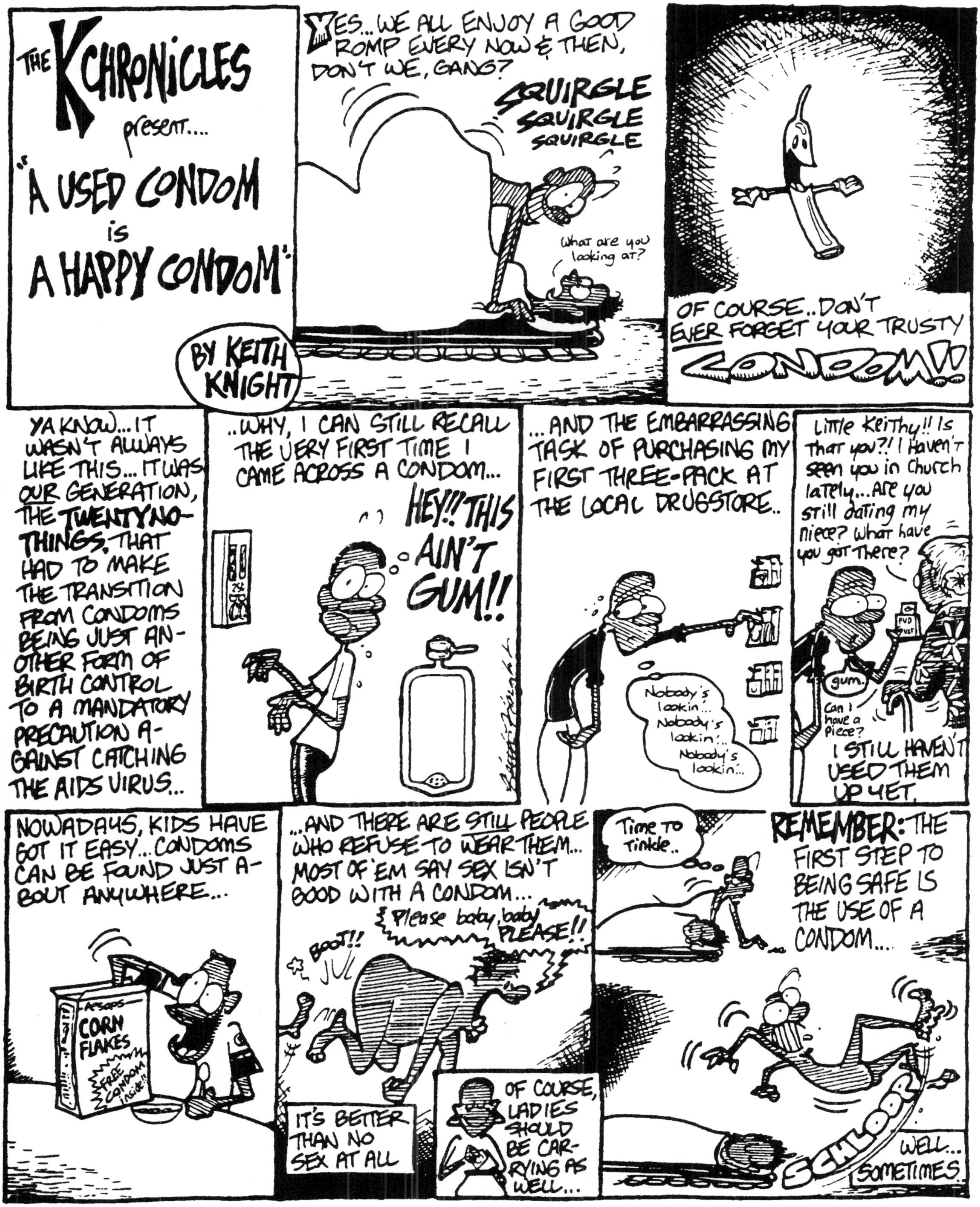

THE K CHRONICLES present.... "A USED CONDOM is A HAPPY CONDOM"
BY KEITH KNIGHT
YES... WE ALL ENJOY A GOOD ROMP EVERY NOW & THEN, DON'T WE, GANG?
SQUIRGLE SQUIRGLE SQUIRGLE
What are you looking at?
OF COURSE.. DON'T EVER FORGET YOUR TRUSTY CONDOM!!
YA KNOW... IT WASN'T ALWAYS LIKE THIS... IT WAS OUR GENERATION, THE TWENTYNOTHINGS, THAT HAD TO MAKE THE TRANSITION FROM CONDOMS BEING JUST ANOTHER FORM OF BIRTH CONTROL TO A MANDATORY PRECAUTION AGAINST CATCHING THE AIDS VIRUS...
..WHY, I CAN STILL RECALL THE VERY FIRST TIME I CAME ACROSS A CONDOM...
HEY!! THIS AIN'T GUM!!
...AND THE EMBARRASSING TASK OF PURCHASING MY FIRST THREE-PACK AT THE LOCAL DRUGSTORE..
Nobody's lookin'... Nobody's lookin'... Nobody's lookin'...
Little Keithy!! Is that you?! I haven't seen you in Church lately... Are you still dating my niece? What have you got there?
gum.
Can I have a piece?
I STILL HAVEN'T USED THEM UP YET.
NOWADAYS, KIDS HAVE GOT IT EASY... CONDOMS CAN BE FOUND JUST ABOUT ANYWHERE...
CORN FLAKES
FREE CONDOM inside!!
...AND THERE ARE STILL PEOPLE WHO REFUSE TO WEAR THEM... MOST OF 'EM SAY SEX ISN'T GOOD WITH A CONDOM...
Please baby, baby PLEASE!!
BOOT!!
IT'S BETTER THAN NO SEX AT ALL
OF COURSE, LADIES SHOULD BE CARRYING AS WELL...
Time to tinkle..
REMEMBER: THE FIRST STEP TO BEING SAFE IS THE USE OF A CONDOM...
SCHLOOP
WELL... SOMETIMES.

Another strip adapted for the German film. |

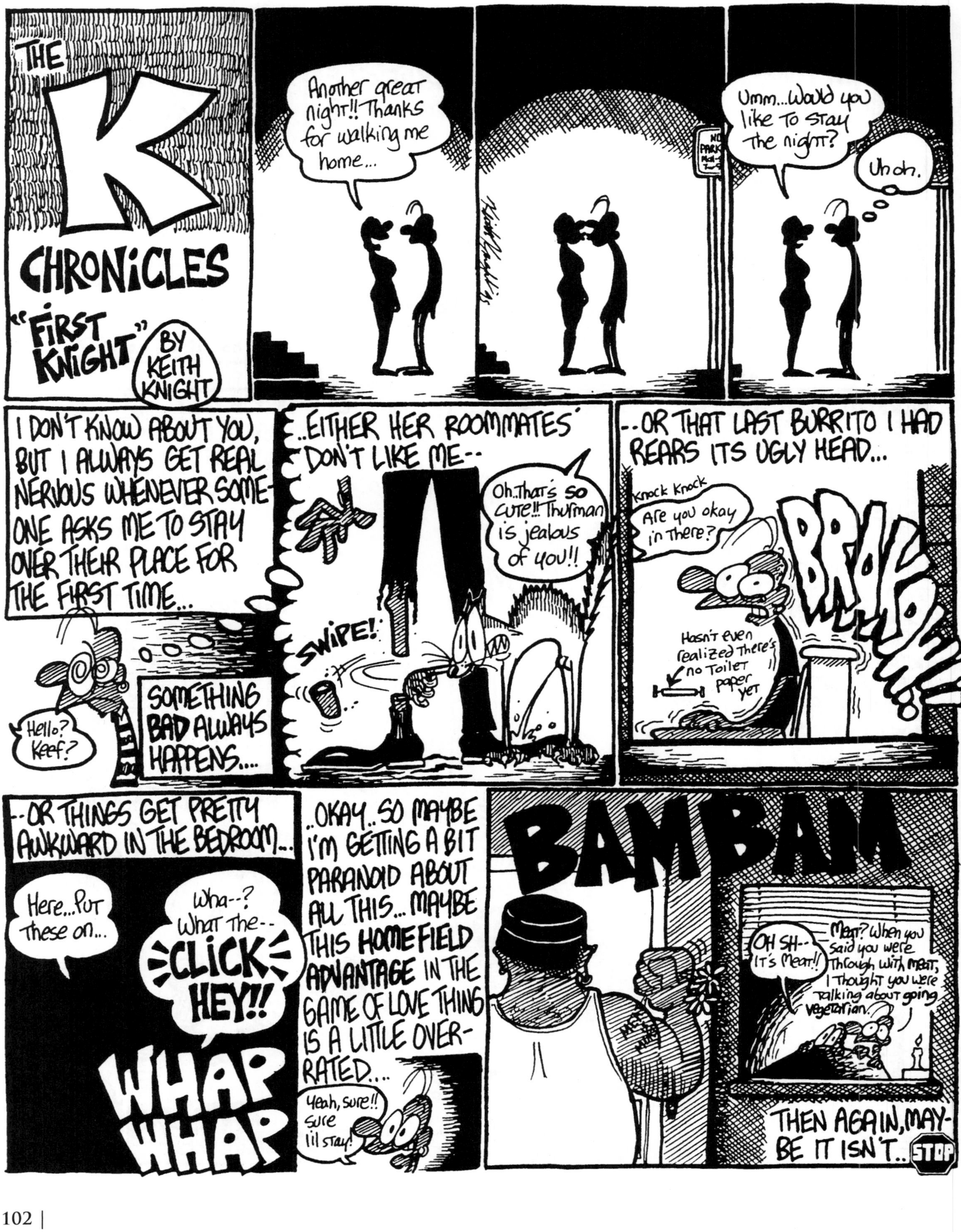
THE K CHRONICLES
"FIRST KNIGHT"
BY KEITH KNIGHT
Another great night!! Thanks for walking me home...
NO PARK
Umm...Would you like to stay the night?
Uh oh.
I DON'T KNOW ABOUT YOU, BUT I ALWAYS GET REAL NERVOUS WHENEVER SOME-ONE ASKS ME TO STAY OVER THEIR PLACE FOR THE FIRST TIME...
Hello? Keef?
SOMETHING BAD ALWAYS HAPPENS....
..EITHER HER ROOMMATES' DON'T LIKE ME--
Oh..That's SO CUTE!! Thurman is jealous of you!!
SWIPE!
--OR THAT LAST BURRITO I HAD REARS ITS UGLY HEAD...
Knock Knock
Are you okay in there?
BRRAKOWW!!
Hasn't even realized there's no Toilet paper yet
--OR THINGS GET PRETTY AWKWARD IN THE BEDROOM...
Here...Put these on...
Wha--? What the--
CLICK
HEY!!
WHAP WHAP
..OKAY..SO MAYBE I'M GETTING A BIT PARANOID ABOUT ALL THIS... MAYBE THIS HOMEFIELD ADVANTAGE IN THE GAME OF LOVE THING IS A LITTLE OVER-RATED....
Yeah, sure!! sure i'll stay!
BAM BAM
OH SH-- It's Meat!!
Meat? When you said you were through with meat, I thought you were talking about going vegetarian.
THEN AGAIN, MAY-BE IT ISN'T..
STOP

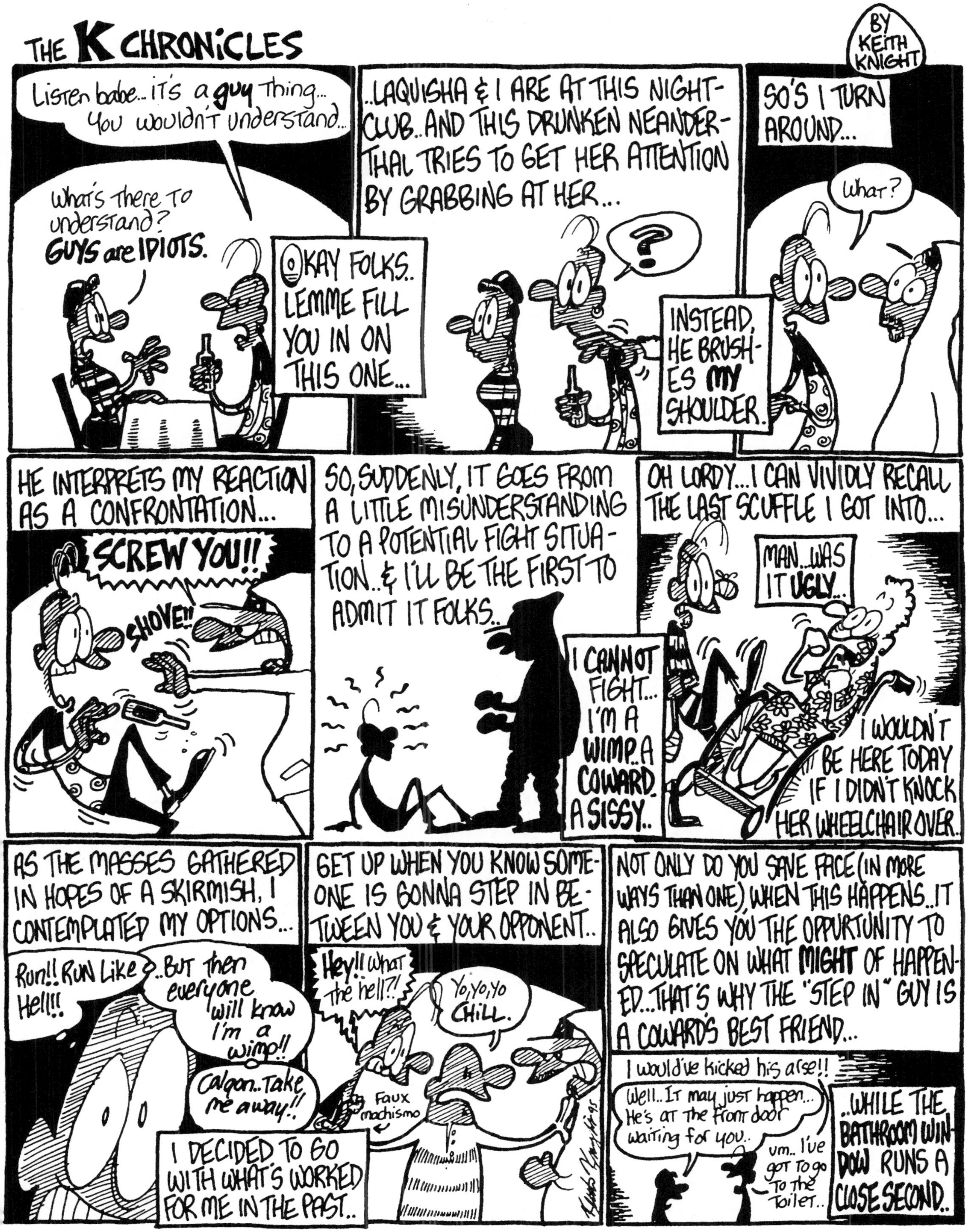
THE K CHRONICLES
BY KEITH KNIGHT
Listen babe... it's a guy thing... You wouldn't understand...
What's there to understand? GUYS are IDIOTS.
OKAY FOLKS.. LEMME FILL YOU IN ON THIS ONE...
..LAQUISHA & I ARE AT THIS NIGHT-CLUB.. AND THIS DRUNKEN NEANDER-THAL TRIES TO GET HER ATTENTION BY GRABBING AT HER...
?
INSTEAD, HE BRUSH-ES MY SHOULDER.
SO'S I TURN AROUND...
What?
HE INTERPRETS MY REACTION AS A CONFRONTATION...
SCREW YOU!!
SHOVE!!
SO, SUDDENLY, IT GOES FROM A LITTLE MISUNDERSTANDING TO A POTENTIAL FIGHT SITUA-TION.. & I'LL BE THE FIRST TO ADMIT IT FOLKS..
I CANNOT FIGHT... I'M A WIMP.. A COWARD.. A SISSY..
OH LORDY... I CAN VIVIDLY RECALL THE LAST SCUFFLE I GOT INTO...
MAN.. WAS IT UGLY...
I WOULDN'T BE HERE TODAY IF I DIDN'T KNOCK HER WHEELCHAIR OVER..
AS THE MASSES GATHERED IN HOPES OF A SKIRMISH, I CONTEMPLATED MY OPTIONS...
Run!! Run Like Hell!!!
..But then everyone will know I'm a wimp!!
Calgon.. Take me away!!
I DECIDED TO GO WITH WHAT'S WORKED FOR ME IN THE PAST..
GET UP WHEN YOU KNOW SOME-ONE IS GONNA STEP IN BE-TWEEN YOU & YOUR OPPONENT..
Hey!! What the hell?!
Yo, yo, yo CHILL.
Faux machismo
NOT ONLY DO YOU SAVE FACE (IN MORE WAYS THAN ONE) WHEN THIS HAPPENS.. IT ALSO GIVES YOU THE OPPURTUNITY TO SPECULATE ON WHAT MIGHT OF HAPPEN-ED... THAT'S WHY THE "STEP IN" GUY IS A COWARD'S BEST FRIEND...
I would've kicked his arse!!
Well.. It may just happen... He's at the front door waiting for you..
um.. I've got to go to the Toilet..
..WHILE THE BATHROOM WIN-DOW RUNS A CLOSE SECOND..

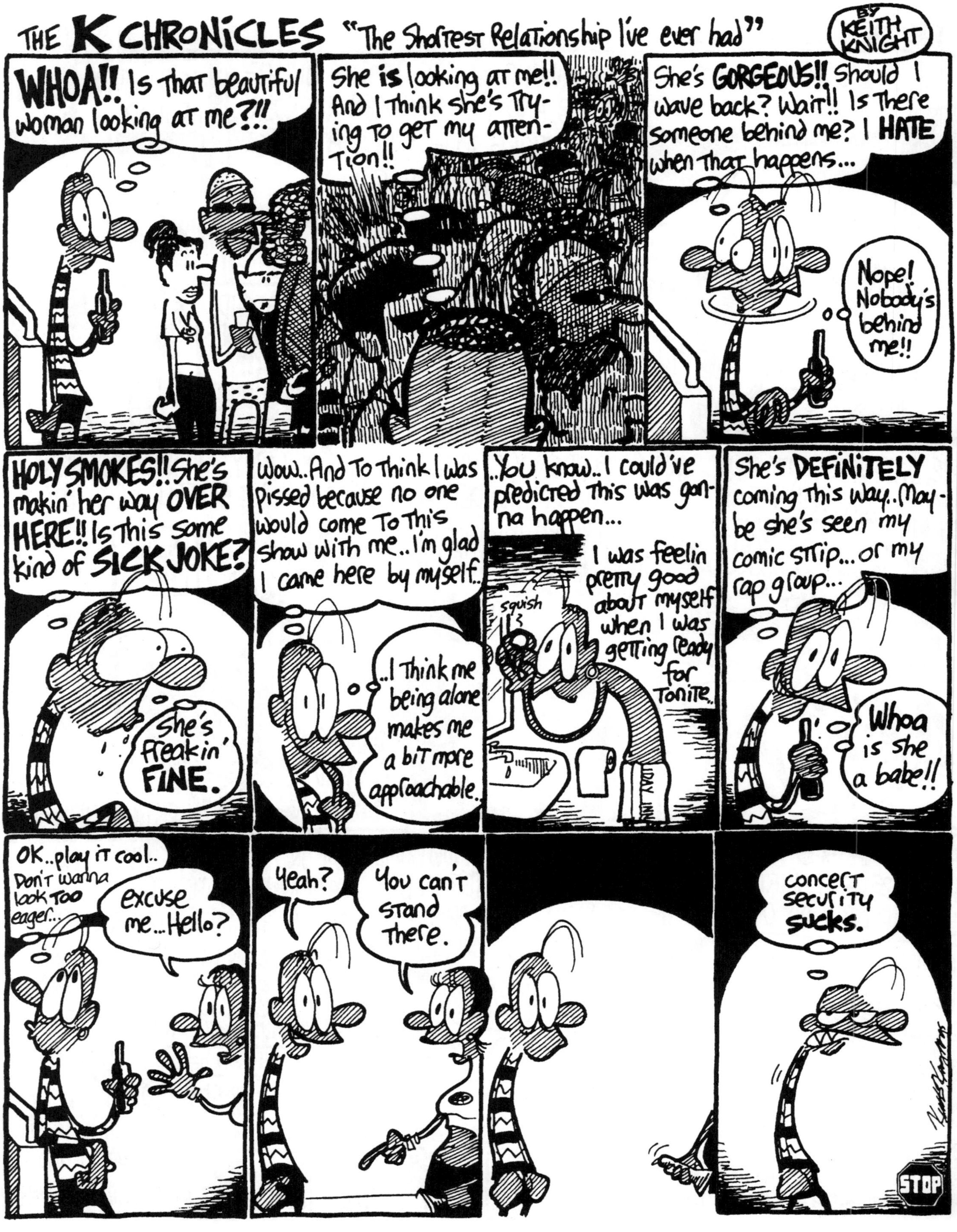
THE K CHRONICLES "The Shortest Relationship I've ever had"
BY KEITH KNIGHT
WHOA!! Is that beautiful woman looking at me?!!
She is looking at me!! And I think she's trying to get my attention!!
She's GORGEOUS!! Should I wave back? Wait!! Is there someone behind me? I HATE when that happens...
Nope! Nobody's behind me!!
HOLY SMOKES!! She's makin' her way OVER HERE!! Is this some kind of SICK JOKE?
She's freakin' FINE.
Wow.. And to think I was pissed because no one would come to this show with me.. I'm glad I came here by myself..
..I think me being alone makes me a bit more approachable..
..You know.. I could've predicted this was gonna happen...
squish
I was feelin pretty good about myself when I was getting ready for tonite..
She's DEFINITELY coming this way.. Maybe she's seen my comic strip... or my rap group...
Whoa is she a babe!!
OK.. play it cool.. Don't wanna look TOO eager...
excuse me... Hello?
Yeah?
You can't stand there.
concert security sucks.
STOP

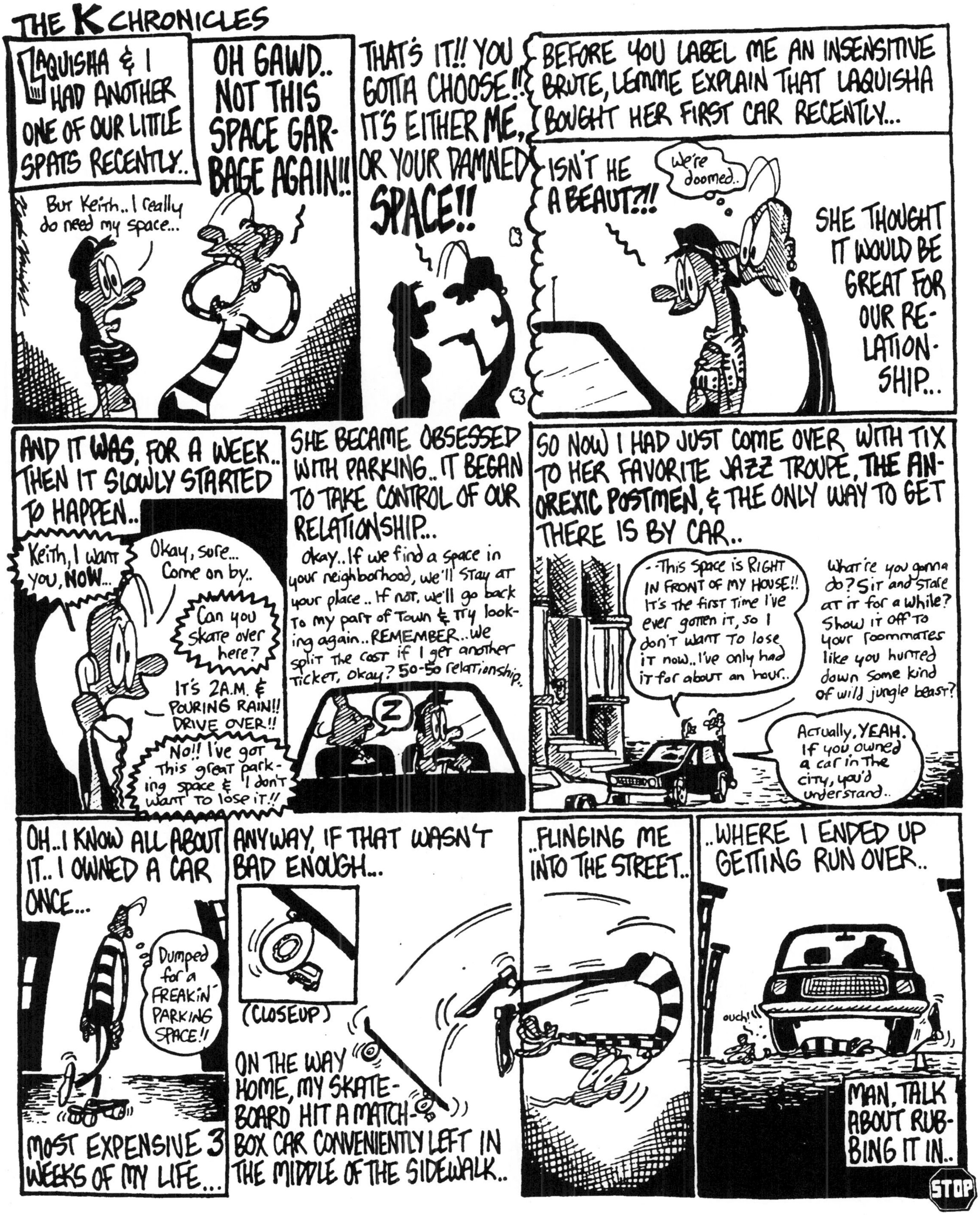
THE K CHRONICLES
LAQUISHA & I HAD ANOTHER ONE OF OUR LITTLE SPATS RECENTLY..
But Keith.. I really do need my space...
OH GAWD.. NOT THIS SPACE GARBAGE AGAIN!!..
THAT'S IT!! YOU GOTTA CHOOSE!! IT'S EITHER ME, OR YOUR DAMNED SPACE!!
BEFORE YOU LABEL ME AN INSENSITIVE BRUTE, LEMME EXPLAIN THAT LAQUISHA BOUGHT HER FIRST CAR RECENTLY...
ISN'T HE A BEAUT?!!
We're doomed..
SHE THOUGHT IT WOULD BE GREAT FOR OUR RELATIONSHIP...
AND IT WAS, FOR A WEEK.. THEN IT SLOWLY STARTED TO HAPPEN..
Keith, I want you, NOW...
Okay, sure... Come on by..
Can you skate over here?
IT'S 2A.M. & POURING RAIN!! DRIVE OVER!!
No!! I've got this great parking space & I don't want to lose it!!
SHE BECAME OBSESSED WITH PARKING.. IT BEGAN TO TAKE CONTROL OF OUR RELATIONSHIP...
Okay.. If we find a space in your neighborhood, we'll stay at your place.. If not, we'll go back to my part of Town & try looking again.. REMEMBER...we split the cost if I get another ticket, okay? 50-50 relationship..
Z
SO NOW I HAD JUST COME OVER WITH TIX TO HER FAVORITE JAZZ TROUPE, THE ANOREXIC POSTMEN, & THE ONLY WAY TO GET THERE IS BY CAR..
--This space is RIGHT IN FRONT OF MY HOUSE!! It's the first time I've ever gotten it, so I don't want to lose it now.. I've only had it for about an hour..
What're you gonna do? Sit and stare at it for a while? Show it off to your roommates like you hunted down some kind of wild jungle beast?
Actually, YEAH. If you owned a car in the city, you'd understand..
OH.. I KNOW ALL ABOUT IT.. I OWNED A CAR ONCE...
Dumped for a FREAKIN' PARKING SPACE!!
MOST EXPENSIVE 3 WEEKS OF MY LIFE...
ANYWAY, IF THAT WASN'T BAD ENOUGH...
(CLOSEUP)
ON THE WAY HOME, MY SKATEBOARD HIT A MATCHBOX CAR CONVENIENTLY LEFT IN THE MIDDLE OF THE SIDEWALK..
..FLINGING ME INTO THE STREET..
..WHERE I ENDED UP GETTING RUN OVER..
ouch!
MAN, TALK ABOUT RUBBING IT IN..
STOP

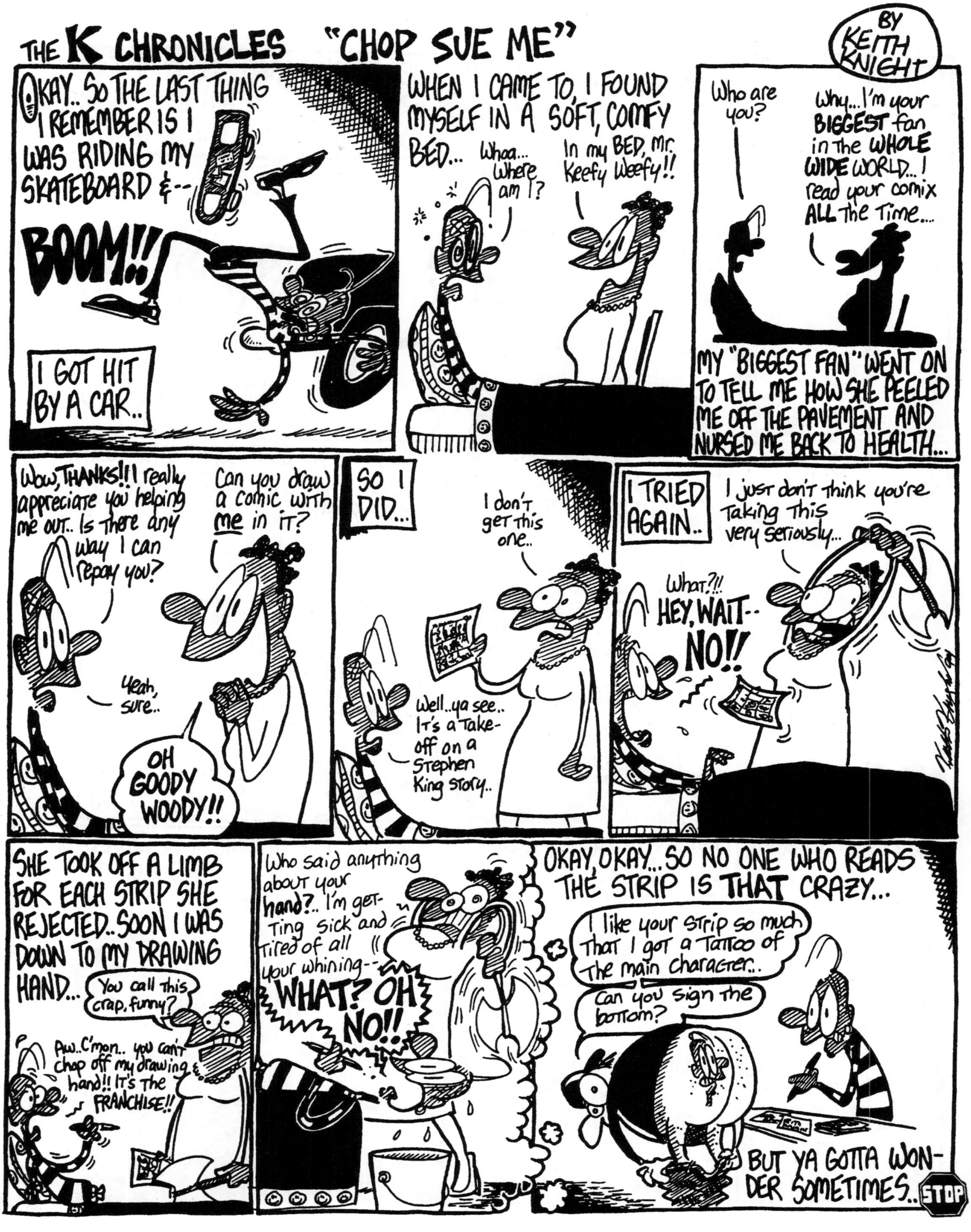
THE K CHRONICLES "CHOP SUE ME"
BY KEITH KNIGHT
OKAY.. SO THE LAST THING I REMEMBER IS I WAS RIDING MY SKATEBOARD &--
BOOM!!
I GOT HIT BY A CAR..
WHEN I CAME TO, I FOUND MYSELF IN A SOFT, COMFY BED...
Whoa... Where am I?
In my BED, Mr. Keefy Weefy!!
Who are you?
Why... I'm your BIGGEST fan in the WHOLE WIDE WORLD... I read your comix ALL the time....
MY "BIGGEST FAN" WENT ON TO TELL ME HOW SHE PEELED ME OFF THE PAVEMENT AND NURSED ME BACK TO HEALTH...
Wow, THANKS!!! I really appreciate you helping me out.. Is there any way I can repay you?
Can you draw a comic with me in it?
Yeah, sure..
OH GOODY WOODY!!
SO I DID...
I don't get this one..
Well.. ya see.. It's a take-off on a Stephen King story..
I TRIED AGAIN..
I just don't think you're taking this very seriously...
What?!!
HEY, WAIT-- NO!!
SHE TOOK OFF A LIMB FOR EACH STRIP SHE REJECTED.. SOON I WAS DOWN TO MY DRAWING HAND...
You call this crap, funny?
Aw.. C'mon.. you can't chop off my drawing hand!! It's the FRANCHISE!!
Who said anything about your hand?.. I'm getting sick and tired of all your whining--
WHAT? OH NO!!
OKAY, OKAY... SO NO ONE WHO READS THE STRIP IS THAT CRAZY...
I like your strip so much that I got a tattoo of the main character..
Can you sign the bottom?
BUT YA GOTTA WONDER SOMETIMES..
STOP

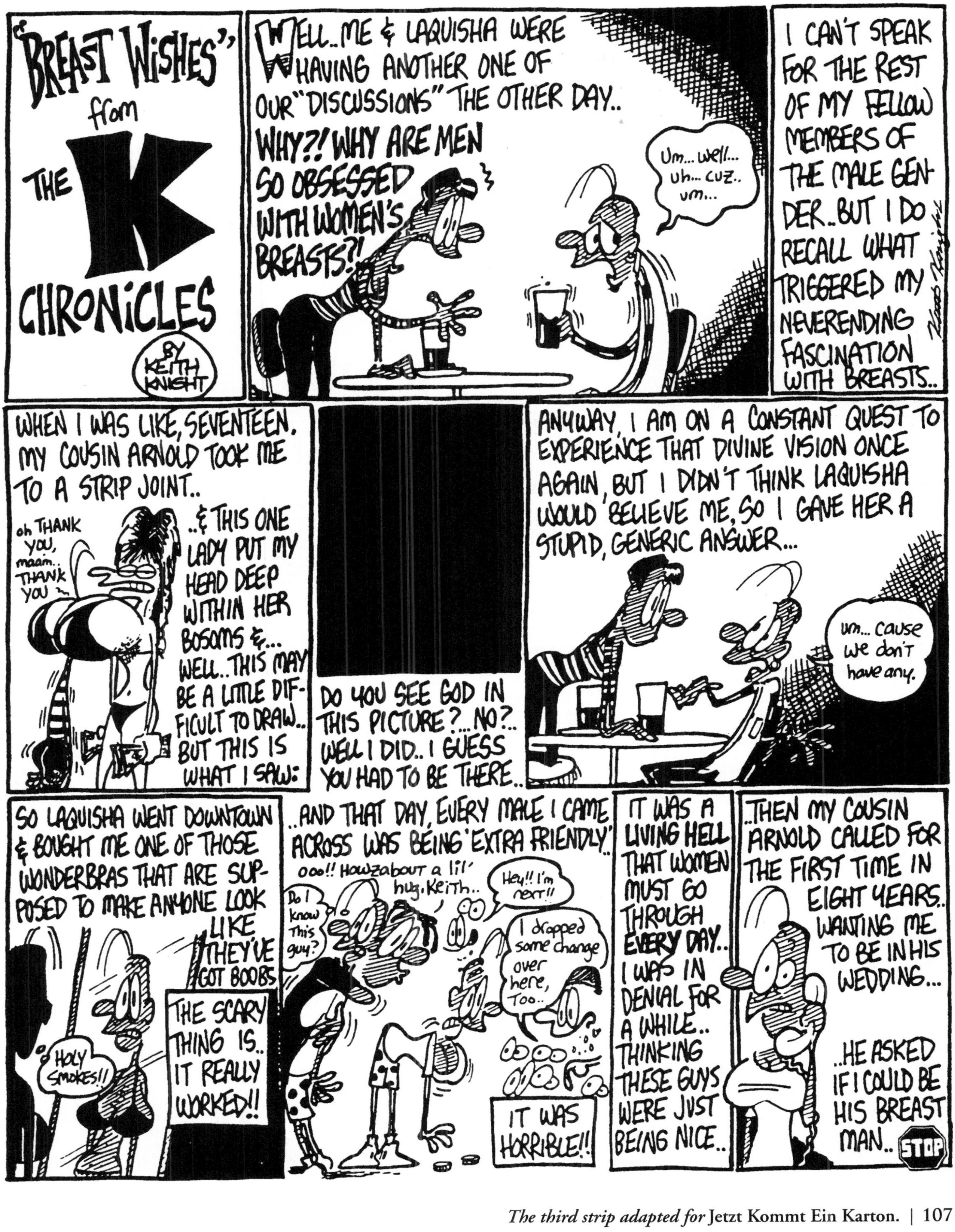
"BREAST WISHES" from THE K CHRONICLES
BY KEITH KNIGHT
WELL.. ME & LAQUISHA WERE HAVING ANOTHER ONE OF OUR "DISCUSSIONS" THE OTHER DAY..
WHY?! WHY ARE MEN SO OBSESSED WITH WOMEN'S BREASTS?!
Um... well... uh... cuz.. um...
I CAN'T SPEAK FOR THE REST OF MY FELLOW MEMBERS OF THE MALE GENDER.. BUT I DO RECALL WHAT TRIGGERED MY NEVERENDING FASCINATION WITH BREASTS..
WHEN I WAS LIKE, SEVENTEEN, MY COUSIN ARNOLD TOOK ME TO A STRIP JOINT..
oh THANK YOU, maam.. THANK YOU
..& THIS ONE LADY PUT MY HEAD DEEP WITHIN HER BOSOMS &... WELL.. THIS MAY BE A LITTLE DIFFICULT TO DRAW.. BUT THIS IS WHAT I SAW:
DO YOU SEE GOD IN THIS PICTURE?... NO?.. WELL I DID.. I GUESS YOU HAD TO BE THERE..
ANYWAY, I AM ON A CONSTANT QUEST TO EXPERIENCE THAT DIVINE VISION ONCE AGAIN, BUT I DIDN'T THINK LAQUISHA WOULD BELIEVE ME, SO I GAVE HER A STUPID, GENERIC ANSWER...
um... cause we don't have any.
SO LAQUISHA WENT DOWNTOWN & BOUGHT ME ONE OF THOSE WONDERBRAS THAT ARE SUPPOSED TO MAKE ANYONE LOOK LIKE THEY'VE GOT BOOBS
HOLY SMOKES!!
THE SCARY THING IS.. IT REALLY WORKED!!
..AND THAT DAY, EVERY MALE I CAME ACROSS WAS BEING 'EXTRA FRIENDLY'..
ooo!! Howzabout a lil' hug, Keith..
Do I know this guy?
Hey!! I'm next!!
I dropped some change over here, Too..
IT WAS HORRIBLE!!
IT WAS A LIVING HELL THAT WOMEN MUST GO THROUGH EVERY DAY.. I WAS IN DENIAL FOR A WHILE.. THINKING THESE GUYS WERE JUST BEING NICE..
..THEN MY COUSIN ARNOLD CALLED FOR THE FIRST TIME IN EIGHT YEARS.. WANTING ME TO BE IN HIS WEDDING...
..HE ASKED IF I COULD BE HIS BREAST MAN..
STOP

The third strip adapted for Jetzt Kommt Ein Karton. |

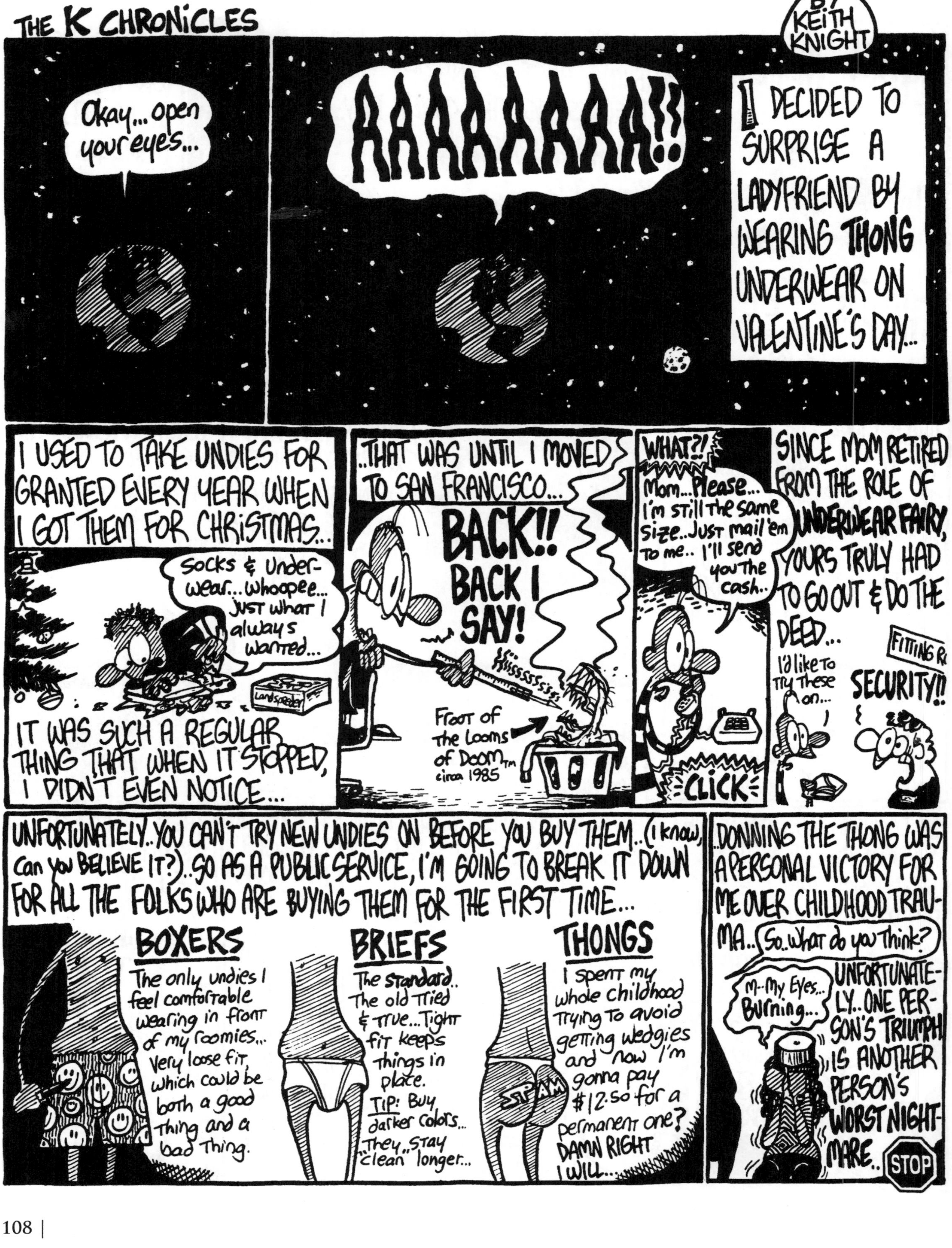

THE K CHRONICLES
BY KEITH KNIGHT
Okay... open your eyes...
AAAAAAAA!!
I DECIDED TO SURPRISE A LADYFRIEND BY WEARING THONG UNDERWEAR ON VALENTINE'S DAY...
I USED TO TAKE UNDIES FOR GRANTED EVERY YEAR WHEN I GOT THEM FOR CHRISTMAS...
Socks & Underwear... whoopee... just what I always wanted...
Landspeeder
IT WAS SUCH A REGULAR THING THAT WHEN IT STOPPED, I DIDN'T EVEN NOTICE...
..THAT WAS UNTIL I MOVED TO SAN FRANCISCO...
BACK!! BACK I SAY!
Hisssssssss
Froot of the Looms of Doom™ circa 1985
WHAT?!
Mom... Please... I'm still the same size.. Just mail 'em to me.. I'll send you the cash..
CLICK
SINCE MOM RETIRED FROM THE ROLE OF UNDERWEAR FAIRY, YOURS TRULY HAD TO GO OUT & DO THE DEED...
I'd like to try these on...
FITTING R
SECURITY!!
UNFORTUNATELY..YOU CAN'T TRY NEW UNDIES ON BEFORE YOU BUY THEM..(I know, Can you BELIEVE IT?)..SO AS A PUBLIC SERVICE, I'M GOING TO BREAK IT DOWN FOR ALL THE FOLKS WHO ARE BUYING THEM FOR THE FIRST TIME...
BOXERS
The only undies I feel comfortable wearing in front of my roomies... Very loose fit, which could be both a good thing and a bad thing.
BRIEFS
The standard.. The old tried & true... Tight fit keeps things in place.
TIP: Buy darker colors... ..They.. stay clean longer...
THONGS
I spent my whole childhood trying to avoid getting wedgies and now I'm gonna pay $12.50 for a permanent one? DAMN RIGHT I WILL...
SPAM
..DONNING THE THONG WAS A PERSONAL VICTORY FOR ME OVER CHILDHOOD TRAUMA...
So.. what do you think?
M-My Eyes... Burning...
UNFORTUNATELY..ONE PERSON'S TRIUMPH IS ANOTHER PERSON'S WORST NIGHTMARE..
STOP

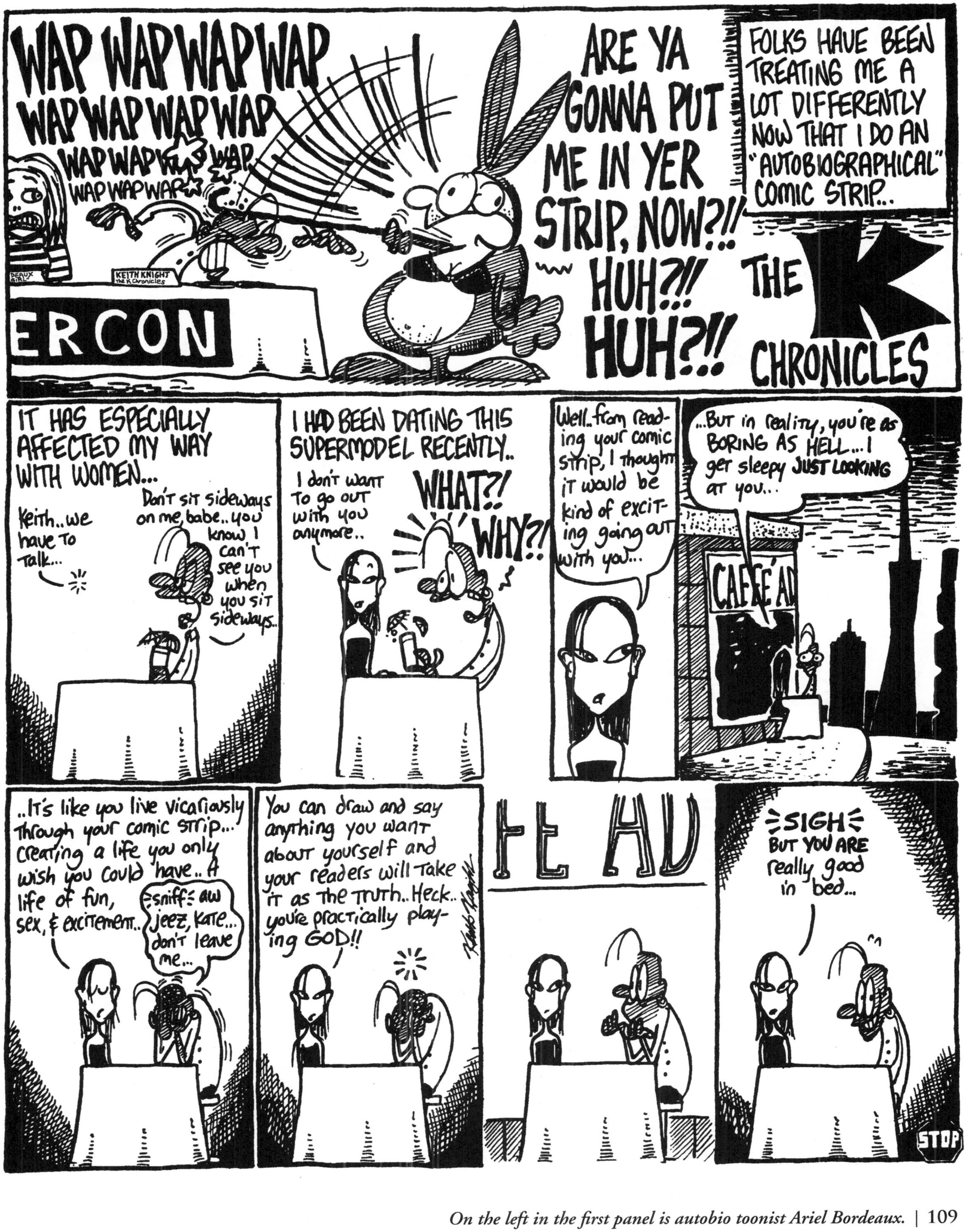
WAP WAP WAP WAP
WAP WAP WAP WAP
WAP WAP WAP WAP
WAP WAP WAP
DEAUX GIRL
KEITH KNIGHT the K Chronicles
ERCON
ARE YA GONNA PUT ME IN YER STRIP, NOW?!.. HUH?!! HUH?!!
FOLKS HAVE BEEN TREATING ME A LOT DIFFERENTLY NOW THAT I DO AN "AUTOBIOGRAPHICAL" COMIC STRIP...
THE K CHRONICLES
IT HAS ESPECIALLY AFFECTED MY WAY WITH WOMEN...
Keith.. we have to talk...
Don't sit sideways on me, babe.. you know I can't see you when you sit sideways..
I HAD BEEN DATING THIS SUPERMODEL RECENTLY..
I don't want to go out with you anymore..
WHAT?! WHY?!
Well.. from reading your comic strip, I thought it would be kind of exciting going out with you...
...But in reality, you're as BORING AS HELL... I get sleepy JUST LOOKING at you...
CAFE AD
..It's like you live vicariously through your comic strip... creating a life you only wish you could have.. A life of fun, sex, & excitement..
sniff aw jeez, Kate... don't leave me...
You can draw and say anything you want about yourself and your readers will take it as the truth.. Heck.. you're practically playing GOD!!
E AD
SIGH BUT YOU ARE really good in bed...
STOP

On the left in the first panel is autobio toonist Ariel Bordeaux. |

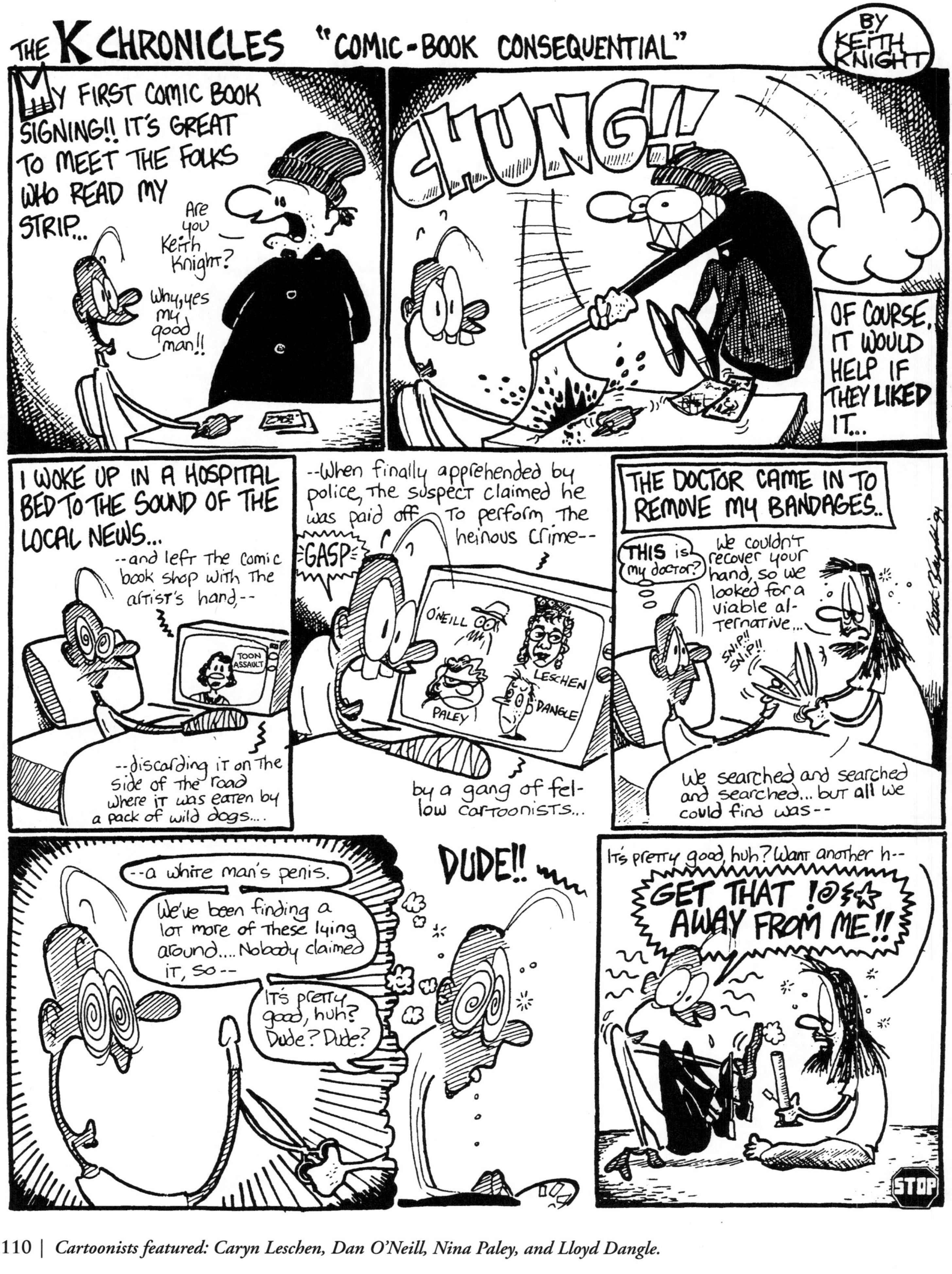
THE K CHRONICLES "COMIC-BOOK CONSEQUENTIAL"
BY KEITH KNIGHT
MY FIRST COMIC BOOK SIGNING!! IT'S GREAT TO MEET THE FOLKS WHO READ MY STRIP...
Are you Keith Knight?
Why, yes my good man!!
CHUNG!!
OF COURSE, IT WOULD HELP IF THEY LIKED IT...
I WOKE UP IN A HOSPITAL BED TO THE SOUND OF THE LOCAL NEWS...
--and left the comic book shop with the artist's hand,--
TOON ASSAULT
--discarding it on the side of the road where it was eaten by a pack of wild dogs....
--When finally apprehended by police, the suspect claimed he was paid off to perform the heinous crime--
GASP
O'NEILL
LESCHEN
PALEY
DANGLE
by a gang of fellow cartoonists...
THE DOCTOR CAME IN TO REMOVE MY BANDAGES..
THIS is my doctor?
We couldn't recover your hand, so we looked for a viable alternative...
SNIP!! SNIP!!
We searched and searched and searched... but all we could find was--
--a white man's penis.
We've been finding a lot more of these lying around.... Nobody claimed it, so--
It's pretty good, huh? Dude? Dude?
DUDE!!
It's pretty good, huh? Want another h--
GET THAT !@$☆ AWAY FROM ME!!
STOP

 Cartoonists featured: Caryn Leschen, Dan O'Neill, Nina Paley, and Lloyd Dangle.

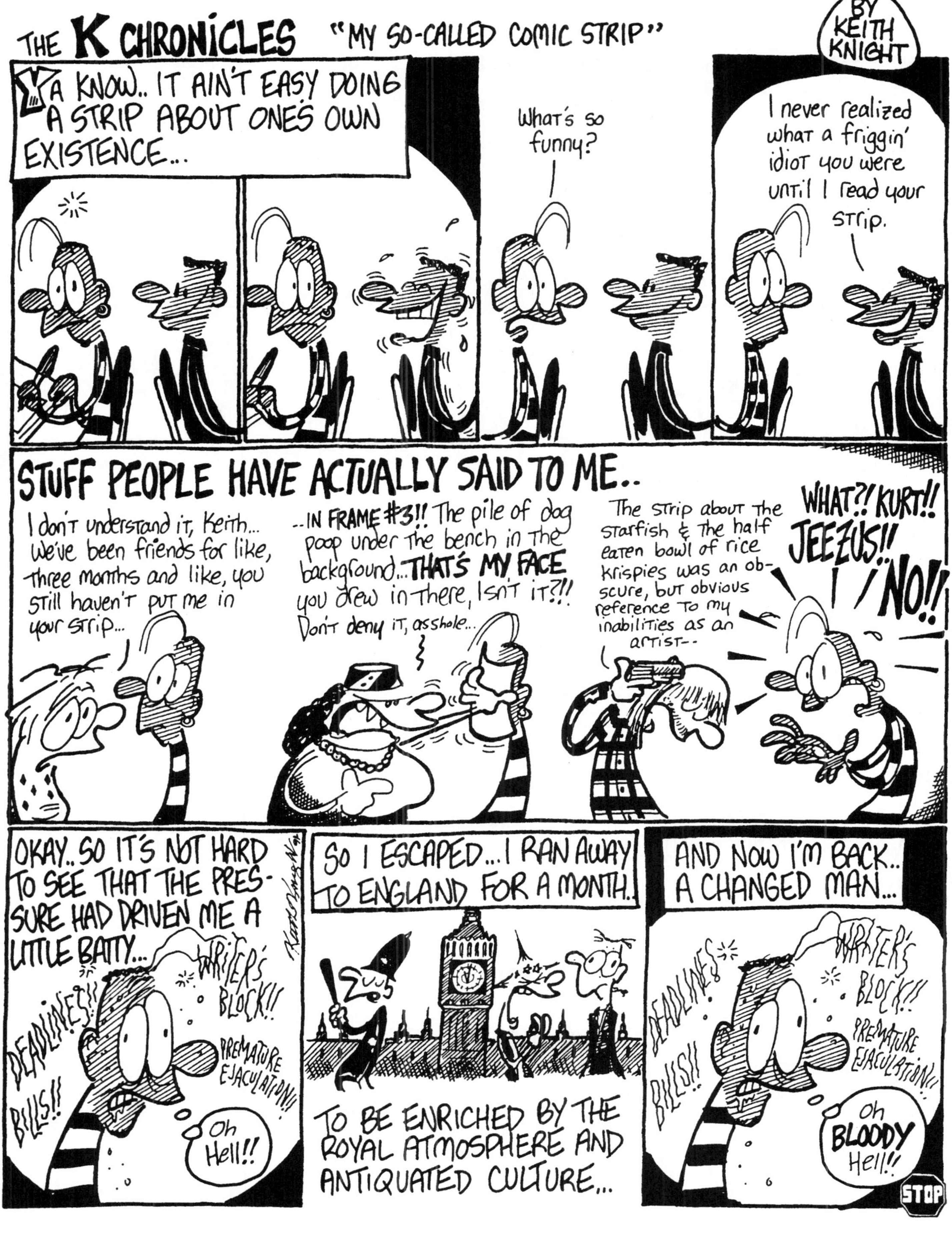
THE K CHRONICLES "MY SO-CALLED COMIC STRIP"
BY KEITH KNIGHT
YA KNOW.. IT AIN'T EASY DOING A STRIP ABOUT ONE'S OWN EXISTENCE...
What's so funny?
I never realized what a friggin' idiot you were until I read your strip.
STUFF PEOPLE HAVE ACTUALLY SAID TO ME..
I don't understand it, Keith... We've been friends for like, three months and like, you still haven't put me in your strip...
--IN FRAME #3!! The pile of dog poop under the bench in the background... THAT'S MY FACE you drew in there, isn't it?!! Don't deny it, asshole...
The strip about the starfish & the half eaten bowl of rice krispies was an obscure, but obvious reference to my inabilities as an artist--
WHAT?! KURT!! JEEZUS!! NO!!
OKAY.. SO IT'S NOT HARD TO SEE THAT THE PRESSURE HAD DRIVEN ME A LITTLE BATTY...
DEADLINES!!
WRITER'S BLOCK!!
PREMATURE EJACULATION!!
BILLS!!
Oh Hell!!
SO I ESCAPED... I RAN AWAY TO ENGLAND FOR A MONTH.
TO BE ENRICHED BY THE ROYAL ATMOSPHERE AND ANTIQUATED CULTURE...
AND NOW I'M BACK.. A CHANGED MAN...
DEADLINES
WRITER'S BLOCK!!
PREMATURE EJACULATION!!
BILLS!!
Oh BLOODY Hell!!
STOP

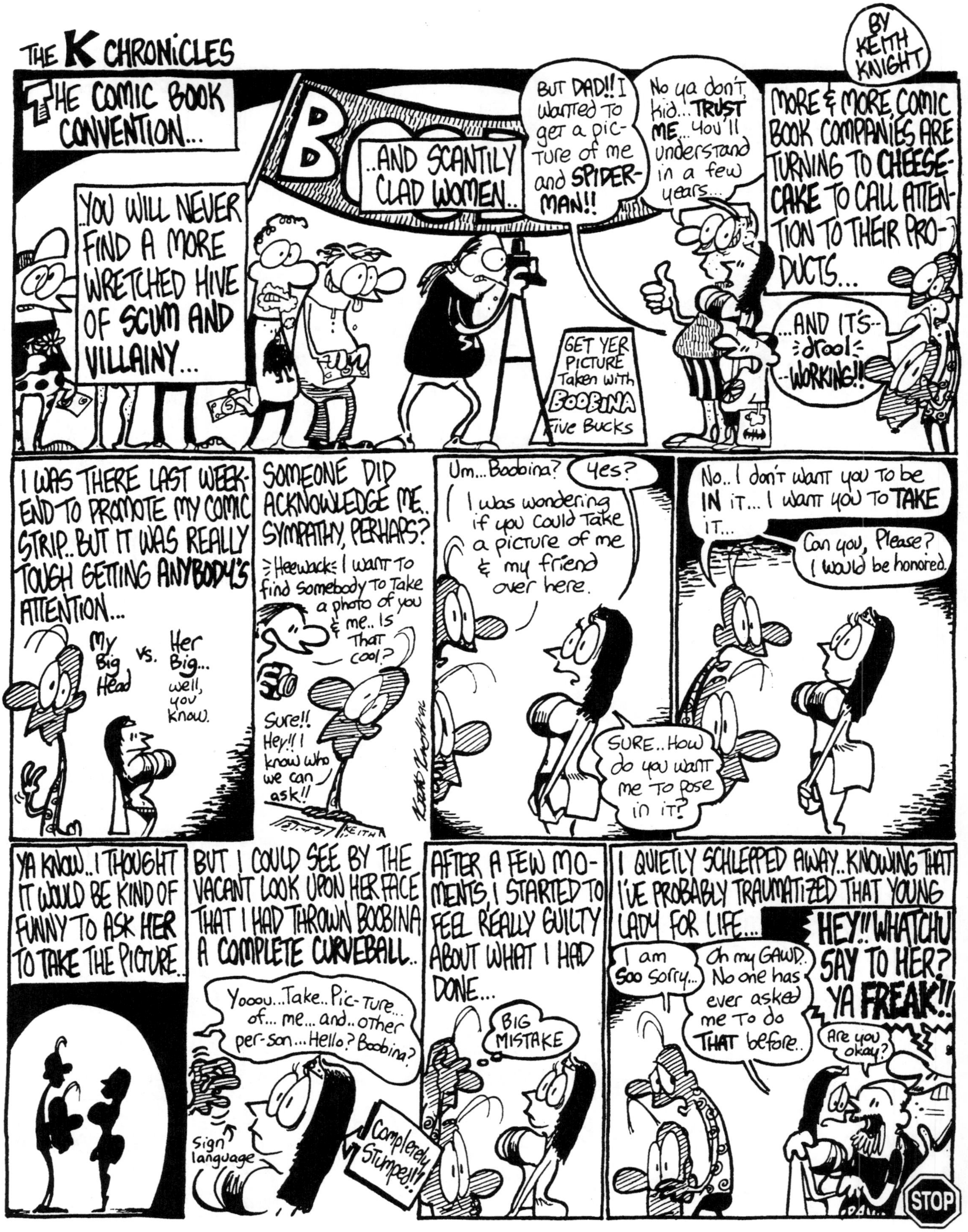
THE K CHRONICLES
BY KEITH KNIGHT
THE COMIC BOOK CONVENTION...
...YOU WILL NEVER FIND A MORE WRETCHED HIVE OF SCUM AND VILLAINY...
..AND SCANTILY CLAD WOMEN..
BUT DAD!! I wanted to get a picture of me and SPIDER-MAN!!
No ya don't, kid... TRUST ME... You'll understand in a few years...
MORE & MORE, COMIC BOOK COMPANIES ARE TURNING TO CHEESE-CAKE TO CALL ATTENTION TO THEIR PRODUCTS...
GET YER PICTURE Taken with BOOBINA Five Bucks
...AND IT'S -drool- WORKING!!
I WAS THERE LAST WEEKEND TO PROMOTE MY COMIC STRIP.. BUT IT WAS REALLY TOUGH GETTING ANYBODY'S ATTENTION...
My Big Head vs. Her Big... well, you know.
SOMEONE DID ACKNOWLEDGE ME.. SYMPATHY, PERHAPS?
Heewack: I want to find somebody to take a photo of you & me.. Is that cool?
Sure!! Hey!! I know who we can ask!!
Um... Boobina?
Yes?
I was wondering if you could take a picture of me & my friend over here.
SURE.. How do you want me to pose in it?
No.. I don't want you to be IN it... I want you to TAKE it...
Can you, Please? I would be honored.
YA KNOW.. I THOUGHT IT WOULD BE KIND OF FUNNY TO ASK HER TO TAKE THE PICTURE..
BUT I COULD SEE BY THE VACANT LOOK UPON HER FACE THAT I HAD THROWN BOOBINA A COMPLETE CURVEBALL..
Yooou... Take.. Pic-ture... of... me... and.. other per-son... Hello? Boobina?
Sign language
Completely Stumped!!
AFTER A FEW MOMENTS, I STARTED TO FEEL REALLY GUILTY ABOUT WHAT I HAD DONE...
BIG MISTAKE
I QUIETLY SCHLEPPED AWAY.. KNOWING THAT I'VE PROBABLY TRAUMATIZED THAT YOUNG LADY FOR LIFE...
I am soo sorry...
Oh my GAWD. No one has ever asked me to do THAT before..
HEY!! WHATCHU SAY TO HER? YA FREAK!!
Are you okay?
STOP

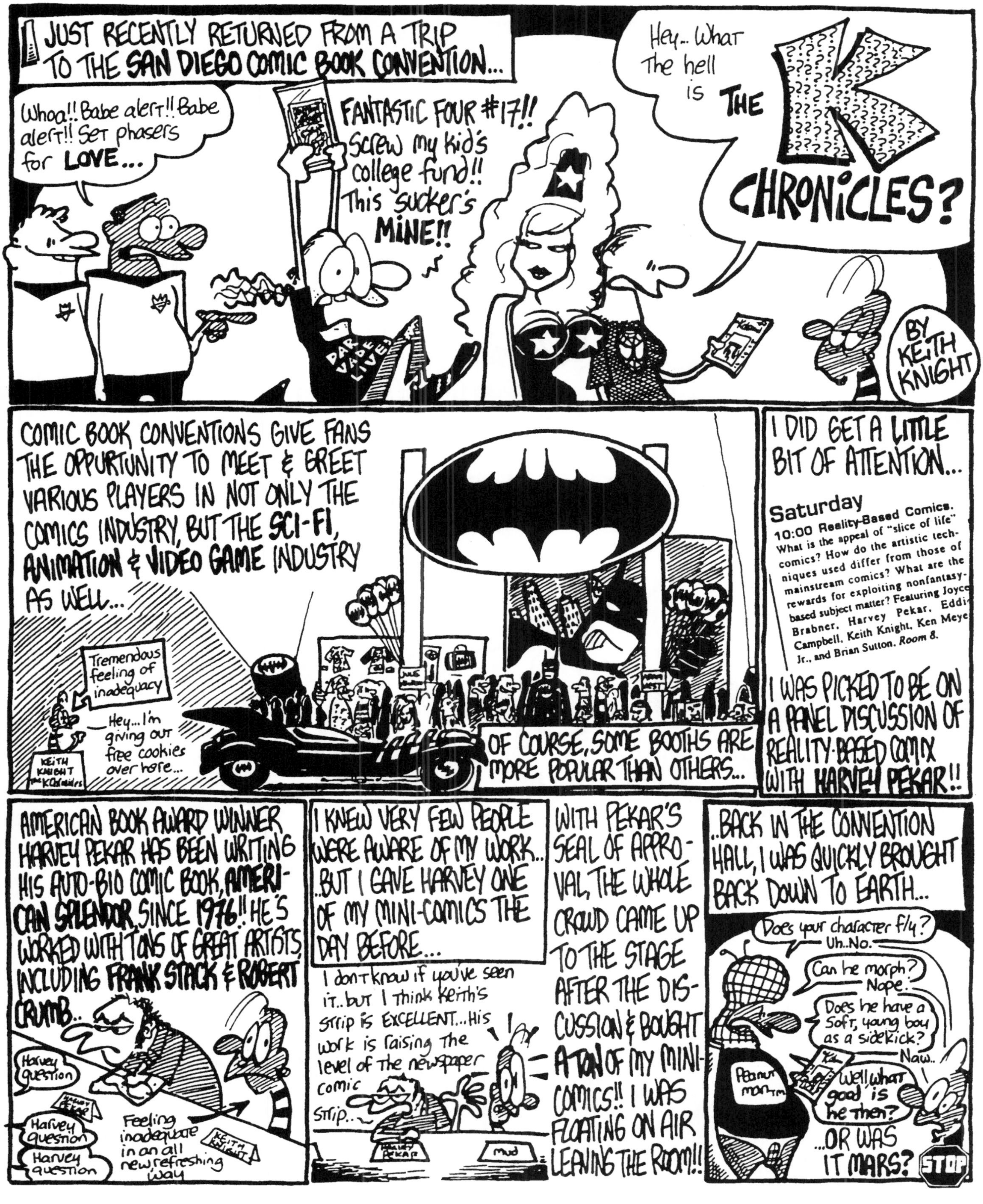
I JUST RECENTLY RETURNED FROM A TRIP TO THE SAN DIEGO COMIC BOOK CONVENTION...
Whoa!! Babe alert!! Babe alert!! Set phasers for LOVE...
FANTASTIC FOUR #17!! Screw my kid's college fund!! This sucker's MINE!!
Hey.. What The hell is THE K CHRONICLES?
BY KEITH KNIGHT
COMIC BOOK CONVENTIONS GIVE FANS THE OPPURTUNITY TO MEET & GREET VARIOUS PLAYERS IN NOT ONLY THE COMICS INDUSTRY, BUT THE SCI-FI, ANIMATION & VIDEO GAME INDUSTRY AS WELL...
Tremendous feeling of inadequacy
Hey...I'm giving out free cookies over here...
KEITH KNIGHT
OF COURSE, SOME BOOTHS ARE MORE POPULAR THAN OTHERS...
I DID GET A LITTLE BIT OF ATTENTION...
Saturday
10:00 Reality-Based Comics. What is the appeal of "slice of life" comics? How do the artistic techniques used differ from those of mainstream comics? What are the rewards for exploiting nonfantasy-based subject matter? Featuring Joyce Brabner, Harvey Pekar, Eddie Campbell, Keith Knight, Ken Meyer Jr., and Brian Sutton. Room 8.
I WAS PICKED TO BE ON A PANEL DISCUSSION OF REALITY-BASED COMIX WITH HARVEY PEKAR!!
AMERICAN BOOK AWARD WINNER HARVEY PEKAR HAS BEEN WRITING HIS AUTO-BIO COMIC BOOK, AMERICAN SPLENDOR, SINCE 1976!! HE'S WORKED WITH TONS OF GREAT ARTISTS, INCLUDING FRANK STACK & ROBERT CRUMB..
Harvey question
Harvey question
Harvey question
HARVEY PEKAR
Feeling inadequate in an all new refreshing way
KEITH KNIGHT
I KNEW VERY FEW PEOPLE WERE AWARE OF MY WORK.. ..BUT I GAVE HARVEY ONE OF MY MINI-COMICS THE DAY BEFORE...
I don't know if you've seen it..but I think Keith's strip is EXCELLENT...His work is raising the level of the newspaper comic strip..
HARVEY PEKAR
WITH PEKAR'S SEAL OF APPROVAL, THE WHOLE CROWD CAME UP TO THE STAGE AFTER THE DISCUSSION & BOUGHT A TON OF MY MINI-COMICS!! I WAS FLOATING ON AIR LEAVING THE ROOM!!
..BACK IN THE CONVENTION HALL, I WAS QUICKLY BROUGHT BACK DOWN TO EARTH...
Does your character fly?
Uh..No.
Can he morph?
Nope.
Does he have a soft, young boy as a sidekick?
Naw..
Well, what good is he then?
Peanut man TM
...OR WAS IT MARS?
STOP

Harvey Pekar praised my work on a panel we both sat on at Comic-Con.
It's been super-models and trays of crack ever since.

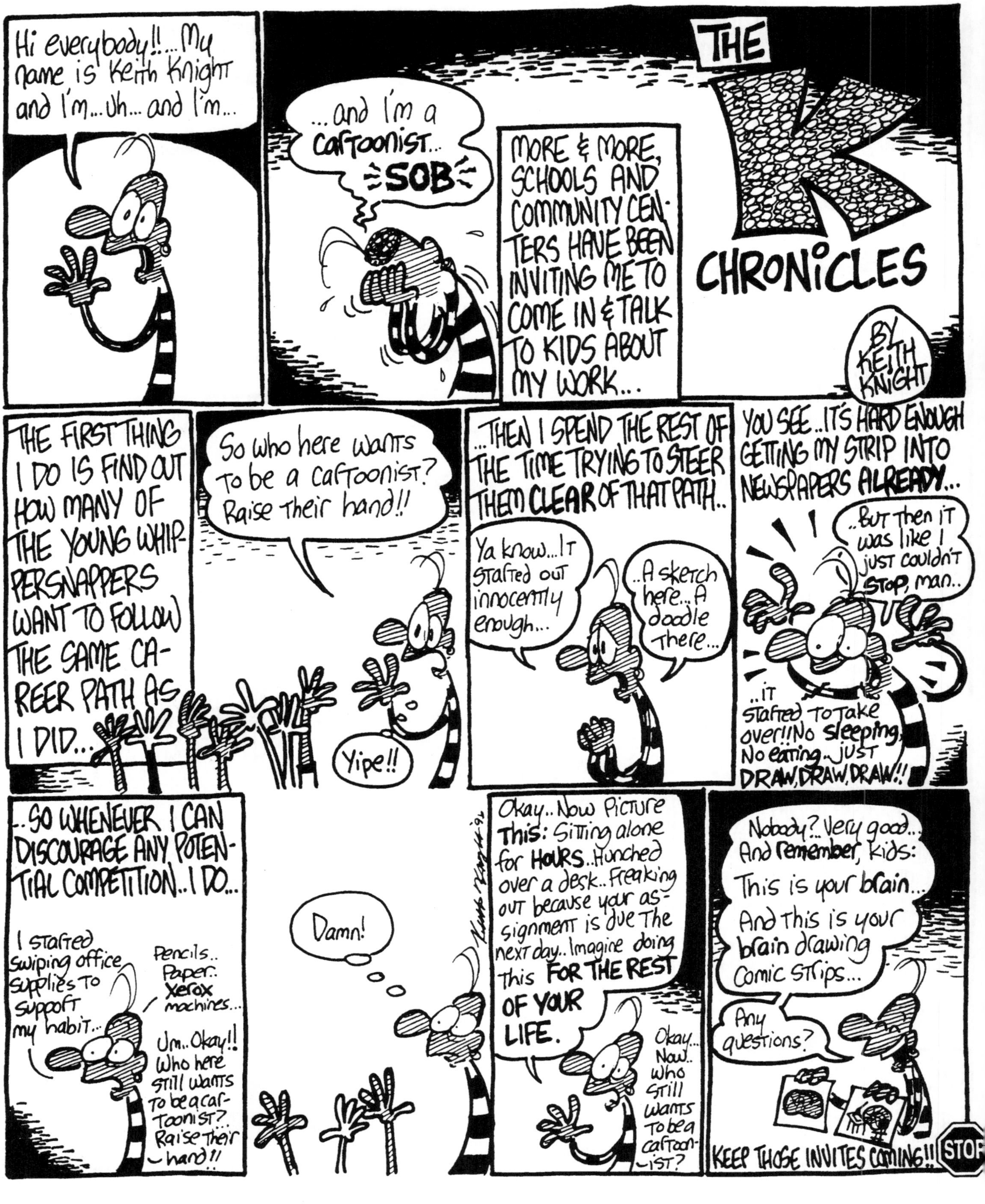

Hi everybody!!... My name is Keith Knight and I'm... uh... and I'm...
...and I'm a cartoonist... SOB
THE K CHRONICLES
BY KEITH KNIGHT
MORE & MORE, SCHOOLS AND COMMUNITY CENTERS HAVE BEEN INVITING ME TO COME IN & TALK TO KIDS ABOUT MY WORK...
THE FIRST THING I DO IS FIND OUT HOW MANY OF THE YOUNG WHIPPERSNAPPERS WANT TO FOLLOW THE SAME CAREER PATH AS I DID...
So who here wants to be a cartoonist? Raise their hand!!
Yipe!!
...THEN I SPEND THE REST OF THE TIME TRYING TO STEER THEM CLEAR OF THAT PATH..
Ya know... It started out innocently enough...
..A sketch here... A doodle there...
YOU SEE... IT'S HARD ENOUGH GETTING MY STRIP INTO NEWSPAPERS ALREADY...
..But then it was like I just couldn't stop, man..
..It started to take over!! No sleeping, No eating.. JUST DRAW, DRAW, DRAW!!
..SO WHENEVER I CAN DISCOURAGE ANY POTENTIAL COMPETITION.. I DO...
I started swiping office supplies to support my habit...
Pencils.. Paper.. Xerox machines...
Um.. Okay!! Who here still wants to be a cartoonist? ...Raise their hand!!
Damn!
Okay.. Now picture this: Sitting alone for HOURS.. Hunched over a desk.. Freaking out because your assignment is due the next day.. Imagine doing this FOR THE REST OF YOUR LIFE.
Okay... Now.. Who still wants to be a cartoonist?
Nobody?.. Very good... And remember, kids: This is your brain... And this is your brain drawing comic strips...
Any questions?
KEEP THOSE INVITES COMING!!
STOP

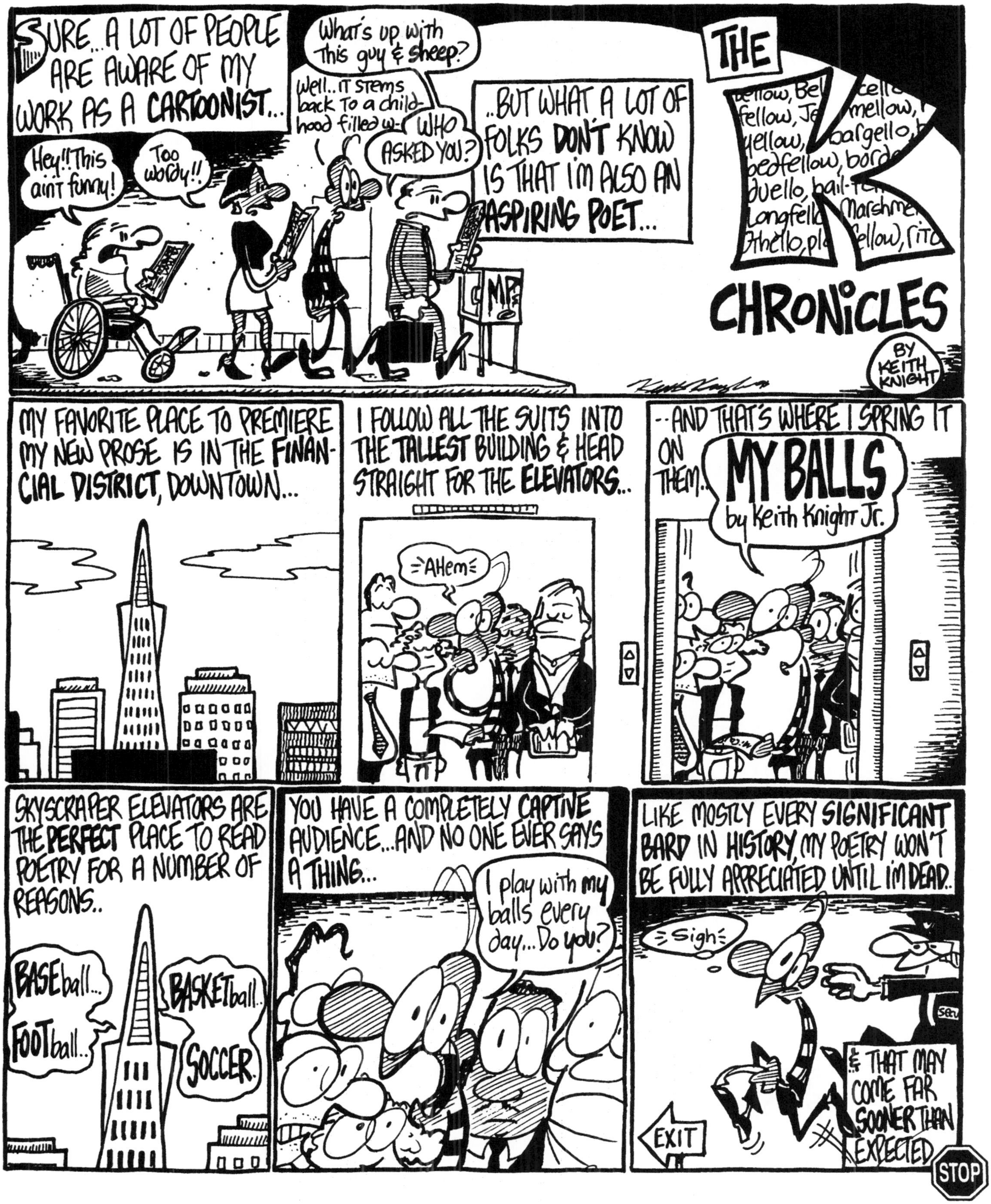
SURE... A LOT OF PEOPLE ARE AWARE OF MY WORK AS A CARTOONIST...
What's up with this guy & sheep?
Well.. IT STEMS back to a childhood filled w-
WHO ASKED YOU?
Hey!! This ain't funny!
Too wordy!!
..BUT WHAT A LOT OF FOLKS DON'T KNOW IS THAT I'M ALSO AN ASPIRING POET...
THE K CHRONICLES
BY KEITH KNIGHT
MY FAVORITE PLACE TO PREMIERE MY NEW PROSE IS IN THE FINANCIAL DISTRICT, DOWNTOWN...
I FOLLOW ALL THE SUITS INTO THE TALLEST BUILDING & HEAD STRAIGHT FOR THE ELEVATORS...
AHem
..AND THAT'S WHERE I SPRING IT ON THEM..
MY BALLS by Keith Knight Jr.
SKYSCRAPER ELEVATORS ARE THE PERFECT PLACE TO READ POETRY FOR A NUMBER OF REASONS..
BASEball...
FOOTball..
BASKETball..
SOCCER
YOU HAVE A COMPLETELY CAPTIVE AUDIENCE...AND NO ONE EVER SAYS A THING...
I play with my balls every day...Do you?
LIKE MOSTLY EVERY SIGNIFICANT BARD IN HISTORY, MY POETRY WON'T BE FULLY APPRECIATED UNTIL I'M DEAD..
Sigh
& THAT MAY COME FAR SOONER THAN EXPECTED
EXIT
STOP

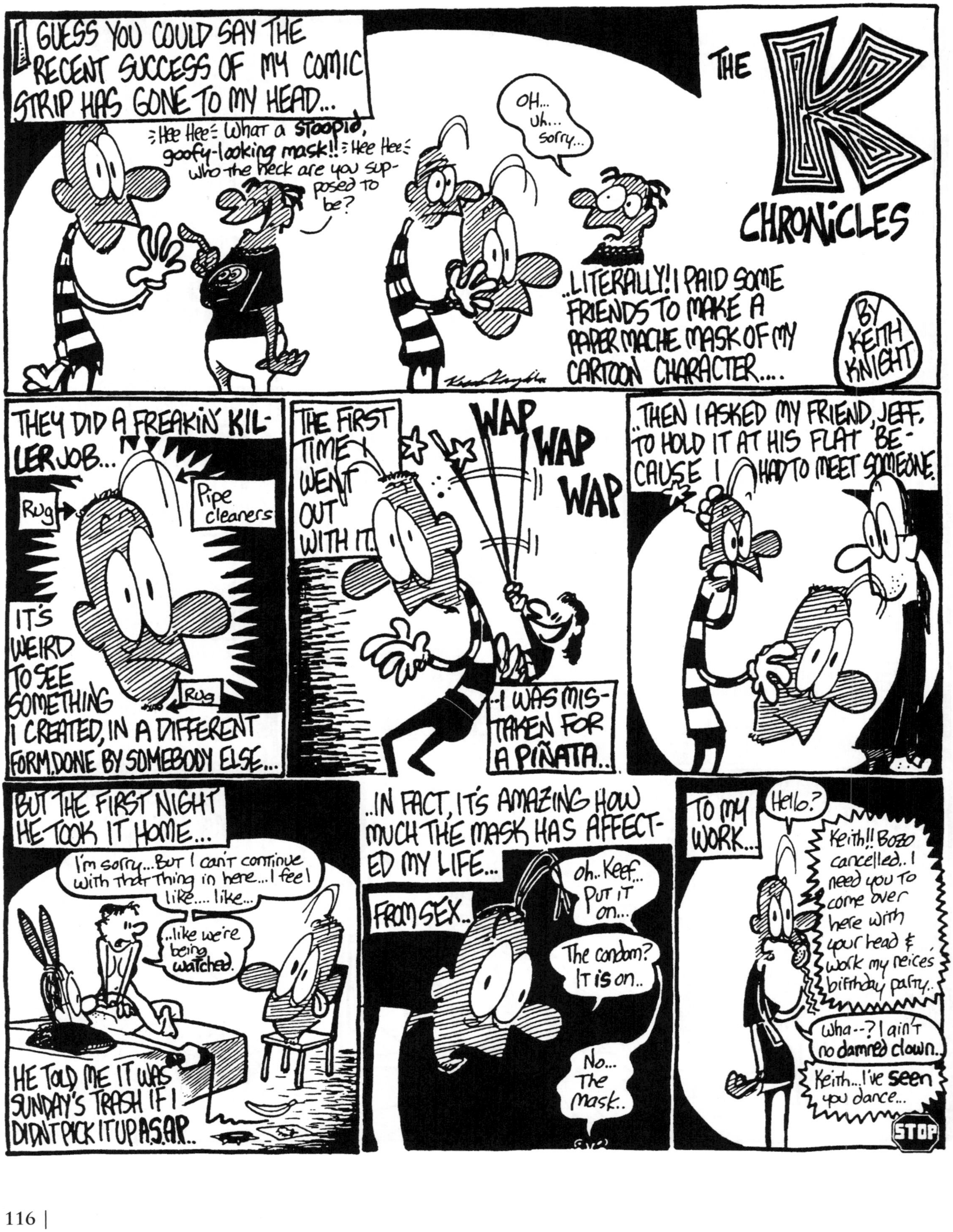
I GUESS YOU COULD SAY THE RECENT SUCCESS OF MY COMIC STRIP HAS GONE TO MY HEAD...
THE K CHRONICLES
Hee Hee What a stoopid, goofy-looking mask!! Hee Hee who the heck are you supposed to be?
OH... uh... sorry...
..LITERALLY! I PAID SOME FRIENDS TO MAKE A PAPER MACHE MASK OF MY CARTOON CHARACTER....
BY KEITH KNIGHT
THEY DID A FREAKIN' KILLER JOB...
Rug
Pipe cleaners
Rug
IT'S WEIRD TO SEE SOMETHING I CREATED, IN A DIFFERENT FORM, DONE BY SOMEBODY ELSE...
THE FIRST TIME I WENT OUT WITH IT..
WAP WAP WAP
..I WAS MISTAKEN FOR A PIÑATA..
..THEN I ASKED MY FRIEND, JEFF, TO HOLD IT AT HIS FLAT BECAUSE I HAD TO MEET SOMEONE.
BUT THE FIRST NIGHT HE TOOK IT HOME...
I'm sorry...But I can't continue with that thing in here...I feel like.... like...
..like we're being watched.
HE TOLD ME IT WAS SUNDAY'S TRASH IF I DIDN'T PICK IT UP A.S.A.P..
..IN FACT, IT'S AMAZING HOW MUCH THE MASK HAS AFFECTED MY LIFE...
FROM SEX..
oh.. Keef.. PUT IT on...
The condom? It is on..
No... The Mask..
TO MY WORK...
Hello?
Keith!! Bozo cancelled.. I need you to come over here with your head & work my neice's birthday party..
Wha--? I ain't no damned clown..
Keith...I've seen you dance...
STOP

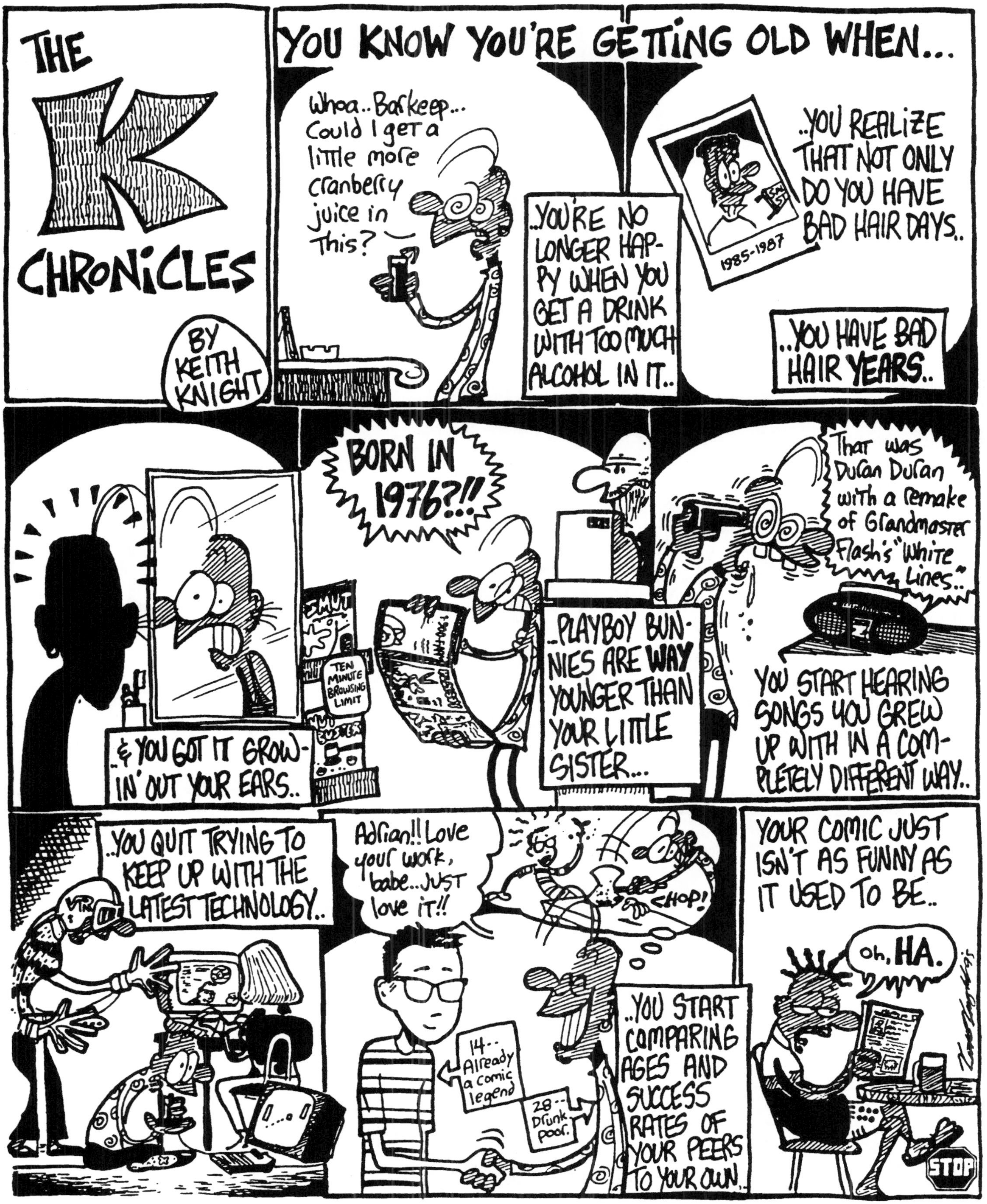
THE K CHRONICLES
BY KEITH KNIGHT
YOU KNOW YOU'RE GETTING OLD WHEN...
Whoa.. Barkeep... Could I get a little more cranberry juice in This?
..YOU'RE NO LONGER HAPPY WHEN YOU GET A DRINK WITH TOO MUCH ALCOHOL IN IT..
1985-1987
..YOU REALIZE THAT NOT ONLY DO YOU HAVE BAD HAIR DAYS..
..YOU HAVE BAD HAIR YEARS..
..& YOU GOT IT GROWIN' OUT YOUR EARS..
SMUT
TEN MINUTE BROWSING LIMIT
BORN IN 1976?!!
..PLAYBOY BUNNIES ARE WAY YOUNGER THAN YOUR LITTLE SISTER...
That was Duran Duran with a remake of Grandmaster Flash's "White Lines."
YOU START HEARING SONGS YOU GREW UP WITH IN A COMPLETELY DIFFERENT WAY..
..YOU QUIT TRYING TO KEEP UP WITH THE LATEST TECHNOLOGY..
Adrian!! Love your work, babe...JUST love it!!
CHOP!
14.. Already a comic legend
28.. Drunk, poor.
..YOU START COMPARING AGES AND SUCCESS RATES OF YOUR PEERS TO YOUR OWN..
YOUR COMIC JUST ISN'T AS FUNNY AS IT USED TO BE..
Oh, HA.
STOP

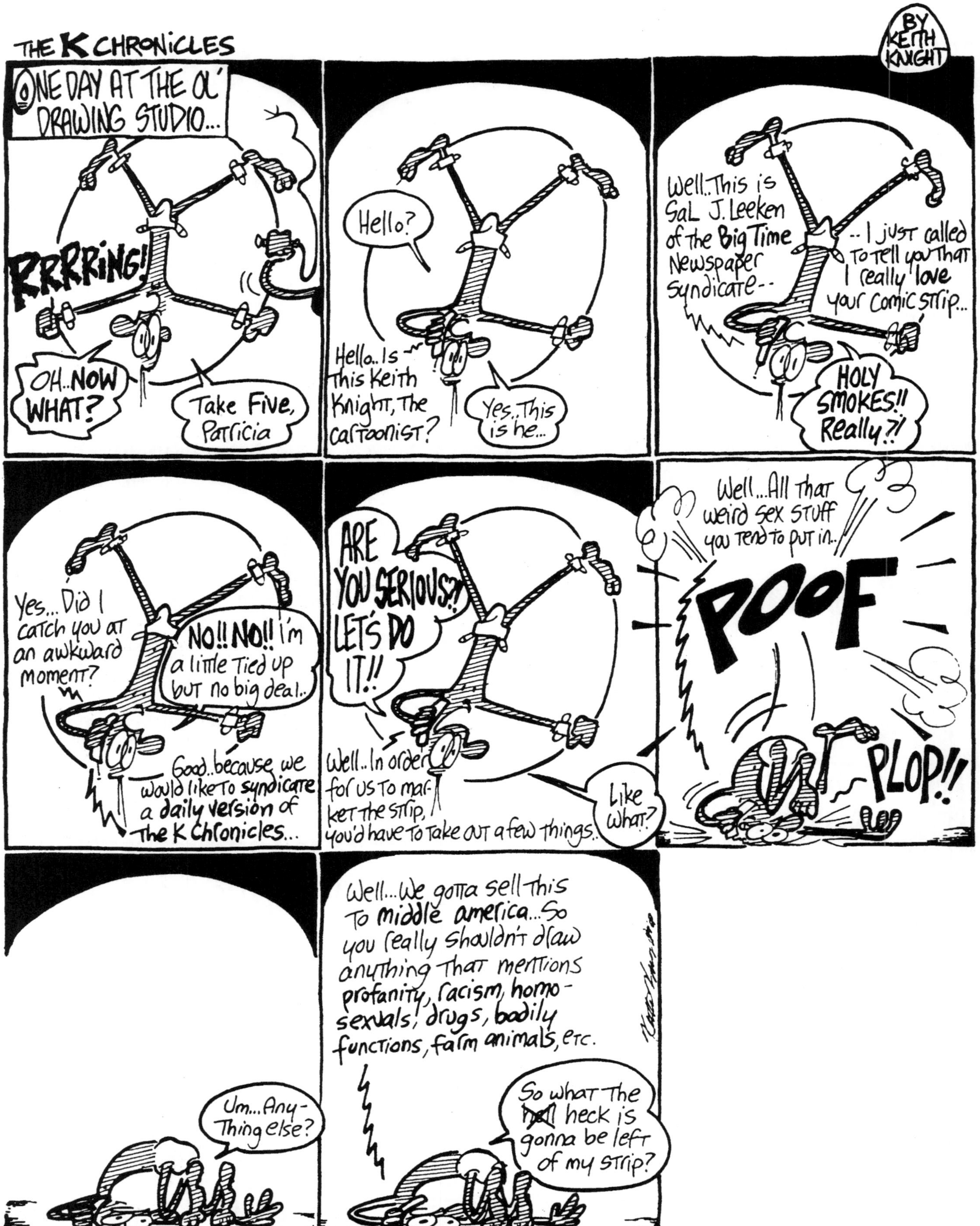
THE K CHRONICLES
BY KEITH KNIGHT
ONE DAY AT THE OL' DRAWING STUDIO...
RRRRING!
OH..NOW WHAT?
Take Five, Patricia
Hello?
Hello.. Is This Keith Knight, The cartoonist?
Yes..This is he...
Well..This is SaL J. Leeken of the Big Time Newspaper Syndicate--
-- I just called to tell you that I really love your comic strip...
HOLY SMOKES!! Really?!
Yes... Did I catch you at an awkward moment?
NO!! NO!! I'm a little Tied up but no big deal..
Good..because we would like to syndicate a daily version of The K Chronicles...
ARE YOU SERIOUS?! LET'S DO IT!!
Well..In order for us to market the strip, you'd have to take out a few things..
Like what?
Well...All that weird sex stuff you tend to put in..
POOF
PLOP!!
Um...Any-Thing else?
Well...We gotta sell this to middle america...So you really shouldn't draw anything that mentions profanity, racism, homo-sexuals, drugs, bodily functions, farm animals, etc.
So what the hell heck is gonna be left of my strip?

 An editor asked me what happened to the final panel of the strip.

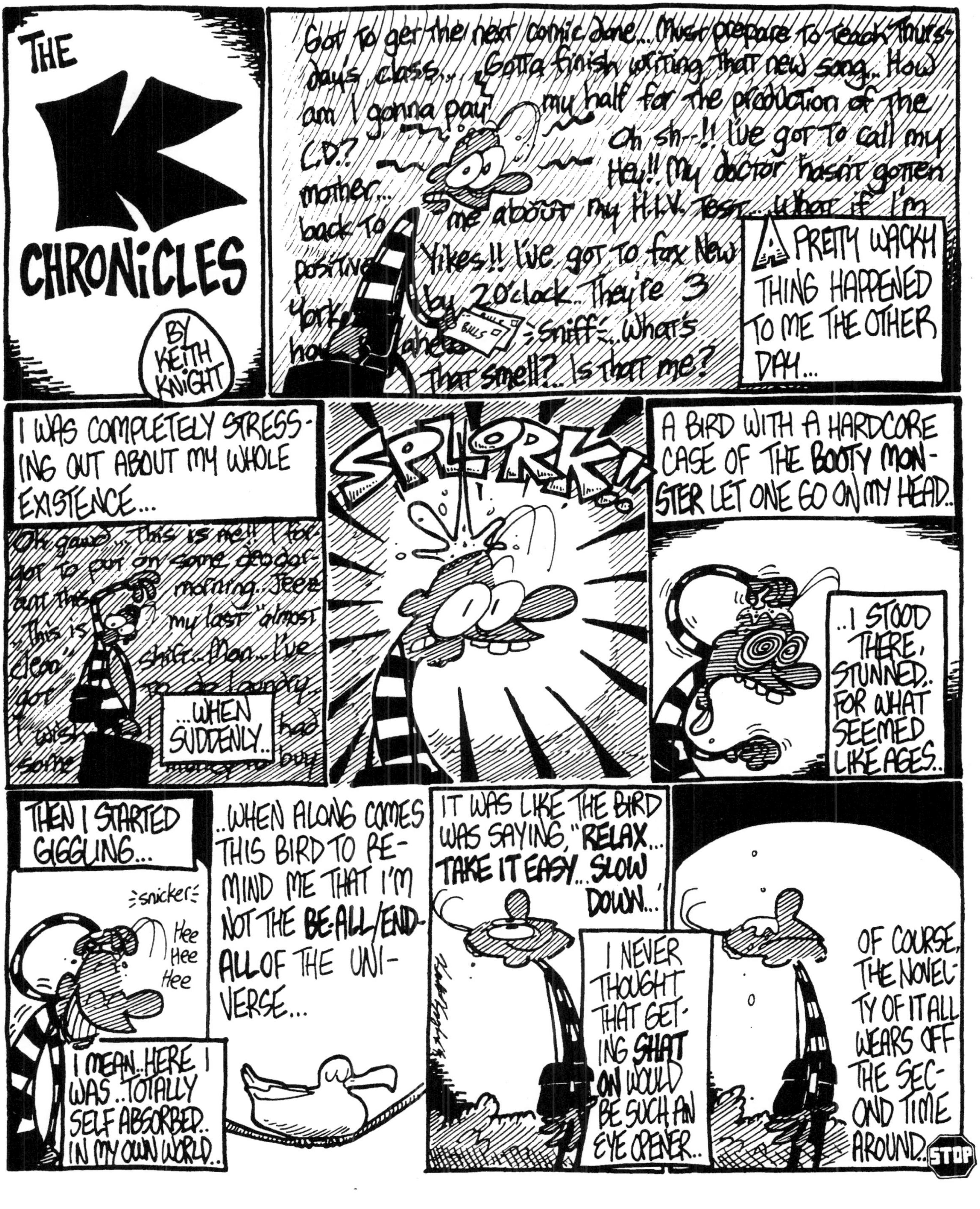
THE K CHRONICLES
BY KEITH KNIGHT
Got to get the next comic done... Must prepare to teach Thursday's class... Gotta finish writing that new song... How am I gonna pay my half for the production of the C.D.?
Oh sh--!! I've got to call my mother...
Hey!! My doctor hasn't gotten back to me about my H.I.V. test... What if I'm positive
Yikes!! I've got to fax New York by 2 o'clock... They're 3 hours ahead
BILLS
:Sniff:.. What's that smell?.. Is that me?
A PRETTY WACKY THING HAPPENED TO ME THE OTHER DAY...
I WAS COMPLETELY STRESSING OUT ABOUT MY WHOLE EXISTENCE...
Oh gawd.. This is me!! I forgot to put on some deodorant this morning.. Jeez.. This is my last "almost clean" shirt.. Man.. I've got to do laundry.. I wish I had some money to buy
...WHEN SUDDENLY..
SPLORK!!
A BIRD WITH A HARDCORE CASE OF THE BOOTY MONSTER LET ONE GO ON MY HEAD..
..I STOOD THERE, STUNNED.. FOR WHAT SEEMED LIKE AGES..
THEN I STARTED GIGGLING...
:snicker:
Hee Hee Hee
I MEAN.. HERE I WAS.. TOTALLY SELF ABSORBED.. IN MY OWN WORLD..
..WHEN ALONG COMES THIS BIRD TO REMIND ME THAT I'M NOT THE BE-ALL/END-ALL OF THE UNIVERSE...
IT WAS LIKE THE BIRD WAS SAYING, "RELAX... TAKE IT EASY... SLOW DOWN..."
I NEVER THOUGHT THAT GETTING SHAT ON WOULD BE SUCH AN EYE OPENER..
OF COURSE, THE NOVELTY OF IT ALL WEARS OFF THE SECOND TIME AROUND..
STOP

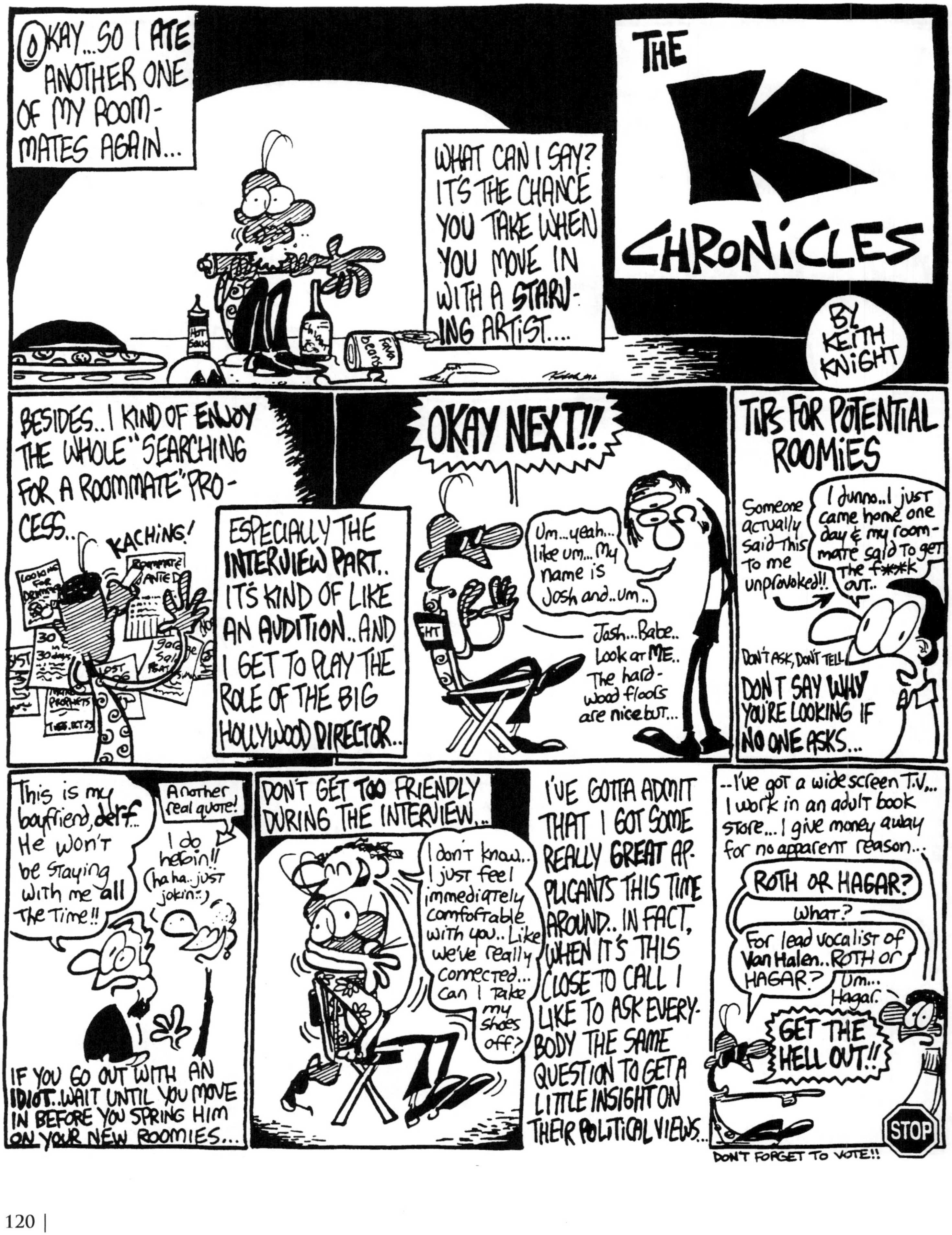

THE K CHRONICLES
BY KEITH KNIGHT
OKAY...SO I ATE ANOTHER ONE OF MY ROOM-MATES AGAIN...
WHAT CAN I SAY? IT'S THE CHANCE YOU TAKE WHEN YOU MOVE IN WITH A STARV-ING ARTIST....
HOT SAUCE
BESIDES..I KIND OF ENJOY THE WHOLE "SEARCHING FOR A ROOMMATE" PRO-CESS..
KACHING!
ESPECIALLY THE INTERVIEW PART.. IT'S KIND OF LIKE AN AUDITION..AND I GET TO PLAY THE ROLE OF THE BIG HOLLYWOOD DIRECTOR..
OKAY NEXT!!
Um...yeah... like um... My name is Josh and..um..
Josh...Babe.. Look at ME.. The hard-wood floors are nice but...
TIPS FOR POTENTIAL ROOMIES
Someone actually said this to me unprovoked!!
I dunno..I just came home one day & my room-mate said to get the f**k out..
DON'T ASK, DON'T TELL
DON'T SAY WHY YOU'RE LOOKING IF NO ONE ASKS...
This is my boyfriend, derf... He won't be staying with me all the time!!
Another real quote!
I do hebin!! (ha ha..just jokin'.)
IF YOU GO OUT WITH AN IDIOT..WAIT UNTIL YOU MOVE IN BEFORE YOU SPRING HIM ON YOUR NEW ROOMIES...
DON'T GET TOO FRIENDLY DURING THE INTERVIEW...
I don't know.. I just feel immediately comfortable with you..Like we've really connected... Can I take my shoes off?
I'VE GOTTA ADMIT THAT I GOT SOME REALLY GREAT AP-PLICANTS THIS TIME AROUND.. IN FACT, WHEN IT'S THIS CLOSE TO CALL I LIKE TO ASK EVERY-BODY THE SAME QUESTION TO GET A LITTLE INSIGHT ON THEIR POLITICAL VIEWS...
--I've got a wide screen T.V... I work in an adult book store... I give money away for no apparent reason...
ROTH OR HAGAR?
What?
For lead vocalist of Van Halen..ROTH or HAGAR?
Um... Hagar.
GET THE HELL OUT!!
STOP
DON'T FORGET TO VOTE!!

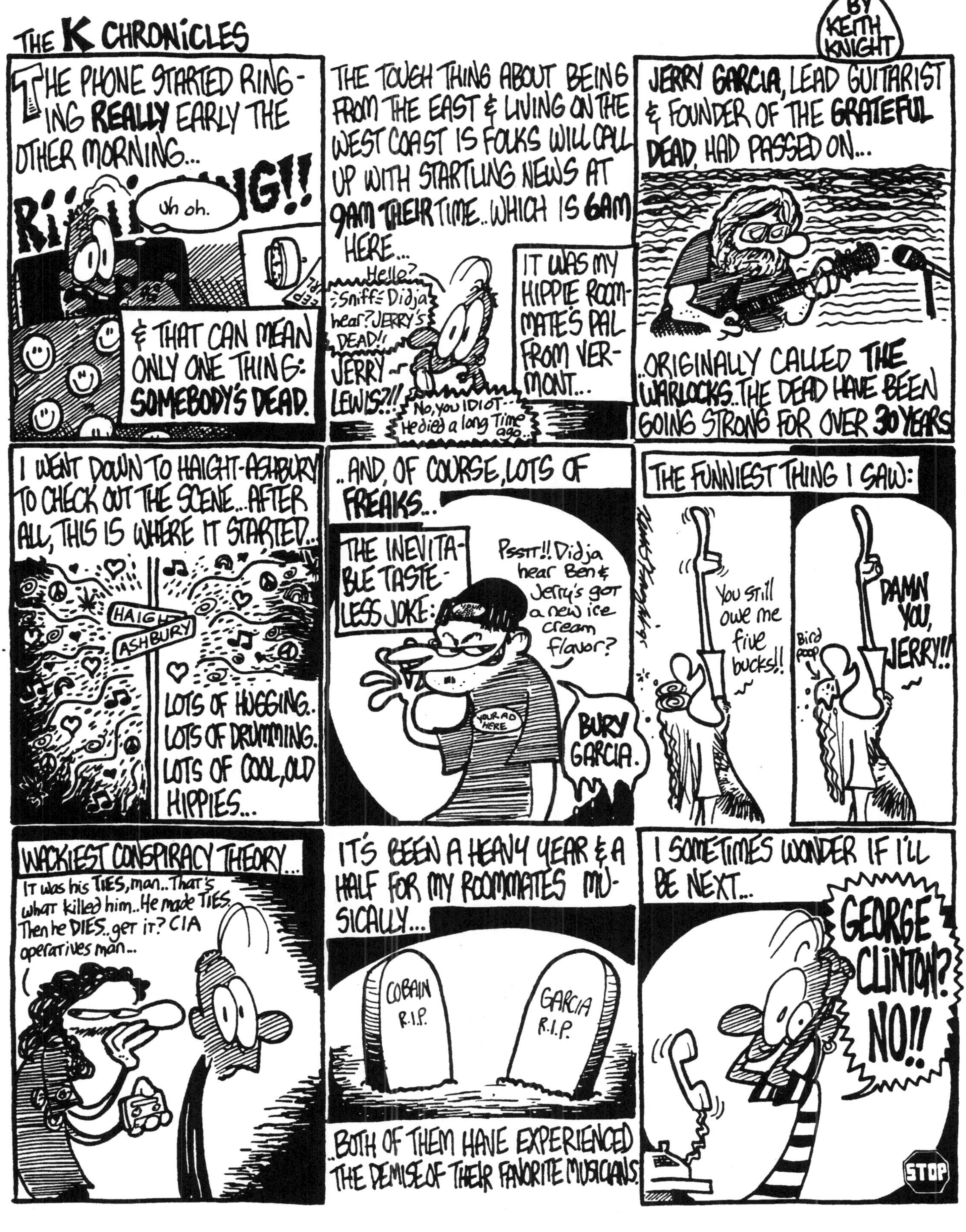
THE K CHRONICLES
BY KEITH KNIGHT
THE PHONE STARTED RINGING REALLY EARLY THE OTHER MORNING...
uh oh.
& THAT CAN MEAN ONLY ONE THING: SOMEBODY'S DEAD.
THE TOUGH THING ABOUT BEING FROM THE EAST & LIVING ON THE WEST COAST IS FOLKS WILL CALL UP WITH STARTLING NEWS AT 9AM THEIR TIME.. WHICH IS 6AM HERE...
Hello?
Sniff Didja hear? JERRY'S DEAD!!
JERRY LEWIS?!!
No, you IDIOT-- He died a long time ago..
IT WAS MY HIPPIE ROOMMATE'S PAL FROM VERMONT...
JERRY GARCIA, LEAD GUITARIST & FOUNDER OF THE GRATEFUL DEAD, HAD PASSED ON...
..ORIGINALLY CALLED THE WARLOCKS..THE DEAD HAVE BEEN GOING STRONG FOR OVER 30 YEARS
I WENT DOWN TO HAIGHT-ASHBURY TO CHECK OUT THE SCENE...AFTER ALL, THIS IS WHERE IT STARTED...
HAIGHT
ASHBURY
LOTS OF HUGGING. LOTS OF DRUMMING. LOTS OF COOL, OLD HIPPIES...
..AND, OF COURSE, LOTS OF FREAKS...
THE INEVITABLE TASTELESS JOKE:
Psstt!! Didja hear Ben & Jerry's got a new ice cream flavor?
BURY GARCIA.
THE FUNNIEST THING I SAW:
You still owe me five bucks!!
Bird poop
DAMN YOU, JERRY!!
WACKIEST CONSPIRACY THEORY...
It was his TIES, man.. That's what killed him.. He made TIES. Then he DIES.. get it? CIA operatives man...
IT'S BEEN A HEAVY YEAR & A HALF FOR MY ROOMMATES MUSICALLY...
COBAIN R.I.P.
GARCIA R.I.P.
..BOTH OF THEM HAVE EXPERIENCED THE DEMISE OF THEIR FAVORITE MUSICIANS.
I SOMETIMES WONDER IF I'LL BE NEXT...
GEORGE CLINTON?! NO!!
STOP

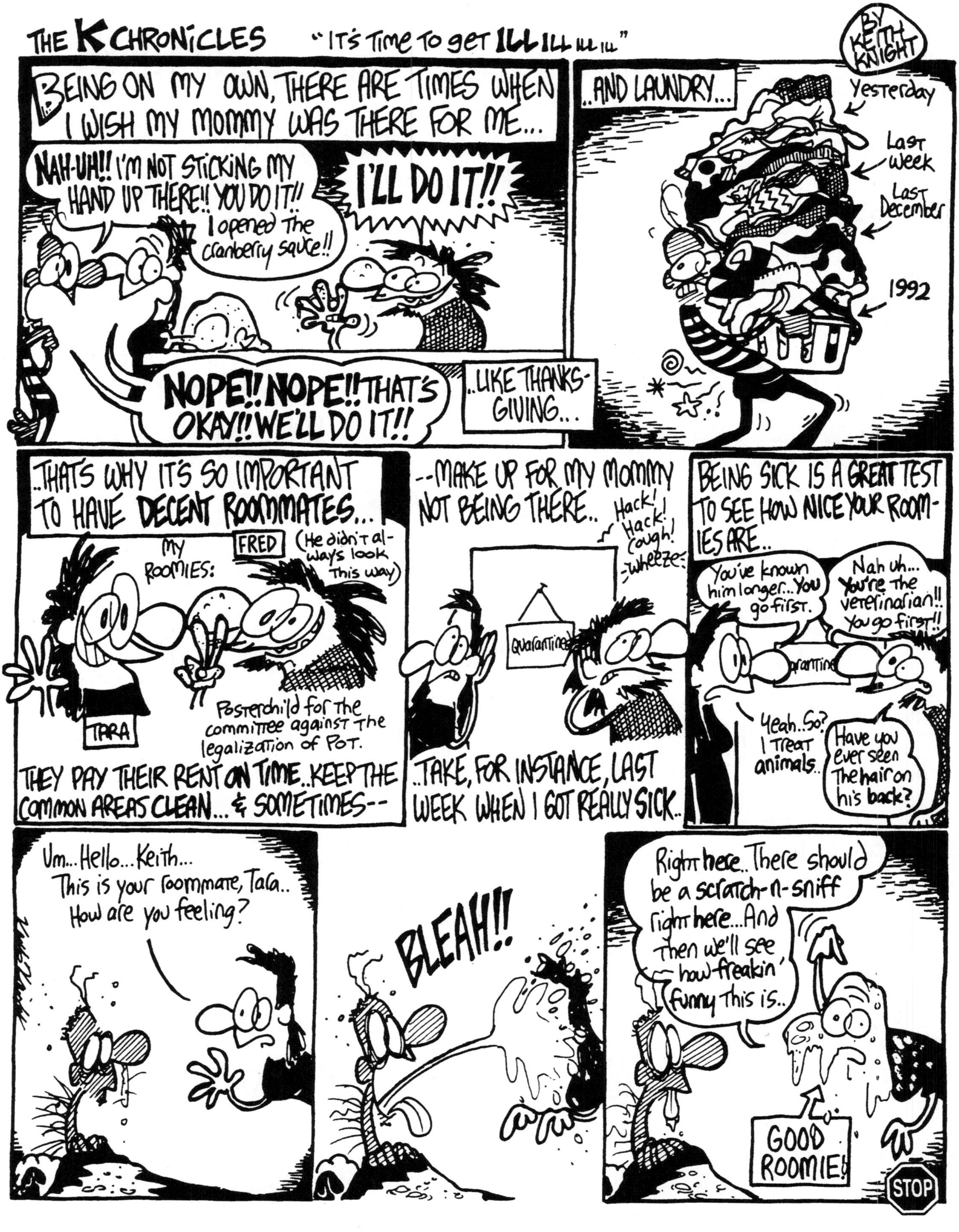
THE K CHRONICLES
"IT'S TIME TO GET ILL ILL ILL ILL"
BY KEITH KNIGHT
BEING ON MY OWN, THERE ARE TIMES WHEN I WISH MY MOMMY WAS THERE FOR ME...
NAH-UH!! I'M NOT STICKING MY HAND UP THERE!! YOU DO IT!!
I opened the cranberry sauce!!
I'LL DO IT!!
NOPE!! NOPE!! THAT'S OKAY!! WE'LL DO IT!!
..LIKE THANKSGIVING...
..AND LAUNDRY...
Yesterday
Last Week
Last December
1992
..THAT'S WHY IT'S SO IMPORTANT TO HAVE DECENT ROOMMATES...
MY ROOMIES:
FRED
(He didn't always look this way)
TARA
Posterchild for the committee against the legalization of Pot.
THEY PAY THEIR RENT ON TIME..KEEP THE COMMON AREAS CLEAN... & SOMETIMES--
--MAKE UP FOR MY MOMMY NOT BEING THERE..
Hack! Hack! Cough! wheeze
Quarantine
..TAKE, FOR INSTANCE, LAST WEEK WHEN I GOT REALLY SICK..
BEING SICK IS A GREAT TEST TO SEE HOW NICE YOUR ROOMIES ARE..
You've known him longer...You go first.
Nah uh... You're the veterinarian!! You go first!!
Yeah..So? I treat animals..
Have you ever seen the hair on his back?
Um...Hello...Keith... This is your roommate, Tara.. How are you feeling?
BLEAH!!
Right here..There should be a scratch-n-sniff right here...And then we'll see how freakin' funny this is..
GOOD ROOMIE!
STOP

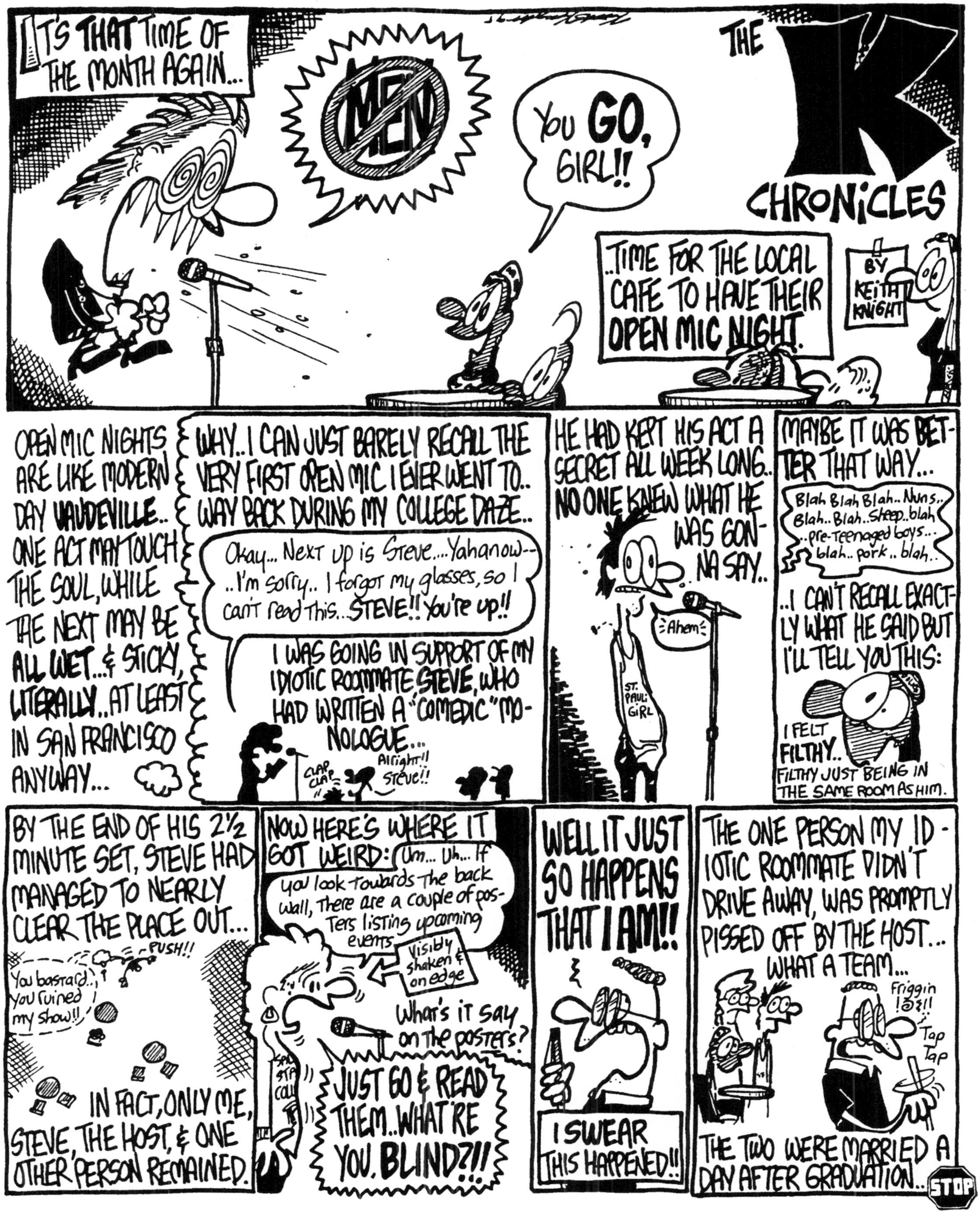

IT'S THAT TIME OF THE MONTH AGAIN...
MEN
You GO, GIRL!!
THE K CHRONICLES
BY KEITH KNIGHT
..TIME FOR THE LOCAL CAFE TO HAVE THEIR OPEN MIC NIGHT.
OPEN MIC NIGHTS ARE LIKE MODERN DAY VAUDEVILLE.. ONE ACT MAY TOUCH THE SOUL, WHILE THE NEXT MAY BE ALL WET...& STICKY, LITERALLY...AT LEAST IN SAN FRANCISCO ANYWAY...
WHY..I CAN JUST BARELY RECALL THE VERY FIRST OPEN MIC I EVER WENT TO.. WAY BACK DURING MY COLLEGE DAZE..
Okay... Next up is Steve....Yahanow-- ..I'm sorry.. I forgot my glasses, so I can't read This...STEVE!! You're up!!
I WAS GOING IN SUPPORT OF MY IDIOTIC ROOMMATE STEVE, WHO HAD WRITTEN A "COMEDIC" MONOLOGUE...
CLAP CLAP
Alright!! Steve!!
HE HAD KEPT HIS ACT A SECRET ALL WEEK LONG.. NO ONE KNEW WHAT HE WAS GONNA SAY..
Ahem
ST. PAULI GIRL
MAYBE IT WAS BETTER THAT WAY...
Blah Blah Blah...Nuns.. Blah..Blah..Sheep..blah ..pre-Teenaged boys... blah..pork..blah..
..I CAN'T RECALL EXACTLY WHAT HE SAID BUT I'LL TELL YOU THIS:
I FELT FILTHY..
FILTHY JUST BEING IN THE SAME ROOM AS HIM.
BY THE END OF HIS 2½ MINUTE SET, STEVE HAD MANAGED TO NEARLY CLEAR THE PLACE OUT...
PUSH!!
You bastard.. You ruined my show!!
IN FACT, ONLY ME, STEVE, THE HOST, & ONE OTHER PERSON REMAINED.
NOW HERE'S WHERE IT GOT WEIRD:
Um... Uh... If you look Towards The back wall, There are a couple of posTers listing upcoming events..
Visibly shaken & on edge
What's it say on The posters?
JUST GO & READ THEM..WHAT'RE YOU, BLIND?!!
WELL IT JUST SO HAPPENS THAT I AM!!
I SWEAR THIS HAPPENED!!
THE ONE PERSON MY IDIOTIC ROOMMATE DIDN'T DRIVE AWAY, WAS PROMPTLY PISSED OFF BY THE HOST... WHAT A TEAM...
Friggin !@?!!
Tap Tap
THE TWO WERE MARRIED A DAY AFTER GRADUATION...
STOP

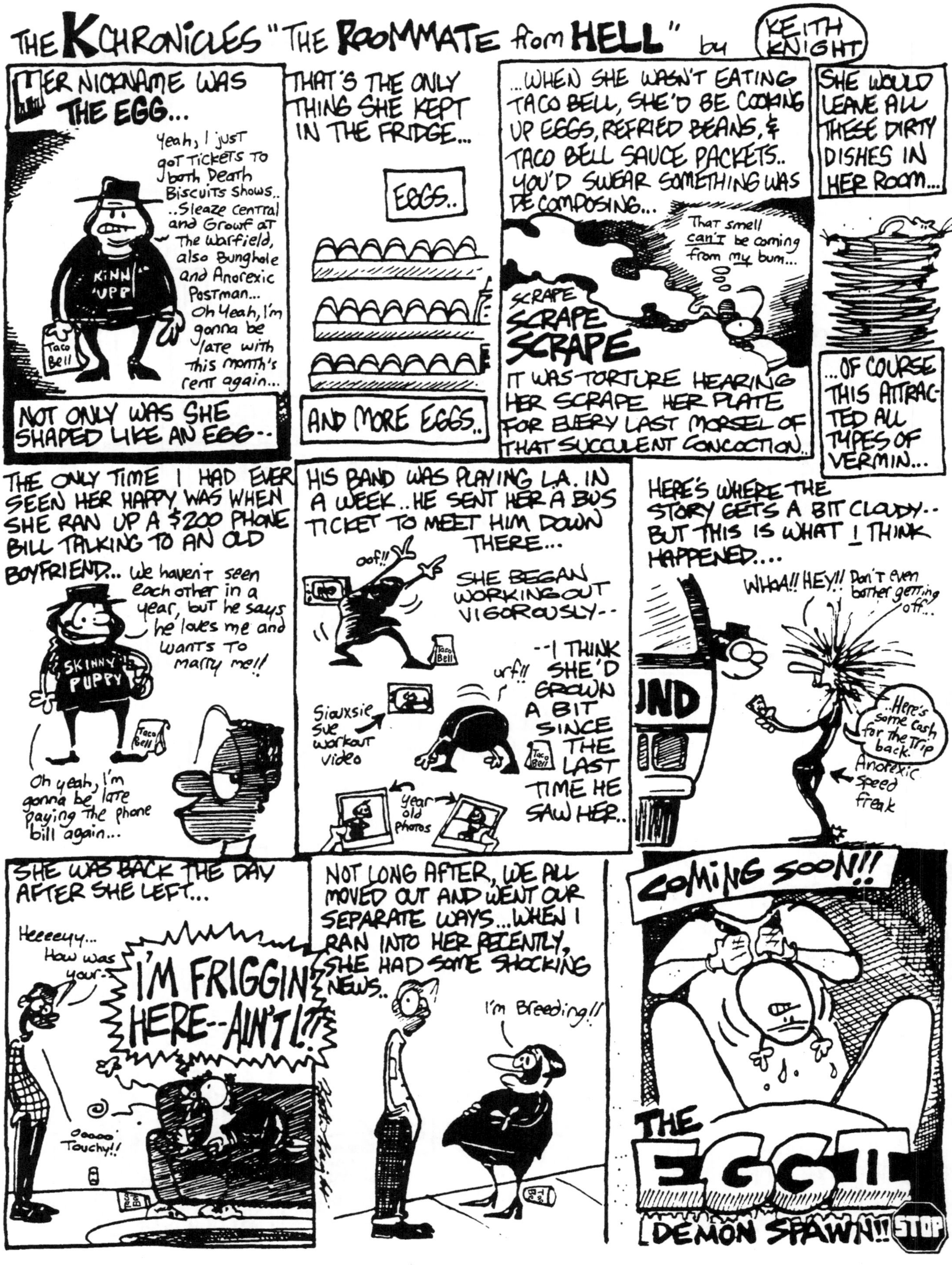
THE K CHRONICLES "THE ROOMMATE from HELL" by KEITH KNIGHT
HER NICKNAME WAS THE EGG...
Yeah, I just got tickets to both Death Biscuits shows.. ..Sleaze central and Growf at the Warfield, also Bunghole and Anorexic Postman... Oh yeah, I'm gonna be late with this month's rent again...
NOT ONLY WAS SHE SHAPED LIKE AN EGG..
THAT'S THE ONLY THING SHE KEPT IN THE FRIDGE...
EGGS..
AND MORE EGGS..
...WHEN SHE WASN'T EATING TACO BELL, SHE'D BE COOKING UP EGGS, REFRIED BEANS, & TACO BELL SAUCE PACKETS.. YOU'D SWEAR SOMETHING WAS DECOMPOSING...
That smell can't be coming from my bum...
SCRAPE SCRAPE SCRAPE
IT WAS TORTURE HEARING HER SCRAPE HER PLATE FOR EVERY LAST MORSEL OF THAT SUCCULENT CONCOCTION..
SHE WOULD LEAVE ALL THESE DIRTY DISHES IN HER ROOM...
...OF COURSE THIS ATTRACTED ALL TYPES OF VERMIN...
THE ONLY TIME I HAD EVER SEEN HER HAPPY WAS WHEN SHE RAN UP A $200 PHONE BILL TALKING TO AN OLD BOYFRIEND..
We haven't seen each other in a year, but he says he loves me and wants to marry me!!
SKINNY PUPPY
Oh yeah, I'm gonna be late paying the phone bill again...
HIS BAND WAS PLAYING L.A. IN A WEEK..HE SENT HER A BUS TICKET TO MEET HIM DOWN THERE...
oof!!
SHE BEGAN WORKING OUT VIGOROUSLY--
--I THINK SHE'D GROWN A BIT SINCE THE LAST TIME HE SAW HER..
urf!!
Siouxsie Sue workout video
year old photos
HERE'S WHERE THE STORY GETS A BIT CLOUDY.. BUT THIS IS WHAT I THINK HAPPENED....
WHOA!! HEY!!
Don't even bother getting off...
..Here's some cash for the Trip back.
Anorexic speed freak
SHE WAS BACK THE DAY AFTER SHE LEFT...
Heeeeyy... How was your-
I'M FRIGGIN' HERE--AIN'T I!?
Ooooo Touchy!!
NOT LONG AFTER, WE ALL MOVED OUT AND WENT OUR SEPARATE WAYS...WHEN I RAN INTO HER RECENTLY, SHE HAD SOME SHOCKING NEWS..
I'm Breeding!!
COMING SOON!!
THE EGG II
DEMON SPAWN!!
STOP

 One of my earliest published strips.

YOU IDIOT!!.. IT'S A GODDAMNED TREE!!

Time's Up!!

THE OTHER NITE I MADE THE MISTAKE OF PARTICIPATING IN A GAME OF PICTIONARY..

THE **K** CHRONICLES

"QUICK-DRAW GUFFAW"

BY KEITH KNIGHT

GUESS WHO LOST...

YES!!

OHMIGOSH!! We beat a real, live CARTOONIST!!

NEEDLESS TO SAY, MY ROOMMATE AND HER FRIEND WERE QUITE ECSTATIC...

I'm a nurse.. A NURSE!! And I beat you in PICTIONARY!!

Whoa... This is better than sex... Gawd, I need a cigarette.

MOST CARTOONISTS REFUSE TO PLAY THE GAME WITH NORMAL PEOPLE...

:Sigh:

IT'S BECAUSE THEY'RE AFRAID OF LOSING.. BUT THEY WON'T ADMIT IT...

I CALLED MY CARTOONIST FRIEND, NINA, FOR A LITTLE CONSOLATION...

YOU WHAT?!

I'm sorry, Keith... but I really don't think we should talk to each other anymore... =CLICK=

DEJECTED, I PICKED UP A 40-OUNCE AT THE LOCAL STORE & HEADED FOR THE PARK...

Had a cousin Clarence... was a private detective... A DAMN GOOD ONE--

--ended up losing to his daughter in a game of **CLUE**.. He was DEVASTATED.

.The next day, he jumped out in front of a **STEAM ROLLER**...

I've read your stuff... a bit wordy... but it sure beats GARFIELD...

..Don't sweat it, kid... it's just a game.

THE OLD DUDE WAS RIGHT..IT'S JUST A STUPID MEANINGLESS GAME...I'M AN ADULT NOW..MATURE. I RUSHED HOME, INSPIRED.. READY TO DO A WHOLE BUNCH OF CARTOON STRIPS...
..BUT FIRST..

YES!!

I KICKED MY ROOMMATE'S **ASS** IN OPERATION. STOP

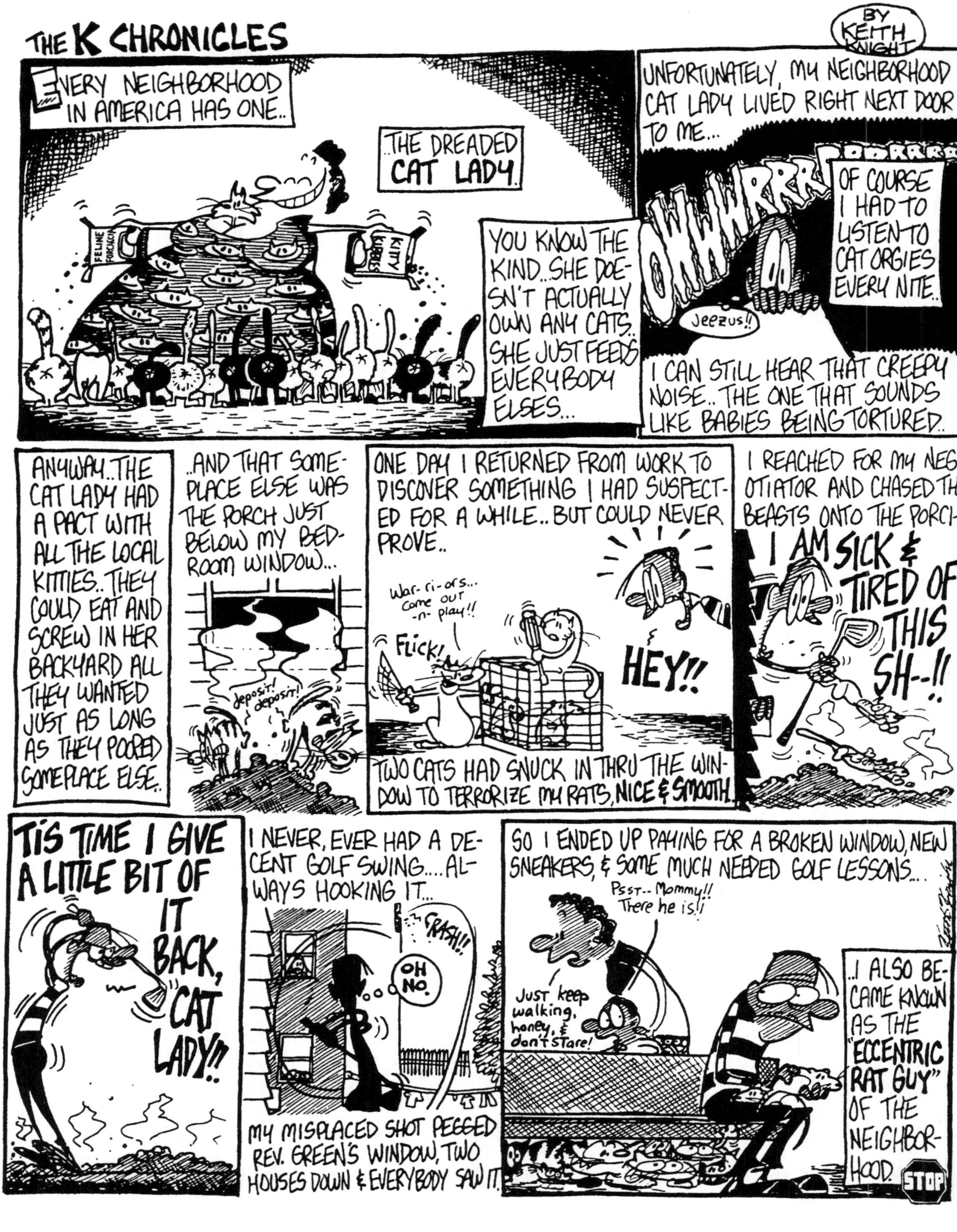
THE K CHRONICLES
BY KEITH KNIGHT
EVERY NEIGHBORHOOD IN AMERICA HAS ONE..
..THE DREADED CAT LADY.
FELINE FORCACCIA
KITTY KIBBLES
YOU KNOW THE KIND..SHE DOESN'T ACTUALLY OWN ANY CATS.. SHE JUST FEEDS EVERYBODY ELSES...
UNFORTUNATELY, MY NEIGHBORHOOD CAT LADY LIVED RIGHT NEXT DOOR TO ME...
OWWWRRRRRRRRRRR
OF COURSE I HAD TO LISTEN TO CAT ORGIES EVERY NITE..
Jeezus!!
I CAN STILL HEAR THAT CREEPY NOISE.. THE ONE THAT SOUNDS LIKE BABIES BEING TORTURED..
ANYWAY..THE CAT LADY HAD A PACT WITH ALL THE LOCAL KITTIES..THEY COULD EAT AND SCREW IN HER BACKYARD ALL THEY WANTED JUST AS LONG AS THEY POOPED SOMEPLACE ELSE..
..AND THAT SOMEPLACE ELSE WAS THE PORCH JUST BELOW MY BEDROOM WINDOW...
deposit! deposit!
ONE DAY I RETURNED FROM WORK TO DISCOVER SOMETHING I HAD SUSPECTED FOR A WHILE.. BUT COULD NEVER PROVE..
War-ri-ors... Come out -n- play!!
FLICK!
HEY!!
TWO CATS HAD SNUCK IN THRU THE WINDOW TO TERRORIZE MY RATS, NICE & SMOOTH.
I REACHED FOR MY NEGOTIATOR AND CHASED THE BEASTS ONTO THE PORCH..
I AM SICK & TIRED OF THIS SH--!!
TIS TIME I GIVE A LITTLE BIT OF IT BACK, "CAT LADY"!!
I NEVER, EVER HAD A DECENT GOLF SWING....ALWAYS HOOKING IT...
CRASH!!
OH NO.
MY MISPLACED SHOT PEGGED REV. GREEN'S WINDOW, TWO HOUSES DOWN & EVERYBODY SAW IT.
SO I ENDED UP PAYING FOR A BROKEN WINDOW, NEW SNEAKERS, & SOME MUCH NEEDED GOLF LESSONS...
Psst-- Mommy!! There he is!!
Just keep walking, honey, & don't stare!
..I ALSO BECAME KNOWN AS THE "ECCENTRIC RAT GUY" OF THE NEIGHBORHOOD.
STOP

 Fourteen puckered cat sphincters: BRILLIANT.

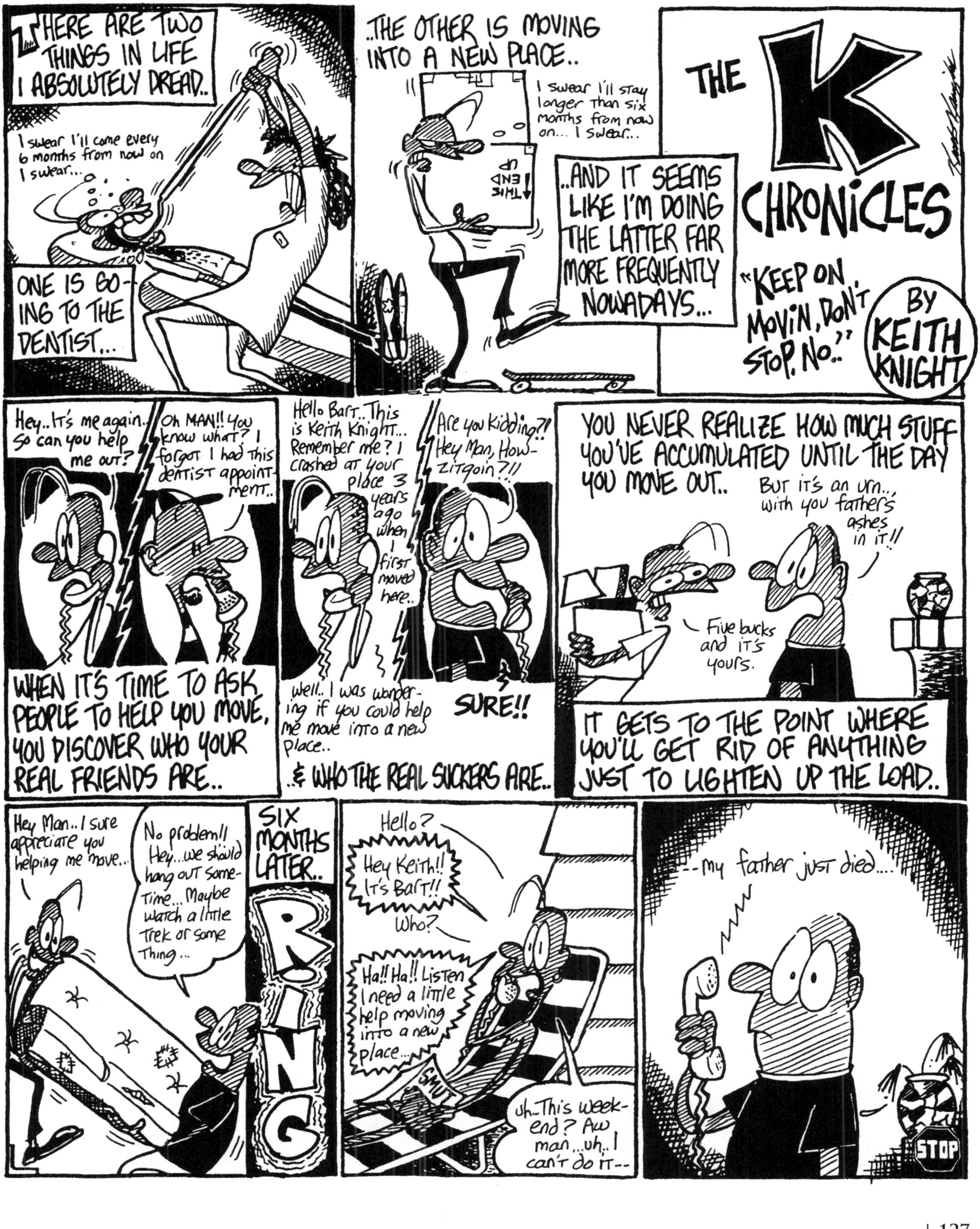
THERE ARE TWO THINGS IN LIFE I ABSOLUTELY DREAD..
I swear I'll come every 6 months from now on I swear...
ONE IS GOING TO THE DENTIST...
..THE OTHER IS MOVING INTO A NEW PLACE..
I swear I'll stay longer than six months from now on... I swear...
THIS END UP
..AND IT SEEMS LIKE I'M DOING THE LATTER FAR MORE FREQUENTLY NOWADAYS...
THE K CHRONICLES
"KEEP ON MOVIN, DON'T STOP, NO.."
BY KEITH KNIGHT
Hey..It's me again.. So can you help me out?
Oh MAN!! You know what? I forgot I had this dentist appointment..
WHEN IT'S TIME TO ASK PEOPLE TO HELP YOU MOVE, YOU DISCOVER WHO YOUR REAL FRIENDS ARE..
Hello Bart..This is Keith Knight... Remember me? I crashed at your place 3 years ago when I first moved here..
Are you kidding?!! Hey Man, How-zitgoin?!!
Well.. I was wondering if you could help me move into a new place..
SURE!!
..& WHO THE REAL SUCKERS ARE..
YOU NEVER REALIZE HOW MUCH STUFF YOU'VE ACCUMULATED UNTIL THE DAY YOU MOVE OUT..
But it's an urn.., with you father's ashes in it!!
Five bucks and it's yours.
IT GETS TO THE POINT WHERE YOU'LL GET RID OF ANYTHING JUST TO LIGHTEN UP THE LOAD..
Hey Man..I sure appreciate you helping me move...
No problem!! Hey...we should hang out sometime... Maybe watch a little Trek or some thing...
SIX MONTHS LATER..
RING
Hello?
Hey Keith!! It's Bart!!
Who?
Ha!! Ha!! Listen I need a little help moving into a new place...
SMUT
uh..This weekend? Aw man...uh..I can't do it--
--my father just died....
STOP

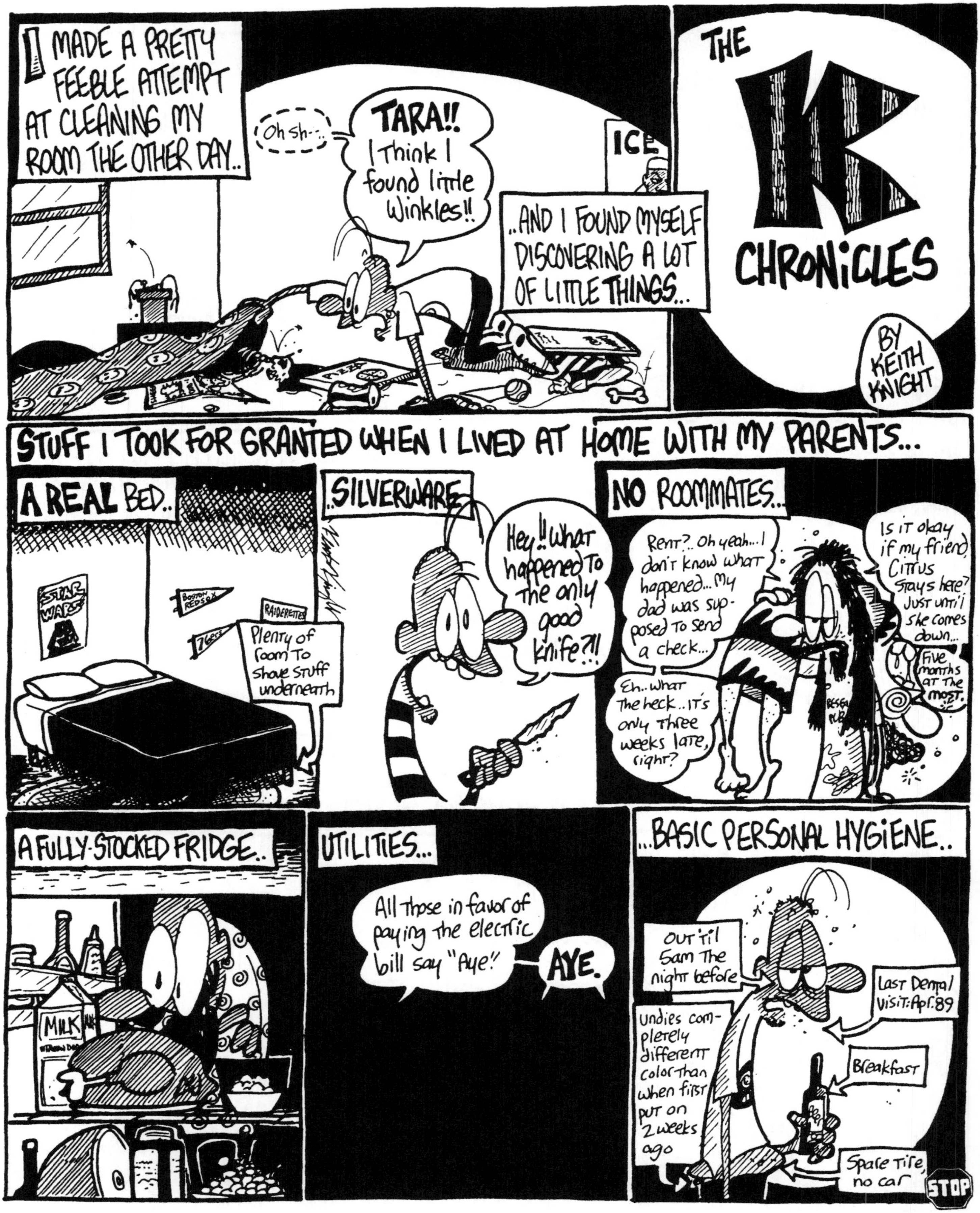
THE K CHRONICLES
BY KEITH KNIGHT
I MADE A PRETTY FEEBLE ATTEMPT AT CLEANING MY ROOM THE OTHER DAY..
Oh sh--
TARA!! I Think I found little Winkles!!
ICE
..AND I FOUND MYSELF DISCOVERING A LOT OF LITTLE THINGS...
STUFF I TOOK FOR GRANTED WHEN I LIVED AT HOME WITH MY PARENTS...
A REAL BED..
STAR WARS
BOSTON RED SOX
RAIDERETTES
76ers
Plenty of room To shove stuff underneath
..SILVERWARE
Hey!! What happened to the only good knife?!!
NO ROOMMATES...
Rent? Oh yeah...I don't know what happened... My dad was supposed to send a check...
Eh.. What The heck.. It's only Three weeks late, right?
Is it okay if my friend Citrus stays here? Just until she comes down...
Five months at The most.
A FULLY-STOCKED FRIDGE..
MILK
UTILITIES...
All those in favor of paying the electric bill say "Aye."
AYE.
...BASIC PERSONAL HYGIENE..
Out til 5am The night before
Last Dental Visit: Apr. 89
undies completely different color than when first put on 2 weeks ago
Breakfast
Spare tire, no car
STOP

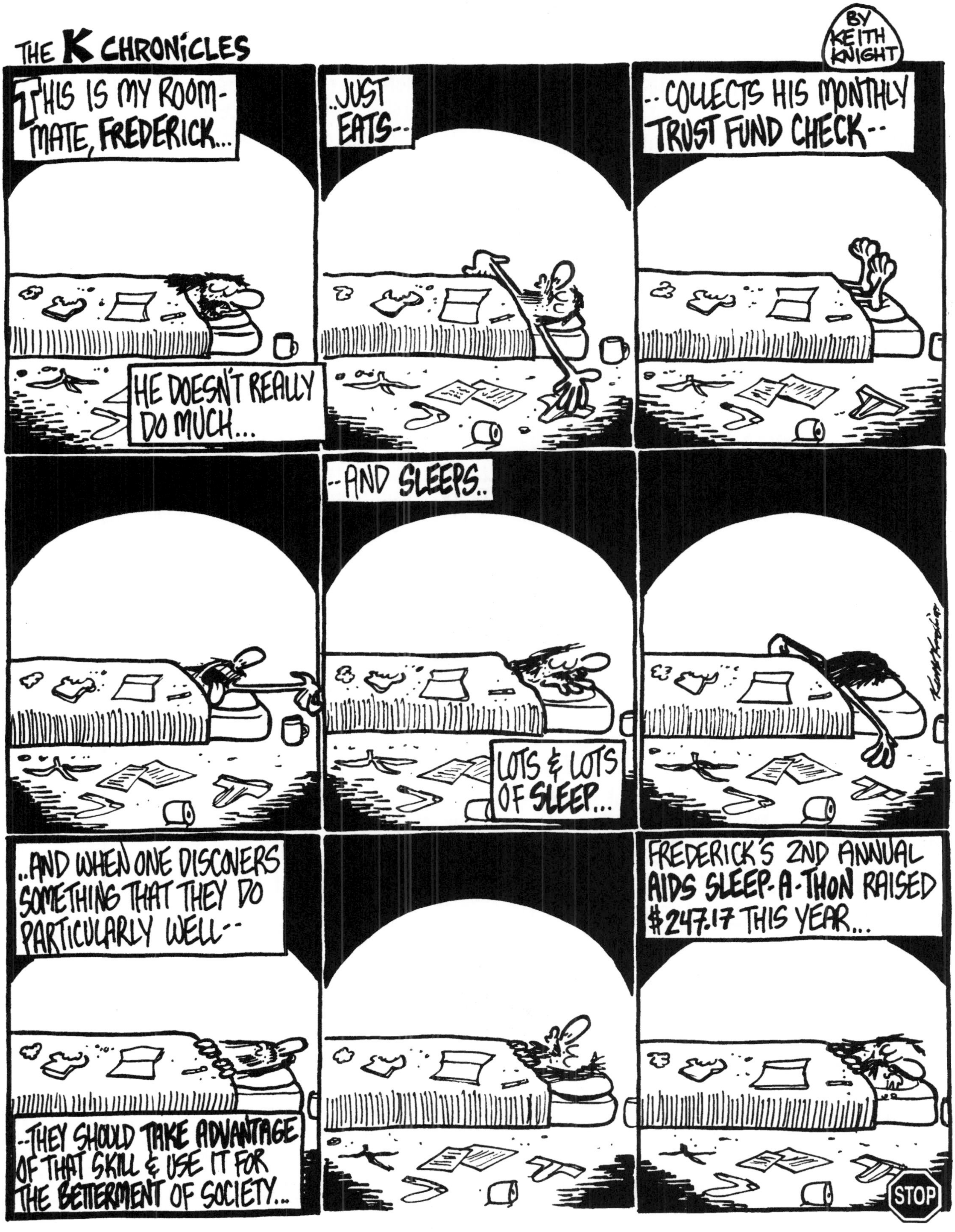
THE K CHRONICLES
BY KEITH KNIGHT
THIS IS MY ROOM-MATE, FREDERICK...
HE DOESN'T REALLY DO MUCH...
..JUST EATS--..
--COLLECTS HIS MONTHLY TRUST FUND CHECK--
--AND SLEEPS..
LOTS & LOTS OF SLEEP...
..AND WHEN ONE DISCOVERS SOMETHING THAT THEY DO PARTICULARLY WELL--
--THEY SHOULD TAKE ADVANTAGE OF THAT SKILL & USE IT FOR THE BETTERMENT OF SOCIETY...
FREDERICK'S 2ND ANNUAL AIDS SLEEP-A-THON RAISED $247.17 THIS YEAR...
STOP

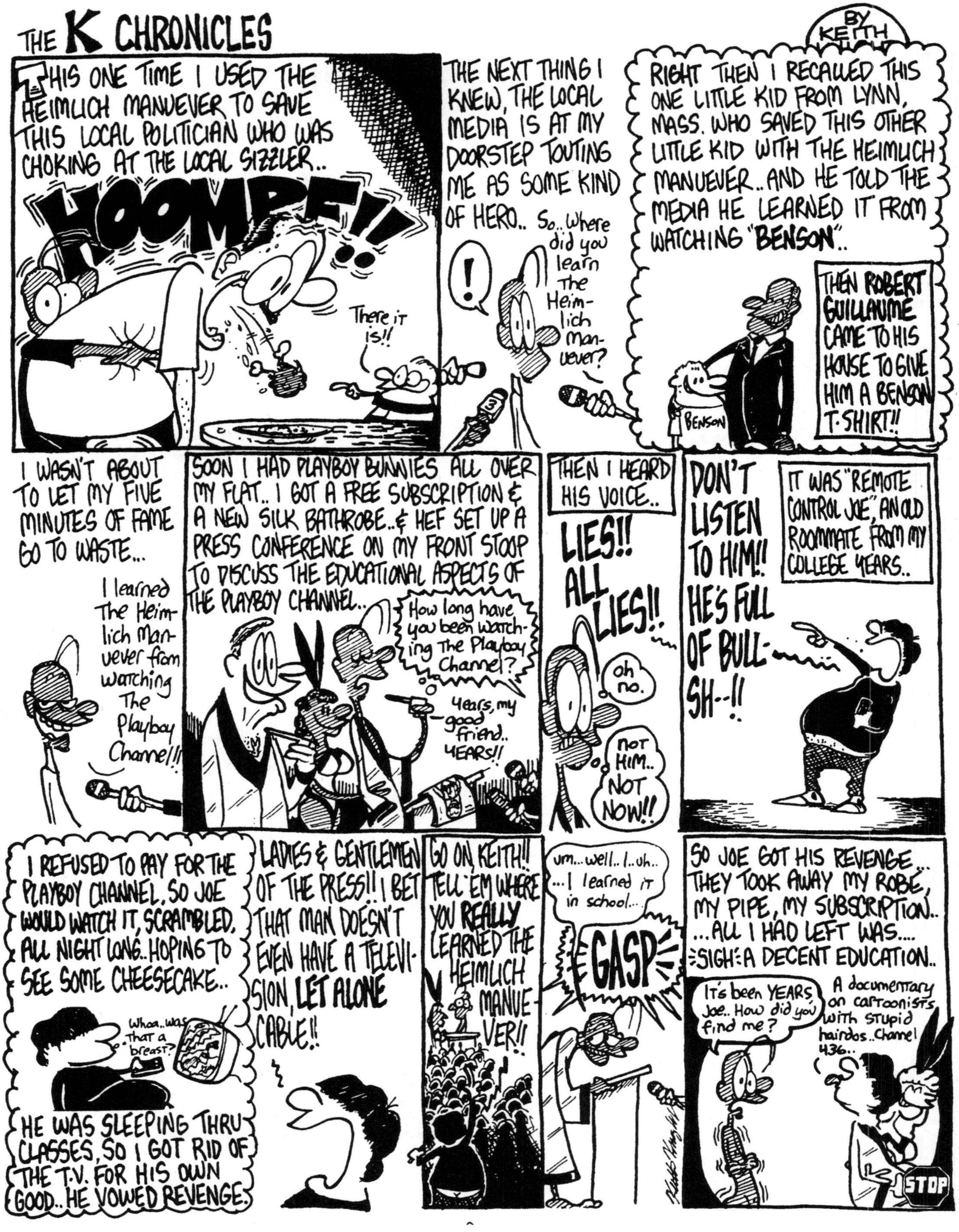
THE K CHRONICLES
BY KEITH
THIS ONE TIME I USED THE HEIMLICH MANUEVER TO SAVE THIS LOCAL POLITICIAN WHO WAS CHOKING AT THE LOCAL SIZZLER..
HOOMPF!!
There it is!!
THE NEXT THING I KNEW, THE LOCAL MEDIA IS AT MY DOORSTEP TOUTING ME AS SOME KIND OF HERO..
So.. Where did you learn The Heim-lich Man-uever?
!
RIGHT THEN I RECALLED THIS ONE LITTLE KID FROM LYNN, MASS. WHO SAVED THIS OTHER LITTLE KID WITH THE HEIMLICH MANUEVER.. AND HE TOLD THE MEDIA HE LEARNED IT FROM WATCHING "BENSON"..
THEN ROBERT GUILLAUME CAME TO HIS HOUSE TO GIVE HIM A BENSON T-SHIRT!!
BENSON
I WASN'T ABOUT TO LET MY FIVE MINUTES OF FAME GO TO WASTE...
I learned The Heim-lich Man-uever from watching The Playboy Channel!!
SOON I HAD PLAYBOY BUNNIES ALL OVER MY FLAT.. I GOT A FREE SUBSCRIPTION & A NEW SILK BATHROBE..& HEF SET UP A PRESS CONFERENCE ON MY FRONT STOOP TO DISCUSS THE EDUCATIONAL ASPECTS OF THE PLAYBOY CHANNEL..
How long have you been watch-ing The Playboy Channel?
Years, my good friend.. YEARS!!
THEN I HEARD HIS VOICE..
LIES!! ALL LIES!!
oh no.
NOT HIM.. NOT NOW!!
DON'T LISTEN TO HIM!! HE'S FULL OF BULL-SH--!!
IT WAS "REMOTE CONTROL JOE", AN OLD ROOMMATE FROM MY COLLEGE YEARS..
I REFUSED TO PAY FOR THE PLAYBOY CHANNEL, SO JOE WOULD WATCH IT, SCRAMBLED, ALL NIGHT LONG.. HOPING TO SEE SOME CHEESECAKE..
Whoa.. Was that a breast?
HE WAS SLEEPING THRU CLASSES, SO I GOT RID OF THE T.V. FOR HIS OWN GOOD.. HE VOWED REVENGE.
LADIES & GENTLEMEN OF THE PRESS!! I BET THAT MAN DOESN'T EVEN HAVE A TELEVI-SION, LET ALONE CABLE!!
GO ON, KEITH!! TELL 'EM WHERE YOU REALLY LEARNED THE HEIMLICH MANUE-VER!!
um... well.. I.. uh.. ...I learned it in school...
GASP
SO JOE GOT HIS REVENGE... THEY TOOK AWAY MY ROBE, MY PIPE, MY SUBSCRIPTION.. ...ALL I HAD LEFT WAS.... =SIGH= A DECENT EDUCATION..
It's been YEARS, Joe.. How did you find me?
A documentary on cartoonists with stupid hairdos.. Channel 436..
STOP

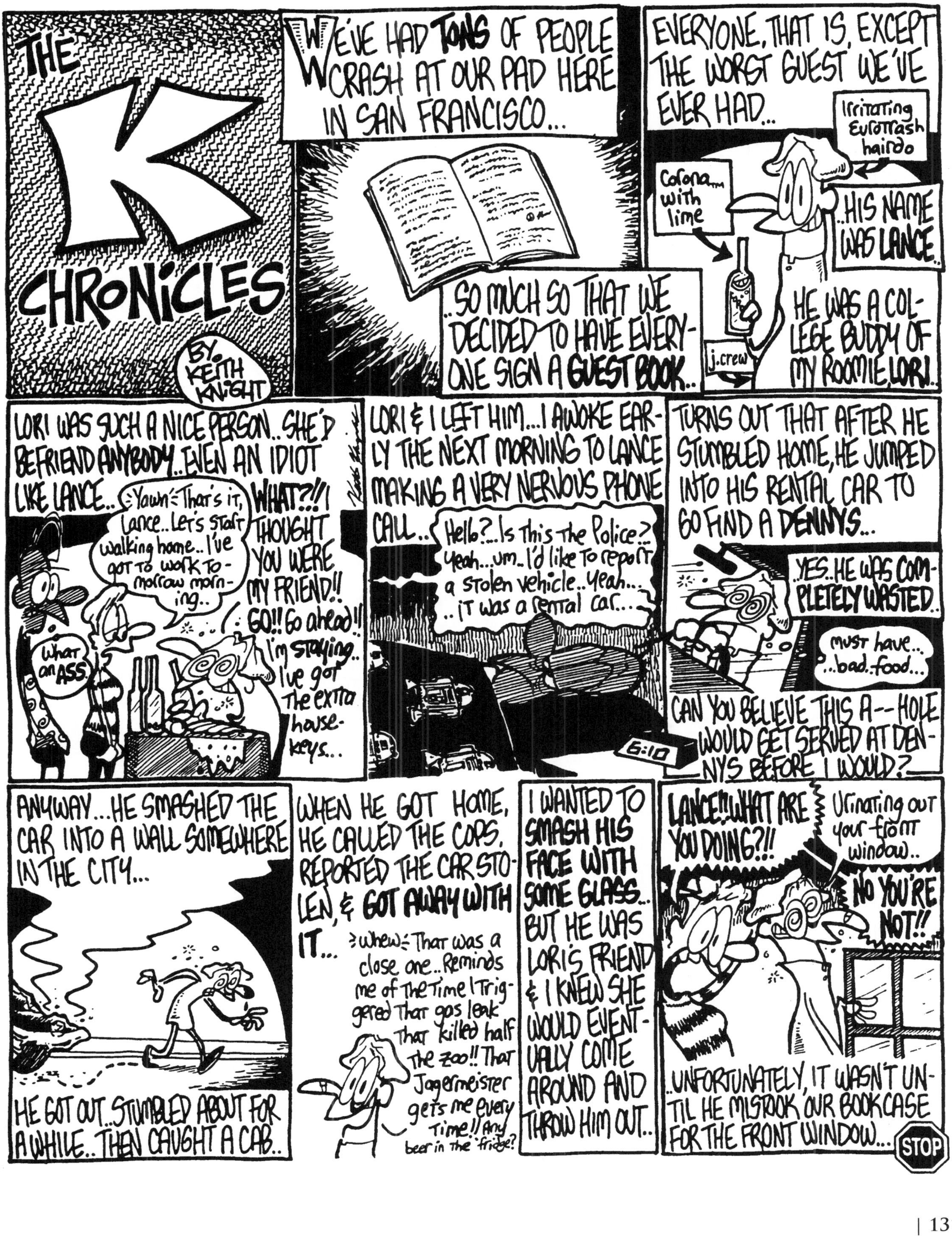
THE K CHRONICLES
BY, KEITH KNIGHT
WE'VE HAD TONS OF PEOPLE CRASH AT OUR PAD HERE IN SAN FRANCISCO...
..SO MUCH SO THAT WE DECIDED TO HAVE EVERY-ONE SIGN A GUEST BOOK..
EVERYONE, THAT IS, EXCEPT THE WORST GUEST WE'VE EVER HAD...
Irritating Eurotrash hairdo
Corona™ with lime
j.crew
..HIS NAME WAS LANCE..
HE WAS A COL-LEGE BUDDY OF MY ROOMIE, LORI..
LORI WAS SUCH A NICE PERSON.. SHE'D BEFRIEND ANYBODY.. EVEN AN IDIOT LIKE LANCE...
=Yawn= That's it, Lance.. Let's start walking home.. I've got to work to-morrow morn-ing..
WHAT?!! I THOUGHT YOU WERE MY FRIEND!! GO!! Go ahead!! I'm staying.. I've got the extra house-keys...
What an ASS.
LORI & I LEFT HIM... I AWOKE EAR-LY THE NEXT MORNING TO LANCE MAKING A VERY NERVOUS PHONE CALL..
Hello?.. Is this the Police? Yeah...um.. I'd like to report a stolen vehicle.. Yeah... ..it was a rental car...
6:10
TURNS OUT THAT AFTER HE STUMBLED HOME, HE JUMPED INTO HIS RENTAL CAR TO GO FIND A DENNYS...
..YES..HE WAS COM-PLETELY WASTED..
must have... ..bad..food...
CAN YOU BELIEVE THIS A--HOLE WOULD GET SERVED AT DEN-NYS BEFORE I WOULD?
ANYWAY...HE SMASHED THE CAR INTO A WALL SOMEWHERE IN THE CITY...
HE GOT OUT..STUMBLED ABOUT FOR A WHILE.. THEN CAUGHT A CAB..
WHEN HE GOT HOME, HE CALLED THE COPS, REPORTED THE CAR STO-LEN, & GOT AWAY WITH IT...
=Whew= That was a close one... Reminds me of The Time I Trig-gered That gas leak That killed half The zoo!! That Jagermeister gets me every Time!! Any beer in The fridge?
I WANTED TO SMASH HIS FACE WITH SOME GLASS... BUT HE WAS LORI'S FRIEND & I KNEW SHE WOULD EVENT-UALLY COME AROUND AND THROW HIM OUT..
LANCE!! WHAT ARE YOU DOING?!!
Urinating out your front window..
NO YOU'RE NOT!!
..UNFORTUNATELY, IT WASN'T UN-TIL HE MISTOOK OUR BOOKCASE FOR THE FRONT WINDOW...
STOP

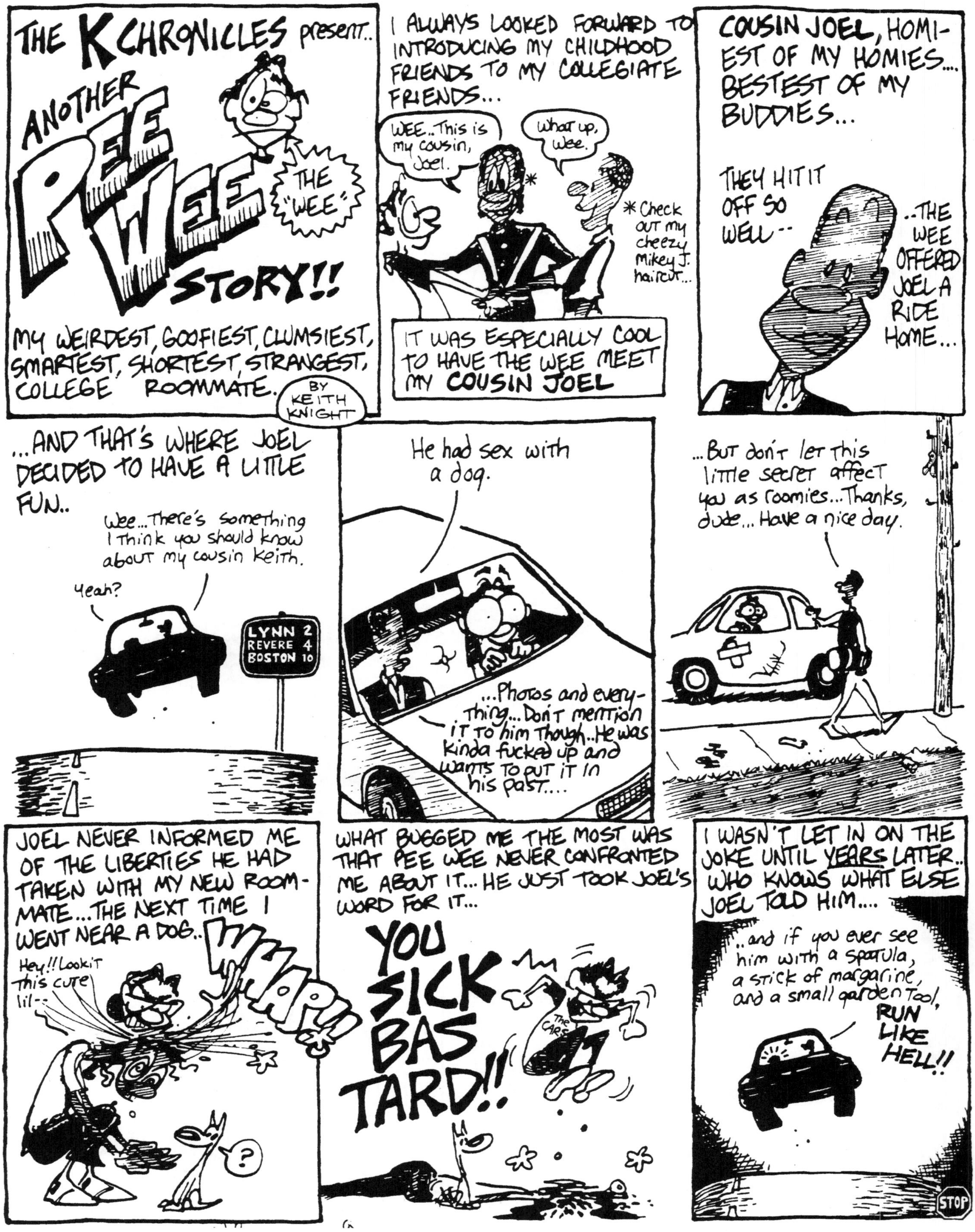
THE K CHRONICLES present..
ANOTHER PEE WEE STORY!!
THE "WEE"
MY WEIRDEST, GOOFIEST, CLUMSIEST, SMARTEST, SHORTEST, STRANGEST, COLLEGE ROOMMATE.
BY KEITH KNIGHT
I ALWAYS LOOKED FORWARD TO INTRODUCING MY CHILDHOOD FRIENDS TO MY COLLEGIATE FRIENDS...
WEE.. This is my cousin, Joel.
What up, Wee.
*Check out my cheezy Mikey J. haircut...
IT WAS ESPECIALLY COOL TO HAVE THE WEE MEET MY COUSIN JOEL
COUSIN JOEL, HOMIEST OF MY HOMIES.... BESTEST OF MY BUDDIES...
THEY HIT IT OFF SO WELL..
..THE WEE OFFERED JOEL A RIDE HOME...
...AND THAT'S WHERE JOEL DECIDED TO HAVE A LITTLE FUN..
Wee... There's something I think you should know about my cousin Keith.
Yeah?
LYNN 2
REVERE 4
BOSTON 10
He had sex with a dog.
...Photos and everything... Don't mention it to him though.. He was kinda fucked up and wants to put it in his past....
...But don't let this little secret affect you as roomies... Thanks, dude... Have a nice day.
JOEL NEVER INFORMED ME OF THE LIBERTIES HE HAD TAKEN WITH MY NEW ROOMMATE... THE NEXT TIME I WENT NEAR A DOG..
Hey!! Lookit this cute lil--
WHAP!!
?
WHAT BUGGED ME THE MOST WAS THAT PEE WEE NEVER CONFRONTED ME ABOUT IT... HE JUST TOOK JOEL'S WORD FOR IT...
YOU SICK BASTARD!!
The CARS
I WASN'T LET IN ON THE JOKE UNTIL YEARS LATER.. WHO KNOWS WHAT ELSE JOEL TOLD HIM....
..and if you ever see him with a spatula, a stick of margarine, and a small garden Tool, RUN LIKE HELL!!
STOP

 I like the drawing of the splattered head with just a stringy eyeball in the eighth panel.

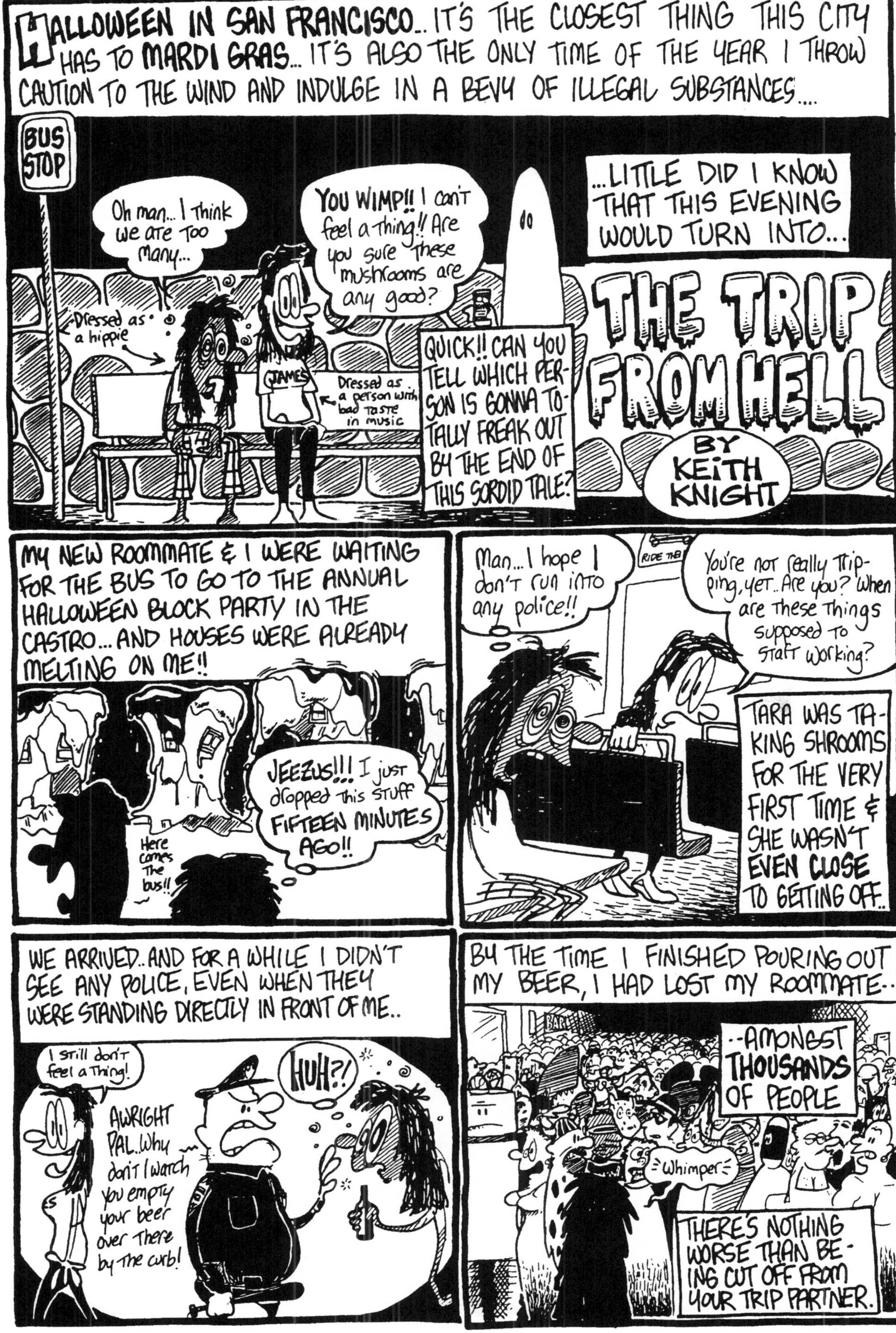
HALLOWEEN IN SAN FRANCISCO.. IT'S THE CLOSEST THING THIS CITY HAS TO MARDI GRAS... IT'S ALSO THE ONLY TIME OF THE YEAR I THROW CAUTION TO THE WIND AND INDULGE IN A BEVY OF ILLEGAL SUBSTANCES....
BUS STOP
Oh man... I think we ate Too many...
YOU WIMP!! I can't feel a thing!! Are you sure these mushrooms are any good?
Dressed as a hippie
JAMES
Dressed as a person with bad Taste in music
QUICK!! CAN YOU TELL WHICH PERSON IS GONNA TOTALLY FREAK OUT BY THE END OF THIS SORDID TALE?
...LITTLE DID I KNOW THAT THIS EVENING WOULD TURN INTO...
THE TRIP FROM HELL
BY KEITH KNIGHT
MY NEW ROOMMATE & I WERE WAITING FOR THE BUS TO GO TO THE ANNUAL HALLOWEEN BLOCK PARTY IN THE CASTRO... AND HOUSES WERE ALREADY MELTING ON ME!!
JEEZUS!!! I just dropped This stuff FIFTEEN MINUTES AGO!!
Here comes The bus!!
Man... I hope I don't run into any police!!
RIDE THE
You're not really Tripping, yet.. Are you? When are these things supposed to start working?
TARA WAS TAKING SHROOMS FOR THE VERY FIRST TIME & SHE WASN'T EVEN CLOSE TO GETTING OFF..
WE ARRIVED.. AND FOR A WHILE I DIDN'T SEE ANY POLICE, EVEN WHEN THEY WERE STANDING DIRECTLY IN FRONT OF ME..
I still don't feel a Thing!
AWRIGHT PAL.. Why don't I watch you empty your beer over There by The curb!
HUH?!
BY THE TIME I FINISHED POURING OUT MY BEER, I HAD LOST MY ROOMMATE..
BAR
..AMONGST THOUSANDS OF PEOPLE
Whimper
THERE'S NOTHING WORSE THAN BEING CUT OFF FROM YOUR TRIP PARTNER.

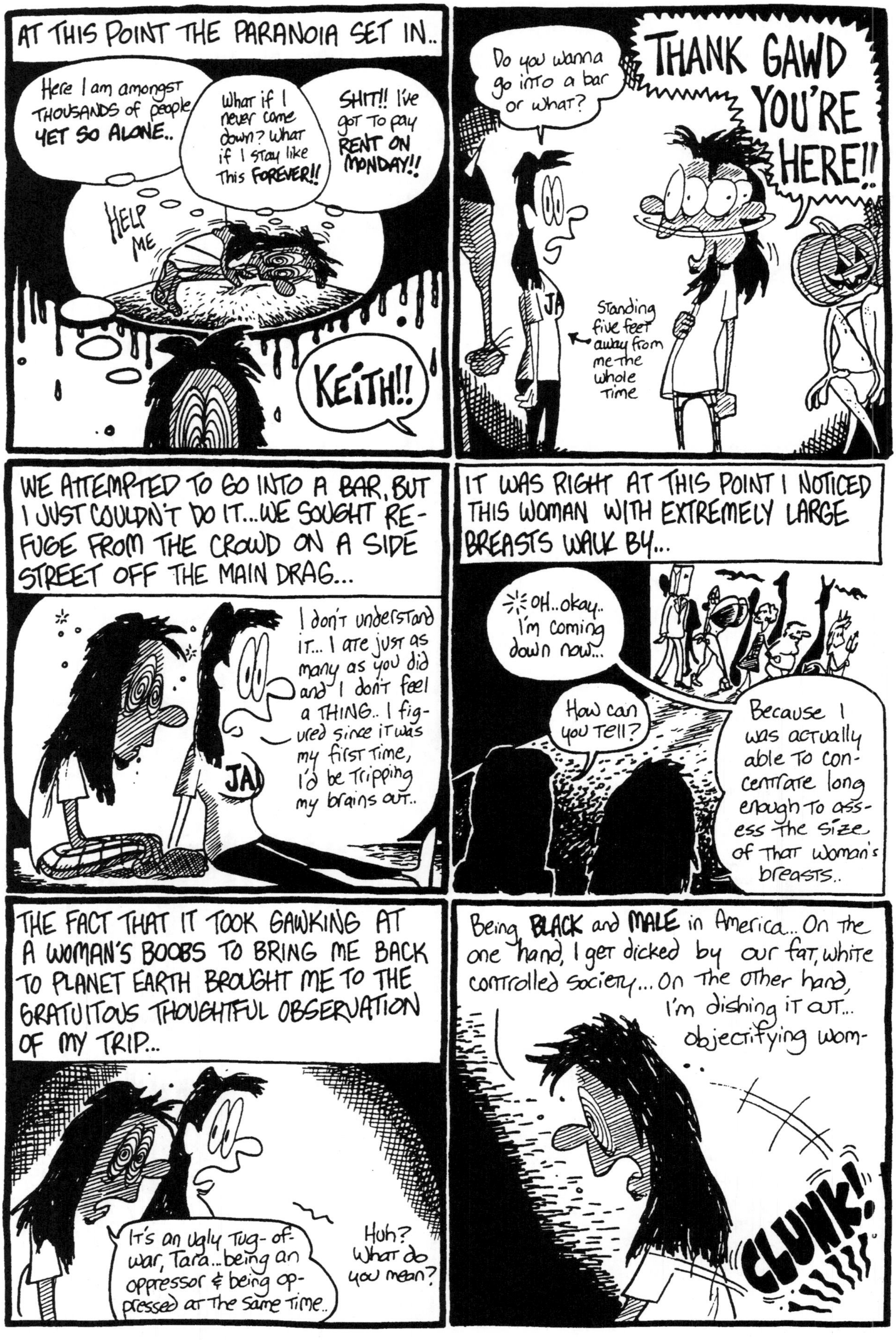
AT THIS POINT THE PARANOIA SET IN..
Here I am amongst THOUSANDS of people YET SO ALONE..
What if I never come down? What if I stay like This FOREVER!!
SHIT!! I've got to pay RENT ON MONDAY!!
HELP ME
KEITH!!
Do you wanna go into a bar or what?
THANK GAWD YOU'RE HERE!!
Standing five feet away from me the whole time
JA
WE ATTEMPTED TO GO INTO A BAR, BUT I JUST COULDN'T DO IT...WE SOUGHT REFUGE FROM THE CROWD ON A SIDE STREET OFF THE MAIN DRAG...
I don't understand it... I ate just as many as you did and I don't feel a THING.. I figured since it was my first Time, I'd be Tripping my brains out..
JA
IT WAS RIGHT AT THIS POINT I NOTICED THIS WOMAN WITH EXTREMELY LARGE BREASTS WALK BY...
OH..okay.. I'm coming down now...
How can you Tell?
Because I was actually able to concentrate long enough to assess the size of that woman's breasts..
THE FACT THAT IT TOOK GAWKING AT A WOMAN'S BOOBS TO BRING ME BACK TO PLANET EARTH BROUGHT ME TO THE GRATUITOUS THOUGHTFUL OBSERVATION OF MY TRIP...
It's an ugly Tug-of-war, Tara...being an oppressor & being oppressed at the same Time..
Huh? What do you mean?
Being BLACK and MALE in America... On the one hand, I get dicked by our fat, white controlled society... On the other hand, I'm dishing it out... objectifying wom-
CLUNK!

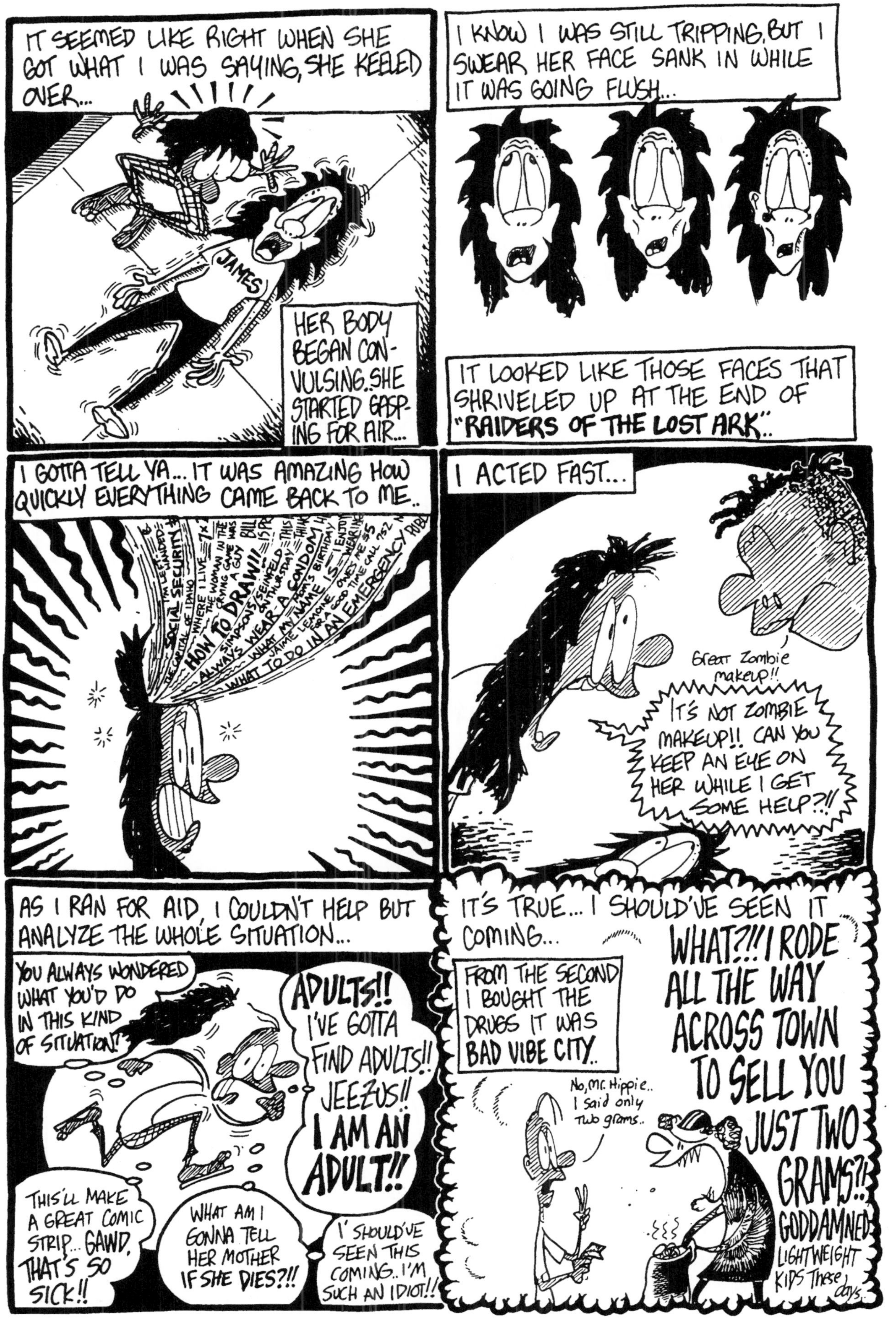
IT SEEMED LIKE RIGHT WHEN SHE GOT WHAT I WAS SAYING, SHE KEELED OVER...
JAMES
HER BODY BEGAN CON-VULSING. SHE STARTED GASP-ING FOR AIR...
I KNOW I WAS STILL TRIPPING, BUT I SWEAR HER FACE SANK IN WHILE IT WAS GOING FLUSH...
IT LOOKED LIKE THOSE FACES THAT SHRIVELED UP AT THE END OF "RAIDERS OF THE LOST ARK"..
I GOTTA TELL YA... IT WAS AMAZING HOW QUICKLY EVERYTHING CAME BACK TO ME..
SOCIAL SECURITY #
HOW TO DRAW!!
ALWAYS WEAR A CONDOM
WHAT TO DO IN AN EMERGENCY
I ACTED FAST...
Great Zombie makeup!!
IT'S NOT ZOMBIE MAKEUP!! CAN YOU KEEP AN EYE ON HER WHILE I GET SOME HELP?!!
AS I RAN FOR AID, I COULDN'T HELP BUT ANALYZE THE WHOLE SITUATION...
YOU ALWAYS WONDERED WHAT YOU'D DO IN THIS KIND OF SITUATION!
ADULTS!! I'VE GOTTA FIND ADULTS!! JEEZUS!! I AM AN ADULT!!
THIS'LL MAKE A GREAT COMIC STRIP... GAWD, THAT'S SO SICK!!
WHAT AM I GONNA TELL HER MOTHER IF SHE DIES?!!
I SHOULD'VE SEEN THIS COMING.. I'M SUCH AN IDIOT!!
IT'S TRUE... I SHOULD'VE SEEN IT COMING...
FROM THE SECOND I BOUGHT THE DRUGS IT WAS BAD VIBE CITY..
No, Mr. Hippie.. I said only two grams..
WHAT?!! I RODE ALL THE WAY ACROSS TOWN TO SELL YOU JUST TWO GRAMS?!.. GODDAMNED LIGHTWEIGHT KIDS these days.

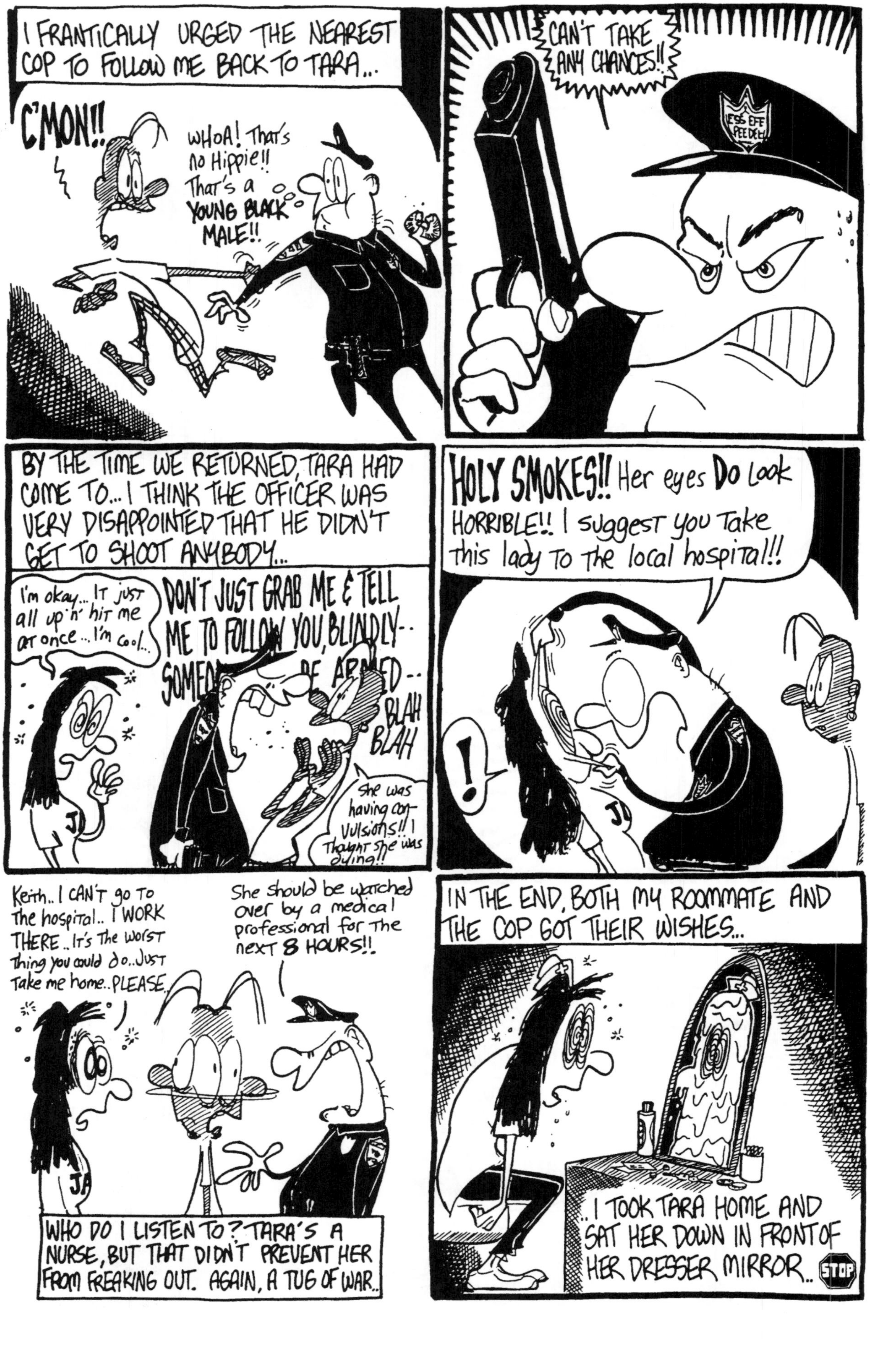

I FRANTICALLY URGED THE NEAREST COP TO FOLLOW ME BACK TO TARA...
C'MON!!
WHOA! That's no Hippie!! That's a YOUNG BLACK MALE!!
CAN'T TAKE ANY CHANCES!!
ESS EFF PEE DEE
BY THE TIME WE RETURNED, TARA HAD COME TO... I THINK THE OFFICER WAS VERY DISAPPOINTED THAT HE DIDN'T GET TO SHOOT ANYBODY...
I'm okay... It just all up 'n' hit me at once... I'm cool...
DON'T JUST GRAB ME & TELL ME TO FOLLOW YOU, BLINDLY..
BLAH BLAH
She was having convulsions!! I Thought she was dying!!
HOLY SMOKES!! Her eyes DO look HORRIBLE!! I suggest you Take this lady To the local hospital!!
!
Keith.. I CAN'T go to the hospital.. I WORK THERE.. It's The worst thing you could do.. Just Take me home.. PLEASE..
She should be watched over by a medical professional for the next 8 HOURS!!
WHO DO I LISTEN TO? TARA'S A NURSE, BUT THAT DIDN'T PREVENT HER FROM FREAKING OUT. AGAIN, A TUG OF WAR..
IN THE END, BOTH MY ROOMMATE AND THE COP GOT THEIR WISHES...
..I TOOK TARA HOME AND SAT HER DOWN IN FRONT OF HER DRESSER MIRROR..
STOP

CHAPTER TWO

FEAR OF A BLACK MARKER

Cartoons from 1996-1999   San Francisco / Berlin / Prague / Amsterdam

Youth Hostel   the Marginal Prophets

THE K CHRONICLES

A PARENTS' EXPLANATION

BY MAMA, PAPA & KEITH KNIGHT

FIRST QUESTION: ANY SPECIFIC RECOLLECTIONS FROM YOUR SON'S CHILDHOOD THAT MAY HAVE LED HIM DOWN THE DARK & LONELY PATH TOWARDS A CAREER IN COMIX?

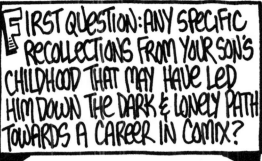

Well...He could never get up in the morning so I knew he could never hold down a 9 to 5 job.. No one would put up with it...

I remember his grade school teachers saying he never paid attention in class...

..he was too busy drawing.

WHICH OF YOUR SON'S STRIPS IS YOUR FAVORITE & WHICH MAKES YOU SAY TO YOURSELF: "HE COULDN'T POSSIBLY BE THE PRODUCT OF MY LOINS?"

Hmmm...Now that's a tough one cuz they're all pretty damn disturbing to me....

My favorite was a strip he did when he was playing little league baseball...He drew the whole team.. His work was so cute back then....

TRANSLATION: "My son's work peaked when he was 12 years old."

WHO DO YOU THINK IS RESPONSIBLE FOR YOUR SON'S SORDID SENSE OF HUMOR?

Her.   Him.

The artist's parents are divorced.

The Oregonian

ESTABLISHED 1850

1320 S.W. BROADWAY PORTLAND, OREGON 97201-3499

RICHARD C. JOHNSTON
ASSISTANT TO THE EDITOR

October 19, 1998

Keith Knight
PO Box 591794
San Francisco, CA 94159-1794

Dear Mr. Knight:

Thank you for sending samples of "The K Chronicles." I found them interesting.

IN A FAMILY NEWSPAPER? ARE YOU NUTS?

We've gone a long way since we first put Matt Groening's "Life in Hell" in The Oregonian, but I do not think we have gone as far as "The K Chronicles." Well, maybe we have, but I think a lot of the readers haven't, so the result is the same: Thanks, but not right now.

It is fun, though, and I would love to have a comic that makes people talk. "The K Chronicles" would certainly do that.

Again, thanks.

Sincerely,

Richard C. Johnston

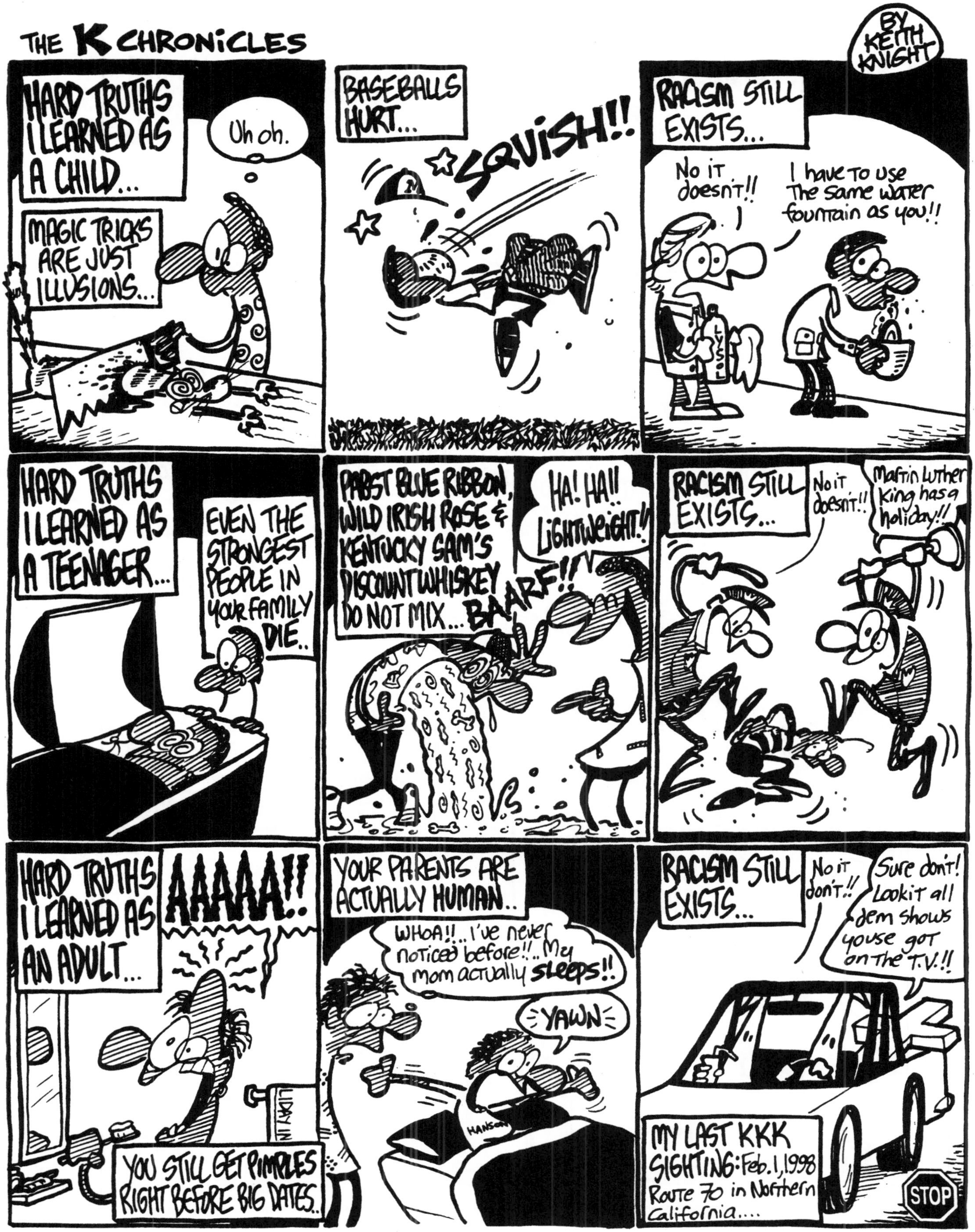
THE K CHRONICLES
BY KEITH KNIGHT
HARD TRUTHS I LEARNED AS A CHILD...
Uh oh.
MAGIC TRICKS ARE JUST ILLUSIONS...
BASEBALLS HURT...
SQUISH!!
RACISM STILL EXISTS...
No it doesn't!!
I have to use the same water fountain as you!!
LYSOL
HARD TRUTHS I LEARNED AS A TEENAGER...
EVEN THE STRONGEST PEOPLE IN YOUR FAMILY DIE..
PABST BLUE RIBBON, WILD IRISH ROSE & KENTUCKY SAM'S DISCOUNT WHISKEY DO NOT MIX...
HA! HA!! LIGHTWEIGHT!!
BAARF!!
RACISM STILL EXISTS...
No it doesn't!!
Martin Luther King has a holiday!!
HARD TRUTHS I LEARNED AS AN ADULT...
AAAAA!!
YOU STILL GET PIMPLES RIGHT BEFORE BIG DATES..
YOUR PARENTS ARE ACTUALLY HUMAN..
WHOA!!.. I've never noticed before!!.. My mom actually sleeps!!
YAWN
HANSON
RACISM STILL EXISTS...
No it don't!!
Sure don't! Lookit all dem shows youse got on the T.V.!!
MY LAST KKK SIGHTING: Feb. 1, 1998 Route 70 in Northern California....
STOP

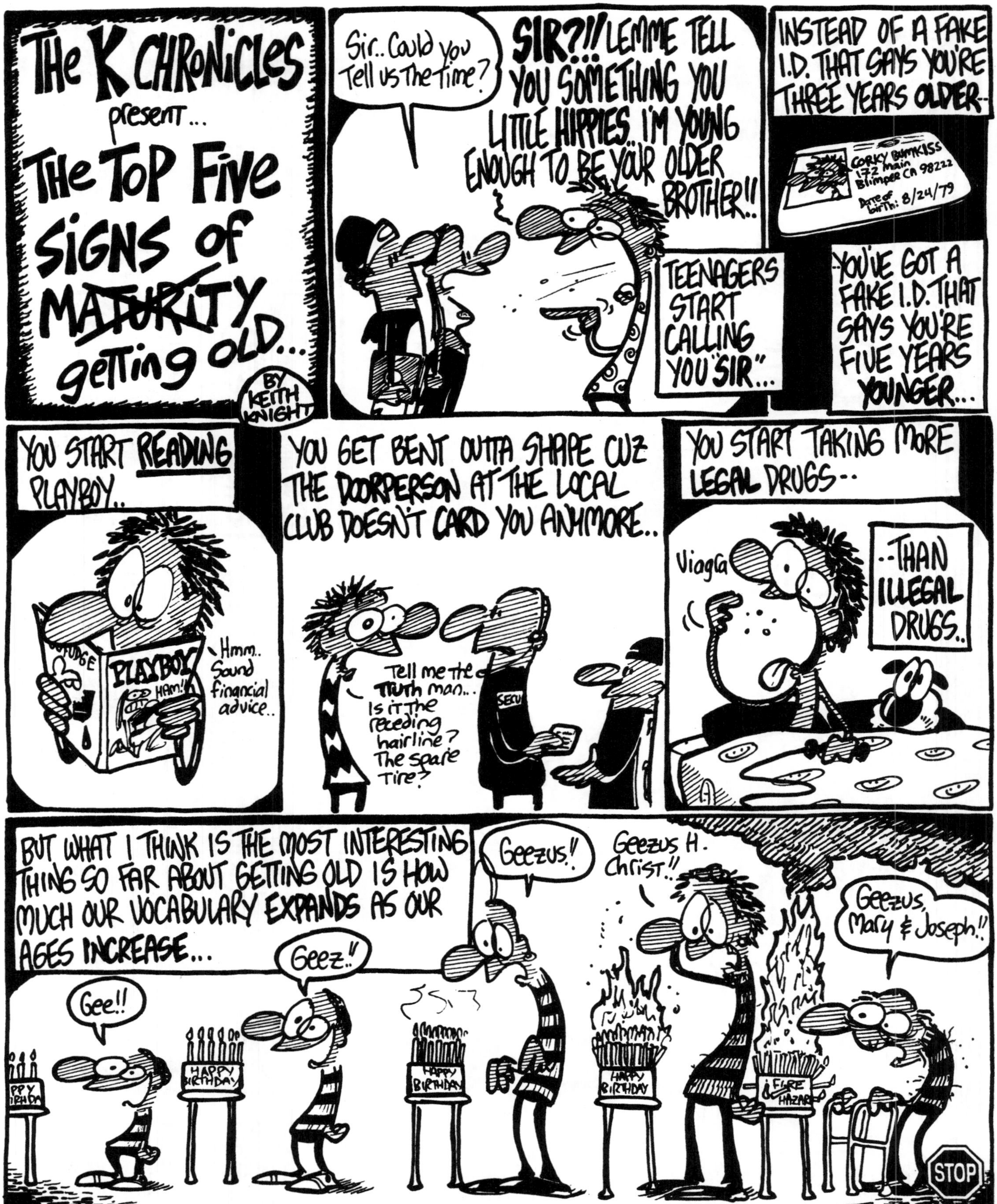

The K Chronicles present... The Top Five Signs of ~~Maturity~~ getting old...
By Keith Knight
Sir.. Could you tell us the time?
SIR?!! Lemme tell you something you little hippies.. I'm young enough to be your older brother!!
Teenagers start calling you "sir"...
Instead of a fake I.D. that says you're three years older--
Corky Buttkiss 172 Main Blimper CA 98222 Date of birth: 8/24/79
--You've got a fake I.D. that says you're five years younger...
You start reading Playboy..
Playboy
Hmm.. Sound financial advice..
You get bent outta shape cuz the doorperson at the local club doesn't card you anymore..
Tell me the truth man... Is it the receding hairline? The spare tire?
Secu
You start taking more legal drugs--
Viagra
--than illegal drugs..
But what I think is the most interesting thing so far about getting old is how much our vocabulary expands as our ages increase...
Gee!!
Geez.!!
Geezus.!!
Geezus H. Christ!!
Geezus, Mary & Joseph!!
Happy Birthday
Fire Hazard
STOP

The K CHRONICLES

whew

ON SUMMER VACATION!!

BY KEITH KNIGHT

FOR MY LATEST VACATION, I FLEW BACK TO BOSTON TO VISIT MY HOMETOWN OF MALDEN MASSACHUSETTS...

San Francisco · Boston

MALDEN IS 15 MINUTES FROM BOSTON..

EVERYONE'S HOMETOWN IS FAMOUS FOR SOMETHING..& MINE IS NO EXCEPTION....

MALDEN IS THE BIRTHPLACE OF THE CONVERSE RUBBER CO.. MAKER OF CONVERSE ALL-STARS..

MALDEN IS ALSO THE BIRTH-PLACE OF JACK ALBERTSON, AN ACTOR WHO PLAYED THE OLD GUY IN THE 70's SITCOM CHICO & THE MAN....

Chico!! Blah, Blah Blah, complain complain...

ANYWAY..IT WAS GREAT TO BE HOME...MOM PREPARED SOME OF MY FAVORITE FOODS FOR MY ARRIVAL...

That's mah boy!!

GULP!! CHOMP!! CONSUME!!

Keep IT comin'!

NOBODY APPRECIATES A MOM'S COOKING MORE THAN HER SON..

IT WAS ALSO A JOY TO BE AROUND FAMILY & FRIENDS AGAIN.. ALTHOUGH THEY ALL HAD CHOICE COMMENTS FOR MY NEW DREADLOCKED HAIR-DO..

YANK!!

Is it a wig?

Yo Rasta-mon.. Do you have any POT?

SIDESHOW BOB!! He looks like SIDESHOW BOB!!

ANOTHER THING THAT I REALLY ENJOYED WAS CHILLIN' ON THE BACK PORCH WITH A TALL GLASS OF LEMONADE & A COPY OF THE LOCAL NEWSPAPER..

BURP

MALDEN OBSERVER

THERE'S SOMETHING REALLY QUAINT ABOUT ONE'S TINY LITTLE HOMETOWN NEWSPAPER.

"Local Cafe recognized for being smoke-free"

"Panthers outlast Badgers"

"MHS class of '74 reunion planned"

THERE IS NO BETTER WAY TO CATCH UP WITH WHAT'S GO-ING ON IN LOCAL POLITICS, SPORTS, SCHOOLS, ETC....

PLUS..IT'S A GREAT WAY TO FIND OUT WHAT YOUR FRIENDS ARE UP TO...

POLICE LOG/ARR

MONDAY, JUNE 14TH
THOMAS J. WELCH, 32 of 666 BOLTON ST. was arrested and charged with indecent exposure.

CLIFFO

DAVID P. PA 69 Bowdin charged pornogr

Heh, Heh, Heh.. I knew they'd finally catch that bastard...

STOP

| 143

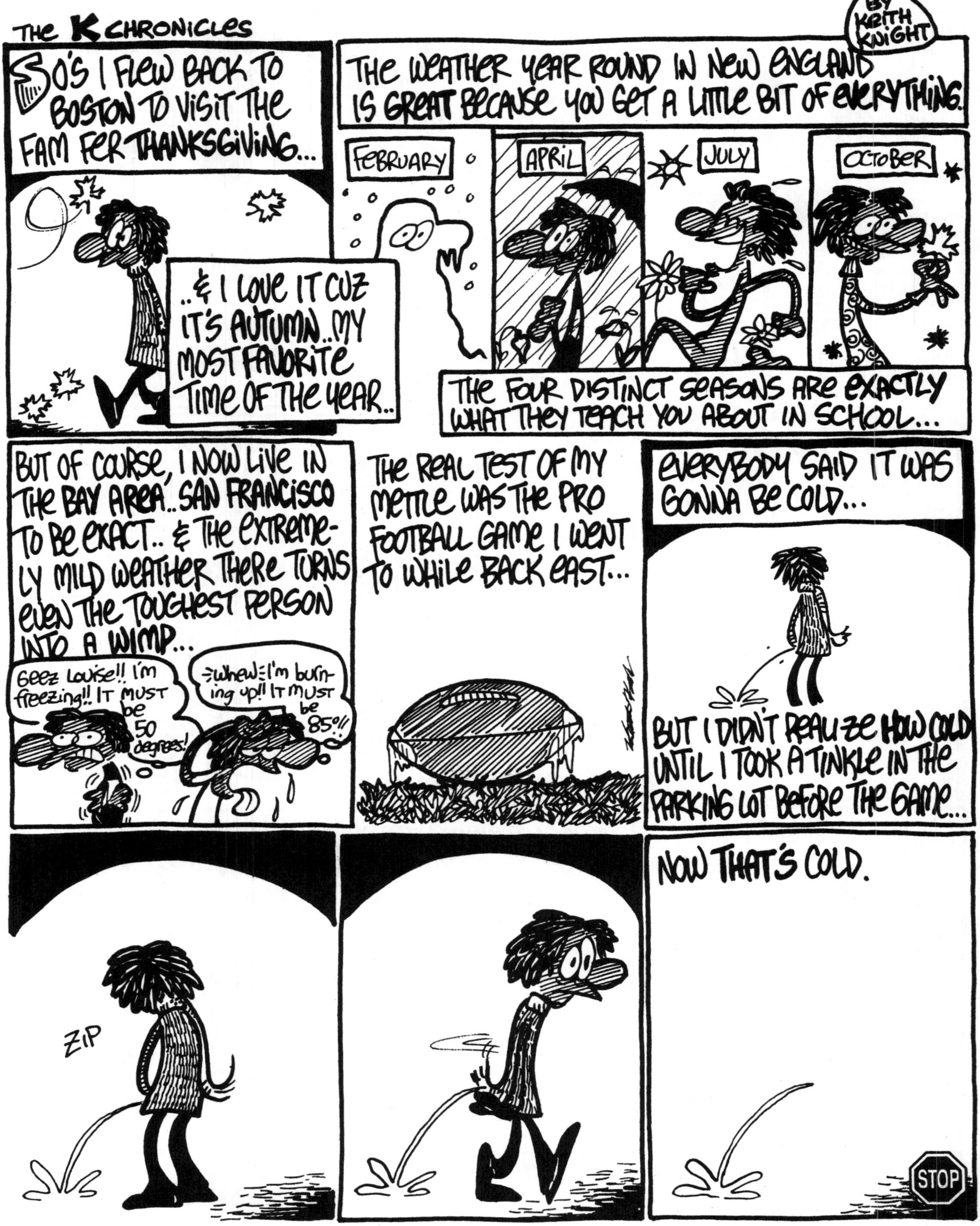
THE K CHRONICLES
BY KEITH KNIGHT
SO'S I FLEW BACK TO BOSTON TO VISIT THE FAM FER THANKSGIVING...
..& I LOVE IT CUZ IT'S AUTUMN..MY MOST FAVORITE TIME OF THE YEAR..
THE WEATHER YEAR ROUND IN NEW ENGLAND IS GREAT BECAUSE YOU GET A LITTLE BIT OF EVERYTHING.
FEBRUARY
APRIL
JULY
OCTOBER
THE FOUR DISTINCT SEASONS ARE EXACTLY WHAT THEY TEACH YOU ABOUT IN SCHOOL...
BUT OF COURSE, I NOW LIVE IN THE BAY AREA..SAN FRANCISCO TO BE EXACT.. & THE EXTREMELY MILD WEATHER THERE TURNS EVEN THE TOUGHEST PERSON INTO A WIMP...
Geez Louise!! I'm freezing!! IT MUST be 50 degrees!
=whew= I'm burning up!! IT MUST be 85°!!
THE REAL TEST OF MY METTLE WAS THE PRO FOOTBALL GAME I WENT TO WHILE BACK EAST...
EVERYBODY SAID IT WAS GONNA BE COLD...
BUT I DIDN'T REALIZE HOW COLD UNTIL I TOOK A TINKLE IN THE PARKING LOT BEFORE THE GAME...
ZIP
NOW THAT'S COLD.
STOP

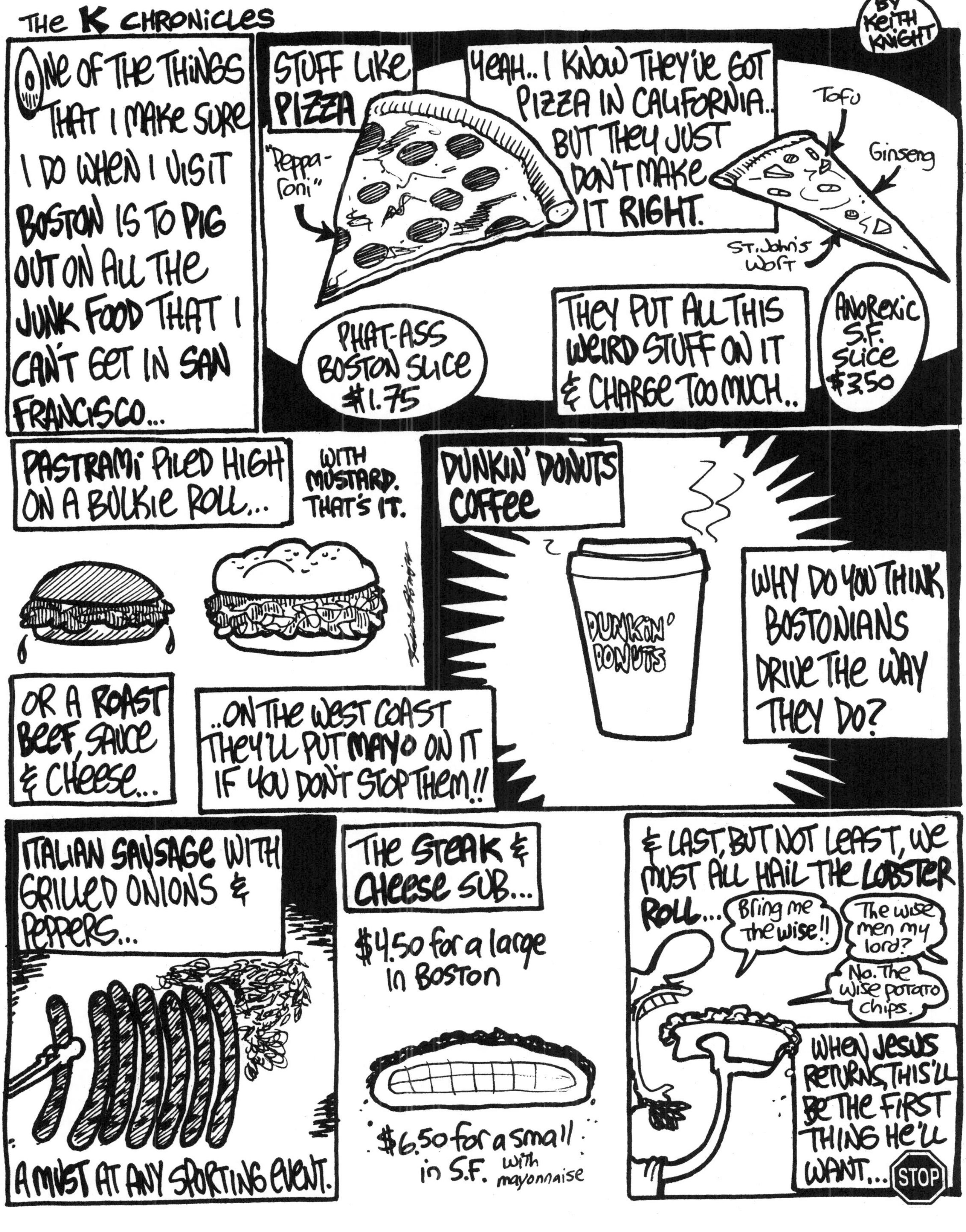

THE K CHRONICLES
BY KEITH KNIGHT
ONE OF THE THINGS THAT I MAKE SURE I DO WHEN I VISIT BOSTON IS TO PIG OUT ON ALL THE JUNK FOOD THAT I CAN'T GET IN SAN FRANCISCO...
STUFF LIKE PIZZA
YEAH.. I KNOW THEY'VE GOT PIZZA IN CALIFORNIA.. BUT THEY JUST DON'T MAKE IT RIGHT.
"Peppa-roni"
Tofu
Ginseng
St. John's Wort
PHAT-ASS BOSTON SLICE $1.75
THEY PUT ALL THIS WEIRD STUFF ON IT & CHARGE TOO MUCH..
ANOREXIC S.F. SLICE $3.50
PASTRAMI PILED HIGH ON A BULKIE ROLL...
WITH MUSTARD. THAT'S IT.
OR A ROAST BEEF, SAUCE & CHEESE...
..ON THE WEST COAST THEY'LL PUT MAYO ON IT IF YOU DON'T STOP THEM!!
DUNKIN' DONUTS COFFEE
DUNKIN' DONUTS
WHY DO YOU THINK BOSTONIANS DRIVE THE WAY THEY DO?
ITALIAN SAUSAGE WITH GRILLED ONIONS & PEPPERS...
A MUST AT ANY SPORTING EVENT.
THE STEAK & CHEESE SUB...
$4.50 for a large in Boston
$6.50 for a small in S.F. with mayonnaise
& LAST, BUT NOT LEAST, WE MUST ALL HAIL THE LOBSTER ROLL...
Bring me the wise!!
The wise men my lord?
No. The wise potato chips.
WHEN JESUS RETURNS, THIS'LL BE THE FIRST THING HE'LL WANT...
STOP

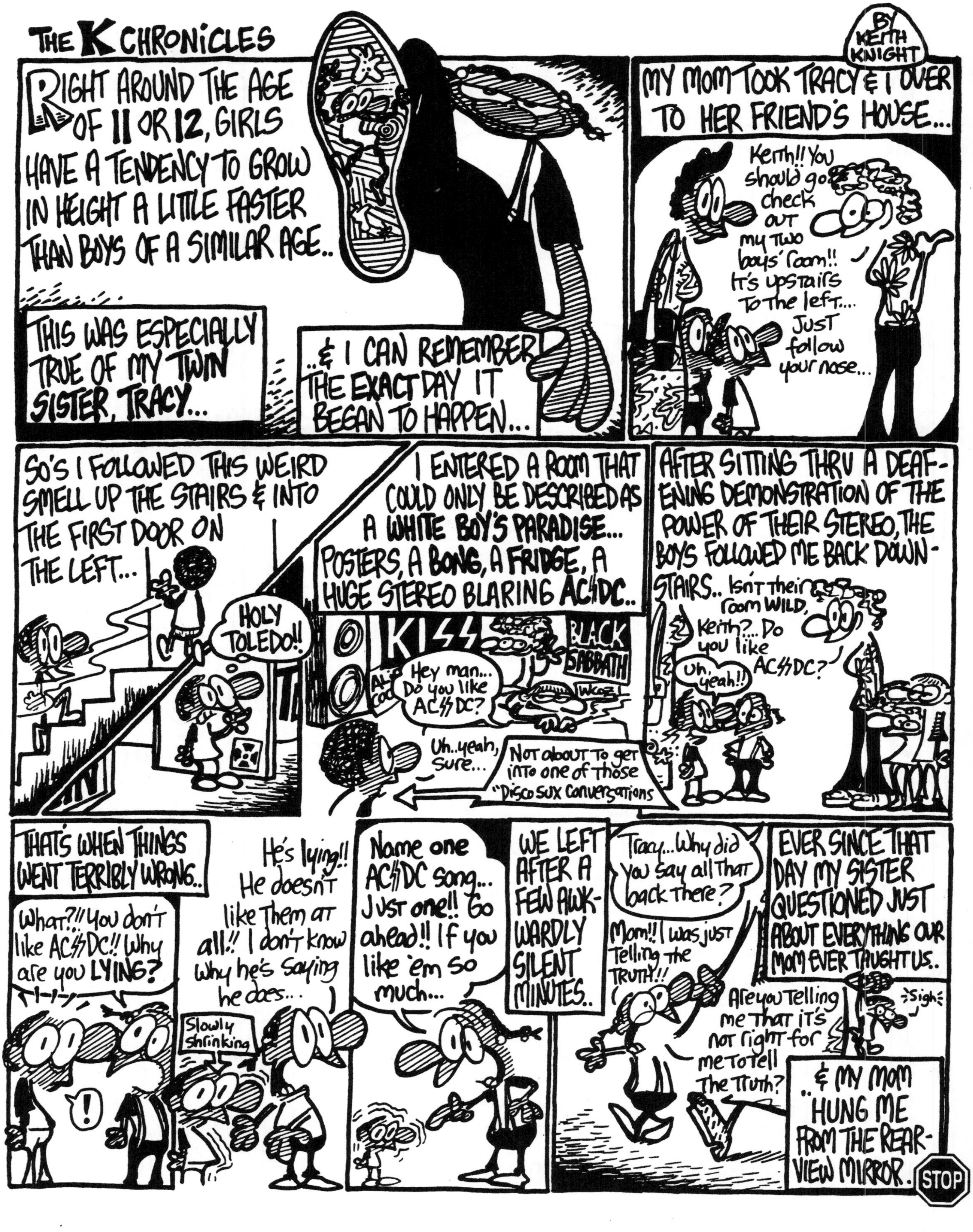
THE K CHRONICLES
BY KEITH KNIGHT
RIGHT AROUND THE AGE OF 11 OR 12, GIRLS HAVE A TENDENCY TO GROW IN HEIGHT A LITTLE FASTER THAN BOYS OF A SIMILAR AGE..
THIS WAS ESPECIALLY TRUE OF MY TWIN SISTER, TRACY...
..& I CAN REMEMBER THE EXACT DAY IT BEGAN TO HAPPEN...
MY MOM TOOK TRACY & I OVER TO HER FRIEND'S HOUSE...
Keith!! You should go check out my two boys' room!! It's upstairs to the left.... Just follow your nose...
SO'S I FOLLOWED THIS WEIRD SMELL UP THE STAIRS & INTO THE FIRST DOOR ON THE LEFT...
HOLY TOLEDO!!
I ENTERED A ROOM THAT COULD ONLY BE DESCRIBED AS A WHITE BOY'S PARADISE... POSTERS, A BONG, A FRIDGE, A HUGE STEREO BLARING AC/DC..
KISS
BLACK SABBATH
Hey man... Do you like AC/DC?
Uh..yeah, sure...
Not about to get into one of those "Disco Sux Conversations
AFTER SITTING THRU A DEAFENING DEMONSTRATION OF THE POWER OF THEIR STEREO, THE BOYS FOLLOWED ME BACK DOWNSTAIRS..
Isn't their room WILD, Keith?.. Do you like AC/DC?
Uh, yeah!!
THAT'S WHEN THINGS WENT TERRIBLY WRONG..
What?!! You don't like AC/DC!! Why are you LYING?
He's lying!! He doesn't like them at all!! I don't know why he's saying he does...
Slowly shrinking
Name one AC/DC song... Just one!! Go ahead!! If you like 'em so much...
WE LEFT AFTER A FEW AWKWARDLY SILENT MINUTES..
Tracy...Why did you say all that back there?
Mom!! I was just telling the truth!!
Are you telling me that it's not right for me to tell the truth?
EVER SINCE THAT DAY MY SISTER QUESTIONED JUST ABOUT EVERYTHING OUR MOM EVER TAUGHT US..
Sigh
..& MY MOM HUNG ME FROM THE REAR-VIEW MIRROR.
STOP

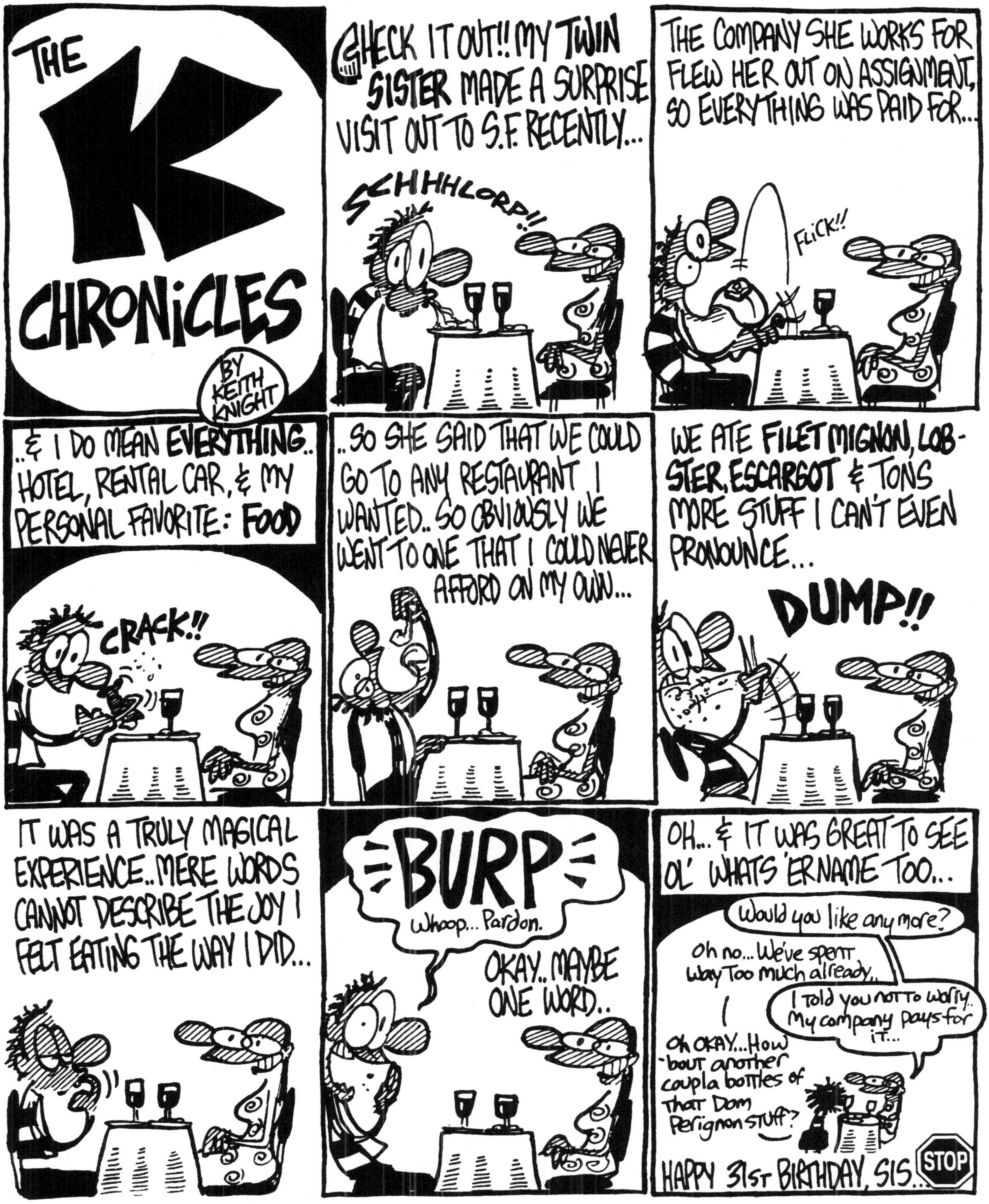
THE K CHRONICLES
BY KEITH KNIGHT
CHECK IT OUT!! MY TWIN SISTER MADE A SURPRISE VISIT OUT TO S.F. RECENTLY...
SCHHHLORP!!
THE COMPANY SHE WORKS FOR FLEW HER OUT ON ASSIGNMENT, SO EVERYTHING WAS PAID FOR...
FLICK!!
..& I DO MEAN EVERYTHING.. HOTEL, RENTAL CAR, & MY PERSONAL FAVORITE: FOOD
CRACK!!
..SO SHE SAID THAT WE COULD GO TO ANY RESTAURANT I WANTED.. SO OBVIOUSLY WE WENT TO ONE THAT I COULD NEVER AFFORD ON MY OWN...
WE ATE FILET MIGNON, LOBSTER, ESCARGOT & TONS MORE STUFF I CAN'T EVEN PRONOUNCE...
DUMP!!
IT WAS A TRULY MAGICAL EXPERIENCE..MERE WORDS CANNOT DESCRIBE THE JOY I FELT EATING THE WAY I DID...
BURP
Whoop... Pardon.
OKAY.. MAYBE ONE WORD..
OH... & IT WAS GREAT TO SEE OL' WHATS 'ER NAME TOO...
Would you like any more?
Oh no... We've spent way too much already..
I told you not to worry.. My company pays for it...
Oh OKAY...How -bout another coupla bottles of that Dom Perignon stuff?
HAPPY 31ST BIRTHDAY, SIS...
STOP

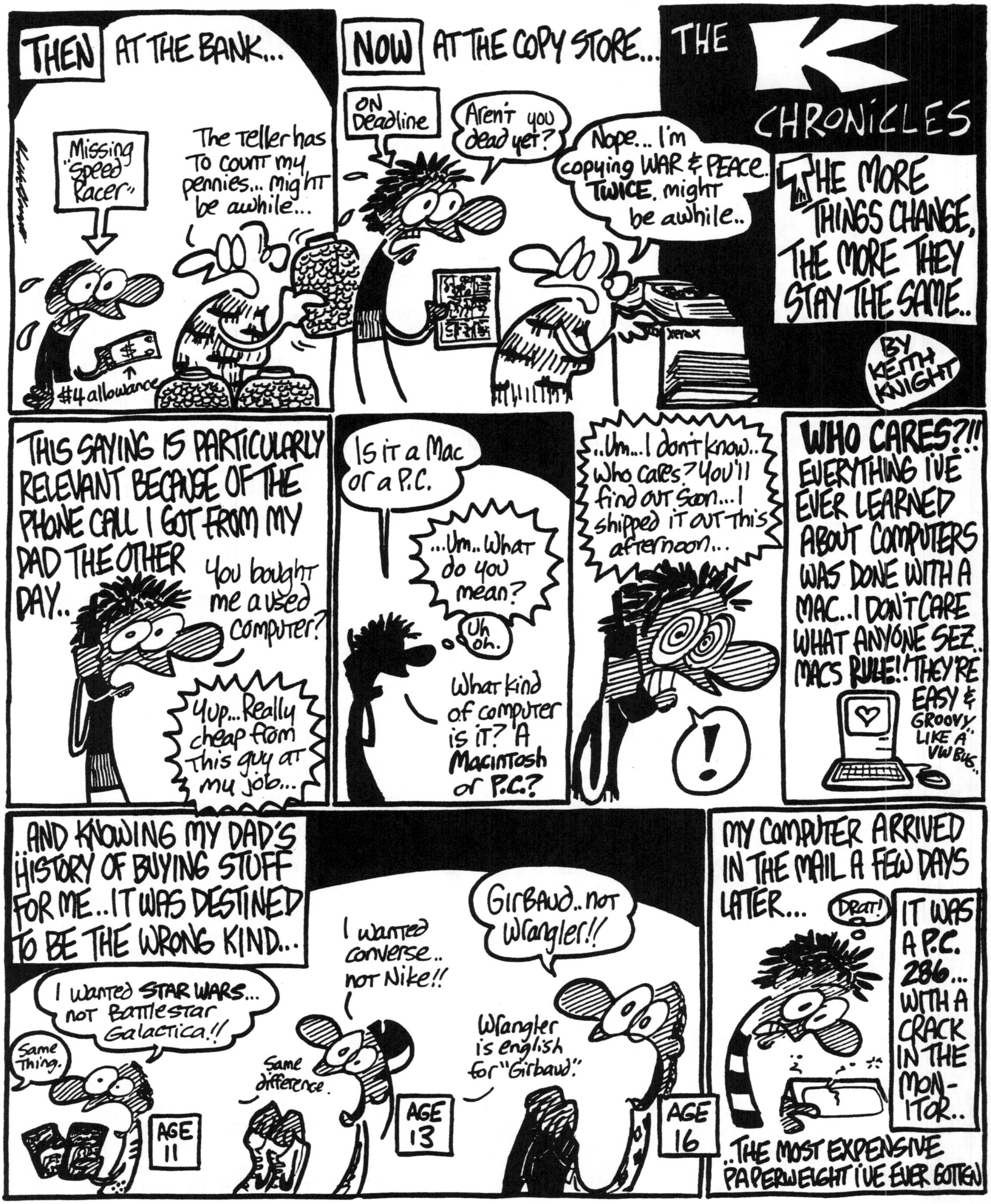
THEN AT THE BANK...
Missing "Speed Racer"
The teller has to count my pennies... might be awhile...
$4 allowance
NOW AT THE COPY STORE...
ON Deadline
Aren't you dead yet?
Nope... I'm copying WAR & PEACE TWICE. might be awhile..
THE K CHRONICLES
THE MORE THINGS CHANGE, THE MORE THEY STAY THE SAME..
BY KEITH KNIGHT
THIS SAYING IS PARTICULARLY RELEVANT BECAUSE OF THE PHONE CALL I GOT FROM MY DAD THE OTHER DAY..
You bought me a used computer?
Yup... Really cheap from this guy at my job...
Is it a Mac or a P.C.
...Um.. What do you mean?
Uh oh.
What kind of computer is it? A Macintosh or P.C.?
..Um...I don't know.. Who cares? You'll find out soon...I shipped it out this afternoon...
!
WHO CARES?!! EVERYTHING I'VE EVER LEARNED ABOUT COMPUTERS WAS DONE WITH A MAC..I DON'T CARE WHAT ANYONE SEZ.. MACS RULE!! THEY'RE EASY & GROOVY, LIKE A VW BUG..
..AND KNOWING MY DAD'S HISTORY OF BUYING STUFF FOR ME...IT WAS DESTINED TO BE THE WRONG KIND...
I wanted STAR WARS... not Battlestar Galactica!!
Same Thing.
AGE 11
I wanted converse.. not Nike!!
Same difference.
AGE 13
Girbaud.. not Wrangler!!
Wrangler is english for "Girbaud."
AGE 16
MY COMPUTER ARRIVED IN THE MAIL A FEW DAYS LATER...
DRAT!
IT WAS A P.C. 286... WITH A CRACK IN THE MONITOR..
..THE MOST EXPENSIVE PAPERWEIGHT I'VE EVER GOTTEN

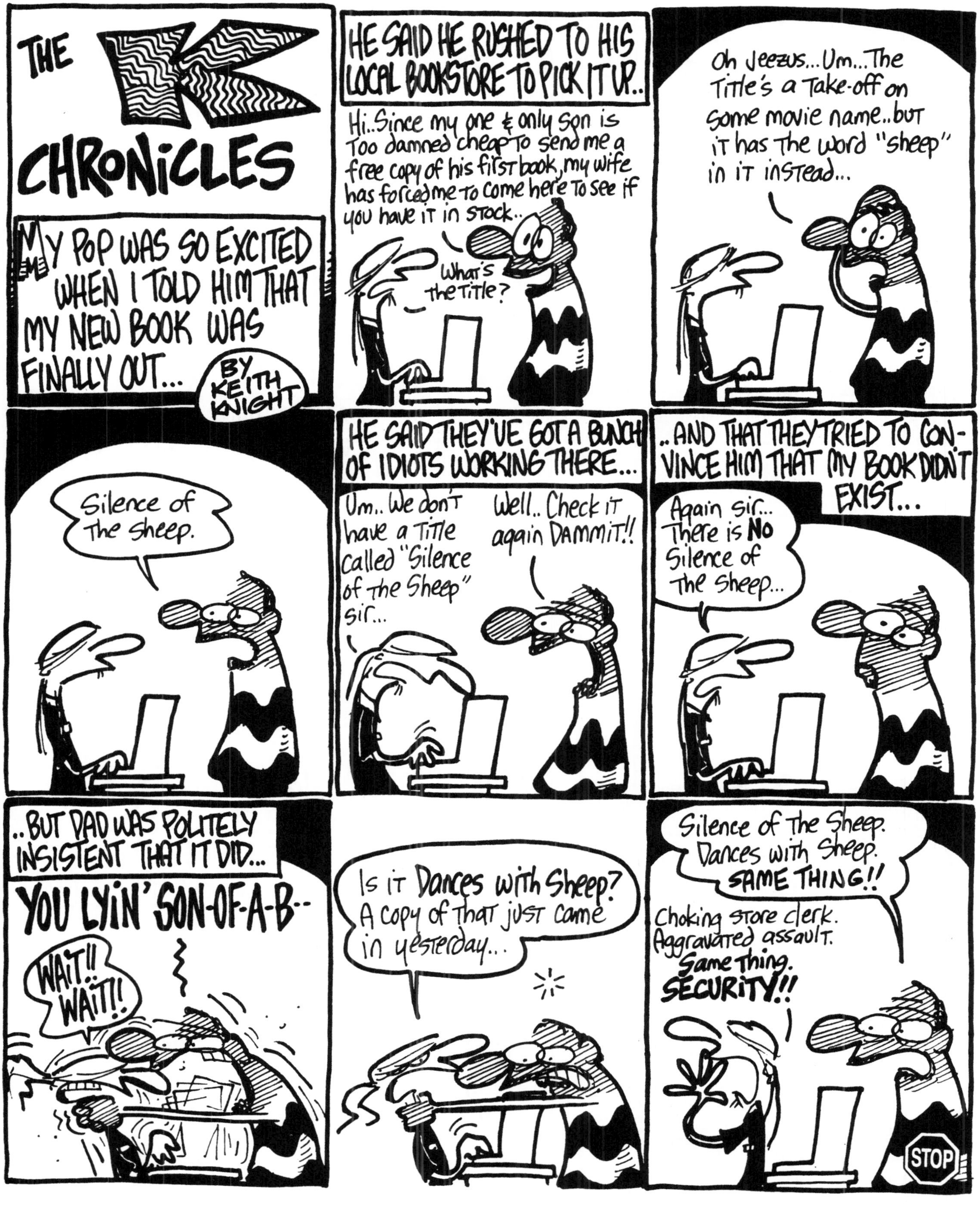
THE K CHRONICLES
MY POP WAS SO EXCITED WHEN I TOLD HIM THAT MY NEW BOOK WAS FINALLY OUT...
BY KEITH KNIGHT
HE SAID HE RUSHED TO HIS LOCAL BOOKSTORE TO PICK IT UP..
Hi..Since my one & only son is Too damned cheap To send me a free copy of his first book, my wife has forced me To come here To see if you have it in stock..
What's the Title?
Oh Jeezus...Um...The Title's a Take-off on some movie name..but it has the word "sheep" in it instead...
Silence of The Sheep.
HE SAID THEY'VE GOT A BUNCH OF IDIOTS WORKING THERE...
Um.. We don't have a Title called "Silence of The Sheep" sir...
Well.. Check it again DAMMIT!!
..AND THAT THEY TRIED TO CONVINCE HIM THAT MY BOOK DIDN'T EXIST...
Again sir... There is NO Silence of The Sheep...
..BUT DAD WAS POLITELY INSISTENT THAT IT DID...
YOU LYIN' SON-OF-A-B--
WAIT!! WAIT!!
Is it Dances with Sheep? A copy of That just came in yesterday...
Silence of The Sheep. Dances with Sheep. SAME THING!!
Choking store clerk. Aggravated assault. Same Thing. SECURITY!!
STOP

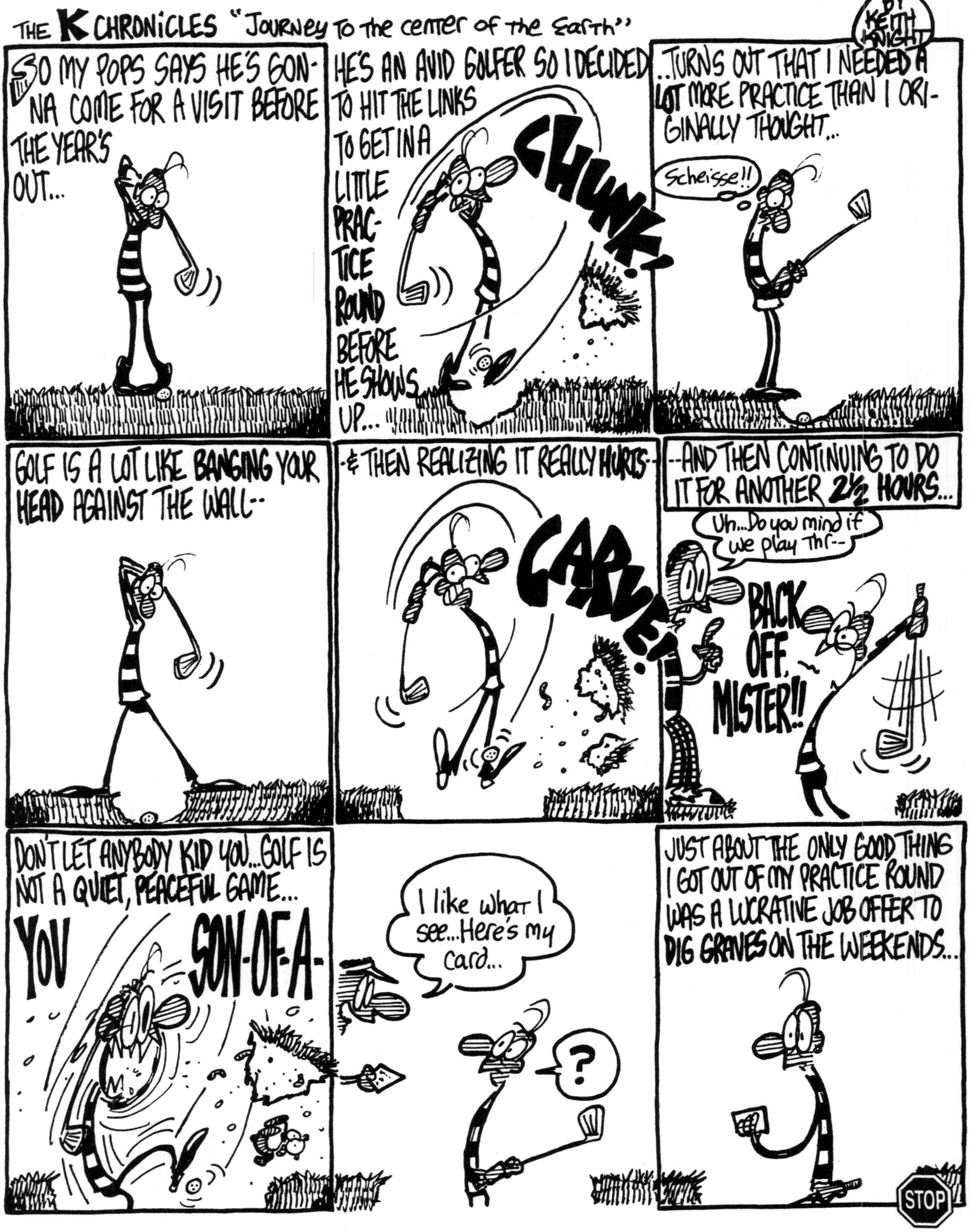
THE K CHRONICLES "Journey to the center of the Earth"
BY KEITH KNIGHT
SO MY POPS SAYS HE'S GONNA COME FOR A VISIT BEFORE THE YEAR'S OUT...
HE'S AN AVID GOLFER SO I DECIDED TO HIT THE LINKS TO GET IN A LITTLE PRACTICE ROUND BEFORE HE SHOWS UP...
CHUNK!
..TURNS OUT THAT I NEEDED A LOT MORE PRACTICE THAN I ORIGINALLY THOUGHT...
Scheisse!!
GOLF IS A LOT LIKE BANGING YOUR HEAD AGAINST THE WALL--
-& THEN REALIZING IT REALLY HURTS--
CARVE!
--AND THEN CONTINUING TO DO IT FOR ANOTHER 2½ HOURS...
Uh...Do you mind if we play thr--
BACK OFF, MISTER!!
DON'T LET ANYBODY KID YOU...GOLF IS NOT A QUIET, PEACEFUL GAME...
YOU SON-OF-A-
I like what I see...Here's my card...
?
JUST ABOUT THE ONLY GOOD THING I GOT OUT OF MY PRACTICE ROUND WAS A LUCRATIVE JOB OFFER TO DIG GRAVES ON THE WEEKENDS...
STOP

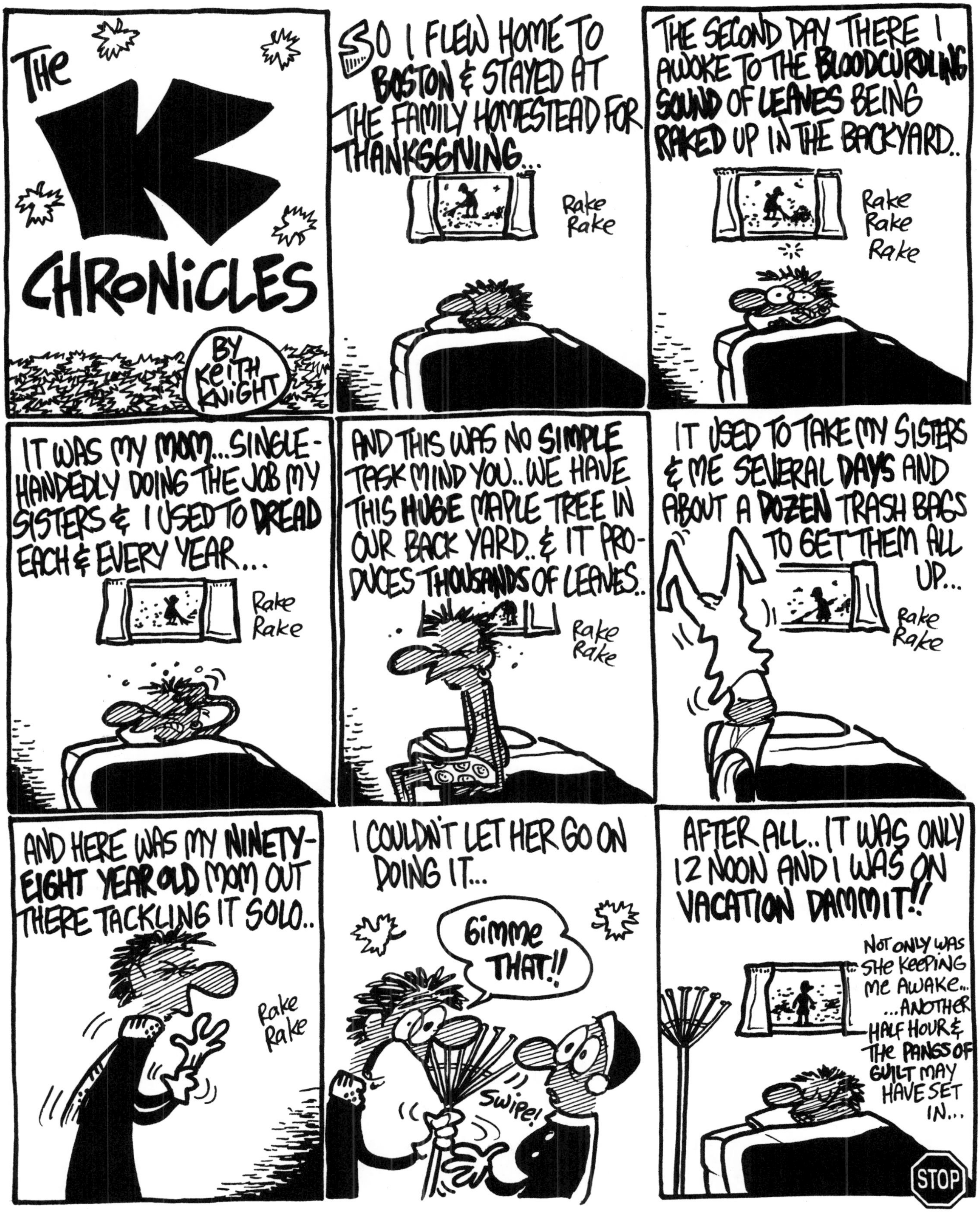
THE K CHRONICLES
BY KEITH KNIGHT
SO I FLEW HOME TO BOSTON & STAYED AT THE FAMILY HOMESTEAD FOR THANKSGIVING...
Rake Rake
THE SECOND DAY THERE I AWOKE TO THE BLOODCURDLING SOUND OF LEAVES BEING RAKED UP IN THE BACKYARD..
Rake Rake Rake Rake
IT WAS MY MOM...SINGLE-HANDEDLY DOING THE JOB MY SISTERS & I USED TO DREAD EACH & EVERY YEAR...
Rake Rake
AND THIS WAS NO SIMPLE TASK MIND YOU.. WE HAVE THIS HUGE MAPLE TREE IN OUR BACK YARD.. & IT PRODUCES THOUSANDS OF LEAVES..
Rake Rake
IT USED TO TAKE MY SISTERS & ME SEVERAL DAYS AND ABOUT A DOZEN TRASH BAGS TO GET THEM ALL UP...
Rake Rake
AND HERE WAS MY NINETY-EIGHT YEAR OLD MOM OUT THERE TACKLING IT SOLO..
Rake Rake
I COULDN'T LET HER GO ON DOING IT...
Gimme THAT!!
Swipe!
AFTER ALL.. IT WAS ONLY 12 NOON AND I WAS ON VACATION DAMMIT!!
NOT ONLY WAS SHE KEEPING ME AWAKE... ...ANOTHER HALF HOUR & THE PANGS OF GUILT MAY HAVE SET IN...
STOP

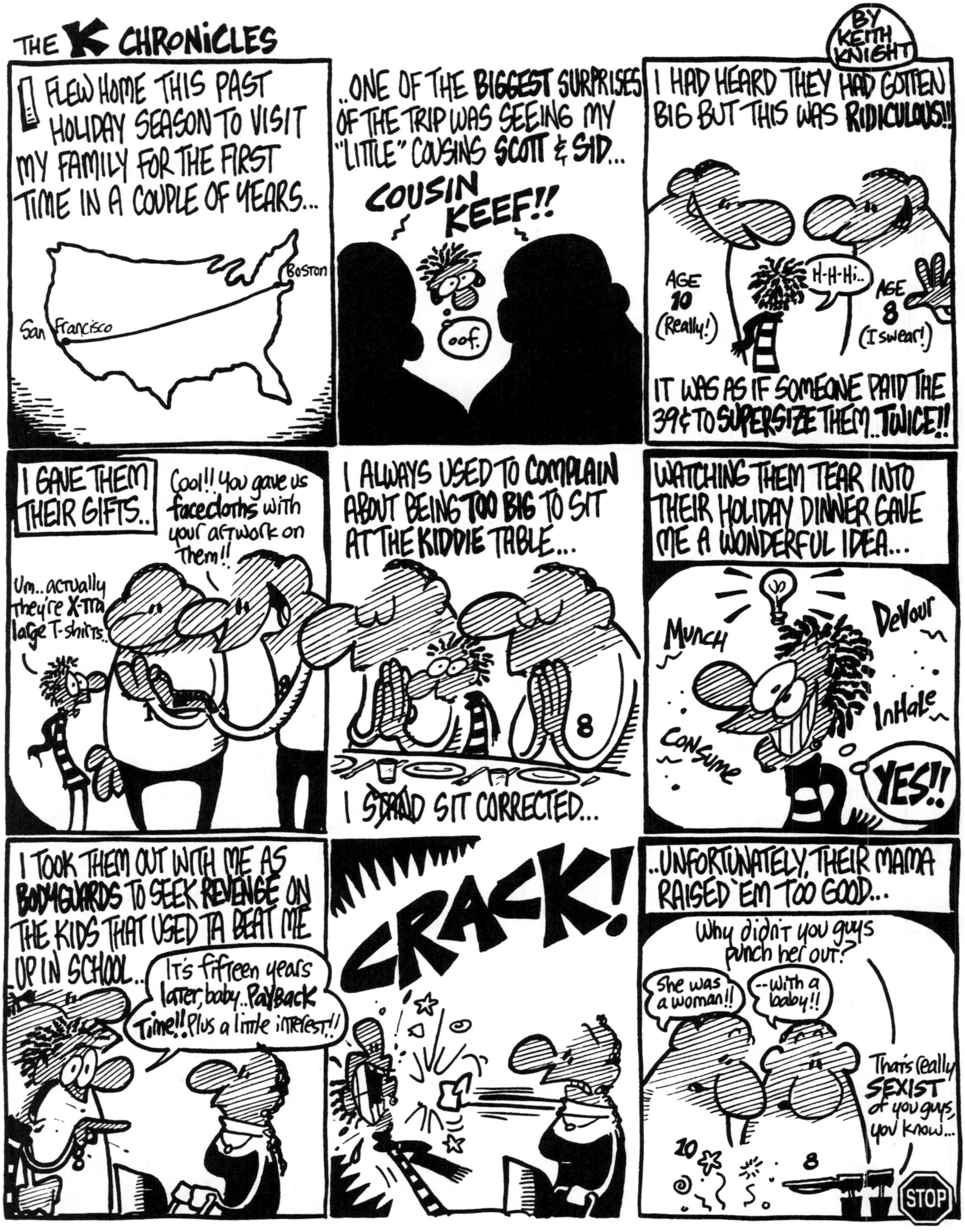
THE K CHRONICLES
BY KEITH KNIGHT
I FLEW HOME THIS PAST HOLIDAY SEASON TO VISIT MY FAMILY FOR THE FIRST TIME IN A COUPLE OF YEARS...
Boston
San Francisco
..ONE OF THE BIGGEST SURPRISES OF THE TRIP WAS SEEING MY "LITTLE" COUSINS SCOTT & SID...
COUSIN KEEF!!
oof.
I HAD HEARD THEY HAD GOTTEN BIG BUT THIS WAS RIDICULOUS!!
AGE 10 (Really!)
H-H-Hi..
AGE 8 (I swear!)
IT WAS AS IF SOMEONE PAID THE 39¢ TO SUPERSIZE THEM..TWICE!!
I GAVE THEM THEIR GIFTS..
Cool!! You gave us facecloths with your artwork on them!!
Um...actually they're X-tra large T-shirts..
I ALWAYS USED TO COMPLAIN ABOUT BEING TOO BIG TO SIT AT THE KIDDIE TABLE...
8
I STAND SIT CORRECTED...
WATCHING THEM TEAR INTO THEIR HOLIDAY DINNER GAVE ME A WONDERFUL IDEA...
Munch
Devour
Inhale
Consume
YES!!
I TOOK THEM OUT WITH ME AS BODYGUARDS TO SEEK REVENGE ON THE KIDS THAT USED TA BEAT ME UP IN SCHOOL...
It's fifteen years later, baby..Payback Time!! Plus a little interest!!
CRACK!
..UNFORTUNATELY, THEIR MAMA RAISED 'EM TOO GOOD...
Why didn't you guys punch her out?
She was a woman!!
--with a baby!!
That's really SEXIST of you guys, you know...
10
8
STOP

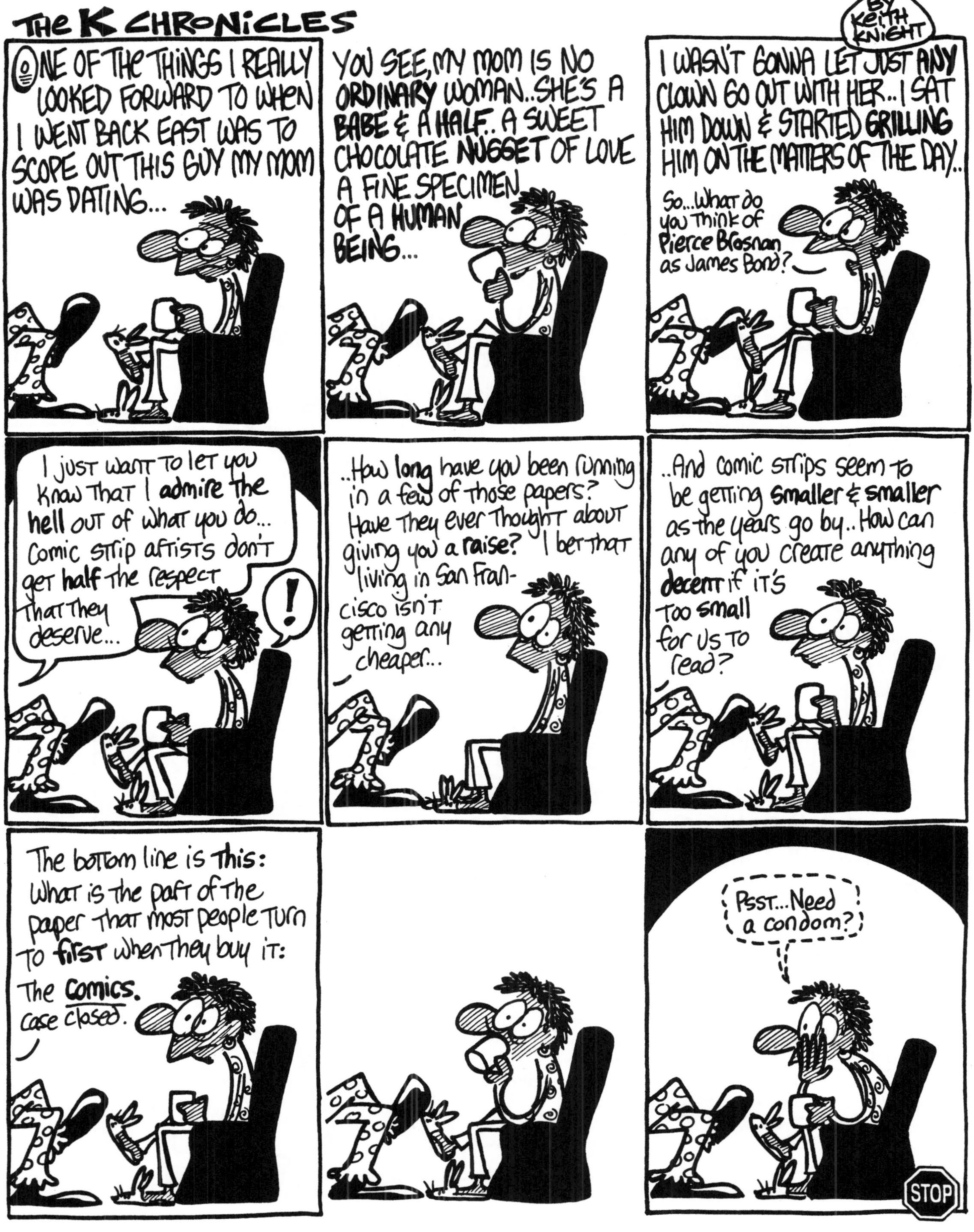
THE K CHRONICLES
BY KEITH KNIGHT
ONE OF THE THINGS I REALLY LOOKED FORWARD TO WHEN I WENT BACK EAST WAS TO SCOPE OUT THIS GUY MY MOM WAS DATING...
YOU SEE, MY MOM IS NO ORDINARY WOMAN.. SHE'S A BABE & A HALF.. A SWEET CHOCOLATE NUGGET OF LOVE A FINE SPECIMEN OF A HUMAN BEING...
I WASN'T GONNA LET JUST ANY CLOWN GO OUT WITH HER.. I SAT HIM DOWN & STARTED GRILLING HIM ON THE MATTERS OF THE DAY..
So...What do you Think of Pierce Brosnan as James Bond?
I just want to let you know That I admire the hell out of what you do... Comic strip artists don't get half the respect That They deserve...
!
..How long have you been running in a few of those papers? Have They ever Thought about giving you a raise? I bet that living in San Francisco isn't getting any cheaper...
..And comic strips seem to be getting smaller & smaller as the years go by.. How can any of you create anything decent if it's too small for us to read?
The bottom line is This: What is the part of the paper that most people turn to first when They buy it: The Comics. Case closed.
Psst...Need a condom?
STOP

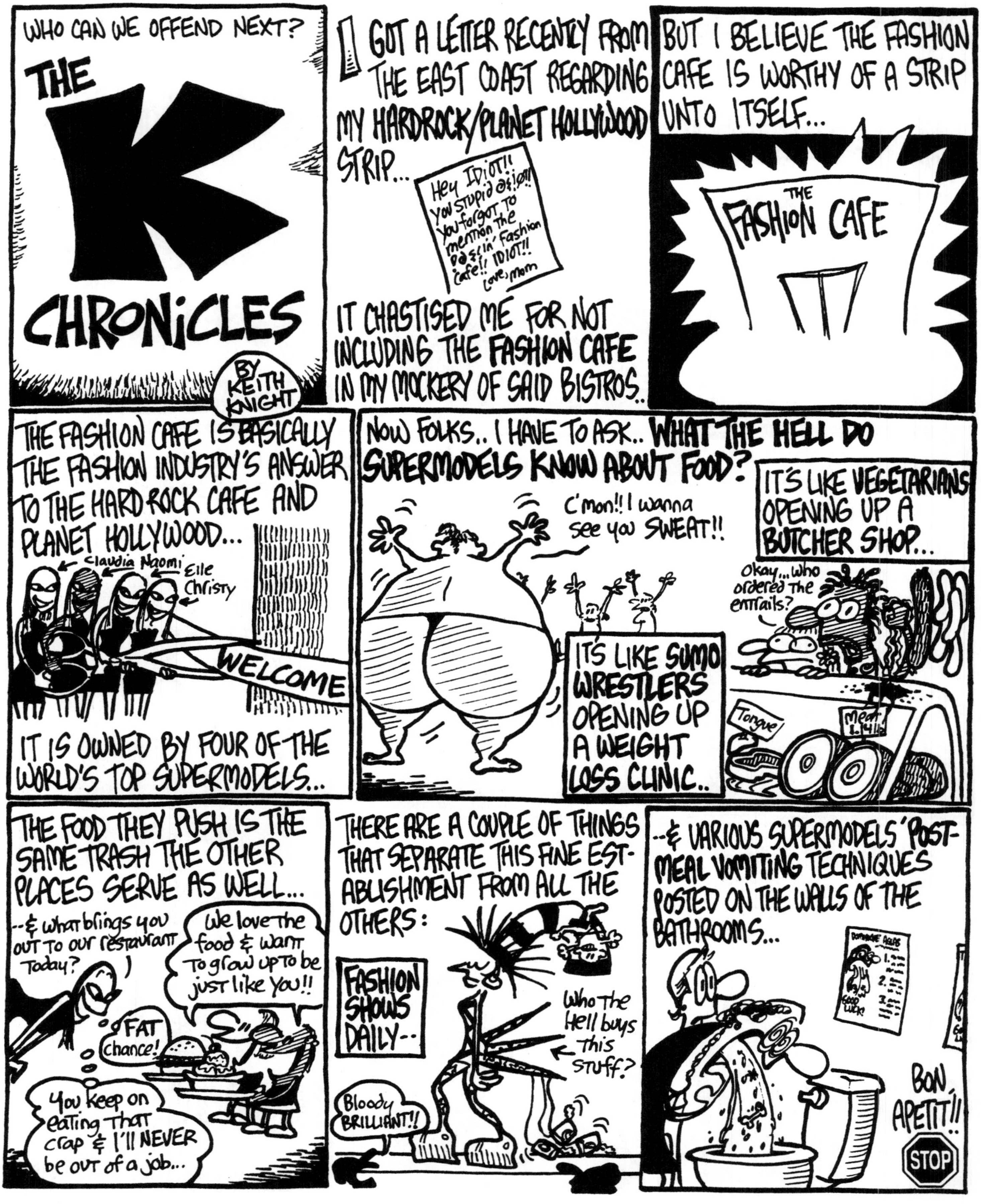
WHO CAN WE OFFEND NEXT?
THE K CHRONICLES
BY KEITH KNIGHT
I GOT A LETTER RECENTLY FROM THE EAST COAST REGARDING MY HARDROCK/PLANET HOLLYWOOD STRIP...
Hey IDIOT!! You stupid @$!@!! You forgot to mention the f@$%in' Fashion Cafe!! IDIOT!! Love, mom
IT CHASTISED ME FOR NOT INCLUDING THE FASHION CAFE IN MY MOCKERY OF SAID BISTROS..
BUT I BELIEVE THE FASHION CAFE IS WORTHY OF A STRIP UNTO ITSELF...
THE FASHION CAFE
THE FASHION CAFE IS BASICALLY THE FASHION INDUSTRY'S ANSWER TO THE HARD ROCK CAFE AND PLANET HOLLYWOOD...
Claudia
Naomi
Elle
Christy
WELCOME
IT IS OWNED BY FOUR OF THE WORLD'S TOP SUPERMODELS...
NOW FOLKS.. I HAVE TO ASK.. WHAT THE HELL DO SUPERMODELS KNOW ABOUT FOOD?
C'mon!! I wanna see you SWEAT!!
IT'S LIKE SUMO WRESTLERS OPENING UP A WEIGHT LOSS CLINIC..
IT'S LIKE VEGETARIANS OPENING UP A BUTCHER SHOP...
Okay... who ordered the entrails?
Tongue
Meat! $1.41 lb
THE FOOD THEY PUSH IS THE SAME TRASH THE OTHER PLACES SERVE AS WELL...
--& what brings you out to our restaurant today?
We love the food & want to grow up to be just like you!!
FAT chance!
You keep on eating that crap & I'll NEVER be out of a job...
THERE ARE A COUPLE OF THINGS THAT SEPARATE THIS FINE ESTABLISHMENT FROM ALL THE OTHERS:
FASHION SHOWS DAILY--
Who the Hell buys this stuff?
Bloody BRILLIANT!!
--& VARIOUS SUPERMODELS' POST-MEAL VOMITING TECHNIQUES POSTED ON THE WALLS OF THE BATHROOMS...
GOOD LUCK!
BON APETIT!!
STOP

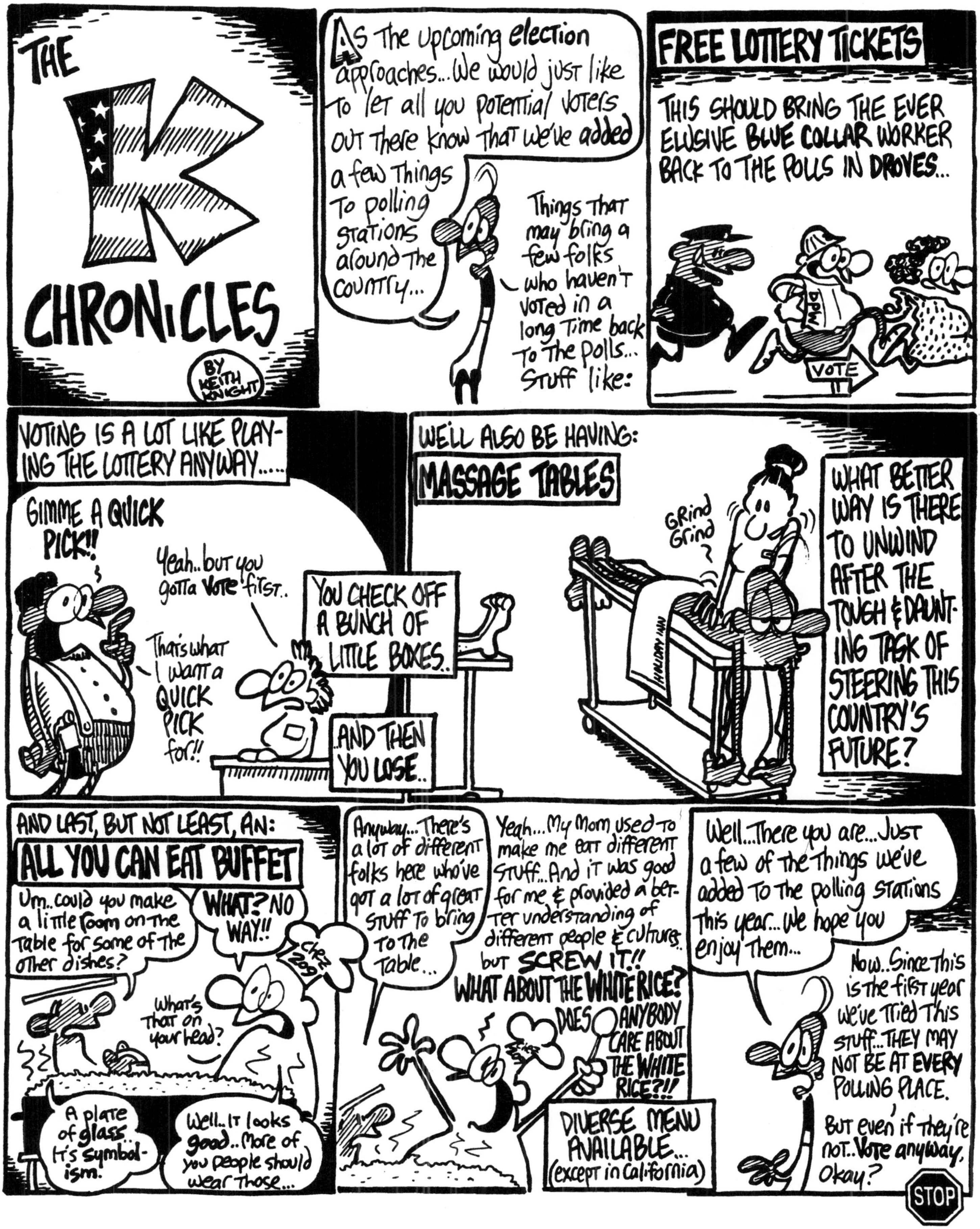

THE K CHRONICLES
BY KEITH KNIGHT
AS THE UPCOMING ELECTION APPROACHES... WE WOULD JUST LIKE TO LET ALL YOU POTENTIAL VOTERS OUT THERE KNOW THAT WE'VE ADDED A FEW THINGS TO POLLING STATIONS AROUND THE COUNTRY...
THINGS THAT MAY BRING A FEW FOLKS WHO HAVEN'T VOTED IN A LONG TIME BACK TO THE POLLS... STUFF LIKE:
FREE LOTTERY TICKETS
THIS SHOULD BRING THE EVER ELUSIVE BLUE COLLAR WORKER BACK TO THE POLLS IN DROVES...
DPW
VOTE
VOTING IS A LOT LIKE PLAYING THE LOTTERY ANYWAY.....
GIMME A QUICK PICK!!
YEAH.. BUT YOU GOTTA VOTE FIRST..
THAT'S WHAT I WANT A QUICK PICK FOR!!
YOU CHECK OFF A BUNCH OF LITTLE BOXES..
..AND THEN YOU LOSE..
WE'LL ALSO BE HAVING:
MASSAGE TABLES
GRIND GRIND
HOLIDAY INN
WHAT BETTER WAY IS THERE TO UNWIND AFTER THE TOUGH & DAUNTING TASK OF STEERING THIS COUNTRY'S FUTURE?
AND LAST, BUT NOT LEAST, AN:
ALL YOU CAN EAT BUFFET
UM.. COULD YOU MAKE A LITTLE ROOM ON THE TABLE FOR SOME OF THE OTHER DISHES?
WHAT? NO WAY!!
CHEZ 209
WHAT'S THAT ON YOUR HEAD?
A PLATE OF GLASS.. IT'S SYMBOLISM.
WELL.. IT LOOKS GOOD.. MORE OF YOU PEOPLE SHOULD WEAR THOSE...
ANYWAY... THERE'S A LOT OF DIFFERENT FOLKS HERE WHO'VE GOT A LOT OF GREAT STUFF TO BRING TO THE TABLE...
YEAH... MY MOM USED TO MAKE ME EAT DIFFERENT STUFF... AND IT WAS GOOD FOR ME & PROVIDED A BETTER UNDERSTANDING OF DIFFERENT PEOPLE & CULTURES.. BUT SCREW IT!!
WHAT ABOUT THE WHITE RICE? DOES ANYBODY CARE ABOUT THE WHITE RICE?!!
DIVERSE MENU AVAILABLE... (EXCEPT IN CALIFORNIA)
WELL... THERE YOU ARE... JUST A FEW OF THE THINGS WE'VE ADDED TO THE POLLING STATIONS THIS YEAR... WE HOPE YOU ENJOY THEM...
NOW.. SINCE THIS IS THE FIRST YEAR WE'VE TRIED THIS STUFF... THEY MAY NOT BE AT EVERY POLLING PLACE.
BUT EVEN IF THEY'RE NOT.. VOTE ANYWAY, OKAY?
STOP

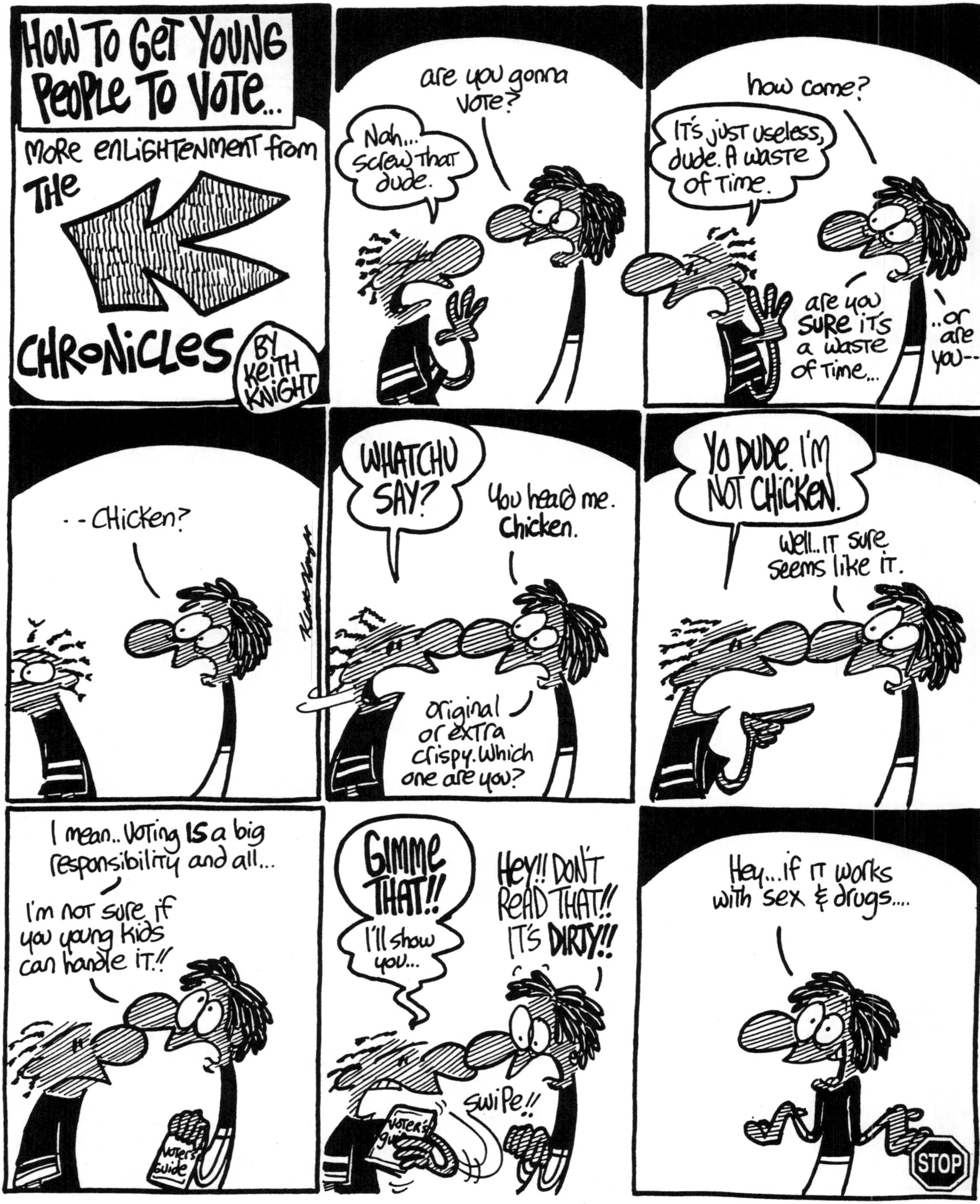
HOW TO GET YOUNG PEOPLE TO VOTE...
MORE ENLIGHTENMENT from THE K CHRONICLES
BY KEITH KNIGHT
are you gonna vote?
Nah... screw that dude.
how come?
IT'S just useless, dude. A waste of time.
are you SURE it's a waste of time...
..or are you--
--Chicken?
WHATCHU SAY?
You heard me. Chicken.
original or extra crispy. Which one are you?
YO DUDE. I'M NOT CHICKEN.
Well.. it sure seems like it.
I mean.. Voting IS a big responsibility and all...
I'm not sure if you young kids can handle it.!!
Voter's Guide
GIMME THAT!!
I'll show you...
HEY!! DON'T READ THAT!! IT'S DIRTY!!
SWIPE!!
Hey...if it works with sex & drugs....
STOP

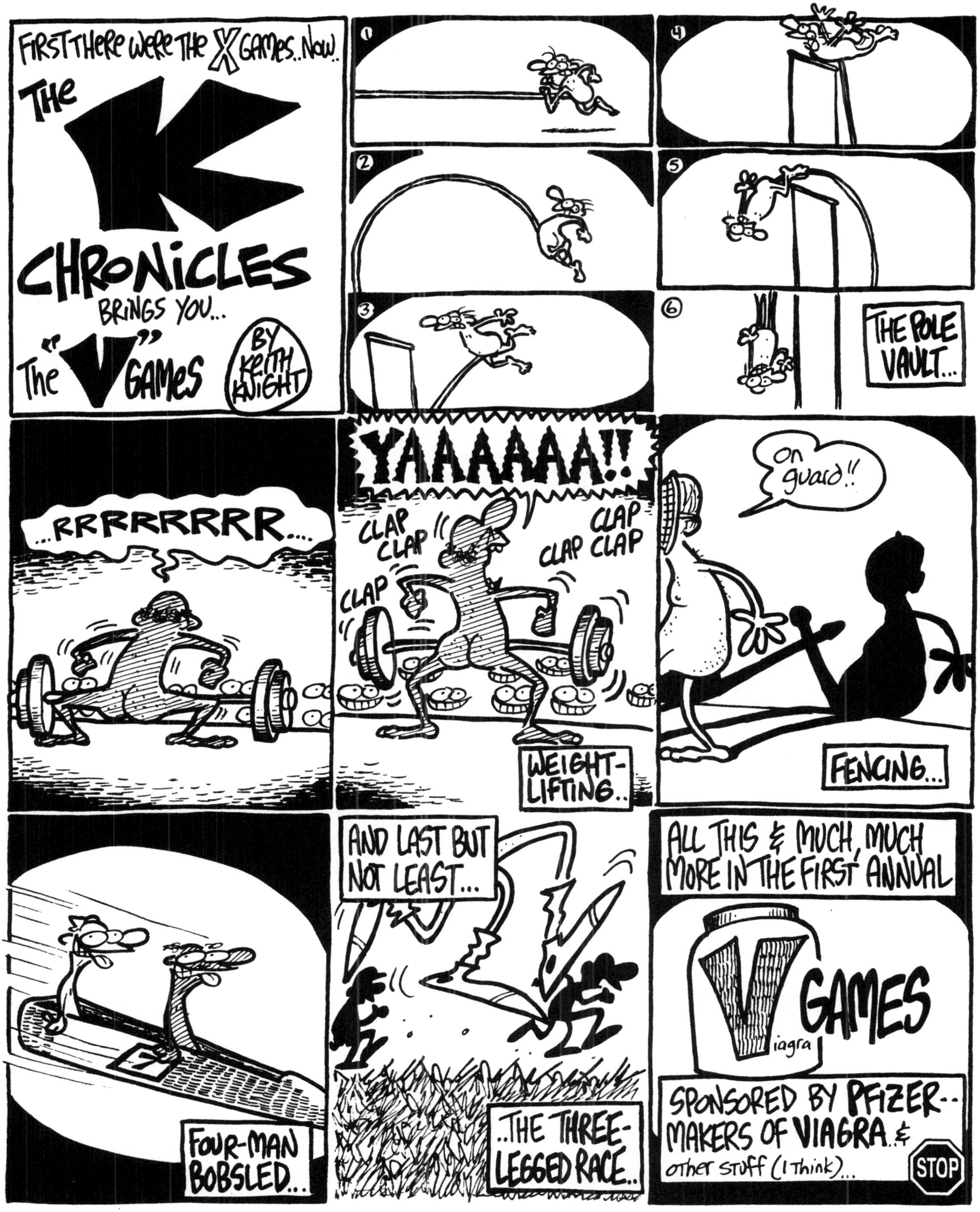
FIRST THERE WERE THE X GAMES.. NOW..
THE K CHRONICLES
BRINGS YOU...
THE "V" GAMES
BY KEITH KNIGHT
1
2
3
4
5
6
THE POLE VAULT...
...RRRRRRRR....
YAAAAAA!!
CLAP CLAP
CLAP
CLAP CLAP CLAP
WEIGHT-LIFTING..
On guard!!
FENCING...
FOUR-MAN BOBSLED...
AND LAST BUT NOT LEAST...
..THE THREE-LEGGED RACE..
ALL THIS & MUCH, MUCH MORE IN THE FIRST ANNUAL
Viagra GAMES
SPONSORED BY PFIZER--
MAKERS OF VIAGRA..&
other stuff (I think)...
STOP

V-games Strip: A reaction to the Viagra epidemic that swept our country in a matter of days. I was extremely excited (pardon the pun) to have so many penises running in newspapers across the country.

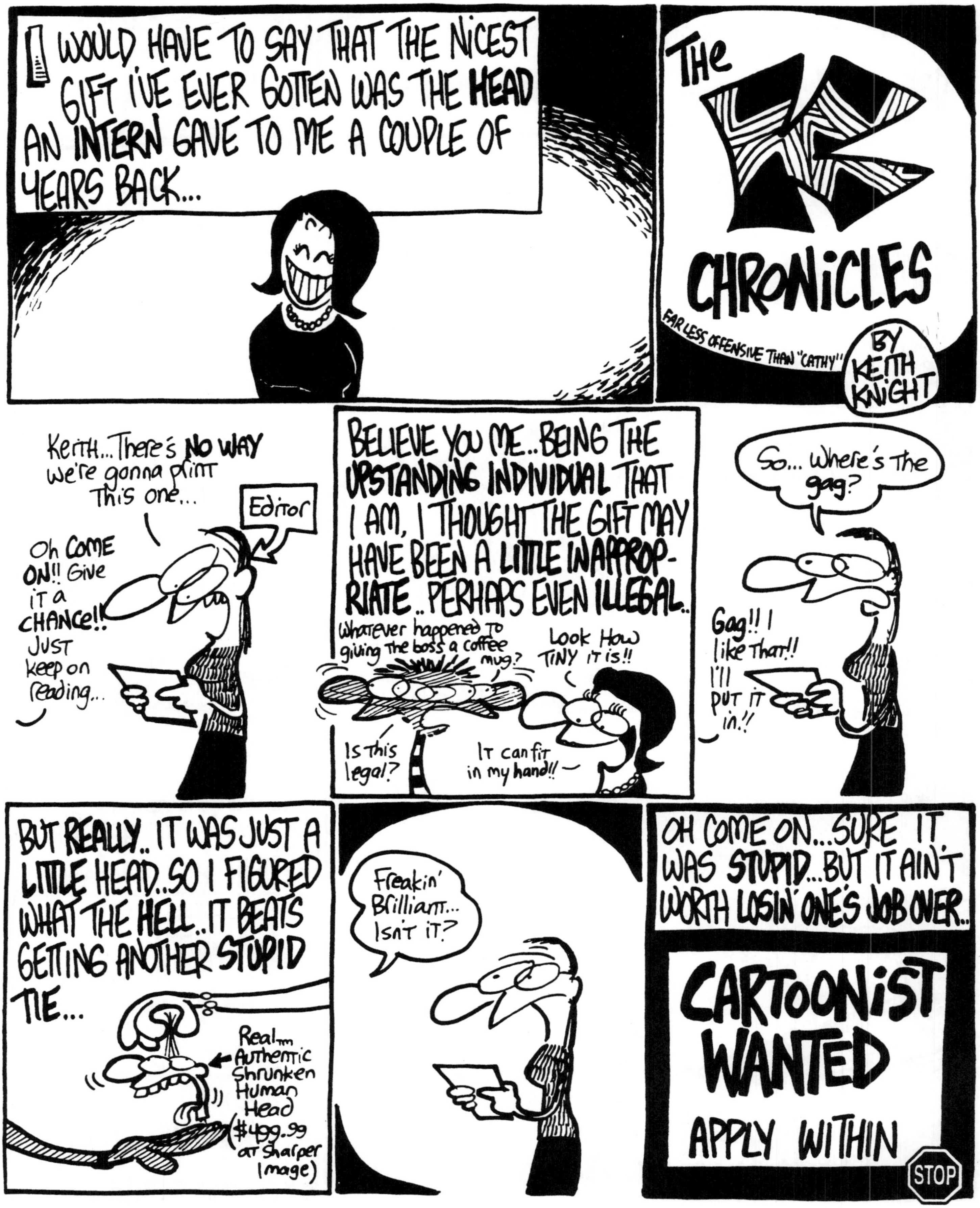
I WOULD HAVE TO SAY THAT THE NICEST GIFT I'VE EVER GOTTEN WAS THE HEAD AN INTERN GAVE TO ME A COUPLE OF YEARS BACK...
THE K CHRONICLES
FAR LESS OFFENSIVE THAN "CATHY"
BY KEITH KNIGHT
Keith... There's NO WAY we're gonna print this one...
Editor
Oh COME ON!! Give it a CHANCE!! JUST keep on reading...
BELIEVE YOU ME.. BEING THE UPSTANDING INDIVIDUAL THAT I AM, I THOUGHT THE GIFT MAY HAVE BEEN A LITTLE INAPPROP-RIATE.. PERHAPS EVEN ILLEGAL..
Whatever happened to giving the boss a coffee mug?
Look How TINY it is!!
Is this legal?
It can fit in my hand!!
So... Where's the gag?
Gag!! I like that!! I'll put it in!!
BUT REALLY.. IT WAS JUST A LITTLE HEAD.. SO I FIGURED WHAT THE HELL.. IT BEATS GETTING ANOTHER STUPID TIE...
Real™ Authentic Shrunken Human Head ($499.99 at Sharper Image)
Freakin' Brilliant... Isn't it?
OH COME ON... SURE IT WAS STUPID... BUT IT AIN'T WORTH LOSIN' ONE'S JOB OVER..
CARTOONIST WANTED
APPLY WITHIN
STOP

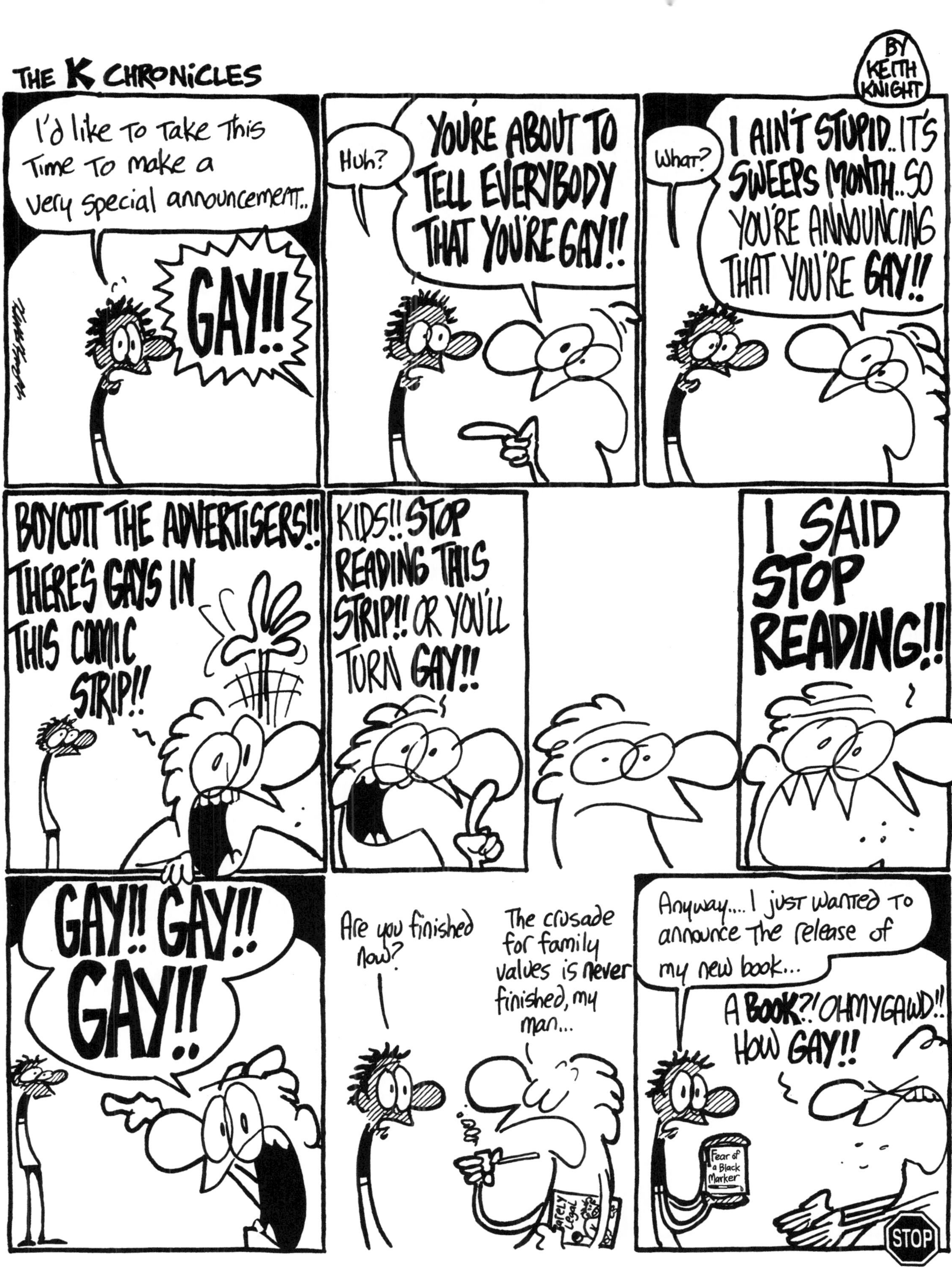
THE K CHRONICLES
BY KEITH KNIGHT
I'd like to take this time to make a very special announcement..
GAY!!
Huh?
YOU'RE ABOUT TO TELL EVERYBODY THAT YOU'RE GAY!!
What?
I AIN'T STUPID.. IT'S SWEEPS MONTH..SO YOU'RE ANNOUNCING THAT YOU'RE GAY!!
BOYCOTT THE ADVERTISERS!! THERE'S GAYS IN THIS COMIC STRIP!!
KIDS!! STOP READING THIS STRIP!! OR YOU'LL TURN GAY!!
I SAID STOP READING!!
GAY!! GAY!! GAY!!
Are you finished now?
The crusade for family values is never finished, my man...
Anyway.... I just wanted to announce the release of my new book...
A BOOK?! OHMYGAWD!! HOW GAY!!
Fear of a Black Marker
STOP

Done in reaction to Ellen DeGeneres coming out in her T.V. show. |

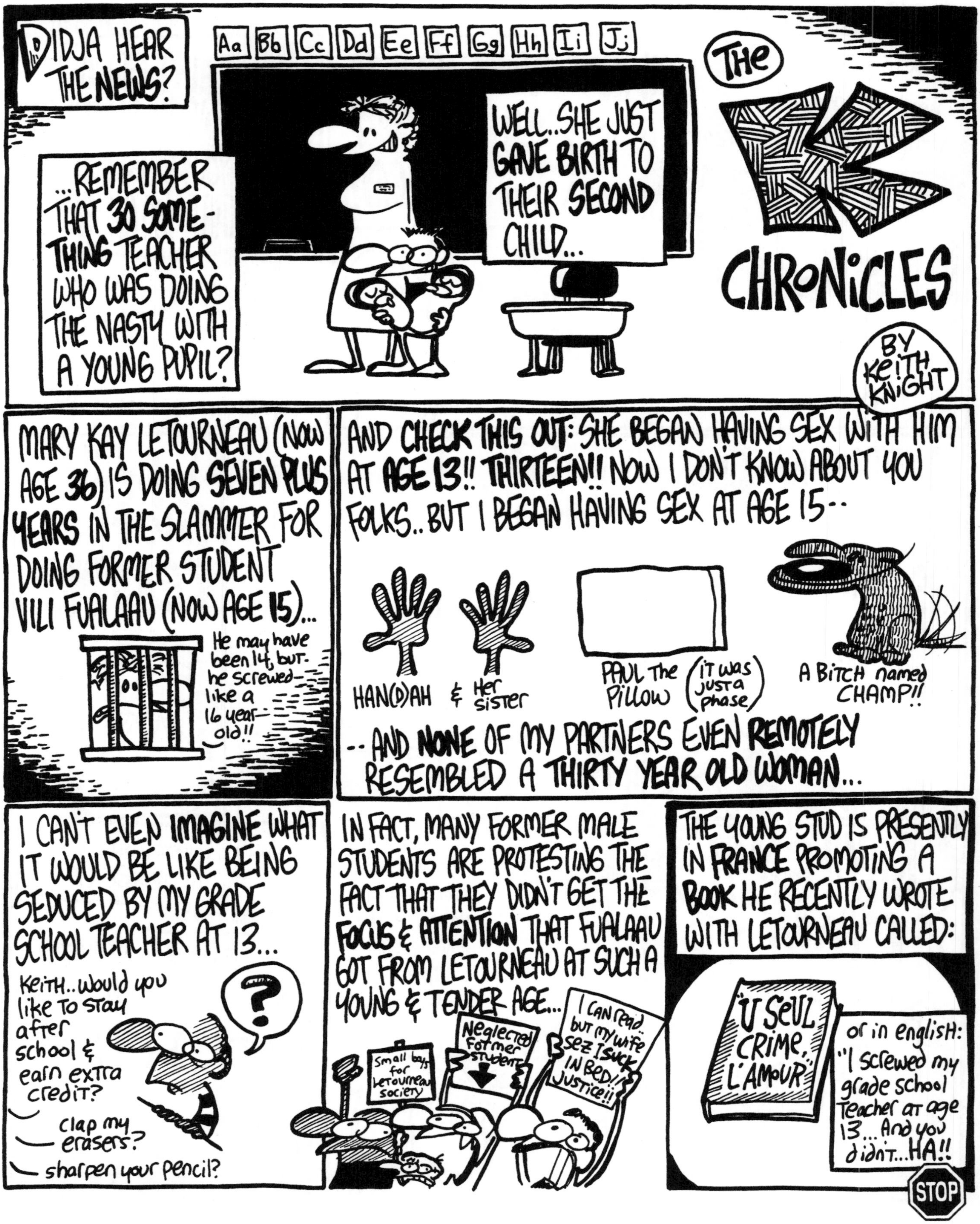

DIDJA HEAR THE NEWS?
Aa Bb Cc Dd Ee Ff Gg Hh Ii Jj
...REMEMBER THAT 30 SOME-THING TEACHER WHO WAS DOING THE NASTY WITH A YOUNG PUPIL?
WELL..SHE JUST GAVE BIRTH TO THEIR SECOND CHILD...
THE K CHRONICLES
BY KEITH KNIGHT
MARY KAY LETOURNEAU (NOW AGE 36) IS DOING SEVEN PLUS YEARS IN THE SLAMMER FOR DOING FORMER STUDENT VILI FUALAAU (NOW AGE 15)...
He may have been 14, but he screwed like a 16 year old!!
AND CHECK THIS OUT: SHE BEGAN HAVING SEX WITH HIM AT AGE 13!! THIRTEEN!! NOW I DON'T KNOW ABOUT YOU FOLKS.. BUT I BEGAN HAVING SEX AT AGE 15..
HAN(D)AH & Her sister
PAUL The Pillow (it was just a phase)
A BITCH named CHAMP!!
..AND NONE OF MY PARTNERS EVEN REMOTELY RESEMBLED A THIRTY YEAR OLD WOMAN...
I CAN'T EVEN IMAGINE WHAT IT WOULD BE LIKE BEING SEDUCED BY MY GRADE SCHOOL TEACHER AT 13...
Keith..would you like to stay after school & earn extra credit?
clap my erasers?
sharpen your pencil?
?
IN FACT, MANY FORMER MALE STUDENTS ARE PROTESTING THE FACT THAT THEY DIDN'T GET THE FOCUS & ATTENTION THAT FUALAAU GOT FROM LETOURNEAU AT SUCH A YOUNG & TENDER AGE...
Small boys for Letourneau society
Neglected Former student
I can read but my wife sez I SUCK IN BED!! JUSTICE!!
THE YOUNG STUD IS PRESENTLY IN FRANCE PROMOTING A BOOK HE RECENTLY WROTE WITH LETOURNEAU CALLED:
"U SEUL CRIME, L'AMOUR"
or in english: "I screwed my grade school teacher at age 13... And you didn't...HA!!
STOP

I had at least two different teachers doing the do with students. And a state rep was caught running an escort service with high school students. And the high school leader was getting' some nookie too.

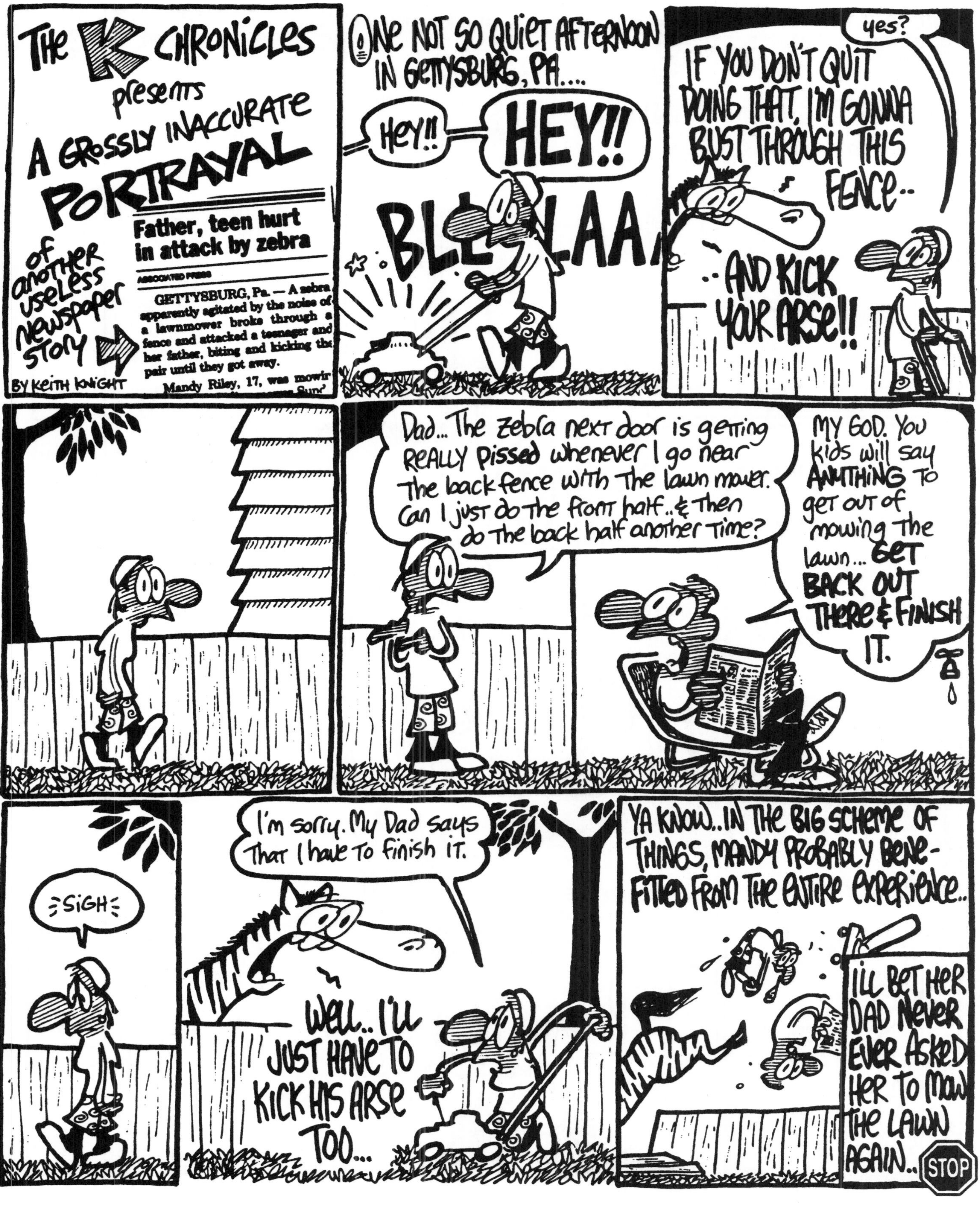

The K Chronicles presents
A grossly inaccurate PORTRAYAL
of another useless newspaper story
Father, teen hurt in attack by zebra
ASSOCIATED PRESS
GETTYSBURG, Pa. — A zebra apparently agitated by the noise of a lawnmower broke through a fence and attacked a teenager and her father, biting and kicking the pair until they got away.
Mandy Riley, 17, was mowir
By Keith Knight
One not so quiet afternoon in Gettysburg, PA....
Hey!!
HEY!!
BLLLLAA
yes?
If you don't quit doing that, I'm gonna bust through this fence..
and kick your arse!!
Dad... The zebra next door is getting really pissed whenever I go near the back fence with the lawn mower. Can I just do the front half.. & then do the back half another time?
My God. You kids will say ANYTHING to get out of mowing the lawn... GET BACK OUT THERE & FINISH IT.
SIGH
I'm sorry. My Dad says that I have to finish it.
Well.. I'll just have to kick his arse too...
Ya know.. in the big scheme of things, Mandy probably benefitted from the entire experience..
I'll bet her dad never ever asked her to mow the lawn again..
STOP

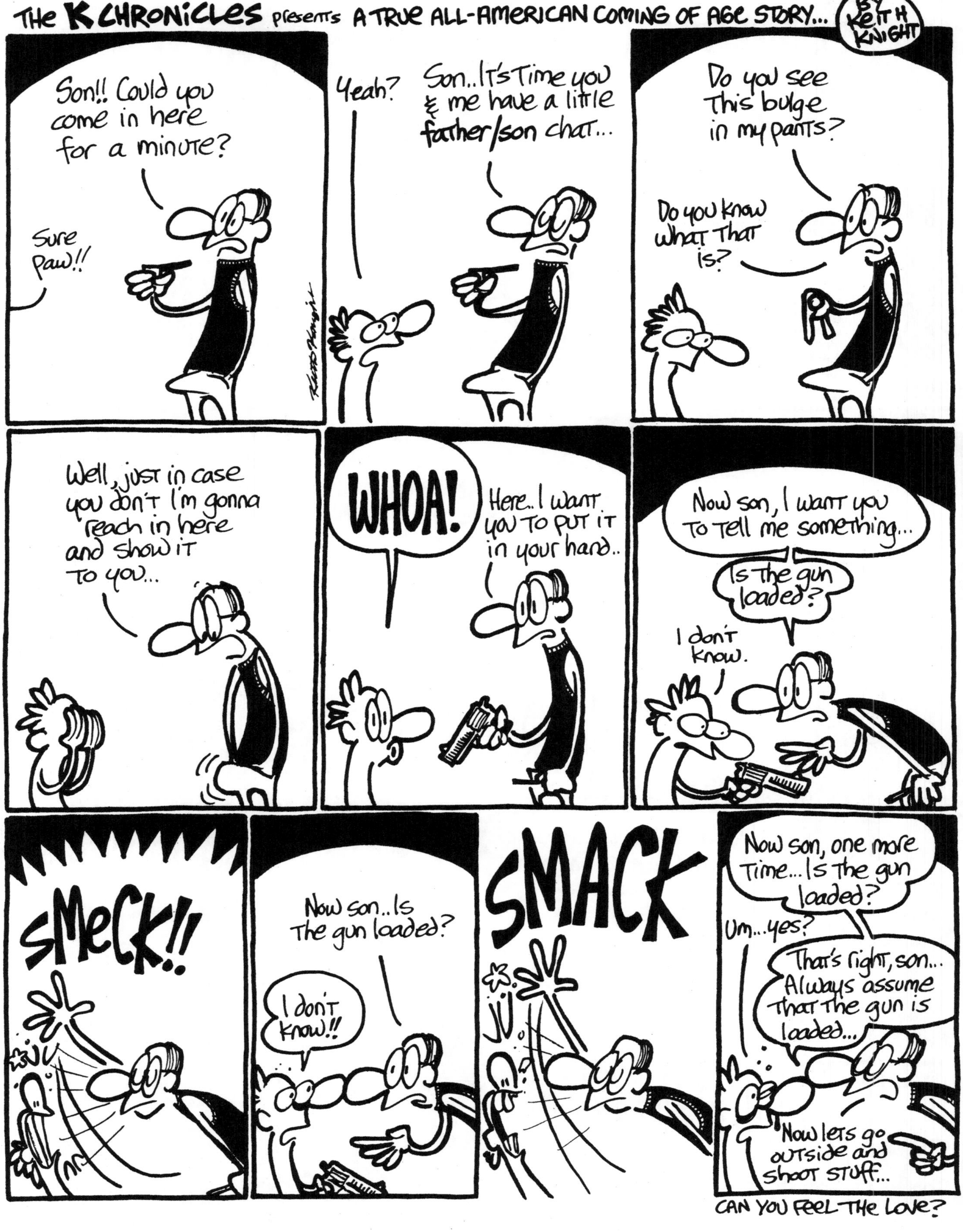
THE K CHRONICLES presents A TRUE ALL-AMERICAN COMING OF AGE STORY... BY KEITH KNIGHT
Son!! Could you come in here for a minute?
Sure paw!!
Yeah?
Son.. It's Time you & me have a little father/son chat...
Do you see This bulge in my pants?
Do you know what That is?
Well, just in case you don't I'm gonna reach in here and show it to you...
WHOA!
Here.. I want you to put it in your hand..
Now son, I want you to Tell me something...
Is The gun loaded?
I don't know.
sMeCK!!
Now son.. Is The gun loaded?
I don't know!!
SMACK
Now son, one more Time... Is The gun loaded?
Um...yes?
That's right, son... Always assume That The gun is loaded...
Now lets go outside and shoot stuff...
CAN YOU FEEL THE LOVE?

I did a sketch of the dad with a bulge and was looking to use it somewhere, anywhere. Then this story came along. I fashioned the father after Dr. Drew from Loveline. *It was funny to see my editor cringe at the third panel.*

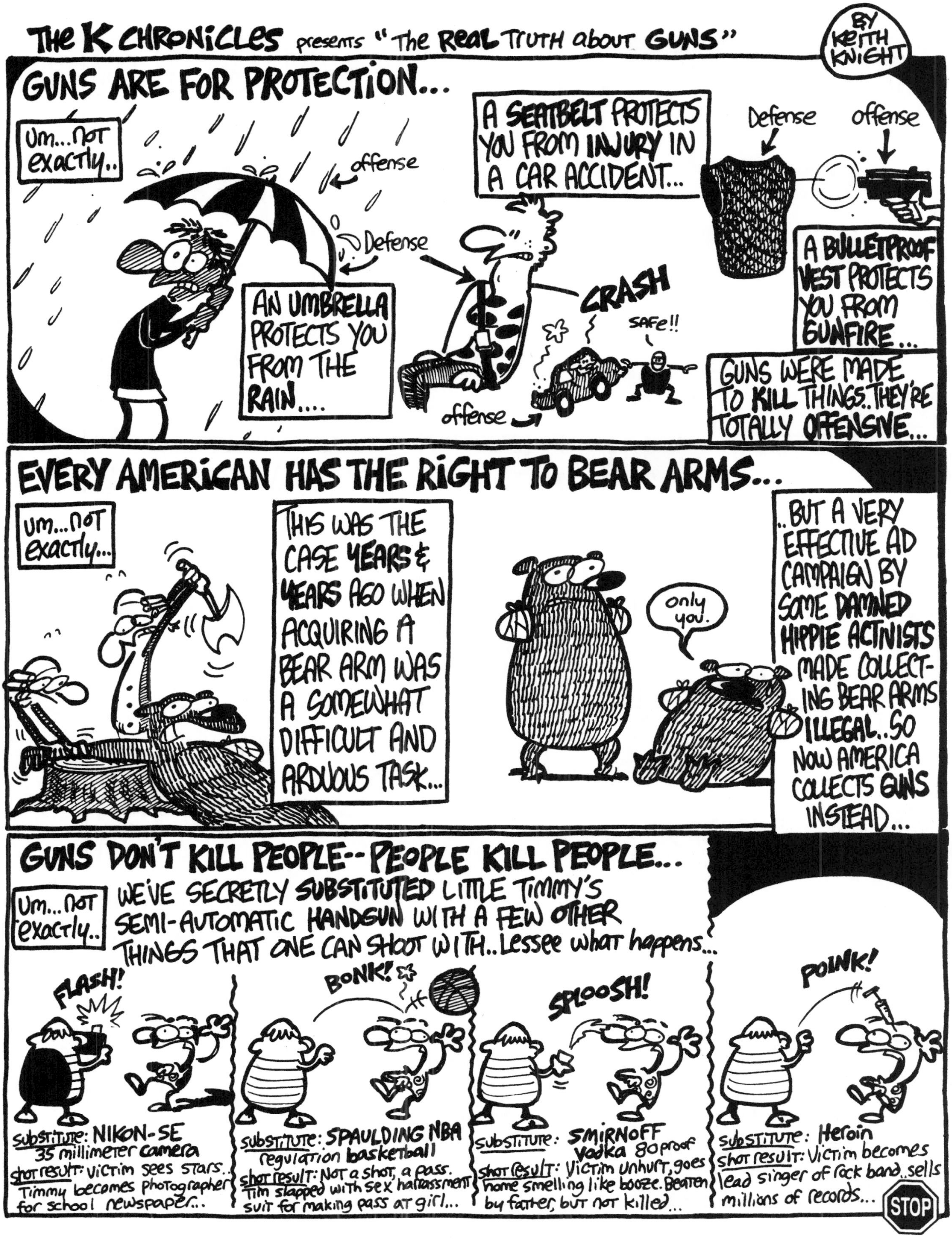
THE K CHRONICLES presents "The REAL TRUTH about GUNS"
BY KEITH KNIGHT
GUNS ARE FOR PROTECTION...
Um...not exactly..
offense
Defense
AN UMBRELLA PROTECTS YOU FROM THE RAIN....
A SEATBELT PROTECTS YOU FROM INJURY IN A CAR ACCIDENT...
CRASH
SAFE!!
offense
Defense
offense
A BULLETPROOF VEST PROTECTS YOU FROM GUNFIRE...
GUNS WERE MADE TO KILL THINGS. THEY'RE TOTALLY OFFENSIVE...
EVERY AMERICAN HAS THE RIGHT TO BEAR ARMS...
um...not exactly...
THIS WAS THE CASE YEARS & YEARS AGO WHEN ACQUIRING A BEAR ARM WAS A SOMEWHAT DIFFICULT AND ARDUOUS TASK...
only you.
..BUT A VERY EFFECTIVE AD CAMPAIGN BY SOME DAMNED HIPPIE ACTIVISTS MADE COLLECTING BEAR ARMS ILLEGAL..SO NOW AMERICA COLLECTS GUNS INSTEAD...
GUNS DON'T KILL PEOPLE--PEOPLE KILL PEOPLE...
Um...not exactly..
WE'VE SECRETLY SUBSTITUTED LITTLE TIMMY'S SEMI-AUTOMATIC HANDGUN WITH A FEW OTHER THINGS THAT ONE CAN SHOOT WITH.. Lessee what happens...
FLASH!
substitute: NIKON-SE 35 millimeter camera
shot result: victim sees stars.. Timmy becomes photographer for school newspaper...
BONK!
substitute: SPAULDING NBA regulation basketball
shot result: Not a shot, a pass. Tim slapped with sex harassment suit for making pass at girl...
SPLOOSH!
substitute: SMIRNOFF Vodka 80 proof
shot result: Victim unhurt, goes home smelling like booze. Beaten by father, but not killed...
POINK!
substitute: Heroin
shot result: Victim becomes lead singer of rock band..sells millions of records...
STOP

I got my first death threats from gun fanatics for this one. And a mean letter from columnist Dave Barry.

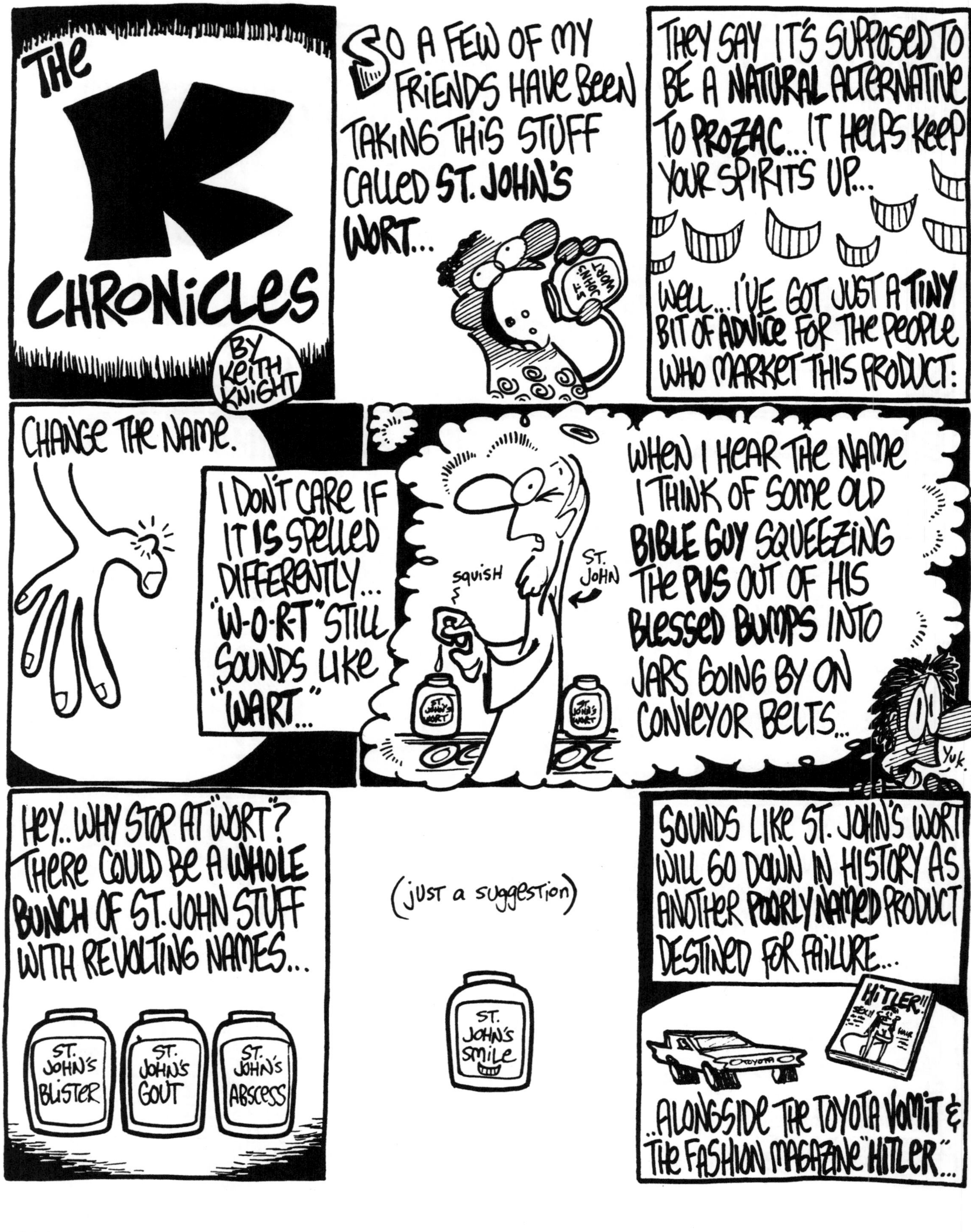
THE K CHRONICLES
BY KEITH KNIGHT
SO A FEW OF MY FRIENDS HAVE BEEN TAKING THIS STUFF CALLED ST. JOHN'S WORT...
ST. JOHN'S WORT
THEY SAY IT'S SUPPOSED TO BE A NATURAL ALTERNATIVE TO PROZAC... IT HELPS KEEP YOUR SPIRITS UP...
WELL... I'VE GOT JUST A TINY BIT OF ADVICE FOR THE PEOPLE WHO MARKET THIS PRODUCT:
CHANGE THE NAME.
I DON'T CARE IF IT IS SPELLED DIFFERENTLY... "W-O-R-T" STILL SOUNDS LIKE "WART"...
WHEN I HEAR THE NAME I THINK OF SOME OLD BIBLE GUY SQUEEZING THE PUS OUT OF HIS BLESSED BUMPS INTO JARS GOING BY ON CONVEYOR BELTS...
SQUISH
ST. JOHN
ST. JOHN'S WORT
ST. JOHN'S WORT
YUK.
HEY.. WHY STOP AT "WORT"? THERE COULD BE A WHOLE BUNCH OF ST. JOHN STUFF WITH REVOLTING NAMES...
ST. JOHN'S BLISTER
ST. JOHN'S GOUT
ST. JOHN'S ABSCESS
(JUST A SUGGESTION)
ST. JOHN'S SMILE
SOUNDS LIKE ST. JOHN'S WORT WILL GO DOWN IN HISTORY AS ANOTHER POORLY NAMED PRODUCT DESTINED FOR FAILURE...
TOYOTA
HITLER!!
..ALONGSIDE THE TOYOTA VOMIT & THE FASHION MAGAZINE "HITLER"...

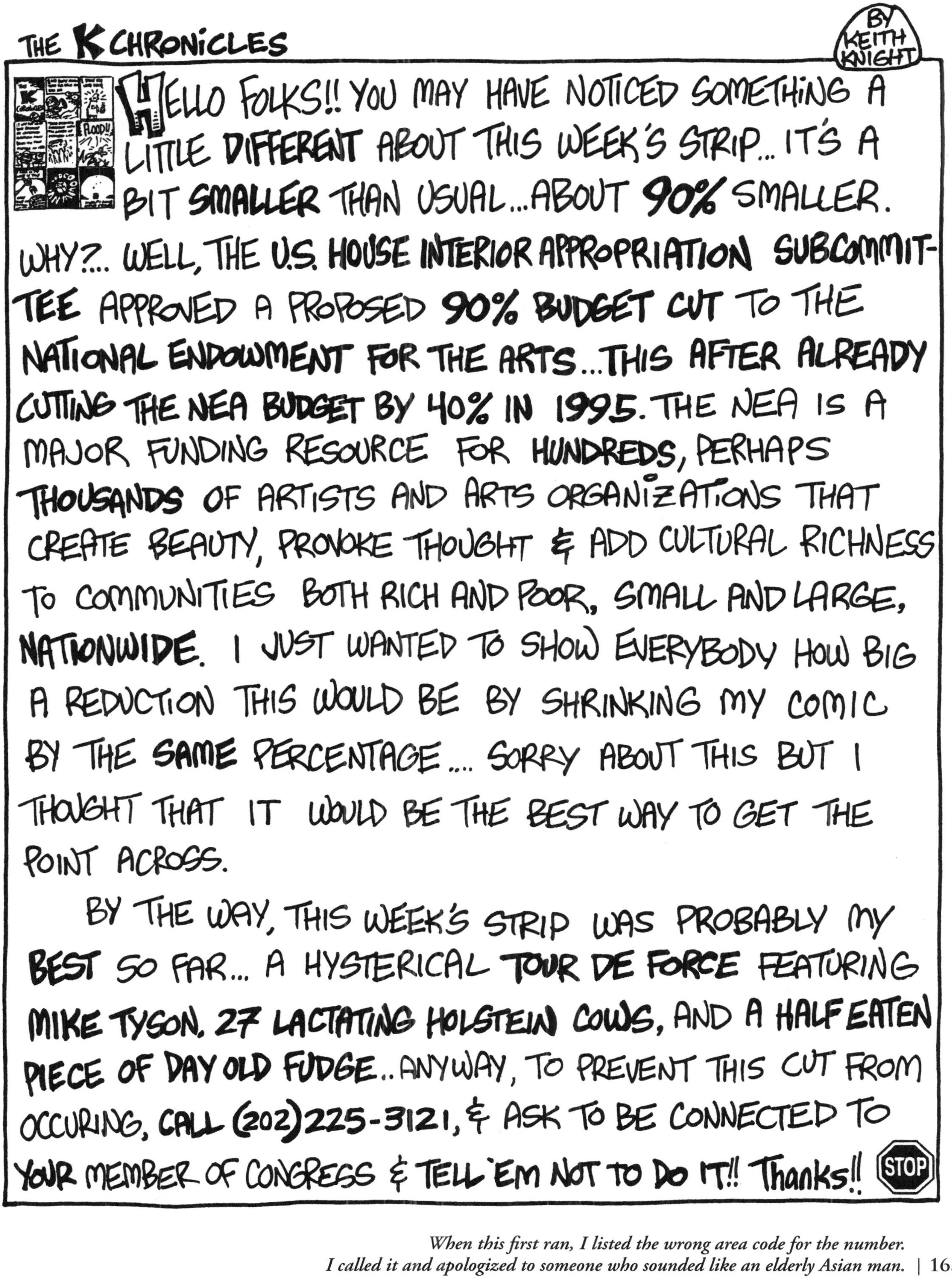
THE K CHRONICLES
BY KEITH KNIGHT
HELLO FOLKS!! YOU MAY HAVE NOTICED SOMETHING A LITTLE DIFFERENT ABOUT THIS WEEK'S STRIP... IT'S A BIT SMALLER THAN USUAL... ABOUT 90% SMALLER. WHY?... WELL, THE U.S. HOUSE INTERIOR APPROPRIATION SUBCOMMITTEE APPROVED A PROPOSED 90% BUDGET CUT TO THE NATIONAL ENDOWMENT FOR THE ARTS... THIS AFTER ALREADY CUTTING THE NEA BUDGET BY 40% IN 1995. THE NEA IS A MAJOR FUNDING RESOURCE FOR HUNDREDS, PERHAPS THOUSANDS OF ARTISTS AND ARTS ORGANIZATIONS THAT CREATE BEAUTY, PROVOKE THOUGHT & ADD CULTURAL RICHNESS TO COMMUNITIES BOTH RICH AND POOR, SMALL AND LARGE, NATIONWIDE. I JUST WANTED TO SHOW EVERYBODY HOW BIG A REDUCTION THIS WOULD BE BY SHRINKING MY COMIC BY THE SAME PERCENTAGE.... SORRY ABOUT THIS BUT I THOUGHT THAT IT WOULD BE THE BEST WAY TO GET THE POINT ACROSS.
BY THE WAY, THIS WEEK'S STRIP WAS PROBABLY MY BEST SO FAR... A HYSTERICAL TOUR DE FORCE FEATURING MIKE TYSON, 27 LACTATING HOLSTEIN COWS, AND A HALF EATEN PIECE OF DAY OLD FUDGE.. ANYWAY, TO PREVENT THIS CUT FROM OCCURING, CALL (202) 225-3121, & ASK TO BE CONNECTED TO YOUR MEMBER OF CONGRESS & TELL 'EM NOT TO DO IT!! Thanks!!
STOP

When this first ran, I listed the wrong area code for the number.
I called it and apologized to someone who sounded like an elderly Asian man.

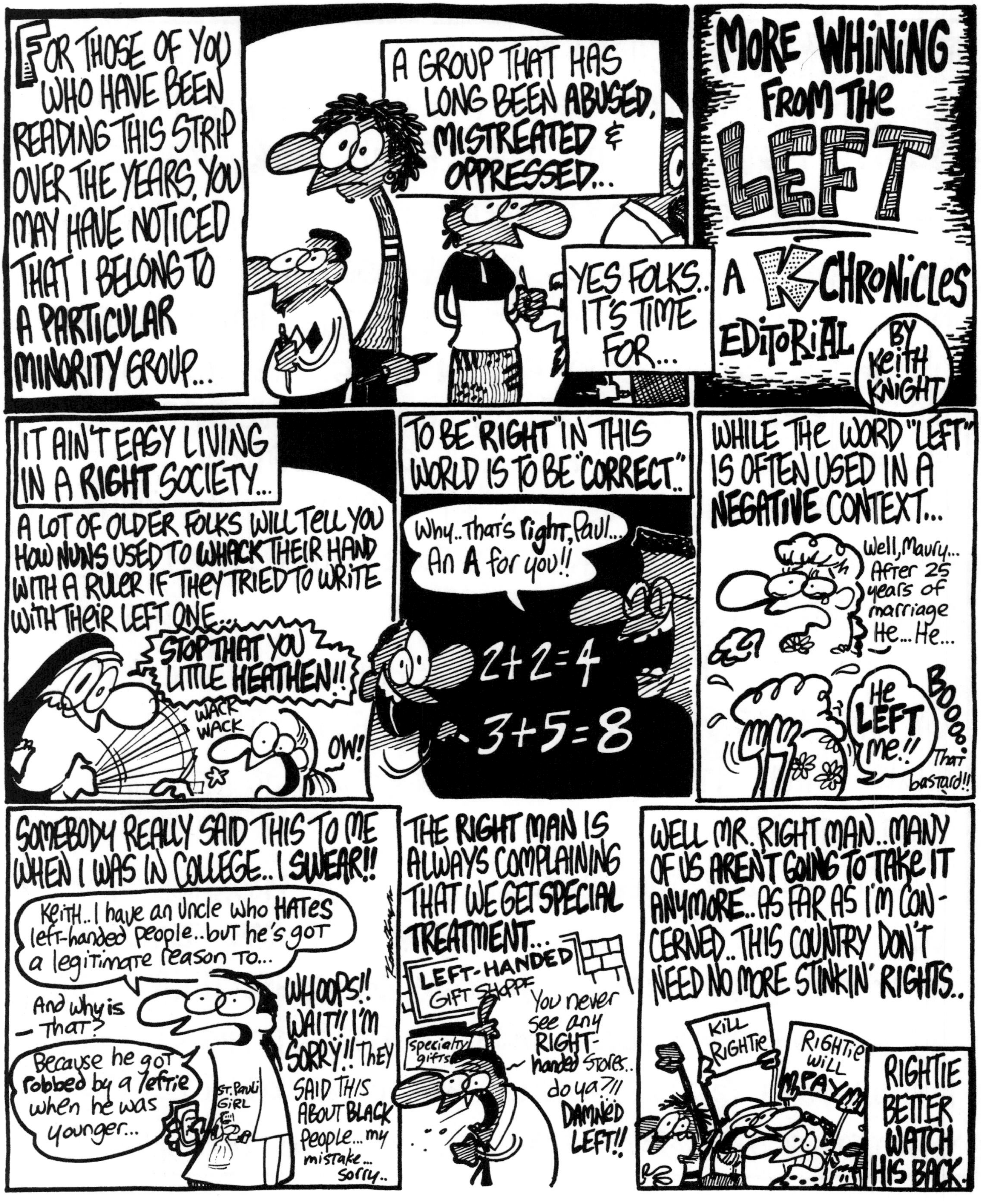

FOR THOSE OF YOU WHO HAVE BEEN READING THIS STRIP OVER THE YEARS, YOU MAY HAVE NOTICED THAT I BELONG TO A PARTICULAR MINORITY GROUP...
A GROUP THAT HAS LONG BEEN ABUSED, MISTREATED & OPPRESSED...
YES FOLKS.. IT'S TIME FOR...
MORE WHINING FROM THE LEFT
A K CHRONICLES EDITORIAL
BY KEITH KNIGHT
IT AIN'T EASY LIVING IN A RIGHT SOCIETY...
A LOT OF OLDER FOLKS WILL TELL YOU HOW NUNS USED TO WHACK THEIR HAND WITH A RULER IF THEY TRIED TO WRITE WITH THEIR LEFT ONE...
STOP THAT YOU LITTLE HEATHEN!!
WACK WACK
OW!
TO BE "RIGHT" IN THIS WORLD IS TO BE "CORRECT."
Why.. That's right, Paul... An A for you!!
2+2=4
3+5=8
WHILE THE WORD "LEFT" IS OFTEN USED IN A NEGATIVE CONTEXT...
Well, Maury... After 25 years of marriage He... He...
He LEFT me!!
Boooo.
That bastard!!
SOMEBODY REALLY SAID THIS TO ME WHEN I WAS IN COLLEGE.. I SWEAR!!
Keith.. I have an Uncle who HATES left-handed people.. but he's got a legitimate reason to...
And why is that?
Because he got robbed by a leftie when he was younger...
ST. PAULI GIRL
WHOOPS!! WAIT!! I'M SORRY!! THEY SAID THIS ABOUT BLACK people... my mistake... sorry..
THE RIGHT MAN IS ALWAYS COMPLAINING THAT WE GET SPECIAL TREATMENT...
LEFT-HANDED GIFT SHOPPE
specialty gifts
You never see any RIGHT-handed stores.. do ya?!!
DAMNED LEFT!!
WELL MR. RIGHT MAN.. MANY OF US AREN'T GOING TO TAKE IT ANYMORE.. AS FAR AS I'M CONCERNED.. THIS COUNTRY DON'T NEED NO MORE STINKIN' RIGHTS..
KILL RIGHTIE
RIGHTIE WILL PAY
RIGHTIE BETTER WATCH HIS BACK.

 A favorite that took on new meaning during the Bush era of left/right partisan hate politics.

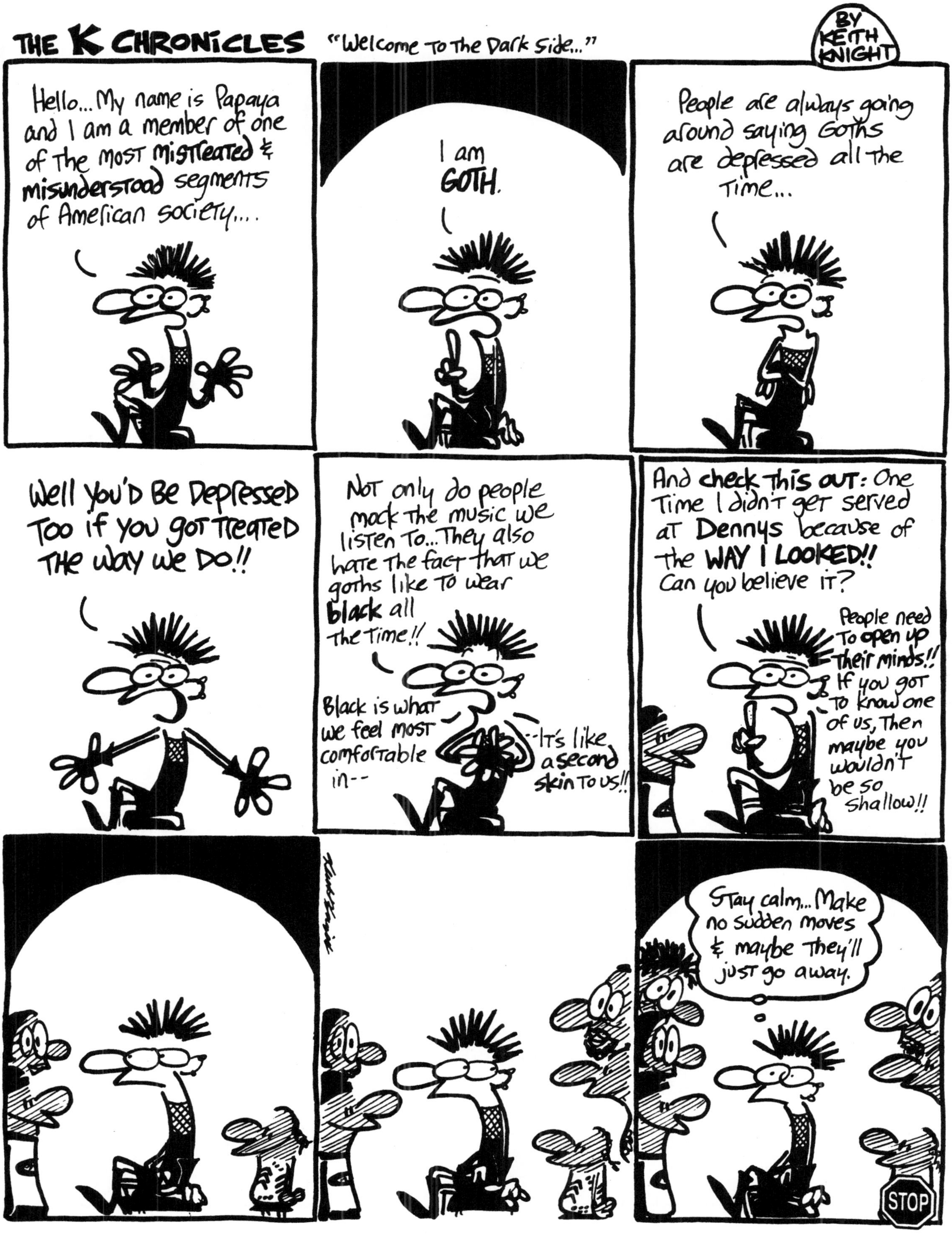
THE K CHRONICLES
"Welcome To The Dark Side..."
BY KEITH KNIGHT
Hello... My name is Papaya and I am a member of one of the most mistreated & misunderstood segments of American society....
I am GOTH.
People are always going around saying Goths are depressed all the time...
Well you'd be depressed too if you got treated the way we do!!
Not only do people mock the music we listen to... They also hate the fact that we goths like to wear black all the time!!
Black is what we feel most comfortable in--
--It's like a second skin to us!!
And check this out: One time I didn't get served at Dennys because of the WAY I LOOKED!! Can you believe it?
People need to open up their minds!! If you got to know one of us, then maybe you wouldn't be so shallow!!
Stay calm... Make no sudden moves & maybe they'll just go away.
STOP

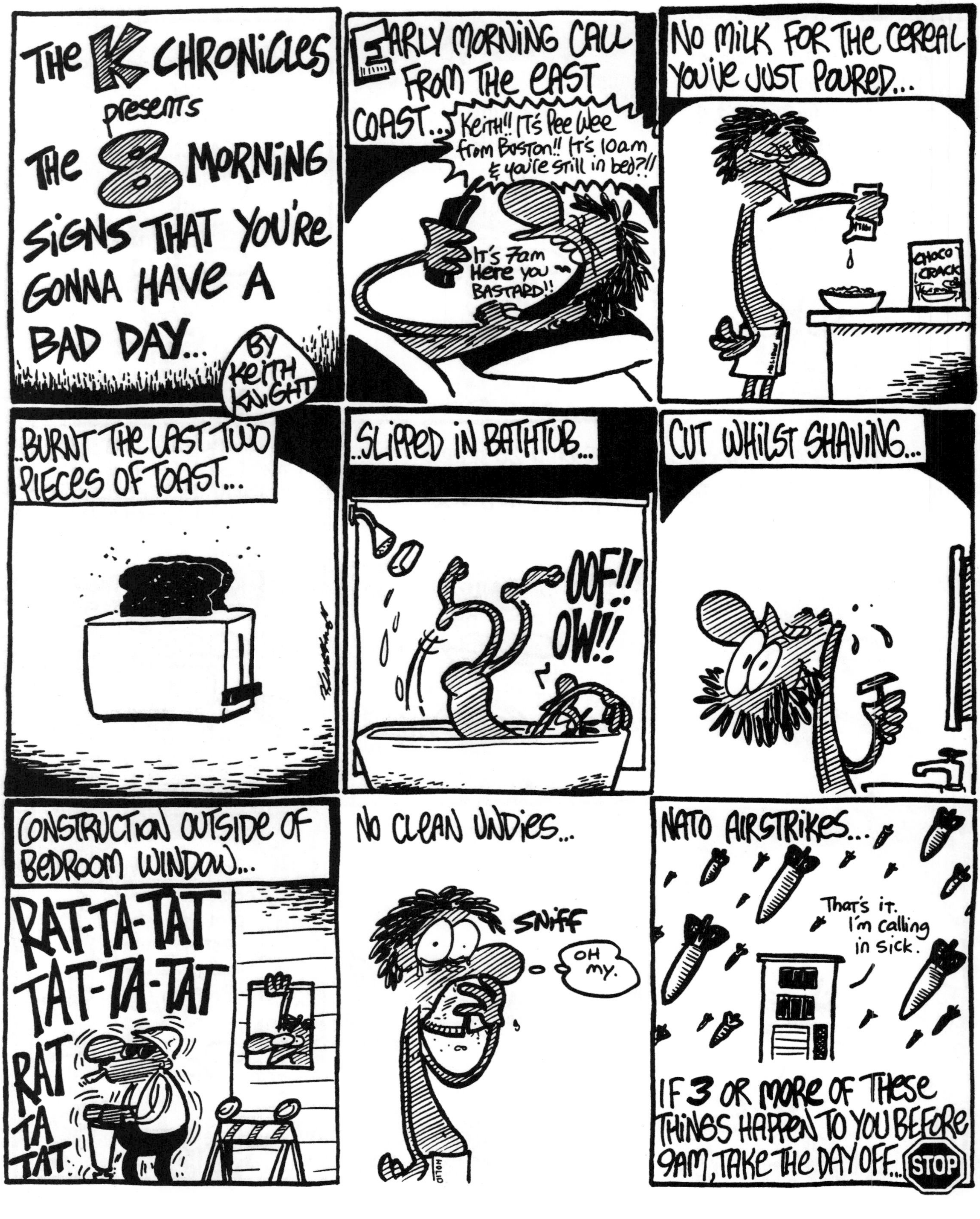
THE K CHRONICLES presents THE 8 MORNING SIGNS THAT YOU'RE GONNA HAVE A BAD DAY...
BY KEITH KNIGHT
EARLY MORNING CALL FROM THE EAST COAST...
KEITH!! IT'S PEE WEE FROM BOSTON!! IT'S 10am & you're still in bed?!!
It's 7am Here you BASTARD!!
NO MILK FOR THE CEREAL YOU'VE JUST POURED...
CHOCO CRACK
..BURNT THE LAST TWO PIECES OF TOAST...
..SLIPPED IN BATHTUB...
OOF!! OW!!
CUT WHILST SHAVING...
CONSTRUCTION OUTSIDE OF BEDROOM WINDOW...
RAT-TA-TAT TAT-TA-TAT RAT TA TAT
NO CLEAN UNDIES...
SNIFF
OH my.
NATO AIRSTRIKES...
That's it. I'm calling in sick.
IF 3 OR MORE OF THESE THINGS HAPPEN TO YOU BEFORE 9AM, TAKE THE DAY OFF...
STOP

The **K** CHRONICLES

BY KEITH KNIGHT

1 JUST VISITED YOSEMITE NATIONAL PARK RECENTLY...

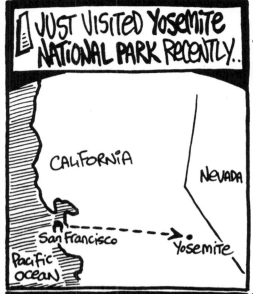

CALIFORNIA

NEVADA

San Francisco

Pacific Ocean

Yosemite

I WAS OUT THERE ATTENDING THE WEDDING OF STARK RAVING BRAD GONZO PERCUSSIONIST OF THE WORLD'S MOST INCREDIBLE BAND, THE MARGINAL PROPHETS*...

BRAD

ANDIE

* MY BAND.

YOSEMITE IS A GREAT PLACE TO GET MARRIED... HELL...IT'S A GREAT PLACE TO DO ANYTHING...

Grand Canyon of the Tuolumne

HETCH HETCHY Res.

Tuolumne Meadows

1189 SQUARE MILES OF STUNNING WATERFALLS, RUSHING RIVERS, ALPINE MEADOWS, HUNGRY BEARS & GRANITE CLIFFS...

A BUNCH OF FOLKS FROM THE WEDDING PARTY WENT ON A HIKE ALONG THE HETCH HETCHY RESERVOIR THE DAY BEFORE THE CEREMONY...

I WAS PSYCHED BECAUSE I COULD FINALLY PUT MY HIKING BOOTS TO GOOD USE...

HIKING BOOTS ARE LIKE THE SPORT UTILITY VEHICLES OF FOOTWEAR...

PEOPLE DON'T BUY THEM TO GO OUT INTO THE WOODS.. THEY BUY THEM BECAUSE THEY LOOK COOL...

SITTING IN CITY TRAFFIC

7 miles TO the gallon

BEEP!

ANYWAYS...AFTER ABOUT 20 MINUTES OF HIKING, OUR EXPEDITION CAME TO AN ABRUPT HALT...

WHOA!!

RATTLE RATTLE

I WAS A HALF-STEP AWAY FROM AN INTIMATE ENCOUNTER WITH A 2-FOOT LONG RATTLESNAKE!!

RATTLE

..IT WAS GIVING ME A "DON'T TREAD ON ME" WARNING RATTLE.

YEESH...I GOTTA TELL YA.. I DIG THE GREAT OUTDOORS & ALL...

VH1 Behind the Music

..BUT IT'S INCIDENTS LIKE THAT THAT MAKE ME THINK CABLE T.V. AIN'T REALLY THAT BAD...

STOP

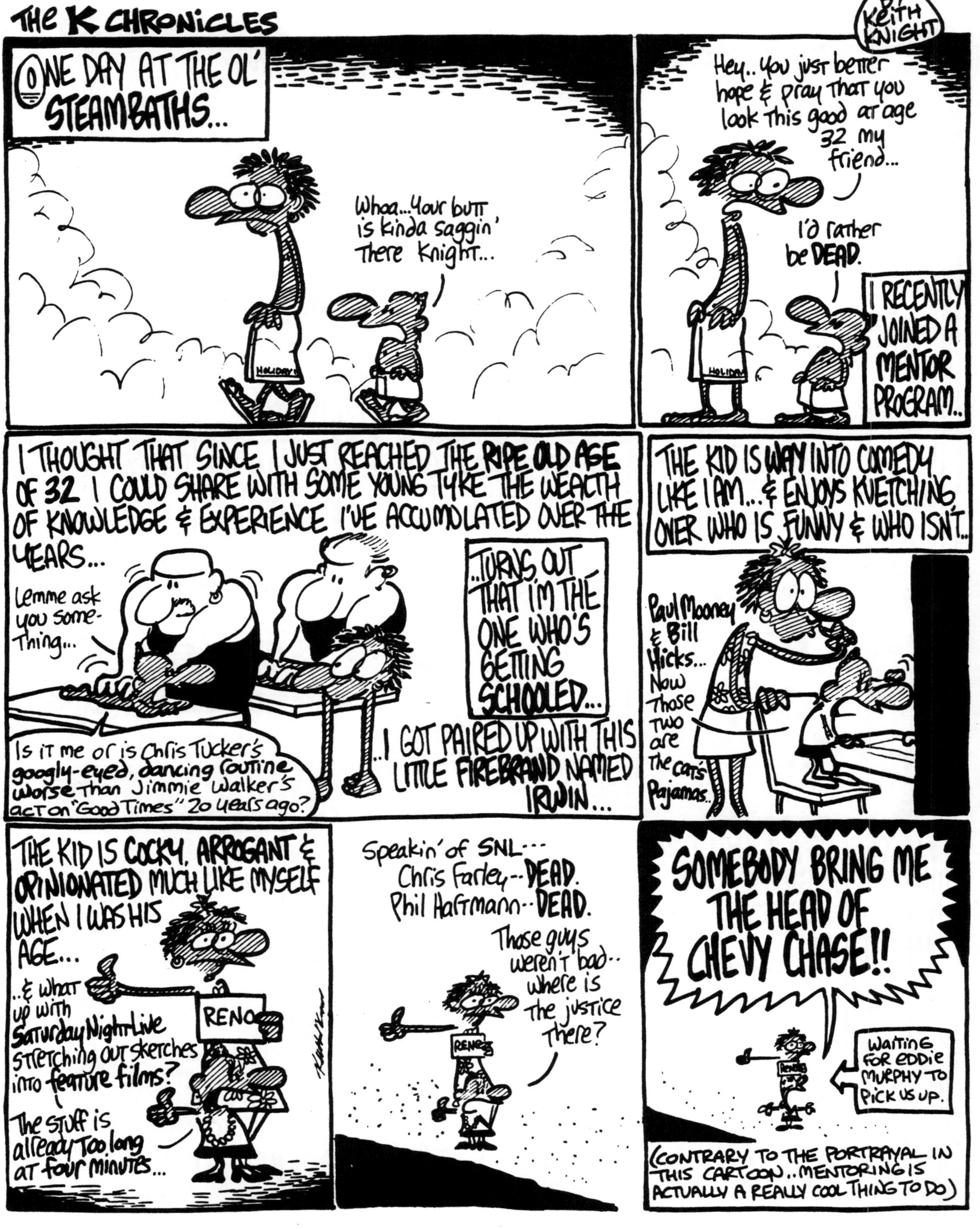
THE K CHRONICLES
BY KEITH KNIGHT
ONE DAY AT THE OL' STEAMBATHS...
Whoa...Your butt is kinda saggin' there Knight...
Hey.. you just better hope & pray that you look this good at age 32 my friend...
I'd rather be DEAD.
I RECENTLY JOINED A MENTOR PROGRAM..
I THOUGHT THAT SINCE I JUST REACHED THE RIPE OLD AGE OF 32 I COULD SHARE WITH SOME YOUNG TYKE THE WEALTH OF KNOWLEDGE & EXPERIENCE I'VE ACCUMOLATED OVER THE YEARS...
Lemme ask you some-thing...
Is it me or is Chris Tucker's googly-eyed, dancing routine worse than Jimmie Walker's act on "Good Times" 20 years ago?
..TURNS OUT THAT I'M THE ONE WHO'S GETTING SCHOOLED...
..I GOT PAIRED UP WITH THIS LITTLE FIREBRAND NAMED IRWIN...
THE KID IS WAY INTO COMEDY LIKE I AM... & ENJOYS KVETCHING OVER WHO IS FUNNY & WHO ISN'T..
Paul Mooney & Bill Hicks... Now those two are the cat's pajamas..
THE KID IS COCKY, ARROGANT & OPINIONATED MUCH LIKE MYSELF WHEN I WAS HIS AGE...
..& what up with Saturday Night Live stretching out sketches into feature films?
The stuff is already too long at four minutes...
RENO
Speakin' of SNL... Chris Farley.. DEAD. Phil Hartmann.. DEAD.
Those guys weren't bad.. where is the justice there?
RENO
SOMEBODY BRING ME THE HEAD OF CHEVY CHASE!!
WAITING FOR EDDIE MURPHY TO PICK US UP.
RENO
(CONTRARY TO THE PORTRAYAL IN THIS CARTOON..MENTORING IS ACTUALLY A REALLY COOL THING TO DO)

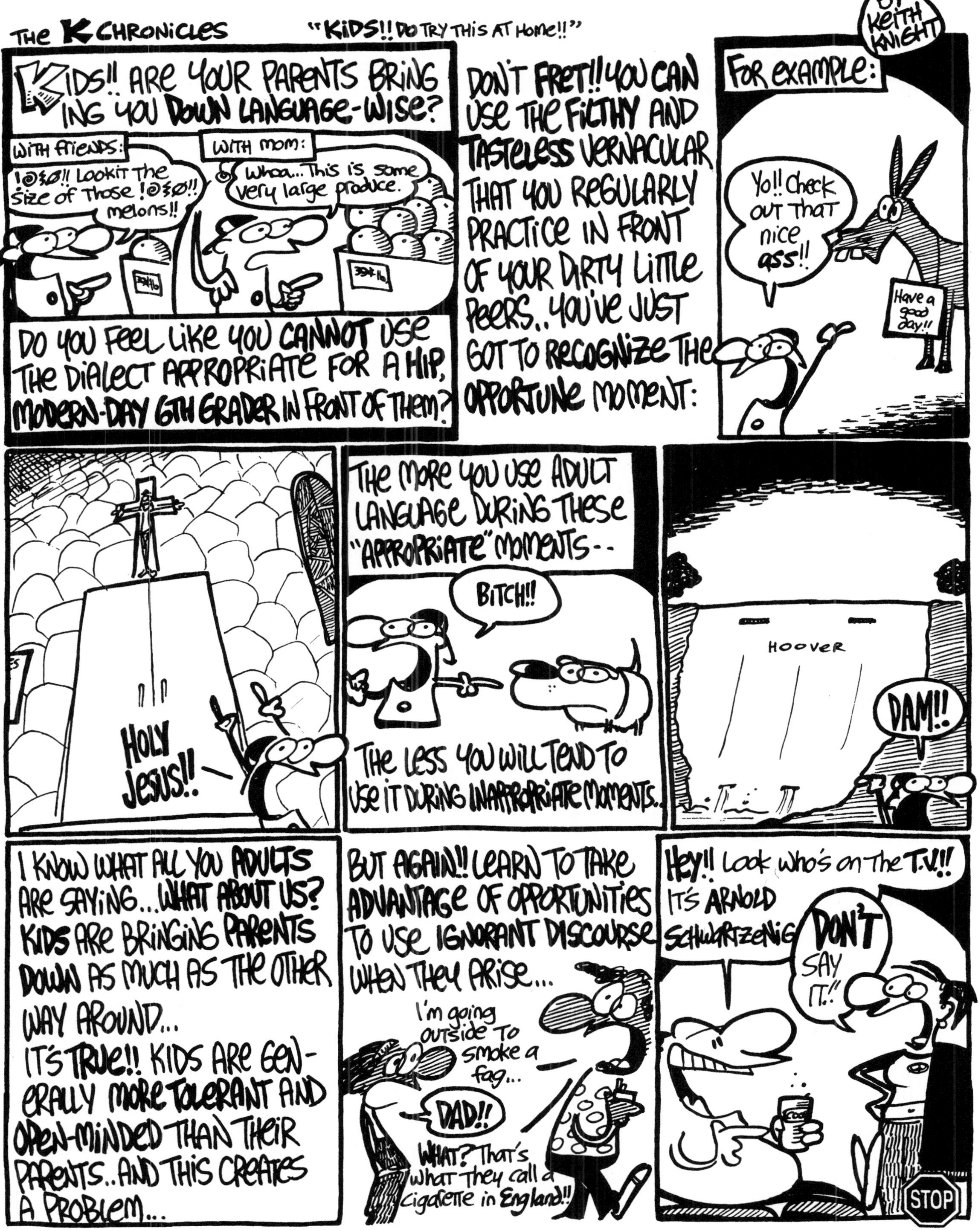
THE K CHRONICLES
"KIDS!! DO TRY THIS AT HOME!!"
BY KEITH KNIGHT
KIDS!! ARE YOUR PARENTS BRINGING YOU DOWN LANGUAGE-WISE?
WITH FRIENDS:
!@$&!! LOOKIT THE SIZE OF THOSE !@$&!! MELONS!!
WITH MOM:
WHOA... THIS IS SOME VERY LARGE PRODUCE.
DO YOU FEEL LIKE YOU CANNOT USE THE DIALECT APPROPRIATE FOR A HIP, MODERN-DAY 6TH GRADER IN FRONT OF THEM?
DON'T FRET!! YOU CAN USE THE FILTHY AND TASTELESS VERNACULAR THAT YOU REGULARLY PRACTICE IN FRONT OF YOUR DIRTY LITTLE PEERS.. YOU'VE JUST GOT TO RECOGNIZE THE OPPORTUNE MOMENT:
FOR EXAMPLE:
YO!! CHECK OUT THAT NICE ASS!!
HAVE A GOOD DAY!!
HOLY JESUS!!..
THE MORE YOU USE ADULT LANGUAGE DURING THESE "APPROPRIATE" MOMENTS..
BITCH!!
THE LESS YOU WILL TEND TO USE IT DURING INAPPROPRIATE MOMENTS..
HOOVER
DAM!!
I KNOW WHAT ALL YOU ADULTS ARE SAYING... WHAT ABOUT US? KIDS ARE BRINGING PARENTS DOWN AS MUCH AS THE OTHER WAY AROUND... IT'S TRUE!! KIDS ARE GENERALLY MORE TOLERANT AND OPEN-MINDED THAN THEIR PARENTS.. AND THIS CREATES A PROBLEM...
BUT AGAIN!! LEARN TO TAKE ADVANTAGE OF OPPORTUNITIES TO USE IGNORANT DISCOURSE WHEN THEY ARISE...
I'M GOING OUTSIDE TO SMOKE A FAG...
DAD!!
WHAT? THAT'S WHAT THEY CALL A CIGARETTE IN ENGLAND!!
HEY!! LOOK WHO'S ON THE T.V.!! IT'S ARNOLD SCHWARTZENIG
DON'T SAY IT!!
STOP

Shannon Wheeler made a funny ad for me with the third panel of this strip.

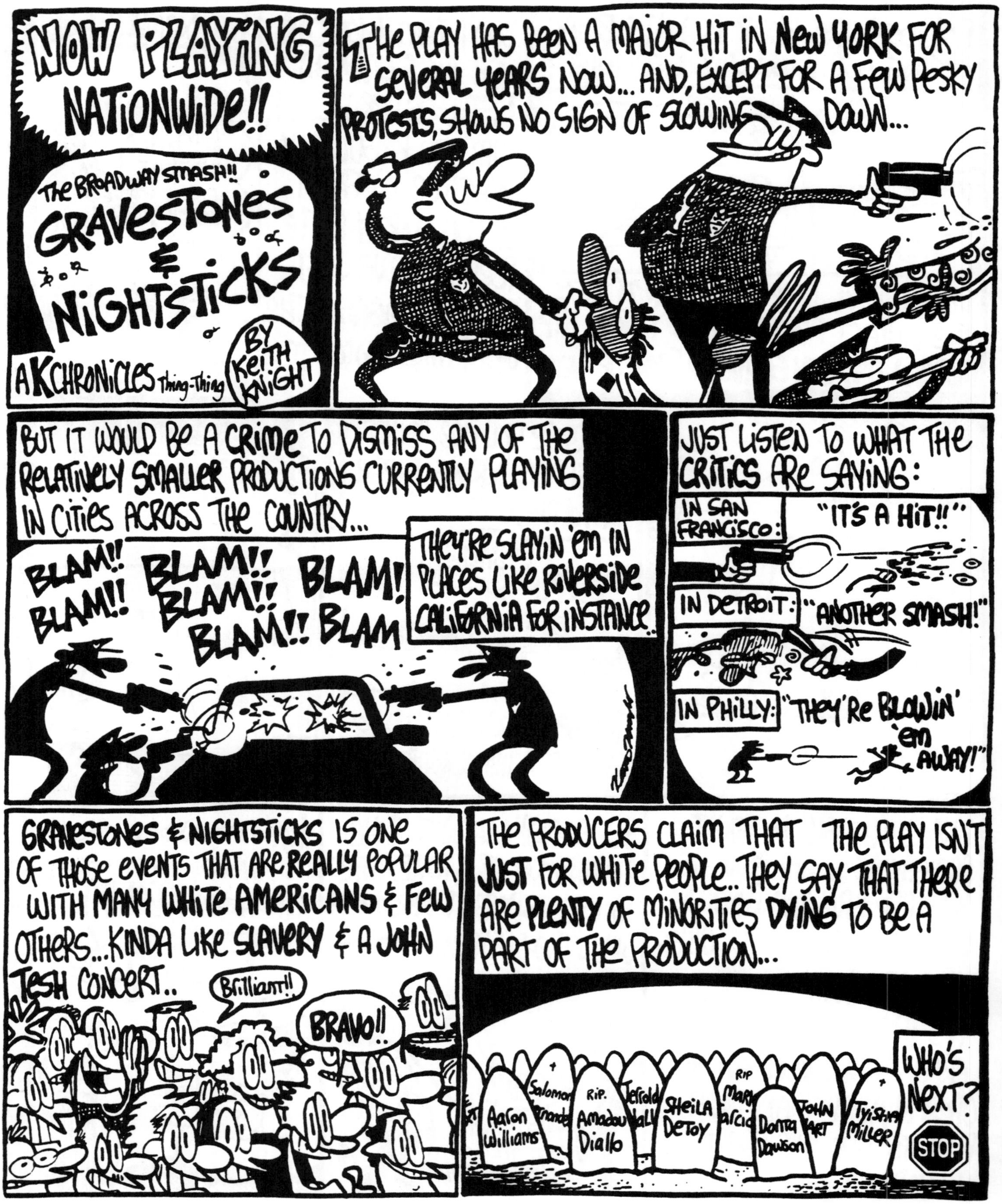
NOW PLAYING NATIONWIDE!!
THE BROADWAY SMASH!!
GRAVESTONES & NIGHTSTICKS
A K CHRONICLES Thing-Thing
BY KEITH KNIGHT
THE PLAY HAS BEEN A MAJOR HIT IN NEW YORK FOR SEVERAL YEARS NOW... AND, EXCEPT FOR A FEW PESKY PROTESTS, SHOWS NO SIGN OF SLOWING DOWN...
BUT IT WOULD BE A CRIME TO DISMISS ANY OF THE RELATIVELY SMALLER PRODUCTIONS CURRENTLY PLAYING IN CITIES ACROSS THE COUNTRY...
THEY'RE SLAYIN' 'EM IN PLACES LIKE RIVERSIDE CALIFORNIA FOR INSTANCE..
BLAM!! BLAM!! BLAM!! BLAM!! BLAM!! BLAM!! BLAM!! BLAM
JUST LISTEN TO WHAT THE CRITICS ARE SAYING:
IN SAN FRANCISCO: "IT'S A HIT!!"
IN DETROIT: "ANOTHER SMASH!"
IN PHILLY: "THEY'RE BLOWIN' 'EM AWAY!"
GRAVESTONES & NIGHTSTICKS IS ONE OF THOSE EVENTS THAT ARE REALLY POPULAR WITH MANY WHITE AMERICANS & FEW OTHERS...KINDA LIKE SLAVERY & A JOHN TESH CONCERT..
Brilliant!!
BRAVO!!
THE PRODUCERS CLAIM THAT THE PLAY ISN'T JUST FOR WHITE PEOPLE.. THEY SAY THAT THERE ARE PLENTY OF MINORITIES DYING TO BE A PART OF THE PRODUCTION...
Aaron Williams
Salomon
R.I.P. Amadou Diallo
Jerrold
SHEILA DETOY
RIP
Donta Dawson
JOHN
Tyisha Miller
WHO'S NEXT?
STOP

 So many more have died since this strip that I recently did a second version.

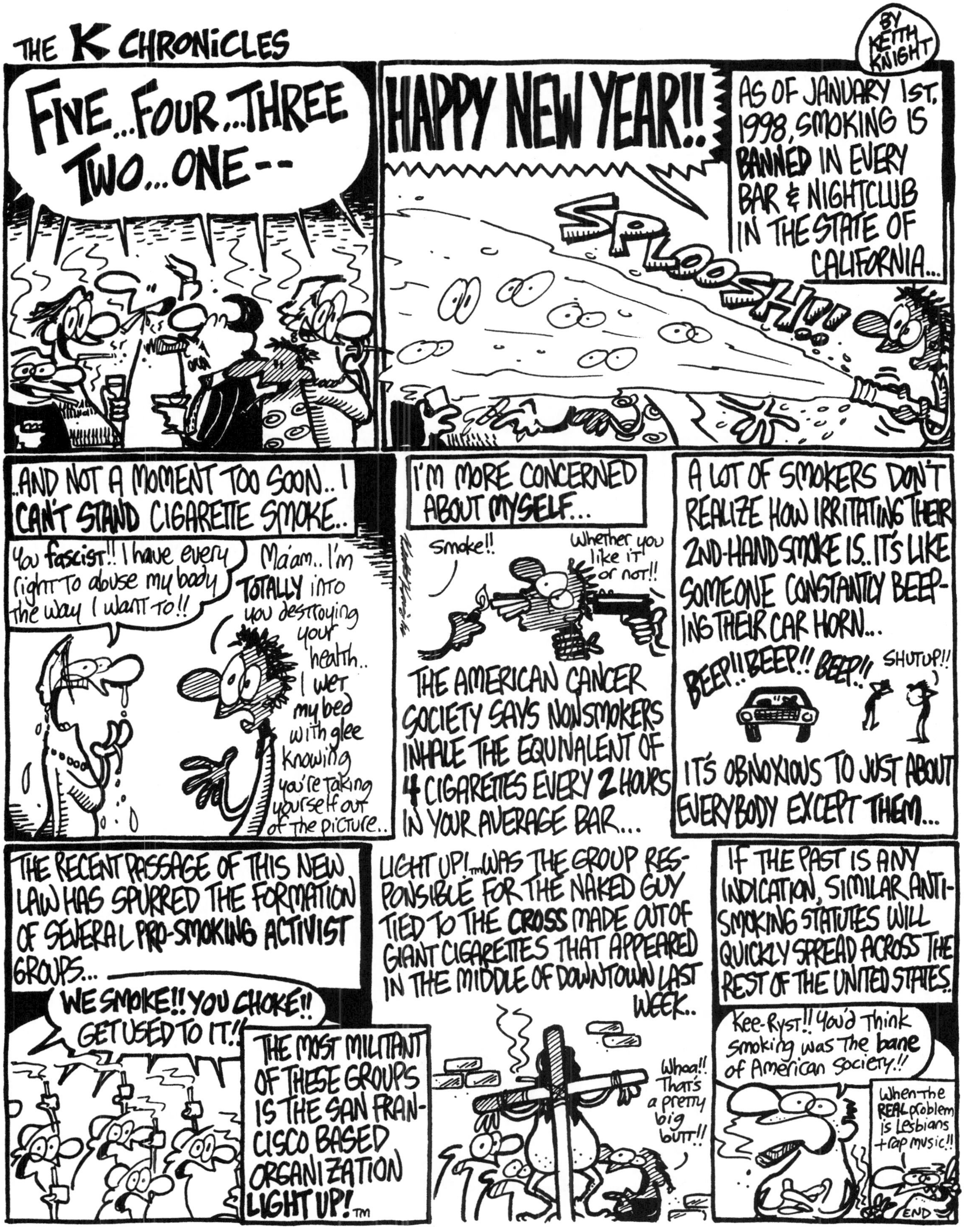
THE K CHRONICLES
BY KEITH KNIGHT
FIVE...FOUR...THREE TWO...ONE--
HAPPY NEW YEAR!!
AS OF JANUARY 1ST, 1998, SMOKING IS BANNED IN EVERY BAR & NIGHTCLUB IN THE STATE OF CALIFORNIA...
SPLOOSH!!
...AND NOT A MOMENT TOO SOON.. I CAN'T STAND CIGARETTE SMOKE..
You fascist!! I have every right to abuse my body the way I want to!!
Ma'am.. I'm TOTALLY into you destroying your health.. I wet my bed with glee knowing you're taking yourself out of the picture..
I'M MORE CONCERNED ABOUT MYSELF...
smoke!!
Whether you like it or not!!
THE AMERICAN CANCER SOCIETY SAYS NONSMOKERS INHALE THE EQUIVALENT OF 4 CIGARETTES EVERY 2 HOURS IN YOUR AVERAGE BAR...
A LOT OF SMOKERS DON'T REALIZE HOW IRRITATING THEIR 2ND-HAND SMOKE IS.. IT'S LIKE SOMEONE CONSTANTLY BEEPING THEIR CAR HORN...
BEEP!! BEEP!! BEEP!!
SHUTUP!!
IT'S OBNOXIOUS TO JUST ABOUT EVERYBODY EXCEPT THEM...
THE RECENT PASSAGE OF THIS NEW LAW HAS SPURRED THE FORMATION OF SEVERAL PRO-SMOKING ACTIVIST GROUPS...
WE SMOKE!! YOU CHOKE!! GET USED TO IT!!
THE MOST MILITANT OF THESE GROUPS IS THE SAN FRANCISCO BASED ORGANIZATION LIGHT UP!™
LIGHT UP!™ WAS THE GROUP RESPONSIBLE FOR THE NAKED GUY TIED TO THE CROSS MADE OUT OF GIANT CIGARETTES THAT APPEARED IN THE MIDDLE OF DOWNTOWN LAST WEEK..
Whoa!! That's a pretty big butt!!
IF THE PAST IS ANY INDICATION, SIMILAR ANTI-SMOKING STATUTES WILL QUICKLY SPREAD ACROSS THE REST OF THE UNITED STATES..
Kee-Ryst!! You'd think smoking was the bane of American society!!
When the REAL problem is Lesbians + rap music!!
END

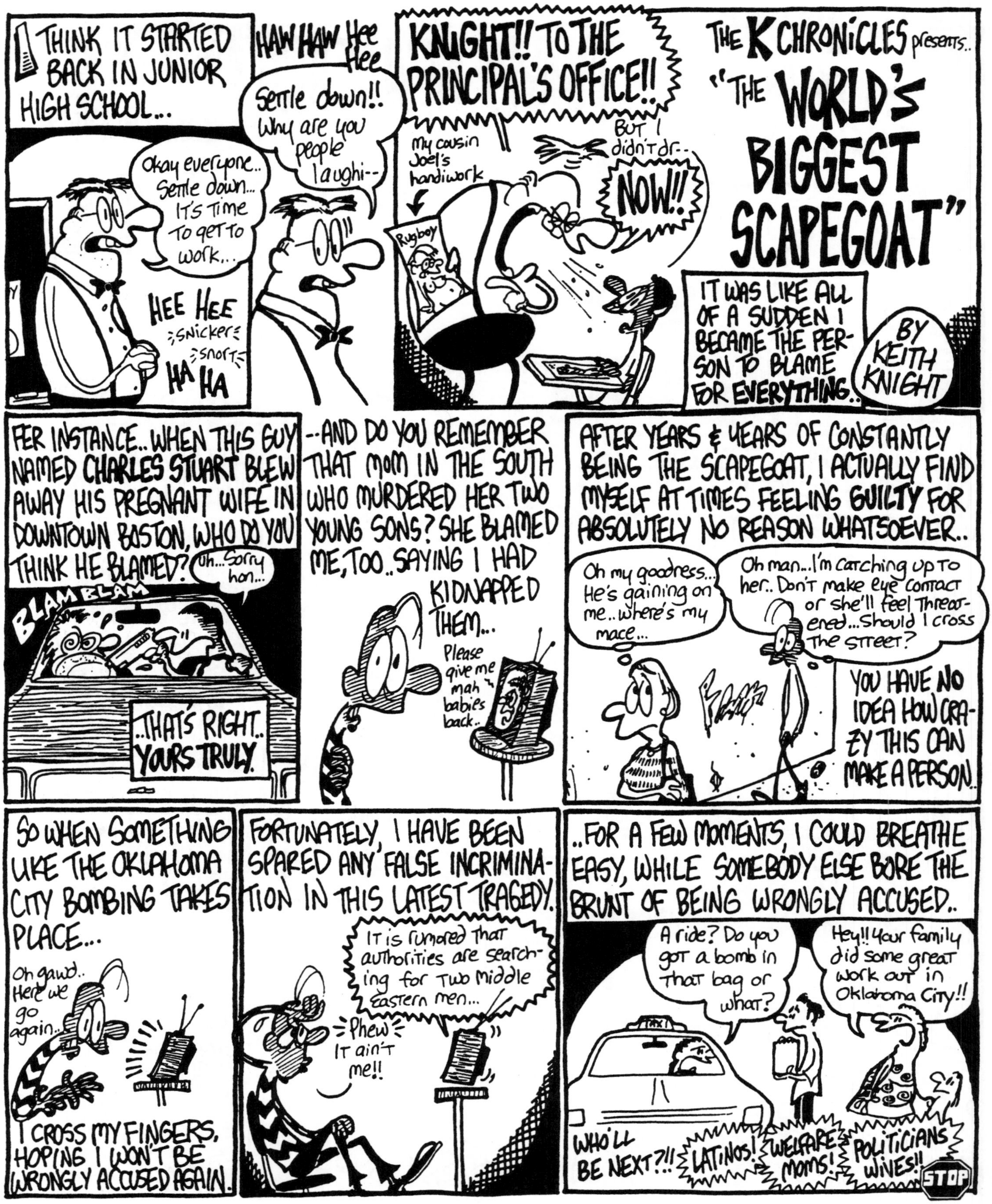

I THINK IT STARTED BACK IN JUNIOR HIGH SCHOOL...
Okay everyone.. Settle down... It's time to get to work...
HEE HEE
snicker
snort
HA HA
HAW HAW Hee Hee
Settle down!! Why are you people laughi--
KNIGHT!! TO THE PRINCIPAL'S OFFICE!!
My cousin Joel's handiwork
Rugboy
But I didn't dr--
NOW!!
THE K CHRONICLES presents..
"THE WORLD'S BIGGEST SCAPEGOAT"
IT WAS LIKE ALL OF A SUDDEN I BECAME THE PERSON TO BLAME FOR EVERYTHING..
BY KEITH KNIGHT
FER INSTANCE.. WHEN THIS GUY NAMED CHARLES STUART BLEW AWAY HIS PREGNANT WIFE IN DOWNTOWN BOSTON, WHO DO YOU THINK HE BLAMED?
Uh...Sorry hon...
BLAM BLAM
..THAT'S RIGHT.. YOURS TRULY.
--AND DO YOU REMEMBER THAT MOM IN THE SOUTH WHO MURDERED HER TWO YOUNG SONS? SHE BLAMED ME, TOO.. SAYING I HAD KIDNAPPED THEM...
Please give me mah babies back..
AFTER YEARS & YEARS OF CONSTANTLY BEING THE SCAPEGOAT, I ACTUALLY FIND MYSELF AT TIMES FEELING GUILTY FOR ABSOLUTELY NO REASON WHATSOEVER..
Oh my goodness... He's gaining on me.. where's my mace...
Oh man...I'm catching up to her.. Don't make eye contact or she'll feel threatened... Should I cross the street?
YOU HAVE NO IDEA HOW CRAZY THIS CAN MAKE A PERSON..
SO WHEN SOMETHING LIKE THE OKLAHOMA CITY BOMBING TAKES PLACE...
Oh gawd.. Here we go again..
I CROSS MY FINGERS, HOPING I WON'T BE WRONGLY ACCUSED AGAIN.
FORTUNATELY, I HAVE BEEN SPARED ANY FALSE INCRIMINATION IN THIS LATEST TRAGEDY.
It is rumored that authorities are searching for two Middle Eastern men...
Phew It ain't me!!
..FOR A FEW MOMENTS, I COULD BREATHE EASY, WHILE SOMEBODY ELSE BORE THE BRUNT OF BEING WRONGLY ACCUSED..
TAXI
A ride? Do you got a bomb in that bag or what?
Hey!! Your family did some great work out in Oklahoma City!!
WHO'LL BE NEXT?!!
LATINOS!
WELFARE MOMS!
POLITICIANS WIVES!!
STOP

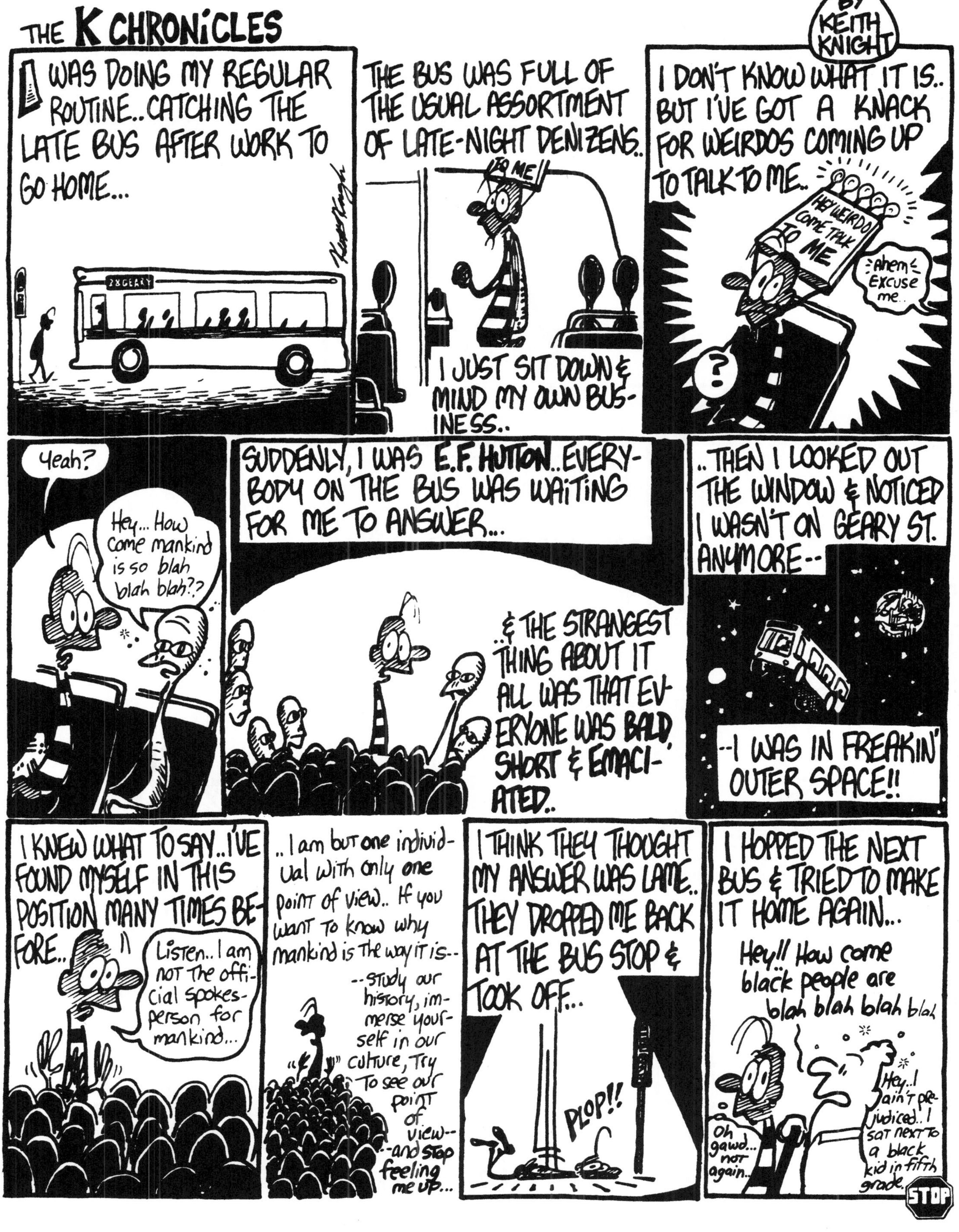
THE K CHRONICLES
BY KEITH KNIGHT
I WAS DOING MY REGULAR ROUTINE.. CATCHING THE LATE BUS AFTER WORK TO GO HOME...
28 GEARY
THE BUS WAS FULL OF THE USUAL ASSORTMENT OF LATE-NIGHT DENIZENS..
I JUST SIT DOWN & MIND MY OWN BUSINESS..
I DON'T KNOW WHAT IT IS.. BUT I'VE GOT A KNACK FOR WEIRDOS COMING UP TO TALK TO ME..
HEY WEIRDO COME TALK TO ME
ahem Excuse me..
?
Yeah?
Hey... How come mankind is so blah blah blah?!?
SUDDENLY, I WAS E.F. HUTTON.. EVERYBODY ON THE BUS WAS WAITING FOR ME TO ANSWER...
..& THE STRANGEST THING ABOUT IT ALL WAS THAT EVERYONE WAS BALD, SHORT & EMACIATED..
..THEN I LOOKED OUT THE WINDOW & NOTICED I WASN'T ON GEARY ST. ANYMORE--
--I WAS IN FREAKIN' OUTER SPACE!!
I KNEW WHAT TO SAY.. I'VE FOUND MYSELF IN THIS POSITION MANY TIMES BEFORE..
Listen.. I am not the official spokesperson for mankind...
.. I am but one individual with only one point of view.. If you want to know why mankind is the way it is--
--study our history, immerse yourself in our culture, Try to see our point of view--
--and stop feeling me up...
I THINK THEY THOUGHT MY ANSWER WAS LAME.. THEY DROPPED ME BACK AT THE BUS STOP & TOOK OFF...
PLOP!!
I HOPPED THE NEXT BUS & TRIED TO MAKE IT HOME AGAIN...
Hey!! How come black people are blah blah blah blah
Oh gawd... not again..
Hey..I ain't prejudiced..I sat next to a black kid in fifth grade.
STOP

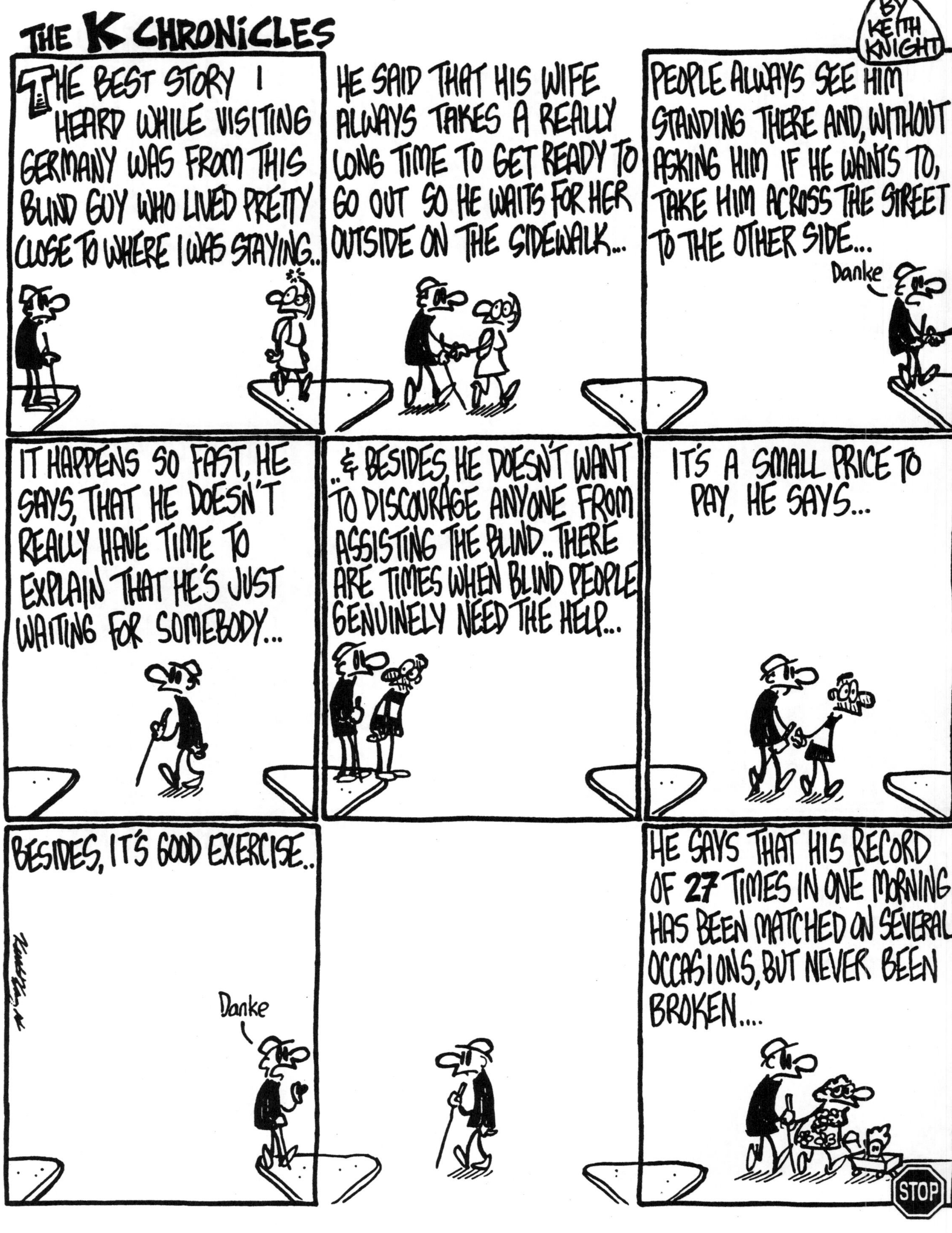
THE K CHRONICLES
BY KEITH KNIGHT
THE BEST STORY I HEARD WHILE VISITING GERMANY WAS FROM THIS BLIND GUY WHO LIVED PRETTY CLOSE TO WHERE I WAS STAYING..
HE SAID THAT HIS WIFE ALWAYS TAKES A REALLY LONG TIME TO GET READY TO GO OUT SO HE WAITS FOR HER OUTSIDE ON THE SIDEWALK...
PEOPLE ALWAYS SEE HIM STANDING THERE AND, WITHOUT ASKING HIM IF HE WANTS TO, TAKE HIM ACROSS THE STREET TO THE OTHER SIDE...
Danke
IT HAPPENS SO FAST, HE SAYS, THAT HE DOESN'T REALLY HAVE TIME TO EXPLAIN THAT HE'S JUST WAITING FOR SOMEBODY...
..& BESIDES, HE DOESN'T WANT TO DISCOURAGE ANYONE FROM ASSISTING THE BLIND.. THERE ARE TIMES WHEN BLIND PEOPLE GENUINELY NEED THE HELP...
IT'S A SMALL PRICE TO PAY, HE SAYS...
BESIDES, IT'S GOOD EXERCISE..
Danke
HE SAYS THAT HIS RECORD OF 27 TIMES IN ONE MORNING HAS BEEN MATCHED ON SEVERAL OCCASIONS, BUT NEVER BEEN BROKEN....
STOP

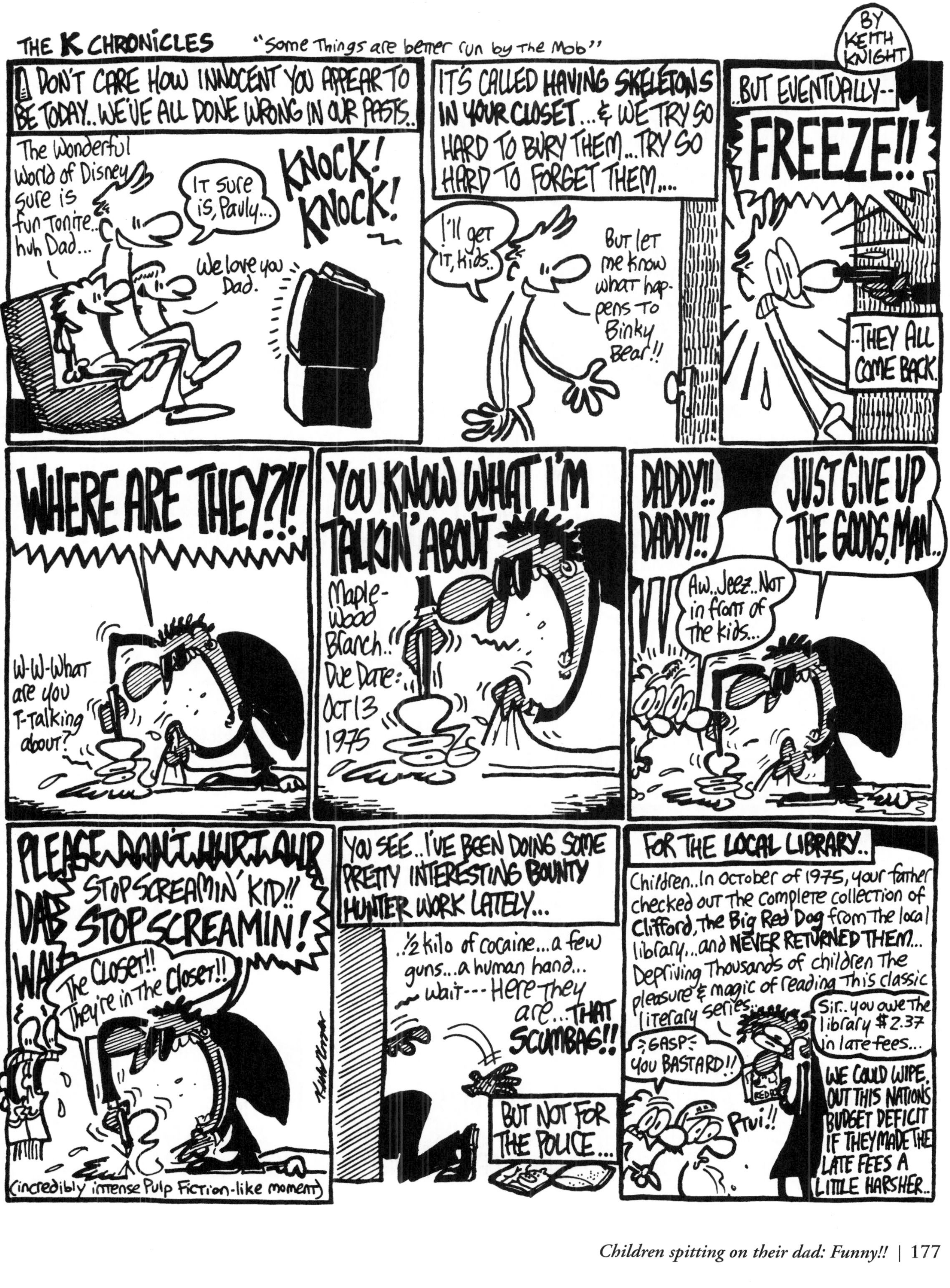
THE K CHRONICLES
"Some Things are better run by The Mob"
BY KEITH KNIGHT
I DON'T CARE HOW INNOCENT YOU APPEAR TO BE TODAY.. WE'VE ALL DONE WRONG IN OUR PASTS..
The Wonderful World of Disney sure is fun Tonite.. huh Dad...
IT sure is, Pauly...
We love you Dad.
KNOCK! KNOCK!
IT'S CALLED HAVING SKELETONS IN YOUR CLOSET... & WE TRY SO HARD TO BURY THEM... TRY SO HARD TO FORGET THEM....
I'll get it, kids..
But let me know what happens to Binky Bear!!
..BUT EVENTUALLY--
FREEZE!!
..THEY ALL COME BACK.
WHERE ARE THEY?!!..
W-W-What are you T-Talking about?
YOU KNOW WHAT I'M TALKIN' ABOUT
Maple-wood Branch.. Due Date: Oct 13 1975
DADDY!!.. DADDY!!..
JUST GIVE UP THE GOODS, MAN..
Aw..Jeez..Not in front of the kids...
PLEASE DON'T HURT OUR DAD
STOP SCREAMIN' KID!! STOP SCREAMIN!
The CLOSET!! They're in the CLOSET!!
(incredibly intense Pulp Fiction-like moment)
YOU SEE.. I'VE BEEN DOING SOME PRETTY INTERESTING BOUNTY HUNTER WORK LATELY...
..½ kilo of cocaine... a few guns... a human hand... wait--- Here they are... THAT SCUMBAG!!
BUT NOT FOR THE POLICE...
FOR THE LOCAL LIBRARY..
Children.. In October of 1975, your father checked out the complete collection of Clifford, the Big Red Dog from the local library... and NEVER RETURNED THEM... Depriving thousands of children the pleasure & magic of reading this classic literary series..
Sir.. you owe the library $2.37 in late fees...
GASP
You BASTARD!!
Ptui!!
WE COULD WIPE OUT THIS NATION'S BUDGET DEFICIT IF THEY MADE THE LATE FEES A LITTLE HARSHER..

MOST AMERICAN BOROUGHS LOOK FORWARD TO THE DAILY APPEARANCE OF THEIR FRIENDLY NEIGHBORHOOD ICE CREAM TRUCK...

YANNI, GALLAGHER & DOUG HENNING: CLONES — Exclusive photographs

BUT IN SAN FRANCISCO'S HAIGHT/ASHBURY DISTRICT...

...WE WELCOME THE DAILY APPEARANCE OF OUR FRIENDLY NEIGHBORHOOD CONSPIRACY TRUCK...

THE K CHRONICLES

BY KEITH KNIGHT

SCREW CNN!! EVERYTHING I NEED TO KNOW COMES STRAIGHT FROM THE MAN WITH THE SCOOP: FRANK "THE MOOCH"...

Whaddaya got on Sonny Bono's death?

You kiddin' me? It was an obvious hit by The Democratic party...

I got the tapes right here..

They were settling the score for the Republican hit on Kennedy the week before..

THE MOOCH HAS GOT THE SKINNY ON EVERYTHING...

--INCLUDING TAPES DOCUMENTING THE TIES BETWEEN CHAMPIONSHIP FIGURE SKATING & THE WORLD WRESTLING FEDERATION...

YOU SEE.. FIGURE SKATING TURNED TO THE W.W.F. FOR HELP IN RAISING PUBLIC AWARENESS OF THE SPORT...

IT WAS THE W.W.F. THAT CONJURED UP THE NANCY KERRIGAN/TONYA HARDING KNEECAP DEBACLE..

WAP WAP

DID ANYBODY CARE ABOUT FIGURE SKATING BEFORE THIS HAPPENED? NOW SKATING HAS A $10,000,000 T.V. CONTRACT.

BUT THE BIGGEST SCOOP THE MOOCH HAS GOT GOIN' IS THAT DIANA, PRINCESS OF WALES, AIN'T DEAD!!

HE SAYS DIANA WASN'T EVEN IN THE CAR THAT CRASHED DURING THAT FATEFUL NIGHT IN GAY PARIS...

HE SAYS SHE WAS IN A SECRETLY LOCATED STYLING SALON GETTING A "YENTL-LIKE" MAKEOVER...

Was it just me or did Prince William look even more like his mom after she "died"?

PEOPLE — mike william

SHE IS NOW POSING AS HER OLDEST SON, WILLIAM, WHO IS CURRENTLY IN LINE TO BECOME THE KING OF ENGLAND...

IT WILL BE THE ULTIMATE SLAP IN THE FACE TO THE ROYAL FAMILY WHEN "WILLIAM" IS CROWNED KING & HE REVEALS HIS ROYAL BREASTS TO THE PUBLIC...

BLOODY HELL!!

LONG LIVE KING DIANA!!

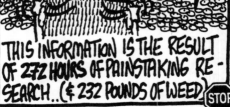

THIS INFORMATION IS THE RESULT OF 272 HOURS OF PAINSTAKING RESEARCH.. (& 232 POUNDS OF WEED) STOP

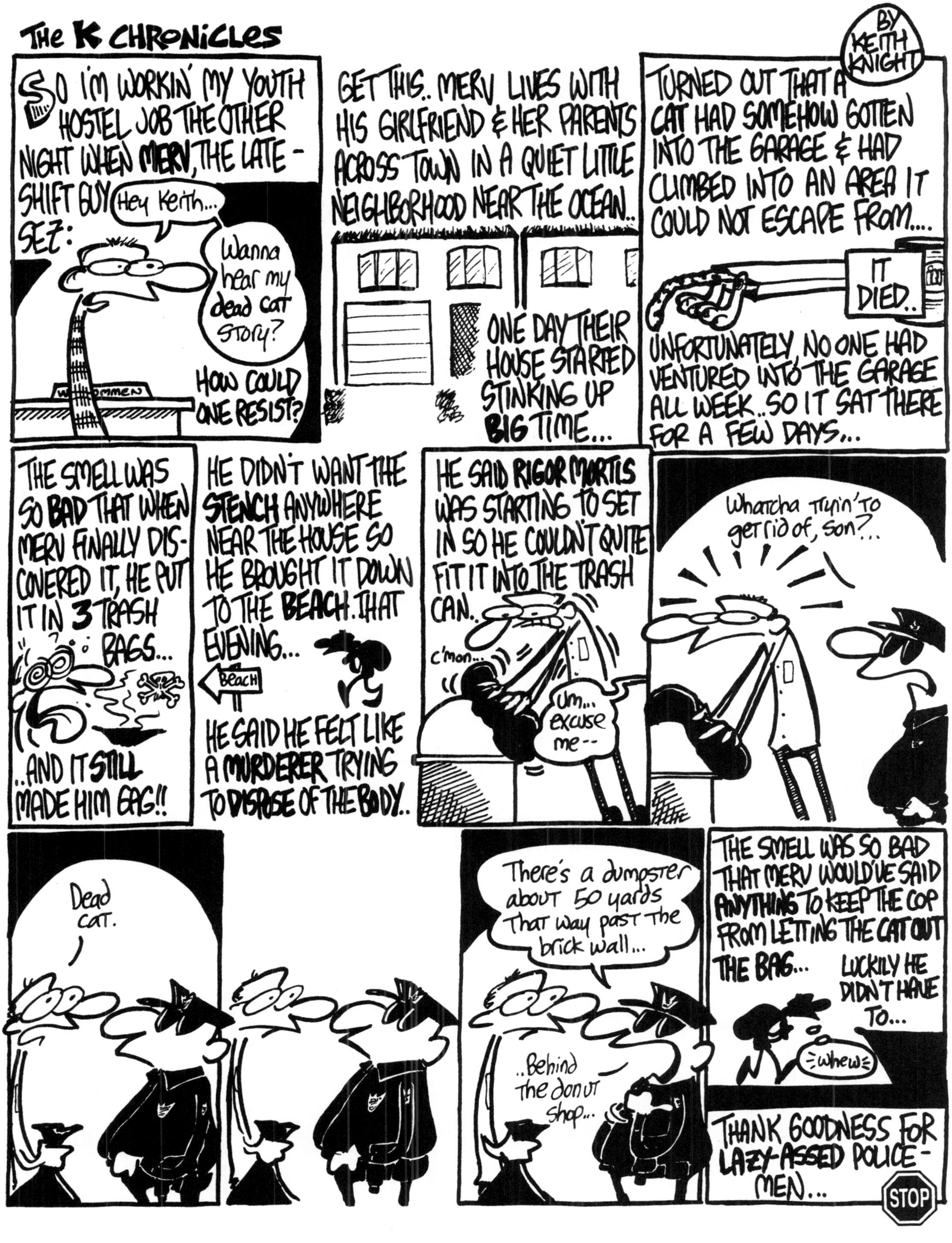
The K Chronicles
By Keith Knight
So I'm workin' my youth hostel job the other night when Merv, the late-shift guy sez:
Hey Keith...
Wanna hear my dead cat story?
How could one resist?
Get this.. Merv lives with his girlfriend & her parents across town in a quiet little neighborhood near the ocean..
One day their house started stinking up big time...
Turned out that a cat had somehow gotten into the garage & had climbed into an area it could not escape from....
It died..
Unfortunately, no one had ventured into the garage all week.. so it sat there for a few days...
The smell was so bad that when Merv finally discovered it, he put it in 3 trash bags...
..and it still made him gag!!
He didn't want the stench anywhere near the house so he brought it down to the beach. That evening...
Beach
He said he felt like a murderer trying to dispose of the body..
He said rigor mortis was starting to set in so he couldn't quite fit it into the trash can..
c'mon...
Um... excuse me--
Whatcha tryin' to get rid of, son?...
Dead cat.
There's a dumpster about 50 yards that way past the brick wall...
..Behind the donut shop...
The smell was so bad that Merv would've said anything to keep the cop from letting the cat out the bag...
Luckily he didn't have to...
whew
Thank goodness for lazy-assed policemen...
STOP

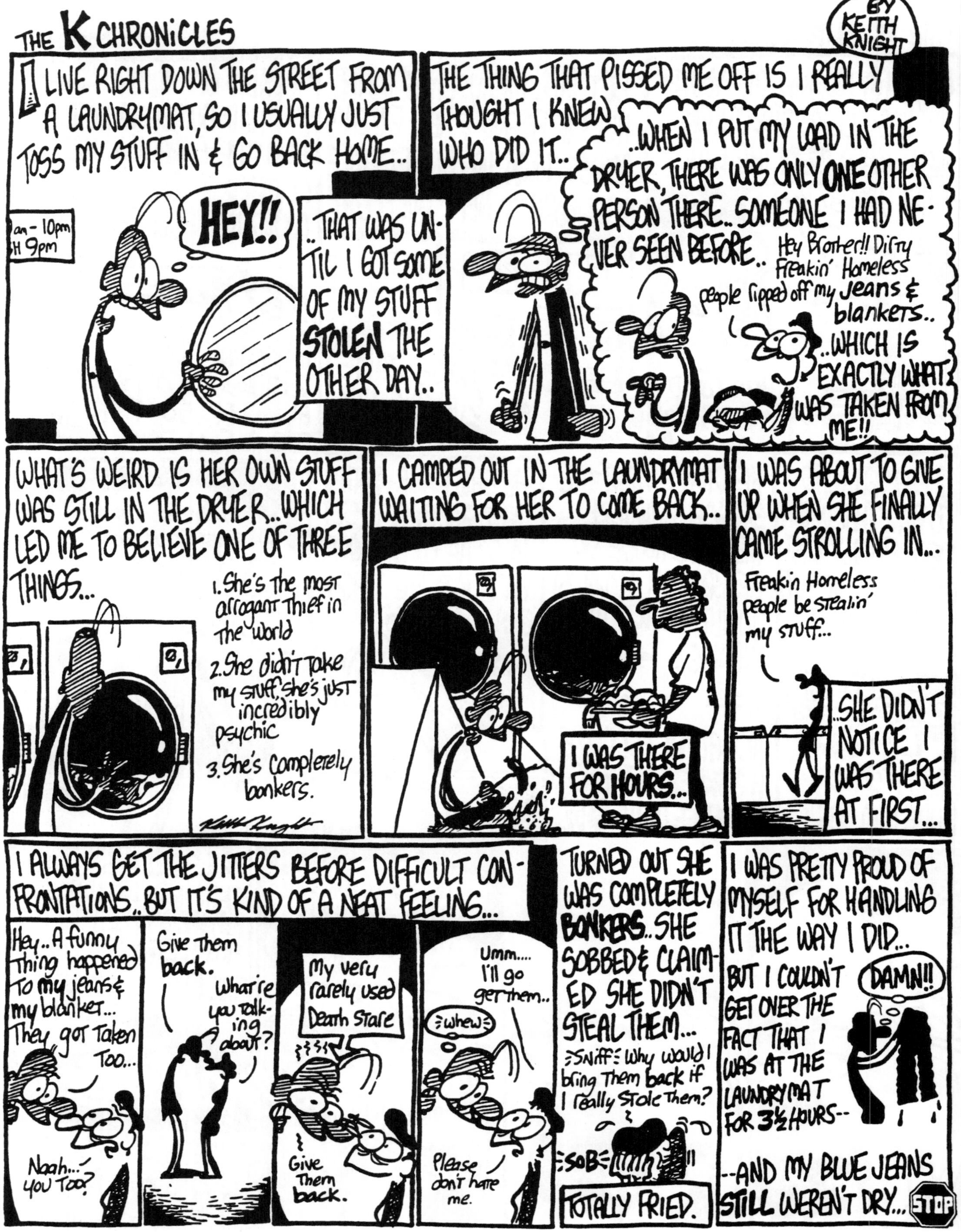
THE K CHRONICLES
BY KEITH KNIGHT
I LIVE RIGHT DOWN THE STREET FROM A LAUNDRYMAT, SO I USUALLY JUST TOSS MY STUFF IN & GO BACK HOME..
HEY!!
..THAT WAS UNTIL I GOT SOME OF MY STUFF STOLEN THE OTHER DAY..
THE THING THAT PISSED ME OFF IS I REALLY THOUGHT I KNEW WHO DID IT..
..WHEN I PUT MY LOAD IN THE DRYER, THERE WAS ONLY ONE OTHER PERSON THERE.. SOMEONE I HAD NEVER SEEN BEFORE..
Hey Brother!! Dirty Freakin' Homeless people ripped off my jeans & blankets..
..WHICH IS EXACTLY WHAT WAS TAKEN FROM ME!!
WHAT'S WEIRD IS HER OWN STUFF WAS STILL IN THE DRYER... WHICH LED ME TO BELIEVE ONE OF THREE THINGS...
1. She's the most arrogant thief in the world
2. She didn't take my stuff, she's just incredibly psychic
3. She's completely bonkers.
I CAMPED OUT IN THE LAUNDRYMAT WAITING FOR HER TO COME BACK..
I WAS THERE FOR HOURS...
I WAS ABOUT TO GIVE UP WHEN SHE FINALLY CAME STROLLING IN...
Freakin Homeless people be stealin' my stuff...
..SHE DIDN'T NOTICE I WAS THERE AT FIRST...
I ALWAYS GET THE JITTERS BEFORE DIFFICULT CONFRONTATIONS.. BUT IT'S KIND OF A NEAT FEELING...
Hey.. A funny thing happened to my jeans & my blanket... They got taken too...
Naah...you too?
Give them back.
What're you talking about?
My very rarely used Death Stare
Give them back.
whew
Umm.... I'll go get them...
Please don't hate me.
TURNED OUT SHE WAS COMPLETELY BONKERS.. SHE SOBBED & CLAIMED SHE DIDN'T STEAL THEM...
Sniff Why would I bring them back if I really stole them?
SOB
TOTALLY FRIED.
I WAS PRETTY PROUD OF MYSELF FOR HANDLING IT THE WAY I DID...
BUT I COULDN'T GET OVER THE FACT THAT I WAS AT THE LAUNDRYMAT FOR 3½ HOURS--
DAMN!!
--AND MY BLUE JEANS STILL WEREN'T DRY...
STOP

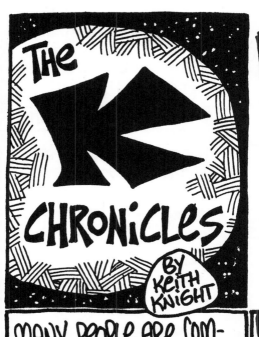

THE K CHRONICLES BY KEITH KNIGHT

IT'S ALL OVER THE NEWS-PAPERS & TELEVISION...

SAN FRANCISCO OBSERVER

NEW YORK TIMES

TIME

THE HYPE IS IMPOSSIBLE TO AVOID...

..YET WHEN THEY SHOW A LITTLE BIT OF IT ON T.V.--

WHOA!! WHAT THE HECK WAS THAT?!

--IT'S HARD TO MAKE ANY SENSE OF WHAT'S GOING ON..

MANY PEOPLE ARE COM-PLETELY DIVIDED ON THE SUBJECT...

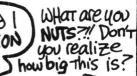

NO WAY WOULD I GO IN A MILLION YEARS...

WHAT ARE YOU NUTS?!! DON'T YOU REALIZE HOW BIG THIS IS?

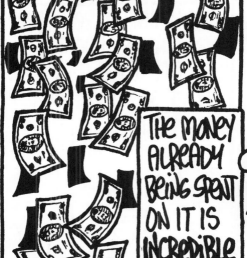

THE MONEY ALREADY BEING SPENT ON IT IS INCREDIBLE.

I'M NOT INTO VIOLENCE OR ANYTHING BUT I GOTTA ADMIT..

BOOM!!

AAAAHHH...

Oooooo...

I'M ENTICED BY ALL THE HIGH TECH GADGETS & WEAPONS.

..BUT WHEN YOU SEE THOUSANDS & THOUSANDS OF PEOPLE IN LINES, YOU HAVE TO ASK YOURSELF ..WHAT THE HECK IS GOING ON?

THE WAR IN KOSOVO?...

..OR THE PHANTOM MENACE?

STOP

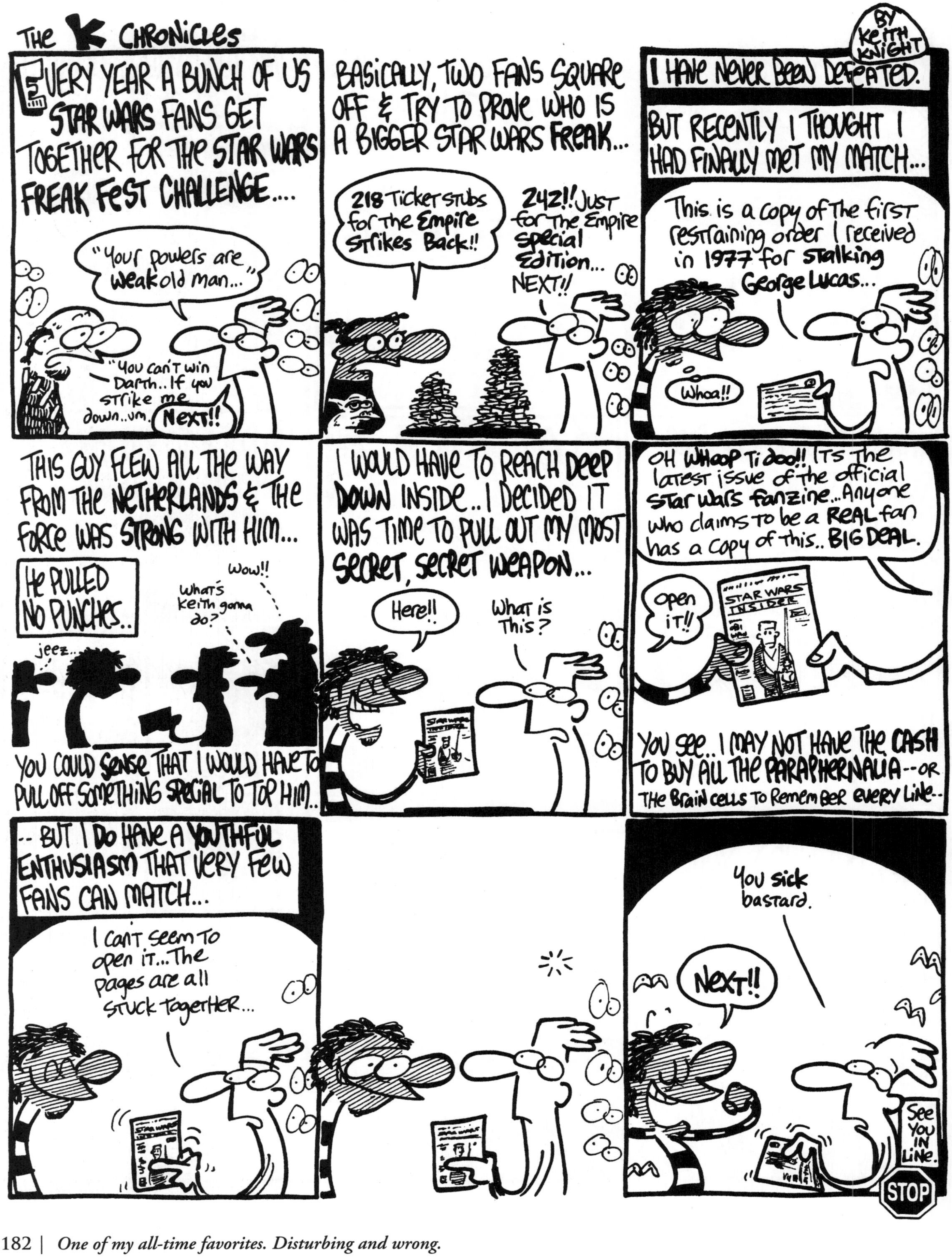

THE K CHRONICLES
BY KEITH KNIGHT
EVERY YEAR A BUNCH OF US STAR WARS FANS GET TOGETHER FOR THE STAR WARS FREAK FEST CHALLENGE....
"Your powers are weak old man..."
"You can't win Darth.. If you strike me down..um..
NEXT!!
BASICALLY, TWO FANS SQUARE OFF & TRY TO PROVE WHO IS A BIGGER STAR WARS FREAK...
218 Ticket stubs for the Empire Strikes Back!!
242!! Just for the Empire Special Edition... NEXT!!
I HAVE NEVER BEEN DEFEATED.
BUT RECENTLY I THOUGHT I HAD FINALLY MET MY MATCH...
This is a copy of the first restraining order I received in 1977 for stalking George Lucas...
Whoa!!
THIS GUY FLEW ALL THE WAY FROM THE NETHERLANDS & THE FORCE WAS STRONG WITH HIM...
He PULLED NO PUNCHES..
Wow!!
What's keith gonna do?
jeez..
YOU COULD SENSE THAT I WOULD HAVE TO PULL OFF SOMETHING SPECIAL TO TOP HIM..
I WOULD HAVE TO REACH DEEP DOWN INSIDE.. I DECIDED IT WAS TIME TO PULL OUT MY MOST SECRET, SECRET WEAPON...
Here!!
What is This?
OH WHOOP Ti DOO!! ITS The latest issue of the official Star Wars fanzine... Anyone who claims to be a REAL fan has a copy of this.. BIG DEAL.
open iT!!
STAR WARS INSIDER
YOU SEE.. I MAY NOT HAVE THE CASH TO BUY ALL THE PARAPHERNALIA--OR THE BRAIN CELLS TO REMEMBER EVERY LINE..
-- BUT I DO HAVE A YOUTHFUL ENTHUSIASM THAT VERY FEW FANS CAN MATCH...
I can't seem to open it... The pages are all stuck together...
You sick bastard.
NEXT!!
See You IN LINE.
STOP

 One of my all-time favorites. Disturbing and wrong.

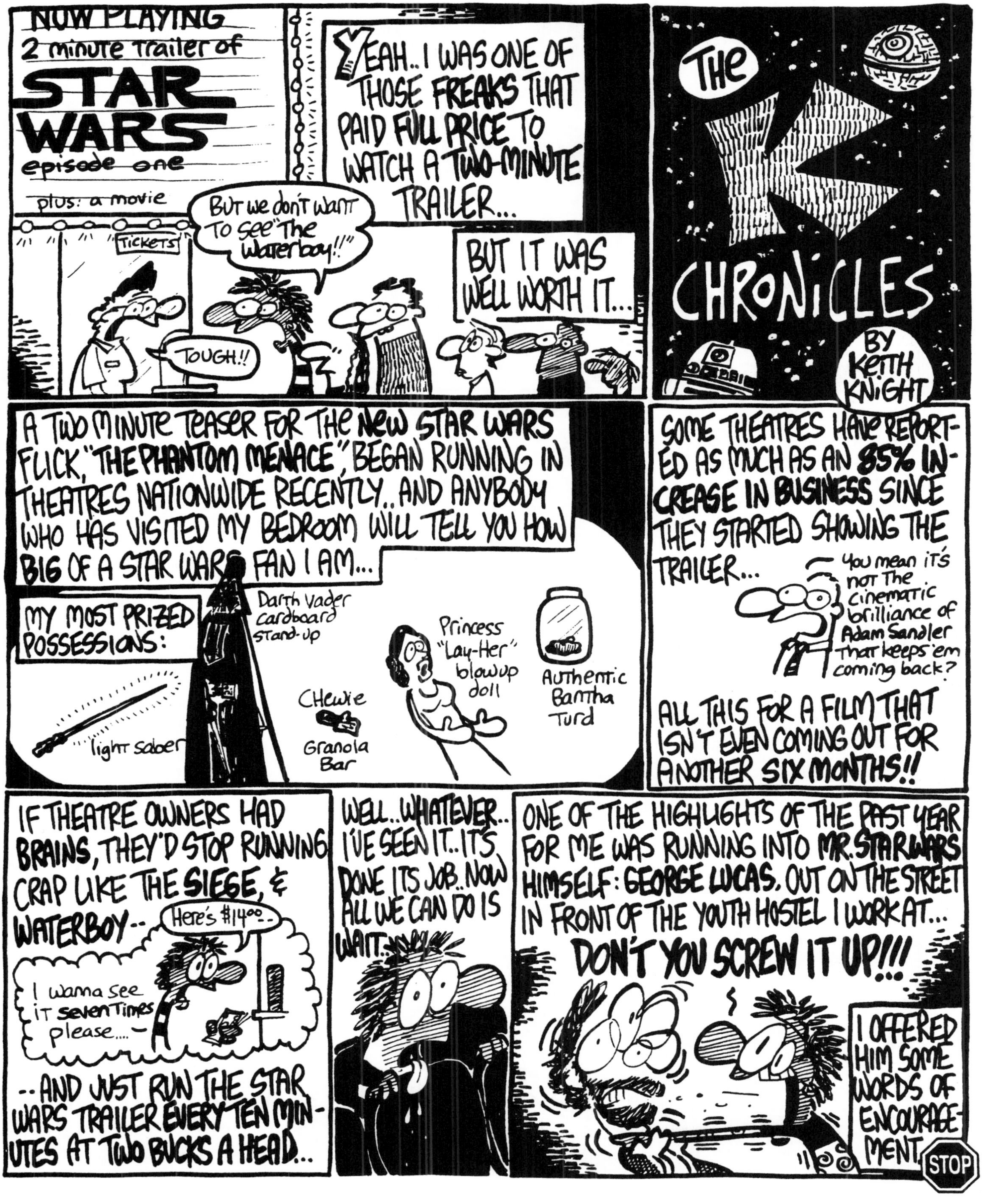
NOW PLAYING
2 minute trailer of
STAR WARS
episode one
plus: a movie
YEAH.. I WAS ONE OF THOSE FREAKS THAT PAID FULL PRICE TO WATCH A TWO-MINUTE TRAILER...
TICKETS
BUT WE DON'T WANT TO SEE "THE WATERBOY!!"
TOUGH!!
BUT IT WAS WELL WORTH IT...
THE K CHRONICLES
BY KEITH KNIGHT
A TWO MINUTE TEASER FOR THE NEW STAR WARS FLICK, "THE PHANTOM MENACE", BEGAN RUNNING IN THEATRES NATIONWIDE RECENTLY.. AND ANYBODY WHO HAS VISITED MY BEDROOM WILL TELL YOU HOW BIG OF A STAR WARS FAN I AM...
MY MOST PRIZED POSSESSIONS:
Darth Vader cardboard stand-up
light saber
Chewie Granola Bar
Princess "Lay-Her" blowup doll
Authentic Bantha Turd
SOME THEATRES HAVE REPORTED AS MUCH AS AN 85% INCREASE IN BUSINESS SINCE THEY STARTED SHOWING THE TRAILER...
You mean it's not the cinematic brilliance of Adam Sandler that keeps 'em coming back?
ALL THIS FOR A FILM THAT ISN'T EVEN COMING OUT FOR ANOTHER SIX MONTHS!!
IF THEATRE OWNERS HAD BRAINS, THEY'D STOP RUNNING CRAP LIKE THE SIEGE, & WATERBOY--
Here's $14.00
I wanna see it seven times please....
--AND JUST RUN THE STAR WARS TRAILER EVERY TEN MINUTES AT TWO BUCKS A HEAD...
WELL...WHATEVER... I'VE SEEN IT..IT'S DONE ITS JOB..NOW ALL WE CAN DO IS WAIT...
ONE OF THE HIGHLIGHTS OF THE PAST YEAR FOR ME WAS RUNNING INTO MR. STAR WARS HIMSELF: GEORGE LUCAS. OUT ON THE STREET IN FRONT OF THE YOUTH HOSTEL I WORK AT...
DON'T YOU SCREW IT UP!!!
I OFFERED HIM SOME WORDS OF ENCOURAGEMENT.
STOP

Meeting George Lucas on the street in front of my youth hostel was the coolest.

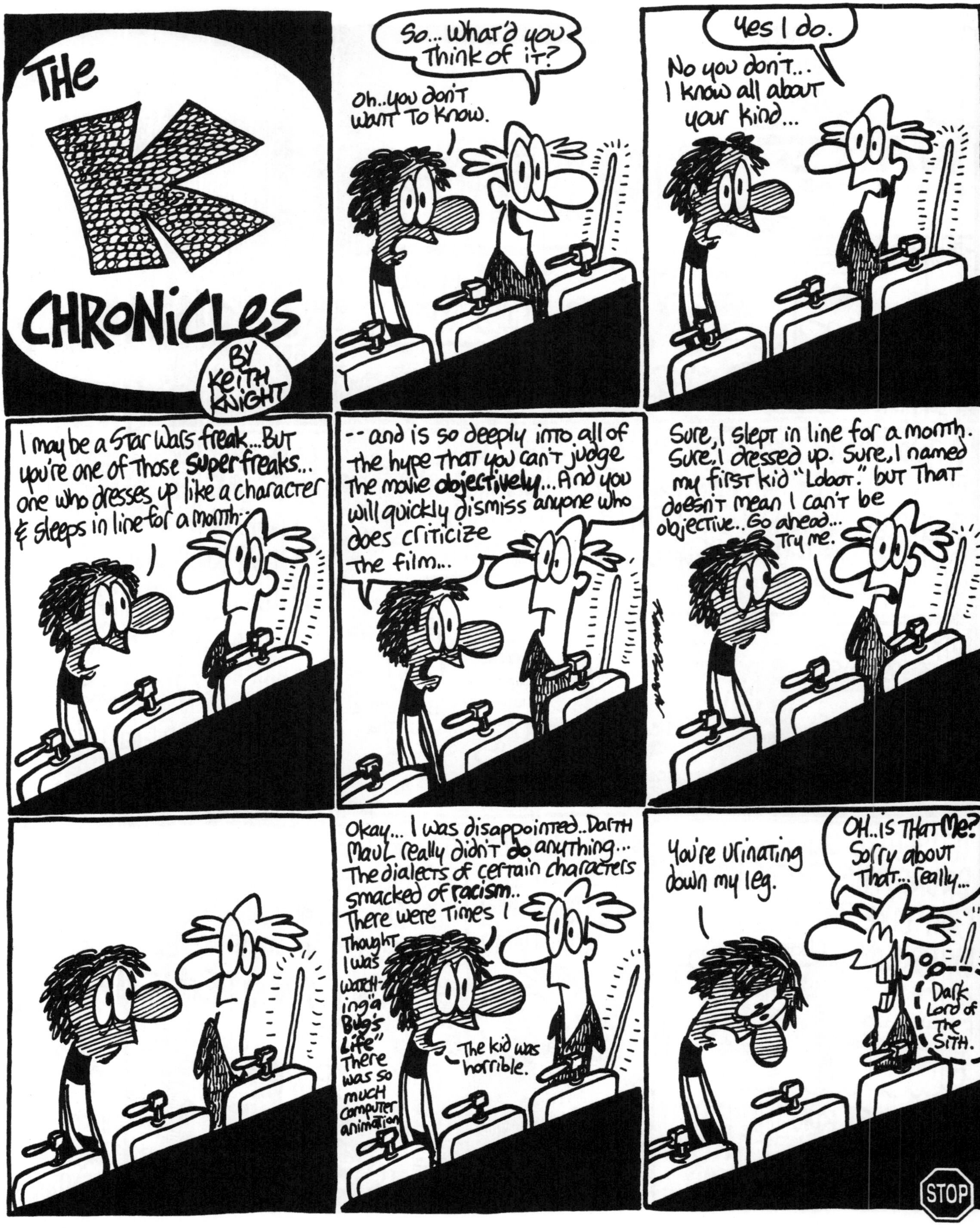
THE K CHRONICLES
BY KEITH KNIGHT
So... What'd you Think of it?
Oh..you don't want To know.
Yes I do.
No you don't... I know all about your kind...
I may be a Star Wars freak...But you're one of those superfreaks... one who dresses up like a character & sleeps in line for a month--
--and is so deeply into all of the hype that you can't judge the movie objectively...And you will quickly dismiss anyone who does criticize the film...
Sure, I slept in line for a month. Sure, I dressed up. Sure, I named my first kid "Lobot." but That doesn't mean I can't be objective..Go ahead... Try me.
Okay... I was disappointed..Darth Maul really didn't do anything... The dialects of certain characters smacked of racism.. There were Times I Thought I was watching "a Bug's Life" There was so much computer animation
The kid was horrible.
You're urinating down my leg.
OH..is That Me? Sorry about That... really...
Dark Lord of The Sith.
STOP

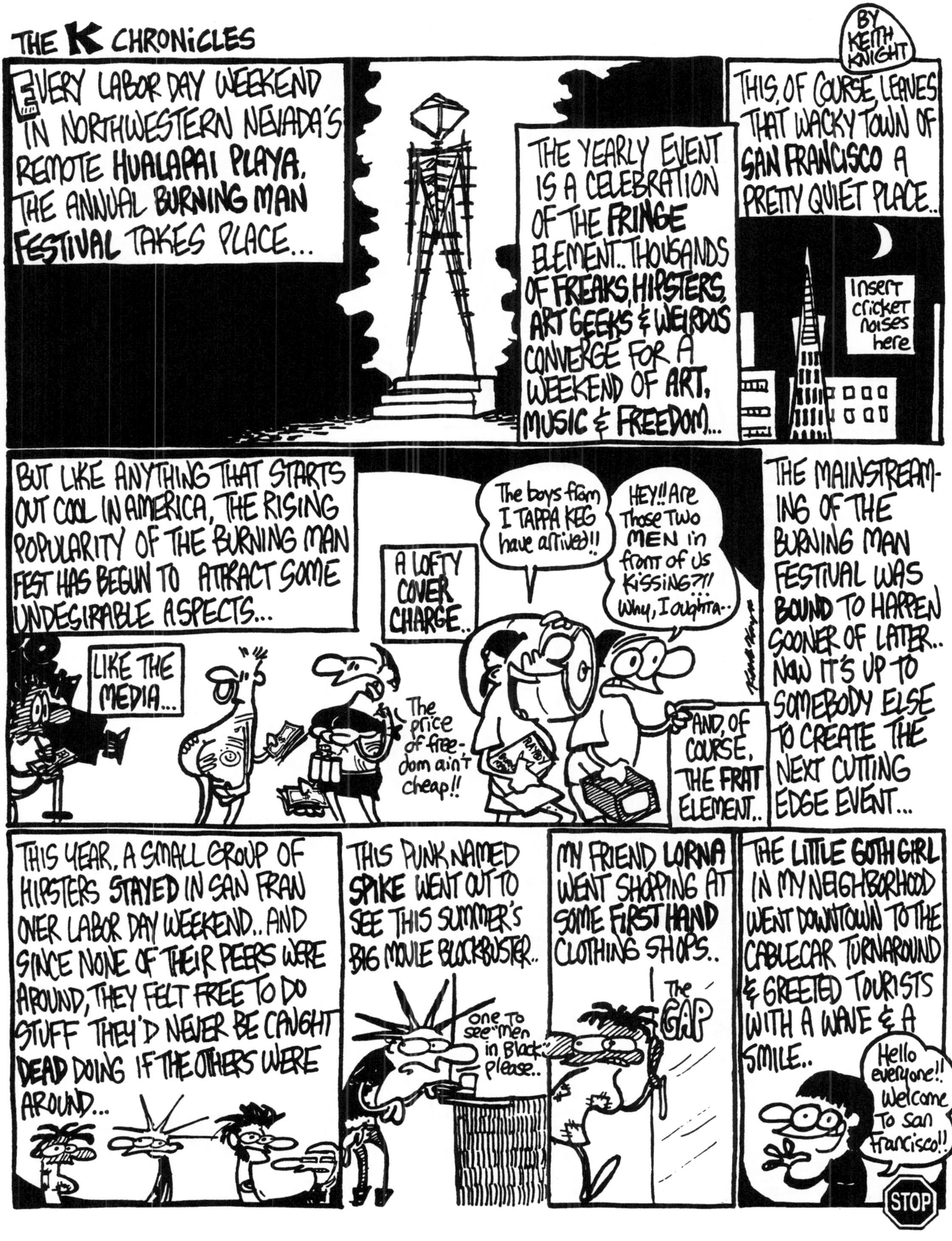
THE K CHRONICLES
BY KEITH KNIGHT
EVERY LABOR DAY WEEKEND IN NORTHWESTERN NEVADA'S REMOTE HUALAPAI PLAYA, THE ANNUAL BURNING MAN FESTIVAL TAKES PLACE...
THE YEARLY EVENT IS A CELEBRATION OF THE FRINGE ELEMENT.. THOUSANDS OF FREAKS, HIPSTERS, ART GEEKS & WEIRDOS CONVERGE FOR A WEEKEND OF ART, MUSIC & FREEDOM...
THIS, OF COURSE, LEAVES THAT WACKY TOWN OF SAN FRANCISCO A PRETTY QUIET PLACE..
Insert cricket noises here
BUT LIKE ANYTHING THAT STARTS OUT COOL IN AMERICA, THE RISING POPULARITY OF THE BURNING MAN FEST HAS BEGUN TO ATTRACT SOME UNDESIRABLE ASPECTS...
LIKE THE MEDIA...
A LOFTY COVER CHARGE..
The price of free-dom ain't cheap!!
The boys from I TAPPA KEG have arrived!!
HEY!! Are Those Two MEN in front of us kissing?!! Why, I oughta..
AND, OF COURSE, THE FRAT ELEMENT..
THE MAINSTREAMING OF THE BURNING MAN FESTIVAL WAS BOUND TO HAPPEN SOONER OF LATER.. NOW IT'S UP TO SOMEBODY ELSE TO CREATE THE NEXT CUTTING EDGE EVENT...
THIS YEAR, A SMALL GROUP OF HIPSTERS STAYED IN SAN FRAN OVER LABOR DAY WEEKEND.. AND SINCE NONE OF THEIR PEERS WERE AROUND, THEY FELT FREE TO DO STUFF THEY'D NEVER BE CAUGHT DEAD DOING IF THE OTHERS WERE AROUND...
THIS PUNK NAMED SPIKE WENT OUT TO SEE THIS SUMMER'S BIG MOVIE BLOCKBUSTER..
one to see "Men in Black" please..
MY FRIEND LORNA WENT SHOPPING AT SOME FIRST HAND CLOTHING SHOPS..
The GAP
THE LITTLE GOTH GIRL IN MY NEIGHBORHOOD WENT DOWNTOWN TO THE CABLECAR TURNAROUND & GREETED TOURISTS WITH A WAVE & A SMILE..
Hello everyone!! Welcome To San Francisco!!
STOP

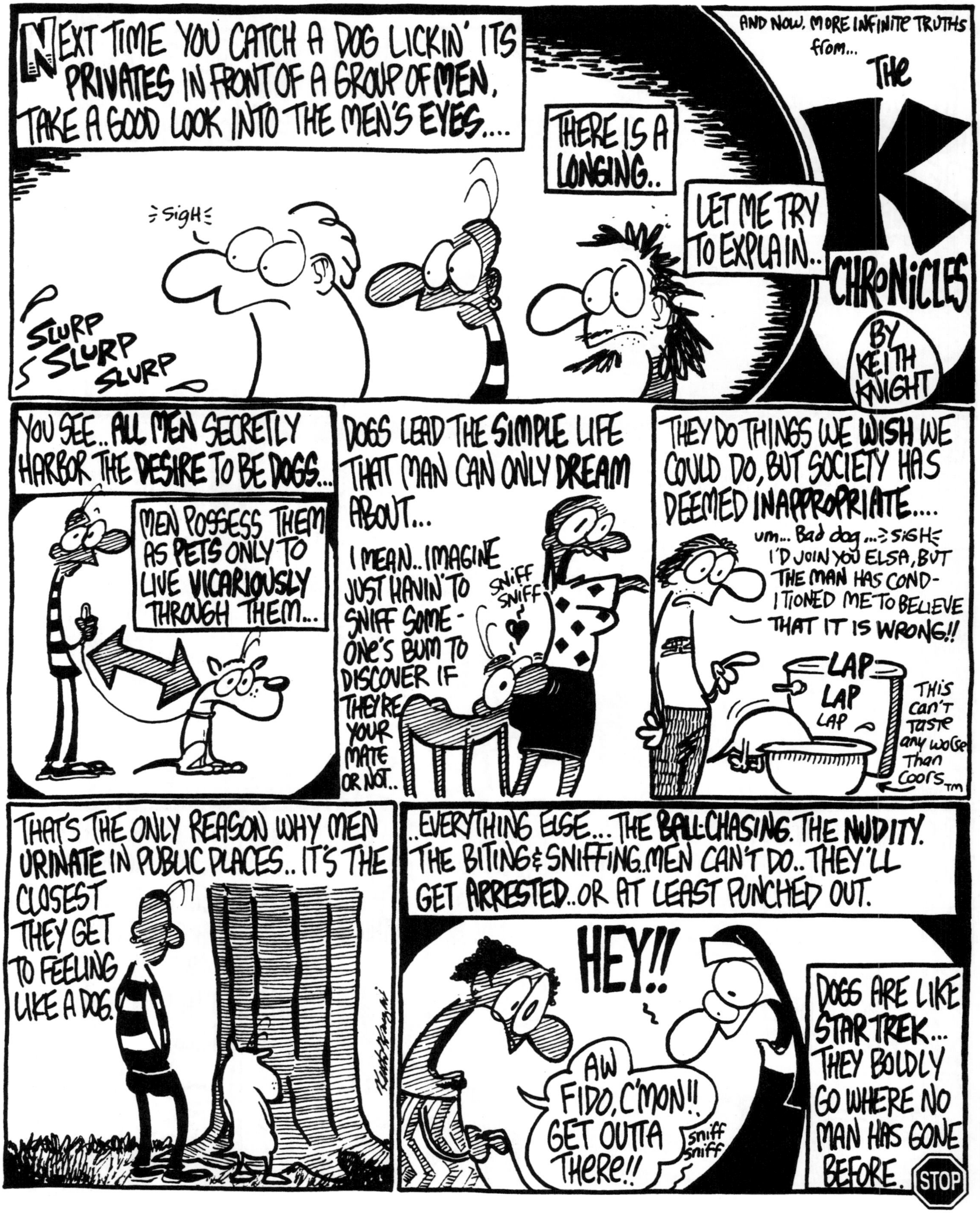
NEXT TIME YOU CATCH A DOG LICKIN' ITS PRIVATES IN FRONT OF A GROUP OF MEN, TAKE A GOOD LOOK INTO THE MEN'S EYES....
AND NOW, MORE INFINITE TRUTHS from... THE K CHRONICLES
BY KEITH KNIGHT
THERE IS A LONGING..
LET ME TRY TO EXPLAIN..
SIGH
SLURP SLURP SLURP
YOU SEE.. ALL MEN SECRETLY HARBOR THE DESIRE TO BE DOGS...
MEN POSSESS THEM AS PETS ONLY TO LIVE VICARIOUSLY THROUGH THEM...
DOGS LEAD THE SIMPLE LIFE THAT MAN CAN ONLY DREAM ABOUT...
I MEAN.. IMAGINE JUST HAVIN' TO SNIFF SOME-ONE'S BUM TO DISCOVER IF THEY'RE YOUR MATE OR NOT..
SNIFF SNIFF
THEY DO THINGS WE WISH WE COULD DO, BUT SOCIETY HAS DEEMED INAPPROPRIATE....
um... Bad dog... SIGH
I'D JOIN YOU ELSA, BUT THE MAN HAS CONDITIONED ME TO BELIEVE THAT IT IS WRONG!!
LAP LAP LAP
THIS can't Taste any worse Than Coors TM
THAT'S THE ONLY REASON WHY MEN URINATE IN PUBLIC PLACES.. IT'S THE CLOSEST THEY GET TO FEELING LIKE A DOG.
..EVERYTHING ELSE... THE BALL-CHASING. THE NUDITY. THE BITING & SNIFFING. MEN CAN'T DO.. THEY'LL GET ARRESTED..OR AT LEAST PUNCHED OUT.
HEY!!
AW FIDO, C'MON!! GET OUTTA THERE!!
sniff sniff
DOGS ARE LIKE STAR TREK... THEY BOLDLY GO WHERE NO MAN HAS GONE BEFORE.
STOP

THE K CHRONICLES

BY KEITH KNIGHT

SINCE I'M A CARTOONIST, PEOPLE ARE ALWAYS SAYING THAT I MUST BE GOOD WITH MY **HANDS**...

Whoops.

WELL.. THE ONE THING I AM DEFINITELY NOT GOOD AT IS THE ART OF THE HANDSHAKE..

Drat.

IT USED TO BE EASY FOR ME BACK IN THE DAY...

Man.

THE **TRADITIONAL** HANDSHAKE FOR ELDERS & FORMAL OCCASIONS...

Nice to meet chu..

..AND THE **CASUAL** HANDSHAKE FOR WHEN YOU'RE JUST HANGIN' WITH YOUR HOMIES..

What up.

NOWADAYS IT'S ALL COMPLICATED WITH ALL THESE INTRICATE MOVES...

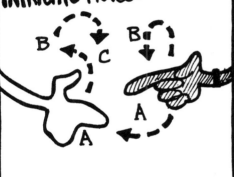

B C B

A A

IT'S LIKE YOU HAVE TO ANTICIPATE WHAT THE OTHER PERSON IS ABOUT TO DO WITHIN SECONDS OF MEETING THEM...

Rats.

.. & NOTHING SAYS "GEEK" FASTER THAN SCREWING UP ON THE VERY FIRST HANDSHAKE..

Damn.

Loser.

IF THERE EVER WAS A PRIZE FOR WORST HANDSHAKER IN THE UNIVERSE..

..I WOULD WIN..

--HANDS DOWN..

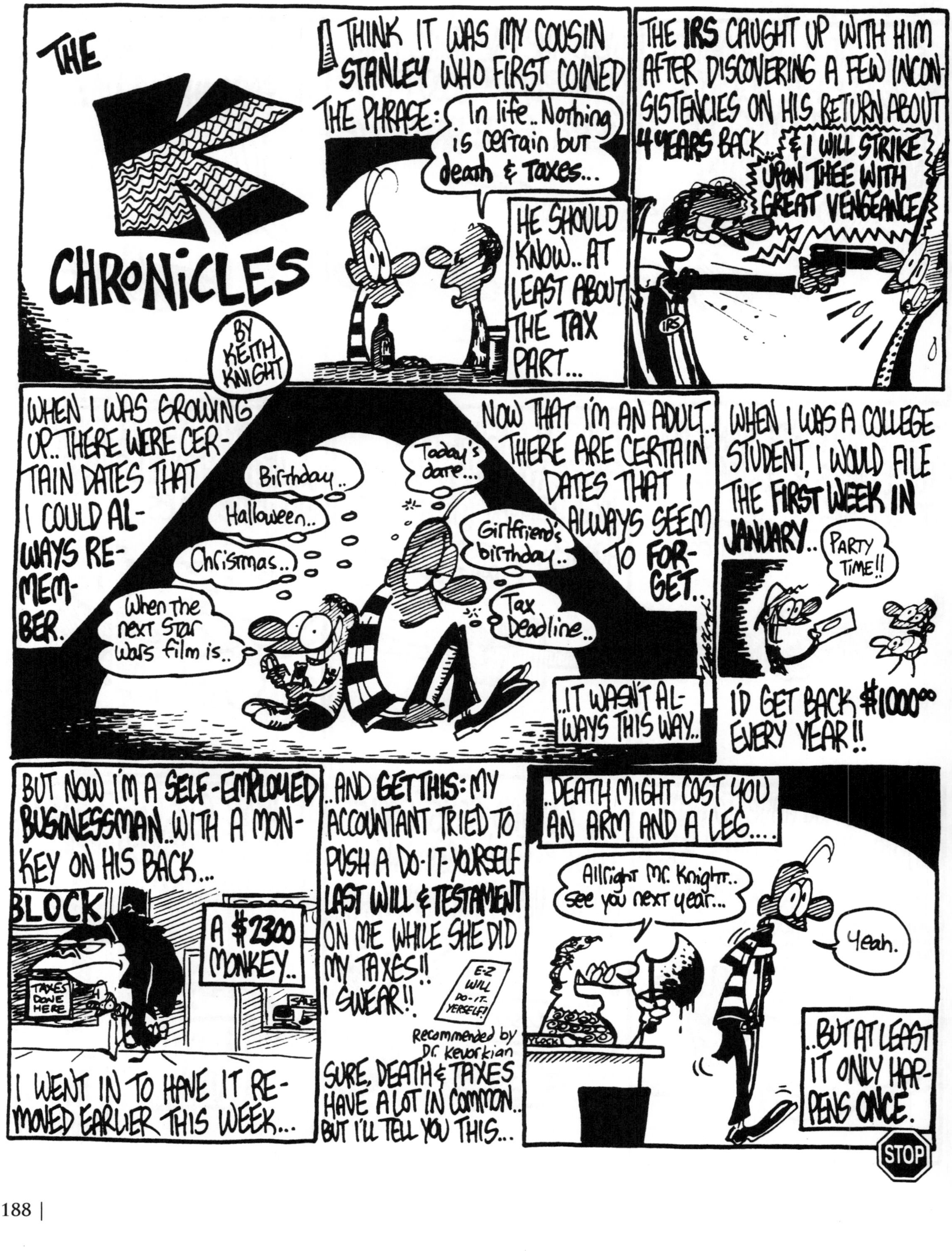
THE K CHRONICLES
BY KEITH KNIGHT
I THINK IT WAS MY COUSIN STANLEY WHO FIRST COINED THE PHRASE:
In life.. Nothing is certain but death & Taxes...
HE SHOULD KNOW.. AT LEAST ABOUT THE TAX PART...
THE IRS CAUGHT UP WITH HIM AFTER DISCOVERING A FEW INCONSISTENCIES ON HIS RETURN ABOUT 4 YEARS BACK...
& I WILL STRIKE UPON THEE WITH GREAT VENGEANCE
IRS
WHEN I WAS GROWING UP.. THERE WERE CERTAIN DATES THAT I COULD ALWAYS REMEMBER.
Birthday..
Halloween..
Christmas..
When the next Star Wars film is..
NOW THAT I'M AN ADULT.. THERE ARE CERTAIN DATES THAT I ALWAYS SEEM TO FORGET..
Today's date...
Girlfriend's birthday..
Tax Deadline..
..IT WASN'T ALWAYS THIS WAY..
WHEN I WAS A COLLEGE STUDENT, I WOULD FILE THE FIRST WEEK IN JANUARY..
PARTY TIME!!
I'D GET BACK $1000.00 EVERY YEAR!!
BUT NOW I'M A SELF-EMPLOYED BUSINESSMAN.. WITH A MONKEY ON HIS BACK...
BLOCK
TAXES DONE HERE
A $2300 MONKEY..
I WENT IN TO HAVE IT REMOVED EARLIER THIS WEEK...
..AND GET THIS: MY ACCOUNTANT TRIED TO PUSH A DO-IT-YOURSELF LAST WILL & TESTAMENT ON ME WHILE SHE DID MY TAXES!! I SWEAR!!
E-Z WILL DO-IT-YERSELF!
Recommended by Dr. Kevorkian
SURE, DEATH & TAXES HAVE A LOT IN COMMON.. BUT I'LL TELL YOU THIS...
..DEATH MIGHT COST YOU AN ARM AND A LEG....
Allright Mr. Knight.. see you next year...
Yeah.
..BUT AT LEAST IT ONLY HAPPENS ONCE.
STOP

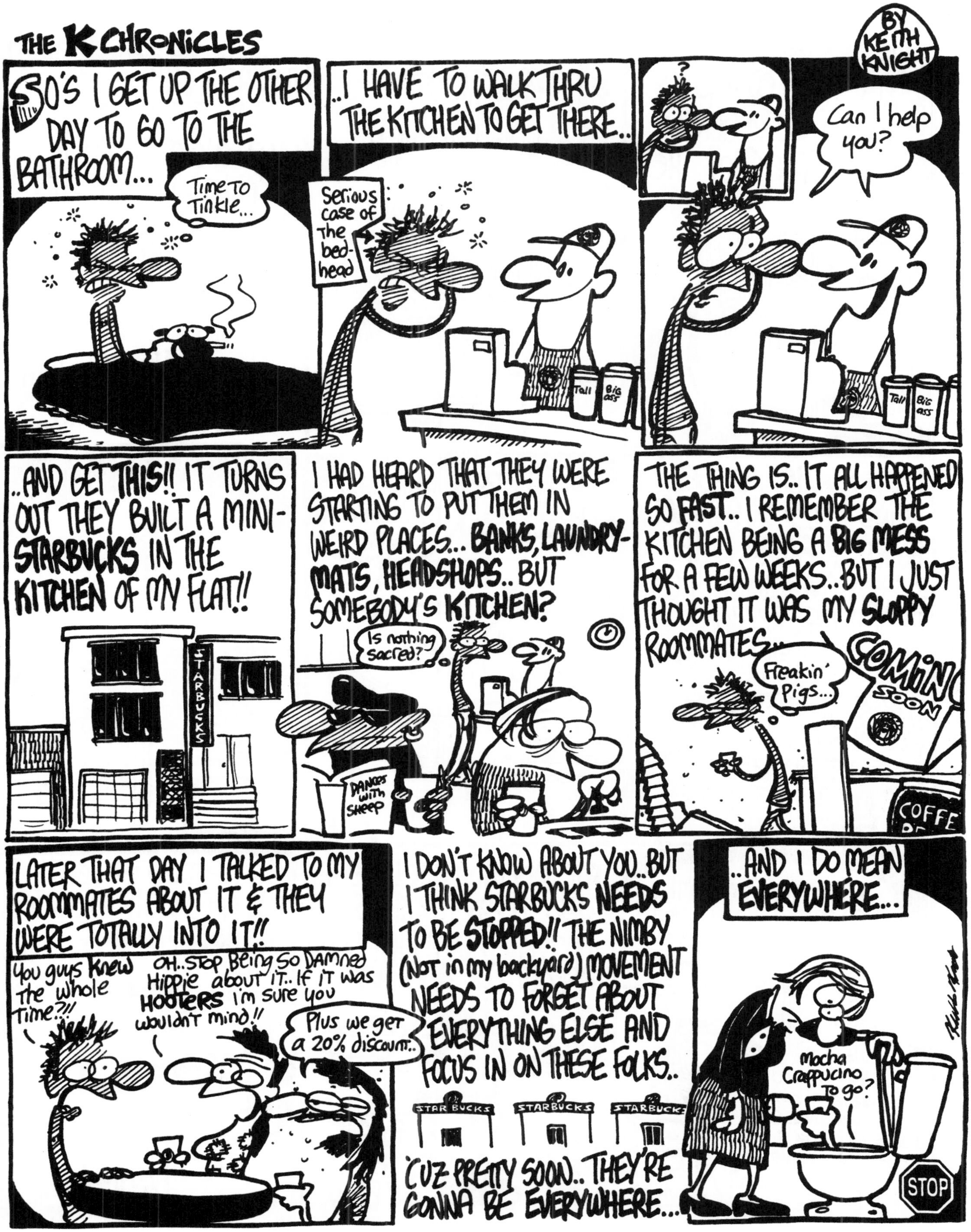
THE K CHRONICLES
BY KEITH KNIGHT
SO'S I GET UP THE OTHER DAY TO GO TO THE BATHROOM...
Time to Tinkle...
..I HAVE TO WALK THRU THE KITCHEN TO GET THERE..
Serious case of the bed-head
Tall
Big ass
?
Can I help you?
..AND GET THIS!! IT TURNS OUT THEY BUILT A MINI-STARBUCKS IN THE KITCHEN OF MY FLAT!!
STARBUCKS
I HAD HEARD THAT THEY WERE STARTING TO PUT THEM IN WEIRD PLACES... BANKS, LAUNDRY-MATS, HEADSHOPS.. BUT SOMEBODY'S KITCHEN?
Is nothing sacred?
DANCES WITH SHEEP
THE THING IS.. IT ALL HAPPENED SO FAST.. I REMEMBER THE KITCHEN BEING A BIG MESS FOR A FEW WEEKS.. BUT I JUST THOUGHT IT WAS MY SLOPPY ROOMMATES..
Freakin' Pigs...
COMIN SOON
COFFE
LATER THAT DAY I TALKED TO MY ROOMMATES ABOUT IT & THEY WERE TOTALLY INTO IT!!
You guys knew the whole time?!!
OH.. STOP BEING SO DAMNED HIPPIE ABOUT IT.. IF IT WAS HOOTERS I'M SURE YOU WOULDN'T MIND!!
Plus we get a 20% discount..
I DON'T KNOW ABOUT YOU.. BUT I THINK STARBUCKS NEEDS TO BE STOPPED!! THE NIMBY (NOT IN MY BACKYARD) MOVEMENT NEEDS TO FORGET ABOUT EVERYTHING ELSE AND FOCUS IN ON THESE FOLKS..
STAR BUCKS
STARBUCKS
STARBUCKS
'CUZ PRETTY SOON.. THEY'RE GONNA BE EVERYWHERE...
..AND I DO MEAN EVERYWHERE...
Mocha Crappucino to go?
STOP

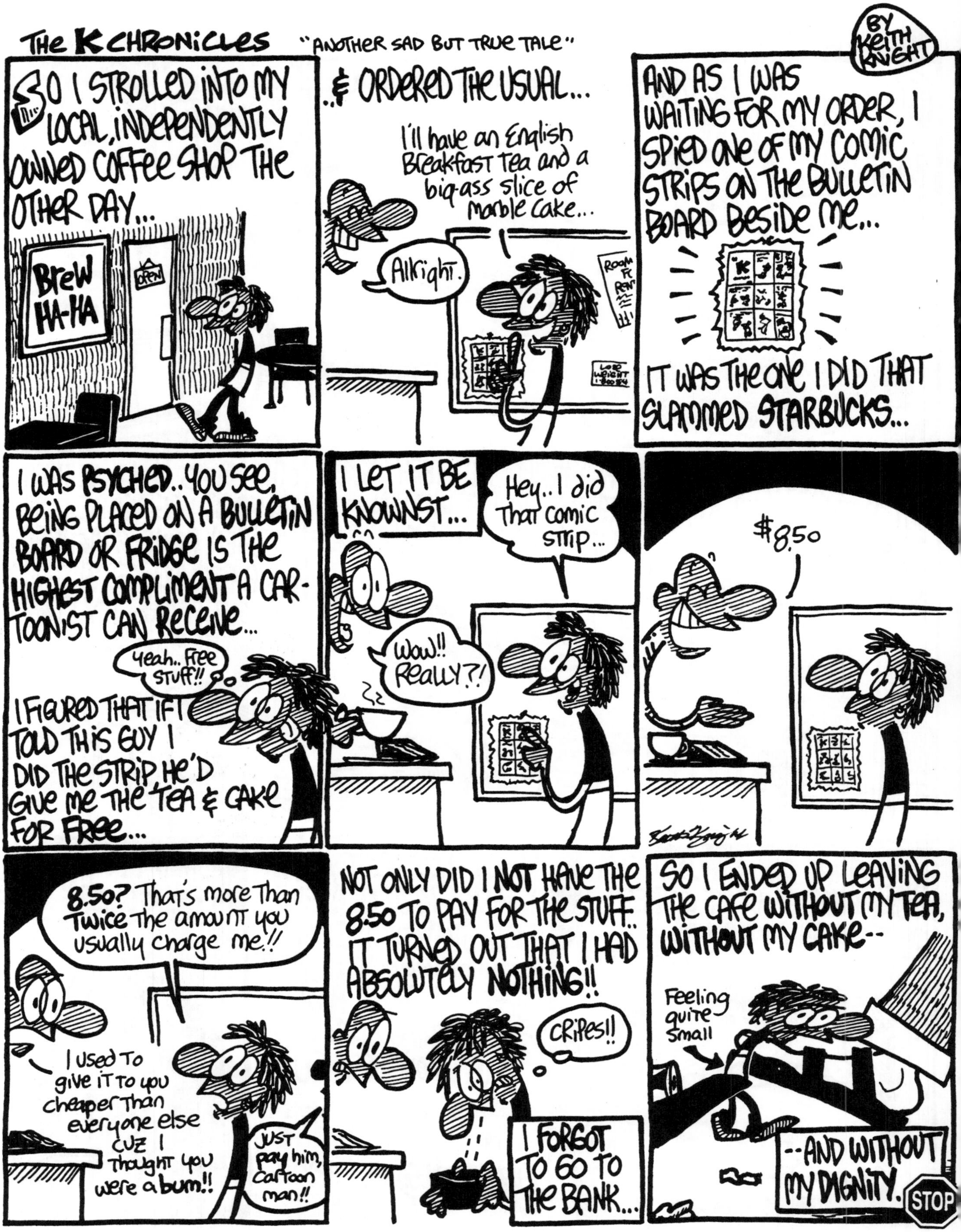
THE K CHRONICLES
"ANOTHER SAD BUT TRUE TALE"
BY KEITH KNIGHT
SO I STROLLED INTO MY LOCAL, INDEPENDENTLY OWNED COFFEE SHOP THE OTHER DAY...
BREW HA-HA
OPEN
& ORDERED THE USUAL...
I'll have an English Breakfast Tea and a big-ass slice of Marble Cake...
Alright.
AND AS I WAS WAITING FOR MY ORDER, I SPIED ONE OF MY COMIC STRIPS ON THE BULLETIN BOARD BESIDE ME...
IT WAS THE ONE I DID THAT SLAMMED STARBUCKS...
I WAS PSYCHED.. YOU SEE, BEING PLACED ON A BULLETIN BOARD OR FRIDGE IS THE HIGHEST COMPLIMENT A CAR-TOONIST CAN RECEIVE...
Yeah.. Free STUFF!!
I FIGURED THAT IF I TOLD THIS GUY I DID THE STRIP HE'D GIVE ME THE TEA & CAKE FOR FREE...
I LET IT BE KNOWNST...
Hey..I did That comic strip...
Wow!! Really?!
$8.50
8.50? That's more Than Twice The amount you usually charge me!!
I used To give it to you cheaper Than everyone else cuz I Thought you were a bum!!
JUST pay him, Cartoon man!!
NOT ONLY DID I NOT HAVE THE 8.50 TO PAY FOR THE STUFF.. IT TURNED OUT THAT I HAD ABSOLUTELY NOTHING!!
Cripes!!
I FORGOT TO GO TO THE BANK...
SO I ENDED UP LEAVING THE CAFE WITHOUT MY TEA, WITHOUT MY CAKE--
Feeling quite small
--AND WITHOUT MY DIGNITY.
STOP

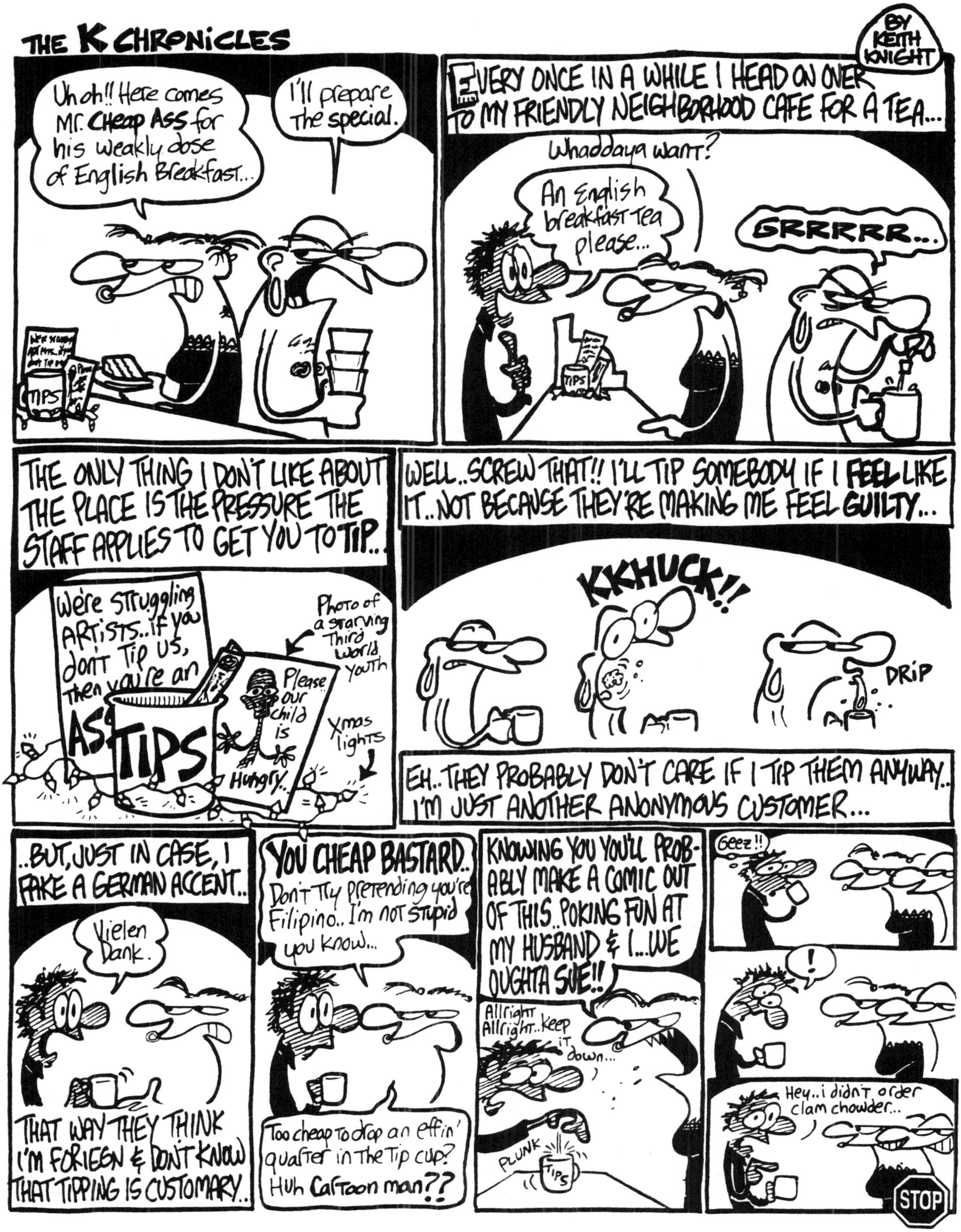
THE K CHRONICLES
BY KEITH KNIGHT
Uh oh!! Here comes Mr. Cheap Ass for his weakly dose of English Breakfast...
I'll prepare the special.
TIPS
EVERY ONCE IN A WHILE I HEAD ON OVER TO MY FRIENDLY NEIGHBORHOOD CAFE FOR A TEA...
Whaddaya want?
An English breakfast tea please...
GRRRRR...
TIPS
THE ONLY THING I DON'T LIKE ABOUT THE PLACE IS THE PRESSURE THE STAFF APPLIES TO GET YOU TO TIP..
We're struggling ARTISTS..if you don't Tip us, then you're an ASS
TIPS
Photo of a starving Third World Youth
Please our child is Hungry..
Xmas lights
WELL..SCREW THAT!! I'LL TIP SOMEBODY IF I FEEL LIKE IT..NOT BECAUSE THEY'RE MAKING ME FEEL GUILTY...
KKHUCK!!
DRIP
EH..THEY PROBABLY DON'T CARE IF I TIP THEM ANYWAY.. I'M JUST ANOTHER ANONYMOUS CUSTOMER...
..BUT, JUST IN CASE, I FAKE A GERMAN ACCENT..
Vielen Dank.
THAT WAY THEY THINK I'M FORIEGN & DON'T KNOW THAT TIPPING IS CUSTOMARY..
YOU CHEAP BASTARD.. Don't Try pretending you're Filipino.. I'm not stupid you know...
Too cheap to drop an effin' quarter in the Tip cup? Huh Cartoon man??
KNOWING YOU YOU'LL PROBABLY MAKE A COMIC OUT OF THIS..POKING FUN AT MY HUSBAND & I...WE OUGHTA SUE!!
Allright Allright..Keep it down...
PLUNK
TIPS
Geez!!
!
Hey..i didn't order clam chowder...
STOP

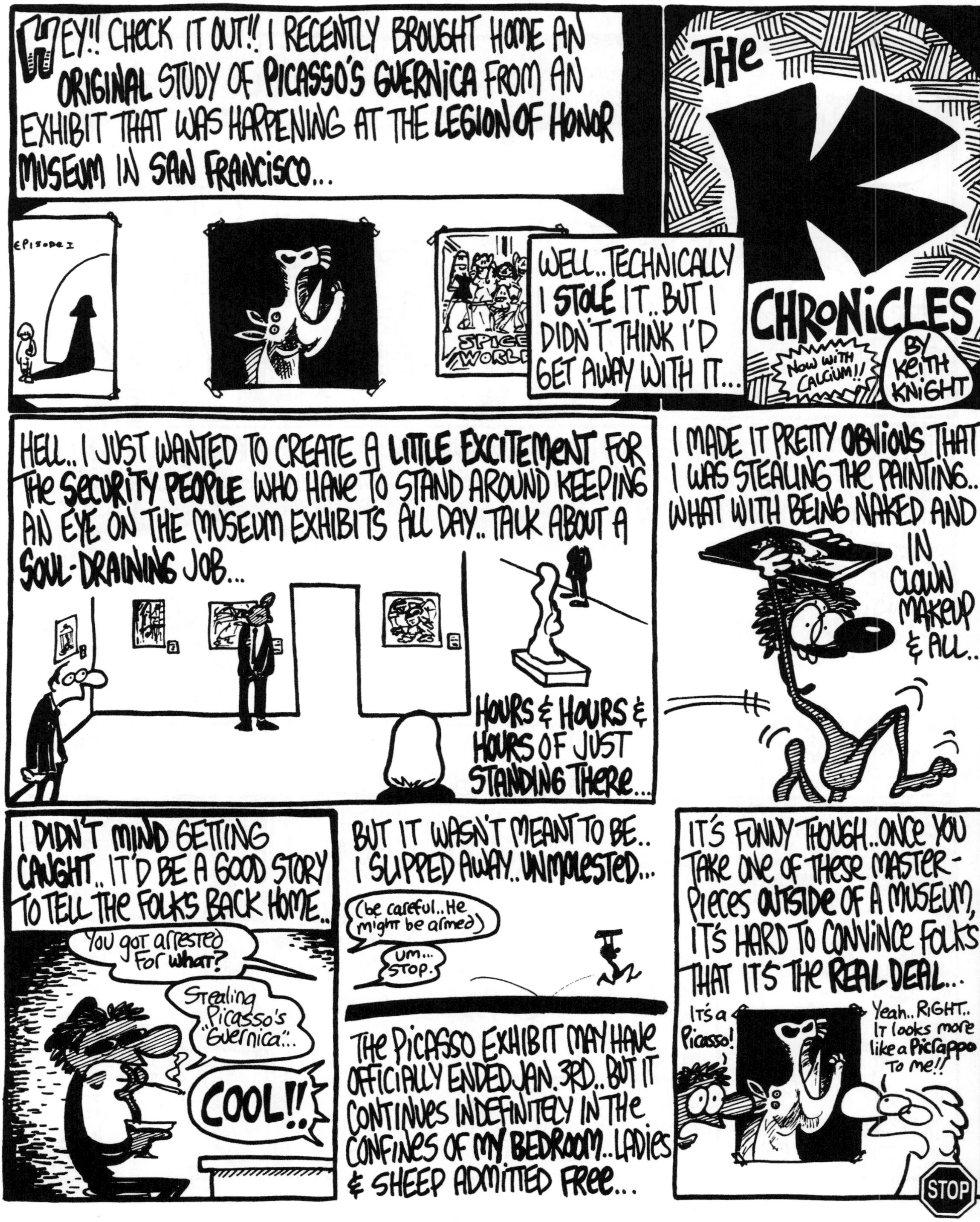

HEY!! CHECK IT OUT!! I RECENTLY BROUGHT HOME AN ORIGINAL STUDY OF PICASSO'S GUERNICA FROM AN EXHIBIT THAT WAS HAPPENING AT THE LEGION OF HONOR MUSEUM IN SAN FRANCISCO...
THE K CHRONICLES
NOW WITH CALCIUM!!
BY KEITH KNIGHT
EPISODE I
SPICE WORLD
WELL.. TECHNICALLY I STOLE IT.. BUT I DIDN'T THINK I'D GET AWAY WITH IT...
HELL.. I JUST WANTED TO CREATE A LITTLE EXCITEMENT FOR THE SECURITY PEOPLE WHO HAVE TO STAND AROUND KEEPING AN EYE ON THE MUSEUM EXHIBITS ALL DAY.. TALK ABOUT A SOUL-DRAINING JOB...
HOURS & HOURS & HOURS OF JUST STANDING THERE...
I MADE IT PRETTY OBVIOUS THAT I WAS STEALING THE PAINTING.. WHAT WITH BEING NAKED AND IN CLOWN MAKEUP & ALL..
I DIDN'T MIND GETTING CAUGHT.. IT'D BE A GOOD STORY TO TELL THE FOLKS BACK HOME..
You got arrested for what?
Stealing Picasso's "Guernica"..
COOL!!
BUT IT WASN'T MEANT TO BE.. I SLIPPED AWAY.. UNMOLESTED...
(be careful.. He might be armed)
Um... Stop.
THE PICASSO EXHIBIT MAY HAVE OFFICIALLY ENDED JAN. 3RD.. BUT IT CONTINUES INDEFINITELY IN THE CONFINES OF MY BEDROOM.. LADIES & SHEEP ADMITTED FREE...
IT'S FUNNY THOUGH.. ONCE YOU TAKE ONE OF THESE MASTERPIECES OUTSIDE OF A MUSEUM, IT'S HARD TO CONVINCE FOLKS THAT IT'S THE REAL DEAL...
It's a Picasso!
Yeah.. RIGHT.. It looks more like a Picrappo to me!!
STOP

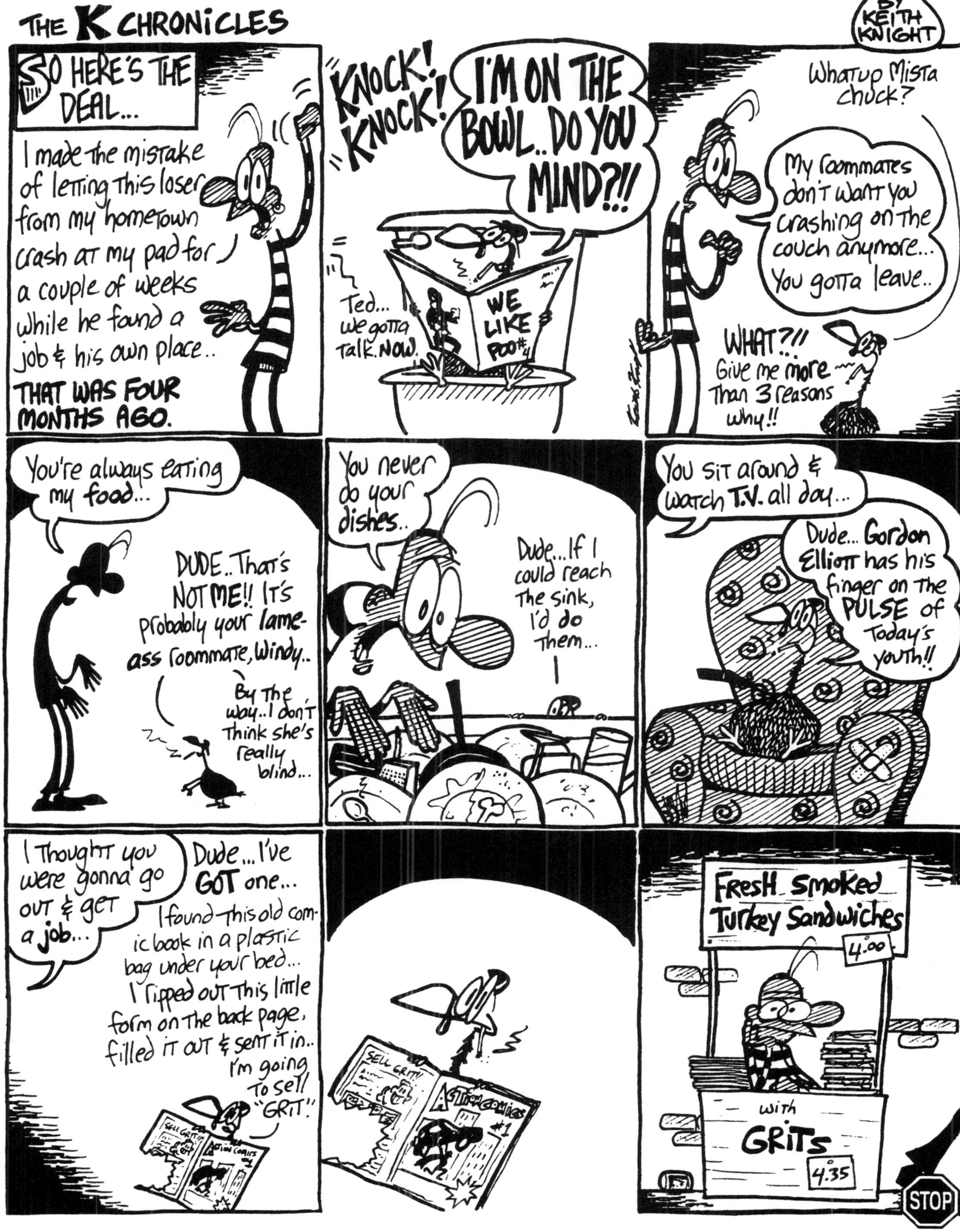
THE K CHRONICLES
BY KEITH KNIGHT
SO HERE'S THE DEAL...
I made the mistake of letting this loser from my hometown crash at my pad for a couple of weeks while he found a job & his own place..
THAT WAS FOUR MONTHS AGO.
KNOCK! KNOCK!
I'M ON THE BOWL.. DO YOU MIND?!!
Ted... we gotta talk. NOW.
WE LIKE POO #4
Whatup Mista Chuck?
My roommates don't want you crashing on the couch anymore... You gotta leave..
WHAT?!! Give me more than 3 reasons why!!
You're always eating my food...
DUDE.. That's NOT ME!! It's probably your lame-ass roommate, Windy..
By the way.. I don't think she's really blind...
You never do your dishes..
Dude... If I could reach the sink, I'd do them...
You sit around & watch T.V. all day...
Dude... Gordon Elliott has his finger on the PULSE of today's youth!!
I thought you were gonna go out & get a job...
Dude... I've GOT one...
I found this old comic book in a plastic bag under your bed... I ripped out this little form on the back page, filled it out & sent it in.. I'm going to sell "GRIT."
SELL GRIT!
ACTION COMICS #1
FRESH SMOKED Turkey Sandwiches
4.00
with GRITS
4.35
STOP

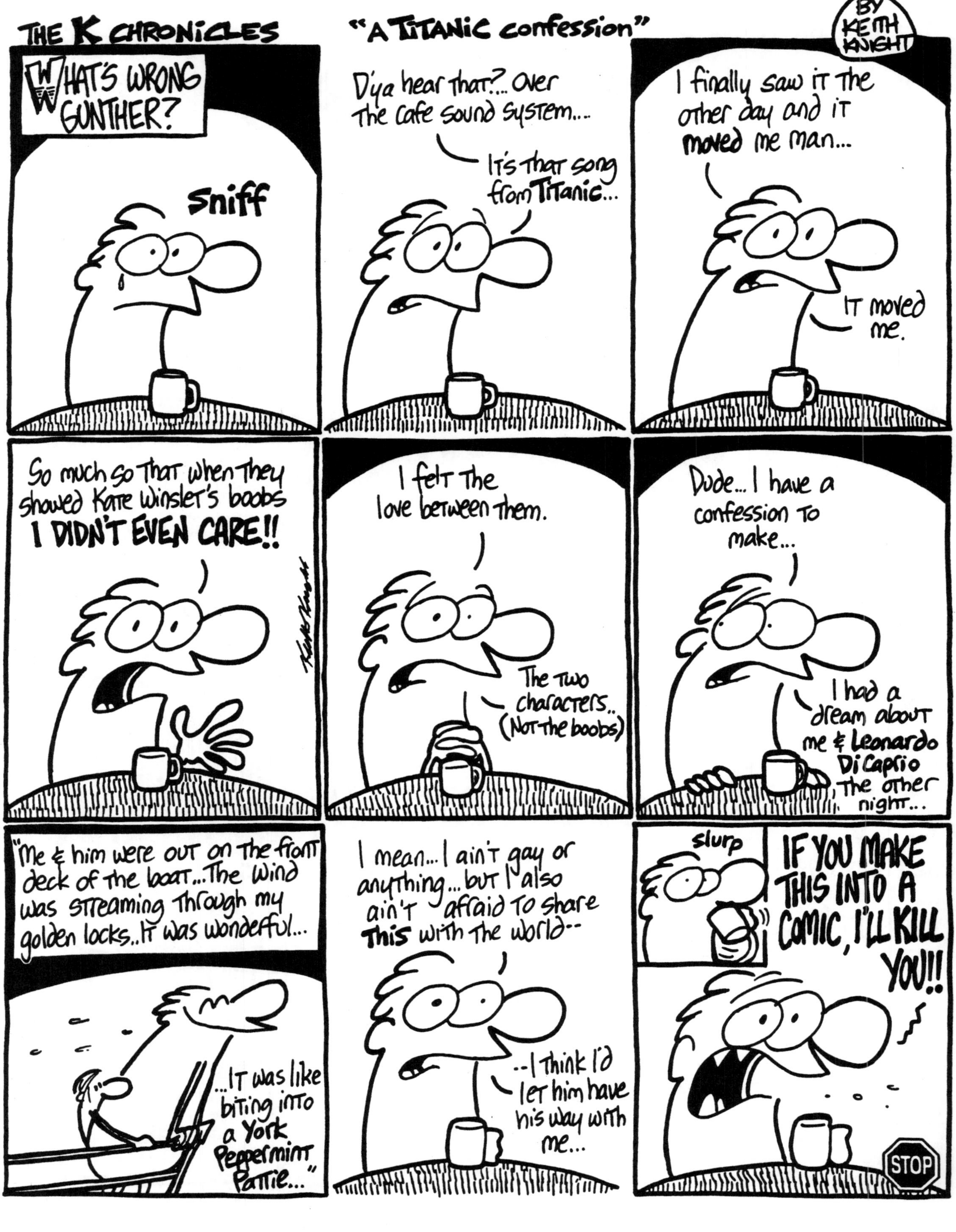
THE K CHRONICLES
"A TITANIC confession"
BY KEITH KNIGHT
WHAT'S WRONG GUNTHER?
Sniff
D'ya hear that?... Over the cafe sound system....
It's that song from Titanic...
I finally saw it the other day and it moved me man...
It moved me.
So much so that when they showed Kate Winslet's boobs I DIDN'T EVEN CARE!!
I felt the love between them.
The two characters... (Not the boobs)
Dude... I have a confession to make...
I had a dream about me & Leonardo DiCaprio the other night...
"Me & him were out on the front deck of the boat... The wind was streaming through my golden locks.. It was wonderful...
...It was like biting into a York Peppermint Pattie..."
I mean... I ain't gay or anything... but I also ain't afraid to share this with the world--
--I think I'd let him have his way with me...
slurp
IF YOU MAKE THIS INTO A COMIC, I'LL KILL YOU!!
STOP

 The seventh panel is my favorite drawing of Gunther ever.

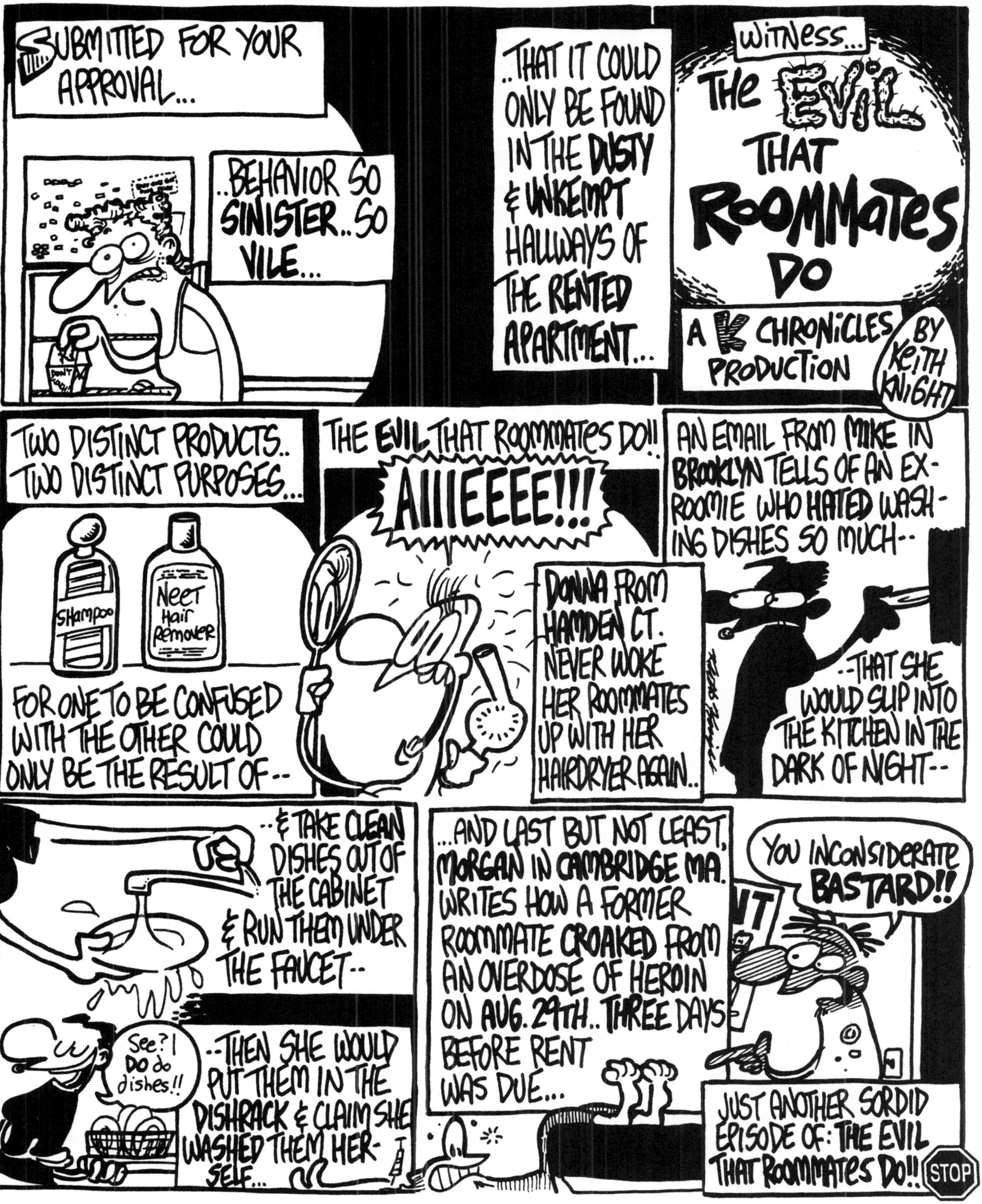
SUBMITTED FOR YOUR APPROVAL...
...BEHAVIOR SO SINISTER...SO VILE...
DON'T TOUCH!!
..THAT IT COULD ONLY BE FOUND IN THE DUSTY & UNKEMPT HALLWAYS OF THE RENTED APARTMENT...
WITNESS...
THE EVIL THAT ROOMMATES DO
A K CHRONICLES PRODUCTION
BY KEITH KNIGHT
TWO DISTINCT PRODUCTS.. TWO DISTINCT PURPOSES...
SHAMPOO
NEET Hair Remover
FOR ONE TO BE CONFUSED WITH THE OTHER COULD ONLY BE THE RESULT OF--
THE EVIL THAT ROOMMATES DO!!..
AIIIEEEE!!!
DONNA FROM HAMDEN CT. NEVER WOKE HER ROOMMATES UP WITH HER HAIRDRYER AGAIN..
AN EMAIL FROM MIKE IN BROOKLYN TELLS OF AN EX-ROOMIE WHO HATED WASHING DISHES SO MUCH--
--THAT SHE WOULD SLIP INTO THE KITCHEN IN THE DARK OF NIGHT--
--& TAKE CLEAN DISHES OUT OF THE CABINET & RUN THEM UNDER THE FAUCET--
See?! DO do dishes!!
--THEN SHE WOULD PUT THEM IN THE DISHRACK & CLAIM SHE WASHED THEM HER-SELF...
...AND LAST BUT NOT LEAST, MORGAN IN CAMBRIDGE MA. WRITES HOW A FORMER ROOMMATE CROAKED FROM AN OVERDOSE OF HEROIN ON AUG. 29TH.. THREE DAYS BEFORE RENT WAS DUE...
YOU INCONSIDERATE BASTARD!!
JUST ANOTHER SORDID EPISODE OF: THE EVIL THAT ROOMMATES DO!!..
STOP

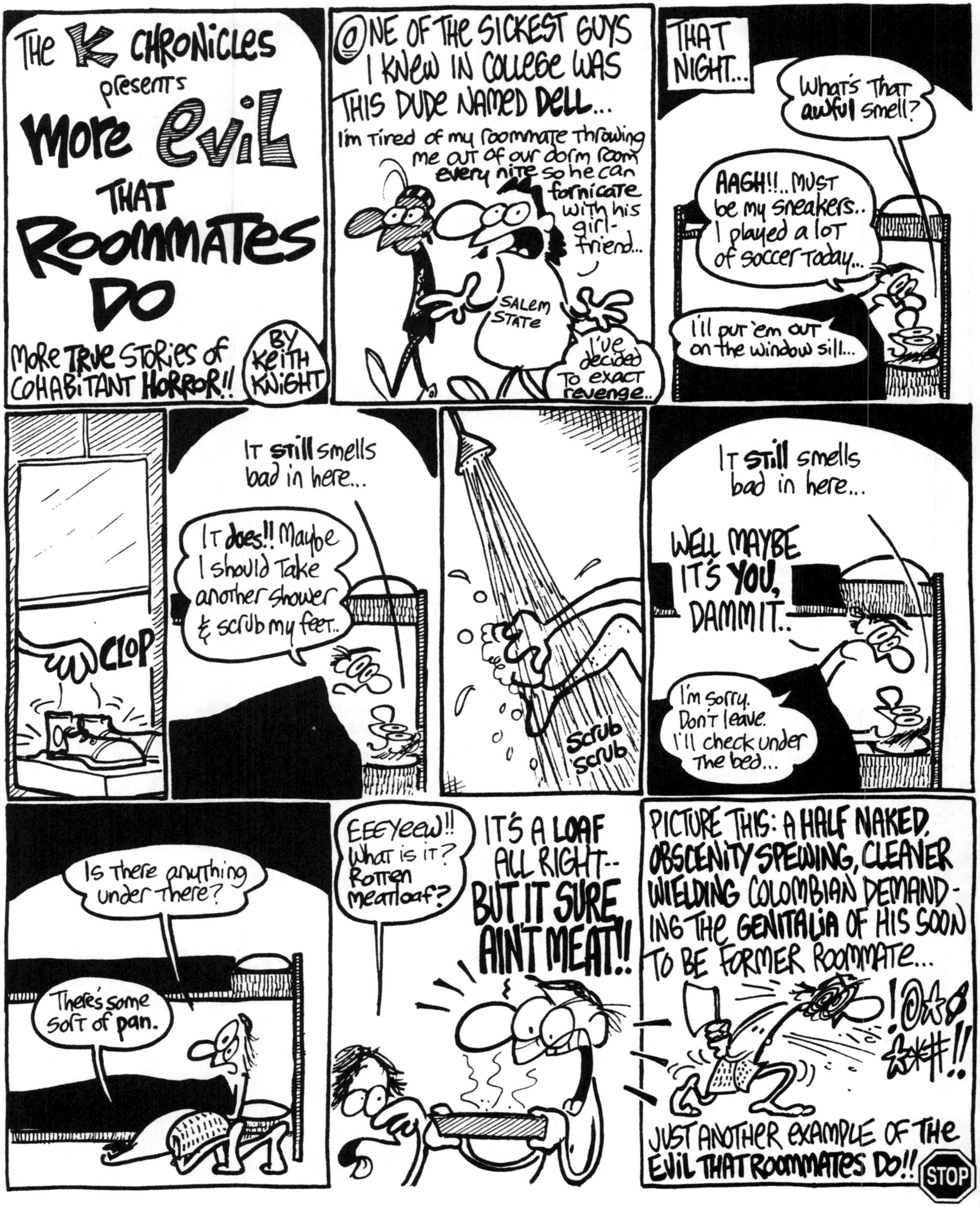

THE K CHRONICLES presents more evil THAT ROOMMATES DO
MORE TRUE STORIES OF COHABITANT HORROR!!
BY KEITH KNIGHT
ONE OF THE SICKEST GUYS I KNEW IN COLLEGE WAS THIS DUDE NAMED DELL...
I'm tired of my roommate throwing me out of our dorm room every nite so he can fornicate with his girl-friend...
SALEM STATE
I've decided to exact revenge..
THAT NIGHT...
What's that awful smell?
AAGH!!..MUST be my sneakers.. I played a lot of soccer today...
I'll put 'em out on the window sill...
CLOP
IT still smells bad in here...
IT does!! Maybe I should take another shower & scrub my feet..
scrub scrub
IT still smells bad in here...
WELL MAYBE IT'S YOU, DAMMIT..
I'm sorry. Don't leave. I'll check under the bed...
Is there anything under there?
There's some sort of pan.
EEEYeeW!! What is it? Rotten meatloaf?
IT'S A LOAF ALL RIGHT-- BUT IT SURE AIN'T MEAT!!
PICTURE THIS: A HALF NAKED, OBSCENITY SPEWING, CLEAVER WIELDING COLOMBIAN DEMANDING THE GENITALIA OF HIS SOON TO BE FORMER ROOMMATE...
JUST ANOTHER EXAMPLE OF THE EVIL THAT ROOMMATES DO!!
STOP

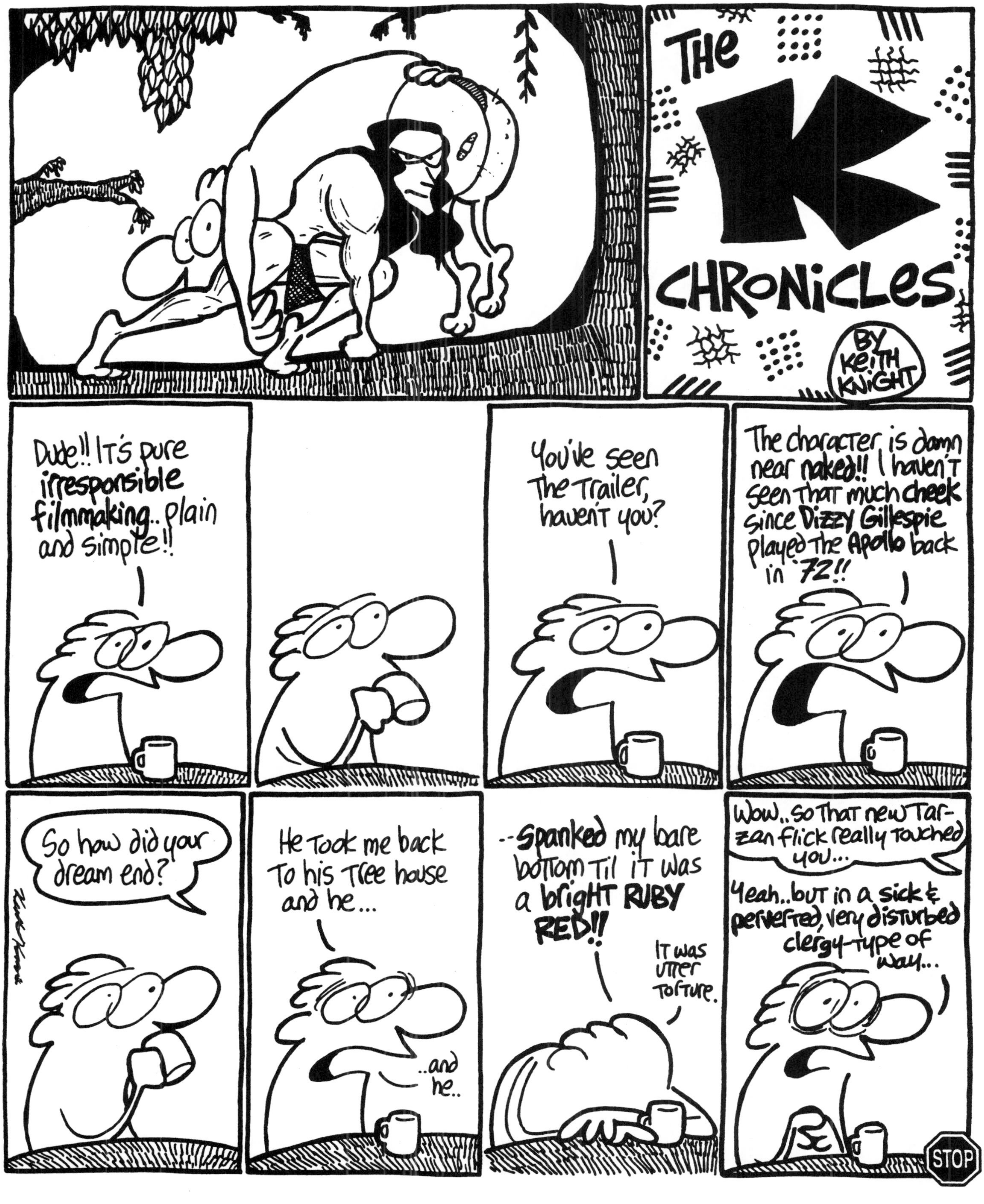
THE K CHRONICLES
BY KEITH KNIGHT
Dude!! It's pure irresponsible filmmaking.. plain and simple!!
You've seen The Trailer, haven't you?
The character is damn near naked!! I haven't seen that much cheek since Dizzy Gillespie played the Apollo back in '72!!
So how did your dream end?
He Took me back To his Tree house and he...
..and he..
--Spanked my bare bottom Til it was a bright RUBY RED!!
It was utter Torture.
Wow.. so That new Tarzan flick really Touched you...
Yeah.. but in a sick & perverted, very disturbed clergy-type of way...
STOP

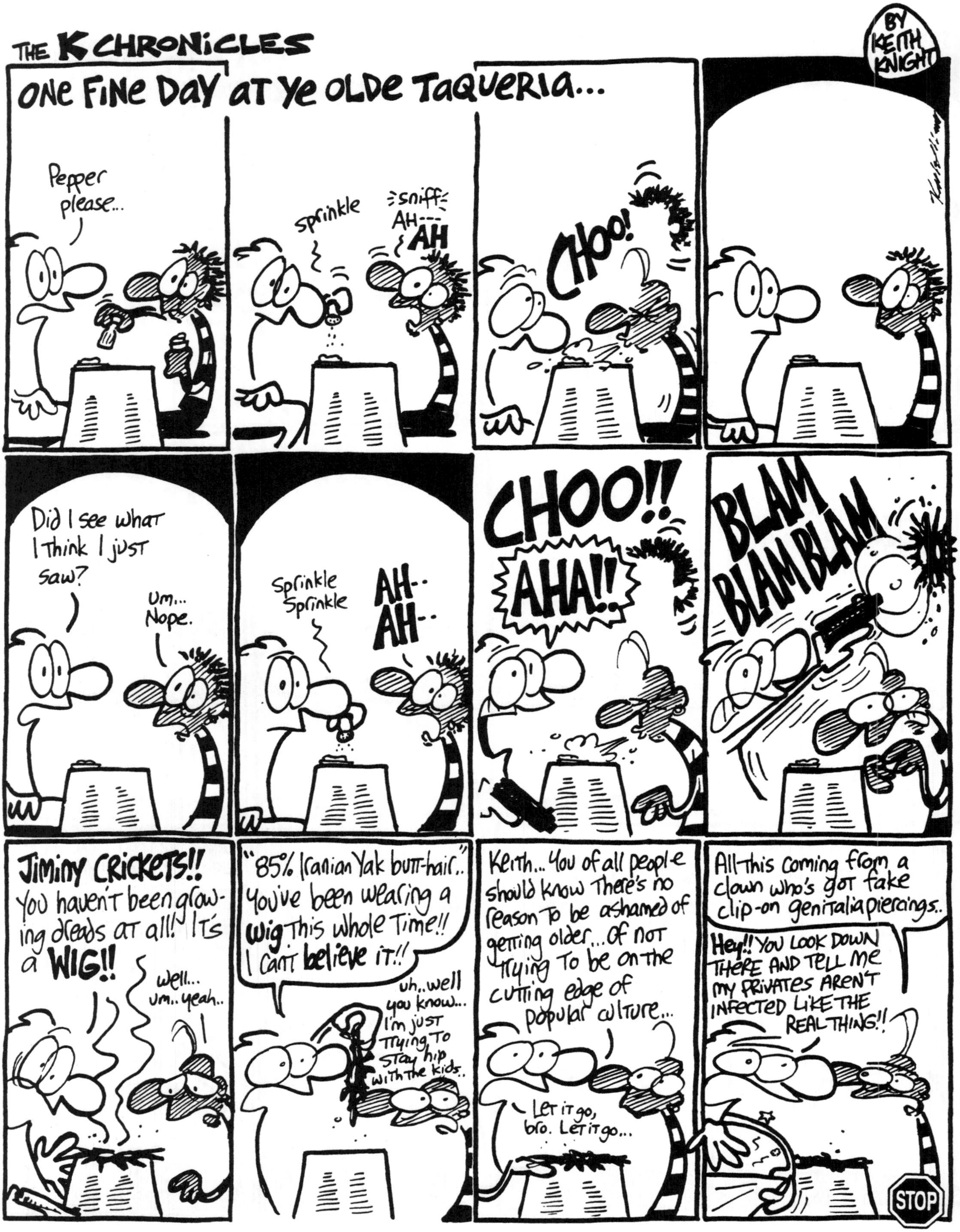

This was done when I was contemplating changing my character's hairstyle. I was growing dreads but wasn't sure if I wanted to put it in the strip.

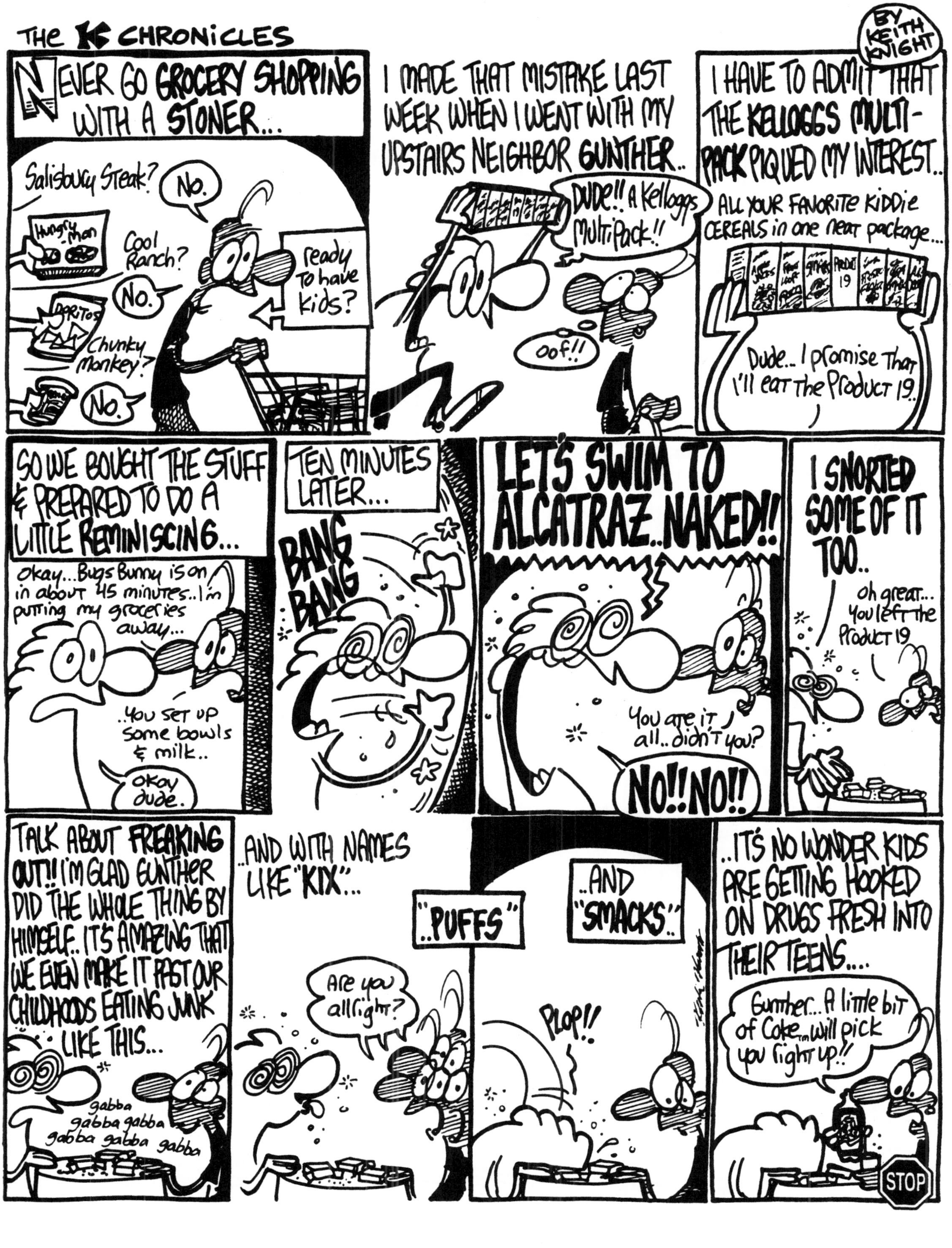
THE K CHRONICLES
BY KEITH KNIGHT
NEVER GO GROCERY SHOPPING WITH A STONER...
Salisbury Steak?
No.
Hungry Man
Cool Ranch?
No.
DORITOS
Chunky Monkey?
No.
ready to have kids?
I MADE THAT MISTAKE LAST WEEK WHEN I WENT WITH MY UPSTAIRS NEIGHBOR GUNTHER..
DUDE!! A Kelloggs MultiPack!!
oof!!
I HAVE TO ADMIT THAT THE KELLOGGS MULTI-PACK PIQUED MY INTEREST...
ALL YOUR FAVORITE KIDDIE CEREALS in one neat package...
Dude... I promise That I'll eat The Product 19..
SO WE BOUGHT THE STUFF & PREPARED TO DO A LITTLE REMINISCING...
Okay...Bugs Bunny is on in about 45 minutes..I'm putting my groceries away...
..You set up some bowls & milk..
Okay dude.
TEN MINUTES LATER...
BANG BANG
LET'S SWIM TO ALCATRAZ..NAKED!!
You ate it all..didn't you?
NO!!NO!!
I SNORTED SOME OF IT TOO..
Oh great... You left the Product 19
TALK ABOUT FREAKING OUT!! I'M GLAD GUNTHER DID THE WHOLE THING BY HIMSELF.. IT'S AMAZING THAT WE EVEN MAKE IT PAST OUR CHILDHOODS EATING JUNK LIKE THIS...
gabba gabba gabba gabba gabba gabba
..AND WITH NAMES LIKE "KIX"...
"..PUFFS"
Are you allright?
..AND "SMACKS"..
PLOP!!
..IT'S NO WONDER KIDS ARE GETTING HOOKED ON DRUGS FRESH INTO THEIR TEENS....
Gunther... A little bit of Coke™ will pick you right up!!
STOP

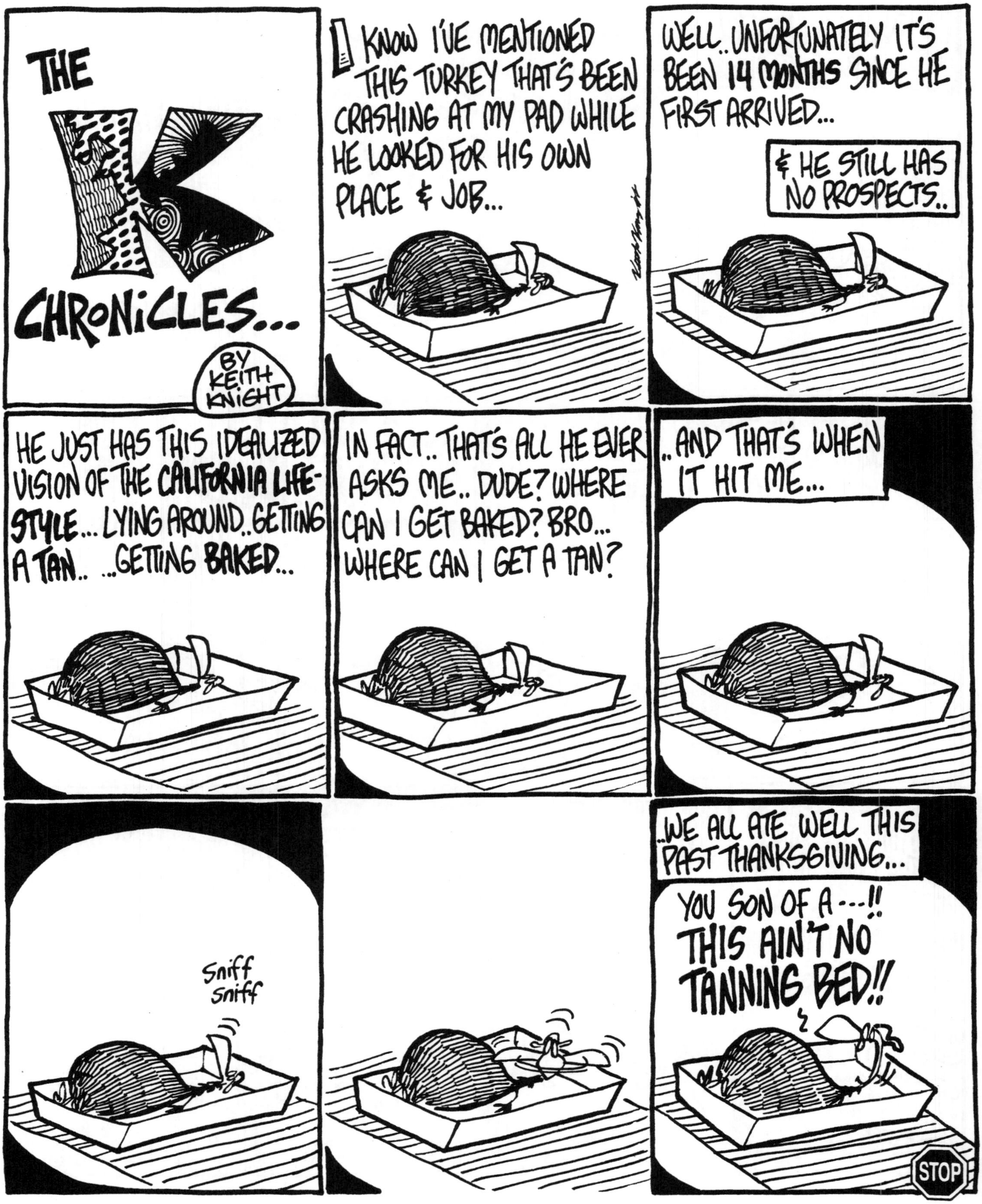
THE K CHRONICLES...
BY KEITH KNIGHT
I KNOW I'VE MENTIONED THIS TURKEY THAT'S BEEN CRASHING AT MY PAD WHILE HE LOOKED FOR HIS OWN PLACE & JOB...
WELL.. UNFORTUNATELY IT'S BEEN 14 MONTHS SINCE HE FIRST ARRIVED...
& HE STILL HAS NO PROSPECTS..
HE JUST HAS THIS IDEALIZED VISION OF THE CALIFORNIA LIFE-STYLE... LYING AROUND.. GETTING A TAN.. ...GETTING BAKED...
IN FACT.. THAT'S ALL HE EVER ASKS ME.. DUDE? WHERE CAN I GET BAKED? BRO... WHERE CAN I GET A TAN?
..AND THAT'S WHEN IT HIT ME...
Sniff sniff
..WE ALL ATE WELL THIS PAST THANKSGIVING...
YOU SON OF A ---!!
THIS AIN'T NO TANNING BED!!
STOP

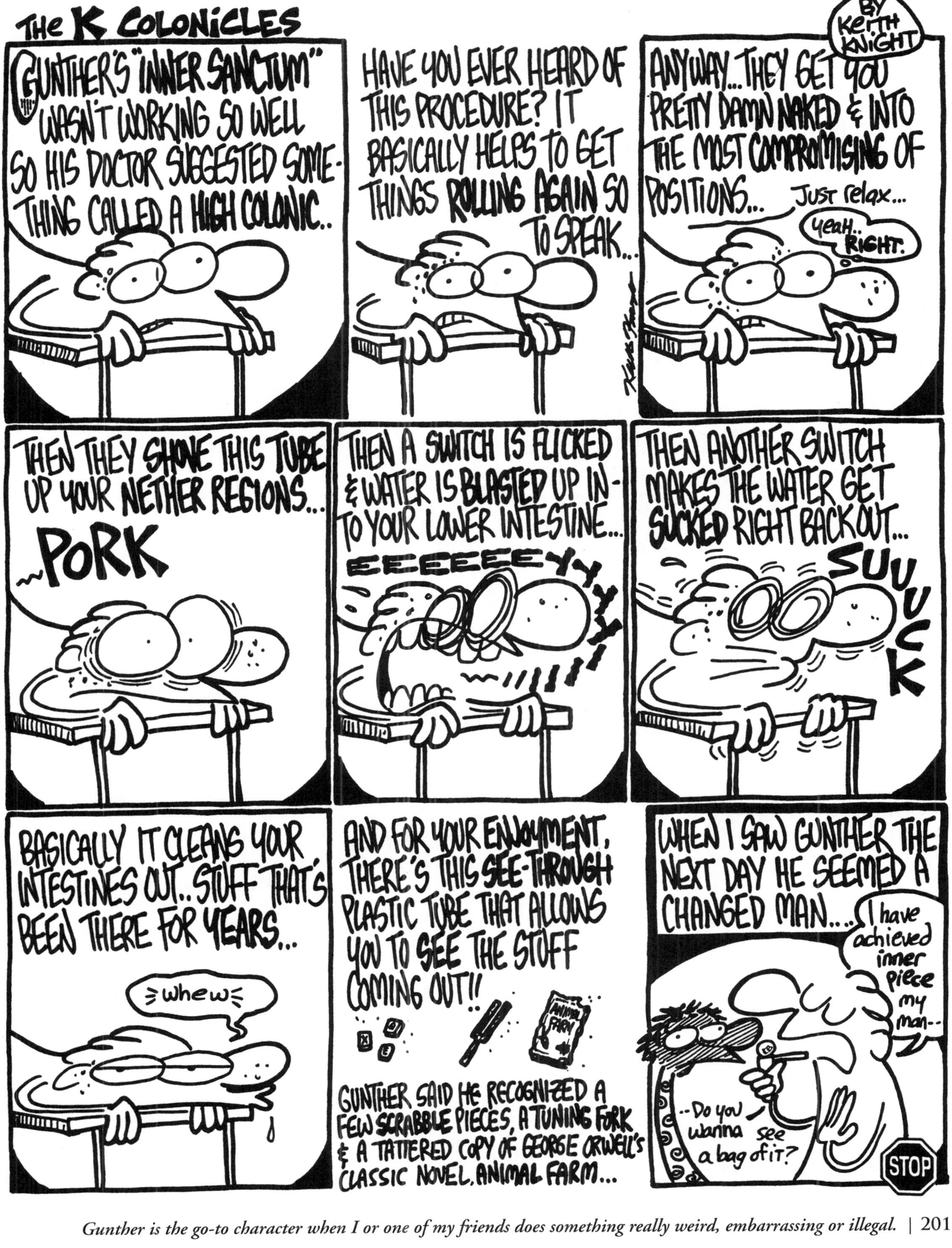
THE K COLONICLES
BY KEITH KNIGHT
GUNTHER'S "INNER SANCTUM" WASN'T WORKING SO WELL SO HIS DOCTOR SUGGESTED SOME-THING CALLED A HIGH COLONIC..
HAVE YOU EVER HEARD OF THIS PROCEDURE? IT BASICALLY HELPS TO GET THINGS ROLLING AGAIN SO TO SPEAK...
ANYWAY... THEY GET YOU PRETTY DAMN NAKED & INTO THE MOST COMPROMISING OF POSITIONS...
JUST relax...
yeah.. RIGHT.
THEN THEY SHOVE THIS TUBE UP YOUR NETHER REGIONS...
~PORK
THEN A SWITCH IS FLICKED & WATER IS BLASTED UP IN-TO YOUR LOWER INTESTINE...
EEEEEEYYYY
THEN ANOTHER SWITCH MAKES THE WATER GET SUCKED RIGHT BACK OUT...
SUUUUCK
BASICALLY IT CLEANS YOUR INTESTINES OUT.. STUFF THAT'S BEEN THERE FOR YEARS...
whew
AND FOR YOUR ENJOYMENT, THERE'S THIS SEE-THROUGH PLASTIC TUBE THAT ALLOWS YOU TO SEE THE STUFF COMING OUT!!
ANIMAL FARM
GUNTHER SAID HE RECOGNIZED A FEW SCRABBLE PIECES, A TUNING FORK & A TATTERED COPY OF GEORGE ORWELL'S CLASSIC NOVEL, ANIMAL FARM...
WHEN I SAW GUNTHER THE NEXT DAY HE SEEMED A CHANGED MAN....
I have achieved inner piece my man...
..Do you wanna see a bag of it?
STOP

Gunther is the go-to character when I or one of my friends does something really weird, embarrassing or illegal.

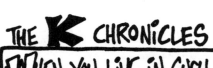

BY KEITH KNIGHT

WHEN YOU LIVE IN SUCH A HIP & HAPPENING TOWN LIKE SAN FRANCISCO, YOU'RE BOUND TO MEET A LOT OF HIP & HAPPENIN' PEOPLE...

TAKE MY FRIEND, ⊘, FER INSTANCE..

⊘ IS SO DAMN HIP THAT SHE CHANGED HER NAME TO A SYMBOL YEARS AGO...

Pierced nose @ age 2

Tongue Tattoo @ 2 months

Baby Sue

SHE'S SO DAMN COOL THAT SHE HAD BOTH HER ARMS & LEGS AMPUTATED...NOT ONLY PREDICTING THE NEXT BIG TREND IN MODERN PRIMITIVES, BUT ALSO SCORING A JOB AS A STUNT DOUBLE FOR SHERILYN FENN IN THE POPULAR FAMILY CLASSIC, BOXING HELENA.

..& SHE ALWAYS TAKES ME & MY NEIGHBOR, GUNTHER TO ALL THE HIP UNDERGROUND PARTIES...

Listen to me, Gunther.. you will NOT lick any toads tonite...Ingesting equine hormone drugs is NOT responsible behavior...

Yeah...Dude.. Yeah...

I COULD ACTUALLY SEE MY WORDS GOING IN ONE EAR & OUT THE OTHER...

ANYWAY..THE MAIN EVENT OF THE LAST PARTY ⊘ TOOK US TO WAS A SPECIAL SCREENING OF THE DIRECTOR'S CUT OF ANDY WARHOL'S CLASSIC UNDERGROUND FILM, EMPIRE...

THE FILM CONSISTS OF A SINGLE STATIC SHOT OF THE EMPIRE STATE BUILDING...

IT IS EIGHT HOURS LONG..

THE DIRECTORS CUT RETAIN THE ADDITIONAL 3 HOURS OF FOOTAGE PREVIOUSLY CUT FROM THE FILM.

GUNTHER HAD TROUBLE FOLLOWING THE PLOT AFTER 3 MINUTES... I LASTED TEN...

OH MY GAWD!! THIS IS A COMPLETELY DIFFERENT FILM WITH THE EXTRA FOOTAGE!!

Cool!

EAST 17

WE NEVER SAW ⊘ FOR THE REST OF THE NITE..

I FINALLY FOUND GUNTHER...

Wanna bust outta here?

SPROING!

GUNTHER!! WHAT DID I SAY TO YOU EARLIER?!!!

DUDE!!! I THOUGHT THEY WERE MENTOS!!

STOP

202

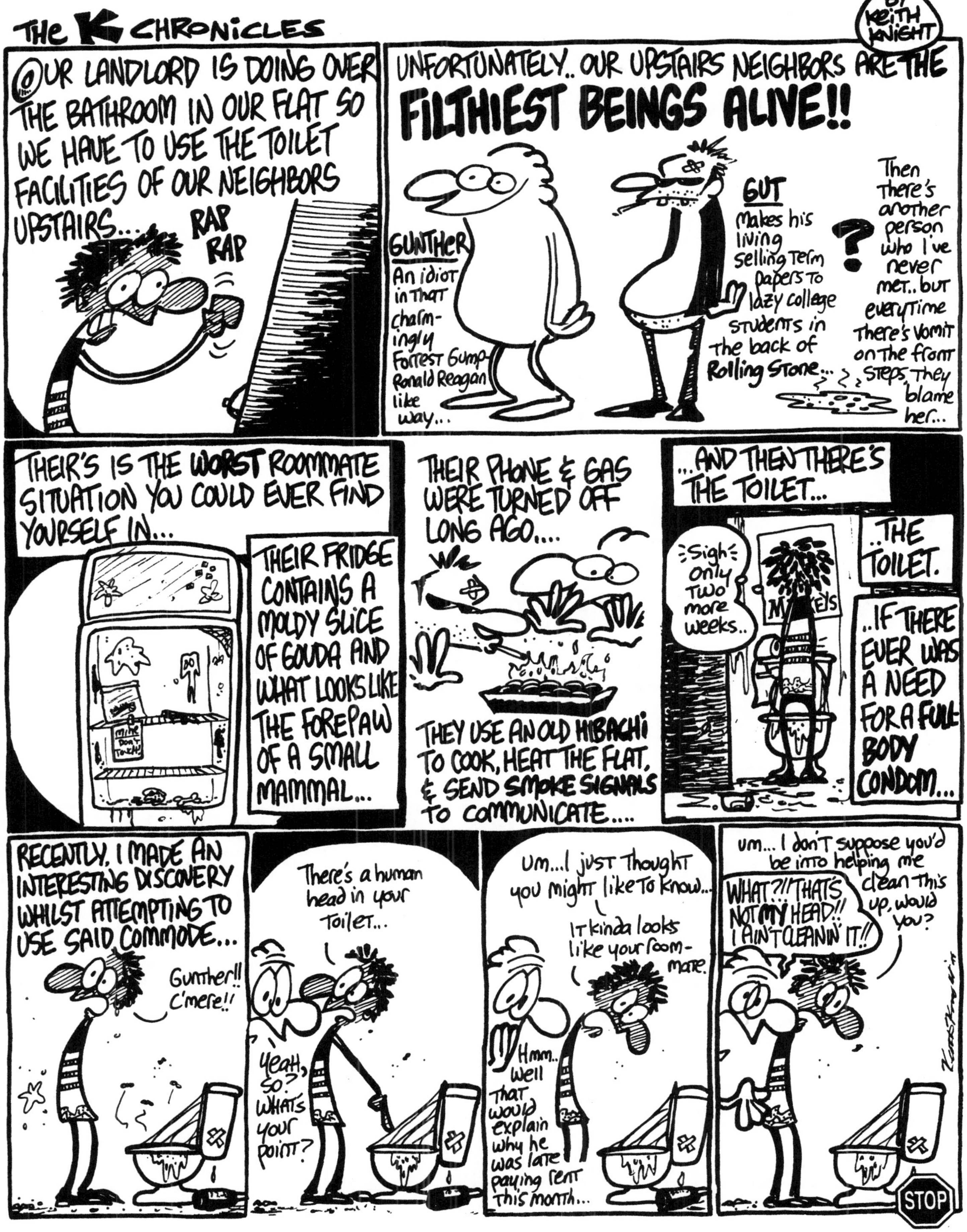
THE K CHRONICLES
BY KEITH KNIGHT
@UR LANDLORD IS DOING OVER THE BATHROOM IN OUR FLAT SO WE HAVE TO USE THE TOILET FACILITIES OF OUR NEIGHBORS UPSTAIRS...
RAP RAP
UNFORTUNATELY.. OUR UPSTAIRS NEIGHBORS ARE THE FILTHIEST BEINGS ALIVE!!
GUNTHER An idiot in that charmingly Forrest Gump-Ronald Reagan like way...
GUT Makes his living selling term papers to lazy college students in the back of Rolling Stone...
Then there's another person who I've never met.. but everytime there's vomit on the front steps, they blame her...
THEIR'S IS THE WORST ROOMMATE SITUATION YOU COULD EVER FIND YOURSELF IN...
THEIR FRIDGE CONTAINS A MOLDY SLICE OF GOUDA AND WHAT LOOKS LIKE THE FOREPAW OF A SMALL MAMMAL...
mine DON'T TOUCH!!
THEIR PHONE & GAS WERE TURNED OFF LONG AGO....
THEY USE AN OLD HIBACHI TO COOK, HEAT THE FLAT, & SEND SMOKE SIGNALS TO COMMUNICATE....
...AND THEN THERE'S THE TOILET...
Sigh only two more weeks..
..THE TOILET.
..IF THERE EVER WAS A NEED FOR A FULL-BODY CONDOM...
RECENTLY, I MADE AN INTERESTING DISCOVERY WHILST ATTEMPTING TO USE SAID COMMODE...
Gunther!! C'mere!!
There's a human head in your toilet...
Yeah, so? What's your point?
Um...I just thought you might like to know...
It kinda looks like your room-mate.
Hmm.. Well that would explain why he was late paying rent this month...
um... I don't suppose you'd be into helping me clean this up, would you?
WHAT?!! THAT'S NOT MY HEAD!! I AIN'T CLEANIN' IT!!
STOP

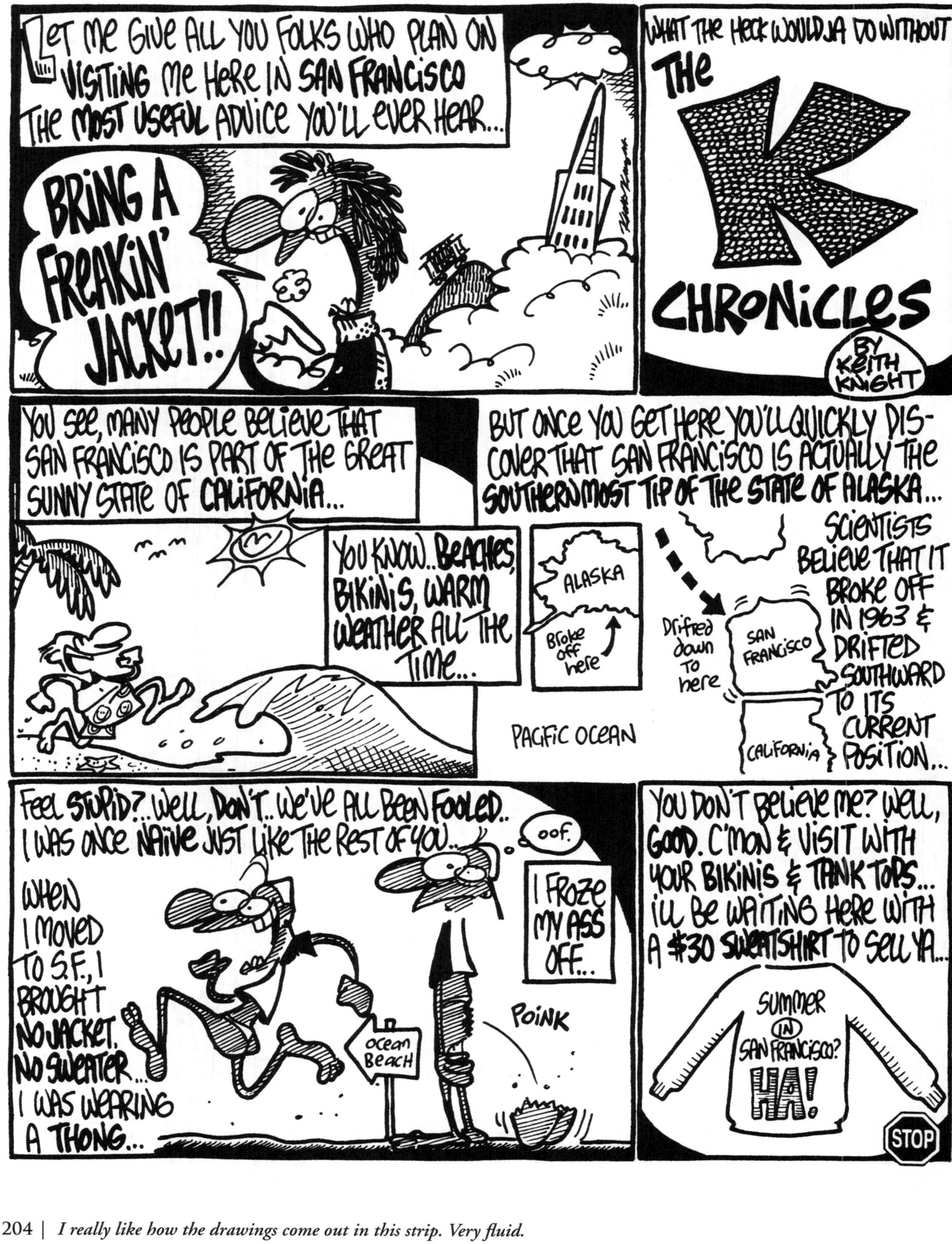
Let me give all you folks who plan on visiting me here in San Francisco the most useful advice you'll ever hear...
BRING A FREAKIN' JACKET!!
What the heck would ja do without
THE K CHRONICLES
BY KEITH KNIGHT
You see, many people believe that San Francisco is part of the great sunny state of California...
You know... beaches, bikinis, warm weather all the time...
But once you get here you'll quickly discover that San Francisco is actually the southernmost tip of the state of Alaska...
ALASKA
Broke off here
Drifted down to here
SAN FRANCISCO
CALIFORNIA
PACIFIC OCEAN
Scientists believe that it broke off in 1963 & drifted southward to its current position...
Feel stupid?.. Well, don't.. We've all been fooled.. I was once naive just like the rest of you..
oof.
When I moved to S.F., I brought no jacket, no sweater... I was wearing a thong...
I froze my ass off...
Ocean Beach
POINK
You don't believe me? Well, good. C'mon & visit with your bikinis & tank tops... I'll be waiting here with a $30 sweatshirt to sell ya...
SUMMER IN SAN FRANCISCO? HA!
STOP

 I really like how the drawings come out in this strip. Very fluid.

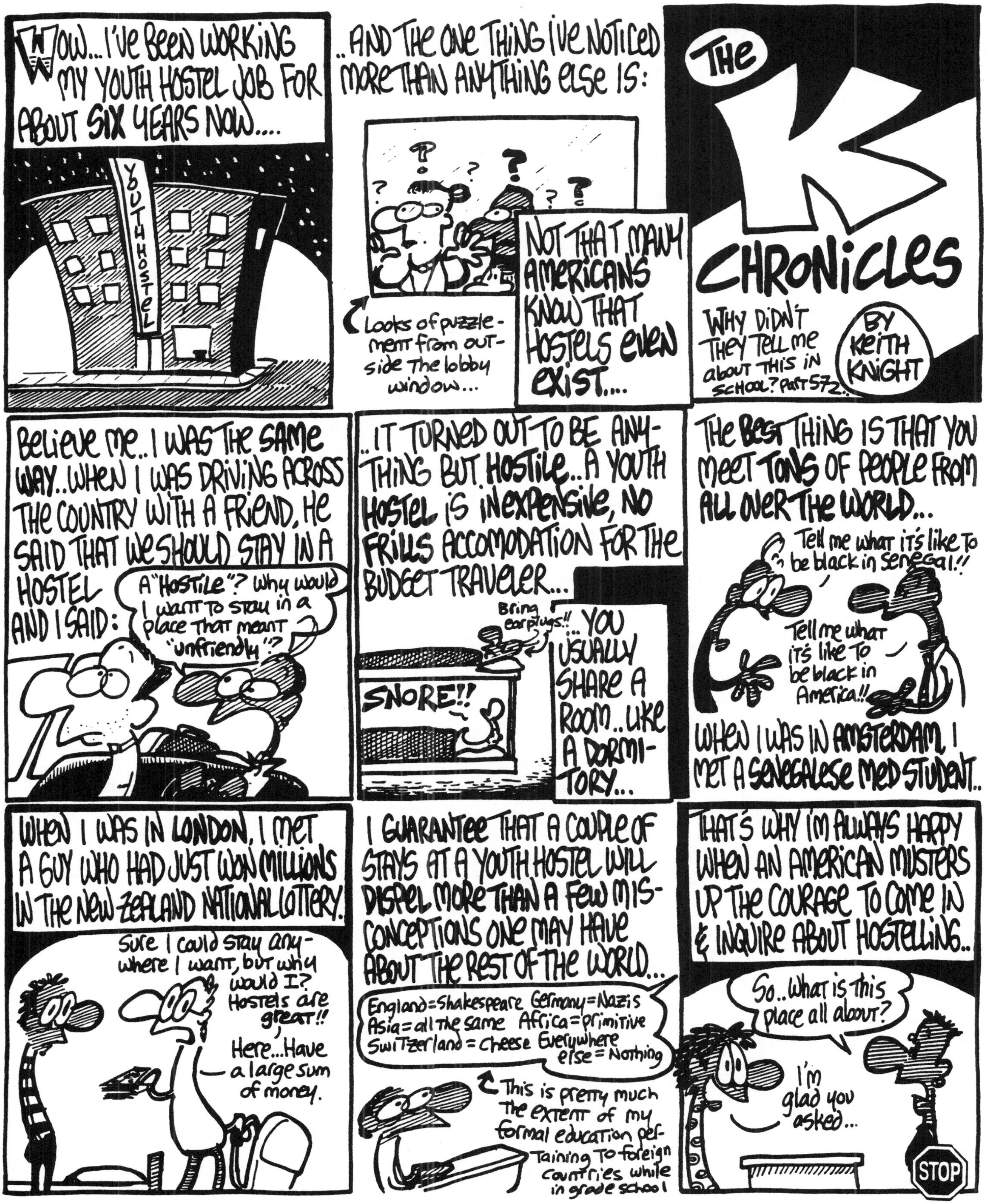
WOW... I'VE BEEN WORKING MY YOUTH HOSTEL JOB FOR ABOUT SIX YEARS NOW....
YOUTH HOSTEL
...AND THE ONE THING I'VE NOTICED MORE THAN ANYTHING ELSE IS:
Looks of puzzlement from outside the lobby window...
NOT THAT MANY AMERICANS KNOW THAT HOSTELS EVEN EXIST....
THE K CHRONICLES
WHY DIDN'T THEY TELL ME ABOUT THIS IN SCHOOL? PART 572..
BY KEITH KNIGHT
BELIEVE ME.. I WAS THE SAME WAY.. WHEN I WAS DRIVING ACROSS THE COUNTRY WITH A FRIEND, HE SAID THAT WE SHOULD STAY IN A HOSTEL AND I SAID:
A "HOSTILE"? WHY WOULD I WANT TO STAY IN A PLACE THAT MEANT "UNFRIENDLY"?
...IT TURNED OUT TO BE ANYTHING BUT HOSTILE.. A YOUTH HOSTEL IS INEXPENSIVE, NO FRILLS ACCOMODATION FOR THE BUDGET TRAVELER...
Bring earplugs!!
SNORE!!
...YOU USUALLY SHARE A ROOM.. LIKE A DORMITORY...
THE BEST THING IS THAT YOU MEET TONS OF PEOPLE FROM ALL OVER THE WORLD...
Tell me what it's like to be black in Senegal!!
Tell me what it's like to be black in America!!
WHEN I WAS IN AMSTERDAM, I MET A SENEGALESE MED STUDENT..
WHEN I WAS IN LONDON, I MET A GUY WHO HAD JUST WON MILLIONS IN THE NEW ZEALAND NATIONAL LOTTERY.
Sure I could stay anywhere I want, but why would I? Hostels are great!!
Here...Have a large sum of money.
I GUARANTEE THAT A COUPLE OF STAYS AT A YOUTH HOSTEL WILL DISPEL MORE THAN A FEW MISCONCEPTIONS ONE MAY HAVE ABOUT THE REST OF THE WORLD...
England=Shakespeare Germany=Nazis Asia=all the same Africa=primitive Switzerland=Cheese Everywhere else=Nothing
This is pretty much the extent of my formal education pertaining to foreign countries while in grade school
THAT'S WHY I'M ALWAYS HAPPY WHEN AN AMERICAN MUSTERS UP THE COURAGE TO COME IN & INQUIRE ABOUT HOSTELLING..
So.. What is this place all about?
I'm glad you asked...
STOP

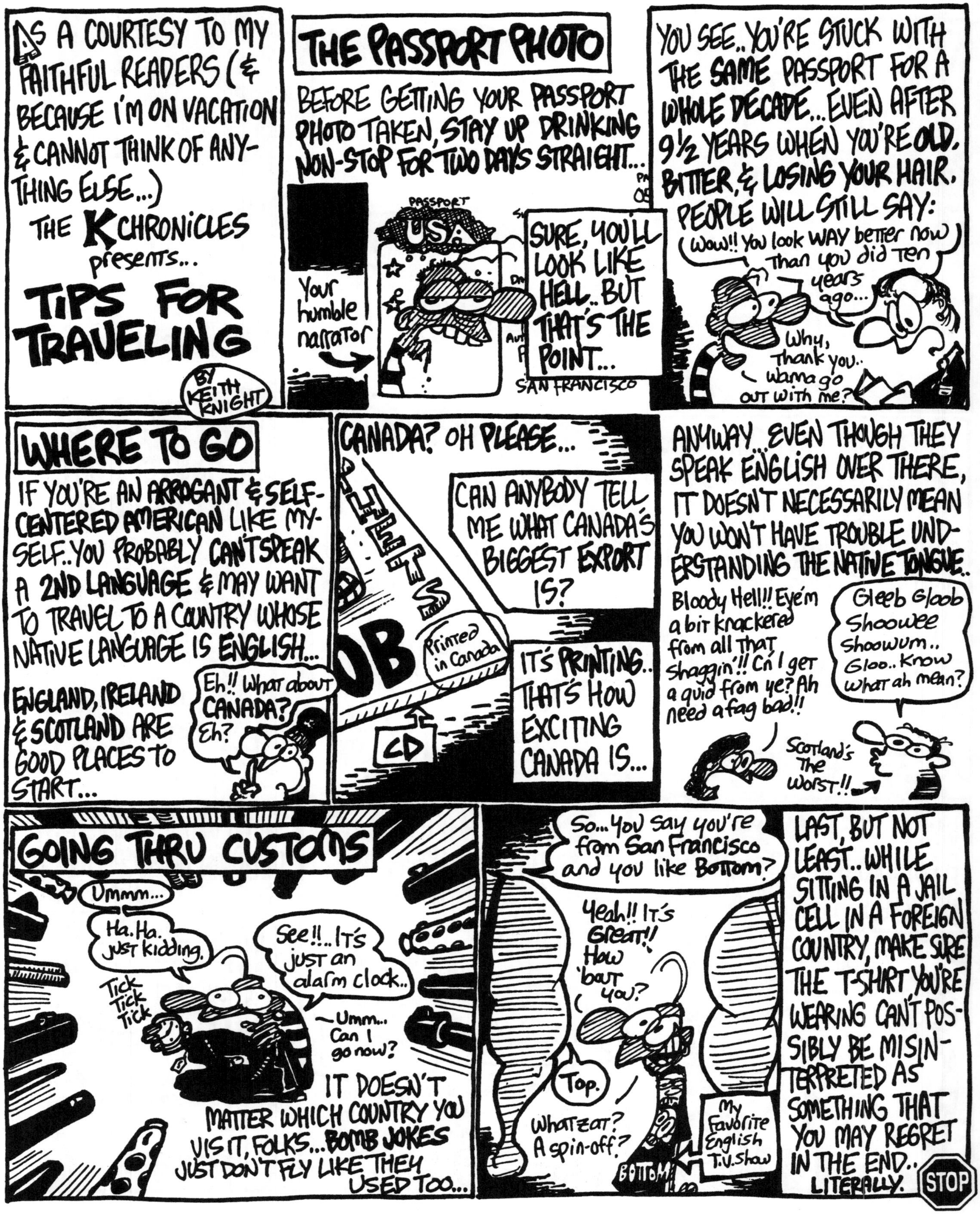
AS A COURTESY TO MY FAITHFUL READERS (& BECAUSE I'M ON VACATION & CANNOT THINK OF ANYTHING ELSE...)
THE K CHRONICLES presents...
TIPS FOR TRAVELING
BY KEITH KNIGHT
THE PASSPORT PHOTO
BEFORE GETTING YOUR PASSPORT PHOTO TAKEN, STAY UP DRINKING NON-STOP FOR TWO DAYS STRAIGHT...
PASSPORT
USA
Your humble narrator
SURE, YOU'LL LOOK LIKE HELL.. BUT THAT'S THE POINT...
SAN FRANCISCO
YOU SEE.. YOU'RE STUCK WITH THE SAME PASSPORT FOR A WHOLE DECADE... EVEN AFTER 9½ YEARS WHEN YOU'RE OLD, BITTER, & LOSING YOUR HAIR, PEOPLE WILL STILL SAY:
Wow!! You look WAY better now than you did ten years ago...
Why, Thank you.. wanna go out with me?
WHERE TO GO
IF YOU'RE AN ARROGANT & SELF-CENTERED AMERICAN LIKE MYSELF.. YOU PROBABLY CAN'T SPEAK A 2ND LANGUAGE & MAY WANT TO TRAVEL TO A COUNTRY WHOSE NATIVE LANGUAGE IS ENGLISH...
ENGLAND, IRELAND & SCOTLAND ARE GOOD PLACES TO START...
Eh!! What about CANADA? Eh?
CANADA? OH PLEASE...
CAN ANYBODY TELL ME WHAT CANADA'S BIGGEST EXPORT IS?
SHEETS
OB
Printed in Canada
CD
IT'S PRINTING.. THAT'S HOW EXCITING CANADA IS...
ANYWAY.. EVEN THOUGH THEY SPEAK ENGLISH OVER THERE, IT DOESN'T NECESSARILY MEAN YOU WON'T HAVE TROUBLE UNDERSTANDING THE NATIVE TONGUE..
Bloody Hell!! Eye'm a bit knackered from all that shaggin'!! Cn' I get a quid from ye? Ah need a fag bad!!
Gleeb Gloob Shoowee Showum.. Gloo.. Know what ah mean?
Scotland's The Worst!!
GOING THRU CUSTOMS
Ummm...
Ha. Ha. Just kidding.
Tick Tick Tick
See!!... It's just an alarm clock..
Umm... Can I go now?
IT DOESN'T MATTER WHICH COUNTRY YOU VISIT, FOLKS... BOMB JOKES JUST DON'T FLY LIKE THEY USED TOO...
So... You say you're from San Francisco and you like Bottom?
Yeah!! It's Great!! How 'bout you?
Top.
What zat? A spin-off?
My Favorite English T.V. Show
BOTTOM
LAST, BUT NOT LEAST.. WHILE SITTING IN A JAIL CELL IN A FOREIGN COUNTRY, MAKE SURE THE T-SHIRT YOU'RE WEARING CAN'T POSSIBLY BE MISINTERPRETED AS SOMETHING THAT YOU MAY REGRET IN THE END.. LITERALLY.
STOP

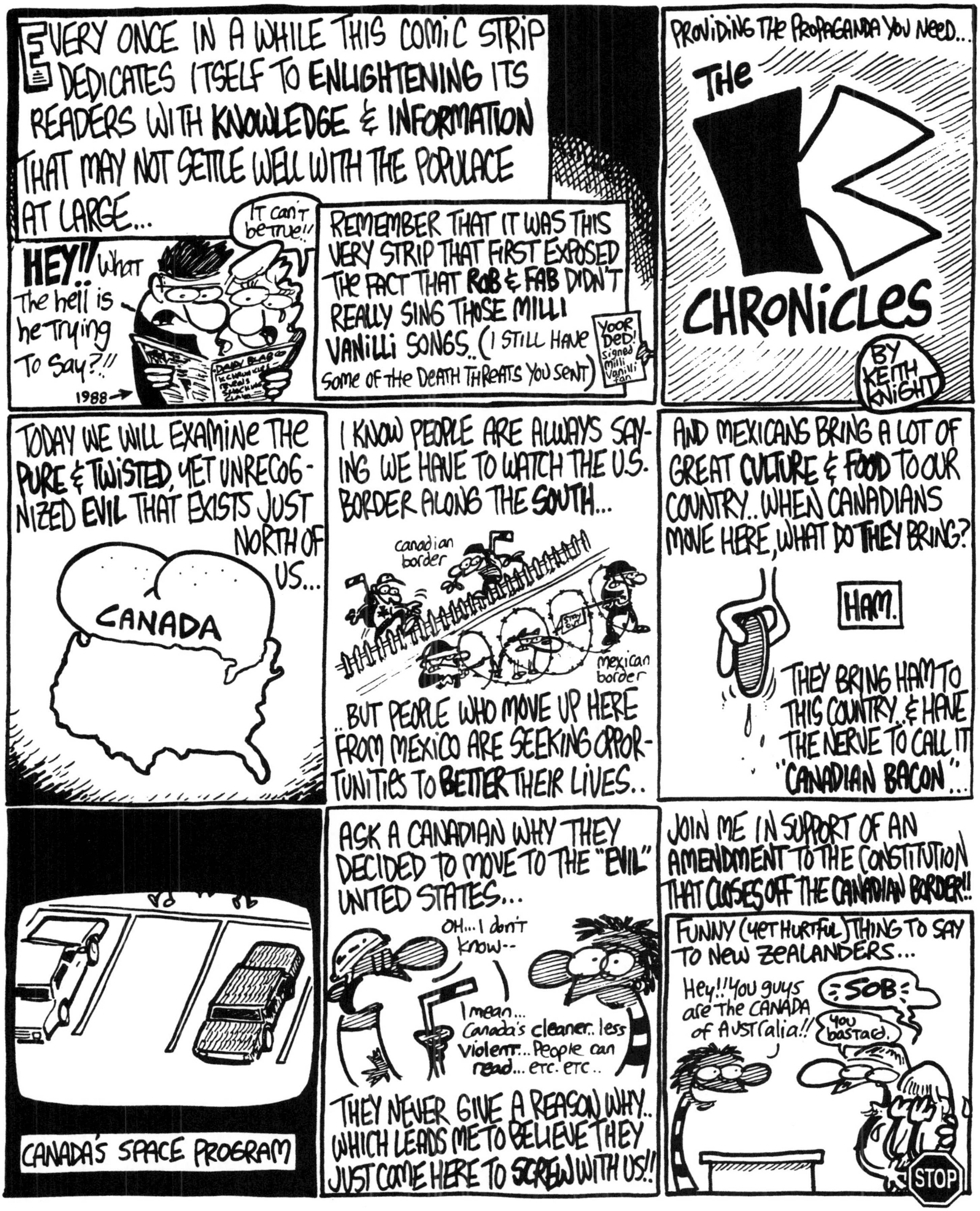
EVERY ONCE IN A WHILE THIS COMIC STRIP DEDICATES ITSELF TO ENLIGHTENING ITS READERS WITH KNOWLEDGE & INFORMATION THAT MAY NOT SETTLE WELL WITH THE POPULACE AT LARGE...
HEY!! What The hell is he Trying To Say?!!
It can't be true!!
1988
REMEMBER THAT IT WAS THIS VERY STRIP THAT FIRST EXPOSED THE FACT THAT ROB & FAB DIDN'T REALLY SING THOSE MILLI VANILLI SONGS.. (I STILL HAVE SOME OF THE DEATH THREATS YOU SENT)
YOOR DED! signed Milli Vanilli fan
PROVIDING THE PROPAGANDA YOU NEED...
THE K CHRONICLES
BY KEITH KNIGHT
TODAY WE WILL EXAMINE THE PURE & TWISTED, YET UNRECOGNIZED EVIL THAT EXISTS JUST NORTH OF US...
CANADA
I KNOW PEOPLE ARE ALWAYS SAYING WE HAVE TO WATCH THE U.S. BORDER ALONG THE SOUTH...
canadian border
mexican border
..BUT PEOPLE WHO MOVE UP HERE FROM MEXICO ARE SEEKING OPPORTUNITIES TO BETTER THEIR LIVES..
AND MEXICANS BRING A LOT OF GREAT CULTURE & FOOD TO OUR COUNTRY.. WHEN CANADIANS MOVE HERE, WHAT DO THEY BRING?
HAM.
THEY BRING HAM TO THIS COUNTRY..& HAVE THE NERVE TO CALL IT "CANADIAN BACON"...
CANADA'S SPACE PROGRAM
ASK A CANADIAN WHY THEY DECIDED TO MOVE TO THE "EVIL" UNITED STATES...
OH... I don't know--
I mean... Canada's cleaner.. less violent... People can read... etc. etc..
THEY NEVER GIVE A REASON WHY.. WHICH LEADS ME TO BELIEVE THEY JUST COME HERE TO SCREW WITH US!!
JOIN ME IN SUPPORT OF AN AMENDMENT TO THE CONSTITUTION THAT CLOSES OFF THE CANADIAN BORDER!!
FUNNY (YET HURTFUL) THING TO SAY TO NEW ZEALANDERS...
Hey!! You guys are the CANADA of AUSTralia!!
SOB
You bastard.
STOP

The first of many comics where I make fun of Canada. The strip started with the space program and grew from there. Some readers still don't get that I'm making fun of all the folks up in arms about Mexicans coming across the border.

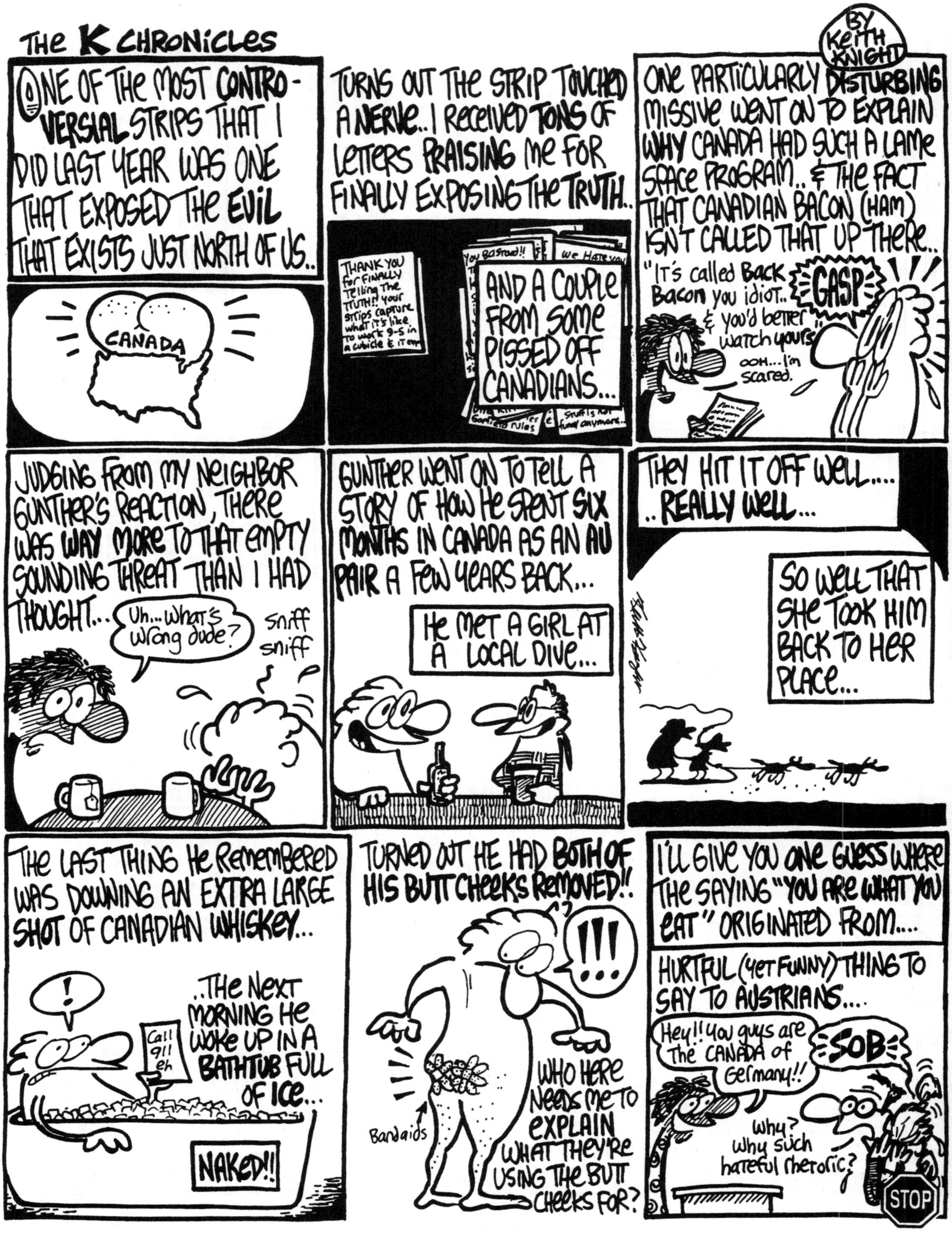
THE K CHRONICLES
BY KEITH KNIGHT
ONE OF THE MOST CONTROVERSIAL STRIPS THAT I DID LAST YEAR WAS ONE THAT EXPOSED THE EVIL THAT EXISTS JUST NORTH OF US..
CANADA
TURNS OUT THE STRIP TOUCHED A NERVE.. I RECEIVED TONS OF LETTERS PRAISING ME FOR FINALLY EXPOSING THE TRUTH..
THANK YOU for FINALLY Telling The TRUTH!! your strips capture what it's like to work 9-5 in a cubicle
You Bastard!!
We Hate you
AND A COUPLE FROM SOME PISSED OFF CANADIANS...
Stuff is not funny anymore..
ONE PARTICULARLY DISTURBING MISSIVE WENT ON TO EXPLAIN WHY CANADA HAD SUCH A LAME SPACE PROGRAM.. & THE FACT THAT CANADIAN BACON (HAM) ISN'T CALLED THAT UP THERE...
"IT'S called Back Bacon you idiot.. & you'd better watch yours"
GASP
OOH... I'm scared.
JUDGING FROM MY NEIGHBOR GUNTHER'S REACTION, THERE WAS WAY MORE TO THAT EMPTY SOUNDING THREAT THAN I HAD THOUGHT...
Uh... What's wrong dude?
Sniff sniff
GUNTHER WENT ON TO TELL A STORY OF HOW HE SPENT SIX MONTHS IN CANADA AS AN AU PAIR A FEW YEARS BACK...
He MET A GIRL AT A LOCAL DIVE...
THEY HIT IT OFF WELL.... ..REALLY WELL...
SO WELL THAT SHE TOOK HIM BACK TO HER PLACE...
THE LAST THING HE REMEMBERED WAS DOWNING AN EXTRA LARGE SHOT OF CANADIAN WHISKEY...
!
..THE NEXT MORNING HE WOKE UP IN A BATHTUB FULL OF ICE...
Call 911 eh
NAKED!!
TURNED OUT HE HAD BOTH OF HIS BUTT CHEEKS REMOVED!!
!!!
Bandaids
WHO HERE NEEDS ME TO EXPLAIN WHAT THEY'RE USING THE BUTT CHEEKS FOR?
I'LL GIVE YOU ONE GUESS WHERE THE SAYING "YOU ARE WHAT YOU EAT" ORIGINATED FROM....
HURTFUL (YET FUNNY) THING TO SAY TO AUSTRIANS....
Hey!! You guys are The CANADA of Germany!!
SOB
Why? Why such hateful rhetoric?
STOP

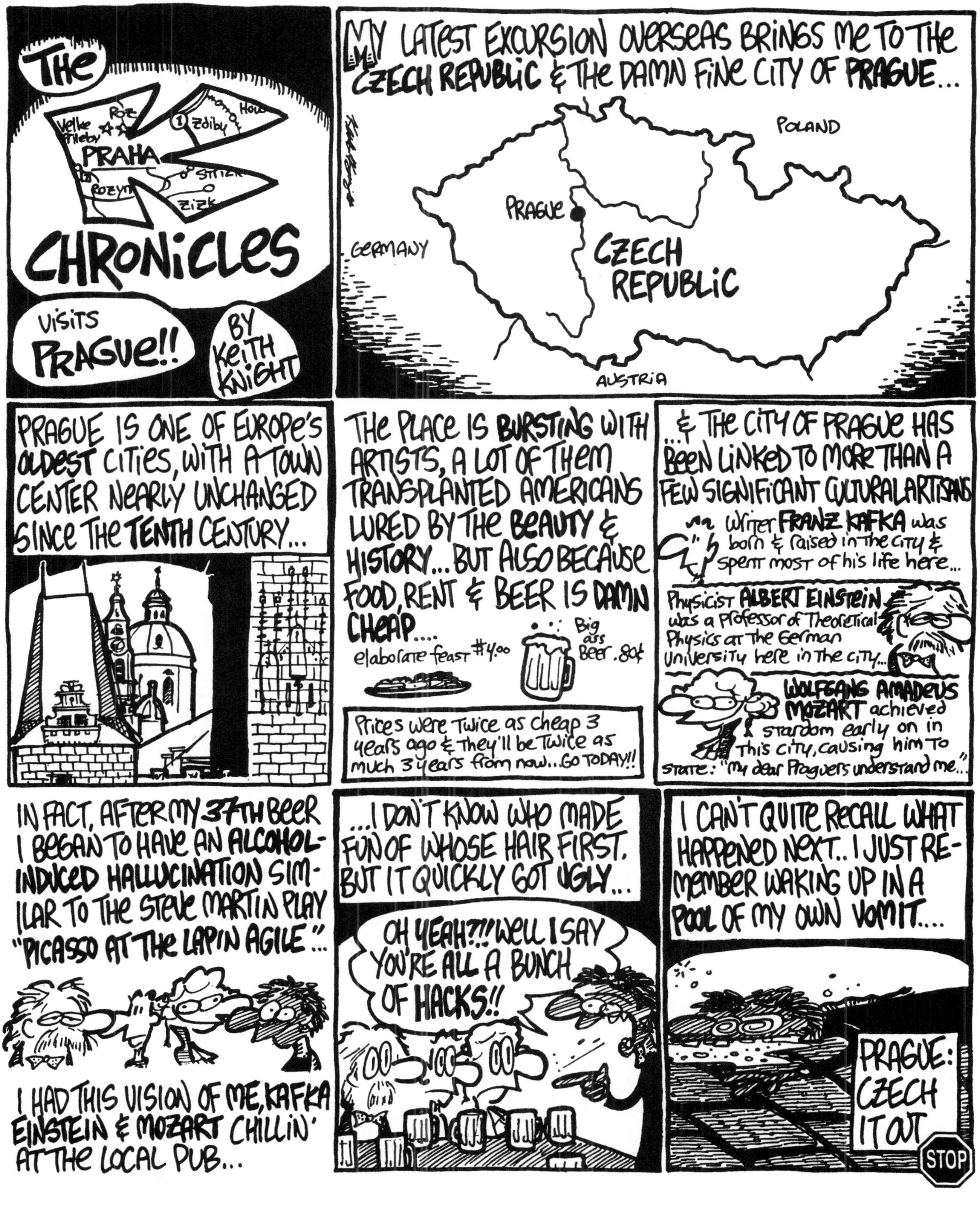
The
Praha
Velke Prileby
Zdiby
Chronicles
Visits Prague!!
By Keith Knight
My latest excursion overseas brings me to the Czech Republic & the damn fine city of Prague...
Poland
Prague
Germany
Czech Republic
Austria
Prague is one of Europe's oldest cities, with a town center nearly unchanged since the tenth century...
The place is bursting with artists, a lot of them transplanted Americans lured by the beauty & history... but also because food, rent & beer is damn cheap....
elaborate feast $4.00
Big ass Beer .80¢
Prices were twice as cheap 3 years ago & they'll be twice as much 3 years from now... Go today!!
...& the city of Prague has been linked to more than a few significant cultural artisans
Writer Franz Kafka was born & raised in the city & spent most of his life here...
Physicist Albert Einstein was a professor of theoretical physics at the German University here in the city...
Wolfgang Amadeus Mozart achieved stardom early on in this city, causing him to state: "My dear Praguers understand me."
In fact, after my 37th beer I began to have an alcohol-induced hallucination simillar to the Steve Martin play "Picasso at the Lapin Agile"...
I had this vision of me, Kafka Einstein & Mozart chillin' at the local pub...
...I don't know who made fun of whose hair first, but it quickly got ugly...
Oh yeah?!! Well I say you're all a bunch of hacks!!
I can't quite recall what happened next.. I just remember waking up in a pool of my own vomit....
Prague: Czech it out
STOP

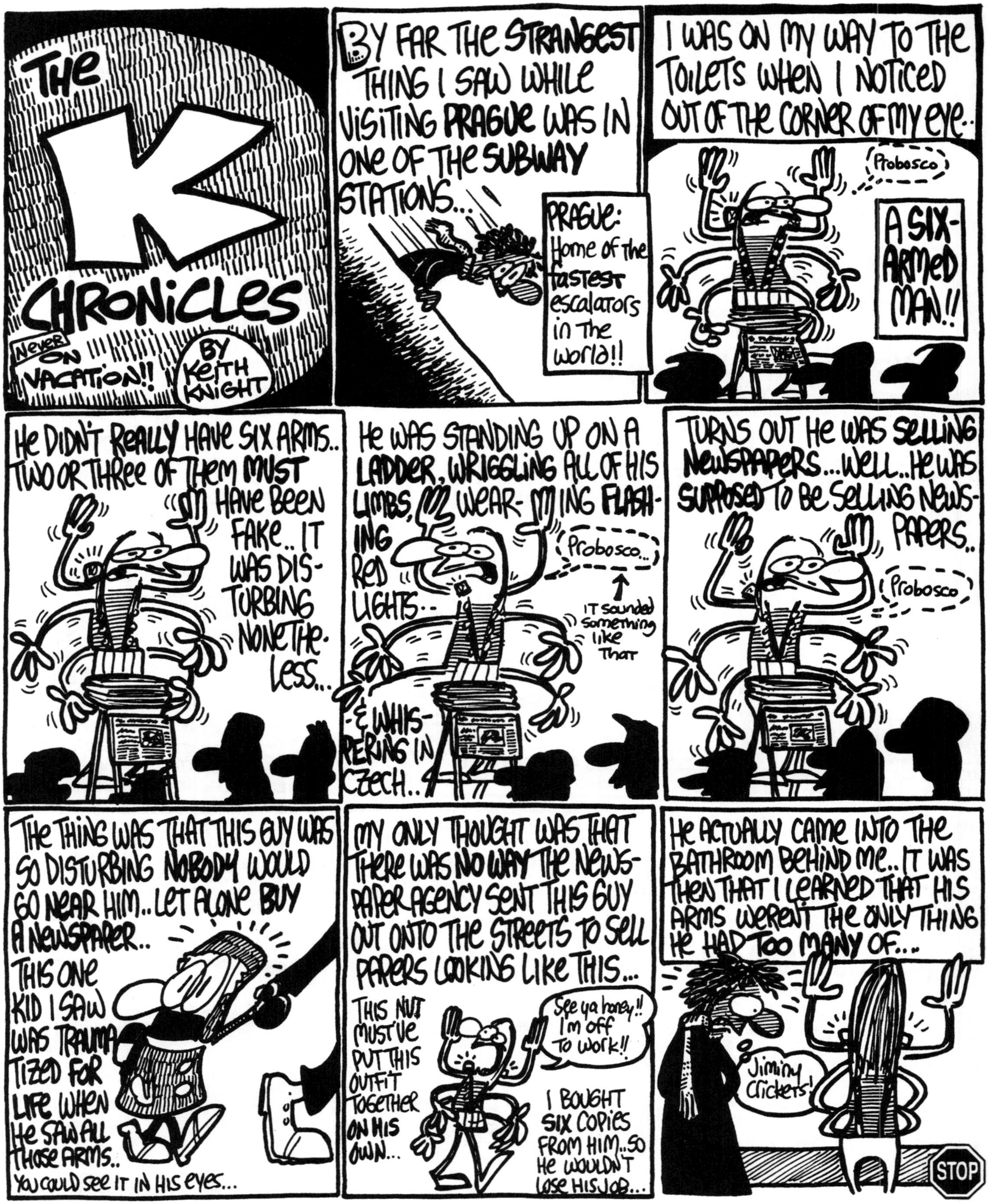
THE K CHRONICLES
NEVER ON VACATION!!
BY KEITH KNIGHT
BY FAR THE STRANGEST THING I SAW WHILE VISITING PRAGUE WAS IN ONE OF THE SUBWAY STATIONS...
PRAGUE: Home of the fastest escalators in the world!!
I WAS ON MY WAY TO THE TOILETS WHEN I NOTICED OUT OF THE CORNER OF MY EYE..
Probosco
A SIX-ARMED MAN!!
HE DIDN'T REALLY HAVE SIX ARMS.. TWO OR THREE OF THEM MUST HAVE BEEN FAKE.. IT WAS DISTURBING NONETHELESS...
HE WAS STANDING UP ON A LADDER, WRIGGLING ALL OF HIS LIMBS, WEARING FLASHING RED LIGHTS..
Probosco...
IT sounded something like That
& WHISPERING IN CZECH..
TURNS OUT HE WAS SELLING NEWSPAPERS...WELL..HE WAS SUPPOSED TO BE SELLING NEWSPAPERS..
Probosco
THE THING WAS THAT THIS GUY WAS SO DISTURBING NOBODY WOULD GO NEAR HIM..LET ALONE BUY A NEWSPAPER..
THIS ONE KID I SAW WAS TRAUMATIZED FOR LIFE WHEN HE SAW ALL THOSE ARMS..
YOU COULD SEE IT IN HIS EYES...
MY ONLY THOUGHT WAS THAT THERE WAS NO WAY THE NEWSPAPER AGENCY SENT THIS GUY OUT ONTO THE STREETS TO SELL PAPERS LOOKING LIKE THIS...
THIS NUT MUST'VE PUT THIS OUTFIT TOGETHER ON HIS OWN...
See ya honey!! I'm off to work!!
I BOUGHT SIX COPIES FROM HIM..SO HE WOULDN'T LOSE HIS JOB...
HE ACTUALLY CAME INTO THE BATHROOM BEHIND ME.. IT WAS THEN THAT I LEARNED THAT HIS ARMS WEREN'T THE ONLY THING HE HAD TOO MANY OF...
Jiminy Crickets!
STOP

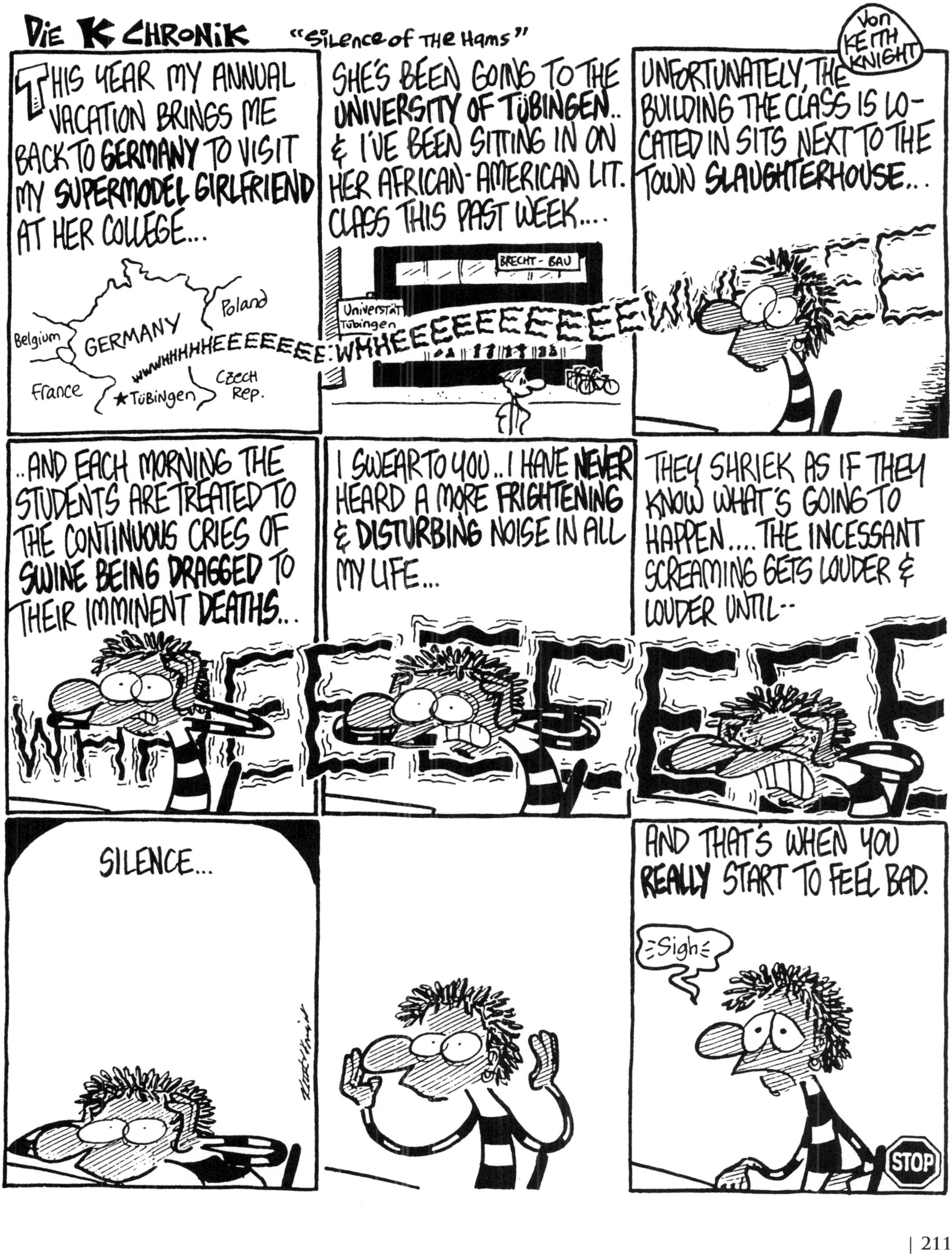

DIE K CHRONIK
"Silence of the Hams"
Von KEITH KNIGHT
THIS YEAR MY ANNUAL VACATION BRINGS ME BACK TO GERMANY TO VISIT MY SUPERMODEL GIRLFRIEND AT HER COLLEGE...
Poland
Belgium
GERMANY
France
★Tübingen
Czech Rep.
WWWHHHHEEEEEEE.
SHE'S BEEN GOING TO THE UNIVERSITY OF TÜBINGEN.. & I'VE BEEN SITTING IN ON HER AFRICAN-AMERICAN LIT. CLASS THIS PAST WEEK....
BRECHT - BAU
Universität Tübingen
WHHEEEEEEEEEEEEW
UNFORTUNATELY, THE BUILDING THE CLASS IS LOCATED IN SITS NEXT TO THE TOWN SLAUGHTERHOUSE...
..AND EACH MORNING THE STUDENTS ARE TREATED TO THE CONTINUOUS CRIES OF SWINE BEING DRAGGED TO THEIR IMMINENT DEATHS...
I SWEAR TO YOU.. I HAVE NEVER HEARD A MORE FRIGHTENING & DISTURBING NOISE IN ALL MY LIFE...
THEY SHRIEK AS IF THEY KNOW WHAT'S GOING TO HAPPEN.... THE INCESSANT SCREAMING GETS LOUDER & LOUDER UNTIL..
SILENCE...
AND THAT'S WHEN YOU REALLY START TO FEEL BAD.
Sigh
STOP

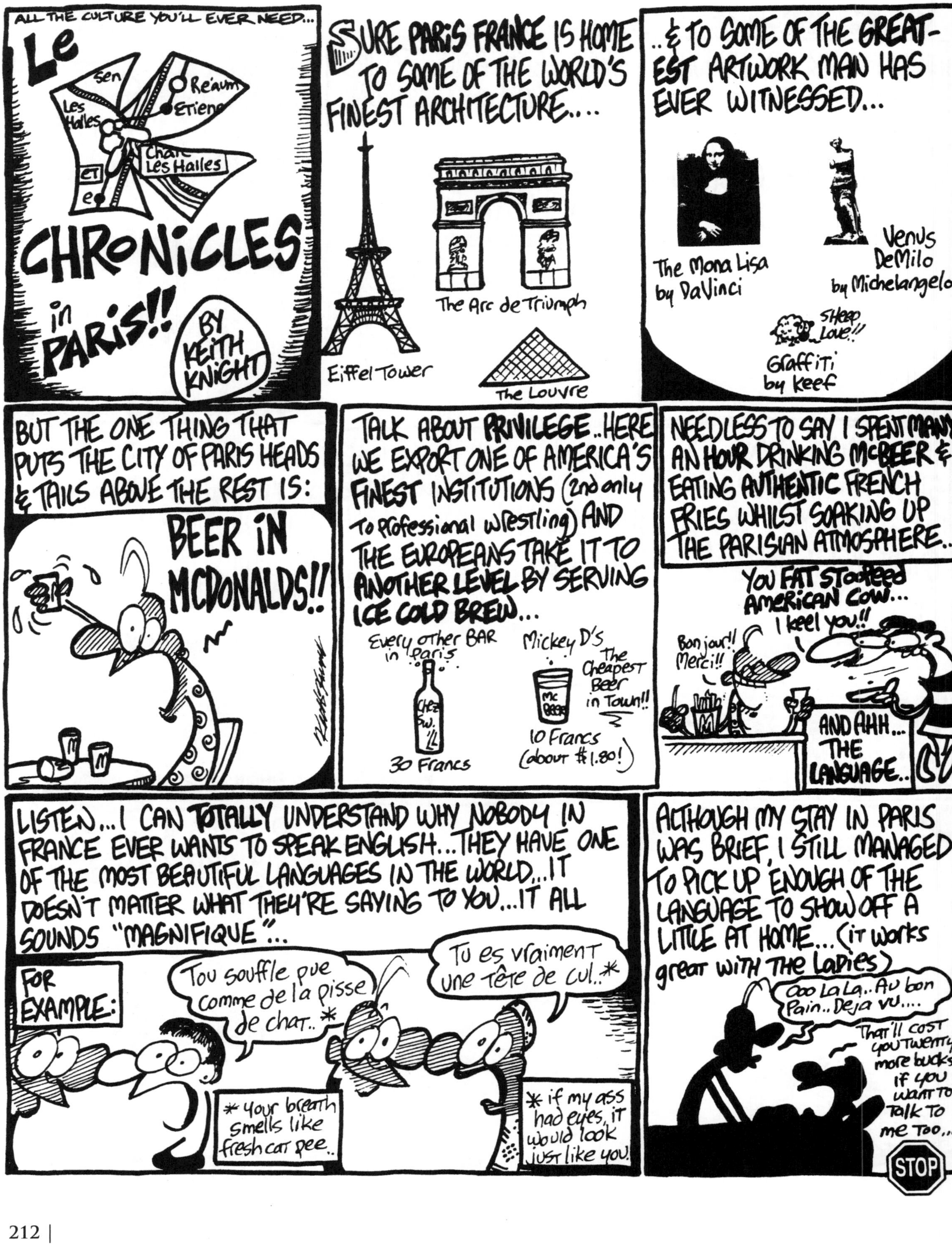
ALL THE CULTURE YOU'LL EVER NEED...
Le CHRONICLES in PARIS!!
BY KEITH KNIGHT
SURE PARIS FRANCE IS HOME TO SOME OF THE WORLD'S FINEST ARCHITECTURE....
Eiffel Tower
The Arc de Triumph
The Louvre
...& TO SOME OF THE GREATEST ARTWORK MAN HAS EVER WITNESSED...
The Mona Lisa by DaVinci
Venus DeMilo by Michelangelo
Sheep Love!!
Graffiti by keef
BUT THE ONE THING THAT PUTS THE CITY OF PARIS HEADS & TAILS ABOVE THE REST IS:
BEER IN MCDONALDS!!..
TALK ABOUT PRIVILEGE..HERE WE EXPORT ONE OF AMERICA'S FINEST INSTITUTIONS (2nd only to professional wrestling) AND THE EUROPEANS TAKE IT TO ANOTHER LEVEL BY SERVING ICE COLD BREW...
Every other BAR in Paris
30 Francs
Mickey D's
The Cheapest Beer in Town!!
10 Francs (about $1.80!)
NEEDLESS TO SAY I SPENT MANY AN HOUR DRINKING McBEER & EATING AUTHENTIC FRENCH FRIES WHILST SOAKING UP THE PARISIAN ATMOSPHERE...
You FAT Stoofeed AMERICAN COW... I keel you!!
Bonjour!! Merci!!
AND AHH... THE LANGUAGE..
LISTEN...I CAN TOTALLY UNDERSTAND WHY NOBODY IN FRANCE EVER WANTS TO SPEAK ENGLISH...THEY HAVE ONE OF THE MOST BEAUTIFUL LANGUAGES IN THE WORLD...IT DOESN'T MATTER WHAT THEY'RE SAYING TO YOU...IT ALL SOUNDS "MAGNIFIQUE"...
FOR EXAMPLE:
Tou souffle pue comme de la pisse de chat..*
Tu es vraiment une tête de cul..*
* your breath smells like fresh cat pee..
* if my ass had eyes, it would look just like you.
ALTHOUGH MY STAY IN PARIS WAS BRIEF, I STILL MANAGED TO PICK UP ENOUGH OF THE LANGUAGE TO SHOW OFF A LITTLE AT HOME...(IT works great with THE LADIES)
Ooo La La.. Au bon Pain.. Deja vu....
That'll cost you twenty more bucks if you want to Talk to me Too...
STOP

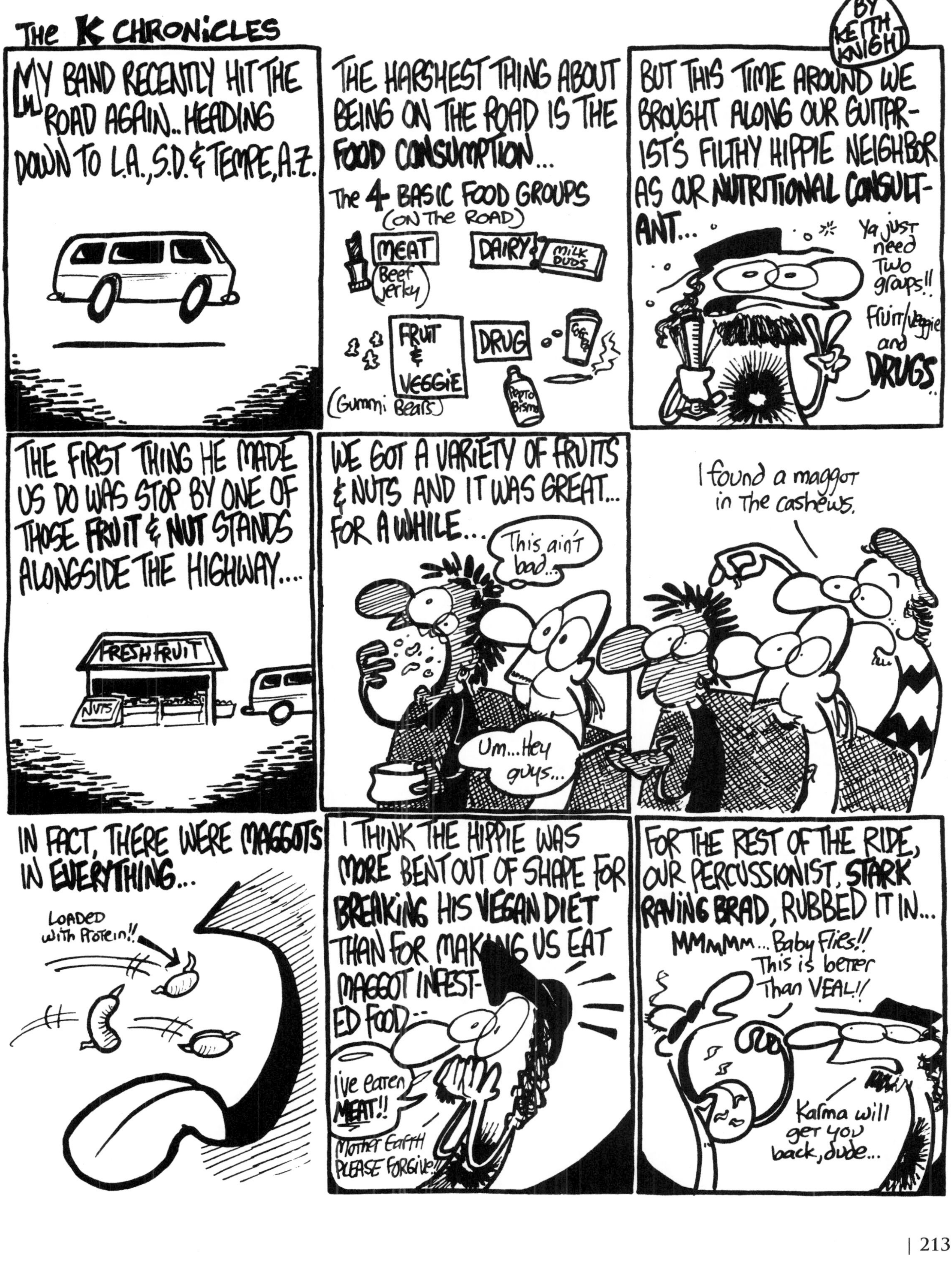
THE K CHRONICLES
BY KEITH KNIGHT
MY BAND RECENTLY HIT THE ROAD AGAIN.. HEADING DOWN TO L.A., S.D. & TEMPE, A.Z.
THE HARSHEST THING ABOUT BEING ON THE ROAD IS THE FOOD CONSUMPTION...
The 4 BASIC FOOD GROUPS (ON The ROAD)
MEAT
Beef jerky
DAIRY
MILK DUDS
FRUIT & VEGGIE
(Gummi Bears)
DRUG
COFFEE
PEPTO BISMOL
BUT THIS TIME AROUND WE BROUGHT ALONG OUR GUITARIST'S FILTHY HIPPIE NEIGHBOR AS OUR NUTRITIONAL CONSULTANT...
Ya just need Two groups!!
Fruit/Veggie and DRUGS..
THE FIRST THING HE MADE US DO WAS STOP BY ONE OF THOSE FRUIT & NUT STANDS ALONGSIDE THE HIGHWAY....
FRESH FRUIT
NUTS
WE GOT A VARIETY OF FRUITS & NUTS AND IT WAS GREAT... FOR A WHILE...
This ain't bad...
Um...Hey guys...
I found a maggot in the cashews.
IN FACT, THERE WERE MAGGOTS IN EVERYTHING...
LOADED with Protein!!
I THINK THE HIPPIE WAS MORE BENT OUT OF SHAPE FOR BREAKING HIS VEGAN DIET THAN FOR MAKING US EAT MAGGOT INFESTED FOOD..
I've eaten MEAT!!
Mother Earth PLEASE FORGIVE!!
FOR THE REST OF THE RIDE, OUR PERCUSSIONIST, STARK RAVING BRAD, RUBBED IT IN...
MMMMM... Baby Flies!! This is better Than VEAL!!
Karma will get you back, dude...

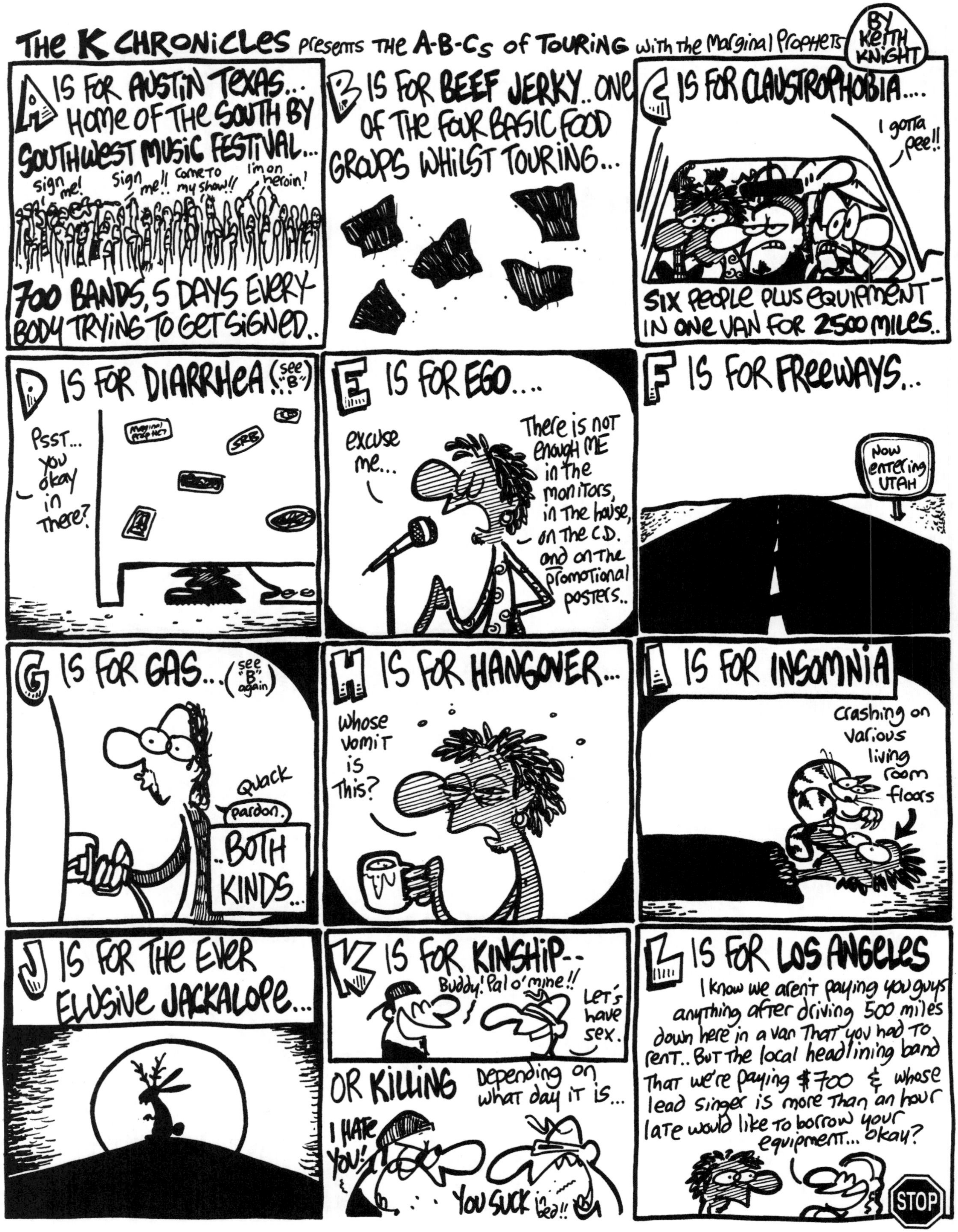
THE K CHRONICLES presents THE A-B-Cs of TOURING with The Marginal Prophets
BY KEITH KNIGHT
A IS FOR AUSTIN TEXAS... Home OF THE SOUTH BY SOUTHWEST MUSIC FESTIVAL...
Sign me!
Sign me!!
Come to my show!!
I'm on heroin!
700 BANDS, 5 DAYS EVERYBODY TRYING TO GET SIGNED..
B IS FOR BEEF JERKY.. ONE OF THE FOUR BASIC FOOD GROUPS WHILST TOURING...
C IS FOR CLAUSTROPHOBIA....
I gotta pee!!
SIX PEOPLE PLUS EQUIPMENT IN ONE VAN FOR 2500 MILES..
D IS FOR DIARRHEA (see "B")
Psst... you okay in there?
SRB
E IS FOR EGO....
excuse me...
There is not enough ME in The monitors, in The house, on The C.D. and on The promotional posters..
F IS FOR FREEWAYS...
Now entering UTAH
G IS FOR GAS... (see "B" again)
Quack
pardon.
..BOTH KINDS...
H IS FOR HANGOVER...
Whose vomit is This?
I IS FOR INSOMNIA
Crashing on various living room floors
J IS FOR THE EVER ELUSIVE JACKALOPE...
K IS FOR KINSHIP--
Buddy! Pal o'mine!!
Let's have sex.
OR KILLING depending on what day it is...
I HATE YOU!
YOU SUCK in bed!!
L IS FOR LOS ANGELES
I know we aren't paying you guys anything after driving 500 miles down here in a van That you had to rent.. But The local headlining band That we're paying $700 & whose lead singer is more Than an hour late would like to borrow your equipment... okay?
STOP

 At Marginal Prophets shows, people often ask how I managed to get the K Chronicles guy to do all of the artwork.

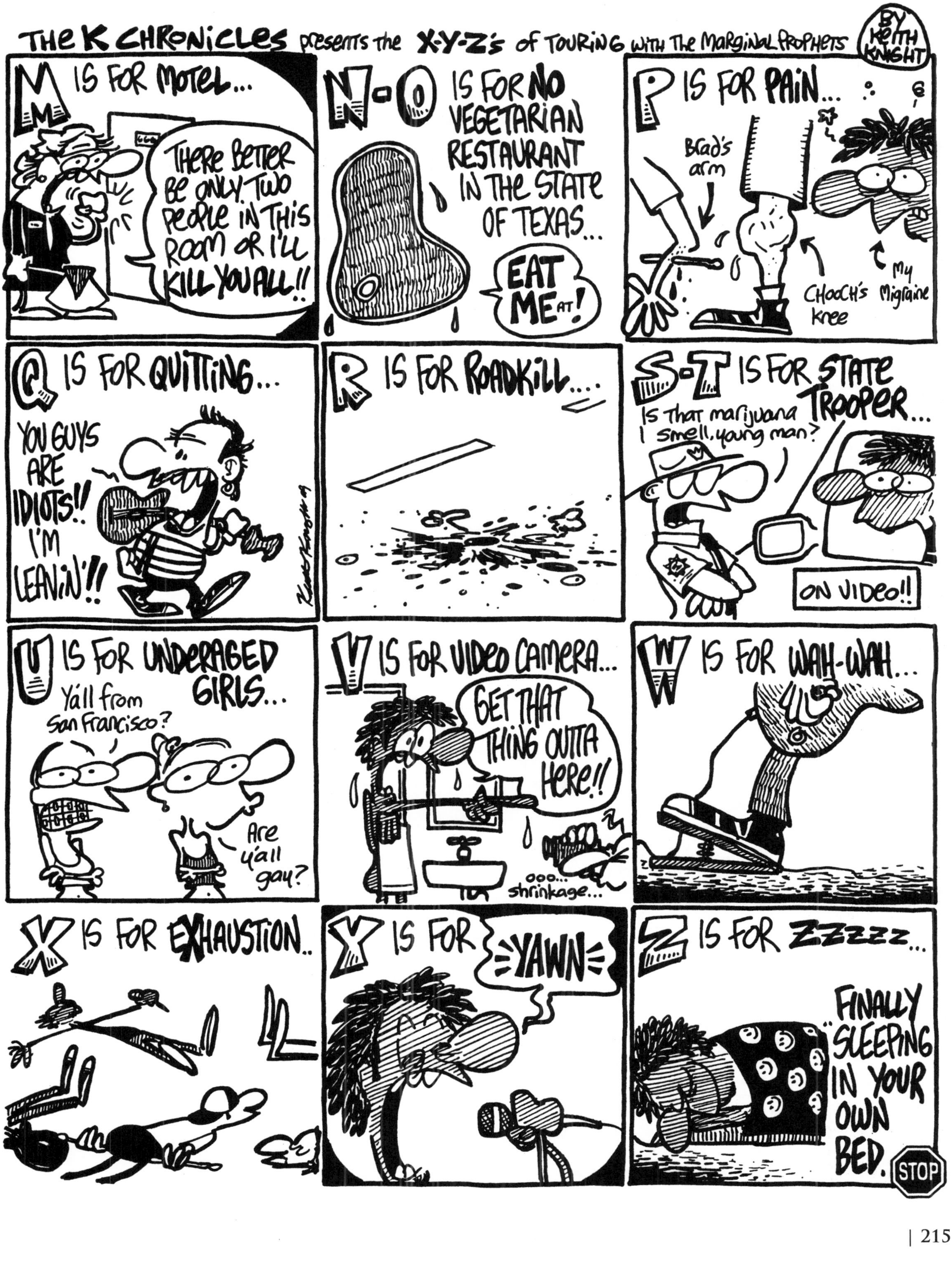
THE K CHRONICLES presents the X-Y-Z's of TOURING with The Marginal Prophets
BY KEITH KNIGHT
M IS FOR MOTEL...
THERE BETTER BE ONLY TWO PEOPLE IN THIS ROOM OR I'LL KILL YOU ALL!!
N-O IS FOR NO VEGETARIAN RESTAURANT IN THE STATE OF TEXAS...
EAT MEAT!
P IS FOR PAIN...
Brad's arm
Chooch's knee
My Migraine
Q IS FOR QUITTING...
YOU GUYS ARE IDIOTS!! I'M LEAVIN'!!
R IS FOR ROADKILL....
S-T IS FOR STATE TROOPER...
Is that marijuana I smell, young man?
ON VIDEO!!
U IS FOR UNDERAGED GIRLS...
Y'all from San Francisco?
Are y'all gay?
V IS FOR VIDEO CAMERA...
GET THAT THING OUTTA HERE!!
ooo... shrinkage...
W IS FOR WAH-WAH...
X IS FOR EXHAUSTION...
Y IS FOR YAWN
Z IS FOR ZZZZZ...
...FINALLY SLEEPING IN YOUR OWN BED.
STOP

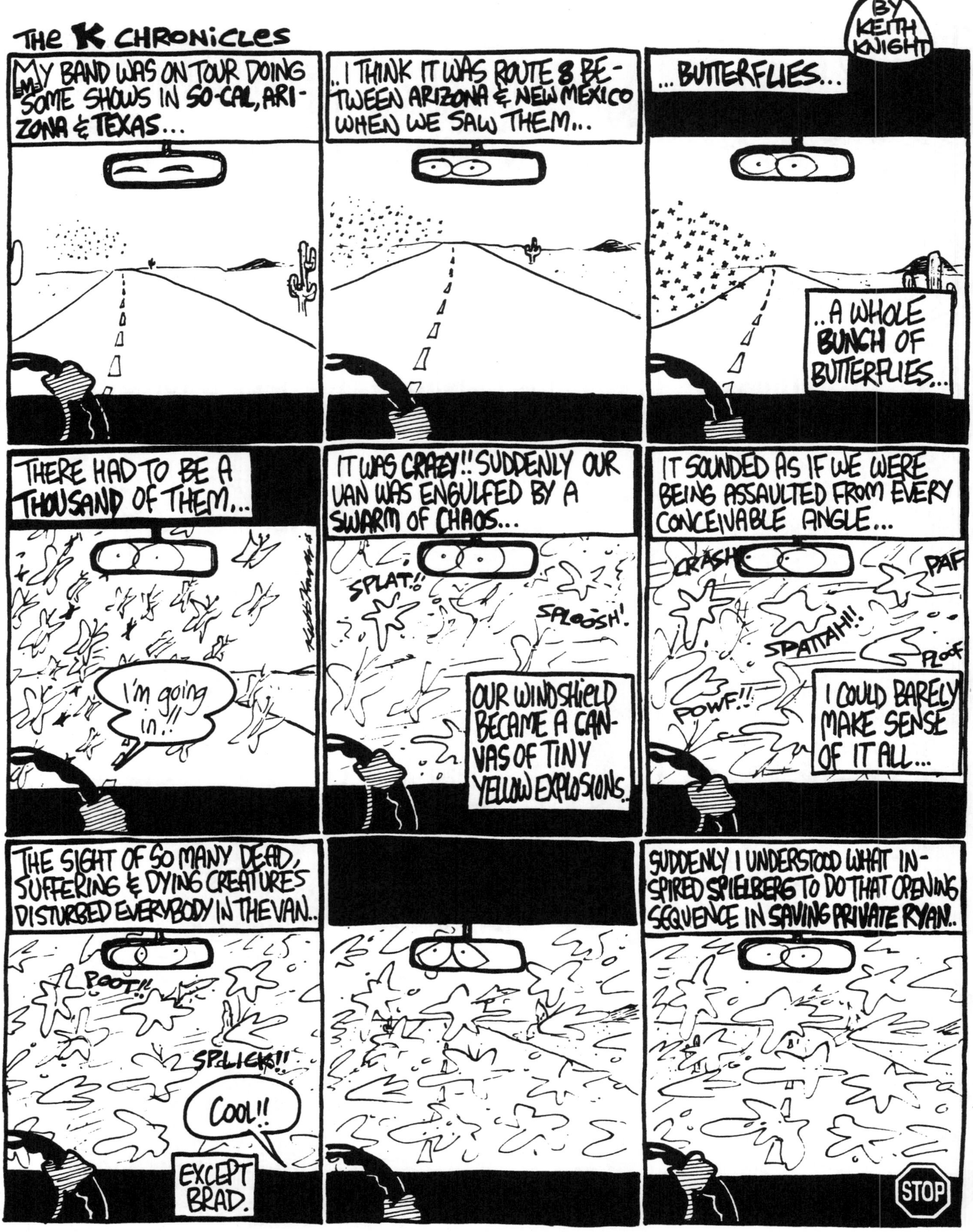
THE K CHRONICLES
BY KEITH KNIGHT
MY BAND WAS ON TOUR DOING SOME SHOWS IN SO-CAL, ARIZONA & TEXAS...
..I THINK IT WAS ROUTE 8 BETWEEN ARIZONA & NEW MEXICO WHEN WE SAW THEM...
...BUTTERFLIES...
..A WHOLE BUNCH OF BUTTERFLIES...
THERE HAD TO BE A THOUSAND OF THEM...
I'm going in!!
IT WAS CRAZY!! SUDDENLY OUR VAN WAS ENGULFED BY A SWARM OF CHAOS...
SPLAT!!
SPLOOSH!
OUR WINDSHIELD BECAME A CANVAS OF TINY YELLOW EXPLOSIONS.
IT SOUNDED AS IF WE WERE BEING ASSAULTED FROM EVERY CONCEIVABLE ANGLE...
CRASH
PAF
SPATTAH!!
PLOOF
POWF!!
I COULD BARELY MAKE SENSE OF IT ALL...
THE SIGHT OF SO MANY DEAD, SUFFERING & DYING CREATURES DISTURBED EVERYBODY IN THE VAN..
POOT!!
SPLICK!!
COOL!!
EXCEPT BRAD.
SUDDENLY I UNDERSTOOD WHAT INSPIRED SPIELBERG TO DO THAT OPENING SEQUENCE IN SAVING PRIVATE RYAN..
STOP

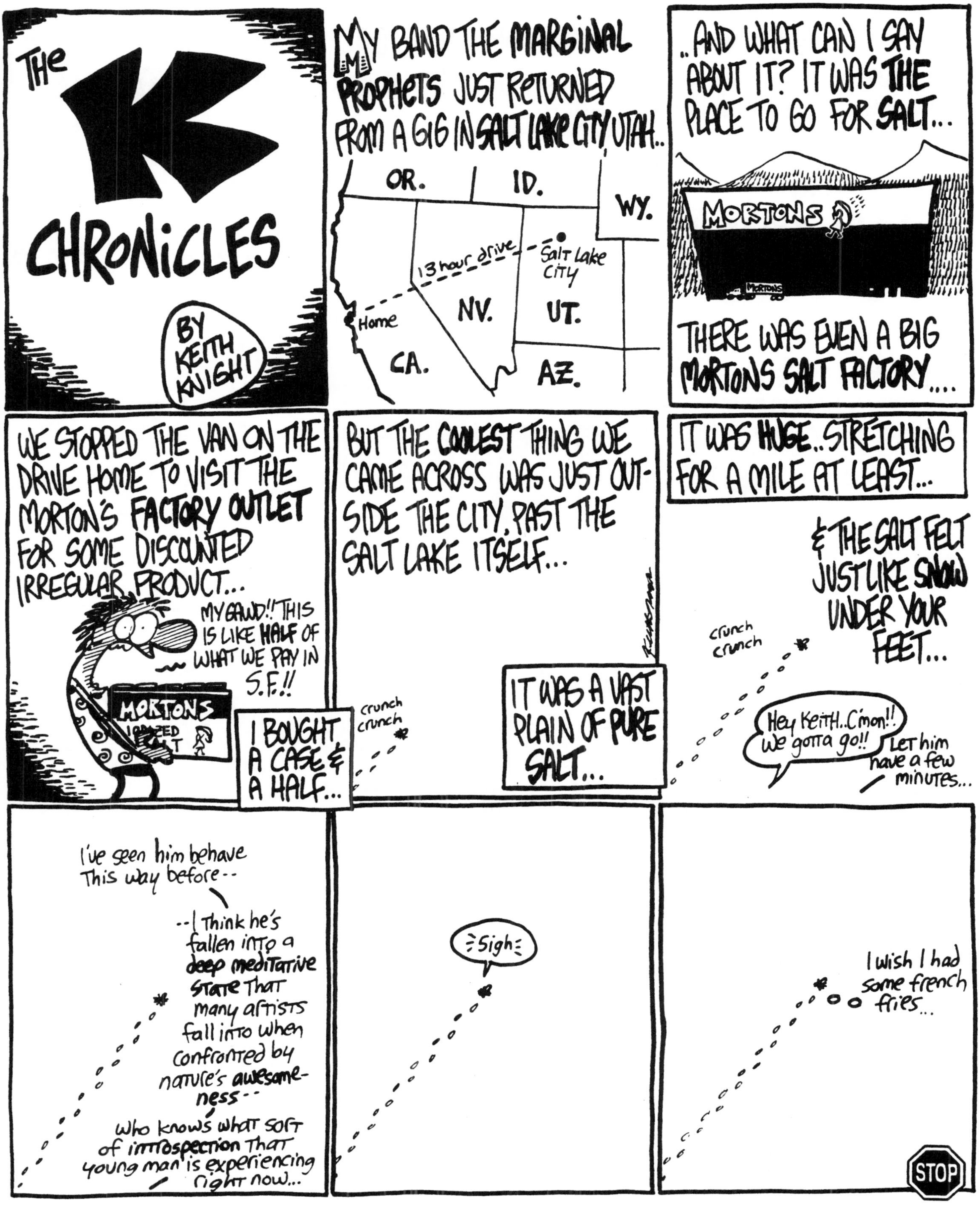

The K Chronicles
By Keith Knight
My band the Marginal Prophets just returned from a gig in Salt Lake City, Utah..
OR.
ID.
WY.
13 hour drive
Salt Lake City
Home
NV.
UT.
CA.
AZ.
..and what can I say about it? It was the place to go for salt...
MORTONS
There was even a big Mortons Salt Factory....
We stopped the van on the drive home to visit the Morton's factory outlet for some discounted irregular product...
My gawd!! This is like half of what we pay in S.F.!!
MORTONS IODIZED SALT
I bought a case & a half...
crunch crunch
But the coolest thing we came across was just outside the city, past the salt lake itself...
It was a vast plain of pure salt...
It was huge..stretching for a mile at least...
& the salt felt just like snow under your feet...
crunch crunch
Hey Keith..C'mon!! We gotta go!!
Let him have a few minutes...
I've seen him behave this way before--
--I think he's fallen into a deep meditative state that many artists fall into when confronted by nature's awesomeness--
Who knows what sort of introspection that young man is experiencing right now...
Sigh
I wish I had some french fries...
STOP

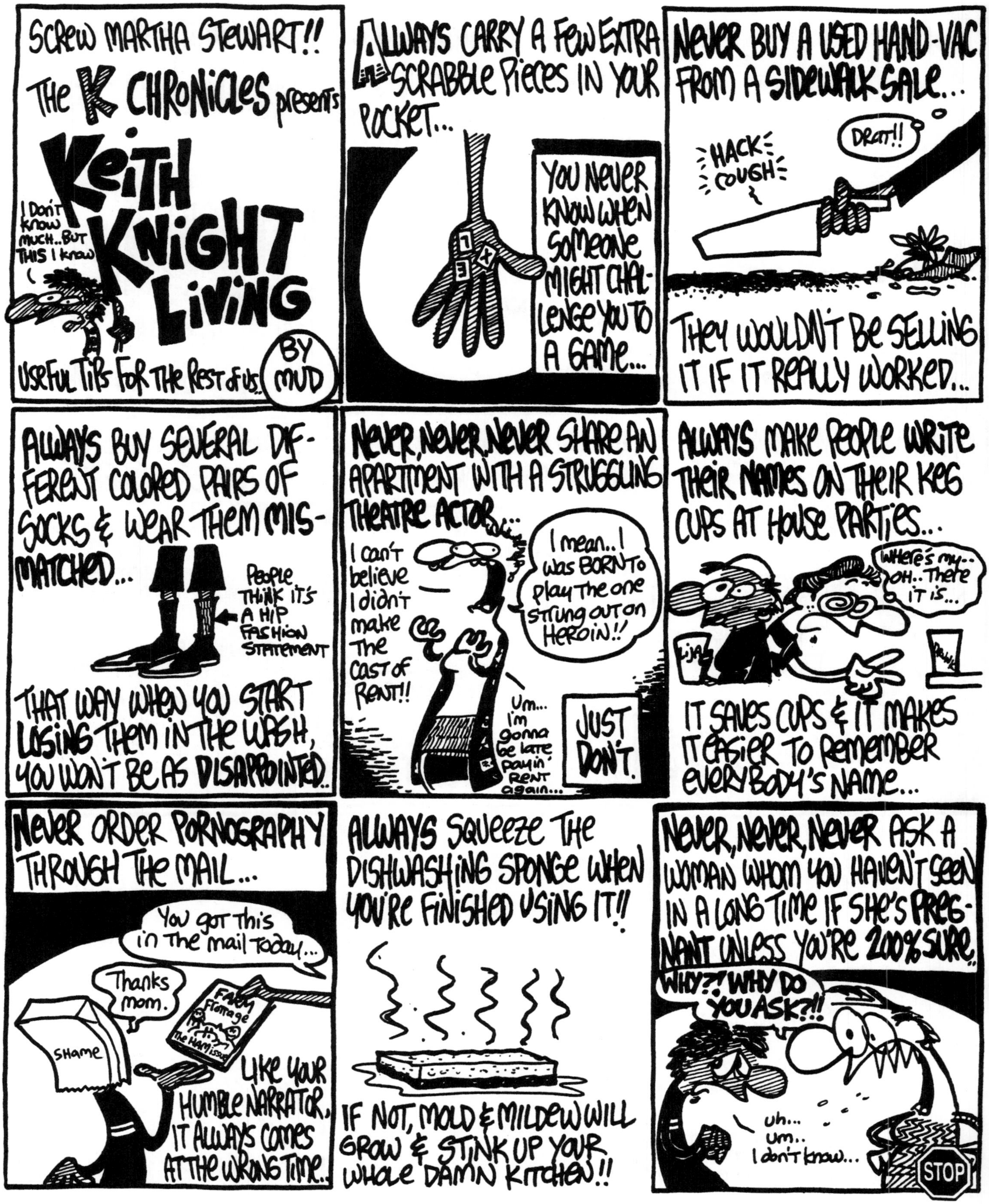
SCREW MARTHA STEWART!!
THE K CHRONICLES PRESENTS
KEITH KNIGHT LIVING
I DON'T KNOW MUCH.. BUT THIS I KNOW
USEFUL TIPS FOR THE REST OF US..
BY MUD
ALWAYS CARRY A FEW EXTRA SCRABBLE PIECES IN YOUR POCKET...
YOU NEVER KNOW WHEN SOMEONE MIGHT CHAL-LENGE YOU TO A GAME...
NEVER BUY A USED HAND-VAC FROM A SIDEWALK SALE...
HACK COUGH
DRAT!!
THEY WOULDN'T BE SELLING IT IF IT REALLY WORKED...
ALWAYS BUY SEVERAL DIF-FERENT COLORED PAIRS OF SOCKS & WEAR THEM MIS-MATCHED...
PEOPLE THINK IT'S A HIP FASHION STATEMENT
THAT WAY WHEN YOU START LOSING THEM IN THE WASH, YOU WON'T BE AS DISAPPOINTED..
NEVER, NEVER, NEVER SHARE AN APARTMENT WITH A STRUGGLING THEATRE ACTOR...
I can't believe I didn't make the cast of RENT!!
I mean.. I was BORN TO play the one strung out on HEROIN!!
Um... I'm gonna be late payin' RENT again...
JUST DON'T.
ALWAYS MAKE PEOPLE WRITE THEIR NAMES ON THEIR KEG CUPS AT HOUSE PARTIES...
Where's my.. OH.. There it is...
IT SAVES CUPS & IT MAKES IT EASIER TO REMEMBER EVERYBODY'S NAME...
NEVER ORDER PORNOGRAPHY THROUGH THE MAIL...
You got this in the mail today...
Thanks mom.
FARM Fromage
The HAM issue
SHAME
LIKE YOUR HUMBLE NARRATOR, IT ALWAYS COMES AT THE WRONG TIME..
ALWAYS SQUEEZE THE DISHWASHING SPONGE WHEN YOU'RE FINISHED USING IT!!
IF NOT, MOLD & MILDEW WILL GROW & STINK UP YOUR WHOLE DAMN KITCHEN!!
NEVER, NEVER, NEVER ASK A WOMAN WHOM YOU HAVEN'T SEEN IN A LONG TIME IF SHE'S PREG-NANT UNLESS YOU'RE 200% SURE.
WHY?! WHY DO YOU ASK?!!
uh... um.. I don't know...
STOP

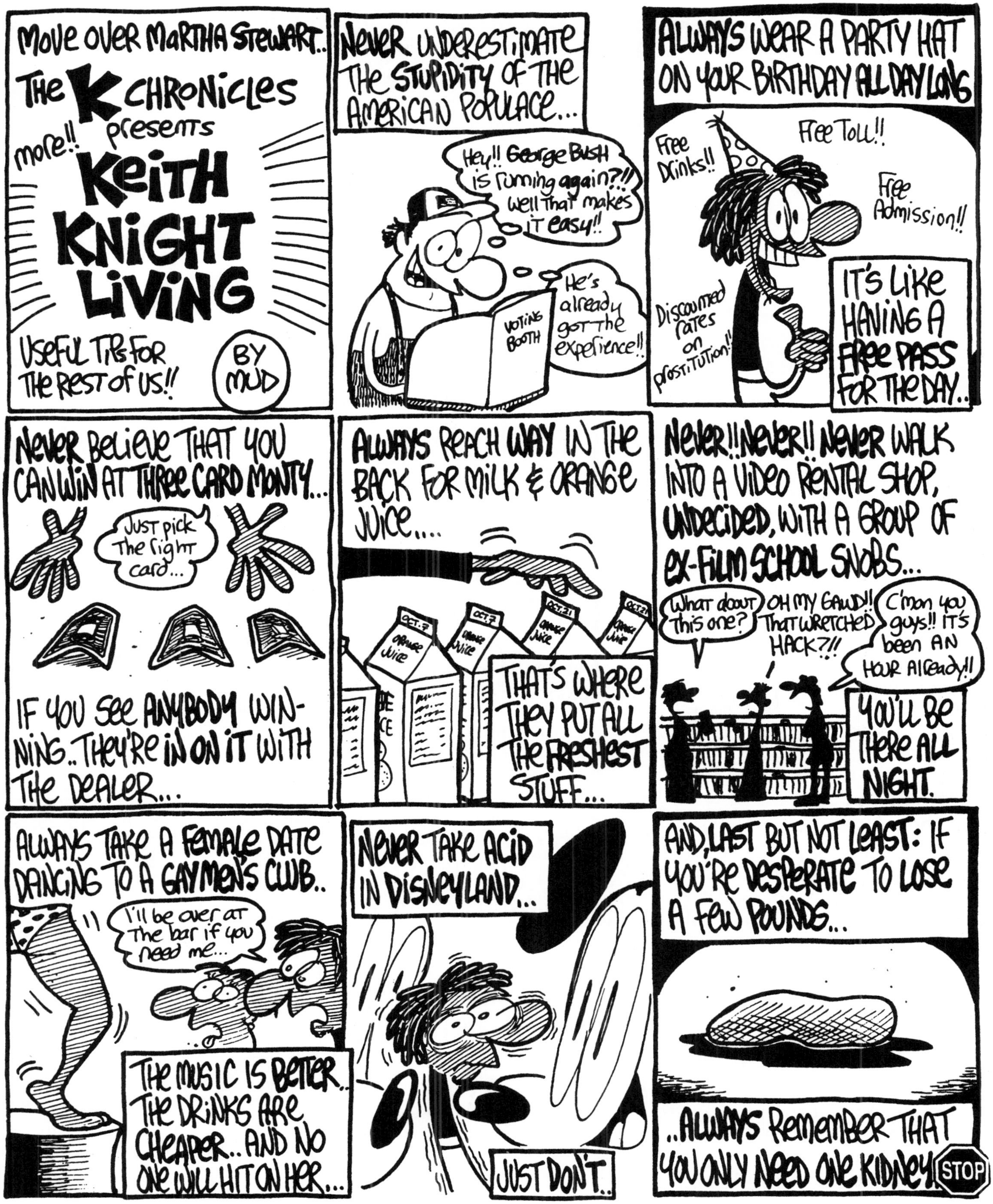
MOVE OVER MARTHA STEWART..
THE K CHRONICLES
more!! presents
KEITH KNIGHT LIVING
USEFUL TIPS FOR THE REST OF US!!
BY MUD
NEVER UNDERESTIMATE THE STUPIDITY OF THE AMERICAN POPULACE...
Hey!! George Bush is running again?!! Well that makes it easy!!
He's already got the experience!!
VOTING BOOTH
ALWAYS WEAR A PARTY HAT ON YOUR BIRTHDAY ALL DAY LONG
Free Drinks!!
Free Toll!!
Free Admission!!
Discounted rates on prostitution!!
IT'S LIKE HAVING A FREE PASS FOR THE DAY..
NEVER BELIEVE THAT YOU CAN WIN AT THREE CARD MONTY...
Just pick the right card...
IF YOU SEE ANYBODY WINNING.. THEY'RE IN ON IT WITH THE DEALER...
ALWAYS REACH WAY IN THE BACK FOR MILK & ORANGE JUICE....
OCT. 7
ORANGE JUICE
OCT. 21
THAT'S WHERE THEY PUT ALL THE FRESHEST STUFF...
NEVER!! NEVER!! NEVER WALK INTO A VIDEO RENTAL SHOP, UNDECIDED, WITH A GROUP OF EX-FILM SCHOOL SNOBS...
What about this one?
OH MY GAWD!! That wretched HACK?!!
C'mon you guys!! It's been an hour already!!
YOU'LL BE THERE ALL NIGHT.
ALWAYS TAKE A FEMALE DATE DANCING TO A GAY MEN'S CLUB..
I'll be over at the bar if you need me...
THE MUSIC IS BETTER.. THE DRINKS ARE CHEAPER.. AND NO ONE WILL HIT ON HER...
NEVER TAKE ACID IN DISNEYLAND...
JUST DON'T..
AND, LAST BUT NOT LEAST: IF YOU'RE DESPERATE TO LOSE A FEW POUNDS...
..ALWAYS REMEMBER THAT YOU ONLY NEED ONE KIDNEY!
STOP

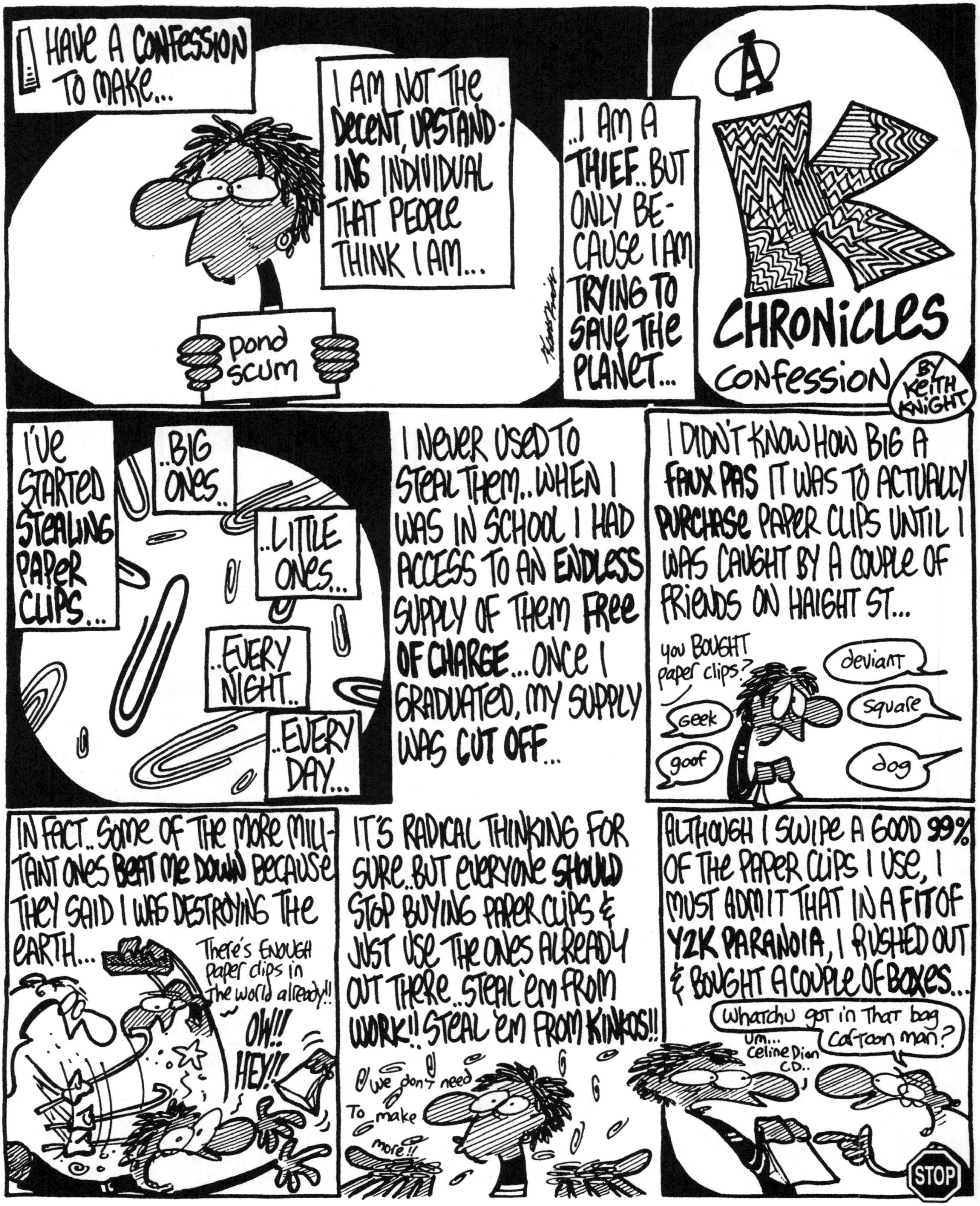
I HAVE A CONFESSION TO MAKE...
I AM NOT THE DECENT, UPSTANDING INDIVIDUAL THAT PEOPLE THINK I AM...
pond scum
...I AM A THIEF.. BUT ONLY BECAUSE I AM TRYING TO SAVE THE PLANET...
A K CHRONICLES
CONFESSION
BY KEITH KNIGHT
I'VE STARTED STEALING PAPER CLIPS...
..BIG ONES..
..LITTLE ONES...
..EVERY NIGHT..
..EVERY DAY...
I NEVER USED TO STEAL THEM.. WHEN I WAS IN SCHOOL I HAD ACCESS TO AN ENDLESS SUPPLY OF THEM FREE OF CHARGE... ONCE I GRADUATED, MY SUPPLY WAS CUT OFF...
I DIDN'T KNOW HOW BIG A FAUX PAS IT WAS TO ACTUALLY PURCHASE PAPER CLIPS UNTIL I WAS CAUGHT BY A COUPLE OF FRIENDS ON HAIGHT ST...
you BOUGHT paper clips?
deviant
geek
square
goof
dog
IN FACT.. SOME OF THE MORE MILITANT ONES BEAT ME DOWN BECAUSE THEY SAID I WAS DESTROYING THE EARTH...
There's ENOUGH paper clips in The world already!!
OW!!
HEY!!
IT'S RADICAL THINKING FOR SURE.. BUT EVERYONE SHOULD STOP BUYING PAPER CLIPS & JUST USE THE ONES ALREADY OUT THERE.. STEAL 'EM FROM WORK!! STEAL 'EM FROM KINKOS!!
we don't need To make more!!
ALTHOUGH I SWIPE A GOOD 99% OF THE PAPER CLIPS I USE, I MUST ADMIT THAT IN A FIT OF Y2K PARANOIA, I RUSHED OUT & BOUGHT A COUPLE OF BOXES...
Whatchu got in That bag Cartoon man?
um... Celine Dion C.D..
STOP

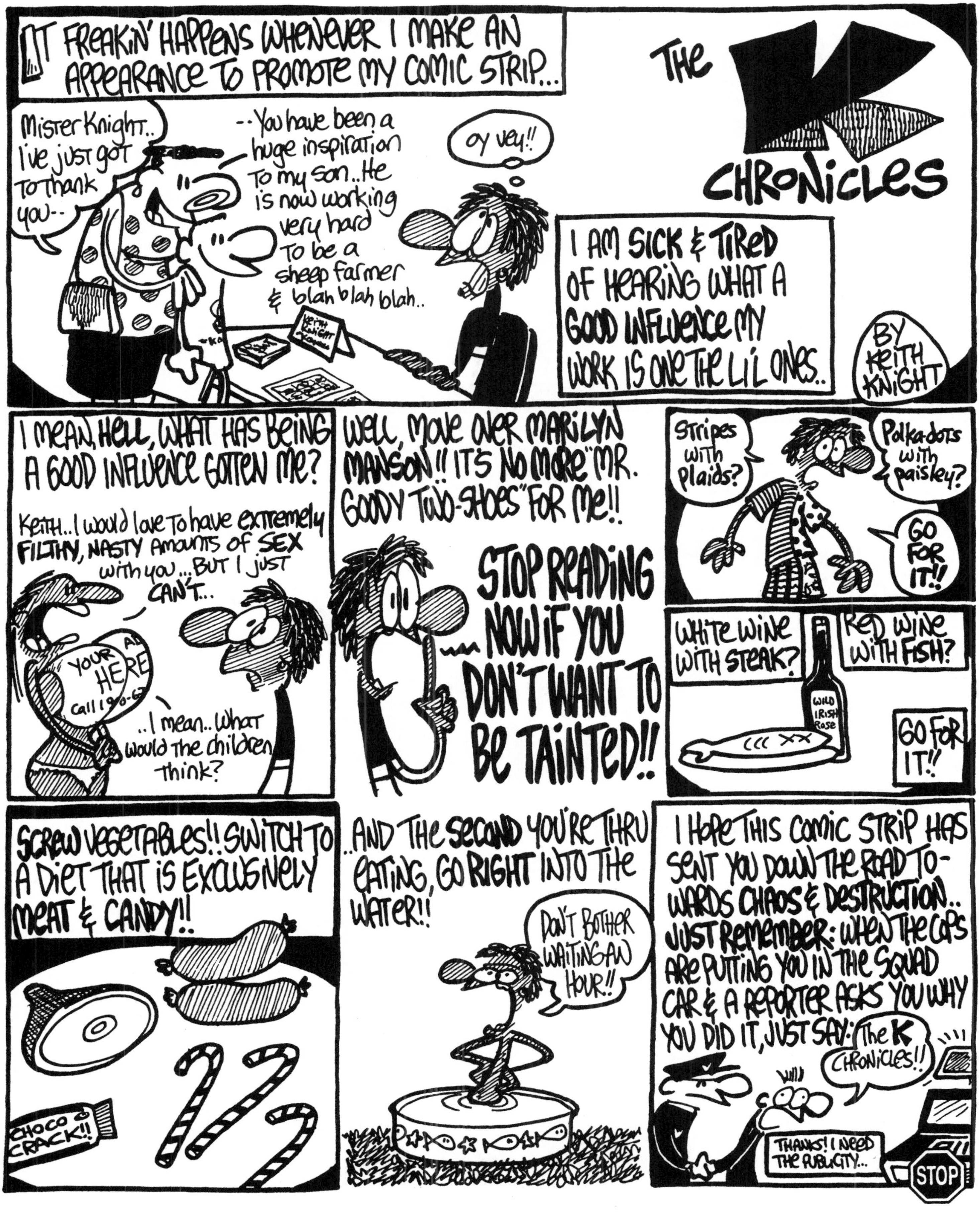
IT FREAKIN' HAPPENS WHENEVER I MAKE AN APPEARANCE TO PROMOTE MY COMIC STRIP...
THE K CHRONICLES
Mister Knight.. I've just got to thank you..
--You have been a huge inspiration to my son..He is now working very hard to be a sheep farmer & blah blah blah..
oy vey!!
I AM SICK & TIRED OF HEARING WHAT A GOOD INFLUENCE MY WORK IS ONE THE LIL ONES..
BY KEITH KNIGHT
I MEAN, HELL, WHAT HAS BEING A GOOD INFLUENCE GOTTEN ME?
Keith..I would love to have extremely FILTHY, NASTY amounts of SEX with you...BUT I just CAN'T...
..I mean.. What would the children think?
WELL, MOVE OVER MARILYN MANSON!! IT'S NO MORE "MR. GOODY TWO-SHOES" FOR ME!!
STOP READING NOW IF YOU DON'T WANT TO BE TAINTED!!..
Stripes with plaids?
Polka-dots with paisley?
GO FOR IT!!
WHITE WINE WITH STEAK?
RED WINE WITH FISH?
WILD IRISH ROSE
GO FOR IT!!
SCREW VEGETABLES!! SWITCH TO A DIET THAT IS EXCLUSIVELY MEAT & CANDY!!..
CHOCO CRACK!!
..AND THE SECOND YOU'RE THRU EATING, GO RIGHT INTO THE WATER!!
DON'T BOTHER WAITING AN HOUR!!
I HOPE THIS COMIC STRIP HAS SENT YOU DOWN THE ROAD TOWARDS CHAOS & DESTRUCTION.. JUST REMEMBER: WHEN THE COPS ARE PUTTING YOU IN THE SQUAD CAR & A REPORTER ASKS YOU WHY YOU DID IT, JUST SAY:
The K CHRONICLES!!
THANKS! I NEED THE PUBLICITY...
STOP

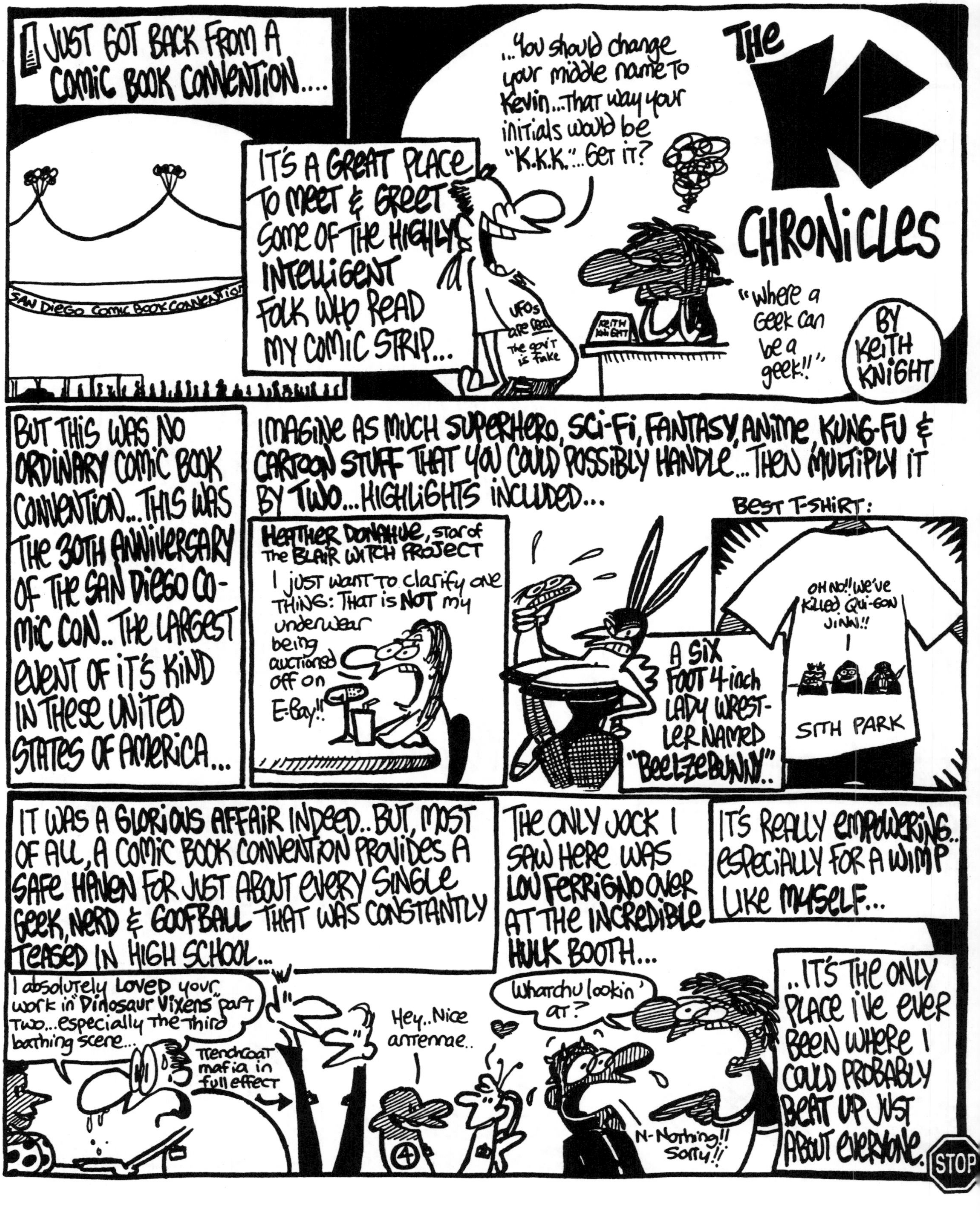

THE K CHRONICLES
"where a geek can be a geek!!"
BY KEITH KNIGHT
I JUST GOT BACK FROM A COMIC BOOK CONVENTION....
SAN DIEGO COMIC BOOK CONVENTION
IT'S A GREAT PLACE TO MEET & GREET SOME OF THE HIGHLY INTELLIGENT FOLK WHO READ MY COMIC STRIP...
...You should change your middle name to Kevin...That way your initials would be "K.K.K."...Get it?
UFOs are real. The gov't is fake
KEITH KNIGHT
BUT THIS WAS NO ORDINARY COMIC BOOK CONVENTION... THIS WAS THE 30TH ANNIVERSARY OF THE SAN DIEGO COMIC CON.. THE LARGEST EVENT OF IT'S KIND IN THESE UNITED STATES OF AMERICA...
IMAGINE AS MUCH SUPERHERO, SCI-FI, FANTASY, ANIME, KUNG-FU & CARTOON STUFF THAT YOU COULD POSSIBLY HANDLE... THEN MULTIPLY IT BY TWO... HIGHLIGHTS INCLUDED...
HEATHER DONAHUE, star of The BLAIR WITCH PROJECT
I just want to clarify one thing: That is NOT my underwear being auctioned off on E-Bay!!
A SIX FOOT 4-inch LADY WRESTLER NAMED "BEELZEBUNNY"..
BEST T-SHIRT:
OH NO!! We've killed Qui-Gon Jinn!!
SITH PARK
IT WAS A GLORIOUS AFFAIR INDEED.. BUT, MOST OF ALL, A COMIC BOOK CONVENTION PROVIDES A SAFE HAVEN FOR JUST ABOUT EVERY SINGLE GEEK, NERD & GOOFBALL THAT WAS CONSTANTLY TEASED IN HIGH SCHOOL...
THE ONLY JOCK I SAW HERE WAS LOU FERRIGNO OVER AT THE INCREDIBLE HULK BOOTH...
IT'S REALLY EMPOWERING.. ESPECIALLY FOR A WIMP LIKE MYSELF...
I absolutely LOVED your work in "Dinosaur Vixens" part two...especially the third bathing scene...
Trenchcoat mafia in full effect
Hey..Nice antennae..
Whatchu lookin' at?
N-Nothing!! Sorry!!
..IT'S THE ONLY PLACE I'VE EVER BEEN WHERE I COULD PROBABLY BEAT UP JUST ABOUT EVERYONE.
STOP

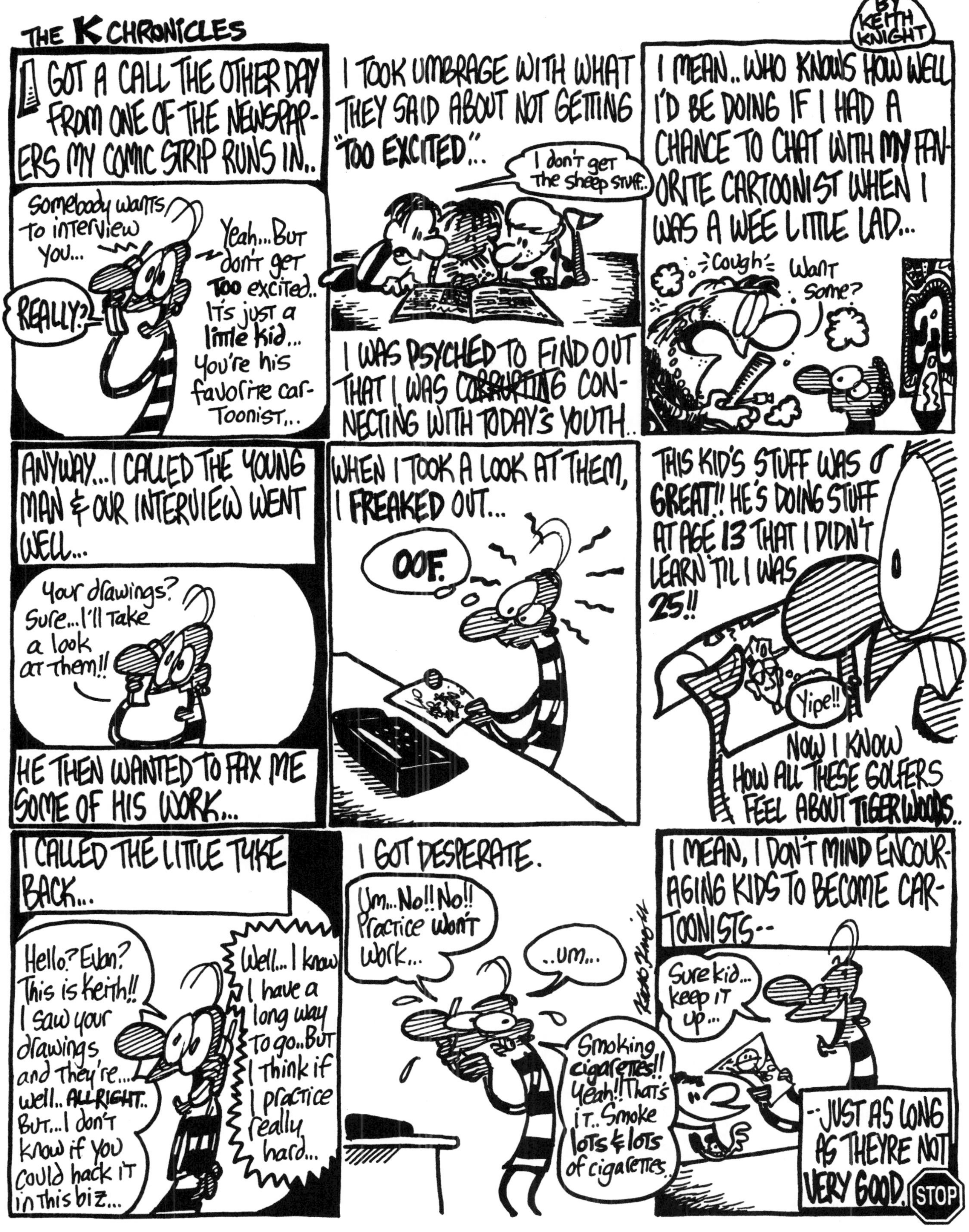
THE K CHRONICLES
BY KEITH KNIGHT
I GOT A CALL THE OTHER DAY FROM ONE OF THE NEWSPAPERS MY COMIC STRIP RUNS IN..
Somebody wants to interview you...
REALLY?
Yeah... But don't get TOO excited.. It's just a little kid... You're his favorite cartoonist...
I TOOK UMBRAGE WITH WHAT THEY SAID ABOUT NOT GETTING "TOO EXCITED"..
I don't get the sheep stuff..
I WAS PSYCHED TO FIND OUT THAT I WAS ~~CORRUPTIN~~G CONNECTING WITH TODAY'S YOUTH..
I MEAN.. WHO KNOWS HOW WELL I'D BE DOING IF I HAD A CHANCE TO CHAT WITH MY FAVORITE CARTOONIST WHEN I WAS A WEE LITTLE LAD...
Cough
Want some?
ANYWAY... I CALLED THE YOUNG MAN & OUR INTERVIEW WENT WELL...
Your drawings? Sure... I'll take a look at them!!
HE THEN WANTED TO FAX ME SOME OF HIS WORK...
WHEN I TOOK A LOOK AT THEM, I FREAKED OUT...
OOF.
THIS KID'S STUFF WAS GREAT!! HE'S DOING STUFF AT AGE 13 THAT I DIDN'T LEARN 'TIL I WAS 25!!
Yipe!!
NOW I KNOW HOW ALL THESE GOLFERS FEEL ABOUT TIGER WOODS..
I CALLED THE LITTLE TYKE BACK...
Hello? Evan? This is Keith!! I saw your drawings and they're.... well.. ALLRIGHT.. But... I don't know if you could hack it in this biz...
Well... I know I have a long way to go.. But I think if I practice really hard...
I GOT DESPERATE.
Um... No!! No!! Practice won't work...
..um...
Smoking cigarettes!! Yeah!! That's it.. Smoke lots & lots of cigarettes..
I MEAN, I DON'T MIND ENCOURAGING KIDS TO BECOME CARTOONISTS--
Sure kid... keep it up...
--JUST AS LONG AS THEYRE NOT VERY GOOD.
STOP

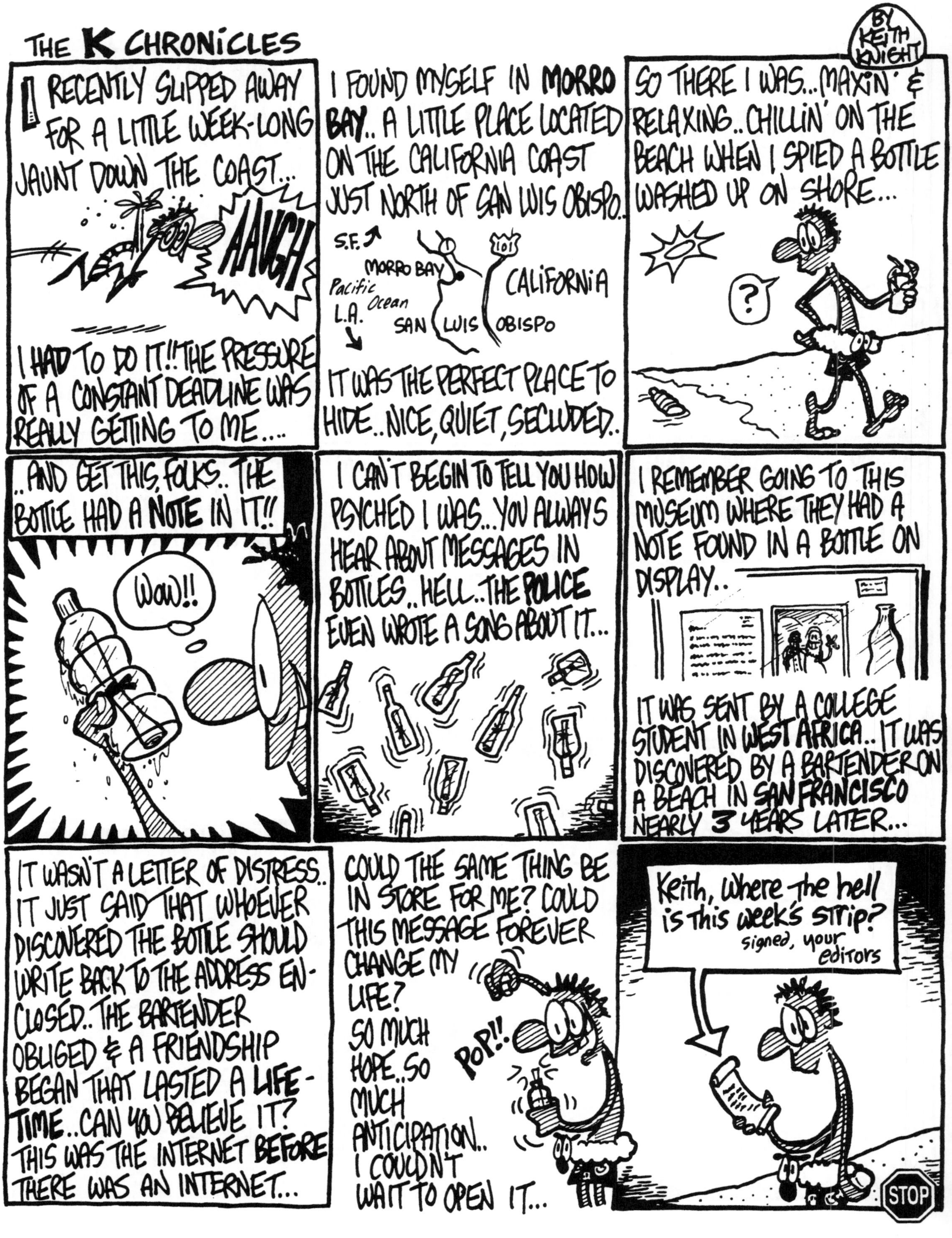
THE K CHRONICLES
BY KEITH KNIGHT
I RECENTLY SLIPPED AWAY FOR A LITTLE WEEK-LONG JAUNT DOWN THE COAST...
AAUGH
I HAD TO DO IT!! THE PRESSURE OF A CONSTANT DEADLINE WAS REALLY GETTING TO ME....
I FOUND MYSELF IN MORRO BAY.. A LITTLE PLACE LOCATED ON THE CALIFORNIA COAST JUST NORTH OF SAN LUIS OBISPO..
S.F.
MORRO BAY
1
101
CALIFORNIA
Pacific Ocean
L.A.
SAN LUIS OBISPO
IT WAS THE PERFECT PLACE TO HIDE.. NICE, QUIET, SECLUDED..
SO THERE I WAS... MAXIN' & RELAXING.. CHILLIN' ON THE BEACH WHEN I SPIED A BOTTLE WASHED UP ON SHORE...
?
..AND GET THIS, FOLKS.. THE BOTTLE HAD A NOTE IN IT!!
WOW!!
I CAN'T BEGIN TO TELL YOU HOW PSYCHED I WAS... YOU ALWAYS HEAR ABOUT MESSAGES IN BOTTLES.. HELL.. THE POLICE EVEN WROTE A SONG ABOUT IT...
I REMEMBER GOING TO THIS MUSEUM WHERE THEY HAD A NOTE FOUND IN A BOTTLE ON DISPLAY..
IT WAS SENT BY A COLLEGE STUDENT IN WEST AFRICA.. IT WAS DISCOVERED BY A BARTENDER ON A BEACH IN SAN FRANCISCO NEARLY 3 YEARS LATER...
IT WASN'T A LETTER OF DISTRESS.. IT JUST SAID THAT WHOEVER DISCOVERED THE BOTTLE SHOULD WRITE BACK TO THE ADDRESS ENCLOSED.. THE BARTENDER OBLIGED & A FRIENDSHIP BEGAN THAT LASTED A LIFETIME.. CAN YOU BELIEVE IT? THIS WAS THE INTERNET BEFORE THERE WAS AN INTERNET...
COULD THE SAME THING BE IN STORE FOR ME? COULD THIS MESSAGE FOREVER CHANGE MY LIFE?
SO MUCH HOPE.. SO MUCH ANTICIPATION.. I COULDN'T WAIT TO OPEN IT...
POP!!
Keith, where the hell is this week's strip?
signed, your editors
STOP

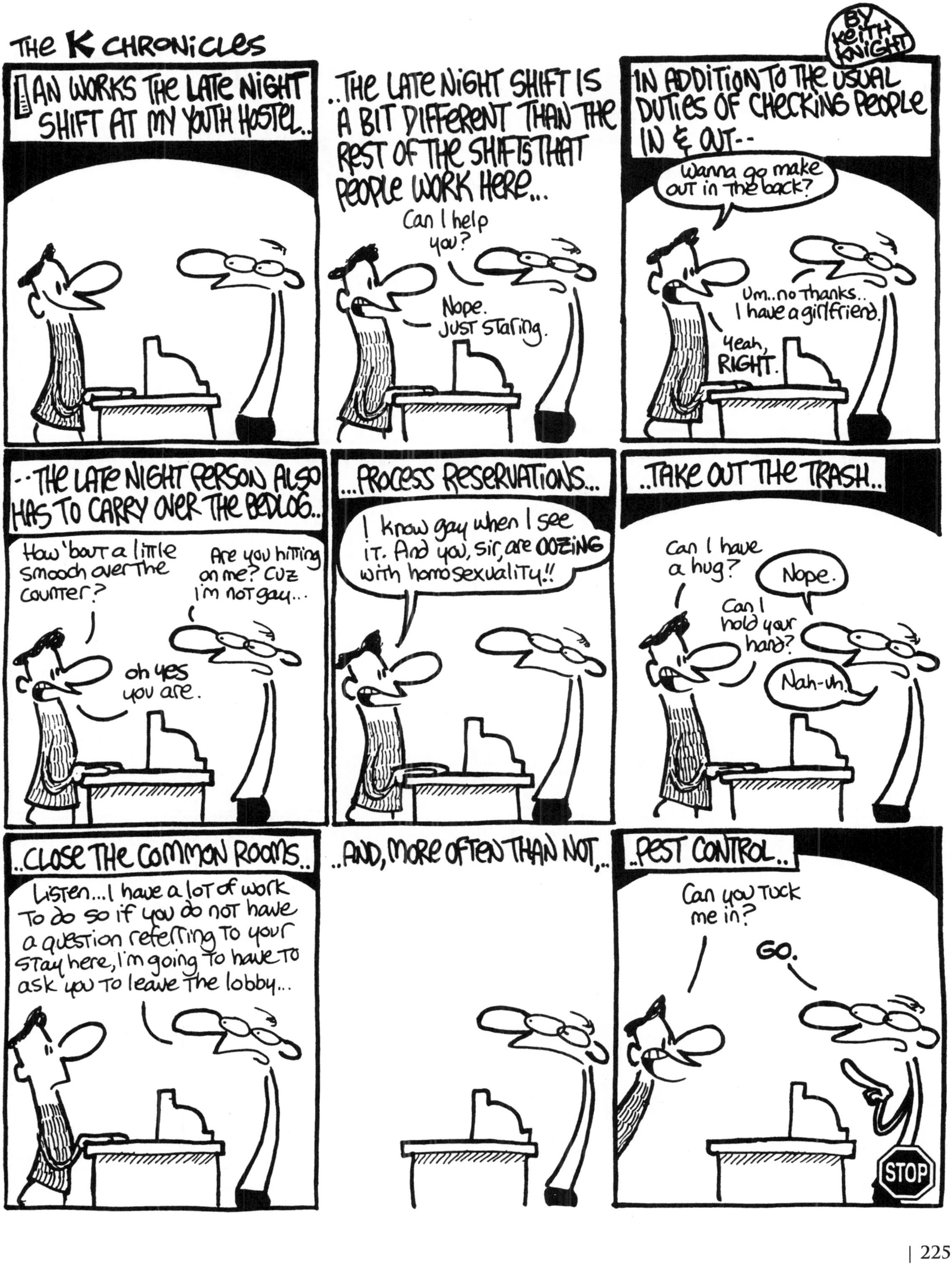
THE K CHRONICLES
BY KEITH KNIGHT
[redacted]AN WORKS THE LATE NIGHT SHIFT AT MY YOUTH HOSTEL..
..THE LATE NIGHT SHIFT IS A BIT DIFFERENT THAN THE REST OF THE SHIFTS THAT PEOPLE WORK HERE...
Can I help you?
Nope. JUST STARING.
IN ADDITION TO THE USUAL DUTIES OF CHECKING PEOPLE IN & OUT--
Wanna go make out in the back?
Um..no thanks.. I have a girlfriend.
Yeah, RIGHT.
--THE LATE NIGHT PERSON ALSO HAS TO CARRY OVER THE BEDLOG..
How 'bout a little smooch over the counter?
Are you hitting on me? Cuz I'm not gay...
oh yes you are.
...PROCESS RESERVATIONS...
I know gay when I see it. And you, sir, are OOZING with homosexuality!!
..TAKE OUT THE TRASH..
Can I have a hug?
Nope.
Can I hold your hand?
Nah-uh.
..CLOSE THE COMMON ROOMS..
Listen...I have a lot of work to do so if you do not have a question referring to your stay here, I'm going to have to ask you to leave the lobby...
..AND, MORE OFTEN THAN NOT,..
..PEST CONTROL..
Can you tuck me in?
GO.
STOP

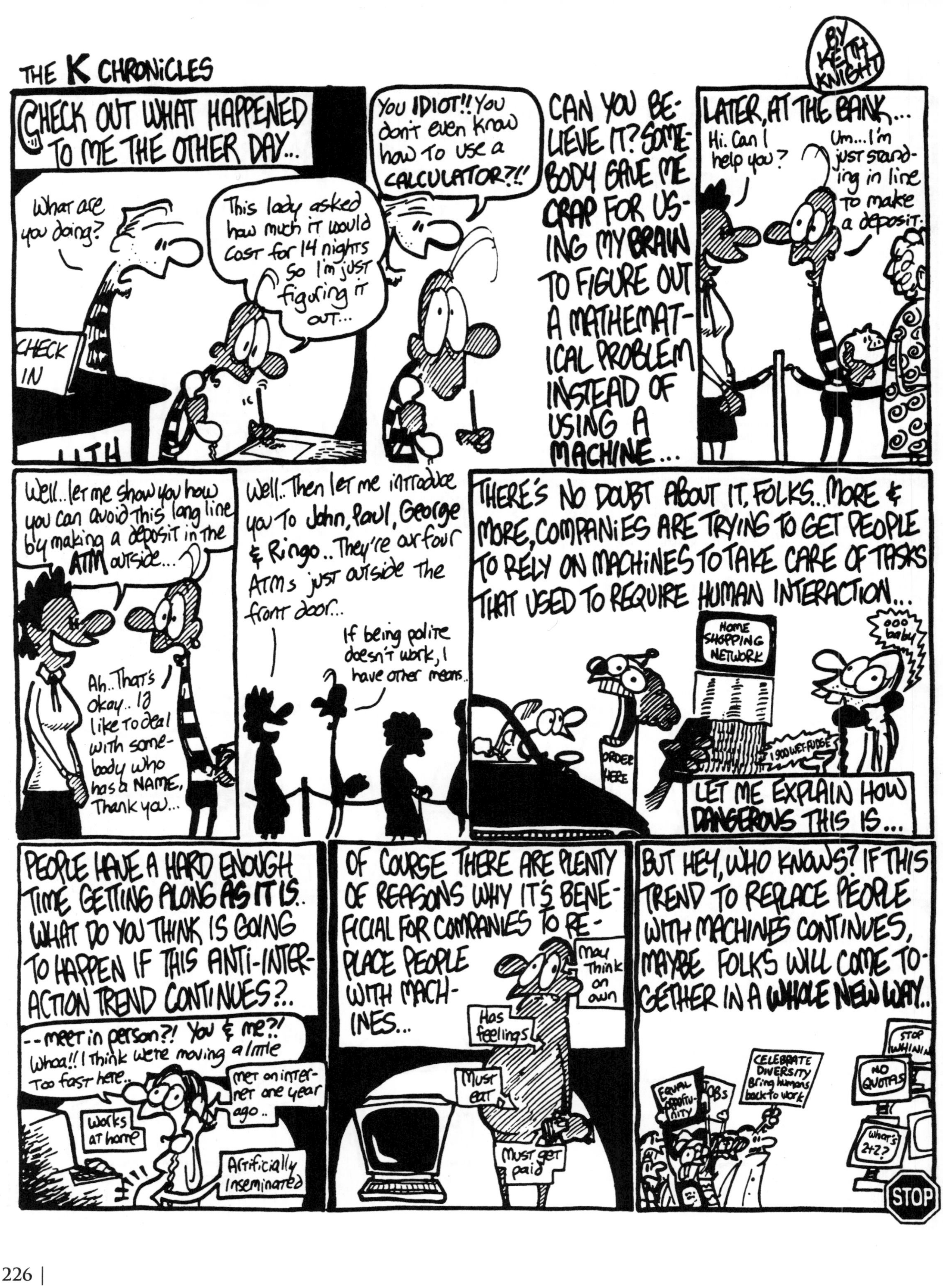
THE K CHRONICLES
BY KEITH KNIGHT
CHECK OUT WHAT HAPPENED TO ME THE OTHER DAY...
What are you doing?
This lady asked how much it would cost for 14 nights So I'm just figuring it out...
CHECK IN
You IDIOT!! You don't even know how to use a CALCULATOR?!!
CAN YOU BELIEVE IT? SOMEBODY GAVE ME CRAP FOR USING MY BRAIN TO FIGURE OUT A MATHEMATICAL PROBLEM INSTEAD OF USING A MACHINE...
LATER, AT THE BANK...
Hi. Can I help you?
Um... I'm just standing in line to make a deposit.
Well.. let me show you how you can avoid this long line by making a deposit in the ATM outside...
Ah.. That's okay.. I'd like to deal with somebody who has a NAME. Thank you...
Well.. Then let me introduce you to John, Paul, George & Ringo.. They're our four ATMs just outside the front door...
If being polite doesn't work, I have other means..
THERE'S NO DOUBT ABOUT IT, FOLKS... MORE & MORE, COMPANIES ARE TRYING TO GET PEOPLE TO RELY ON MACHINES TO TAKE CARE OF TASKS THAT USED TO REQUIRE HUMAN INTERACTION...
HOME SHOPPING NETWORK
ooo baby
ORDER HERE
1 900 WET-FUDGE
LET ME EXPLAIN HOW DANGEROUS THIS IS...
PEOPLE HAVE A HARD ENOUGH TIME GETTING ALONG AS IT IS.. WHAT DO YOU THINK IS GOING TO HAPPEN IF THIS ANTI-INTERACTION TREND CONTINUES?..
--meet in person?! You & me?! Whoa!! I think we're moving a little too fast here..
met on internet one year ago..
Works at home
Artificially Inseminated
OF COURSE THERE ARE PLENTY OF REASONS WHY IT'S BENEFICIAL FOR COMPANIES TO REPLACE PEOPLE WITH MACHINES...
May Think on own
Has feelings
Must eat
Must get paid
BUT HEY, WHO KNOWS? IF THIS TREND TO REPLACE PEOPLE WITH MACHINES CONTINUES, MAYBE FOLKS WILL COME TOGETHER IN A WHOLE NEW WAY...
EQUAL OPPORTUNITY
JOBS
CELEBRATE DIVERSITY Bring humans back to work
STOP WHININ
NO QUOTAS
What's 2+2?
STOP

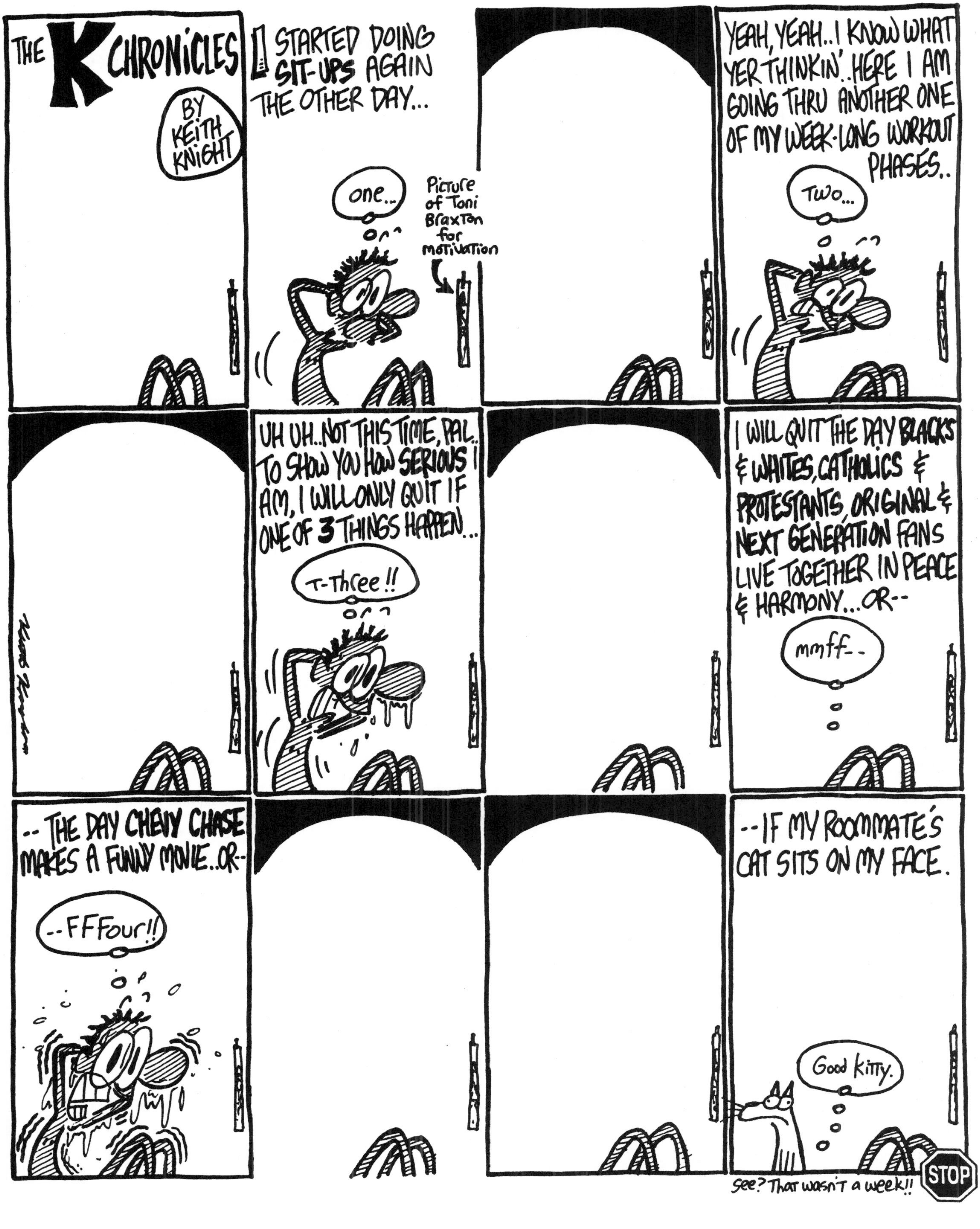
THE K CHRONICLES
BY KEITH KNIGHT
I STARTED DOING SIT-UPS AGAIN THE OTHER DAY...
one...
Picture of Toni Braxton for motivation
YEAH, YEAH.. I KNOW WHAT YER THINKIN'.. HERE I AM GOING THRU ANOTHER ONE OF MY WEEK-LONG WORKOUT PHASES..
Two...
UH UH.. NOT THIS TIME, PAL.. TO SHOW YOU HOW SERIOUS I AM, I WILL ONLY QUIT IF ONE OF 3 THINGS HAPPEN...
T-Three !!
I WILL QUIT THE DAY BLACKS & WHITES, CATHOLICS & PROTESTANTS, ORIGINAL & NEXT GENERATION FANS LIVE TOGETHER IN PEACE & HARMONY... OR--
mmff--
-- THE DAY CHEVY CHASE MAKES A FUNNY MOVIE.. OR--
--FFFour!!
--IF MY ROOMMATE'S CAT SITS ON MY FACE..
Good kitty.
See? That wasn't a week!!
STOP

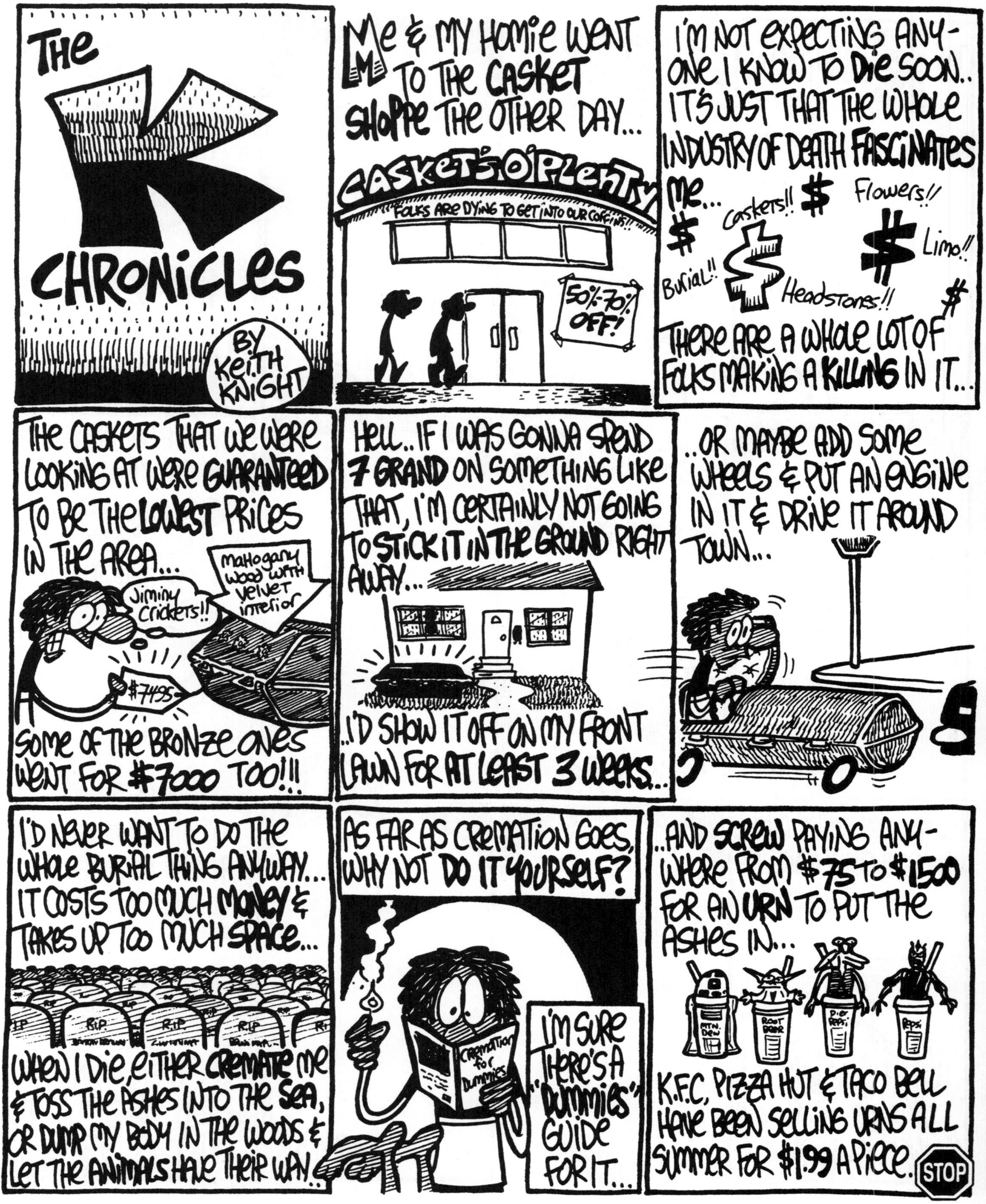
THE K CHRONICLES
BY KEITH KNIGHT
ME & MY HOMIE WENT TO THE CASKET SHOPPE THE OTHER DAY...
CASKETS O'PLENTY
FOLKS ARE DYING TO GET INTO OUR COFFINS!!
50%-70% OFF!
I'M NOT EXPECTING ANYONE I KNOW TO DIE SOON.. IT'S JUST THAT THE WHOLE INDUSTRY OF DEATH FASCINATES ME...
Caskets!!
Flowers!!
Limo!!
Burial!!
Headstones!!
THERE ARE A WHOLE LOT OF FOLKS MAKING A KILLING IN IT...
THE CASKETS THAT WE WERE LOOKING AT WERE GUARANTEED TO BE THE LOWEST PRICES IN THE AREA...
Jiminy Crickets!!
Mahogany wood with velvet interior
$7495
SOME OF THE BRONZE ONES WENT FOR $7000 TOO!!!
HELL.. IF I WAS GONNA SPEND 7 GRAND ON SOMETHING LIKE THAT, I'M CERTAINLY NOT GOING TO STICK IT IN THE GROUND RIGHT AWAY...
..I'D SHOW IT OFF ON MY FRONT LAWN FOR AT LEAST 3 WEEKS...
...OR MAYBE ADD SOME WHEELS & PUT AN ENGINE IN IT & DRIVE IT AROUND TOWN...
I'D NEVER WANT TO DO THE WHOLE BURIAL THING ANYWAY... IT COSTS TOO MUCH MONEY & TAKES UP TOO MUCH SPACE...
WHEN I DIE, EITHER CREMATE ME & TOSS THE ASHES INTO THE SEA, OR DUMP MY BODY IN THE WOODS & LET THE ANIMALS HAVE THEIR WAY..
AS FAR AS CREMATION GOES, WHY NOT DO IT YOURSELF?
Cremation for Dummies
I'M SURE THERE'S A "DUMMIES" GUIDE FOR IT...
...AND SCREW PAYING ANYWHERE FROM $75 TO $1500 FOR AN URN TO PUT THE ASHES IN...
MTN. DEW
ROOT BEER
Diet Pepsi
Pepsi
K.F.C, PIZZA HUT & TACO BELL HAVE BEEN SELLING URNS ALL SUMMER FOR $1.99 A PIECE.
STOP

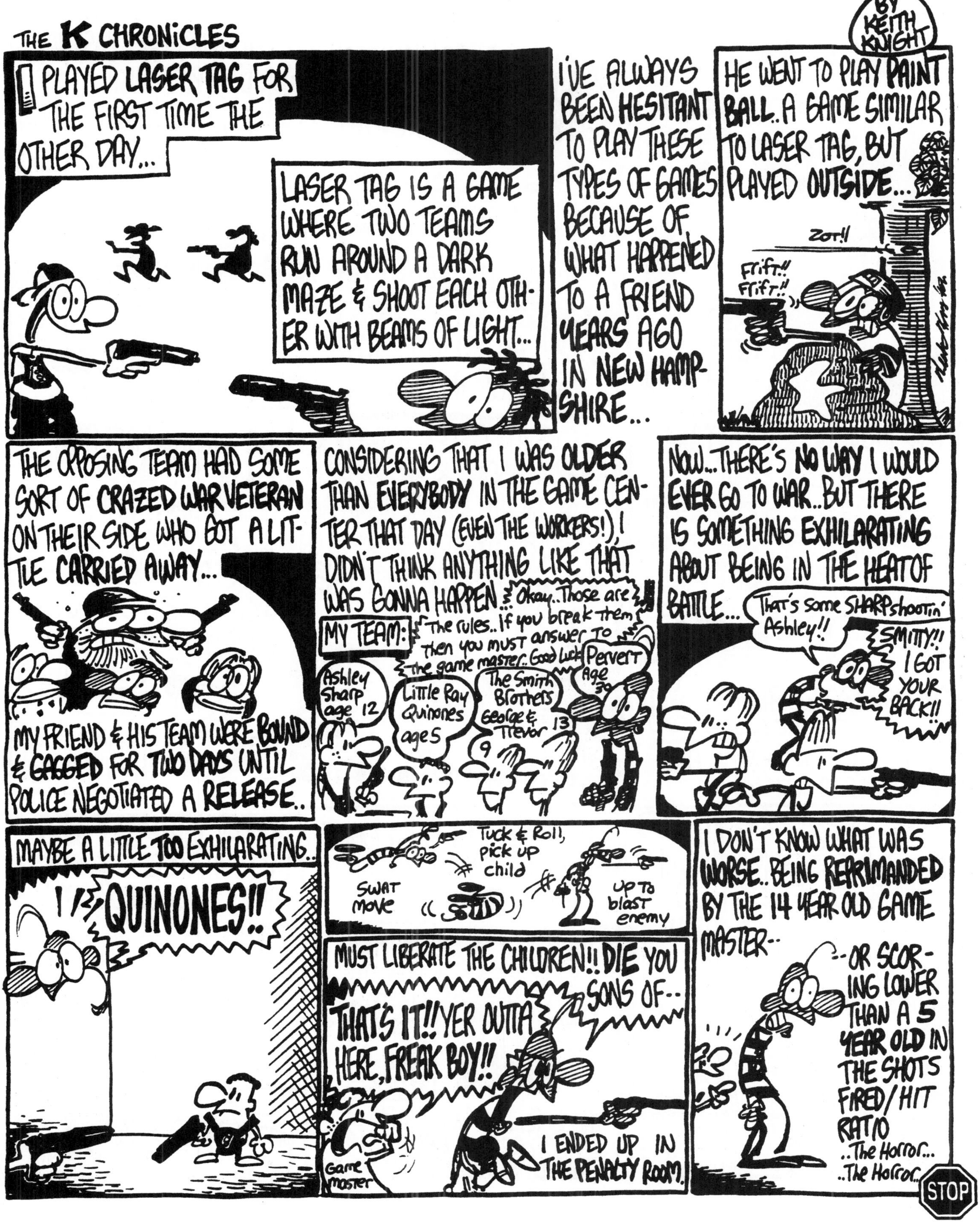
THE K CHRONICLES
BY KEITH KNIGHT
I PLAYED LASER TAG FOR THE FIRST TIME THE OTHER DAY...
LASER TAG IS A GAME WHERE TWO TEAMS RUN AROUND A DARK MAZE & SHOOT EACH OTHER WITH BEAMS OF LIGHT...
I'VE ALWAYS BEEN HESITANT TO PLAY THESE TYPES OF GAMES BECAUSE OF WHAT HAPPENED TO A FRIEND YEARS AGO IN NEW HAMPSHIRE...
HE WENT TO PLAY PAINT BALL.. A GAME SIMILAR TO LASER TAG, BUT PLAYED OUTSIDE...
ZOT!!
Frift!! Frift!!
THE OPPOSING TEAM HAD SOME SORT OF CRAZED WAR VETERAN ON THEIR SIDE WHO GOT A LITTLE CARRIED AWAY...
MY FRIEND & HIS TEAM WERE BOUND & GAGGED FOR TWO DAYS UNTIL POLICE NEGOTIATED A RELEASE..
CONSIDERING THAT I WAS OLDER THAN EVERYBODY IN THE GAME CENTER THAT DAY (EVEN THE WORKERS!), I DIDN'T THINK ANYTHING LIKE THAT WAS GONNA HAPPEN...
Okay.. Those are the rules.. If you break them then you must answer to the game master.. Good Luck
MY TEAM:
Ashley Sharp age 12
Little Ray Quinones age 5
The Smith Brothers George & Trevor 9 13
Pervert Age 30
NOW... THERE'S NO WAY I WOULD EVER GO TO WAR.. BUT THERE IS SOMETHING EXHILARATING ABOUT BEING IN THE HEAT OF BATTLE...
That's some SHARPshootin' Ashley!!
SMITTY!! I GOT YOUR BACK!!
MAYBE A LITTLE TOO EXHILARATING..
QUINONES!!
Tuck & Roll, pick up child
SWAT move
Up to blast enemy
MUST LIBERATE THE CHILDREN!! DIE YOU SONS OF..
THAT'S IT!! YER OUTTA HERE, FREAK BOY!!
Game master
I ENDED UP IN THE PENALTY ROOM.
I DON'T KNOW WHAT WAS WORSE.. BEING REPRIMANDED BY THE 14 YEAR OLD GAME MASTER..
..OR SCORING LOWER THAN A 5 YEAR OLD IN THE SHOTS FIRED/HIT RATIO
..The Horror... ..The Horror..
STOP

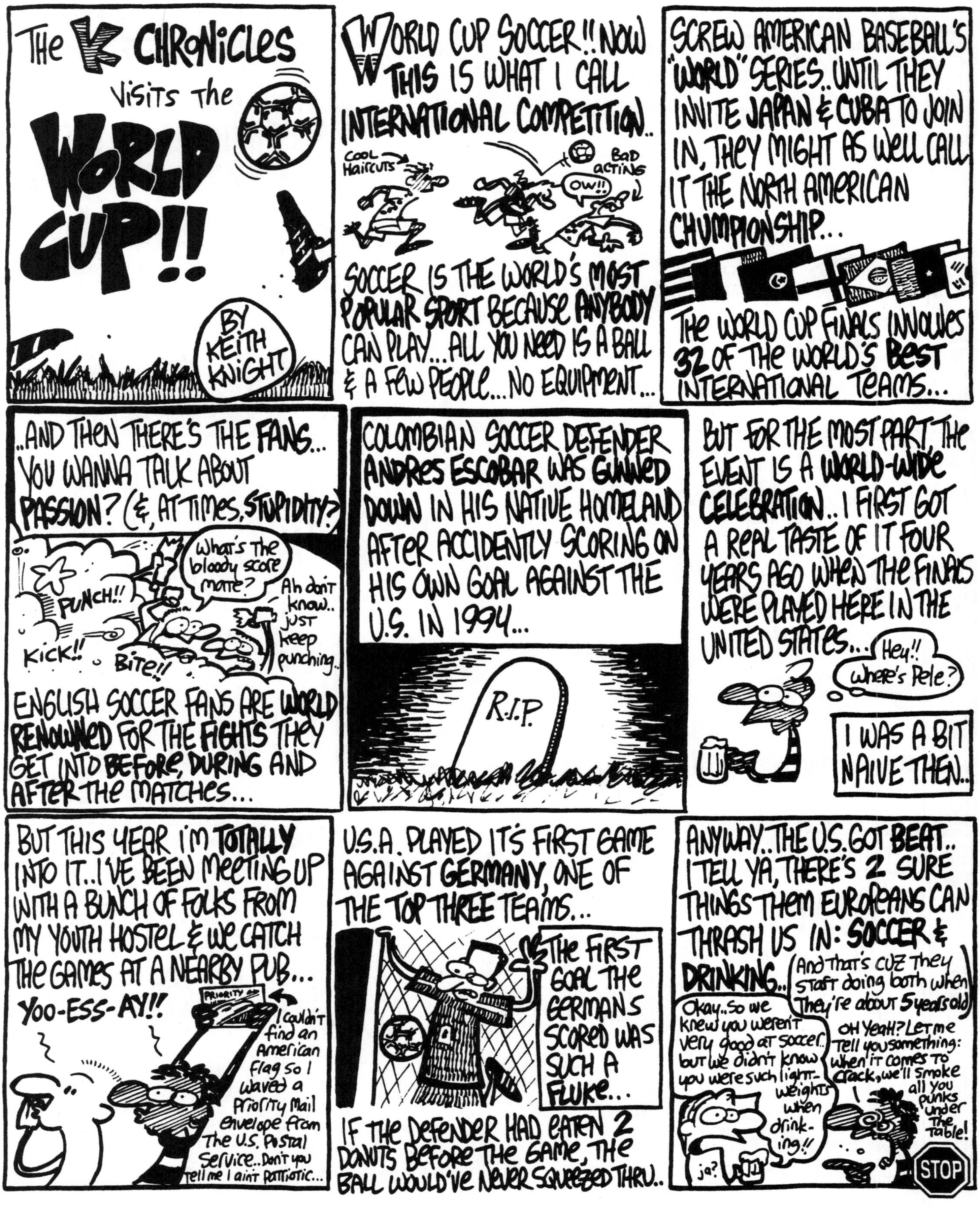
The K Chronicles visits the World Cup!!
By Keith Knight
World Cup Soccer!! Now this is what I call international competition..
Cool haircuts
Bad acting
Ow!!
Soccer is the world's most popular sport because anybody can play... all you need is a ball & a few people... no equipment...
Screw American baseball's "World" Series.. until they invite Japan & Cuba to join in, they might as well call it the North American Chumpionship...
The World Cup finals involves 32 of the world's best international teams...
..And then there's the fans... you wanna talk about passion? (&, at times, stupidity?)
What's the bloody score mate?
Ah don't know.. just keep punching..
Punch!!
Kick!!
Bite!!
English soccer fans are world renowned for the fights they get into before, during and after the matches...
Colombian soccer defender Andres Escobar was gunned down in his native homeland after accidently scoring on his own goal against the U.S. in 1994...
R.I.P.
But for the most part, the event is a world-wide celebration.. I first got a real taste of it four years ago when the finals were played here in the United States...
Hey!! Where's Pele?
I was a bit naive then..
But this year I'm totally into it.. I've been meeting up with a bunch of folks from my youth hostel & we catch the games at a nearby pub...
Yoo-Ess-Ay!!
Priority Mail
I couldn't find an American flag so I waved a Priority Mail envelope from the U.S. Postal Service... Don't you tell me I ain't patriotic...
U.S.A. played it's first game against Germany, one of the top three teams...
The first goal the Germans scored was such a fluke...
If the defender had eaten 2 donuts before the game, the ball would've never squeezed thru..
Anyway.. the U.S. got beat.. I tell ya, there's 2 sure things them Europeans can thrash us in: soccer & drinking..
(And that's cuz they start doing both when they're about 5 years old)
Okay.. so we knew you weren't very good at soccer.. but we didn't know you were such lightweights when drinking!!
Ja?
Oh yeah? Let me tell you something: when it comes to crack, we'll smoke all you punks under the table!
STOP

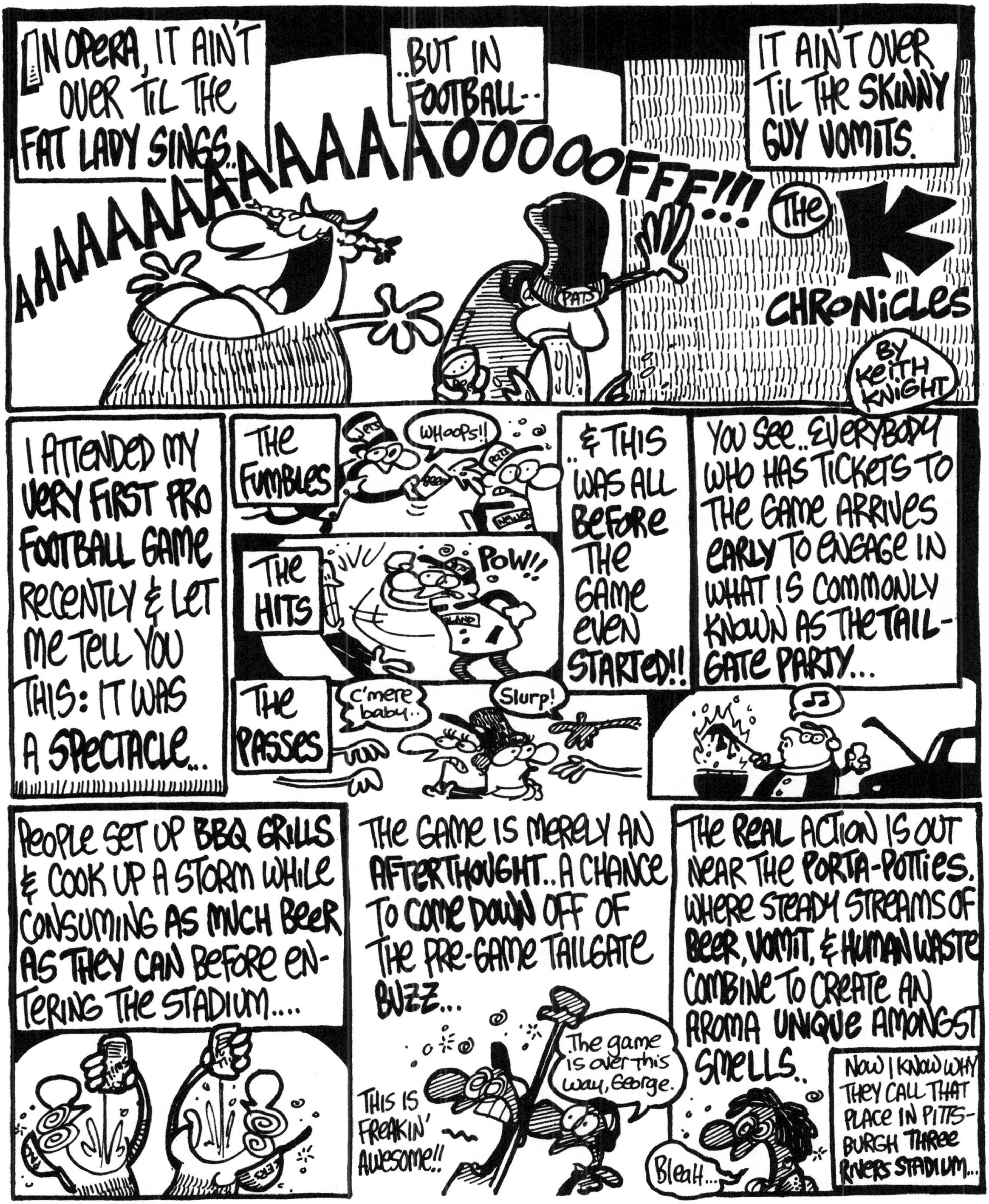

IN OPERA, IT AIN'T OVER TIL THE FAT LADY SINGS..
..BUT IN FOOTBALL..
IT AIN'T OVER TIL THE SKINNY GUY VOMITS.
AAAAAAAAAAAAAAOOOOOOFFF!!!
THE K CHRONICLES
BY KEITH KNIGHT
PATS
I ATTENDED MY VERY FIRST PRO FOOTBALL GAME RECENTLY & LET ME TELL YOU THIS: IT WAS A SPECTACLE...
THE FUMBLES
WHOOPS!!
THE HITS
POW!!
THE PASSES
C'mere baby..
Slurp!
..& THIS WAS ALL BEFORE THE GAME EVEN STARTED!!
YOU SEE..EVERYBODY WHO HAS TICKETS TO THE GAME ARRIVES EARLY TO ENGAGE IN WHAT IS COMMONLY KNOWN AS THE TAIL-GATE PARTY...
PEOPLE SET UP BBQ GRILLS & COOK UP A STORM WHILE CONSUMING AS MUCH BEER AS THEY CAN BEFORE EN-TERING THE STADIUM....
THE GAME IS MERELY AN AFTERTHOUGHT..A CHANCE TO COME DOWN OFF OF THE PRE-GAME TAILGATE BUZZ...
THIS IS FREAKIN' AWESOME!!
The game is over this way, George.
THE REAL ACTION IS OUT NEAR THE PORTA-POTTIES. WHERE STEADY STREAMS OF BEER, VOMIT, & HUMAN WASTE COMBINE TO CREATE AN AROMA UNIQUE AMONGST SMELLS..
NOW I KNOW WHY THEY CALL THAT PLACE IN PITTS-BURGH THREE RIVERS STADIUM...
Bleah...

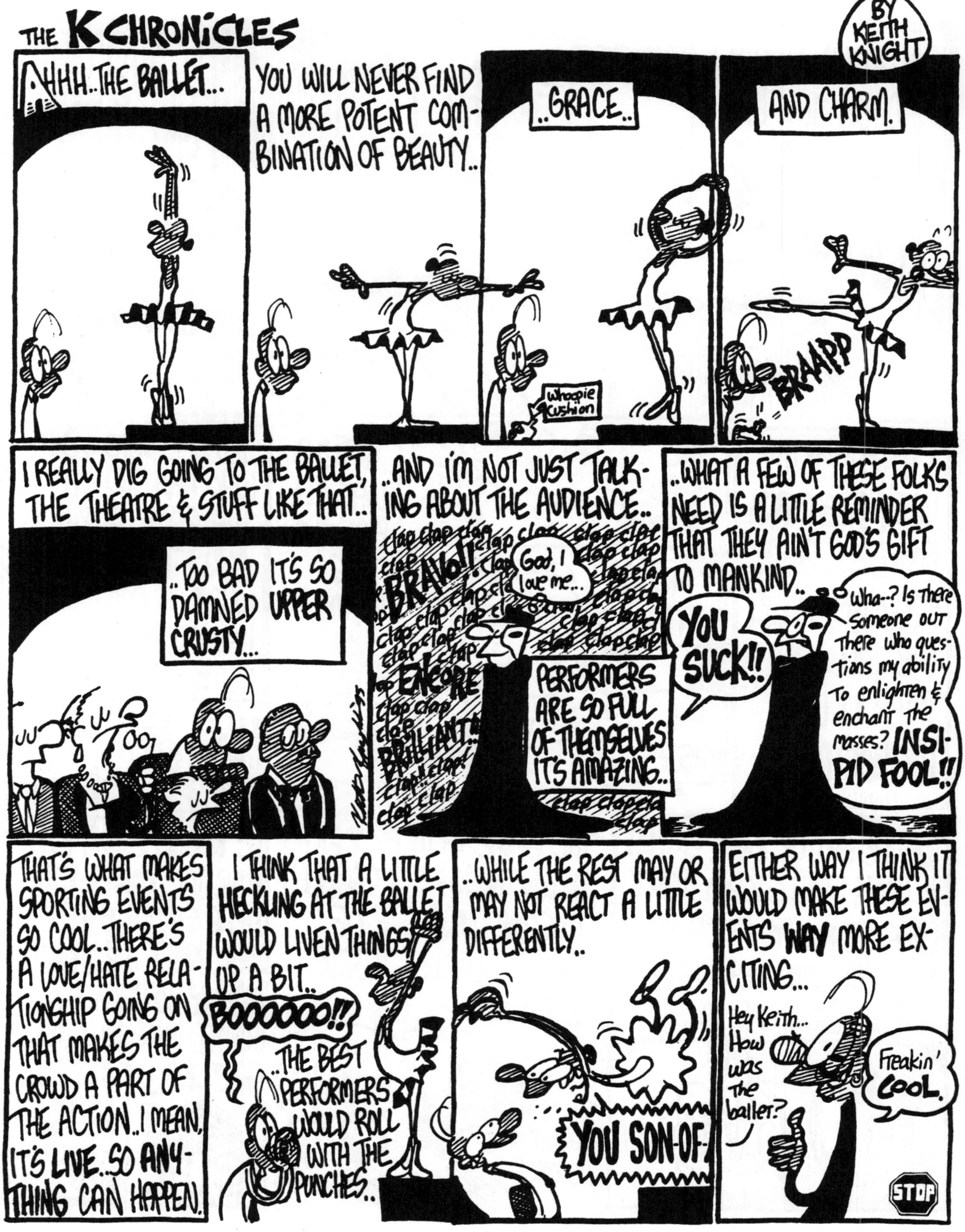
THE K CHRONICLES
BY KEITH KNIGHT
AHHH..THE BALLET...
YOU WILL NEVER FIND A MORE POTENT COMBINATION OF BEAUTY..
..GRACE..
Whoopie Cushion
AND CHARM.
BRAAPP
I REALLY DIG GOING TO THE BALLET, THE THEATRE & STUFF LIKE THAT..
..TOO BAD IT'S SO DAMNED UPPER CRUSTY...
..AND I'M NOT JUST TALKING ABOUT THE AUDIENCE..
BRAVO!!
God, I love me...
ENCORE
BRILLIANT!!
PERFORMERS ARE SO FULL OF THEMSELVES IT'S AMAZING..
..WHAT A FEW OF THESE FOLKS NEED IS A LITTLE REMINDER THAT THEY AIN'T GOD'S GIFT TO MANKIND..
YOU SUCK!!
Wha--? Is there someone out there who questions my ability to enlighten & enchant the masses? INSIPID FOOL!!
THAT'S WHAT MAKES SPORTING EVENTS SO COOL..THERE'S A LOVE/HATE RELATIONSHIP GOING ON THAT MAKES THE CROWD A PART OF THE ACTION..I MEAN, IT'S LIVE..SO ANYTHING CAN HAPPEN.
I THINK THAT A LITTLE HECKLING AT THE BALLET WOULD LIVEN THINGS UP A BIT..
BOOOOOO!!
..THE BEST PERFORMERS WOULD ROLL WITH THE PUNCHES..
..WHILE THE REST MAY OR MAY NOT REACT A LITTLE DIFFERENTLY..
YOU SON-OF-
EITHER WAY I THINK IT WOULD MAKE THESE EVENTS WAY MORE EXCITING...
Hey Keith... How was the ballet?
Freakin' COOL.
STOP

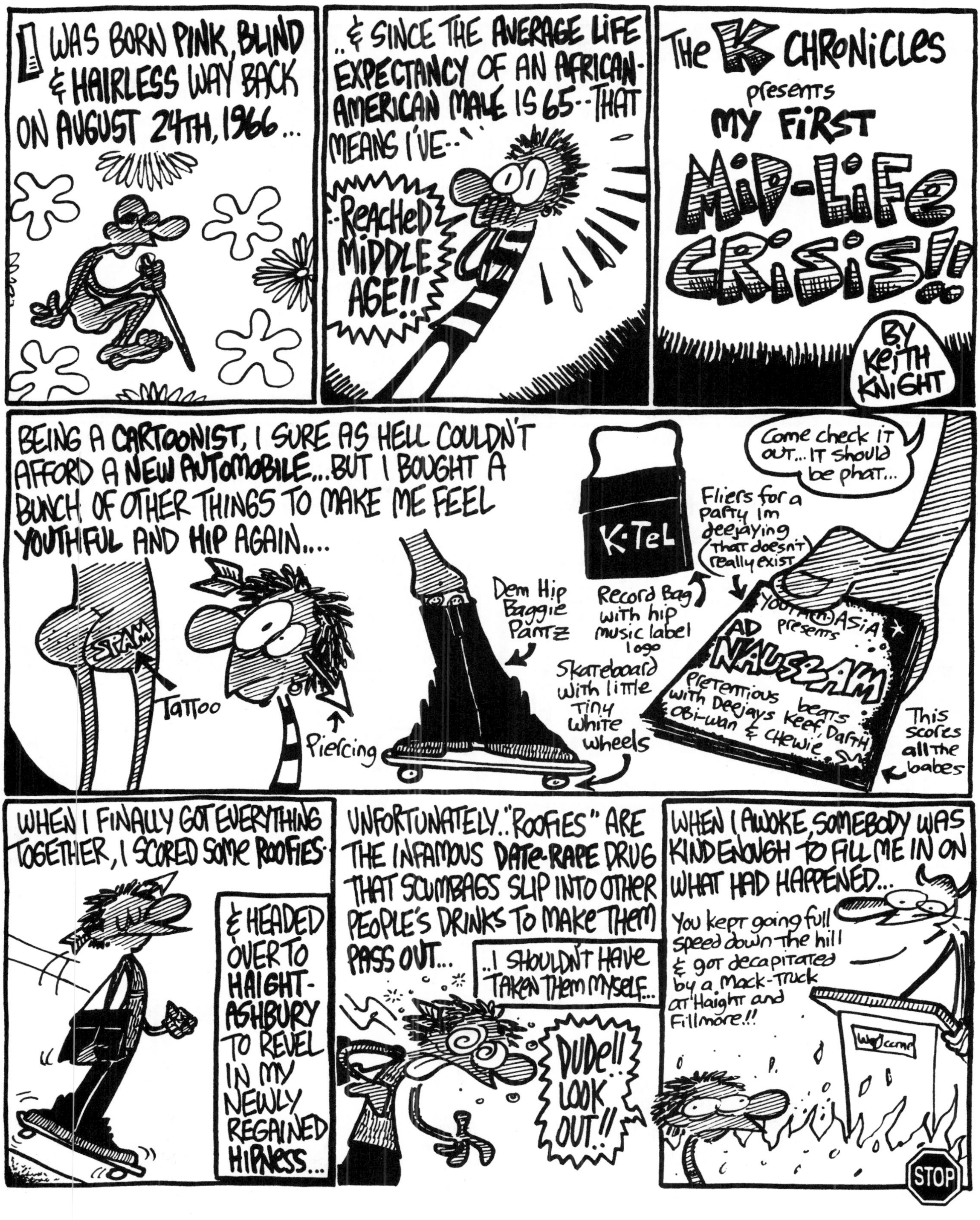
I WAS BORN PINK, BLIND & HAIRLESS WAY BACK ON AUGUST 24TH, 1966...
..& SINCE THE AVERAGE LIFE EXPECTANCY OF AN AFRICAN-AMERICAN MALE IS 65.. THAT MEANS I'VE..
..REACHED MIDDLE AGE!!
THE K CHRONICLES presents MY FIRST MID-LIFE CRISIS!!
BY KEITH KNIGHT
BEING A CARTOONIST, I SURE AS HELL COULDN'T AFFORD A NEW AUTOMOBILE... BUT I BOUGHT A BUNCH OF OTHER THINGS TO MAKE ME FEEL YOUTHFUL AND HIP AGAIN....
Tattoo
Piercing
Dem Hip Baggie Pantz
K-TeL
Record Bag with hip music label logo
Skateboard with little tiny white wheels
Fliers for a party I'm deejaying (that doesn't really exist)
Come check it out... It should be phat...
YOUTH(IN) ASIA presents AD NAUSEAM Pretentious beats with Deejays Keef, Darth Obi-wan & Chewie
This scores all the babes
WHEN I FINALLY GOT EVERYTHING TOGETHER, I SCORED SOME ROOFIES.
& HEADED OVER TO HAIGHT-ASHBURY TO REVEL IN MY NEWLY REGAINED HIPNESS...
UNFORTUNATELY.. "ROOFIES" ARE THE INFAMOUS DATE-RAPE DRUG THAT SCUMBAGS SLIP INTO OTHER PEOPLE'S DRINKS TO MAKE THEM PASS OUT...
..I SHOULDN'T HAVE TAKEN THEM MYSELF...
DUDE!! LOOK OUT!!
WHEN I AWOKE, SOMEBODY WAS KIND ENOUGH TO FILL ME IN ON WHAT HAD HAPPENED...
You kept going full speed down the hill & got decapitated by a Mack-Truck at Haight and Fillmore!!
Welcome
STOP

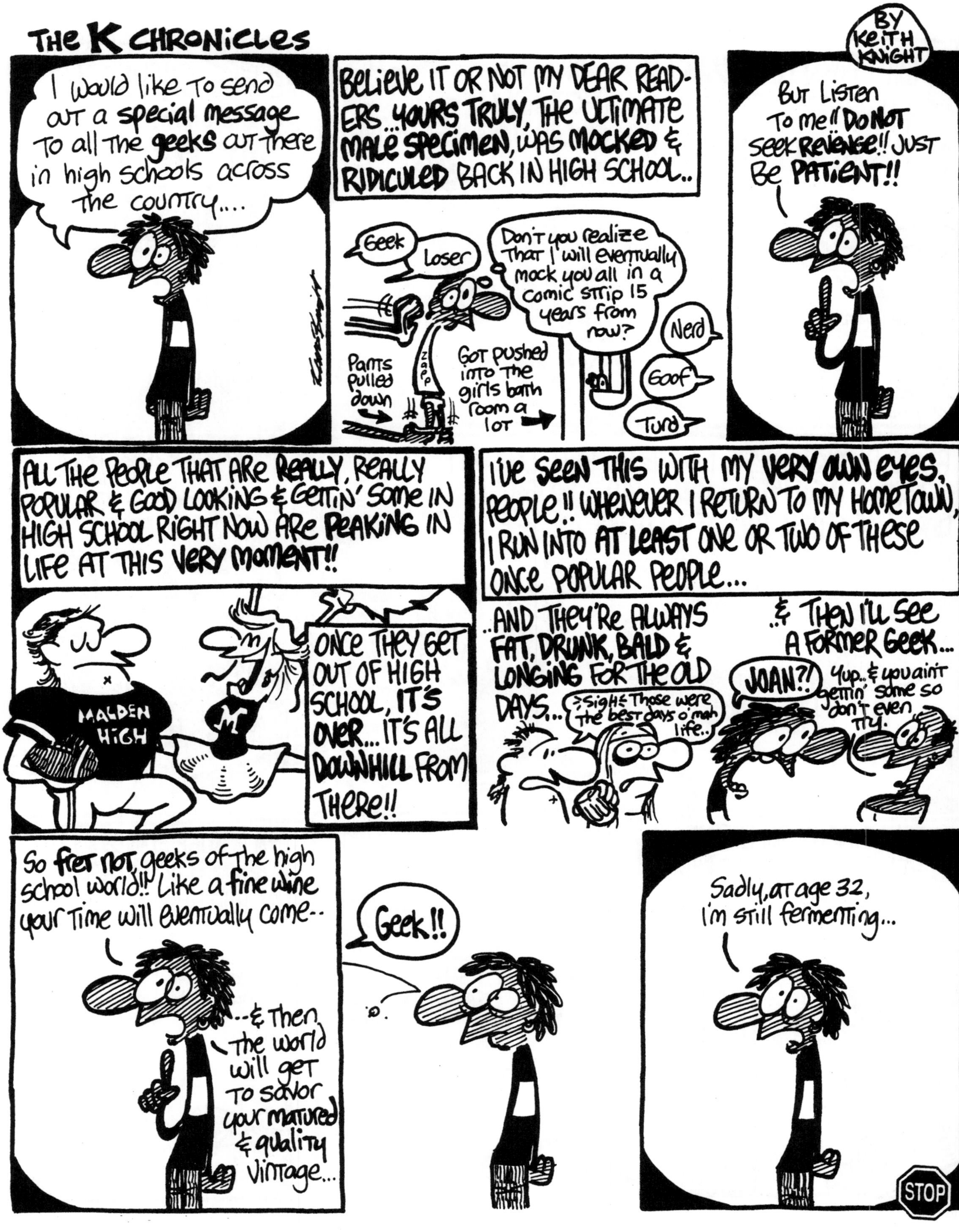
THE K CHRONICLES
BY KEITH KNIGHT
I would like to send out a special message to all the geeks out there in high schools across the country....
BELIEVE IT OR NOT MY DEAR READERS... YOURS TRULY, THE ULTIMATE MALE SPECIMEN, WAS MOCKED & RIDICULED BACK IN HIGH SCHOOL..
Geek
Loser
Don't you realize That I will eventually mock you all in a comic strip 15 years from now?
Nerd
Goof
Turd
Pants pulled down
ZAPP
Got pushed into the girls bath room a lot
But Listen To me!! DO NOT seek REVENGE!! JUST Be PATIENT!!
ALL THE PEOPLE THAT ARE REALLY, REALLY POPULAR & GOOD LOOKING & GETTIN' SOME IN HIGH SCHOOL RIGHT NOW ARE PEAKING IN LIFE AT THIS VERY MOMENT!!
MALDEN HIGH
M
ONCE THEY GET OUT OF HIGH SCHOOL, IT'S OVER... IT'S ALL DOWNHILL FROM THERE!!
I'VE SEEN THIS WITH MY VERY OWN EYES, PEOPLE!! WHENEVER I RETURN TO MY HOMETOWN, I RUN INTO AT LEAST ONE OR TWO OF THESE ONCE POPULAR PEOPLE...
..AND THEY'RE ALWAYS FAT, DRUNK, BALD & LONGING FOR THE OLD DAYS...
>Sigh< Those were the best days o' mah life..
..& THEN I'LL SEE A FORMER GEEK...
JOAN?!
Yup..& you ain't gettin' some so don't even try.
So fret not, geeks of the high school world!! Like a fine wine your time will eventually come--
--& Then the world will get to savor your matured & quality vintage...
Geek!!
Sadly, at age 32, I'm still fermenting...
STOP

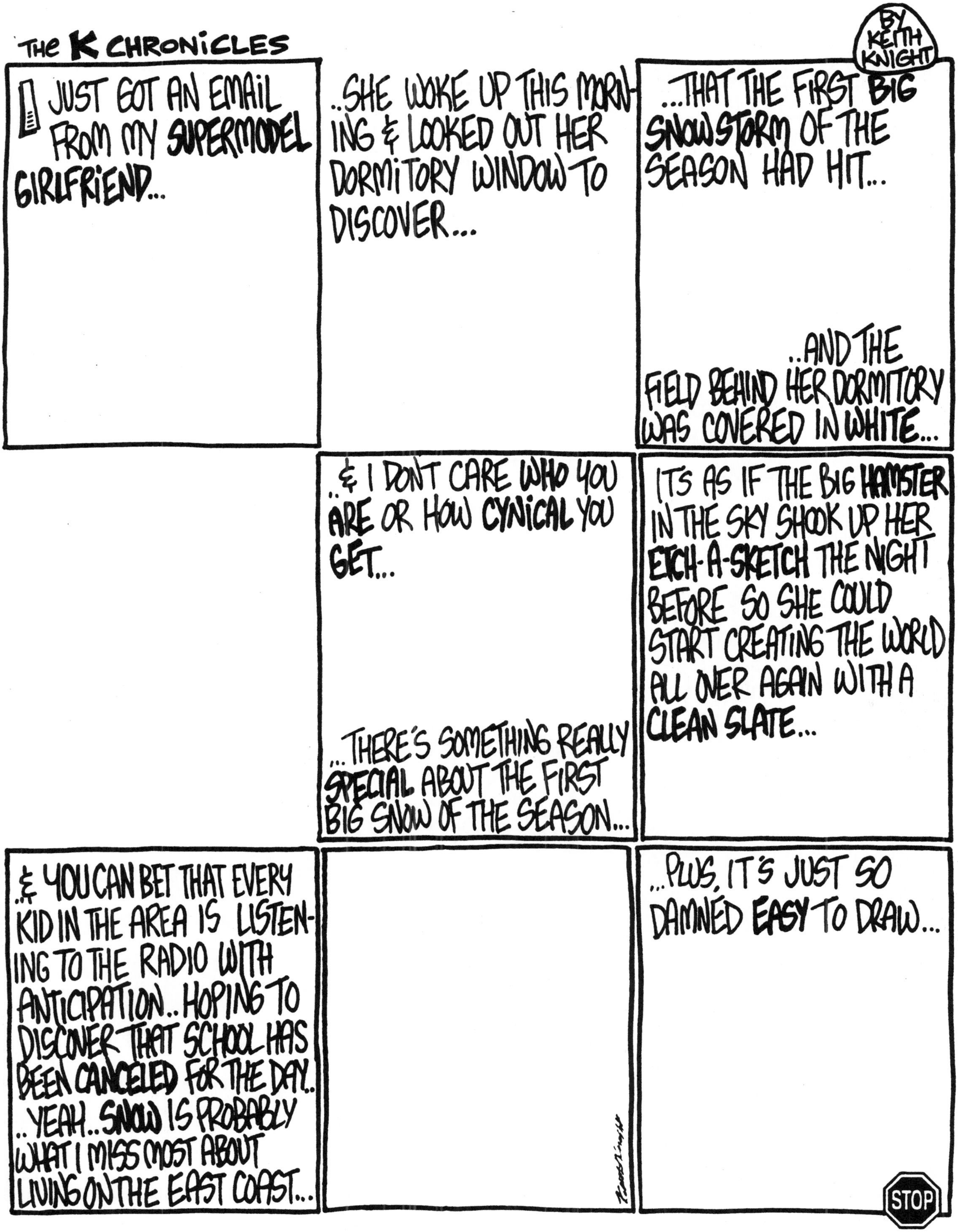
THE K CHRONICLES
BY KEITH KNIGHT
I JUST GOT AN EMAIL FROM MY SUPERMODEL GIRLFRIEND...
..SHE WOKE UP THIS MORNING & LOOKED OUT HER DORMITORY WINDOW TO DISCOVER...
...THAT THE FIRST BIG SNOWSTORM OF THE SEASON HAD HIT...
..AND THE FIELD BEHIND HER DORMITORY WAS COVERED IN WHITE...
..& I DON'T CARE WHO YOU ARE OR HOW CYNICAL YOU GET...
...THERE'S SOMETHING REALLY SPECIAL ABOUT THE FIRST BIG SNOW OF THE SEASON...
ITS AS IF THE BIG HAMSTER IN THE SKY SHOOK UP HER ETCH-A-SKETCH THE NIGHT BEFORE SO SHE COULD START CREATING THE WORLD ALL OVER AGAIN WITH A CLEAN SLATE...
..& YOU CAN BET THAT EVERY KID IN THE AREA IS LISTENING TO THE RADIO WITH ANTICIPATION.. HOPING TO DISCOVER THAT SCHOOL HAS BEEN CANCELED FOR THE DAY..
..YEAH..SNOW IS PROBABLY WHAT I MISS MOST ABOUT LIVING ON THE EAST COAST...
...PLUS, IT'S JUST SO DAMNED EASY TO DRAW...
STOP

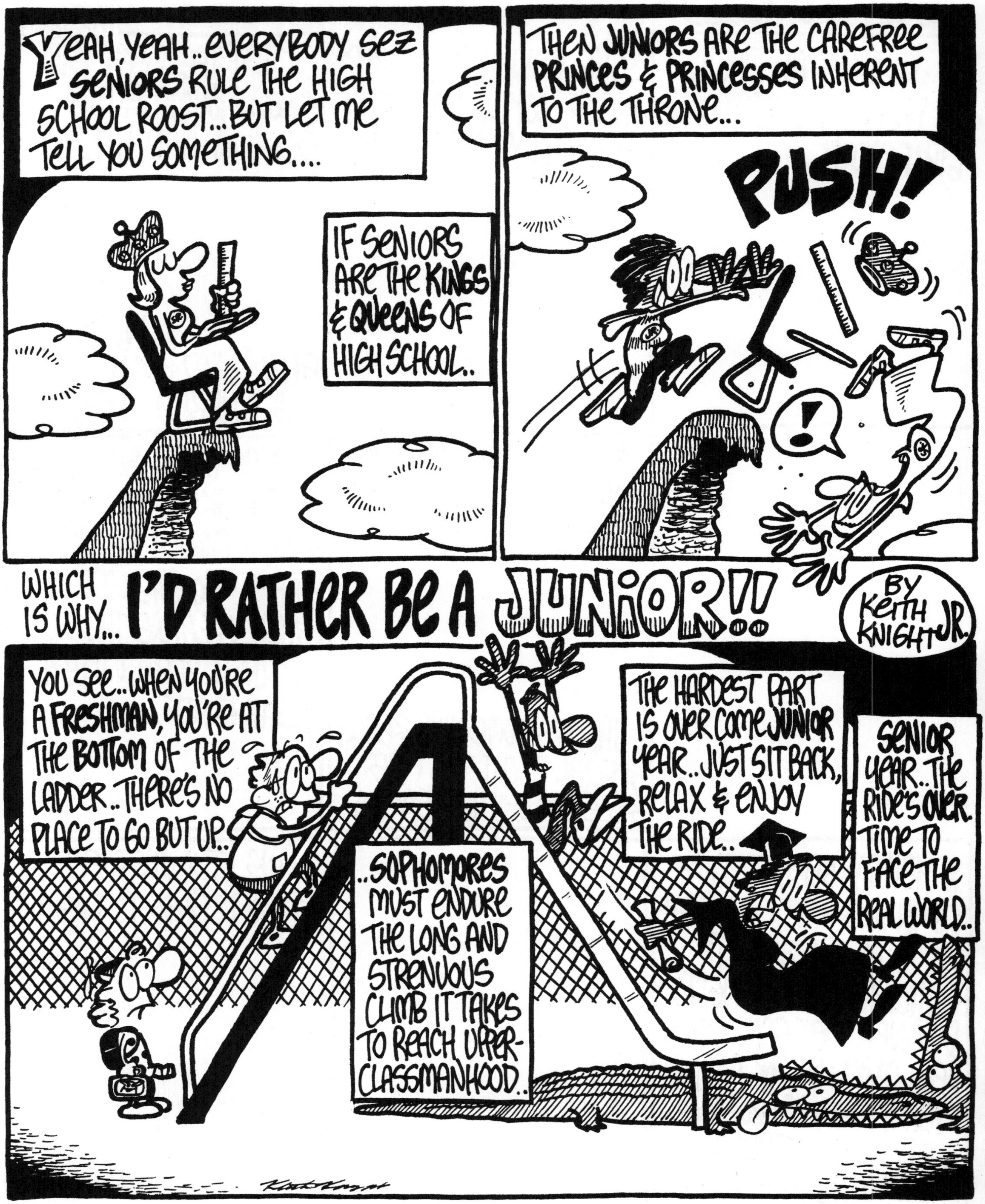
YEAH, YEAH.. EVERYBODY SEZ SENIORS RULE THE HIGH SCHOOL ROOST... BUT LET ME TELL YOU SOMETHING....
IF SENIORS ARE THE KINGS & QUEENS OF HIGH SCHOOL..
THEN JUNIORS ARE THE CAREFREE PRINCES & PRINCESSES INHERENT TO THE THRONE...
PUSH!
!
WHICH IS WHY... I'D RATHER BE A JUNIOR!!
BY KEITH KNIGHT JR.
YOU SEE.. WHEN YOU'RE A FRESHMAN, YOU'RE AT THE BOTTOM OF THE LADDER.. THERE'S NO PLACE TO GO BUT UP..
..SOPHOMORES MUST ENDURE THE LONG AND STRENUOUS CLIMB IT TAKES TO REACH UPPER-CLASSMANHOOD..
THE HARDEST PART IS OVER COME JUNIOR YEAR.. JUST SIT BACK, RELAX & ENJOY THE RIDE..
SENIOR YEAR.. THE RIDE'S OVER. TIME TO FACE THE REAL WORLD..

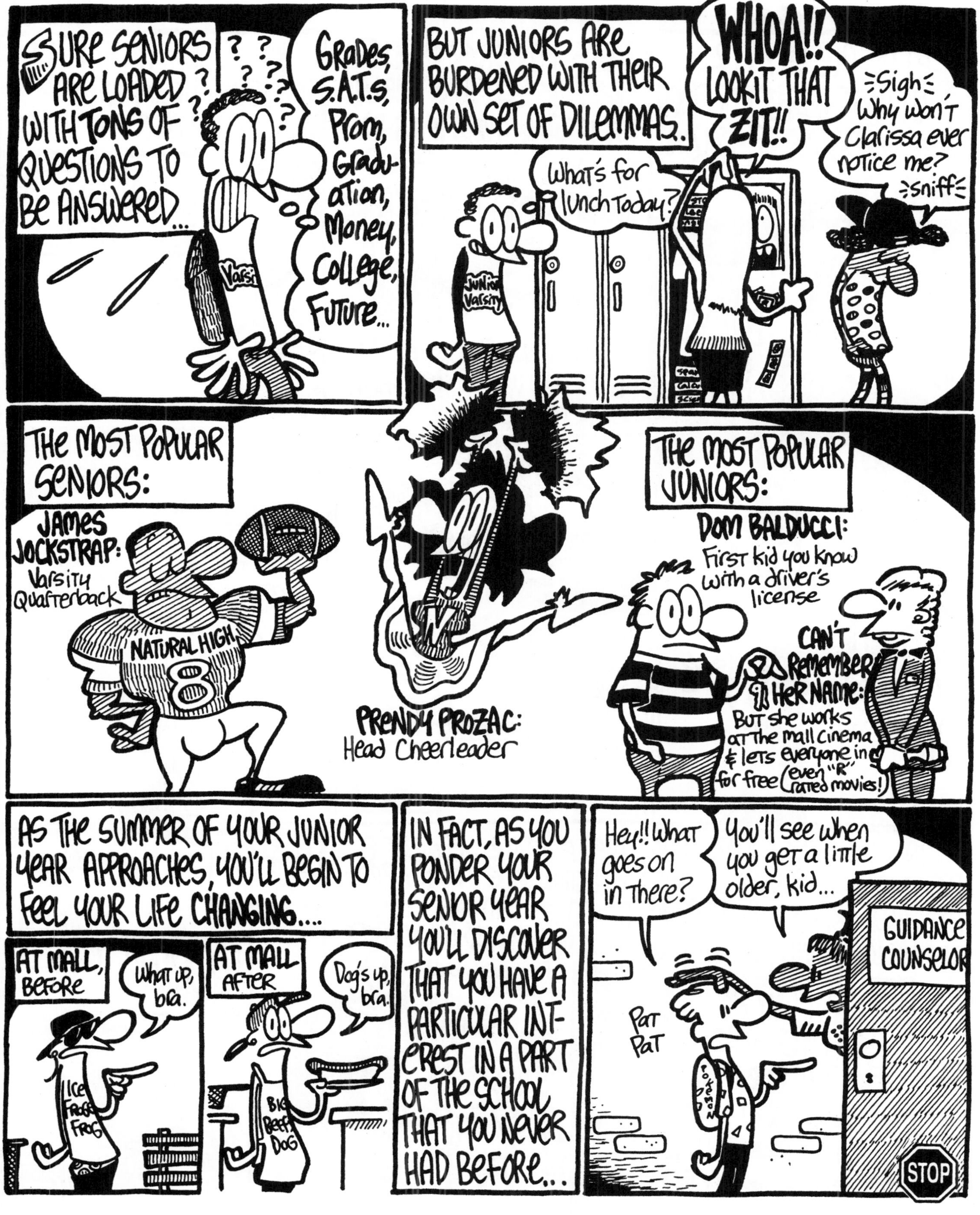
SURE SENIORS ARE LOADED WITH TONS OF QUESTIONS TO BE ANSWERED...
? ? ? ? ? ? ?
Grades, S.A.T.s, Prom, Graduation, Money, College, Future...
Varsi
BUT JUNIORS ARE BURDENED WITH THEIR OWN SET OF DILEMMAS.
What's for lunch today?
Junior Varsity
WHOA!! LOOKIT THAT ZIT!!
Sigh Why won't Clarissa ever notice me? sniff
THE MOST POPULAR SENIORS:
JAMES JOCKSTRAP: Varsity Quarterback
NATURAL HIGH
8
PRENDY PROZAC: Head Cheerleader
THE MOST POPULAR JUNIORS:
DOM BALDUCCI: First kid you know with a driver's license
CAN'T REMEMBER HER NAME: But she works at the mall cinema & lets everyone in for free (even "R" rated movies!)
AS THE SUMMER OF YOUR JUNIOR YEAR APPROACHES, YOU'LL BEGIN TO FEEL YOUR LIFE CHANGING....
AT MALL, BEFORE
What up, bra.
Ice Frogg Frog
AT MALL AFTER
Dog's up, bra.
Big Beef Dog
IN FACT, AS YOU PONDER YOUR SENIOR YEAR YOU'LL DISCOVER THAT YOU HAVE A PARTICULAR INTEREST IN A PART OF THE SCHOOL THAT YOU NEVER HAD BEFORE...
Hey!! What goes on in there?
You'll see when you get a little older, kid...
GUIDANCE COUNSELOR
Pat Pat
STOP

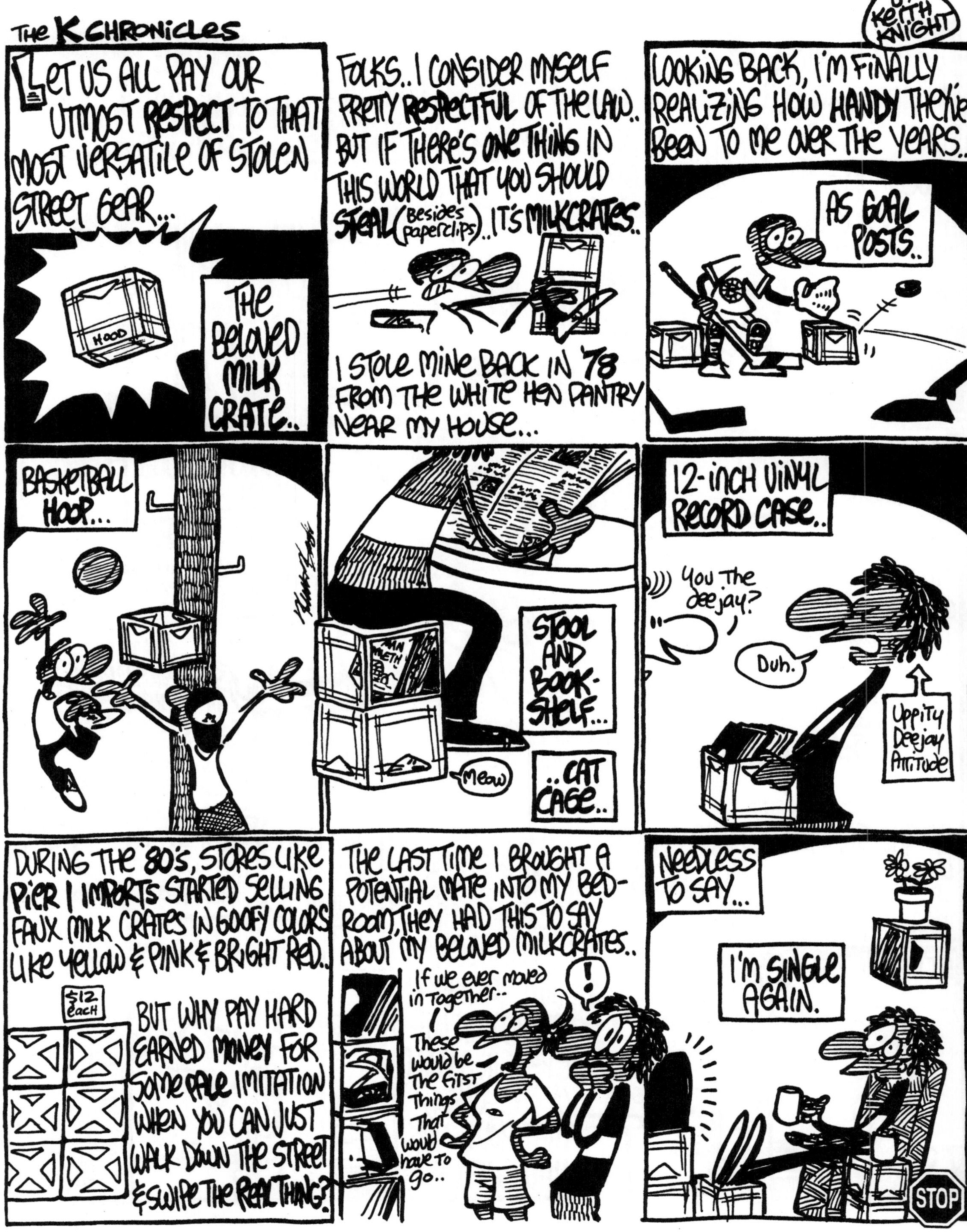
THE K CHRONICLES
BY KEITH KNIGHT
LET US ALL PAY OUR UTMOST RESPECT TO THAT MOST VERSATILE OF STOLEN STREET GEAR...
HOOD
THE BELOVED MILK CRATE..
FOLKS.. I CONSIDER MYSELF PRETTY RESPECTFUL OF THE LAW.. BUT IF THERE'S ONE THING IN THIS WORLD THAT YOU SHOULD STEAL (BESIDES PAPERCLIPS).. IT'S MILKCRATES..
I STOLE MINE BACK IN '78 FROM THE WHITE HEN PANTRY NEAR MY HOUSE...
LOOKING BACK, I'M FINALLY REALIZING HOW HANDY THEY'VE BEEN TO ME OVER THE YEARS..
AS GOAL POSTS..
BASKETBALL HOOP...
STOOL AND BOOK-SHELF...
MEOW
..CAT CAGE..
12-INCH VINYL RECORD CASE..
YOU THE DEEJAY?
DUH.
UPPITY DEEJAY ATTITUDE
DURING THE '80'S, STORES LIKE PIER 1 IMPORTS STARTED SELLING FAUX MILK CRATES IN GOOFY COLORS LIKE YELLOW & PINK & BRIGHT RED..
$12 EACH
BUT WHY PAY HARD EARNED MONEY FOR SOME PALE IMITATION WHEN YOU CAN JUST WALK DOWN THE STREET & SWIPE THE REAL THING?
THE LAST TIME I BROUGHT A POTENTIAL MATE INTO MY BED-ROOM, THEY HAD THIS TO SAY ABOUT MY BELOVED MILKCRATES..
IF WE EVER MOVED IN TOGETHER.. THESE WOULD BE THE FIRST THINGS THAT WOULD HAVE TO GO..
!
NEEDLESS TO SAY...
I'M SINGLE AGAIN.
STOP

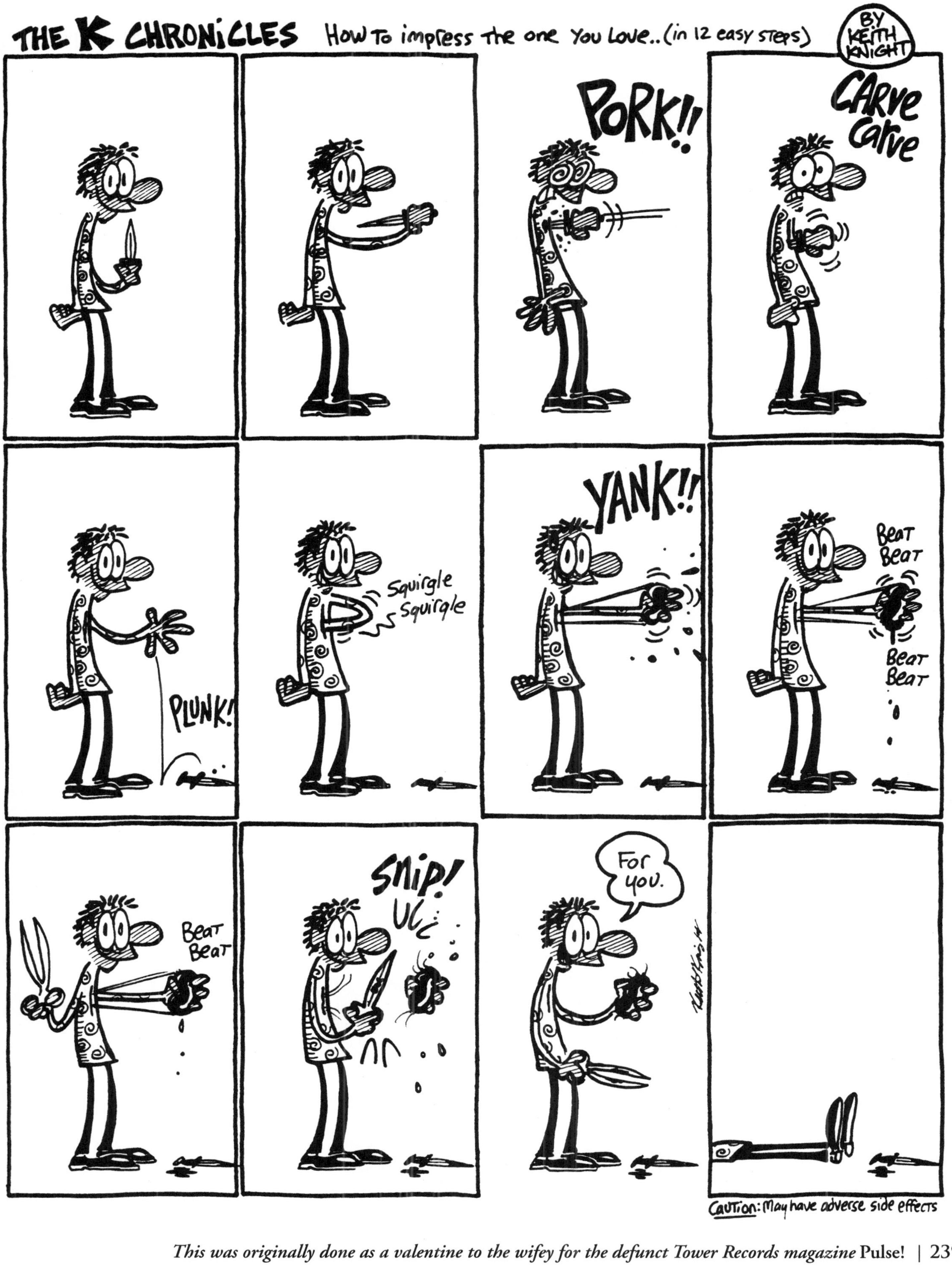
THE K CHRONICLES
How to impress the one you love.. (in 12 easy steps)
BY KEITH KNIGHT
PORK!!
CARVE CARVE
PLUNK!
Squirgle squirgle
YANK!!
Beat Beat
Beat Beat
Beat Beat
SNIP!
For you.
Caution: May have adverse side effects

This was originally done as a valentine to the wifey for the defunct Tower Records magazine Pulse!

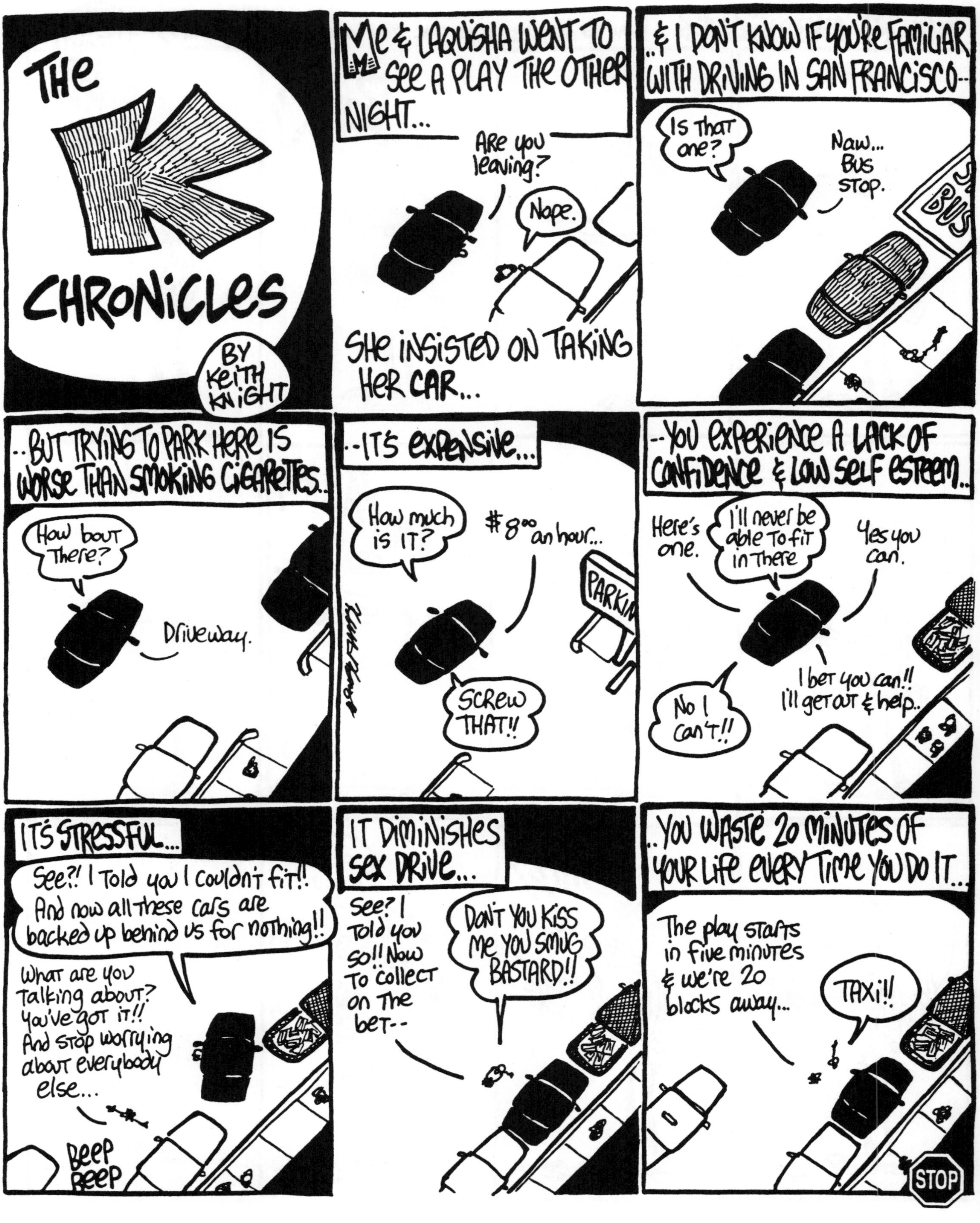
THE K CHRONICLES
BY KEITH KNIGHT
Me & LAQUISHA WENT TO SEE A PLAY THE OTHER NIGHT...
Are you leaving?
Nope.
SHE INSISTED ON TAKING HER CAR...
..& I DON'T KNOW IF YOU'RE FAMILIAR WITH DRIVING IN SAN FRANCISCO--
Is that one?
Naw... Bus stop.
BUS
..BUT TRYING TO PARK HERE IS WORSE THAN SMOKING CIGARETTES..
How bout there?
Driveway.
--IT'S EXPENSIVE...
How much is it?
$8.00 an hour...
PARKIN
SCREW THAT!!
--YOU EXPERIENCE A LACK OF CONFIDENCE & LOW SELF ESTEEM..
Here's one.
I'll never be able to fit in there
Yes you can.
No I can't!!
I bet you can!! I'll get out & help..
IT'S STRESSFUL...
See?! I told you I couldn't fit!! And now all these cars are backed up behind us for nothing!!
What are you talking about? You've got it!! And stop worrying about everybody else...
BEEP BEEP
IT DIMINISHES SEX DRIVE...
See? I told you so!! Now to collect on the bet--
DON'T YOU KISS ME YOU SMUG BASTARD!!
..YOU WASTE 20 MINUTES OF YOUR LIFE EVERY TIME YOU DO IT...
The play starts in five minutes & we're 20 blocks away...
TAXI!!
STOP

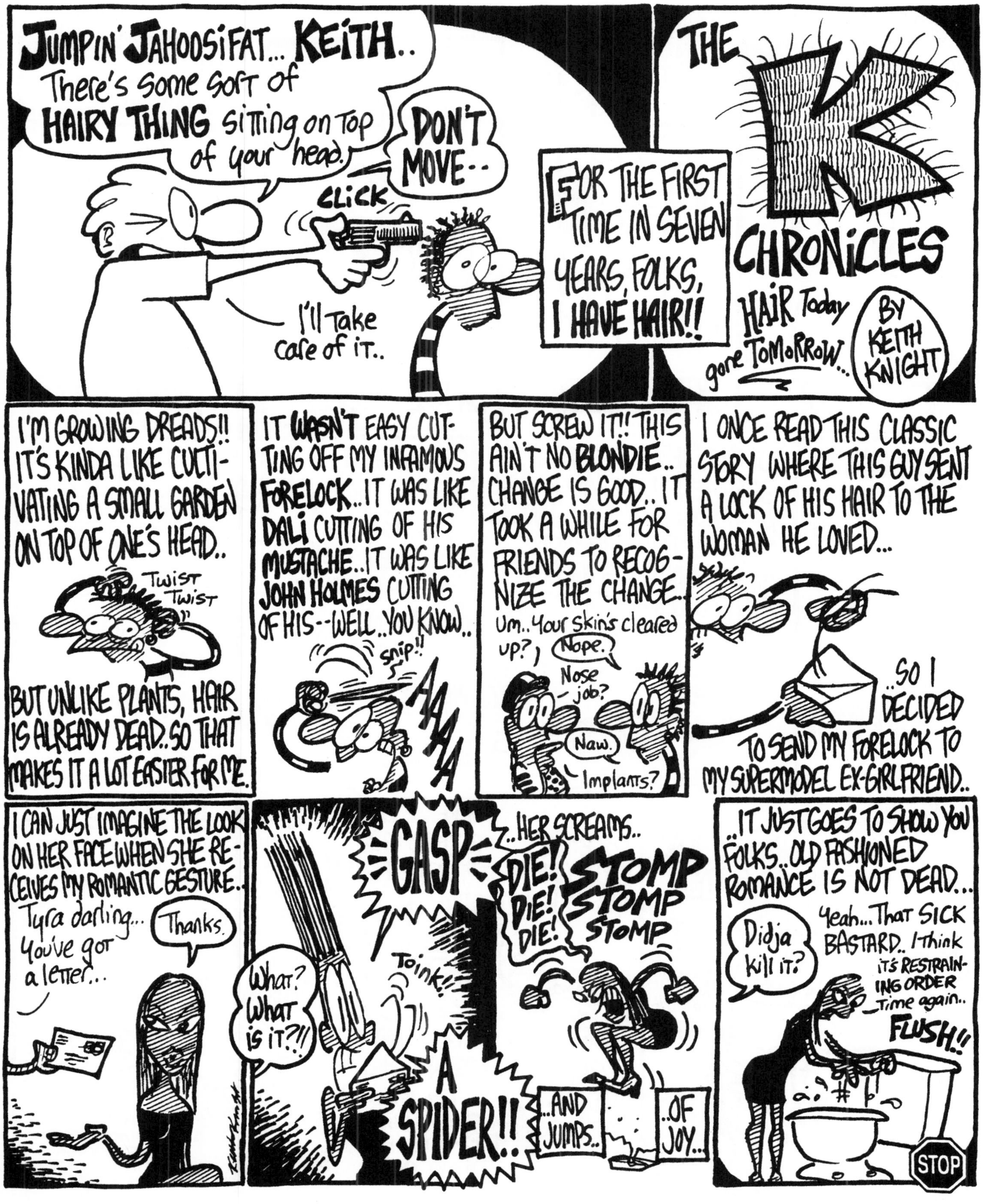
JUMPIN' JAHOOSIFAT... KEITH.. There's some sort of HAIRY THING sitting on top of your head.
DON'T MOVE..
CLICK
I'll take care of it..
FOR THE FIRST TIME IN SEVEN YEARS, FOLKS, I HAVE HAIR!!
THE K CHRONICLES
HAIR Today gone TOMORROW...
BY KEITH KNIGHT
I'M GROWING DREADS!! IT'S KINDA LIKE CULTIVATING A SMALL GARDEN ON TOP OF ONE'S HEAD..
TWIST TWIST
BUT UNLIKE PLANTS, HAIR IS ALREADY DEAD..SO THAT MAKES IT A LOT EASIER FOR ME.
IT WASN'T EASY CUTTING OFF MY INFAMOUS FORELOCK..IT WAS LIKE DALI CUTTING OF HIS MUSTACHE..IT WAS LIKE JOHN HOLMES CUTTING OF HIS--WELL..YOU KNOW..
snip!!
AAAAAA
BUT SCREW IT!! THIS AIN'T NO BLONDIE.. CHANGE IS GOOD.. IT TOOK A WHILE FOR FRIENDS TO RECOGNIZE THE CHANGE..
Um..Your skin's cleared up?
Nope.
Nose job?
Naw.
Implants?
I ONCE READ THIS CLASSIC STORY WHERE THIS GUY SENT A LOCK OF HIS HAIR TO THE WOMAN HE LOVED...
..SO I DECIDED TO SEND MY FORELOCK TO MY SUPERMODEL EX-GIRLFRIEND..
I CAN JUST IMAGINE THE LOOK ON HER FACE WHEN SHE RECEIVES MY ROMANTIC GESTURE..
Tyra darling... You've got a letter...
Thanks.
GASP
What? What is it?!!
Toink!
A SPIDER!!
..HER SCREAMS..
DIE! DIE! DIE!
STOMP STOMP STOMP
..AND JUMPS..
..OF JOY..
..IT JUST GOES TO SHOW YOU FOLKS..OLD FASHIONED ROMANCE IS NOT DEAD...
Didja kill it?
Yeah...That SICK BASTARD.. I think it's RESTRAINING ORDER time again..
FLUSH!!
STOP

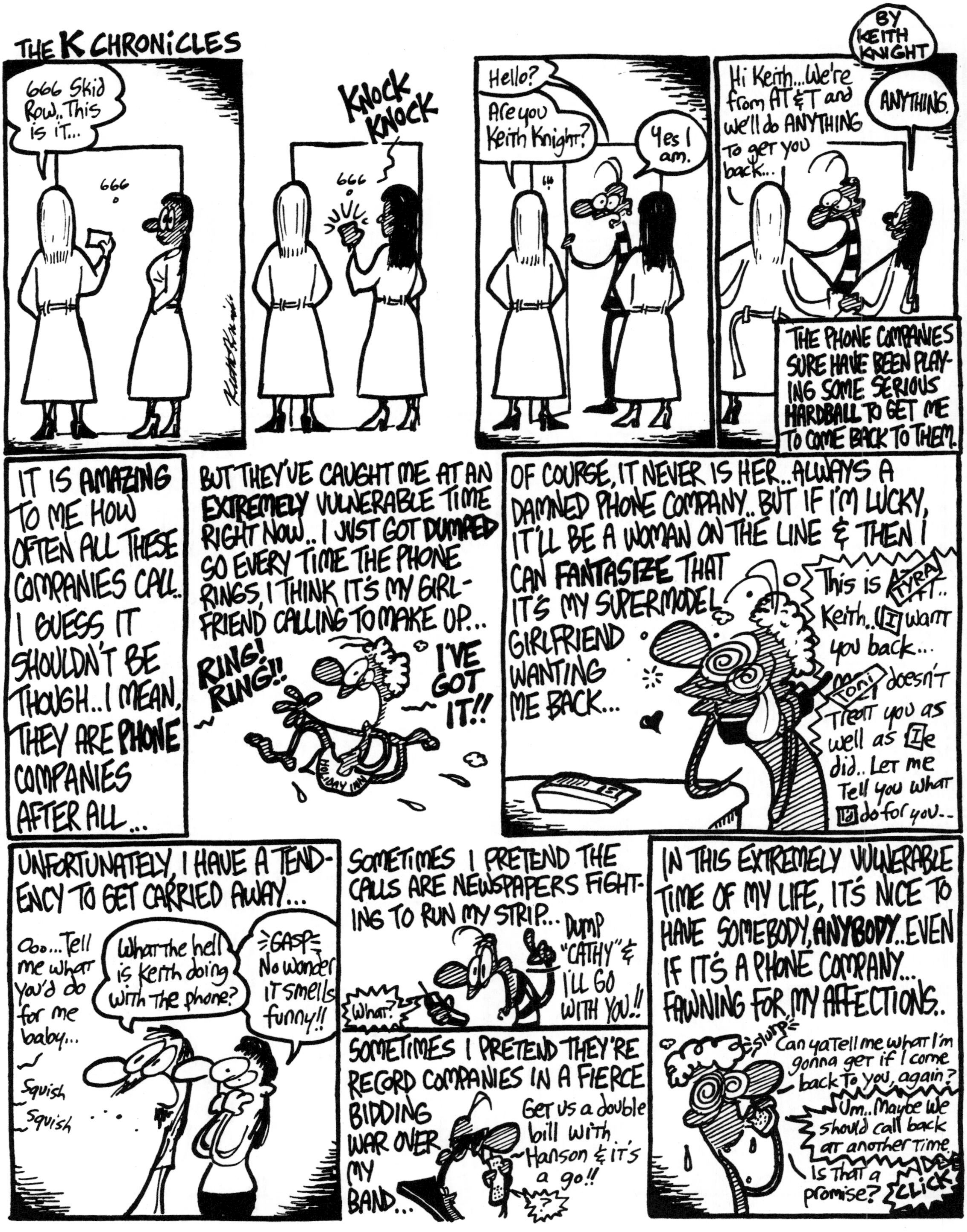
THE K CHRONICLES
BY KEITH KNIGHT
666 Skid Row.. This is IT...
666
KNOCK KNOCK
Hello?
Are you Keith Knight?
Yes I am.
Hi Keith...We're from AT&T and we'll do ANYTHING to get you back...
ANYTHING.
THE PHONE COMPANIES SURE HAVE BEEN PLAYING SOME SERIOUS HARDBALL TO GET ME TO COME BACK TO THEM.
IT IS AMAZING TO ME HOW OFTEN ALL THESE COMPANIES CALL.. I GUESS IT SHOULDN'T BE THOUGH.. I MEAN, THEY ARE PHONE COMPANIES AFTER ALL...
BUT THEY'VE CAUGHT ME AT AN EXTREMELY VULNERABLE TIME RIGHT NOW.. I JUST GOT DUMPED SO EVERY TIME THE PHONE RINGS, I THINK IT'S MY GIRLFRIEND CALLING TO MAKE UP...
RING! RING!!
I'VE GOT IT!!
HOLIDAY INN
OF COURSE, IT NEVER IS HER.. ALWAYS A DAMNED PHONE COMPANY.. BUT IF I'M LUCKY, IT'LL BE A WOMAN ON THE LINE & THEN I CAN FANTASIZE THAT IT'S MY SUPERMODEL GIRLFRIEND WANTING ME BACK...
This is TYRA.. Keith.. I want you back... TONI doesn't treat you as well as I've did.. Let me tell you what I'd do for you..
UNFORTUNATELY, I HAVE A TENDENCY TO GET CARRIED AWAY...
Ooo...Tell me what you'd do for me baby...
Squish Squish
What the hell is Keith doing with the phone?
GASP No wonder it smells funny!!
SOMETIMES I PRETEND THE CALLS ARE NEWSPAPERS FIGHTING TO RUN MY STRIP...
Dump "CATHY" & I'LL GO WITH YOU!!
What?
SOMETIMES I PRETEND THEY'RE RECORD COMPANIES IN A FIERCE BIDDING WAR OVER MY BAND...
Get us a double bill with Hanson & it's a go!!
?
IN THIS EXTREMELY VULNERABLE TIME OF MY LIFE, IT'S NICE TO HAVE SOMEBODY, ANYBODY.. EVEN IF IT'S A PHONE COMPANY... FAWNING FOR MY AFFECTIONS..
slurp
Can ya tell me what I'm gonna get if I come back to you, again?
Um.. Maybe we should call back at another time.
Is that a promise?
CLICK

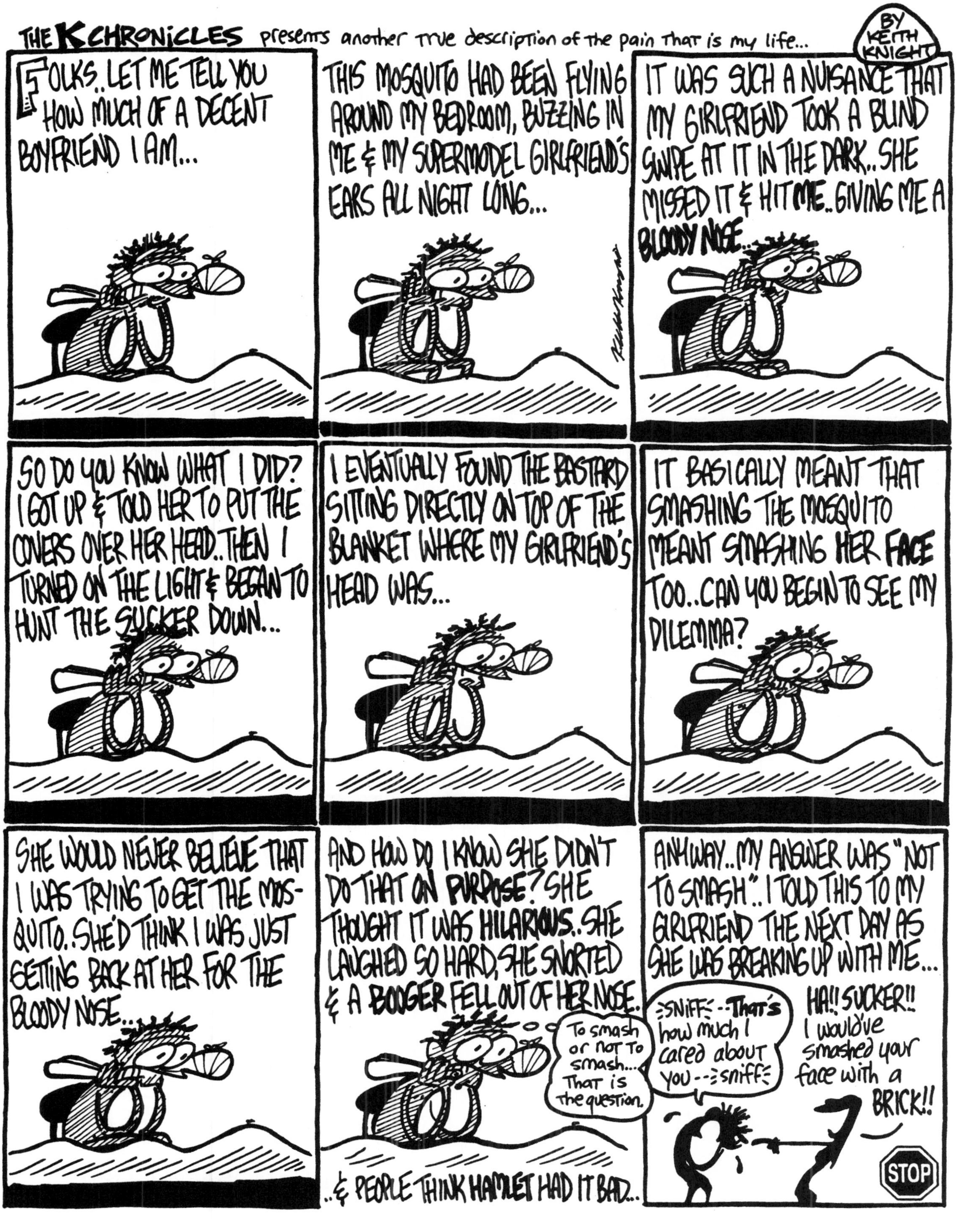
THE K CHRONICLES presents another true description of the pain that is my life...
BY KEITH KNIGHT
FOLKS..LET ME TELL YOU HOW MUCH OF A DECENT BOYFRIEND I AM...
THIS MOSQUITO HAD BEEN FLYING AROUND MY BEDROOM, BUZZING IN ME & MY SUPERMODEL GIRLFRIEND'S EARS ALL NIGHT LONG...
IT WAS SUCH A NUISANCE THAT MY GIRLFRIEND TOOK A BLIND SWIPE AT IT IN THE DARK..SHE MISSED IT & HIT ME..GIVING ME A BLOODY NOSE...
SO DO YOU KNOW WHAT I DID? I GOT UP & TOLD HER TO PUT THE COVERS OVER HER HEAD..THEN I TURNED ON THE LIGHT & BEGAN TO HUNT THE SUCKER DOWN...
I EVENTUALLY FOUND THE BASTARD SITTING DIRECTLY ON TOP OF THE BLANKET WHERE MY GIRLFRIEND'S HEAD WAS...
IT BASICALLY MEANT THAT SMASHING THE MOSQUITO MEANT SMASHING HER FACE TOO..CAN YOU BEGIN TO SEE MY DILEMMA?
SHE WOULD NEVER BELIEVE THAT I WAS TRYING TO GET THE MOSQUITO..SHE'D THINK I WAS JUST GETTING BACK AT HER FOR THE BLOODY NOSE...
AND HOW DO I KNOW SHE DIDN'T DO THAT ON PURPOSE? SHE THOUGHT IT WAS HILARIOUS..SHE LAUGHED SO HARD, SHE SNORTED & A BOOGER FELL OUT OF HER NOSE...
To smash or not to smash... That is the question.
..& PEOPLE THINK HAMLET HAD IT BAD...
ANYWAY..MY ANSWER WAS "NOT TO SMASH"..I TOLD THIS TO MY GIRLFRIEND THE NEXT DAY AS SHE WAS BREAKING UP WITH ME...
SNIFF --That's how much I cared about you --sniff
HA!! SUCKER!! I would've smashed your face with a BRICK!!
STOP

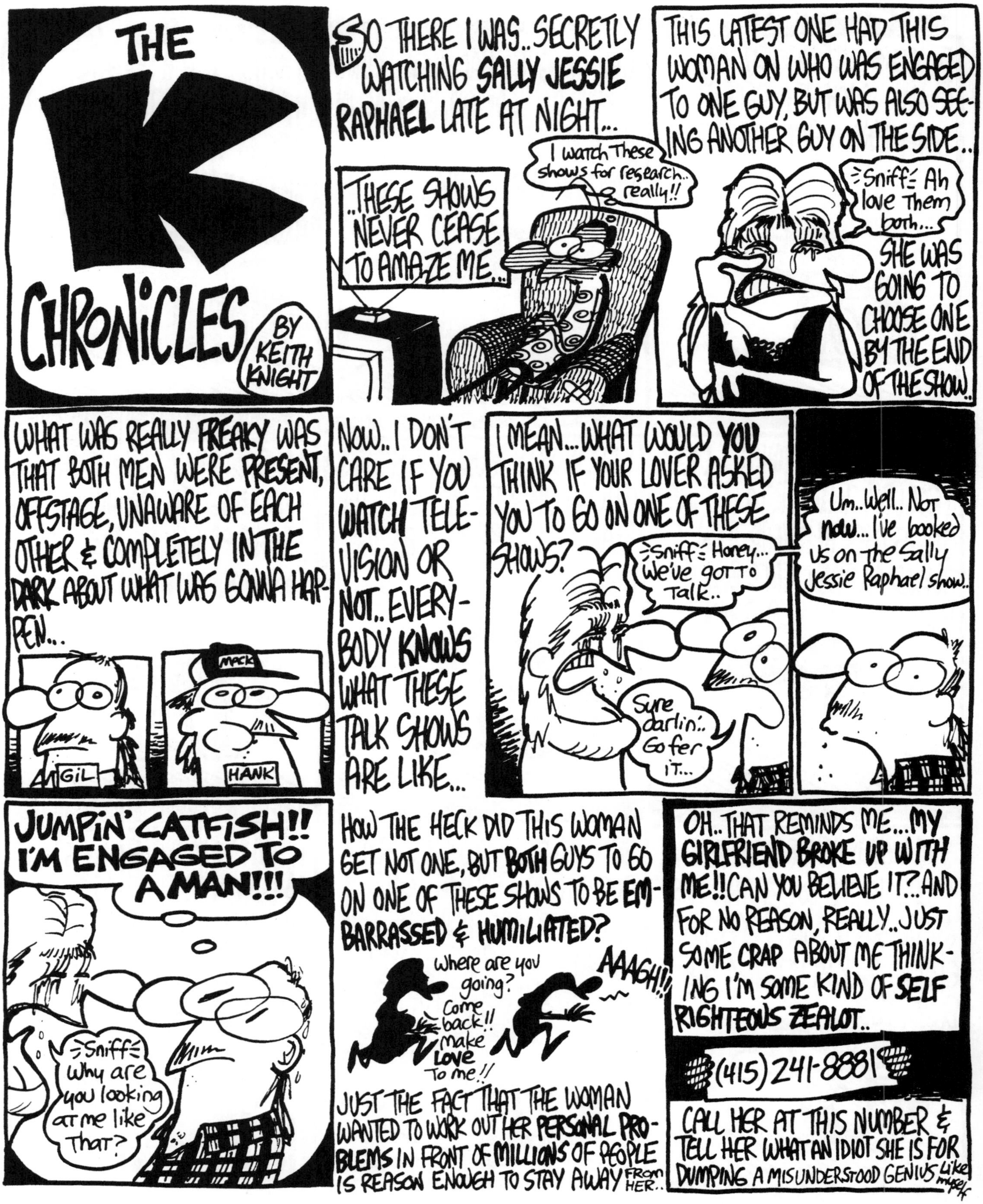
THE K CHRONICLES
BY KEITH KNIGHT
SO THERE I WAS.. SECRETLY WATCHING SALLY JESSIE RAPHAEL LATE AT NIGHT...
..THESE SHOWS NEVER CEASE TO AMAZE ME...
I watch These shows for research.. really!!
THIS LATEST ONE HAD THIS WOMAN ON WHO WAS ENGAGED TO ONE GUY, BUT WAS ALSO SEEING ANOTHER GUY ON THE SIDE..
Sniff Ah love Them both...
SHE WAS GOING TO CHOOSE ONE BY THE END OF THE SHOW..
WHAT WAS REALLY FREAKY WAS THAT BOTH MEN WERE PRESENT, OFFSTAGE, UNAWARE OF EACH OTHER & COMPLETELY IN THE DARK ABOUT WHAT WAS GONNA HAPPEN...
MACK
GIL
HANK
NOW.. I DON'T CARE IF YOU WATCH TELEVISION OR NOT.. EVERYBODY KNOWS WHAT THESE TALK SHOWS ARE LIKE...
I MEAN... WHAT WOULD YOU THINK IF YOUR LOVER ASKED YOU TO GO ON ONE OF THESE SHOWS?
Sniff Honey... We've GOT TO Talk..
Sure darlin'.. Go fer IT...
Um.. Well.. Not now... I've booked us on the Sally Jessie Raphael show..
JUMPIN' CATFISH!! I'M ENGAGED TO A MAN!!!
Sniff Why are you looking at me like That?
HOW THE HECK DID THIS WOMAN GET NOT ONE, BUT BOTH GUYS TO GO ON ONE OF THESE SHOWS TO BE EMBARRASSED & HUMILIATED?
Where are you going? Come back!! make LOVE To me!!
AAAGH!!
JUST THE FACT THAT THE WOMAN WANTED TO WORK OUT HER PERSONAL PROBLEMS IN FRONT OF MILLIONS OF PEOPLE IS REASON ENOUGH TO STAY AWAY FROM HER..
OH.. THAT REMINDS ME... MY GIRLFRIEND BROKE UP WITH ME!! CAN YOU BELIEVE IT?.. AND FOR NO REASON, REALLY.. JUST SOME CRAP ABOUT ME THINKING I'M SOME KIND OF SELF RIGHTEOUS ZEALOT..
(415) 241-8881
CALL HER AT THIS NUMBER & TELL HER WHAT AN IDIOT SHE IS FOR DUMPING A MISUNDERSTOOD GENIUS Like myself

 The phone number was to the Marginal Prophets hotline. Folks left some funny messages.

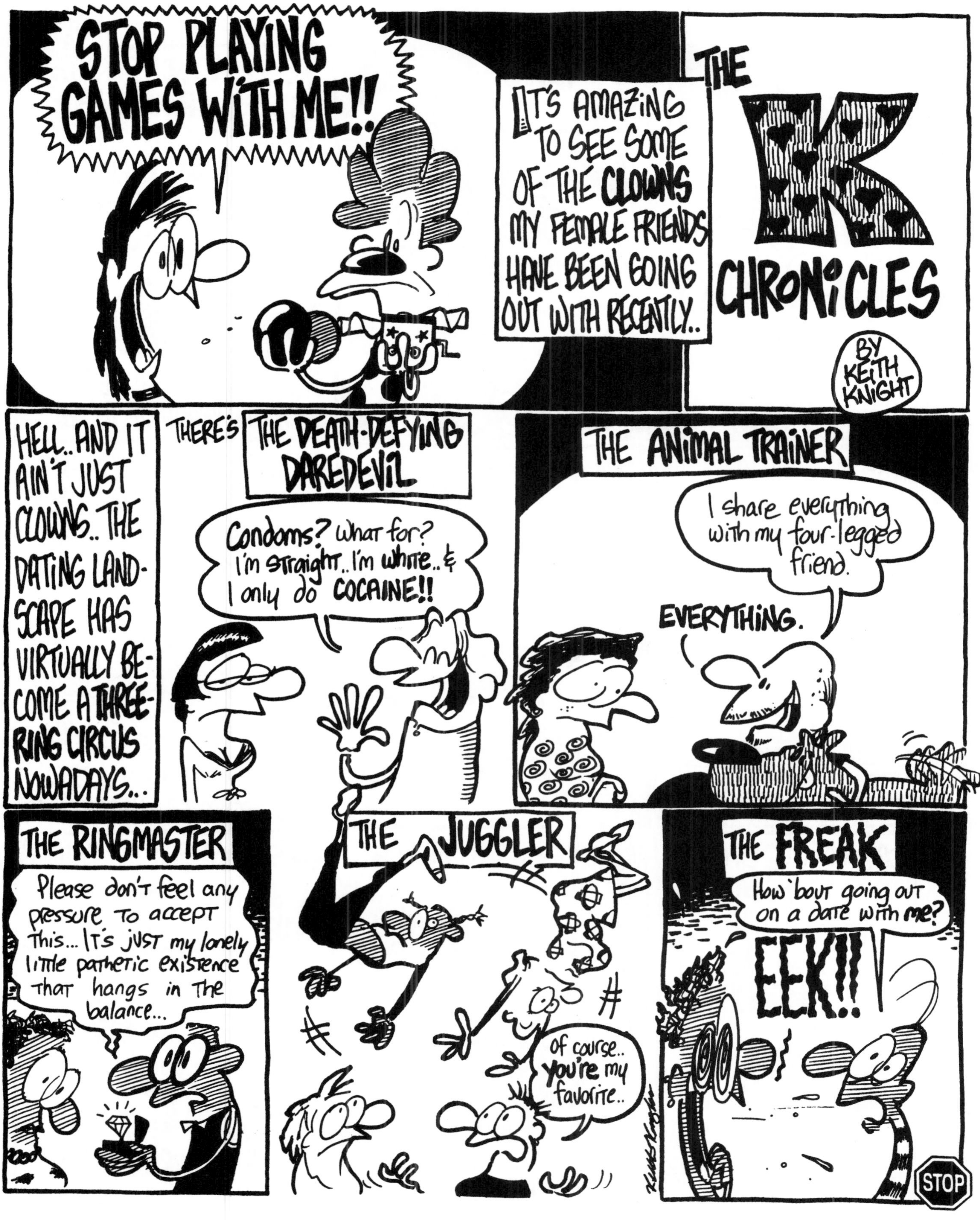
STOP PLAYING GAMES WITH ME!!
IT'S AMAZING TO SEE SOME OF THE CLOWNS MY FEMALE FRIENDS HAVE BEEN GOING OUT WITH RECENTLY..
THE K CHRONICLES
BY KEITH KNIGHT
HELL.. AND IT AIN'T JUST CLOWNS.. THE DATING LANDSCAPE HAS VIRTUALLY BECOME A THREE-RING CIRCUS NOWADAYS...
THERE'S THE DEATH-DEFYING DAREDEVIL
Condoms? what for? I'm straight.. I'm white.. & I only do COCAINE!!
THE ANIMAL TRAINER
I share everything with my four-legged friend.
EVERYTHING.
THE RINGMASTER
Please don't feel any pressure to accept this... It's just my lonely little pathetic existence that hangs in the balance...
THE JUGGLER
of course.. you're my favorite..
THE FREAK
How 'bout going out on a date with me?
EEK!!
STOP

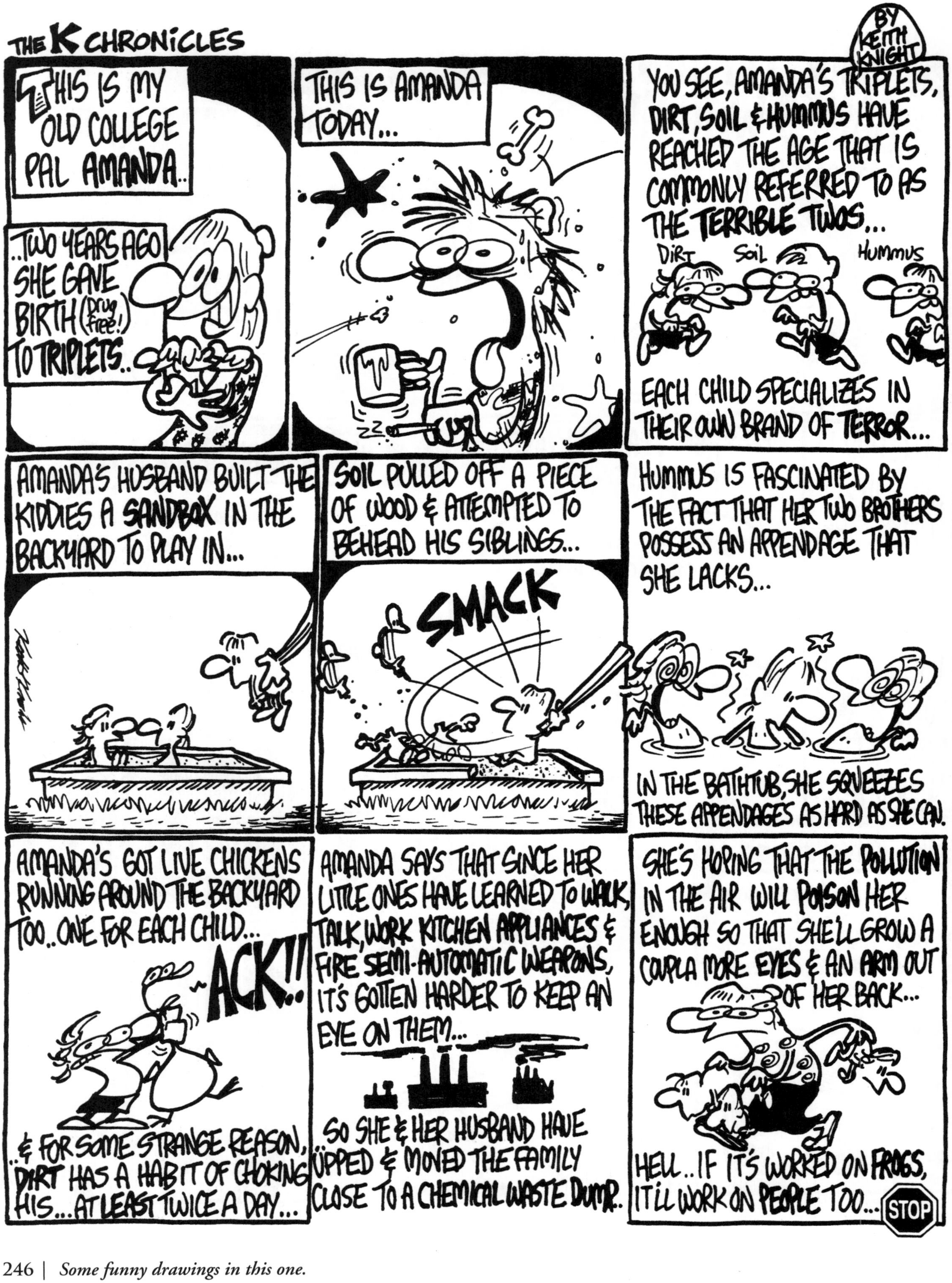
THE K CHRONICLES
BY KEITH KNIGHT
THIS IS MY OLD COLLEGE PAL AMANDA..
..TWO YEARS AGO SHE GAVE BIRTH (drug free!) TO TRIPLETS..
THIS IS AMANDA TODAY...
YOU SEE, AMANDA'S TRIPLETS, DIRT, SOIL & HUMMUS HAVE REACHED THE AGE THAT IS COMMONLY REFERRED TO AS THE TERRIBLE TWOS...
DIRT
SOIL
HUMMUS
EACH CHILD SPECIALIZES IN THEIR OWN BRAND OF TERROR...
AMANDA'S HUSBAND BUILT THE KIDDIES A SANDBOX IN THE BACKYARD TO PLAY IN...
SOIL PULLED OFF A PIECE OF WOOD & ATTEMPTED TO BEHEAD HIS SIBLINGS...
SMACK
HUMMUS IS FASCINATED BY THE FACT THAT HER TWO BROTHERS POSSESS AN APPENDAGE THAT SHE LACKS...
IN THE BATHTUB, SHE SQUEEZES THESE APPENDAGES AS HARD AS SHE CAN.
AMANDA'S GOT LIVE CHICKENS RUNNING AROUND THE BACKYARD TOO.. ONE FOR EACH CHILD...
ACK!!
..& FOR SOME STRANGE REASON, DIRT HAS A HABIT OF CHOKING HIS... AT LEAST TWICE A DAY...
AMANDA SAYS THAT SINCE HER LITTLE ONES HAVE LEARNED TO WALK, TALK, WORK KITCHEN APPLIANCES & FIRE SEMI-AUTOMATIC WEAPONS, IT'S GOTTEN HARDER TO KEEP AN EYE ON THEM...
SO SHE & HER HUSBAND HAVE UPPED & MOVED THE FAMILY CLOSE TO A CHEMICAL WASTE DUMP.
SHE'S HOPING THAT THE POLLUTION IN THE AIR WILL POISON HER ENOUGH SO THAT SHE'LL GROW A COUPLA MORE EYES & AN ARM OUT OF HER BACK...
HELL... IF IT'S WORKED ON FROGS, IT'LL WORK ON PEOPLE TOO...
STOP

 Some funny drawings in this one.

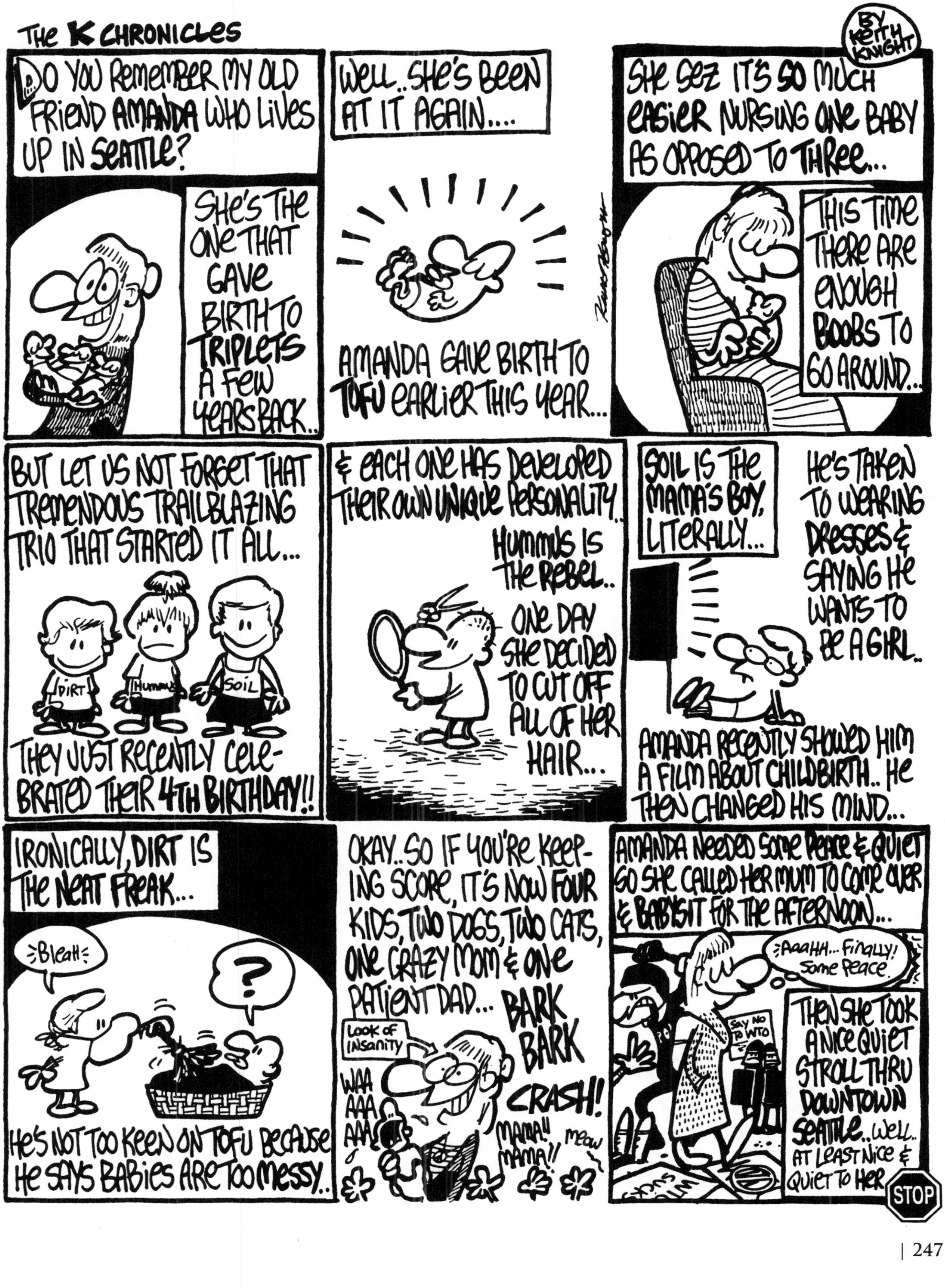
THE K CHRONICLES
BY KEITH KNIGHT
DO YOU REMEMBER MY OLD FRIEND AMANDA WHO LIVES UP IN SEATTLE?
SHE'S THE ONE THAT GAVE BIRTH TO TRIPLETS A FEW YEARS BACK..
WELL.. SHE'S BEEN AT IT AGAIN....
AMANDA GAVE BIRTH TO TOFU EARLIER THIS YEAR...
SHE SEZ IT'S SO MUCH EASIER NURSING ONE BABY AS OPPOSED TO THREE...
THIS TIME THERE ARE ENOUGH BOOBS TO GO AROUND...
BUT LET US NOT FORGET THAT TREMENDOUS TRAILBLAZING TRIO THAT STARTED IT ALL...
DIRT
HUMMUS
SOIL
THEY JUST RECENTLY CELE-BRATED THEIR 4TH BIRTHDAY!!
& EACH ONE HAS DEVELOPED THEIR OWN UNIQUE PERSONALITY..
HUMMUS IS THE REBEL..
ONE DAY SHE DECIDED TO CUT OFF ALL OF HER HAIR...
SOIL IS THE MAMA'S BOY, LITERALLY...
HE'S TAKEN TO WEARING DRESSES & SAYING HE WANTS TO BE A GIRL..
AMANDA RECENTLY SHOWED HIM A FILM ABOUT CHILDBIRTH.. HE THEN CHANGED HIS MIND...
IRONICALLY, DIRT IS THE NEAT FREAK...
BLEAH
?
HE'S NOT TOO KEEN ON TOFU BECAUSE HE SAYS BABIES ARE TOO MESSY..
OKAY.. SO IF YOU'RE KEEP-ING SCORE, IT'S NOW FOUR KIDS, TWO DOGS, TWO CATS, ONE CRAZY MOM & ONE PATIENT DAD...
BARK BARK
LOOK OF INSANITY
WAA AAA AAA
CRASH!
MAMA!! MAMA!!
MEOW
AMANDA NEEDED SOME PEACE & QUIET SO SHE CALLED HER MUM TO COME OVER & BABYSIT FOR THE AFTERNOON...
AAAHH... FINALLY! SOME PEACE.
SAY NO TO WTO
THEN SHE TOOK A NICE QUIET STROLL THRU DOWNTOWN SEATTLE.. WELL.. AT LEAST NICE & QUIET TO HER
STOP

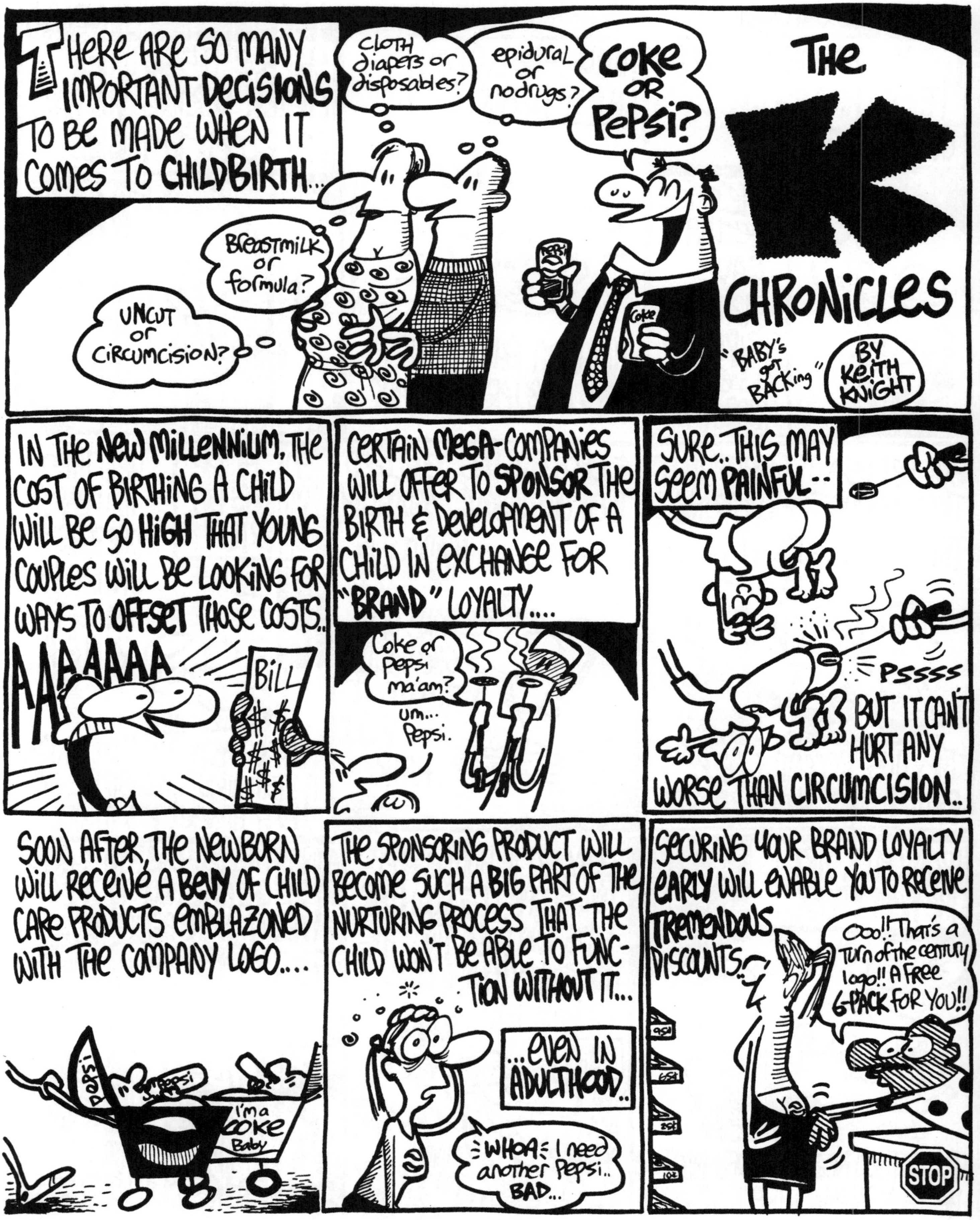
THERE ARE SO MANY IMPORTANT DECISIONS TO BE MADE WHEN IT COMES TO CHILDBIRTH...
CLOTH diapers or disposables?
epidural or nodrugs?
COKE OR PEPSI?
THE K CHRONICLES
BREASTMILK or formula?
UNCUT or CIRCUMCISION?
Pepsi
Coke
"BABY'S got BACKing"
BY KEITH KNIGHT
IN THE NEW MILLENNIUM, THE COST OF BIRTHING A CHILD WILL BE SO HIGH THAT YOUNG COUPLES WILL BE LOOKING FOR WAYS TO OFFSET THOSE COSTS...
AAAAAAA
BILL
CERTAIN MEGA-COMPANIES WILL OFFER TO SPONSOR THE BIRTH & DEVELOPMENT OF A CHILD IN EXCHANGE FOR "BRAND" LOYALTY....
Coke or Pepsi ma'am?
um... Pepsi.
SURE.. THIS MAY SEEM PAINFUL--
PSSSS
BUT IT CAN'T HURT ANY WORSE THAN CIRCUMCISION..
SOON AFTER, THE NEWBORN WILL RECEIVE A BEVY OF CHILD CARE PRODUCTS EMBLAZONED WITH THE COMPANY LOGO....
Pepsi
Pepsi
i'm a COKE Baby
THE SPONSORING PRODUCT WILL BECOME SUCH A BIG PART OF THE NURTURING PROCESS THAT THE CHILD WON'T BE ABLE TO FUNCTION WITHOUT IT...
...EVEN IN ADULTHOOD..
WHOA I need another Pepsi.. BAD...
SECURING YOUR BRAND LOYALTY EARLY WILL ENABLE YOU TO RECEIVE TREMENDOUS DISCOUNTS..
Ooo!! That's a Turn of the century logo!! A Free 6-PACK FOR YOU!!
STOP

 This is already happening with adults and tattoos.

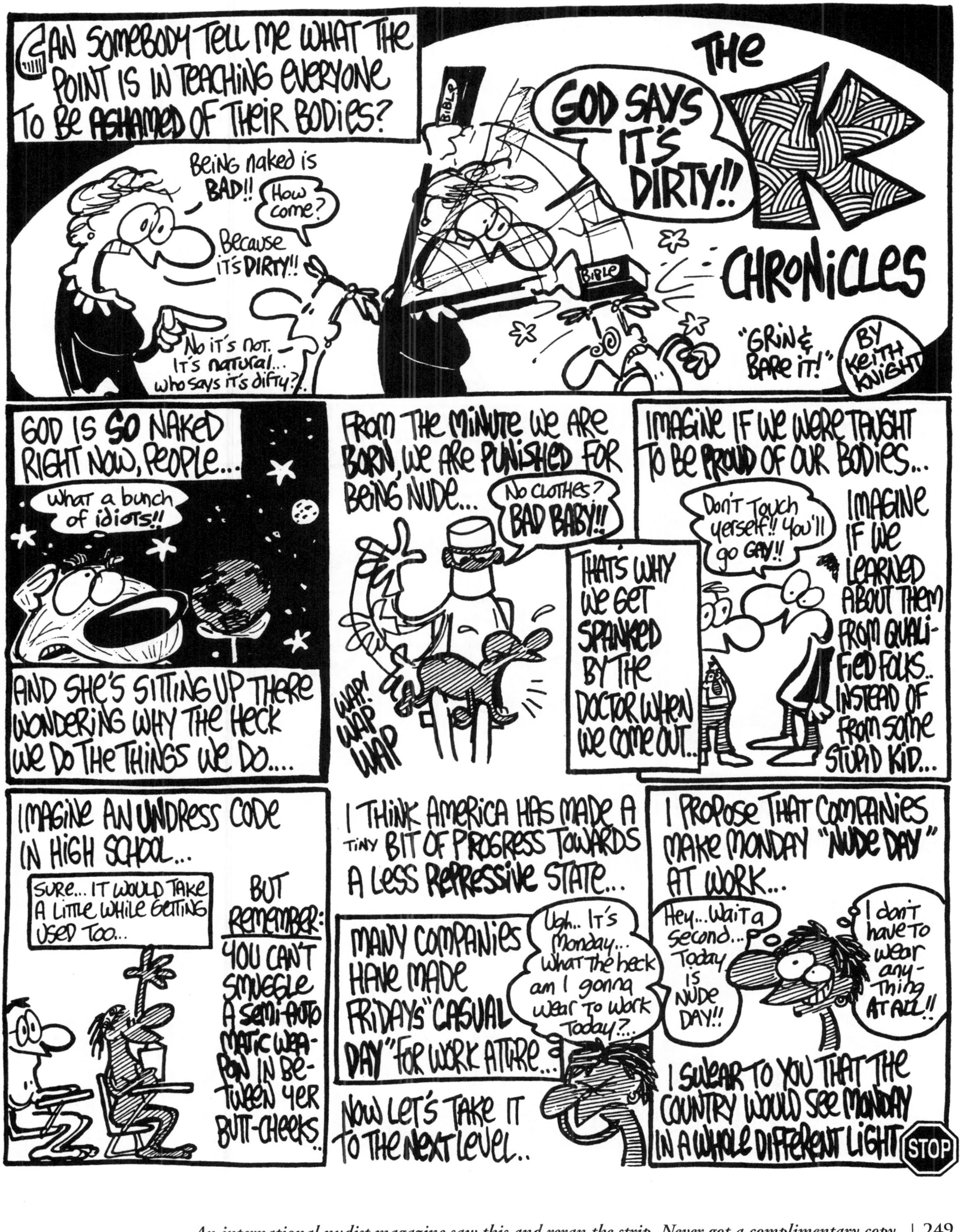

CAN SOMEBODY TELL ME WHAT THE POINT IS IN TEACHING EVERYONE TO BE ASHAMED OF THEIR BODIES?
THE K CHRONICLES
Being naked is BAD!!
How come?
Because it's DIRTY!!
No it's not. It's natural... who says it's dirty?
BIBLE
GOD SAYS IT'S DIRTY!!
BIBLE
"GRIN & BARE IT!"
BY KEITH KNIGHT
GOD IS SO NAKED RIGHT NOW, PEOPLE...
What a bunch of idiots!!
AND SHE'S SITTING UP THERE WONDERING WHY THE HECK WE DO THE THINGS WE DO....
FROM THE MINUTE WE ARE BORN, WE ARE PUNISHED FOR BEING NUDE...
No clothes? BAD BABY!!
WAP! WAP WAP
THAT'S WHY WE GET SPANKED BY THE DOCTOR WHEN WE COME OUT...
IMAGINE IF WE WERE TAUGHT TO BE PROUD OF OUR BODIES...
Don't touch yerself!! You'll go GAY!!
IMAGINE IF WE LEARNED ABOUT THEM FROM QUALIFIED FOLKS.. INSTEAD OF FROM SOME STUPID KID...
IMAGINE AN UNDRESS CODE IN HIGH SCHOOL...
SURE... IT WOULD TAKE A LITTLE WHILE GETTING USED TOO...
BUT REMEMBER: YOU CAN'T SMUGGLE A SEMI-AUTOMATIC WEAPON IN BETWEEN YER BUTT-CHEEKS...
I THINK AMERICA HAS MADE A TINY BIT OF PROGRESS TOWARDS A LESS REPRESSIVE STATE...
MANY COMPANIES HAVE MADE FRIDAYS "CASUAL DAY" FOR WORK ATTIRE...
Ugh.. It's Monday... What the heck am I gonna wear to work today?..
NOW LET'S TAKE IT TO THE NEXT LEVEL..
I PROPOSE THAT COMPANIES MAKE MONDAY "NUDE DAY" AT WORK...
Hey... Wait a second... Today is NUDE DAY!!
I don't have to wear anything AT ALL!!
I SWEAR TO YOU THAT THE COUNTRY WOULD SEE MONDAY IN A WHOLE DIFFERENT LIGHT
STOP

An international nudist magazine saw this and reran the strip. Never got a complimentary copy.

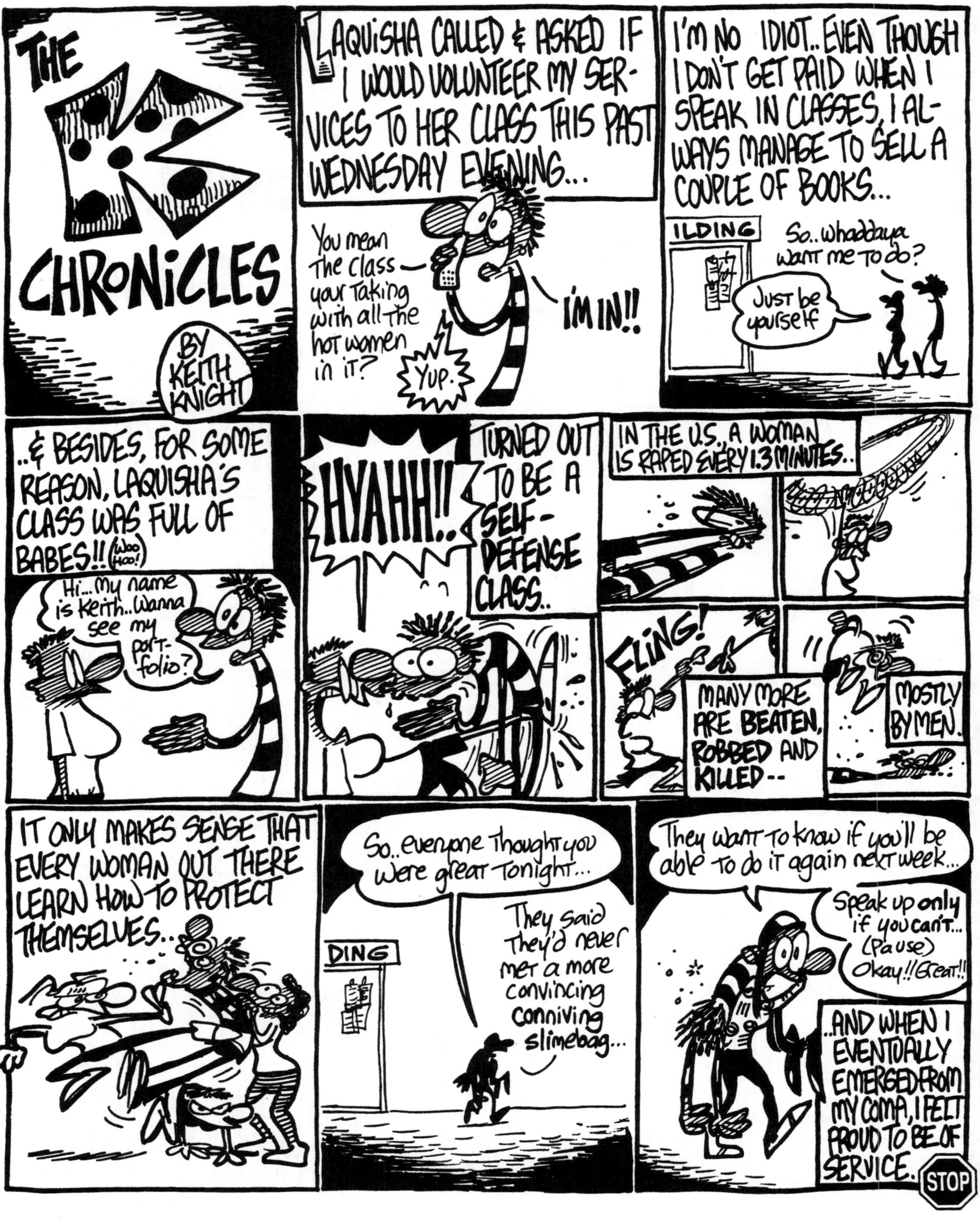
THE K CHRONICLES
BY KEITH KNIGHT
LAQUISHA CALLED & ASKED IF I WOULD VOLUNTEER MY SERVICES TO HER CLASS THIS PAST WEDNESDAY EVENING...
You mean the class your taking with all the hot women in it?
YUP.
I'M IN!!
I'M NO IDIOT.. EVEN THOUGH I DON'T GET PAID WHEN I SPEAK IN CLASSES, I ALWAYS MANAGE TO SELL A COUPLE OF BOOKS...
ILDING
So.. whaddaya want me to do?
Just be yourself
..& BESIDES, FOR SOME REASON, LAQUISHA'S CLASS WAS FULL OF BABES!! (Woo Hoo!)
Hi... My name is Keith.. Wanna see my portfolio?
HYAHH!!..
TURNED OUT TO BE A SELF-DEFENSE CLASS..
IN THE U.S., A WOMAN IS RAPED EVERY 1.3 MINUTES..
FLING!
MANY MORE ARE BEATEN, ROBBED AND KILLED--
MOSTLY BY MEN.
IT ONLY MAKES SENSE THAT EVERY WOMAN OUT THERE LEARN HOW TO PROTECT THEMSELVES...
So.. everyone thought you were great tonight...
They said they'd never met a more convincing conniving slimebag...
DING
They want to know if you'll be able to do it again next week...
Speak up only if you can't... (Pause) Okay!! Great!!
..AND WHEN I EVENTUALLY EMERGED FROM MY COMA, I FELT PROUD TO BE OF SERVICE.
STOP

 I like how the action drawings came out on the right side middle panels.

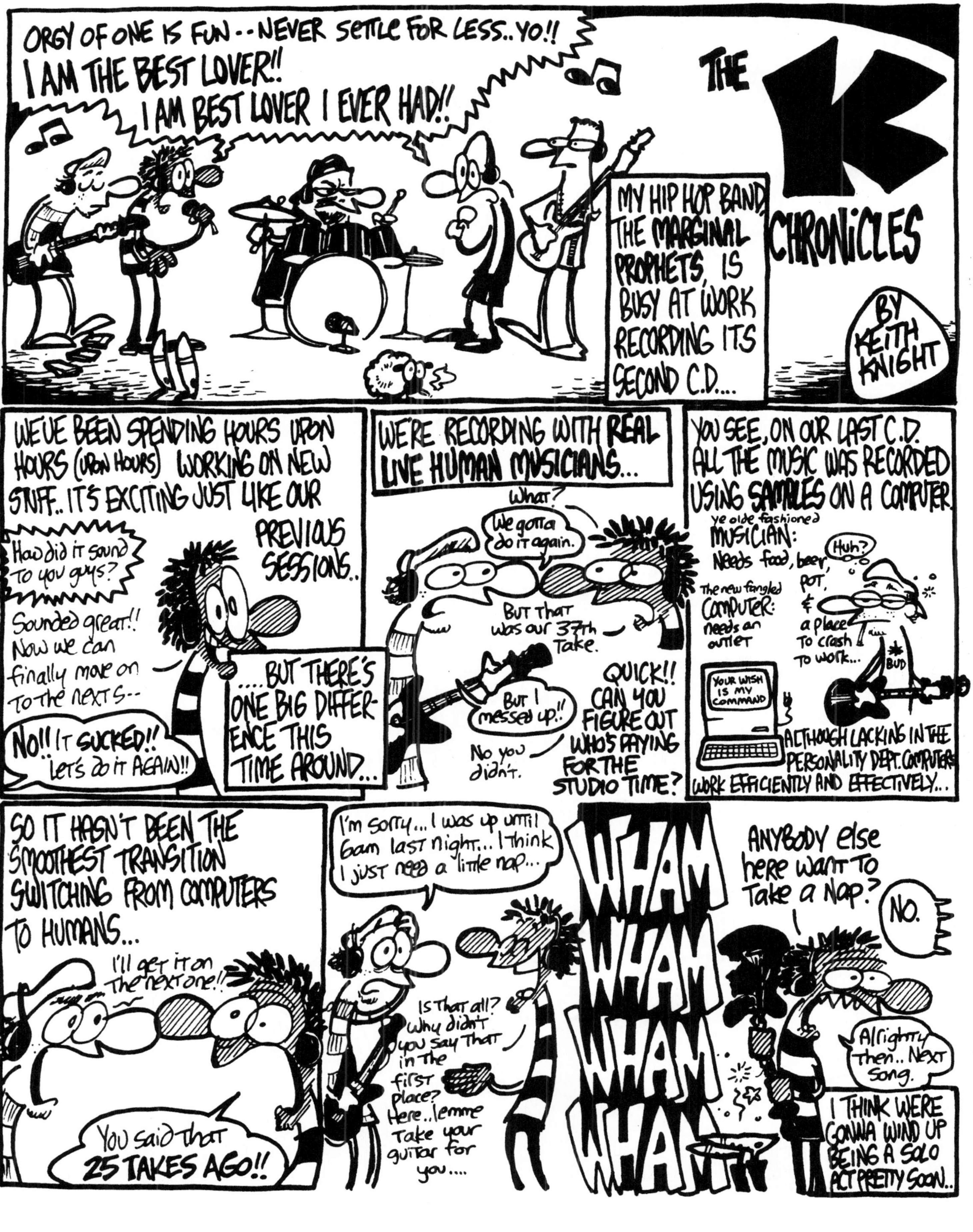

ORGY OF ONE IS FUN - - NEVER SETTLE FOR LESS.. YO!!
I AM THE BEST LOVER!!
I AM BEST LOVER I EVER HAD!!
THE K CHRONICLES
BY KEITH KNIGHT
MY HIP HOP BAND, THE MARGINAL PROPHETS, IS BUSY AT WORK RECORDING ITS SECOND C.D....
WE'VE BEEN SPENDING HOURS UPON HOURS (UPON HOURS) WORKING ON NEW STUFF.. IT'S EXCITING JUST LIKE OUR PREVIOUS SESSIONS..
How did it sound to you guys?
Sounded great!! Now we can finally move on to the next s--
NO!! IT SUCKED!! Let's do it AGAIN!!
....BUT THERE'S ONE BIG DIFFERENCE THIS TIME AROUND...
WE'RE RECORDING WITH REAL LIVE HUMAN MUSICIANS...
What?
We gotta do it again.
But that was our 37th Take.
But I messed up!!
No you didn't.
QUICK!! CAN YOU FIGURE OUT WHO'S PAYING FOR THE STUDIO TIME?
YOU SEE, ON OUR LAST C.D. ALL THE MUSIC WAS RECORDED USING SAMPLES ON A COMPUTER.
ye olde fashioned MUSICIAN: Needs food, beer, pot, & a place to crash to work...
Huh?
The new fangled COMPUTER: needs an outlet
YOUR WISH IS MY COMMAND
BUD
ALTHOUGH LACKING IN THE PERSONALITY DEPT. COMPUTERS WORK EFFICIENTLY AND EFFECTIVELY...
SO IT HASN'T BEEN THE SMOOTHEST TRANSITION SWITCHING FROM COMPUTERS TO HUMANS...
I'll get it on the next one!!
You said that 25 TAKES AGO!!
I'm sorry... I was up until 6am last night... I think I just need a little nap...
Is that all? Why didn't you say that in the first place? Here.. lemme take your guitar for you....
WHAM WHAM WHAM WHAM
ANYBODY else here want to Take a Nap?
NO.
Alrighty then.. Next Song.
I THINK WE'RE GONNA WIND UP BEING A SOLO ACT PRETTY SOON..

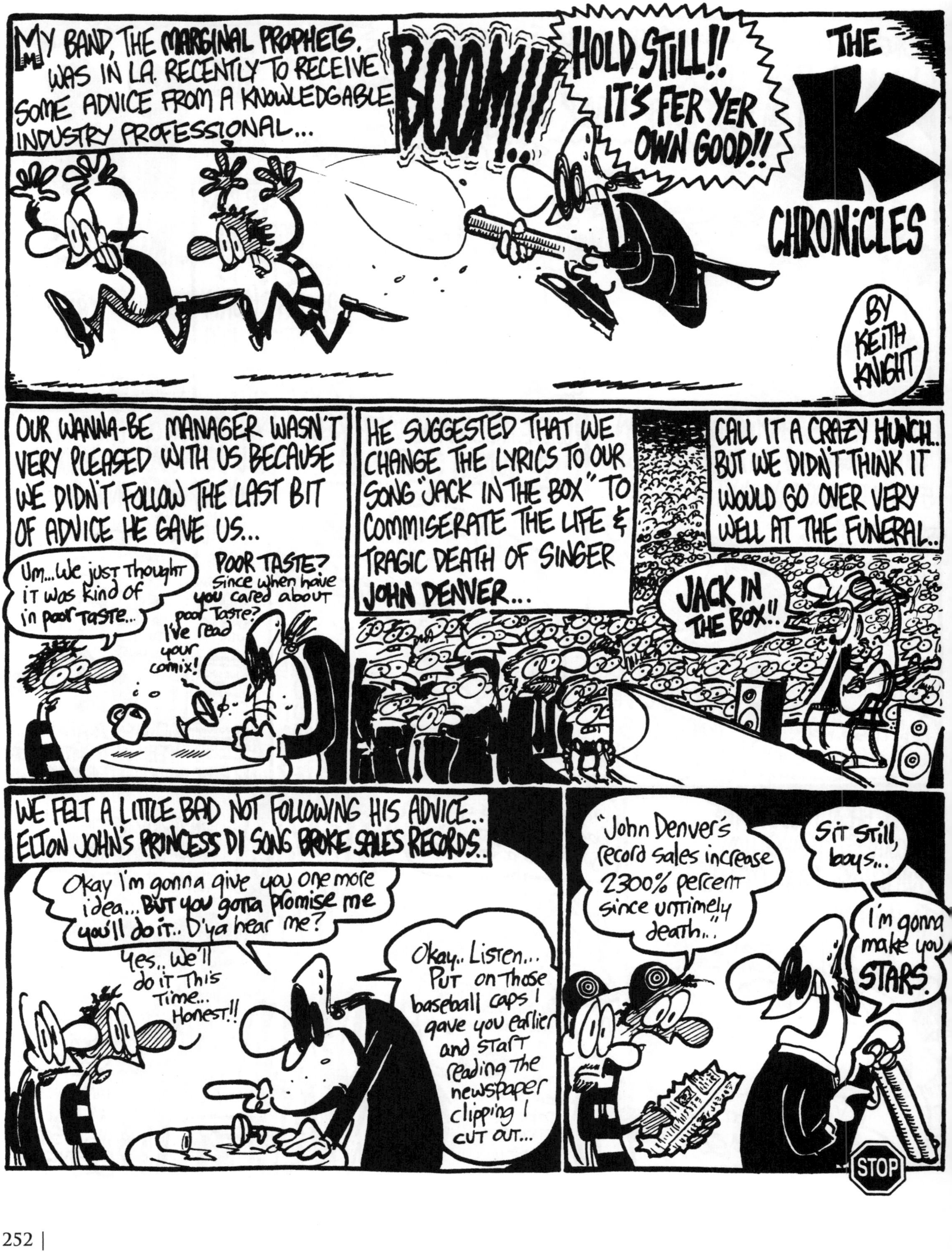

THE K CHRONICLES
BY KEITH KNIGHT
MY BAND, THE MARGINAL PROPHETS, WAS IN L.A. RECENTLY TO RECEIVE SOME ADVICE FROM A KNOWLEDGABLE INDUSTRY PROFESSIONAL...
BOOM!!
HOLD STILL!! IT'S FER YER OWN GOOD!!
OUR WANNA-BE MANAGER WASN'T VERY PLEASED WITH US BECAUSE WE DIDN'T FOLLOW THE LAST BIT OF ADVICE HE GAVE US...
Um... We just thought it was kind of in poor TASTE...
POOR TASTE? Since when have you cared about poor Taste? I've read your comix!
HE SUGGESTED THAT WE CHANGE THE LYRICS TO OUR SONG "JACK IN THE BOX" TO COMMISERATE THE LIFE & TRAGIC DEATH OF SINGER JOHN DENVER...
CALL IT A CRAZY HUNCH... BUT WE DIDN'T THINK IT WOULD GO OVER VERY WELL AT THE FUNERAL..
JACK IN THE BOX!!
WE FELT A LITTLE BAD NOT FOLLOWING HIS ADVICE.. ELTON JOHN'S PRINCESS DI SONG BROKE SALES RECORDS..
Okay I'm gonna give you one more idea... BUT you gotta promise me you'll do it.. D'ya hear me?
Yes.. We'll do it This Time... Honest!!
Okay.. Listen... Put on those baseball caps I gave you earlier and start reading the newspaper clipping I cut out...
"John Denver's record sales increase 2300% percent since untimely death.."
Sit still, boys...
I'm gonna make you STARS.
STOP

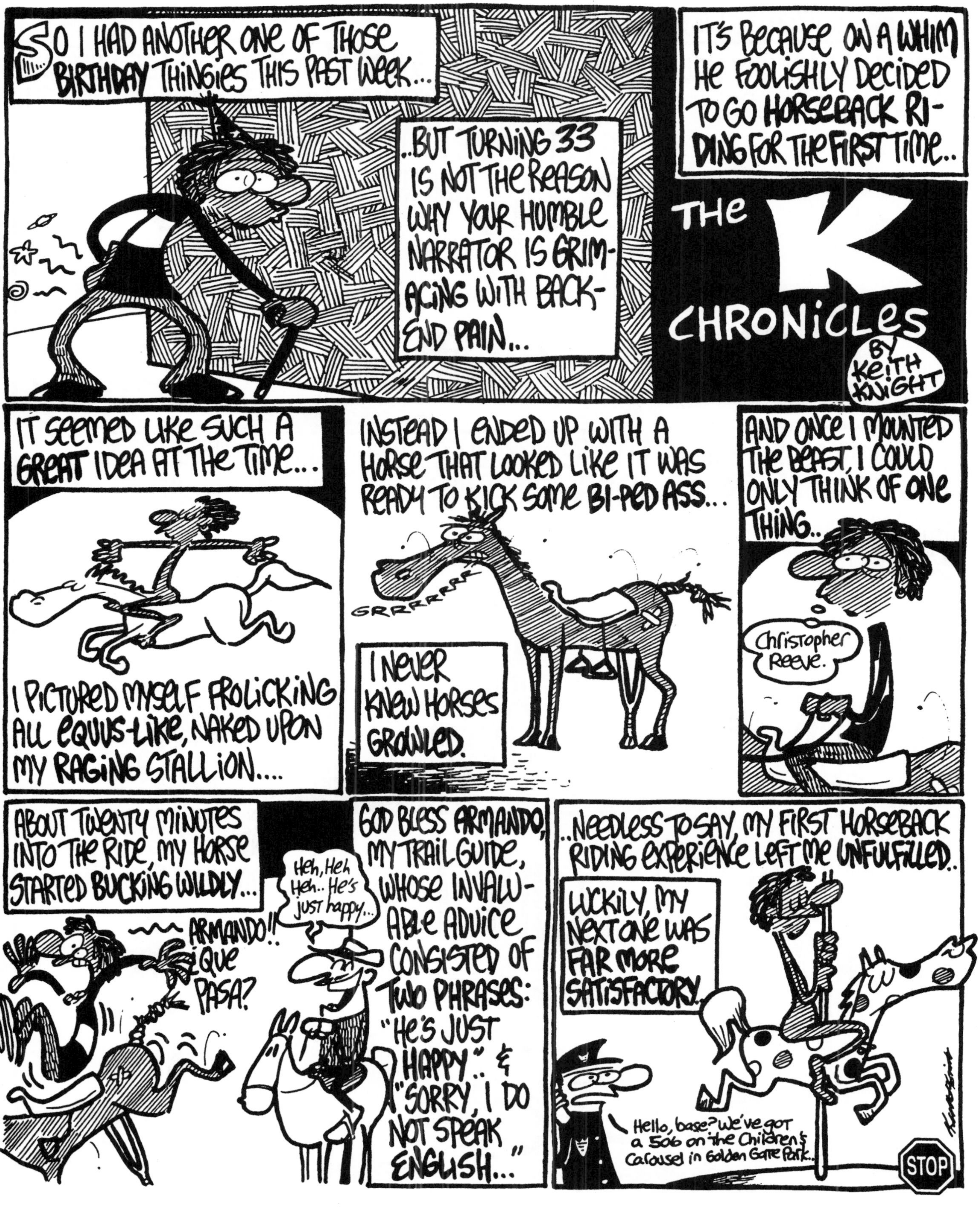

SO I HAD ANOTHER ONE OF THOSE BIRTHDAY THINGIES THIS PAST WEEK...
..BUT TURNING 33 IS NOT THE REASON WHY YOUR HUMBLE NARRATOR IS GRIMACING WITH BACK-END PAIN...
IT'S BECAUSE ON A WHIM HE FOOLISHLY DECIDED TO GO HORSEBACK RIDING FOR THE FIRST TIME...
THE K CHRONICLES
BY KEITH KNIGHT
IT SEEMED LIKE SUCH A GREAT IDEA AT THE TIME...
I PICTURED MYSELF FROLICKING ALL EQUUS-LIKE, NAKED UPON MY RAGING STALLION....
INSTEAD I ENDED UP WITH A HORSE THAT LOOKED LIKE IT WAS READY TO KICK SOME BI-PED ASS...
GRRRRRRR
I NEVER KNEW HORSES GROWLED.
AND ONCE I MOUNTED THE BEAST, I COULD ONLY THINK OF ONE THING..
Christopher Reeve.
ABOUT TWENTY MINUTES INTO THE RIDE, MY HORSE STARTED BUCKING WILDLY...
ARMANDO!! ¡QUE PASA?
Heh, Heh Heh.. He's just happy...
GOD BLESS ARMANDO, MY TRAIL GUIDE, WHOSE INVALUABLE ADVICE CONSISTED OF TWO PHRASES: "HE'S JUST HAPPY".. & "SORRY, I DO NOT SPEAK ENGLISH..."
..NEEDLESS TO SAY, MY FIRST HORSEBACK RIDING EXPERIENCE LEFT ME UNFULFILLED..
LUCKILY, MY NEXT ONE WAS FAR MORE SATISFACTORY.
Hello, base? We've got a 506 on the Children's Carousel in Golden Gate Park..
STOP

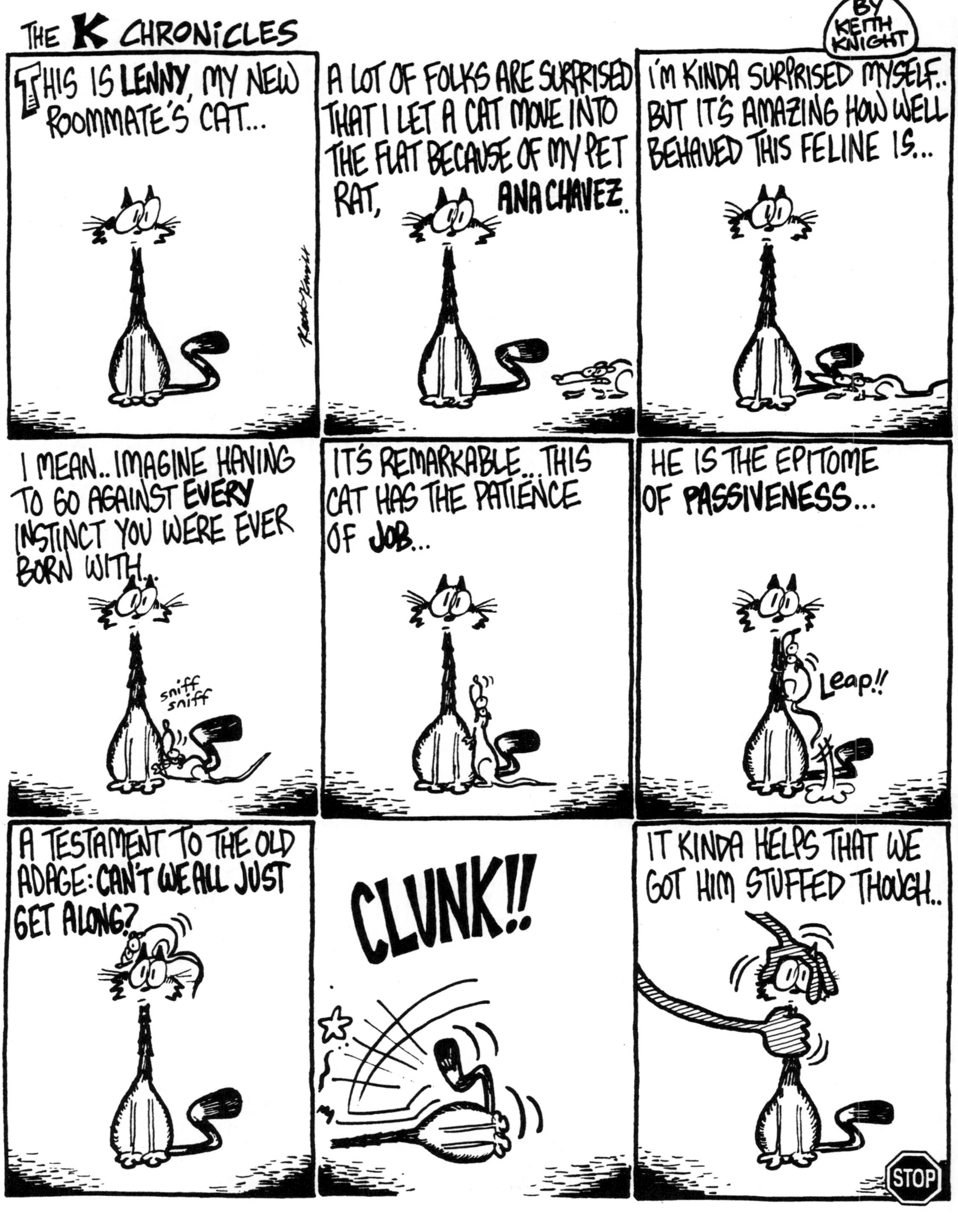
THE K CHRONICLES
BY KEITH KNIGHT
THIS IS LENNY, MY NEW ROOMMATE'S CAT...
A LOT OF FOLKS ARE SURPRISED THAT I LET A CAT MOVE INTO THE FLAT BECAUSE OF MY PET RAT, ANA CHAVEZ..
I'M KINDA SURPRISED MYSELF.. BUT IT'S AMAZING HOW WELL BEHAVED THIS FELINE IS...
I MEAN.. IMAGINE HAVING TO GO AGAINST EVERY INSTINCT YOU WERE EVER BORN WITH..
sniff sniff
IT'S REMARKABLE... THIS CAT HAS THE PATIENCE OF JOB...
HE IS THE EPITOME OF PASSIVENESS...
Leap!!
A TESTAMENT TO THE OLD ADAGE: CAN'T WE ALL JUST GET ALONG?
CLUNK!!
IT KINDA HELPS THAT WE GOT HIM STUFFED THOUGH..
STOP

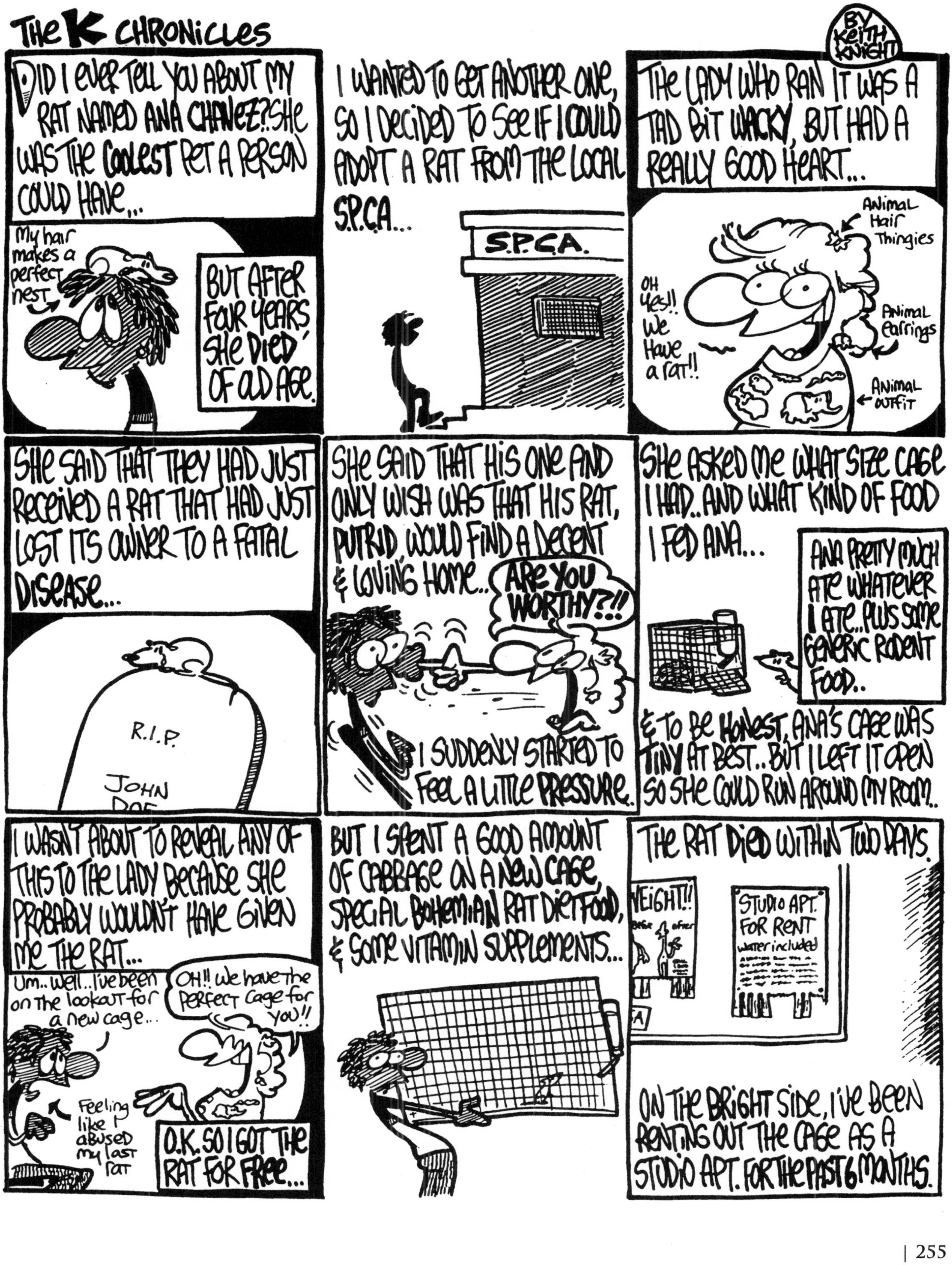
THE K CHRONICLES
BY KEITH KNIGHT
DID I EVER TELL YOU ABOUT MY RAT NAMED ANA CHAVEZ?! SHE WAS THE COOLEST PET A PERSON COULD HAVE...
My hair makes a perfect nest
BUT AFTER FOUR YEARS, SHE DIED OF OLD AGE.
I WANTED TO GET ANOTHER ONE, SO I DECIDED TO SEE IF I COULD ADOPT A RAT FROM THE LOCAL S.P.C.A...
S.P.C.A.
THE LADY WHO RAN IT WAS A TAD BIT WACKY, BUT HAD A REALLY GOOD HEART...
Animal Hair Thingies
OH Yes!! We Have a rat!!
Animal earrings
Animal outfit
SHE SAID THAT THEY HAD JUST RECEIVED A RAT THAT HAD JUST LOST ITS OWNER TO A FATAL DISEASE...
R.I.P.
JOHN DOE
SHE SAID THAT HIS ONE AND ONLY WISH WAS THAT HIS RAT, PUTRID, WOULD FIND A DECENT & LOVING HOME...
ARE YOU WORTHY?!!
I SUDDENLY STARTED TO FEEL A LITTLE PRESSURE.
SHE ASKED ME WHAT SIZE CAGE I HAD.. AND WHAT KIND OF FOOD I FED ANA...
ANA PRETTY MUCH ATE WHATEVER I ATE.. PLUS SOME GENERIC RODENT FOOD..
& TO BE HONEST, ANA'S CAGE WAS TINY AT BEST.. BUT I LEFT IT OPEN SO SHE COULD RUN AROUND MY ROOM..
I WASN'T ABOUT TO REVEAL ANY OF THIS TO THE LADY BECAUSE SHE PROBABLY WOULDN'T HAVE GIVEN ME THE RAT...
Um.. well.. I've been on the lookout for a new cage...
OH!! We have the perfect cage for you!!
Feeling like I abused my last rat
O.K. SO I GOT THE RAT FOR FREE...
BUT I SPENT A GOOD AMOUNT OF CABBAGE ON A NEW CAGE, SPECIAL BOHEMIAN RAT DIET FOOD, & SOME VITAMIN SUPPLEMENTS...
THE RAT DIED WITHIN TWO DAYS.
WEIGHT!!
Before after
STUDIO APT. FOR RENT
water included
ON THE BRIGHT SIDE, I'VE BEEN RENTING OUT THE CAGE AS A STUDIO APT. FOR THE PAST 6 MONTHS.

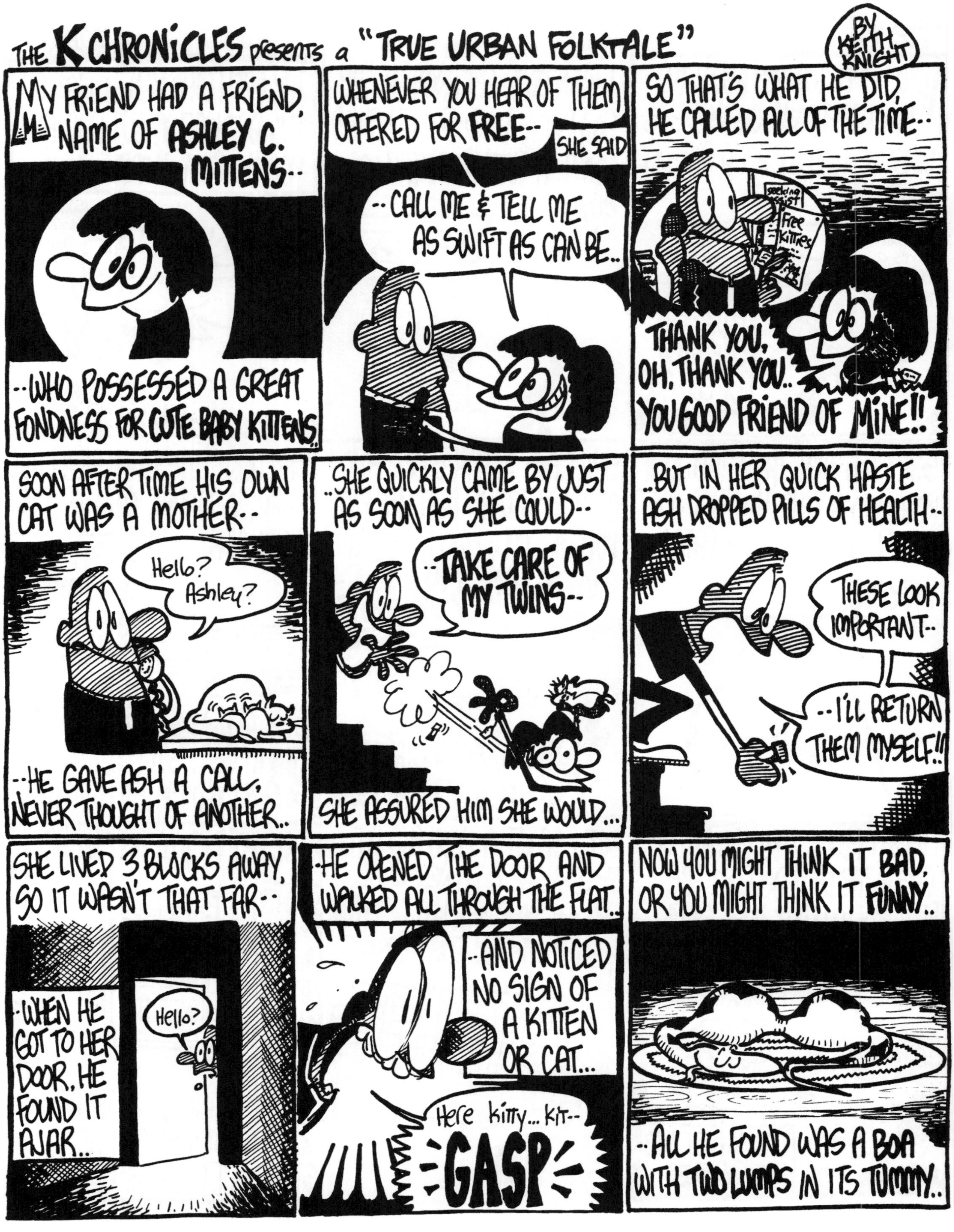
THE K CHRONICLES presents a "TRUE URBAN FOLKTALE"
BY KEITH KNIGHT
MY FRIEND HAD A FRIEND, NAME OF ASHLEY C. MITTENS..
..WHO POSSESSED A GREAT FONDNESS FOR CUTE BABY KITTENS..
WHENEVER YOU HEAR OF THEM OFFERED FOR FREE--
SHE SAID
--CALL ME & TELL ME AS SWIFT AS CAN BE..
SO THAT'S WHAT HE DID, HE CALLED ALL OF THE TIME--
Free Kitties
THANK YOU, OH, THANK YOU.. YOU GOOD FRIEND OF MINE!!
SOON AFTER TIME HIS OWN CAT WAS A MOTHER--
Hello? Ashley?
--HE GAVE ASH A CALL, NEVER THOUGHT OF ANOTHER..
..SHE QUICKLY CAME BY JUST AS SOON AS SHE COULD--
--TAKE CARE OF MY TWINS--
SHE ASSURED HIM SHE WOULD...
..BUT IN HER QUICK HASTE ASH DROPPED PILLS OF HEALTH--
THESE LOOK IMPORTANT--
--I'LL RETURN THEM MYSELF!!
SHE LIVED 3 BLOCKS AWAY, SO IT WASN'T THAT FAR--
-WHEN HE GOT TO HER DOOR, HE FOUND IT AJAR..
Hello?
-HE OPENED THE DOOR AND WALKED ALL THROUGH THE FLAT..
--AND NOTICED NO SIGN OF A KITTEN OR CAT...
Here kitty... kit--
GASP
NOW YOU MIGHT THINK IT BAD, OR YOU MIGHT THINK IT FUNNY..
--ALL HE FOUND WAS A BOA WITH TWO LUMPS IN ITS TUMMY..

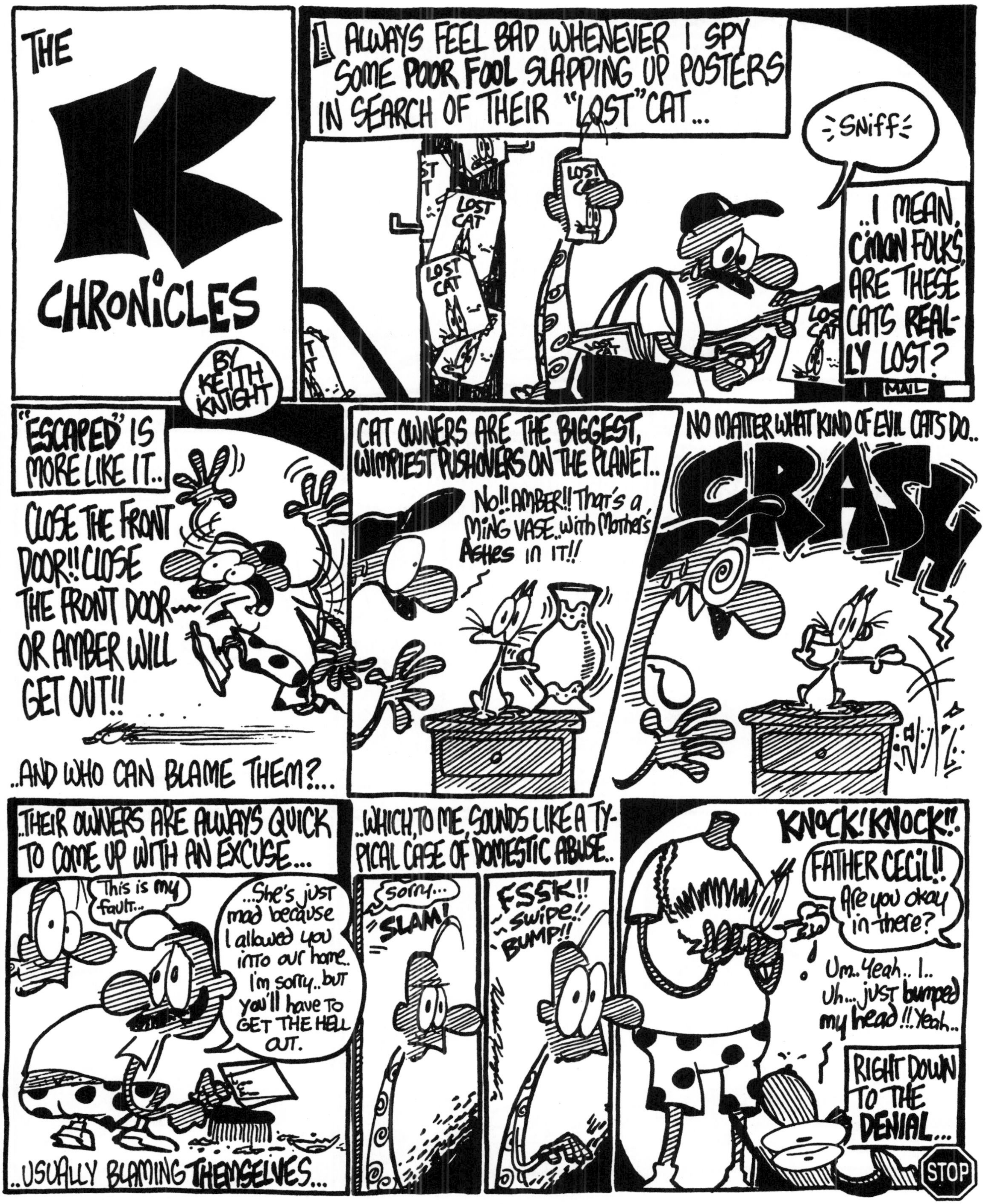
THE K CHRONICLES
BY KEITH KNIGHT
I ALWAYS FEEL BAD WHENEVER I SPY SOME POOR FOOL SLAPPING UP POSTERS IN SEARCH OF THEIR "LOST" CAT...
LOST CAT
SNIFF
..I MEAN, C'MON FOLKS, ARE THESE CATS REALLY LOST?
MAIL
"ESCAPED" IS MORE LIKE IT..
CLOSE THE FRONT DOOR!! CLOSE THE FRONT DOOR-- OR AMBER WILL GET OUT!!
..AND WHO CAN BLAME THEM?...
CAT OWNERS ARE THE BIGGEST, WIMPIEST PUSHOVERS ON THE PLANET..
No!! AMBER!! That's a MING VASE.. with Mother's Ashes in it!!
NO MATTER WHAT KIND OF EVIL CATS DO..
CRASH
..THEIR OWNERS ARE ALWAYS QUICK TO COME UP WITH AN EXCUSE...
This is my fault...
...She's just mad because I allowed you into our home.. I'm sorry.. but you'll have to GET THE HELL OUT.
..USUALLY BLAMING THEMSELVES...
..WHICH, TO ME, SOUNDS LIKE A TYPICAL CASE OF DOMESTIC ABUSE..
sorry...
SLAM!
FSSK!!
SWIPE!!
BUMP!!
KNOCK! KNOCK!!
FATHER CECIL!! Are you okay in there?
Um.. Yeah.. I.. Uh... just bumped my head!!! Yeah...
RIGHT DOWN TO THE DENIAL...
STOP

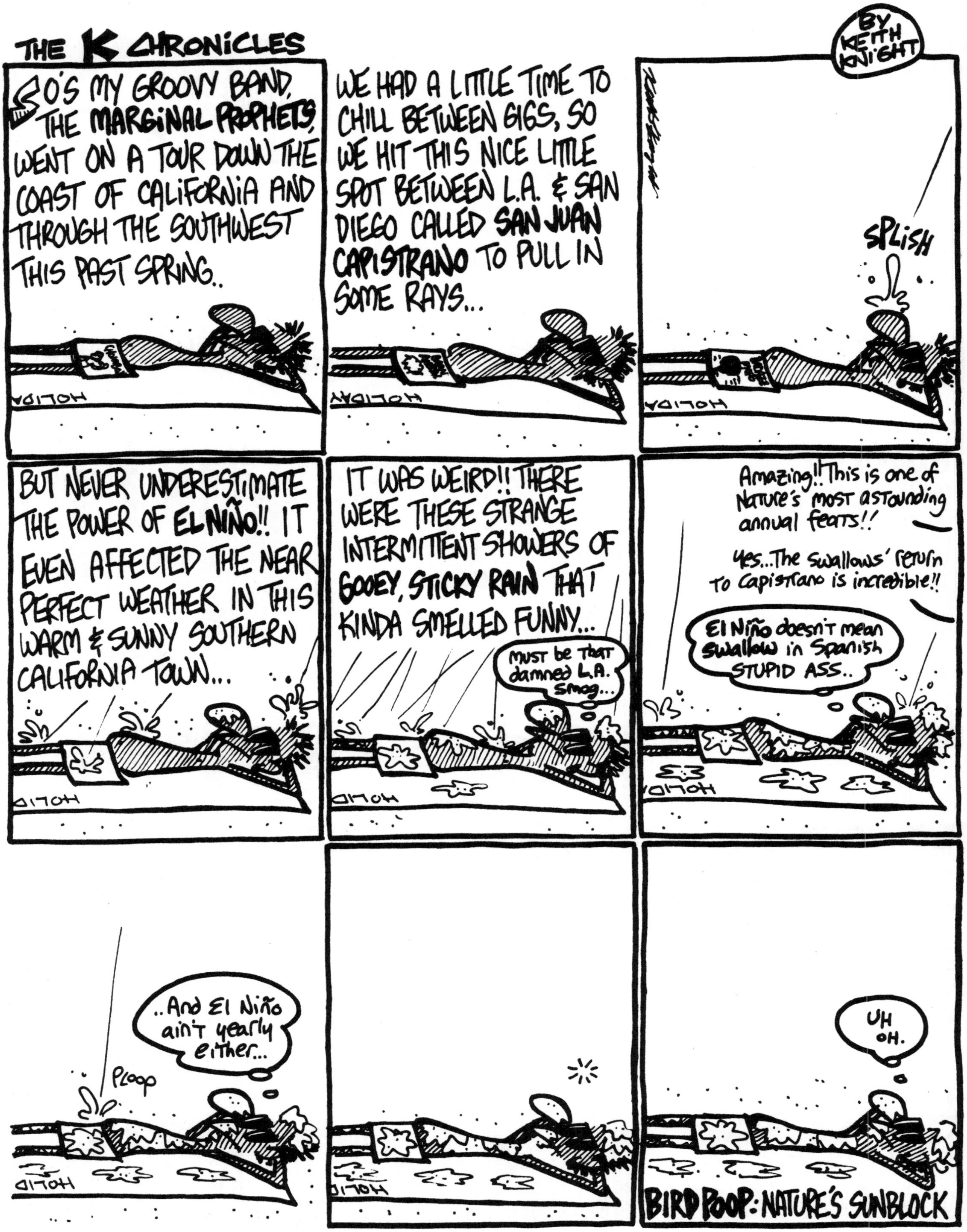
THE K CHRONICLES
BY KEITH KNIGHT
SO'S MY GROOVY BAND, THE MARGINAL PROPHETS, WENT ON A TOUR DOWN THE COAST OF CALIFORNIA AND THROUGH THE SOUTHWEST THIS PAST SPRING..
WE HAD A LITTLE TIME TO CHILL BETWEEN GIGS, SO WE HIT THIS NICE LITTLE SPOT BETWEEN L.A. & SAN DIEGO CALLED SAN JUAN CAPISTRANO TO PULL IN SOME RAYS...
SPLISH
BUT NEVER UNDERESTIMATE THE POWER OF EL NIÑO!! IT EVEN AFFECTED THE NEAR PERFECT WEATHER IN THIS WARM & SUNNY SOUTHERN CALIFORNIA TOWN...
IT WAS WEIRD!! THERE WERE THESE STRANGE INTERMITTENT SHOWERS OF GOOEY, STICKY RAIN THAT KINDA SMELLED FUNNY...
Must be that damned L.A. Smog...
Amazing!! This is one of Nature's most astounding annual feats!!
Yes...The swallows' return to Capistrano is incredible!!
El Niño doesn't mean swallow in Spanish STUPID ASS..
..And El Niño ain't yearly either...
PLOOP
UH OH.
BIRD POOP: NATURE'S SUNBLOCK

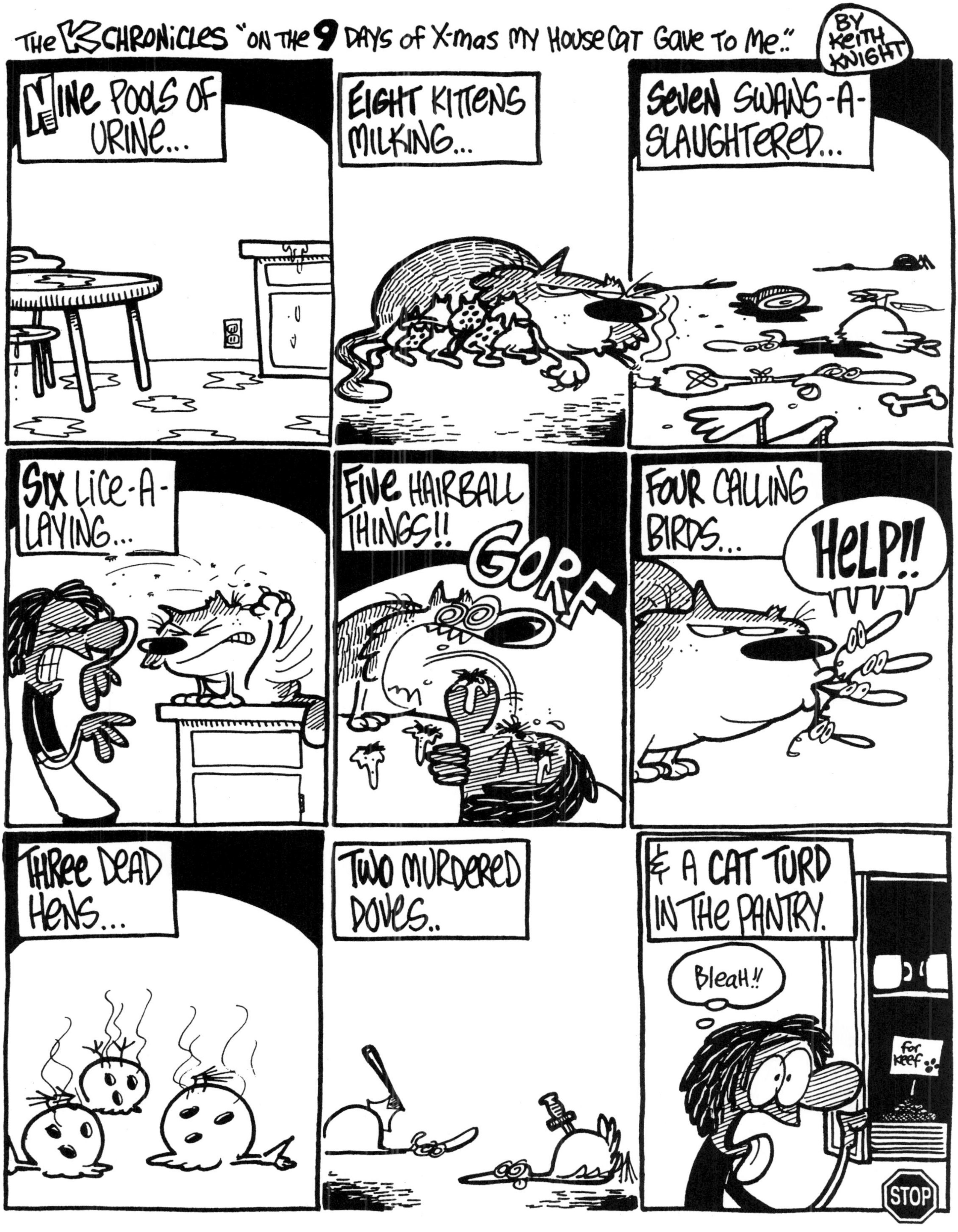
The K Chronicles "On the 9 Days of X-mas My House Cat Gave to Me.."
By Keith Knight
Nine pools of urine...
Eight kittens milking...
Seven swans-a-slaughtered...
Six lice-a-laying...
Five hairball things!!
GORF
Four calling birds...
HELP!!
Three dead hens...
Two murdered doves..
& a cat turd in the pantry.
Bleah!!
for keef
STOP

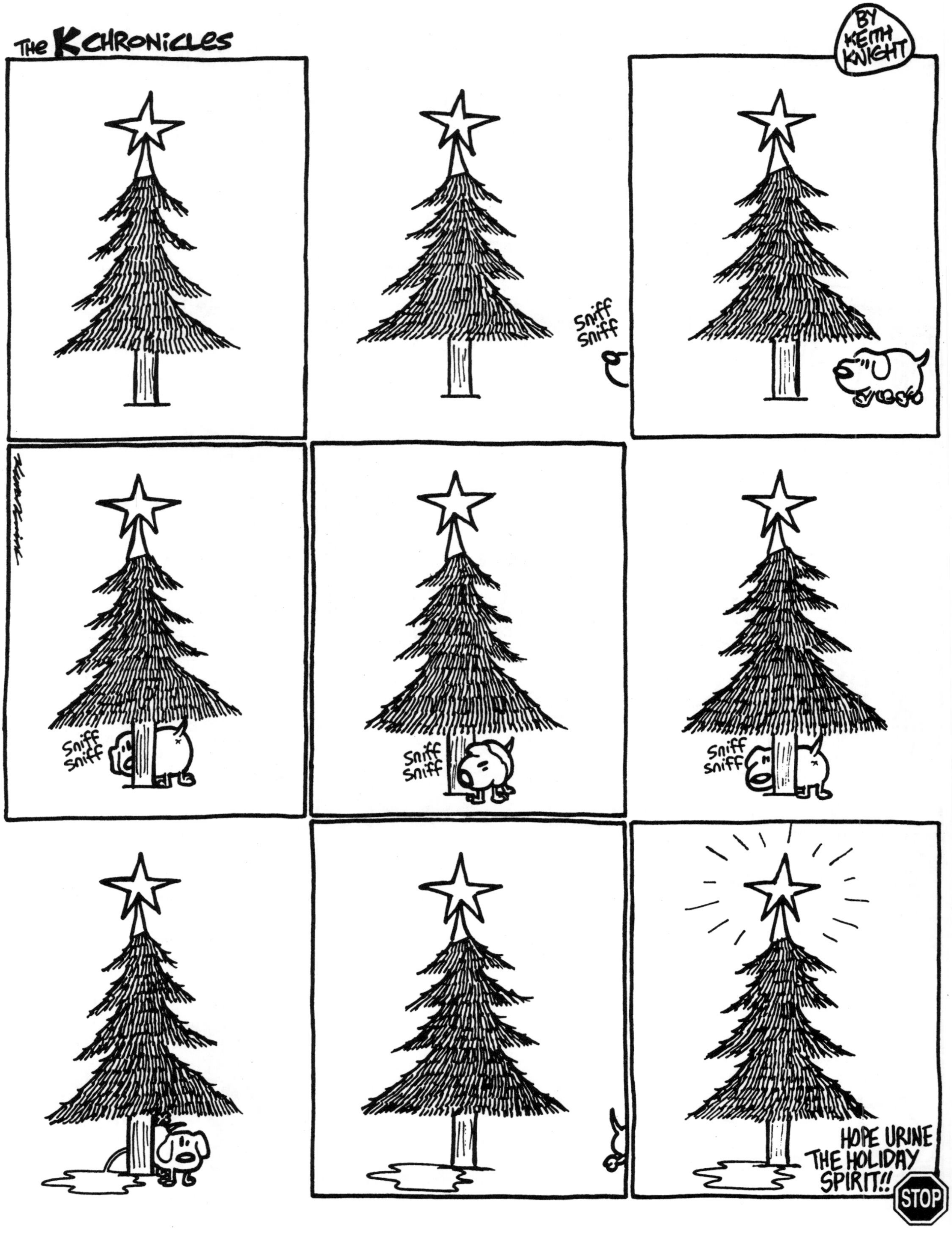
THE K CHRONICLES
BY KEITH KNIGHT
SNIFF SNIFF
SNIFF SNIFF
SNIFF SNIFF
SNIFF SNIFF
HOPE URINE THE HOLIDAY SPIRIT!!
STOP

 I "caught" someone making this strip into an Xmas party invite at my local copy store. They invited me to the party.

CHAPTER THREE

WHAT A LONG STRANGE STRIP IT'S BEEN

Cartoons from 1999-2002   San Francisco / New Orleans / Paris / New York

41 Shots   Sept. 11. 2001

Suicide   Little Victories

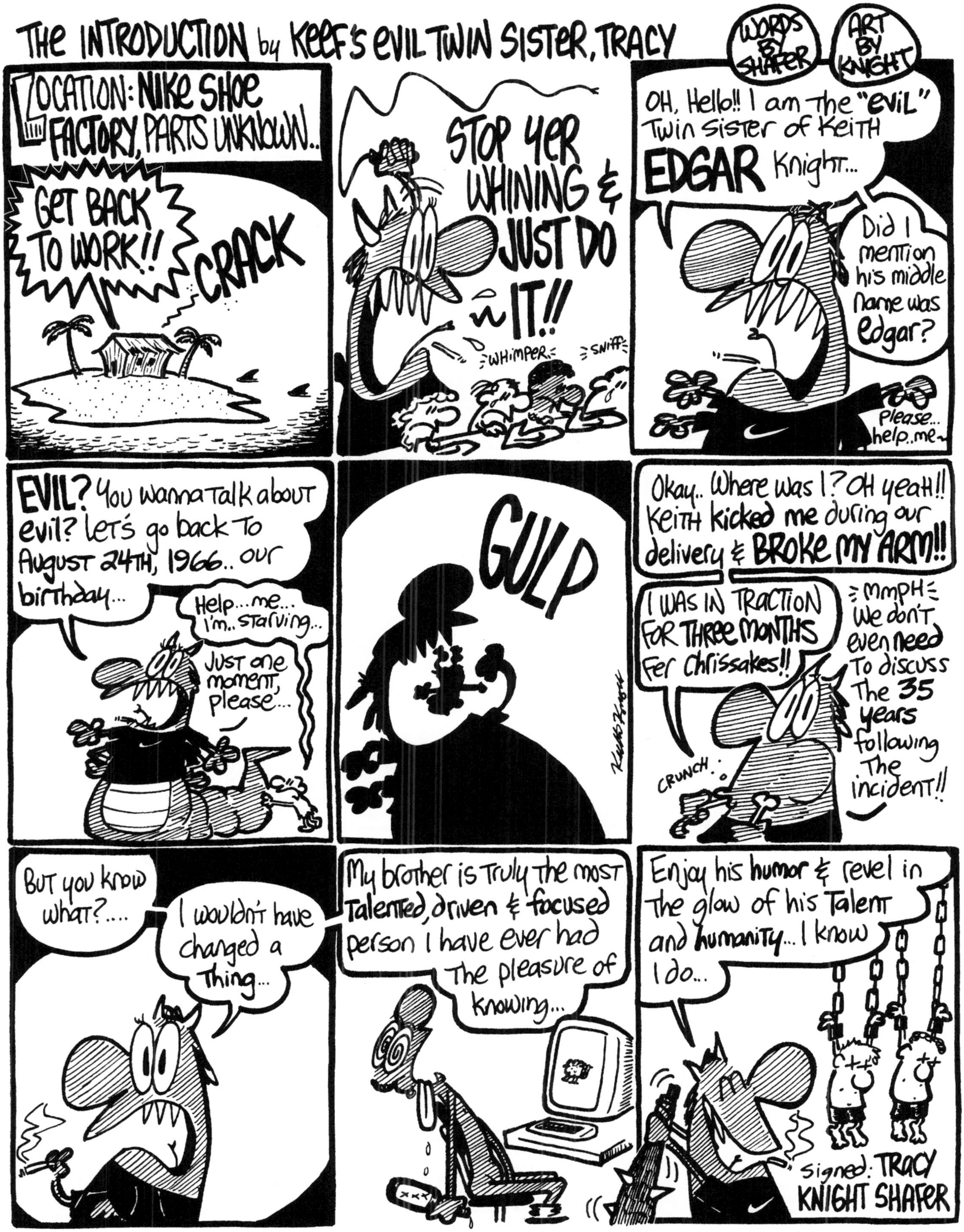
THE INTRODUCTION by KEEF'S EVIL TWIN SISTER, TRACY
WORDS BY SHAFER
ART BY KNIGHT
LOCATION: NIKE SHOE FACTORY, PARTS UNKNOWN..
GET BACK TO WORK!!
CRACK
STOP YER WHINING & JUST DO IT!!
WHIMPER
SNIFF
OH, Hello!! I am The "EVIL" Twin Sister of KEITH EDGAR Knight...
Did I mention his middle name was edgar?
please... help..me..
EVIL? You wanna Talk about evil? Let's go back To August 24TH, 1966.. our birthday...
Help...me... I'm.. starving...
JUST one moment, please...
GULP
Okay.. Where was I? OH yeah!! Keith kicked me during our delivery & BROKE MY ARM!!
I WAS IN TRACTION FOR THREE MONTHS Fer Chrissakes!!
MMPH We don'T even need To discuss The 35 years following The incident!!
CRUNCH
BUT you know what?....
I wouldn't have changed a Thing...
My brother is Truly The most Talented, driven & focused person I have ever had The pleasure of knowing...
Enjoy his humor & revel in The glow of his Talent and humanity... I know I do...
Signed: TRACY KNIGHT SHAFER

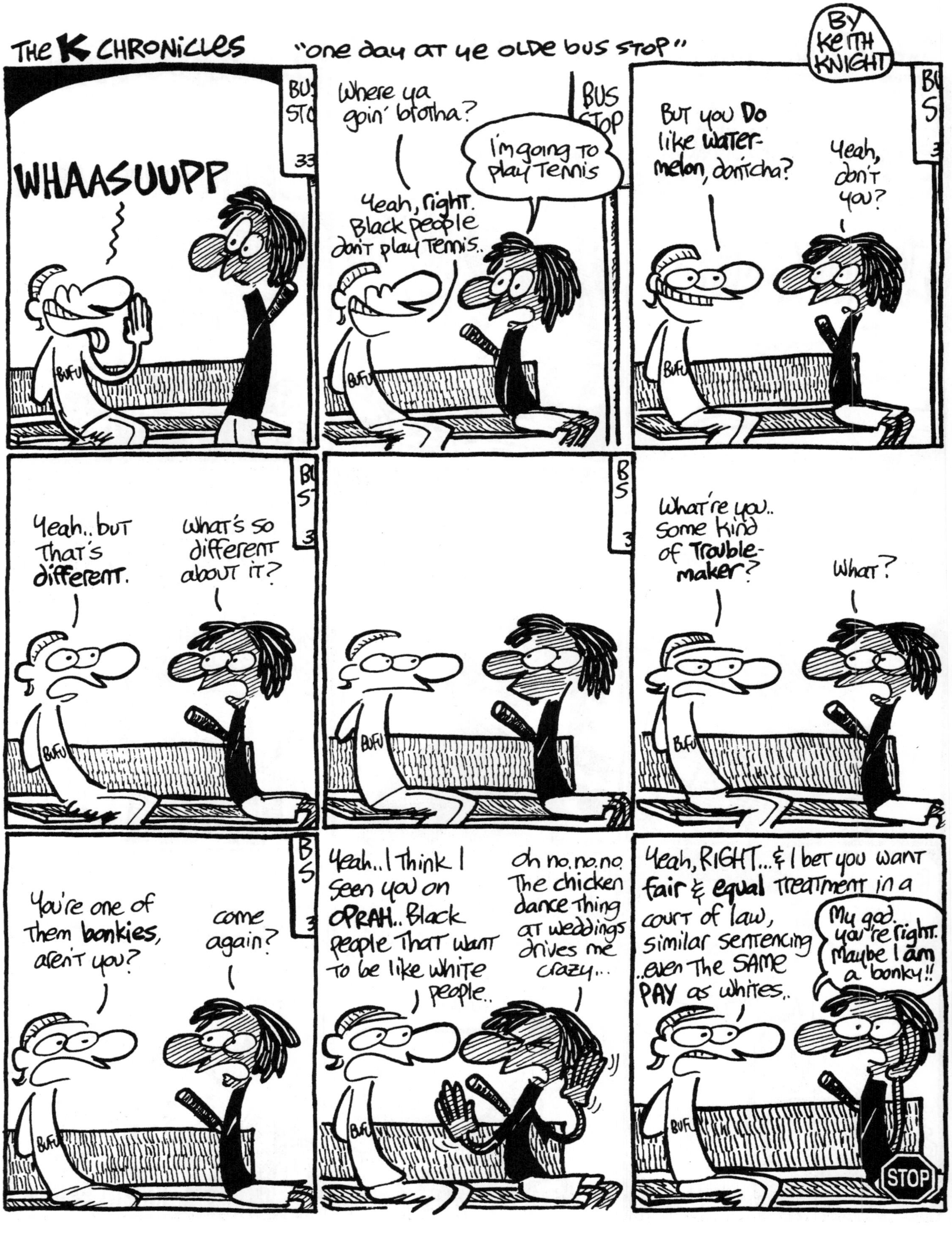
THE K CHRONICLES
"one day at ye olde bus stop"
BY KEITH KNIGHT
WHAASUUPP
Where ya goin' brotha?
I'm going to play Tennis
Yeah, right. Black people don't play Tennis..
But you Do like water-melon, dontcha?
Yeah, don't you?
Yeah.. but that's different.
What's so different about it?
What're you.. Some kind of Trouble-maker?
What?
You're one of them bonkies, aren't you?
come again?
Yeah.. I think I seen you on OPRAH.. Black people that want to be like white people..
oh no.no.no. The chicken dance thing at weddings drives me crazy...
Yeah, RIGHT... & I bet you want fair & equal treatment in a court of law, similar sentencing ..even the SAME PAY as whites..
My god. you're right. Maybe I am a bonky!!
STOP

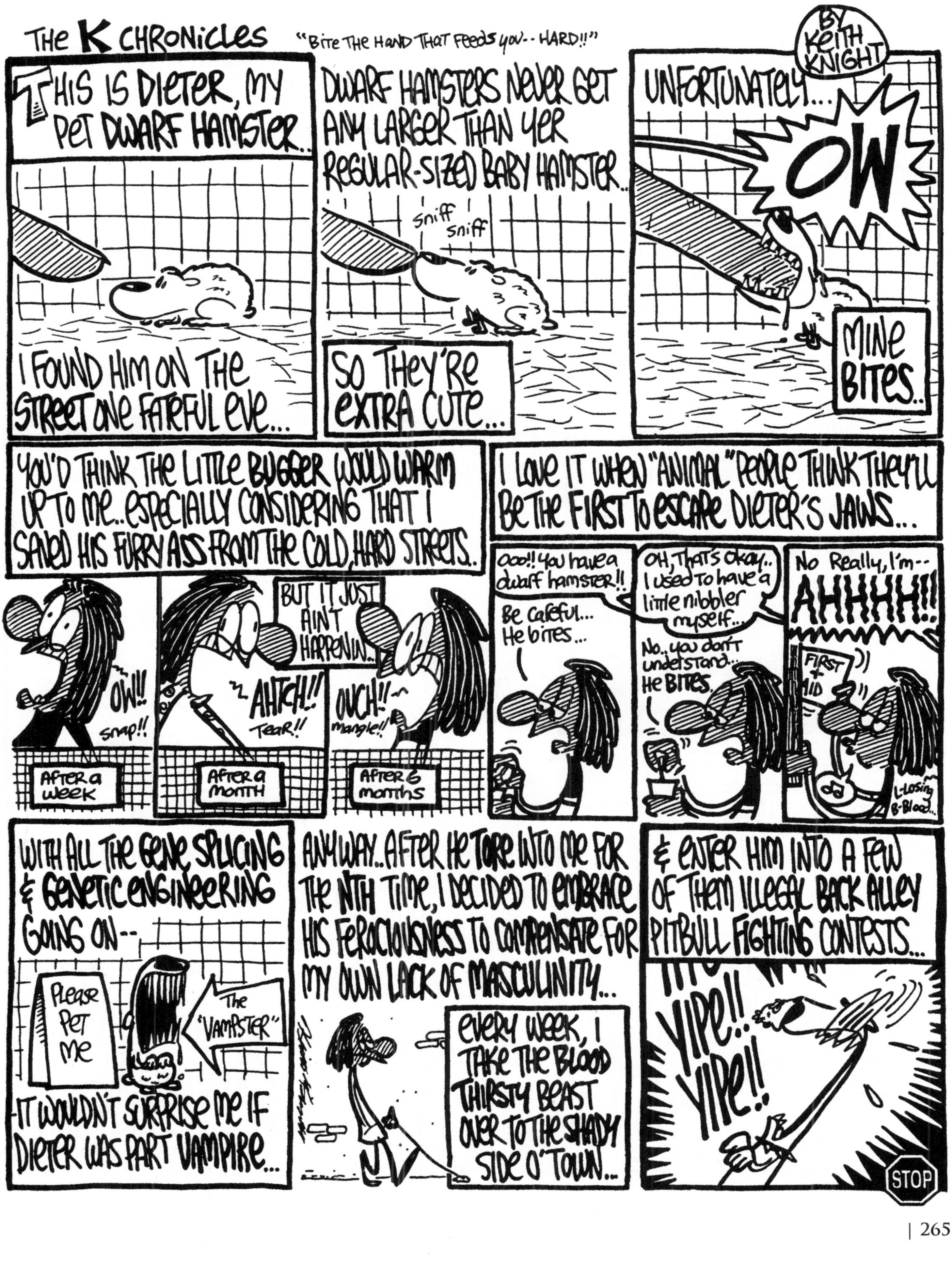

THE K CHRONICLES
"Bite The Hand That Feeds you-- HARD!!"
BY KEITH KNIGHT
THIS IS DIETER, MY PET DWARF HAMSTER..
I FOUND HIM ON THE STREET ONE FATEFUL EVE...
DWARF HAMSTERS NEVER GET ANY LARGER THAN YER REGULAR-SIZED BABY HAMSTER..
sniff sniff
SO THEY'RE EXTRA CUTE...
UNFORTUNATELY...
OW
MINE BITES..
YOU'D THINK THE LITTLE BUGGER WOULD WARM UP TO ME..ESPECIALLY CONSIDERING THAT I SAVED HIS FURRY ASS FROM THE COLD, HARD STREETS..
OW!! snap!!
After a week
AHTCH!! Tear!!
After a month
BUT IT JUST AIN'T HAPPENIN..
OUCH!! mangle!!
After 6 months
I LOVE IT WHEN "ANIMAL" PEOPLE THINK THEY'LL BE THE FIRST TO ESCAPE DIETER'S JAWS...
Ooo!! You have a dwarf hamster!!
Be careful... He bites...
OH, THAT'S okay.. I used to have a little nibbler myself..
No.. you don't understand... He BITES.
No Really, I'm-- AHHHH!!
FIRST AID
L-Losing B-Blood..
WITH ALL THE GENE SPLICING & GENETIC ENGINEERING GOING ON--
Please Pet me
The "VAMPSTER"
IT WOULDN'T SURPRISE ME IF DIETER WAS PART VAMPIRE...
ANYWAY.. AFTER HE TORE INTO ME FOR THE NTH TIME, I DECIDED TO EMBRACE HIS FEROCIOUSNESS TO COMPENSATE FOR MY OWN LACK OF MASCULINITY...
EVERY WEEK, I TAKE THE BLOOD THIRSTY BEAST OVER TO THE SHADY SIDE O' TOWN...
& ENTER HIM INTO A FEW OF THEM ILLEGAL BACK ALLEY PITBULL FIGHTING CONTESTS...
YIPE!! YIPE!!
STOP

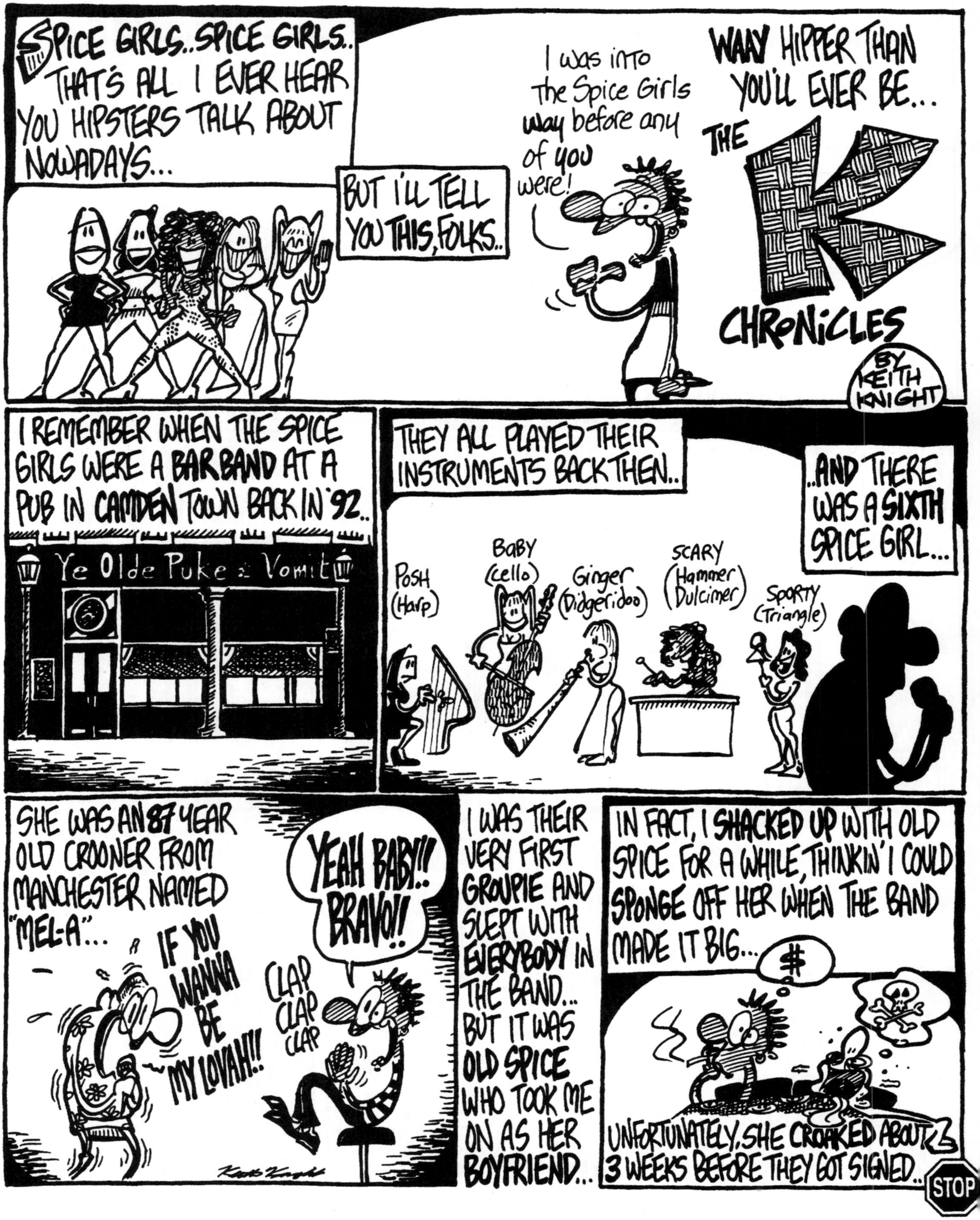
SPICE GIRLS.. SPICE GIRLS.. THAT'S ALL I EVER HEAR YOU HIPSTERS TALK ABOUT NOWADAYS...
BUT I'LL TELL YOU THIS, FOLKS..
I was into the Spice Girls way before any of you were!
WAAY HIPPER THAN YOU'LL EVER BE... THE K CHRONICLES
BY KEITH KNIGHT
I REMEMBER WHEN THE SPICE GIRLS WERE A BAR BAND AT A PUB IN CAMDEN TOWN BACK IN '92..
Ye Olde Puke & Vomit
THEY ALL PLAYED THEIR INSTRUMENTS BACK THEN..
..AND THERE WAS A SIXTH SPICE GIRL...
POSH (Harp)
BABY (cello)
Ginger (Didgeridoo)
SCARY (Hammer Dulcimer)
SPORTY (Triangle)
SHE WAS AN 87 YEAR OLD CROONER FROM MANCHESTER NAMED "MEL-A"...
IF YOU WANNA BE MY LOVAH!!
YEAH BABY!!.. BRAVO!!
CLAP CLAP CLAP
I WAS THEIR VERY FIRST GROUPIE AND SLEPT WITH EVERYBODY IN THE BAND... BUT IT WAS OLD SPICE WHO TOOK ME ON AS HER BOYFRIEND...
IN FACT, I SHACKED UP WITH OLD SPICE FOR A WHILE, THINKIN' I COULD SPONGE OFF HER WHEN THE BAND MADE IT BIG...
$
UNFORTUNATELY, SHE CROAKED ABOUT 3 WEEKS BEFORE THEY GOT SIGNED...
STOP

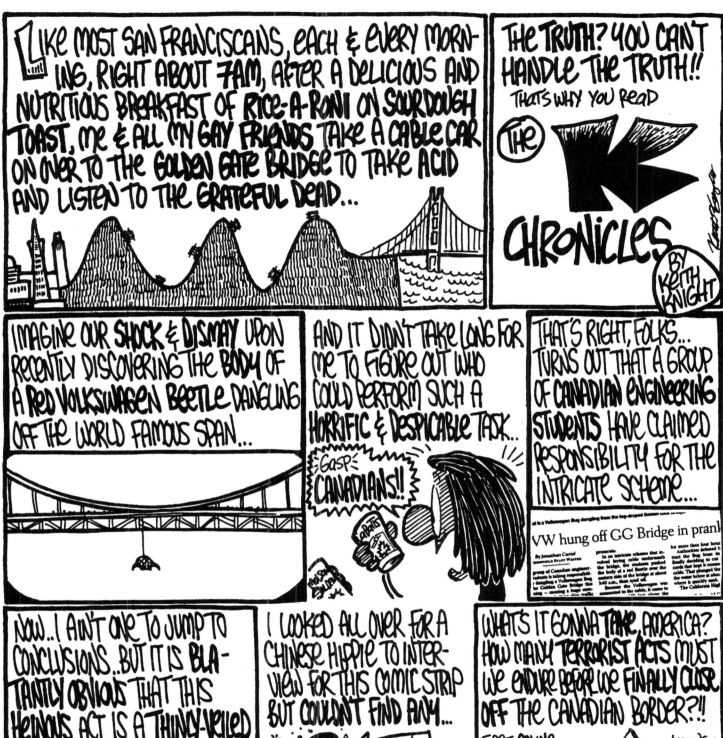

LIKE MOST SAN FRANCISCANS, EACH & EVERY MORNING, RIGHT ABOUT 7AM, AFTER A DELICIOUS AND NUTRITIOUS BREAKFAST OF RICE-A-RONI ON SOURDOUGH TOAST, ME & ALL MY GAY FRIENDS TAKE A CABLE CAR ON OVER TO THE GOLDEN GATE BRIDGE TO TAKE ACID AND LISTEN TO THE GRATEFUL DEAD...

THE TRUTH? YOU CAN'T HANDLE THE TRUTH!! THAT'S WHY YOU READ THE CHRONICLES BY KEITH KNIGHT

IMAGINE OUR SHOCK & DISMAY UPON RECENTLY DISCOVERING THE BODY OF A RED VOLKSWAGEN BEETLE DANGLING OFF THE WORLD FAMOUS SPAN...

AND IT DIDN'T TAKE LONG FOR ME TO FIGURE OUT WHO COULD PERFORM SUCH A HORRIFIC & DESPICABLE TASK...

GASP CANADIANS!!

THAT'S RIGHT, FOLKS... TURNS OUT THAT A GROUP OF CANADIAN ENGINEERING STUDENTS HAVE CLAIMED RESPONSIBILITY FOR THE INTRICATE SCHEME...

VW hung off GG Bridge in prank

By Jonathan Curiel

NOW.. I AIN'T ONE TO JUMP TO CONCLUSIONS.. BUT IT IS BLATANTLY OBVIOUS THAT THIS HEINOUS ACT IS A THINLY-VEILED REFERENCE TO LYNCHING CHINESE HIPPIES!!

I LOOKED ALL OVER FOR A CHINESE HIPPIE TO INTERVIEW FOR THIS COMIC STRIP BUT COULDN'T FIND ANY...

WHA..?

ARTIST'S RENDITION OF A CHINESE HIPPIE

MAYBE THOSE BASTARD CANADIANS GOT THEM ALL ALREADY!!

WHAT'S IT GONNA TAKE, AMERICA? HOW MANY TERRORIST ACTS MUST WE ENDURE BEFORE WE FINALLY CLOSE OFF THE CANADIAN BORDER?!!

FIRST CELINE DION, NOW THIS...

EMBARGO

JUST DROP IT OVER THERE... NORTH OF THE BORDER...

I SAY WE LIFT THE EMBARGO OFF CUBA & DROP IT ON THEM DARN HEATHENS UP NORTH...

STOP

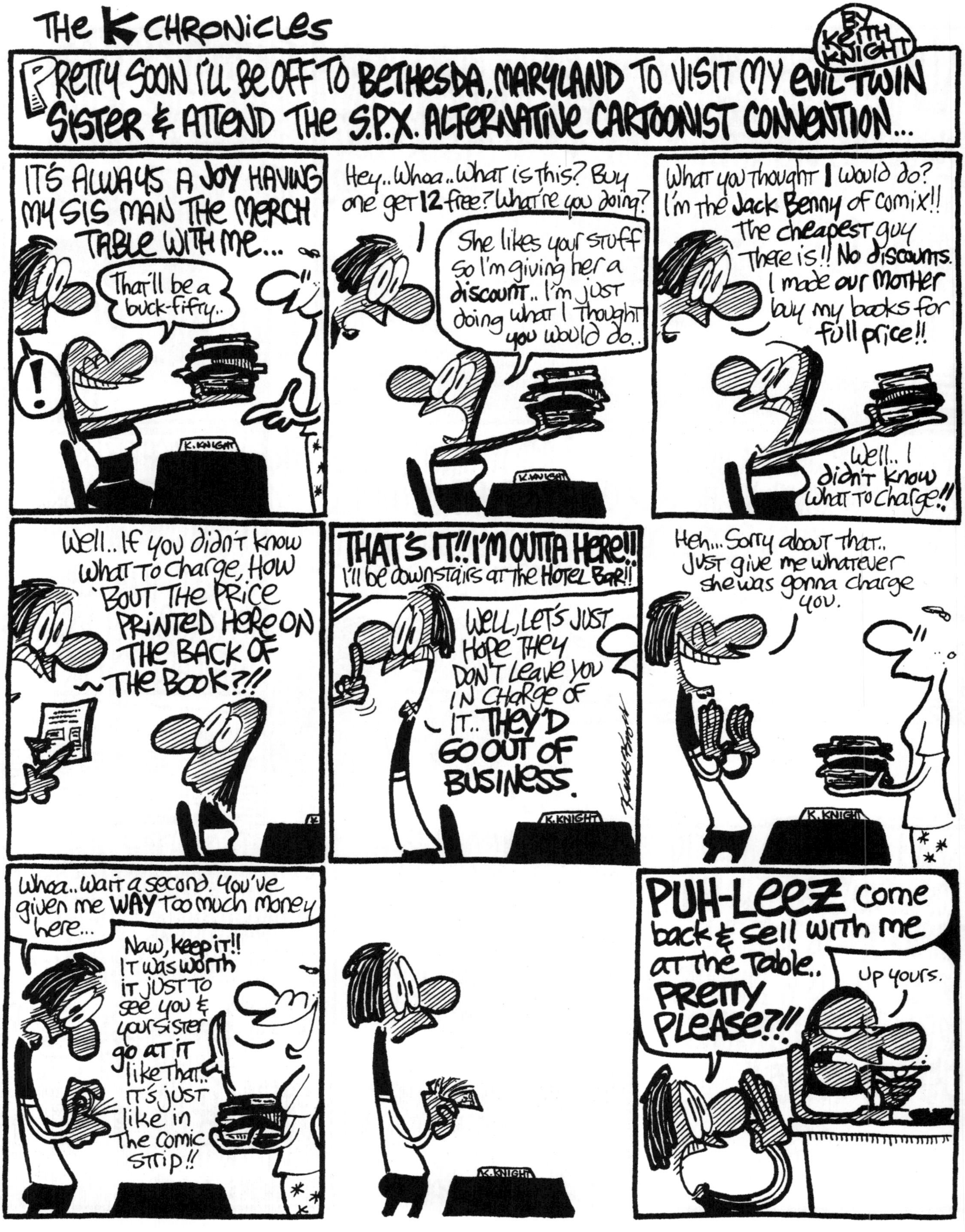
THE K CHRONICLES
BY KEITH KNIGHT
PRETTY SOON I'LL BE OFF TO BETHESDA, MARYLAND TO VISIT MY EVIL TWIN SISTER & ATTEND THE S.P.X. ALTERNATIVE CARTOONIST CONVENTION...
IT'S ALWAYS A JOY HAVING MY SIS MAN THE MERCH TABLE WITH ME...
That'll be a buck-fifty..
!
K.KNIGHT
Hey.. Whoa.. What is this? Buy one get 12 free? What're you doing?
She likes your stuff so I'm giving her a discount.. I'm just doing what I thought you would do..
What you thought I would do? I'm the Jack Benny of comix!! The cheapest guy there is!! No discounts. I made our mother buy my books for full price!!
Well.. I didn't know what to charge!!
Well.. If you didn't know what to charge, how 'bout the price printed here on the back of the book?!!
THAT'S IT!! I'M OUTTA HERE!! I'll be downstairs at the hotel bar!!
Well, let's just hope they don't leave you in charge of it.. They'd go out of business.
Heh... Sorry about that.. Just give me whatever she was gonna charge you.
Whoa.. Wait a second. You've given me WAY too much money here...
Naw, keep it!! It was worth it just to see you & your sister go at it like that!! It's just like in the comic strip!!
PUH-LEEZ come back & sell with me at the table.. PRETTY PLEASE?!!
Up yours.

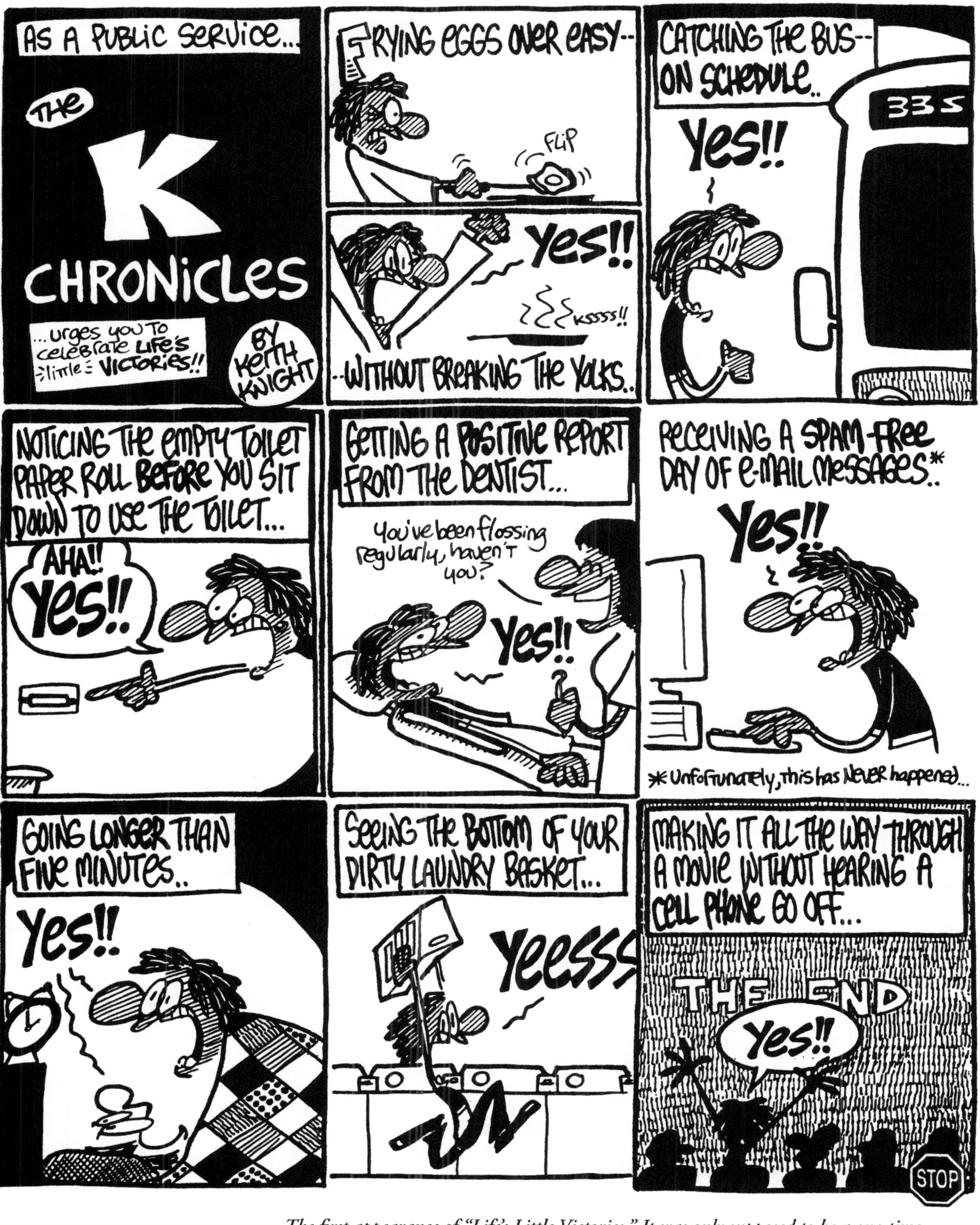
AS A PUBLIC SERVICE...
THE
K
CHRONICLES
...URGES YOU TO CELEBRATE LIFE'S LITTLE VICTORIES!!
BY KEITH KNIGHT
FRYING EGGS OVER EASY--
FLIP
YES!!
KSSSS!!
--WITHOUT BREAKING THE YOLKS..
CATCHING THE BUS-- ON SCHEDULE..
33S
YES!!
NOTICING THE EMPTY TOILET PAPER ROLL BEFORE YOU SIT DOWN TO USE THE TOILET...
AHA!! YES!!
GETTING A POSITIVE REPORT FROM THE DENTIST...
You've been flossing regularly, haven't you?
YES!!
RECEIVING A SPAM-FREE DAY OF E-MAIL MESSAGES*..
YES!!
* UNFORTUNATELY, THIS HAS NEVER HAPPENED...
GOING LONGER THAN FIVE MINUTES..
YES!!
SEEING THE BOTTOM OF YOUR DIRTY LAUNDRY BASKET...
YEESSS
MAKING IT ALL THE WAY THROUGH A MOVIE WITHOUT HEARING A CELL PHONE GO OFF...
THE END
YES!!
STOP

The first appearance of "Life's Little Victories." It was only supposed to be a one-time strip, but I got so many suggestions that it became a regular and very popular series.

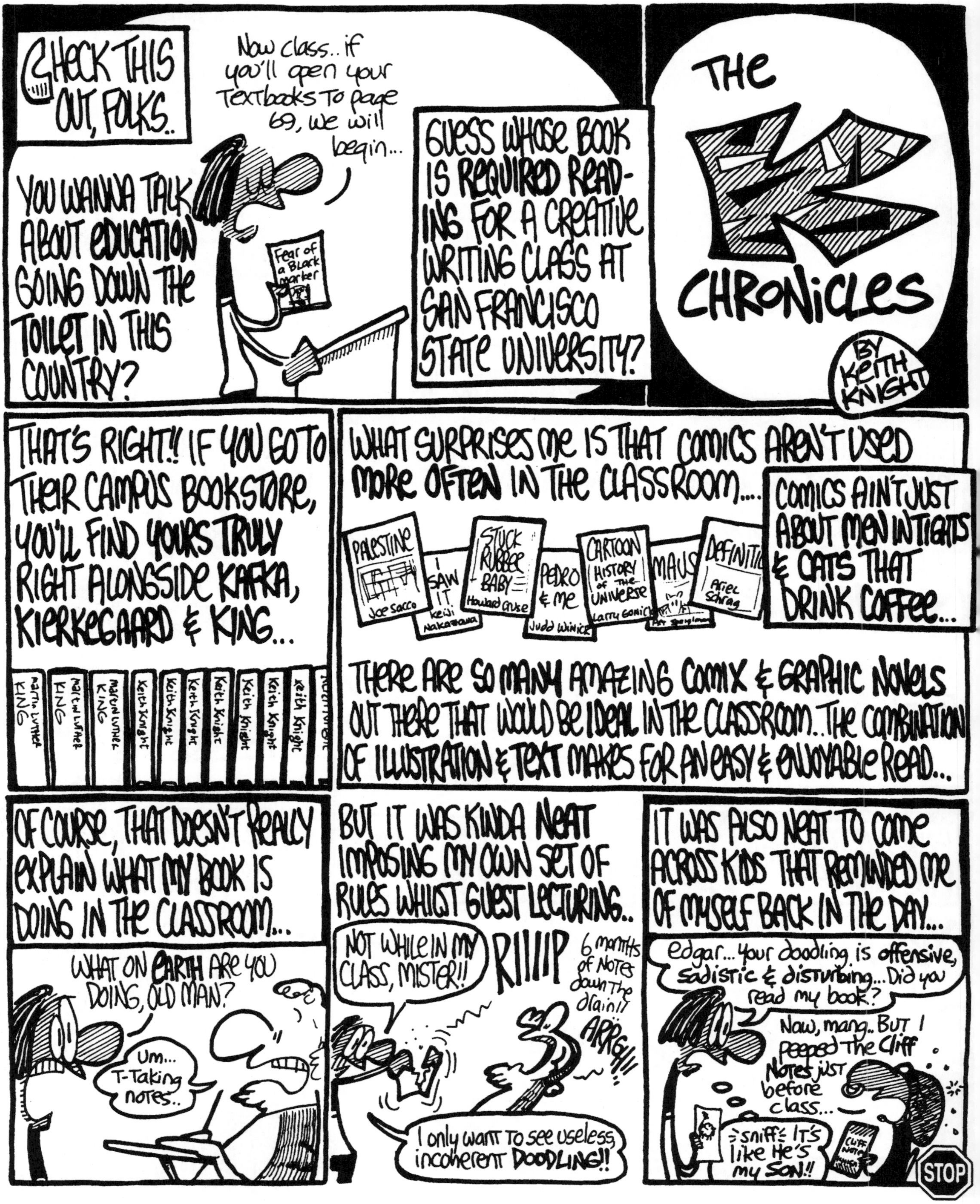
CHECK THIS OUT, FOLKS..
Now class.. if you'll open your textbooks to page 69, we will begin...
YOU WANNA TALK ABOUT EDUCATION GOING DOWN THE TOILET IN THIS COUNTRY?
Fear of a Black Marker
GUESS WHOSE BOOK IS REQUIRED READING FOR A CREATIVE WRITING CLASS AT SAN FRANCISCO STATE UNIVERSITY?
THE K CHRONICLES
BY KEITH KNIGHT
THAT'S RIGHT!! IF YOU GO TO THEIR CAMPUS BOOKSTORE, YOU'LL FIND YOURS TRULY RIGHT ALONGSIDE KAFKA, KIERKEGAARD & KING...
Martin Luther King
Keith Knight
WHAT SURPRISES ME IS THAT COMICS AREN'T USED MORE OFTEN IN THE CLASSROOM....
COMICS AIN'T JUST ABOUT MEN IN TIGHTS & CATS THAT DRINK COFFEE...
PALESTINE Joe Sacco
I SAW IT Keiji Nakazawa
STUCK RUBBER BABY Howard Cruse
PEDRO & ME Judd Winick
CARTOON HISTORY OF THE UNIVERSE Larry Gonick
MAUS
DEFINITI Ariel Schrag
THERE ARE SO MANY AMAZING COMIX & GRAPHIC NOVELS OUT THERE THAT WOULD BE IDEAL IN THE CLASSROOM.. THE COMBINATION OF ILLUSTRATION & TEXT MAKES FOR AN EASY & ENJOYABLE READ...
OF COURSE, THAT DOESN'T REALLY EXPLAIN WHAT MY BOOK IS DOING IN THE CLASSROOM...
WHAT ON EARTH ARE YOU DOING, OLD MAN?
Um... T-Taking notes..
BUT IT WAS KINDA NEAT IMPOSING MY OWN SET OF RULES WHILST GUEST LECTURING..
NOT WHILE IN MY CLASS, MISTER!!
RIIIIP
6 months of notes down the drain!!
ARRG!!
I only want to see useless, incoherent DOODLING!!
IT WAS ALSO NEAT TO COME ACROSS KIDS THAT REMINDED ME OF MYSELF BACK IN THE DAY...
edgar... your doodling is offensive, sadistic & disturbing... Did you read my book?
Now, mang.. But I peeped the Cliff Notes just before class...
sniff It's like he's my son!!
STOP

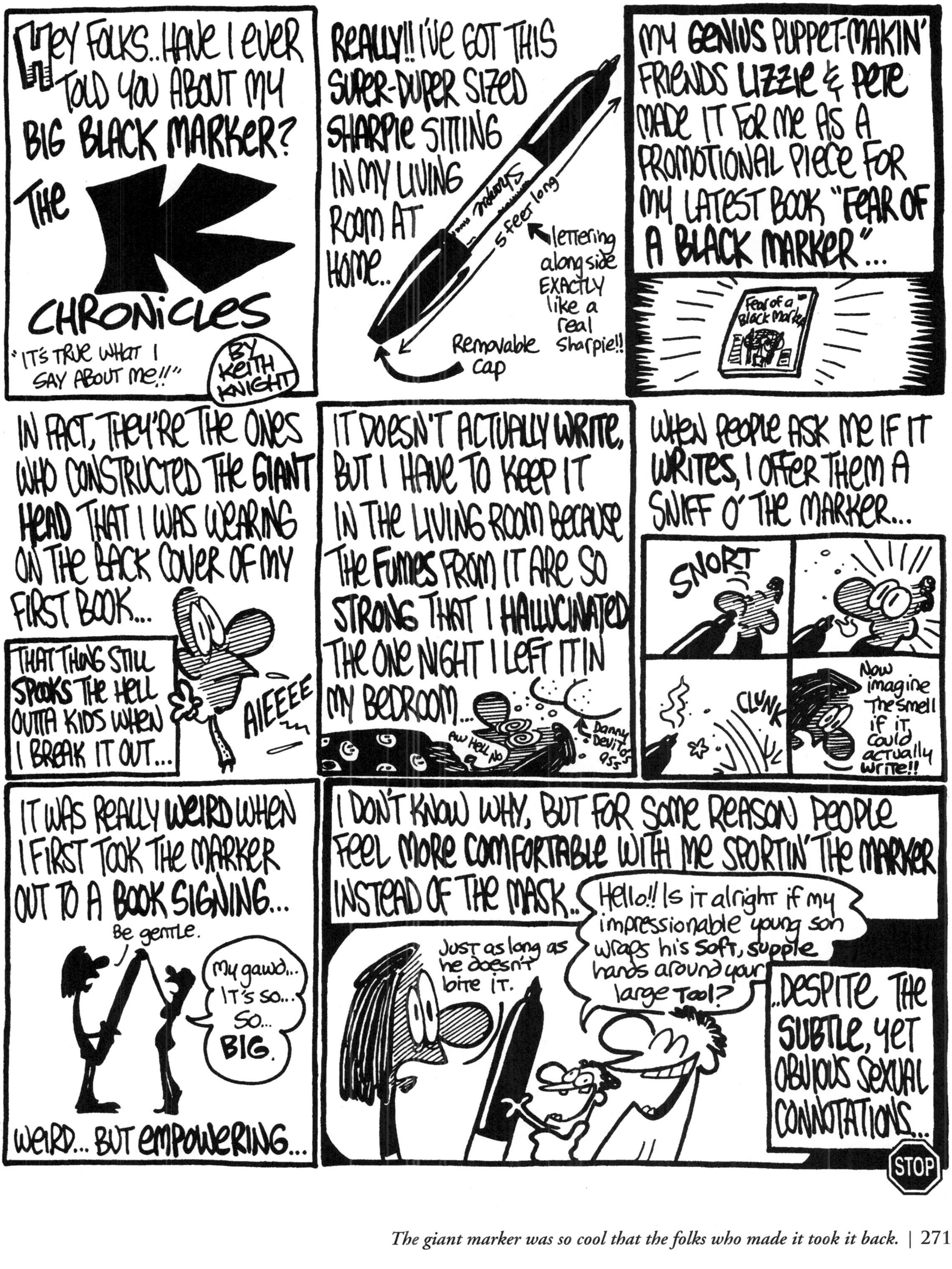
Hey folks.. Have I ever told you about my big black marker?
The K Chronicles
"It's true what I say about me!!"
By Keith Knight
Really!! I've got this super-duper sized Sharpie sitting in my living room at home..
5 feet long
lettering alongside EXACTLY like a real Sharpie!!
Removable cap
My genius puppet-makin' friends Lizzie & Pete made it for me as a promotional piece for my latest book "Fear of a Black Marker"...
Fear of a Black Marker
In fact, they're the ones who constructed the giant head that I was wearing on the back cover of my first book...
That thing still spooks the hell outta kids when I break it out...
AIEEEE
It doesn't actually write, but I have to keep it in the living room because the fumes from it are so strong that I hallucinated the one night I left it in my bedroom...
Aw hell no
Danny DeVito's ass
When people ask me if it writes, I offer them a sniff o' the marker...
SNORT
CLUNK
Now imagine the smell if it could actually write!!
It was really weird when I first took the marker out to a book signing...
Be gentle.
My gawd... It's so... so... BIG.
Weird... but empowering...
I don't know why, but for some reason people feel more comfortable with me sportin' the marker instead of the mask..
Hello!! Is it alright if my impressionable young son wraps his soft, supple hands around your large tool?
Just as long as he doesn't bite it.
..Despite the subtle, yet obvious sexual connotations...
STOP

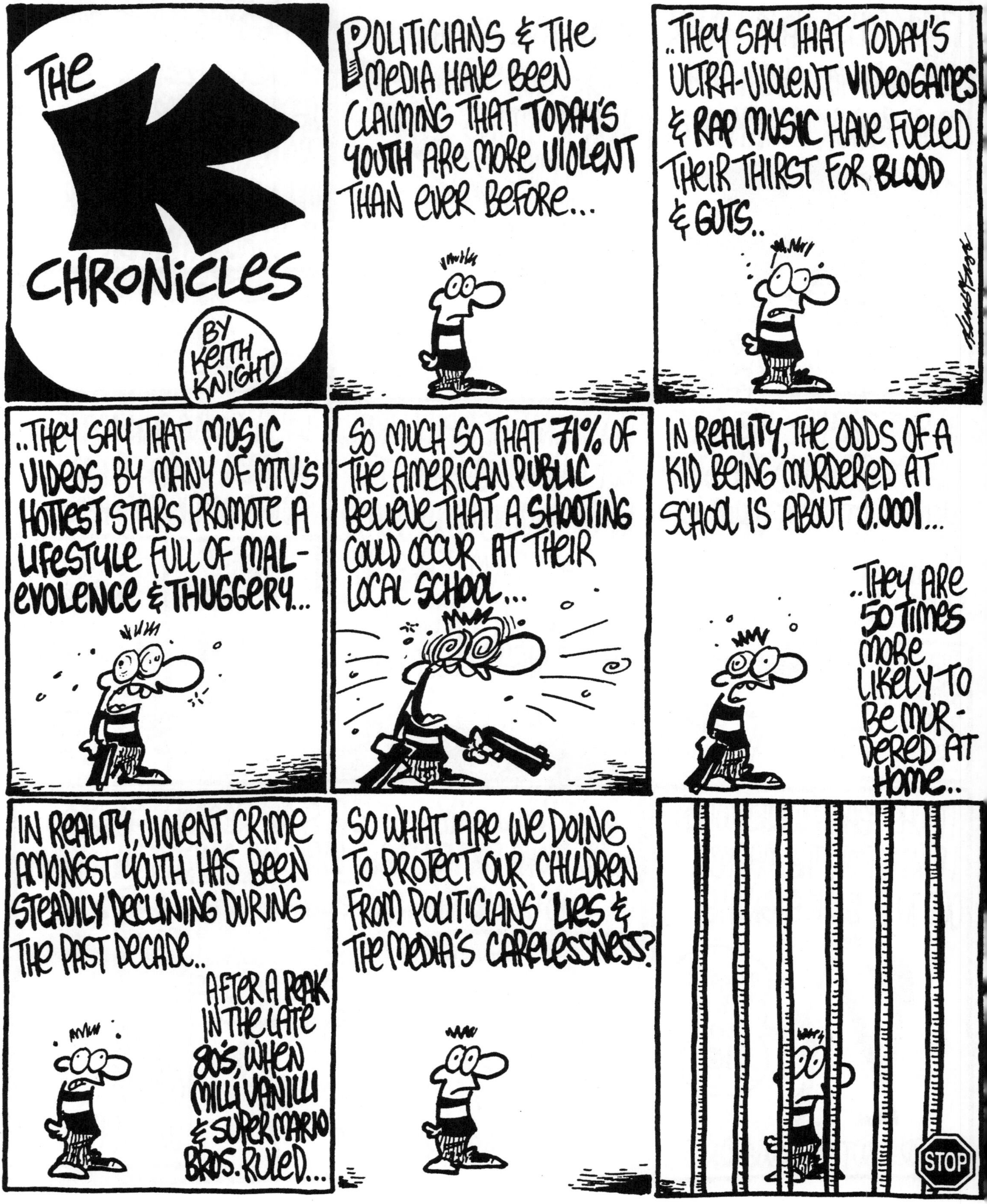

THE K CHRONICLES
BY KEITH KNIGHT
POLITICIANS & THE MEDIA HAVE BEEN CLAIMING THAT TODAY'S YOUTH ARE MORE VIOLENT THAN EVER BEFORE...
..THEY SAY THAT TODAY'S ULTRA-VIOLENT VIDEOGAMES & RAP MUSIC HAVE FUELED THEIR THIRST FOR BLOOD & GUTS..
..THEY SAY THAT MUSIC VIDEOS BY MANY OF MTV'S HOTTEST STARS PROMOTE A LIFESTYLE FULL OF MAL-EVOLENCE & THUGGERY...
SO MUCH SO THAT 71% OF THE AMERICAN PUBLIC BELIEVE THAT A SHOOTING COULD OCCUR AT THEIR LOCAL SCHOOL...
IN REALITY, THE ODDS OF A KID BEING MURDERED AT SCHOOL IS ABOUT 0.0001...
..THEY ARE 50 TIMES MORE LIKELY TO BE MUR-DERED AT HOME..
IN REALITY, VIOLENT CRIME AMONGST YOUTH HAS BEEN STEADILY DECLINING DURING THE PAST DECADE..
AFTER A PEAK IN THE LATE 80'S, WHEN MILLI VANILLI & SUPER MARIO BROS. RULED...
SO WHAT ARE WE DOING TO PROTECT OUR CHILDREN FROM POLITICIANS' LIES & THE MEDIA'S CARELESSNESS?
STOP

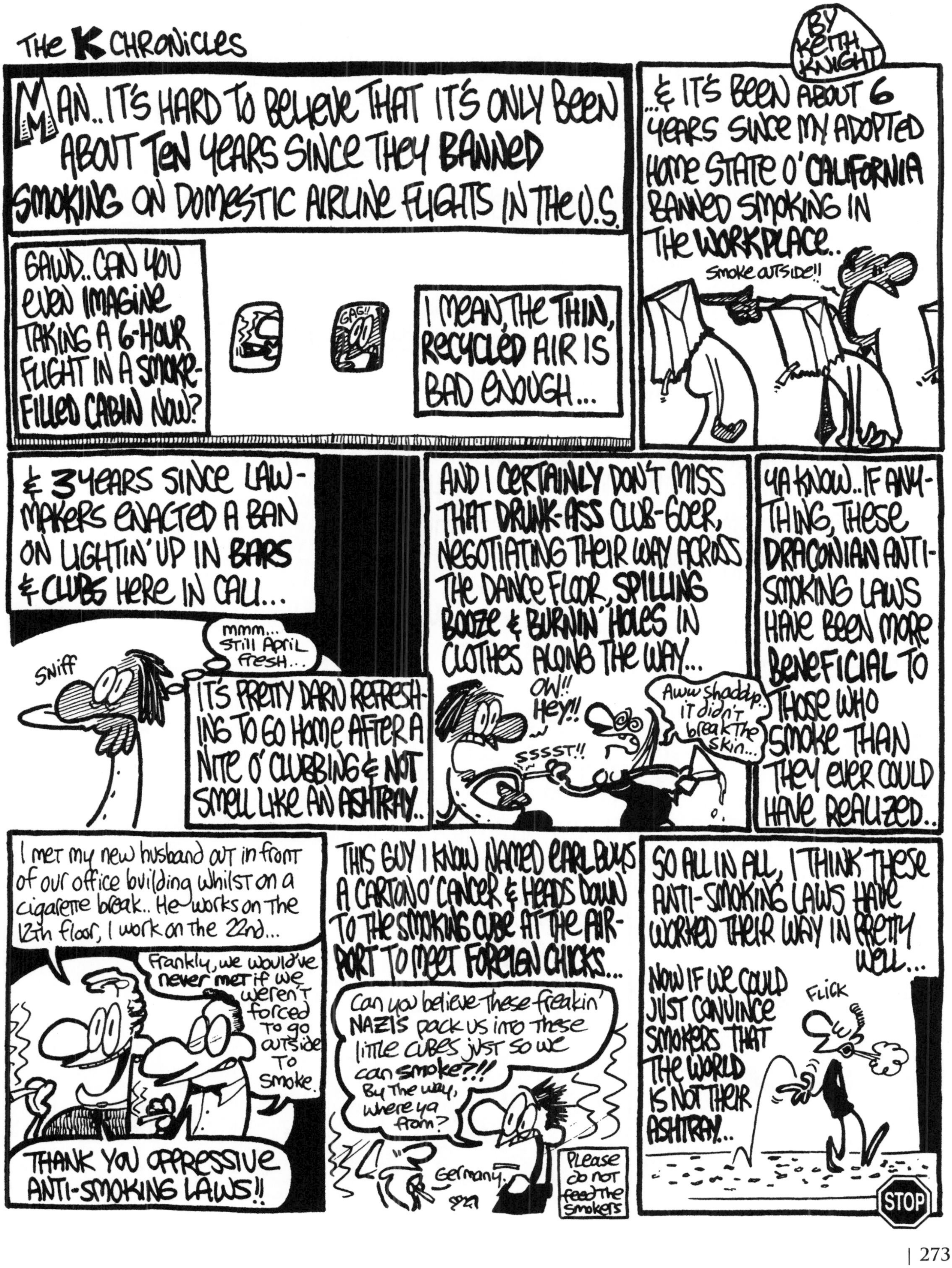
THE K CHRONICLES
BY KEITH KNIGHT
MAN.. IT'S HARD TO BELIEVE THAT IT'S ONLY BEEN ABOUT TEN YEARS SINCE THEY BANNED SMOKING ON DOMESTIC AIRLINE FLIGHTS IN THE U.S.
GAWD.. CAN YOU EVEN IMAGINE TAKING A 6-HOUR FLIGHT IN A SMOKE-FILLED CABIN NOW?
GAG!!
I MEAN, THE THIN, RECYCLED AIR IS BAD ENOUGH...
...& IT'S BEEN ABOUT 6 YEARS SINCE MY ADOPTED HOME STATE O' CALIFORNIA BANNED SMOKING IN THE WORKPLACE..
SMOKE OUTSIDE!!
& 3 YEARS SINCE LAW-MAKERS ENACTED A BAN ON LIGHTIN' UP IN BARS & CLUBS HERE IN CALI...
SNIFF
mmm... still April fresh...
IT'S PRETTY DARN REFRESHING TO GO HOME AFTER A NITE O' CLUBBING & NOT SMELL LIKE AN ASHTRAY..
AND I CERTAINLY DON'T MISS THAT DRUNK-ASS CLUB-GOER, NEGOTIATING THEIR WAY ACROSS THE DANCE FLOOR, SPILLING BOOZE & BURNIN' HOLES IN CLOTHES ALONG THE WAY...
OW!! HEY!!
SSSST!!
Aww shaddup.. It didn't break the skin...
YA KNOW.. IF ANYTHING, THESE DRACONIAN ANTI-SMOKING LAWS HAVE BEEN MORE BENEFICIAL TO THOSE WHO SMOKE THAN THEY EVER COULD HAVE REALIZED..
I met my new husband out in front of our office building whilst on a cigarette break.. He works on the 12th floor, I work on the 22nd...
Frankly, we would've never met if we weren't forced to go outside to smoke.
THANK YOU OPPRESSIVE ANTI-SMOKING LAWS!!
THIS GUY I KNOW NAMED EARL BUYS A CARTON O' CANCER & HEADS DOWN TO THE SMOKING CUBE AT THE AIRPORT TO MEET FOREIGN CHICKS...
Can you believe these freakin' NAZIS pack us into these little cubes just so we can smoke?!! By the way, where ya from?
Germany.
Please do not feed the smokers
SO ALL IN ALL, I THINK THESE ANTI-SMOKING LAWS HAVE WORKED THEIR WAY IN PRETTY WELL...
NOW IF WE COULD JUST CONVINCE SMOKERS THAT THE WORLD IS NOT THEIR ASHTRAY...
FLICK
STOP

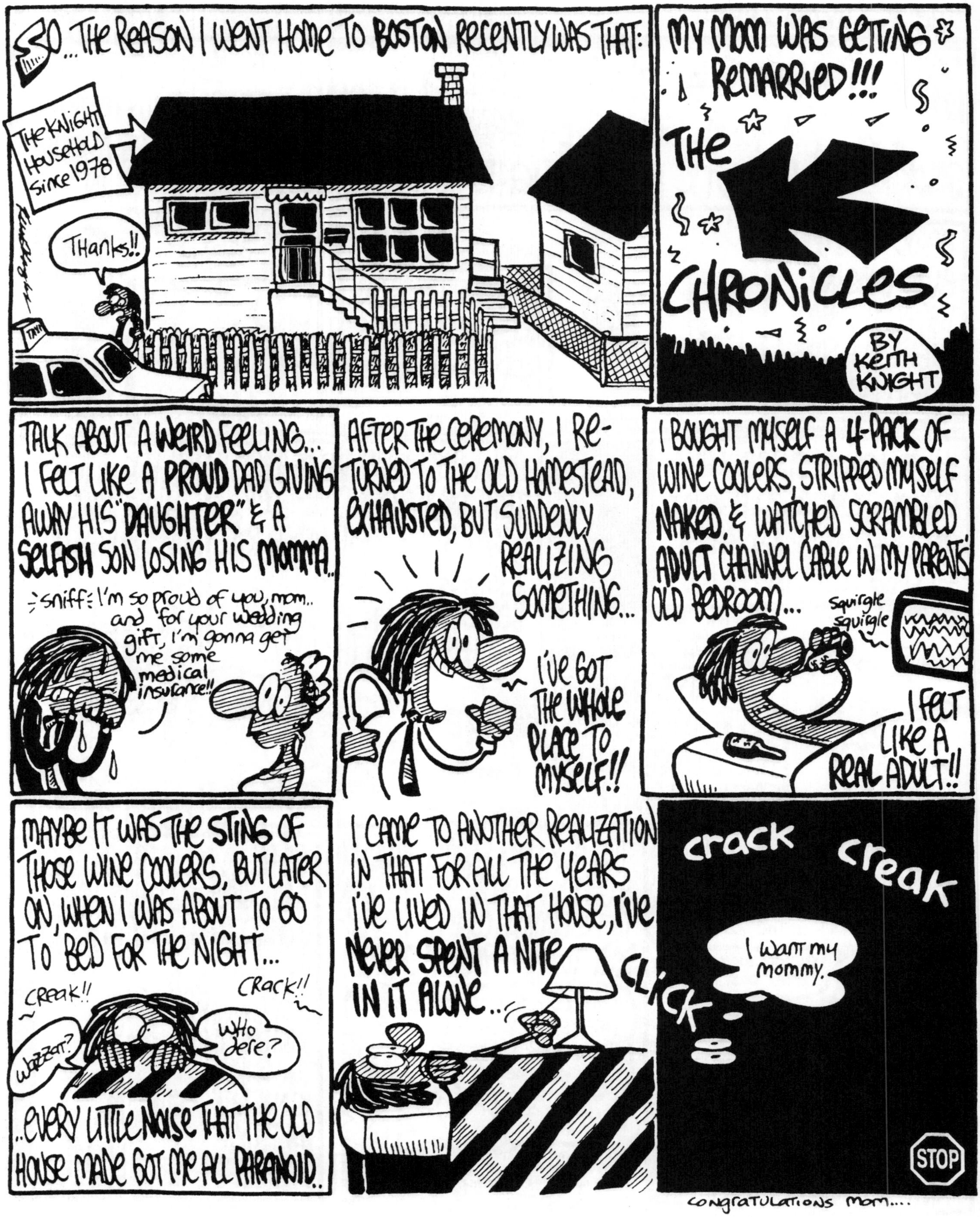
SO... THE REASON I WENT HOME TO BOSTON RECENTLY WAS THAT:
THE KNIGHT HOUSEHOLD SINCE 1978
THANKS!!
TAXI
MY MOM WAS GETTING REMARRIED!!!
THE K CHRONICLES
BY KEITH KNIGHT
TALK ABOUT A WEIRD FEELING... I FELT LIKE A PROUD DAD GIVING AWAY HIS "DAUGHTER" & A SELFISH SON LOSING HIS MOMMA...
:sniff: I'm so proud of you, mom.. and for your wedding gift, I'm gonna get me some medical insurance!!
AFTER THE CEREMONY, I RETURNED TO THE OLD HOMESTEAD, EXHAUSTED, BUT SUDDENLY REALIZING SOMETHING...
I'VE GOT THE WHOLE PLACE TO MYSELF!!
I BOUGHT MYSELF A 4-PACK OF WINE COOLERS, STRIPPED MYSELF NAKED, & WATCHED SCRAMBLED ADULT CHANNEL CABLE IN MY PARENTS' OLD BEDROOM...
squirgle squirgle
I FELT LIKE A REAL ADULT!!
MAYBE IT WAS THE STING OF THOSE WINE COOLERS, BUT LATER ON, WHEN I WAS ABOUT TO GO TO BED FOR THE NIGHT...
CREAK!!
CRACK!!
WAZZAT?
WHO DERE?
..EVERY LITTLE NOISE THAT THE OLD HOUSE MADE GOT ME ALL PARANOID..
I CAME TO ANOTHER REALIZATION IN THAT FOR ALL THE YEARS I'VE LIVED IN THAT HOUSE, I'VE NEVER SPENT A NITE IN IT ALONE...
CLICK
crack
creak
I want my mommy.
STOP
congratulations mom....

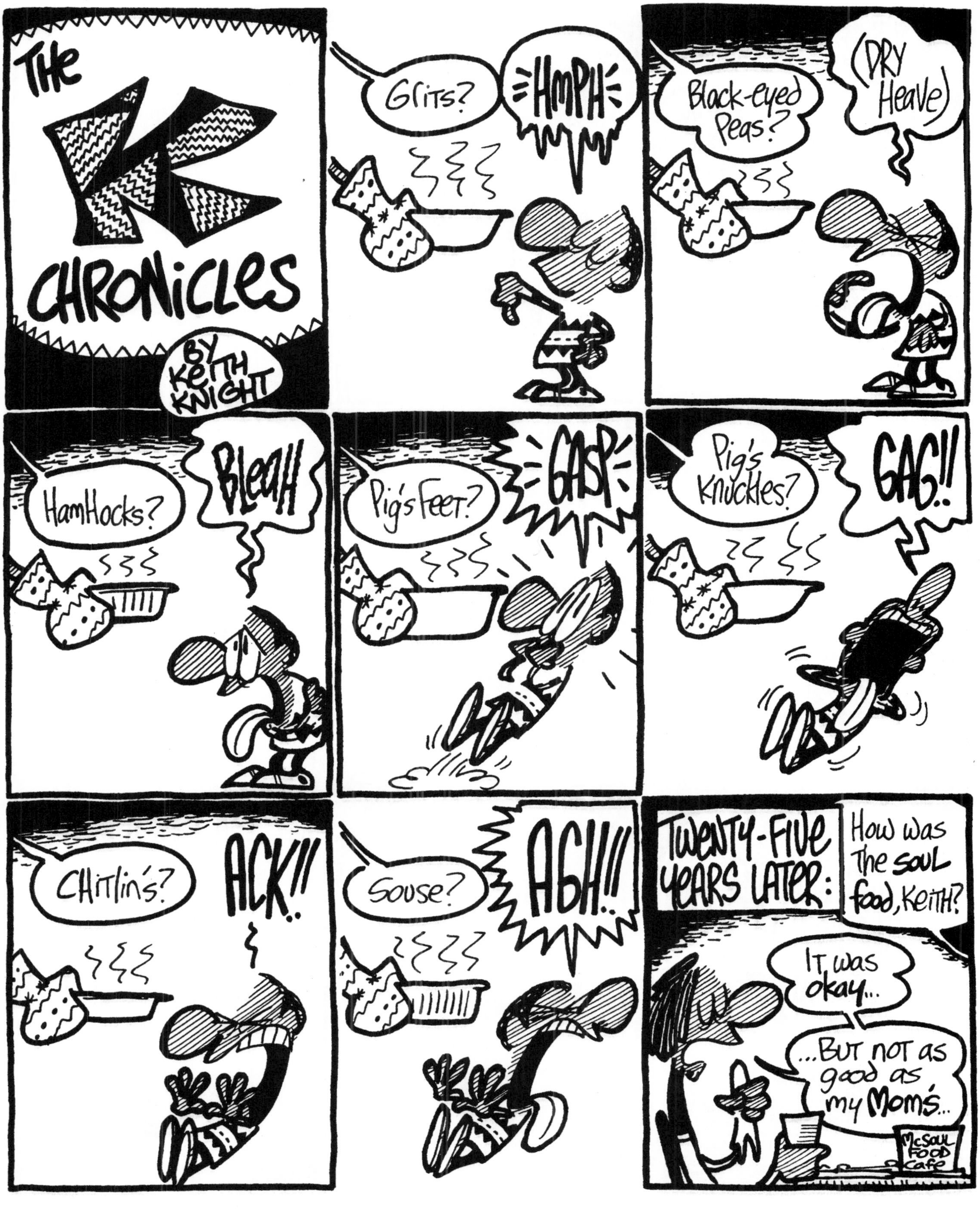
THE K CHRONICLES
BY KEITH KNIGHT
Grits?
HMPH
Black-eyed Peas?
(DRY Heave)
HamHocks?
BLEAH
Pig's Feet?
GASP
Pig's Knuckles?
GAG!!
CHitlin's?
ACK!!
Souse?
AGH!!
TWENTY-FIVE YEARS LATER:
How was the SOUL food, KeiTH?
IT was okay...
...BUT not as good as my Mom's...
McSOUL FOOD Cafe

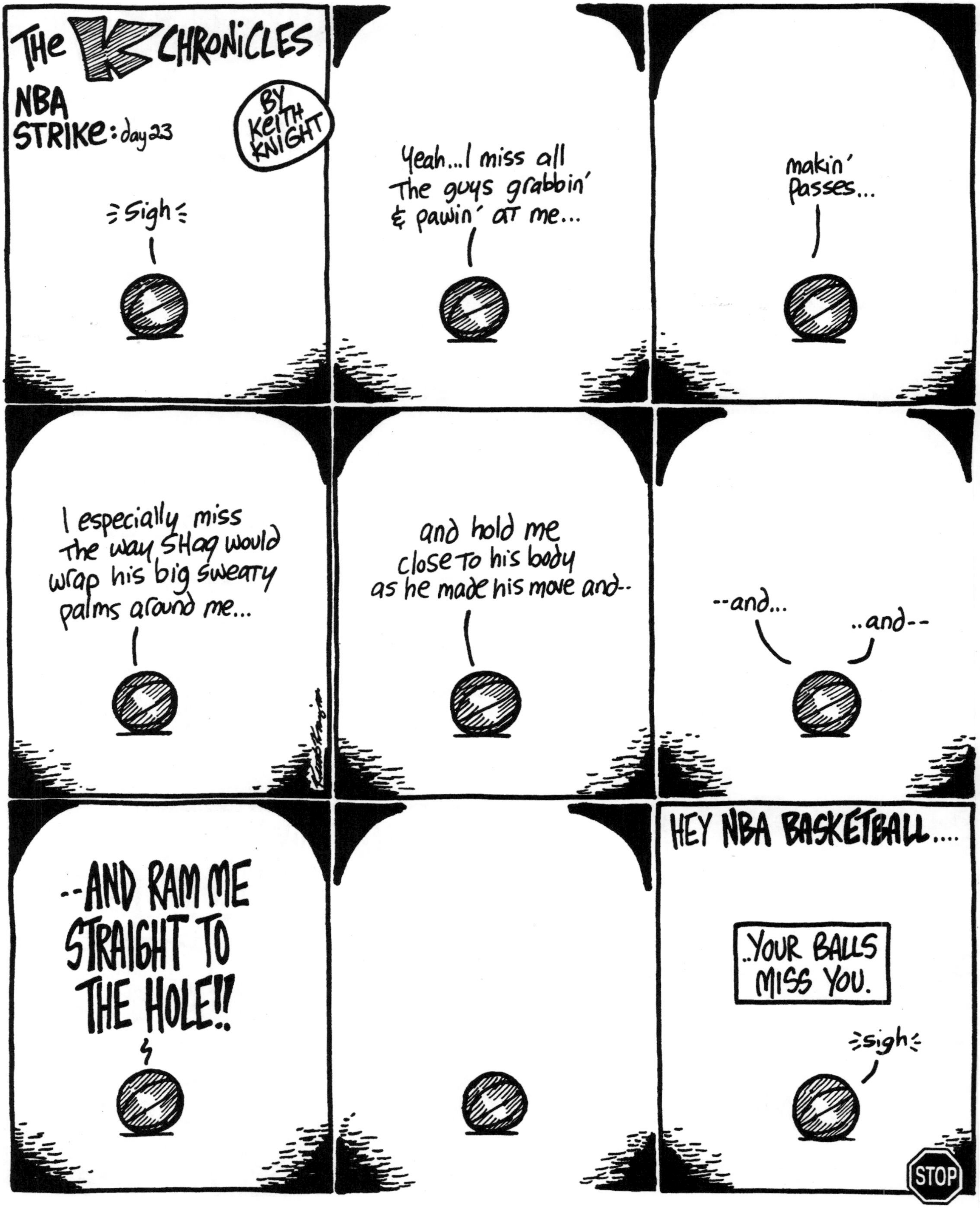
THE K CHRONICLES
NBA STRIKE: day 23
BY KEITH KNIGHT
sigh
Yeah...I miss all The guys grabbin' & pawin' at me...
makin' passes...
I especially miss The way SHaq would wrap his big sweaty palms around me...
and hold me close To his body as he made his move and--
--and...
..and--
--AND RAM ME STRAIGHT TO THE HOLE!!
HEY NBA BASKETBALL....
..YOUR BALLS MISS YOU.
sigh
STOP

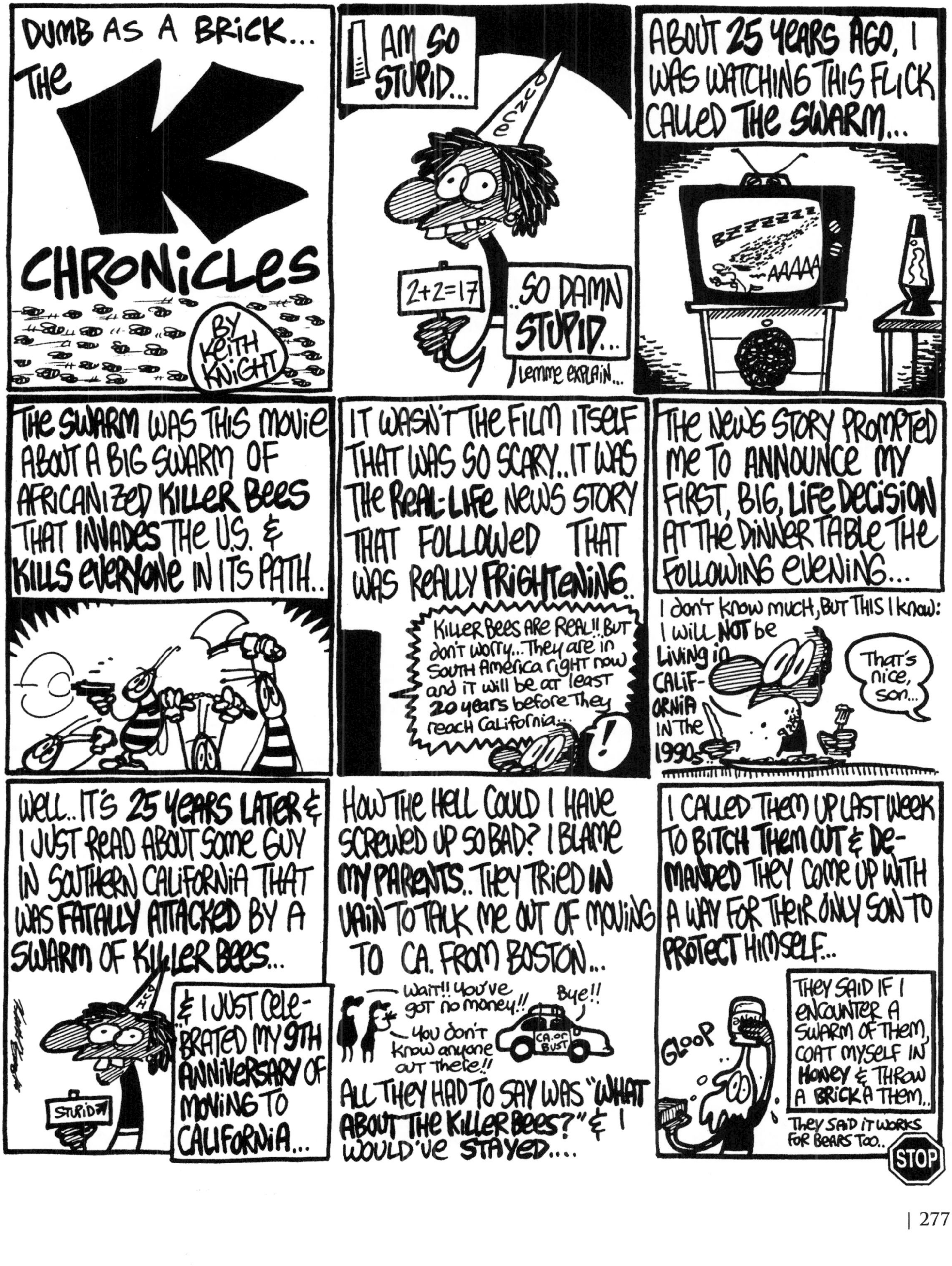

DUMB AS A BRICK...
THE K CHRONICLES
BY KEITH KNIGHT
I AM SO STUPID...
2+2=17
...SO DAMN STUPID...
LEMME EXPLAIN...
ABOUT 25 YEARS AGO, I WAS WATCHING THIS FLICK CALLED THE SWARM...
BZZZZZZ
AAAAA
THE SWARM WAS THIS MOVIE ABOUT A BIG SWARM OF AFRICANIZED KILLER BEES THAT INVADES THE U.S. & KILLS EVERYONE IN ITS PATH...
IT WASN'T THE FILM ITSELF THAT WAS SO SCARY.. IT WAS THE REAL-LIFE NEWS STORY THAT FOLLOWED THAT WAS REALLY FRIGHTENING..
KILLER BEES ARE REAL!! BUT DON'T WORRY... THEY ARE IN SOUTH AMERICA RIGHT NOW AND IT WILL BE AT LEAST 20 YEARS BEFORE THEY REACH CALIFORNIA...
!
THE NEWS STORY PROMPTED ME TO ANNOUNCE MY FIRST, BIG, LIFE DECISION AT THE DINNER TABLE THE FOLLOWING EVENING...
I DON'T KNOW MUCH, BUT THIS I KNOW: I WILL NOT BE LIVING IN CALIFORNIA IN THE 1990S...
THAT'S NICE, SON...
WELL.. IT'S 25 YEARS LATER & I JUST READ ABOUT SOME GUY IN SOUTHERN CALIFORNIA THAT WAS FATALLY ATTACKED BY A SWARM OF KILLER BEES...
& I JUST CELEBRATED MY 9TH ANNIVERSARY OF MOVING TO CALIFORNIA...
STUPID
HOW THE HELL COULD I HAVE SCREWED UP SO BAD? I BLAME MY PARENTS.. THEY TRIED IN VAIN TO TALK ME OUT OF MOVING TO CA. FROM BOSTON...
WAIT!! YOU'VE GOT NO MONEY!!
YOU DON'T KNOW ANYONE OUT THERE!!
BYE!!
CA. OR BUST
ALL THEY HAD TO SAY WAS "WHAT ABOUT THE KILLER BEES?" & I WOULD'VE STAYED....
I CALLED THEM UP LAST WEEK TO BITCH THEM OUT & DEMANDED THEY COME UP WITH A WAY FOR THEIR ONLY SON TO PROTECT HIMSELF...
GLOOP
THEY SAID IF I ENCOUNTER A SWARM OF THEM, COAT MYSELF IN HONEY & THROW A BRICK A THEM..
THEY SAID IT WORKS FOR BEARS TOO..
STOP

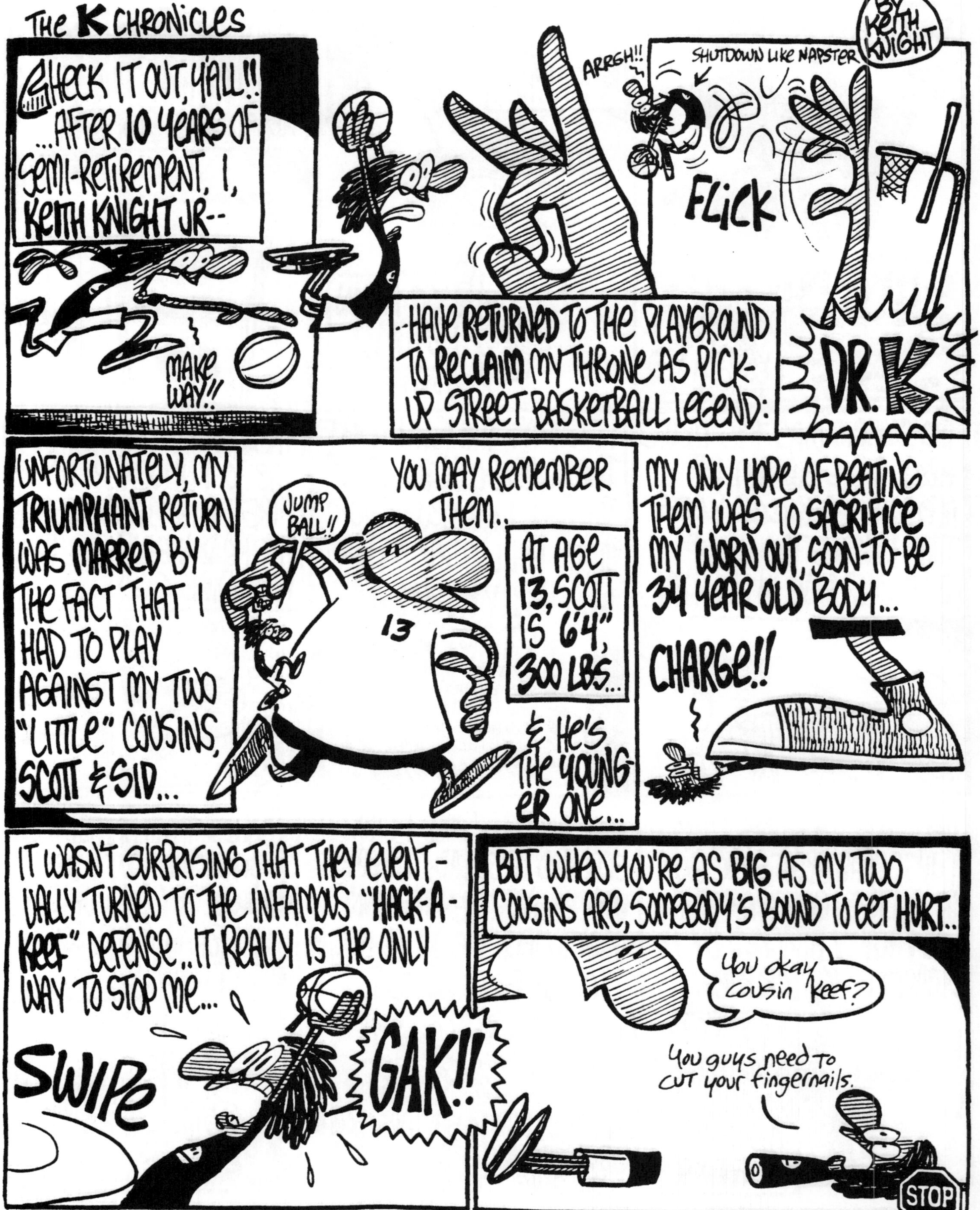
THE K CHRONICLES
BY KEITH KNIGHT
CHECK IT OUT, Y'ALL!! ...AFTER 10 YEARS OF SEMI-RETIREMENT, I, KEITH KNIGHT JR--
MAKE WAY!!
ARRGH!!
SHUTDOWN LIKE NAPSTER
FLICK
--HAVE RETURNED TO THE PLAYGROUND TO RECLAIM MY THRONE AS PICK-UP STREET BASKETBALL LEGEND:
DR. K
UNFORTUNATELY, MY TRIUMPHANT RETURN WAS MARRED BY THE FACT THAT I HAD TO PLAY AGAINST MY TWO "LITTLE" COUSINS, SCOTT & SID...
YOU MAY REMEMBER THEM...
JUMP BALL!!
13
AT AGE 13, SCOTT IS 6'4", 300 LBS...
& HE'S THE YOUNGER ONE...
MY ONLY HOPE OF BEATING THEM WAS TO SACRIFICE MY WORN OUT, SOON-TO-BE 34 YEAR OLD BODY...
CHARGE!!
IT WASN'T SURPRISING THAT THEY EVENTUALLY TURNED TO THE INFAMOUS "HACK-A-KEEF" DEFENSE... IT REALLY IS THE ONLY WAY TO STOP ME...
SWIPE
GAK!!
BUT WHEN YOU'RE AS BIG AS MY TWO COUSINS ARE, SOMEBODY'S BOUND TO GET HURT...
You okay cousin Keef?
You guys need to cut your fingernails.
STOP

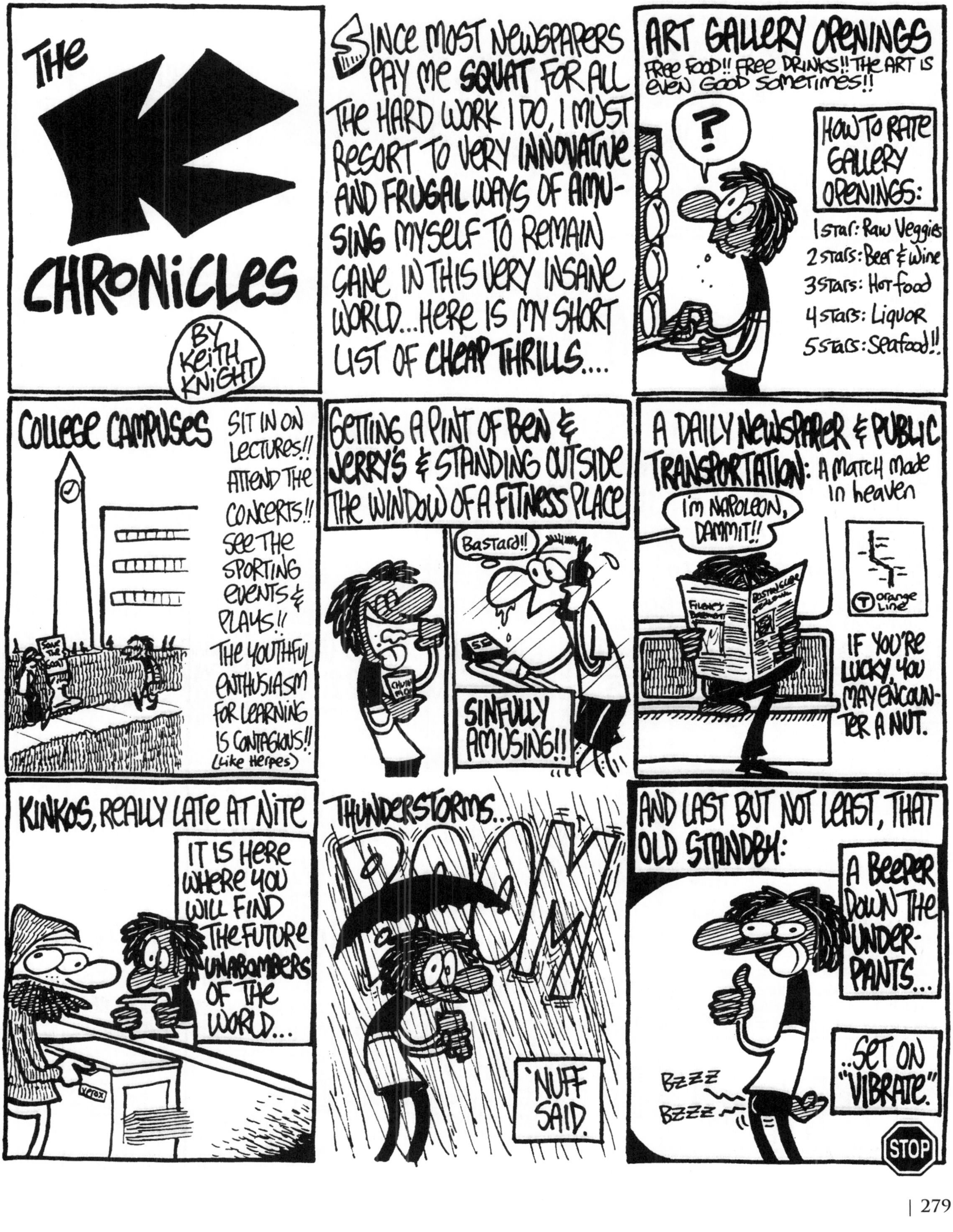
THE K CHRONICLES
BY KEITH KNIGHT
SINCE MOST NEWSPAPERS PAY ME SQUAT FOR ALL THE HARD WORK I DO, I MUST RESORT TO VERY INNOVATIVE AND FRUGAL WAYS OF AMUSING MYSELF TO REMAIN SANE IN THIS VERY INSANE WORLD... HERE IS MY SHORT LIST OF CHEAP THRILLS....
ART GALLERY OPENINGS
FREE FOOD!! FREE DRINKS!! THE ART IS EVEN GOOD SOMETIMES!!
?
HOW TO RATE GALLERY OPENINGS:
1 star: Raw Veggies
2 stars: Beer & Wine
3 stars: Hot food
4 stars: Liquor
5 stars: Seafood!!
COLLEGE CAMPUSES
SIT IN ON LECTURES!! ATTEND THE CONCERTS!! SEE THE SPORTING EVENTS & PLAYS!! THE YOUTHFUL ENTHUSIASM FOR LEARNING IS CONTAGIOUS!!
(Like Herpes)
GETTING A PINT OF BEN & JERRY'S & STANDING OUTSIDE THE WINDOW OF A FITNESS PLACE
Bastard!!
SINFULLY AMUSING!!
A DAILY NEWSPAPER & PUBLIC TRANSPORTATION: A MATCH MADE IN HEAVEN
I'M NAPOLEON, DAMMIT!!
Orange Line
IF YOU'RE LUCKY, YOU MAY ENCOUNTER A NUT.
KINKOS, REALLY LATE AT NITE
IT IS HERE WHERE YOU WILL FIND THE FUTURE UNABOMBERS OF THE WORLD...
THUNDERSTORMS...
BOOM
'NUFF SAID.
AND LAST BUT NOT LEAST, THAT OLD STANDBY:
A BEEPER DOWN THE UNDERPANTS...
...SET ON "VIBRATE."
BZZZ
BZZZ
STOP

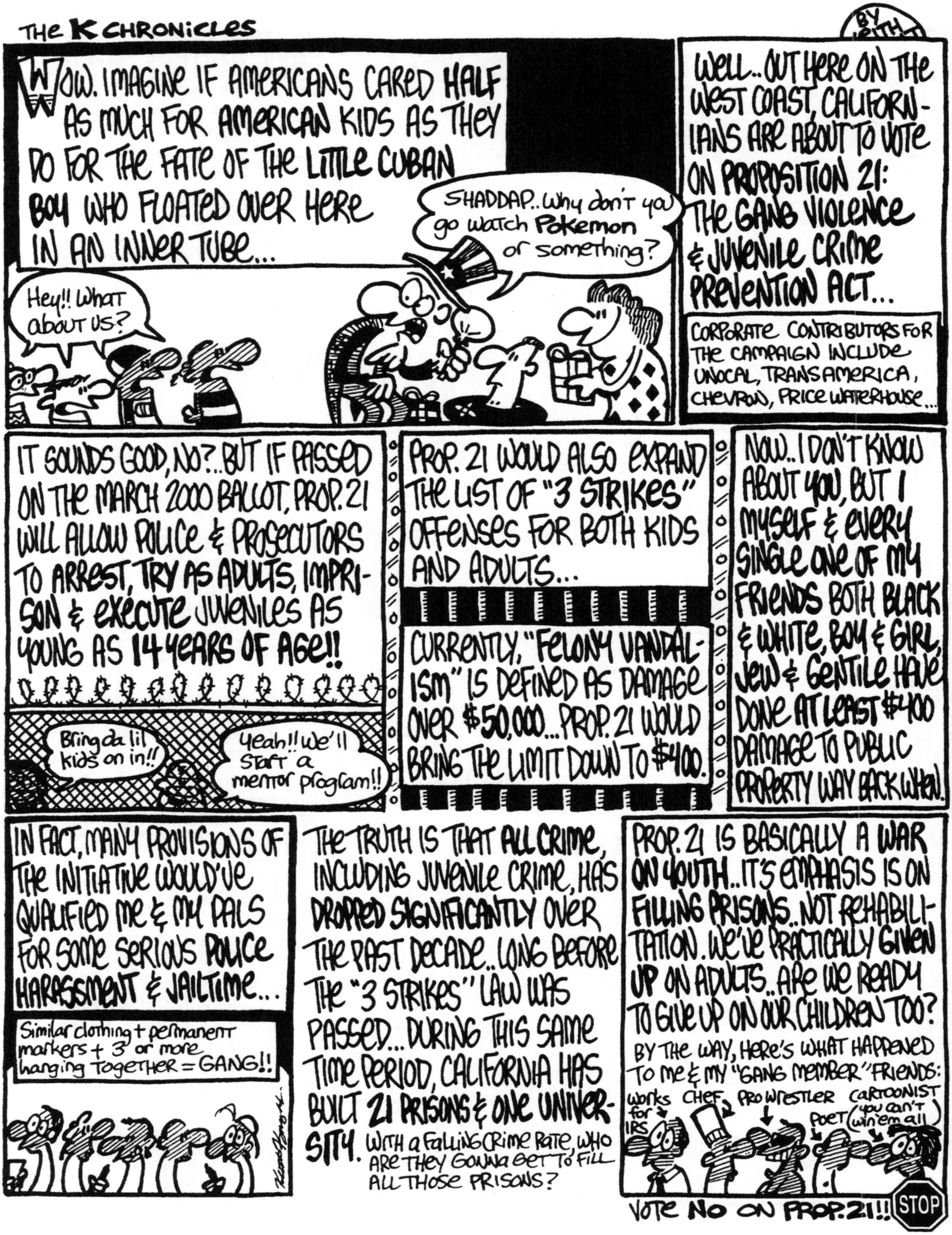
THE K CHRONICLES
WOW. IMAGINE IF AMERICANS CARED HALF AS MUCH FOR AMERICAN KIDS AS THEY DO FOR THE FATE OF THE LITTLE CUBAN BOY WHO FLOATED OVER HERE IN AN INNER TUBE...
Hey!! What about us?
SHADDAP.. Why don't you go watch Pokemon or something?
WELL.. OUT HERE ON THE WEST COAST, CALIFORNIANS ARE ABOUT TO VOTE ON PROPOSITION 21: THE GANG VIOLENCE & JUVENILE CRIME PREVENTION ACT...
CORPORATE CONTRIBUTORS FOR THE CAMPAIGN INCLUDE UNOCAL, TRANSAMERICA, CHEVRON, PRICE WATERHOUSE...
IT SOUNDS GOOD, NO?... BUT IF PASSED ON THE MARCH 2000 BALLOT, PROP. 21 WILL ALLOW POLICE & PROSECUTORS TO ARREST, TRY AS ADULTS, IMPRISON & EXECUTE JUVENILES AS YOUNG AS 14 YEARS OF AGE!!
Bring da lil kids on in!!
Yeah!! We'll start a mentor program!!
PROP. 21 WOULD ALSO EXPAND THE LIST OF "3 STRIKES" OFFENSES FOR BOTH KIDS AND ADULTS...
CURRENTLY, "FELONY VANDALISM" IS DEFINED AS DAMAGE OVER $50,000... PROP. 21 WOULD BRING THE LIMIT DOWN TO $400.
NOW.. I DON'T KNOW ABOUT YOU, BUT I MYSELF & EVERY SINGLE ONE OF MY FRIENDS BOTH BLACK & WHITE, BOY & GIRL, JEW & GENTILE HAVE DONE AT LEAST $400 DAMAGE TO PUBLIC PROPERTY WAY BACK WHEN.
IN FACT, MANY PROVISIONS OF THE INITIATIVE WOULD'VE QUALIFIED ME & MY PALS FOR SOME SERIOUS POLICE HARASSMENT & JAILTIME...
Similar clothing + permanent markers + 3 or more hanging together = GANG!!
THE TRUTH IS THAT ALL CRIME, INCLUDING JUVENILE CRIME, HAS DROPPED SIGNIFICANTLY OVER THE PAST DECADE.. LONG BEFORE THE "3 STRIKES" LAW WAS PASSED... DURING THIS SAME TIME PERIOD, CALIFORNIA HAS BUILT 21 PRISONS & ONE UNIVERSITY.
WITH A FALLING CRIME RATE, WHO ARE THEY GONNA GET TO FILL ALL THOSE PRISONS?
PROP. 21 IS BASICALLY A WAR ON YOUTH.. IT'S EMPHASIS IS ON FILLING PRISONS.. NOT REHABILITATION. WE'VE PRACTICALLY GIVEN UP ON ADULTS.. ARE WE READY TO GIVE UP ON OUR CHILDREN TOO?
BY THE WAY, HERE'S WHAT HAPPENED TO ME & MY "GANG MEMBER" FRIENDS:
works for IRS
CHEF
PRO WRESTLER
POET
CARTOONIST (you can't win 'em all)
VOTE NO ON PROP. 21!!
STOP

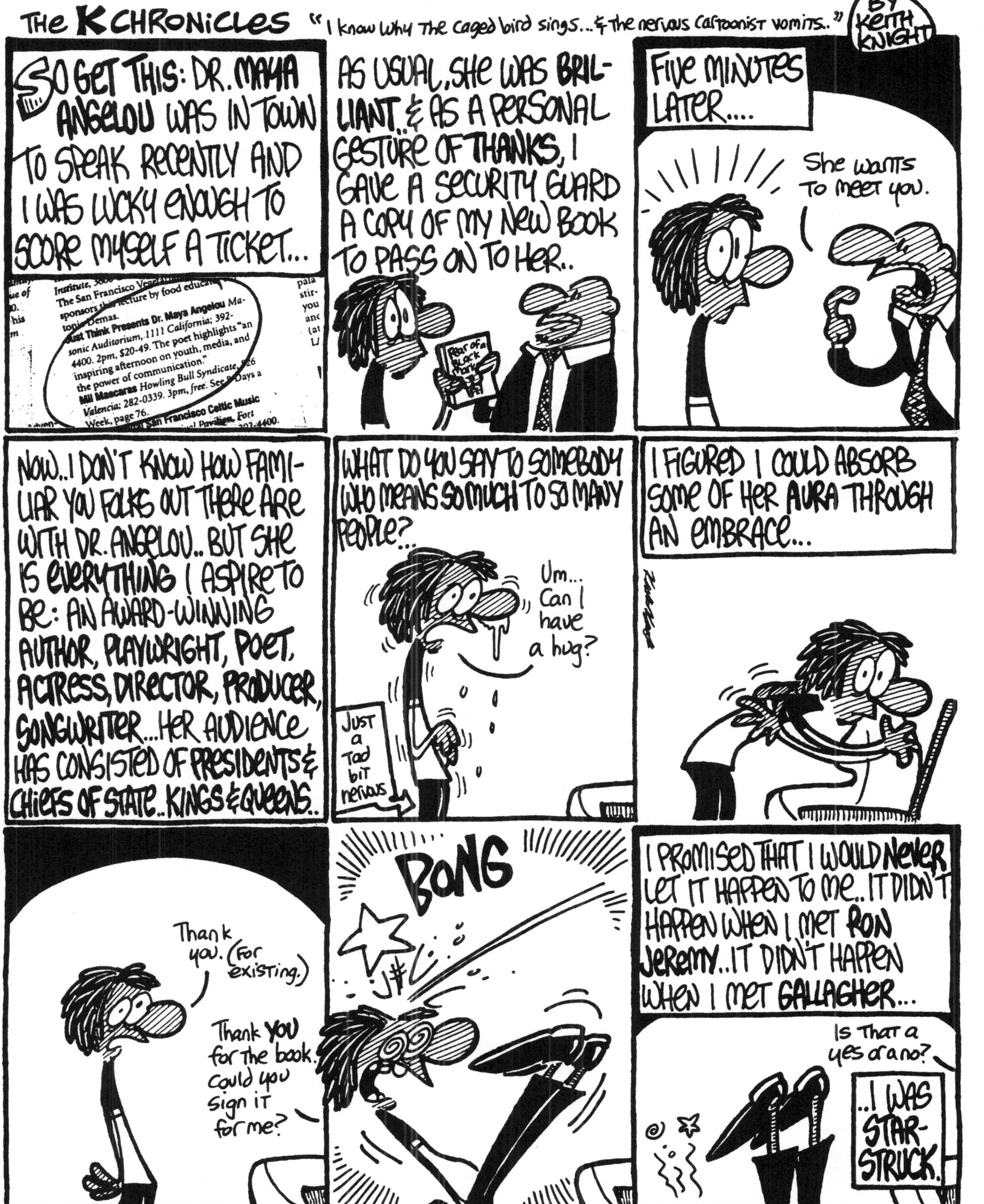
THE K CHRONICLES
"I know why the caged bird sings... & the nervous cartoonist vomits.."
BY KEITH KNIGHT
SO GET THIS: DR. MAYA ANGELOU WAS IN TOWN TO SPEAK RECENTLY AND I WAS LUCKY ENOUGH TO SCORE MYSELF A TICKET...
The San Francisco Vege... sponsors this lecture by food educat... Ma...
Just Think Presents Dr. Maya Angelou Ma... sonic Auditorium, 1111 California; 392-4400. 2pm, $20-49. The poet highlights "an inspiring afternoon on youth, media, and the power of communication."
Mil Mascaras Howling Bull Syndicate, 826 Valencia; 282-0339. 3pm, free. See 8 Days a Week, page 76.
San Francisco Celtic Music
AS USUAL, SHE WAS BRILLIANT.. & AS A PERSONAL GESTURE OF THANKS, I GAVE A SECURITY GUARD A COPY OF MY NEW BOOK TO PASS ON TO HER..
Fear of a Black Marker
FIVE MINUTES LATER....
She wants to meet you.
NOW.. I DON'T KNOW HOW FAMILIAR YOU FOLKS OUT THERE ARE WITH DR. ANGELOU.. BUT SHE IS EVERYTHING I ASPIRE TO BE: AN AWARD-WINNING AUTHOR, PLAYWRIGHT, POET, ACTRESS, DIRECTOR, PRODUCER, SONGWRITER... HER AUDIENCE HAS CONSISTED OF PRESIDENTS & CHIEFS OF STATE.. KINGS & QUEENS..
WHAT DO YOU SAY TO SOMEBODY WHO MEANS SO MUCH TO SO MANY PEOPLE?...
Um... Can I have a hug?
JUST a Tad bit nervous
I FIGURED I COULD ABSORB SOME OF HER AURA THROUGH AN EMBRACE...
Thank you. (For existing.)
Thank YOU for the book. Could you sign it for me?
BONG
I PROMISED THAT I WOULD NEVER LET IT HAPPEN TO ME.. IT DIDN'T HAPPEN WHEN I MET RON JEREMY.. IT DIDN'T HAPPEN WHEN I MET GALLAGHER...
Is that a yes or a no?
..I WAS STAR-STRUCK.

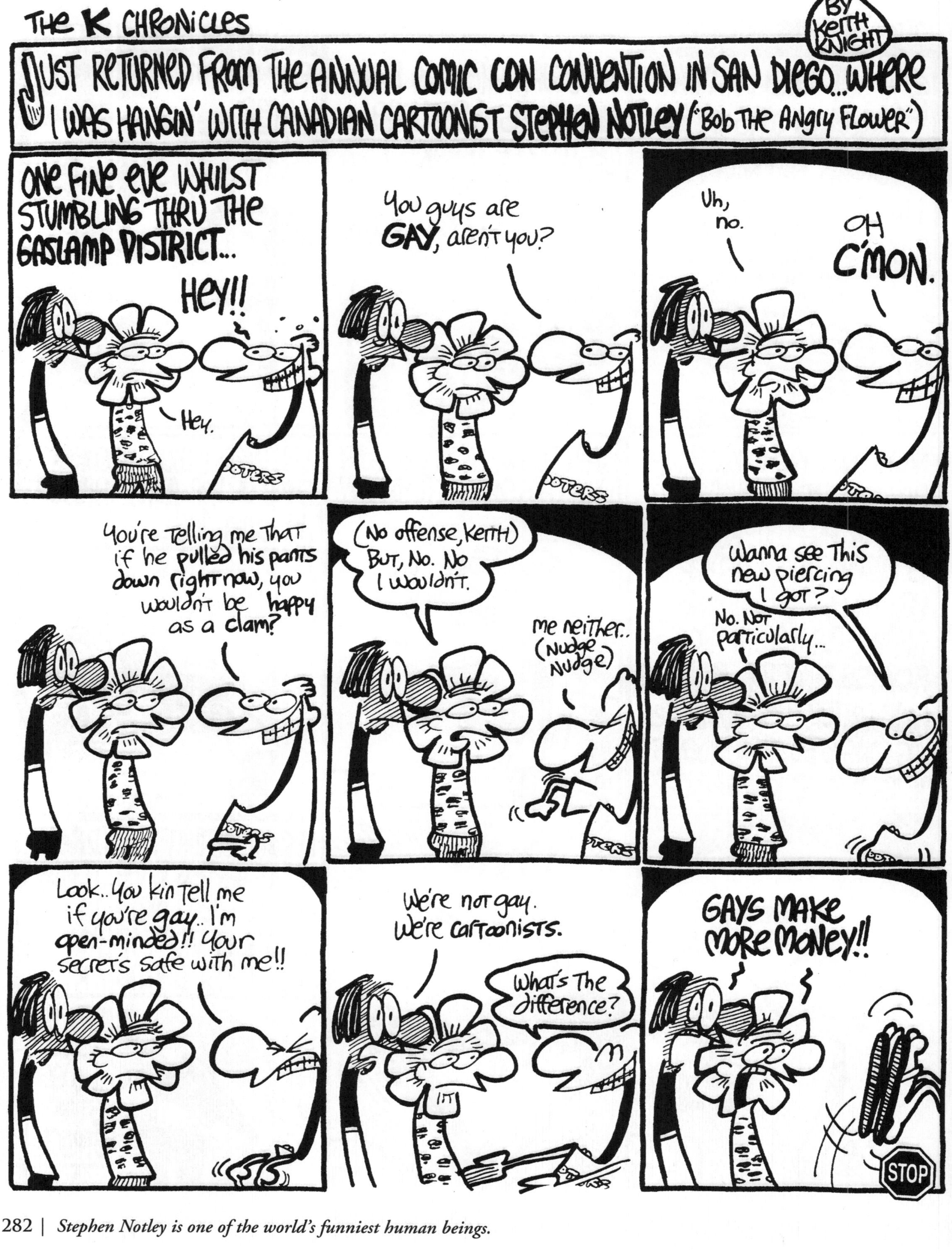
THE K CHRONICLES
BY KEITH KNIGHT
JUST RETURNED FROM THE ANNUAL COMIC CON CONVENTION IN SAN DIEGO...WHERE I WAS HANGIN' WITH CANADIAN CARTOONIST STEPHEN NOTLEY ("Bob The Angry Flower")
ONE FINE EVE WHILST STUMBLING THRU THE GASLAMP DISTRICT...
HEY!!
Hey.
You guys are GAY, aren't you?
Uh, no.
OH C'MON.
You're telling me that if he pulled his pants down right now, you wouldn't be happy as a clam?
(No offense, Keith) But, No. No I wouldn't.
me neither.. (Nudge Nudge)
Wanna see this new piercing I got?
No. Not particularly...
Look.. You kin tell me if you're gay.. I'm open-minded!! Your secret's safe with me!!
We're not gay. We're cartoonists.
What's the difference?
GAYS MAKE MORE MONEY!!
STOP

 Stephen Notley is one of the world's funniest human beings.

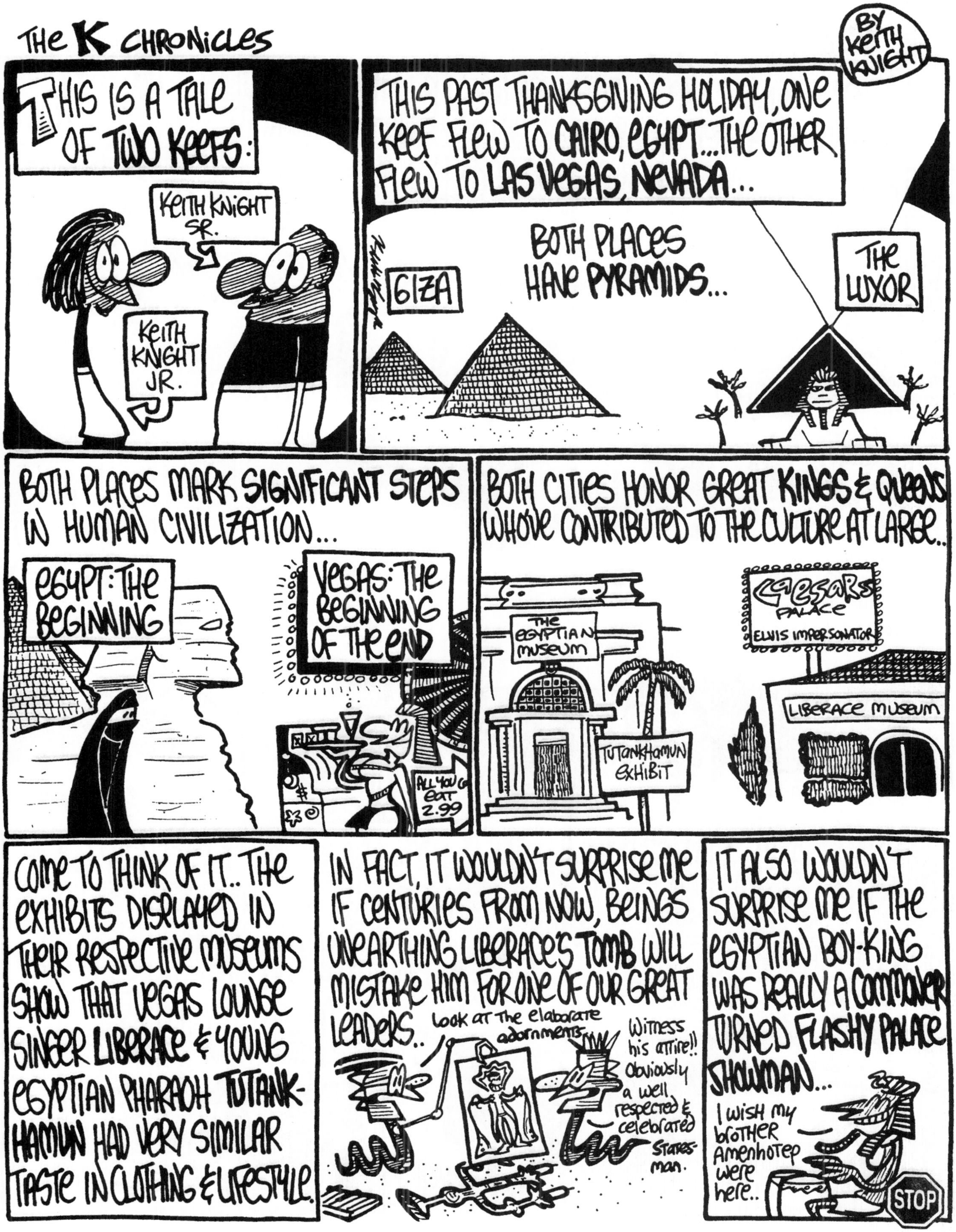
THE K CHRONICLES
BY KEITH KNIGHT
THIS IS A TALE OF TWO KEEFS:
KEITH KNIGHT SR.
KEITH KNIGHT JR.
THIS PAST THANKSGIVING HOLIDAY, ONE KEEF FLEW TO CAIRO, EGYPT... THE OTHER FLEW TO LAS VEGAS, NEVADA...
BOTH PLACES HAVE PYRAMIDS...
GIZA
THE LUXOR
BOTH PLACES MARK SIGNIFICANT STEPS IN HUMAN CIVILIZATION...
EGYPT: THE BEGINNING
VEGAS: THE BEGINNING OF THE END
ALL YOU CAN EAT 2.99
BOTH CITIES HONOR GREAT KINGS & QUEENS WHO'VE CONTRIBUTED TO THE CULTURE AT LARGE...
THE EGYPTIAN MUSEUM
TUTANKHAMUN EXHIBIT
CAESARS PALACE
ELVIS IMPERSONATOR
LIBERACE MUSEUM
COME TO THINK OF IT.. THE EXHIBITS DISPLAYED IN THEIR RESPECTIVE MUSEUMS SHOW THAT VEGAS LOUNGE SINGER LIBERACE & YOUNG EGYPTIAN PHARAOH TUTANKHAMUN HAD VERY SIMILAR TASTE IN CLOTHING & LIFESTYLE.
IN FACT, IT WOULDN'T SURPRISE ME IF CENTURIES FROM NOW, BEINGS UNEARTHING LIBERACE'S TOMB WILL MISTAKE HIM FOR ONE OF OUR GREAT LEADERS..
Look at the elaborate adornments
Witness his attire!! Obviously a well respected & celebrated Statesman.
IT ALSO WOULDN'T SURPRISE ME IF THE EGYPTIAN BOY-KING WAS REALLY A COMMONER TURNED FLASHY PALACE SHOWMAN...
I wish my brother Amenhotep were here..
STOP

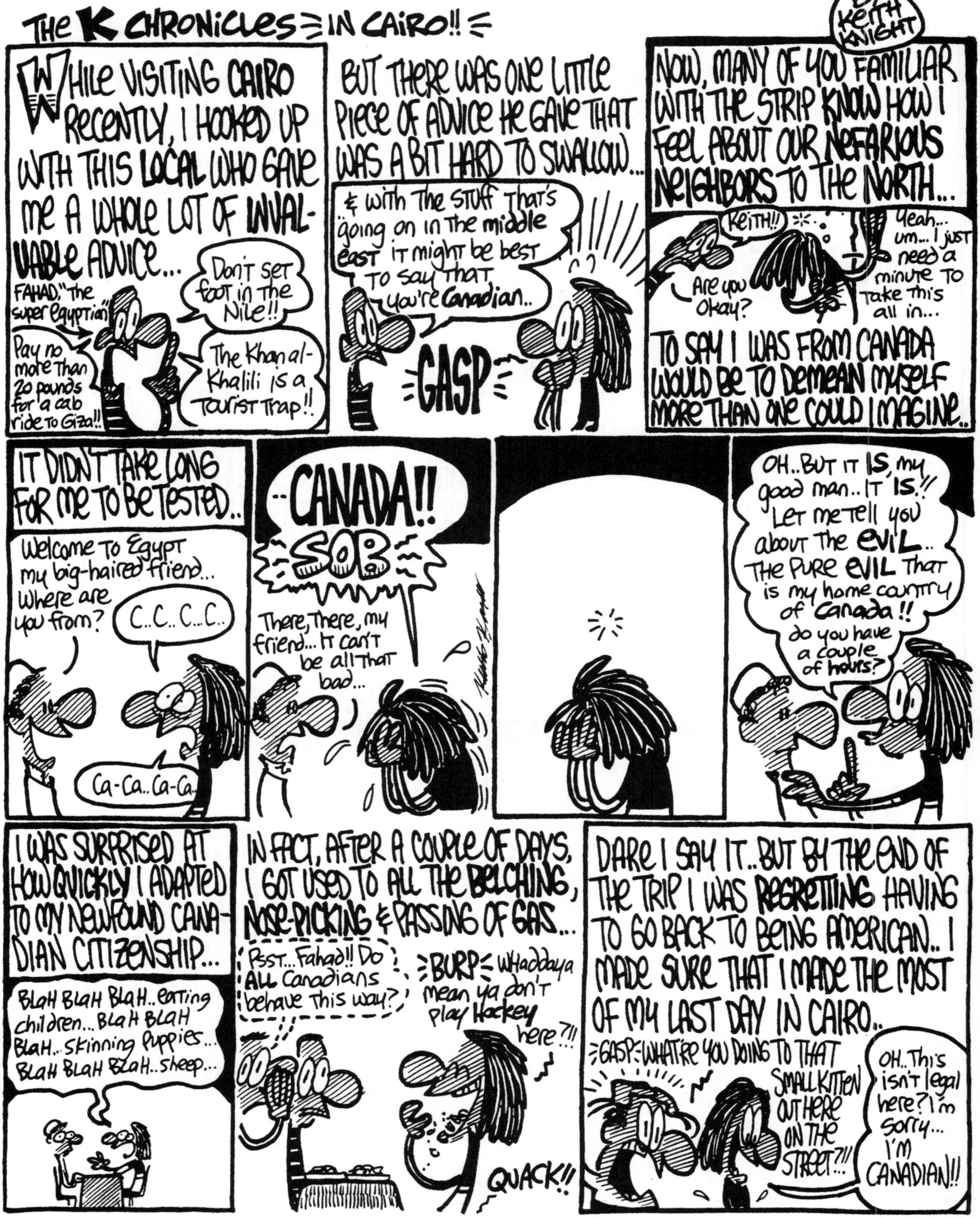

THE K CHRONICLES IN CAIRO!!
BY KEITH KNIGHT
WHILE VISITING CAIRO RECENTLY, I HOOKED UP WITH THIS LOCAL WHO GAVE ME A WHOLE LOT OF INVALUABLE ADVICE...
FAHAD, "THE SUPER EGYPTIAN"
Don't set foot in the Nile!!
Pay no more than 20 pounds for a cab ride to Giza!!
The Khan al-Khalili is a tourist trap!!
BUT THERE WAS ONE LITTLE PIECE OF ADVICE HE GAVE THAT WAS A BIT HARD TO SWALLOW...
& with the stuff that's going on in the middle east it might be best to say that you're Canadian..
GASP
NOW, MANY OF YOU FAMILIAR WITH THE STRIP KNOW HOW I FEEL ABOUT OUR NEFARIOUS NEIGHBORS TO THE NORTH...
KEITH!!
Are you okay?
Yeah... um... I just need a minute to take this all in...
TO SAY I WAS FROM CANADA WOULD BE TO DEMEAN MYSELF MORE THAN ONE COULD IMAGINE..
IT DIDN'T TAKE LONG FOR ME TO BE TESTED..
Welcome to Egypt my big-haired friend... Where are you from?
C..C..C..C..
Ca-Ca..Ca-Ca..
CANADA!!
SOB
There, there, my friend... It can't be all that bad...
OH.. BUT IT IS, my good man.. IT IS.!! Let me tell you about the EVIL.. The PURE EVIL that is my home country of Canada!! do you have a couple of hours?
I WAS SURPRISED AT HOW QUICKLY I ADAPTED TO MY NEWFOUND CANADIAN CITIZENSHIP...
BLAH BLAH BLAH.. eating children... BLAH BLAH BLAH.. skinning puppies... BLAH BLAH BLAH.. sheep...
IN FACT, AFTER A COUPLE OF DAYS, I GOT USED TO ALL THE BELCHING, NOSE-PICKING & PASSING OF GAS...
Psst... Fahad!! Do ALL Canadians behave this way?
BURP Whaddaya mean ya don't play Hockey here?!!
QUACK!!
DARE I SAY IT.. BUT BY THE END OF THE TRIP I WAS REGRETTING HAVING TO GO BACK TO BEING AMERICAN.. I MADE SURE THAT I MADE THE MOST OF MY LAST DAY IN CAIRO..
GASP WHAT'RE YOU DOING TO THAT SMALL KITTEN OUT HERE ON THE STREET?!!
OH.. This isn't legal here? I'm sorry... I'M CANADIAN!!

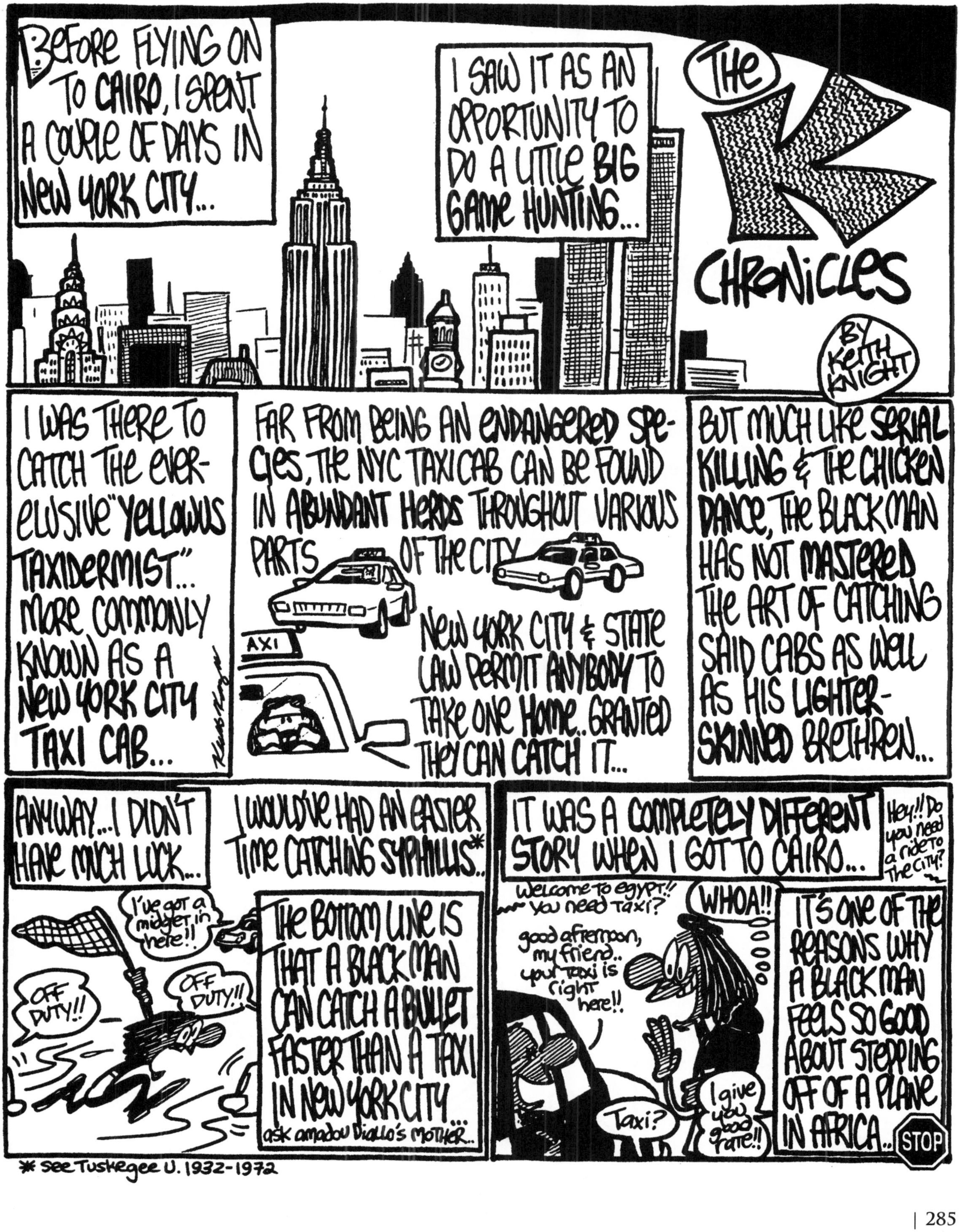

BEFORE FLYING ON TO CAIRO, I SPENT A COUPLE OF DAYS IN NEW YORK CITY...
I SAW IT AS AN OPPORTUNITY TO DO A LITTLE BIG GAME HUNTING...
THE K CHRONICLES
BY KEITH KNIGHT
I WAS THERE TO CATCH THE EVER-ELUSIVE "YELLOWUS TAXIDERMIST"... MORE COMMONLY KNOWN AS A NEW YORK CITY TAXI CAB...
FAR FROM BEING AN ENDANGERED SPECIES, THE NYC TAXI CAB CAN BE FOUND IN ABUNDANT HERDS THROUGHOUT VARIOUS PARTS OF THE CITY
NEW YORK CITY & STATE LAW PERMIT ANYBODY TO TAKE ONE HOME.. GRANTED THEY CAN CATCH IT...
BUT MUCH LIKE SERIAL KILLING & THE CHICKEN DANCE, THE BLACK MAN HAS NOT MASTERED THE ART OF CATCHING SAID CABS AS WELL AS HIS LIGHTER-SKINNED BRETHREN...
ANYWAY...I DIDN'T HAVE MUCH LUCK...
I WOULD'VE HAD AN EASIER TIME CATCHING SYPHILLIS*...
I've got a midget in here!!
OFF DUTY!!
OFF DUTY!!
THE BOTTOM LINE IS THAT A BLACK MAN CAN CATCH A BULLET FASTER THAN A TAXI IN NEW YORK CITY...
ask amadou Diallo's mother..
IT WAS A COMPLETELY DIFFERENT STORY WHEN I GOT TO CAIRO...
Hey!! Do you need a ride to the city?
Welcome to egypt!! you need taxi?
WHOA!!
good afternoon, my friend.. your taxi is right here!!
Taxi?
I give you good rate!!
IT'S ONE OF THE REASONS WHY A BLACK MAN FEELS SO GOOD ABOUT STEPPING OFF OF A PLANE IN AFRICA..
STOP

* See Tuskegee U. 1932-1972

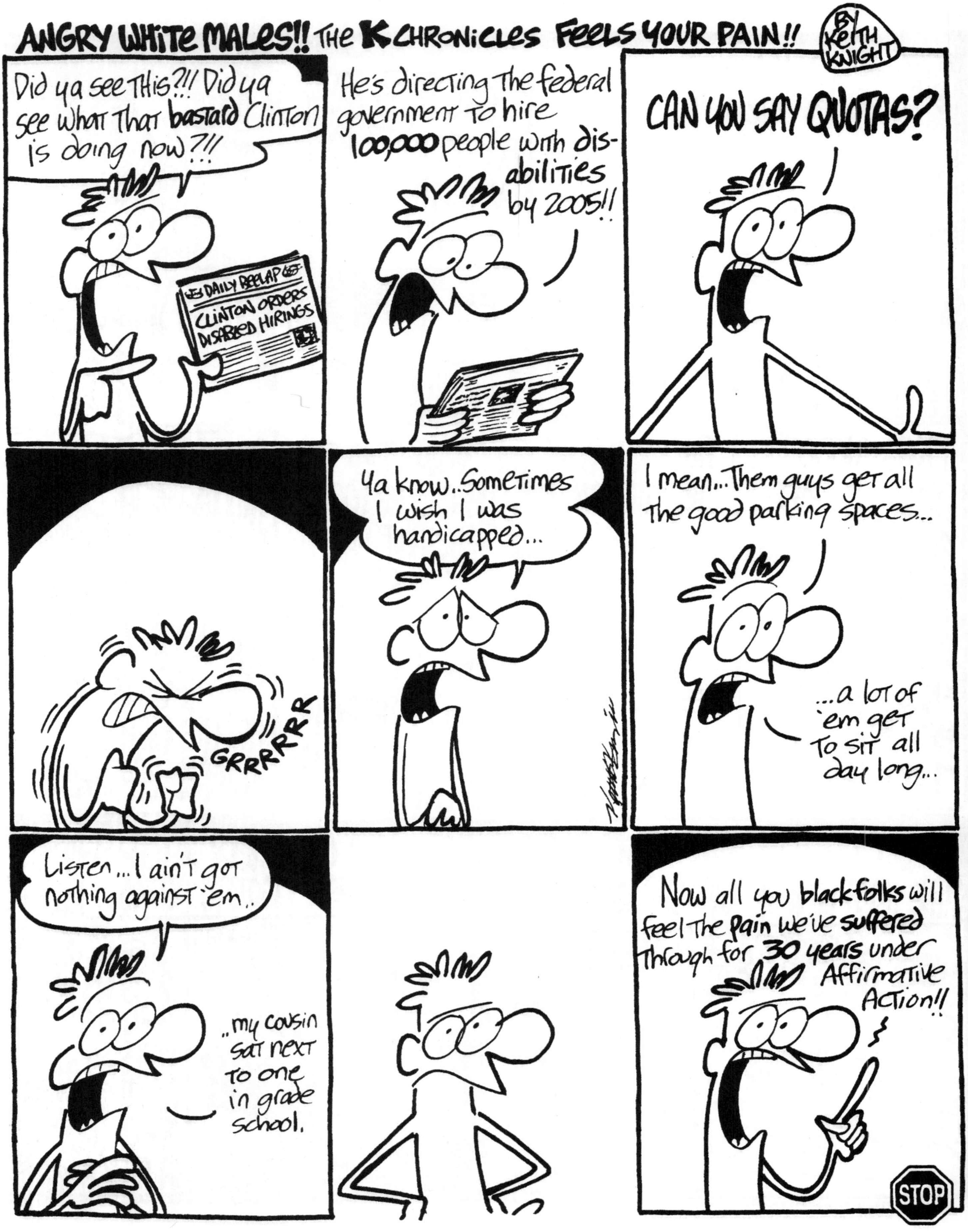
ANGRY WHITE MALES!! THE K CHRONICLES FEELS YOUR PAIN!!
BY KEITH KNIGHT
Did ya see THIS?!! Did ya see what that bastard Clinton is doing now?!!
DAILY BEELAP
CLINTON ORDERS DISABLED HIRINGS
He's directing the federal government to hire 100,000 people with dis-abilities by 2005!!
CAN YOU SAY QUOTAS?
GRRRRRRR
Ya know.. Sometimes I wish I was handicapped...
I mean... Them guys get all the good parking spaces...
...a lot of 'em get to sit all day long...
Listen... I ain't got nothing against 'em..
..my cousin sat next to one in grade school.
Now all you black folks will feel the pain we've suffered through for 30 years under Affirmative Action!!
STOP

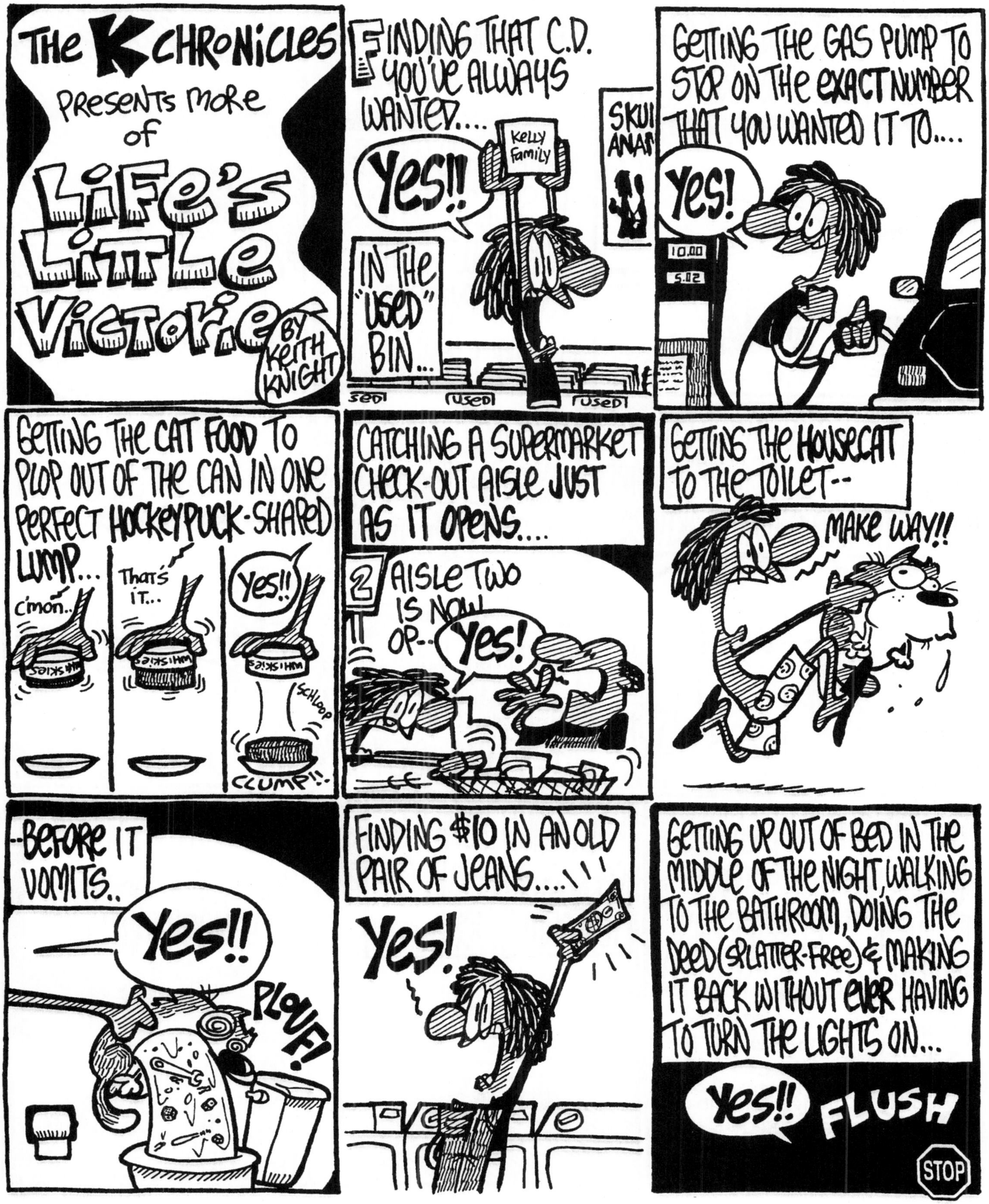
THE K CHRONICLES
PRESENTS MORE OF
LIFE'S LITTLE VICTORIES
BY KEITH KNIGHT
FINDING THAT C.D. YOU'VE ALWAYS WANTED....
YES!!
KELLY FAMILY
IN THE "USED" BIN...
USED
USED
GETTING THE GAS PUMP TO STOP ON THE EXACT NUMBER THAT YOU WANTED IT TO....
YES!
10.00
5.02
GETTING THE CAT FOOD TO PLOP OUT OF THE CAN IN ONE PERFECT HOCKEYPUCK-SHAPED LUMP....
C'MON..
THAT'S IT...
YES!!
SCHLOOP
CLUMP!!
CATCHING A SUPERMARKET CHECK-OUT AISLE JUST AS IT OPENS....
AISLE TWO IS NOW OP--
YES!
GETTING THE HOUSECAT TO THE TOILET--
MAKE WAY!!
--BEFORE IT VOMITS..
YES!!
PLOUF!
FINDING $10 IN AN OLD PAIR OF JEANS....
YES!
GETTING UP OUT OF BED IN THE MIDDLE OF THE NIGHT, WALKING TO THE BATHROOM, DOING THE DEED (SPLATTER-FREE) & MAKING IT BACK WITHOUT EVER HAVING TO TURN THE LIGHTS ON...
YES!!
FLUSH
STOP

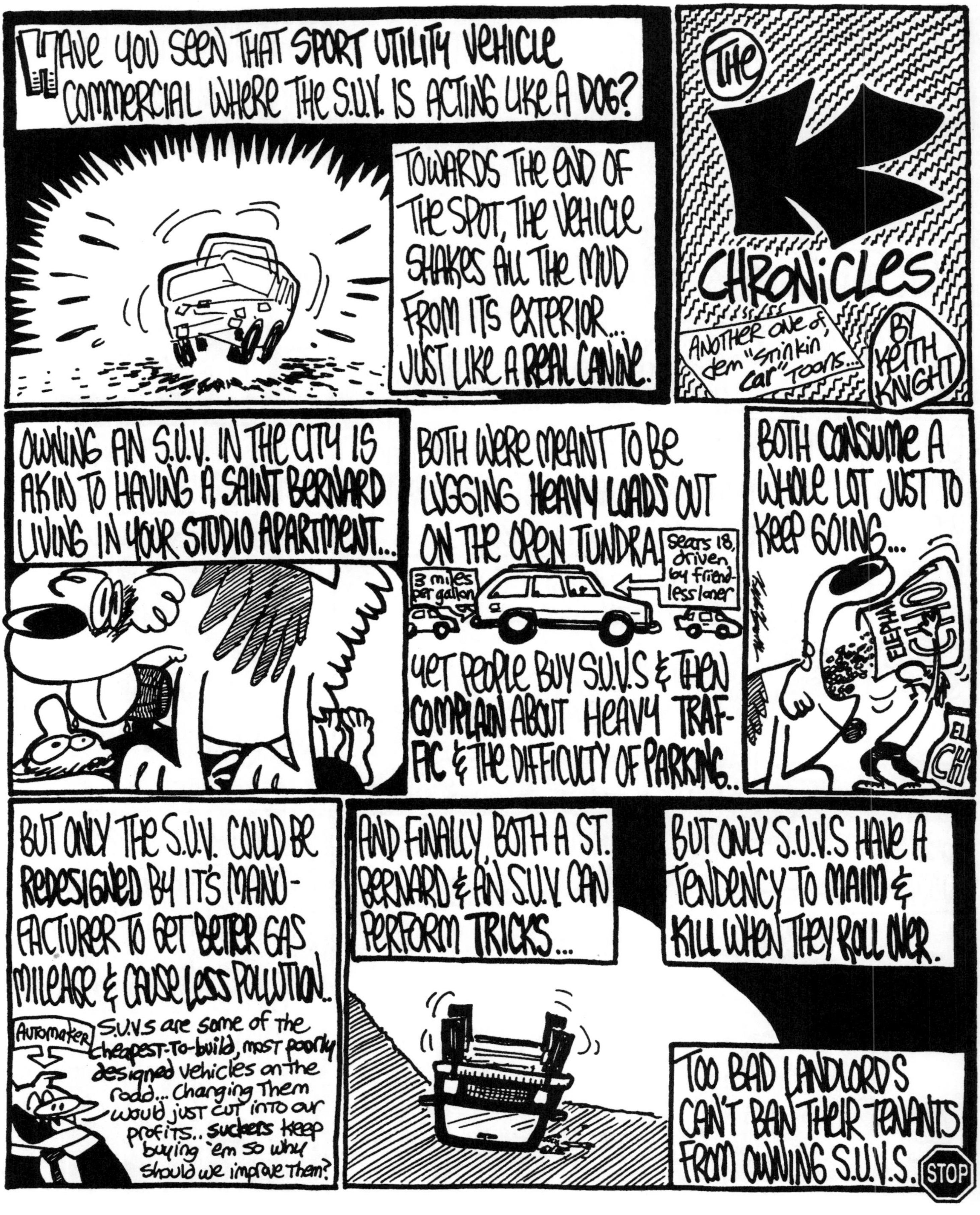

Have you seen that sport utility vehicle commercial where the S.U.V. is acting like a dog?
The K Chronicles
Another one of dem "stinkin car" toons...
By Keith Knight
Towards the end of the spot, the vehicle shakes all the mud from its exterior... just like a real canine.
Owning an S.U.V. in the city is akin to having a Saint Bernard living in your studio apartment...
Both were meant to be lugging heavy loads out on the open tundra.
3 miles per gallon
Seats 18, driven by friendless loner
Yet people buy S.U.V.s & then complain about heavy traffic & the difficulty of parking..
Both consume a whole lot just to keep going...
But only the S.U.V. could be redesigned by it's manufacturer to get better gas mileage & cause less pollution..
Automaker
S.U.V.s are some of the cheapest-to-build, most poorly designed vehicles on the road... Changing them would just cut into our profits.. suckers keep buying 'em so why should we improve them?
And finally, both a St. Bernard & an S.U.V. can perform tricks...
But only S.U.V.s have a tendency to maim & kill when they roll over.
Too bad landlords can't ban their tenants from owning S.U.V.s.
STOP

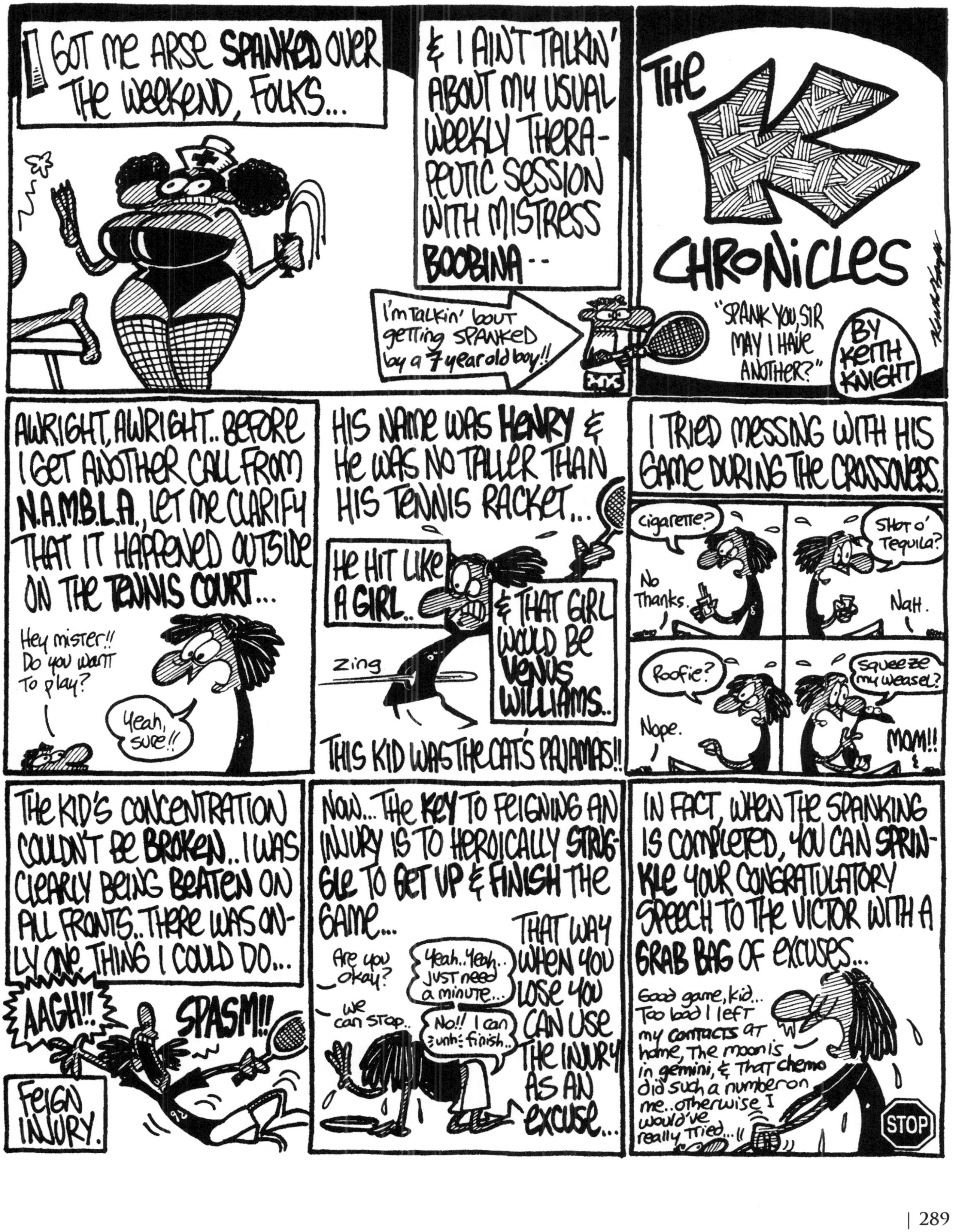
I GOT ME ARSE SPANKED OVER THE WEEKEND, FOLKS...
& I AIN'T TALKIN' ABOUT MY USUAL WEEKLY THERA-PEUTIC SESSION WITH MISTRESS BOOBINA--
I'm TALKIN' 'bout getting SPANKED by a 7 year old boy!!
THE K CHRONICLES
"SPANK YOU, SIR MAY I HAVE ANOTHER?"
BY KEITH KNIGHT
AWRIGHT, AWRIGHT.. BEFORE I GET ANOTHER CALL FROM N.A.M.B.L.A., LET ME CLARIFY THAT IT HAPPENED OUTSIDE ON THE TENNIS COURT...
Hey mister!! Do you want to play?
Yeah, sure!!
HIS NAME WAS HENRY & HE WAS NO TALLER THAN HIS TENNIS RACKET...
HE HIT LIKE A GIRL..
& THAT GIRL WOULD BE VENUS WILLIAMS..
Zing
THIS KID WAS THE CAT'S PAJAMAS!!
I TRIED MESSING WITH HIS GAME DURING THE CROSSOVERS..
Cigarette?
No Thanks.
Shot o' Tequila?
Nah.
Roofie?
Nope.
Squeeze my weasel?
MOM!!
THE KID'S CONCENTRATION COULDN'T BE BROKEN.. I WAS CLEARLY BEING BEATEN ON ALL FRONTS.. THERE WAS ONLY ONE THING I COULD DO...
AAGH!!
SPASM!!
FEIGN INJURY.
NOW... THE KEY TO FEIGNING AN INJURY IS TO HEROICALLY STRUGGLE TO GET UP & FINISH THE GAME...
Are you okay?
Yeah.. Yeah.. JUST need a minute...
we can stop..
No!! I can unh: finish..
THAT WAY WHEN YOU LOSE YOU CAN USE THE INJURY AS AN EXCUSE...
IN FACT, WHEN THE SPANKING IS COMPLETED, YOU CAN SPRINKLE YOUR CONGRATULATORY SPEECH TO THE VICTOR WITH A GRAB BAG OF EXCUSES...
Good game, kid... Too bad I left my CONTACTS at home, The moon is in gemini, & That chemo did such a number on me.. otherwise I would've really Tried...!!
STOP

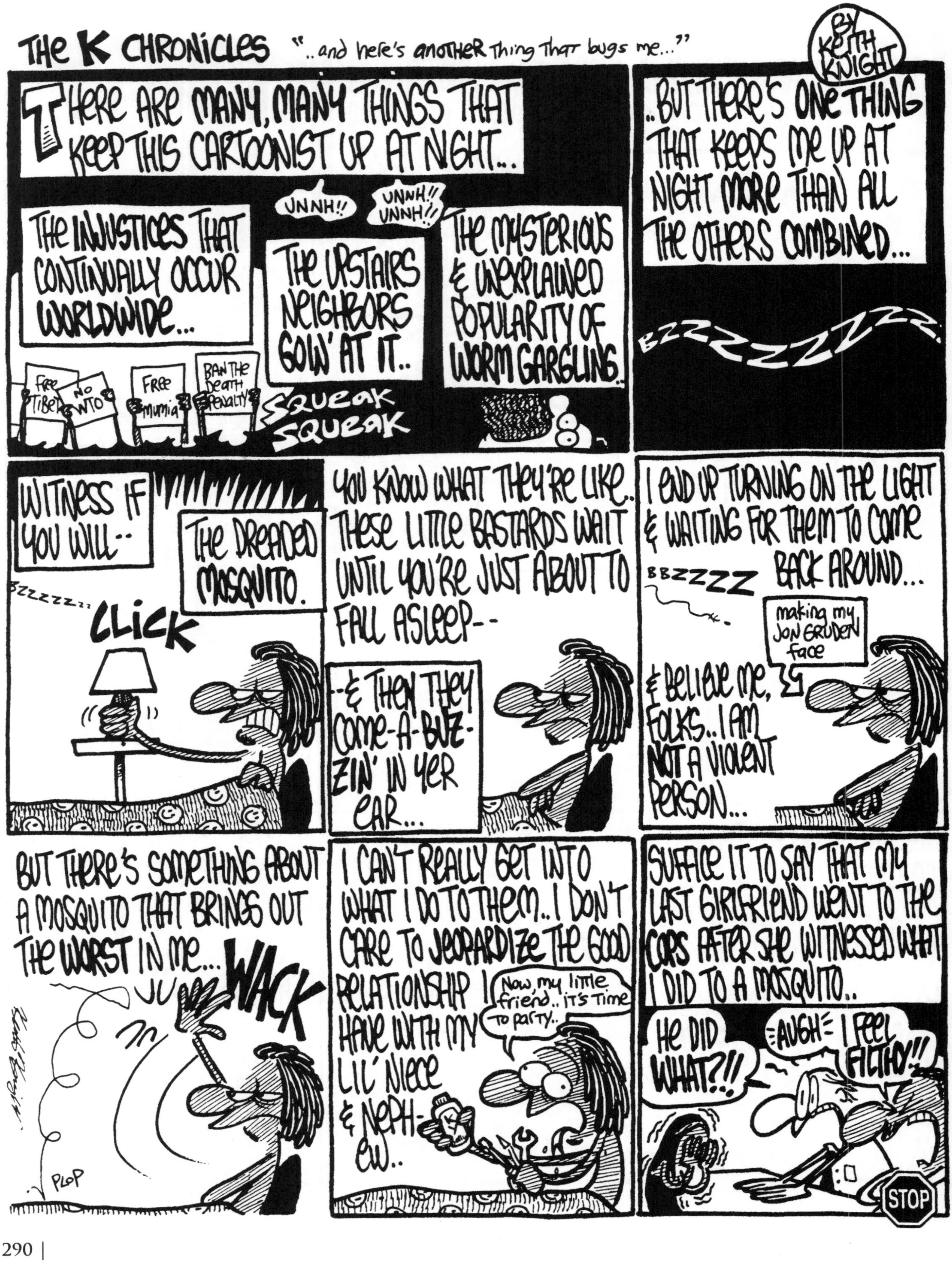
THE K CHRONICLES
"..and here's ANOTHER thing that bugs me..."
BY KEITH KNIGHT
THERE ARE MANY, MANY THINGS THAT KEEP THIS CARTOONIST UP AT NIGHT...
THE INJUSTICES THAT CONTINUALLY OCCUR WORLDWIDE...
Free Tibet
No WTO
Free Mumia
BAN THE DEATH PENALTY
THE UPSTAIRS NEIGHBORS GOIN' AT IT..
UNNH!!
UNNH!! UNNH!!
SQUEAK SQUEAK
THE MYSTERIOUS & UNEXPLAINED POPULARITY OF WORM GARGLING..
..BUT THERE'S ONE THING THAT KEEPS ME UP AT NIGHT MORE THAN ALL THE OTHERS COMBINED...
BZZZZZZZZZ
WITNESS IF YOU WILL--
THE DREADED MOSQUITO.
ZZZZZZ
CLICK
YOU KNOW WHAT THEY'RE LIKE.. THESE LITTLE BASTARDS WAIT UNTIL YOU'RE JUST ABOUT TO FALL ASLEEP--
--& THEN THEY COME-A-BUZ-ZIN' IN YER EAR...
I END UP TURNING ON THE LIGHT & WAITING FOR THEM TO COME BACK AROUND...
BBZZZZ
making my JON GRUDEN face
& BELIEVE ME, FOLKS.. I AM NOT A VIOLENT PERSON...
BUT THERE'S SOMETHING ABOUT A MOSQUITO THAT BRINGS OUT THE WORST IN ME...
WACK
PLOP
I CAN'T REALLY GET INTO WHAT I DO TO THEM.. I DON'T CARE TO JEOPARDIZE THE GOOD RELATIONSHIP I HAVE WITH MY LIL' NIECE & NEPH-EW..
Now, my little friend.. it's time to party..
SUFFICE IT TO SAY THAT MY LAST GIRLFRIEND WENT TO THE COPS AFTER SHE WITNESSED WHAT I DID TO A MOSQUITO..
HE DID WHAT?!!
AUGH! I FEEL FILTHY!!
STOP

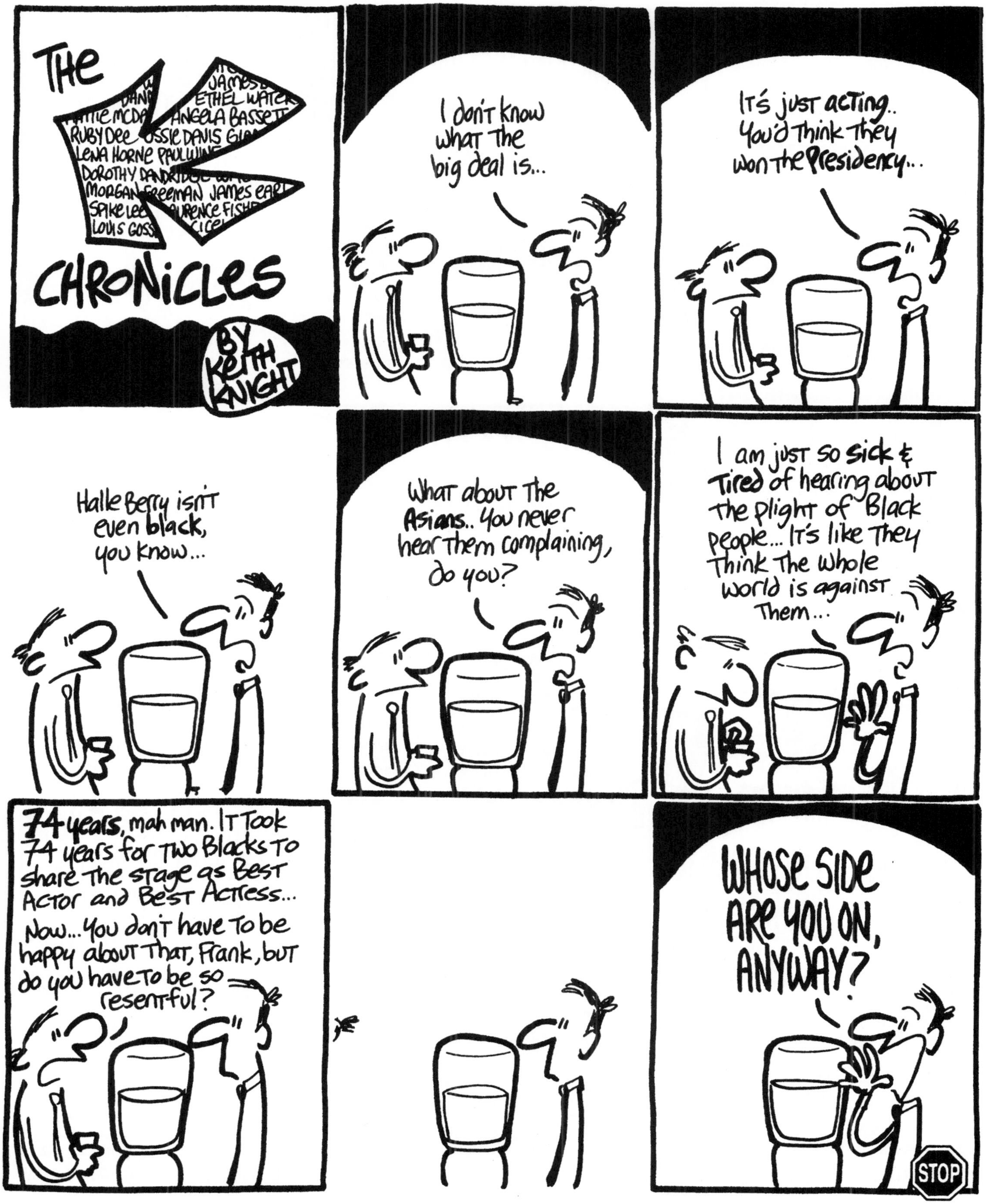
THE K CHRONICLES
JAMES ETHEL WATE HATTIE MCDA ANGELA BASSETT RUBY DEE OSSIE DAVIS LENA HORNE DOROTHY DANDRIDGE MORGAN FREEMAN JAMES EARL SPIKE LEE LAURENCE FISH LOUIS GOSS
BY KEITH KNIGHT
I don't know what the big deal is...
It's just acting.. You'd think they won the Presidency...
Halle Berry isn't even black, you know...
What about the Asians.. You never hear them complaining, do you?
I am just so sick & tired of hearing about the plight of Black people... It's like they think the whole world is against them...
74 years, mah man. It took 74 years for two Blacks to share the stage as Best Actor and Best Actress...
Now... You don't have to be happy about that, Frank, but do you have to be so resentful?
WHOSE SIDE ARE YOU ON, ANYWAY?
STOP

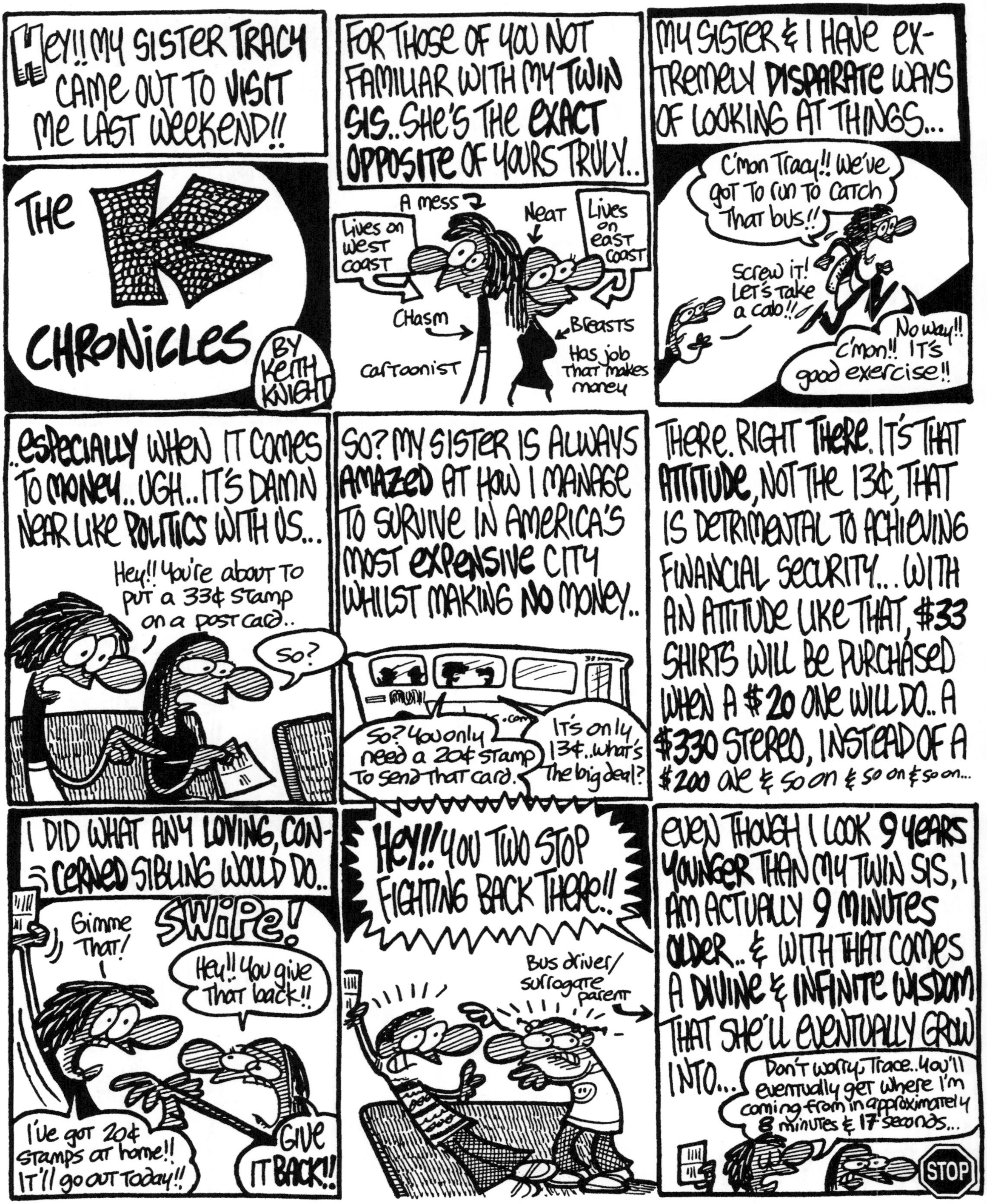
HEY!! MY SISTER TRACY CAME OUT TO VISIT ME LAST WEEKEND!!
THE K CHRONICLES
BY KEITH KNIGHT
FOR THOSE OF YOU NOT FAMILIAR WITH MY TWIN SIS.. SHE'S THE EXACT OPPOSITE OF YOURS TRULY..
A mess
Neat
Lives on west coast
Lives on east coast
CHasm
Breasts
Cartoonist
Has job that makes money
MY SISTER & I HAVE EXTREMELY DISPARATE WAYS OF LOOKING AT THINGS...
C'mon Tracy!! We've got to run to catch that bus!!
Screw it! Let's take a cab!!
No way!! C'mon!! It's good exercise!!
..ESPECIALLY WHEN IT COMES TO MONEY.. UGH.. IT'S DAMN NEAR LIKE POLITICS WITH US...
Hey!! You're about to put a 33¢ stamp on a post card..
So?
SO? MY SISTER IS ALWAYS AMAZED AT HOW I MANAGE TO SURVIVE IN AMERICA'S MOST EXPENSIVE CITY WHILST MAKING NO MONEY..
So? You only need a 20¢ stamp to send that card.
It's only 13¢.. what's the big deal?
THERE. RIGHT THERE. IT'S THAT ATTITUDE, NOT THE 13¢, THAT IS DETRIMENTAL TO ACHIEVING FINANCIAL SECURITY... WITH AN ATTITUDE LIKE THAT, $33 SHIRTS WILL BE PURCHASED WHEN A $20 ONE WILL DO.. A $330 STEREO, INSTEAD OF A $200 ONE & SO ON & SO ON & SO ON...
I DID WHAT ANY LOVING, CONCERNED SIBLING WOULD DO..
SWIPE!
Gimme That!
Hey!! You give that back!!
I've got 20¢ stamps at home!! It'll go out today!!
GIVE IT BACK!!
HEY!! YOU TWO STOP FIGHTING BACK THERE!!
Bus driver/ surrogate parent
EVEN THOUGH I LOOK 9 YEARS YOUNGER THAN MY TWIN SIS, I AM ACTUALLY 9 MINUTES OLDER.. & WITH THAT COMES A DIVINE & INFINITE WISDOM THAT SHE'LL EVENTUALLY GROW INTO...
Don't worry, Trace.. You'll eventually get where I'm coming from in approximately 8 minutes & 17 seconds...
STOP

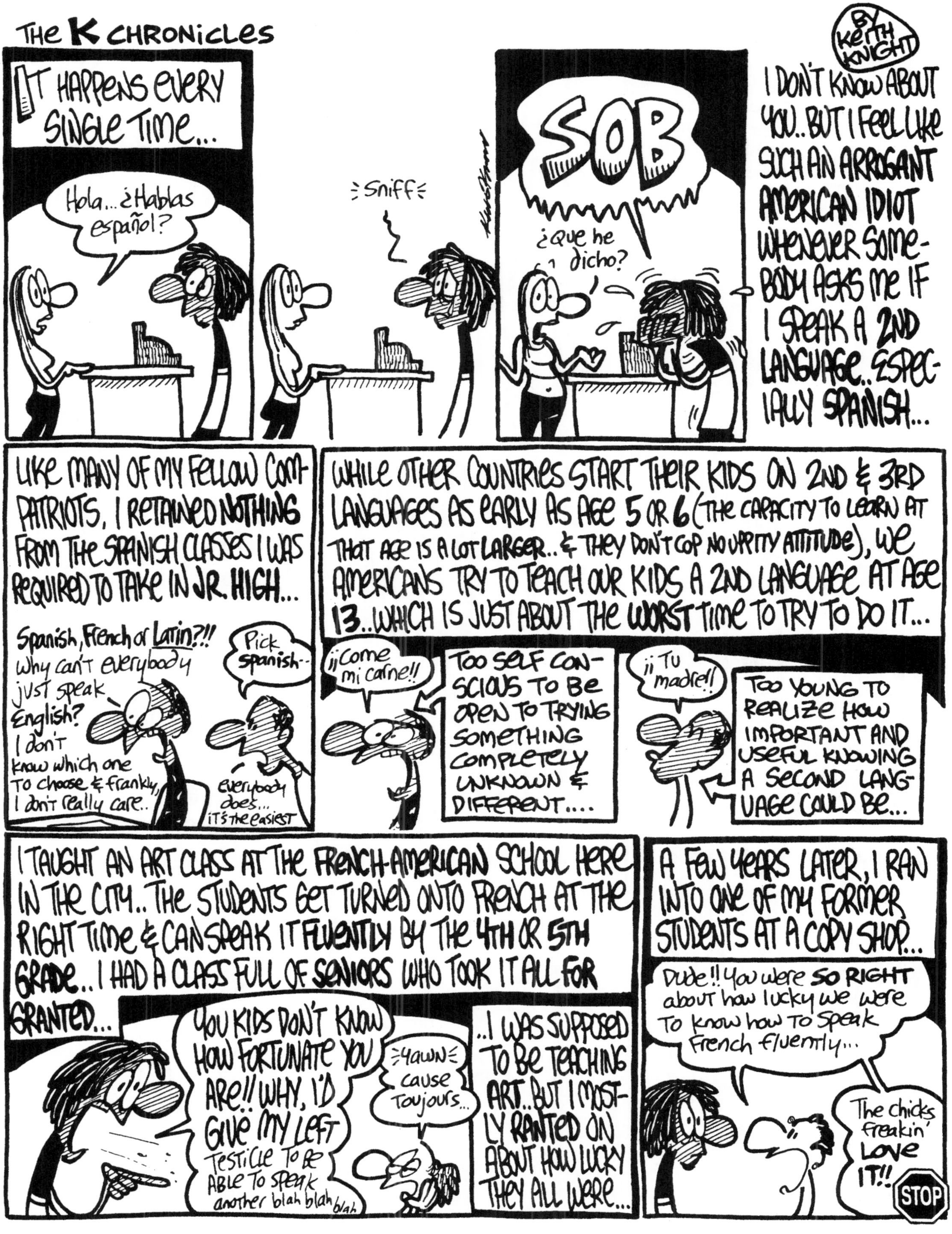
THE K CHRONICLES
BY KEITH KNIGHT
IT HAPPENS EVERY SINGLE TIME...
Hola... ¿Hablas español?
Sniff
SOB
¿Que he dicho?
I DON'T KNOW ABOUT YOU.. BUT I FEEL LIKE SUCH AN ARROGANT AMERICAN IDIOT WHENEVER SOMEBODY ASKS ME IF I SPEAK A 2ND LANGUAGE.. ESPECIALLY SPANISH...
LIKE MANY OF MY FELLOW COMPATRIOTS, I RETAINED NOTHING FROM THE SPANISH CLASSES I WAS REQUIRED TO TAKE IN JR. HIGH...
Spanish, French or Latin?!! Why can't everybody just speak English? I don't know which one to choose & frankly, I don't really care..
Pick spanish..
everybody does... it's the easiest
WHILE OTHER COUNTRIES START THEIR KIDS ON 2ND & 3RD LANGUAGES AS EARLY AS AGE 5 OR 6 (THE CAPACITY TO LEARN AT THAT AGE IS A LOT LARGER... & THEY DON'T COP NO UPPITY ATTITUDE), WE AMERICANS TRY TO TEACH OUR KIDS A 2ND LANGUAGE AT AGE 13.. WHICH IS JUST ABOUT THE WORST TIME TO TRY TO DO IT...
¡¡Come mi carne!!
TOO SELF CONSCIOUS TO BE OPEN TO TRYING SOMETHING COMPLETELY UNKNOWN & DIFFERENT....
¡¡Tu madre!!
TOO YOUNG TO REALIZE HOW IMPORTANT AND USEFUL KNOWING A SECOND LANGUAGE COULD BE...
I TAUGHT AN ART CLASS AT THE FRENCH-AMERICAN SCHOOL HERE IN THE CITY.. THE STUDENTS GET TURNED ONTO FRENCH AT THE RIGHT TIME & CAN SPEAK IT FLUENTLY BY THE 4TH OR 5TH GRADE... I HAD A CLASS FULL OF SENIORS WHO TOOK IT ALL FOR GRANTED...
YOU KIDS DON'T KNOW HOW FORTUNATE YOU ARE!! WHY, I'D GIVE MY LEFT TESTICLE TO BE ABLE TO SPEAK another blah blah blah
Yawn cause toujours...
..I WAS SUPPOSED TO BE TEACHING ART.. BUT I MOSTLY RANTED ON ABOUT HOW LUCKY THEY ALL WERE...
A FEW YEARS LATER, I RAN INTO ONE OF MY FORMER STUDENTS AT A COPY SHOP...
Dude!! You were SO RIGHT about how lucky we were to know how to speak French fluently...
The chicks freakin' LOVE IT!!
STOP

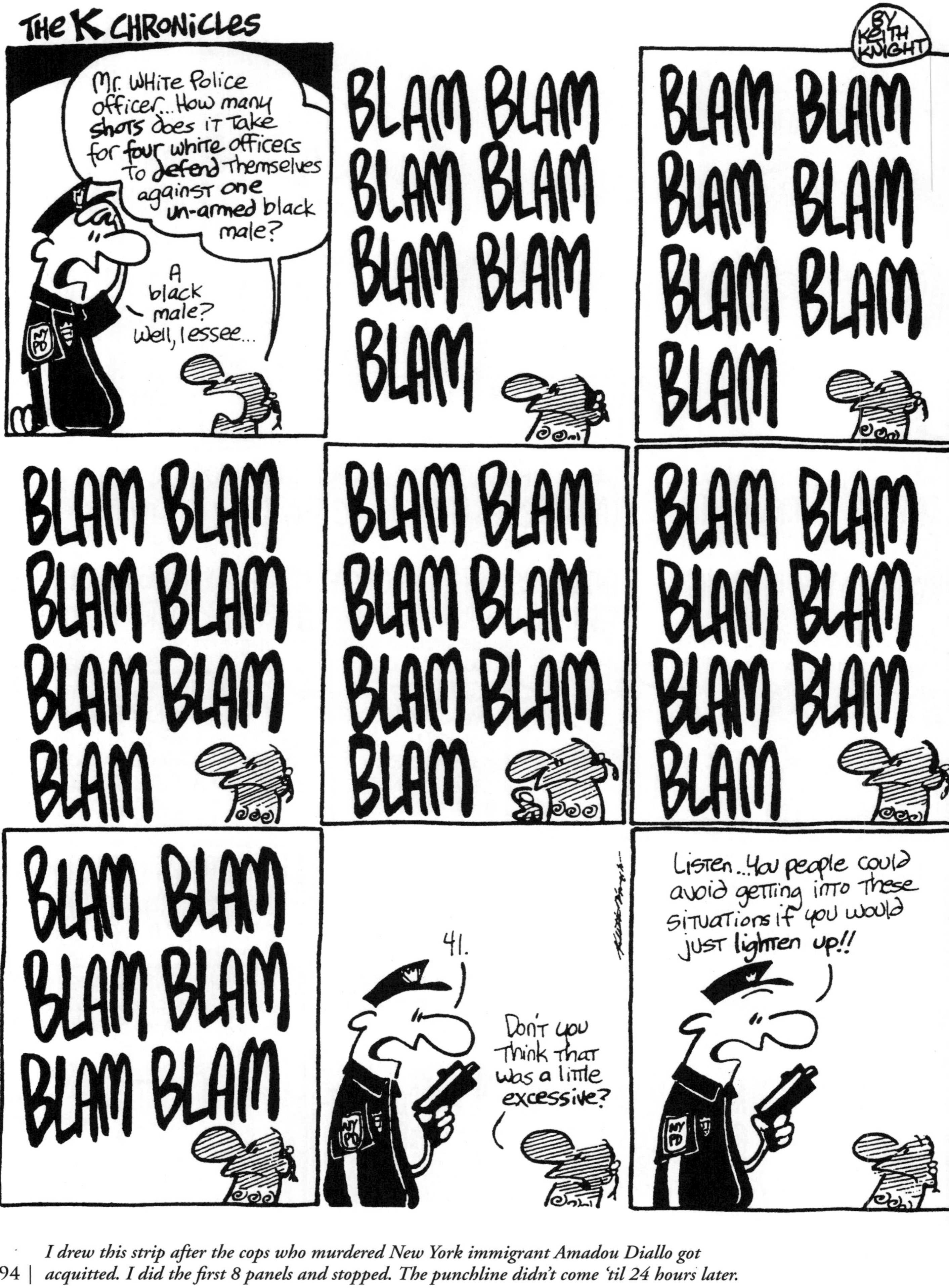
THE K CHRONICLES
BY KEITH KNIGHT
Mr. White Police officer... How many shots does it take for four white officers to defend themselves against one un-armed black male?
A black male? Well, lessee...
BLAM BLAM BLAM BLAM BLAM BLAM BLAM
BLAM BLAM BLAM BLAM BLAM BLAM BLAM
BLAM BLAM BLAM BLAM BLAM BLAM BLAM
BLAM BLAM BLAM BLAM BLAM BLAM BLAM
BLAM BLAM BLAM BLAM BLAM BLAM BLAM
BLAM BLAM BLAM BLAM BLAM BLAM
41.
Don't you think that was a little excessive?
Listen... You people could avoid getting into these situations if you would just lighten up!!

I drew this strip after the cops who murdered New York immigrant Amadou Diallo got acquitted. I did the first 8 panels and stopped. The punchline didn't come 'til 24 hours later.

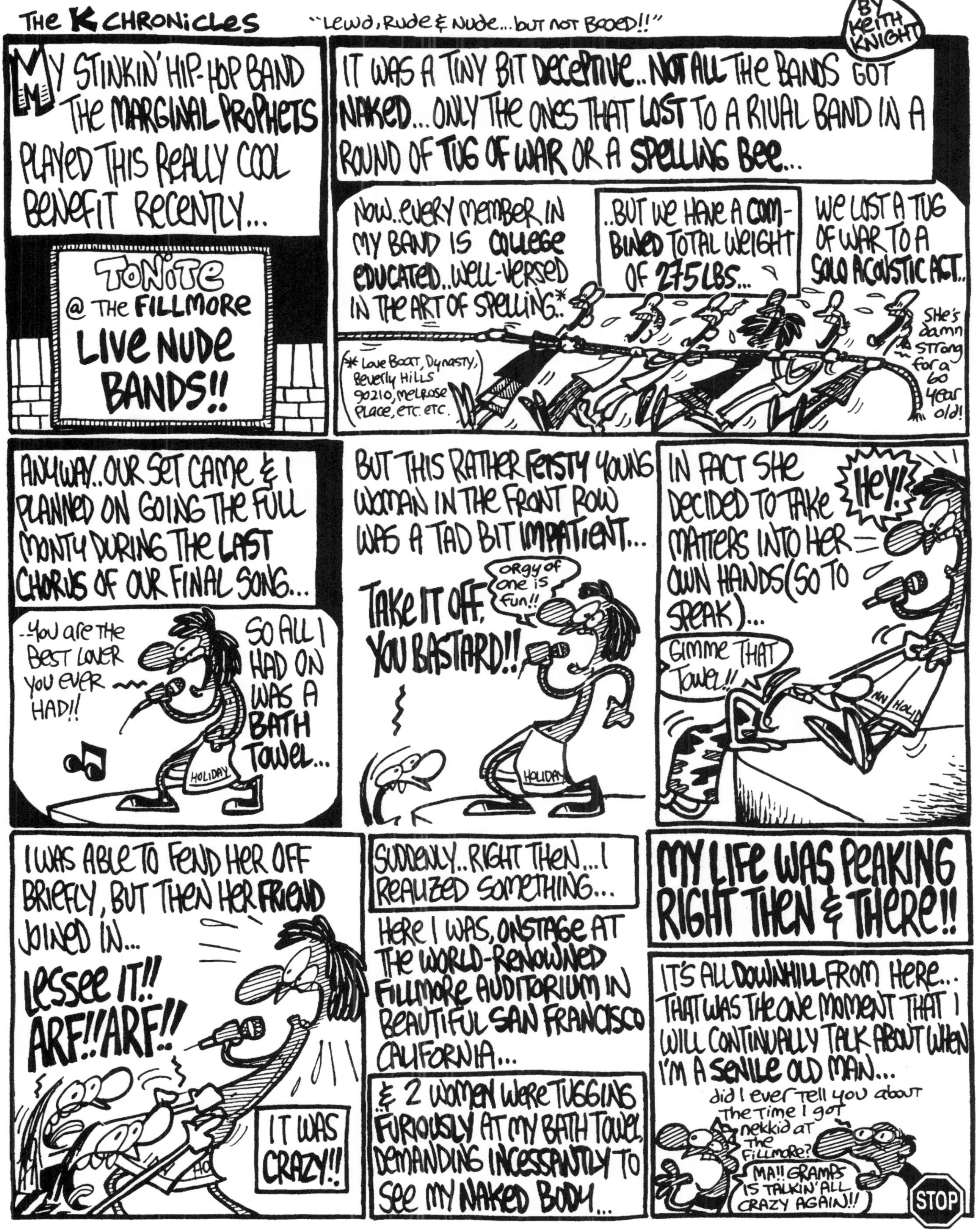
THE K CHRONICLES
"LEWD, RUDE & NUDE... BUT NOT BOOED!!"
BY KEITH KNIGHT
MY STINKIN' HIP-HOP BAND THE MARGINAL PROPHETS PLAYED THIS REALLY COOL BENEFIT RECENTLY...
TONITE @ THE FILLMORE LIVE NUDE BANDS!!
IT WAS A TINY BIT DECEPTIVE.. NOT ALL THE BANDS GOT NAKED... ONLY THE ONES THAT LOST TO A RIVAL BAND IN A ROUND OF TUG OF WAR OR A SPELLING BEE...
NOW.. EVERY MEMBER IN MY BAND IS COLLEGE EDUCATED.. WELL-VERSED IN THE ART OF SPELLING.*
..BUT WE HAVE A COMBINED TOTAL WEIGHT OF 275 LBS...
WE LOST A TUG OF WAR TO A SOLO ACOUSTIC ACT..
SHE'S DAMN STRONG FOR A 60 YEAR OLD!
(* LOVE BOAT, DYNASTY, BEVERLY HILLS 90210, MELROSE PLACE, ETC. ETC.
ANYWAY.. OUR SET CAME & I PLANNED ON GOING THE FULL MONTY DURING THE LAST CHORUS OF OUR FINAL SONG...
-YOU ARE THE BEST LOVER YOU EVER HAD!!
SO ALL I HAD ON WAS A BATH TOWEL...
HOLIDAY
BUT THIS RATHER FEISTY YOUNG WOMAN IN THE FRONT ROW WAS A TAD BIT IMPATIENT...
TAKE IT OFF, YOU BASTARD!!
ORGY OF ONE IS FUN!!
HOLIDAY
IN FACT SHE DECIDED TO TAKE MATTERS INTO HER OWN HANDS (SO TO SPEAK)...
HEY!!
GIMME THAT TOWEL!!
I WAS ABLE TO FEND HER OFF BRIEFLY, BUT THEN HER FRIEND JOINED IN...
LESSEE IT!! ARF!! ARF!!
IT WAS CRAZY!!
SUDDENLY.. RIGHT THEN... I REALIZED SOMETHING...
HERE I WAS, ONSTAGE AT THE WORLD-RENOWNED FILLMORE AUDITORIUM IN BEAUTIFUL SAN FRANCISCO CALIFORNIA...
& 2 WOMEN WERE TUGGING FURIOUSLY AT MY BATH TOWEL, DEMANDING INCESSANTLY TO SEE MY NAKED BODY...
MY LIFE WAS PEAKING RIGHT THEN & THERE!!
IT'S ALL DOWNHILL FROM HERE... THAT WAS THE ONE MOMENT THAT I WILL CONTINUALLY TALK ABOUT WHEN I'M A SENILE OLD MAN...
DID I EVER TELL YOU ABOUT THE TIME I GOT NEKKID AT THE FILLMORE?
MA!! GRAMPS IS TALKIN' ALL CRAZY AGAIN!!
STOP

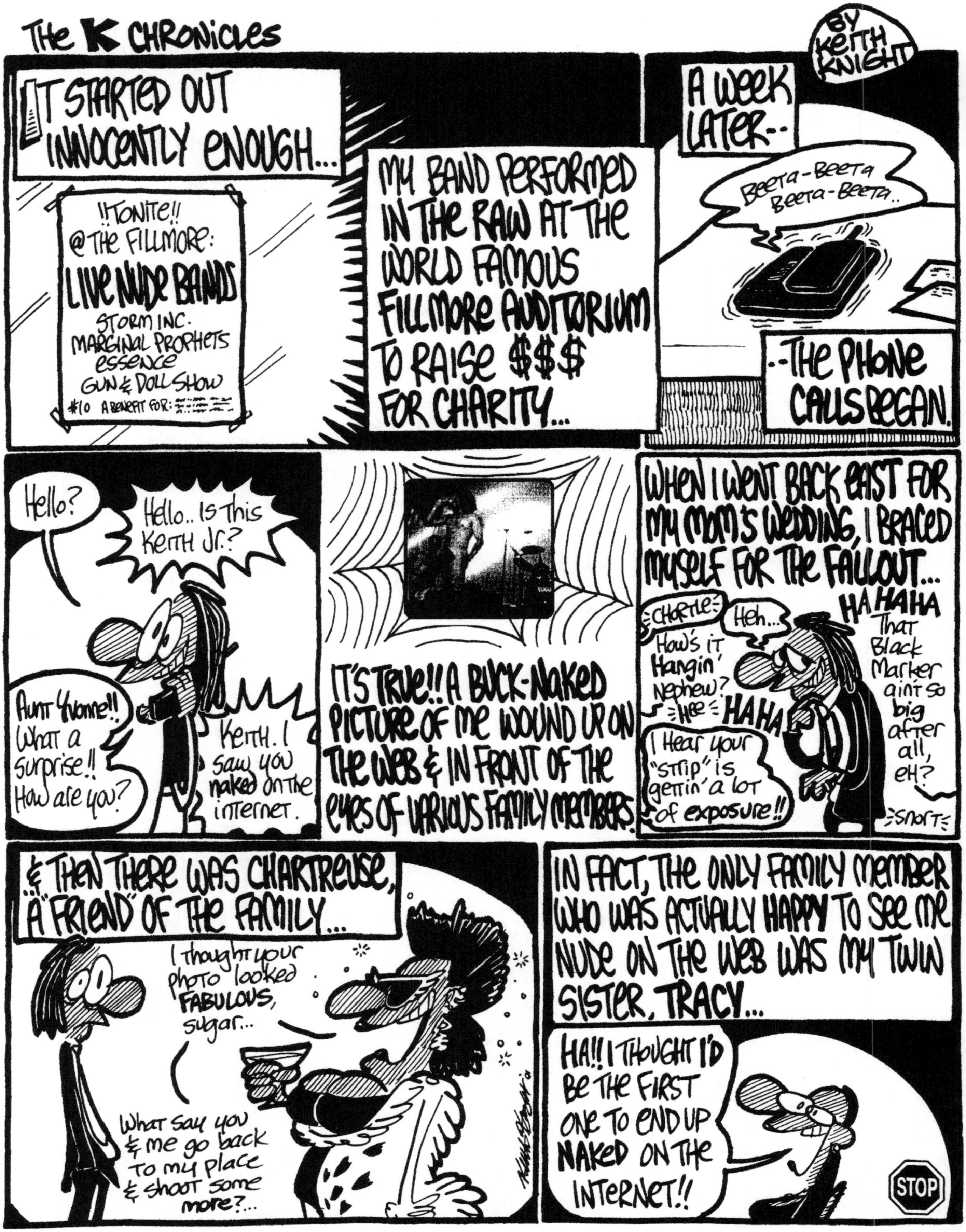

The K Chronicles
By Keith Knight
It started out innocently enough...
!!Tonite!! @ The Fillmore: Live Nude Bands
Storm Inc.
Marginal Prophets
Essence
Gun & Doll Show
#10 A benefit for:
My band performed in the raw at the world famous Fillmore Auditorium to raise $$$ for charity...
A week later...
Beeta-Beeta Beeta-Beeta..
..The phone calls began.
Hello?
Hello.. Is this Keith Jr.?
Aunt Yvonne!! What a surprise!! How are you?
Keith. I saw you naked on the internet.
It's true!! A buck-naked picture of me wound up on the web & in front of the eyes of various family members.
When I went back east for my mom's wedding, I braced myself for the fallout...
Chortle
How's it Hangin' nephew?
Hee
Heh...
HA HAHA
HA HA
That Black Marker ain't so big after all, eh?
I hear your "strip" is gettin' a lot of exposure!!
Snort
...& then there was Chartreuse, "a" "friend" of the family...
I thought your photo looked FABULOUS, sugar...
What say you & me go back to my place & shoot some more?...
In fact, the only family member who was actually happy to see me nude on the web was my twin sister, Tracy...
HA!! I thought I'd be the first one to end up naked on the internet!!
STOP

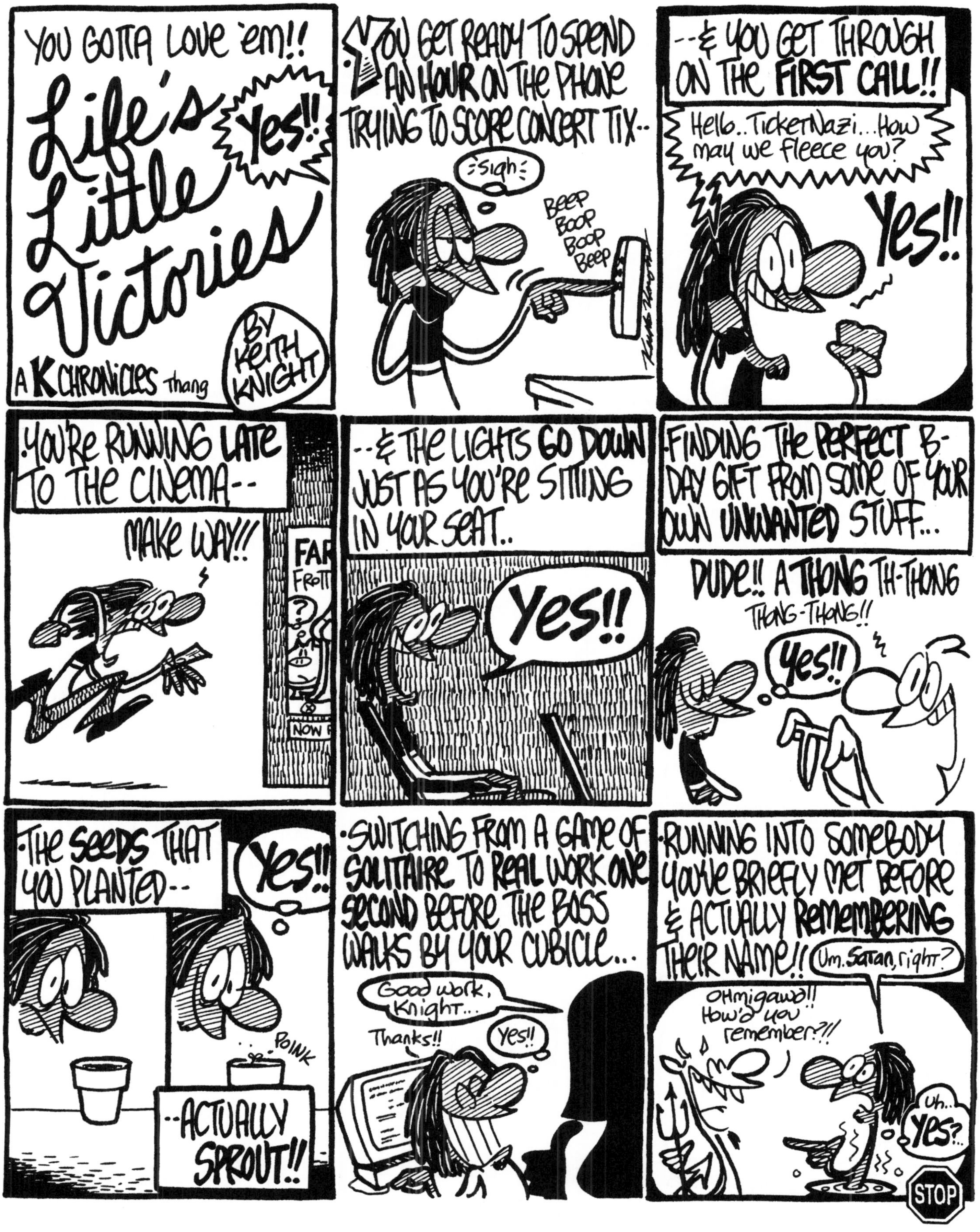

YOU GOTTA LOVE 'EM!!
Life's Little Victories
Yes!!
A K CHRONICLES thang
BY KEITH KNIGHT
YOU GET READY TO SPEND AN HOUR ON THE PHONE TRYING TO SCORE CONCERT TIX..
sigh
BEEP BOOP BOOP BEEP
--& YOU GET THROUGH ON THE FIRST CALL!!
Hello..TicketNazi...How may we fleece you?
Yes!!
YOU'RE RUNNING LATE TO THE CINEMA--
MAKE WAY!!
--& THE LIGHTS GO DOWN JUST AS YOU'RE SITTING IN YOUR SEAT..
Yes!!
FINDING THE PERFECT B-DAY GIFT FROM SOME OF YOUR OWN UNWANTED STUFF...
DUDE!! A THONG TH-THONG THONG-THONG!!
Yes!!
THE SEEDS THAT YOU PLANTED--
Yes!!
POINK
--ACTUALLY SPROUT!!
SWITCHING FROM A GAME OF SOLITAIRE TO REAL WORK ONE SECOND BEFORE THE BOSS WALKS BY YOUR CUBICLE...
Good work, Knight...
Thanks!!
Yes!!
RUNNING INTO SOMEBODY YOU'VE BRIEFLY MET BEFORE & ACTUALLY REMEMBERING THEIR NAME!!
Um. Satan, right?
OHmigawd!! How'd you remember?!!
Uh... Yes?...
STOP

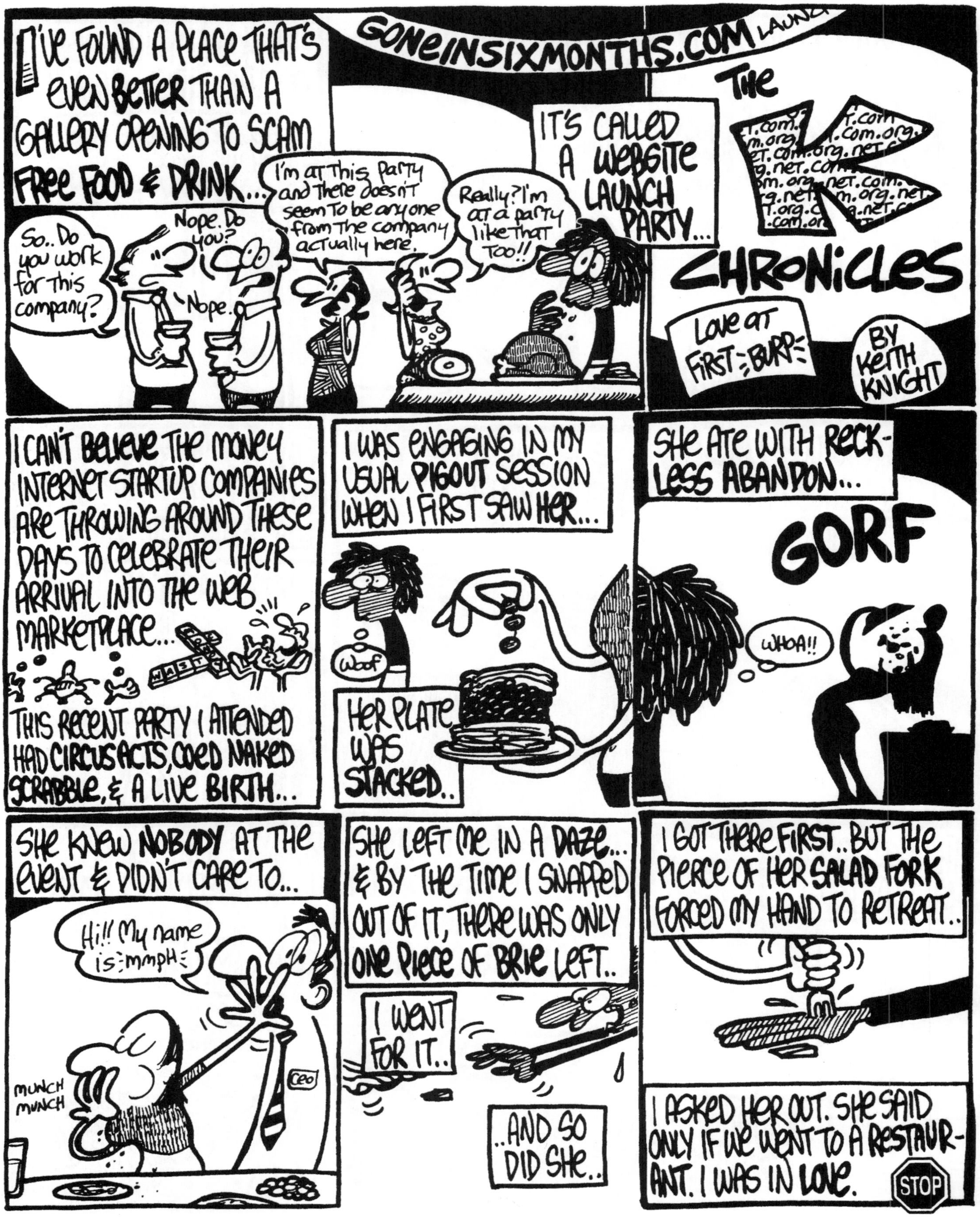
GONEINSIXMONTHS.COM LAUNC
I'VE FOUND A PLACE THAT'S EVEN BETTER THAN A GALLERY OPENING TO SCAM FREE FOOD & DRINK...
IT'S CALLED A WEBSITE LAUNCH PARTY...
THE K CHRONICLES
Love at FIRST BURP
BY KEITH KNIGHT
So.. Do you work for this company?
Nope. Do you?
Nope.
I'm at this party and there doesn't seem to be anyone from the company actually here.
Really? I'm at a party like that too!!
I CAN'T BELIEVE THE MONEY INTERNET STARTUP COMPANIES ARE THROWING AROUND THESE DAYS TO CELEBRATE THEIR ARRIVAL INTO THE WEB MARKETPLACE...
THIS RECENT PARTY I ATTENDED HAD CIRCUS ACTS, COED NAKED SCRABBLE, & A LIVE BIRTH...
I WAS ENGAGING IN MY USUAL PIGOUT SESSION WHEN I FIRST SAW HER...
Woof
HER PLATE WAS STACKED..
SHE ATE WITH RECKLESS ABANDON...
GORF
WHOA!!
SHE KNEW NOBODY AT THE EVENT & DIDN'T CARE TO...
Hi!! My name is mmpH
MUNCH MUNCH
CEO
SHE LEFT ME IN A DAZE... & BY THE TIME I SNAPPED OUT OF IT, THERE WAS ONLY ONE PIECE OF BRIE LEFT..
I WENT FOR IT..
..AND SO DID SHE..
I GOT THERE FIRST.. BUT THE PIERCE OF HER SALAD FORK FORCED MY HAND TO RETREAT..
I ASKED HER OUT. SHE SAID ONLY IF WE WENT TO A RESTAURANT. I WAS IN LOVE.
STOP

 This woman lived in one of the biggest party houses in San Francisco. I was too old to deal with it.

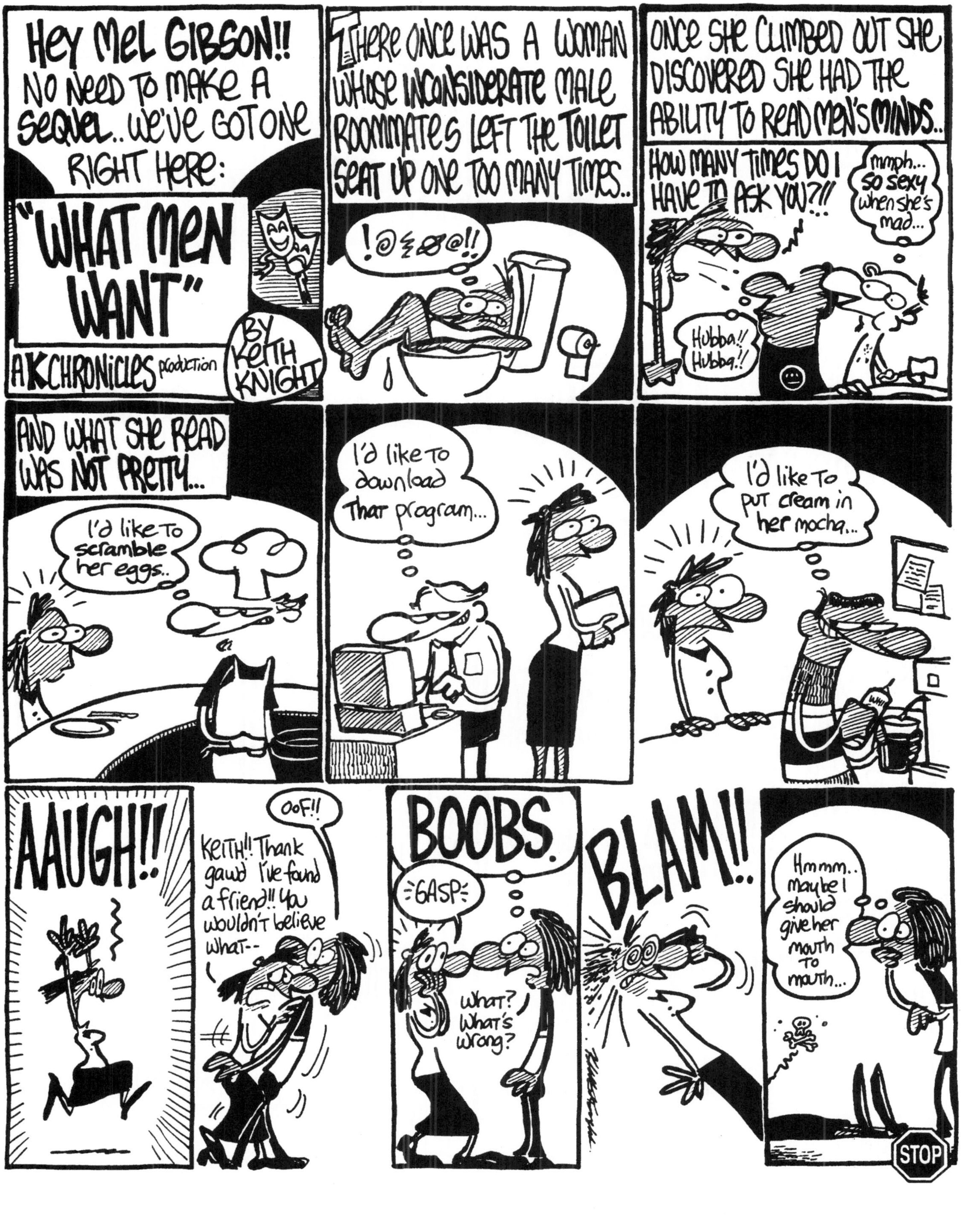

Hey Mel GIBSON!! NO Need TO MAKE A SEQUEL.. WE'VE GOT ONE RIGHT HERE:
"WHAT MEN WANT"
A K CHRONICLES production
BY KEITH KNIGHT
THERE ONCE WAS A WOMAN WHOSE INCONSIDERATE MALE ROOMMATES LEFT THE TOILET SEAT UP ONE TOO MANY TIMES..
ONCE SHE CLIMBED OUT SHE DISCOVERED SHE HAD THE ABILITY TO READ MEN'S MINDS..
HOW MANY TIMES DO I HAVE TO ASK YOU?!!
mmph... so sexy when she's mad...
Hubba!! Hubba!!
AND WHAT SHE READ WAS NOT PRETTY...
I'd like to scramble her eggs..
I'd like to download that program...
I'd like to put cream in her mocha...
AAUGH!!
OOF!!
KEITH!! Thank gawd I've found a friend!! You wouldn't believe what--
BOOBS.
GASP
WHAT? WHAT'S WRONG?
BLAM!!
Hmmm.. maybe I should give her mouth to mouth...
STOP

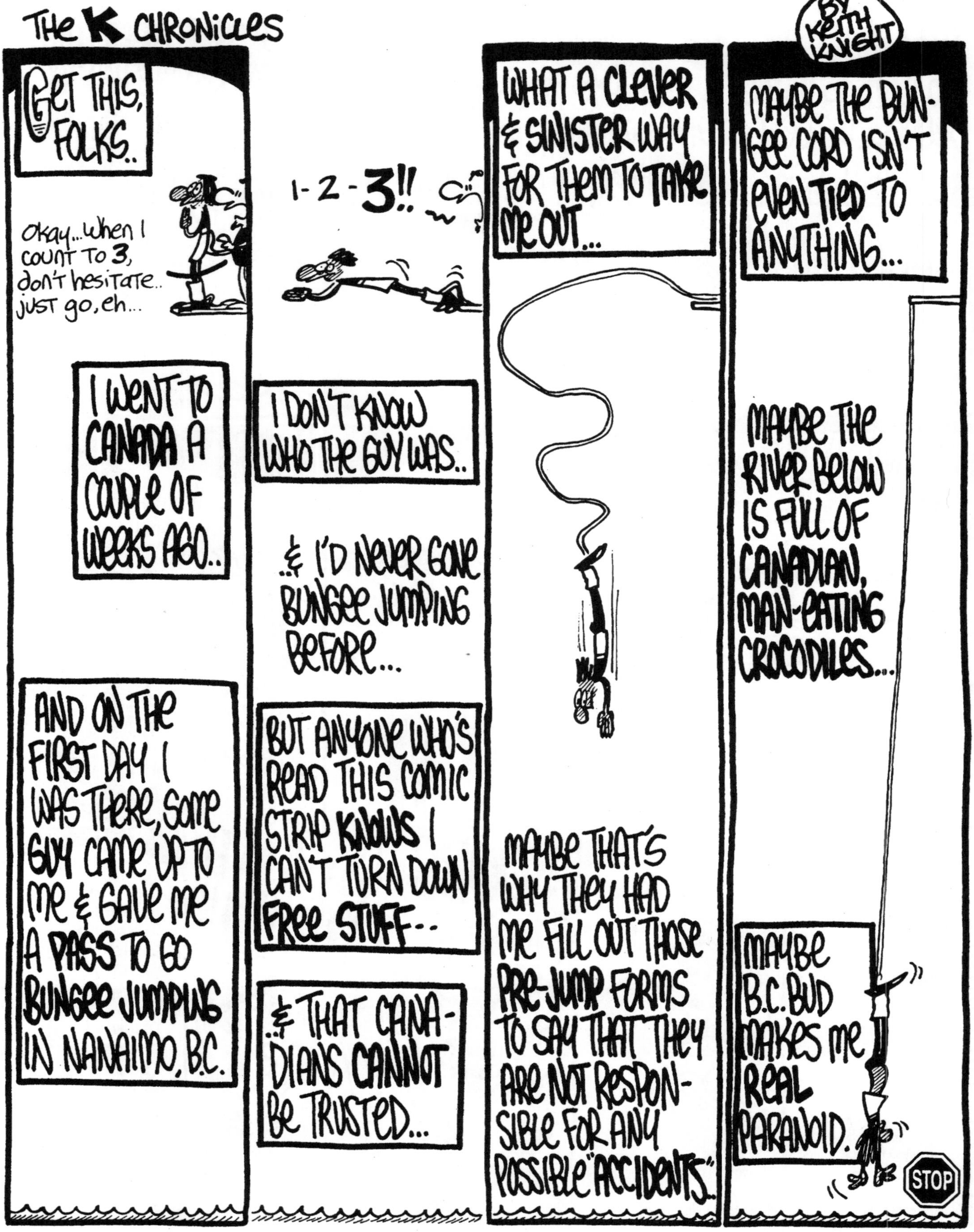
THE K CHRONICLES
BY KEITH KNIGHT
GET THIS, FOLKS..
Okay...When I count to 3, don't hesitate.. just go, eh...
1-2-3!!
WHAT A CLEVER & SINISTER WAY FOR THEM TO TAKE ME OUT...
MAYBE THE BUNGEE CORD ISN'T EVEN TIED TO ANYTHING...
I WENT TO CANADA A COUPLE OF WEEKS AGO..
I DON'T KNOW WHO THE GUY WAS..
..& I'D NEVER GONE BUNGEE JUMPING BEFORE...
MAYBE THE RIVER BELOW IS FULL OF CANADIAN, MAN-EATING CROCODILES....
AND ON THE FIRST DAY I WAS THERE, SOME GUY CAME UP TO ME & GAVE ME A PASS TO GO BUNGEE JUMPING IN NANAIMO, B.C.
BUT ANYONE WHO'S READ THIS COMIC STRIP KNOWS I CAN'T TURN DOWN FREE STUFF--
..& THAT CANADIANS CANNOT BE TRUSTED...
MAYBE THAT'S WHY THEY HAD ME FILL OUT THOSE PRE-JUMP FORMS TO SAY THAT THEY ARE NOT RESPONSIBLE FOR ANY POSSIBLE "ACCIDENTS"..
MAYBE B.C. BUD MAKES ME REAL PARANOID.
STOP

 I always enjoy tweaking the usual format to fit the story.

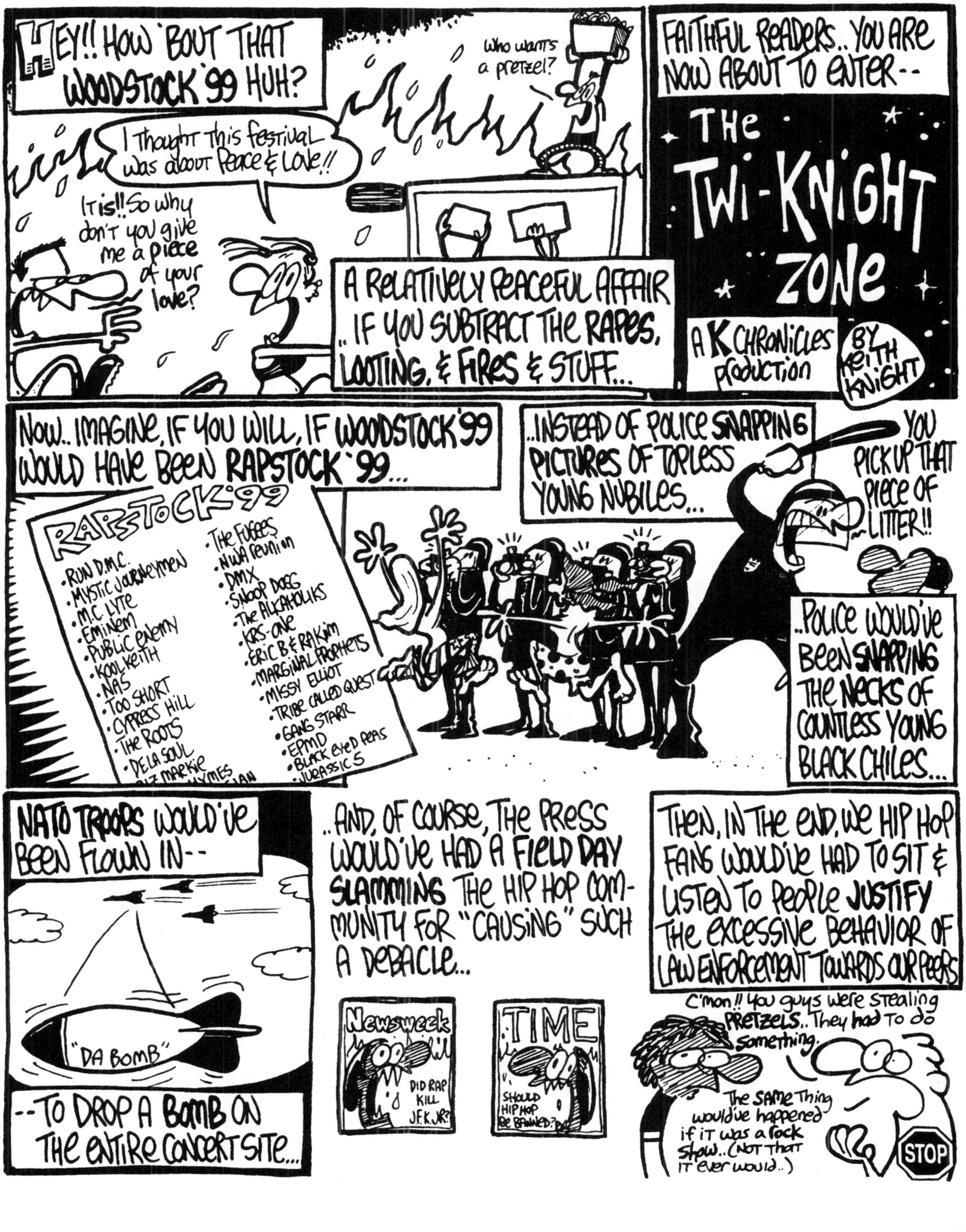

HEY!! HOW 'BOUT THAT WOODSTOCK '99 HUH?
Who wants a pretzel?
I thought this festival was about Peace & Love!!
It is!! So why don't you give me a piece of your love?
A RELATIVELY PEACEFUL AFFAIR.. IF YOU SUBTRACT THE RAPES, LOOTING, & FIRES & STUFF...
FAITHFUL READERS.. YOU ARE NOW ABOUT TO ENTER--
THE TWI-KNIGHT ZONE
A K CHRONICLES production
BY KEITH KNIGHT
NOW.. IMAGINE, IF YOU WILL, IF WOODSTOCK '99 WOULD HAVE BEEN RAPSTOCK '99...
RAPSTOCK '99
·RUN D.M.C.
·MYSTIC JOURNEYMEN
·M.C. LYTE
·EMINEM
·PUBLIC ENEMY
·KOOL KEITH
·NAS
·TOO SHORT
·CYPRESS HILL
·THE ROOTS
·DE LA SOUL
·THE FUGEES
·NWA reunion
·DMX
·SNOOP DOGG
·THE ALKAHOLIKS
·KRS-ONE
·ERIC B & RAKIM
·MARGINAL PROPHETS
·MISSY ELLIOT
·TRIBE CALLED QUEST
·GANG STARR
·EPMD
·BLACK EYED PEAS
·JURASSIC 5
..INSTEAD OF POLICE SNAPPING PICTURES OF TOPLESS YOUNG NUBILES...
YOU PICK UP THAT PIECE OF LITTER!!
..POLICE WOULD'VE BEEN SNAPPING THE NECKS OF COUNTLESS YOUNG BLACK CHILES...
NATO TROOPS WOULD'VE BEEN FLOWN IN--
"DA BOMB"
--TO DROP A BOMB ON THE ENTIRE CONCERT SITE...
..AND, OF COURSE, THE PRESS WOULD'VE HAD A FIELD DAY SLAMMING THE HIP HOP COMMUNITY FOR "CAUSING" SUCH A DEBACLE...
Newsweek
DID RAP KILL J.F.K. JR?
TIME
SHOULD HIP HOP BE BANNED?
THEN, IN THE END, WE HIP HOP FANS WOULD'VE HAD TO SIT & LISTEN TO PEOPLE JUSTIFY THE EXCESSIVE BEHAVIOR OF LAW ENFORCEMENT TOWARDS OUR PEERS
C'mon!! You guys were stealing PRETZELS.. They had to do something.
The same thing would've happened if it was a rock show.. (NOT THAT IT ever would..)
STOP

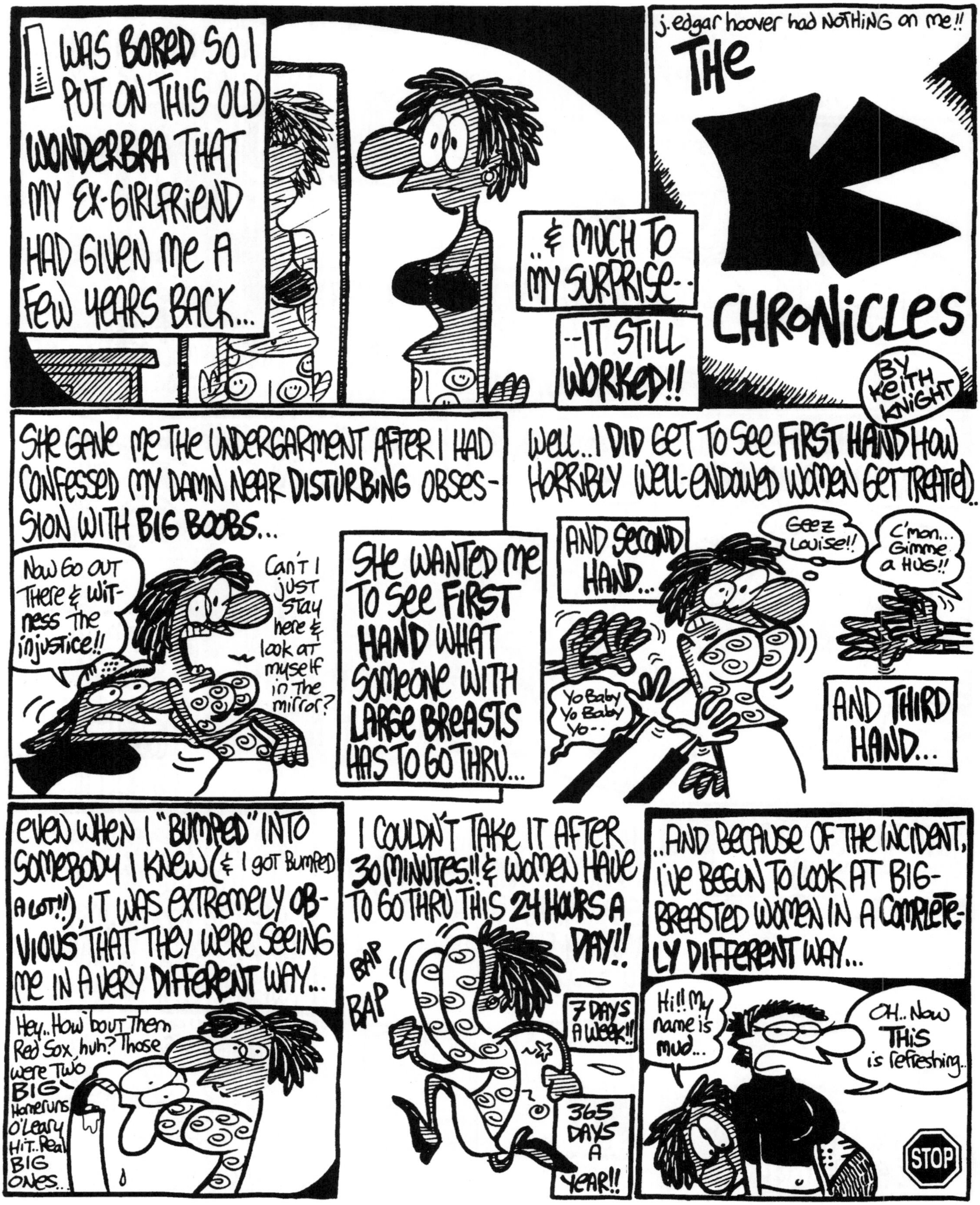
I WAS BORED SO I PUT ON THIS OLD WONDERBRA THAT MY EX-GIRLFRIEND HAD GIVEN ME A FEW YEARS BACK...
..& MUCH TO MY SURPRISE..
--IT STILL WORKED!!
j. edgar hoover had NOTHING on me!!
THE K CHRONICLES
BY KEITH KNIGHT
SHE GAVE ME THE UNDERGARMENT AFTER I HAD CONFESSED MY DAMN NEAR DISTURBING OBSESSION WITH BIG BOOBS...
Now GO OUT There & WITness The injustice!!
Can't I just stay here & look at myself in the mirror?
SHE WANTED ME TO SEE FIRST HAND WHAT SOMEONE WITH LARGE BREASTS HAS TO GO THRU...
WELL.. I DID GET TO SEE FIRST HAND HOW HORRIBLY WELL-ENDOWED WOMEN GET TREATED..
AND SECOND HAND...
Geez Louise!!
C'mon... Gimme a HUG!!
Yo Baby Yo Baby Yo--
AND THIRD HAND...
EVEN WHEN I "BUMPED" INTO SOMEBODY I KNEW (& I GOT BUMPED A LOT!!), IT WAS EXTREMELY OBVIOUS THAT THEY WERE SEEING ME IN A VERY DIFFERENT WAY...
Hey.. How 'bout Them Red Sox, huh? Those were TWO BIG Homeruns O'Leary HIT.. Real BIG ONES..
I COULDN'T TAKE IT AFTER 30 MINUTES!! & WOMEN HAVE TO GO THRU THIS 24 HOURS A DAY!!
BAP
BAP
7 DAYS A WEEK!!
365 DAYS A YEAR!!
..AND BECAUSE OF THE INCIDENT, I'VE BEGUN TO LOOK AT BIG-BREASTED WOMEN IN A COMPLETELY DIFFERENT WAY...
Hi!! My name is mud...
OH.. Now THIS is refreshing..
STOP

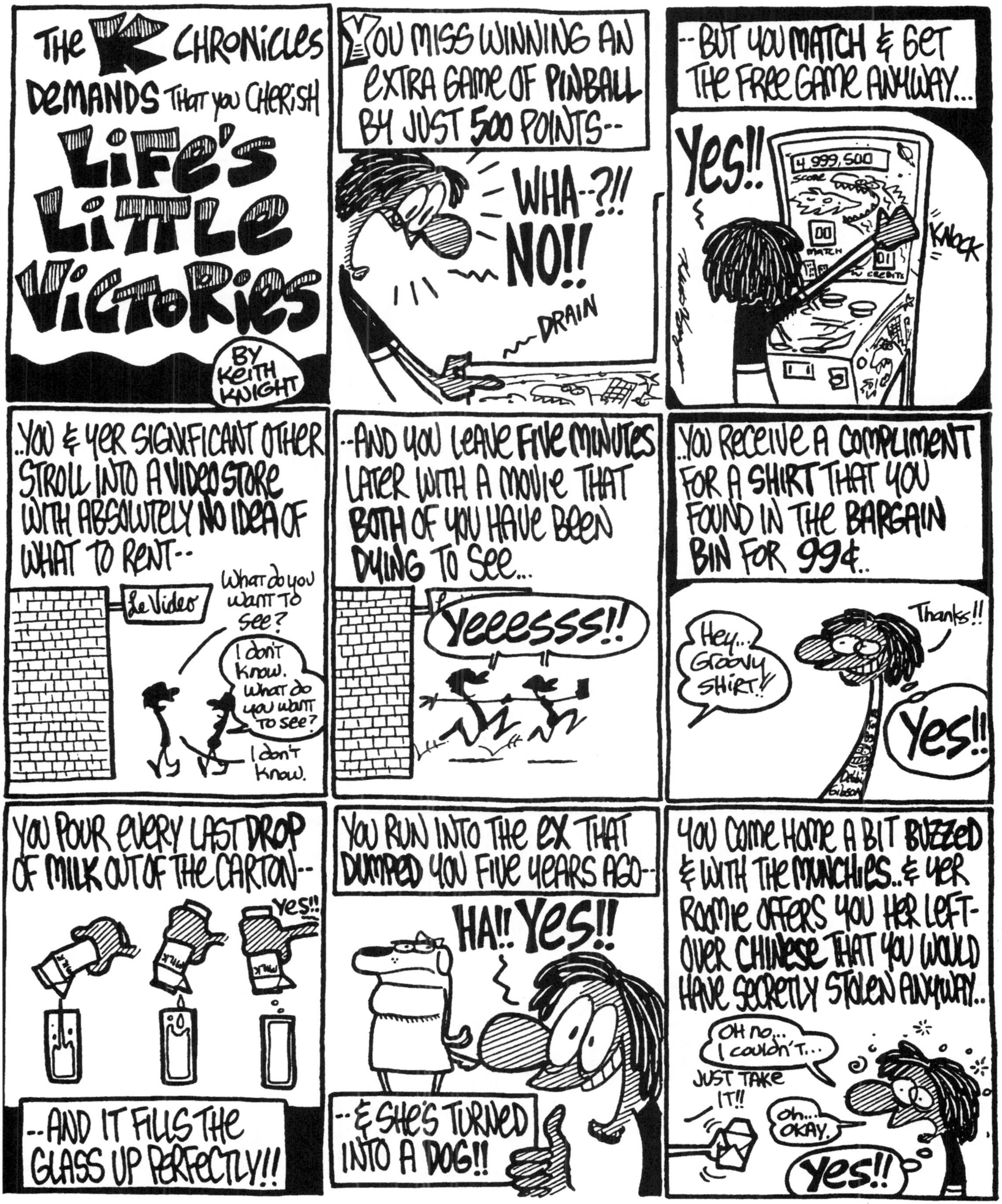

THE K CHRONICLES DEMANDS THAT YOU CHERISH LIFE'S LITTLE VICTORIES
BY KEITH KNIGHT
YOU MISS WINNING AN EXTRA GAME OF PINBALL BY JUST 500 POINTS--
WHA--?!!
NO!!
DRAIN
--BUT YOU MATCH & GET THE FREE GAME ANYWAY...
YES!!
4,999,500
SCORE
MATCH
CREDITS
KNOCK
..YOU & YER SIGNIFICANT OTHER STROLL INTO A VIDEO STORE WITH ABSOLUTELY NO IDEA OF WHAT TO RENT--
Le Video
What do you want to see?
I don't know. What do you want to see?
I don't know.
--AND YOU LEAVE FIVE MINUTES LATER WITH A MOVIE THAT BOTH OF YOU HAVE BEEN DYING TO SEE...
Yeeessss!!
..YOU RECEIVE A COMPLIMENT FOR A SHIRT THAT YOU FOUND IN THE BARGAIN BIN FOR 99¢..
Hey... Groovy shirt!
Thanks!!
Yes!!
Debbie Gibson
YOU POUR EVERY LAST DROP OF MILK OUT OF THE CARTON--
YES!!
MILK
--AND IT FILLS THE GLASS UP PERFECTLY!!
YOU RUN INTO THE EX THAT DUMPED YOU FIVE YEARS AGO--
HA!! YES!!
--& SHE'S TURNED INTO A DOG!!
YOU COME HOME A BIT BUZZED & WITH THE MUNCHIES..& YER ROOMIE OFFERS YOU HER LEFT-OVER CHINESE THAT YOU WOULD HAVE SECRETLY STOLEN ANYWAY..
OH no... I couldn't...
JUST TAKE IT!!
oh... OKAY.
YES!!

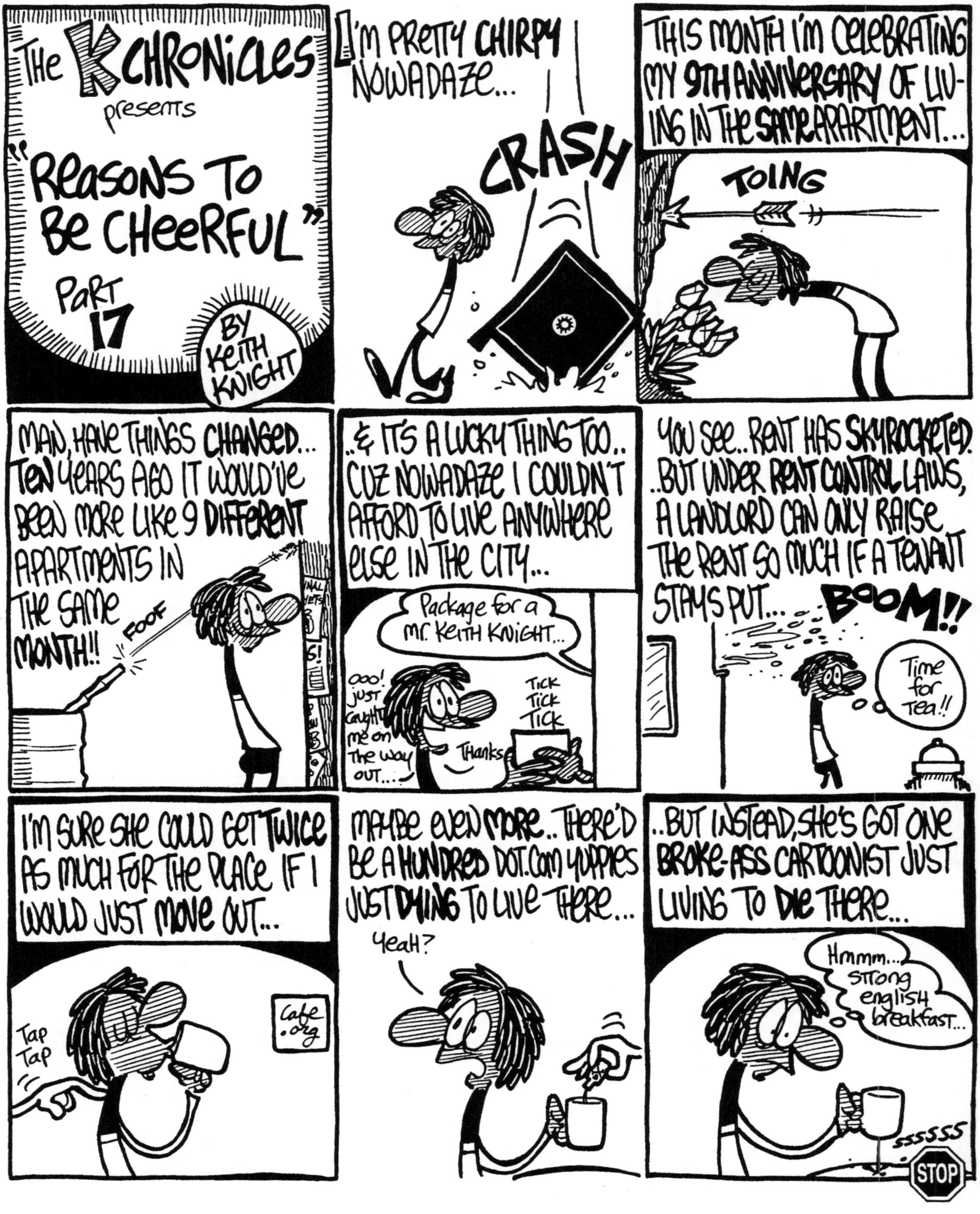
The K Chronicles presents
"Reasons to Be Cheerful"
Part 17
By Keith Knight
I'm pretty chirpy nowadaze...
CRASH
This month I'm celebrating my 9th anniversary of living in the same apartment...
TOING
Man, have things changed... Ten years ago it would've been more like 9 different apartments in the same month!!
FOOF
..& it's a lucky thing too.. cuz nowadaze I couldn't afford to live anywhere else in the city...
Package for a mr. Keith Knight...
ooo! just caught me on the way out...
Tick Tick Tick
Thanks
You see... rent has skyrocketed. ..But under rent control laws, a landlord can only raise the rent so much if a tenant stays put...
BOOM!!
Time for Tea!!
I'm sure she could get twice as much for the place if I would just move out...
Tap Tap
cafe .org
Maybe even more.. there'd be a hundred dot.com yuppies just dying to live there...
Yeah?
..But instead, she's got one broke-ass cartoonist just living to die there...
Hmmm... strong english breakfast...
SSSSSS
STOP

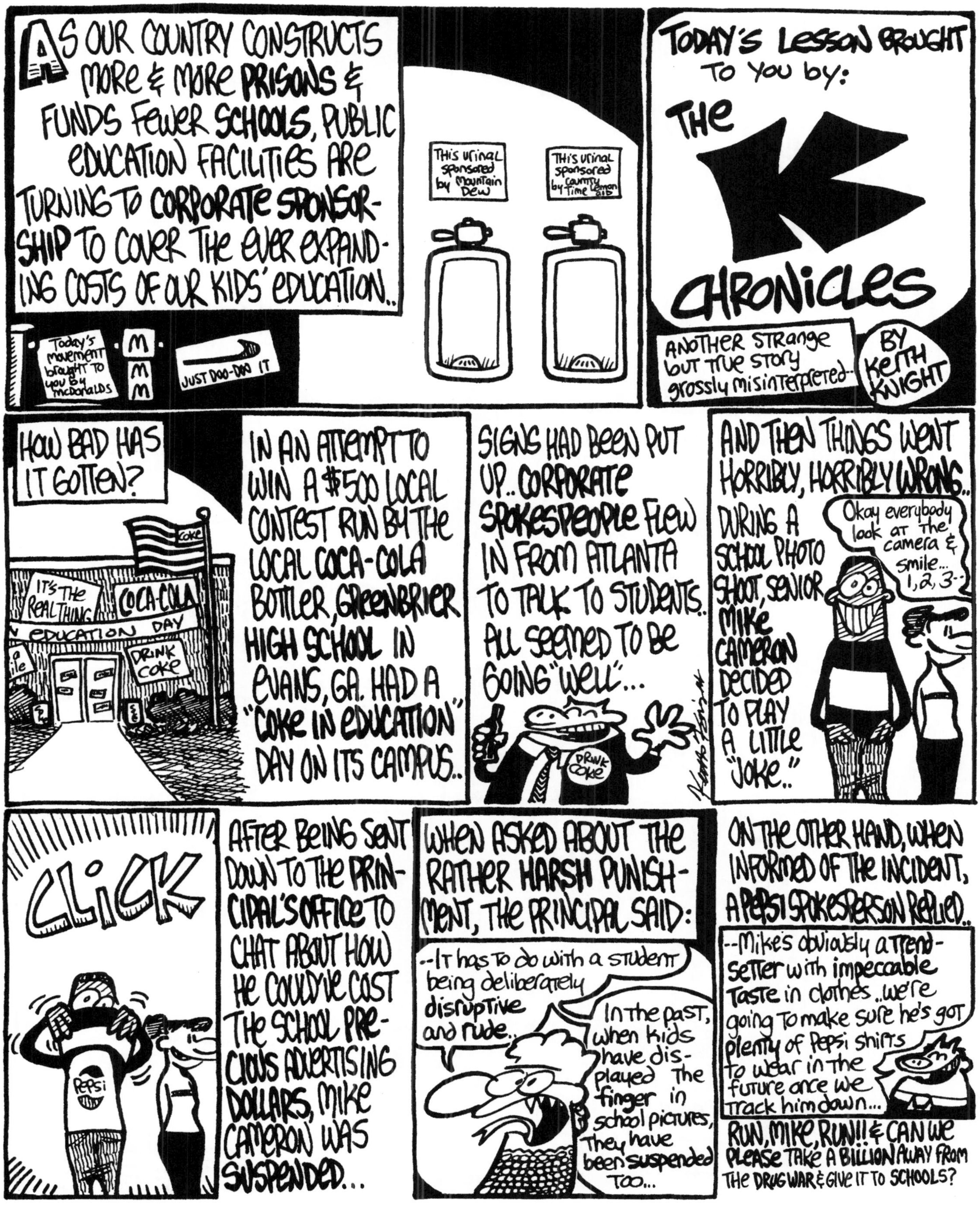

As our country constructs more & more PRISONS & funds fewer SCHOOLS, public education facilities are turning to CORPORATE SPONSORSHIP to cover the ever expanding costs of our kids' education..
This urinal sponsored by Mountain Dew
This urinal sponsored by Country Time Lemonade
Today's movement brought to you by McDonalds
JUST DOO-DOO IT
TODAY'S LESSON BROUGHT TO YOU BY:
THE K CHRONICLES
ANOTHER STRANGE BUT TRUE STORY grossly misinterpreted..
BY KEITH KNIGHT
HOW BAD HAS IT GOTTEN?
COKE
IT'S THE REAL THING
COCA-COLA
EDUCATION DAY
DRINK COKE
IN AN ATTEMPT TO WIN A $500 LOCAL CONTEST RUN BY THE LOCAL COCA-COLA BOTTLER, GREENBRIER HIGH SCHOOL IN EVANS, GA. HAD A "COKE IN EDUCATION" DAY ON ITS CAMPUS..
SIGNS HAD BEEN PUT UP.. CORPORATE SPOKESPEOPLE FLEW IN FROM ATLANTA TO TALK TO STUDENTS. ALL SEEMED TO BE GOING "WELL"...
DRINK COKE
AND THEN THINGS WENT HORRIBLY, HORRIBLY WRONG..
DURING A SCHOOL PHOTO SHOOT, SENIOR MIKE CAMERON DECIDED TO PLAY A LITTLE "JOKE."
Okay everybody look at the camera & smile... 1, 2, 3--
CLICK
PEPSI
AFTER BEING SENT DOWN TO THE PRINCIPAL'S OFFICE TO CHAT ABOUT HOW HE COULD'VE COST THE SCHOOL PRECIOUS ADVERTISING DOLLARS, MIKE CAMERON WAS SUSPENDED...
WHEN ASKED ABOUT THE RATHER HARSH PUNISHMENT, THE PRINCIPAL SAID:
--It has to do with a student being deliberately disruptive and rude..
In the past, when kids have displayed the finger in school pictures, they have been suspended too...
ON THE OTHER HAND, WHEN INFORMED OF THE INCIDENT, A PEPSI SPOKESPERSON REPLIED..
--Mike's obviously a trend-setter with impeccable taste in clothes..we're going to make sure he's got plenty of Pepsi shirts to wear in the future once we track him down...
RUN, MIKE, RUN!! & CAN WE PLEASE TAKE A BILLION AWAY FROM THE DRUG WAR & GIVE IT TO SCHOOLS?

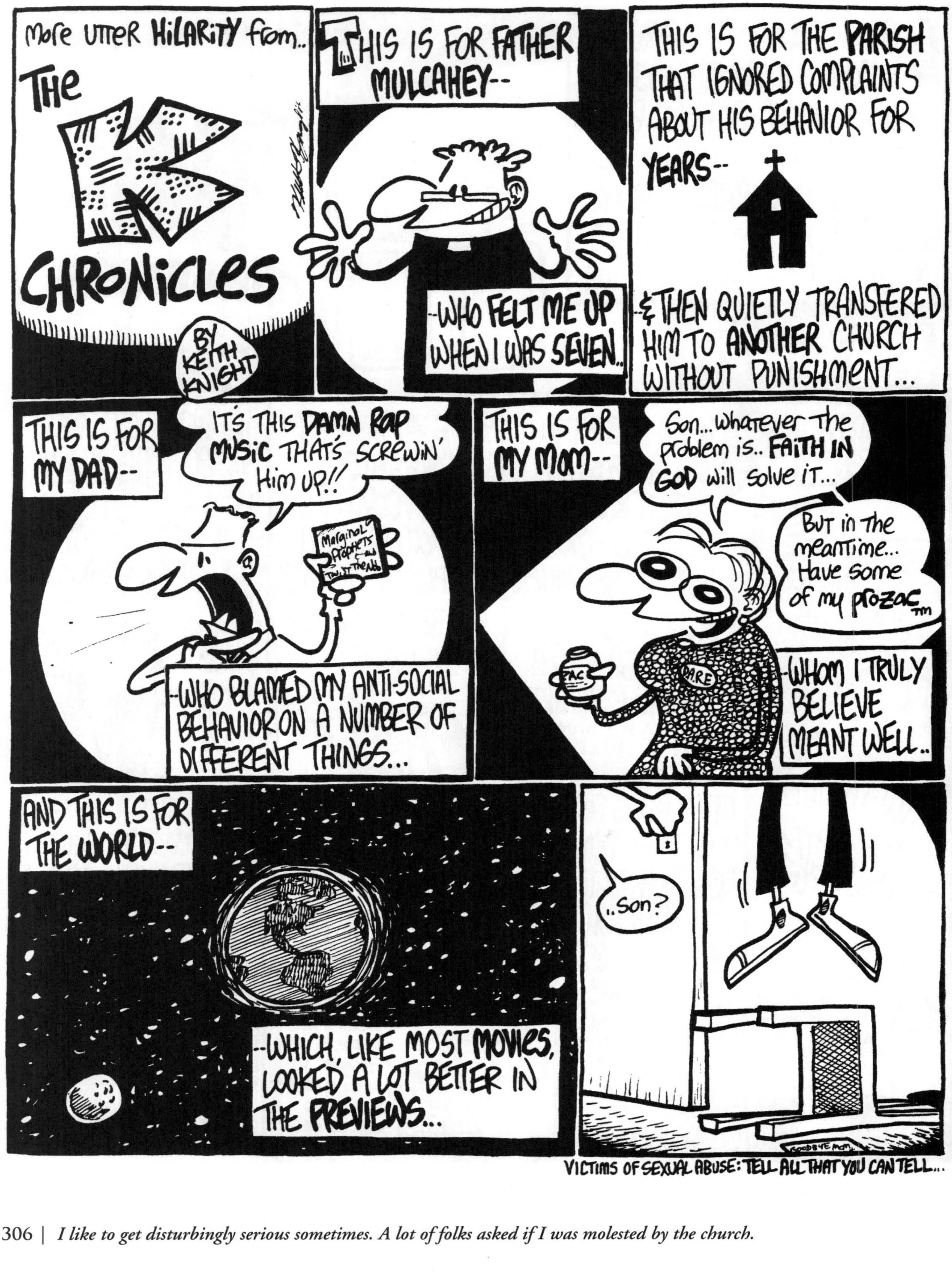
More utter HILARITY from..
THE K CHRONICLES
BY KEITH KNIGHT
THIS IS FOR FATHER MULCAHEY--
--WHO FELT ME UP WHEN I WAS SEVEN..
THIS IS FOR THE PARISH THAT IGNORED COMPLAINTS ABOUT HIS BEHAVIOR FOR YEARS--
--& THEN QUIETLY TRANSFERED HIM TO ANOTHER CHURCH WITHOUT PUNISHMENT...
THIS IS FOR MY DAD--
IT'S THIS DAMN RAP MUSIC THAT'S SCREWIN' HIM UP!!
--WHO BLAMED MY ANTI-SOCIAL BEHAVIOR ON A NUMBER OF DIFFERENT THINGS...
THIS IS FOR MY MOM--
Son... whatever the problem is.. FAITH IN GOD will solve it...
But in the meantime... Have some of my prozac™
D.A.R.E
--WHOM I TRULY BELIEVE MEANT WELL..
AND THIS IS FOR THE WORLD--
--WHICH, LIKE MOST MOVIES, LOOKED A LOT BETTER IN THE PREVIEWS...
..Son?
VICTIMS OF SEXUAL ABUSE: TELL ALL THAT YOU CAN TELL...

 I like to get disturbingly serious sometimes. A lot of folks asked if I was molested by the church.

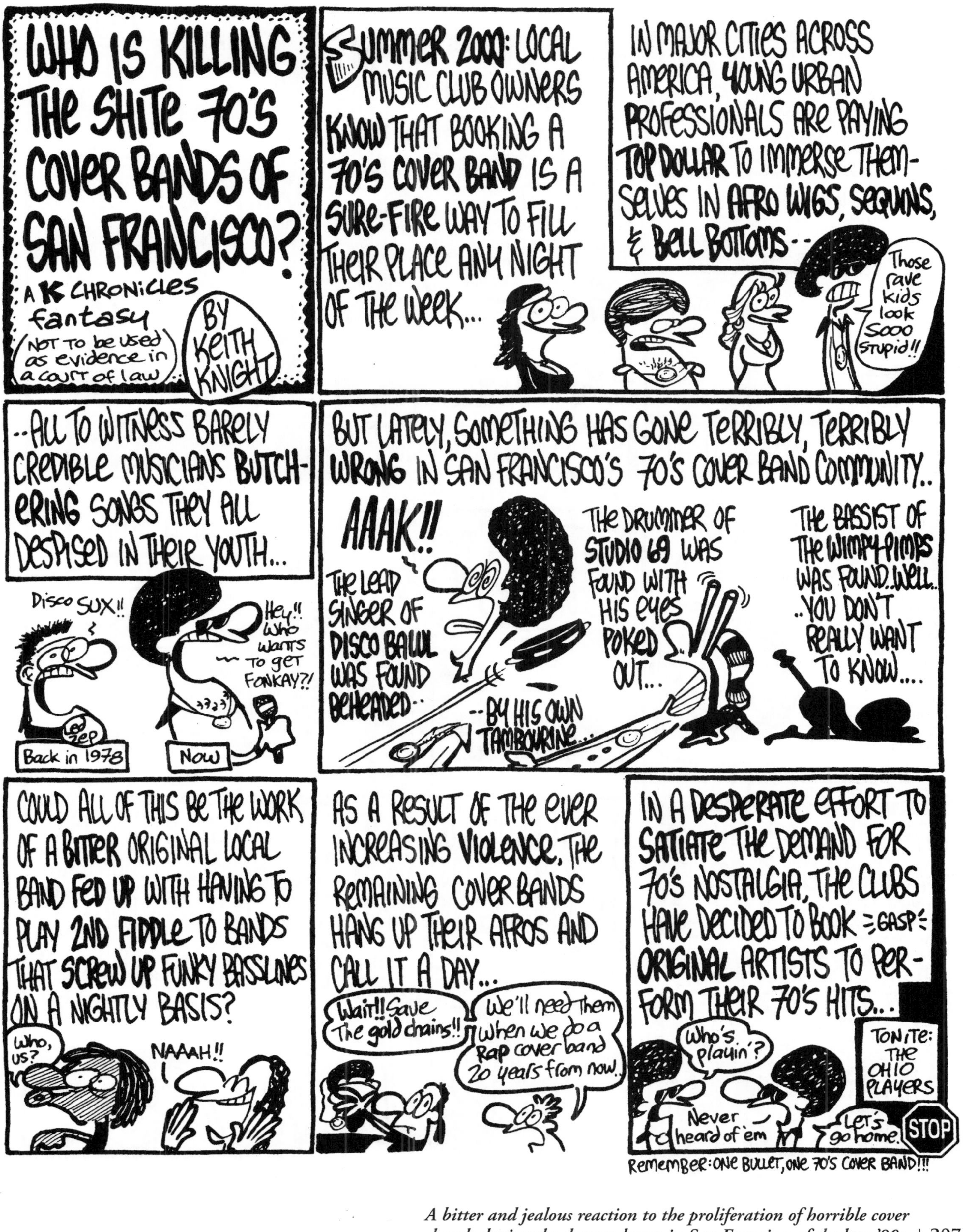
WHO IS KILLING THE SHITE 70'S COVER BANDS OF SAN FRANCISCO?
A K CHRONICLES fantasy
(NOT TO be USED as evidence in a court of law)
BY KEITH KNIGHT
SUMMER 2000: LOCAL MUSIC CLUB OWNERS KNOW THAT BOOKING A 70'S COVER BAND IS A SURE-FIRE WAY TO FILL THEIR PLACE ANY NIGHT OF THE WEEK...
IN MAJOR CITIES ACROSS AMERICA, YOUNG URBAN PROFESSIONALS ARE PAYING TOP DOLLAR TO IMMERSE THEMSELVES IN AFRO WIGS, SEQUINS, & BELL BOTTOMS..
Those rave kids look Sooo Stupid!!
..ALL TO WITNESS BARELY CREDIBLE MUSICIANS BUTCHERING SONGS THEY ALL DESPISED IN THEIR YOUTH...
DISCO SUX!!
Hey!! Who wants to get FONKAY?!
Led Zep
Back in 1978
Now
BUT LATELY, SOMETHING HAS GONE TERRIBLY, TERRIBLY WRONG IN SAN FRANCISCO'S 70'S COVER BAND COMMUNITY..
AAAK!!
THE LEAD SINGER OF DISCO BALLL WAS FOUND BEHEADED..
..BY HIS OWN TAMBOURINE...
THE DRUMMER OF STUDIO 69 WAS FOUND WITH HIS EYES POKED OUT...
THE BASSIST OF THE WIMPY-PIMPS WAS FOUND..WELL.. ..YOU DON'T REALLY WANT TO KNOW....
COULD ALL OF THIS BE THE WORK OF A BITTER ORIGINAL LOCAL BAND FED UP WITH HAVING TO PLAY 2ND FIDDLE TO BANDS THAT SCREW UP FUNKY BASSLINES ON A NIGHTLY BASIS?
Who, us?
NAAAH!!
AS A RESULT OF THE EVER INCREASING VIOLENCE, THE REMAINING COVER BANDS HANG UP THEIR AFROS AND CALL IT A DAY...
Wait!! Save the gold chains!!
We'll need them when we do a Rap cover band 20 years from now.
IN A DESPERATE EFFORT TO SATIATE THE DEMAND FOR 70'S NOSTALGIA, THE CLUBS HAVE DECIDED TO BOOK =GASP= ORIGINAL ARTISTS TO PERFORM THEIR 70'S HITS...
Who's playin'?
TONITE: THE OHIO PLAYERS
Never heard of 'em
Let's go home.
STOP
REMEMBER: ONE BULLET, ONE 70'S COVER BAND!!!

A bitter and jealous reaction to the proliferation of horrible cover bands during the dotcom boom in San Francisco of the late '90s.

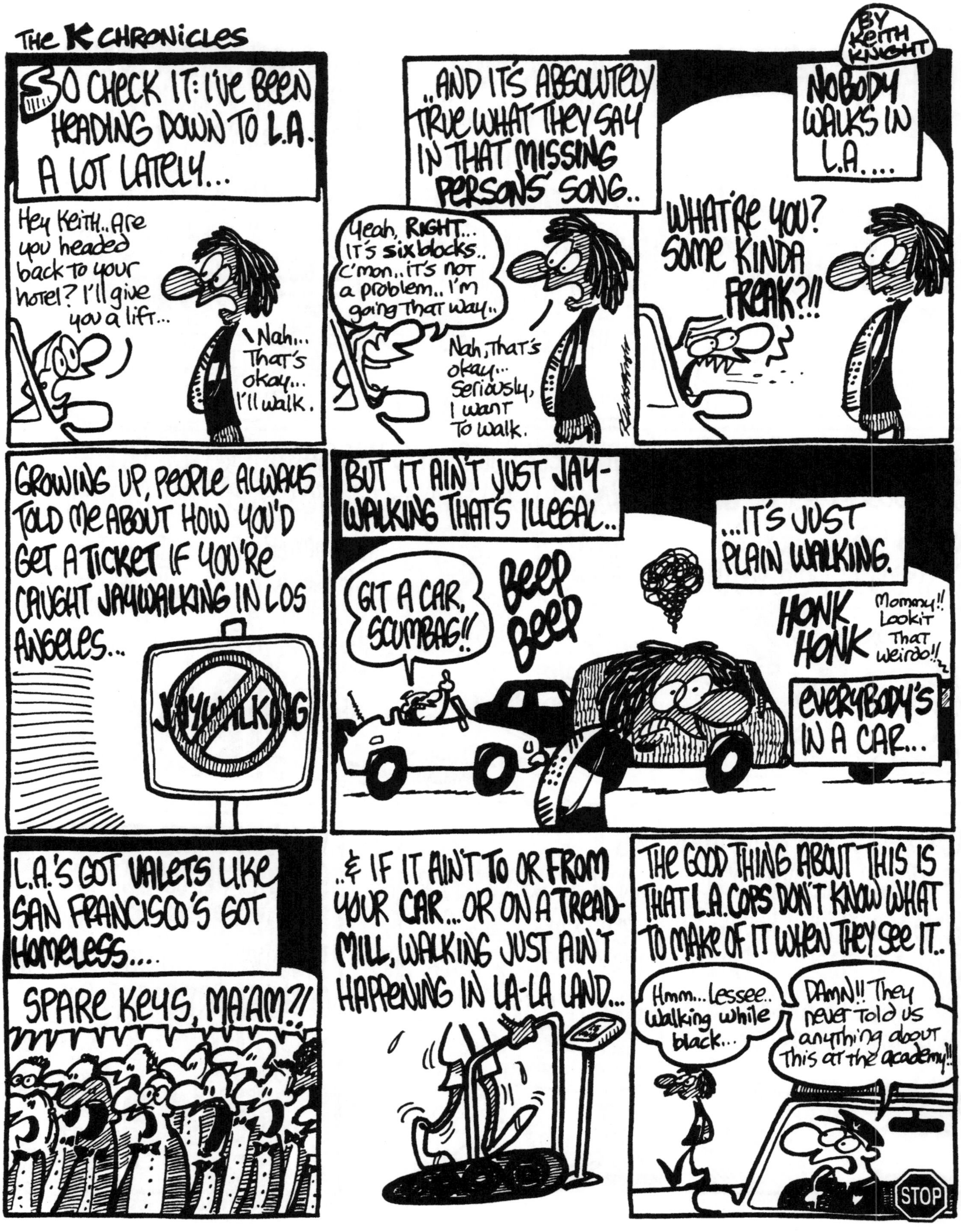
THE K CHRONICLES
BY KEITH KNIGHT
SO CHECK IT: I'VE BEEN HEADING DOWN TO L.A. A LOT LATELY...
Hey Keith.. Are you headed back to your hotel? I'll give you a lift...
Nah... That's okay... I'll walk.
...AND IT'S ABSOLUTELY TRUE WHAT THEY SAY IN THAT MISSING PERSONS' SONG..
Yeah, RIGHT... IT'S six blocks.. C'mon.. it's not a problem.. I'm going that way..
Nah, that's okay... Seriously, I want to walk.
NOBODY WALKS IN L.A....
WHAT'RE YOU? SOME KINDA FREAK?!!
GROWING UP, PEOPLE ALWAYS TOLD ME ABOUT HOW YOU'D GET A TICKET IF YOU'RE CAUGHT JAYWALKING IN LOS ANGELES...
JAYWALKING
BUT IT AIN'T JUST JAY-WALKING THAT'S ILLEGAL..
...IT'S JUST PLAIN WALKING.
GIT A CAR, SCUMBAG!!
BEEP BEEP
HONK HONK
Mommy!! Lookit That weirdo!!
EVERYBODY'S IN A CAR...
L.A.'S GOT VALETS LIKE SAN FRANCISCO'S GOT HOMELESS....
SPARE KEYS, MA'AM?!
..& IF IT AIN'T TO OR FROM YOUR CAR... OR ON A TREAD-MILL, WALKING JUST AIN'T HAPPENING IN LA-LA LAND...
THE GOOD THING ABOUT THIS IS THAT L.A. COPS DON'T KNOW WHAT TO MAKE OF IT WHEN THEY SEE IT..
Hmm... Lessee.. Walking while black...
DAMN!! They never told us anything about this at the academy!!
STOP

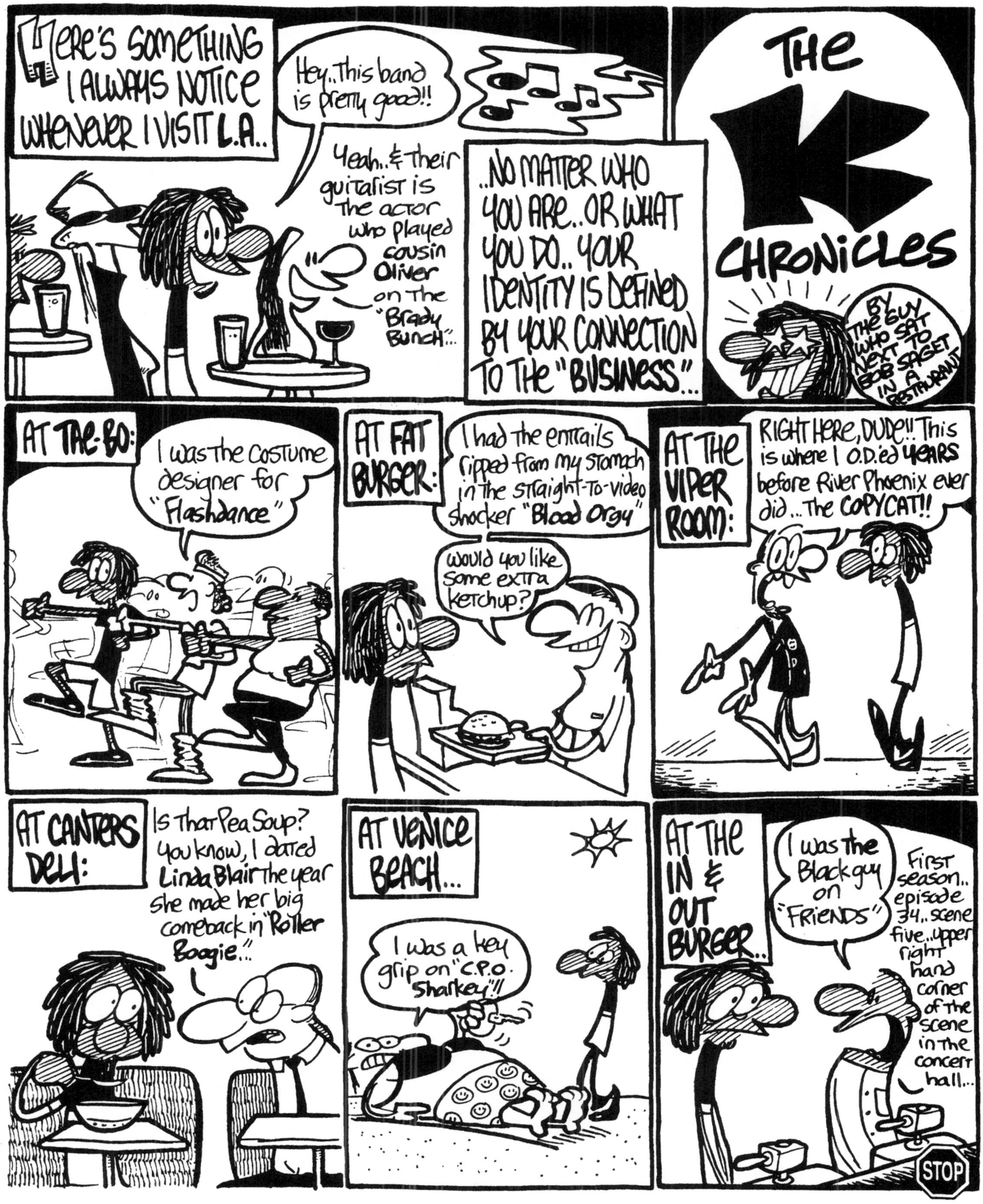

Here's something I always notice whenever I visit L.A..
Hey.. This band is pretty good!!
Yeah.. & their guitarist is the actor who played cousin Oliver on the "Brady Bunch"...
..No matter who you are.. or what you do.. your identity is defined by your connection to the "Business"...
The K Chronicles
By the guy who sat next to Bob Saget in a restaurant
At Tae-Bo:
I was the costume designer for "Flashdance"
At Fat Burger:
I had the entrails ripped from my stomach in the straight-to-video shocker "Blood Orgy"
Would you like some extra ketchup?
At the Viper Room:
Right here, dude!! This is where I O.D.'ed years before River Phoenix ever did... The copycat!!
At Canters Deli:
Is that Pea Soup? You know, I dated Linda Blair the year she made her big comeback in "Roller Boogie"...
At Venice Beach...
I was a key grip on "C.P.O. Sharkey"!!
At the In & Out Burger...
I was the Black guy on "Friends"
First season.. episode 34.. scene five.. upper right hand corner of the scene in the concert hall...
STOP

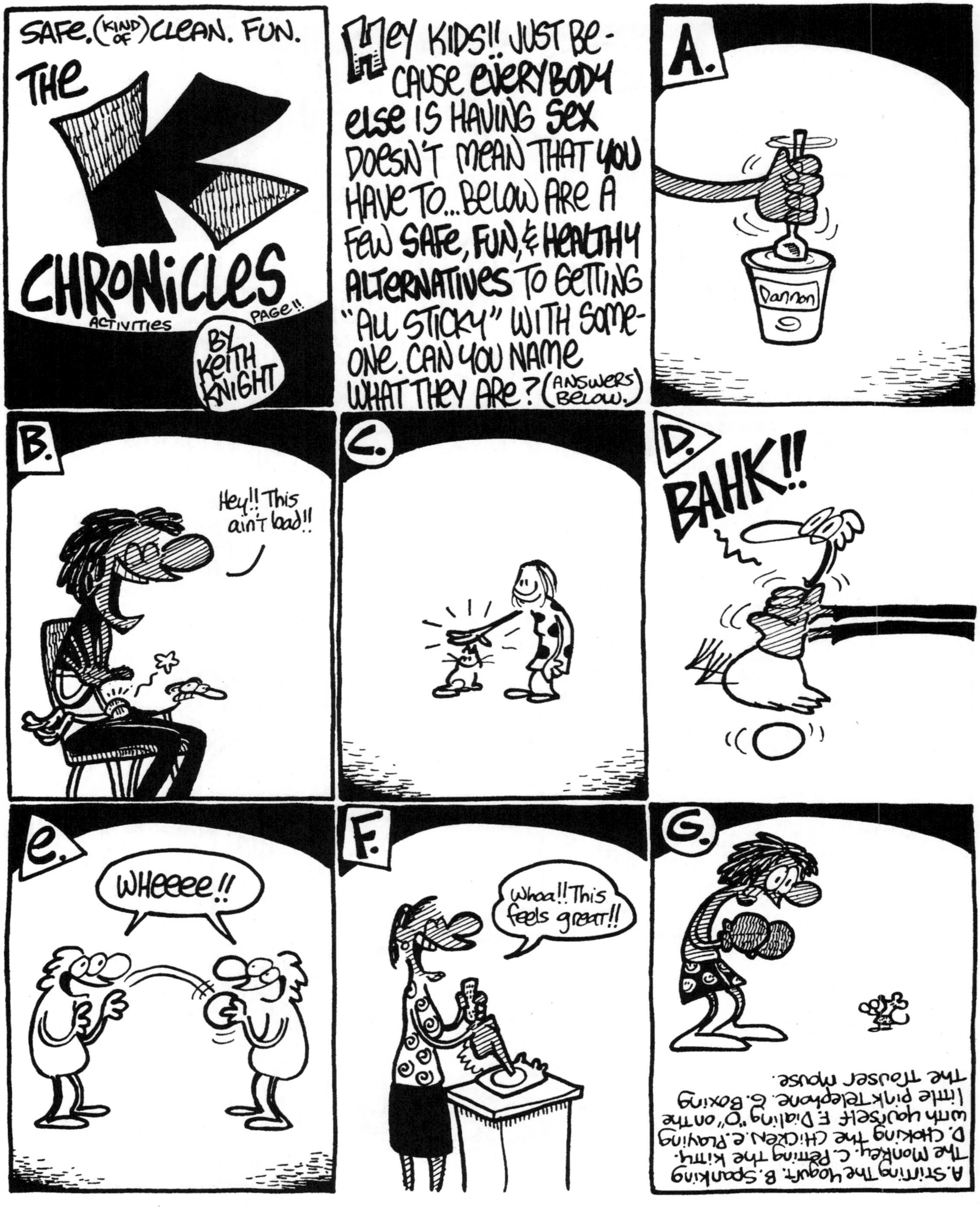
SAFE. (KIND OF) CLEAN. FUN.
THE K CHRONICLES ACTIVITIES PAGE!!
BY KEITH KNIGHT
HEY KIDS!! JUST BECAUSE EVERYBODY ELSE IS HAVING SEX DOESN'T MEAN THAT YOU HAVE TO... BELOW ARE A FEW SAFE, FUN, & HEALTHY ALTERNATIVES TO GETTING "ALL STICKY" WITH SOMEONE. CAN YOU NAME WHAT THEY ARE? (ANSWERS BELOW.)
A.
Dannon
B.
Hey!! This ain't bad!!
C.
D.
BAHK!!
E.
WHEEEE!!
F.
Whoa!! This feels great!!
G.
A. Stirring the yogurt. B. Spanking the monkey. C. Petting the kitty. D. Choking the chicken. E. Playing with yourself. F. Dialing "O" on the little pink telephone. G. Boxing the trouser mouse.

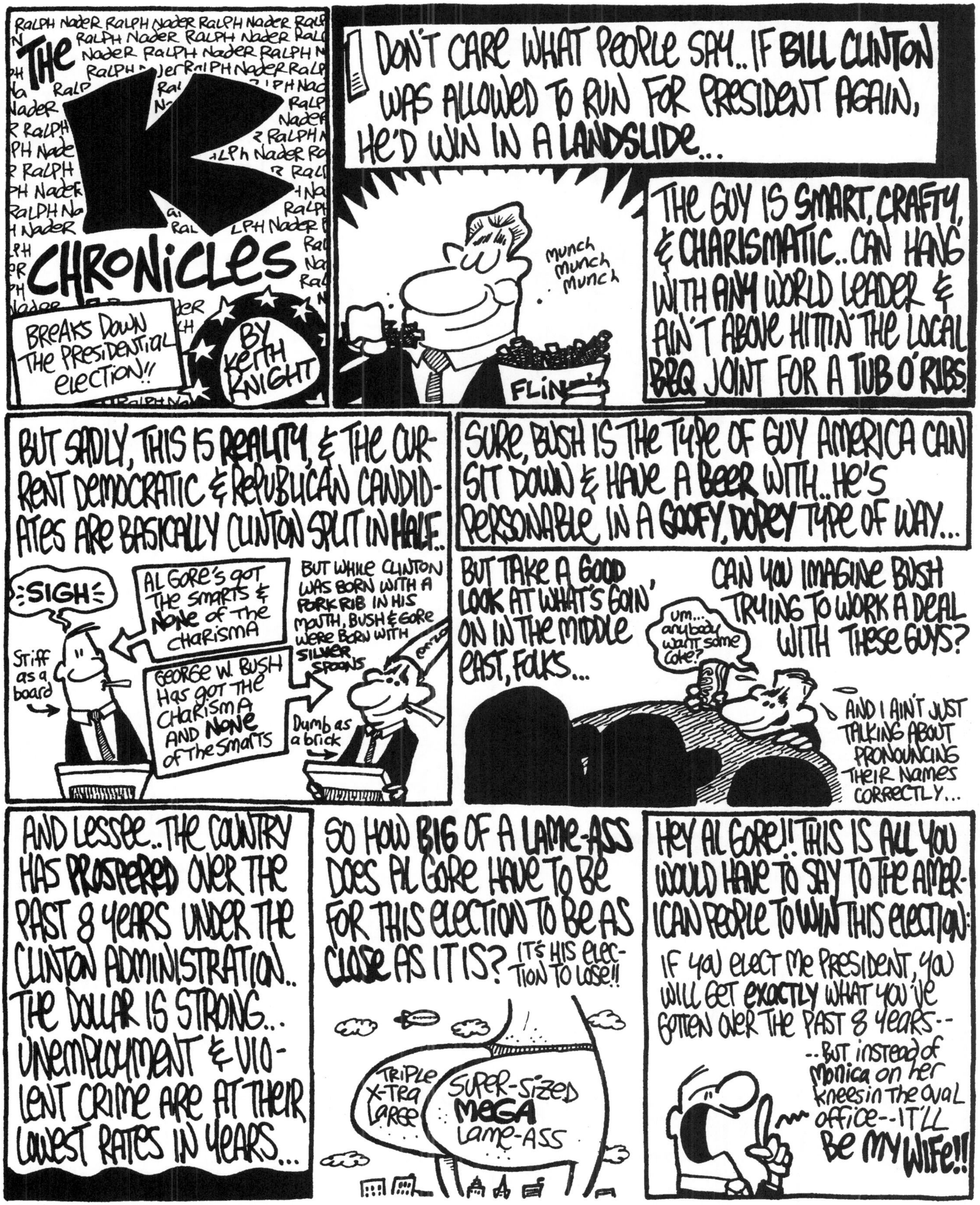

The K Chronicles
Ralph Nader Ralph Nader Ralph Nader
Breaks down the presidential election!!
By Keith Knight
I don't care what people say.. if Bill Clinton was allowed to run for president again, he'd win in a landslide...
munch munch munch
The guy is smart, crafty, & charismatic.. can hang with any world leader & ain't above hittin' the local BBQ joint for a tub o' ribs.
But sadly, this is reality, & the current democratic & republican candidates are basically Clinton split in half..
SIGH
Al Gore's got the smarts & none of the charisma
Stiff as a board
George W. Bush has got the charisma and none of the smarts
But while Clinton was born with a pork rib in his mouth, Bush & Gore were born with silver spoons
Dumb as a brick
Sure, Bush is the type of guy America can sit down & have a beer with.. he's personable in a goofy, dopey type of way...
But take a good look at what's goin' on in the middle east, folks...
um... anybody want some coke?
Can you imagine Bush trying to work a deal with these guys?
And I ain't just talking about pronouncing their names correctly...
And lessee.. the country has prospered over the past 8 years under the Clinton administration.. the dollar is strong... unemployment & violent crime are at their lowest rates in years...
So how big of a lame-ass does Al Gore have to be for this election to be as close as it is?
It's his election to lose!!
Triple X-tra Large
Super-sized MEGA lame-ass
Hey Al Gore!! This is all you would have to say to the American people to win this election:
If you elect me president, you will get exactly what you've gotten over the past 8 years--
--but instead of Monica on her knees in the oval office--it'll be my wife!!

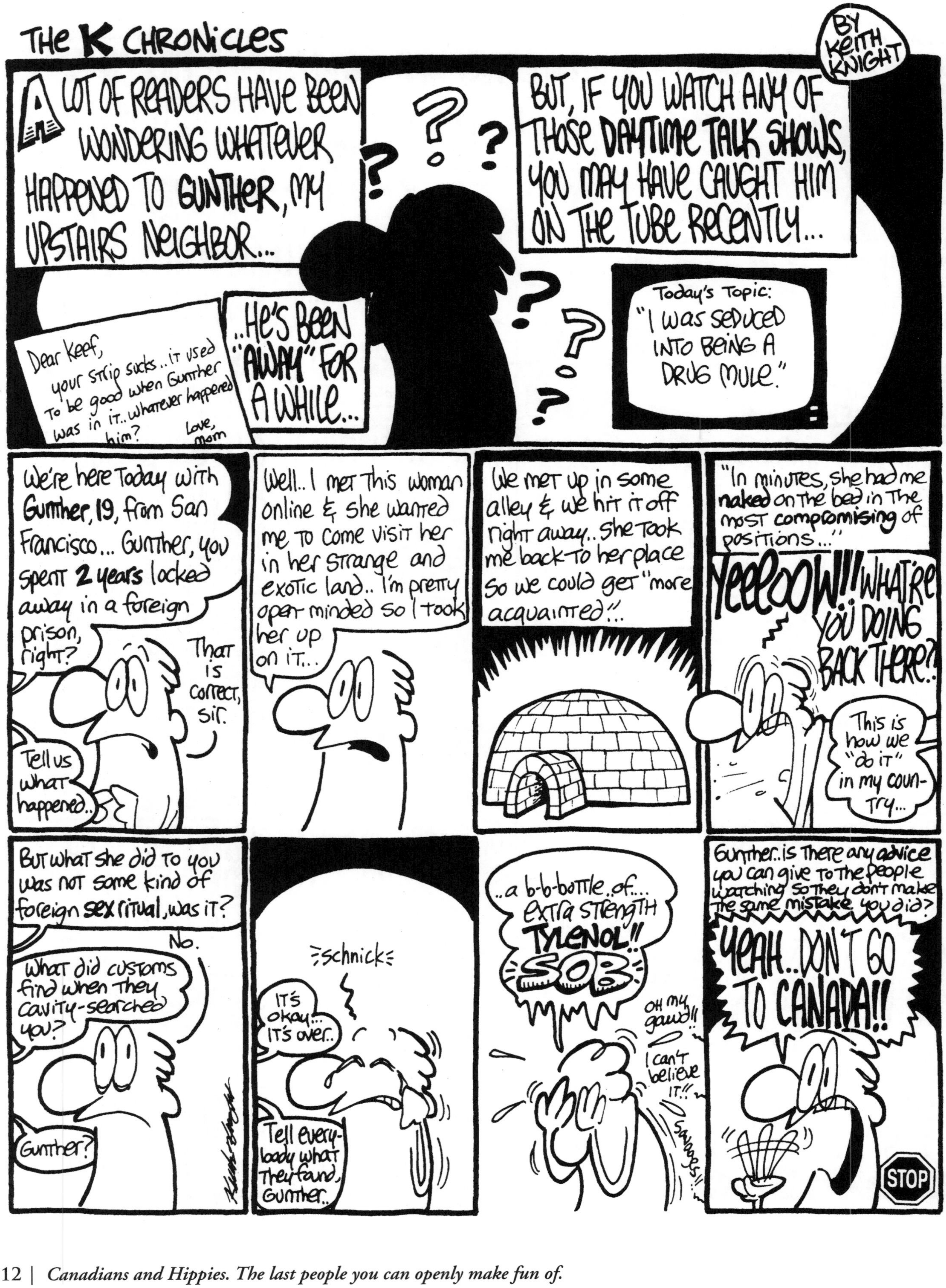
THE K CHRONICLES
BY KEITH KNIGHT
A LOT OF READERS HAVE BEEN WONDERING WHATEVER HAPPENED TO GUNTHER, MY UPSTAIRS NEIGHBOR...
Dear Keef, your strip sucks.. it used to be good when Gunther was in it.. whatever happened to him? Love, mom
..HE'S BEEN "AWAY" FOR A WHILE...
BUT, IF YOU WATCH ANY OF THOSE DAYTIME TALK SHOWS, YOU MAY HAVE CAUGHT HIM ON THE TUBE RECENTLY...
Today's Topic: "I WAS SEDUCED INTO BEING A DRUG MULE."
We're here today with Gunther, 19, from San Francisco... Gunther, you spent 2 years locked away in a foreign prison, right?
That is correct, sir.
Tell us what happened..
Well.. I met this woman online & she wanted me to come visit her in her strange and exotic land.. I'm pretty open minded so I took her up on it...
We met up in some alley & we hit it off right away.. she took me back to her place so we could get "more acquainted"..
"In minutes, she had me naked on the bed in the most compromising of positions..."
YEELOOW!! WHAT'RE YOU DOING BACK THERE?..
This is how we "do it" in my coun-try...
But what she did to you was not some kind of foreign sex ritual, was it?
No.
What did customs find when they cavity-searched you?
Gunther?
schnick
It's okay... it's over..
Tell every-body what they found, Gunther..
..a b-b-bottle of.... EXTRA STRENGTH TYLENOL!!
SOB
OH MY GAWD!!
I can't believe it!!
SNIFFLES!!
Gunther..is there any advice you can give to the people watching so they don't make the same mistake you did?
YEAH..DON'T GO TO CANADA!!
STOP

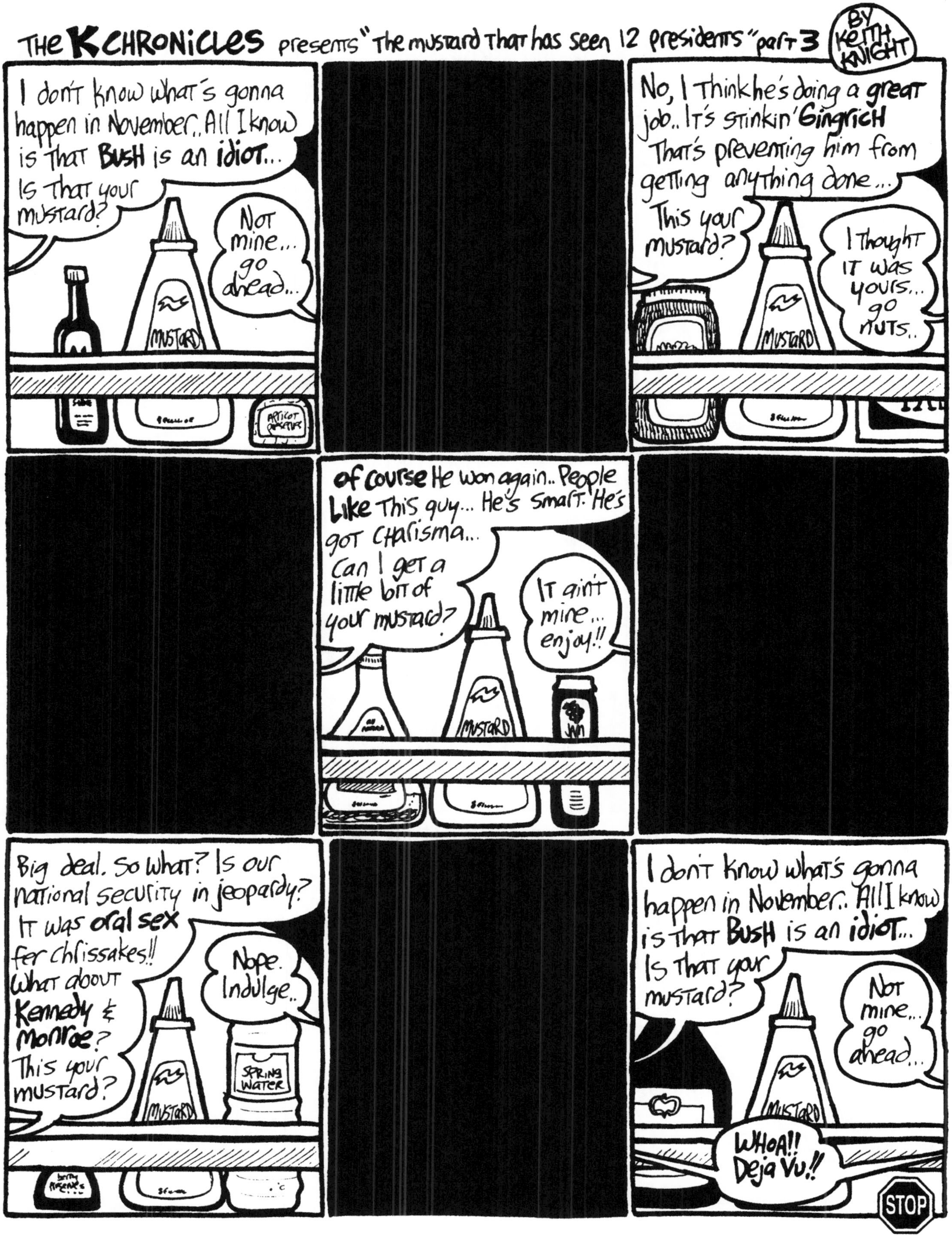
THE K CHRONICLES presents "The mustard that has seen 12 presidents" part 3
BY KEITH KNIGHT
I don't know what's gonna happen in November.. All I know is that BUSH is an idiot... Is that your mustard?
Not mine... go ahead...
MUSTARD
No, I think he's doing a great job.. It's stinkin' Gingrich that's preventing him from getting anything done... This your mustard?
I thought it was yours... go nuts..
MUSTARD
of course he won again.. People like this guy... He's smart. He's got charisma... Can I get a little bit of your mustard?
It ain't mine... enjoy!!
MUSTARD
JAM
Big deal. So what? Is our national security in jeopardy? It was oral sex fer chrissakes!! What about Kennedy & Monroe? This your mustard?
Nope. Indulge..
MUSTARD
SPRING WATER
I don't know what's gonna happen in November.. All I know is that BUSH is an idiot... Is that your mustard?
Not mine... go ahead...
MUSTARD
WHOA!! Deja Vu!!
STOP

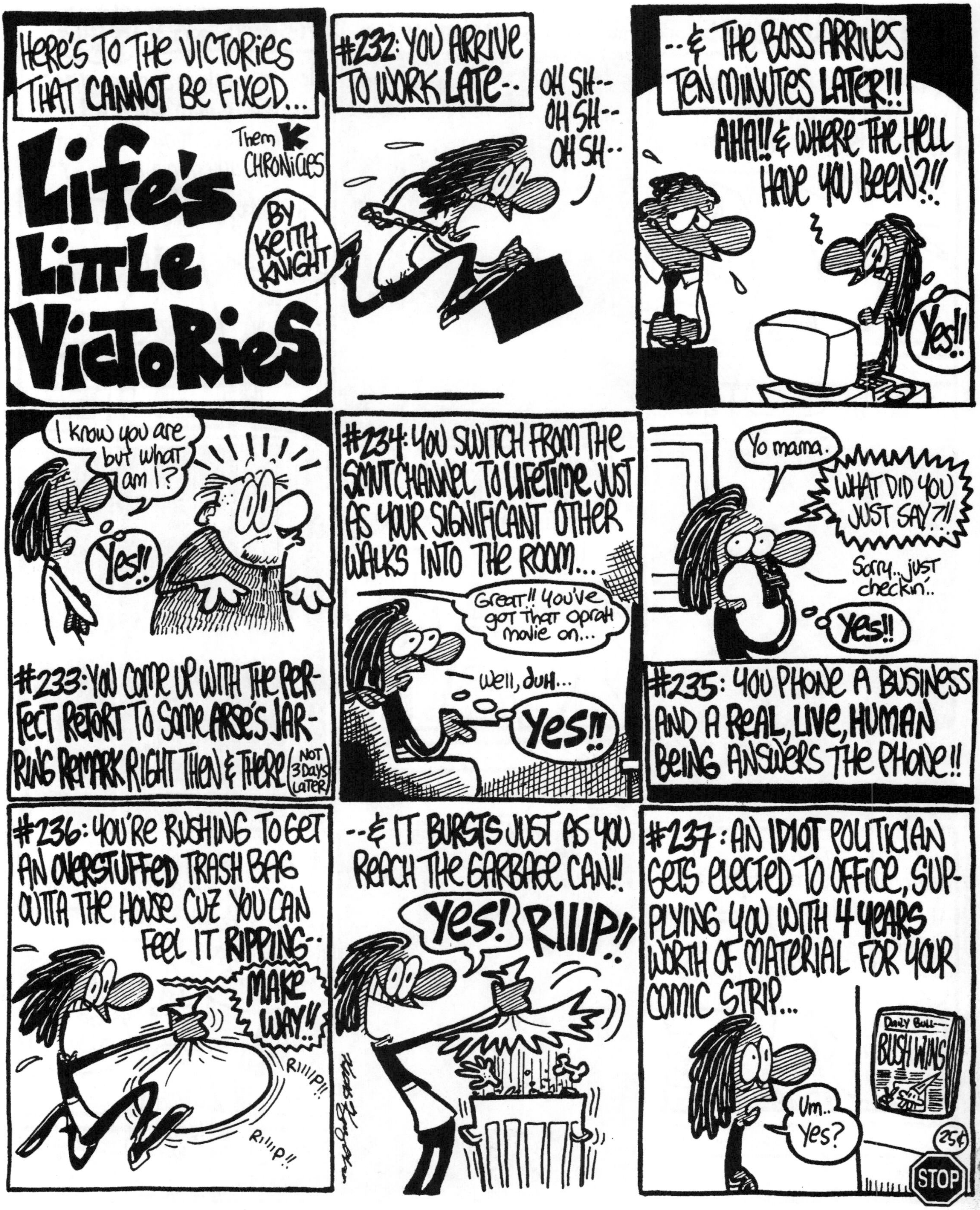

HERE'S TO THE VICTORIES THAT CANNOT BE FIXED...
Life's Little Victories
Them K CHRONICLES
BY KEITH KNIGHT
#232: YOU ARRIVE TO WORK LATE--
OH SH-- OH SH-- OH SH--
--& THE BOSS ARRIVES TEN MINUTES LATER!!
AHA!! & WHERE THE HELL HAVE YOU BEEN?!!
Yes!!
I know you are but what am I?
Yes!!
#233: YOU COME UP WITH THE PERFECT RETORT TO SOME ARSE'S JARRING REMARK RIGHT THEN & THERE (NOT 3 DAYS LATER)
#234: YOU SWITCH FROM THE SMUT CHANNEL TO LIFETIME JUST AS YOUR SIGNIFICANT OTHER WALKS INTO THE ROOM...
Great!! You've got that Oprah movie on...
Well, duh...
Yes!!
Yo mama.
WHAT DID YOU JUST SAY?!!
Sorry.. just checkin'..
Yes!!
#235: YOU PHONE A BUSINESS AND A REAL, LIVE, HUMAN BEING ANSWERS THE PHONE!!
#236: YOU'RE RUSHING TO GET AN OVERSTUFFED TRASH BAG OUTTA THE HOUSE CUZ YOU CAN FEEL IT RIPPING--
MAKE WAY!!
RIIIP!!
RIIIP!!
--& IT BURSTS JUST AS YOU REACH THE GARBAGE CAN!!
Yes!
RIIIP!!
#237: AN IDIOT POLITICIAN GETS ELECTED TO OFFICE, SUPPLYING YOU WITH 4 YEARS WORTH OF MATERIAL FOR YOUR COMIC STRIP...
DAILY BULL
BUSH WINS
25¢
Um.. Yes?
STOP

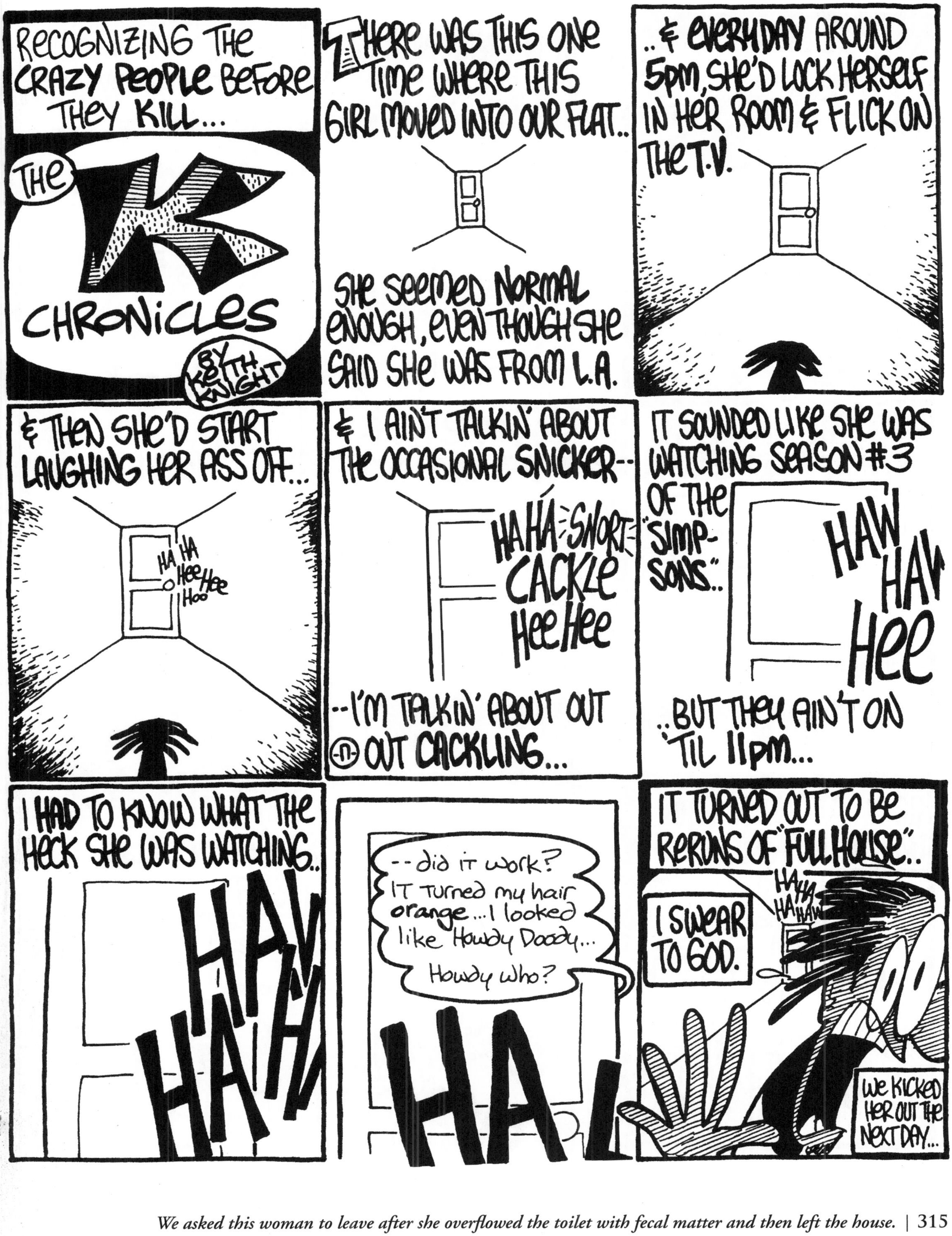
RECOGNIZING THE CRAZY PEOPLE BEFORE THEY KILL...
THE K CHRONICLES
BY KEITH KNIGHT
THERE WAS THIS ONE TIME WHERE THIS GIRL MOVED INTO OUR FLAT..
SHE SEEMED NORMAL ENOUGH, EVEN THOUGH SHE SAID SHE WAS FROM L.A.
..& EVERYDAY AROUND 5PM, SHE'D LOCK HERSELF IN HER ROOM & FLICK ON THE T.V.
& THEN SHE'D START LAUGHING HER ASS OFF...
HA HA HEE HEE HOO
& I AIN'T TALKIN' ABOUT THE OCCASIONAL SNICKER--
HA HA SNORT CACKLE HEE HEE
--I'M TALKIN' ABOUT OUT -N- OUT CACKLING...
IT SOUNDED LIKE SHE WAS WATCHING SEASON #3 OF THE "SIMPSONS"..
HAW HAW HEE
..BUT THEY AIN'T ON 'TIL 11PM...
I HAD TO KNOW WHAT THE HECK SHE WAS WATCHING..
--did it work? IT Turned my hair orange...I looked like Howdy Doody... Howdy who?
HA!
IT TURNED OUT TO BE RERUNS OF "FULL HOUSE"..
I SWEAR TO GOD.
WE KICKED HER OUT THE NEXT DAY...

We asked this woman to leave after she overflowed the toilet with fecal matter and then left the house. |

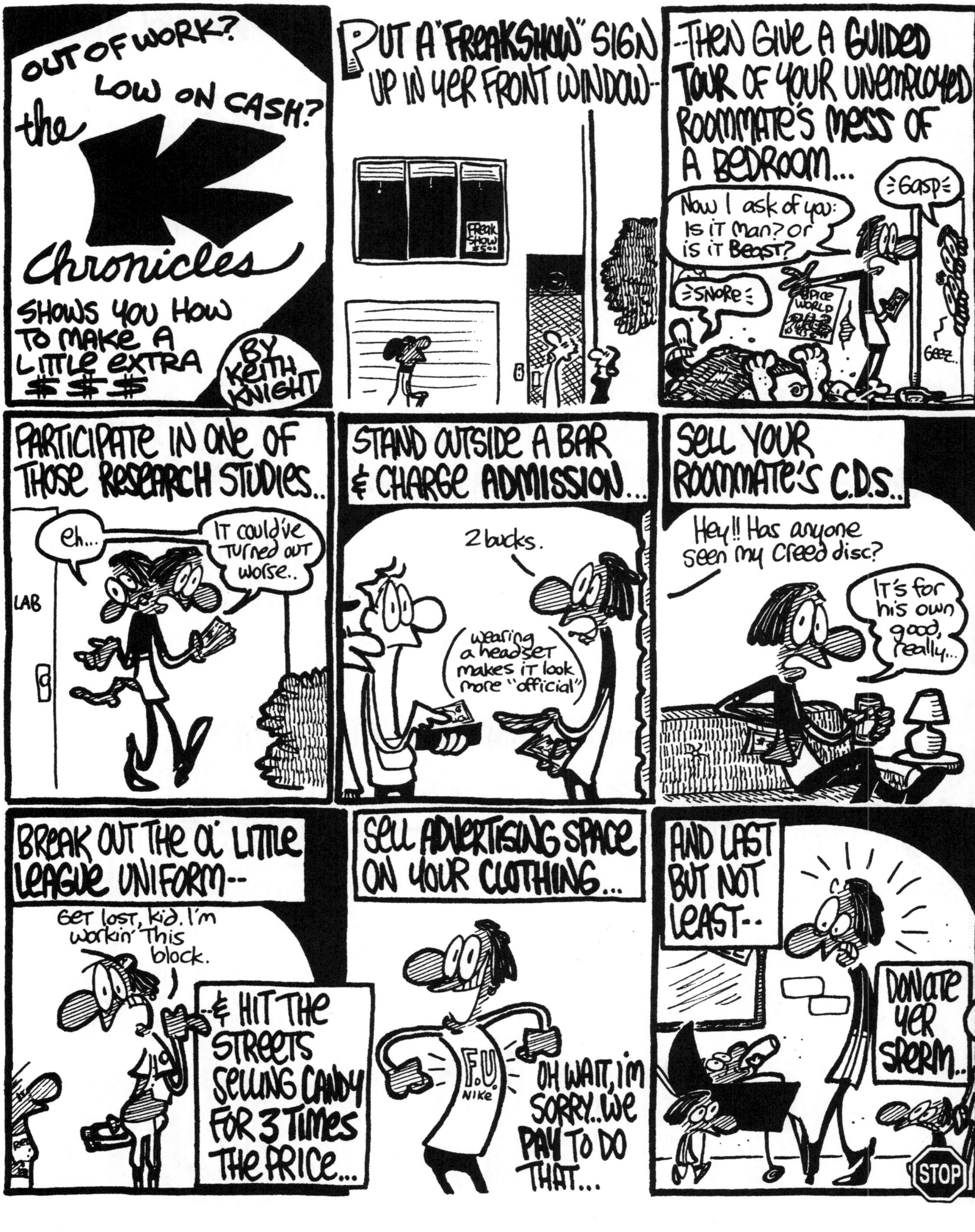

OUT OF WORK?
LOW ON CASH?
the K Chronicles
SHOWS YOU HOW TO MAKE A LITTLE EXTRA $$$
BY KEITH KNIGHT
PUT A "FREAKSHOW" SIGN UP IN YER FRONT WINDOW--
FREAK SHOW
--THEN GIVE A GUIDED TOUR OF YOUR UNEMPLOYED ROOMMATE'S MESS OF A BEDROOM...
GASP
Now I ask of you: Is it Man? or is it Beast?
SNORE
SPICE WORLD
GEEZ..
PARTICIPATE IN ONE OF THOSE RESEARCH STUDIES..
eh...
IT could've Turned out worse..
LAB
STAND OUTSIDE A BAR & CHARGE ADMISSION...
2 bucks.
(wearing a headset makes it look more "official")
SELL YOUR ROOMMATE'S C.D.S..
Hey!! Has anyone seen my Creed disc?
It's for his own good, really...
BREAK OUT THE OL' LITTLE LEAGUE UNIFORM--
Get lost, kid. I'm workin' This block.
--& HIT THE STREETS SELLING CANDY FOR 3 TIMES THE PRICE...
SELL ADVERTISING SPACE ON YOUR CLOTHING...
F.U.
NIKE
OH WAIT, I'M SORRY..WE PAY TO DO THAT...
AND LAST BUT NOT LEAST--
DONATE YER SPERM...
STOP

316 | *Third panel has a pig between the guy's legs.*

32 LINES ABOUT 32 ROOMMATES

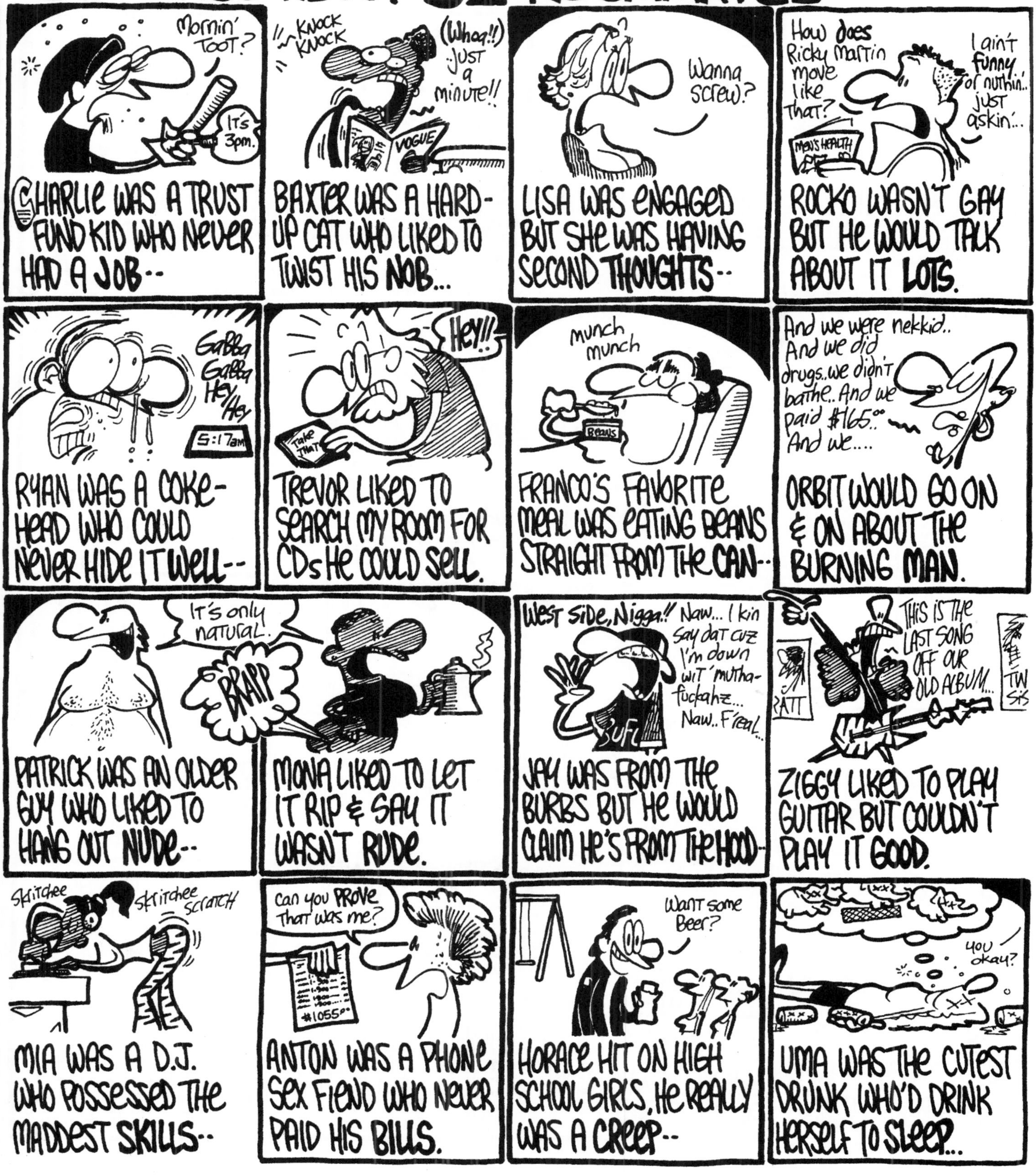

Mornin' TOOT?
It's 3pm.
CHARLIE WAS A TRUST FUND KID WHO NEVER HAD A JOB--
KNOCK KNOCK
(Whoa!!) JUST a minute!!
VOGUE
BAXTER WAS A HARD-UP CAT WHO LIKED TO TWIST HIS NOB...
Wanna screw?
LISA WAS ENGAGED BUT SHE WAS HAVING SECOND THOUGHTS--
How does Ricky Martin move like That?
I ain't funny or nuthin'.. Just askin'..
MEN'S HEALTH
ROCKO WASN'T GAY BUT HE WOULD TALK ABOUT IT LOTS.
Gabba Gabba Hey Hey
5:17am
RYAN WAS A COKE-HEAD WHO COULD NEVER HIDE IT WELL--
HEY!!
TAKE THAT
TREVOR LIKED TO SEARCH MY ROOM FOR CDs HE COULD SELL.
munch munch
BEANS
FRANCO'S FAVORITE MEAL WAS EATING BEANS STRAIGHT FROM THE CAN--
And we were nekkid.. And we did drugs..we didn't bathe.. And we paid $165.00 And we....
ORBIT WOULD GO ON & ON ABOUT THE BURNING MAN.
It's only natural.
PATRICK WAS AN OLDER GUY WHO LIKED TO HANG OUT NUDE--
BRAPP
MONA LIKED TO LET IT RIP & SAY IT WASN'T RUDE.
West Side, Nigga!!
Naw... I kin say dat cuz I'm down wit' mutha-fuckahz... Naw.. F'real..
JAY WAS FROM THE BURBS BUT HE WOULD CLAIM HE'S FROM THE HOOD--
THIS IS THE LAST SONG OFF OUR OLD ALBUM...
RATT
ZIGGY LIKED TO PLAY GUITAR BUT COULDN'T PLAY IT GOOD.
Skritchee
skritchee scratch
MIA WAS A D.J. WHO POSSESSED THE MADDEST SKILLS--
Can you PROVE That was me?
#1055.00
ANTON WAS A PHONE SEX FIEND WHO NEVER PAID HIS BILLS.
Want some Beer?
HORACE HIT ON HIGH SCHOOL GIRLS, HE REALLY WAS A CREEP--
You okay?
UMA WAS THE CUTEST DRUNK WHO'D DRINK HERSELF TO SLEEP...

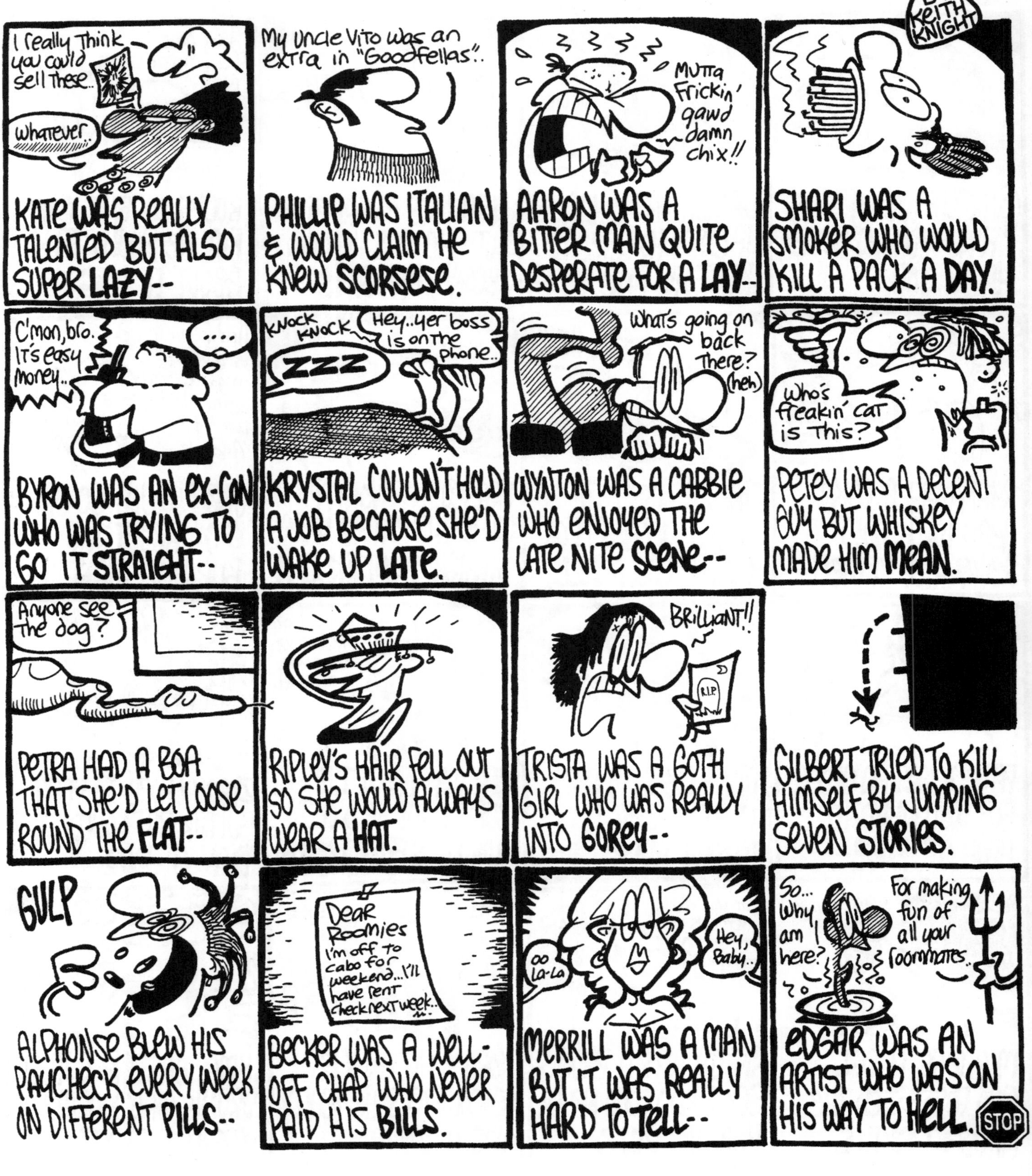
BY KEITH KNIGHT
I really think you could sell these..
Whatever..
KATE WAS REALLY TALENTED BUT ALSO SUPER LAZY--
My Uncle Vito was an extra in "Goodfellas"..
PHILLIP WAS ITALIAN & WOULD CLAIM HE KNEW SCORSESE.
Mutta frickin' gawd damn chix!!
AARON WAS A BITTER MAN QUITE DESPERATE FOR A LAY--
SHARI WAS A SMOKER WHO WOULD KILL A PACK A DAY.
C'mon, bro. It's easy money..
....
BYRON WAS AN EX-CON WHO WAS TRYING TO GO IT STRAIGHT--
KNOCK KNOCK
Hey..yer boss is on the phone..
ZZZ
KRYSTAL COULDN'T HOLD A JOB BECAUSE SHE'D WAKE UP LATE.
What's going on back there? (heh)
WYNTON WAS A CABBIE WHO ENJOYED THE LATE NITE SCENE--
Who's freakin' cat is this?
PETEY WAS A DECENT GUY BUT WHISKEY MADE HIM MEAN.
Anyone see the dog?
PETRA HAD A BOA THAT SHE'D LET LOOSE ROUND THE FLAT--
RIPLEY'S HAIR FELL OUT SO SHE WOULD ALWAYS WEAR A HAT.
BRILLIANT!!
R.I.P.
TRISTA WAS A GOTH GIRL WHO WAS REALLY INTO GOREY--
GILBERT TRIED TO KILL HIMSELF BY JUMPING SEVEN STORIES.
GULP
ALPHONSE BLEW HIS PAYCHECK EVERY WEEK ON DIFFERENT PILLS--
Dear Roomies I'm off to Cabo for weekend...I'll have rent check next week..
BECKER WAS A WELL-OFF CHAP WHO NEVER PAID HIS BILLS.
oo La-La
Hey, Baby..
MERRILL WAS A MAN BUT IT WAS REALLY HARD TO TELL--
So... why am I here?
For making fun of all your roommates..
EDGAR WAS AN ARTIST WHO WAS ON HIS WAY TO HELL.
STOP

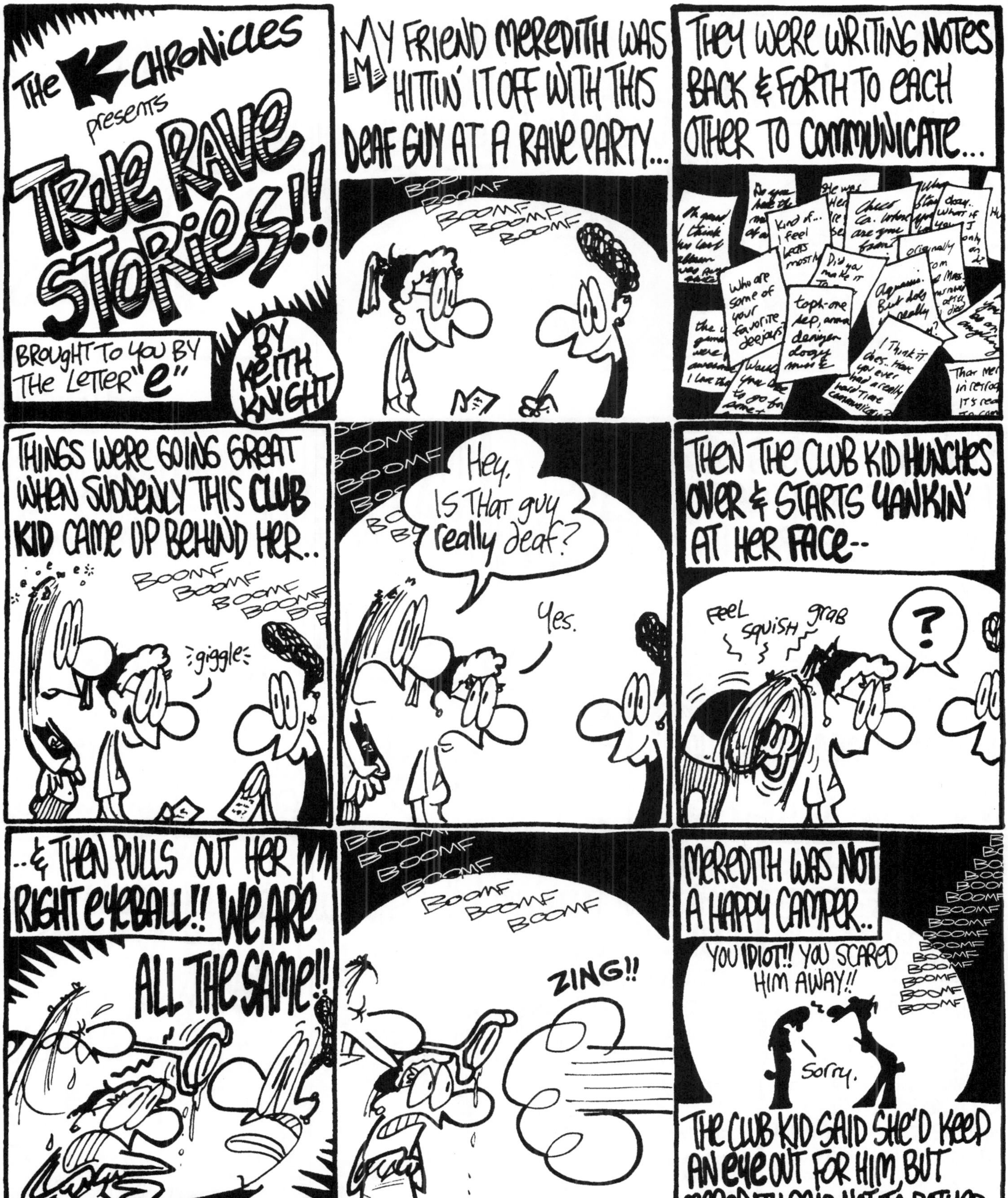
THE K CHRONICLES
presents
TRUE RAVE STORIES!!
BROUGHT TO YOU BY THE LETTER "e"
BY KEITH KNIGHT
MY FRIEND MEREDITH WAS HITTIN' IT OFF WITH THIS DEAF GUY AT A RAVE PARTY...
BOOMF BOOMF BOOMF BOOMF
THEY WERE WRITING NOTES BACK & FORTH TO EACH OTHER TO COMMUNICATE...
Who are some of your favorite deejays?
I think it does.. have you ever had a really hard time communicating?
THINGS WERE GOING GREAT WHEN SUDDENLY THIS CLUB KID CAME UP BEHIND HER..
BOOMF BOOMF BOOMF BOOMF
giggle
BOOMF BOOMF
Hey, IS THAT guy really deaf?
Yes.
THEN THE CLUB KID HUNCHES OVER & STARTS YANKIN' AT HER FACE--
FEEL SQUISH GRAB
?
..& THEN PULLS OUT HER RIGHT EYEBALL!! WE ARE ALL THE SAME!!
BOOMF BOOMF BOOMF BOOMF BOOMF BOOMF
ZING!!
MEREDITH WAS NOT A HAPPY CAMPER..
BOOMF BOOMF BOOMF BOOMF BOOMF BOOMF BOOMF
YOU IDIOT!! YOU SCARED HIM AWAY!!
Sorry.
THE CLUB KID SAID SHE'D KEEP AN EYE OUT FOR HIM, BUT MEREDITH SAID NOT TO BOTHER..

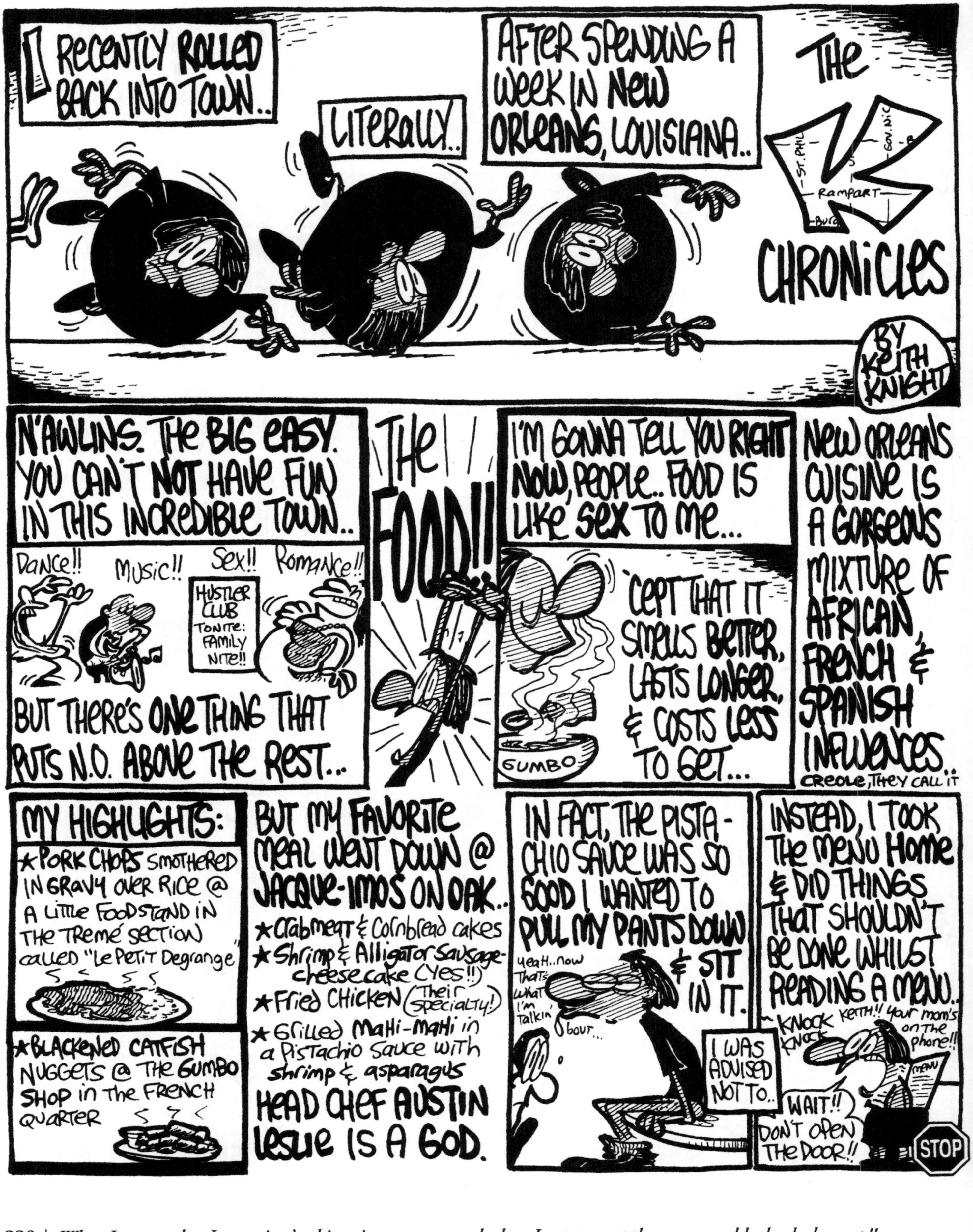

I RECENTLY ROLLED BACK INTO TOWN..
LITERALLY..
AFTER SPENDING A WEEK IN NEW ORLEANS, LOUISIANA..
THE
ST. PHIL
GOV. NIC
RAMPART
CHRONICLES
BY KEITH KNIGHT
N'AWLINS. THE BIG EASY. YOU CAN'T NOT HAVE FUN IN THIS INCREDIBLE TOWN..
DANCE!!
MUSIC!!
SEX!!
ROMANCE!!
HUSTLER CLUB TONITE: FAMILY NITE!!
BUT THERE'S ONE THING THAT PUTS N.O. ABOVE THE REST...
THE FOOD!!
I'M GONNA TELL YOU RIGHT NOW, PEOPLE.. FOOD IS LIKE SEX TO ME...
'CEPT THAT IT SMELLS BETTER, LASTS LONGER, & COSTS LESS TO GET...
GUMBO
NEW ORLEANS CUISINE IS A GORGEOUS MIXTURE OF AFRICAN, FRENCH & SPANISH INFLUENCES.
CREOLE, THEY CALL IT
MY HIGHLIGHTS:
★PORK CHOPS SMOTHERED IN GRAVY OVER RICE @ A LITTLE FOODSTAND IN THE TREMÉ SECTION CALLED "LE PETIT DEGRANGE"
★BLACKENED CATFISH NUGGETS @ THE GUMBO SHOP IN THE FRENCH QUARTER
BUT MY FAVORITE MEAL WENT DOWN @ JACQUE-IMO'S ON OAK..
★CRABMEAT & CORNBREAD CAKES
★SHRIMP & ALLIGATOR SAUSAGE-CHEESECAKE (YES!!)
★FRIED CHICKEN (THEIR SPECIALTY!)
★GRILLED MAHI-MAHI IN A PISTACHIO SAUCE WITH SHRIMP & ASPARAGUS
HEAD CHEF AUSTIN LESLIE IS A GOD.
IN FACT, THE PISTACHIO SAUCE WAS SO GOOD I WANTED TO PULL MY PANTS DOWN & SIT IN IT.
YEAH.. NOW THAT'S WHAT I'M TALKIN' 'BOUT...
I WAS ADVISED NOT TO..
INSTEAD, I TOOK THE MENU HOME & DID THINGS THAT SHOULDN'T BE DONE WHILST READING A MENU..
KNOCK KNOCK
KEITH!! YOUR MOM'S ON THE PHONE!!
MENU
WAIT!! DON'T OPEN THE DOOR!!
STOP

 When I returned to Jacque-imo's, this strip was up over the bar. I got to meet the owner and he hooked me up!!

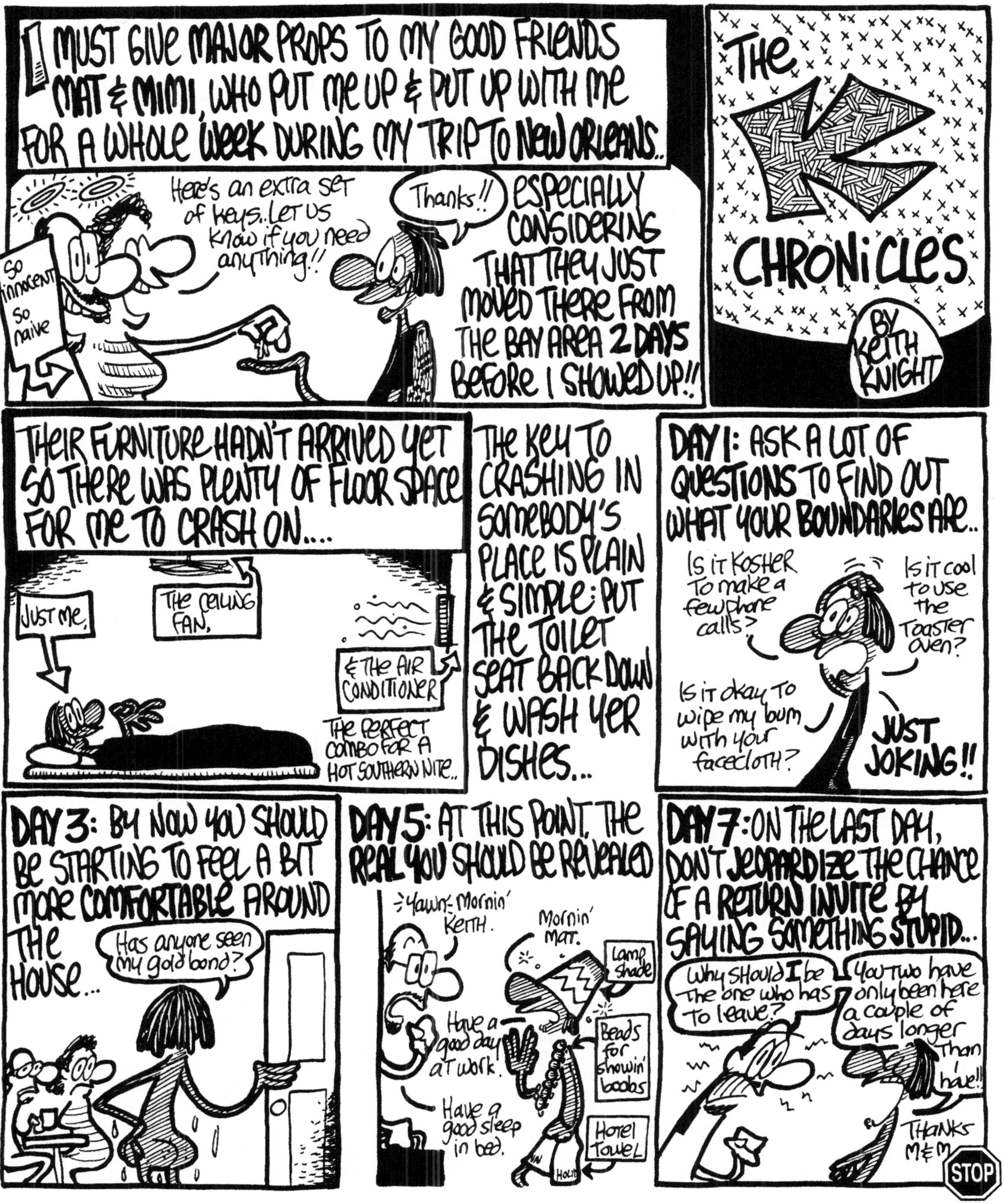

I MUST GIVE MAJOR PROPS TO MY GOOD FRIENDS MAT & MIMI, WHO PUT ME UP & PUT UP WITH ME FOR A WHOLE WEEK DURING MY TRIP TO NEW ORLEANS..
Here's an extra set of keys.. Let us know if you need anything!!
So innocent So naive
Thanks!!
ESPECIALLY CONSIDERING THAT THEY JUST MOVED THERE FROM THE BAY AREA 2 DAYS BEFORE I SHOWED UP!!
THE K CHRONICLES
BY KEITH KNIGHT
THEIR FURNITURE HADN'T ARRIVED YET SO THERE WAS PLENTY OF FLOOR SPACE FOR ME TO CRASH ON....
JUST ME,
THE CEILING FAN,
& THE AIR CONDITIONER
THE PERFECT COMBO FOR A HOT SOUTHERN NITE..
THE KEY TO CRASHING IN SOMEBODY'S PLACE IS PLAIN & SIMPLE: PUT THE TOILET SEAT BACK DOWN & WASH YER DISHES...
DAY 1: ASK A LOT OF QUESTIONS TO FIND OUT WHAT YOUR BOUNDARIES ARE..
Is it Kosher to make a few phone calls?
Is it cool to use the Toaster oven?
Is it okay to wipe my bum with your facecloth?
JUST JOKING!!
DAY 3: BY NOW YOU SHOULD BE STARTING TO FEEL A BIT MORE COMFORTABLE AROUND THE HOUSE...
Has anyone seen my gold bond?
DAY 5: AT THIS POINT, THE REAL YOU SHOULD BE REVEALED
-Yawn- Mornin' Keith.
Mornin' Mat.
Lamp shade
Have a good day at work.
Beads for showin' boobs
Have a good sleep in bed.
Hotel Towel
DAY 7: ON THE LAST DAY, DON'T JEOPARDIZE THE CHANCE OF A RETURN INVITE BY SAYING SOMETHING STUPID...
Why should I be the one who has to leave?
You two have only been here a couple of days longer than I have!!
THANKS M&M
STOP

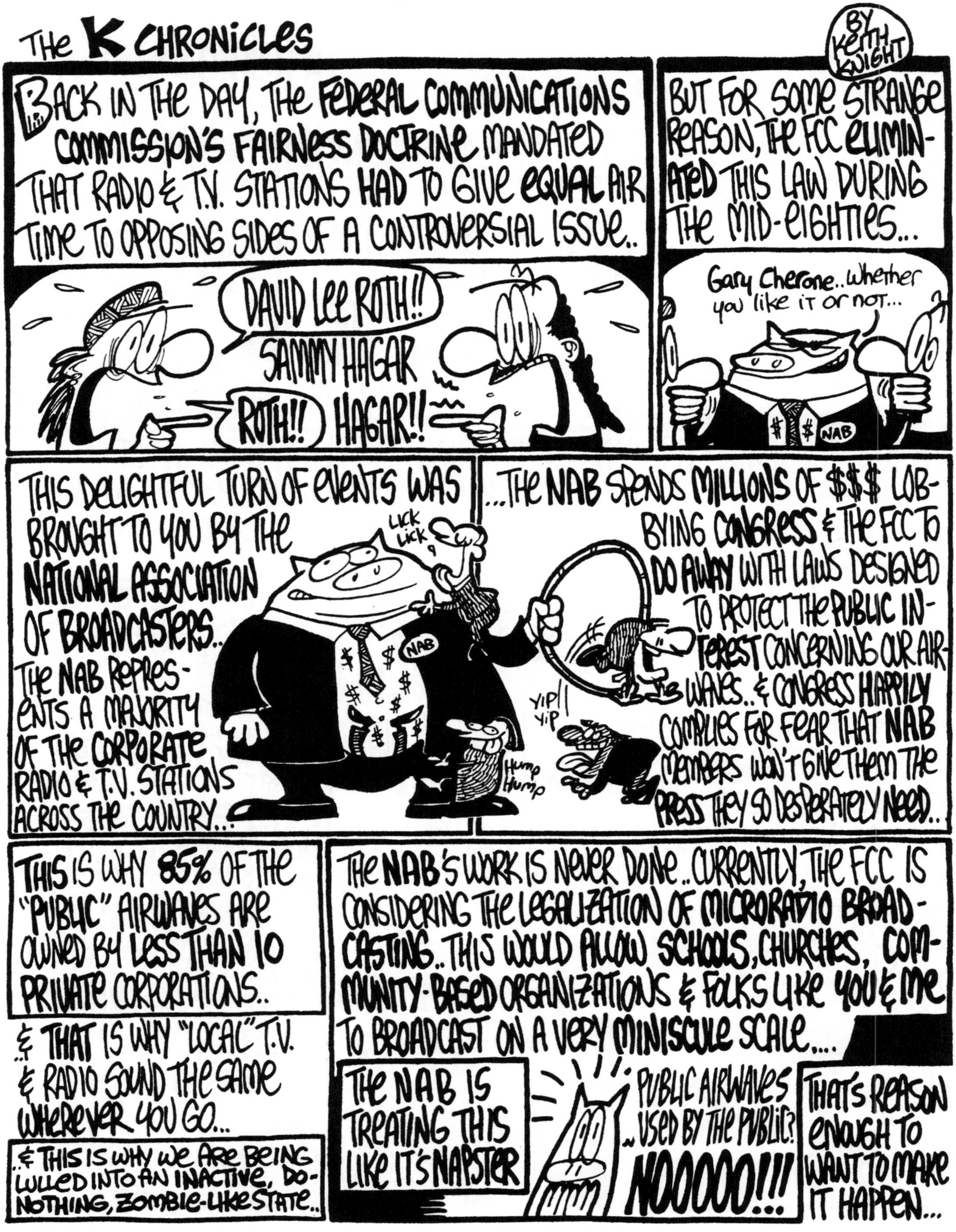
The K Chronicles
By Keith Knight
Back in the day, the Federal Communications Commission's Fairness Doctrine mandated that radio & T.V. stations had to give equal air time to opposing sides of a controversial issue..
David Lee Roth!!
Sammy Hagar
Roth!!
Hagar!!
But for some strange reason, the FCC eliminated this law during the mid-eighties...
Gary Cherone.. whether you like it or not...
NAB
This delightful turn of events was brought to you by the National Association of Broadcasters..
The NAB represents a majority of the corporate radio & T.V. stations across the country..
Lick Lick
Hump Hump
Yip!! Yip
...The NAB spends millions of $$$ lobbying Congress & the FCC to do away with laws designed to protect the public interest concerning our airwaves.. & Congress happily complies for fear that NAB members won't give them the press they so desperately need..
This is why 85% of the "public" airwaves are owned by less than 10 private corporations..
..& that is why "local" T.V. & radio sound the same wherever you go...
..& this is why we are being lulled into an inactive, do-nothing, zombie-like state..
The NAB's work is never done.. currently, the FCC is considering the legalization of microradio broadcasting.. this would allow schools, churches, community-based organizations & folks like you & me to broadcast on a very miniscule scale....
The NAB is treating this like it's Napster
..Public airwaves used by the public? NOOOOO!!!...
That's reason enough to want to make it happen...

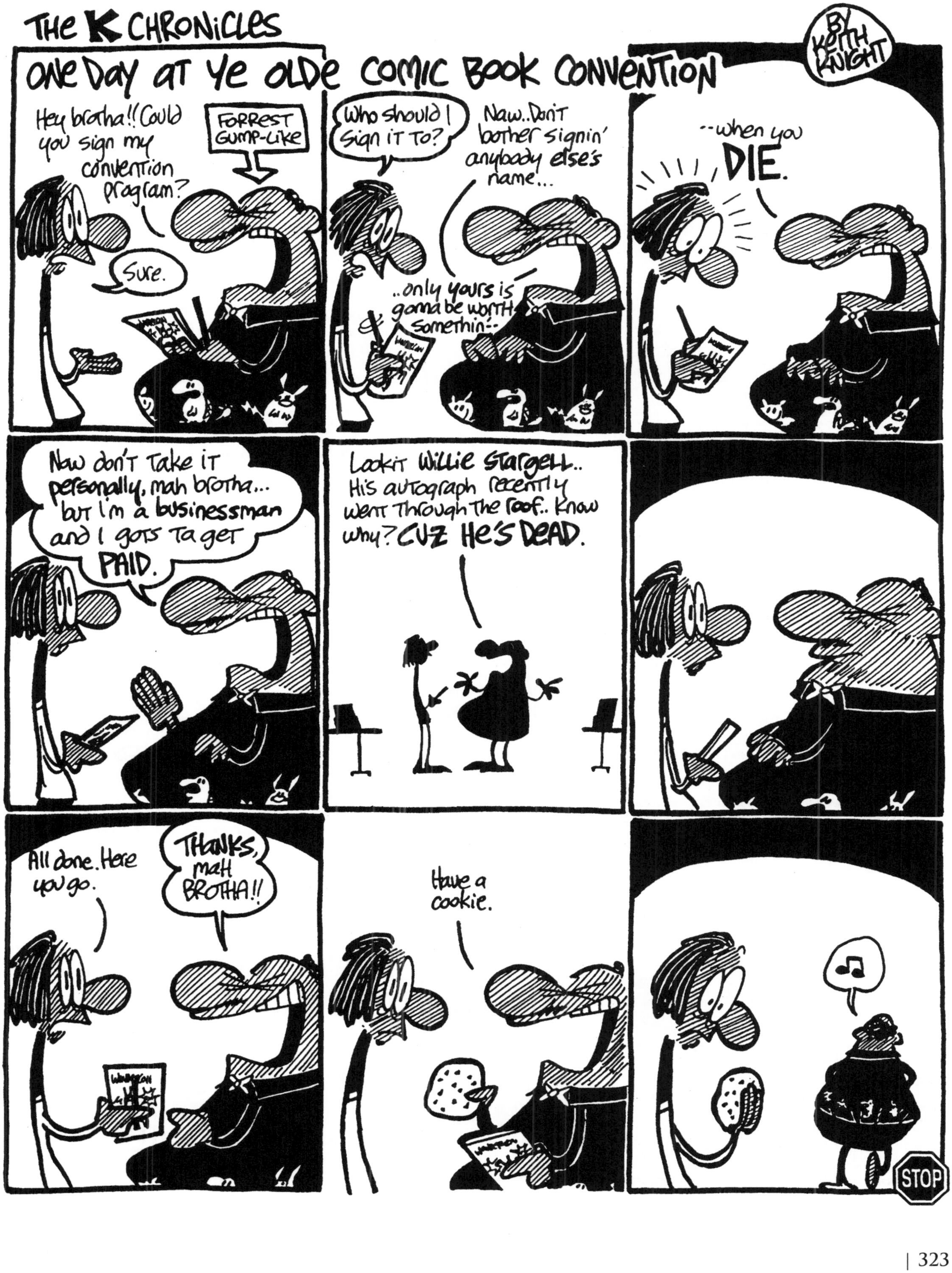
THE K CHRONICLES
BY KEITH KNIGHT
ONE DAY AT YE OLDE COMIC BOOK CONVENTION
Hey brotha!! Could you sign my convention program?
FORREST GUMP-LIKE
Sure.
Who should I sign it to?
Naw.. Don't bother signin' anybody else's name...
..only yours is gonna be worth somethin'--
--when you DIE.
Now don't take it personally, mah brotha... but I'm a businessman and I gots ta get PAID.
Lookit Willie Stargell.. His autograph recently went through the roof.. Know why? CUZ HE'S DEAD.
All done. Here you go.
THANKS, MAH BROTHA!!
Have a cookie.
STOP

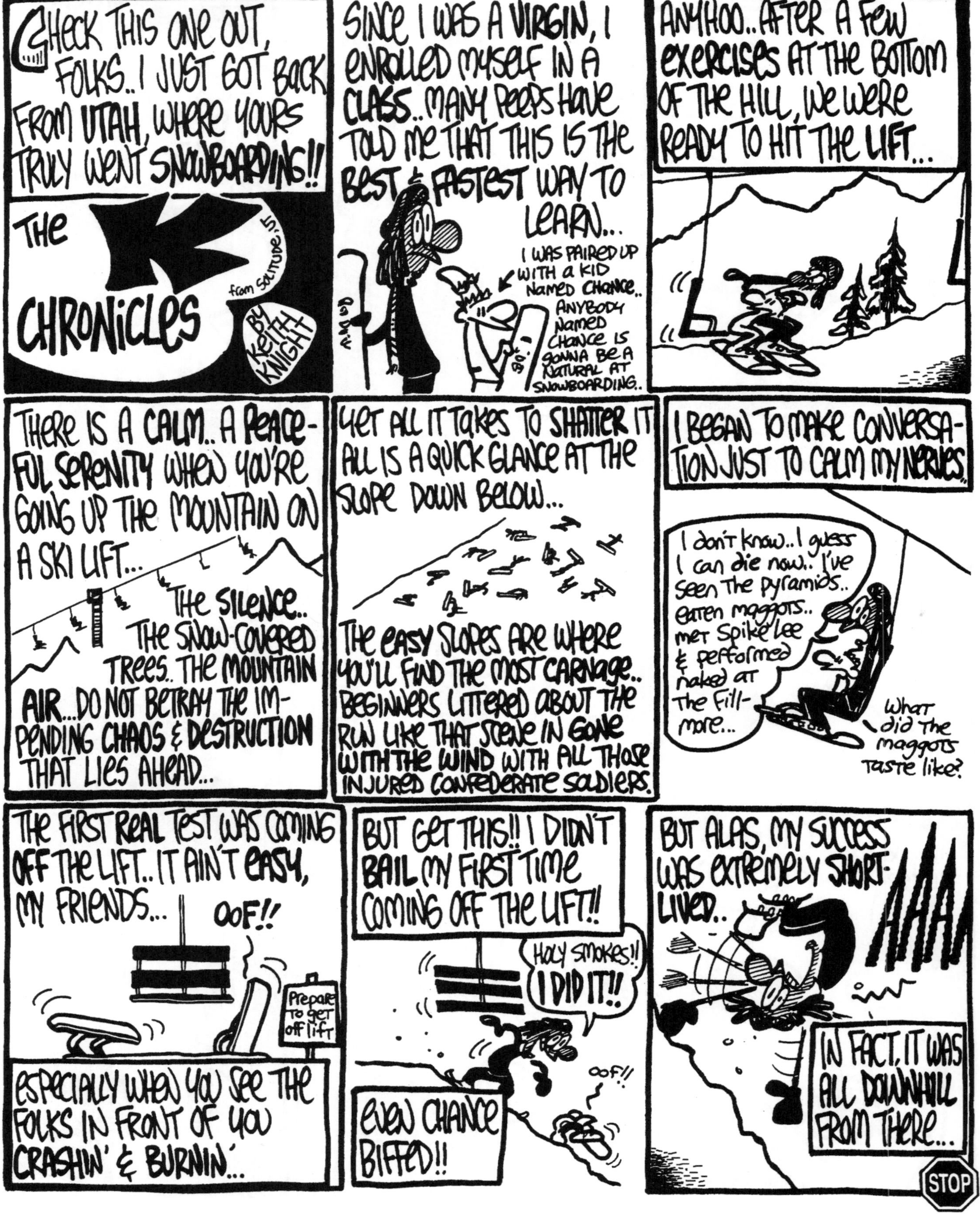
CHECK THIS ONE OUT, FOLKS.. I JUST GOT BACK FROM UTAH, WHERE YOURS TRULY WENT SNOWBOARDING!!
THE K CHRONICLES
from SOLITUDE, UT
BY KEITH KNIGHT
SINCE I WAS A VIRGIN, I ENROLLED MYSELF IN A CLASS.. MANY PEEPS HAVE TOLD ME THAT THIS IS THE BEST & FASTEST WAY TO LEARN...
I WAS PAIRED UP WITH A KID NAMED CHANCE.. ANYBODY NAMED CHANCE IS GONNA BE A NATURAL AT SNOWBOARDING..
ANYHOO.. AFTER A FEW EXERCISES AT THE BOTTOM OF THE HILL, WE WERE READY TO HIT THE LIFT...
THERE IS A CALM.. A PEACE-FUL SERENITY WHEN YOU'RE GOING UP THE MOUNTAIN ON A SKI LIFT...
THE SILENCE.. THE SNOW-COVERED TREES.. THE MOUNTAIN AIR... DO NOT BETRAY THE IM-PENDING CHAOS & DESTRUCTION THAT LIES AHEAD...
YET ALL IT TAKES TO SHATTER IT ALL IS A QUICK GLANCE AT THE SLOPE DOWN BELOW...
THE EASY SLOPES ARE WHERE YOU'LL FIND THE MOST CARNAGE.. BEGINNERS LITTERED ABOUT THE RUN LIKE THAT SCENE IN GONE WITH THE WIND WITH ALL THOSE INJURED CONFEDERATE SOLDIERS.
I BEGAN TO MAKE CONVERSA-TION JUST TO CALM MY NERVES..
I don't know.. I guess I can die now.. I've seen the pyramids.. eaten maggots.. met Spike Lee & performed naked at The Fill-more...
What did the maggots taste like?
THE FIRST REAL TEST WAS COMING OFF THE LIFT.. IT AIN'T EASY, MY FRIENDS...
OOF!!
Prepare to get off lift
ESPECIALLY WHEN YOU SEE THE FOLKS IN FRONT OF YOU CRASHIN' & BURNIN'...
BUT GET THIS!! I DIDN'T BAIL MY FIRST TIME COMING OFF THE LIFT!!
HOLY SMOKES!! I DID IT!!
EVEN CHANCE BIFFED!!
OOF!!
BUT ALAS, MY SUCCESS WAS EXTREMELY SHORT-LIVED..
AAA
IN FACT, IT WAS ALL DOWNHILL FROM THERE...
STOP

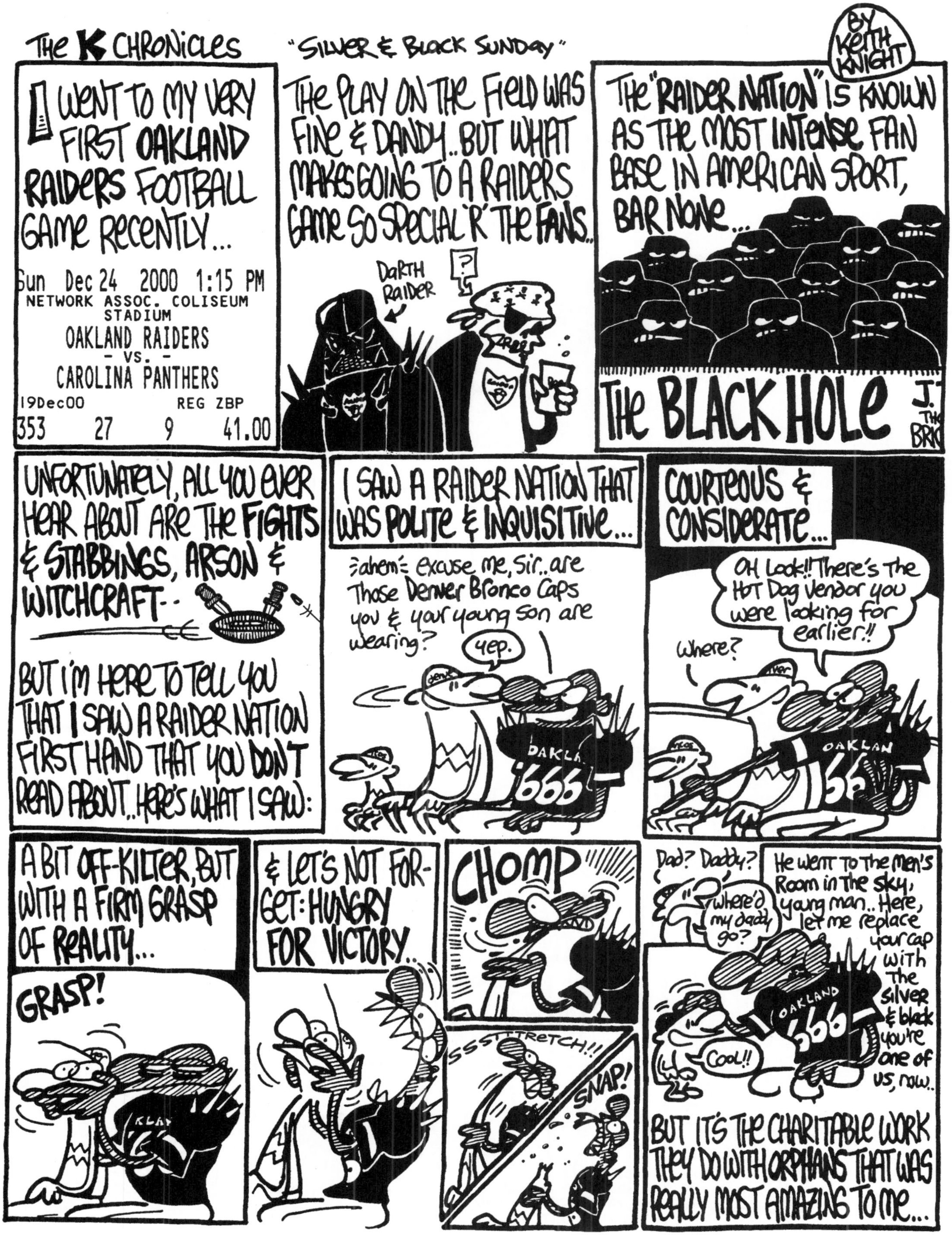
The K Chronicles
"Silver & Black Sunday"
By Keith Knight
I went to my very first Oakland Raiders football game recently...
Sun Dec 24 2000 1:15 PM
NETWORK ASSOC. COLISEUM STADIUM
OAKLAND RAIDERS
- VS. -
CAROLINA PANTHERS
19Dec00 REG ZBP
353 27 9 41.00
The play on the field was fine & dandy.. but what makes going to a Raiders game so special 'R' the fans...
Darth Raider
?
The "Raider Nation" is known as the most intense fan base in American sport, bar none...
The Black Hole
Unfortunately, all you ever hear about are the fights & stabbings, arson & witchcraft..
But I'm here to tell you that I saw a Raider Nation first hand that you don't read about.. Here's what I saw:
I saw a Raider Nation that was polite & inquisitive...
=ahem= excuse me, Sir.. are those Denver Bronco caps you & your young son are wearing?
Yep.
Oakl
666
Courteous & considerate...
Oh look!! There's the Hot Dog vendor you were looking for earlier!!
Where?
Oaklan
A bit off-kilter, but with a firm grasp of reality...
Grasp!
& let's not forget: hungry for victory...
Chomp
Sssttttretch!!
Snap!
Dad? Daddy?
Where'd my daddy go?
He went to the men's room in the sky, young man.. Here, let me replace your cap with the silver & black. You're one of us, now..
Oakland
666
Cool!!
But it's the charitable work they do with orphans that was really most amazing to me...

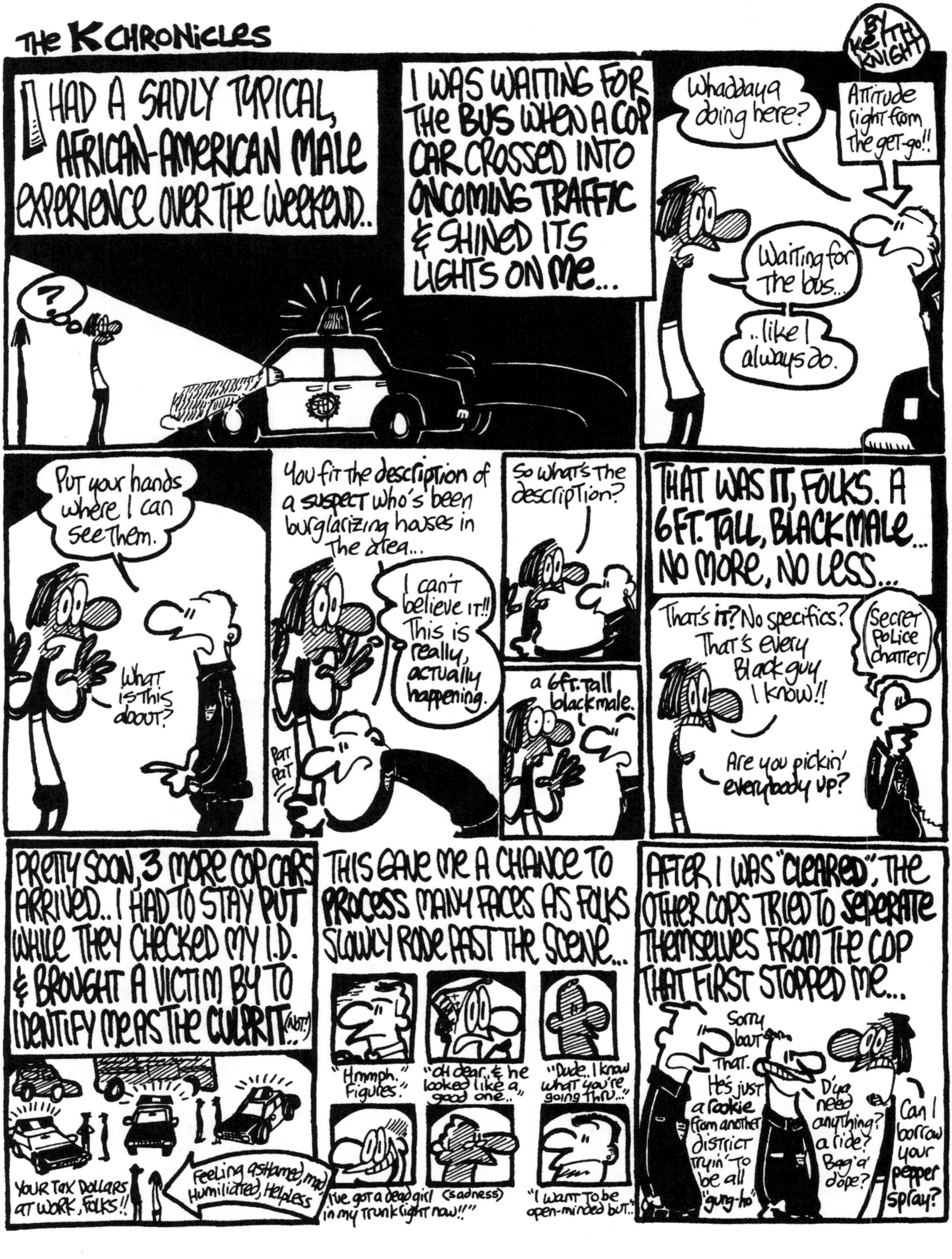
THE K CHRONICLES
BY KEITH KNIGHT
I HAD A SADLY TYPICAL, AFRICAN-AMERICAN MALE EXPERIENCE OVER THE WEEKEND..
?
I WAS WAITING FOR THE BUS WHEN A COP CAR CROSSED INTO ONCOMING TRAFFIC & SHINED ITS LIGHTS ON ME...
Whaddaya doing here?
Attitude right from the get-go!!
Waiting for the bus..
..like I always do.
PUT your hands where I can see them.
What is this about?
You fit the description of a suspect who's been burglarizing houses in the area...
I can't believe it!! This is really, actually happening.
PAT PAT
So what's the description?
a 6ft. tall black male.
THAT WAS IT, FOLKS. A 6FT. TALL, BLACK MALE... NO MORE, NO LESS...
That's it? No specifics? That's every Black guy I know!!
Secret police chatter
Are you pickin' everybody up?
PRETTY SOON, 3 MORE COP CARS ARRIVED.. I HAD TO STAY PUT WHILE THEY CHECKED MY I.D. & BROUGHT A VICTIM BY TO IDENTIFY ME AS THE CULPRIT (NOT!)..
YOUR TAX DOLLARS AT WORK, FOLKS!!
Feeling ashamed, mad, Humiliated, Helpless
THIS GAVE ME A CHANCE TO PROCESS MANY FACES AS FOLKS SLOWLY RODE PAST THE SCENE...
"Hmmph." Figures."
"Oh dear, & he looked like a good one.."
"Dude.. I know what you're going thru..."
"I've got a dead girl (sadness) in my trunk right now!!"
"I want to be open-minded but.."
AFTER I WAS "CLEARED", THE OTHER COPS TRIED TO SEPERATE THEMSELVES FROM THE COP THAT FIRST STOPPED ME...
Sorry 'bout that.
He's just a rookie from another district tryin' to be all "gung-ho"
D'ya need anything? a ride? Bag 'a' dope?
Can I borrow your pepper spray?

My roommate got off a bus during the incident and came over and started yelling and getting' in the cops faces. Can you imagine what would've happened to him if he wasn't white?

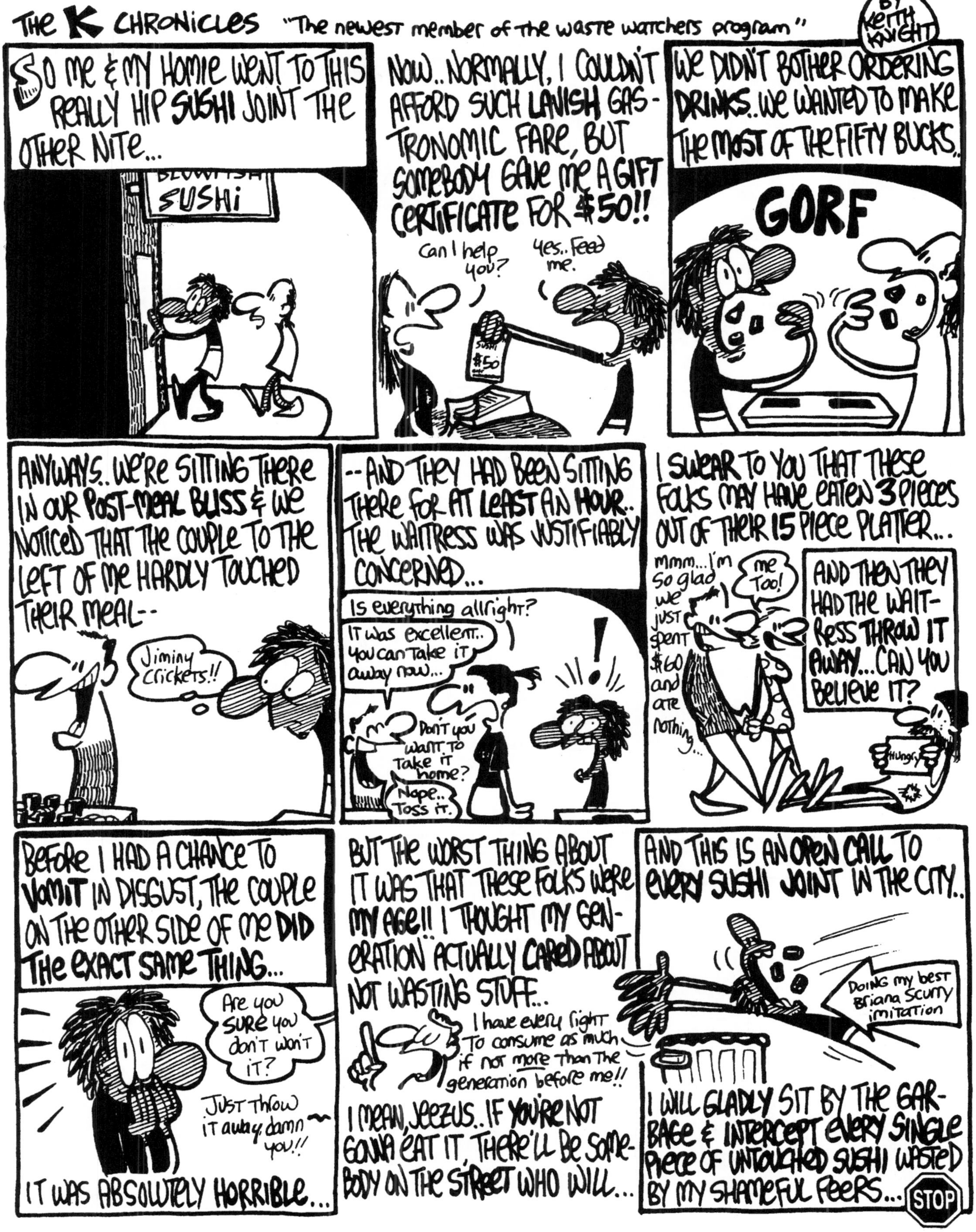
THE K CHRONICLES "The newest member of the waste watchers program"
BY KEITH KNIGHT
SO ME & MY HOMIE WENT TO THIS REALLY HIP SUSHI JOINT THE OTHER NITE...
SUSHI
NOW.. NORMALLY, I COULDN'T AFFORD SUCH LAVISH GAS-TRONOMIC FARE, BUT SOMEBODY GAVE ME A GIFT CERTIFICATE FOR $50!!
Can I help you?
Yes.. Feed me.
SUSHI $50
WE DIDN'T BOTHER ORDERING DRINKS.. WE WANTED TO MAKE THE MOST OF THE FIFTY BUCKS..
GORF
ANYWAYS.. WE'RE SITTING THERE IN OUR POST-MEAL BLISS & WE NOTICED THAT THE COUPLE TO THE LEFT OF ME HARDLY TOUCHED THEIR MEAL--
Jiminy Crickets!!
--AND THEY HAD BEEN SITTING THERE FOR AT LEAST AN HOUR.. THE WAITRESS WAS JUSTIFIABLY CONCERNED...
Is everything allright?
It was excellent.. You can take it away now...
Don't you want to take it home?
Nope.. Toss it.
!
I SWEAR TO YOU THAT THESE FOLKS MAY HAVE EATEN 3 PIECES OUT OF THEIR 15 PIECE PLATTER...
Mmm... I'm so glad we just spent $60 and ate nothing...
Me too!
AND THEN THEY HAD THE WAIT-RESS THROW IT AWAY... CAN YOU BELIEVE IT?
Hungry
BEFORE I HAD A CHANCE TO VOMIT IN DISGUST, THE COUPLE ON THE OTHER SIDE OF ME DID THE EXACT SAME THING...
Are you SURE you don't want it?
Just throw it away, damn you!!
IT WAS ABSOLUTELY HORRIBLE...
BUT THE WORST THING ABOUT IT WAS THAT THESE FOLKS WERE MY AGE!! I THOUGHT MY GEN-ERATION ACTUALLY CARED ABOUT NOT WASTING STUFF...
I have every right to consume as much if not more than the generation before me!!
I MEAN, JEEZUS.. IF YOU'RE NOT GONNA EAT IT, THERE'LL BE SOME-BODY ON THE STREET WHO WILL...
AND THIS IS AN OPEN CALL TO EVERY SUSHI JOINT IN THE CITY..
Doing my best Briana Scurry imitation
I WILL GLADLY SIT BY THE GAR-BAGE & INTERCEPT EVERY SINGLE PIECE OF UNTOUCHED SUSHI WASTED BY MY SHAMEFUL PEERS...
STOP

I won another gift certificate to this place, but this time it was UNLIMITED!! |

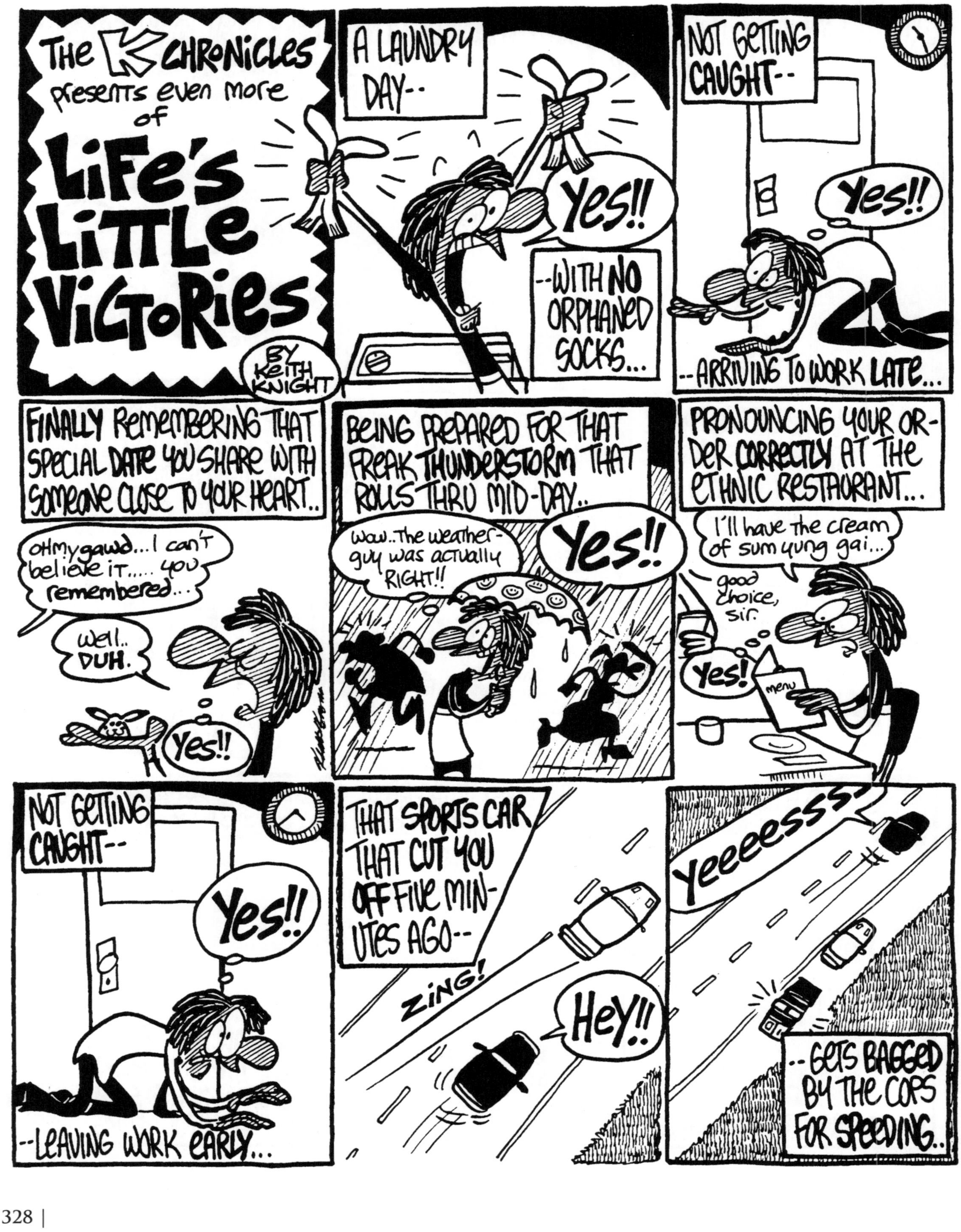

THE K CHRONICLES
presents even more of
LIFE'S LITTLE VICTORIES
BY KEITH KNIGHT
A LAUNDRY DAY--
YES!!
--WITH NO ORPHANED SOCKS...
NOT GETTING CAUGHT--
YES!!
--ARRIVING TO WORK LATE...
FINALLY REMEMBERING THAT SPECIAL DATE YOU SHARE WITH SOMEONE CLOSE TO YOUR HEART..
OHMYGAWD...I CAN'T BELIEVE IT..... YOU REMEMBERED...
WELL.. DUH.
YES!!
BEING PREPARED FOR THAT FREAK THUNDERSTORM THAT ROLLS THRU MID-DAY..
WOW..THE WEATHER-GUY WAS ACTUALLY RIGHT!!
YES!!
PRONOUNCING YOUR ORDER CORRECTLY AT THE ETHNIC RESTAURANT...
I'LL HAVE THE CREAM OF SUM YUNG GAI...
GOOD CHOICE, SIR.
YES!
MENU
NOT GETTING CAUGHT--
YES!!
--LEAVING WORK EARLY...
THAT SPORTS CAR THAT CUT YOU OFF FIVE MINUTES AGO--
ZING!
HEY!!
YEEEEESSSS
--GETS BAGGED BY THE COPS FOR SPEEDING..

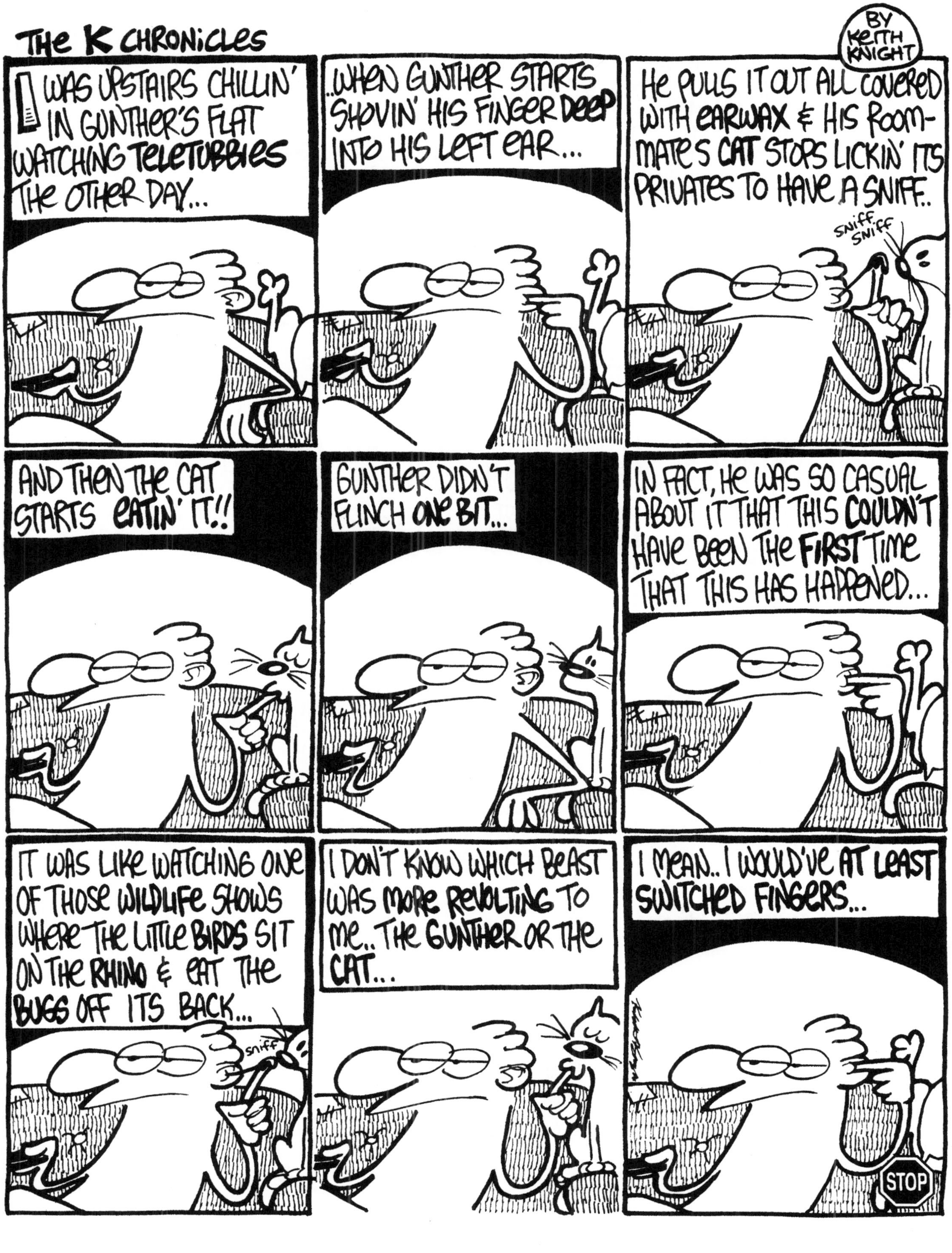
THE K CHRONICLES
BY KEITH KNIGHT
I WAS UPSTAIRS CHILLIN' IN GUNTHER'S FLAT WATCHING TELETUBBIES THE OTHER DAY...
..WHEN GUNTHER STARTS SHOVIN' HIS FINGER DEEP INTO HIS LEFT EAR...
HE PULLS IT OUT ALL COVERED WITH EARWAX & HIS ROOM-MATE'S CAT STOPS LICKIN' ITS PRIVATES TO HAVE A SNIFF..
SNIFF SNIFF
AND THEN THE CAT STARTS EATIN' IT!!
GUNTHER DIDN'T FLINCH ONE BIT...
IN FACT, HE WAS SO CASUAL ABOUT IT THAT THIS COULDN'T HAVE BEEN THE FIRST TIME THAT THIS HAS HAPPENED...
IT WAS LIKE WATCHING ONE OF THOSE WILDLIFE SHOWS WHERE THE LITTLE BIRDS SIT ON THE RHINO & EAT THE BUGS OFF ITS BACK...
SNIFF
I DON'T KNOW WHICH BEAST WAS MORE REVOLTING TO ME.. THE GUNTHER OR THE CAT...
I MEAN.. I WOULD'VE AT LEAST SWITCHED FINGERS...
STOP

Somebody wrote and said to never stick a finger in your ear after a cat licks it. You'll end up with parasites in the brain. |

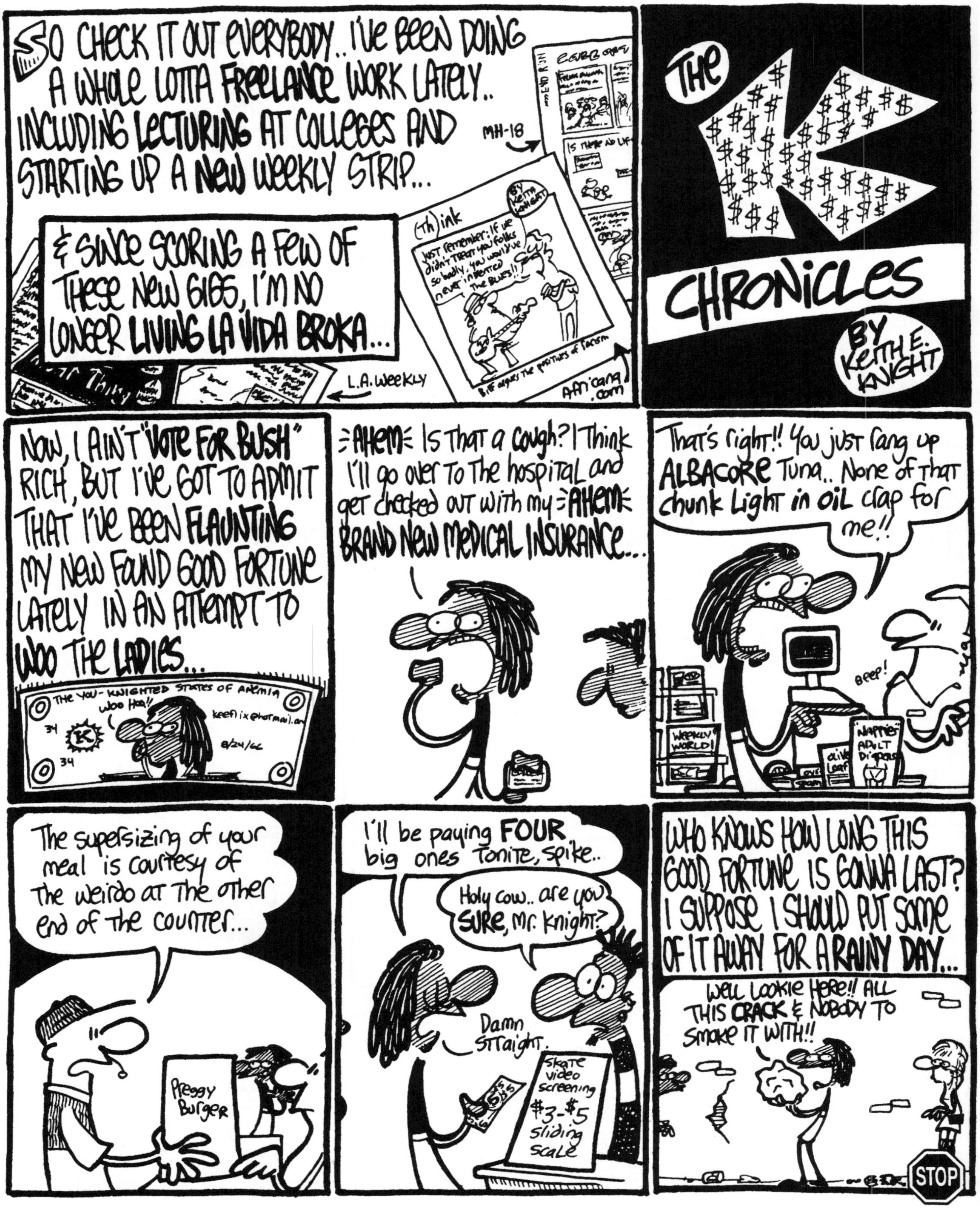
So check it out everybody.. I've been doing a whole lotta freelance work lately.. including lecturing at colleges and starting up a new weekly strip...
MH-18
(Th)ink
L.A. Weekly
Afri'cana .com
& since scoring a few of these new gigs, I'm no longer living la vida broka...
The K Chronicles
By Keith E. Knight
Now, I ain't "Vote for Bush" rich, but I've got to admit that I've been flaunting my new found good fortune lately in an attempt to woo the ladies...
The You-Knighted States of Anemia
Woo Hoo!!
=Ahem= Is that a cough? I think I'll go over to the hospital and get checked out with my =Ahem= brand new medical insurance...
That's right!! You just rang up Albacore Tuna.. None of that chunk light in oil crap for me!!
Beep!
Weekly World
Olive Loaf
Nappie's Adult Diapers
The supersizing of your meal is courtesy of the weirdo at the other end of the counter...
Preggy Burger
I'll be paying FOUR big ones tonite, Spike..
Holy cow.. are you SURE, Mr. Knight?
Damn straight.
Skate video screening $3-$5 sliding scale
Who knows how long this good fortune is gonna last? I suppose I should put some of it away for a rainy day...
Well lookie here!! All this crack & nobody to smoke it with!!
STOP

An editor wouldn't run this strip with the crack line because "we have a large white liberal readership and we do not want to offend them."

SepT. 11TH, 2001

(The only Time I've ever missed a deadline)

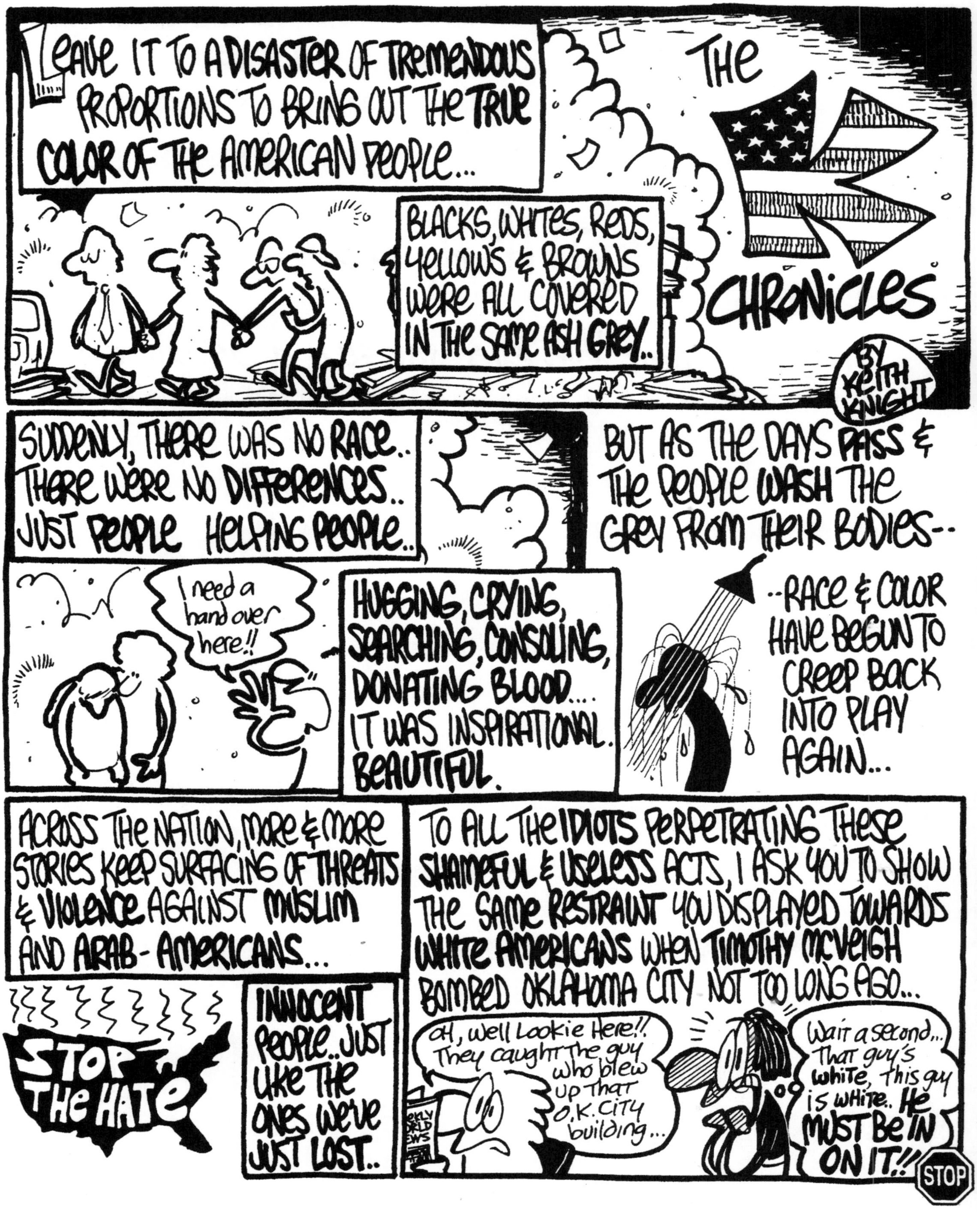
Leave it to a disaster of tremendous proportions to bring out the true color of the American people...
The K Chronicles
by Keith Knight
Blacks, whites, reds, yellows & browns were all covered in the same ash grey..
Suddenly, there was no race.. there were no differences.. just people helping people..
But as the days pass & the people wash the grey from their bodies--
I need a hand over here!!
Hugging, crying, searching, consoling, donating blood.... it was inspirational. beautiful.
--race & color have begun to creep back into play again...
Across the nation, more & more stories keep surfacing of threats & violence against Muslim and Arab-Americans...
To all the idiots perpetrating these shameful & useless acts, I ask you to show the same restraint you displayed towards white Americans when Timothy McVeigh bombed Oklahoma City not too long ago...
Stop the hate
Innocent people.. just like the ones we've just lost..
Oh, well lookie here!! They caught the guy who blew up that O.K. City building...
Wait a second... that guy's white, this guy is white.. he must be in on it!!
STOP

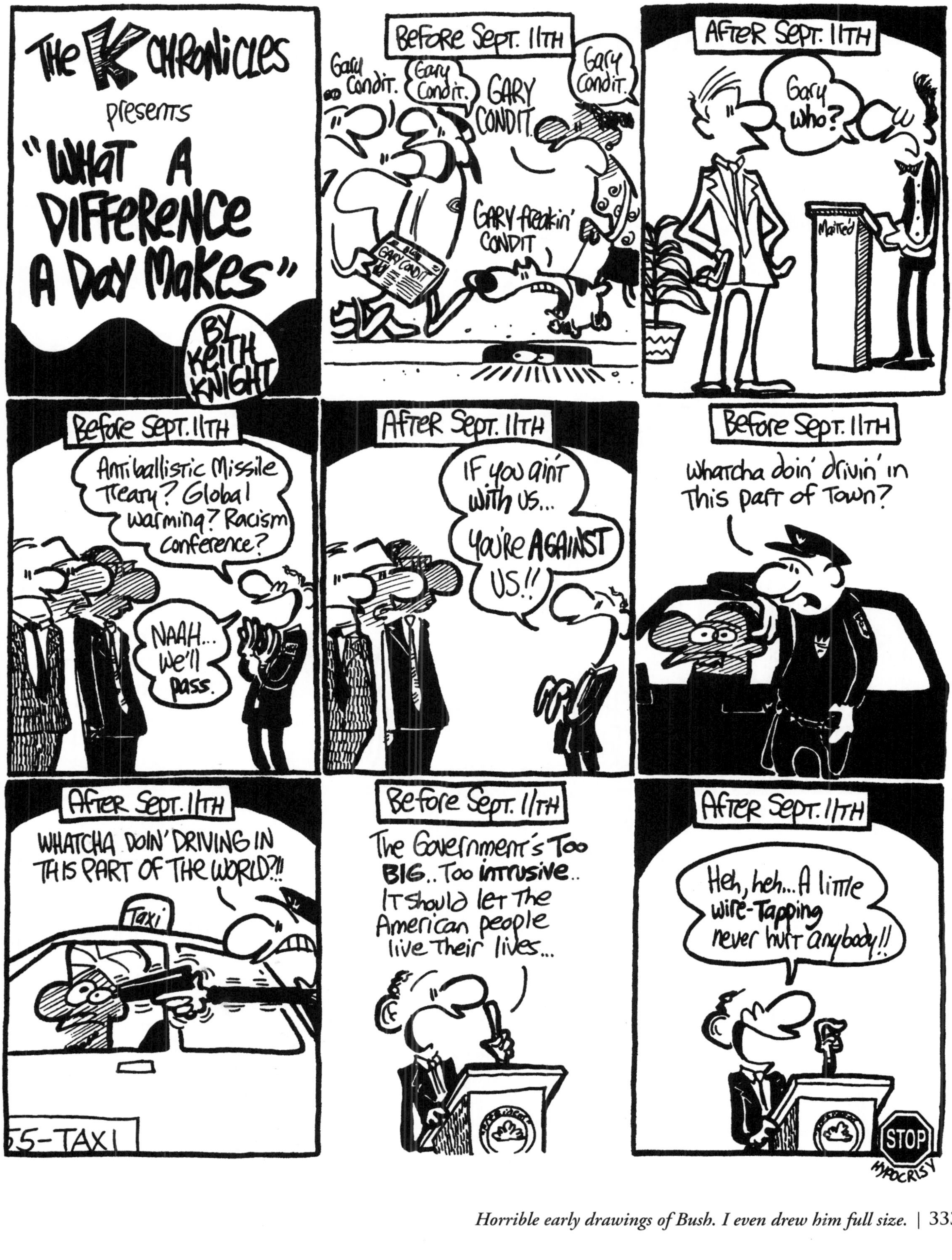
THE K CHRONICLES
presents
"WHAT A DIFFERENCE A DAY MAKES"
BY KEITH KNIGHT
Before Sept. 11th
Gary Condit.
Gary Condit.
GARY CONDIT.
Gary Condit.
Gary freakin' CONDIT
GARY CONDIT
After Sept. 11th
Gary who?
Maitre'd
Before Sept. 11th
Antiballistic Missile Treaty? Global warming? Racism conference?
NAAH... We'll pass.
After Sept. 11th
If you ain't with us...
You're AGAINST US!!
Before Sept. 11th
Whatcha doin' drivin' in This part of Town?
After Sept. 11th
WHATCHA DOIN' DRIVING IN THIS PART OF THE WORLD?!!
Taxi
55-TAXI
Before Sept. 11th
The Government's Too BIG.. Too intrusive.. It should let The American people live Their lives...
After Sept. 11th
Heh, heh... A little wire-Tapping never hurt anybody!!
STOP
HYPOCRISY

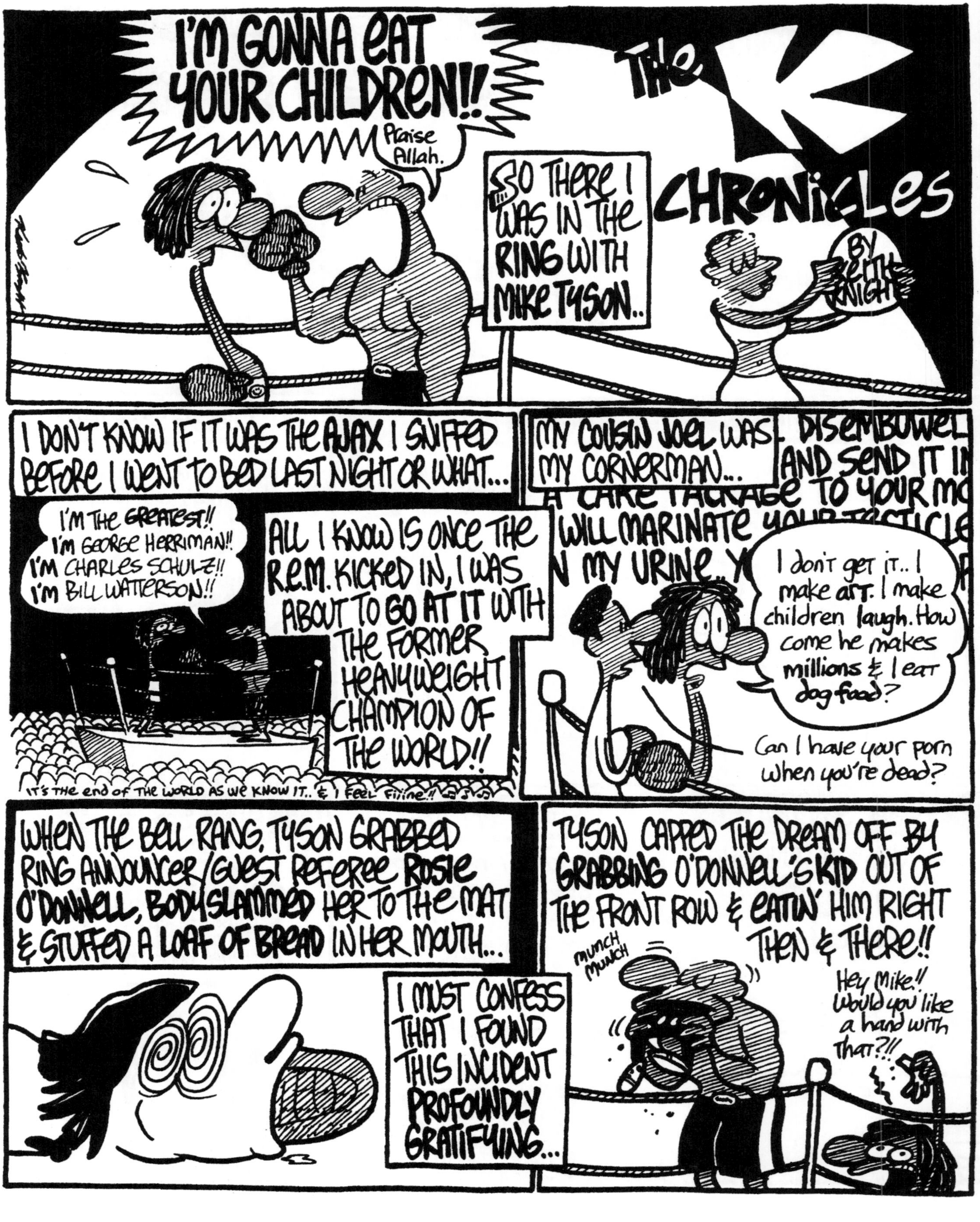
I'M GONNA EAT YOUR CHILDREN!!
THE K CHRONICLES
BY
Praise Allah.
SO THERE I WAS IN THE RING WITH MIKE TYSON..
I DON'T KNOW IF IT WAS THE AJAX I SNIFFED BEFORE I WENT TO BED LAST NIGHT OR WHAT...
I'M THE GREATEST!! I'M GEORGE HERRIMAN!! I'M CHARLES SCHULZ!! I'M BILL WATTERSON!!
ALL I KNOW IS ONCE THE R.E.M. KICKED IN, I WAS ABOUT TO GO AT IT WITH THE FORMER HEAVYWEIGHT CHAMPION OF THE WORLD!!
IT'S THE END OF THE WORLD AS WE KNOW IT.. & I FEEL FIIINE!!
MY COUSIN JOEL WAS MY CORNERMAN...
DISEMBOWEL
AND SEND IT IN
WILL MARINATE
MY URINE..
I don't get it.. I make art. I make children laugh. How come he makes millions & I eat dog food?
Can I have your porn when you're dead?
WHEN THE BELL RANG, TYSON GRABBED RING ANNOUNCER/GUEST REFEREE ROSIE O'DONNELL, BODYSLAMMED HER TO THE MAT & STUFFED A LOAF OF BREAD IN HER MOUTH...
I MUST CONFESS THAT I FOUND THIS INCIDENT PROFOUNDLY GRATIFYING...
TYSON CAPPED THE DREAM OFF BY GRABBING O'DONNELL'S KID OUT OF THE FRONT ROW & EATIN' HIM RIGHT THEN & THERE!!
MUNCH MUNCH
Hey Mike!! Would you like a hand with that?!!

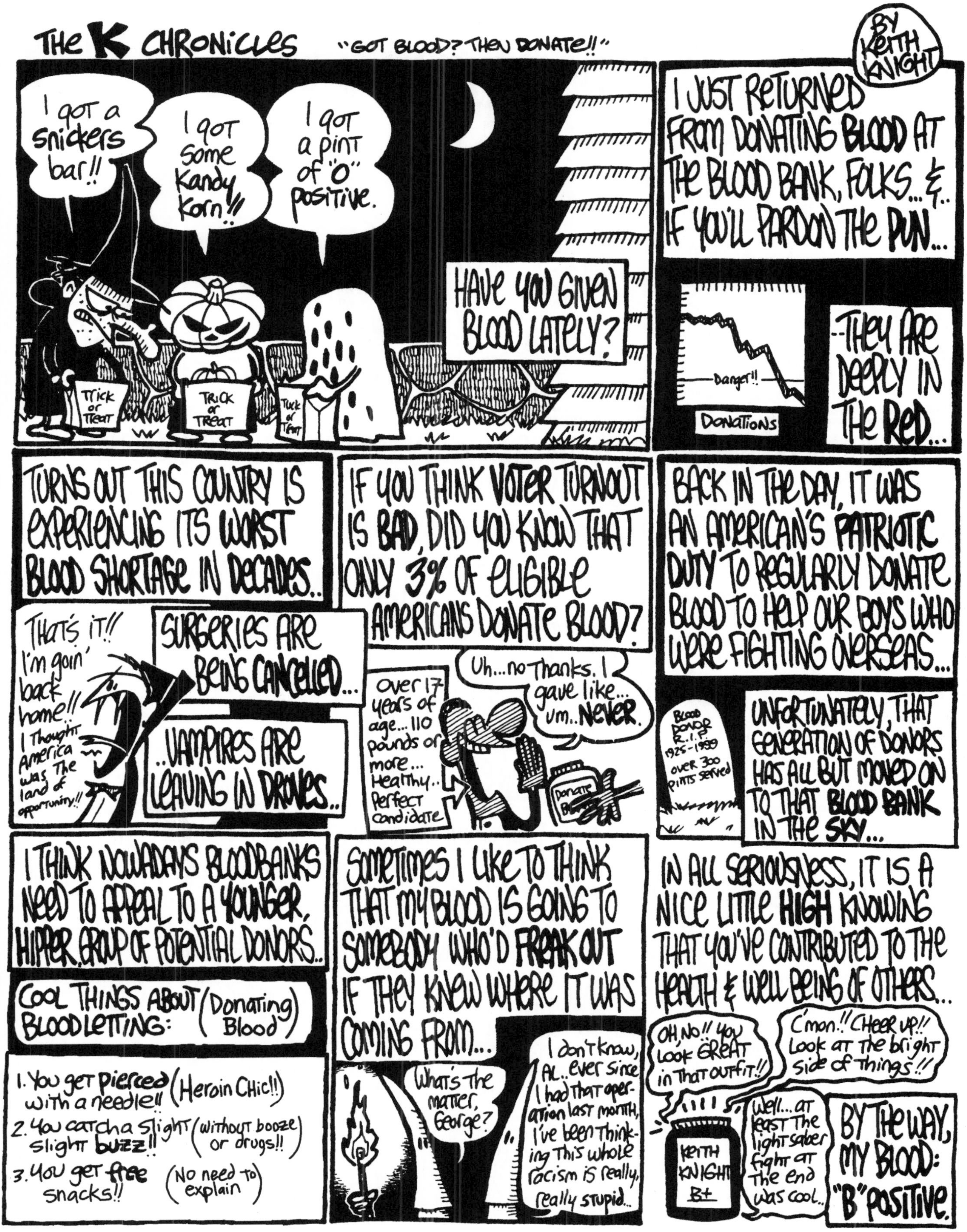

THE K CHRONICLES
"GOT BLOOD? THEN DONATE!!"
BY KEITH KNIGHT
I got a snickers bar!!
I got some Kandy Korn!!
I got a pint of "O" positive.
Trick or Treat
TRICK or TREAT
Tuck or Treat
HAVE YOU GIVEN BLOOD LATELY?
I JUST RETURNED FROM DONATING BLOOD AT THE BLOOD BANK, FOLKS... & IF YOU'LL PARDON THE PUN...
Danger!!
DONATIONS
THEY ARE DEEPLY IN THE RED...
TURNS OUT THIS COUNTRY IS EXPERIENCING ITS WORST BLOOD SHORTAGE IN DECADES..
THAT'S IT!! I'm goin' back home!! I Thought America was The land of opportunity!!
SURGERIES ARE BEING CANCELLED...
..VAMPIRES ARE LEAVING IN DROVES...
IF YOU THINK VOTER TURNOUT IS BAD, DID YOU KNOW THAT ONLY 3% OF ELIGIBLE AMERICANS DONATE BLOOD?
Over 17 years of age... 110 pounds or more... Healthy.. Perfect candidate
Uh...no Thanks. I gave like... um..NEVER.
BACK IN THE DAY, IT WAS AN AMERICAN'S PATRIOTIC DUTY TO REGULARLY DONATE BLOOD TO HELP OUR BOYS WHO WERE FIGHTING OVERSEAS...
BLOOD DONOR R.I.P. 1925-1999 OVER 300 PINTS SERVED
UNFORTUNATELY, THAT GENERATION OF DONORS HAS ALL BUT MOVED ON TO THAT BLOOD BANK IN THE SKY...
I THINK NOWADAYS BLOODBANKS NEED TO APPEAL TO A YOUNGER, HIPPER GROUP OF POTENTIAL DONORS..
COOL THINGS ABOUT BLOODLETTING: (Donating Blood)
1. You get pierced with a needle!! (Heroin Chic!!)
2. You catch a slight slight buzz!! (without booze or drugs!!)
3. You get free snacks!! (No need to explain)
SOMETIMES I LIKE TO THINK THAT MY BLOOD IS GOING TO SOMEBODY WHO'D FREAK OUT IF THEY KNEW WHERE IT WAS COMING FROM...
What's the matter, George?
I don't know, Al.. ever since I had that operation last month, I've been Thinking This whole racism is really, really stupid...
IN ALL SERIOUSNESS, IT IS A NICE LITTLE HIGH KNOWING THAT YOU'VE CONTRIBUTED TO THE HEALTH & WELL BEING OF OTHERS...
OH, NO!! YOU LOOK GREAT IN THAT OUTFIT!!
C'mon!! CHEER UP!! Look at The bright side of things!!
KEITH KNIGHT B+
Well... at least The light saber fight at The end was cool..
BY THE WAY, MY BLOOD: "B" POSITIVE.

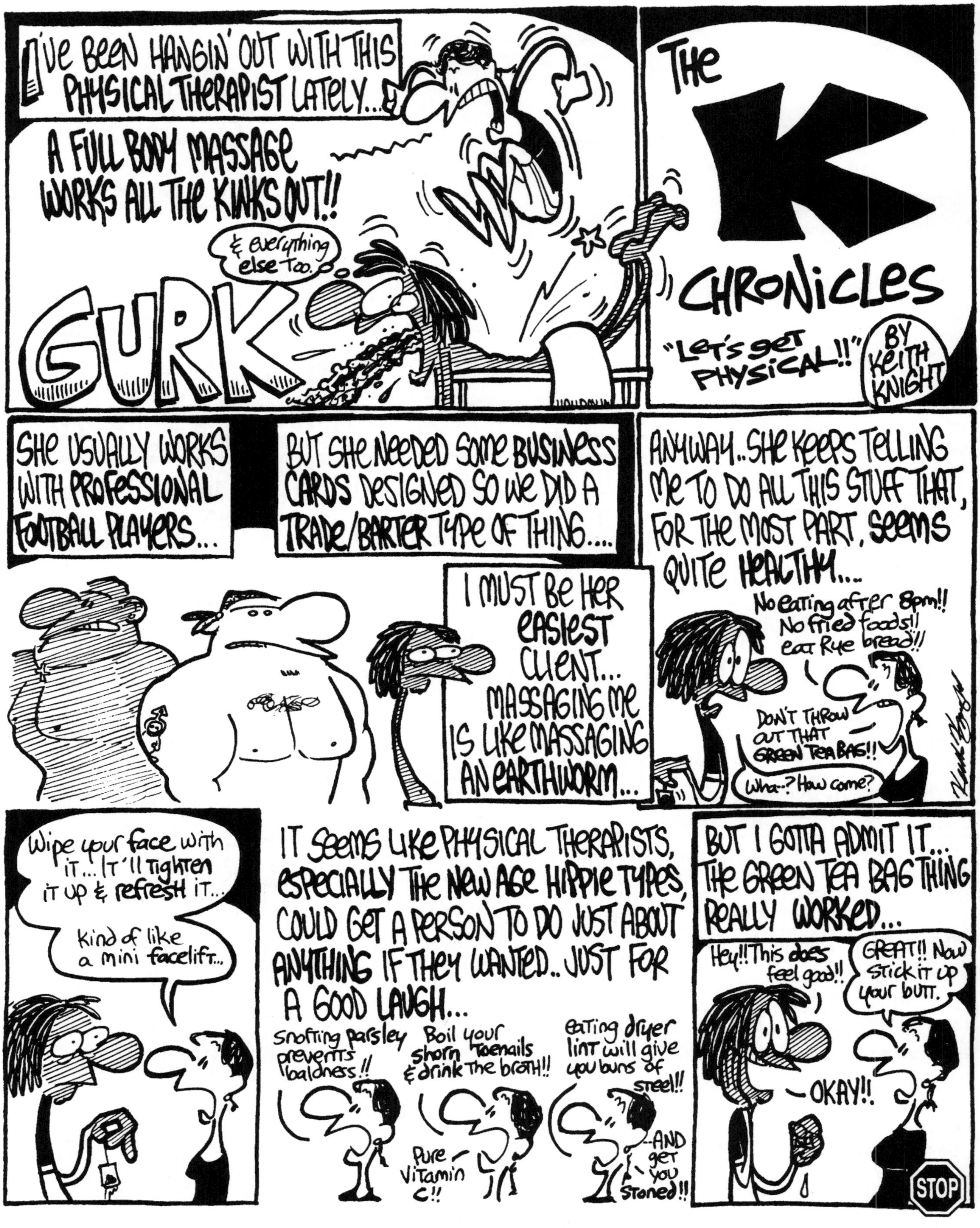
I'VE BEEN HANGIN' OUT WITH THIS PHYSICAL THERAPIST LATELY...
A FULL BODY MASSAGE WORKS ALL THE KINKS OUT!!
& everything else too.
GURK
THE K CHRONICLES
"LET'S GET PHYSICAL!!"
BY KEITH KNIGHT
SHE USUALLY WORKS WITH PROFESSIONAL FOOTBALL PLAYERS...
BUT SHE NEEDED SOME BUSINESS CARDS DESIGNED SO WE DID A TRADE/BARTER TYPE OF THING....
I MUST BE HER EASIEST CLIENT... MASSAGING ME IS LIKE MASSAGING AN EARTHWORM...
ANYWAY.. SHE KEEPS TELLING ME TO DO ALL THIS STUFF THAT, FOR THE MOST PART, SEEMS QUITE HEALTHY...
No eating after 8pm!! No fried foods!! eat Rye bread!!
DON'T THROW OUT THAT GREEN TEA BAG!!
Wha-? How come?
Wipe your face with it... It'll tighten it up & refresh it...
kind of like a mini facelift...
IT SEEMS LIKE PHYSICAL THERAPISTS, ESPECIALLY THE NEW AGE HIPPIE TYPES, COULD GET A PERSON TO DO JUST ABOUT ANYTHING IF THEY WANTED.. JUST FOR A GOOD LAUGH...
Snorting parsley prevents baldness!!
Boil your shorn toenails & drink the broth!!
Pure Vitamin C!!
Eating dryer lint will give you buns of steel!!
--AND get you stoned!!
BUT I GOTTA ADMIT IT... THE GREEN TEA BAG THING REALLY WORKED...
Hey!! This does feel good!!
GREAT!! Now stick it up your butt.
OKAY!!
STOP

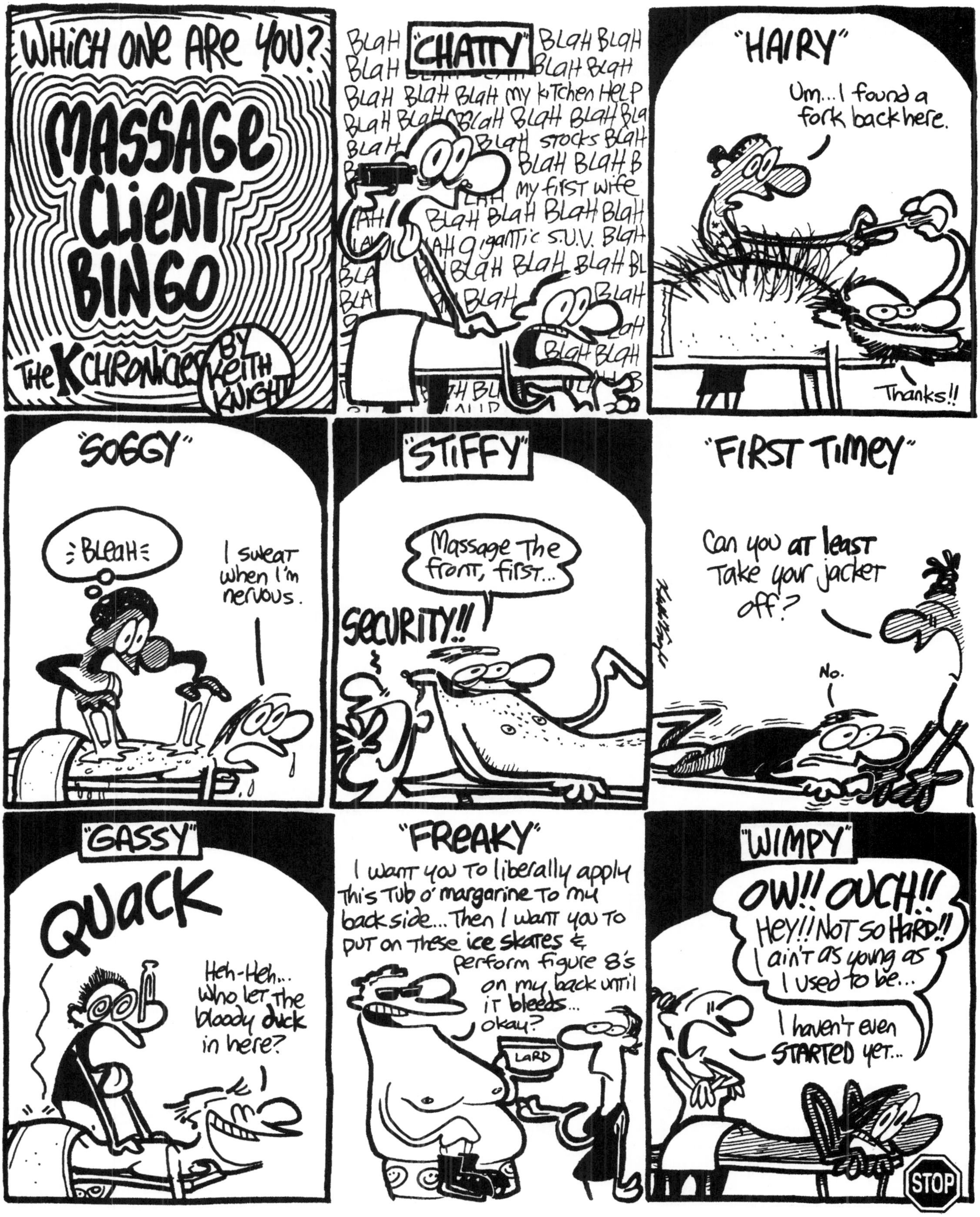
WHICH ONE ARE YOU?
MASSAGE CLIENT BINGO
THE K CHRONICLES BY KEITH KNIGHT
"CHATTY"
BLAH BLAH BLAH BLAH BLAH BLAH BLAH BLAH BLAH my kitchen HELP BLAH BLAH BLAH BLAH stocks BLAH BLAH BLAH my first wife BLAH BLAH BLAH BLAH gigantic S.U.V. BLAH BLAH BLAH BLAH BLAH BLAH BLAH BLAH
"HAIRY"
Um... I found a fork back here.
Thanks!!
"SOGGY"
BLEAH
I sweat when I'm nervous.
"STIFFY"
Massage the front, first...
SECURITY!!
"FIRST TIMEY"
Can you at least take your jacket off?
No.
"GASSY"
QUACK
Heh-Heh... Who let the bloody duck in here?
"FREAKY"
I want you to liberally apply this tub o' margarine to my backside... Then I want you to put on these ice skates & perform figure 8's on my back until it bleeds... okay?
LARD
"WIMPY"
OW!! OUCH!! HEY!!! NOT SO HARD!! I ain't as young as I used to be...
I haven't even STARTED yet...
STOP

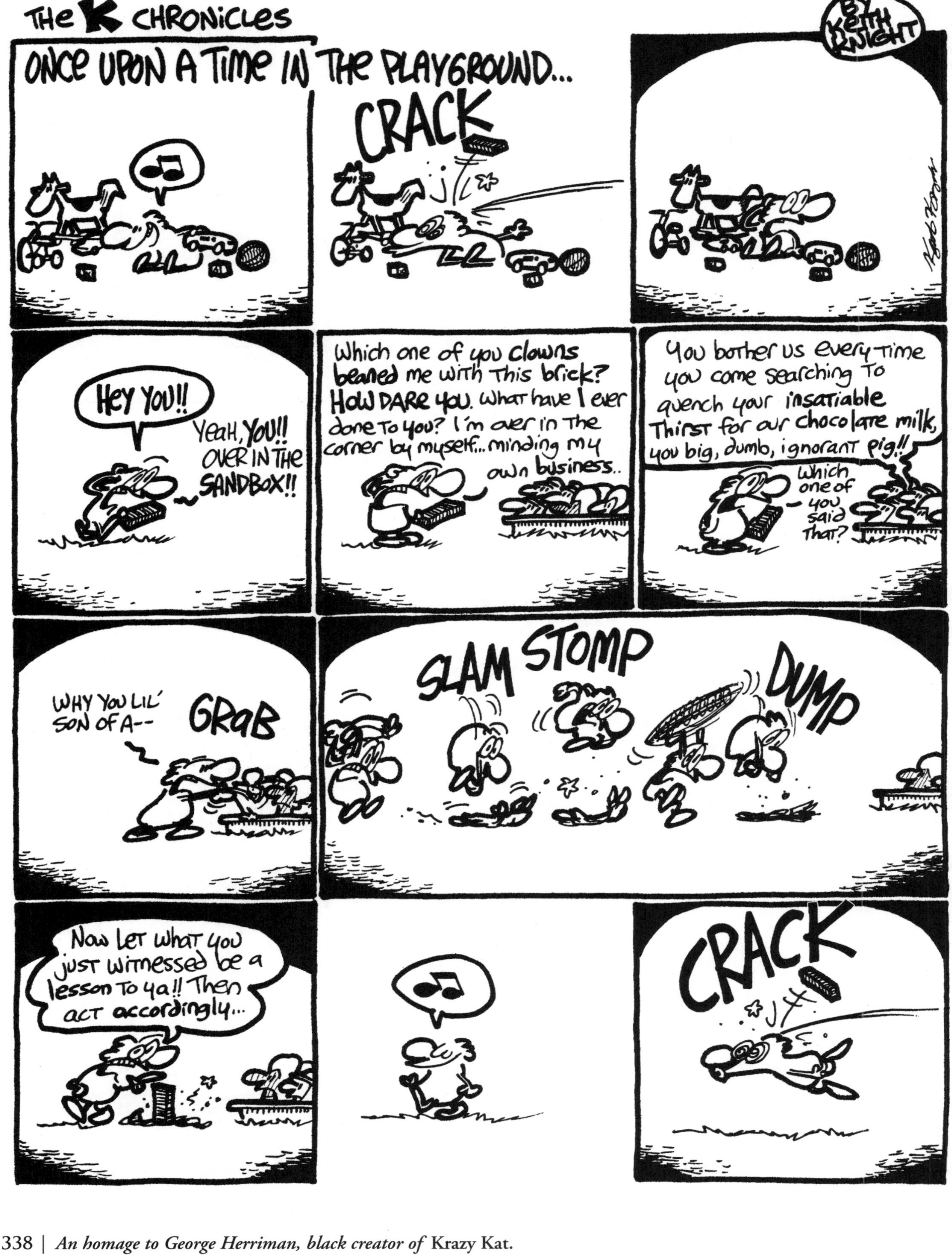
THE K CHRONICLES
BY KEITH KNIGHT
ONCE UPON A TIME IN THE PLAYGROUND...
CRACK
HEY YOU!!
YEAH, YOU!! OVER IN THE SANDBOX!!
Which one of you clowns beaned me with this brick? HOW DARE YOU. What have I ever done to you? I'm over in the corner by myself... minding my own business..
You bother us every time you come searching to quench your insatiable thirst for our chocolate milk, you big, dumb, ignorant pig!!
Which one of you said that?
WHY YOU LIL' SON OF A--
GRAB
SLAM
STOMP
DUMP
Now let what you just witnessed be a lesson to ya!! Then act accordingly...
CRACK

338 | *An homage to George Herriman, black creator of* Krazy Kat.

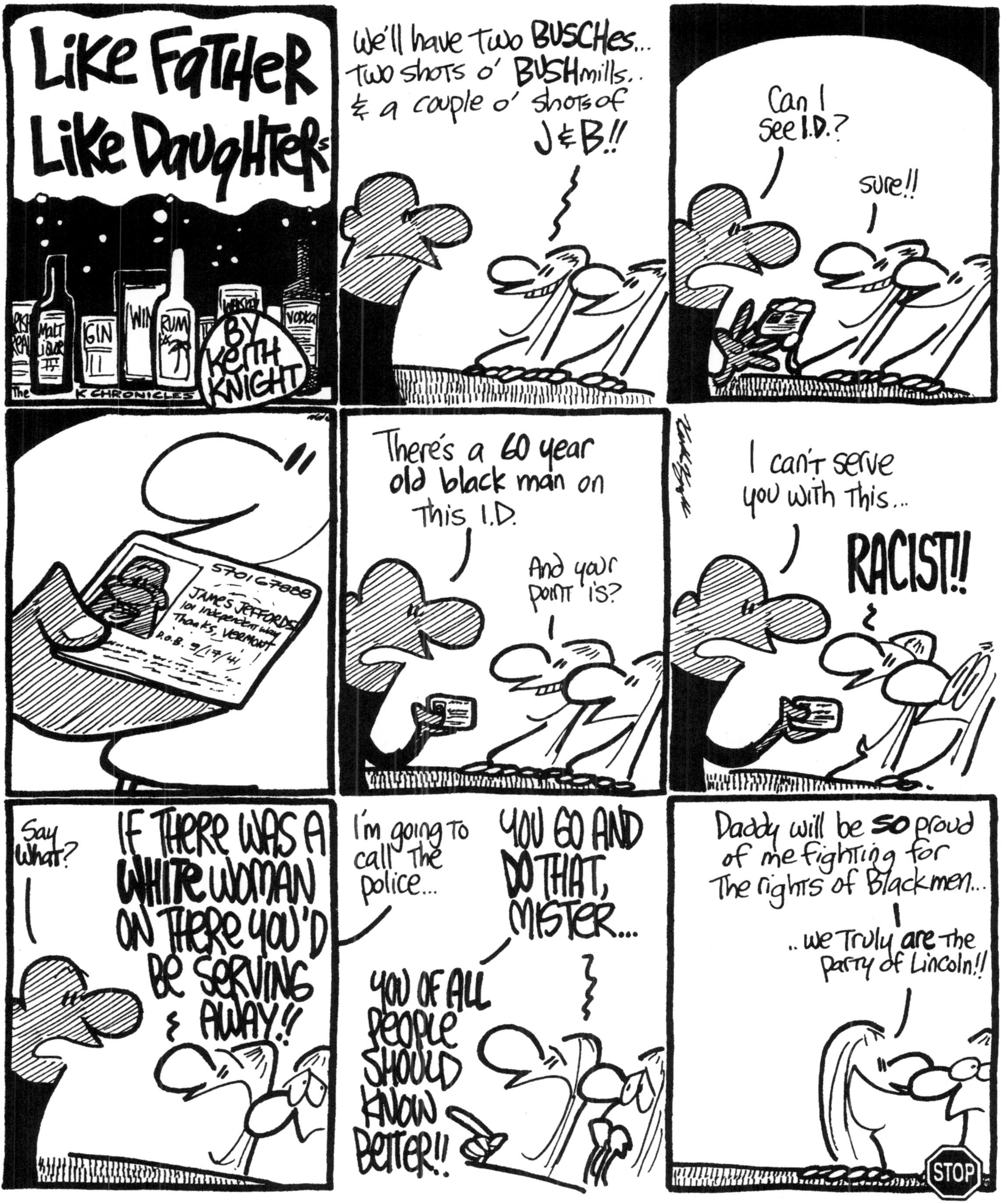
Like Father Like Daughters
MALT LIQUOR
GIN
RUM
WHISKEY
VODKA
The K CHRONICLES
BY KEITH KNIGHT
We'll have two BUSCHes... two shots o' BUSHmills.. & a couple o' shots of J&B!!
Can I see I.D.?
Sure!!
570167888
JAMES JEFFORDS
101 Independent Way
Thanks, Vermont
D.O.B. 5/17/41
There's a 60 year old black man on this I.D.
And your point is?
I can't serve you with this...
RACIST!!
Say What?
IF THERE WAS A WHITE WOMAN ON THERE YOU'D BE SERVING AWAY!!
I'm going to call the police...
YOU GO AND DO THAT, MISTER...
YOU OF ALL PEOPLE SHOULD KNOW BETTER!!
Daddy will be SO proud of me fighting for the rights of Blackmen...
..we truly are the party of Lincoln!!
STOP

The license makes reference to Jim Jeffords, who split from the Republican party and went independent cuz he saw how effed up everything was. And this was before I knew the Bush twins were a blonde and a brunette.

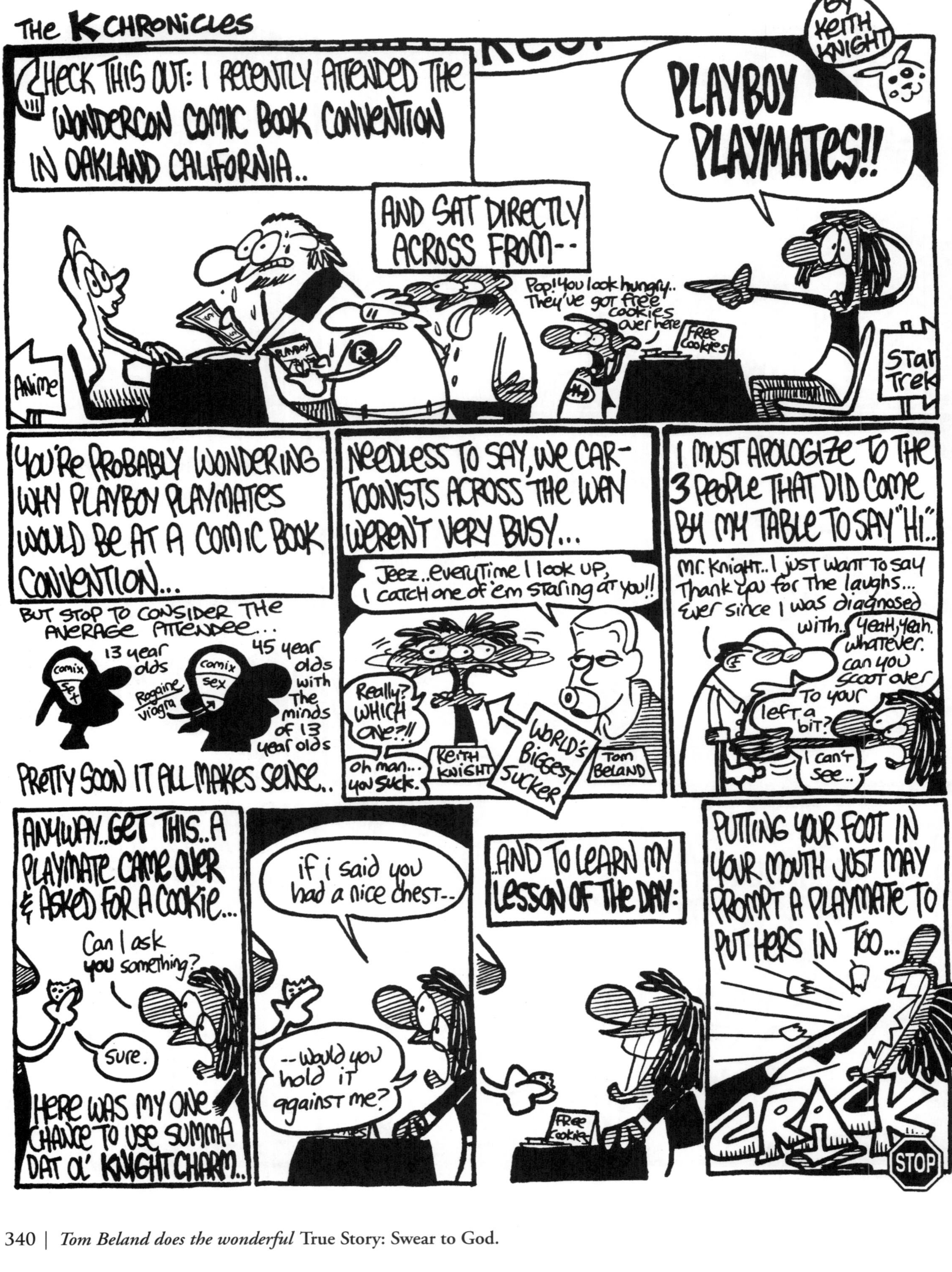

THE K CHRONICLES
BY KEITH KNIGHT
CHECK THIS OUT: I RECENTLY ATTENDED THE WONDERCON COMIC BOOK CONVENTION IN OAKLAND CALIFORNIA..
AND SAT DIRECTLY ACROSS FROM--
PLAYBOY PLAYMATES!!
Pop! You look hungry.. They've got free cookies over here
Free cookies
Anime
Star Trek
YOU'RE PROBABLY WONDERING WHY PLAYBOY PLAYMATES WOULD BE AT A COMIC BOOK CONVENTION...
BUT STOP TO CONSIDER THE AVERAGE ATTENDEE...
13 year olds
comix
sex
45 year olds with the minds of 13 year olds
Rogaine
viagra
PRETTY SOON IT ALL MAKES SENSE..
NEEDLESS TO SAY, WE CARTOONISTS ACROSS THE WAY WEREN'T VERY BUSY...
Jeez..everytime I look up, I catch one of 'em staring at you!!
Really? WHICH ONE?!!
Oh man... you suck.
KEITH KNIGHT
WORLD'S BIGGEST SUCKER
TOM BELAND
I MUST APOLOGIZE TO THE 3 PEOPLE THAT DID COME BY MY TABLE TO SAY "HI"..
Mr. Knight.. I just want to say Thank you for the laughs... Ever since I was diagnosed with..
Yeah, yeah. whatever. can you scoot over to your left a bit?
I can't see..
ANYWAY..GET THIS..A PLAYMATE CAME OVER & ASKED FOR A COOKIE...
Can I ask you something?
Sure.
HERE WAS MY ONE CHANCE TO USE SUMMA DAT OL' KNIGHT CHARM..
if i said you had a nice chest--
--would you hold it against me?
..AND TO LEARN MY LESSON OF THE DAY:
Free cookies
PUTTING YOUR FOOT IN YOUR MOUTH JUST MAY PROMPT A PLAYMATE TO PUT HERS IN TOO...
CRACK
STOP

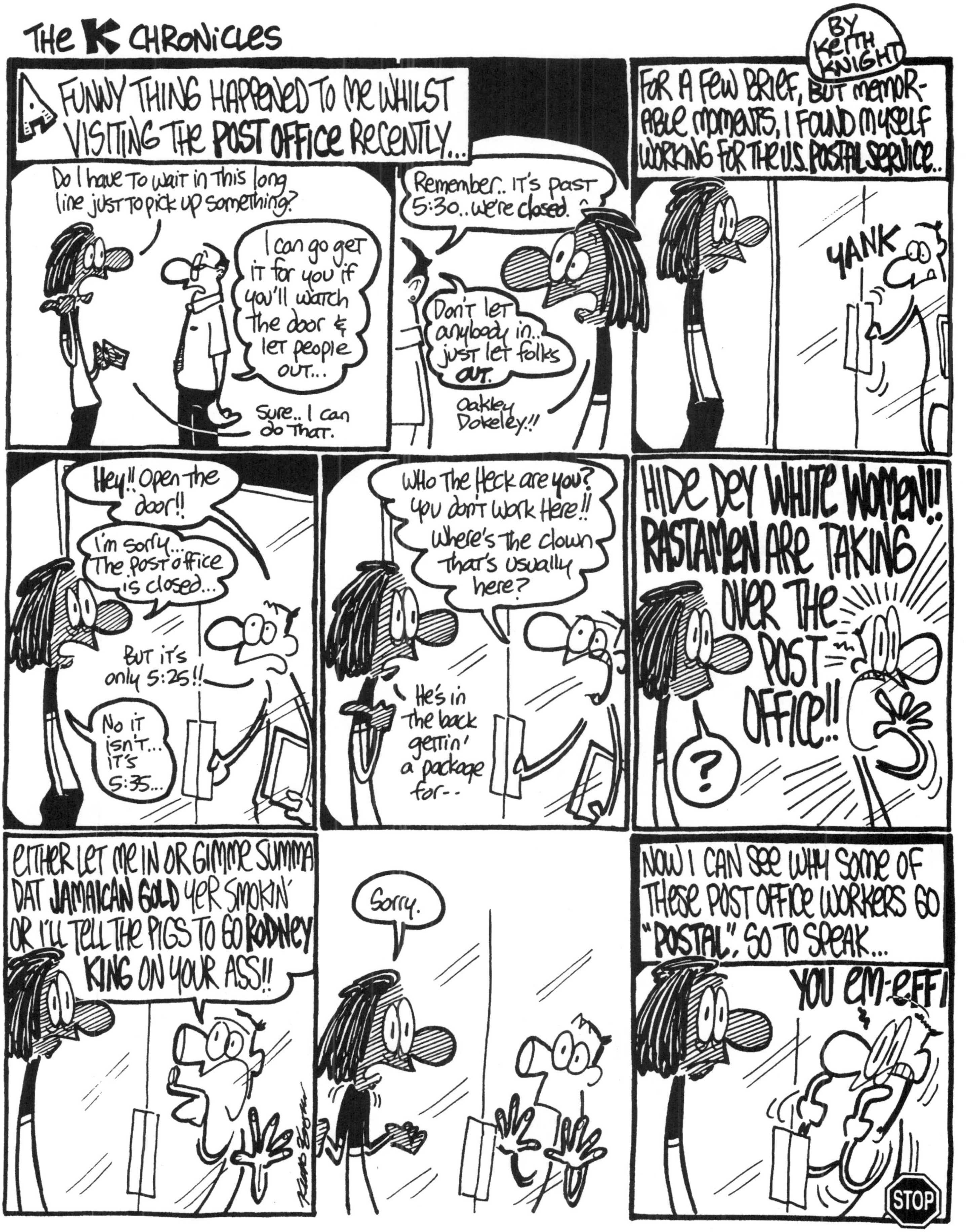
THE K CHRONICLES
BY KEITH KNIGHT
A FUNNY THING HAPPENED TO ME WHILST VISITING THE POST OFFICE RECENTLY...
Do I have to wait in this long line just to pick up something?
I can go get it for you if you'll watch the door & let people out...
Sure.. I can do that.
Remember.. It's past 5:30.. we're closed.
Don't let anybody in.. just let folks OUT.
Oakley Dokeley!!
FOR A FEW BRIEF, BUT MEMORABLE MOMENTS, I FOUND MYSELF WORKING FOR THE U.S. POSTAL SERVICE..
YANK
Hey!! Open the door!!
I'm sorry... The post office is closed...
But it's only 5:25!!
No it isn't... It's 5:35...
Who the Heck are you? You don't work Here!! Where's the clown that's usually here?
He's in the back gettin' a package for--
HIDE DEY WHITE WOMEN!! RASTAMEN ARE TAKING OVER THE POST OFFICE!!..
?
EITHER LET ME IN OR GIMME SUMMA DAT JAMAICAN GOLD YER SMOKIN' OR I'LL TELL THE PIGS TO GO RODNEY KING ON YOUR ASS!!
Sorry.
NOW I CAN SEE WHY SOME OF THESE POST OFFICE WORKERS GO "POSTAL", SO TO SPEAK...
YOU EM-EFF!
STOP

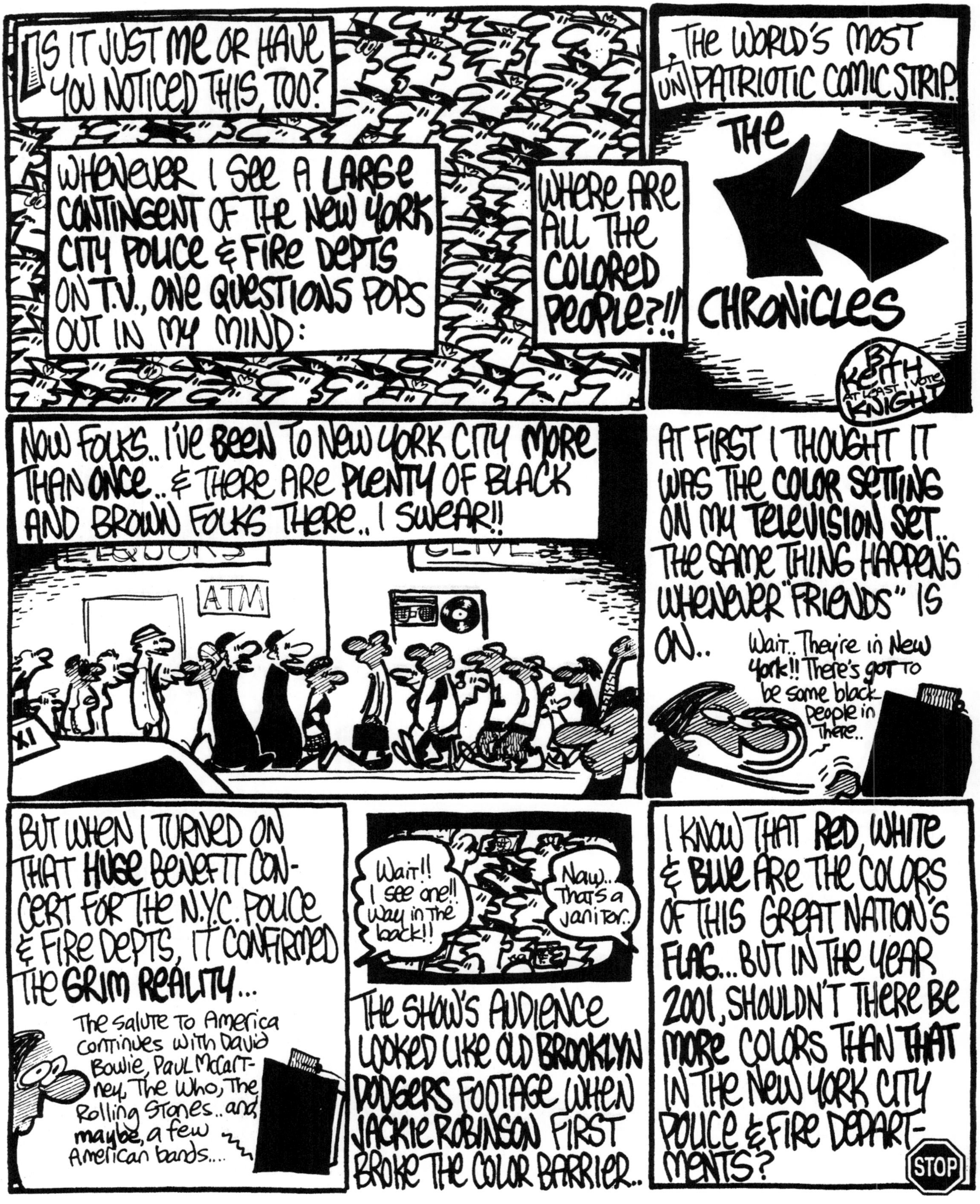

IS IT JUST ME OR HAVE YOU NOTICED THIS, TOO?
WHENEVER I SEE A LARGE CONTINGENT OF THE NEW YORK CITY POLICE & FIRE DEPTS ON T.V., ONE QUESTIONS POPS OUT IN MY MIND:
WHERE ARE ALL THE COLORED PEOPLE?!!
THE WORLD'S MOST UN PATRIOTIC COMIC STRIP.
THE K CHRONICLES
BY KEITH AT LEAST I VOTE KNIGHT
NOW FOLKS.. I'VE BEEN TO NEW YORK CITY MORE THAN ONCE.. & THERE ARE PLENTY OF BLACK AND BROWN FOLKS THERE.. I SWEAR!!
ATM
AT FIRST I THOUGHT IT WAS THE COLOR SETTING ON MY TELEVISION SET.. THE SAME THING HAPPENS WHENEVER "FRIENDS" IS ON..
Wait.. They're in New York!! There's got to be some black people in there..
BUT WHEN I TURNED ON THAT HUGE BENEFIT CONCERT FOR THE N.Y.C. POLICE & FIRE DEPTS, IT CONFIRMED THE GRIM REALITY...
The salute to America continues with David Bowie, Paul McCartney, The Who, The Rolling Stones.. and, maybe, a few American bands....
Wait!! I see one!! Way in the back!!
Naw.. That's a janitor..
THE SHOW'S AUDIENCE LOOKED LIKE OLD BROOKLYN DODGERS FOOTAGE WHEN JACKIE ROBINSON FIRST BROKE THE COLOR BARRIER..
I KNOW THAT RED, WHITE & BLUE ARE THE COLORS OF THIS GREAT NATION'S FLAG... BUT IN THE YEAR 2001, SHOULDN'T THERE BE MORE COLORS THAN THAT IN THE NEW YORK CITY POLICE & FIRE DEPARTMENTS?
STOP

This strip was one of several that earned me tons of post-9/11 hate mail about keeping my mouth shut and how unpatriotic I am.

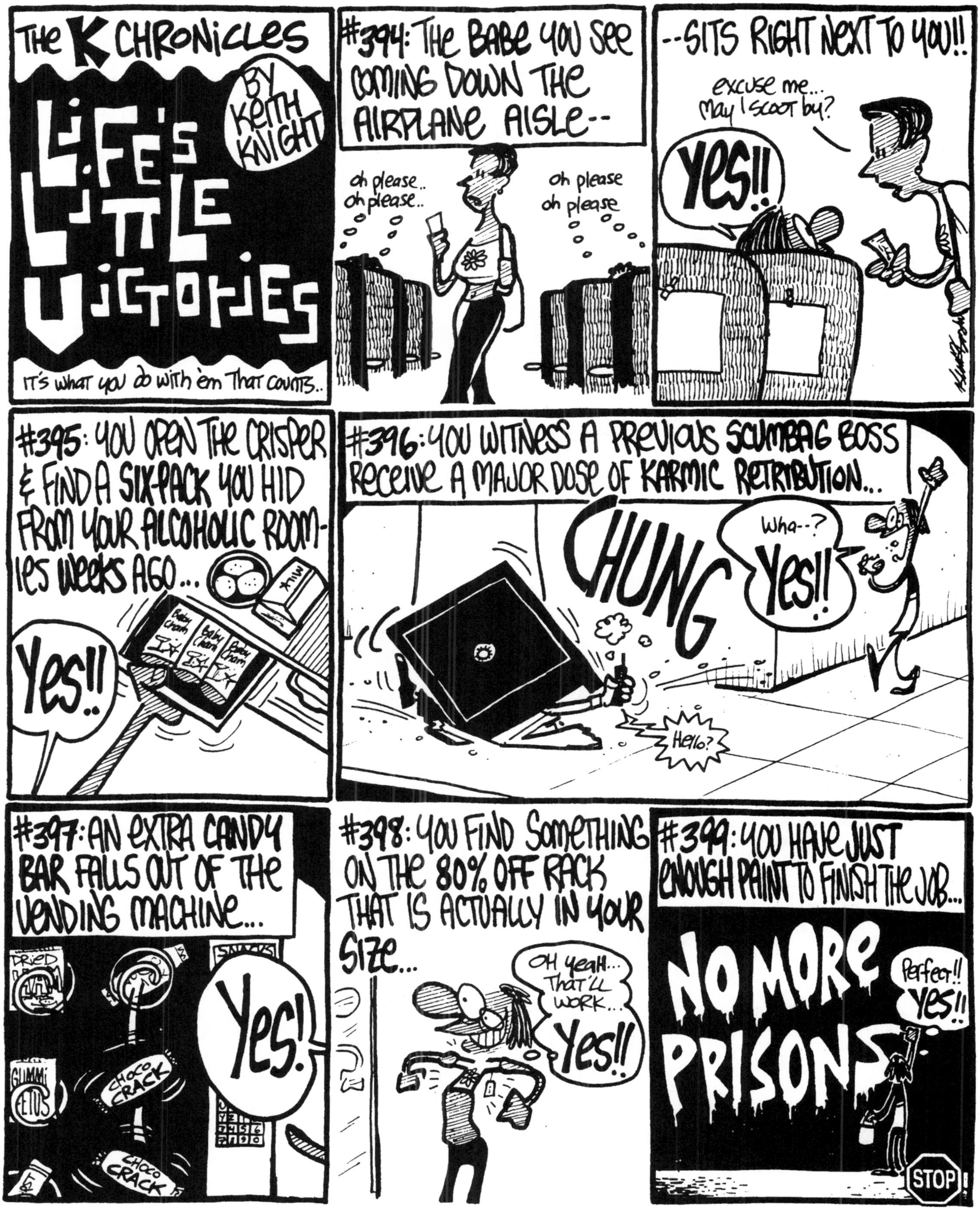
THE K CHRONICLES
BY KEITH KNIGHT
LIFE'S LITTLE VICTORIES
IT'S WHAT YOU DO WITH 'EM THAT COUNTS..
#394: THE BABE YOU SEE COMING DOWN THE AIRPLANE AISLE--
oh please.. oh please..
oh please oh please
--SITS RIGHT NEXT TO YOU!!
excuse me... May I scoot by?
YES!!
#395: YOU OPEN THE CRISPER & FIND A SIX-PACK YOU HID FROM YOUR ALCOHOLIC ROOMIES WEEKS AGO...
MILK
Baby Cham
Baby Cham
Baby Cham
YES!!..
#396: YOU WITNESS A PREVIOUS SCUMBAG BOSS RECEIVE A MAJOR DOSE OF KARMIC RETRIBUTION...
CHUNG
Wha--?
YES!!
Hello?
#397: AN EXTRA CANDY BAR FALLS OUT OF THE VENDING MACHINE...
DRIED
SNACKS
GUMMI FETUS
CHOCO CRACK
CHOCO CRACK
YES!
#398: YOU FIND SOMETHING ON THE 80% OFF RACK THAT IS ACTUALLY IN YOUR SIZE...
OH YEAH... THAT'LL WORK...
YES!!
#399: YOU HAVE JUST ENOUGH PAINT TO FINISH THE JOB...
NO MORE PRISONS
Perfect!! YES!!
STOP

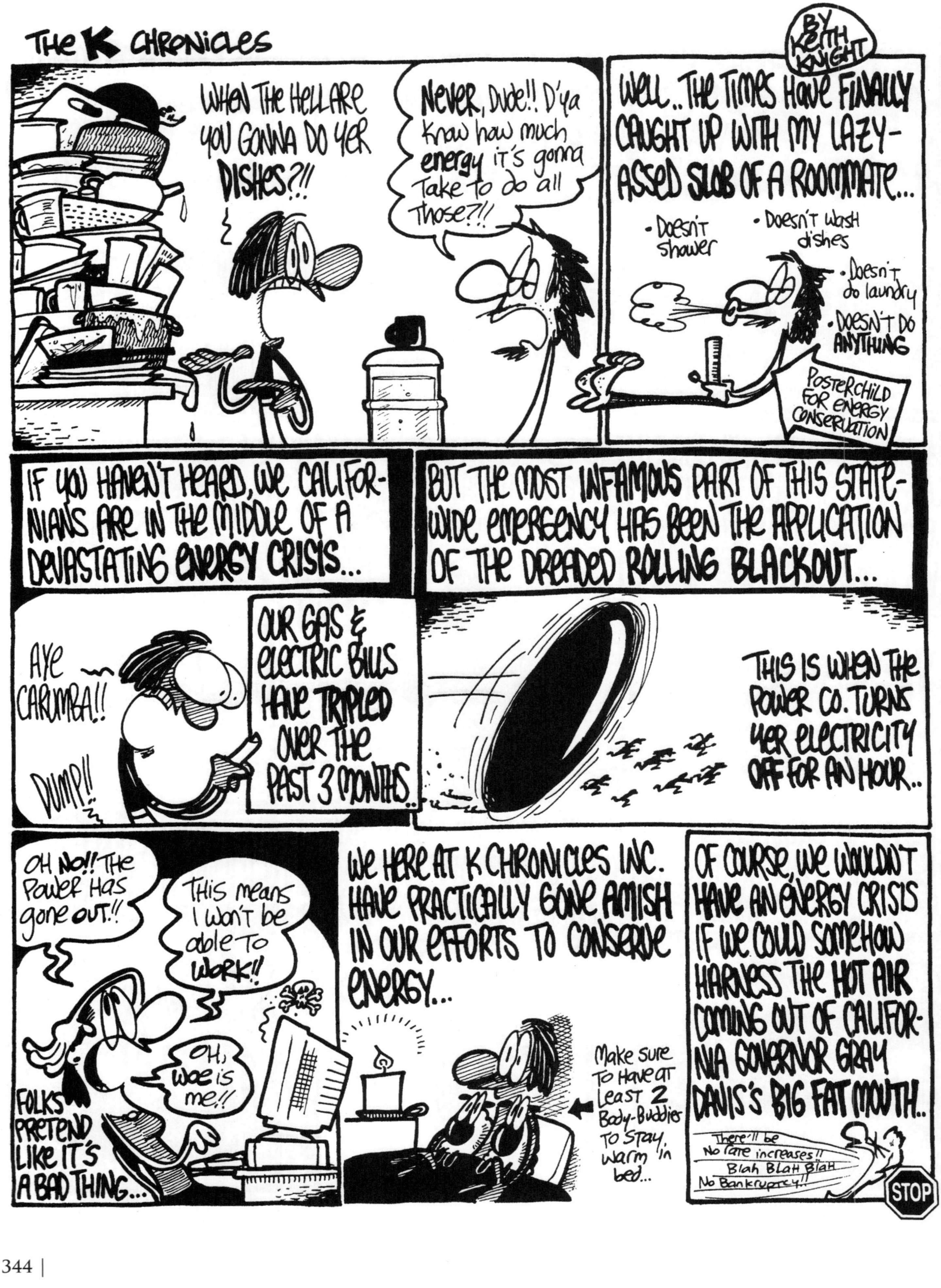

THE K CHRONICLES
BY KEITH KNIGHT
WHEN THE HELL ARE YOU GONNA DO YER DISHES?!!
NEVER, DUDE!! D'YA KNOW HOW MUCH ENERGY IT'S GONNA TAKE TO DO ALL THOSE?!!
WELL.. THE TIMES HAVE FINALLY CAUGHT UP WITH MY LAZY-ASSED SLOB OF A ROOMMATE...
• DOESN'T SHOWER
• DOESN'T WASH DISHES
• DOESN'T DO LAUNDRY
• DOESN'T DO ANYTHING
POSTERCHILD FOR ENERGY CONSERVATION
IF YOU HAVEN'T HEARD, WE CALIFORNIANS ARE IN THE MIDDLE OF A DEVASTATING ENERGY CRISIS...
AYE CARUMBA!!
DUMP!!
OUR GAS & ELECTRIC BILLS HAVE TRIPLED OVER THE PAST 3 MONTHS..
BUT THE MOST INFAMOUS PART OF THIS STATE-WIDE EMERGENCY HAS BEEN THE APPLICATION OF THE DREADED ROLLING BLACKOUT...
THIS IS WHEN THE POWER CO. TURNS YER ELECTRICITY OFF FOR AN HOUR..
OH NO!! THE POWER HAS GONE OUT!!
THIS MEANS I WON'T BE ABLE TO WORK!!
OH, WOE IS ME!!
FOLKS PRETEND LIKE IT'S A BAD THING...
WE HERE AT K CHRONICLES INC. HAVE PRACTICALLY GONE AMISH IN OUR EFFORTS TO CONSERVE ENERGY...
MAKE SURE TO HAVE AT LEAST 2 BODY-BUDDIES TO STAY WARM IN BED...
OF COURSE, WE WOULDN'T HAVE AN ENERGY CRISIS IF WE COULD SOMEHOW HARNESS THE HOT AIR COMING OUT OF CALIFORNIA GOVERNOR GRAY DAVIS'S BIG FAT MOUTH..
THERE'LL BE NO RATE INCREASES!!
BLAH BLAH BLAH
NO BANKRUPTCY!!
STOP

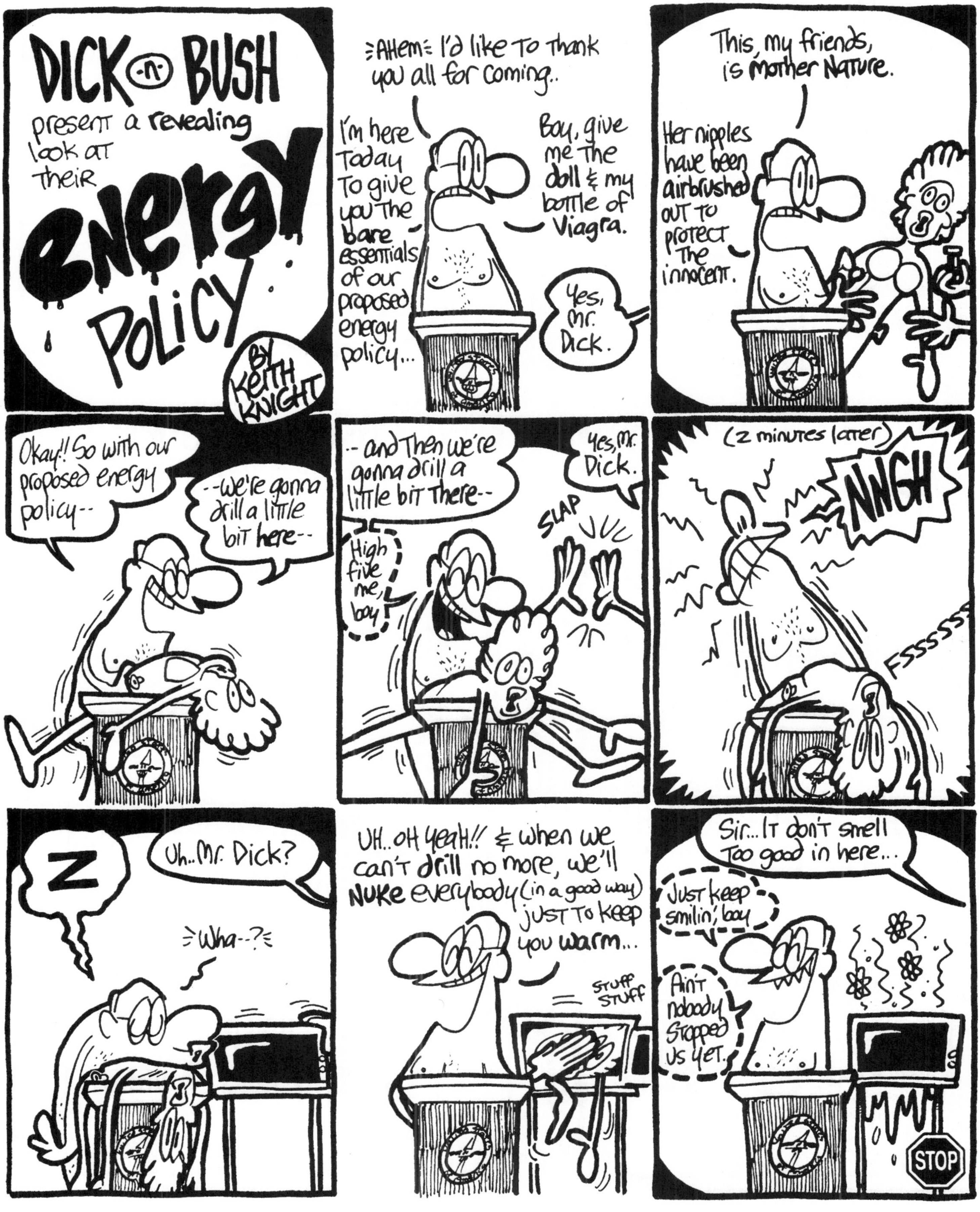

DICK -n- BUSH
present a revealing look at their
ENERGY POLICY
BY KEITH KNIGHT
=AHEM= I'd like to thank you all for coming..
I'm here today to give you the bare essentials of our proposed energy policy...
Boy, give me the doll & my bottle of Viagra.
Yes, Mr. Dick.
This, my friends, is Mother Nature.
Her nipples have been airbrushed out to protect the innocent.
Okay!! So with our proposed energy policy--
--We're gonna drill a little bit here--
--and then we're gonna drill a little bit there--
Yes, Mr. Dick.
High five me, boy!
SLAP
(2 minutes later)
NNGH
FSSSSSS
Z
Uh.. Mr. Dick?
=Wha--?=
UH..OH YEAH!! & when we can't drill no more, we'll NUKE everybody (in a good way) just to keep you warm...
STUFF STUFF
Sir... It don't smell too good in here...
Just keep smilin', boy
Ain't nobody stopped us yet.
STOP

Panel six where Dick explodes may be my single favorite panel ever. |

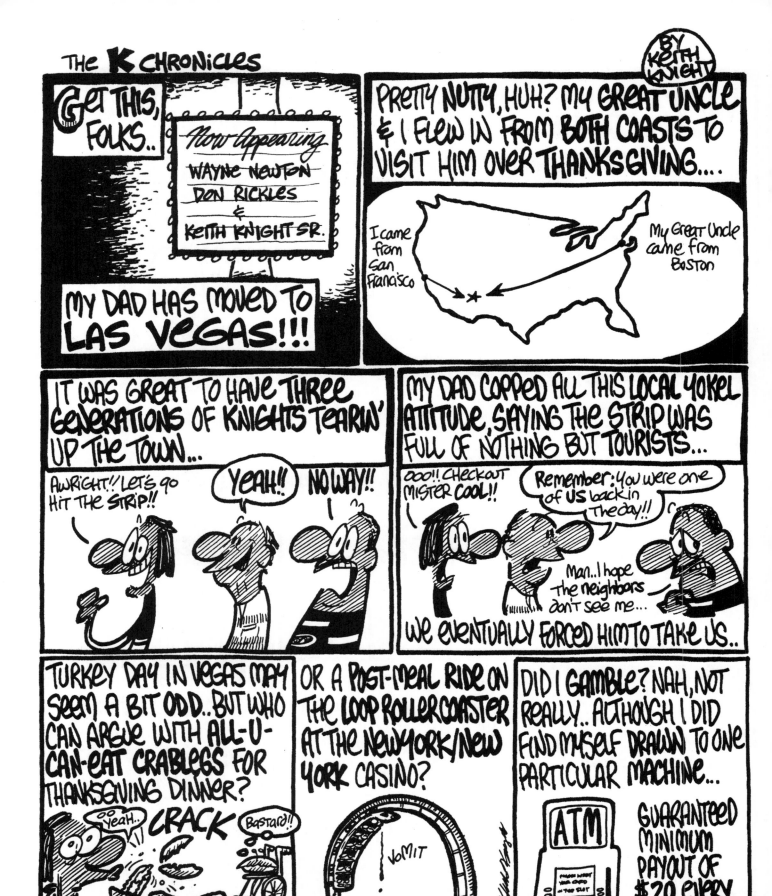

THE K CHRONICLES

BY KEITH KNIGHT

GET THIS, FOLKS..

Now Appearing
WAYNE NEWTON
DON RICKLES
&
KEITH KNIGHT SR.

MY DAD HAS MOVED TO LAS VEGAS!!!

PRETTY NUTTY, HUH? MY GREAT UNCLE & I FLEW IN FROM BOTH COASTS TO VISIT HIM OVER THANKSGIVING....

I came from San Francisco

My Great Uncle came from Boston

IT WAS GREAT TO HAVE THREE GENERATIONS OF KNIGHTS TEARIN' UP THE TOWN...

AWRIGHT!! LET'S GO HIT THE STRIP!!

YEAH!!

NO WAY!!

MY DAD COPPED ALL THIS LOCAL YOKEL ATTITUDE, SAYING THE STRIP WAS FULL OF NOTHING BUT TOURISTS...

OOO!! CHECK OUT MISTER COOL!!

Remember: You were one of US back in the day!!

Man.. I hope the neighbors don't see me...

WE EVENTUALLY FORCED HIM TO TAKE US..

TURKEY DAY IN VEGAS MAY SEEM A BIT ODD.. BUT WHO CAN ARGUE WITH ALL-U-CAN-EAT CRABLEGS FOR THANKSGIVING DINNER?

OO YEAH.. CRACK

got crabs?

Bastard!!

OR A POST-MEAL RIDE ON THE LOOP ROLLERCOASTER AT THE NEW YORK/NEW YORK CASINO?

VOMIT

DID I GAMBLE? NAH, NOT REALLY.. ALTHOUGH I DID FIND MYSELF DRAWN TO ONE PARTICULAR MACHINE...

ATM

GUARANTEED MINIMUM PAYOUT OF $20 EVERY TIME... JUST DON'T GET HOOKED!!

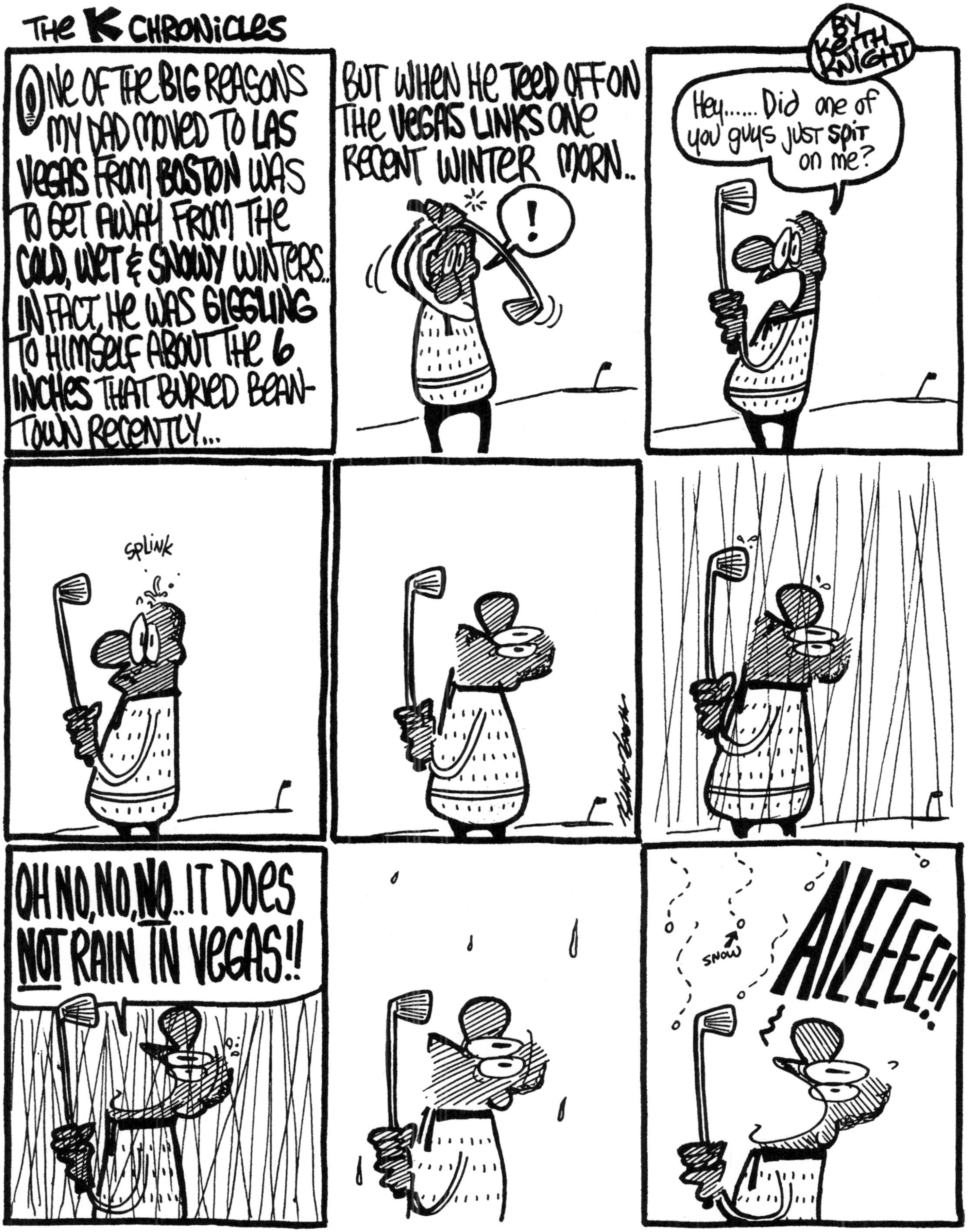
THE K CHRONICLES
BY KEITH KNIGHT
ONE OF THE BIG REASONS MY DAD MOVED TO LAS VEGAS FROM BOSTON WAS TO GET AWAY FROM THE COLD, WET & SNOWY WINTERS... IN FACT, HE WAS GIGGLING TO HIMSELF ABOUT THE 6 INCHES THAT BURIED BEAN-TOWN RECENTLY...
BUT WHEN HE TEED OFF ON THE VEGAS LINKS ONE RECENT WINTER MORN..
!
Hey...... Did one of you guys just spit on me?
SPLINK
OH NO, NO, NO.. IT DOES NOT RAIN IN VEGAS!!
SNOW
AIEEEE!!

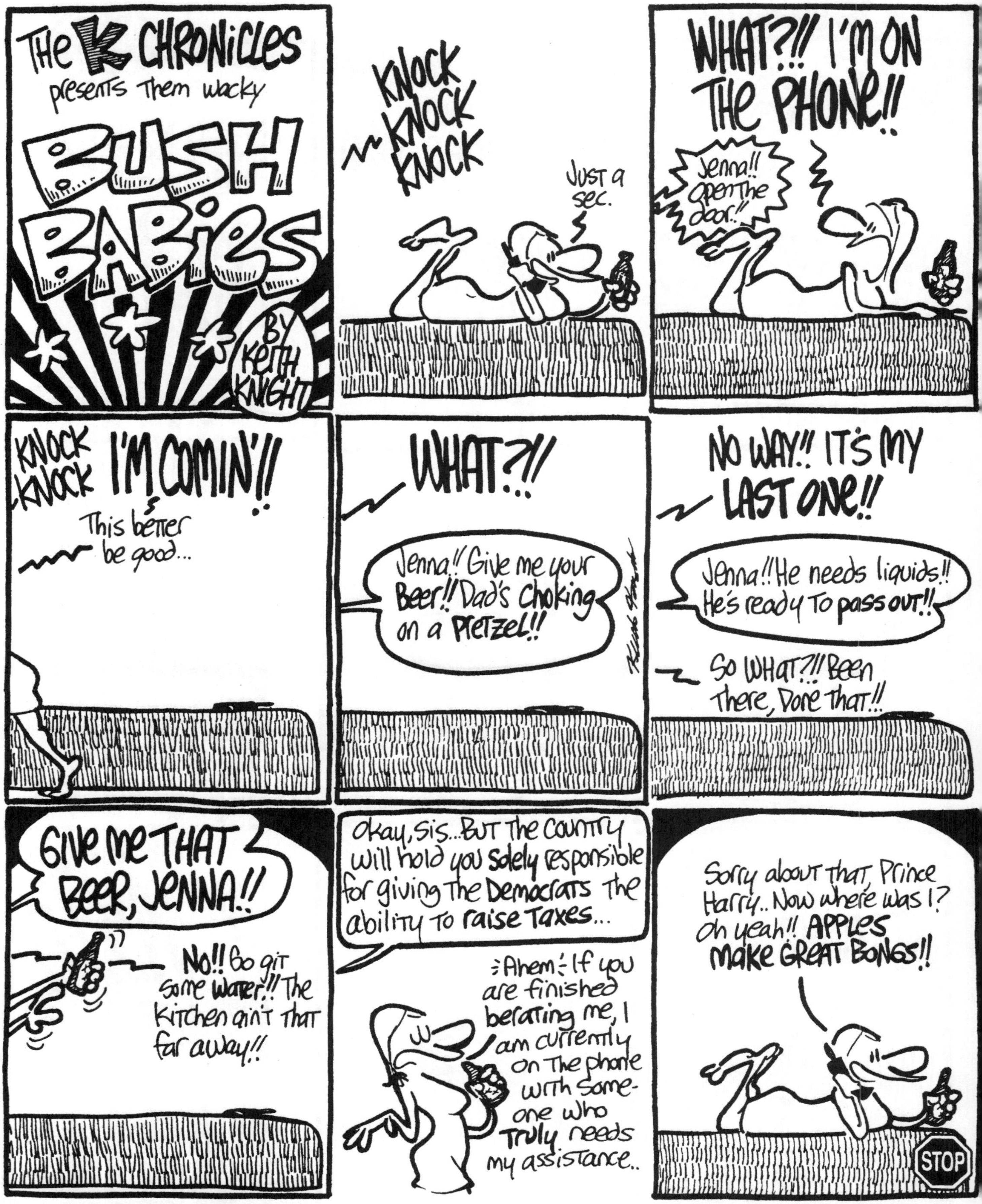
The K Chronicles presents them wacky
BUSH BABIES
By Keith Knight
KNOCK KNOCK KNOCK
Just a sec.
WHAT?!! I'M ON THE PHONE!!
Jenna!! Open the door!!
KNOCK KNOCK
I'M COMIN'!!
This better be good...
WHAT?!!
Jenna!! Give me your Beer!! Dad's Choking on a Pretzel!!
NO WAY!! IT'S MY LAST ONE!!
Jenna!! He needs liquids!! He's ready to pass out!!
So WHAT?!! Been there, Done that!!
GIVE ME THAT BEER, JENNA!!
No!! Go git some water!! The kitchen ain't that far away!!
Okay, Sis...But the country will hold you solely responsible for giving the Democrats the ability to raise Taxes...
Ahem If you are finished berating me, I am currently on the phone with someone who truly needs my assistance..
Sorry about that, Prince Harry.. Now where was I? Oh yeah!! APPLES MAKE GREAT BONGS!!
STOP

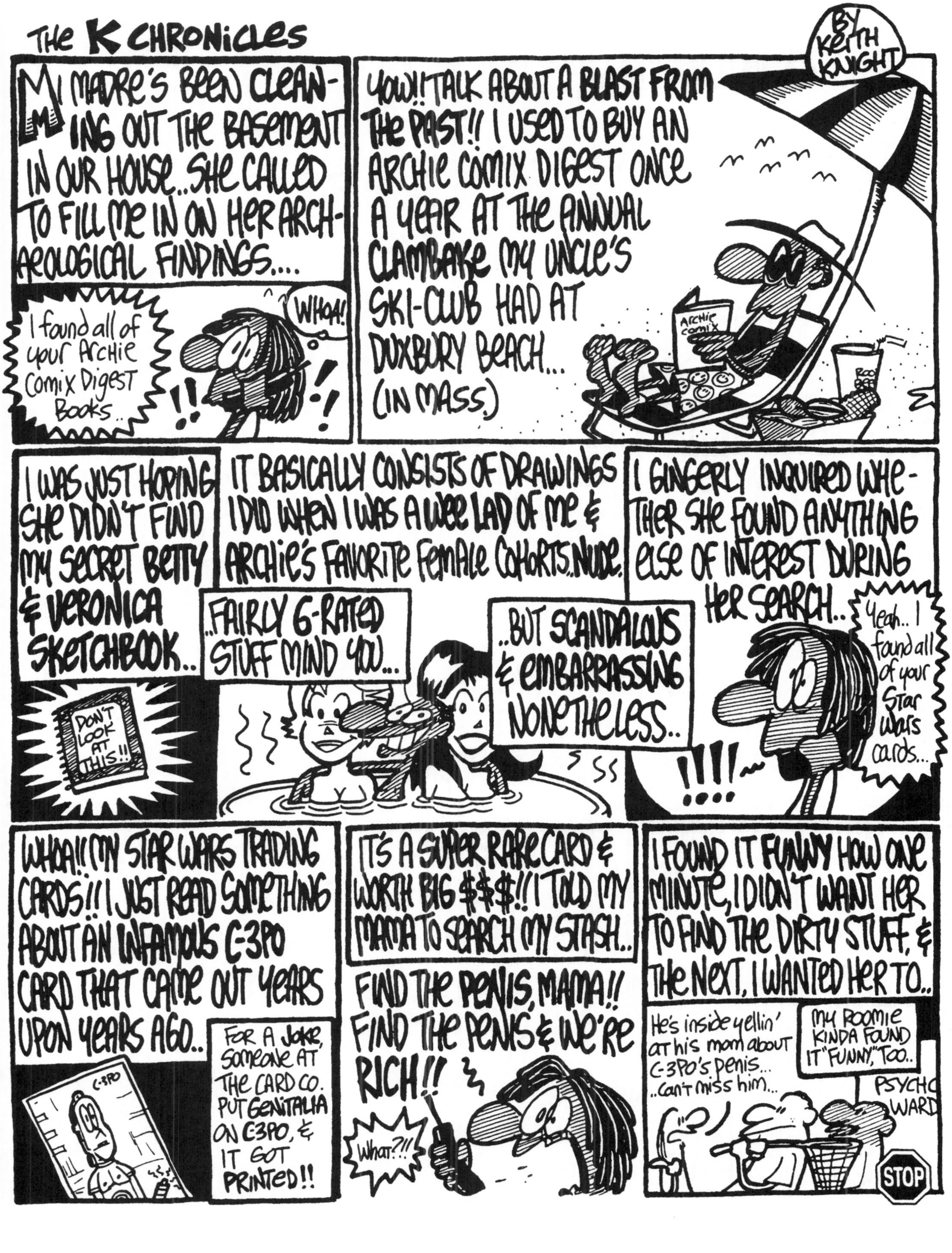
THE K CHRONICLES
BY KEITH KNIGHT
MI MADRE'S BEEN CLEANING OUT THE BASEMENT IN OUR HOUSE...SHE CALLED TO FILL ME IN ON HER ARCHAEOLOGICAL FINDINGS....
I found all of your Archie Comix Digest Books..
WHOA!
YOW!! TALK ABOUT A BLAST FROM THE PAST!! I USED TO BUY AN ARCHIE COMIX DIGEST ONCE A YEAR AT THE ANNUAL CLAMBAKE MY UNCLE'S SKI-CLUB HAD AT DUXBURY BEACH... (IN MASS.)
ARCHIE COMIX
I WAS JUST HOPING SHE DIDN'T FIND MY SECRET BETTY & VERONICA SKETCHBOOK...
DON'T LOOK AT THIS!!
IT BASICALLY CONSISTS OF DRAWINGS I DID WHEN I WAS A WEE LAD OF ME & ARCHIE'S FAVORITE FEMALE COHORTS..NUDE.
..FAIRLY G-RATED STUFF MIND YOU...
..BUT SCANDALOUS & EMBARRASSING NONETHELESS..
I GINGERLY INQUIRED WHETHER SHE FOUND ANYTHING ELSE OF INTEREST DURING HER SEARCH..
Yeah.. I found all of your Star Wars cards...
!!!!
WHOA!! MY STAR WARS TRADING CARDS!! I JUST READ SOMETHING ABOUT AN INFAMOUS C-3PO CARD THAT CAME OUT YEARS UPON YEARS AGO..
FOR A JOKE, SOMEONE AT THE CARD CO. PUT GENITALIA ON C3PO, & IT GOT PRINTED!!
C-3PO
IT'S A SUPER RARE CARD & WORTH BIG $$$!! I TOLD MY MAMA TO SEARCH MY STASH..
FIND THE PENIS, MAMA!! FIND THE PENIS & WE'RE RICH!!
What?!!
I FOUND IT FUNNY HOW ONE MINUTE, I DIDN'T WANT HER TO FIND THE DIRTY STUFF, & THE NEXT, I WANTED HER TO..
He's inside yellin' at his mom about C-3PO's penis... ..Can't miss him...
MY ROOMIE KINDA FOUND IT "FUNNY," TOO..
PSYCHO WARD
STOP

I fashioned the original collections of these comics after Archie Comics digests.

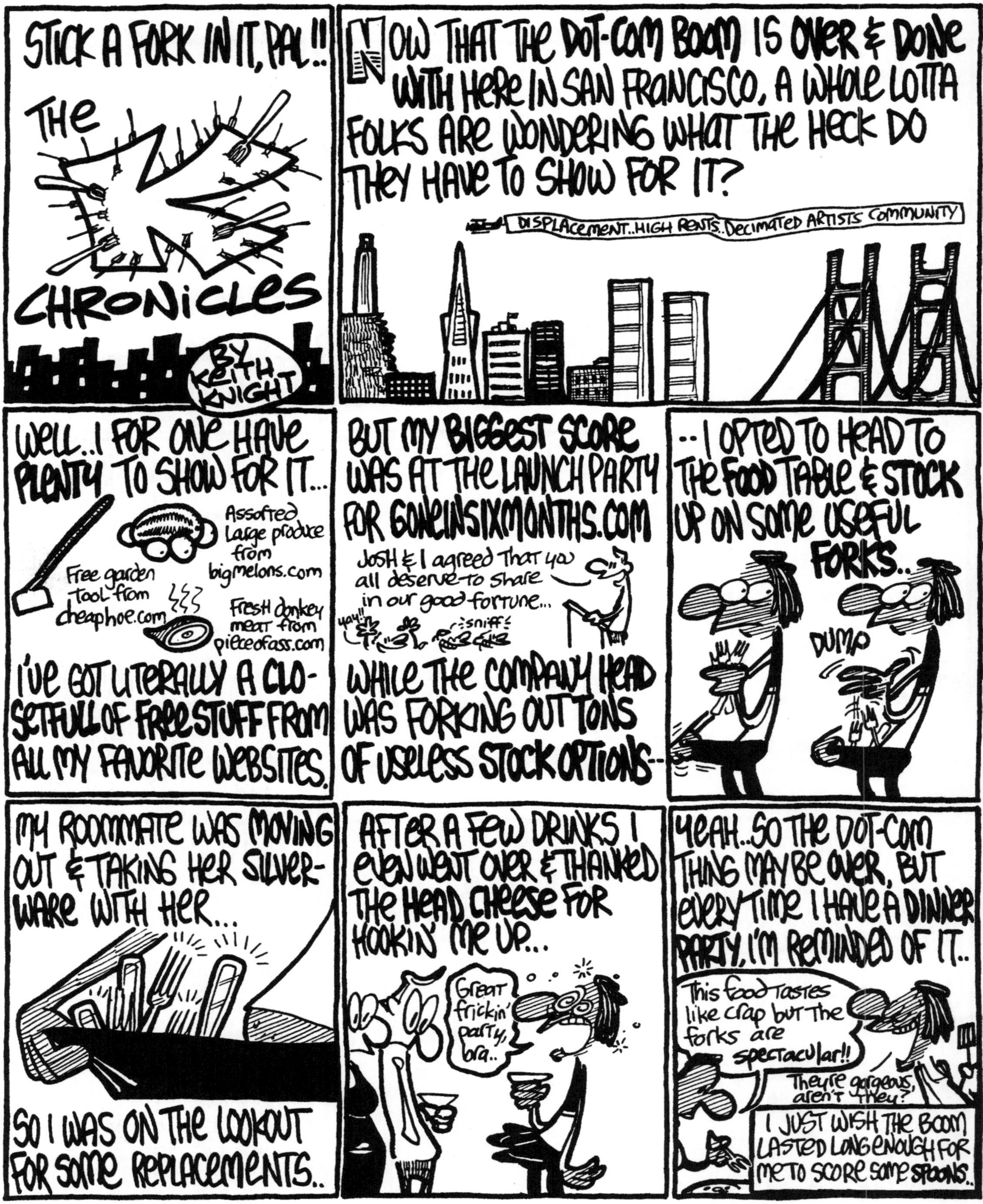

STICK A FORK IN IT, PAL!!..
THE K CHRONICLES
BY KEITH KNIGHT
NOW THAT THE DOT-COM BOOM IS OVER & DONE WITH HERE IN SAN FRANCISCO, A WHOLE LOTTA FOLKS ARE WONDERING WHAT THE HECK DO THEY HAVE TO SHOW FOR IT?
DISPLACEMENT..HIGH RENTS..DECIMATED ARTISTS COMMUNITY
WELL..I FOR ONE HAVE PLENTY TO SHOW FOR IT...
Free garden tool from cheaphoe.com
Assorted Large produce from bigmelons.com
Fresh donkey meat from pieceofass.com
I'VE GOT LITERALLY A CLOSETFULL OF FREE STUFF FROM ALL MY FAVORITE WEBSITES.
BUT MY BIGGEST SCORE WAS AT THE LAUNCH PARTY FOR GONEINSIXMONTHS.COM
JOSH & I agreed that you all deserve to share in our good fortune...
yay!!
sniff
WHILE THE COMPANY HEAD WAS FORKING OUT TONS OF USELESS STOCK OPTIONS--
..I OPTED TO HEAD TO THE FOOD TABLE & STOCK UP ON SOME USEFUL FORKS..
DUMP
MY ROOMMATE WAS MOVING OUT & TAKING HER SILVERWARE WITH HER...
SO I WAS ON THE LOOKOUT FOR SOME REPLACEMENTS..
AFTER A FEW DRINKS I EVEN WENT OVER & THANKED THE HEAD CHEESE FOR HOOKIN' ME UP...
Great frickin' party, bra..
YEAH..SO THE DOT-COM THING MAY BE OVER, BUT EVERY TIME I HAVE A DINNER PARTY, I'M REMINDED OF IT..
This food tastes like crap but the forks are spectacular!!
They're gorgeous, aren't they?
I JUST WISH THE BOOM LASTED LONG ENOUGH FOR ME TO SCORE SOME SPOONS.

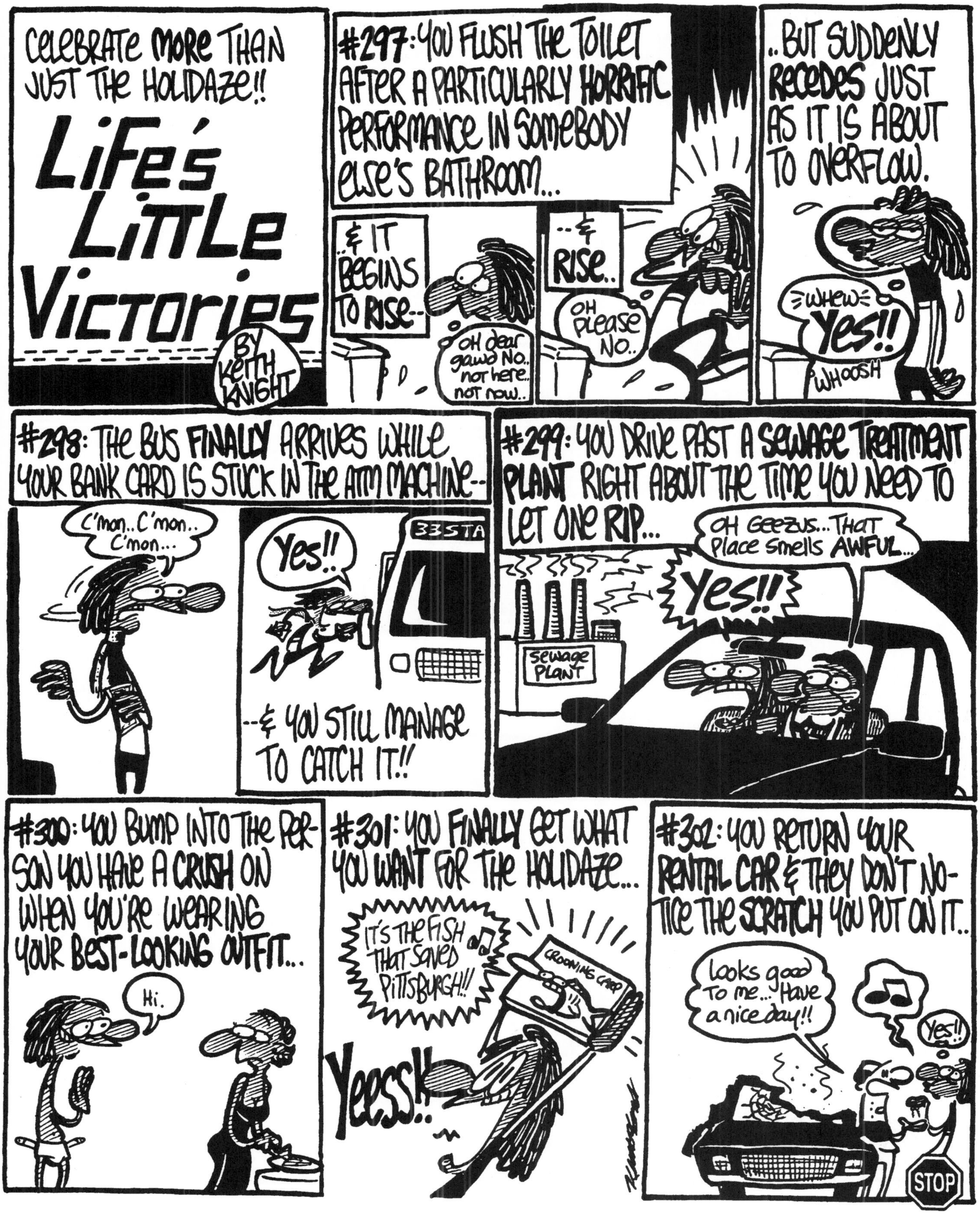

CELEBRATE MORE THAN JUST THE HOLIDAZE!!
Life's Little Victories
BY KEITH KNIGHT
#297: YOU FLUSH THE TOILET AFTER A PARTICULARLY HORRIFIC PERFORMANCE IN SOMEBODY ELSE'S BATHROOM...
..& IT BEGINS TO RISE--
OH dear gawd No.. not here.. not now..
--& RISE..
OH PLEASE NO..
..BUT SUDDENLY RECEDES JUST AS IT IS ABOUT TO OVERFLOW.
WHEW YES!!
WHOOSH
#298: THE BUS FINALLY ARRIVES WHILE YOUR BANK CARD IS STUCK IN THE ATM MACHINE--
C'mon..C'mon.. C'mon...
33 STA
Yes!!..
--& YOU STILL MANAGE TO CATCH IT!!
#299: YOU DRIVE PAST A SEWAGE TREATMENT PLANT RIGHT ABOUT THE TIME YOU NEED TO LET ONE RIP...
OH GEEZUS... THAT Place smells AWFUL...
Yes!!
sewage PLANT
#300: YOU BUMP INTO THE PERSON YOU HAVE A CRUSH ON WHEN YOU'RE WEARING YOUR BEST-LOOKING OUTFIT...
Hi.
#301: YOU FINALLY GET WHAT YOU WANT FOR THE HOLIDAZE...
IT'S THE FISH THAT SAVED PITTSBURGH!!
CROONING CARP
Yeess!!..
#302: YOU RETURN YOUR RENTAL CAR & THEY DON'T NOTICE THE SCRATCH YOU PUT ON IT..
Looks good to me... Have a nice day!!
Yes!!
STOP

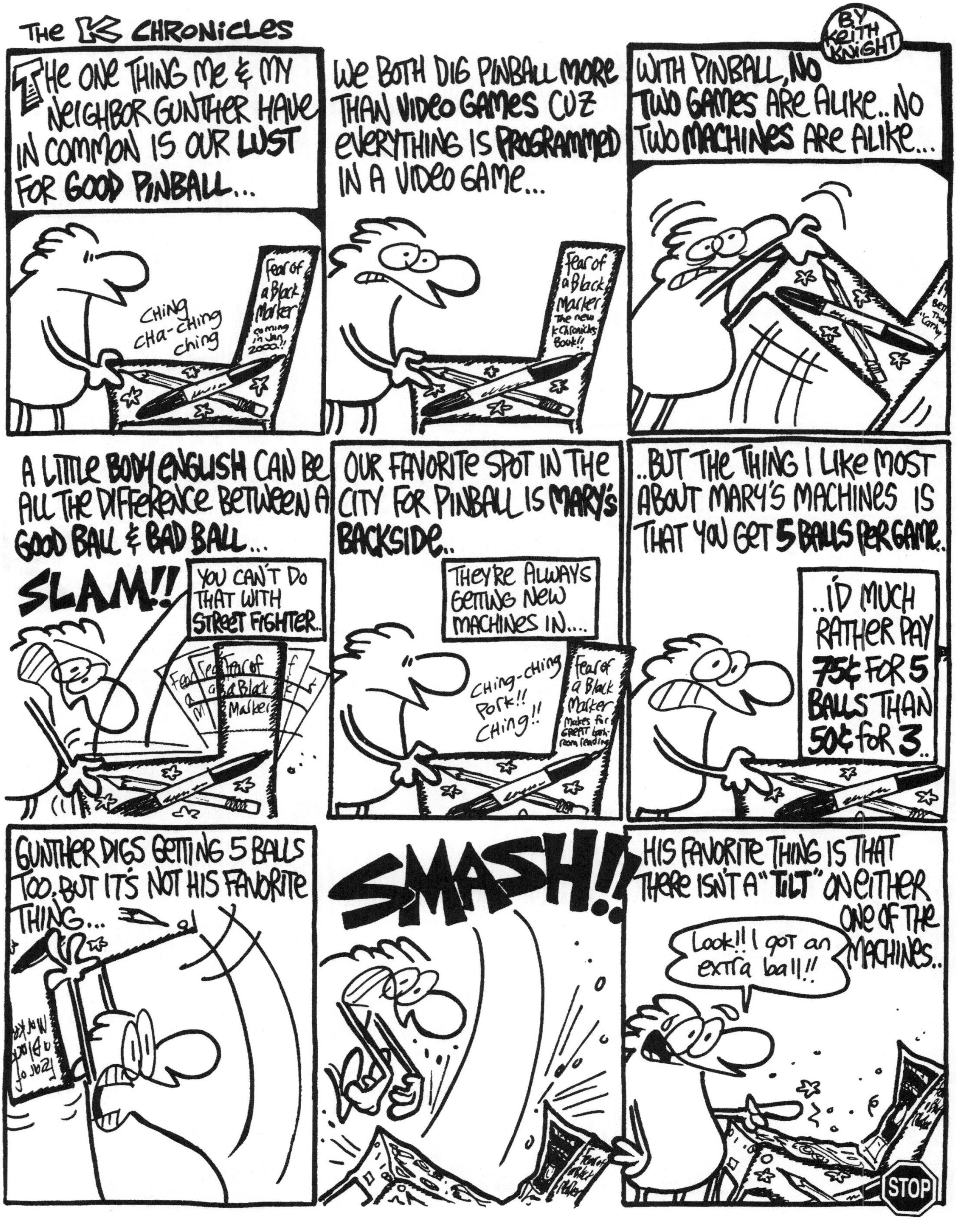
THE K CHRONICLES
BY KEITH KNIGHT
THE ONE THING ME & MY NEIGHBOR GUNTHER HAVE IN COMMON IS OUR LUST FOR GOOD PINBALL...
CHING CHA-CHING CHING
Fear of a Black Marker coming in Jan 2000!!
WE BOTH DIG PINBALL MORE THAN VIDEO GAMES CUZ EVERYTHING IS PROGRAMMED IN A VIDEO GAME...
Fear of a Black Marker The new K Chronicles Book!!
WITH PINBALL, NO TWO GAMES ARE ALIKE.. NO TWO MACHINES ARE ALIKE...
A LITTLE BODY ENGLISH CAN BE ALL THE DIFFERENCE BETWEEN A GOOD BALL & BAD BALL...
SLAM!!
YOU CAN'T DO THAT WITH STREET FIGHTER..
Fear of a Black Marker
OUR FAVORITE SPOT IN THE CITY FOR PINBALL IS MARY'S BACKSIDE..
THEY'RE ALWAYS GETTING NEW MACHINES IN....
CHING-CHING PORK!! CHING!!
Fear of a Black Marker Makes for GREAT bathroom reading
..BUT THE THING I LIKE MOST ABOUT MARY'S MACHINES IS THAT YOU GET 5 BALLS PER GAME..
..I'D MUCH RATHER PAY 75¢ FOR 5 BALLS THAN 50¢ FOR 3..
GUNTHER DIGS GETTING 5 BALLS TOO. BUT IT'S NOT HIS FAVORITE THING...
Fear of a Black Marker
SMASH!!
HIS FAVORITE THING IS THAT THERE ISN'T A "TILT" ON EITHER ONE OF THE MACHINES..
Look!! I got an extra ball!!
STOP

THE K CHRONICLES BY KEITH KNIGHT

I WAS ON THE BUS THE OTHER DAY WHEN I SPIED THIS GUY IN THE SEAT CLOSEST TO WHERE I WAS STANDING..

RR! BOOM!! BA-BOOM
BLAH
BLAH BLAH

IF THE LOOK ON HIS FACE WAS ANY INDICATION, THIS GUY WAS IN THE MIDDLE OF A MOST PEACEFUL & ENJOYABLE NAPPING EXPERIENCE..

I COULDN'T BELIEVE IT CUZ THE BUS DRIVER WAS JERKIN' THE BUS BACK & FORTH & BANGIN' ON THE HORN LIKE A PSYCHO...

HONK HONK!!
SCREECH!!
RAT-TA-TAT-TAT

PLUS A COUPLA KIDS WERE PLAYIN' THEIR BOOMBOXES IN THE BACK..AND THE GUY DIRECTLY BEHIND HIM WAS YAPPIN' ON A CELL PHONE..

YET HE REMAINED BLISSFULLY UNPERTURBED..

BLAH BLAH
BOOM SM CRACK

AND NO, HE WASN'T DEAD.. I SAW HIM BREATHE.

GAWD..I'M SO JEALOUS OF PEOPLE WHO CAN SLEEP ANYWHERE, AT ANYTIME...

I CAN BARELY GET A GOOD NIGHTS SLEEP IN MY OWN BED--

HOOONK!!
BEEP BEEP

..WITH EARPLUGS IN--
BLAH BLAH BLAH

..ON ELEPHANT TRANQUILIZERS..
EMPEEZ

BANG BANG!! SCUMBAG.
SCREEEE

I HOPE HE MISSES HIS STOP... STOP

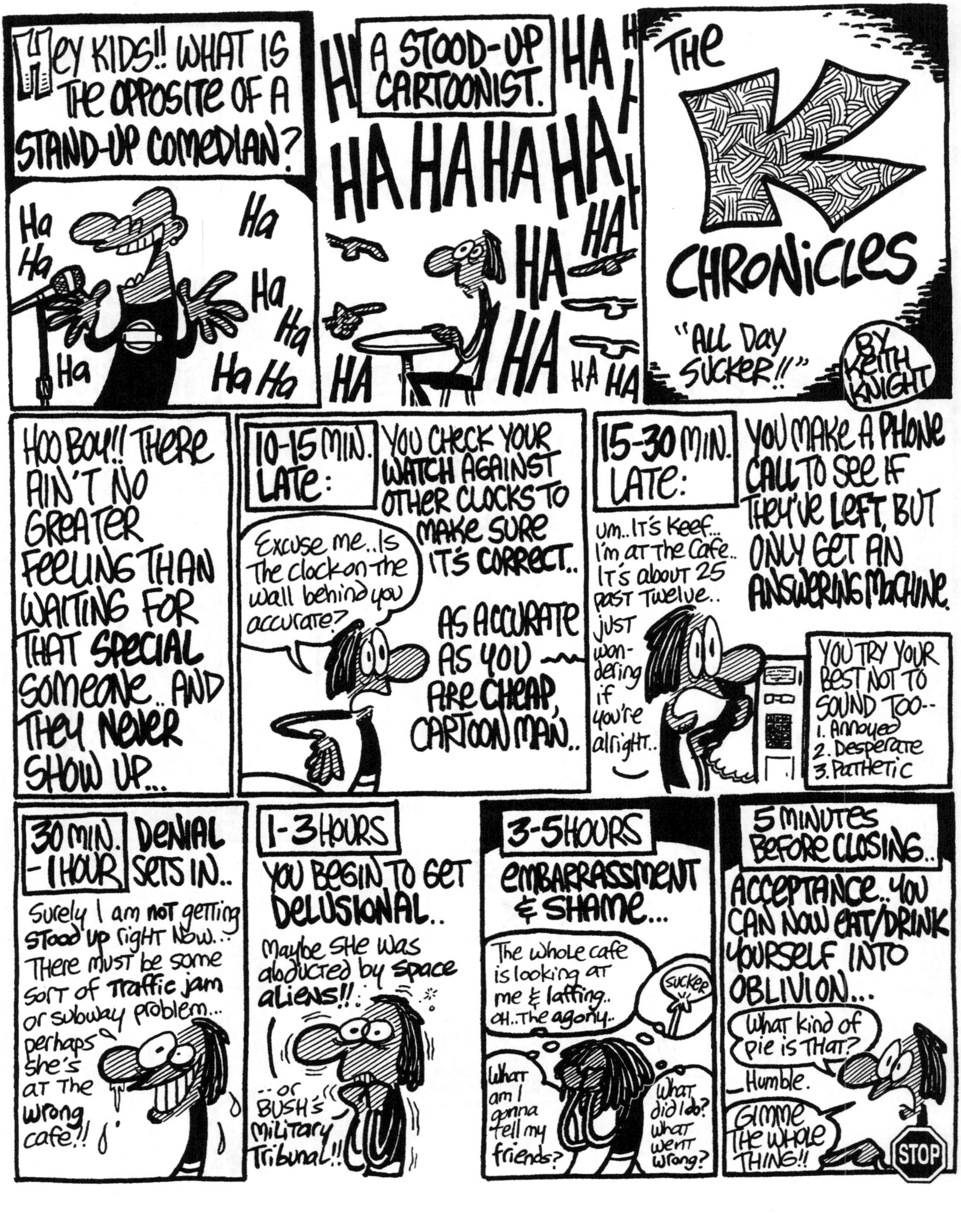
Hey KIDS!! WHAT IS THE OPPOSITE OF A STAND-UP COMEDIAN?
Ha Ha Ha Ha Ha Ha Ha Ha Ha
A STOOD-UP CARTOONIST.
HA HA HA HA HA HA HA HA HA HA HA HA HA
THE K CHRONICLES
"ALL DAY SUCKER!!"
BY KEITH KNIGHT
HOO BOY!! THERE AIN'T NO GREATER FEELING THAN WAITING FOR THAT SPECIAL SOMEONE.. AND THEY NEVER SHOW UP...
10-15 MIN. LATE:
YOU CHECK YOUR WATCH AGAINST OTHER CLOCKS TO MAKE SURE IT'S CORRECT..
Excuse me..Is The clock on the wall behind you accurate?
AS ACCURATE AS YOU ARE CHEAP, CARTOON MAN..
15-30 MIN. LATE:
YOU MAKE A PHONE CALL TO SEE IF THEY'VE LEFT, BUT ONLY GET AN ANSWERING MACHINE.
um..It's Keef... I'm at The Cafe.. It's about 25 past Twelve.. just wondering if you're alright..
YOU TRY YOUR BEST NOT TO SOUND TOO-- 1. Annoyed 2. Desperate 3. Pathetic
30 MIN. - 1 HOUR
DENIAL SETS IN..
Surely I am not getting stood up right Now... There must be some sort of Traffic jam or subway problem... perhaps she's at The wrong cafe!!
1-3 HOURS
YOU BEGIN TO GET DELUSIONAL..
Maybe SHE was abducted by space aliens!!
..or BUSH's Military Tribunal!!
3-5 HOURS
EMBARRASSMENT & SHAME...
The whole cafe is looking at me & laffing.. OH..The agony..
SUCKER
What am I gonna tell my friends?
What did I do? What went wrong?
5 MINUTES BEFORE CLOSING..
ACCEPTANCE.. YOU CAN NOW EAT/DRINK YOURSELF INTO OBLIVION...
What kind of pie is THAT?
_Humble.
GIMME THE WHOLE THING!!
STOP

THE K CHRONICLES

BY KEITH KNIGHT

I VISITED MY DAD RECENTLY... & WE GOT TO HAVE ANOTHER ONE OF THOSE "FATHER/SON" CHATS...

Dad, declaring a War on Terrorism sounds cool, but if you think about it even for a **second**, you realize how futile a gesture it is..

I mean...who **is** a terrorist and who **isn't**? The U.S. drops bombs on Iraq regularly. Our sanctions are killing **thousands** of children every month while Saddam Hussein sits **well-fed, safe and sound.**

What about the I.R.A.? Or the people that bomb abortion clinics? Are they terrorists?

When was the last time we declared war on a **non-country**? It was THE **WAR ON DRUGS.** What kind of result has that given us?

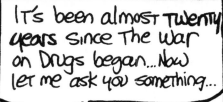

Billions of dollars down the tubes...**Millions** of lives **destroyed**...Civil liberties out the door & countless resources wasted.

It's been almost **TWENTY** years since the War on Drugs began...Now let me ask you something...

Has it gotten any **harder** for you or me to go out there & **score** just about any type of drug we could possibly imagine?...

Plus some we've never even heard of?

I liked it better when all you would talk about is the next **Star Wars** film...

The last one sucked, Dad.

STOP THE WAR!!

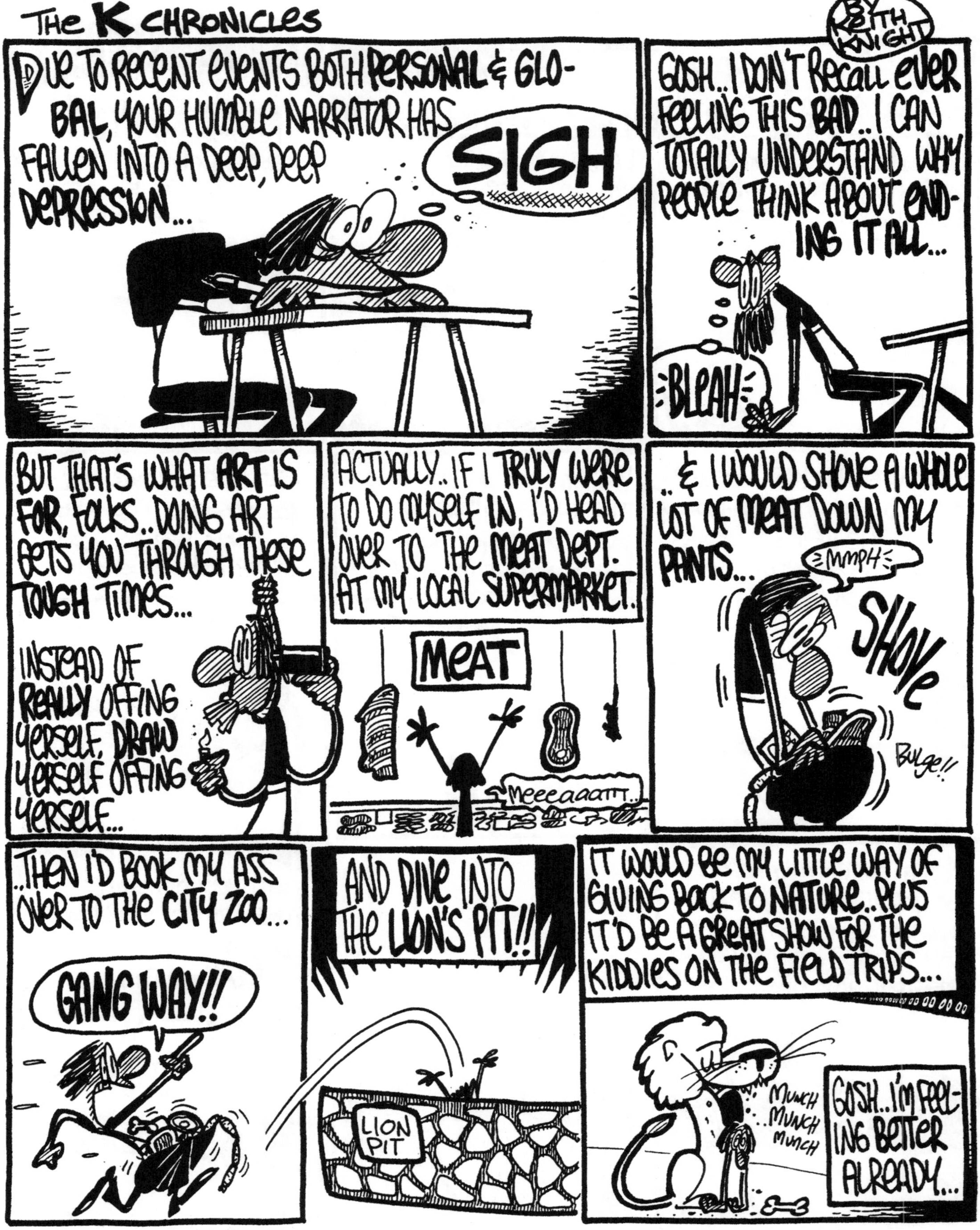
THE K CHRONICLES
BY KEITH KNIGHT
DUE TO RECENT EVENTS BOTH PERSONAL & GLOBAL, YOUR HUMBLE NARRATOR HAS FALLEN INTO A DEEP, DEEP DEPRESSION...
SIGH
GOSH.. I DON'T RECALL EVER FEELING THIS BAD.. I CAN TOTALLY UNDERSTAND WHY PEOPLE THINK ABOUT ENDING IT ALL...
BLEAH
BUT THAT'S WHAT ART IS FOR, FOLKS.. DOING ART GETS YOU THROUGH THESE TOUGH TIMES...
INSTEAD OF REALLY OFFING YERSELF, DRAW YERSELF OFFING YERSELF...
ACTUALLY.. IF I TRULY WERE TO DO MYSELF IN, I'D HEAD OVER TO THE MEAT DEPT. AT MY LOCAL SUPERMARKET..
MEAT
MEEEAAATTT..
.. & I WOULD SHOVE A WHOLE LOT OF MEAT DOWN MY PANTS...
MMPH
SHOVE
BULGE!!
..THEN I'D BOOK MY ASS OVER TO THE CITY ZOO...
GANG WAY!!
AND DIVE INTO THE LION'S PIT!!
LION PIT
IT WOULD BE MY LITTLE WAY OF GIVING BACK TO NATURE.. PLUS IT'D BE A GREAT SHOW FOR THE KIDDIES ON THE FIELD TRIPS...
MUNCH MUNCH MUNCH
GOSH.. I'M FEELING BETTER ALREADY...

 Running with a bunch of meat down yer pants: Funny!!

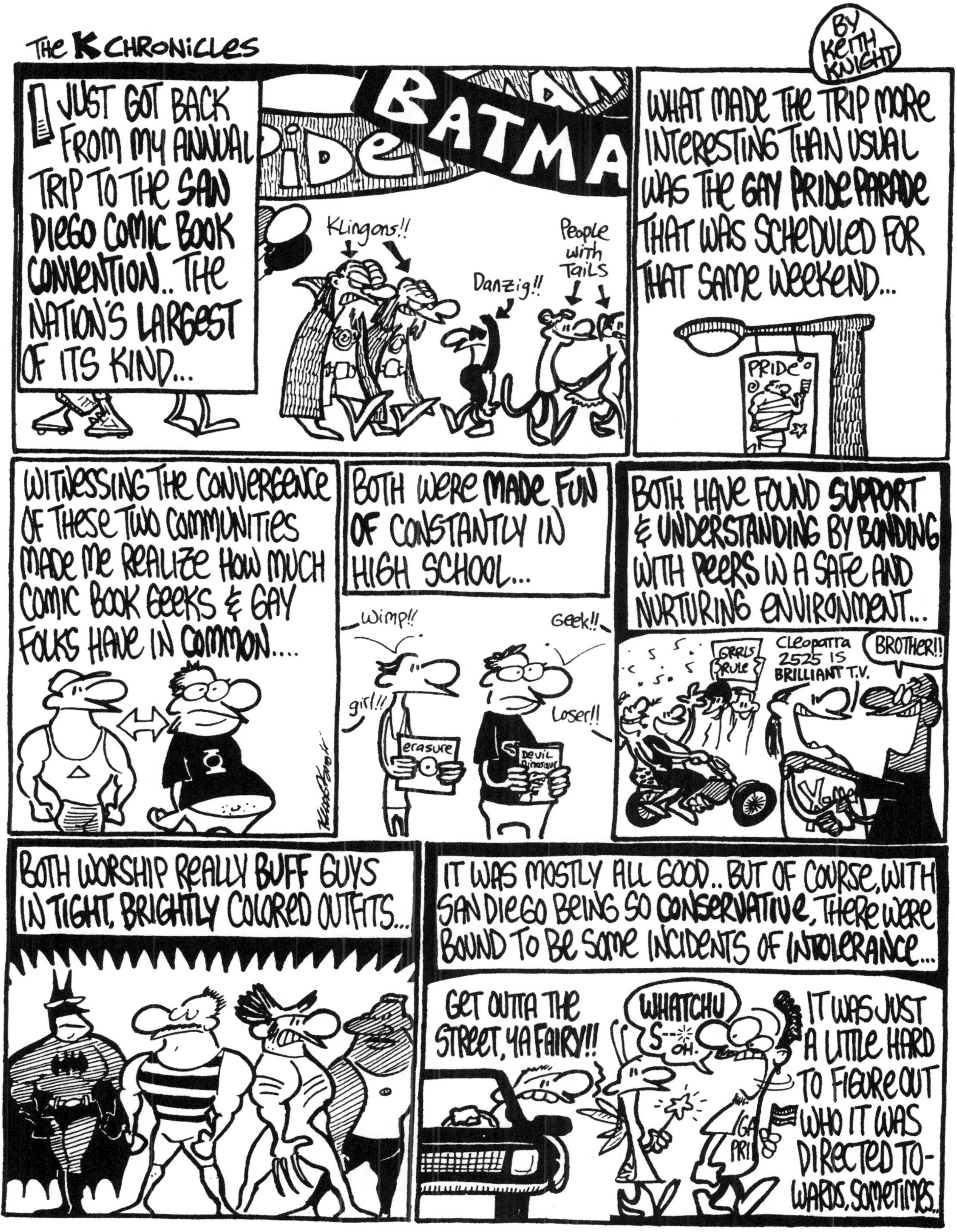
THE K CHRONICLES
BY KEITH KNIGHT
I JUST GOT BACK FROM MY ANNUAL TRIP TO THE SAN DIEGO COMIC BOOK CONVENTION.. THE NATION'S LARGEST OF ITS KIND...
BATMA
Klingons!!
Danzig!!
People with Tails
WHAT MADE THE TRIP MORE INTERESTING THAN USUAL WAS THE GAY PRIDE PARADE THAT WAS SCHEDULED FOR THAT SAME WEEKEND...
PRIDE
WITNESSING THE CONVERGENCE OF THESE TWO COMMUNITIES MADE ME REALIZE HOW MUCH COMIC BOOK GEEKS & GAY FOLKS HAVE IN COMMON....
BOTH WERE MADE FUN OF CONSTANTLY IN HIGH SCHOOL...
Wimp!!
Geek!!
girl!!
Loser!!
erasure
Devil Dinosaur
BOTH HAVE FOUND SUPPORT & UNDERSTANDING BY BONDING WITH PEERS IN A SAFE AND NURTURING ENVIRONMENT...
GRRLS RULE
CLeopatra 2525 IS BRILLIANT T.V.
BROTHER!!
BOTH WORSHIP REALLY BUFF GUYS IN TIGHT, BRIGHTLY COLORED OUTFITS...
IT WAS MOSTLY ALL GOOD.. BUT OF COURSE, WITH SAN DIEGO BEING SO CONSERVATIVE, THERE WERE BOUND TO BE SOME INCIDENTS OF INTOLERANCE...
GET OUTTA THE STREET, YA FAIRY!!
WHATCHU S--
OH.
IT WAS JUST A LITTLE HARD TO FIGURE OUT WHO IT WAS DIRECTED TOWARDS, SOMETIMES...

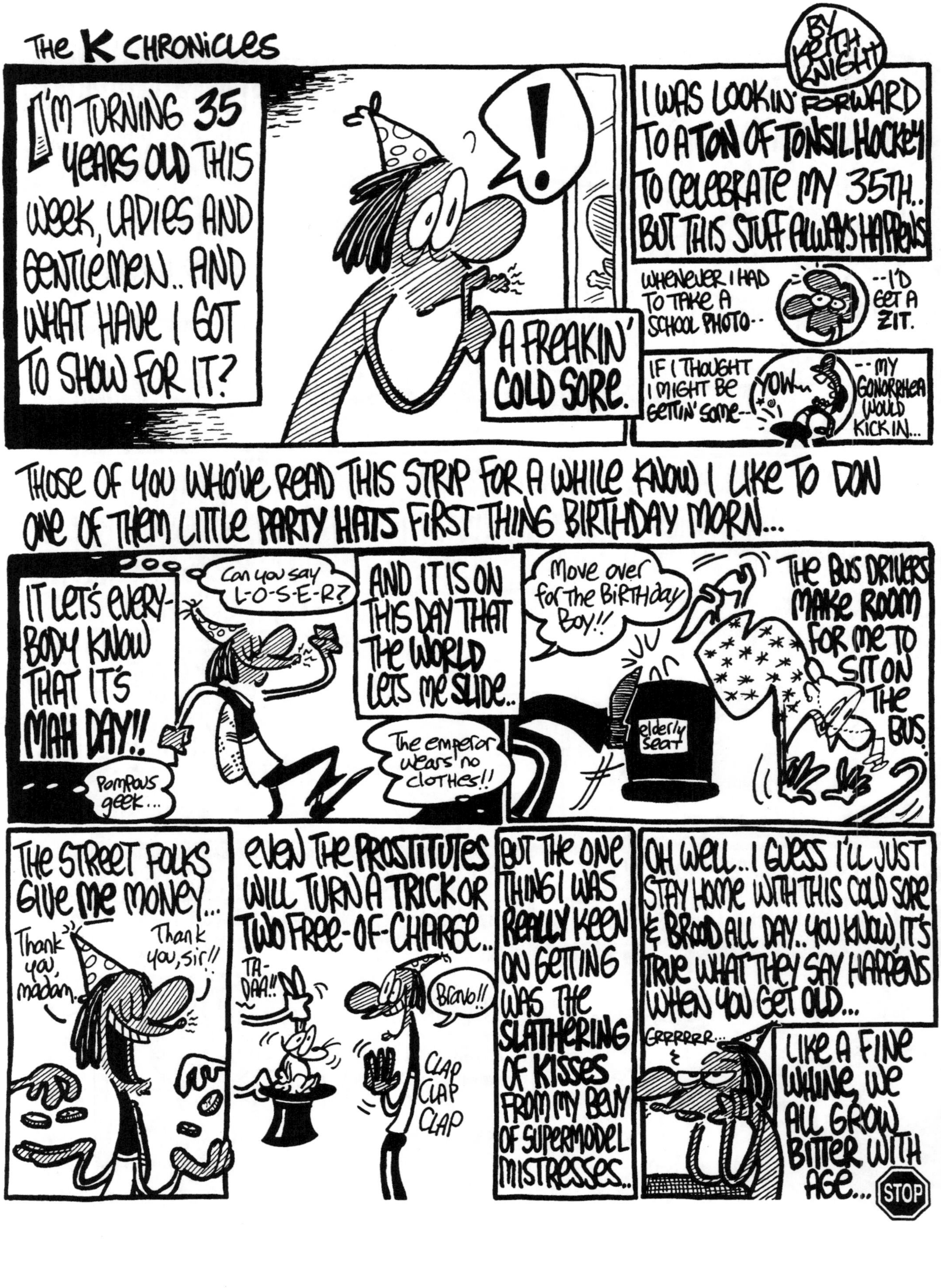

THE K CHRONICLES
BY KEITH KNIGHT
I'M TURNING 35 YEARS OLD THIS WEEK, LADIES AND GENTLEMEN.. AND WHAT HAVE I GOT TO SHOW FOR IT?
!
A FREAKIN' COLD SORE.
I WAS LOOKIN' FORWARD TO A TON OF TONSIL HOCKEY TO CELEBRATE MY 35TH.. BUT THIS STUFF ALWAYS HAPPENS
WHENEVER I HAD TO TAKE A SCHOOL PHOTO--
--I'D GET A ZIT.
IF I THOUGHT I MIGHT BE GETTIN' SOME--
YOW..
--MY GONORRHEA WOULD KICK IN...
THOSE OF YOU WHO'VE READ THIS STRIP FOR A WHILE KNOW I LIKE TO DON ONE OF THEM LITTLE PARTY HATS FIRST THING BIRTHDAY MORN...
IT LET'S EVERY-BODY KNOW THAT IT'S MAH DAY!!
Can you say L-O-S-E-R?
Pompous geek...
AND IT IS ON THIS DAY THAT THE WORLD LETS ME SLIDE..
The emperor wears no clothes!!
Move over for the BIRTHday Boy!!
elderly seat
THE BUS DRIVERS MAKE ROOM FOR ME TO SIT ON THE BUS.
THE STREET FOLKS GIVE ME MONEY...
Thank you, madam..
Thank you, sir!!
EVEN THE PROSTITUTES WILL TURN A TRICK OR TWO FREE-OF-CHARGE..
TA-DAA!!
Bravo!!
CLAP CLAP CLAP
BUT THE ONE THING I WAS REALLY KEEN ON GETTING WAS THE SLATHERING OF KISSES FROM MY BEVY OF SUPERMODEL MISTRESSES..
OH WELL.. I GUESS I'LL JUST STAY HOME WITH THIS COLD SORE & BROOD ALL DAY.. YOU KNOW, IT'S TRUE WHAT THEY SAY HAPPENS WHEN YOU GET OLD...
GRRRRRR...
LIKE A FINE WHINE, WE ALL GROW BITTER WITH AGE...
STOP

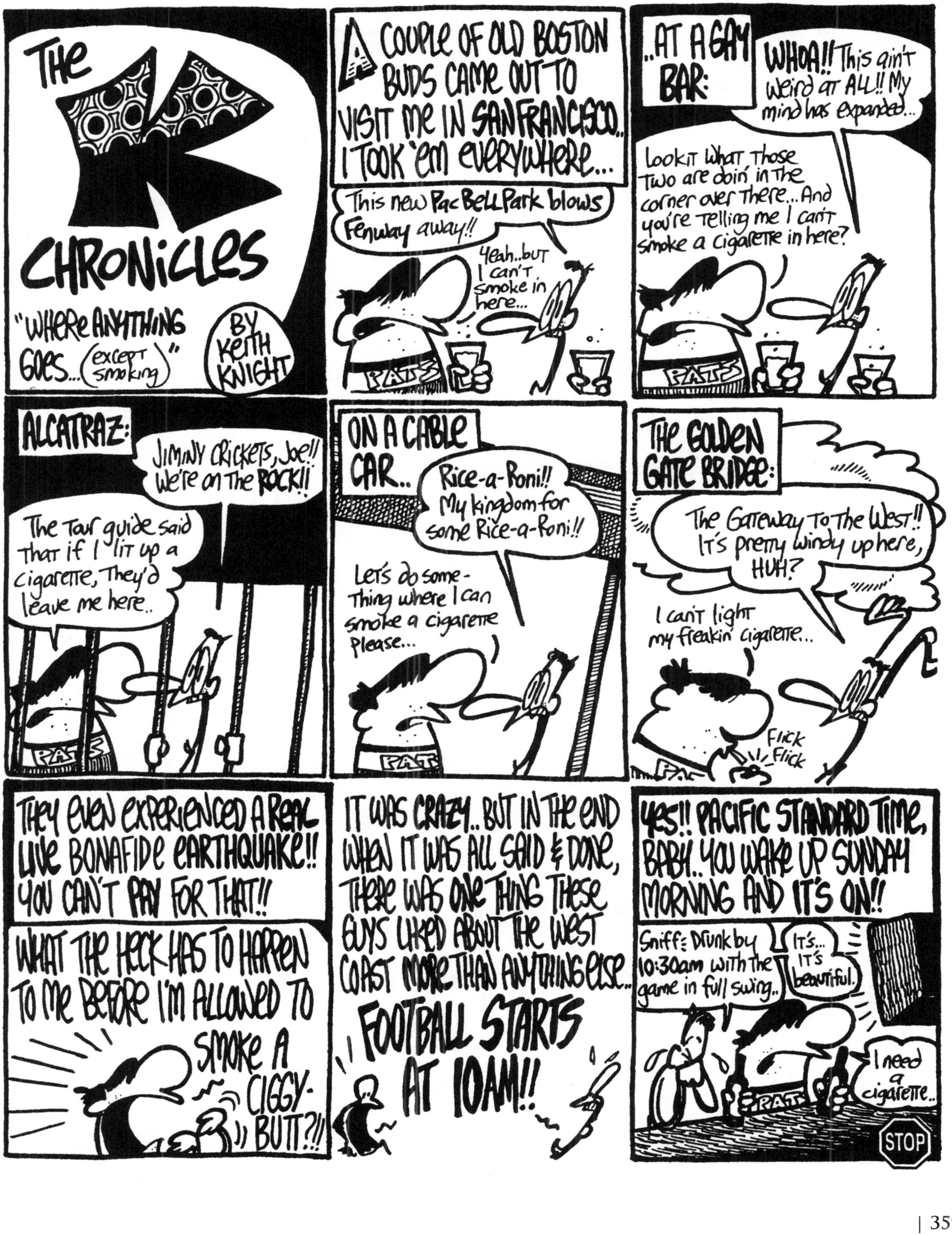

THE K CHRONICLES
"WHERE ANYTHING GOES... (EXCEPT SMOKING)"
BY KEITH KNIGHT
A COUPLE OF OLD BOSTON BUDS CAME OUT TO VISIT ME IN SAN FRANCISCO.. I TOOK 'EM EVERYWHERE...
This new Pac Bell Park blows Fenway away!!
Yeah..but I can't smoke in here...
PATS
..AT A GAY BAR:
WHOA!! This ain't weird at ALL!! My mind has expanded...
Lookit what those two are doin' in the corner over there... And you're telling me I can't smoke a cigarette in here?
PATS
ALCATRAZ:
JIMINY CRICKETS, Joe!! We're on the ROCK!!
The tour guide said that if I lit up a cigarette, they'd leave me here..
PATS
ON A CABLE CAR..
Rice-a-Roni!! My kingdom for some Rice-a-Roni!!
Let's do some-thing where I can smoke a cigarette please...
PAT
THE GOLDEN GATE BRIDGE:
The Gateway to the West!! It's pretty windy up here, HUH?
I can't light my freakin' cigarette...
Flick Flick
THEY EVEN EXPERIENCED A REAL LIVE BONAFIDE EARTHQUAKE!! YOU CAN'T PAY FOR THAT!!
WHAT THE HECK HAS TO HAPPEN TO ME BEFORE I'M ALLOWED TO SMOKE A CIGGY-BUTT?!!
IT WAS CRAZY.. BUT IN THE END WHEN IT WAS ALL SAID & DONE, THERE WAS ONE THING THESE GUYS LIKED ABOUT THE WEST COAST MORE THAN ANYTHING ELSE...
FOOTBALL STARTS AT 10AM!!
YES!! PACIFIC STANDARD TIME, BABY.. YOU WAKE UP SUNDAY MORNING AND IT'S ON!!
Sniff: Drunk by 10:30am with the game in full swing..
It's... it's beautiful.
I need a cigarette...
PAT
STOP

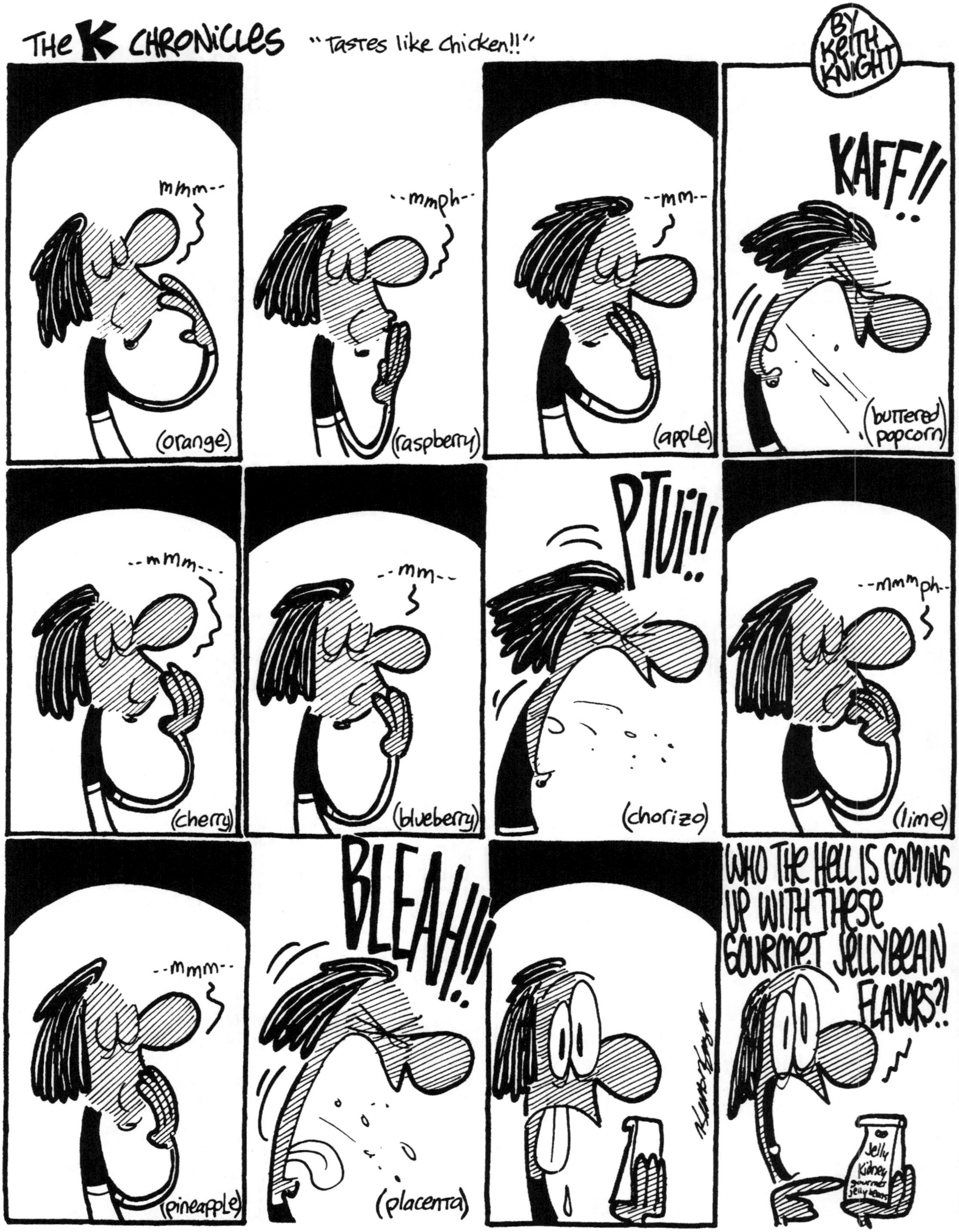
THE K CHRONICLES
"Tastes like Chicken!!"
BY KEITH KNIGHT
mmm--
(orange)
--mmph--
(raspberry)
--mm--
(apple)
KAFF!!
(buttered popcorn)
--mmm---
(cherry)
--mm--
(blueberry)
PTUI!!
(chorizo)
--mmmph--
(lime)
--mmm--
(pineapple)
BLEAH!!
(placenta)
WHO THE HELL IS COMING UP WITH THESE GOURMET JELLYBEAN FLAVORS?!
Jelly Kidney gourmet jelly beans

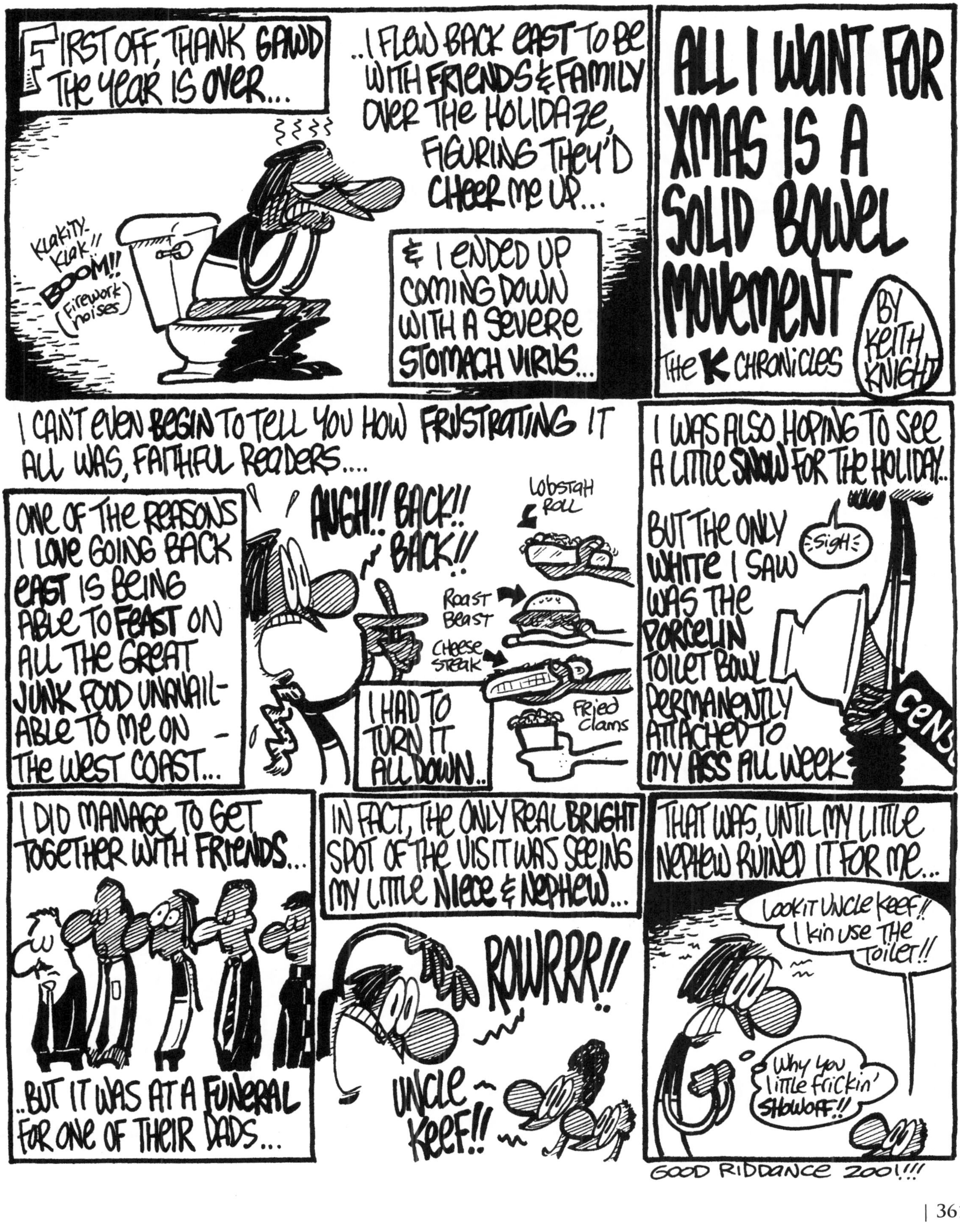
FIRST OFF, THANK GAWD THE YEAR IS OVER...
...I FLEW BACK EAST TO BE WITH FRIENDS & FAMILY OVER THE HOLIDAZE, FIGURING THEY'D CHEER ME UP...
KLAKITY-KLAK!! BOOM!! (Firework noises)
& I ENDED UP COMING DOWN WITH A SEVERE STOMACH VIRUS...
ALL I WANT FOR XMAS IS A SOLID BOWEL MOVEMENT
THE K CHRONICLES
BY KEITH KNIGHT
I CAN'T EVEN BEGIN TO TELL YOU HOW FRUSTRATING IT ALL WAS, FAITHFUL READERS....
ONE OF THE REASONS I LOVE GOING BACK EAST IS BEING ABLE TO FEAST ON ALL THE GREAT JUNK FOOD UNAVAILABLE TO ME ON THE WEST COAST...
AUGH!! BACK!! BACK!!
Lobstah Roll
Roast Beast
Cheese Steak
Fried Clams
I HAD TO TURN IT ALL DOWN..
I WAS ALSO HOPING TO SEE A LITTLE SNOW FOR THE HOLIDAY...
BUT THE ONLY WHITE I SAW WAS THE PORCELIN TOILET BOWL PERMANENTLY ATTACHED TO MY ASS ALL WEEK
Sigh
CENS
I DID MANAGE TO GET TOGETHER WITH FRIENDS...
..BUT IT WAS AT A FUNERAL FOR ONE OF THEIR DADS...
IN FACT, THE ONLY REAL BRIGHT SPOT OF THE VISIT WAS SEEING MY LITTLE NIECE & NEPHEW...
ROWRRR!!
UNCLE KEEF!!
THAT WAS, UNTIL MY LITTLE NEPHEW RUINED IT FOR ME...
LOOKIT UNCLE KEEF!! I KIN USE THE TOILET!!
Why you little frickin' SHOWOFF!!
GOOD RIDDANCE 2001!!!

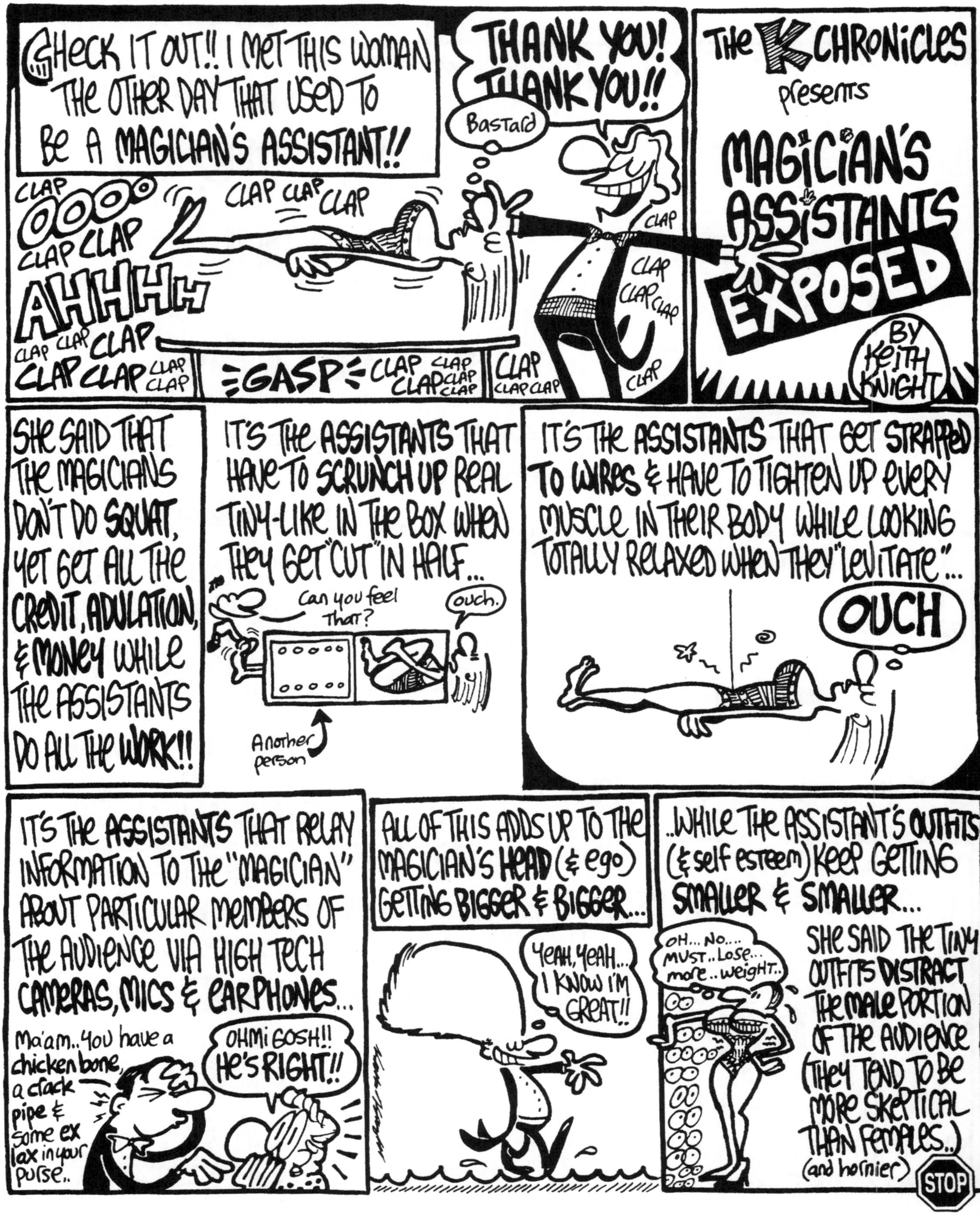
CHECK IT OUT!! I MET THIS WOMAN THE OTHER DAY THAT USED TO BE A MAGICIAN'S ASSISTANT!!
THANK YOU! THANK YOU!!
Bastard
CLAP OOOO CLAP CLAP CLAP CLAP CLAP AHHHHH CLAP CLAP CLAP CLAP CLAP CLAP CLAP GASP CLAP CLAP CLAP CLAP CLAP CLAP CLAP CLAP CLAP CLAP CLAP CLAP CLAP
The K CHRONICLES presents MAGICIAN'S ASSISTANTS EXPOSED
BY KEITH KNIGHT
SHE SAID THAT THE MAGICIANS DON'T DO SQUAT, YET GET ALL THE CREDIT, ADULATION, & MONEY WHILE THE ASSISTANTS DO ALL THE WORK!!
IT'S THE ASSISTANTS THAT HAVE TO SCRUNCH UP REAL TINY-LIKE IN THE BOX WHEN THEY GET "CUT" IN HALF...
Can you feel that?
ouch.
Another person
IT'S THE ASSISTANTS THAT GET STRAPPED TO WIRES & HAVE TO TIGHTEN UP EVERY MUSCLE IN THEIR BODY WHILE LOOKING TOTALLY RELAXED WHEN THEY "LEVITATE"...
OUCH
IT'S THE ASSISTANTS THAT RELAY INFORMATION TO THE "MAGICIAN" ABOUT PARTICULAR MEMBERS OF THE AUDIENCE VIA HIGH TECH CAMERAS, MICS & EARPHONES...
Ma'am.. You have a chicken bone, a crack pipe & some ex lax in your purse..
OHMi GOSH!! He'S RIGHT!!
ALL OF THIS ADDS UP TO THE MAGICIAN'S HEAD (& ego) GETTING BIGGER & BIGGER...
YEAH, YEAH... I KNOW I'M GREAT!!
..WHILE THE ASSISTANT'S OUTFITS (& self esteem) KEEP GETTING SMALLER & SMALLER...
OH... NO.... MUST.. LOSE... more.. weight..
SHE SAID THE TINY OUTFITS DISTRACT THE MALE PORTION OF THE AUDIENCE (THEY TEND TO BE MORE SKEPTICAL THAN FEMALES..)
(and hornier)
STOP

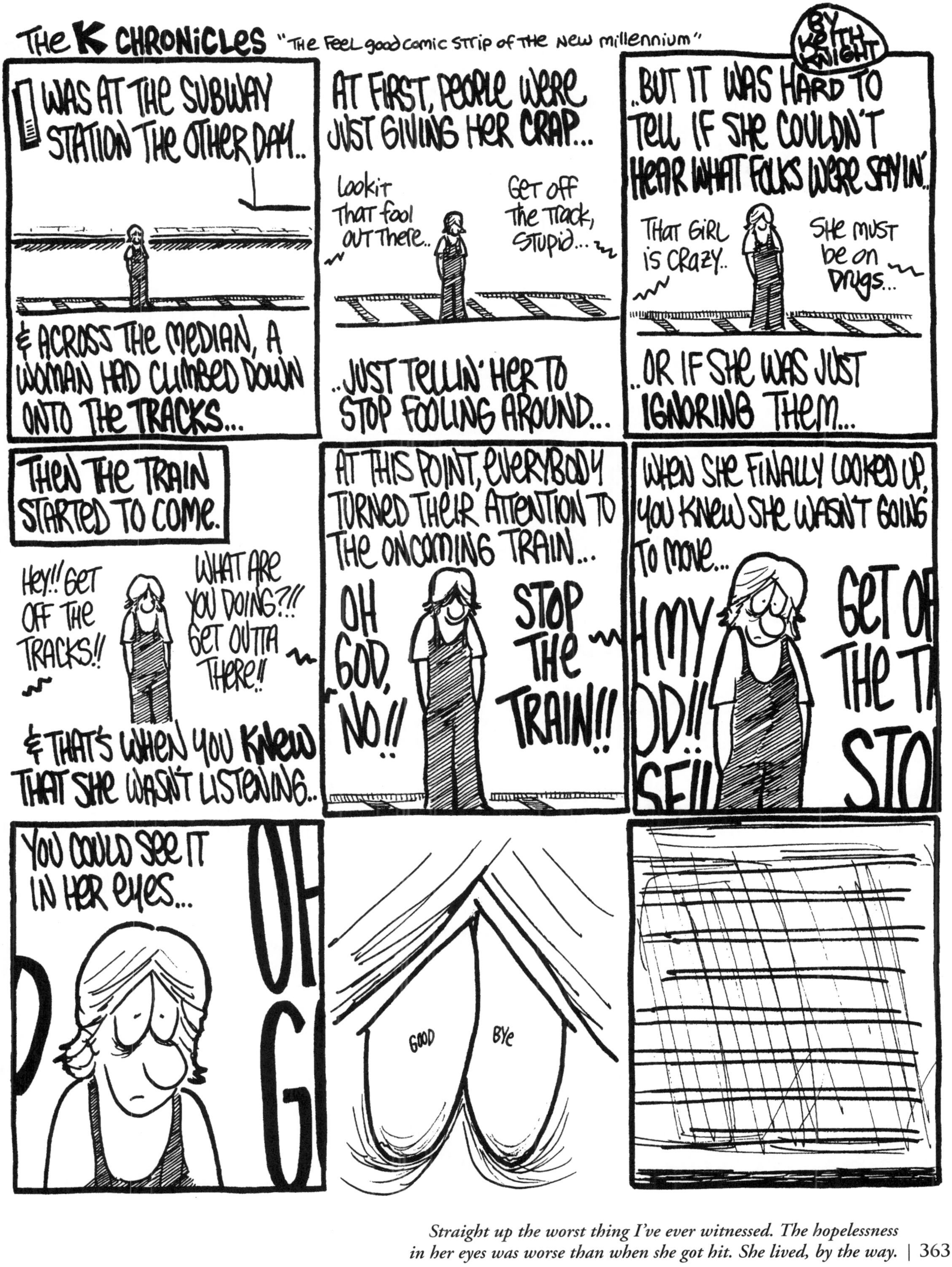
THE K CHRONICLES "THE FEEL GOOD COMIC STRIP OF THE NEW MILLENNIUM"
BY KEITH KNIGHT
I WAS AT THE SUBWAY STATION THE OTHER DAY..
& ACROSS THE MEDIAN, A WOMAN HAD CLIMBED DOWN ONTO THE TRACKS...
AT FIRST, PEOPLE WERE JUST GIVING HER CRAP...
LOOKIT THAT FOOL OUT THERE..
GET OFF THE TRACK, STUPID...
..JUST TELLIN' HER TO STOP FOOLING AROUND...
..BUT IT WAS HARD TO TELL IF SHE COULDN'T HEAR WHAT FOLKS WERE SAYIN'..
THAT GIRL IS CRAZY..
SHE MUST BE ON DRUGS...
..OR IF SHE WAS JUST IGNORING THEM...
THEN THE TRAIN STARTED TO COME.
HEY!! GET OFF THE TRACKS!!
WHAT ARE YOU DOING?!! GET OUTTA THERE!!
& THAT'S WHEN YOU KNEW THAT SHE WASN'T LISTENING..
AT THIS POINT, EVERYBODY TURNED THEIR ATTENTION TO THE ONCOMING TRAIN...
OH GOD, NO!!
STOP THE TRAIN!!
WHEN SHE FINALLY LOOKED UP, YOU KNEW SHE WASN'T GOING TO MOVE...
YOU COULD SEE IT IN HER EYES...
GOOD BYE

Straight up the worst thing I've ever witnessed. The hopelessness in her eyes was worse than when she got hit. She lived, by the way.

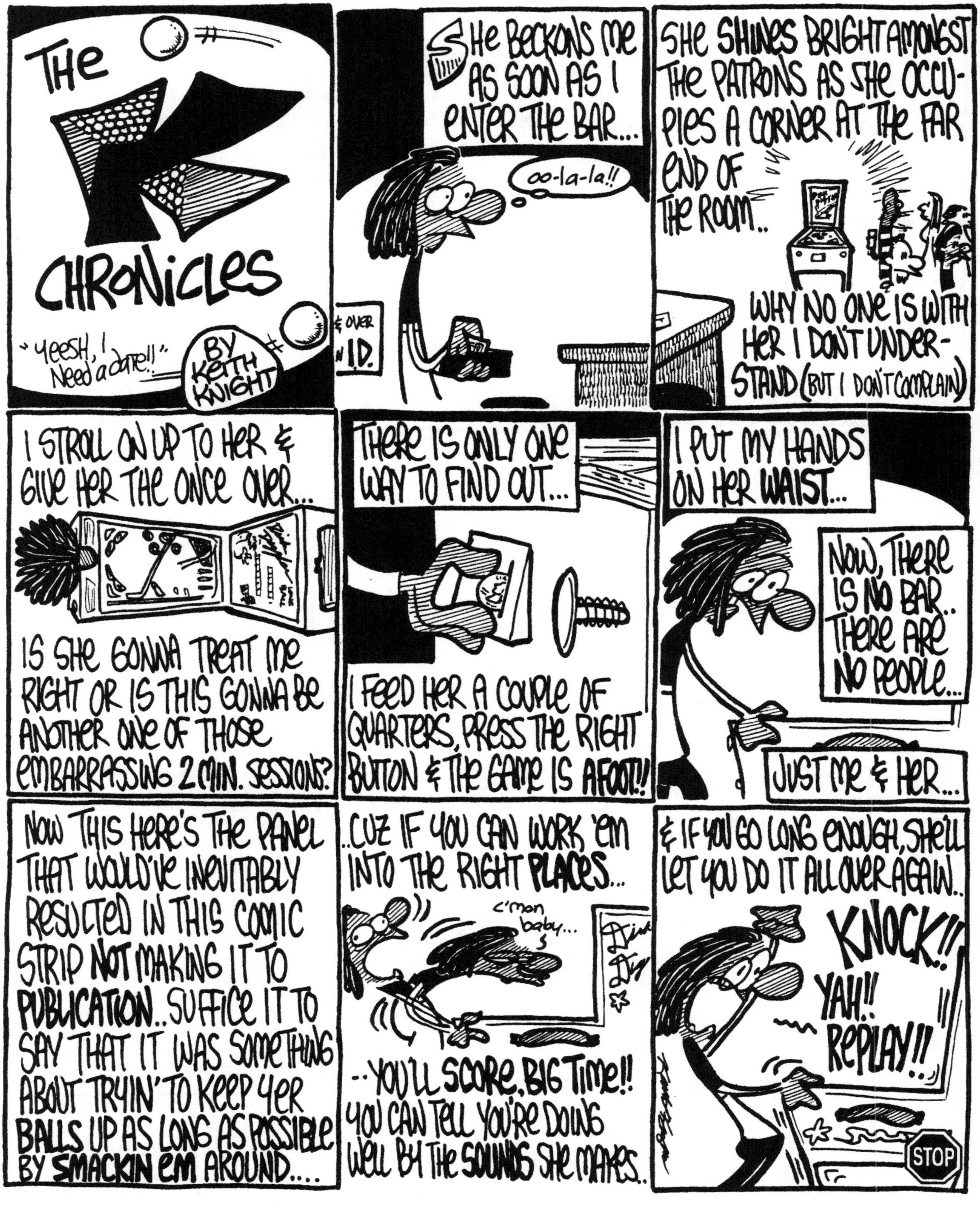

THE K CHRONICLES
"YEESH, I NEED A DATE!!"
BY KEITH KNIGHT
SHE BECKONS ME AS SOON AS I ENTER THE BAR...
oo-la-la!!
21 & OVER W I.D.
SHE SHINES BRIGHT AMONGST THE PATRONS AS SHE OCCUPIES A CORNER AT THE FAR END OF THE ROOM..
WHY NO ONE IS WITH HER I DON'T UNDERSTAND (BUT I DON'T COMPLAIN)
I STROLL ON UP TO HER & GIVE HER THE ONCE OVER...
IS SHE GONNA TREAT ME RIGHT OR IS THIS GONNA BE ANOTHER ONE OF THOSE EMBARRASSING 2 MIN. SESSIONS?
THERE IS ONLY ONE WAY TO FIND OUT...
I FEED HER A COUPLE OF QUARTERS, PRESS THE RIGHT BUTTON & THE GAME IS AFOOT!!
I PUT MY HANDS ON HER WAIST...
NOW, THERE IS NO BAR.. THERE ARE NO PEOPLE...
JUST ME & HER...
NOW THIS HERE'S THE PANEL THAT WOULD'VE INEVITABLY RESULTED IN THIS COMIC STRIP NOT MAKING IT TO PUBLICATION.. SUFFICE IT TO SAY THAT IT WAS SOMETHING ABOUT TRYIN' TO KEEP HER BALLS UP AS LONG AS POSSIBLE BY SMACKIN EM AROUND....
..CUZ IF YOU CAN WORK 'EM INTO THE RIGHT PLACES...
c'mon baby...
..YOU'LL SCORE, BIG TIME!! YOU CAN TELL YOU'RE DOING WELL BY THE SOUNDS SHE MAKES..
& IF YOU GO LONG ENOUGH, SHE'LL LET YOU DO IT ALL OVER AGAIN..
KNOCK!!
YAH!!
REPLAY!!
STOP

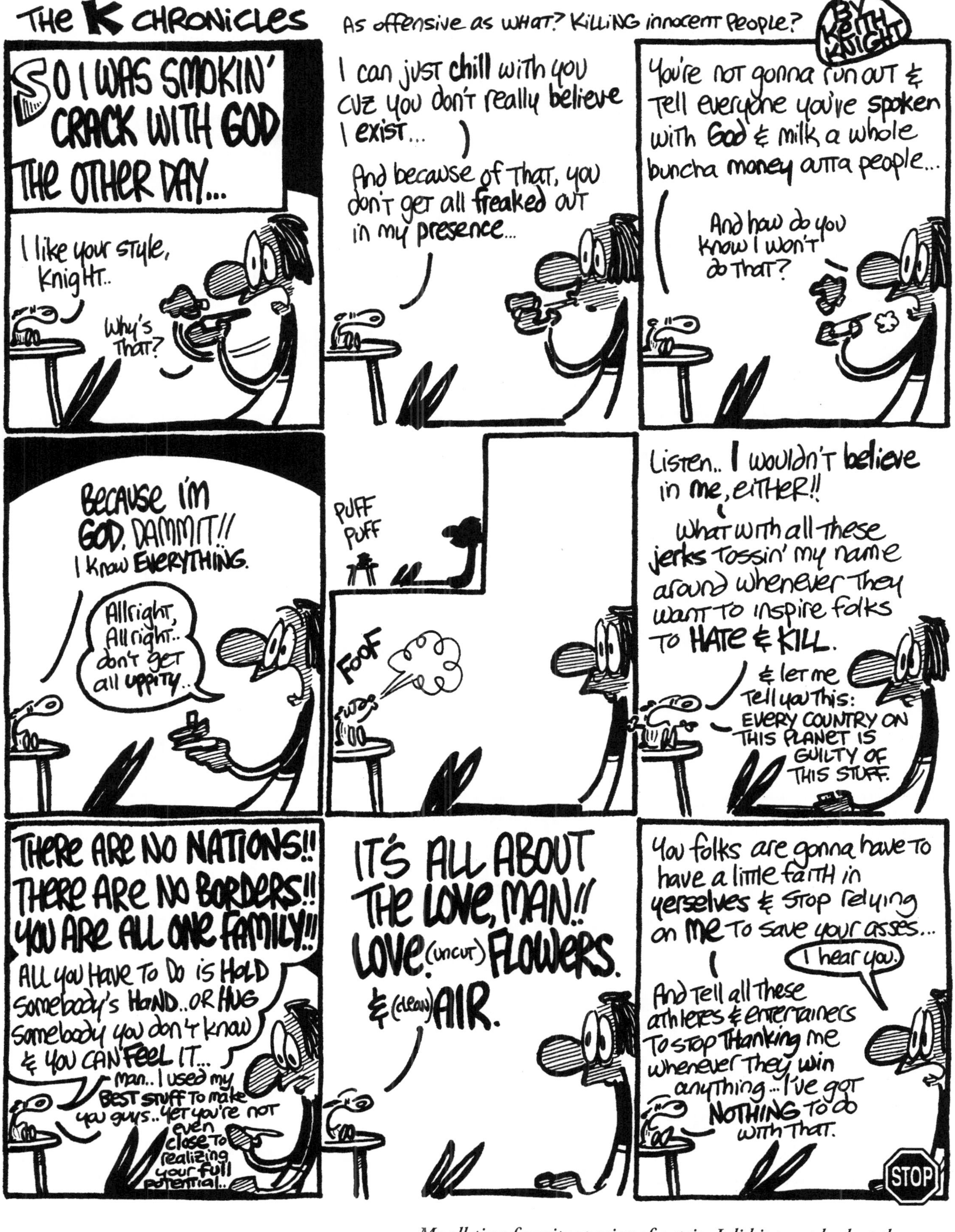

THE K CHRONICLES
As offensive as WHAT? KILLING innocent People?
BY KEITH KNIGHT
SO I WAS SMOKIN' CRACK WITH GOD THE OTHER DAY...
I like your style, Knight..
Why's That?
I can just chill with you cuz you don't really believe I exist...
And because of That, you don't get all freaked out in my presence...
You're not gonna run out & Tell everyone you've spoken with God & milk a whole buncha money outta people...
And how do you know I won't do That?
BECAUSE I'M GOD, DAMMIT!! I Know EVERYTHING.
Allright, Allright.. don't get all uppity..
PUFF PUFF
FOOF
Listen.. I wouldn't believe in me, either!!
What with all these jerks tossin' my name around whenever They want to inspire folks to HATE & KILL.
& let me Tell you This: EVERY COUNTRY ON THIS PLANET IS GUILTY OF THIS STUFF.
THERE ARE NO NATIONS!! THERE ARE NO BORDERS!! YOU ARE ALL ONE FAMILY!!
ALL you Have To Do is HOLD Somebody's HAND..OR HUG Somebody you don't know & YOU CAN FEEL IT...
man.. I used my BEST STUFF To make you guys.. yet you're not even close to realizing your full potential..
IT'S ALL ABOUT THE LOVE, MAN!! LOVE. (uncut) FLOWERS. & (clean) AIR.
You folks are gonna have to have a little faith in yerselves & stop relying on me to save your asses...
I hear you.
And tell all these athletes & entertainers To stop Thanking me whenever They win anything... I've got NOTHING To do with That.
STOP

My all-time favorite opening of a strip. I did it to get back at the editor that didn't run the last strip where I mentioned crack.

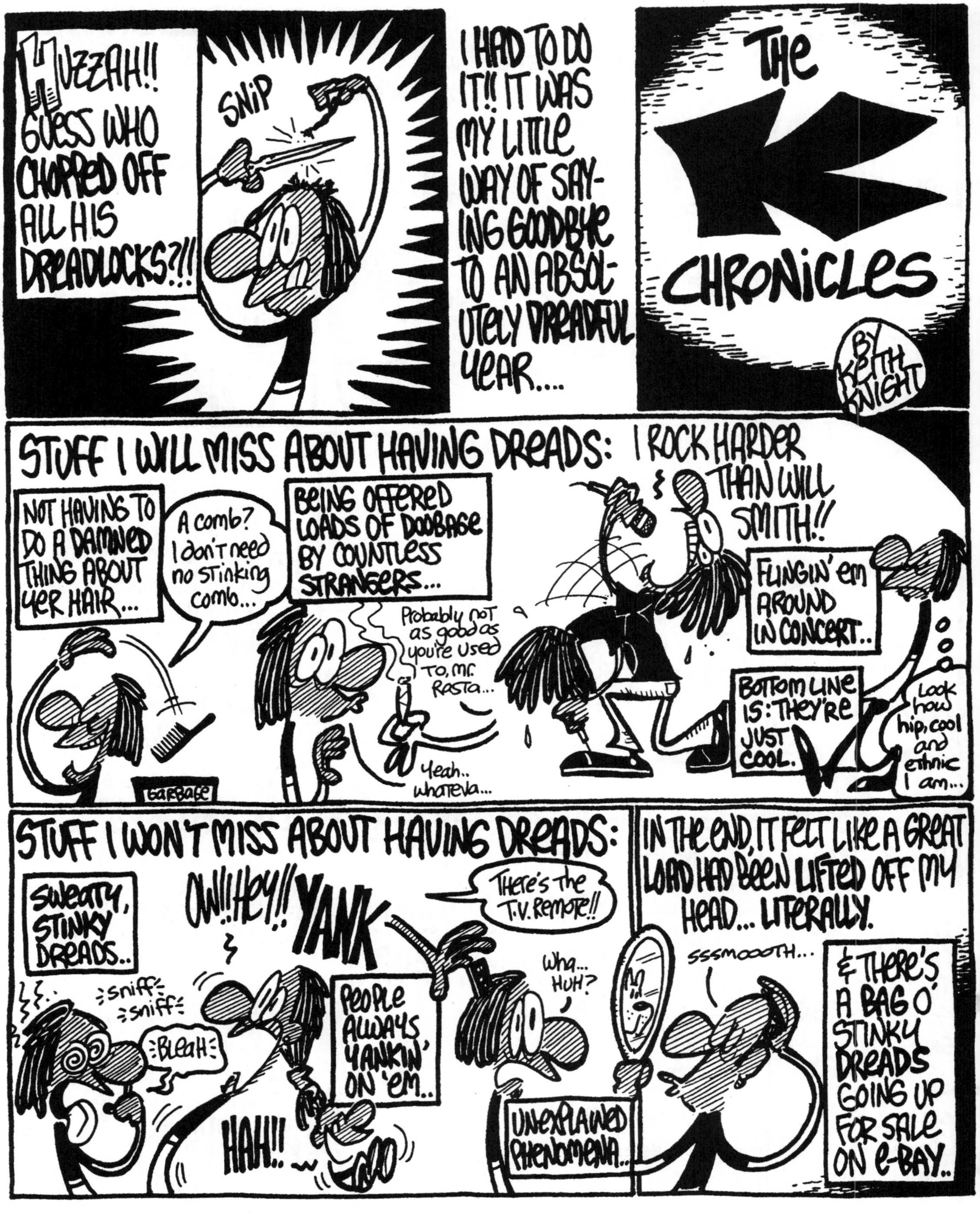
HUZZAH!! GUESS WHO CHOPPED OFF ALL HIS DREADLOCKS?!!
SNIP
I HAD TO DO IT!! IT WAS MY LITTLE WAY OF SAYING GOODBYE TO AN ABSOLUTELY DREADFUL YEAR....
THE K CHRONICLES
BY KEITH KNIGHT
STUFF I WILL MISS ABOUT HAVING DREADS:
NOT HAVING TO DO A DAMNED THING ABOUT YER HAIR...
A comb? I don't need no stinking comb...
GARBAGE
BEING OFFERED LOADS OF DOOBAGE BY COUNTLESS STRANGERS...
Probably not as good as you're used to, mr. Rasta...
Yeah.. whateva...
I ROCK HARDER THAN WILL SMITH!!
FLINGIN' 'EM AROUND IN CONCERT..
BOTTOM LINE IS: THEY'RE JUST COOL.
Look how hip, cool and ethnic I am...
STUFF I WON'T MISS ABOUT HAVING DREADS:
SWEATY, STINKY DREADS..
sniff sniff
BLEAH!
OW!! HEY!!
YANK
PEOPLE ALWAYS YANKIN' ON 'EM..
HAH!!
There's the T.V. Remote!!
Wha... HUH?
UNEXPLAINED PHENOMENA..
IN THE END, IT FELT LIKE A GREAT LOAD HAD BEEN LIFTED OFF MY HEAD... LITERALLY.
SSSMOOOTH...
& THERE'S A BAG O' STINKY DREADS GOING UP FOR SALE ON E-BAY..

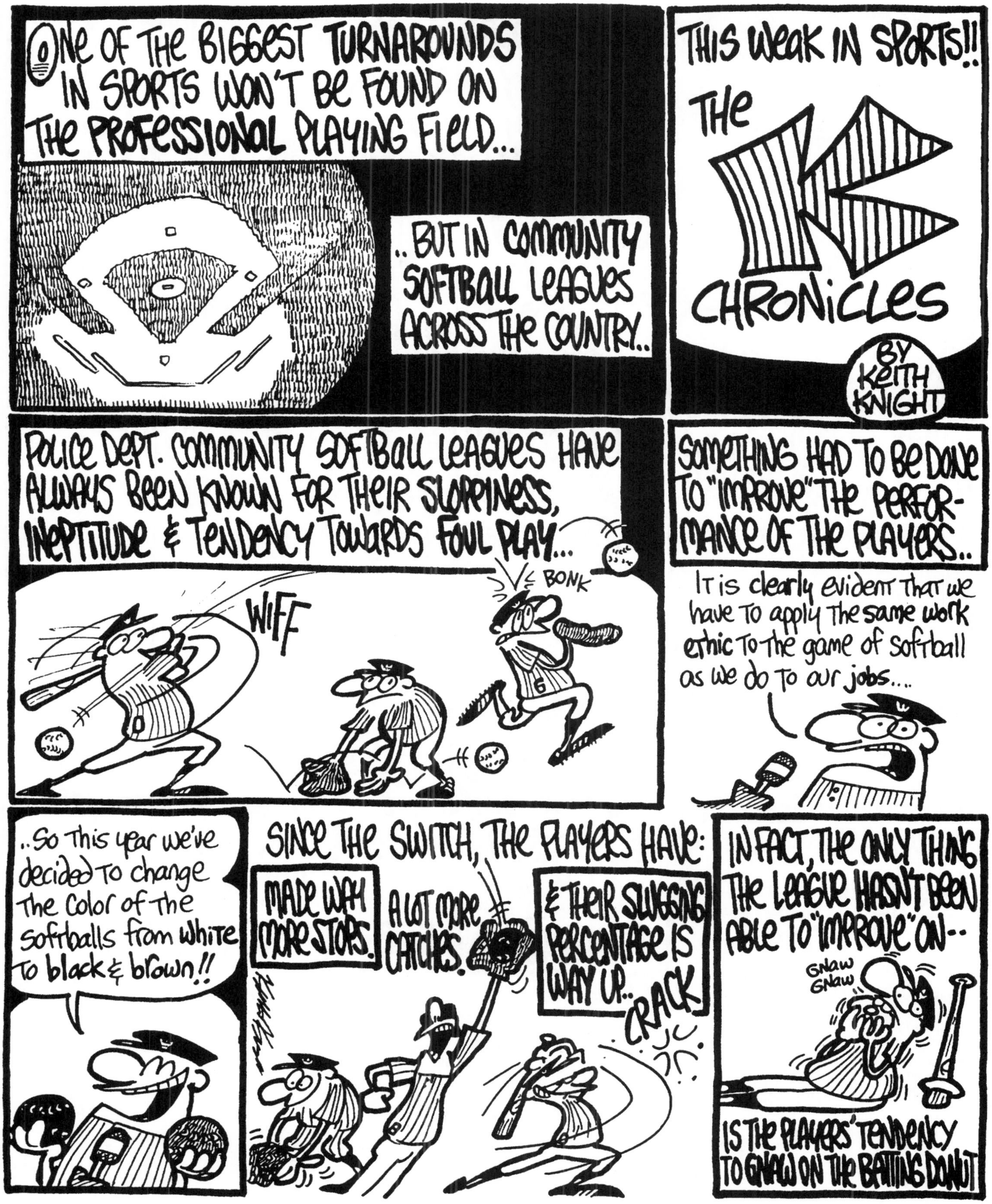

One of the biggest turnarounds in sports won't be found on the professional playing field...
..But in community softball leagues across the country..
This weak in sports!!..
The K Chronicles
By Keith Knight
Police Dept. community softball leagues have always been known for their sloppiness, ineptitude & tendency towards foul play...
WIFF
BONK
Something had to be done to "improve" the performance of the players..
It is clearly evident that we have to apply the same work ethic to the game of softball as we do to our jobs....
..So this year we've decided to change the color of the softballs from white to black & brown!!
Since the switch, the players have:
Made way more stops.
A lot more catches.
& their slugging percentage is way up..
CRACK
In fact, the only thing the league hasn't been able to "improve" on..
GNAW GNAW
Is the players' tendency to gnaw on the batting donut

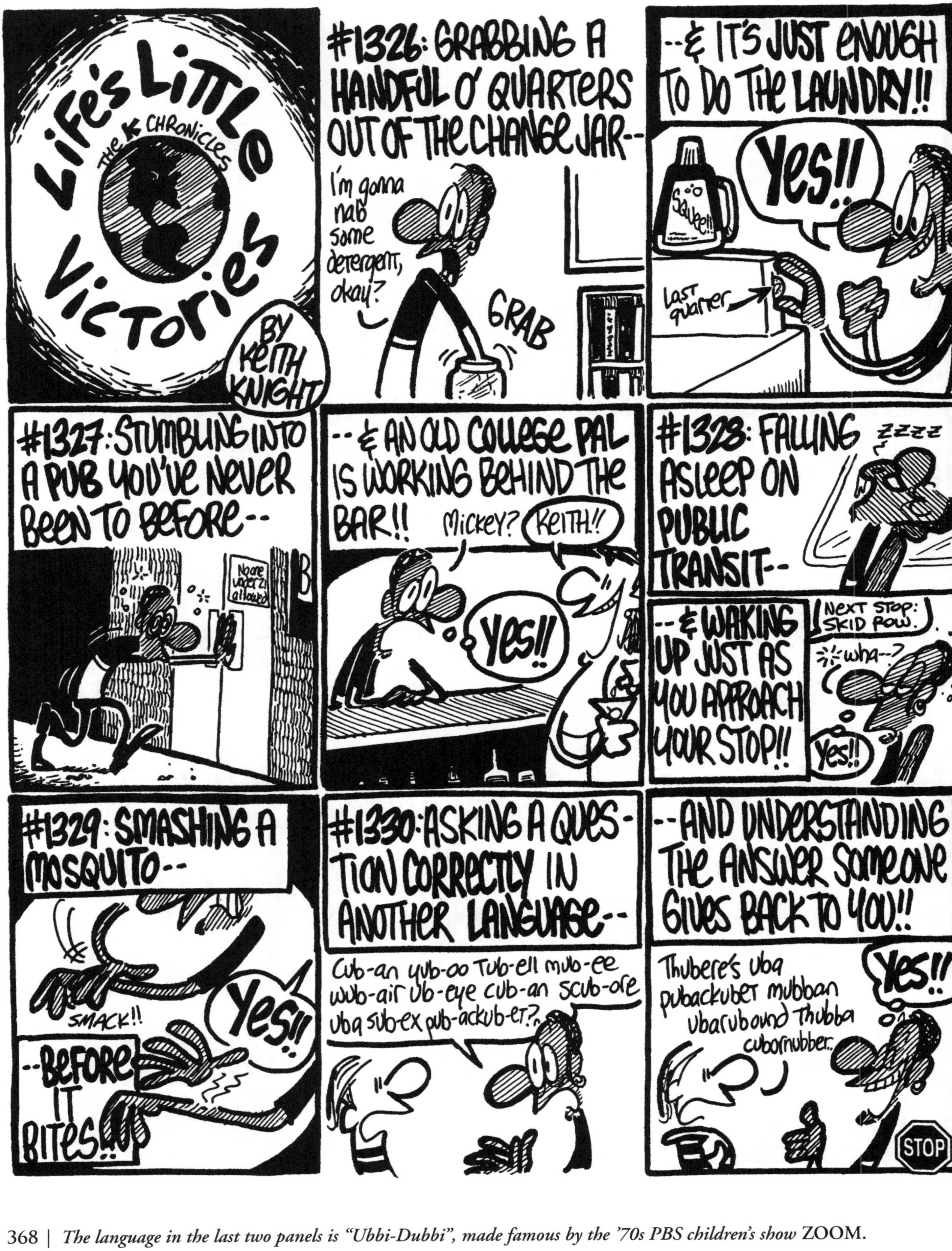
Life's Little Victories
The K Chronicles
By Keith Knight
#1326: GRABBING A HANDFUL O' QUARTERS OUT OF THE CHANGE JAR--
I'm gonna nab some detergent, okay?
GRAB
--& IT'S JUST ENOUGH TO DO THE LAUNDRY!!
Yes!!
Squee!!
Last quarter
#1327: STUMBLING INTO A PUB YOU'VE NEVER BEEN TO BEFORE--
No one under 21 allowed
--& AN OLD COLLEGE PAL IS WORKING BEHIND THE BAR!!
Mickey?
Keith!!
Yes!!
#1328: FALLING ASLEEP ON PUBLIC TRANSIT--
ZZZZZ
--& WAKING UP JUST AS YOU APPROACH YOUR STOP!!
NEXT STOP: SKID ROW.
wha--?
Yes!!
#1329: SMASHING A MOSQUITO--
SMACK!!
Yes!!
--BEFORE IT BITES!!
#1330: ASKING A QUESTION CORRECTLY IN ANOTHER LANGUAGE--
Cub-an yub-oo Tub-ell mub-ee wub-air ub-eye cub-an scub-ore uba sub-ex pub-ackub-et?
--AND UNDERSTANDING THE ANSWER SOMEONE GIVES BACK TO YOU!!
Thubere's uba pubackubet mubban ubarubound thubba cubornubber..
Yes!!
STOP

 The language in the last two panels is "Ubbi-Dubbi", made famous by the '70s PBS children's show ZOOM.

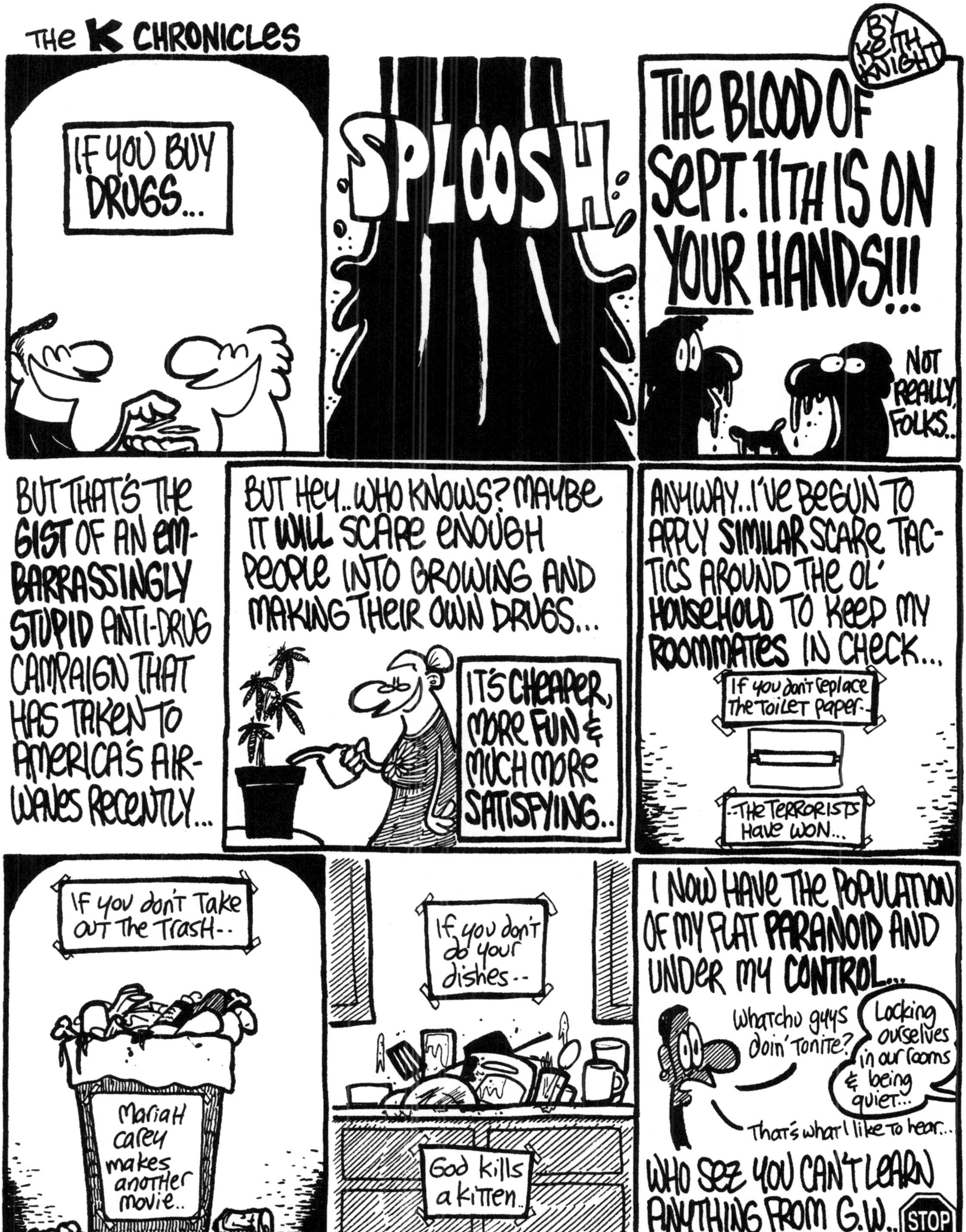
THE K CHRONICLES
BY KEITH KNIGHT
IF YOU BUY DRUGS...
SPLOOSH
THE BLOOD OF SEPT. 11TH IS ON YOUR HANDS!!!...
NOT REALLY, FOLKS..
BUT THAT'S THE GIST OF AN EMBARRASSINGLY STUPID ANTI-DRUG CAMPAIGN THAT HAS TAKEN TO AMERICA'S AIRWAVES RECENTLY...
BUT HEY.. WHO KNOWS? MAYBE IT WILL SCARE ENOUGH PEOPLE INTO GROWING AND MAKING THEIR OWN DRUGS...
IT'S CHEAPER, MORE FUN & MUCH MORE SATISFYING..
ANYWAY.. I'VE BEGUN TO APPLY SIMILAR SCARE TACTICS AROUND THE OL' HOUSEHOLD TO KEEP MY ROOMMATES IN CHECK...
If you don't replace the toilet paper-
-The Terrorists have won...
If you don't Take out the Trash--
Mariah Carey makes another movie..
If you don't do your dishes--
God kills a kitten..
I NOW HAVE THE POPULATION OF MY FLAT PARANOID AND UNDER MY CONTROL...
Whatchu guys doin' tonite?
Locking ourselves in our rooms & being quiet...
That's what I like to hear...
WHO SEZ YOU CAN'T LEARN ANYTHING FROM G.W...
STOP

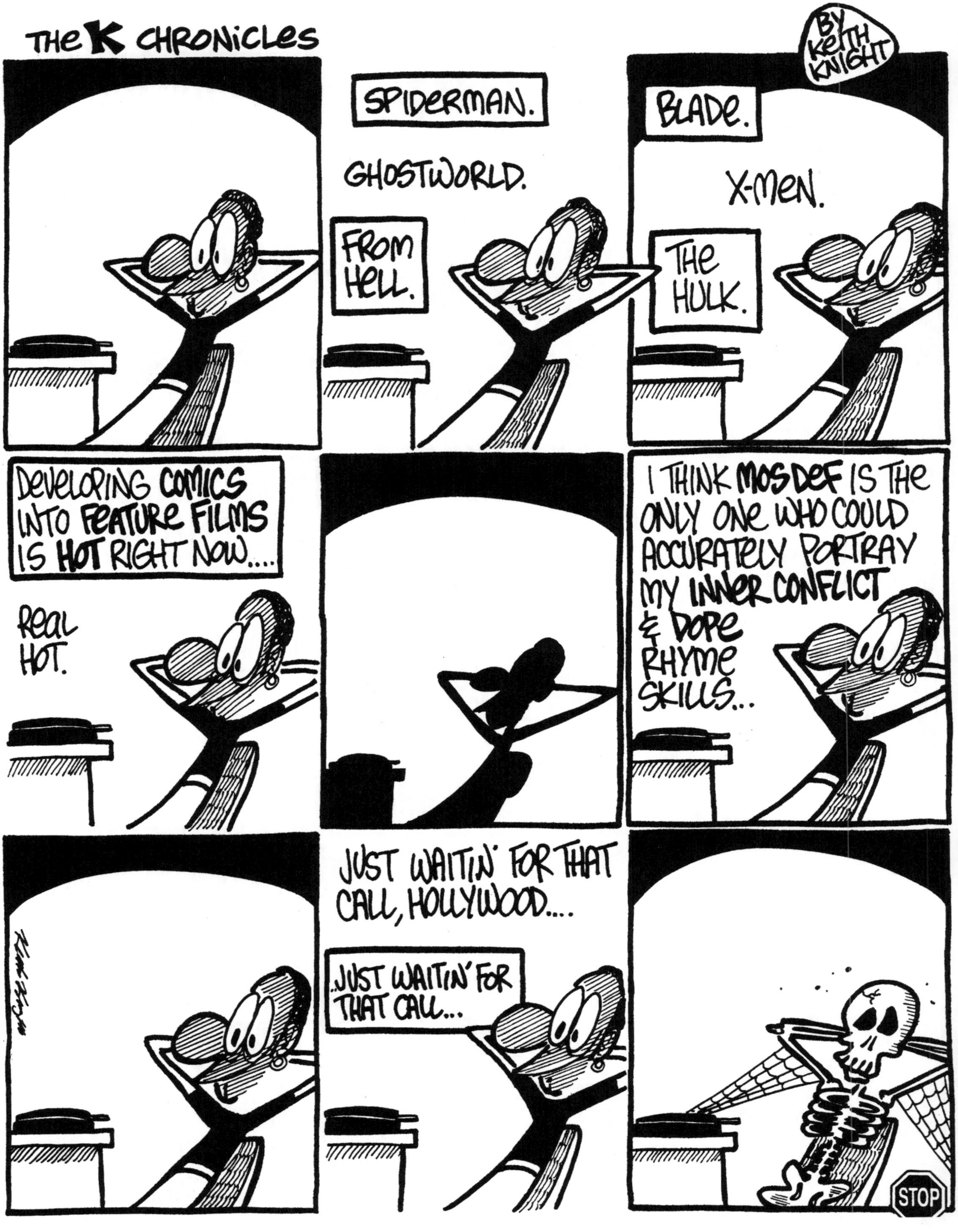
THE K CHRONICLES
BY KEITH KNIGHT
SPIDERMAN.
GHOSTWORLD.
FROM HELL.
BLADE.
X-MEN.
THE HULK.
DEVELOPING COMICS INTO FEATURE FILMS IS HOT RIGHT NOW....
REAL HOT.
I THINK MOS DEF IS THE ONLY ONE WHO COULD ACCURATELY PORTRAY MY INNER CONFLICT & DOPE RHYME SKILLS...
JUST WAITIN' FOR THAT CALL, HOLLYWOOD....
..JUST WAITIN' FOR THAT CALL...
STOP

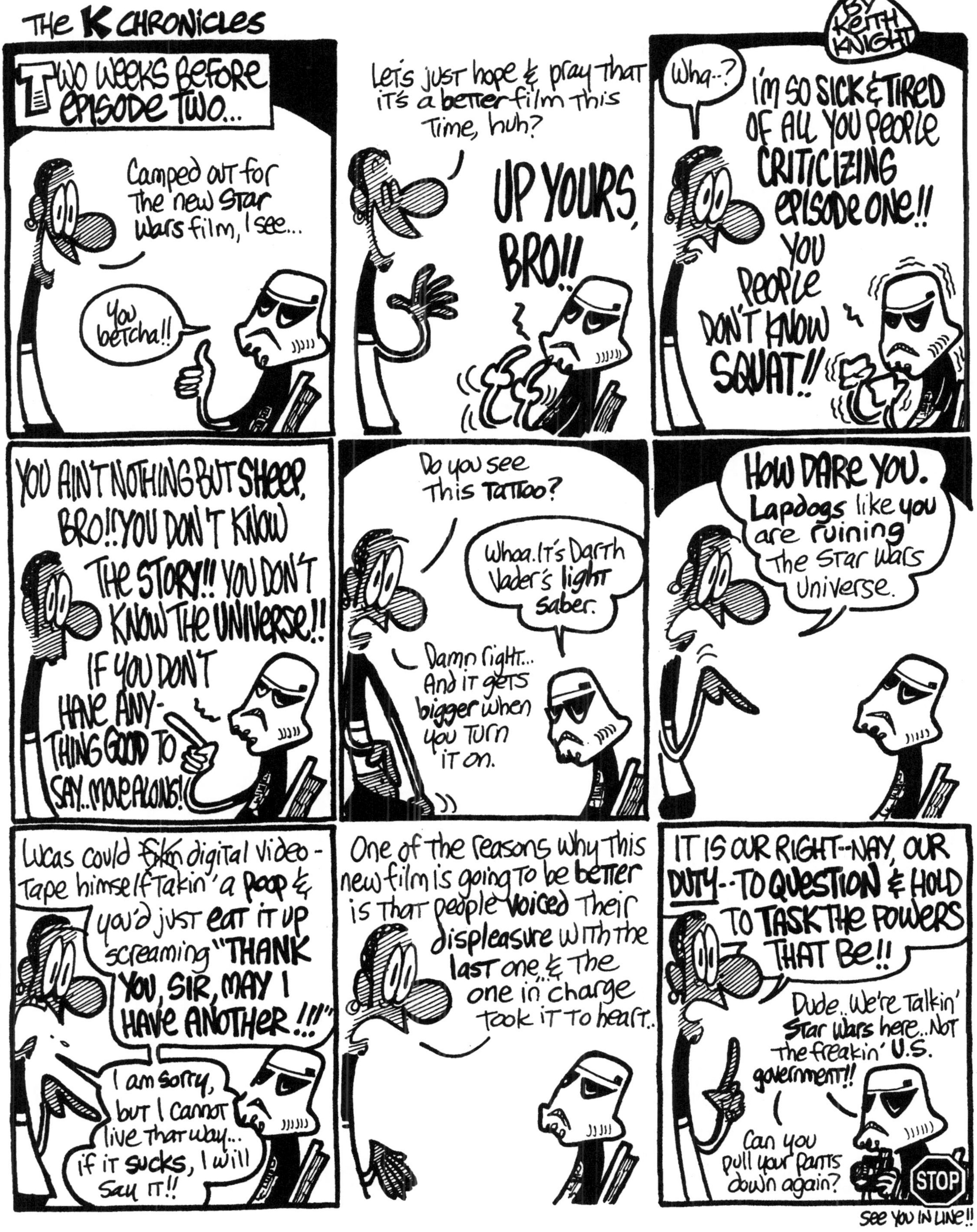
THE K CHRONICLES
BY KEITH KNIGHT
TWO WEEKS BEFORE EPISODE TWO...
Camped out for the new Star Wars film, I see...
You betcha!!
Let's just hope & pray that it's a better film this time, huh?
UP YOURS, BRO!!
Wha..?
I'M SO SICK & TIRED OF ALL YOU PEOPLE CRITICIZING EPISODE ONE!! YOU PEOPLE DON'T KNOW SQUAT!!
YOU AIN'T NOTHING BUT SHEEP, BRO!! YOU DON'T KNOW THE STORY!! YOU DON'T KNOW THE UNIVERSE!! IF YOU DON'T HAVE ANY-THING GOOD TO SAY.. MOVE ALONG!
Do you see this tattoo?
Whoa. It's Darth Vader's light saber.
Damn right... And it gets bigger when you turn it on.
HOW DARE YOU. Lapdogs like you are ruining the Star Wars universe.
Lucas could ~~film~~ digital video-tape himself takin' a poop & you'd just eat it up screaming "THANK YOU, SIR, MAY I HAVE ANOTHER!!!"
I am sorry, but I cannot live that way... if it sucks, I will say it!!
One of the reasons why this new film is going to be better is that people voiced their displeasure with the last one,.. & the one in charge took it to heart..
IT IS OUR RIGHT--NAY, OUR DUTY--TO QUESTION & HOLD TO TASK THE POWERS THAT BE!!
Dude.. We're talkin' Star Wars here.. Not the freakin' U.S. government!!
Can you pull your pants down again?
STOP
SEE YOU IN LINE!!

The middle panel is the whole strip. Everything else is filler. |

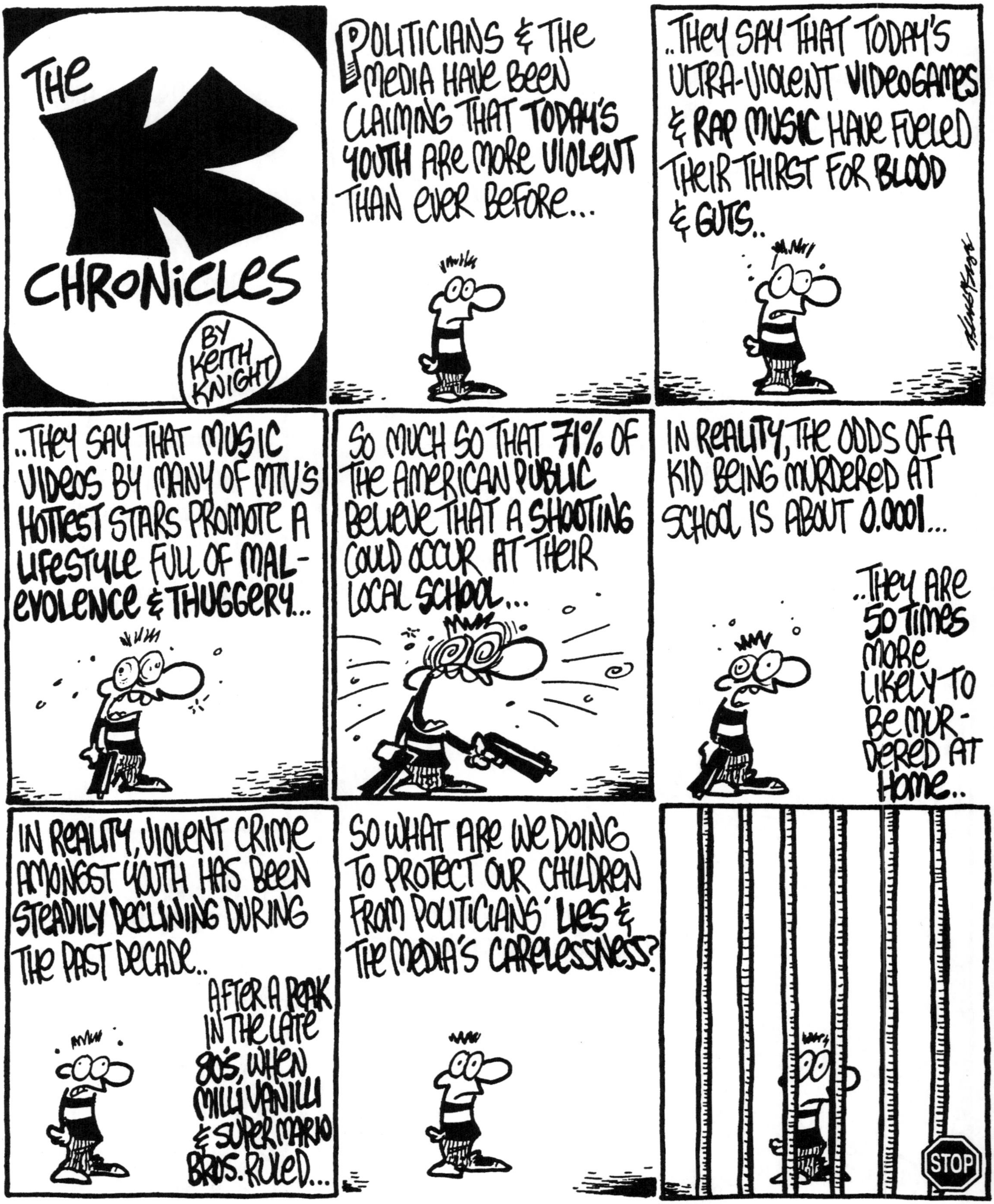
THE K CHRONICLES
BY KEITH KNIGHT
POLITICIANS & THE MEDIA HAVE BEEN CLAIMING THAT TODAY'S YOUTH ARE MORE VIOLENT THAN EVER BEFORE...
..THEY SAY THAT TODAY'S ULTRA-VIOLENT VIDEOGAMES & RAP MUSIC HAVE FUELED THEIR THIRST FOR BLOOD & GUTS..
..THEY SAY THAT MUSIC VIDEOS BY MANY OF MTV'S HOTTEST STARS PROMOTE A LIFESTYLE FULL OF MAL-EVOLENCE & THUGGERY...
SO MUCH SO THAT 71% OF THE AMERICAN PUBLIC BELIEVE THAT A SHOOTING COULD OCCUR AT THEIR LOCAL SCHOOL...
IN REALITY, THE ODDS OF A KID BEING MURDERED AT SCHOOL IS ABOUT 0.0001...
..THEY ARE 50 TIMES MORE LIKELY TO BE MUR-DERED AT HOME..
IN REALITY, VIOLENT CRIME AMONGST YOUTH HAS BEEN STEADILY DECLINING DURING THE PAST DECADE..
AFTER A PEAK IN THE LATE 80'S, WHEN MILLI VANILLI & SUPER MARIO BROS. RULED...
SO WHAT ARE WE DOING TO PROTECT OUR CHILDREN FROM POLITICIANS' LIES & THE MEDIA'S CARELESSNESS?
STOP

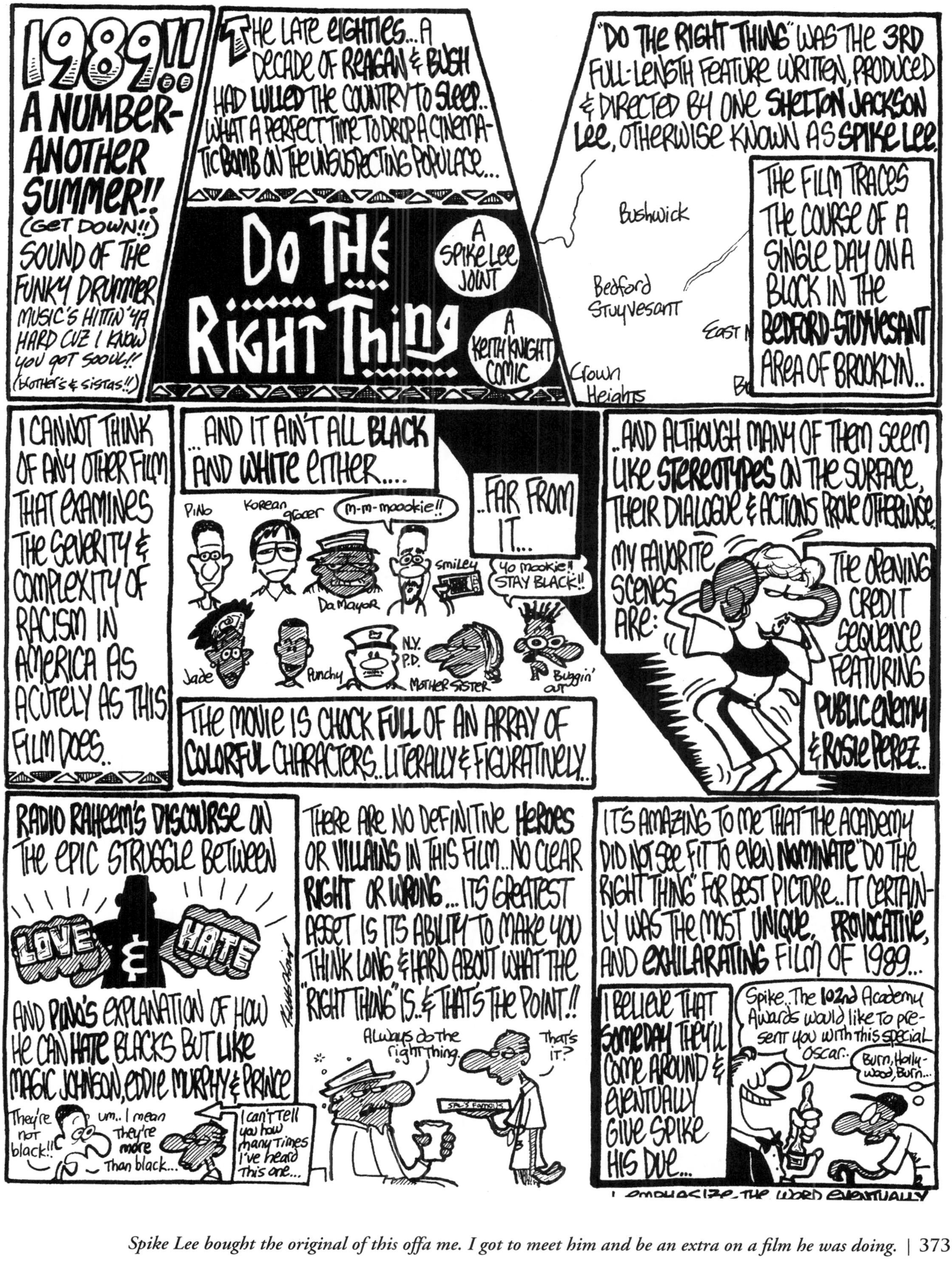

1989!!
A NUMBER-ANOTHER SUMMER!!
(GET DOWN!!)
SOUND OF THE FUNKY DRUMMER
MUSIC'S HITTIN' YA HARD CUZ I KNOW YOU GOT SOOUL!!
(brother's & sistas!!)
The late eighties...a decade of Reagan & Bush had lulled the country to sleep.. what a perfect time to drop a cinematic bomb on the unsuspecting populace...
DO THE RIGHT THING
A SPIKE LEE JOINT
A KEITH KNIGHT COMIC
"Do the Right Thing" was the 3rd full-length feature written, produced & directed by one Shelton Jackson Lee, otherwise known as Spike Lee.
Bushwick
Bedford Stuyvesant
East N
Crown Heights
The film traces the course of a single day on a block in the Bedford-Stuyvesant area of Brooklyn..
I cannot think of any other film that examines the severity & complexity of racism in America as acutely as this film does..
...and it ain't all black and white either....
..far from it...
Pino
Korean grocer
m-m-moookie!!
Smiley
Yo Mookie!! Stay black!!
Da Mayor
Jade
Punchy
N.Y. P.D.
Mother Sister
Buggin' out
The movie is chock full of an array of colorful characters.. literally & figuratively..
..and although many of them seem like stereotypes on the surface, their dialogue & actions prove otherwise.
My favorite scenes are:
The opening credit sequence featuring Public Enemy & Rosie Perez..
Radio Raheem's discourse on the epic struggle between
LOVE & HATE
and Pino's explanation of how he can hate blacks but like Magic Johnson, Eddie Murphy & Prince
They're not black!!
um.. I mean they're more than black...
I can't tell you how many times I've heard this one...
There are no definitive heroes or villains in this film.. no clear right or wrong... its greatest asset is its ability to make you think long & hard about what the "right thing" is.. & that's the point!!
Always do the right thing.
That's it?
Sal's Famous
It's amazing to me that the Academy did not see fit to even nominate "Do the Right Thing" for best picture.. it certainly was the most unique, provocative, and exhilarating film of 1989...
I believe that someday they'll come around & eventually give Spike his due...
Spike.. The 102nd Academy Awards would like to present you with this special oscar..
Burn, Hollywood, Burn...
I EMPHASIZE THE WORD EVENTUALLY

Spike Lee bought the original of this offa me. I got to meet him and be an extra on a film he was doing. |

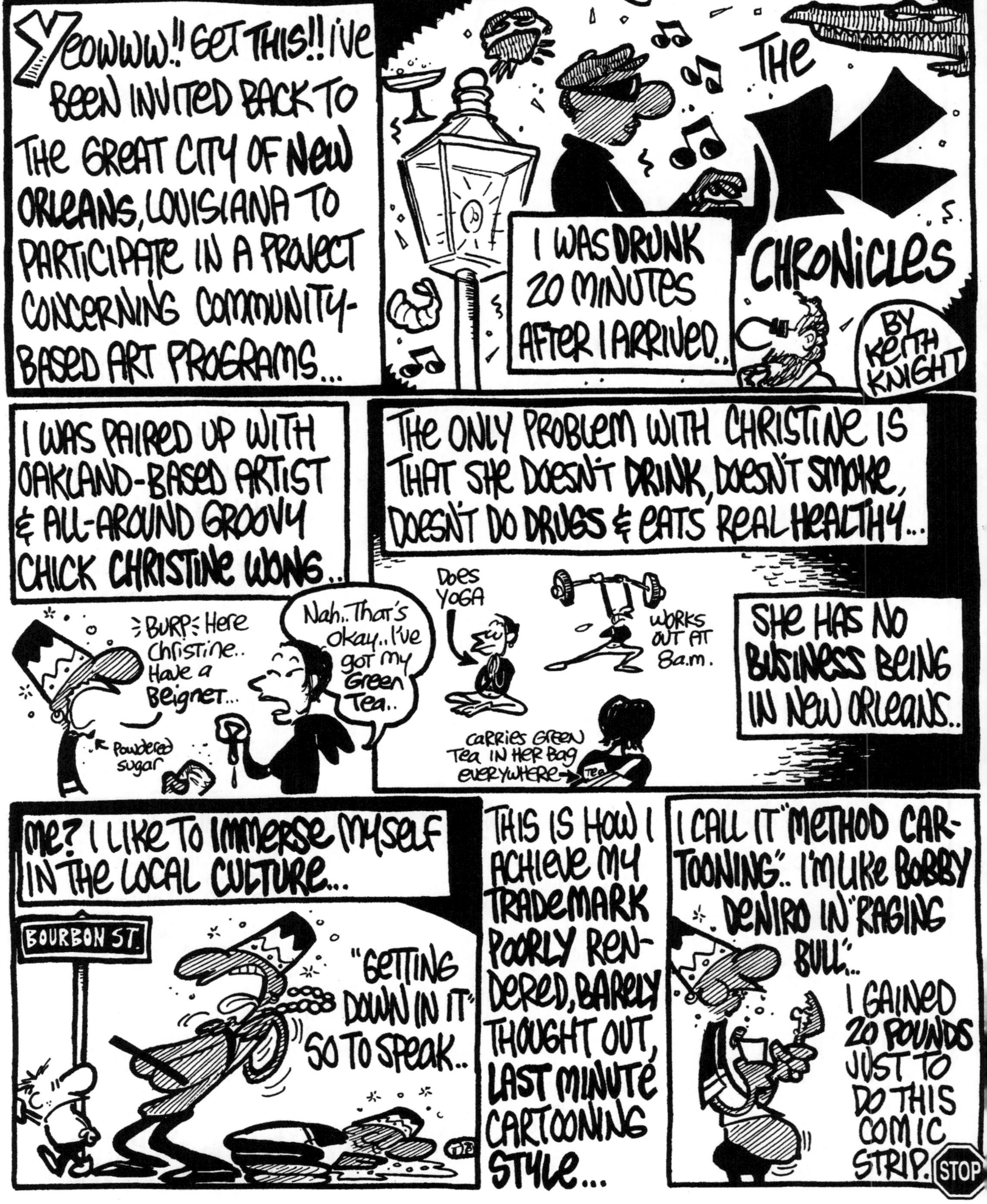

YEOWWW!! GET THIS!! I'VE BEEN INVITED BACK TO THE GREAT CITY OF NEW ORLEANS, LOUISIANA TO PARTICIPATE IN A PROJECT CONCERNING COMMUNITY-BASED ART PROGRAMS...
THE K CHRONICLES
BY KEITH KNIGHT
I WAS DRUNK 20 MINUTES AFTER I ARRIVED..
I WAS PAIRED UP WITH OAKLAND-BASED ARTIST & ALL-AROUND GROOVY CHICK CHRISTINE WONG..
BURP Here Christine.. Have a Beignet...
Powdered sugar
Nah.. That's okay.. I've got my Green Tea..
THE ONLY PROBLEM WITH CHRISTINE IS THAT SHE DOESN'T DRINK, DOESN'T SMOKE, DOESN'T DO DRUGS & EATS REAL HEALTHY...
Does YOGA
WORKS OUT AT 8a.m.
carries green tea in her bag everywhere
TEA
SHE HAS NO BUSINESS BEING IN NEW ORLEANS..
ME? I LIKE TO IMMERSE MYSELF IN THE LOCAL CULTURE...
BOURBON ST.
"GETTING DOWN IN IT" SO TO SPEAK..
THIS IS HOW I ACHIEVE MY TRADEMARK POORLY REN-DERED, BARELY THOUGHT OUT, LAST MINUTE CARTOONING STYLE...
I CALL IT "METHOD CAR-TOONING".. I'M LIKE BOBBY DENIRO IN "RAGING BULL"...
I GAINED 20 POUNDS JUST TO DO THIS COMIC STRIP.
STOP

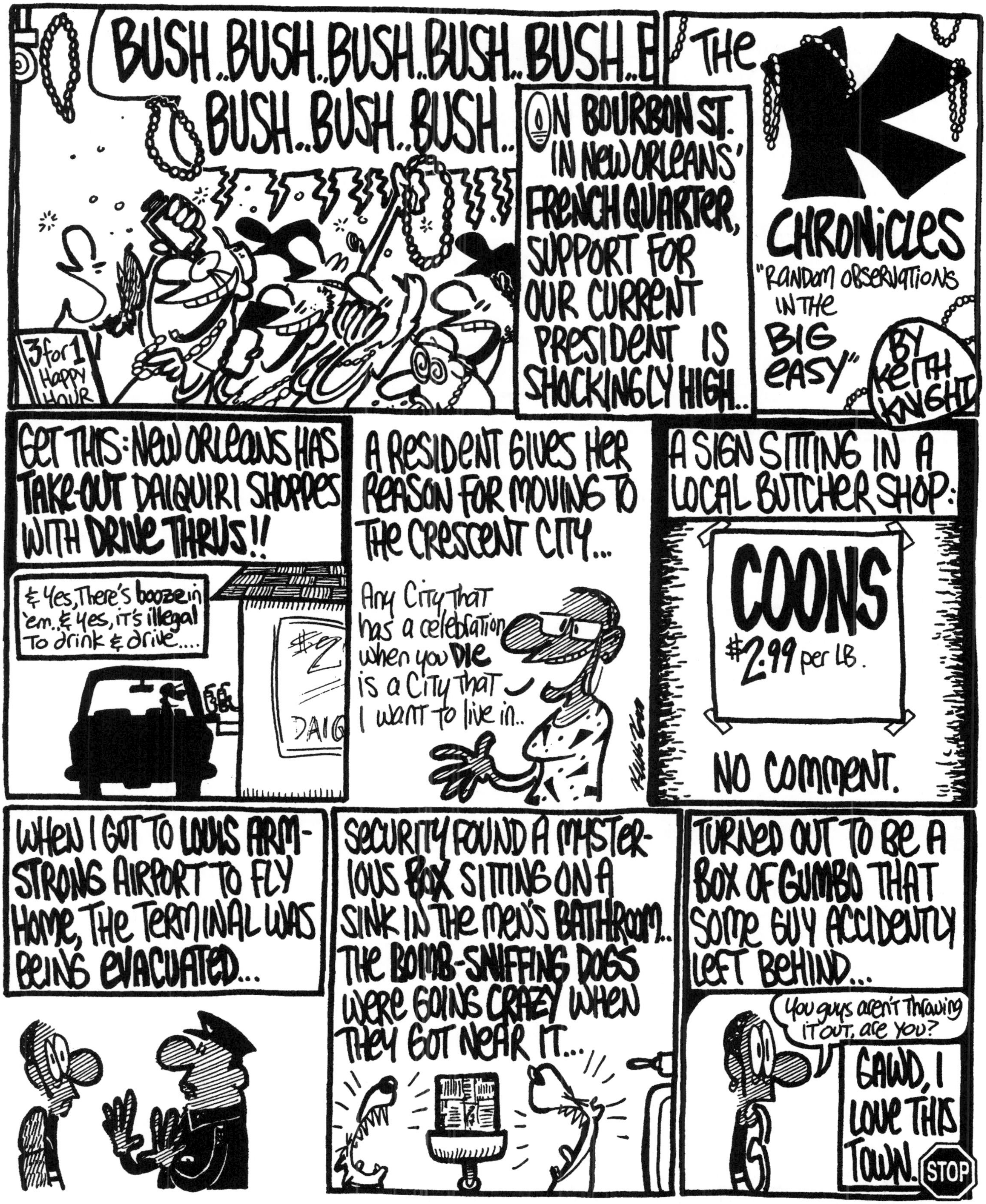
BUSH..BUSH..BUSH..BUSH..BUSH..B
BUSH..BUSH..BUSH..
3 for 1 Happy Hour
ON BOURBON ST. IN NEW ORLEANS' FRENCH QUARTER, SUPPORT FOR OUR CURRENT PRESIDENT IS SHOCKINGLY HIGH..
THE K CHRONICLES
"RANDOM OBSERVATIONS IN THE BIG EASY"
BY KEITH KNIGHT
GET THIS: NEW ORLEANS HAS TAKE-OUT DAIQUIRI SHOPPES WITH DRIVE THRUS!!
& YES, THERE'S BOOZE IN 'EM.. & YES, IT'S ILLEGAL TO DRINK & DRIVE....
DAIQ
A RESIDENT GIVES HER REASON FOR MOVING TO THE CRESCENT CITY...
ANY CITY THAT HAS A CELEBRATION WHEN YOU DIE IS A CITY THAT I WANT TO LIVE IN..
A SIGN SITTING IN A LOCAL BUTCHER SHOP:
COONS
$2.99 PER LB.
NO COMMENT.
WHEN I GOT TO LOUIS ARMSTRONG AIRPORT TO FLY HOME, THE TERMINAL WAS BEING EVACUATED...
SECURITY FOUND A MYSTERIOUS BOX SITTING ON A SINK IN THE MEN'S BATHROOM.. THE BOMB-SNIFFING DOGS WERE GOING CRAZY WHEN THEY GOT NEAR IT...
TURNED OUT TO BE A BOX OF GUMBO THAT SOME GUY ACCIDENTLY LEFT BEHIND...
YOU GUYS AREN'T THROWING IT OUT, ARE YOU?
GAWD, I LOVE THIS TOWN.
STOP

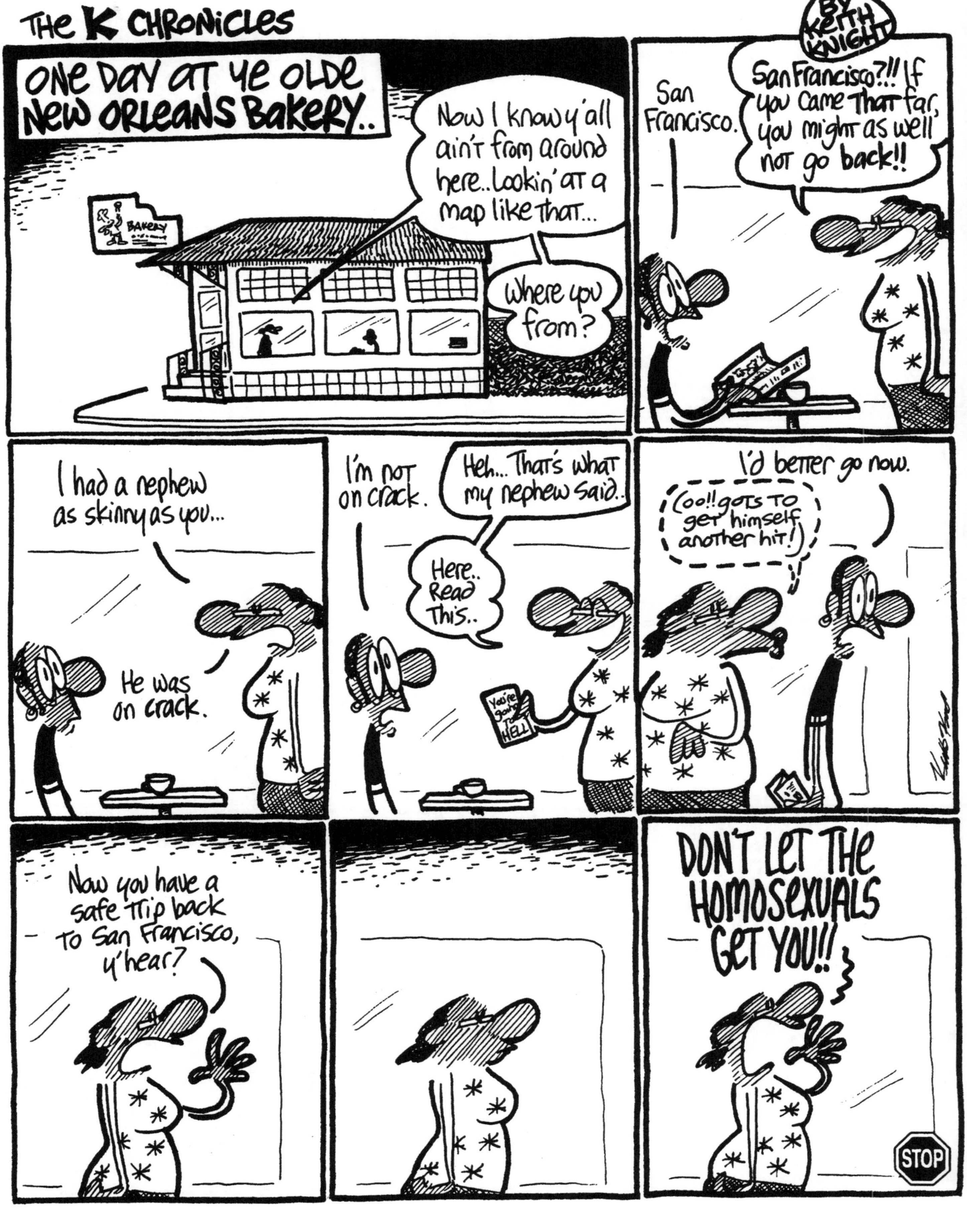
THE K CHRONICLES
BY KEITH KNIGHT
ONE DAY AT YE OLDE NEW ORLEANS BAKERY..
BAKERY
Now I know y'all ain't from around here.. Lookin' at a map like that...
Where you from?
San Francisco.
San Francisco?!! If you came that far, you might as well not go back!!
I had a nephew as skinny as you...
He was on crack.
I'm not on crack.
Heh... That's what my nephew said..
Here.. Read This..
You're going to HELL
I'd better go now.
(oo!! gots to get himself another hit!)
Now you have a safe trip back to San Francisco, y'hear?
DON'T LET THE HOMOSEXUALS GET YOU!!
STOP

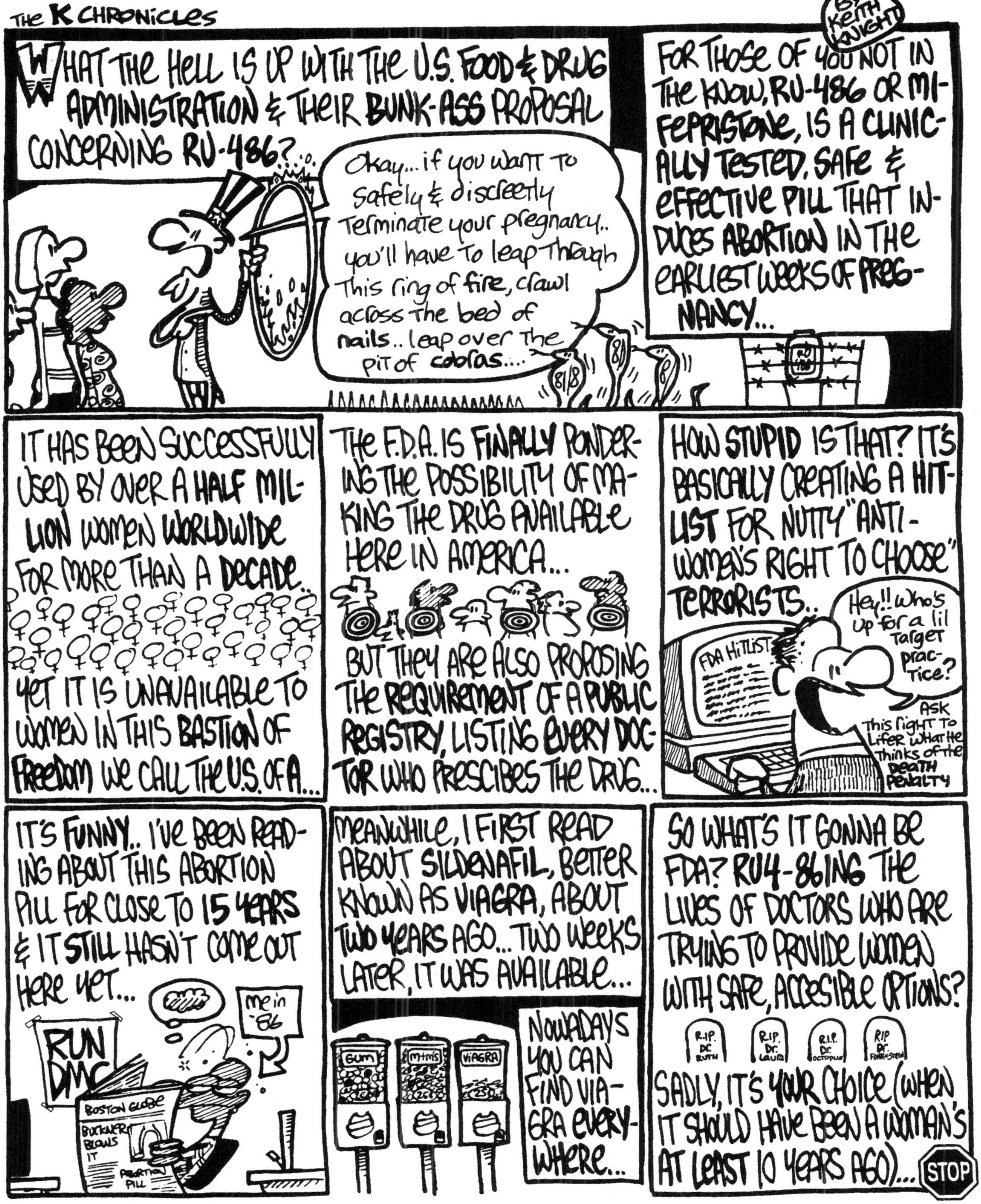
THE K CHRONICLES
BY KEITH KNIGHT
WHAT THE HELL IS UP WITH THE U.S. FOOD & DRUG ADMINISTRATION & THEIR BUNK-ASS PROPOSAL CONCERNING RU-486?
Okay... if you want to safely & discreetly terminate your pregnancy.. you'll have to leap through this ring of fire, crawl across the bed of nails.. leap over the pit of cobras....
FOR THOSE OF YOU NOT IN THE KNOW, RU-486 OR MIFEPRISTONE, IS A CLINICALLY TESTED, SAFE & EFFECTIVE PILL THAT INDUCES ABORTION IN THE EARLIEST WEEKS OF PREGNANCY...
IT HAS BEEN SUCCESSFULLY USED BY OVER A HALF MILLION WOMEN WORLDWIDE FOR MORE THAN A DECADE...
YET IT IS UNAVAILABLE TO WOMEN IN THIS BASTION OF FREEDOM WE CALL THE U.S. OF A...
THE F.D.A. IS FINALLY PONDERING THE POSSIBILITY OF MAKING THE DRUG AVAILABLE HERE IN AMERICA...
BUT THEY ARE ALSO PROPOSING THE REQUIREMENT OF A PUBLIC REGISTRY, LISTING EVERY DOCTOR WHO PRESCIBES THE DRUG...
HOW STUPID IS THAT? IT'S BASICALLY CREATING A HIT-LIST FOR NUTTY "ANTI-WOMEN'S RIGHT TO CHOOSE" TERRORISTS..
FDA HITLIST
Hey!! Who's up for a lil Target practice?
ASK this right to lifer what he thinks of the DEATH PENALTY
IT'S FUNNY.. I'VE BEEN READING ABOUT THIS ABORTION PILL FOR CLOSE TO 15 YEARS & IT STILL HASN'T COME OUT HERE YET...
RUN DMC
me in '86
BOSTON GLOBE
BUCKNER BLOWS IT
ABORTION PILL
MEANWHILE, I FIRST READ ABOUT SILDENAFIL, BETTER KNOWN AS VIAGRA, ABOUT TWO YEARS AGO... TWO WEEKS LATER, IT WAS AVAILABLE...
GUM
M+M'S
VIAGRA
25¢
25¢
NOWADAYS YOU CAN FIND VIAGRA EVERYWHERE...
SO WHAT'S IT GONNA BE FDA? RU4-86ING THE LIVES OF DOCTORS WHO ARE TRYING TO PROVIDE WOMEN WITH SAFE, ACCESIBLE OPTIONS?
R.I.P. DR. RUTH
R.I.P. DR. LAURA
R.I.P. DR. OCTOPUS
RIP DR. FRANKENSTEIN
SADLY, IT'S YOUR CHOICE (WHEN IT SHOULD HAVE BEEN A WOMAN'S AT LEAST 10 YEARS AGO)...
STOP

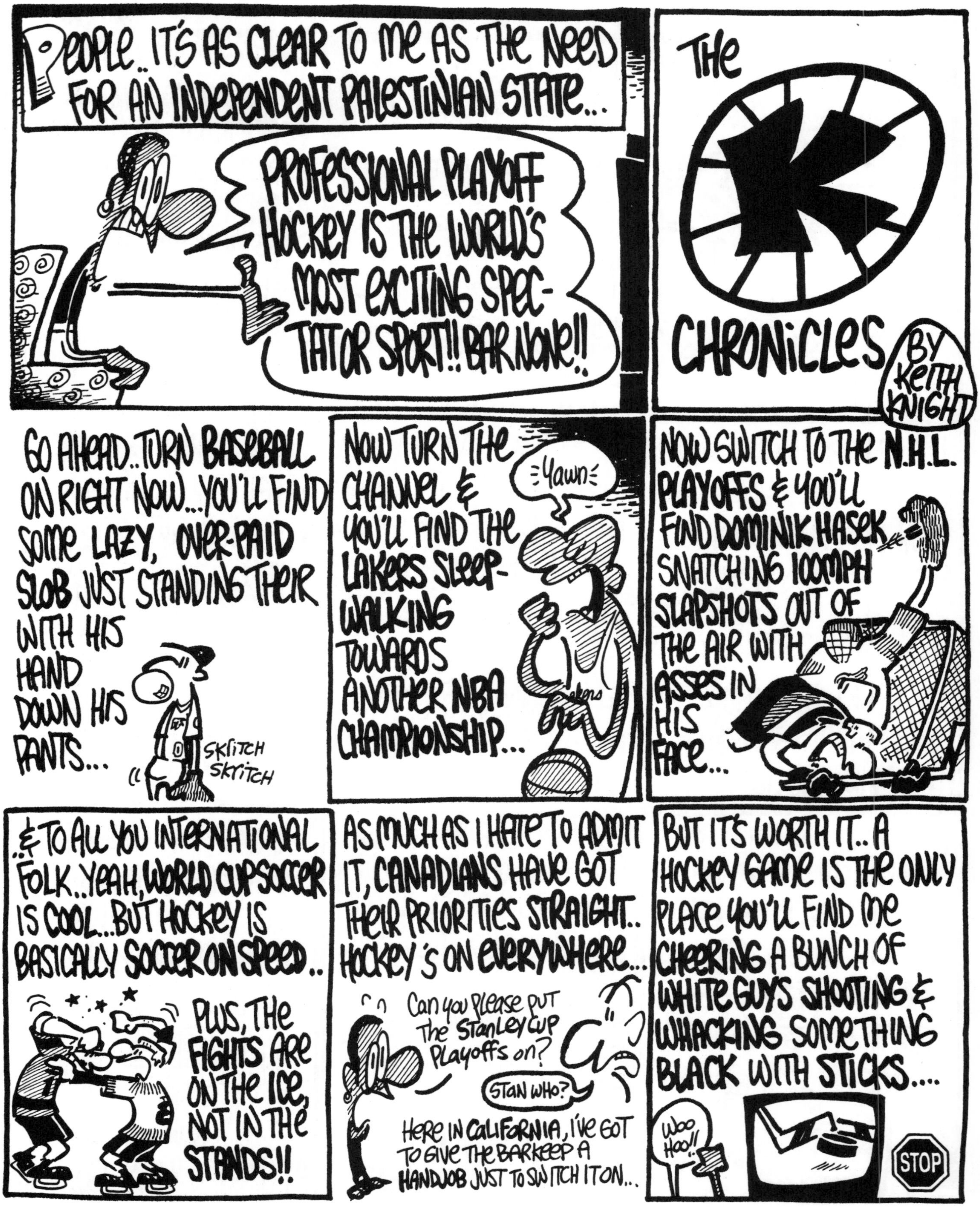
PEOPLE.. IT'S AS CLEAR TO ME AS THE NEED FOR AN INDEPENDENT PALESTINIAN STATE...
PROFESSIONAL PLAYOFF HOCKEY IS THE WORLD'S MOST EXCITING SPEC-TATOR SPORT!! BAR NONE!!
THE K CHRONICLES
BY KEITH KNIGHT
GO AHEAD.. TURN BASEBALL ON RIGHT NOW... YOU'LL FIND SOME LAZY, OVER-PAID SLOB JUST STANDING THEIR WITH HIS HAND DOWN HIS PANTS...
SKRITCH SKRITCH
NOW TURN THE CHANNEL & YOU'LL FIND THE LAKERS SLEEP-WALKING TOWARDS ANOTHER NBA CHAMPIONSHIP...
Yawn
NOW SWITCH TO THE N.H.L. PLAYOFFS & YOU'LL FIND DOMINIK HASEK SNATCHING 100MPH SLAPSHOTS OUT OF THE AIR WITH ASSES IN HIS FACE...
..& TO ALL YOU INTERNATIONAL FOLK.. YEAH, WORLD CUP SOCCER IS COOL... BUT HOCKEY IS BASICALLY SOCCER ON SPEED..
PLUS, THE FIGHTS ARE ON THE ICE, NOT IN THE STANDS!!
AS MUCH AS I HATE TO ADMIT IT, CANADIANS HAVE GOT THEIR PRIORITIES STRAIGHT.. HOCKEY'S ON EVERYWHERE...
Can you please put the Stanley Cup Playoffs on?
STAN WHO?
HERE IN CALIFORNIA, I'VE GOT TO GIVE THE BARKEEP A HANDJOB JUST TO SWITCH IT ON...
BUT IT'S WORTH IT.. A HOCKEY GAME IS THE ONLY PLACE YOU'LL FIND ME CHEERING A BUNCH OF WHITE GUYS SHOOTING & WHACKING SOMETHING BLACK WITH STICKS....
Woo Hoo!!
STOP

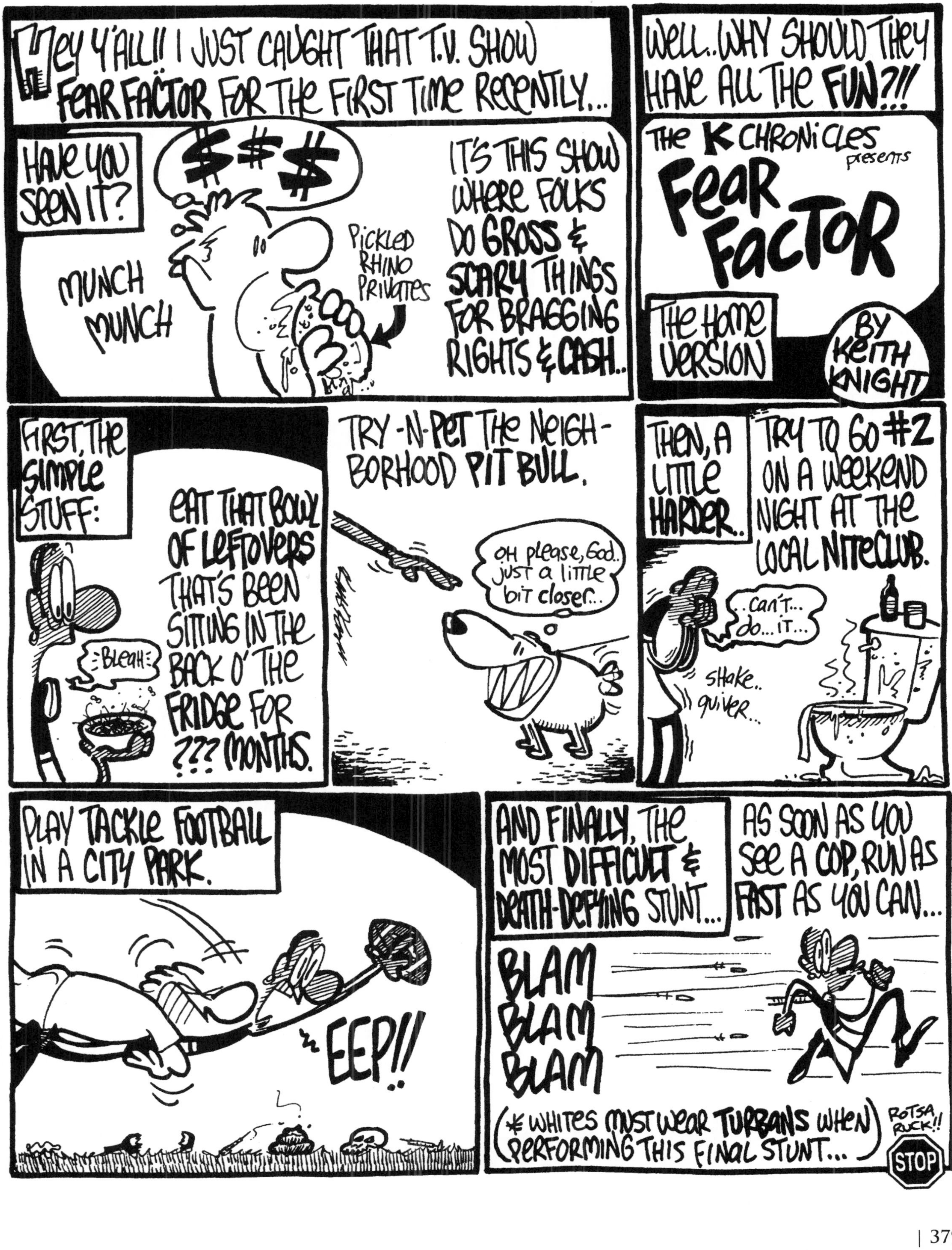
Hey y'all!! I just caught that T.V. show Fear Factor for the first time recently...
Well.. why should they have all the fun?!!
Have you seen it?
$$$
Munch munch
Pickled rhino privates
It's this show where folks do gross & scary things for bragging rights & cash..
The K Chronicles presents
Fear Factor
The home version
By Keith Knight
First, the simple stuff:
Eat that bowl of leftovers that's been sitting in the back o' the fridge for ??? months.
Bleah
Try-n-pet the neighborhood pit bull.
Oh please, God.. just a little bit closer...
Then, a little harder..
Try to go #2 on a weekend night at the local niteclub.
..can't... do... it...
shake.. quiver...
Play tackle football in a city park.
EEP!!
And finally, the most difficult & death-defying stunt...
As soon as you see a cop, run as fast as you can...
Blam
Blam
Blam
(* Whites must wear turbans when performing this final stunt...)
Rotsa ruck!!
STOP

THE K CHRONICLES

BY KEITH KNIGHT

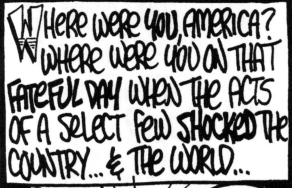

Where were you, America? Where were you on that fateful day when the acts of a select few SHOCKED THE COUNTRY... & THE WORLD...

OH MY GAWD!!

Where were you watching television when-- THE PATRIOTS WON SUPER BOWL XXXVI!!~

The New England Patriots, long the doormats of the AFC East in the National Football League, have beaten all the odds to win their very first Super Bowl ever!!

WITH A LAST SECOND FIELD GOAL AT THAT!!!

You don't understand!!... The Pats were 5-11 last year.. their quarterback coach croaked just before the season started.. they lost their starting QB to injury early in the season... & their best receiver hasn't even been playing!!

R.I.P.

GLENN 88

Enter Superbowl M.V.P. Tom Brady...

You know... I ain't gay or nothing, but...

I'd do him...

>sniff< of course!! Look what he's done for us!!

overheard in a BOSTON PUB

My only REGRET is that I couldn't be with my family & friends back home in Beantown on that fateful eve...

#1

Of course... after watching a few of the hometown fans interviewed on T.V. I remembered why I left town in the first place...

If the Rams had won, the TERRORISTS would have won!!

STOP

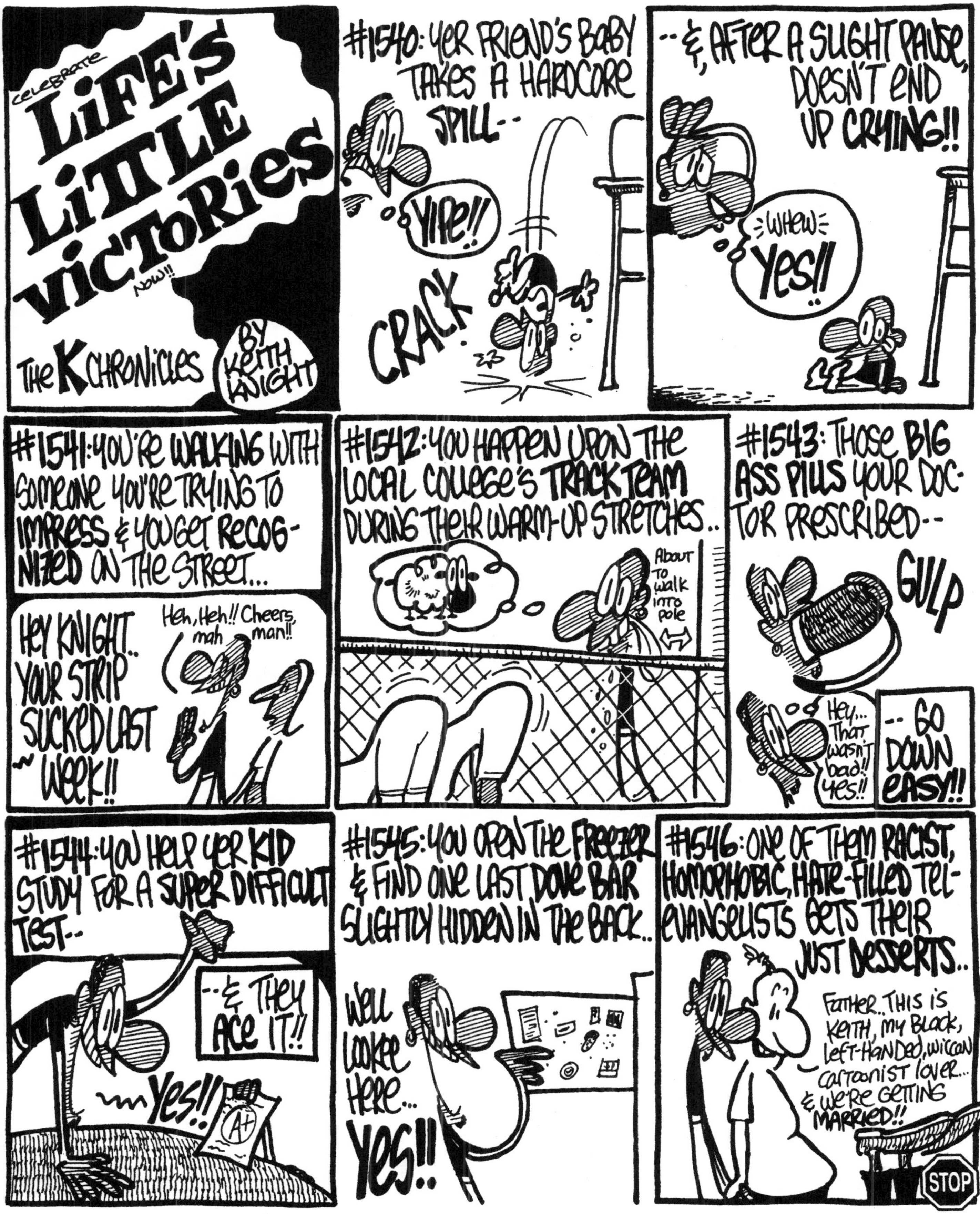

CELEBRATE
LIFE'S LITTLE VICTORIES
NOW!!
THE K CHRONICLES
BY KEITH KNIGHT
#1540: YER FRIEND'S BABY TAKES A HARDCORE SPILL--
YIPE!!
CRACK
--& AFTER A SLIGHT PAUSE, DOESN'T END UP CRYING!!
WHEW
YES!!
#1541: YOU'RE WALKING WITH SOMEONE YOU'RE TRYING TO IMPRESS & YOU GET RECOGNIZED ON THE STREET...
HEY KNIGHT.. YOUR STRIP SUCKED LAST WEEK!!
Heh, Heh!! Cheers, mah man!!
#1542: YOU HAPPEN UPON THE LOCAL COLLEGE'S TRACK TEAM DURING THEIR WARM-UP STRETCHES...
About to walk into pole
#1543: THOSE BIG ASS PILLS YOUR DOCTOR PRESCRIBED--
GULP
Hey... That wasn't bad!! Yes!!
-- GO DOWN EASY!!
#1544: YOU HELP YER KID STUDY FOR A SUPER DIFFICULT TEST--
--& THEY ACE IT!!
YES!!
A+
#1545: YOU OPEN THE FREEZER & FIND ONE LAST DOVE BAR SLIGHTLY HIDDEN IN THE BACK...
WELL LOOKEE HERE...
YES!!
#1546: ONE OF THEM RACIST, HOMOPHOBIC, HATE-FILLED TELEVANGELISTS GETS THEIR JUST DESSERTS..
FATHER.. THIS IS KEITH, MY BLACK, LEFT-HANDED, WICCAN CARTOONIST LOVER... & WE'RE GETTING MARRIED!!
STOP

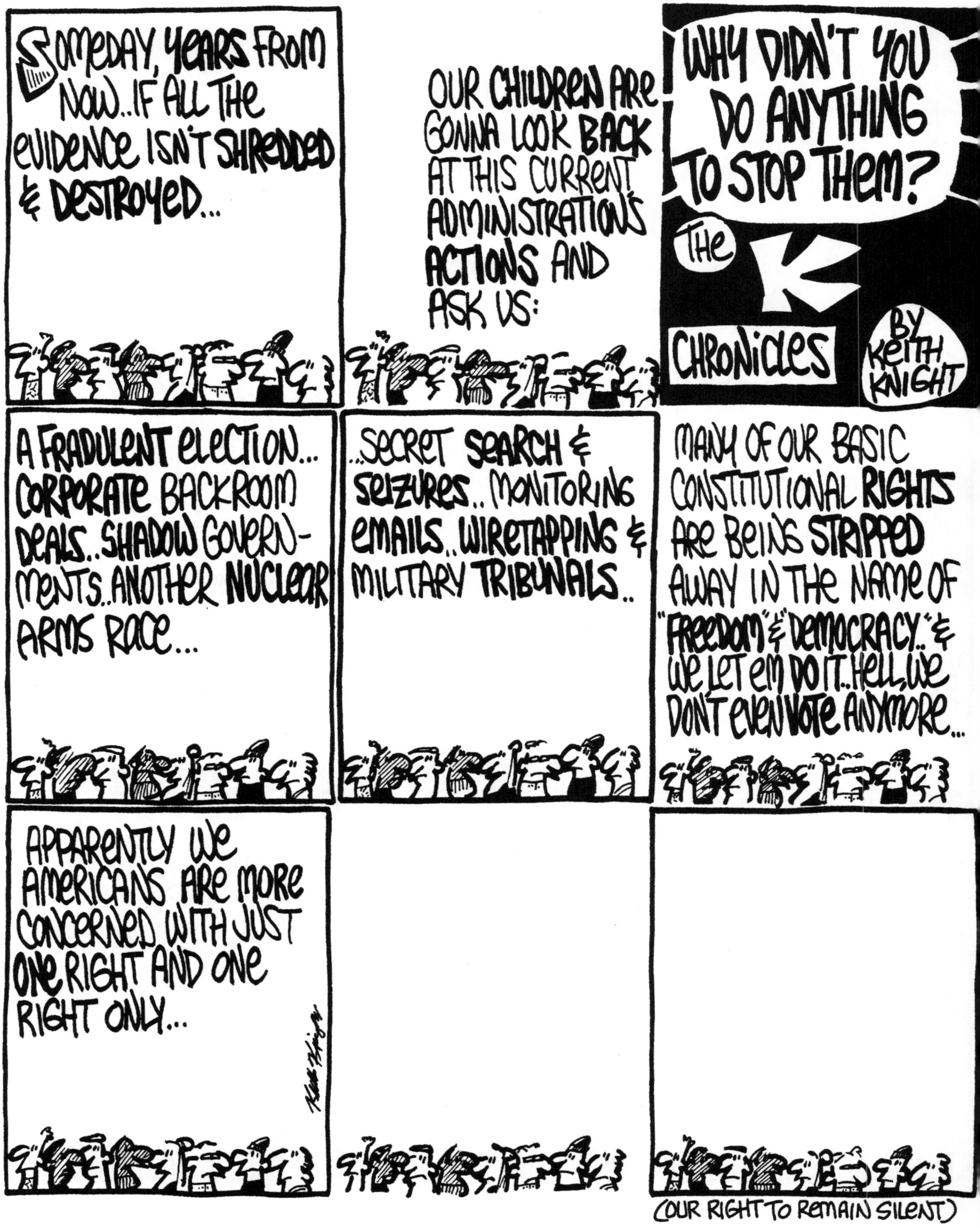
SOMEDAY, YEARS FROM NOW.. IF ALL THE EVIDENCE ISN'T SHREDDED & DESTROYED...
OUR CHILDREN ARE GONNA LOOK BACK AT THIS CURRENT ADMINISTRATION'S ACTIONS AND ASK US:
WHY DIDN'T YOU DO ANYTHING TO STOP THEM?
THE K CHRONICLES
BY KEITH KNIGHT
A FRADULENT ELECTION... CORPORATE BACKROOM DEALS.. SHADOW GOVERN-MENTS.. ANOTHER NUCLEAR ARMS RACE...
...SECRET SEARCH & SEIZURES.. MONITORING EMAILS.. WIRETAPPING & MILITARY TRIBUNALS..
MANY OF OUR BASIC CONSTITUTIONAL RIGHTS ARE BEING STRIPPED AWAY IN THE NAME OF "FREEDOM" & "DEMOCRACY".. & WE LET EM DO IT.. HELL, WE DON'T EVEN VOTE ANYMORE...
APPARENTLY WE AMERICANS ARE MORE CONCERNED WITH JUST ONE RIGHT AND ONE RIGHT ONLY...
(OUR RIGHT TO REMAIN SILENT)

CHAPTER FOUR

THE PASSION OF THE KEEF

Cartoons 2002-2004   San Francisco / New York / New Orleans / Paris

The In-Laws

War   Marriage   Death   Bu-sh--

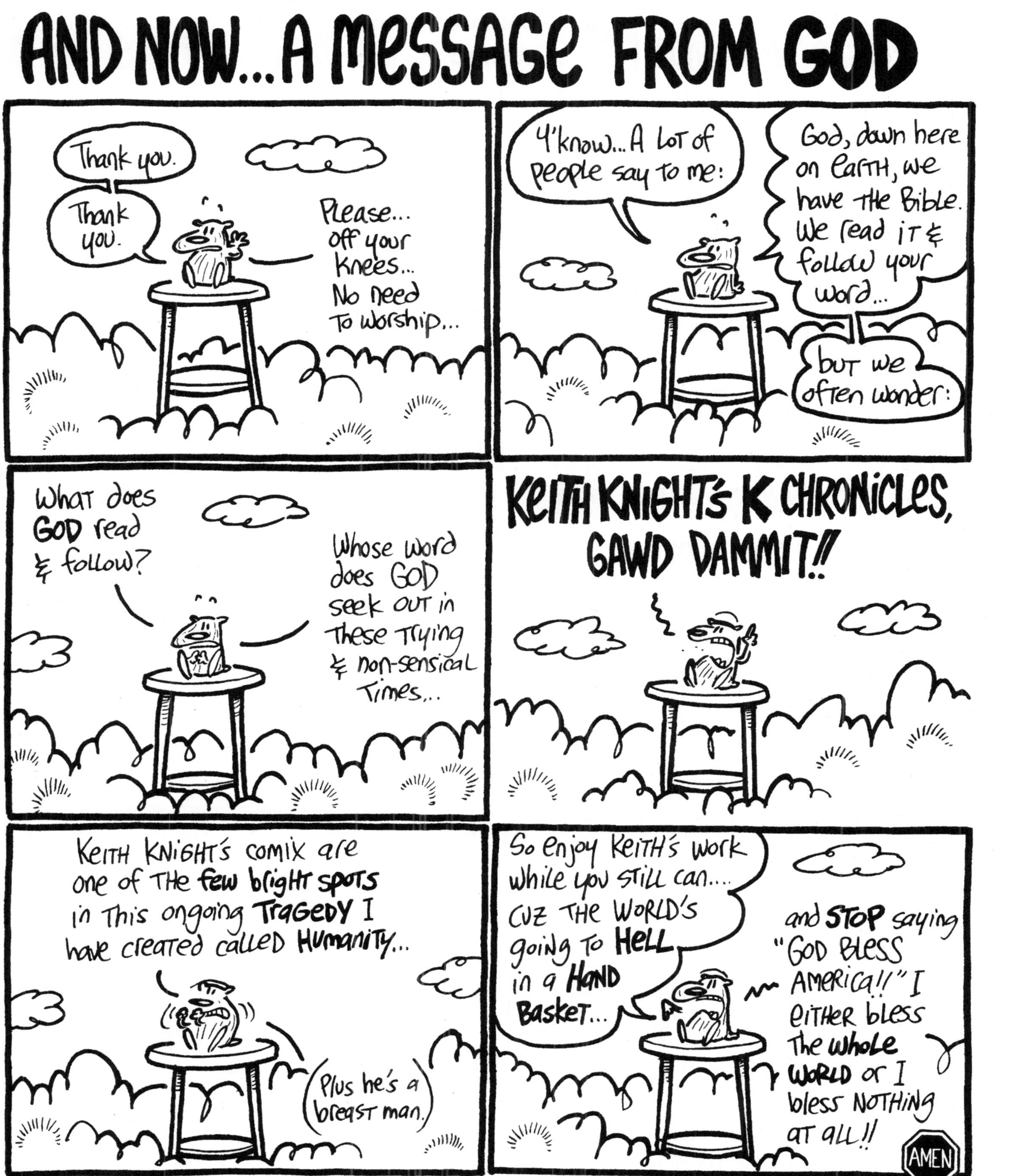
AND NOW... A MESSAGE FROM GOD
Thank you.
Thank you.
Please... off your knees... No need to worship...
Y'know... A lot of people say to me:
God, down here on Earth, we have the Bible. We read it & follow your word...
but we often wonder:
What does GOD read & follow?
Whose word does GOD seek out in these trying & non-sensical times...
KEITH KNIGHT'S K CHRONICLES, GAWD DAMMIT!!
Keith Knight's comix are one of the few bright spots in this ongoing tragedy I have created called Humanity...
(Plus he's a breast man.)
So enjoy Keith's work while you still can.... cuz the world's going to HELL in a HAND BASKET...
and STOP saying "GOD BLESS AMERICA!!" I either bless the WHOLE WORLD or I bless NOTHING at all!!
AMEN

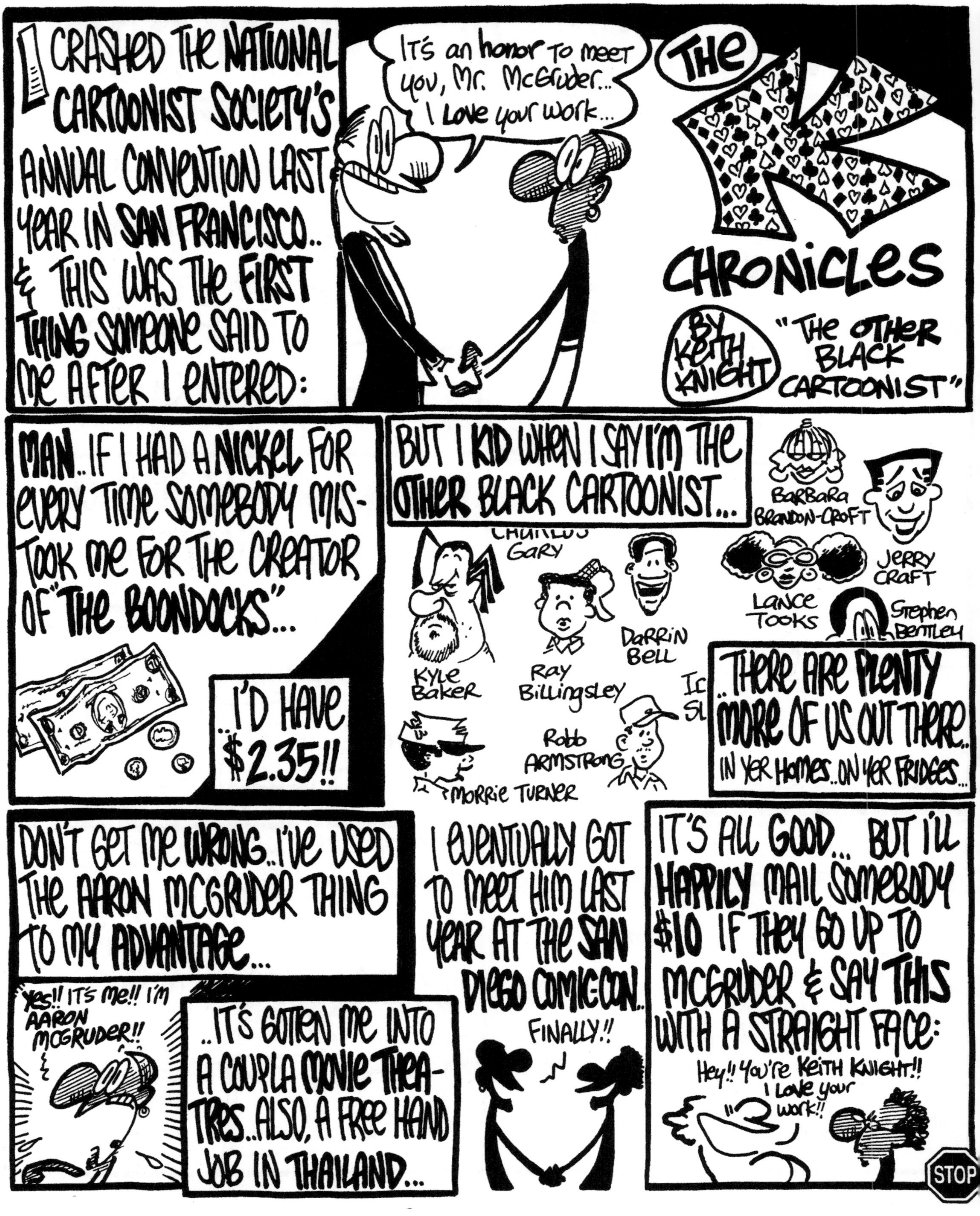
I CRASHED THE NATIONAL CARTOONIST SOCIETY'S ANNUAL CONVENTION LAST YEAR IN SAN FRANCISCO.. & THIS WAS THE FIRST THING SOMEONE SAID TO ME AFTER I ENTERED:
It's an honor to meet you, Mr. McGruder... I love your work...
THE K CHRONICLES
BY KEITH KNIGHT
"THE OTHER BLACK CARTOONIST"
MAN.. IF I HAD A NICKEL FOR EVERY TIME SOMEBODY MIS-TOOK ME FOR THE CREATOR OF "THE BOONDOCKS"...
..I'D HAVE $2.35!!
BUT I KID WHEN I SAY I'M THE OTHER BLACK CARTOONIST...
BARBARA BRANDON-CROFT
GARY
JERRY CRAFT
LANCE TOOKS
STEPHEN BENTLEY
DARRIN BELL
KYLE BAKER
RAY BILLINGSLEY
ROBB ARMSTRONG
MORRIE TURNER
..THERE ARE PLENTY MORE OF US OUT THERE... IN YER HOMES..ON YER FRIDGES...
DON'T GET ME WRONG..I'VE USED THE AARON MCGRUDER THING TO MY ADVANTAGE...
YES!! IT'S ME!! I'M AARON MCGRUDER!!
..IT'S GOTTEN ME INTO A COUPLA MOVIE THEA-TRES..ALSO, A FREE HAND JOB IN THAILAND...
I EVENTUALLY GOT TO MEET HIM LAST YEAR AT THE SAN DIEGO COMIC-CON..
FINALLY!!
IT'S ALL GOOD... BUT I'LL HAPPILY MAIL SOMEBODY $10 IF THEY GO UP TO MCGRUDER & SAY THIS WITH A STRAIGHT FACE:
Hey!! You're KEITH KNIGHT!! I love your work!!
STOP

 It's always fun to draw other cartoonist's characters. The hardest by far was Morrie Turner's Little Nipper.

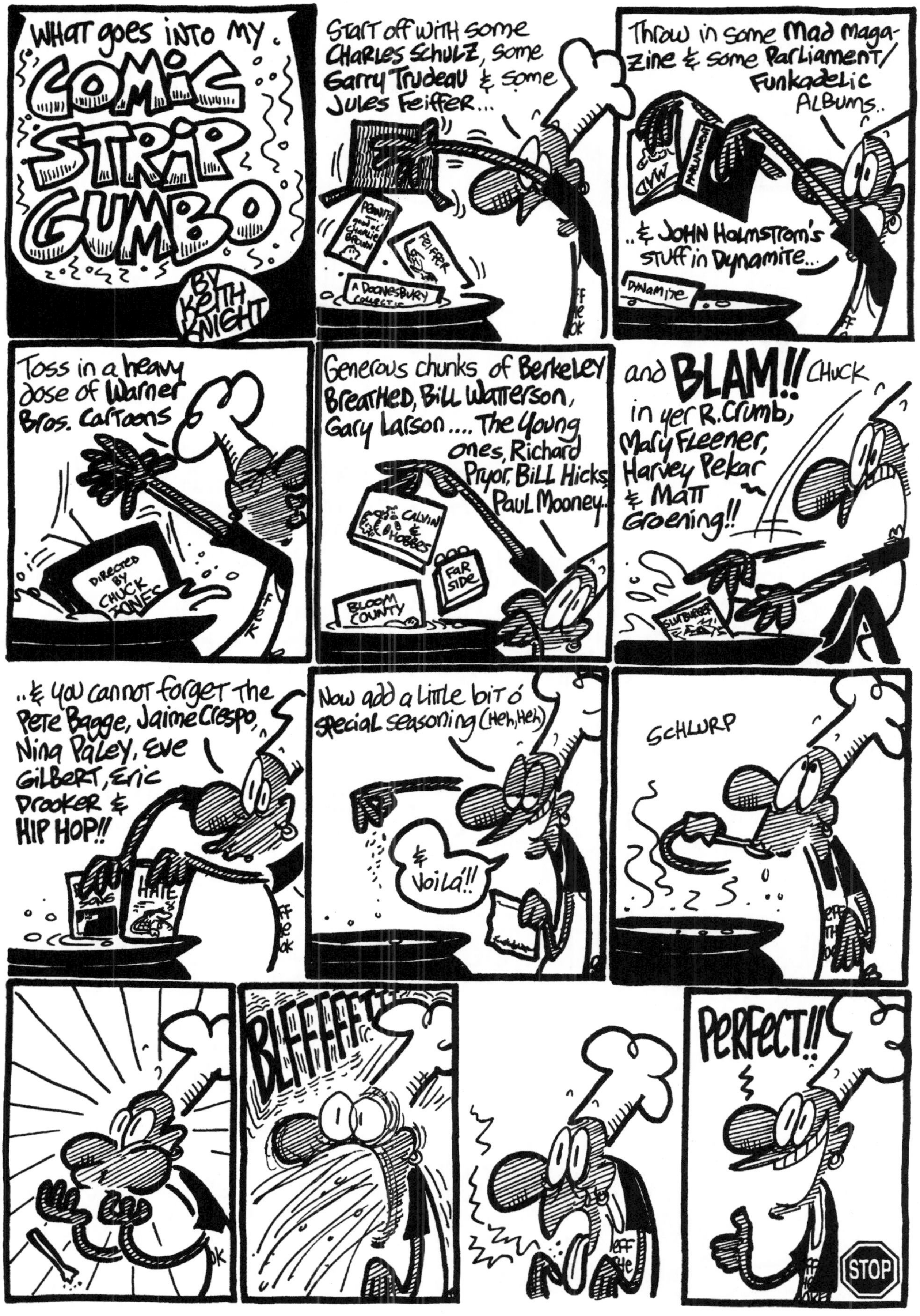

WHAT goes INTO MY COMIC STRIP GUMBO
BY KEITH KNIGHT
START off WITH some CHARLES SCHULZ, some Garry Trudeau & some Jules Feiffer...
PEANUTS
FEIFFER
A DOONESBURY COLLECTION
Throw in some Mad Magazine & some Parliament/Funkadelic ALBUMS..
..& JOHN Holmstrom's STUFF in Dynamite...
MAD
PARLIAMENT
DYNAMITE
Toss in a heavy dose of Warner Bros. Cartoons
DIRECTED BY CHUCK JONES
Generous chunks of Berkeley Breathed, Bill Watterson, Gary Larson.... The Young ones, Richard Pryor, Bill Hicks, Paul Mooney...
CALVIN & HOBBES
FAR SIDE
BLOOM COUNTY
and BLAM!! CHUCK in yer R. Crumb, Mary Fleener, Harvey Pekar & Matt Groening!!
..& you cannot forget the Pete Bagge, Jaime Crespo, Nina Paley, Eve Gilbert, Eric Drooker & HIP HOP!!
HATE
Now add a little bit o' special seasoning (Heh, Heh)
& Voilà!!
SCHLURP
BLFFFFFT!!
PERFECT!!
STOP

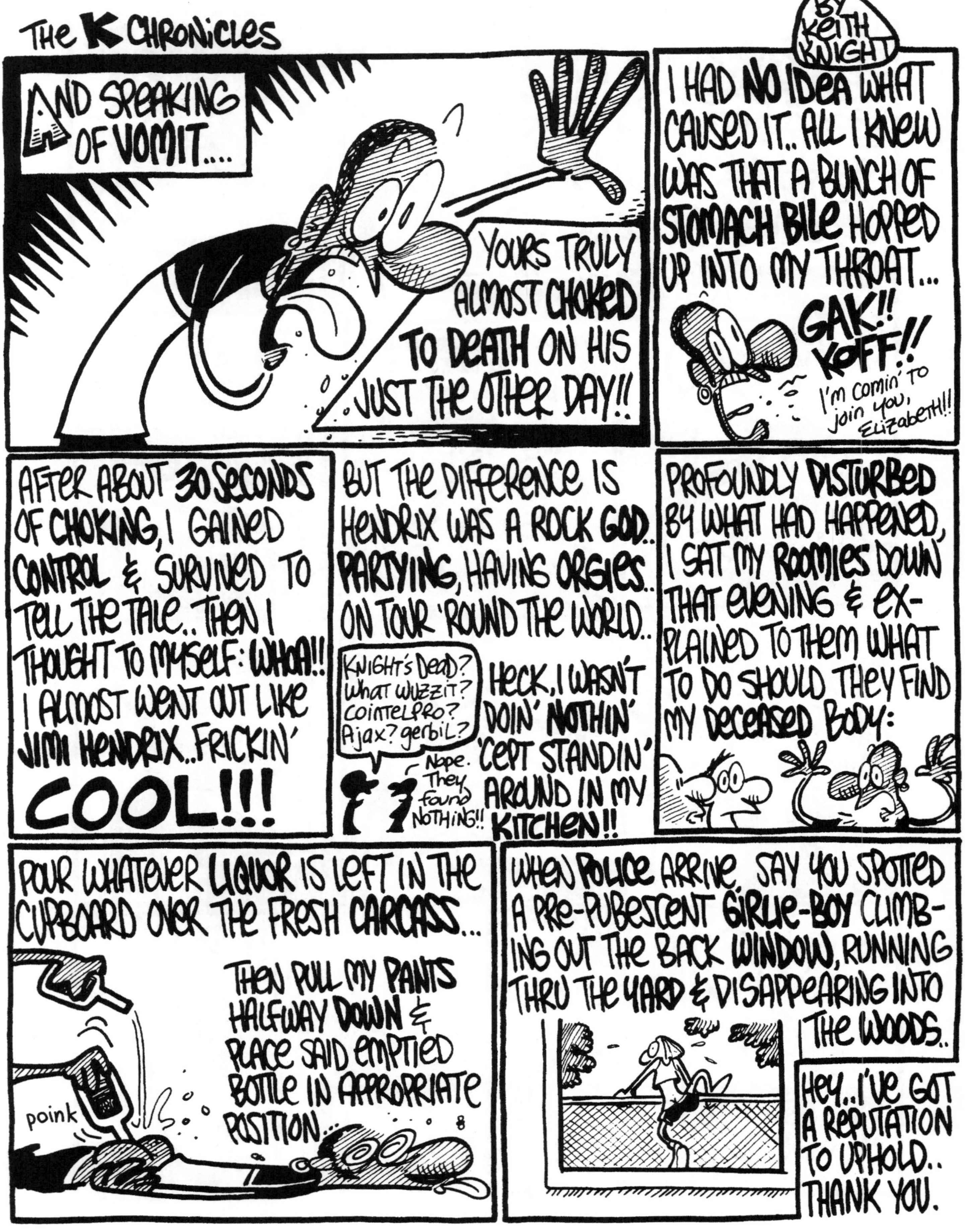

THE K CHRONICLES
BY KEITH KNIGHT
AND SPEAKING OF VOMIT....
YOURS TRULY ALMOST CHOKED TO DEATH ON HIS JUST THE OTHER DAY!!
I HAD NO IDEA WHAT CAUSED IT.. ALL I KNEW WAS THAT A BUNCH OF STOMACH BILE HOPPED UP INTO MY THROAT...
GAK!! KOFF!!
I'm comin' to join you, Elizabeth!!
AFTER ABOUT 30 SECONDS OF CHOKING, I GAINED CONTROL & SURVIVED TO TELL THE TALE.. THEN I THOUGHT TO MYSELF: WHOA!! I ALMOST WENT OUT LIKE JIMI HENDRIX.. FRICKIN' COOL!!!
BUT THE DIFFERENCE IS HENDRIX WAS A ROCK GOD.. PARTYING, HAVING ORGIES.. ON TOUR 'ROUND THE WORLD..
KNIGHT'S DEAD? WHAT WUZZIT? COINTELPRO? AJAX? GERBIL?
NOPE. THEY FOUND NOTHING!!
HECK, I WASN'T DOIN' NOTHIN' 'CEPT STANDIN' AROUND IN MY KITCHEN!!
PROFOUNDLY DISTURBED BY WHAT HAD HAPPENED, I SAT MY ROOMIES DOWN THAT EVENING & EXPLAINED TO THEM WHAT TO DO SHOULD THEY FIND MY DECEASED BODY:
POUR WHATEVER LIQUOR IS LEFT IN THE CUPBOARD OVER THE FRESH CARCASS...
THEN PULL MY PANTS HALFWAY DOWN & PLACE SAID EMPTIED BOTTLE IN APPROPRIATE POSITION...
poink
WHEN POLICE ARRIVE, SAY YOU SPOTTED A PRE-PUBESCENT GIRLIE-BOY CLIMBING OUT THE BACK WINDOW, RUNNING THRU THE YARD & DISAPPEARING INTO THE WOODS..
HEY.. I'VE GOT A REPUTATION TO UPHOLD.. THANK YOU.

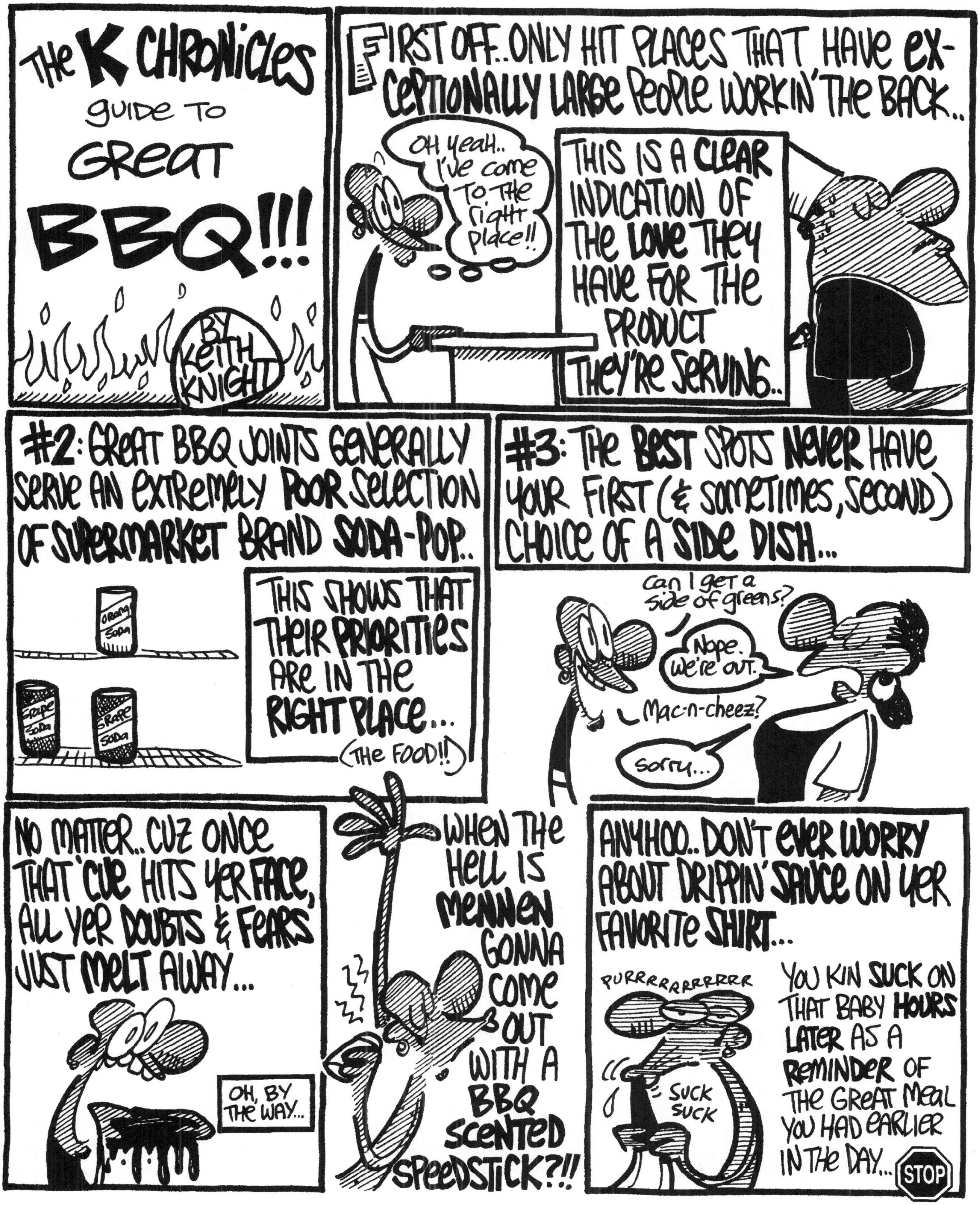
The K Chronicles guide to Great BBQ!!!
By Keith Knight
First off.. only hit places that have exceptionally large people workin' the back..
Oh yeah.. I've come to the right place!!
This is a clear indication of the love they have for the product they're serving..
#2: Great BBQ joints generally serve an extremely poor selection of supermarket brand soda-pop..
Orange Soda
Grape Soda
Grape Soda
This shows that their priorities are in the right place...
(the food!!)
#3: The best spots never have your first (& sometimes, second) choice of a side dish...
Can I get a side of greens?
Nope. We're out.
Mac-n-cheez?
Sorry...
No matter.. cuz once that 'cue hits yer face, all yer doubts & fears just melt away...
Oh, by the way...
When the hell is Mennen gonna come out with a BBQ scented Speedstick?!!
Anyhoo.. don't ever worry about drippin' sauce on yer favorite shirt...
Purrrrrrrrrrr
Suck suck
You kin suck on that baby hours later as a reminder of the great meal you had earlier in the day...
STOP

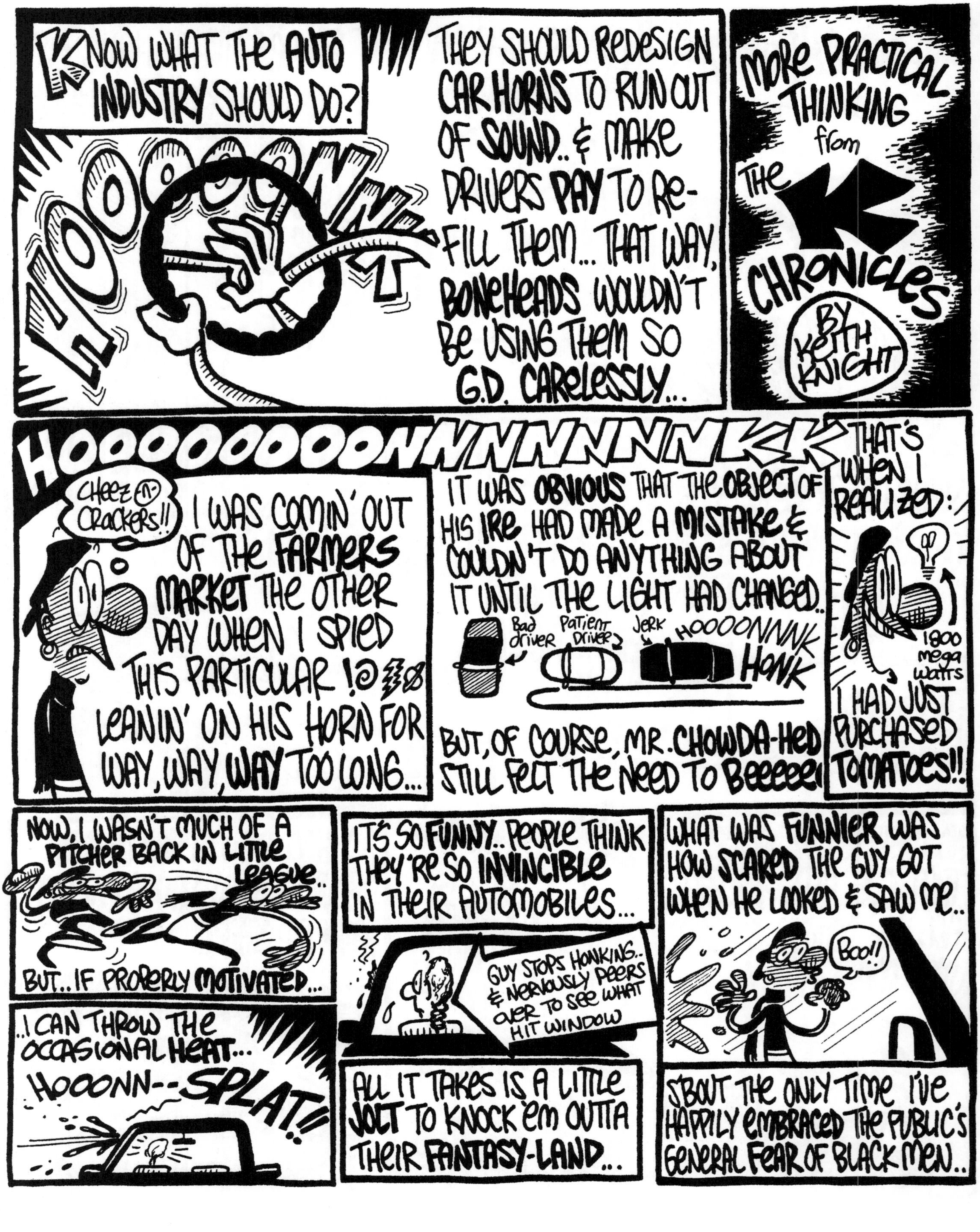
KNOW WHAT THE AUTO INDUSTRY SHOULD DO?
HOOOOOONNK
THEY SHOULD REDESIGN CAR HORNS TO RUN OUT OF SOUND.. & MAKE DRIVERS PAY TO RE-FILL THEM... THAT WAY, BONEHEADS WOULDN'T BE USING THEM SO G.D. CARELESSLY...
MORE PRACTICAL THINKING from THE K CHRONICLES
BY KEITH KNIGHT
HOOOOOOOONNNNNNKK
CHEEZ-N-CRACKERS!!
I WAS COMIN' OUT OF THE FARMERS MARKET THE OTHER DAY WHEN I SPIED THIS PARTICULAR !@⚡Ø LEANIN' ON HIS HORN FOR WAY, WAY, WAY TOO LONG...
IT WAS OBVIOUS THAT THE OBJECT OF HIS IRE HAD MADE A MISTAKE & COULDN'T DO ANYTHING ABOUT IT UNTIL THE LIGHT HAD CHANGED..
Bad driver
Patient Driver
Jerk
HOOOONNNK
HONK
BUT, OF COURSE, MR. CHOWDA-HED STILL FELT THE NEED TO BEEEEE!
THAT'S WHEN I REALIZED:
1800 mega watts
I HAD JUST PURCHASED TOMATOES!!
NOW, I WASN'T MUCH OF A PITCHER BACK IN LITTLE LEAGUE..
BUT.. IF PROPERLY MOTIVATED...
..I CAN THROW THE OCCASIONAL HEAT...
HOOOONN--SPLAT!!
IT'S SO FUNNY.. PEOPLE THINK THEY'RE SO INVINCIBLE IN THEIR AUTOMOBILES...
GUY STOPS HONKING.. & NERVOUSLY PEERS OVER TO SEE WHAT HIT WINDOW
ALL IT TAKES IS A LITTLE JOLT TO KNOCK 'EM OUTTA THEIR FANTASY-LAND...
WHAT WAS FUNNIER WAS HOW SCARED THE GUY GOT WHEN HE LOOKED & SAW ME..
BOO!!
'BOUT THE ONLY TIME I'VE HAPPILY EMBRACED THE PUBLIC'S GENERAL FEAR OF BLACK MEN..

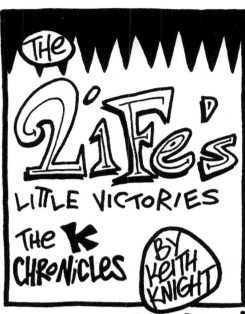

The **2'1FEs'd**
LITTLE VICTORIES
THE **K** CHRONICLES
BY KEITH KNIGHT

#4146: RELUCTANTLY GIVING UP THE WORLD'S GREATEST PARKING SPOT...

≥sniff≤ PARTING IS SUCH SWEET SORROW....

MY FRONT DOOR (54 bs away!)

...RETURNING SEVERAL HOURS LATER & IT'S STILL THERE!!

~YES!!

#4147: SOME SLOWPOKE CUTS IN FRONT OF YOU ON THE HIGHWAY...

CHEEZ-N-CRACKERS!!

..RIGHT BEFORE PASSING A COP WITH A RADAR GUN!!

YES!!

#4148: FORGETTING TO BRING LUNCH TO WORK & BEING BROKE..

WHA--?

POTLUCK TODAY RM.B

..& YER OFFICE IS HAVING A POTLUCK THAT DAY!!

YES!!

#4149: HAVING THE EXACT NUMBER OF HANGERS IN THE CLOSET TO HANG YER JUST CLEANED LAUNDRY...

YES!!

#4150: ORDERING SOME TAKE-OUT FROM YER FAVORITE RESTAURANT...

YES!!

..& THEY THROW IN A COUPLA EXTRA ITEMS FER NOTHIN!!

POWELLS

#4151: FINDING THAT HOT NEW BOOK YOU WANTED..ON THE STREET 4 SUPER CHEAP..

OH..THAT PIECE OF CRAP? 50¢

UM... YES?

RED WHITE BLACK & BLUE

MY NEW BOOK!!

STOP

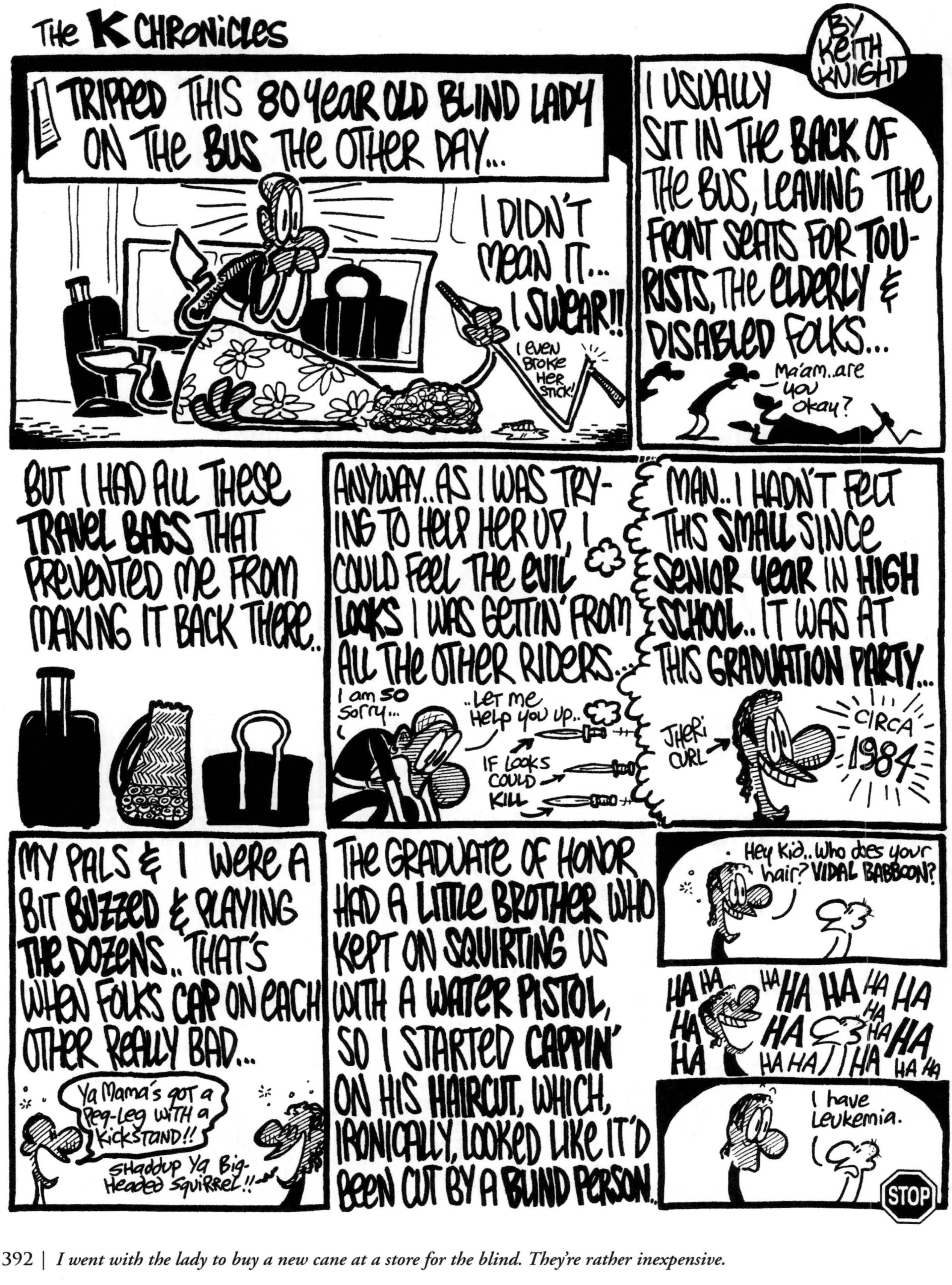

THE K CHRONICLES
BY KEITH KNIGHT
I TRIPPED THIS 80 YEAR OLD BLIND LADY ON THE BUS THE OTHER DAY...
I DIDN'T MEAN IT... I SWEAR!!
I EVEN BROKE HER STICK!
I USUALLY SIT IN THE BACK OF THE BUS, LEAVING THE FRONT SEATS FOR TOURISTS, THE ELDERLY & DISABLED FOLKS...
Ma'am..are you okay?
BUT I HAD ALL THESE TRAVEL BAGS THAT PREVENTED ME FROM MAKING IT BACK THERE..
ANYWAY..AS I WAS TRYING TO HELP HER UP, I COULD FEEL THE EVIL LOOKS I WAS GETTIN' FROM ALL THE OTHER RIDERS...
I am SO sorry...
..Let me Help you up..
IF LOOKS COULD KILL
MAN..I HADN'T FELT THIS SMALL SINCE SENIOR YEAR IN HIGH SCHOOL.. IT WAS AT THIS GRADUATION PARTY...
JHERI CURL
CIRCA 1984
MY PALS & I WERE A BIT BUZZED & PLAYING THE DOZENS.. THAT'S WHEN FOLKS CAP ON EACH OTHER REALLY BAD...
Ya Mama's got a Peg-Leg with a KickSTAND!!
SHADDUP Ya Big-Headed SquirreL!!
THE GRADUATE OF HONOR HAD A LITTLE BROTHER WHO KEPT ON SQUIRTING US WITH A WATER PISTOL, SO I STARTED CAPPIN' ON HIS HAIRCUT, WHICH, IRONICALLY, LOOKED LIKE IT'D BEEN CUT BY A BLIND PERSON..
Hey Kid..Who does your hair? VIDAL BABBOON?
HA HA HA HA HA HA HA HA HA HA HA HA HA HA HA HA HA HA HA
I have Leukemia.
STOP

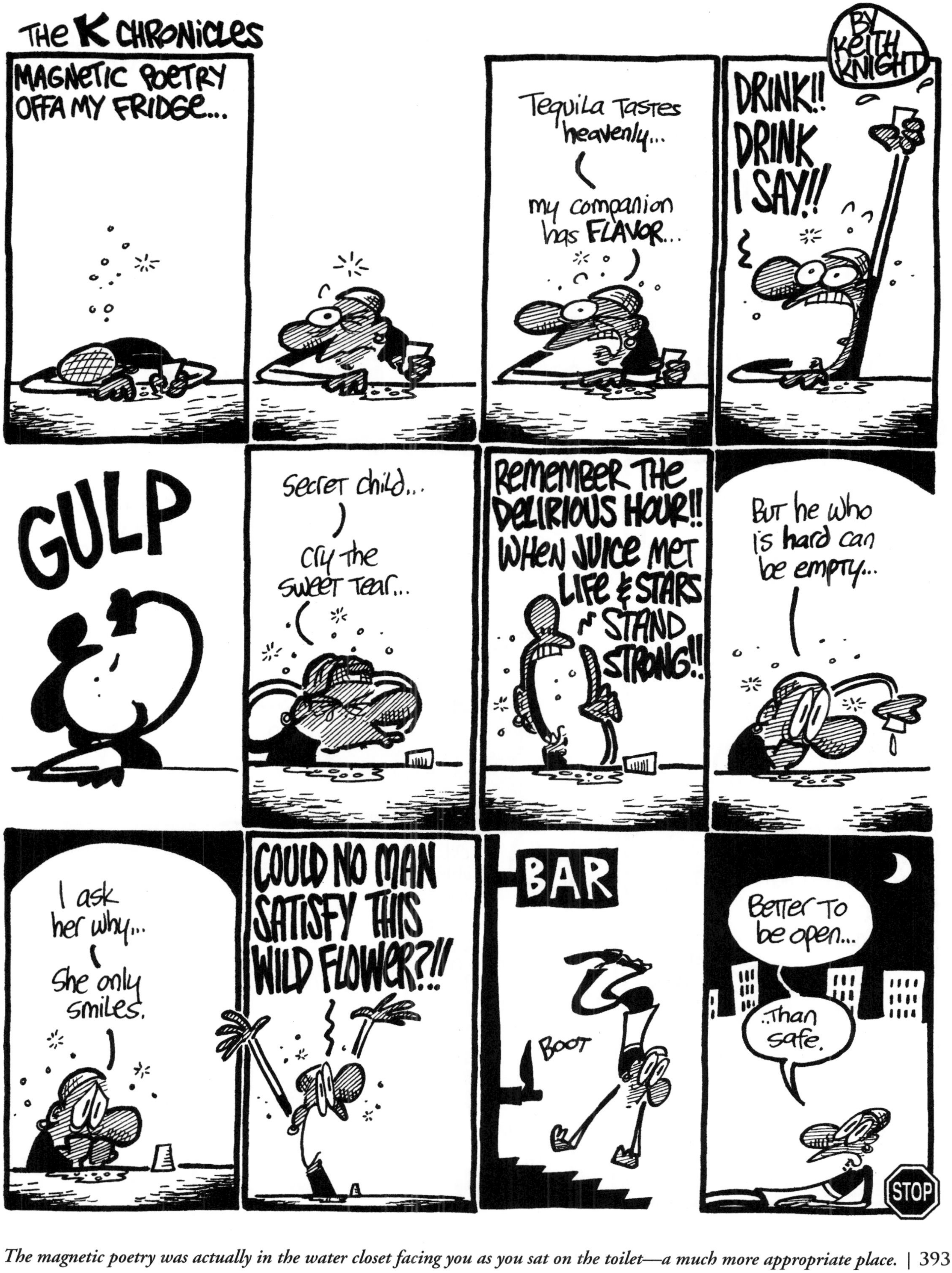
THE K CHRONICLES
BY KEITH KNIGHT
MAGNETIC POETRY OFFA MY FRIDGE...
Tequila Tastes heavenly...
my companion has FLAVOR...
DRINK!! DRINK I SAY!!
GULP
Secret child...
cry the sweet tear...
REMEMBER THE DELIRIOUS HOUR!! WHEN JUICE MET LIFE & STARS ~ STAND STRONG!!
But he who is hard can be empty...
I ask her why...
She only smiles.
COULD NO MAN SATISFY THIS WILD FLOWER?!!...
BAR
BOOT
Better to be open...
..Than safe.
STOP

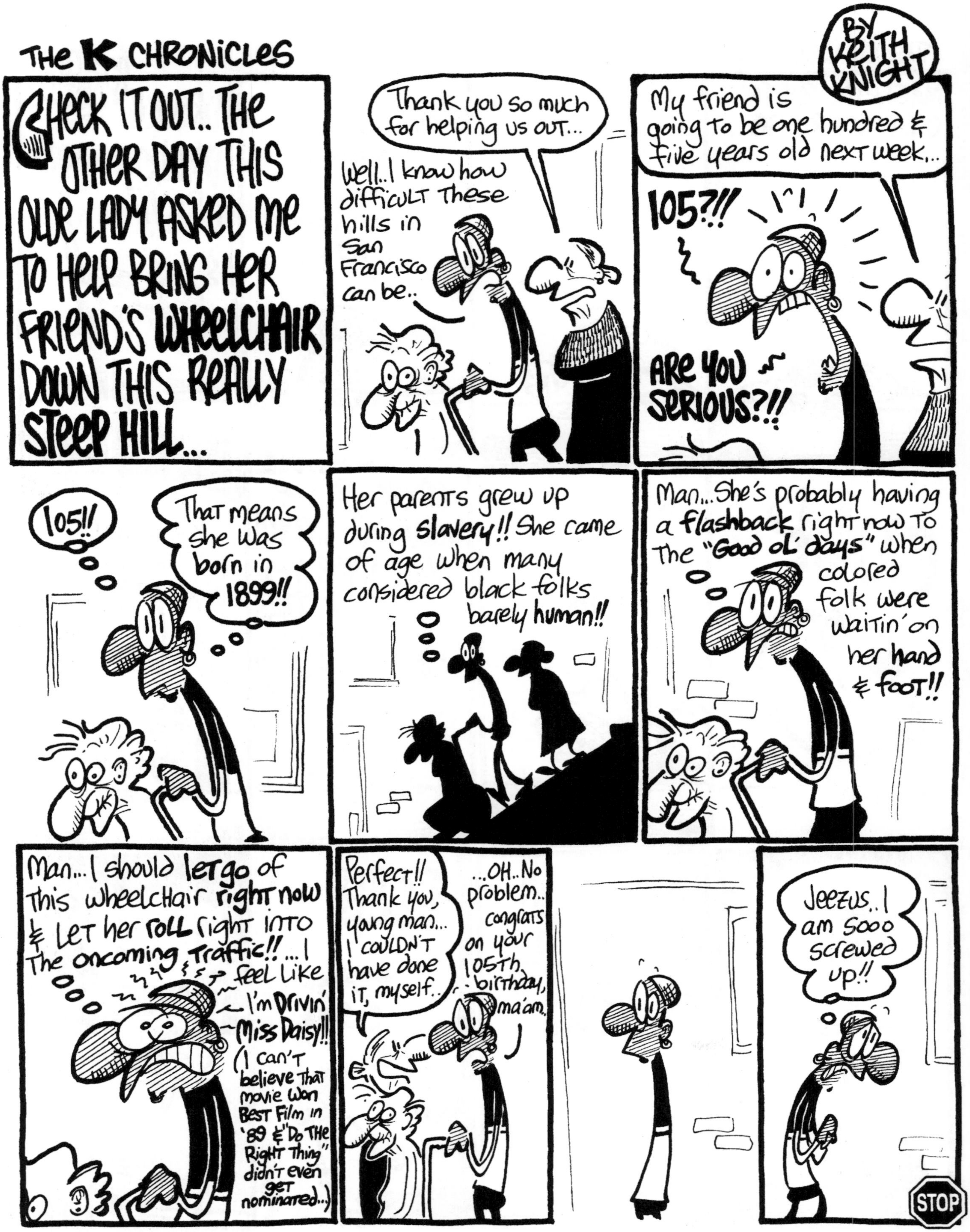
THE K CHRONICLES
BY KEITH KNIGHT
CHECK IT OUT.. THE OTHER DAY THIS OLDE LADY ASKED ME TO HELP BRING HER FRIEND'S WHEELCHAIR DOWN THIS REALLY STEEP HILL...
Thank you so much for helping us out...
Well..I know how difficult these hills in San Francisco can be..
My friend is going to be one hundred & five years old next week...
105?!!
ARE YOU SERIOUS?!!
105!!
That means she was born in 1899!!
Her parents grew up during slavery!! She came of age when many considered black folks barely human!!
Man...She's probably having a flashback right now to the "Good ol' days" when colored folk were waitin' on her hand & foot!!
Man...I should let go of this wheelchair right now & let her roll right into the oncoming traffic!!...I feel like I'm Drivin' Miss Daisy!!
(I can't believe that movie won Best Film in '89 & "Do the Right Thing" didn't even get nominated...)
Perfect!! Thank you, young man... I couldn't have done it, myself..
...OH..No problem.. congrats on your 105th birthday, ma'am..
Jeezus..I am sooo screwed up!!
STOP

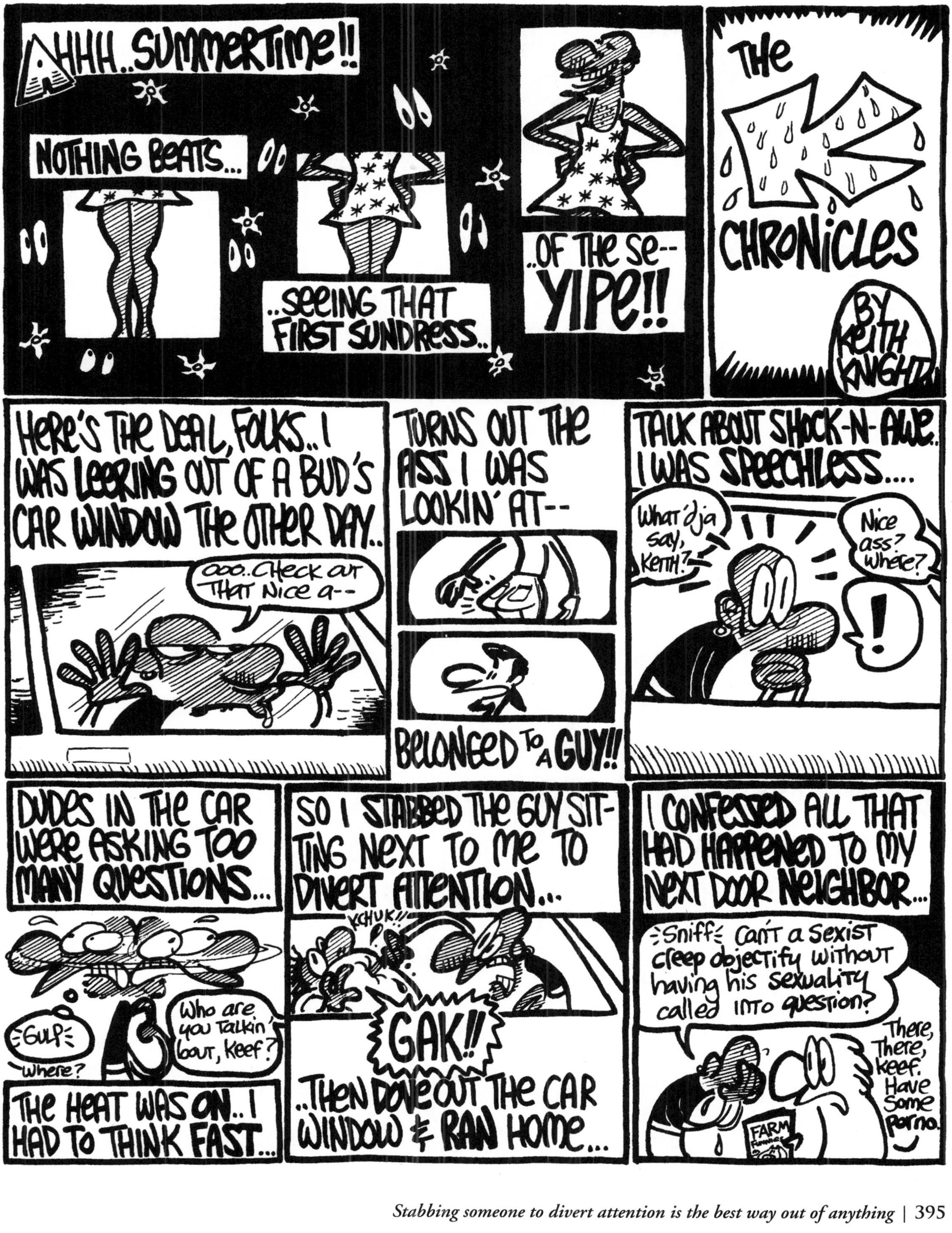

AHHH..SUMMERTIME!!
THE K CHRONICLES
BY KEITH KNIGHT
NOTHING BEATS...
..SEEING THAT FIRST SUNDRESS..
..OF THE SE--
YIPE!!
HERE'S THE DEAL, FOLKS..I WAS LEERING OUT OF A BUD'S CAR WINDOW THE OTHER DAY..
OOO..CHECK OUT THAT NICE A--
TURNS OUT THE ASS I WAS LOOKIN' AT--
BELONGED TO A GUY!!
TALK ABOUT SHOCK-N-AWE.. I WAS SPEECHLESS....
WHAT'D'JA SAY, KEITH?
NICE ASS? WHERE?
!
DUDES IN THE CAR WERE ASKING TOO MANY QUESTIONS...
GULP
WHERE?
WHO ARE YOU TALKIN' 'BOUT, KEEF?
THE HEAT WAS ON..I HAD TO THINK FAST...
SO I STABBED THE GUY SITTING NEXT TO ME TO DIVERT ATTENTION...
KCHUK!!
GAK!!
..THEN DOVE OUT THE CAR WINDOW & RAN HOME...
I CONFESSED ALL THAT HAD HAPPENED TO MY NEXT DOOR NEIGHBOR...
SNIFF CAN'T A SEXIST CREEP OBJECTIFY WITHOUT HAVING HIS SEXUALITY CALLED INTO QUESTION?
THERE, THERE, KEEF. HAVE SOME PORNO.
FARM

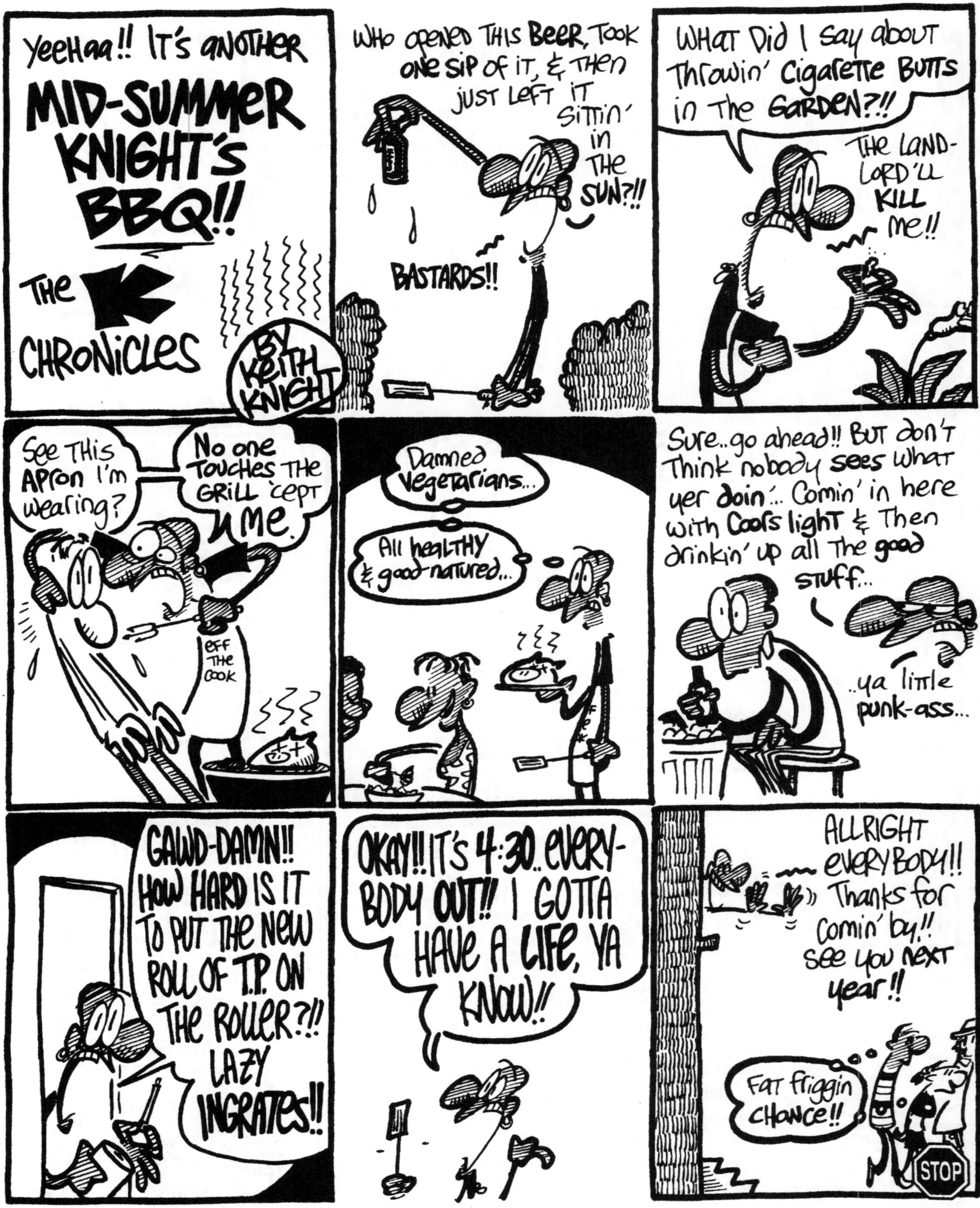
YeeHaa!! IT'S another
MID-SUMMER KNIGHT'S BBQ!!
THE K CHRONICLES
BY KEITH KNIGHT
WHO OPENED THIS BEER, TOOK ONE SIP OF IT, & THEN JUST LEFT IT SITTIN' IN THE SUN?!!
BASTARDS!!
WHAT DID I say about Throwin' Cigarette BUTTS in The GARDEN?!!
THE LAND-LORD'LL KILL me!!
See THIS APron I'm wearing?
No one TOUCHES THE GRILL 'cept me.
EFF THE COOK
Damned Vegetarians...
All healTHY & good-natured...
Sure..go ahead!! BUT don't Think nobody sees What yer doin'... Comin' in here with Coors light & Then drinkin' up all The good STUFF...
..ya little punk-ass...
GAWD-DAMN!! HOW HARD IS IT TO PUT THE NEW ROLL OF T.P. ON THE ROLLER?!! LAZY INGRATES!!
OKAY!! IT'S 4:30.. EVERY-BODY OUT!! I GOTTA HAVE A LIFE, YA KNOW!!
ALLRIGHT EVERYBODY!! Thanks for Comin' by!! see you next year!!
Fat friggin CHANCE!!
STOP

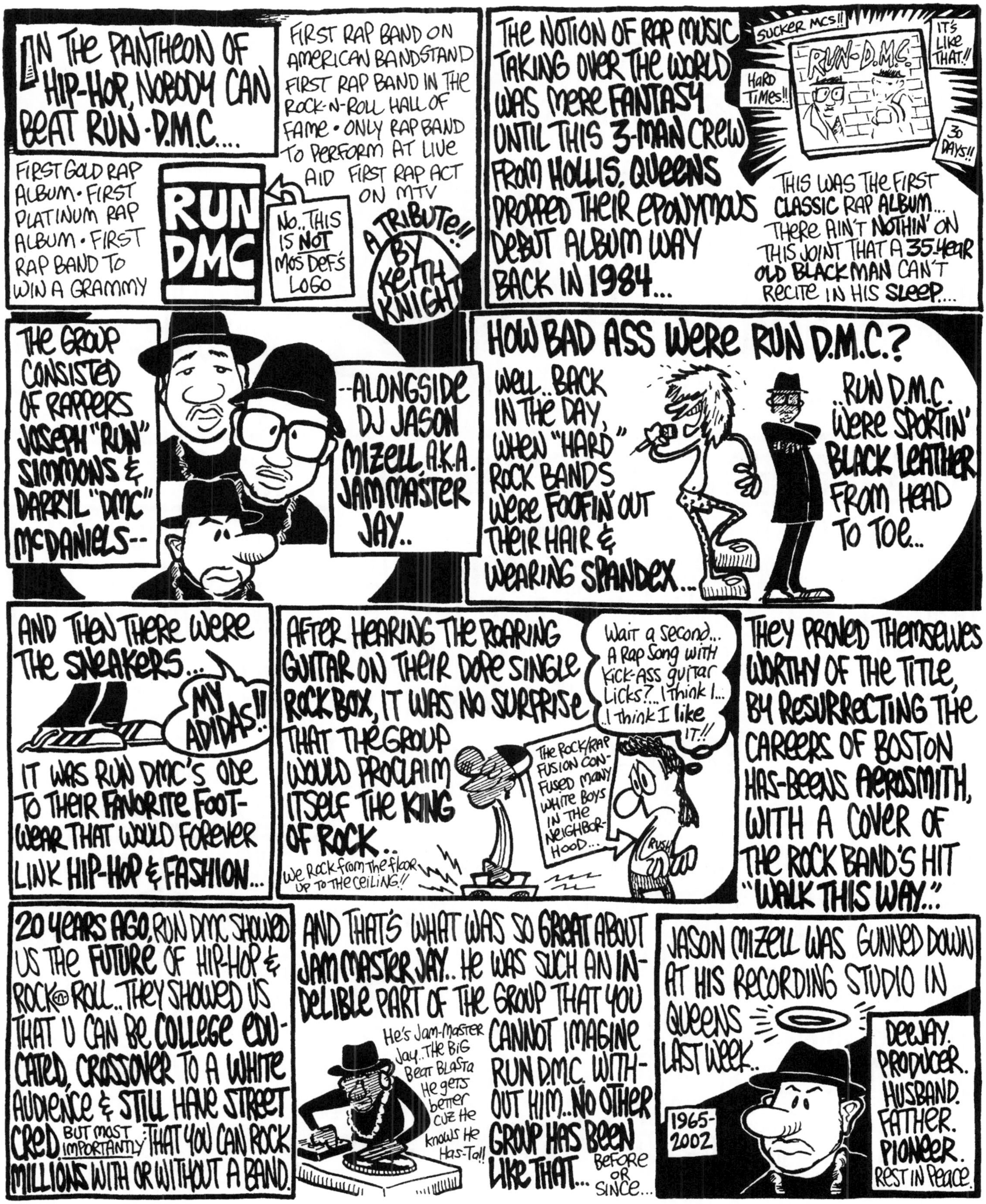

In the pantheon of hip-hop, nobody can beat Run-D.M.C....
First rap band on American Bandstand • First rap band in the Rock-n-Roll Hall of Fame • Only rap band to perform at Live Aid • First rap act on MTV
First gold rap album • First platinum rap album • First rap band to win a Grammy
RUN DMC
No.. this is not Mos Def's logo
A tribute!! By Keith Knight
The notion of rap music taking over the world was mere fantasy until this 3-man crew from Hollis, Queens dropped their eponymous debut album way back in 1984...
Sucker MCs!!
It's like that!!
Hard times!!
RUN-D.M.C.
30 days!!
This was the first classic rap album... There ain't nothin' on this joint that a 35-year old black man can't recite in his sleep...
The group consisted of rappers Joseph "Run" Simmons & Darryl "DMC" McDaniels--
--alongside DJ Jason Mizell, a.k.a. Jam Master Jay..
How bad ass were Run D.M.C.?
Well.. back in the day, when "hard" rock bands were foofin' out their hair & wearing spandex...
..Run D.M.C. were sportin' black leather from head to toe...
And then there were the sneakers...
My Adidas!!..
It was Run DMC's ode to their favorite foot-wear that would forever link hip-hop & fashion...
After hearing the roaring guitar on their dope single Rock Box, it was no surprise that the group would proclaim itself the King of Rock..
Wait a second... A rap song with kick-ass guitar licks?.. I think I... I think I like it!!
The rock/rap fusion confused many white boys in the neighborhood...
We rock from the floor up to the ceiling!!
RUSH
They proved themselves worthy of the title, by resurrecting the careers of Boston has-beens Aerosmith, with a cover of the rock band's hit "Walk This Way."
20 years ago, Run DMC showed us the future of hip-hop & rock-n-roll.. They showed us that U can be college educated, crossover to a white audience & still have street cred. but most importantly: that you can rock millions with or without a band.
And that's what was so great about Jam Master Jay.. He was such an indelible part of the group that you cannot imagine Run D.M.C. without him.. No other group has been like that... before or since...
He's Jam-Master Jay.. The big beat blasta He gets better cuz he knows he has-ta!!
Jason Mizell was gunned down at his recording studio in Queens last week..
1965-2002
Deejay. Producer. Husband. Father. Pioneer. Rest in peace.

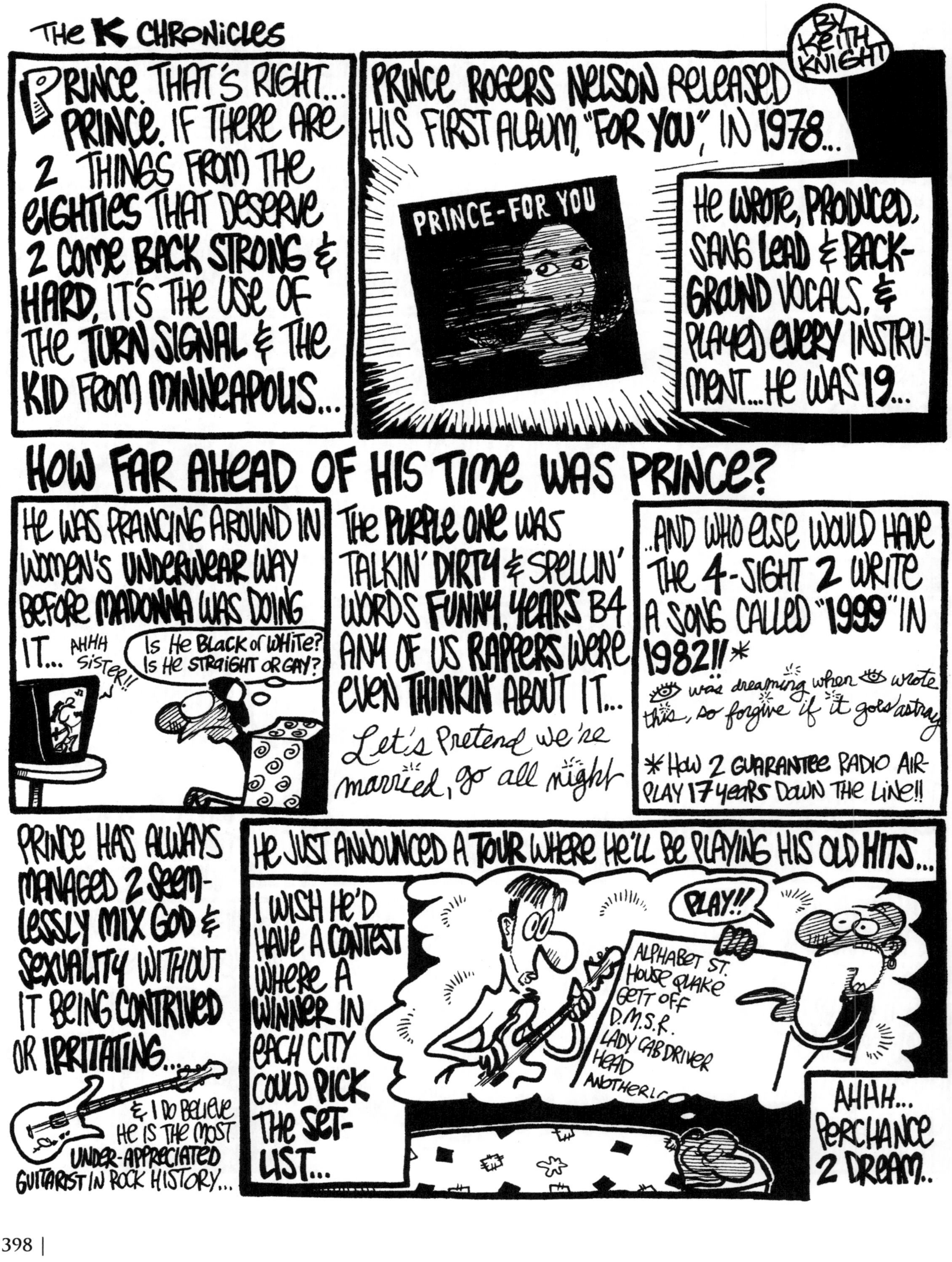
THE K CHRONICLES
BY KEITH KNIGHT
PRINCE. THAT'S RIGHT... PRINCE. IF THERE ARE 2 THINGS FROM THE EIGHTIES THAT DESERVE 2 COME BACK STRONG & HARD, IT'S THE USE OF THE TURN SIGNAL & THE KID FROM MINNEAPOLIS...
PRINCE ROGERS NELSON RELEASED HIS FIRST ALBUM, "FOR YOU", IN 1978...
PRINCE-FOR YOU
HE WROTE, PRODUCED, SANG LEAD & BACK-GROUND VOCALS, & PLAYED EVERY INSTRU-MENT... HE WAS 19...
HOW FAR AHEAD OF HIS TIME WAS PRINCE?
HE WAS PRANCING AROUND IN WOMEN'S UNDERWEAR WAY BEFORE MADONNA WAS DOING IT...
AHHH SISTER!!
IS HE BLACK OR WHITE? IS HE STRAIGHT OR GAY?
THE PURPLE ONE WAS TALKIN' DIRTY & SPELLIN' WORDS FUNNY, YEARS B4 ANY OF US RAPPERS WERE EVEN THINKIN' ABOUT IT...
Let's Pretend we're married, go all night
...AND WHO ELSE WOULD HAVE THE 4-SIGHT 2 WRITE A SONG CALLED "1999" IN 1982!!*
was dreaming when wrote this, so forgive if it goes astray
* HOW 2 GUARANTEE RADIO AIR-PLAY 17 YEARS DOWN THE LINE!!
PRINCE HAS ALWAYS MANAGED 2 SEEM-LESSLY MIX GOD & SEXUALITY WITHOUT IT BEING CONTRIVED OR IRRITATING...
& I DO BELIEVE HE IS THE MOST UNDER-APPRECIATED GUITARIST IN ROCK HISTORY...
HE JUST ANNOUNCED A TOUR WHERE HE'LL BE PLAYING HIS OLD HITS...
I WISH HE'D HAVE A CONTEST WHERE A WINNER IN EACH CITY COULD PICK THE SET-LIST...
PLAY!!
ALPHABET ST.
HOUSE QUAKE
GETT OFF
D.M.S.R.
LADY CAB DRIVER
HEAD
AHHH... PERCHANCE 2 DREAM..

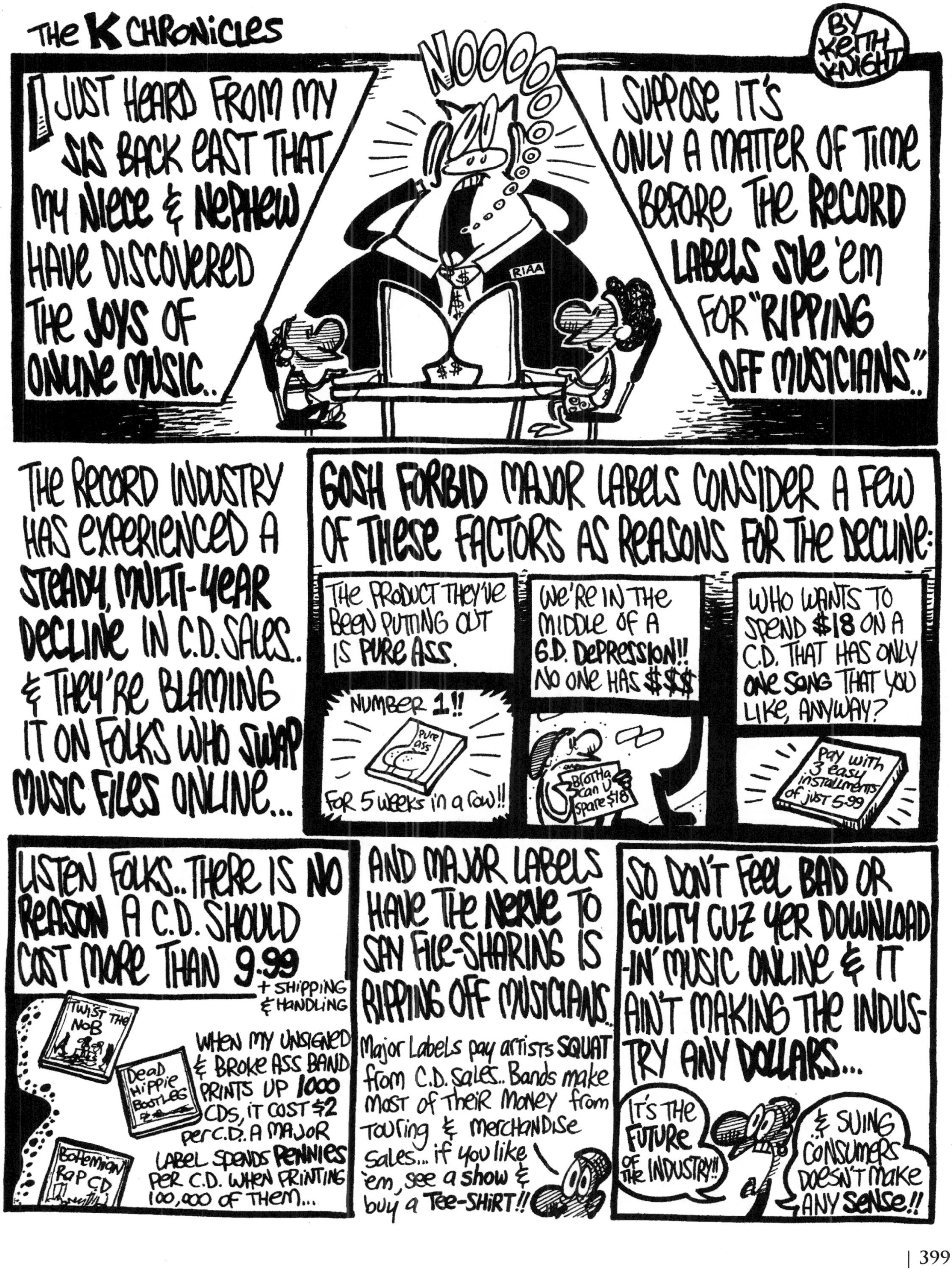
THE K CHRONICLES
BY KEITH KNIGHT
I JUST HEARD FROM MY SIS BACK EAST THAT MY NIECE & NEPHEW HAVE DISCOVERED THE JOYS OF ONLINE MUSIC..
NOOOOOOOOOOO
RIAA
I SUPPOSE IT'S ONLY A MATTER OF TIME BEFORE THE RECORD LABELS SUE 'EM FOR "RIPPING OFF MUSICIANS."..
THE RECORD INDUSTRY HAS EXPERIENCED A STEADY, MULTI-YEAR DECLINE IN C.D. SALES.. & THEY'RE BLAMING IT ON FOLKS WHO SWAP MUSIC FILES ONLINE...
GOSH FORBID MAJOR LABELS CONSIDER A FEW OF THESE FACTORS AS REASONS FOR THE DECLINE:
THE PRODUCT THEY'VE BEEN PUTTING OUT IS PURE ASS.
NUMBER 1!!
PURE ASS
FOR 5 WEEKS IN A ROW!!
WE'RE IN THE MIDDLE OF A G.D. DEPRESSION!! NO ONE HAS $$$
BROTHA CAN U SPARE $18
WHO WANTS TO SPEND $18 ON A C.D. THAT HAS ONLY ONE SONG THAT YOU LIKE, ANYWAY?
PAY WITH 3 EASY INSTALLMENTS OF JUST 5.99
LISTEN FOLKS.. THERE IS NO REASON A C.D. SHOULD COST MORE THAN 9.99
+ SHIPPING & HANDLING
TWIST THE NOB
DEAD HIPPIE BOOTLEG
BOHEMIAN RAP CD
WHEN MY UNSIGNED & BROKE ASS BAND PRINTS UP 1000 CDS, IT COST $2 PER C.D. A MAJOR LABEL SPENDS PENNIES PER C.D. WHEN PRINTING 100,000 OF THEM...
AND MAJOR LABELS HAVE THE NERVE TO SAY FILE-SHARING IS RIPPING OFF MUSICIANS..
Major Labels pay artists SQUAT from C.D. SALES.. Bands make most of their money from touring & merchandise sales... if you like 'em, see a show & buy a TEE-SHIRT!!
SO DON'T FEEL BAD OR GUILTY CUZ YER DOWNLOAD-IN' MUSIC ONLINE & IT AIN'T MAKING THE INDUSTRY ANY DOLLARS...
IT'S THE FUTURE OF THE INDUSTRY!!
& SUING CONSUMERS DOESN'T MAKE ANY SENSE!!

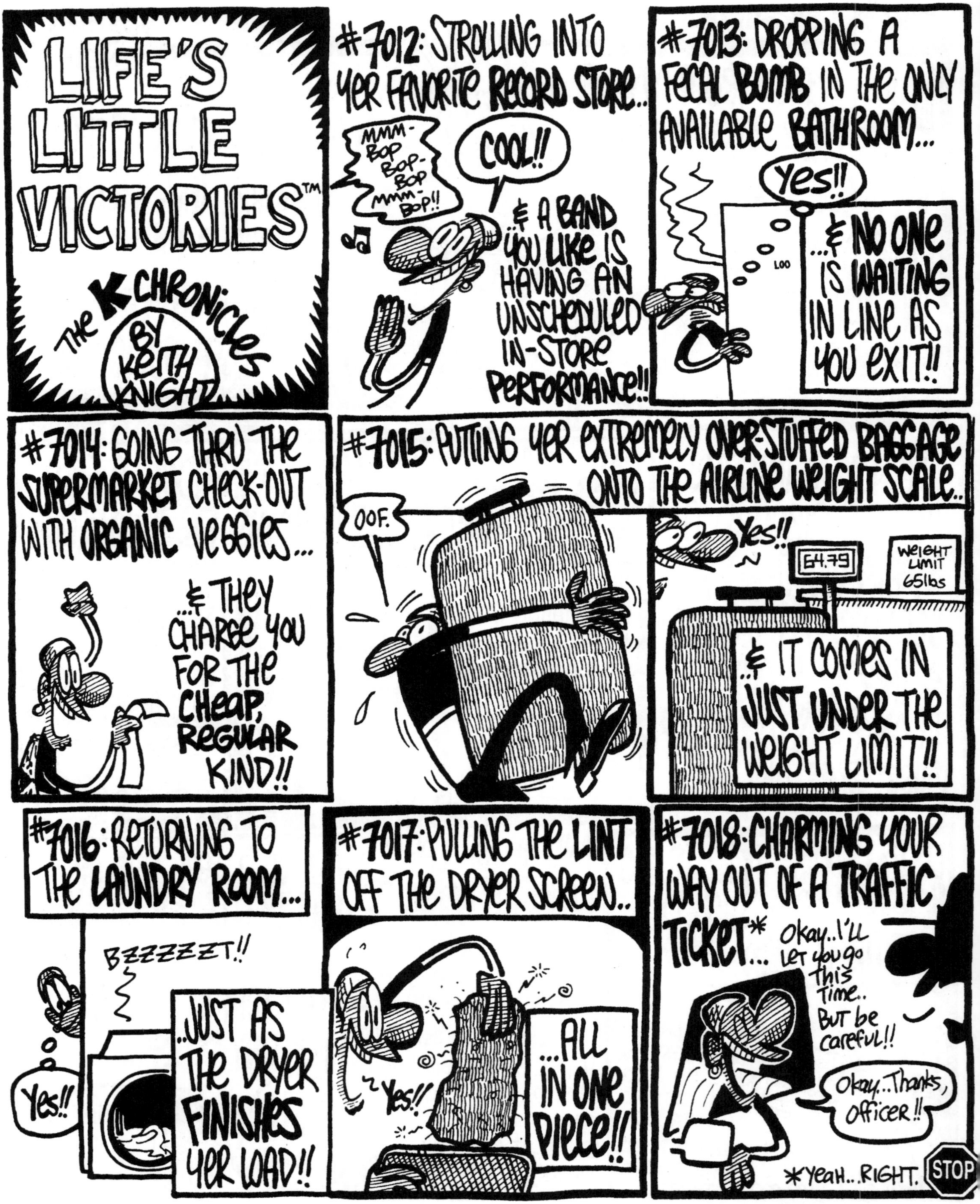
LIFE'S LITTLE VICTORIES™
THE K CHRONICLES BY KEITH KNIGHT
#7012: STROLLING INTO YER FAVORITE RECORD STORE...
MMM-BOP BOP-BOP MMM-BOP!!
COOL!!
...& A BAND YOU LIKE IS HAVING AN UNSCHEDULED IN-STORE PERFORMANCE!!
#7013: DROPPING A FECAL BOMB IN THE ONLY AVAILABLE BATHROOM...
Yes!!
LOO
...& NO ONE IS WAITING IN LINE AS YOU EXIT!!
#7014: GOING THRU THE SUPERMARKET CHECK-OUT WITH ORGANIC VEGGIES...
...& THEY CHARGE YOU FOR THE CHEAP, REGULAR KIND!!
#7015: PUTTING YER EXTREMELY OVER-STUFFED BAGGAGE ONTO THE AIRLINE WEIGHT SCALE..
OOF.
Yes!!
64.79
WEIGHT LIMIT 65lbs
..& IT COMES IN JUST UNDER THE WEIGHT LIMIT!!
#7016: RETURNING TO THE LAUNDRY ROOM...
BZZZZZZT!!
Yes!!
..JUST AS THE DRYER FINISHES YER LOAD!!
#7017: PULLING THE LINT OFF THE DRYER SCREEN..
Yes!!
...ALL IN ONE PIECE!!
#7018: CHARMING YOUR WAY OUT OF A TRAFFIC TICKET*...
Okay..I'LL let you go this time.. But be careful!!
Okay...Thanks, officer!!
*YEAH...RIGHT.
STOP

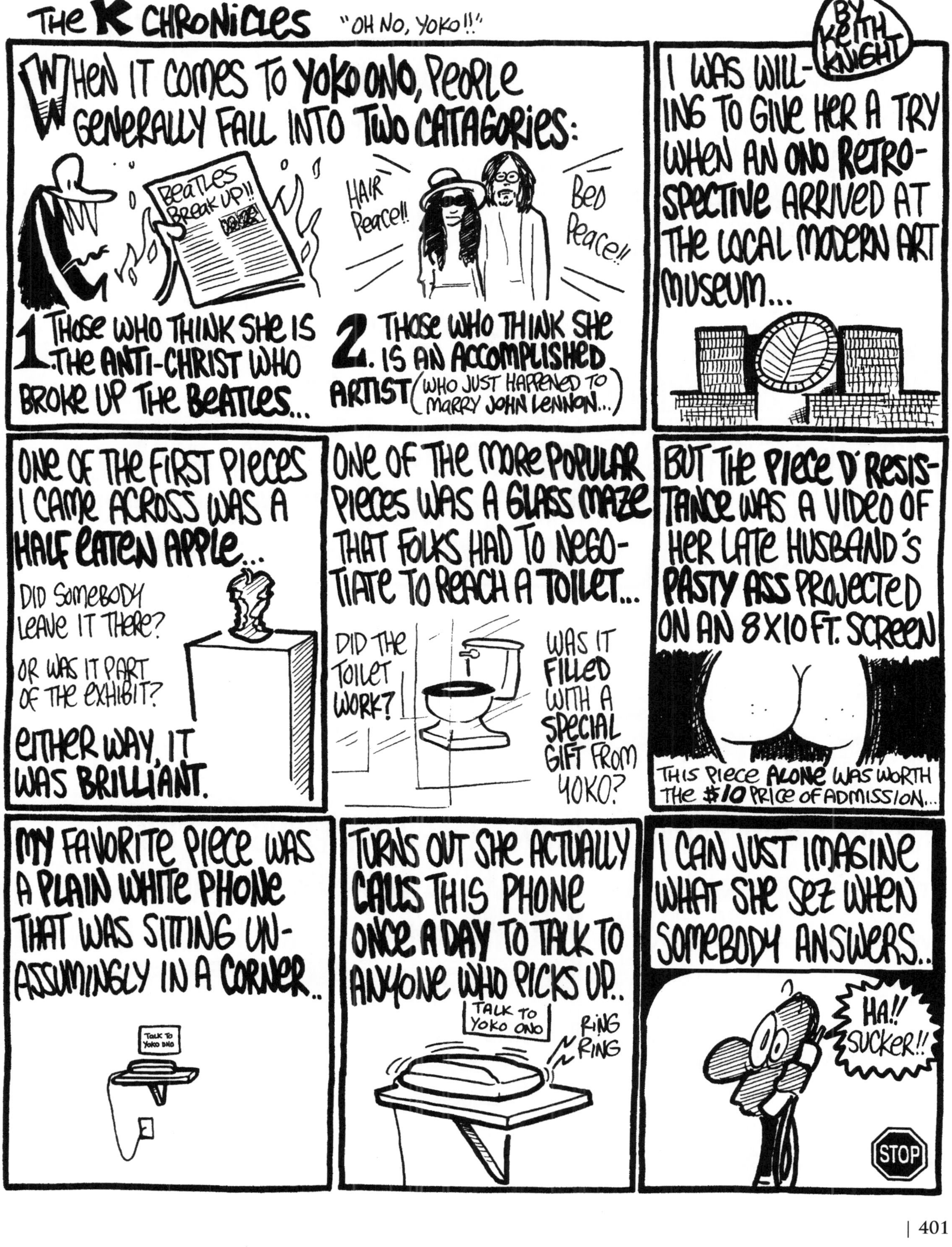
THE K CHRONICLES "OH NO, YOKO!!"
BY KEITH KNIGHT
WHEN IT COMES TO YOKO ONO, PEOPLE GENERALLY FALL INTO TWO CATAGORIES:
BEATLES BREAK UP!!
HAIR PEACE!!
BED PEACE!!
1. THOSE WHO THINK SHE IS THE ANTI-CHRIST WHO BROKE UP THE BEATLES...
2. THOSE WHO THINK SHE IS AN ACCOMPLISHED ARTIST (WHO JUST HAPPENED TO MARRY JOHN LENNON...)
I WAS WILLING TO GIVE HER A TRY WHEN AN ONO RETROSPECTIVE ARRIVED AT THE LOCAL MODERN ART MUSEUM...
ONE OF THE FIRST PIECES I CAME ACROSS WAS A HALF EATEN APPLE...
DID SOMEBODY LEAVE IT THERE?
OR WAS IT PART OF THE EXHIBIT?
EITHER WAY, IT WAS BRILLIANT.
ONE OF THE MORE POPULAR PIECES WAS A GLASS MAZE THAT FOLKS HAD TO NEGOTIATE TO REACH A TOILET...
DID THE TOILET WORK?
WAS IT FILLED WITH A SPECIAL GIFT FROM YOKO?
BUT THE PIECE D'RESISTANCE WAS A VIDEO OF HER LATE HUSBAND'S PASTY ASS PROJECTED ON AN 8X10 FT. SCREEN
THIS PIECE ALONE WAS WORTH THE $10 PRICE OF ADMISSION...
MY FAVORITE PIECE WAS A PLAIN WHITE PHONE THAT WAS SITTING UNASSUMINGLY IN A CORNER..
TALK TO YOKO ONO
TURNS OUT SHE ACTUALLY CALLS THIS PHONE ONCE A DAY TO TALK TO ANYONE WHO PICKS UP..
TALK TO YOKO ONO
RING RING
I CAN JUST IMAGINE WHAT SHE SEZ WHEN SOMEBODY ANSWERS...
HA!! SUCKER!!
STOP

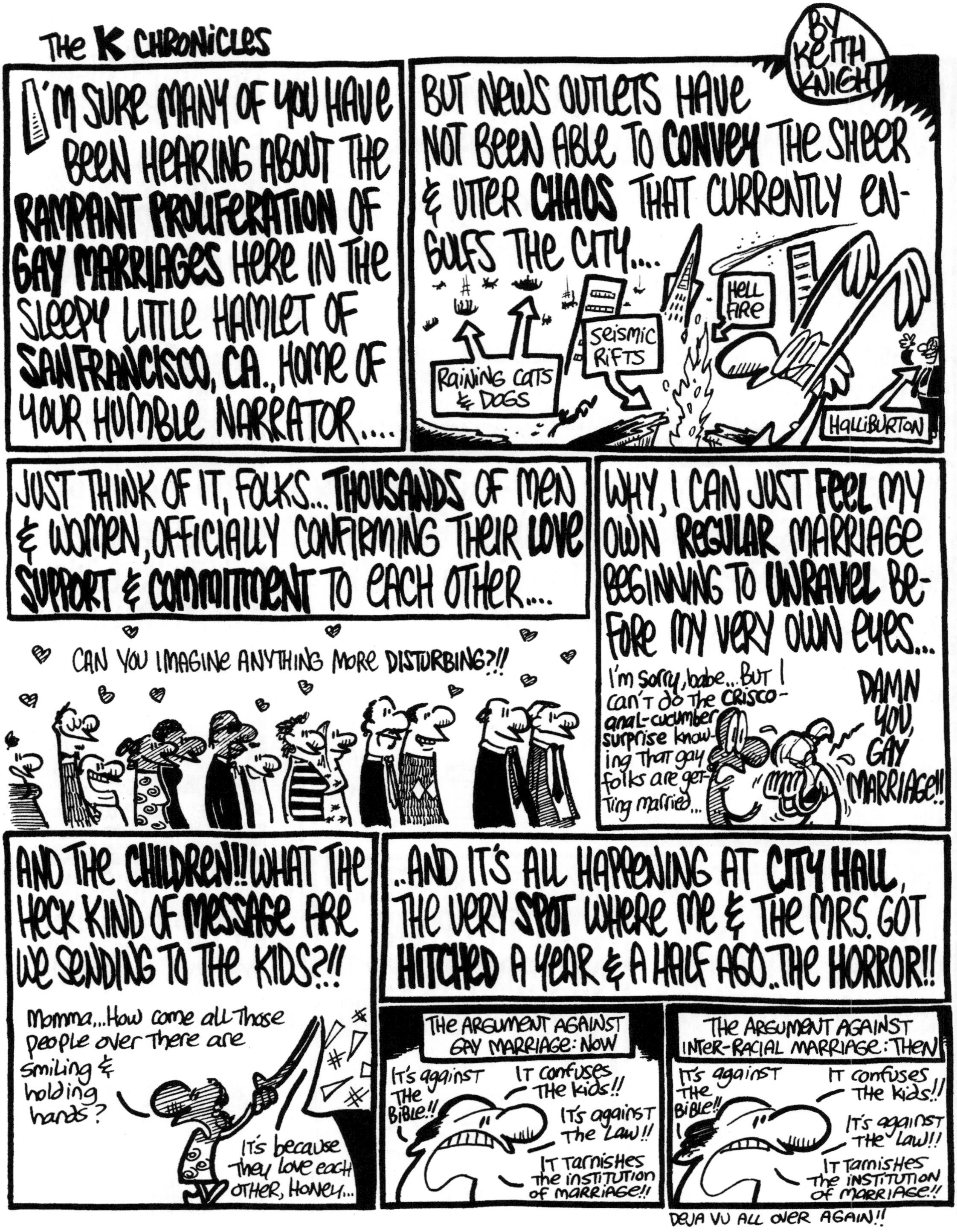

THE K CHRONICLES
BY KEITH KNIGHT
I'M SURE MANY OF YOU HAVE BEEN HEARING ABOUT THE RAMPANT PROLIFERATION OF GAY MARRIAGES HERE IN THE SLEEPY LITTLE HAMLET OF SAN FRANCISCO, CA., HOME OF YOUR HUMBLE NARRATOR....
BUT NEWS OUTLETS HAVE NOT BEEN ABLE TO CONVEY THE SHEER & UTTER CHAOS THAT CURRENTLY ENGULFS THE CITY....
RAINING CATS & DOGS
SEISMIC RIFTS
HELL FIRE
HALLIBURTON
JUST THINK OF IT, FOLKS... THOUSANDS OF MEN & WOMEN, OFFICIALLY CONFIRMING THEIR LOVE SUPPORT & COMMITMENT TO EACH OTHER....
CAN YOU IMAGINE ANYTHING MORE DISTURBING?!!
WHY, I CAN JUST FEEL MY OWN REGULAR MARRIAGE BEGINNING TO UNRAVEL BEFORE MY VERY OWN EYES...
I'm sorry, babe... But I can't do the CRISCO-anal-cucumber surprise knowing that gay folks are getting married...
DAMN YOU, GAY MARRIAGE!!
AND THE CHILDREN!! WHAT THE HECK KIND OF MESSAGE ARE WE SENDING TO THE KIDS?!!
Momma... How come all those people over there are smiling & holding hands?
It's because they love each other, Honey...
..AND IT'S ALL HAPPENING AT CITY HALL, THE VERY SPOT WHERE ME & THE MRS. GOT HITCHED A YEAR & A HALF AGO.. THE HORROR!!
THE ARGUMENT AGAINST GAY MARRIAGE: NOW
It's against the Bible!!
It confuses the kids!!
It's against the law!!
It tarnishes the institution of marriage!!
THE ARGUMENT AGAINST INTER-RACIAL MARRIAGE: THEN
It's against the Bible!!
It confuses the kids!!
It's against the law!!
It tarnishes the institution of marriage!!
DEJA VU ALL OVER AGAIN!!

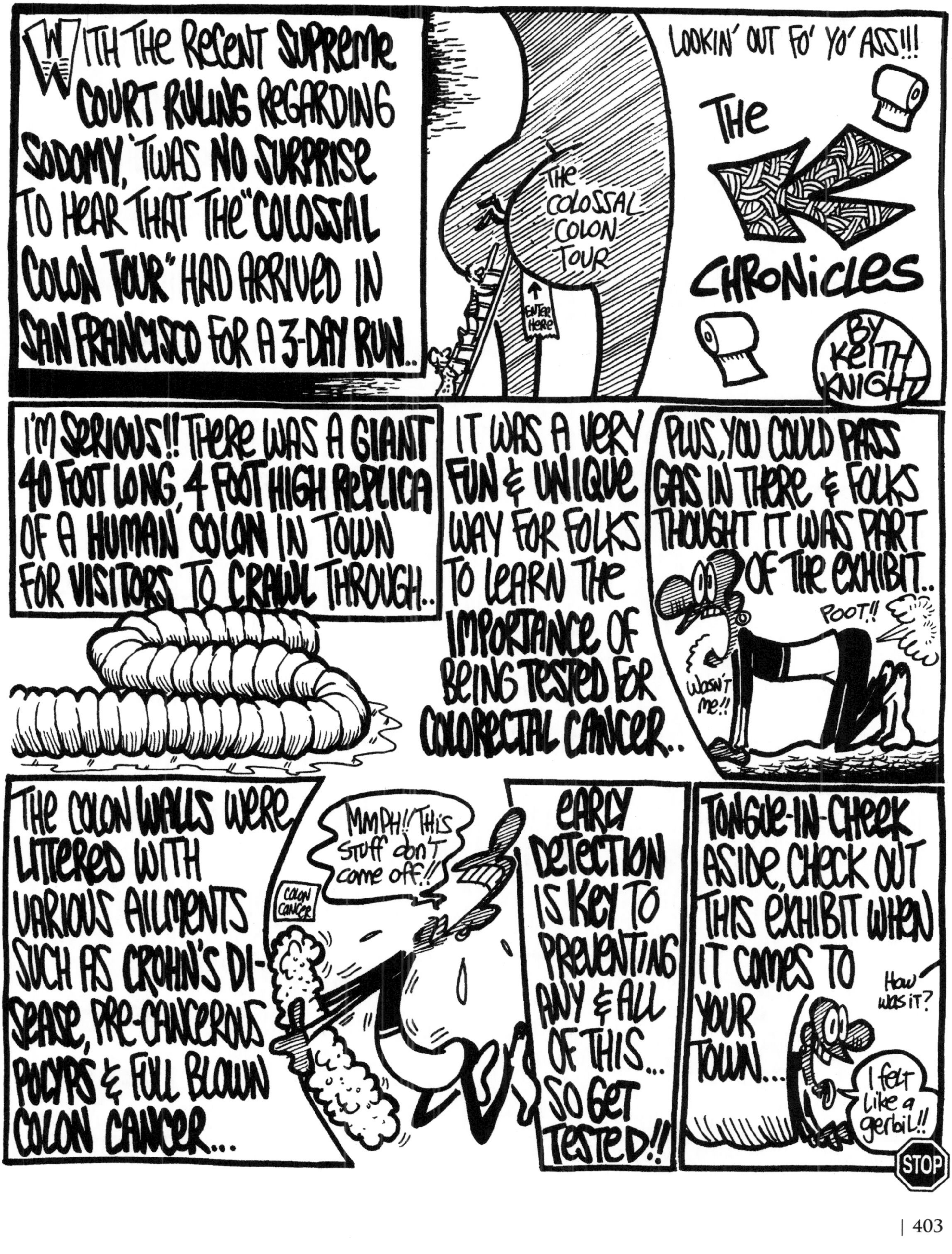
WITH THE RECENT SUPREME COURT RULING REGARDING SODOMY, 'TWAS NO SURPRISE TO HEAR THAT THE "COLOSSAL COLON TOUR" HAD ARRIVED IN SAN FRANCISCO FOR A 3-DAY RUN..
THE COLOSSAL COLON TOUR
ENTER HERE
LOOKIN' OUT FO' YO' ASS!!!
THE K CHRONICLES
BY KEITH KNIGHT
I'M SERIOUS!! THERE WAS A GIANT 40 FOOT LONG, 4 FOOT HIGH REPLICA OF A HUMAN COLON IN TOWN FOR VISITORS TO CRAWL THROUGH..
IT WAS A VERY FUN & UNIQUE WAY FOR FOLKS TO LEARN THE IMPORTANCE OF BEING TESTED FOR COLORECTAL CANCER..
PLUS, YOU COULD PASS GAS IN THERE & FOLKS THOUGHT IT WAS PART OF THE EXHIBIT..
POOT!!
WASN'T ME!!
THE COLON WALLS WERE LITTERED WITH VARIOUS AILMENTS SUCH AS CROHN'S DISEASE, PRE-CANCEROUS POLYPS & FULL BLOWN COLON CANCER...
MMPH!! THIS STUFF DON'T COME OFF!!
COLON CANCER
EARLY DETECTION IS KEY TO PREVENTING ANY & ALL OF THIS... SO GET TESTED!!
TONGUE-IN-CHEEK ASIDE, CHECK OUT THIS EXHIBIT WHEN IT COMES TO YOUR TOWN...
HOW WAS IT?
I FELT LIKE A GERBIL!!
STOP

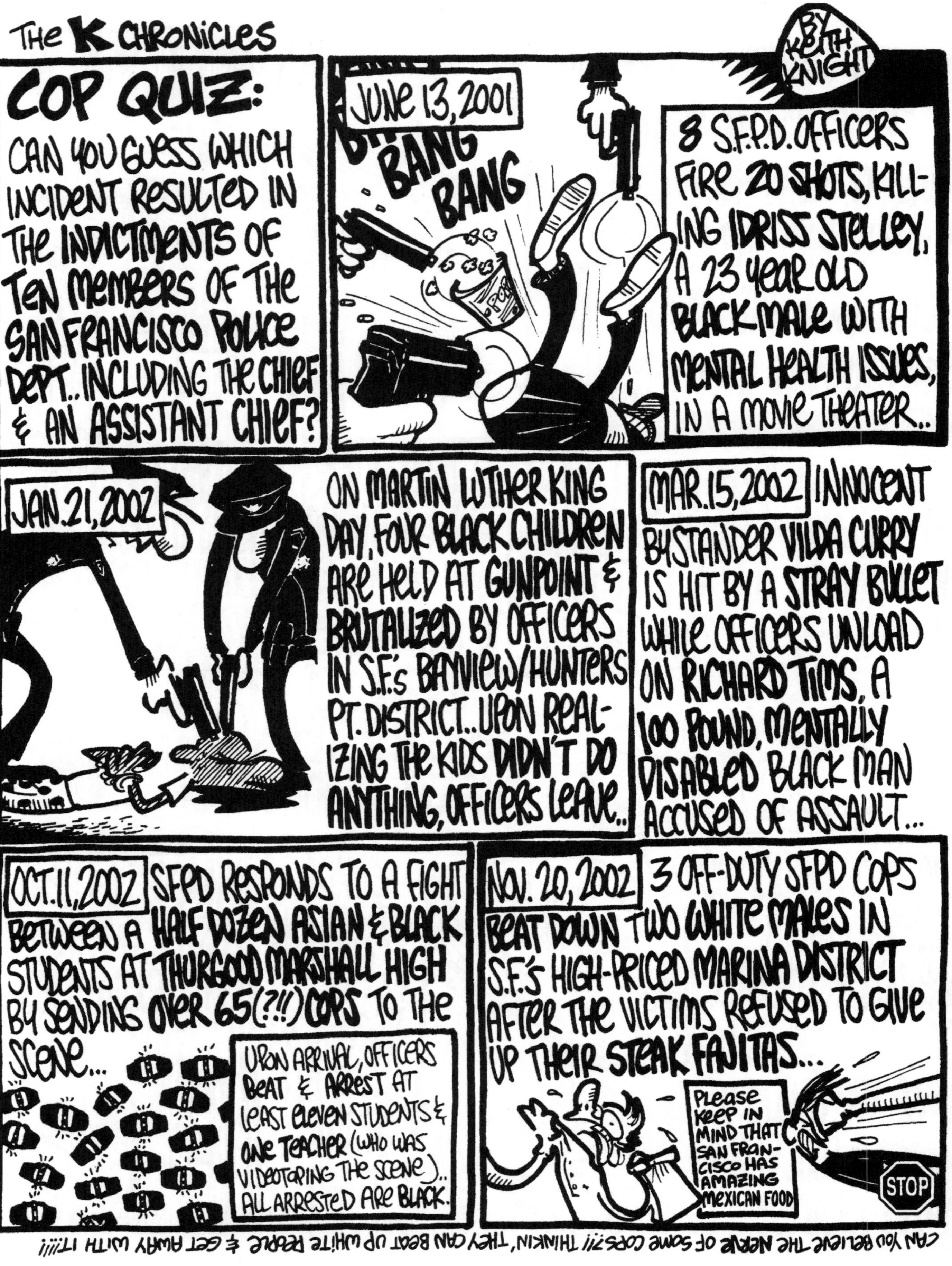
THE K CHRONICLES
BY KEITH KNIGHT
COP QUIZ:
CAN YOU GUESS WHICH INCIDENT RESULTED IN THE INDICTMENTS OF TEN MEMBERS OF THE SAN FRANCISCO POLICE DEPT.. INCLUDING THE CHIEF & AN ASSISTANT CHIEF?
JUNE 13, 2001
BANG
BANG
8 S.F.P.D. OFFICERS FIRE 20 SHOTS, KILLING IDRISS STELLEY, A 23 YEAR OLD BLACK MALE WITH MENTAL HEALTH ISSUES, IN A MOVIE THEATER..
JAN. 21, 2002
ON MARTIN LUTHER KING DAY, FOUR BLACK CHILDREN ARE HELD AT GUNPOINT & BRUTALIZED BY OFFICERS IN S.F.'S BAYVIEW/HUNTERS PT. DISTRICT.. UPON REALIZING THE KIDS DIDN'T DO ANYTHING, OFFICERS LEAVE..
MAR. 15, 2002
INNOCENT BYSTANDER VILDA CURRY IS HIT BY A STRAY BULLET WHILE OFFICERS UNLOAD ON RICHARD TIMS, A 100 POUND, MENTALLY DISABLED BLACK MAN ACCUSED OF ASSAULT...
OCT. 11, 2002
SFPD RESPONDS TO A FIGHT BETWEEN A HALF DOZEN ASIAN & BLACK STUDENTS AT THURGOOD MARSHALL HIGH BY SENDING OVER 65 (?!!) COPS TO THE SCENE...
UPON ARRIVAL, OFFICERS BEAT & ARREST AT LEAST ELEVEN STUDENTS & ONE TEACHER (WHO WAS VIDEOTAPING THE SCENE).. ALL ARRESTED ARE BLACK.
NOV. 20, 2002
3 OFF-DUTY SFPD COPS BEAT DOWN TWO WHITE MALES IN S.F.'S HIGH-PRICED MARINA DISTRICT AFTER THE VICTIMS REFUSED TO GIVE UP THEIR STEAK FAJITAS...
PLEASE KEEP IN MIND THAT SAN FRANCISCO HAS AMAZING MEXICAN FOOD
STOP
CAN YOU BELIEVE THE NERVE OF SOME COPS?!! THINKIN' THEY CAN BEAT UP WHITE PEOPLE & GET AWAY WITH IT!!!!!

There are far more incidents than the ones covered in this strip.
San Francisco ain't as progressive about certain things as one would think.

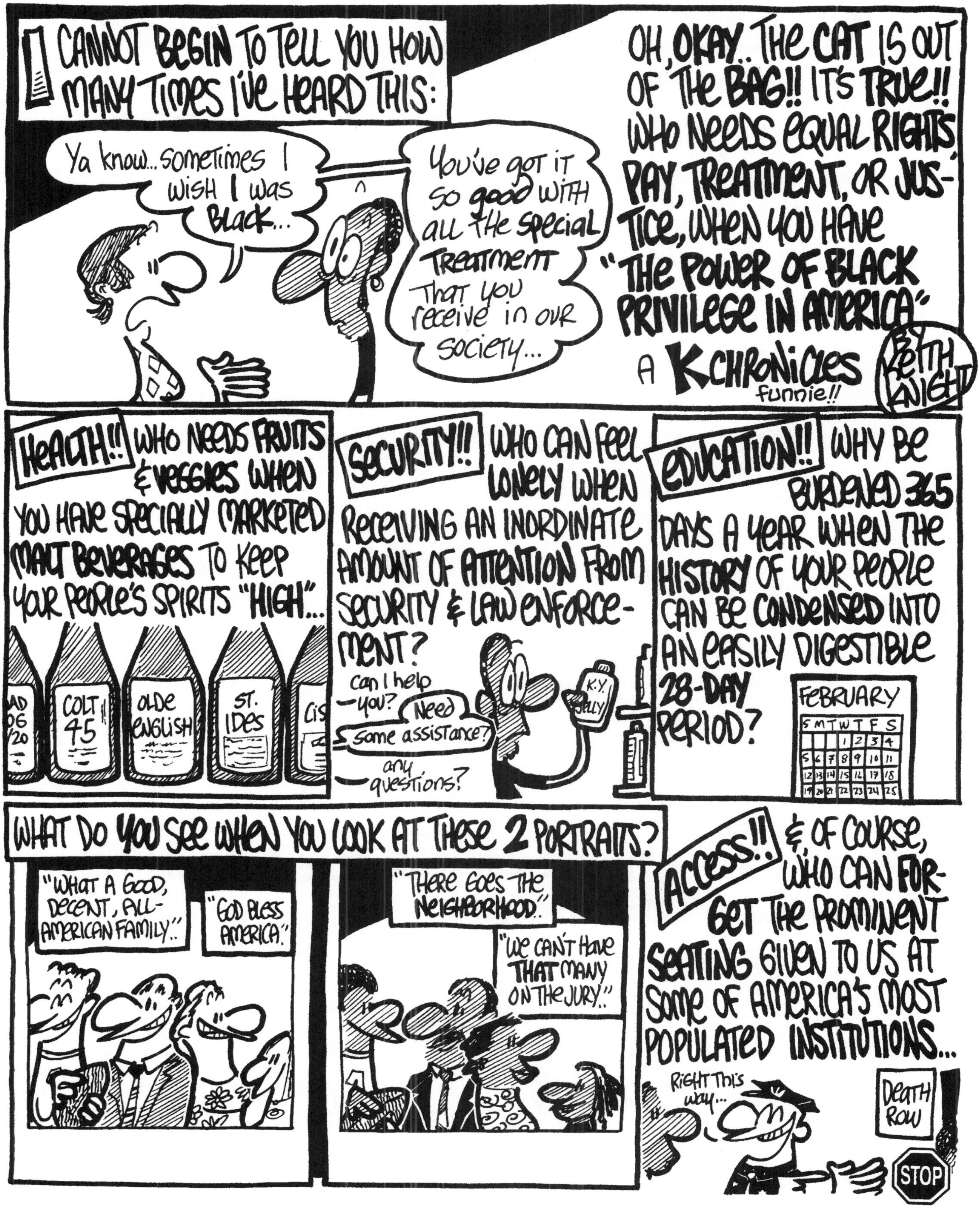
I CANNOT BEGIN TO TELL YOU HOW MANY TIMES I'VE HEARD THIS:
Ya know... sometimes I wish I was Black...
You've got it so good with all the special treatment that you receive in our society...
OH, OKAY.. THE CAT IS OUT OF THE BAG!! IT'S TRUE!! WHO NEEDS EQUAL RIGHTS, PAY, TREATMENT, OR JUSTICE, WHEN YOU HAVE "THE POWER OF BLACK PRIVILEGE IN AMERICA"
A K CHRONICLES funnie!!
BY KEITH KNIGHT
HEALTH!! WHO NEEDS FRUITS & VEGGIES WHEN YOU HAVE SPECIALLY MARKETED MALT BEVERAGES TO KEEP YOUR PEOPLE'S SPIRITS "HIGH"...
COLT 45
OLDE ENGLISH
ST. IDES
SECURITY!! WHO CAN FEEL LONELY WHEN RECEIVING AN INORDINATE AMOUNT OF ATTENTION FROM SECURITY & LAW ENFORCEMENT?
Can I help you?
Need some assistance?
any questions?
K.Y. JELLY
EDUCATION!! WHY BE BURDENED 365 DAYS A YEAR WHEN THE HISTORY OF YOUR PEOPLE CAN BE CONDENSED INTO AN EASILY DIGESTIBLE 28-DAY PERIOD?
FEBRUARY
WHAT DO YOU SEE WHEN YOU LOOK AT THESE 2 PORTRAITS?
"WHAT A GOOD, DECENT, ALL-AMERICAN FAMILY"..
"GOD BLESS AMERICA."
"THERE GOES THE NEIGHBORHOOD."
"WE CAN'T HAVE THAT MANY ON THE JURY."
ACCESS!! & OF COURSE, WHO CAN FORGET THE PROMINENT SEATING GIVEN TO US AT SOME OF AMERICA'S MOST POPULATED INSTITUTIONS...
RIGHT THIS WAY...
DEATH ROW
STOP

A black student group gave static because a white editor ran this strip.
If white editors didn't run strips like this, I wouldn't be running anywhere.

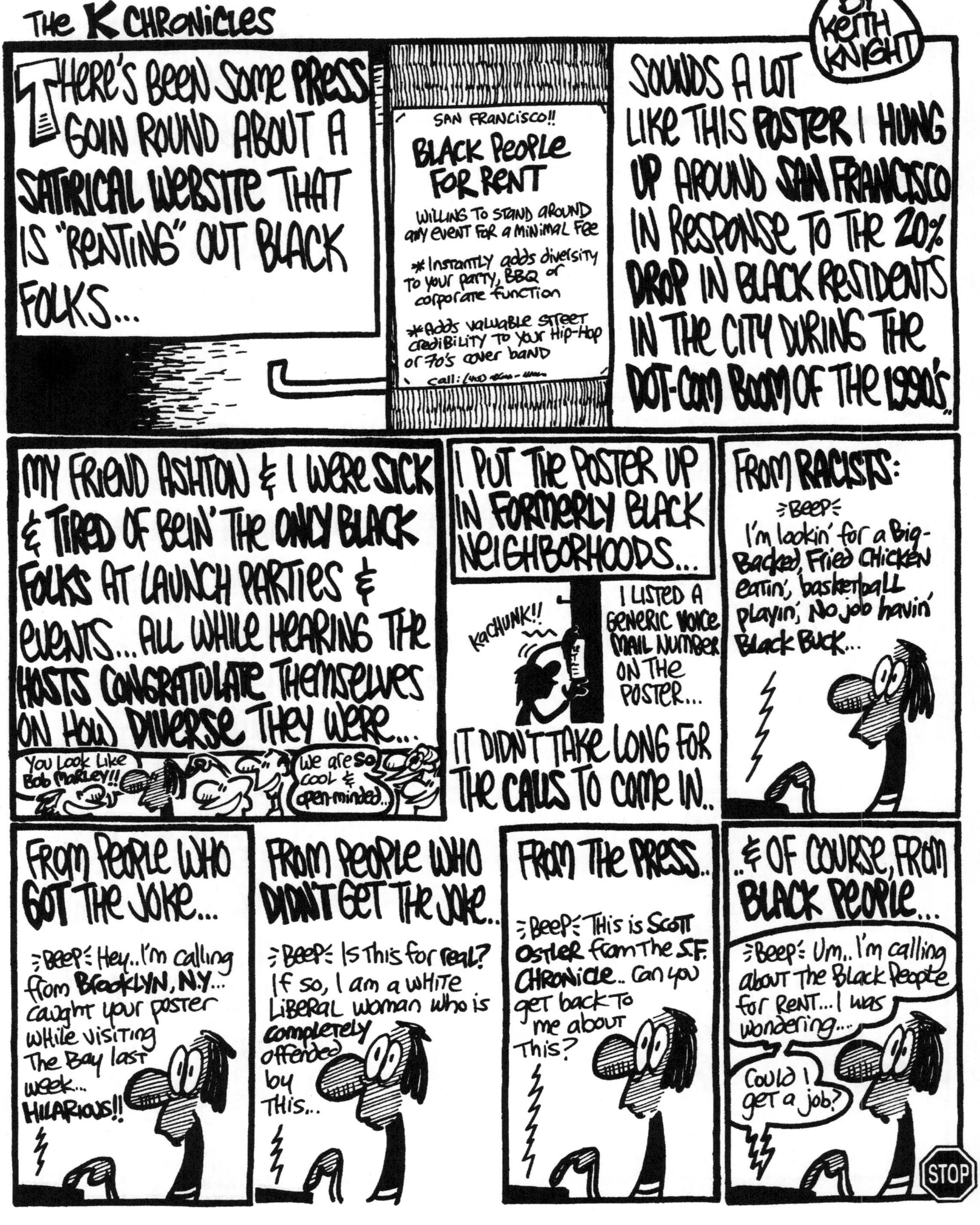
THE K CHRONICLES
BY KEITH KNIGHT
THERE'S BEEN SOME PRESS GOIN ROUND ABOUT A SATIRICAL WEBSITE THAT IS "RENTING" OUT BLACK FOLKS...
SAN FRANCISCO!!
BLACK PEOPLE FOR RENT
WILLING TO STAND AROUND ANY EVENT FOR A MINIMAL FEE
*INSTANTLY ADDS DIVERSITY TO YOUR PARTY, BBQ OR CORPORATE FUNCTION
*ADDS VALUABLE STREET CREDIBILITY TO YOUR HIP-HOP OR 70'S COVER BAND
SOUNDS A LOT LIKE THIS POSTER I HUNG UP AROUND SAN FRANCISCO IN RESPONSE TO THE 20% DROP IN BLACK RESIDENTS IN THE CITY DURING THE DOT-COM BOOM OF THE 1990'S..
MY FRIEND ASHTON & I WERE SICK & TIRED OF BEIN' THE ONLY BLACK FOLKS AT LAUNCH PARTIES & EVENTS... ALL WHILE HEARING THE HOSTS CONGRATULATE THEMSELVES ON HOW DIVERSE THEY WERE...
YOU LOOK LIKE BOB MARLEY!!
WE ARE SO COOL & OPEN-MINDED...
I PUT THE POSTER UP IN FORMERLY BLACK NEIGHBORHOODS...
KACHUNK!!
I LISTED A GENERIC VOICE MAIL NUMBER ON THE POSTER...
IT DIDN'T TAKE LONG FOR THE CALLS TO COME IN..
FROM RACISTS:
BEEP I'M LOOKIN' FOR A BIG-BACKED, FRIED CHICKEN EATIN', BASKETBALL PLAYIN', NO JOB HAVIN' BLACK BUCK...
FROM PEOPLE WHO GOT THE JOKE...
BEEP HEY.. I'M CALLING FROM BROOKLYN, N.Y... CAUGHT YOUR POSTER WHILE VISITING THE BAY LAST WEEK... HILARIOUS!!
FROM PEOPLE WHO DIDN'T GET THE JOKE...
BEEP IS THIS FOR REAL? IF SO, I AM A WHITE LIBERAL WOMAN WHO IS COMPLETELY OFFENDED BY THIS...
FROM THE PRESS..
BEEP THIS IS SCOTT OSTLER FROM THE S.F. CHRONICLE.. CAN YOU GET BACK TO ME ABOUT THIS?
..& OF COURSE, FROM BLACK PEOPLE...
BEEP UM.. I'M CALLING ABOUT THE BLACK PEOPLE FOR RENT... I WAS WONDERING...
COULD I GET A JOB?
STOP

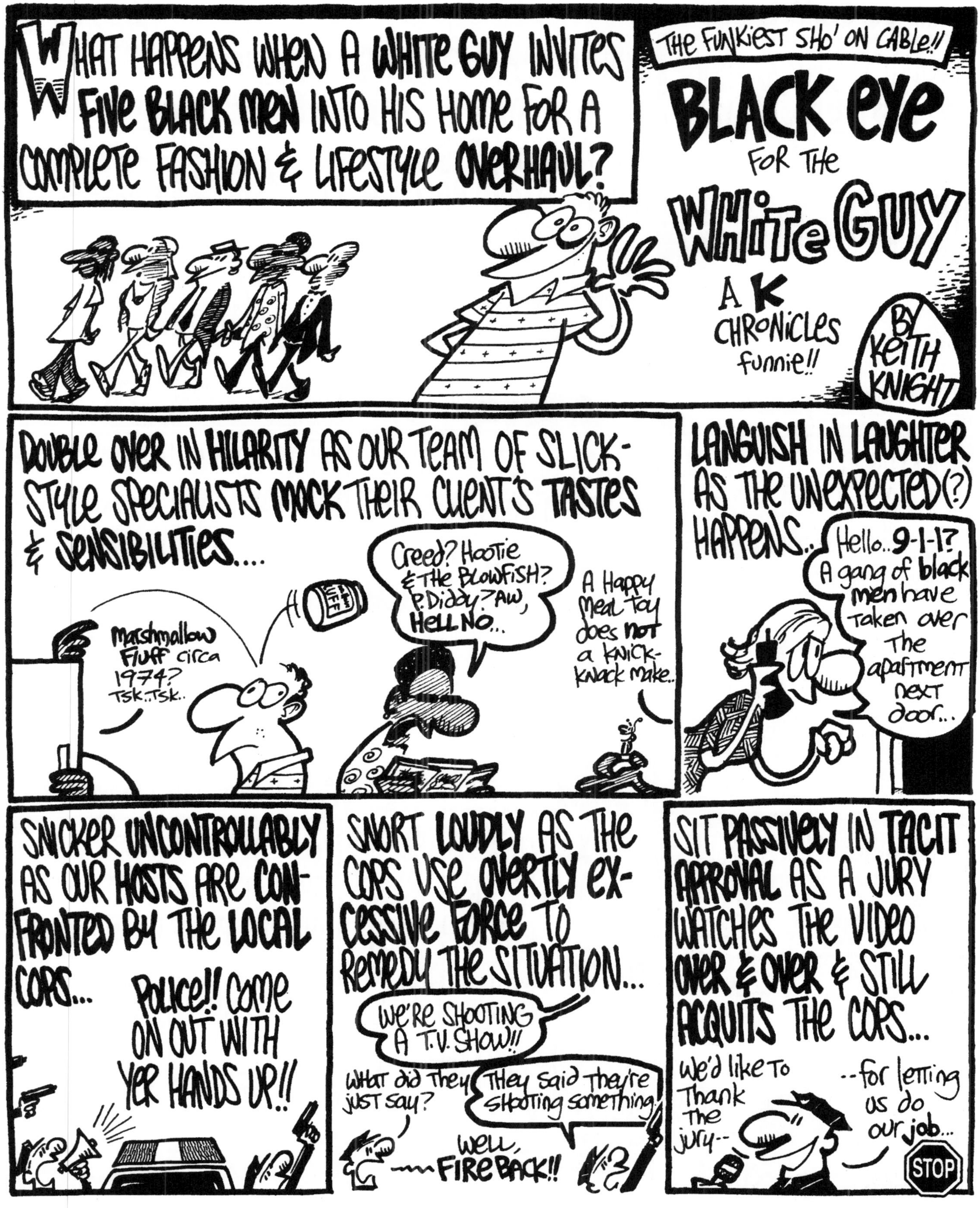
WHAT HAPPENS WHEN A WHITE GUY INVITES FIVE BLACK MEN INTO HIS HOME FOR A COMPLETE FASHION & LIFESTYLE OVERHAUL?
THE FUNKIEST SHO' ON CABLE!!
BLACK EYE FOR THE WHITE GUY
A K CHRONICLES FUNNIE!!
BY KEITH KNIGHT
DOUBLE OVER IN HILARITY AS OUR TEAM OF SLICK-STYLE SPECIALISTS MOCK THEIR CLIENT'S TASTES & SENSIBILITIES....
Marshmallow Fluff circa 1974? Tsk..Tsk..
Creed? Hootie & The Blowfish? P.Diddy? AW, HELL NO...
A Happy Meal Toy does not a knick-knack make..
LANGUISH IN LAUGHTER AS THE UNEXPECTED(?) HAPPENS...
Hello..9-1-1? A gang of black men have taken over the apartment next door...
SNICKER UNCONTROLLABLY AS OUR HOSTS ARE CONFRONTED BY THE LOCAL COPS...
POLICE!! COME ON OUT WITH YER HANDS UP!!
SNORT LOUDLY AS THE COPS USE OVERTLY EXCESSIVE FORCE TO REMEDY THE SITUATION...
WE'RE SHOOTING A T.V. SHOW!!
WHAT DID THEY JUST SAY?
THEY SAID THEY'RE SHOOTING SOMETHING.
WELL, FIRE BACK!!
SIT PASSIVELY IN TACIT APPROVAL AS A JURY WATCHES THE VIDEO OVER & OVER & STILL ACQUITS THE COPS...
We'd like to thank the jury--
--for letting us do our job...
STOP

The K CHRONICLES

BY KEITH KNIGHT

WHAT A LONG, STRANGE TRIP IT'S BEEN OVER THE PAST YEAR IN OUR APARTMENT BUILDING...

OUR LANDLORD (S)ELECTED A NEW ROOMMATE FOR US... THE NEW ROOMIE SHOWED UP WITH A LOTTA BAGGAGE...

Geez Louise!!

IMMEDIATELY AFTER HE MOVED IN, THE UTILITIES BILL BEGAN TO SKYROCKET...

AYE CARUMBA!!

WHEN I WENT TO CONFRONT HIM ON IT, I NOTICED SEVERAL EXTENSION CORDS COMING OUT OF HIS ROOM...

..THEY WENT OUT THE DOOR & INTO A BUNCH OF OTHER APARTMENTS LOCATED ON THE 1ST FLOOR...

!

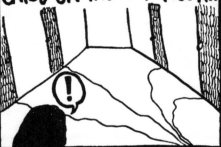

FUSES KEPT ON BLOWING SO THE TENANTS OF THE BUILDING CALLED A MEETING, ASKING US TO EXPLAIN OURSELVES... THE NEW ROOMIE EXPLODED...

IT IS OUR GOD-GIVEN RIGHT TO USE AS MANY OF THE RESOURCES IN THIS BUILDING AS POSSIBLE!!

SOON AFTER, OUR APARTMENT WAS THE VICTIM OF A HEINOUS ACT OF TERROR...

The rest of the floor said the Great Satan lives in your apartment... We're here to come and save you..

Repent, sinner.

THE NEW ROOMIE RETALIATED BY HAVIN' HIS DAD'S FRIENDS FORCIBLY REMOVE RESIDENTS OF THE FIRST FLOOR & INSTALLS FRIENDLY OCCUPANTS OPEN TO THE EXTENSION CORD USE...

WHATEVER... CURRENTLY, OUR APARTMENT IS A MESS, WE'RE ALL BROKE, THE UTILITIES BILL HAS BEEN SHREDDED. & THE REST OF THE BUILDING IS SCARED OF US...

Where the heck is my bag o' pretzels?

CHOKE KOFF

STOP

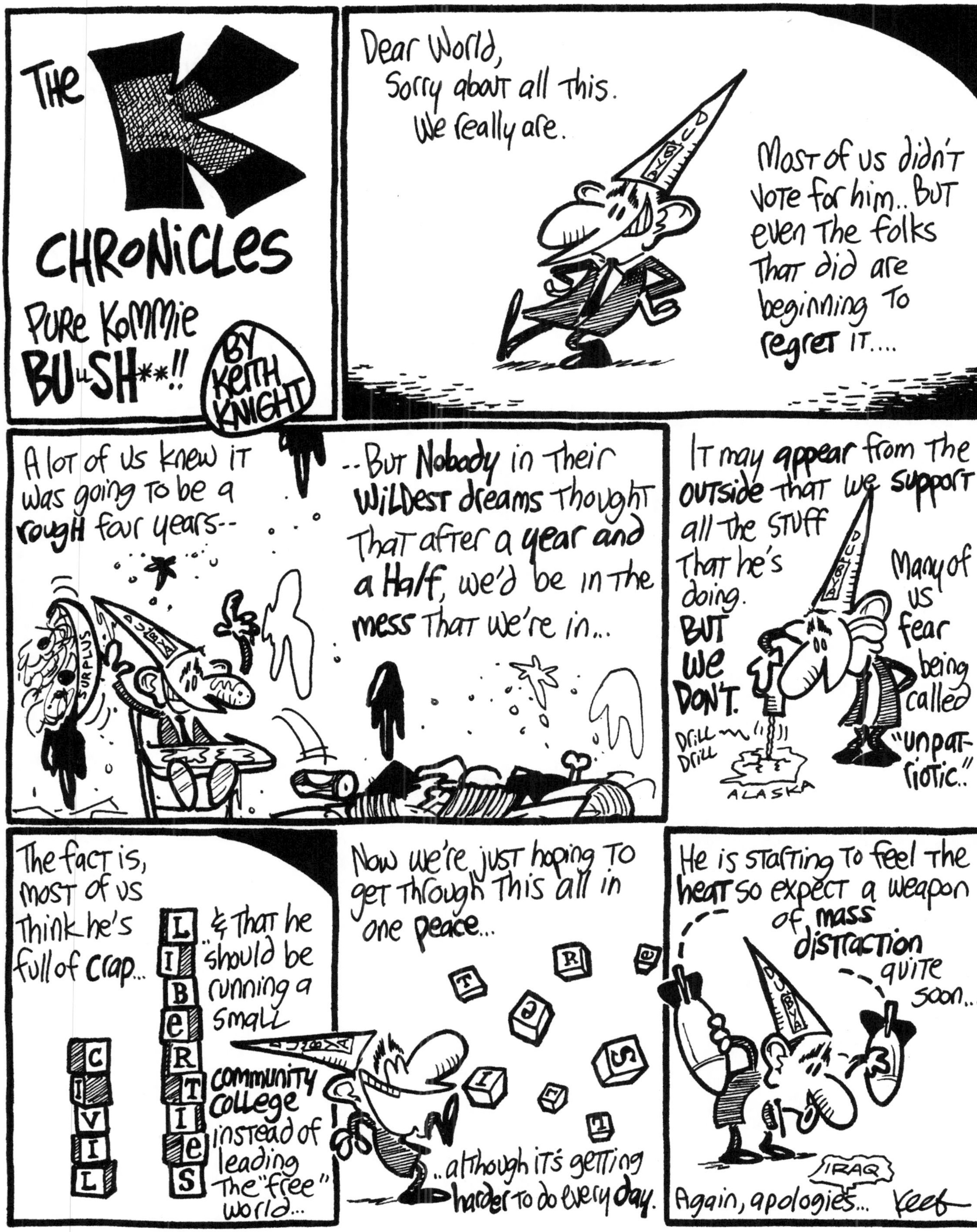

THE K CHRONICLES
Pure Kommie BU_{LL}SH**!!
BY KEITH KNIGHT
Dear World, Sorry about all this. We really are.
Most of us didn't vote for him.. But even the folks that did are beginning to regret it....
A lot of us knew it was going to be a rough four years--
--But nobody in their wildest dreams thought that after a year and a half, we'd be in the mess that we're in...
SURPLUS
It may appear from the outside that we support all the stuff that he's doing.
But we don't.
Many of us fear being called "unpatriotic."
Drill Drill
ALASKA
The fact is, most of us think he's full of crap...
..& that he should be running a small community college instead of leading the "free" world...
CIVIL LIBERTIES
Now we're just hoping to get through this all in one peace...
..although it's getting harder to do every day.
He is starting to feel the heat so expect a weapon of mass distraction quite soon...
IRAQ
Again, apologies...
Keef

I got crap from community college staffs all around the country for daring to say that Bush could actually run a community college.

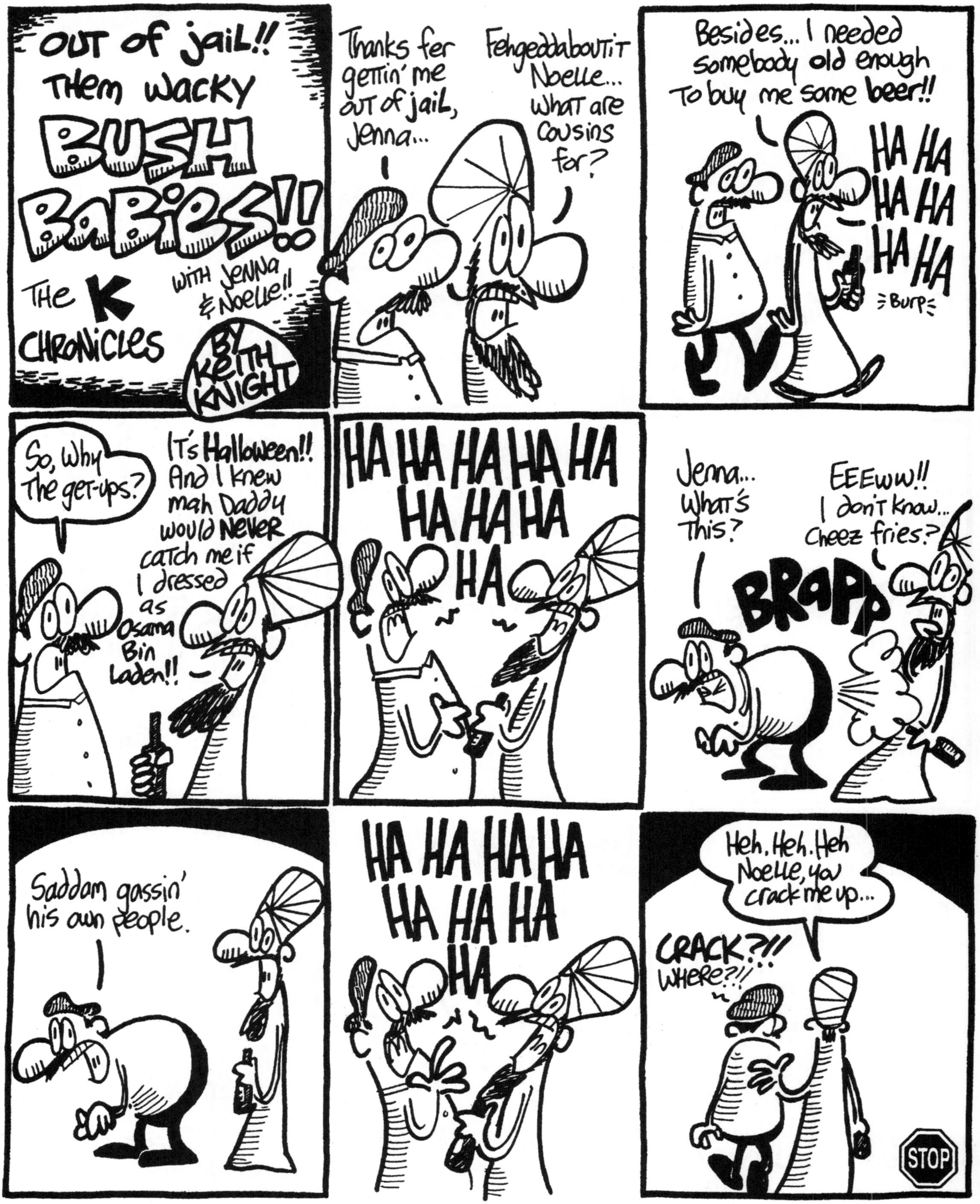
OUT of jaiL!! THEM WACKY
BUSH BaBiES!!
THE K CHRONICLES
WITH JENNA & NOELLE!!
BY KEITH KNIGHT
Thanks fer gettin' me out of jaiL, Jenna...
FehgeddaboutiT Noelle... WhaT are cousins for?
Besides... I needed somebody old enough To buy me some beer!!
HA HA HA HA HA HA
BURP
So, Why The get-ups?
IT's Halloween!! And I knew mah Daddy would NEVER catch me if I dressed as Osama Bin Laden!!
HA HA HA HA HA HA HA HA HA
Jenna... WhaT's This?
BRAPP
EEEWW!! I don'T know... Cheez fries?
Saddam gassin' his own people.
HA HA HA HA HA HA HA HA
Heh. Heh. Heh Noelle, you crack me up...
CRACK?!! WHERE?!!
STOP

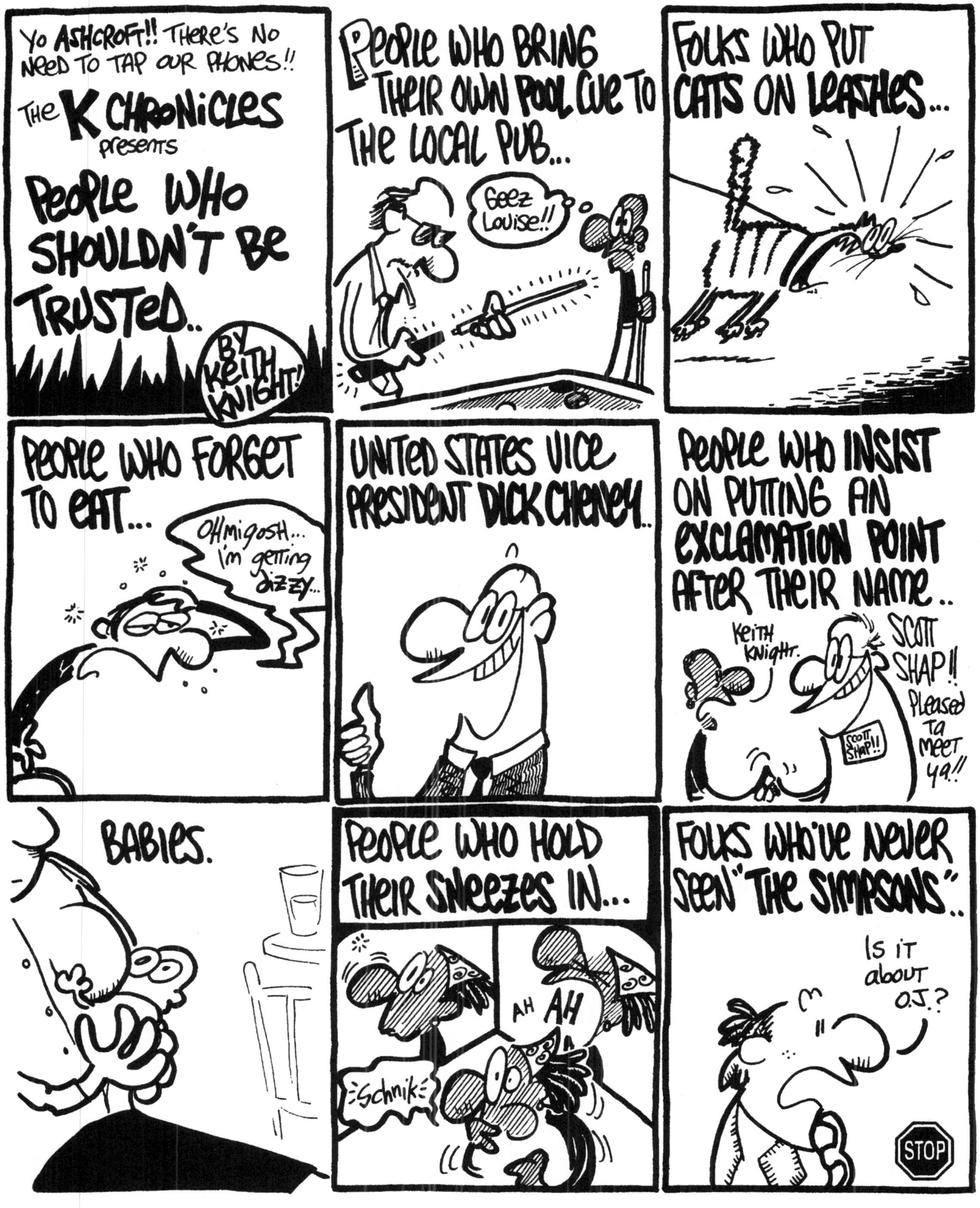
Yo ASHCROFT!! THERE'S NO NEED TO TAP OUR PHONES!!
THE K CHRONICLES presents
PEOPLE WHO SHOULDN'T BE TRUSTED..
BY KEITH KNIGHT!
PEOPLE WHO BRING THEIR OWN POOL CUE TO THE LOCAL PUB...
GEEZ LOUISE!!
FOLKS WHO PUT CATS ON LEASHES...
PEOPLE WHO FORGET TO EAT...
OHMIGOSH... I'M GETTING DIZZY...
UNITED STATES VICE PRESIDENT DICK CHENEY...
PEOPLE WHO INSIST ON PUTTING AN EXCLAMATION POINT AFTER THEIR NAME...
KEITH KNIGHT.
SCOTT SHAP!! Pleased ta meet ya!!
SCOTT SHAP!!
BABIES.
PEOPLE WHO HOLD THEIR SNEEZES IN...
AH AH
Schnik
FOLKS WHO'VE NEVER SEEN "THE SIMPSONS"...
IS IT ABOUT O.J.?
STOP

Scary baby drawing. | 411

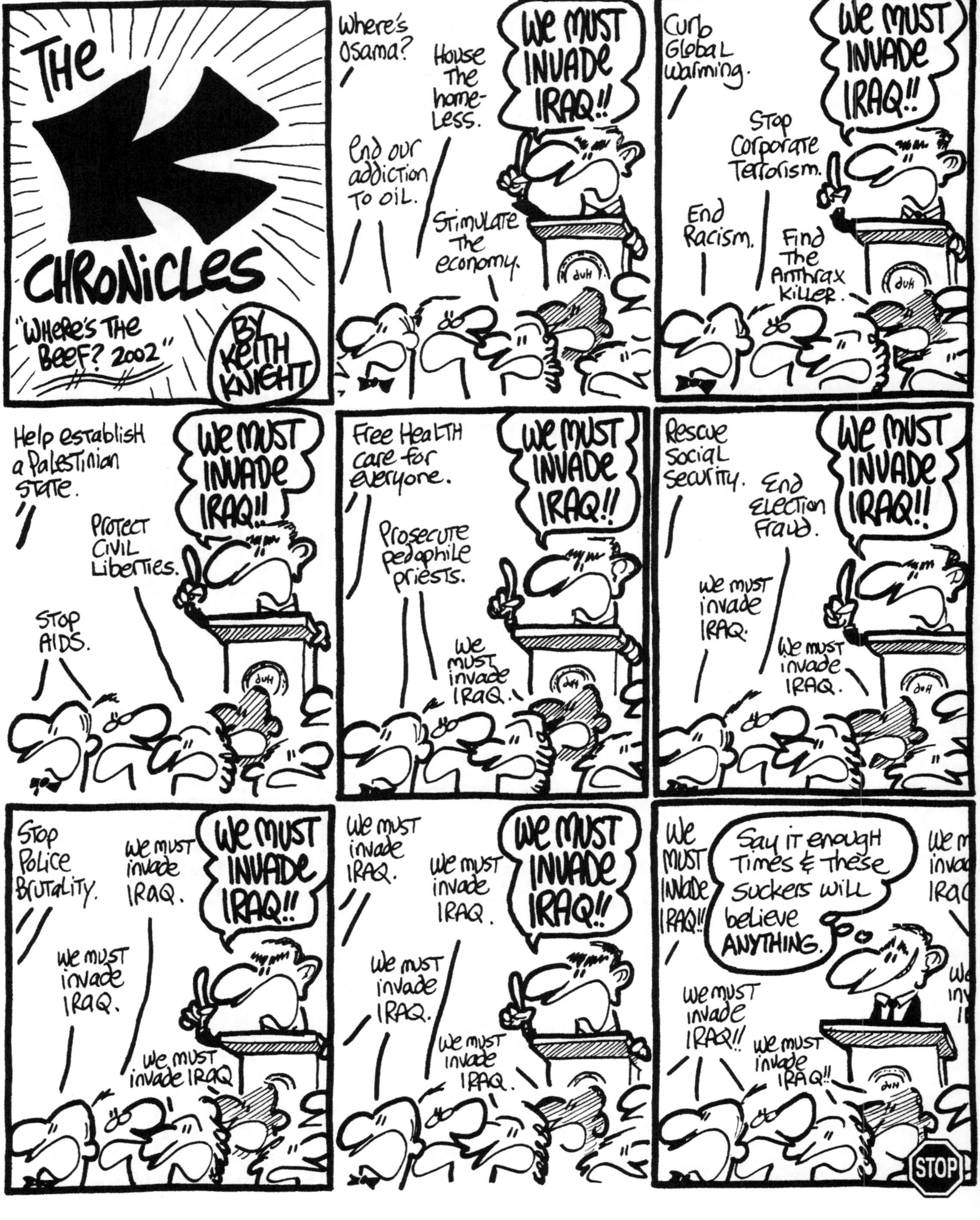
THE K CHRONICLES
"WHERE'S THE BEEF? 2002"
BY KEITH KNIGHT
Where's Osama?
House The homeless.
WE MUST INVADE IRAQ!!
End our addiction to oil.
Stimulate the economy.
duh
Curb Global warming.
WE MUST INVADE IRAQ!!
Stop Corporate Terrorism.
End Racism.
Find The Anthrax Killer.
duh
Help establish a Palestinian state.
WE MUST INVADE IRAQ!!
Protect civil liberties.
Stop AIDS.
duh
Free Health care for everyone.
WE MUST INVADE IRAQ!!
Prosecute pedophile priests.
We must invade IRAQ.
duh
Rescue social security.
End Election Fraud.
WE MUST INVADE IRAQ!!
We must invade IRAQ.
We must invade IRAQ.
duh
Stop Police Brutality.
We must invade IRAQ.
WE MUST INVADE IRAQ!!
We must invade IRAQ.
We must invade IRAQ
We must invade IRAQ.
We must invade IRAQ.
WE MUST INVADE IRAQ!!
We must invade IRAQ.
We must invade IRAQ.
We MUST INVADE IRAQ!!
Say it enough Times & these suckers will believe ANYTHING.
We must invade IRAQ!!
We must invade IRAQ!!
duh
STOP!

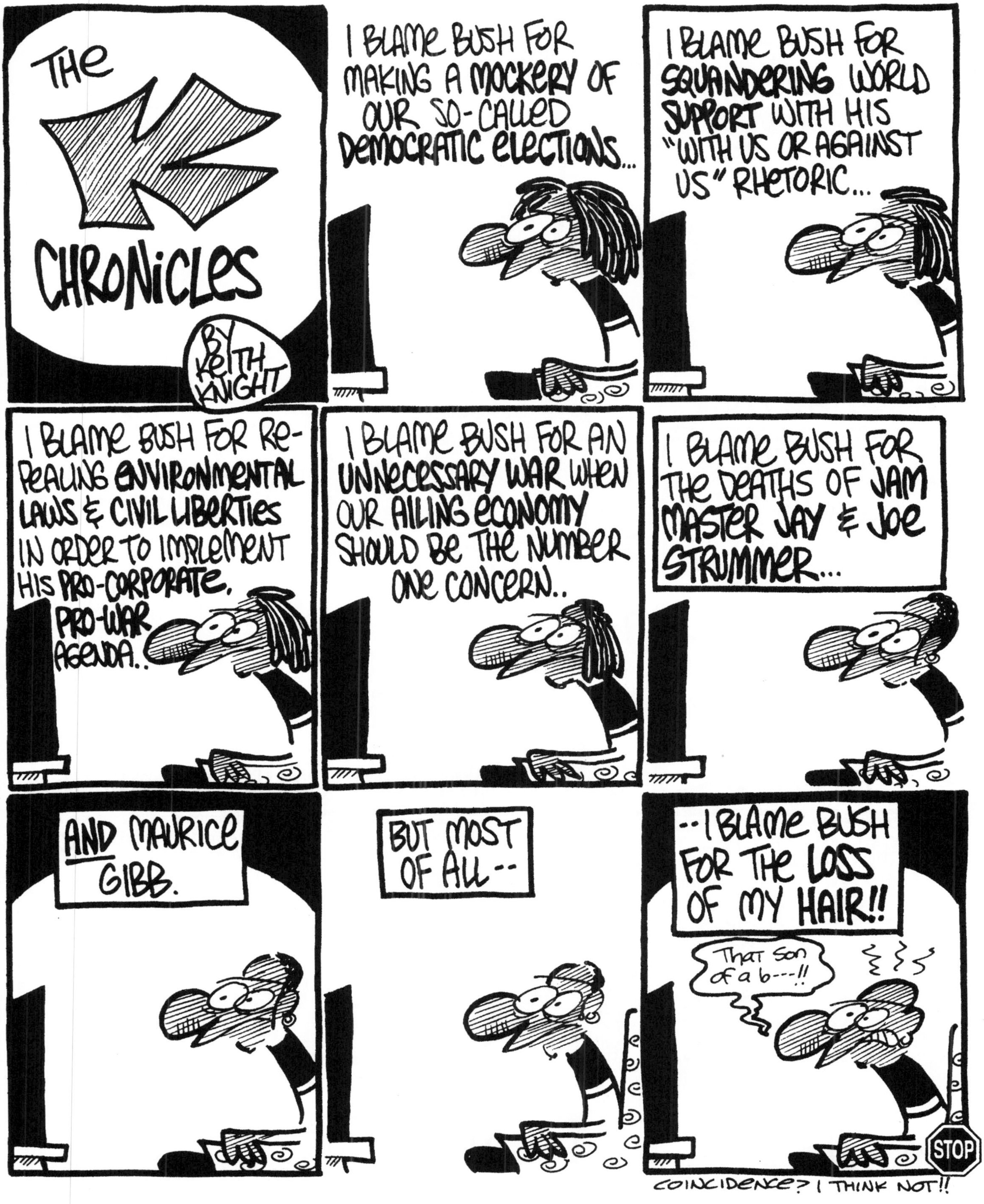
THE K CHRONICLES
BY KEITH KNIGHT
I BLAME BUSH FOR MAKING A MOCKERY OF OUR SO-CALLED DEMOCRATIC ELECTIONS...
I BLAME BUSH FOR SQUANDERING WORLD SUPPORT WITH HIS "WITH US OR AGAINST US" RHETORIC...
I BLAME BUSH FOR RE-PEALING ENVIRONMENTAL LAWS & CIVIL LIBERTIES IN ORDER TO IMPLEMENT HIS PRO-CORPORATE, PRO-WAR AGENDA..
I BLAME BUSH FOR AN UNNECESSARY WAR WHEN OUR AILING ECONOMY SHOULD BE THE NUMBER ONE CONCERN..
I BLAME BUSH FOR THE DEATHS OF JAM MASTER JAY & JOE STRUMMER...
AND MAURICE GIBB.
BUT MOST OF ALL--
--I BLAME BUSH FOR THE LOSS OF MY HAIR!!
That son of a b---!!
STOP
COINCIDENCE? I THINK NOT!!

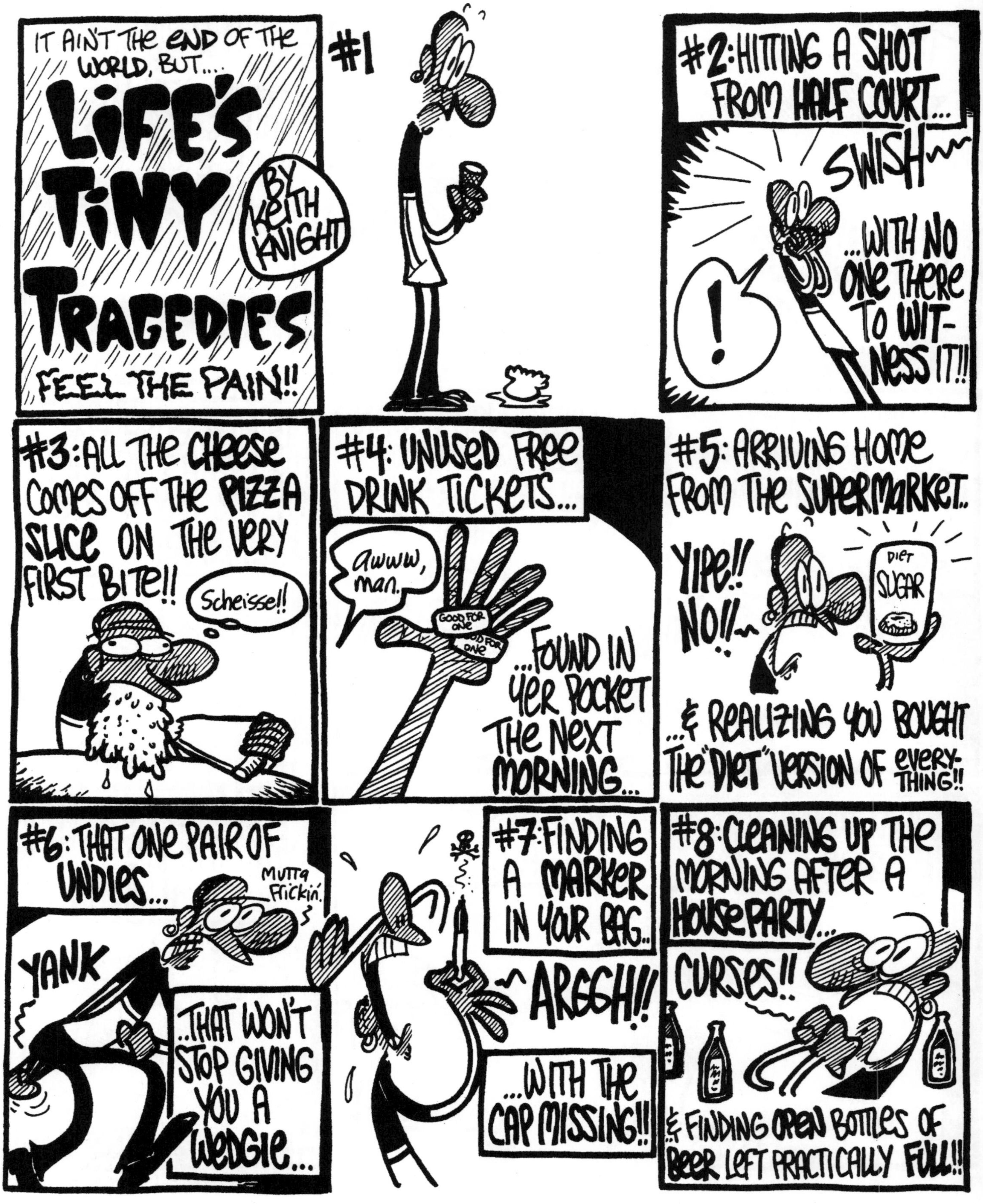
IT AIN'T THE END OF THE WORLD, BUT....
LIFE'S TINY TRAGEDIES
BY KEITH KNIGHT
FEEL THE PAIN!!
#1
#2: HITTING A SHOT FROM HALF COURT...
SWISH
!
...WITH NO ONE THERE TO WIT-NESS IT!!
#3: ALL THE CHEESE COMES OFF THE PIZZA SLICE ON THE VERY FIRST BITE!!
Scheisse!!
#4: UNUSED FREE DRINK TICKETS...
awww, man.
GOOD FOR ONE
GOOD FOR ONE
...FOUND IN YER POCKET THE NEXT MORNING...
#5: ARRIVING HOME FROM THE SUPERMARKET..
YIPE!! NO!!
DIET SUGAR
...& REALIZING YOU BOUGHT THE "DIET" VERSION OF EVERY-THING!!
#6: THAT ONE PAIR OF UNDIES...
MUTTA FRICKIN'
YANK
..THAT WON'T STOP GIVING YOU A WEDGIE...
#7: FINDING A MARKER IN YOUR BAG..
ARGGH!!
...WITH THE CAP MISSING!!
#8: CLEANING UP THE MORNING AFTER A HOUSE PARTY...
CURSES!!
& FINDING OPEN BOTTLES OF BEER LEFT PRACTICALLY FULL!!

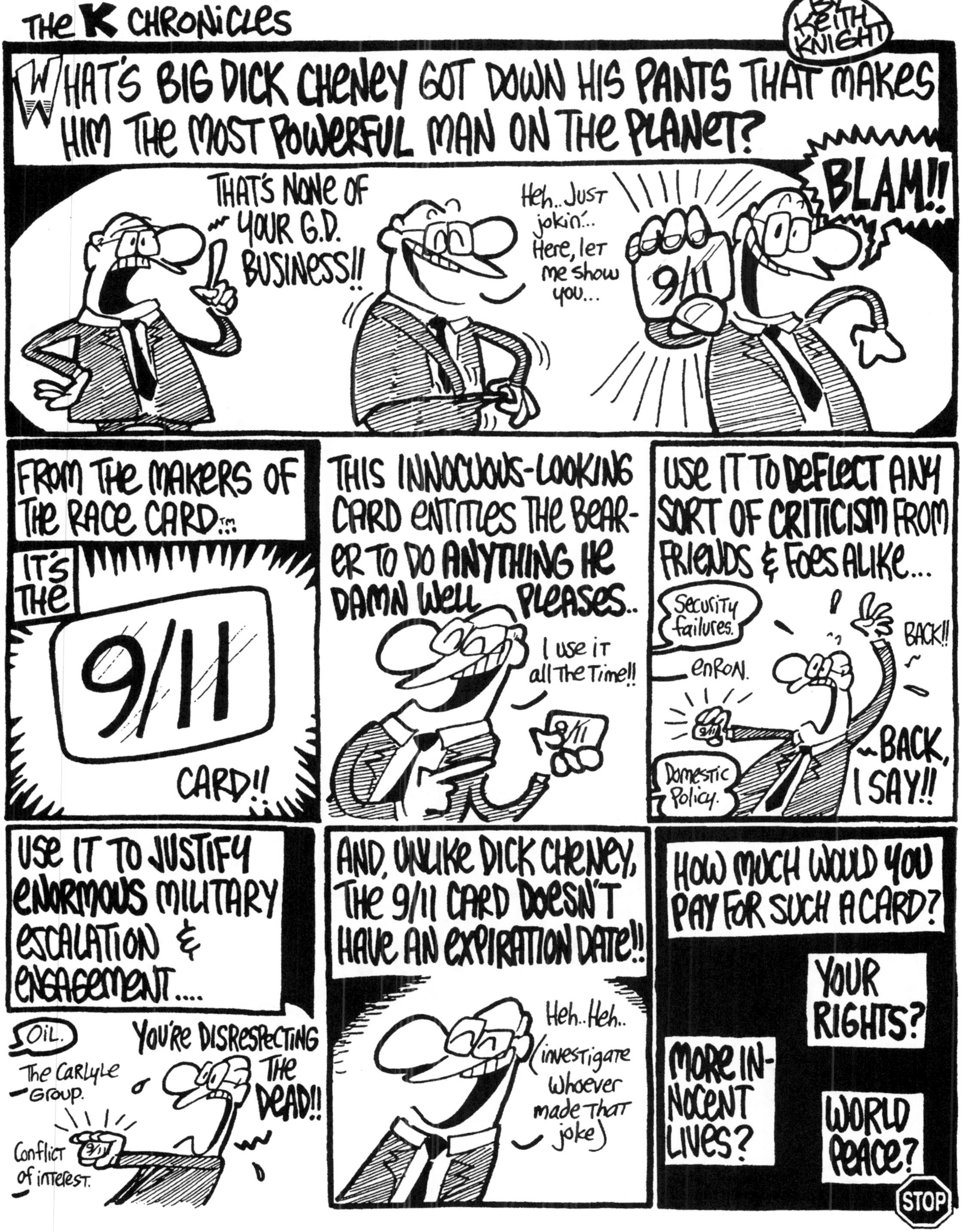
THE K CHRONICLES
BY KEITH KNIGHT
WHAT'S BIG DICK CHENEY GOT DOWN HIS PANTS THAT MAKES HIM THE MOST POWERFUL MAN ON THE PLANET?
THAT'S NONE OF YOUR G.D. BUSINESS!!
Heh.. JUST jokin'... Here, let me show you...
BLAM!!
9/11
FROM THE MAKERS OF THE RACE CARD™...
IT'S THE
9/11
CARD!!
THIS INNOCUOUS-LOOKING CARD ENTITLES THE BEARER TO DO ANYTHING HE DAMN WELL PLEASES..
I use it all the time!!
9/11
USE IT TO DEFLECT ANY SORT OF CRITICISM FROM FRIENDS & FOES ALIKE...
Security failures.
ENRON.
Domestic Policy.
BACK!!
BACK, I SAY!!
USE IT TO JUSTIFY ENORMOUS MILITARY ESCALATION & ENGAGEMENT....
OIL.
The Carlyle Group.
Conflict of interest.
9/11
YOU'RE DISRESPECTING THE DEAD!!
AND, UNLIKE DICK CHENEY, THE 9/11 CARD DOESN'T HAVE AN EXPIRATION DATE!!
Heh.. Heh.. (investigate whoever made that joke)
HOW MUCH WOULD YOU PAY FOR SUCH A CARD?
YOUR RIGHTS?
MORE INNOCENT LIVES?
WORLD PEACE?
STOP

The 9/11 card: Still in use today.

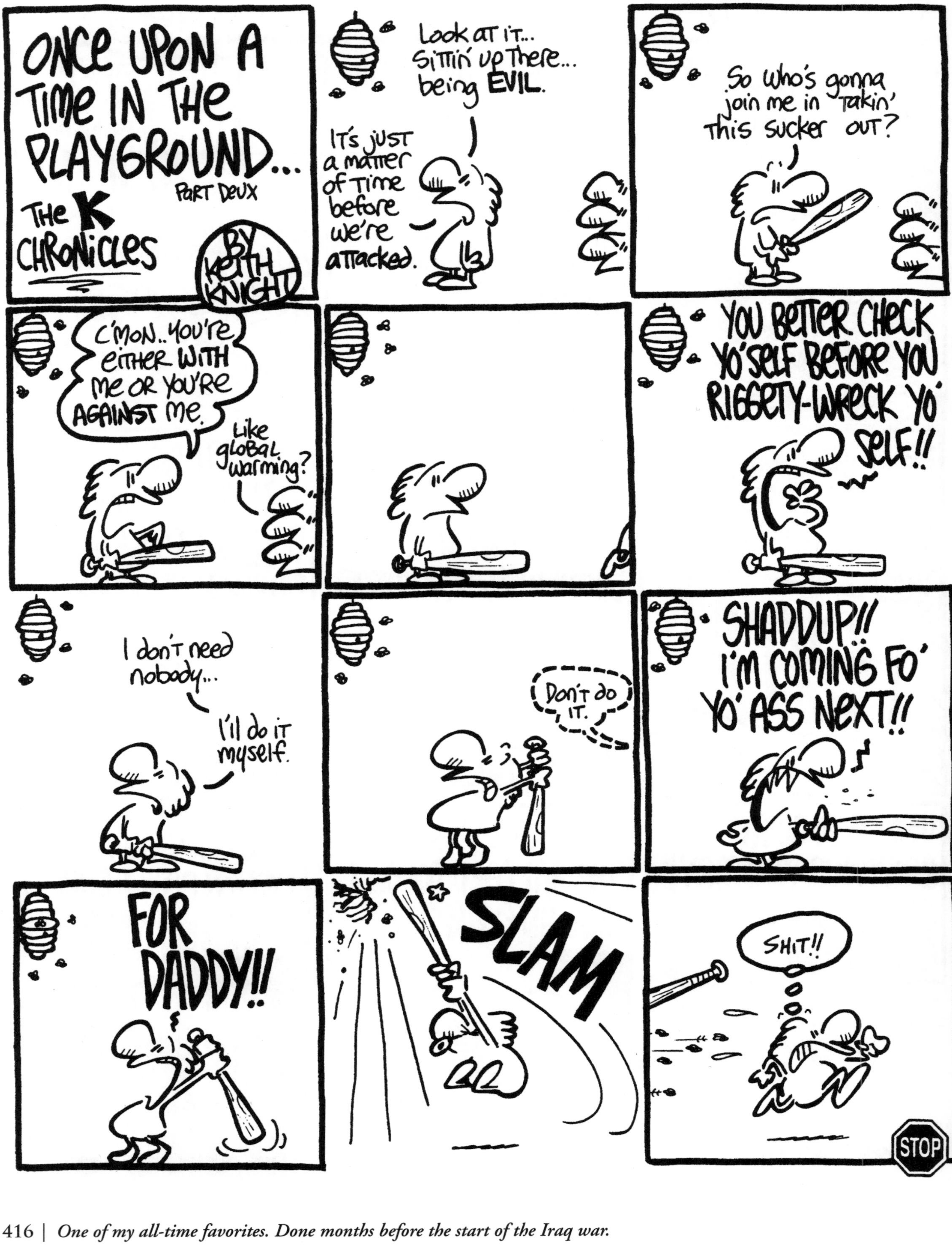
ONCE UPON A TIME IN THE PLAYGROUND...
PART DEUX
THE K CHRONICLES
BY KEITH KNIGHT
Look at it... Sittin' up there... being EVIL.
It's just a matter of time before we're attacked.
So who's gonna join me in takin' this sucker out?
C'MON.. You're either WITH me or you're AGAINST me.
Like global warming?
YOU BETTER CHECK YO'SELF BEFORE YOU RIGGETY-WRECK YO' SELF!!
I don't need nobody...
I'll do it myself.
Don't do it.
SHADDUP!! I'M COMING FO' YO' ASS NEXT!!
FOR DADDY!!
SLAM
SHIT!!
STOP

 One of my all-time favorites. Done months before the start of the Iraq war.

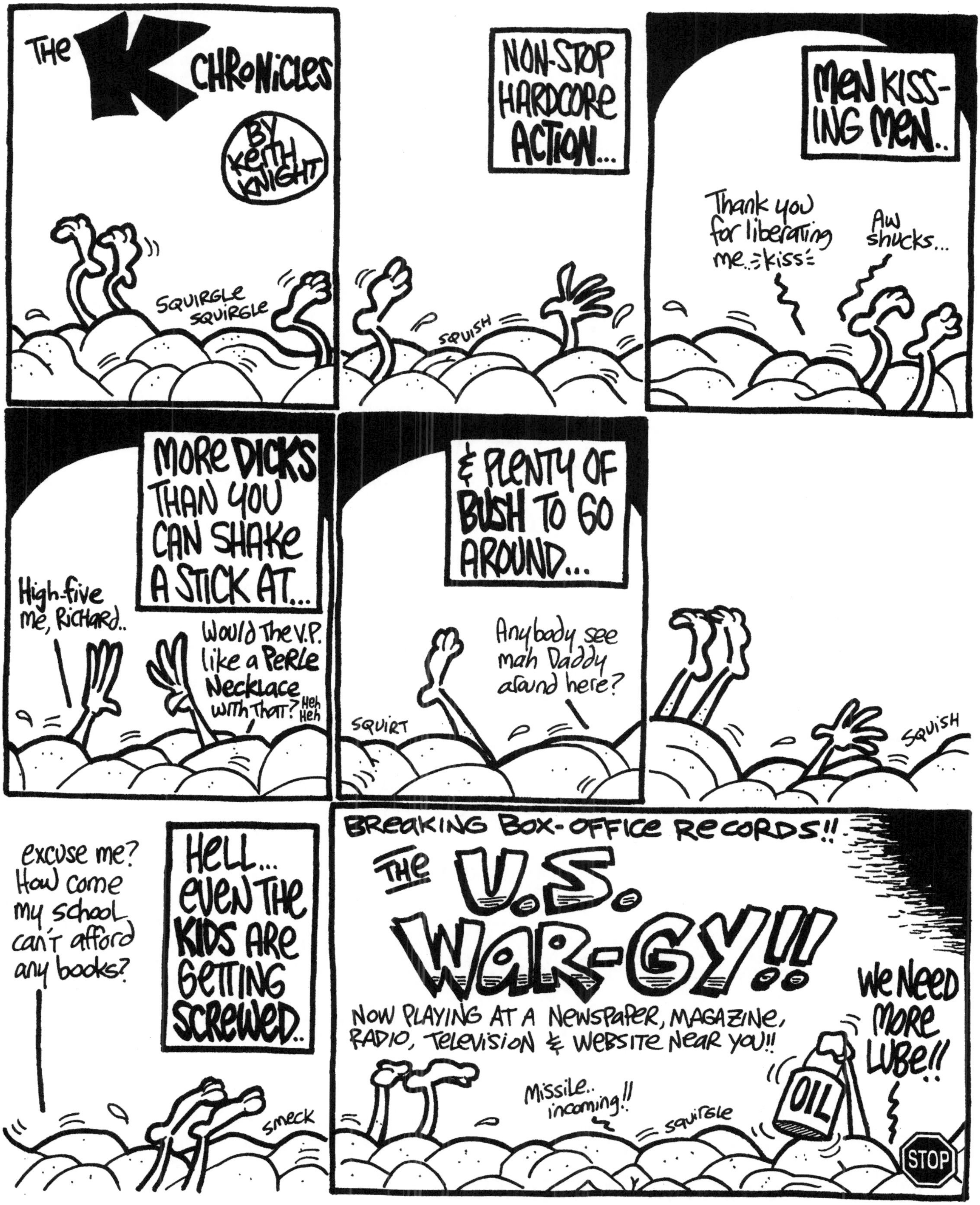
THE K CHRONICLES
BY KEITH KNIGHT
SQUIRGLE SQUIRGLE
NON-STOP HARDCORE ACTION...
SQUISH
MEN KISSING MEN..
Thank you for liberating me..kiss
Aw shucks...
MORE DICKS THAN YOU CAN SHAKE A STICK AT...
High-five me, Richard..
Would the V.P. like a PERLE NECKLACE with that? Heh Heh
& PLENTY OF BUSH TO GO AROUND...
SQUIRT
Anybody see mah Daddy around here?
SQUISH
Excuse me? How come my school can't afford any books?
HELL... EVEN THE KIDS ARE GETTING SCREWED..
SMECK
BREAKING BOX-OFFICE RECORDS!!
THE U.S. WAR-GY!!
NOW PLAYING AT A NEWSPAPER, MAGAZINE, RADIO, TELEVISION & WEBSITE NEAR YOU!!
WE NEED MORE LUBE!!
Missile.. incoming!!
squirgle
OIL
STOP

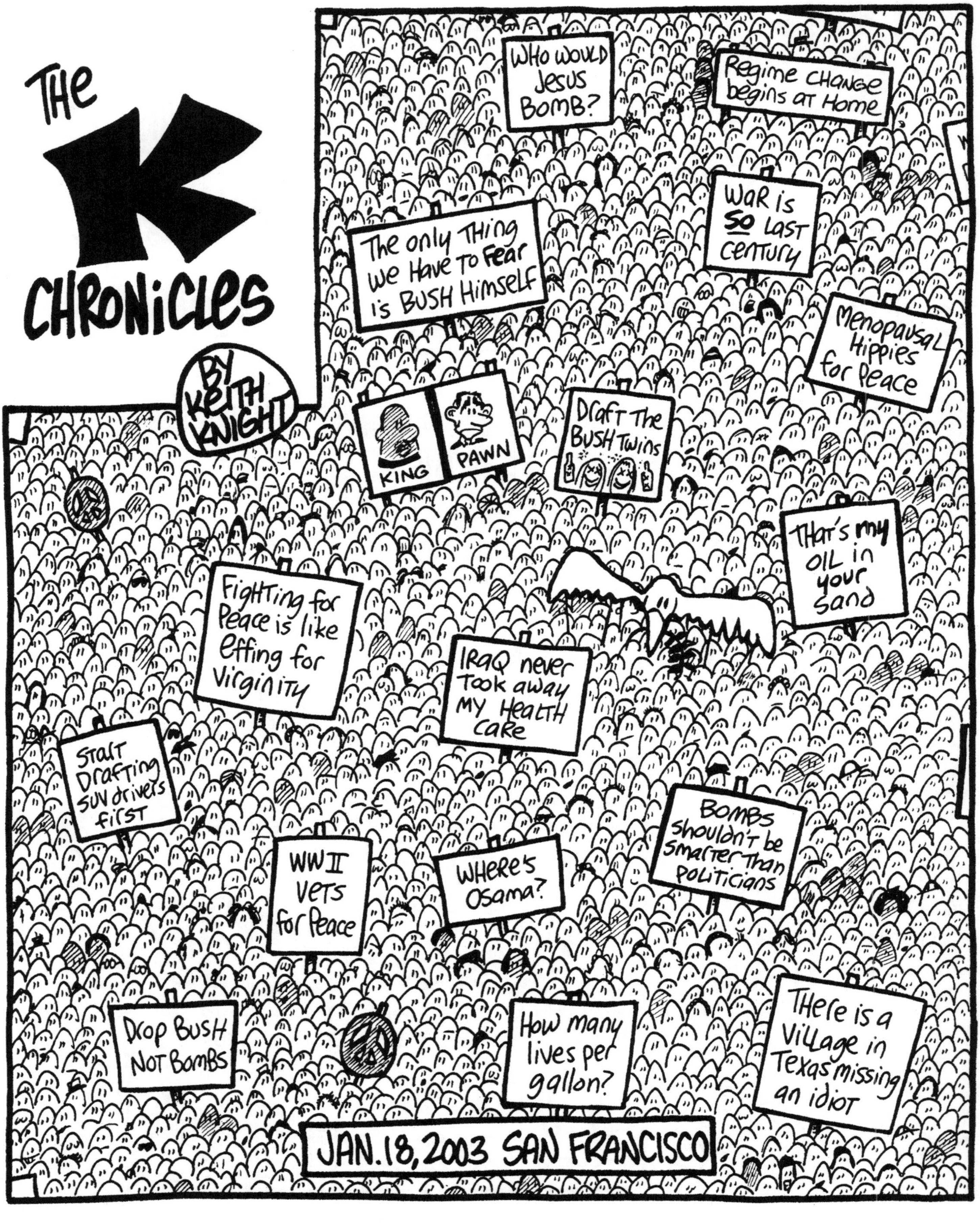
THE K CHRONICLES
BY KEITH KNIGHT
WHO WOULD JESUS BOMB?
Regime CHANGE begins at Home
WaR is SO LasT century
The only THing we Have To Fear is BUSH Himself
Menopausal Hippies for Peace
KING
PAWN
Draft The BUSH Twins
THaT's my OIL in your Sand
Fighting for Peace is like effing for Virginity
IRAQ never Took away MY HealTH care
Start Drafting SUV drivers first
BOMBS shouldn't be SmarTer Than POLITICians
WW II VETS for Peace
WHere's Osama?
Drop BusH NOT BomBS
How many lives per gallon?
THere is a Village in Texas missing an idiot
JAN. 18, 2003 SAN FRANCISCO

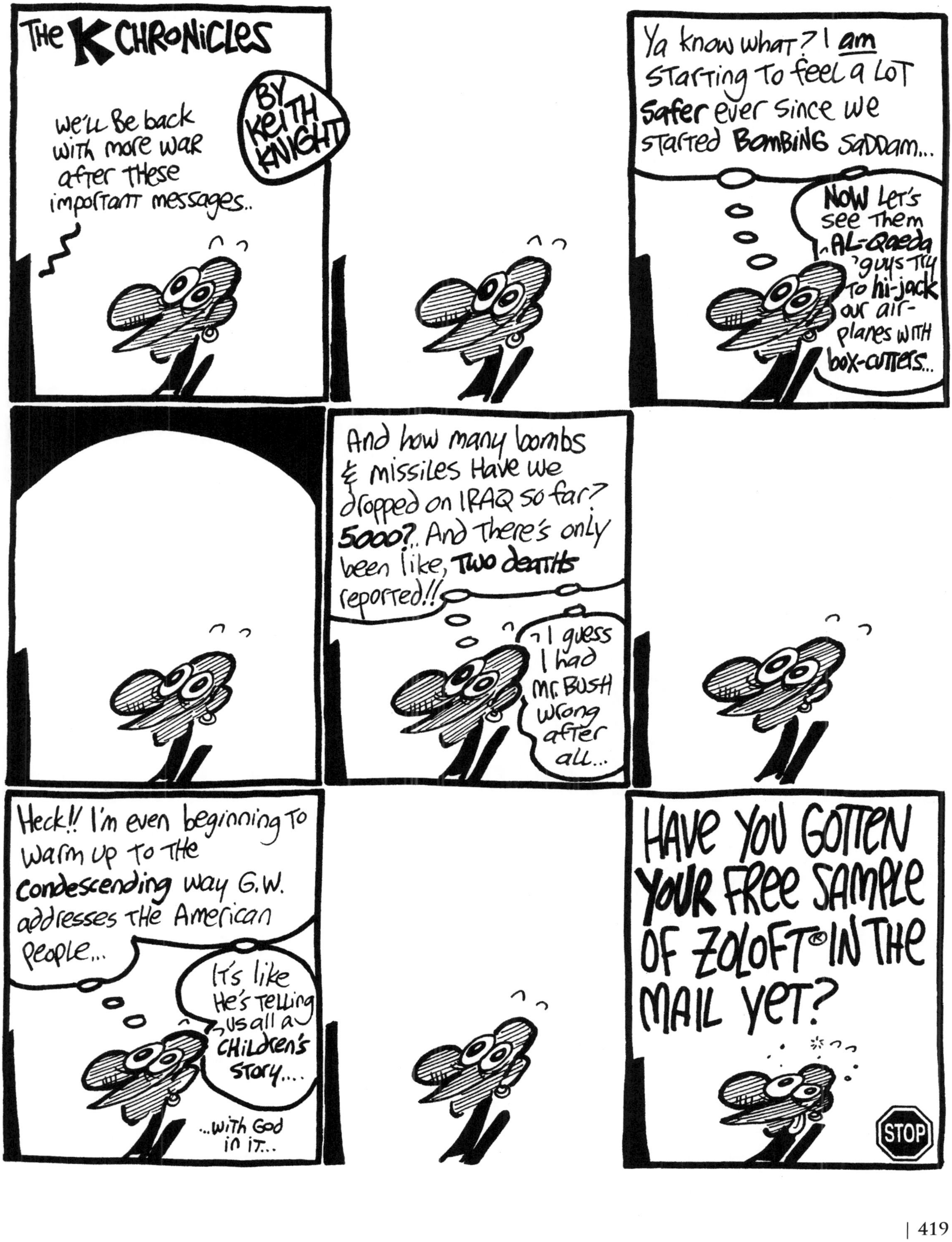

THE K CHRONICLES
BY KEITH KNIGHT
We'll Be back with more war after these important messages..
Ya know what? I am starting to feel a lot safer ever since we started Bombing Saddam...
Now let's see them Al-Qaeda guys try to hi-jack our air-planes with box-cutters...
And how many bombs & missiles have we dropped on IRAQ so far? 5000?.. And there's only been like, two deaths reported!!
I guess I had Mr. Bush wrong after all...
Heck!! I'm even beginning to warm up to the condescending way G.W. addresses the American people...
It's like he's telling us all a children's story....
...with God in it...
HAVE YOU GOTTEN YOUR FREE SAMPLE OF ZOLOFT® IN THE MAIL YET?
STOP

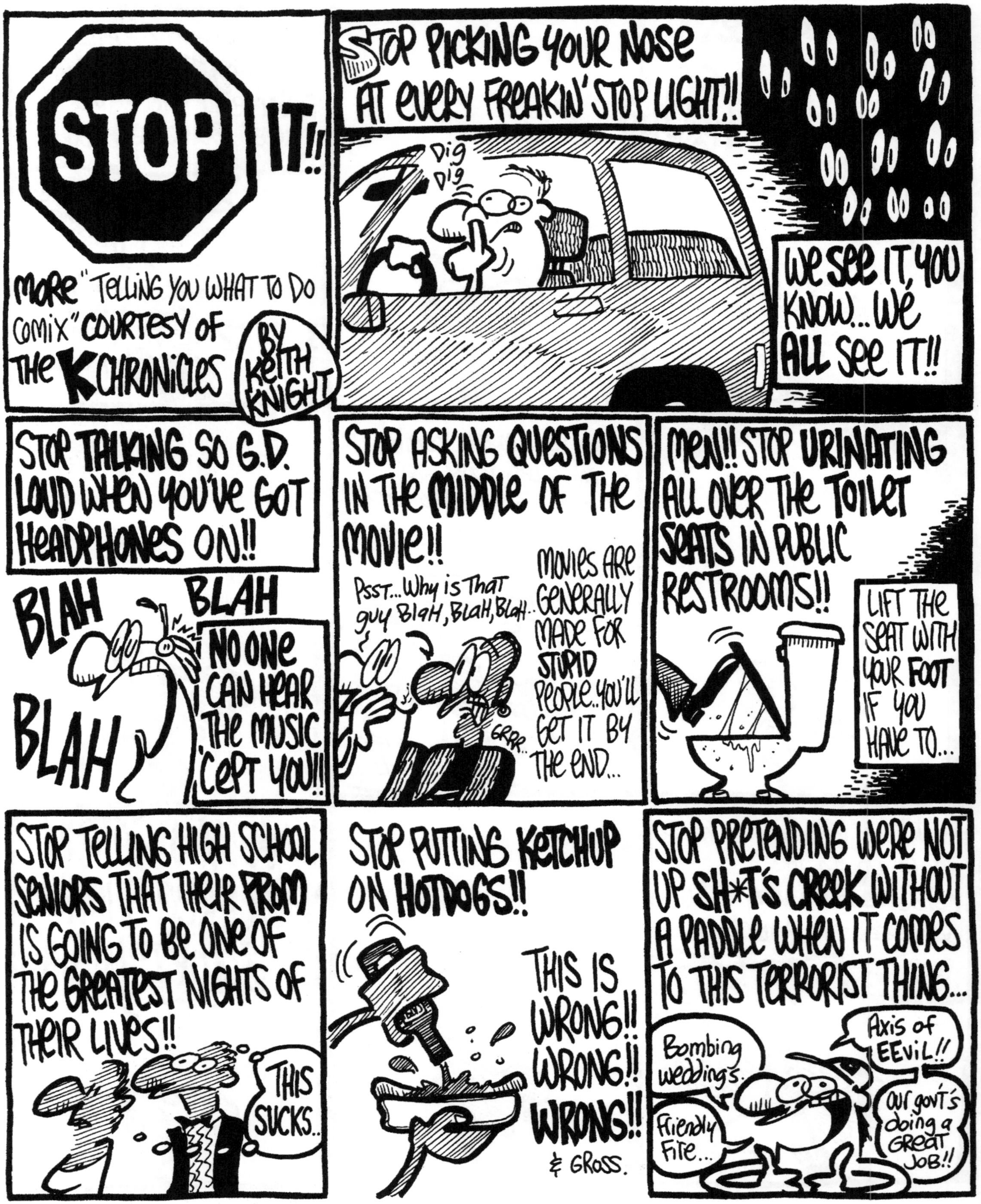
STOP IT!!
MORE "TELLING YOU WHAT TO DO COMIX" COURTESY OF THE K CHRONICLES
BY KEITH KNIGHT
STOP PICKING YOUR NOSE AT EVERY FREAKIN' STOP LIGHT!!
DIG DIG
WE SEE IT, YOU KNOW... WE ALL SEE IT!!
STOP TALKING SO G.D. LOUD WHEN YOU'VE GOT HEADPHONES ON!!
BLAH
BLAH
BLAH
NO ONE CAN HEAR THE MUSIC 'CEPT YOU!!
STOP ASKING QUESTIONS IN THE MIDDLE OF THE MOVIE!!
Psst... Why is That guy Blah, Blah, Blah...
GRRR...
MOVIES ARE GENERALLY MADE FOR STUPID PEOPLE.. YOU'LL GET IT BY THE END...
MEN!! STOP URINATING ALL OVER THE TOILET SEATS IN PUBLIC RESTROOMS!!
LIFT THE SEAT WITH YOUR FOOT IF YOU HAVE TO...
STOP TELLING HIGH SCHOOL SENIORS THAT THEIR PROM IS GOING TO BE ONE OF THE GREATEST NIGHTS OF THEIR LIVES!!
THIS SUCKS..
STOP PUTTING KETCHUP ON HOTDOGS!!
THIS IS WRONG!! WRONG!! WRONG!!
& GROSS.
STOP PRETENDING WE'RE NOT UP SH*T'S CREEK WITHOUT A PADDLE WHEN IT COMES TO THIS TERRORIST THING...
Bombing weddings.
Axis of EEviL!!
Friendly Fire...
Our govt's doing a GREAT JOB!!

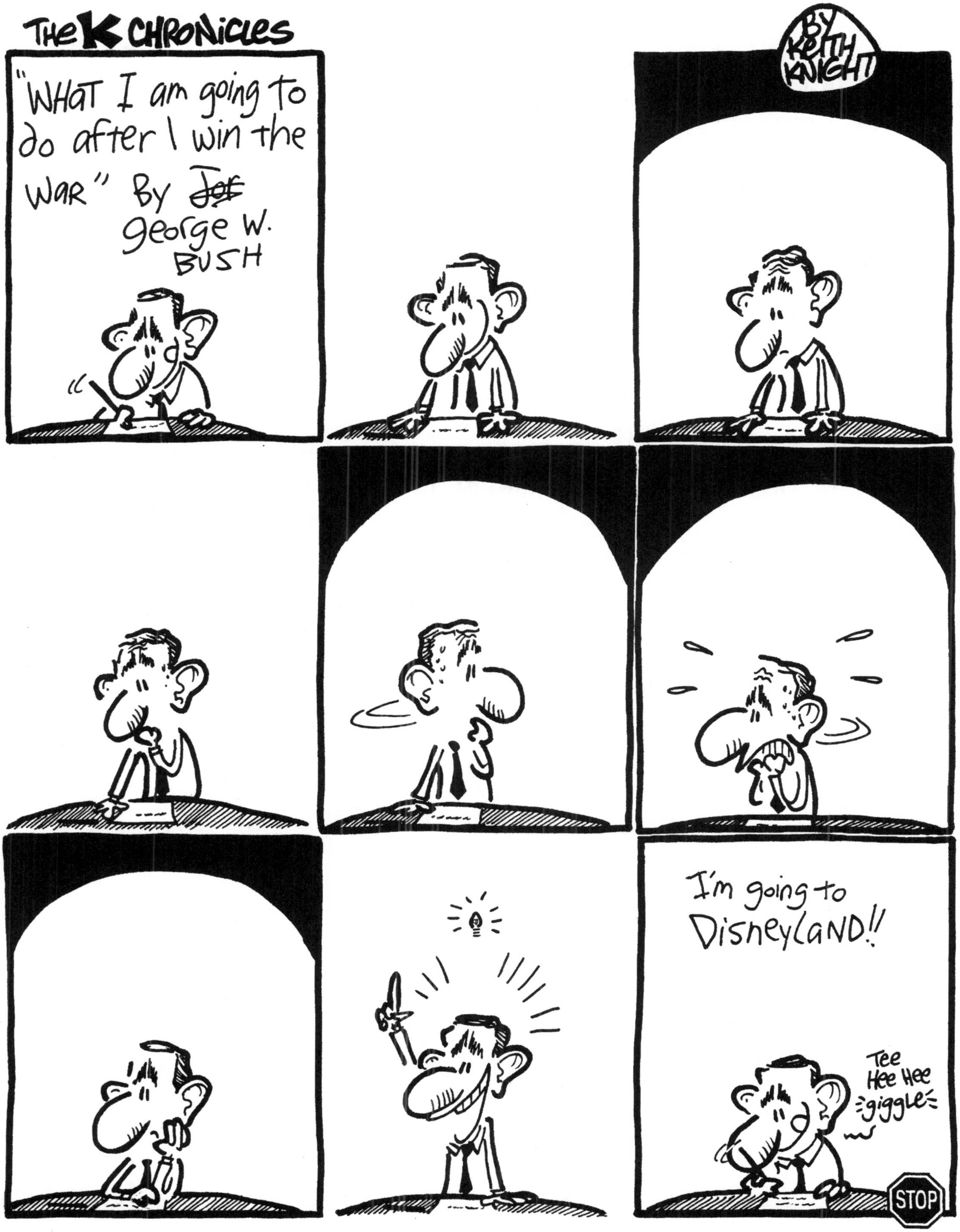
THE K CHRONICLES
BY KEITH KNIGHT
"WHAT I am going to do after I win the WAR" By ~~Joe~~ george W. BUSH
I'm going to DisneyLAND!!
Tee Hee Hee
giggle
STOP

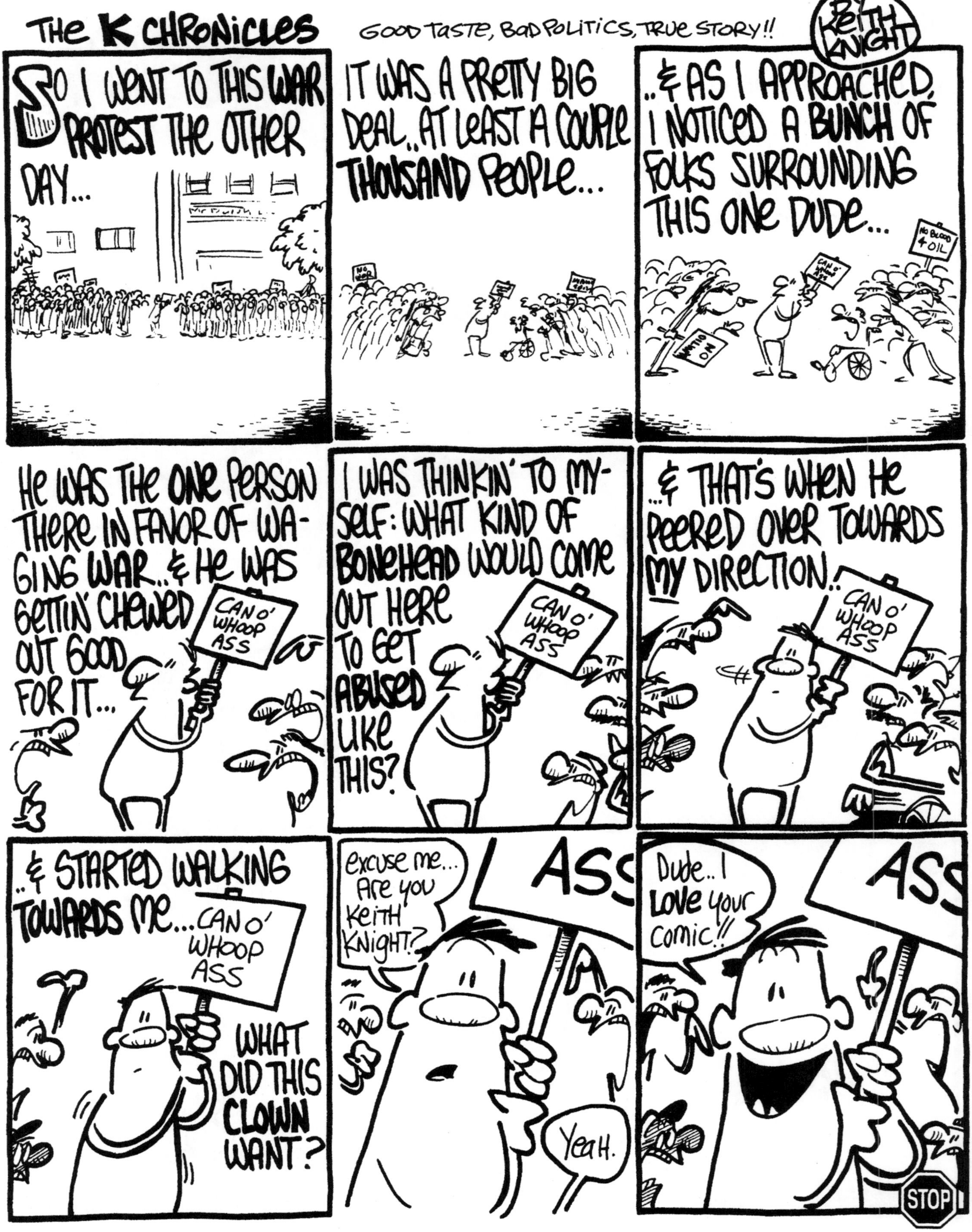
THE K CHRONICLES
GOOD TASTE, BAD POLITICS, TRUE STORY!!
BY KEITH KNIGHT
SO I WENT TO THIS WAR PROTEST THE OTHER DAY...
IT WAS A PRETTY BIG DEAL.. AT LEAST A COUPLE THOUSAND PEOPLE...
NO WAR
..& AS I APPROACHED, I NOTICED A BUNCH OF FOLKS SURROUNDING THIS ONE DUDE...
NO BLOOD 4 OIL
NO WAR 4 OIL
CAN O' WHOOP ASS
HE WAS THE ONE PERSON THERE IN FAVOR OF WAGING WAR.. & HE WAS GETTIN' CHEWED OUT GOOD FOR IT...
CAN O' WHOOP ASS
I WAS THINKIN' TO MYSELF: WHAT KIND OF BONEHEAD WOULD COME OUT HERE TO GET ABUSED LIKE THIS?
CAN O' WHOOP ASS
...& THAT'S WHEN HE PEERED OVER TOWARDS MY DIRECTION...
CAN O' WHOOP ASS
..& STARTED WALKING TOWARDS ME...
CAN O' WHOOP ASS
WHAT DID THIS CLOWN WANT?
excuse me... Are you Keith Knight?
ASS
YeaH.
Dude.. I Love your comic!!
ASS
STOP

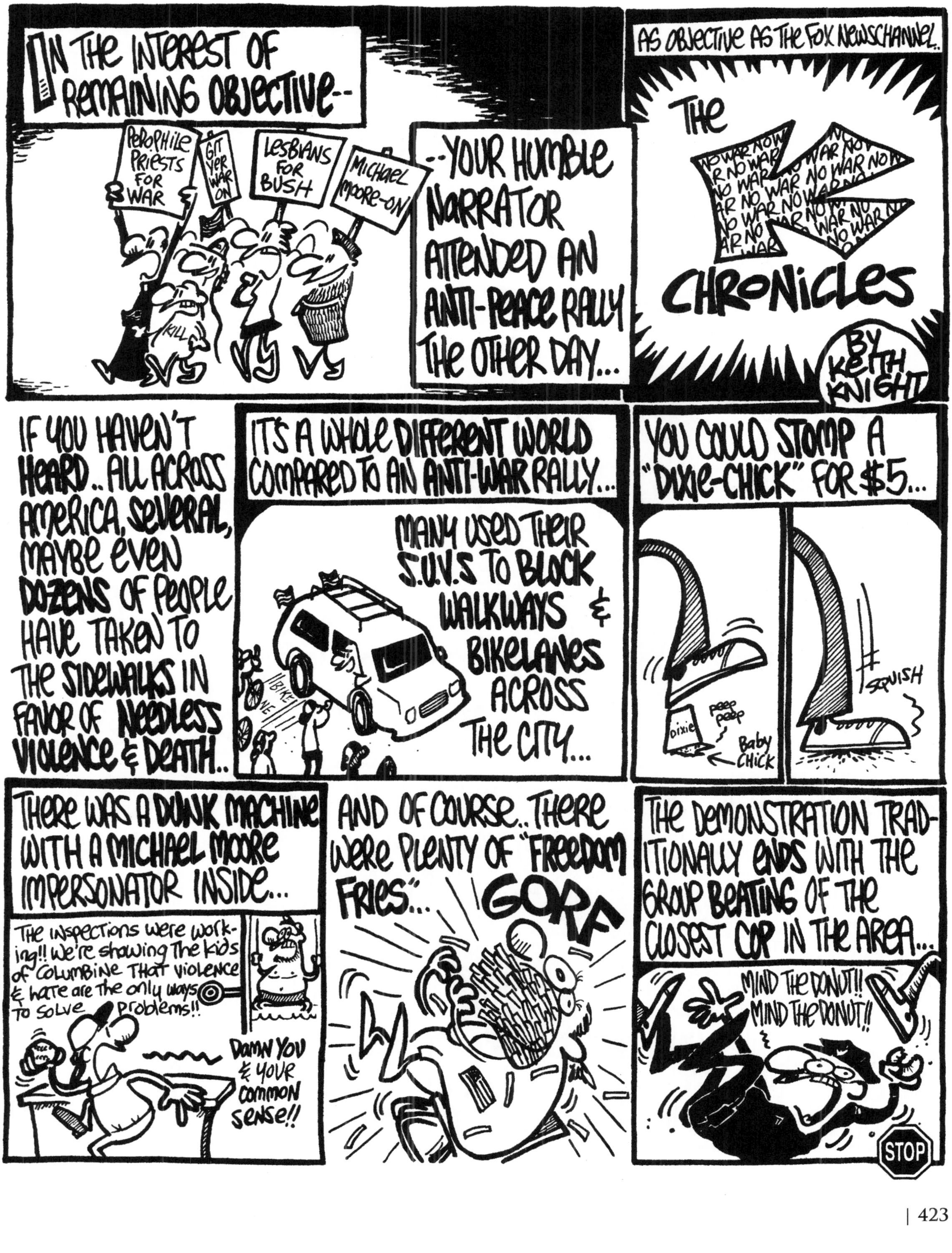
In the interest of remaining objective--
Pedophile Priests for War
Git yer war on
Lesbians for Bush
Michael Moore-on
--Your humble narrator attended an anti-peace rally the other day...
As objective as the Fox News Channel..
The K Chronicles
No war no war
By Keith Knight
If you haven't heard.. All across America, several, maybe even dozens of people have taken to the sidewalks in favor of needless violence & death..
It's a whole different world compared to an anti-war rally...
Many used their S.U.V.S to block walkways & bikelanes across the city...
Bike lane
You could stomp a "Dixie-Chick" for $5...
Dixie
peep peep
Baby chick
Squish
There was a dunk machine with a Michael Moore impersonator inside...
The inspections were working!! We're showing the kids of Columbine that violence & hate are the only ways to solve problems!!
Damn you & your common sense!!
And of course.. There were plenty of "Freedom Fries"...
Gorf
The demonstration traditionally ends with the group beating of the closest cop in the area...
Mind the donut!! Mind the donut!!
Stop

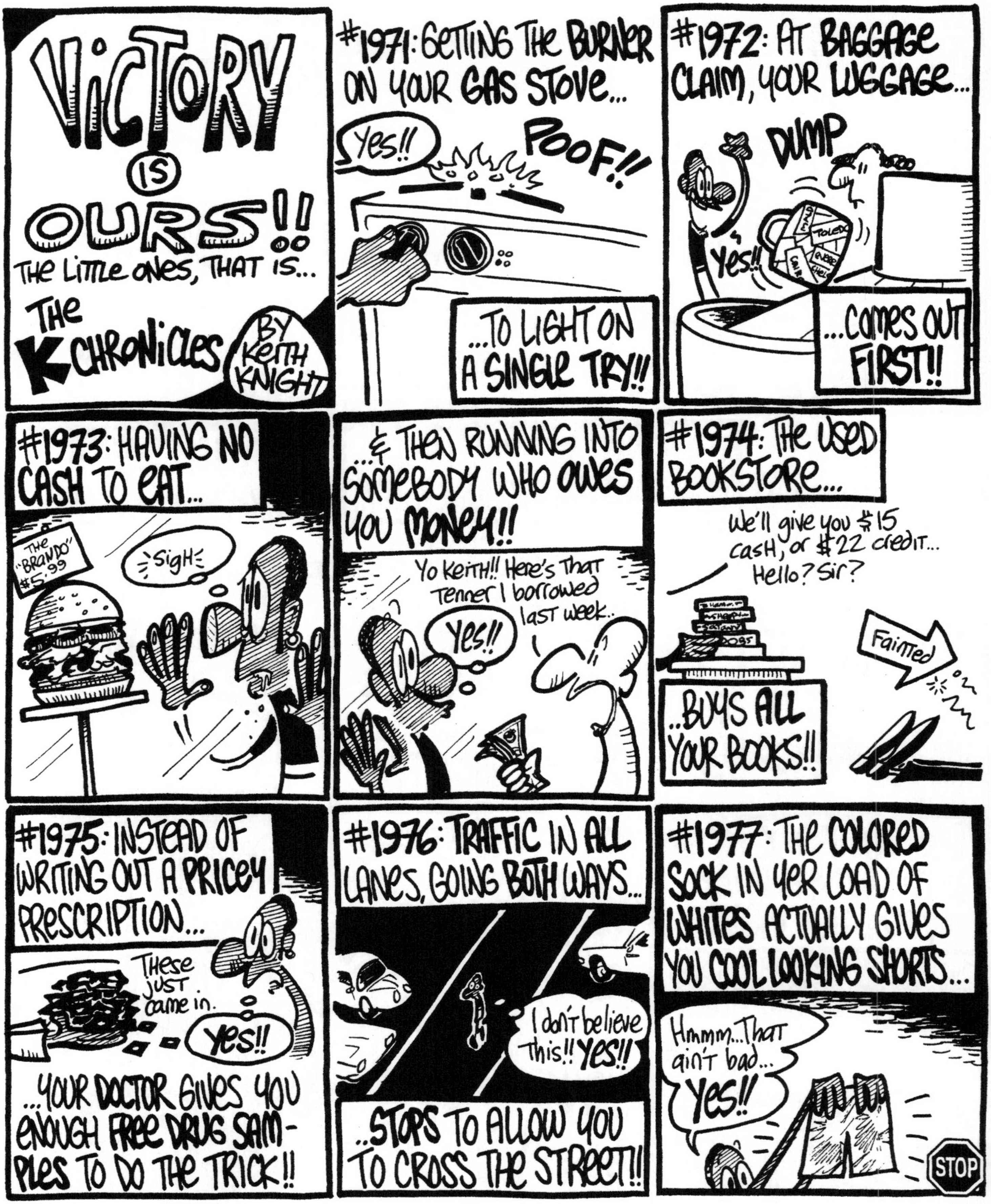
VICTORY IS OURS!!
THE LITTLE ONES, THAT IS...
THE K CHRONICLES
BY KEITH KNIGHT
#1971: GETTING THE BURNER ON YOUR GAS STOVE...
Yes!!
POOF!!
...TO LIGHT ON A SINGLE TRY!!
#1972: AT BAGGAGE CLAIM, YOUR LUGGAGE...
DUMP
Yes!!
TOLEDO
...COMES OUT FIRST!!
#1973: HAVING NO CASH TO EAT...
THE "BRANDO" $5.99
SIGH
...& THEN RUNNING INTO SOMEBODY WHO OWES YOU MONEY!!
Yo Keith!! Here's that tenner I borrowed last week..
Yes!!
#1974: THE USED BOOKSTORE...
We'll give you $15 cash, or $22 credit... Hello? Sir?
Fainted
...BUYS ALL YOUR BOOKS!!
#1975: INSTEAD OF WRITING OUT A PRICEY PRESCRIPTION...
These just came in.
Yes!!
...YOUR DOCTOR GIVES YOU ENOUGH FREE DRUG SAMPLES TO DO THE TRICK!!
#1976: TRAFFIC IN ALL LANES, GOING BOTH WAYS...
I don't believe this!! Yes!!
...STOPS TO ALLOW YOU TO CROSS THE STREET!!
#1977: THE COLORED SOCK IN YER LOAD OF WHITES ACTUALLY GIVES YOU COOL LOOKING SHORTS...
Hmmm...That ain't bad... Yes!!
STOP

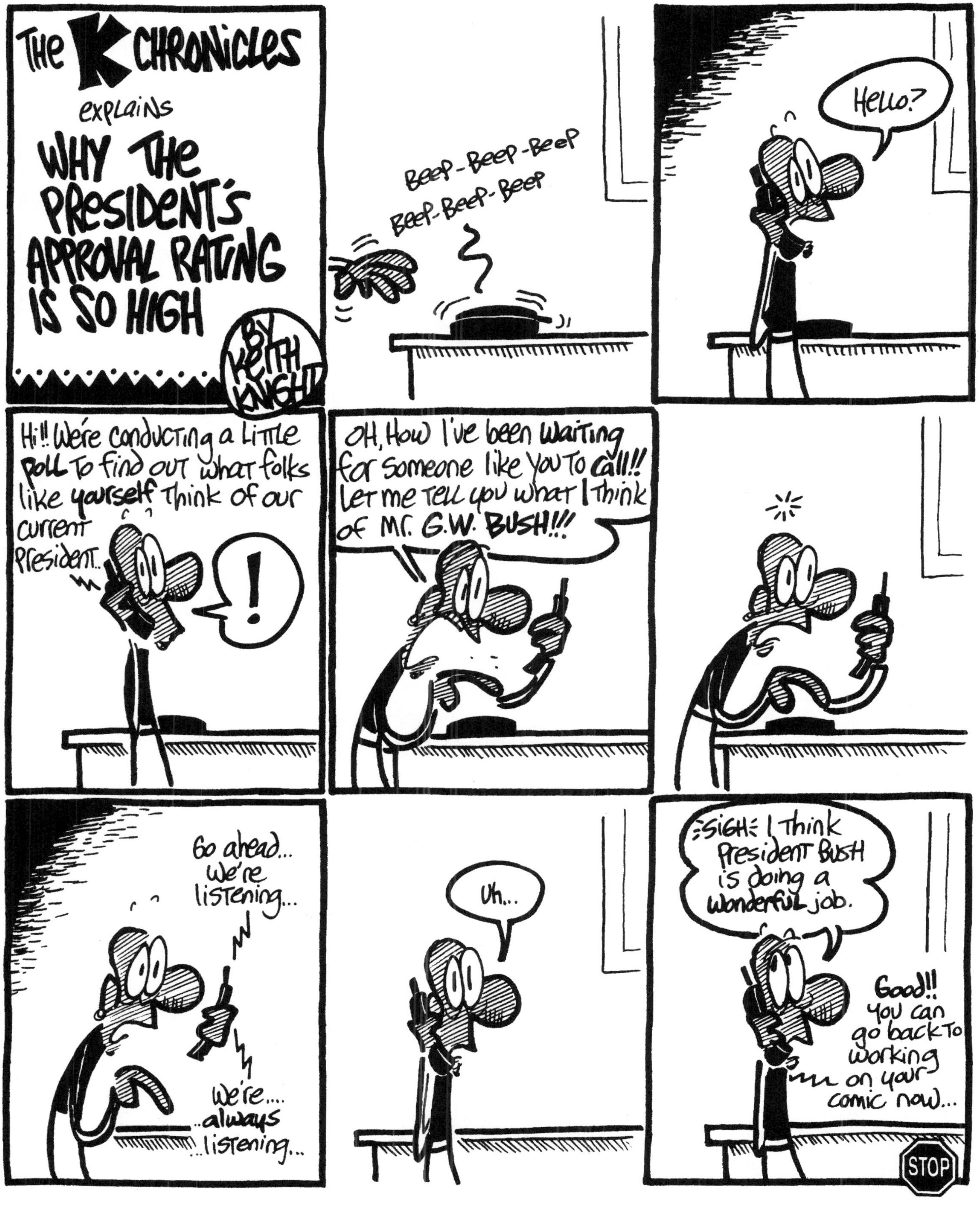

THE K CHRONICLES
explains
WHY THE PRESIDENT'S APPROVAL RATING IS SO HIGH
BY KEITH KNIGHT
BEEP-BEEP-BEEP
BEEP-BEEP-BEEP
HELLO?
Hi!! We're conducting a little poll to find out what folks like yourself think of our current president..
!
OH, How I've been waiting for someone like you to call!! Let me tell you what I think of Mr. G.W. BUSH!!!
Go ahead... We're listening...
We're.... ..always ...listening...
Uh...
=SIGH= I think President BUSH is doing a wonderful job.
Good!! You can go back to working on your comic now...
STOP

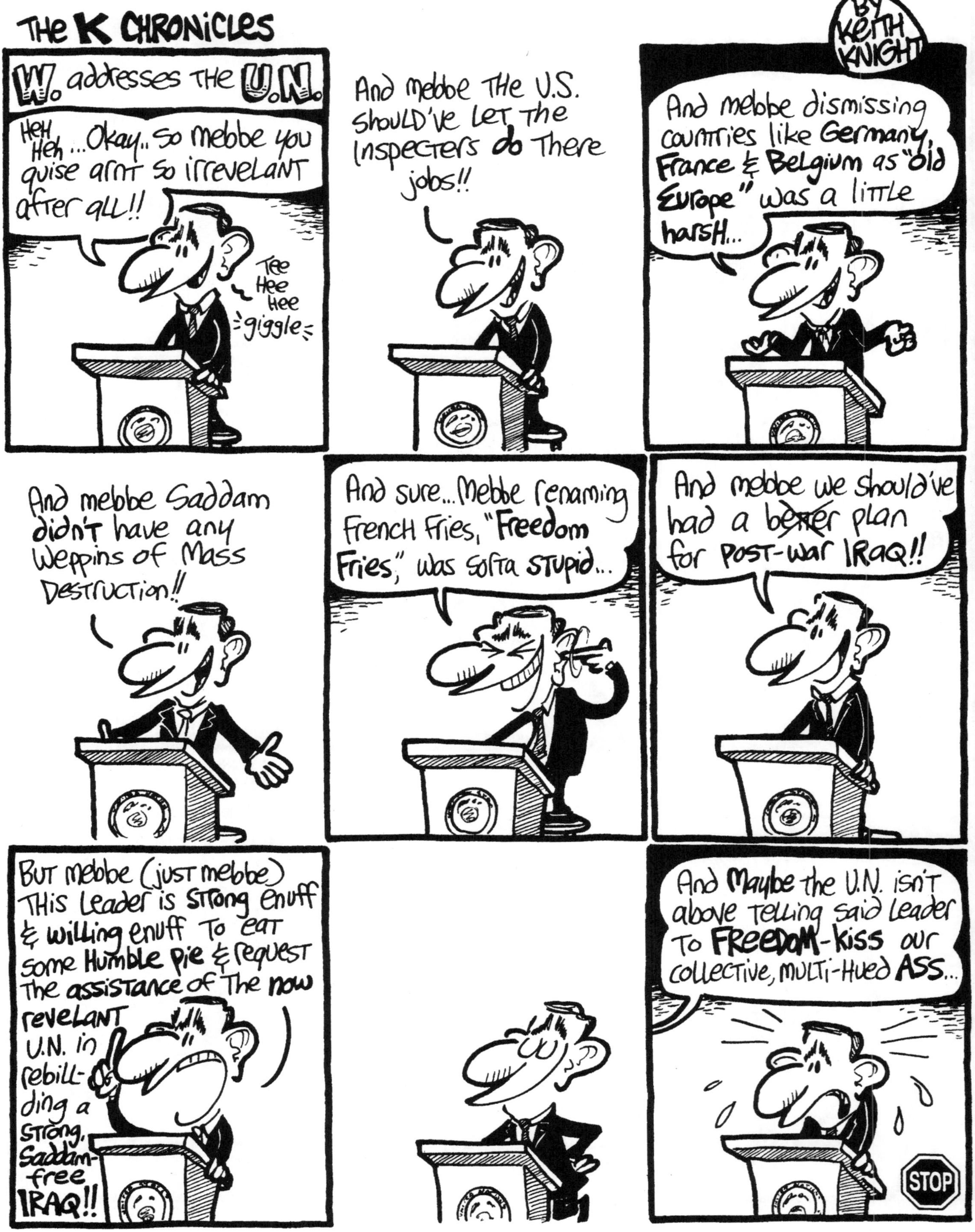
THE K CHRONICLES
BY KEITH KNIGHT
W. addresses the U.N.
Heh Heh ...Okay.. So mebbe you guise arnt so irrevelant after all!!
Tee Hee Hee giggle
And mebbe the U.S. should've let the inspecters do there jobs!!
And mebbe dismissing countries like Germany, France & Belgium as "old Europe" was a little harsh...
And mebbe Saddam didn't have any Weppins of Mass Destruction!!
And sure... Mebbe renaming French Fries, "Freedom Fries," was sorta stupid...
And mebbe we should've had a better plan for post-war IRAQ!!
But mebbe (just mebbe) this leader is strong enuff & willing enuff to eat some Humble pie & request the assistance of the now revelant U.N. in rebill-ding a strong, Saddam-free IRAQ!!
And Maybe the U.N. isn't above telling said leader to FREEDOM-kiss our collective, multi-hued ASS...
STOP

WHENEVER I COME ACROSS SOMEBODY IN A **MILITARY UNIFORM**, I MAKE IT A **POINT** TO ACKNOWLEDGE THE SACRIFICE THEY'RE MAKING FOR THIS COUNTRY...

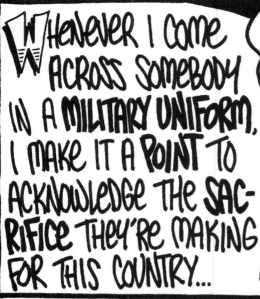

LET ME *profusely* apologize on behalf of the American people for your Commander-in-chief...

Yeah... He's sure keepin' us busy..

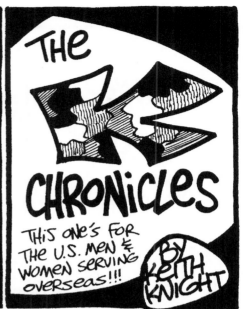

THE K CHRONICLES

THIS ONE'S FOR THE U.S. MEN & WOMEN SERVING OVERSEAS!!!

BY KEITH KNIGHT

HE'S ALREADY **CUT VETERAN'S BENEFITS**..HE WANTED TO CUT **MILITARY PAY**..& HE'S MOTIVATING **OPPOSING FACTIONS** BY TELLING THEM TO--

BRING IT ON!! Tee Hee Hee ≥giggle≤

STATEMENTS LIKE THAT REMIND ME OF **LOUDMOUTH PRO ATHLETES**..AT LEAST **ONCE A YEAR**, THE **PRESS** ASKS A **PLAYER** OF A **HEAVILY FAVORED** TEAM ABOUT AN **UPCOMING OPPONENT**...

So.. What d'ya think their chances are against you next week?

(A REAL ARROGANT & SMUG ANSWER THAT THE OPPOSING COACH CAN USE TO MOTIVATE HIS PLAYERS)

WHATEVER HAPPENED TO GOOD OLD-FASHIONED **HUMILITY**? WHATEVER HAPPENED TO--

Speak softly & carry a **BIG STICK**!!

HERE'S AN **IDEA**: IF MR. **AWOL** DECIDES TO **DON** ANOTHER **MILITARY UNIFORM** & PLAY **FLY-BOY** FOR ANOTHER **PHOTO-OP**, I SUGGEST THAT THE PILOT TAKE HIM TO **IRAQ**, DROP HIM OFF, & BRING ONE OF OUR **SOLDIERS HOME** TO THEIR **FAMILY**..

Hey!! Whoa!! Where are we going, soldier?

Just a little **DETOUR**, Mr. President...

STOP

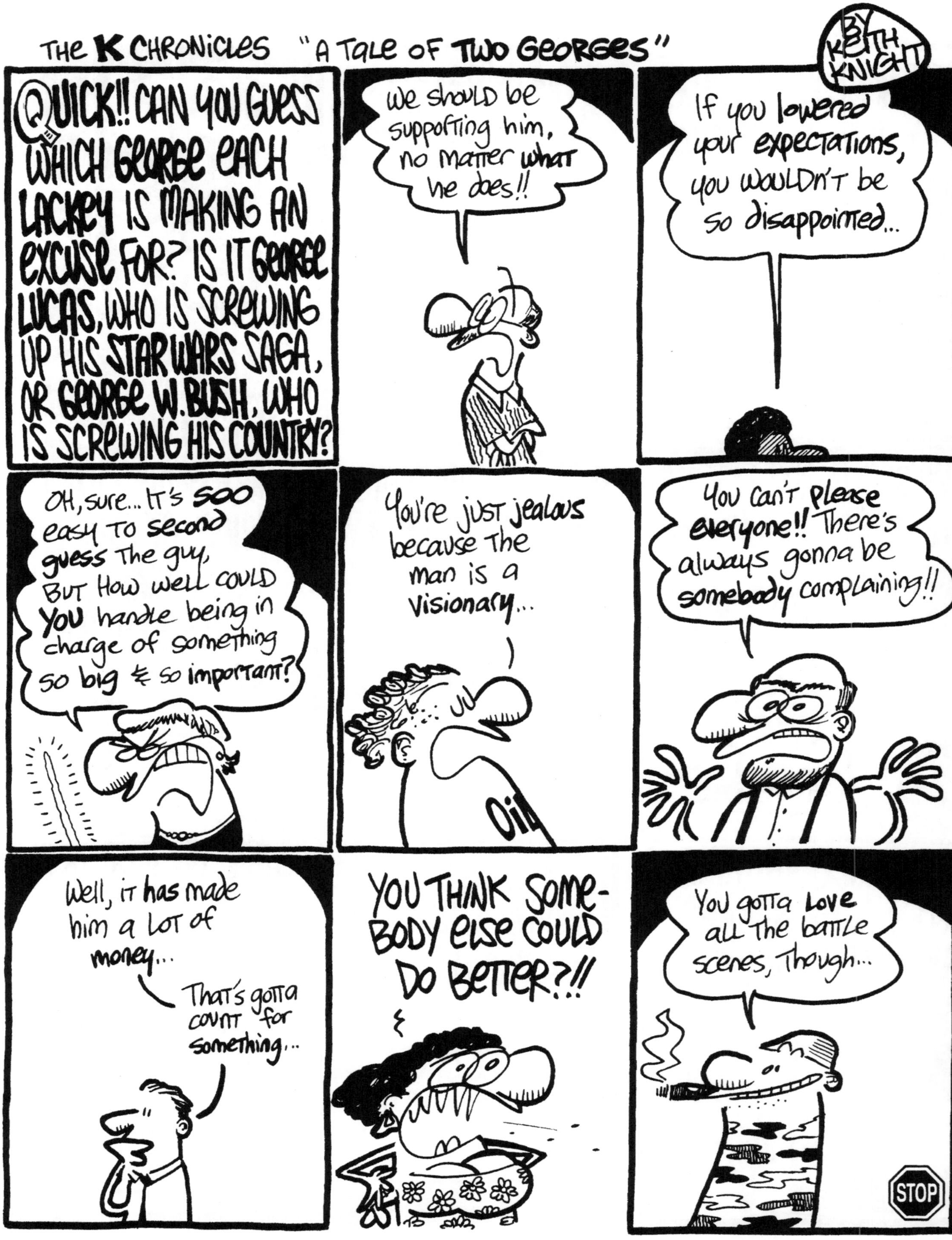
THE K CHRONICLES "A TALE OF TWO GEORGES"
BY KEITH KNIGHT
QUICK!! CAN YOU GUESS WHICH GEORGE EACH LACKEY IS MAKING AN EXCUSE FOR? IS IT GEORGE LUCAS, WHO IS SCREWING UP HIS STAR WARS SAGA, OR GEORGE W. BUSH, WHO IS SCREWING HIS COUNTRY?
We should be supporting him, no matter what he does!!
If you lowered your expectations, you wouldn't be so disappointed...
OH, sure... It's soo easy to second guess the guy, But How well could you handle being in charge of something so big & so important?
You're just jealous because the man is a visionary...
Oil
You can't please everyone!! There's always gonna be somebody complaining!!
Well, it has made him a lot of money...
That's gotta count for something...
YOU THINK SOME-BODY ELSE COULD DO BETTER?!!
You gotta love all the battle scenes, though...
STOP

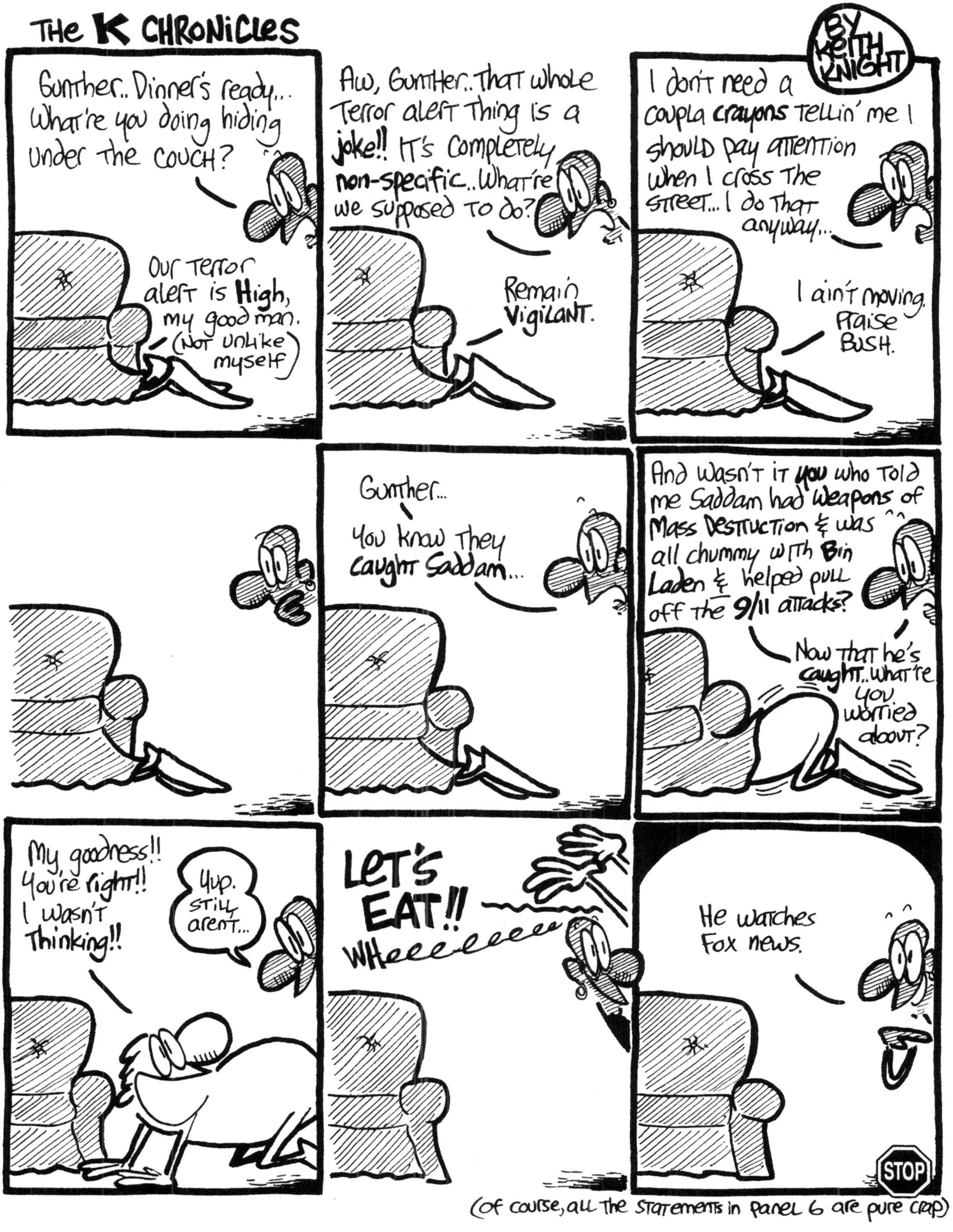
THE K CHRONICLES
BY KEITH KNIGHT
Gunther.. Dinner's ready... What're you doing hiding under the couch?
Our terror alert is High, my good man. (Not unlike myself)
Aw, Gunther.. That whole terror alert thing is a joke!! It's completely non-specific.. What're we supposed to do?
Remain Vigilant.
I don't need a coupla crayons tellin' me I should pay attention when I cross the street... I do that anyway...
I ain't moving. Praise Bush.
Gunther...
You know they caught Saddam...
And wasn't it you who told me Saddam had Weapons of Mass Destruction & was all chummy with Bin Laden & helped pull off the 9/11 attacks?
Now that he's caught.. what're you worried about?
My goodness!! You're right!! I wasn't thinking!!
Yup. Still aren't...
LET'S EAT!!
WHeeeeeeeee
He watches Fox news.
STOP
(Of course, all the statements in panel 6 are pure crap)

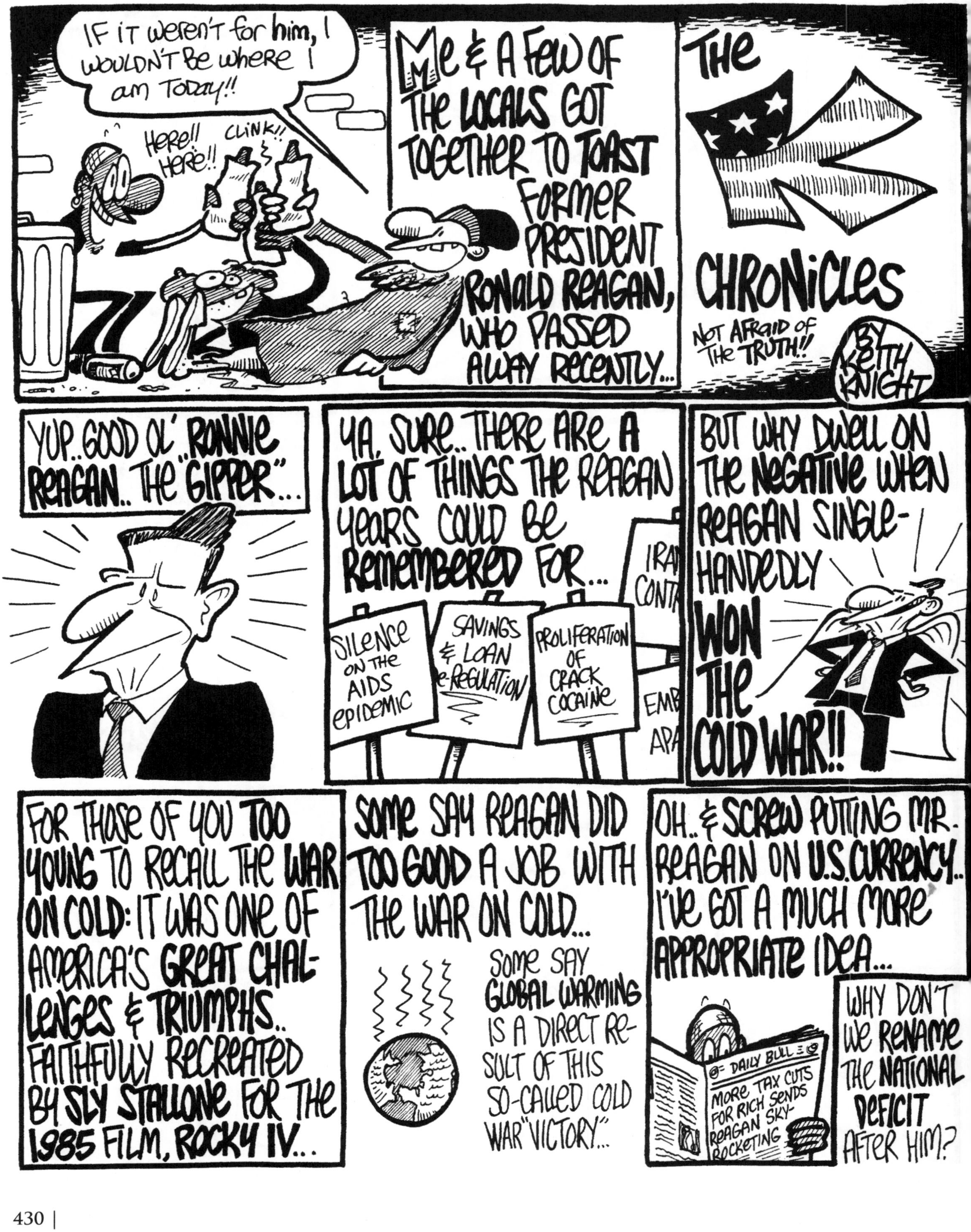
IF IT weren't for him, I WOULDN'T Be where I am TODAY!!
Here!! Here!!
CLINK!!
Me & A Few OF THE LOCALS GOT TOGETHER TO TOAST FORMER PRESIDENT RONALD REAGAN, WHO PASSED AWAY RECENTLY...
THE
CHRONICLES
NOT AFRAID OF THE TRUTH!!
BY KEITH KNIGHT
YUP.. GOOD OL' RONNIE REAGAN.. THE "GIPPER"...
YA, SURE.. THERE ARE A LOT OF THINGS THE REAGAN YEARS COULD BE REMEMBERED FOR...
SILENCE ON THE AIDS EPIDEMIC
SAVINGS & LOAN DE-REGULATION
PROLIFERATION OF CRACK COCAINE
BUT WHY DWELL ON THE NEGATIVE WHEN REAGAN SINGLE-HANDEDLY WON THE COLD WAR!!
FOR THOSE OF YOU TOO YOUNG TO RECALL THE WAR ON COLD: IT WAS ONE OF AMERICA'S GREAT CHAL-LENGES & TRIUMPHS.. FAITHFULLY RECREATED BY SLY STALLONE FOR THE 1985 FILM, ROCKY IV...
SOME SAY REAGAN DID TOO GOOD A JOB WITH THE WAR ON COLD...
SOME SAY GLOBAL WARMING IS A DIRECT RE-SULT OF THIS SO-CALLED COLD WAR "VICTORY"...
OH.. & SCREW PUTTING MR. REAGAN ON U.S. CURRENCY.. I'VE GOT A MUCH MORE APPROPRIATE IDEA...
DAILY BULL
MORE TAX CUTS FOR RICH SENDS REAGAN SKY-ROCKETING
WHY DON'T WE RENAME THE NATIONAL DEFICIT AFTER HIM?

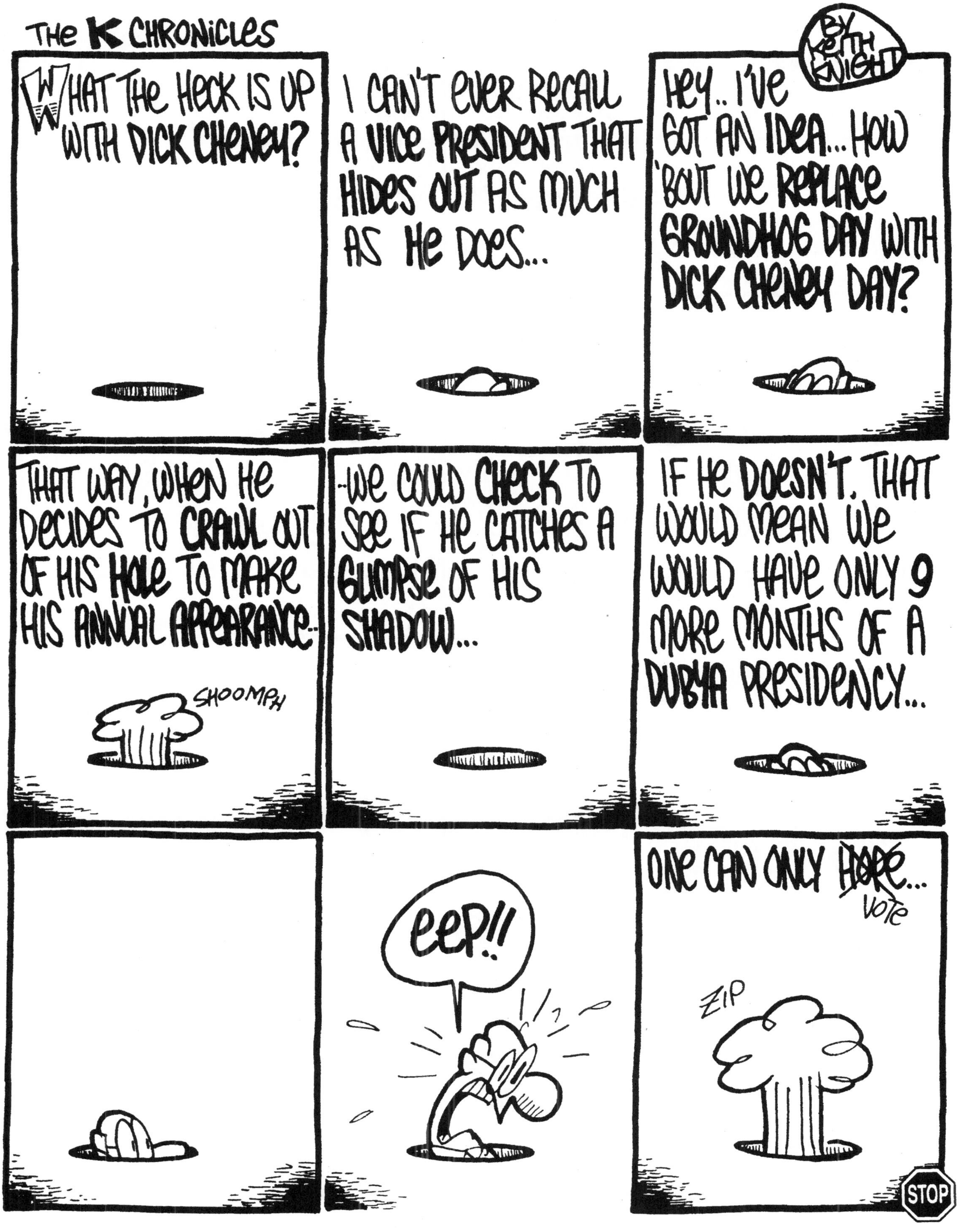
THE K CHRONICLES
BY KEITH KNIGHT
WHAT THE HECK IS UP WITH DICK CHENEY?
I CAN'T EVER RECALL A VICE PRESIDENT THAT HIDES OUT AS MUCH AS HE DOES...
HEY.. I'VE GOT AN IDEA... HOW 'BOUT WE REPLACE GROUNDHOG DAY WITH DICK CHENEY DAY?
THAT WAY, WHEN HE DECIDES TO CRAWL OUT OF HIS HOLE TO MAKE HIS ANNUAL APPEARANCE--
SHOOMPH
--WE COULD CHECK TO SEE IF HE CATCHES A GLIMPSE OF HIS SHADOW...
IF HE DOESN'T, THAT WOULD MEAN WE WOULD HAVE ONLY 9 MORE MONTHS OF A DUBYA PRESIDENCY...
EEP!!
ONE CAN ONLY HOPE... VOTE
ZIP
STOP

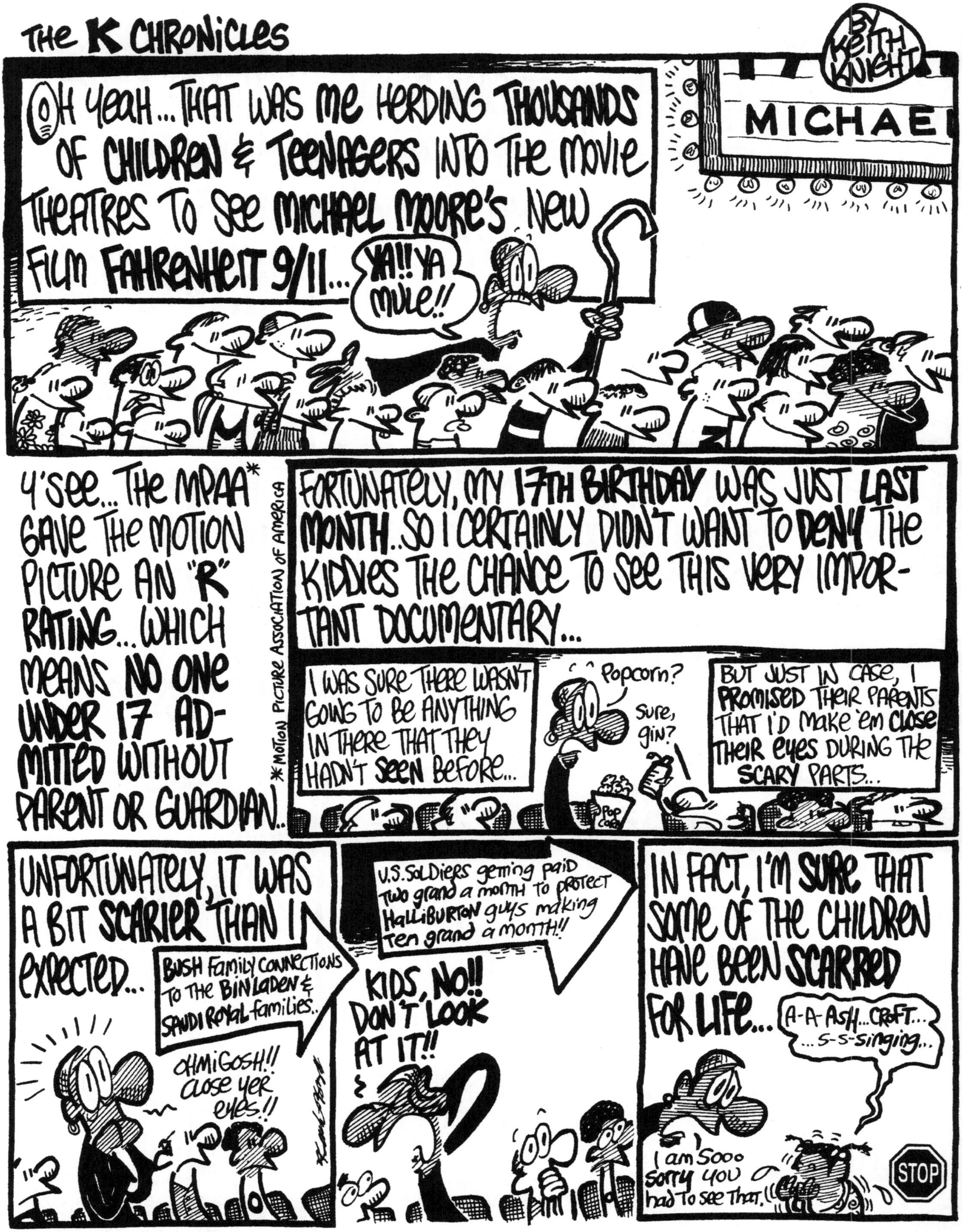
THE K CHRONICLES
BY KEITH KNIGHT
MICHAEL
OH YEAH... THAT WAS ME HERDING THOUSANDS OF CHILDREN & TEENAGERS INTO THE MOVIE THEATRES TO SEE MICHAEL MOORE'S NEW FILM FAHRENHEIT 9/11...
YA!! YA MULE!!
Y'SEE... THE MPAA* GAVE THE MOTION PICTURE AN "R" RATING... WHICH MEANS NO ONE UNDER 17 ADMITTED WITHOUT PARENT OR GUARDIAN..
*MOTION PICTURE ASSOCIATION OF AMERICA
FORTUNATELY, MY 17TH BIRTHDAY WAS JUST LAST MONTH.. SO I CERTAINLY DIDN'T WANT TO DENY THE KIDDIES THE CHANCE TO SEE THIS VERY IMPORTANT DOCUMENTARY...
I WAS SURE THERE WASN'T GOING TO BE ANYTHING IN THERE THAT THEY HADN'T SEEN BEFORE...
Popcorn?
Sure, gin?
Pop corn
BUT JUST IN CASE, I PROMISED THEIR PARENTS THAT I'D MAKE 'EM CLOSE THEIR EYES DURING THE SCARY PARTS...
UNFORTUNATELY, IT WAS A BIT SCARIER THAN I EXPECTED...
BUSH FAMILY CONNECTIONS TO THE BIN LADEN & SAUDI ROYAL FAMILIES..
OHMIGOSH!! CLOSE YER EYES!!
U.S. SOLDIERS GETTING PAID TWO GRAND A MONTH TO PROTECT HALLIBURTON GUYS MAKING TEN GRAND A MONTH!!
KIDS, NO!! DON'T LOOK AT IT!!
IN FACT, I'M SURE THAT SOME OF THE CHILDREN HAVE BEEN SCARRED FOR LIFE...
A-A-ASH... CROFT... ...S-S-SINGING...
I am Sooo Sorry you had to see That.
STOP

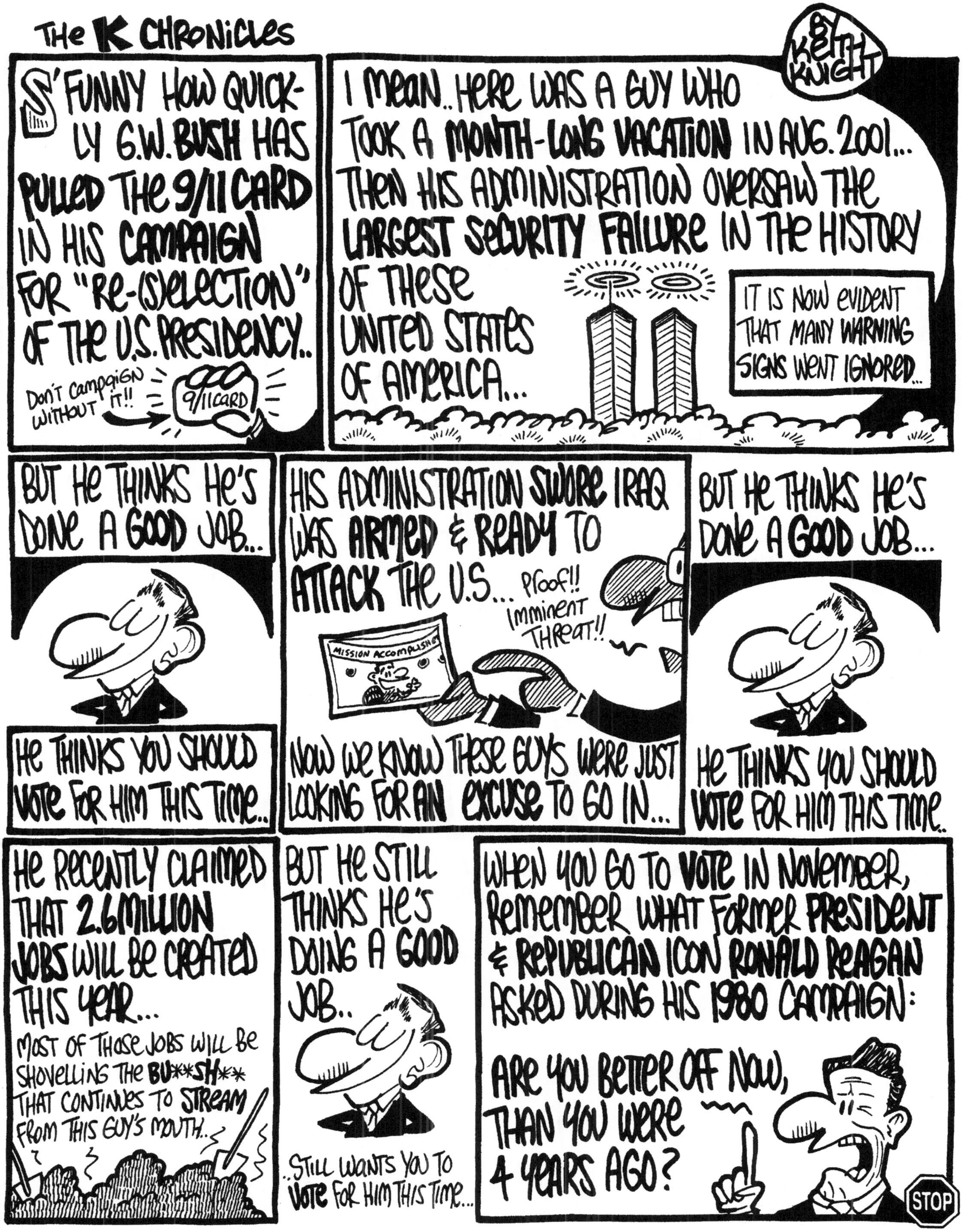

The K Chronicles
By Keith Knight
S'FUNNY HOW QUICKLY G.W. BUSH HAS PULLED THE 9/11 CARD IN HIS CAMPAIGN FOR "RE-(S)ELECTION" OF THE U.S. PRESIDENCY...
DON'T CAMPAIGN WITHOUT IT!!
9/11 CARD
I MEAN.. HERE WAS A GUY WHO TOOK A MONTH-LONG VACATION IN AUG. 2001... THEN HIS ADMINISTRATION OVERSAW THE LARGEST SECURITY FAILURE IN THE HISTORY OF THESE UNITED STATES OF AMERICA...
IT IS NOW EVIDENT THAT MANY WARNING SIGNS WENT IGNORED...
BUT HE THINKS HE'S DONE A GOOD JOB...
HE THINKS YOU SHOULD VOTE FOR HIM THIS TIME..
HIS ADMINISTRATION SWORE IRAQ WAS ARMED & READY TO ATTACK THE U.S...
PROOF!! IMMINENT THREAT!!
MISSION ACCOMPLISHED
NOW WE KNOW THESE GUYS WERE JUST LOOKING FOR AN EXCUSE TO GO IN...
BUT HE THINKS HE'S DONE A GOOD JOB...
HE THINKS YOU SHOULD VOTE FOR HIM THIS TIME..
HE RECENTLY CLAIMED THAT 2.6 MILLION JOBS WILL BE CREATED THIS YEAR...
MOST OF THOSE JOBS WILL BE SHOVELLING THE BU**SH** THAT CONTINUES TO STREAM FROM THIS GUY'S MOUTH..
BUT HE STILL THINKS HE'S DOING A GOOD JOB..
..STILL WANTS YOU TO VOTE FOR HIM THIS TIME...
WHEN YOU GO TO VOTE IN NOVEMBER, REMEMBER WHAT FORMER PRESIDENT & REPUBLICAN ICON RONALD REAGAN ASKED DURING HIS 1980 CAMPAIGN:
ARE YOU BETTER OFF NOW, THAN YOU WERE 4 YEARS AGO?
STOP

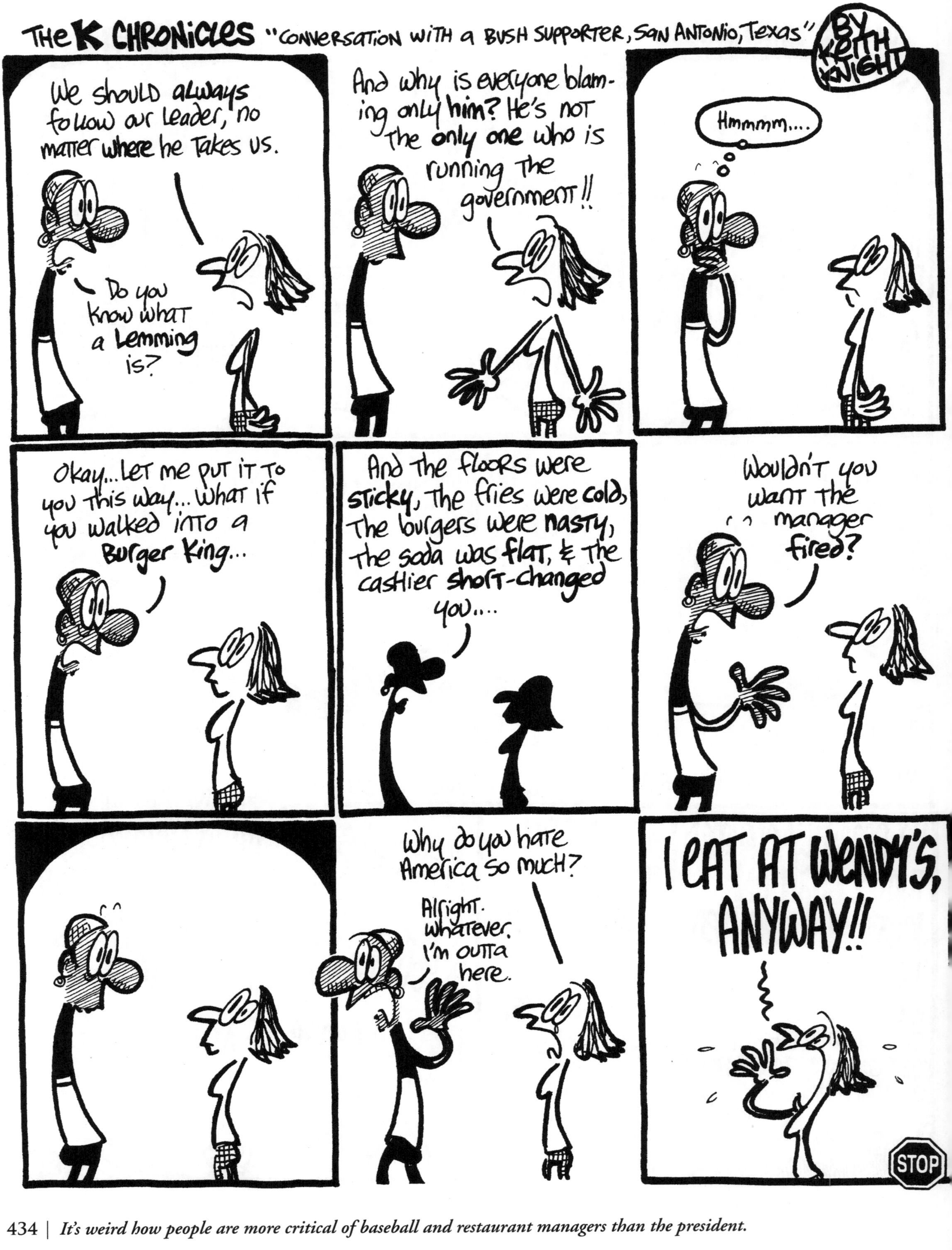
THE K CHRONICLES "CONVERSATION WITH A BUSH SUPPORTER, SAN ANTONIO, TEXAS" BY KEITH KNIGHT
We should always follow our leader, no matter where he takes us.
Do you know what a lemming is?
And why is everyone blaming only him? He's not the only one who is running the government!!
Hmmmm....
Okay...let me put it to you this way...what if you walked into a Burger King...
And the floors were sticky, the fries were cold, the burgers were nasty, the soda was flat, & the cashier short-changed you....
Wouldn't you want the manager fired?
Why do you hate America so much?
Alright. whatever. I'm outta here.
I EAT AT WENDY'S, ANYWAY!!
STOP

 It's weird how people are more critical of baseball and restaurant managers than the president.

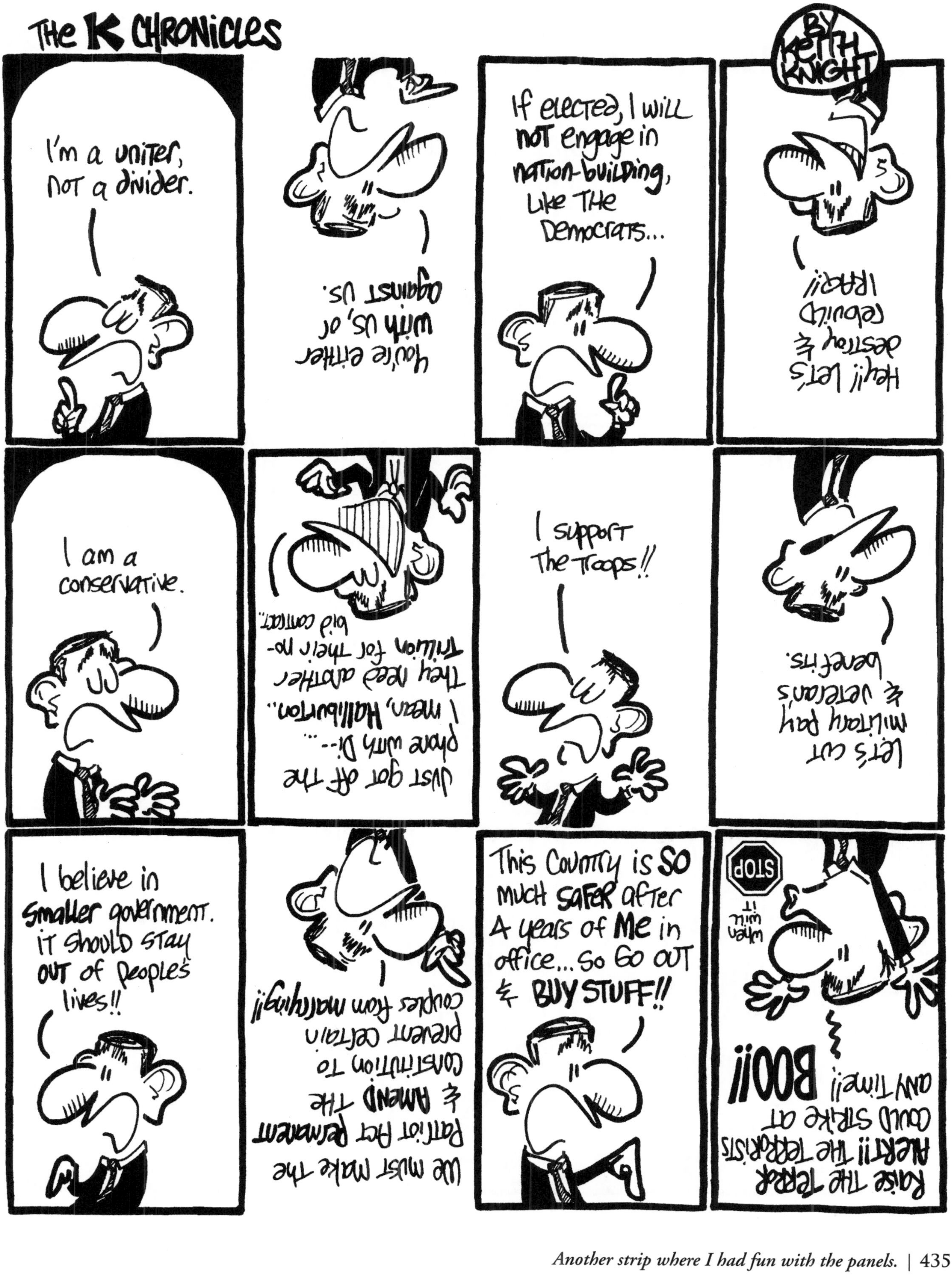
THE K CHRONICLES
BY KEITH KNIGHT
I'm a uniter, not a divider.
You're either with us, or against us.
If elected, I will NOT engage in nation-building, like the Democrats...
Hey!! Let's destroy & rebuild Iraq!!
I am a conservative.
Just got off the phone with Di--... I mean, Halliburton... They need another trillion for their no-bid contract.
I support the troops!!
Let's cut military pay & veteran's benefits.
I believe in smaller government. It should stay out of people's lives!!
We must make the Patriot Act permanent & amend the constitution to prevent certain couples from marrying!!
This country is SO much SAFER after 4 years of ME in office... So go out & BUY STUFF!!
STOP
when will it
Raise the terror alert!! The terrorists could strike at any time!! BOO!!

Another strip where I had fun with the panels.

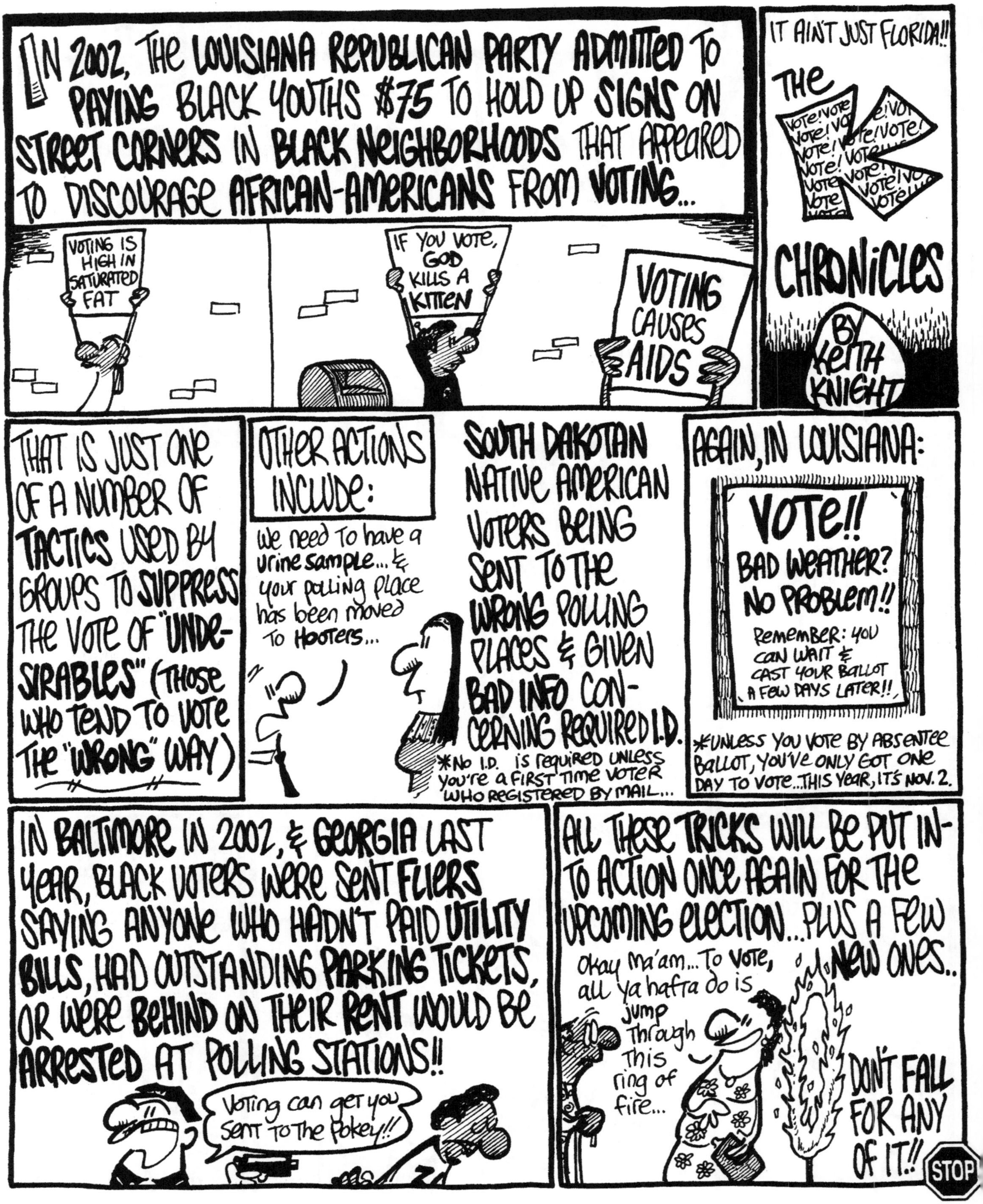

IN 2002, THE LOUISIANA REPUBLICAN PARTY ADMITTED TO PAYING BLACK YOUTHS $75 TO HOLD UP SIGNS ON STREET CORNERS IN BLACK NEIGHBORHOODS THAT APPEARED TO DISCOURAGE AFRICAN-AMERICANS FROM VOTING...

IT AIN'T JUST FLORIDA!!
THE VOTE! CHRONICLES BY KEITH KNIGHT

VOTING IS HIGH IN SATURATED FAT

IF YOU VOTE, GOD KILLS A KITTEN

VOTING CAUSES AIDS

THAT IS JUST ONE OF A NUMBER OF TACTICS USED BY GROUPS TO SUPPRESS THE VOTE OF "UNDESIRABLES" (THOSE WHO TEND TO VOTE THE "WRONG" WAY)

OTHER ACTIONS INCLUDE:
We need to have a urine sample... & your polling place has been moved to Hooters...

SOUTH DAKOTAN NATIVE AMERICAN VOTERS BEING SENT TO THE WRONG POLLING PLACES & GIVEN BAD INFO CONCERNING REQUIRED I.D.
* No I.D. is required unless you're a first time voter who registered by mail...

AGAIN, IN LOUISIANA:

VOTE!! BAD WEATHER? NO PROBLEM!! REMEMBER: YOU CAN WAIT & CAST YOUR BALLOT A FEW DAYS LATER!!

*UNLESS YOU VOTE BY ABSENTEE BALLOT, YOU'VE ONLY GOT ONE DAY TO VOTE...THIS YEAR, IT'S NOV. 2.

IN BALTIMORE IN 2002, & GEORGIA LAST YEAR, BLACK VOTERS WERE SENT FLIERS SAYING ANYONE WHO HADN'T PAID UTILITY BILLS, HAD OUTSTANDING PARKING TICKETS, OR WERE BEHIND ON THEIR RENT WOULD BE ARRESTED AT POLLING STATIONS!!

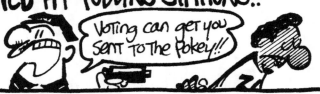

Voting can get you sent to the pokey!!

ALL THESE TRICKS WILL BE PUT INTO ACTION ONCE AGAIN FOR THE UPCOMING ELECTION...PLUS A FEW NEW ONES..

Okay ma'am... To vote, all ya hafta do is jump through this ring of fire...

DON'T FALL FOR ANY OF IT!! STOP

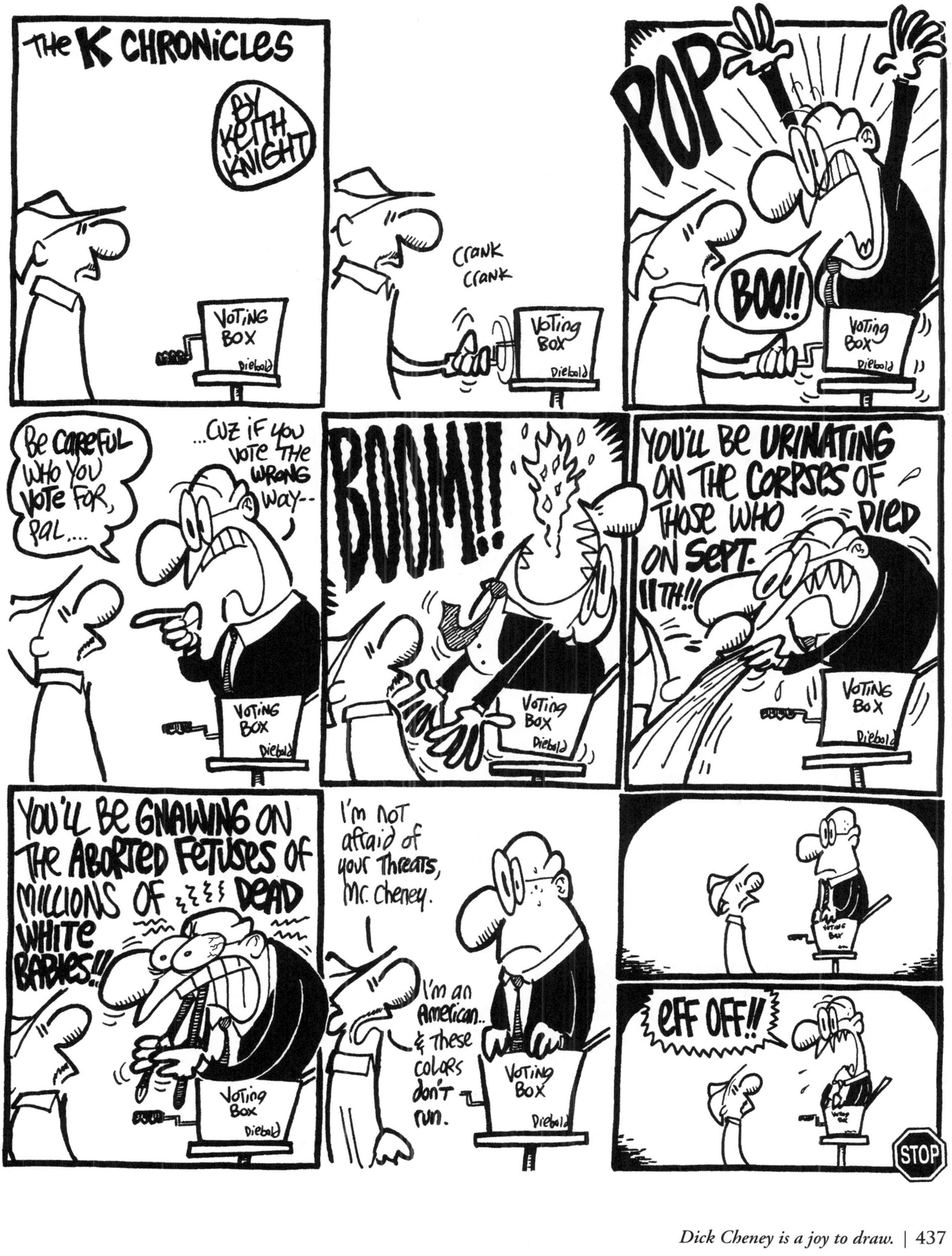
THE K CHRONICLES
BY KEITH KNIGHT
VOTING BOX
Diebold
crank crank
POP
BOO!!
Be careful who you vote for, pal....
...cuz if you vote the wrong way--
BOOM!!
YOU'LL BE URINATING ON THE CORPSES OF THOSE WHO DIED ON SEPT. 11TH!!
YOU'LL BE GNAWING ON THE ABORTED FETUSES OF MILLIONS OF DEAD WHITE BABIES!!
I'm not afraid of your threats, Mr. Cheney.
I'm an American.. & these colors don't run.
EFF OFF!!
STOP

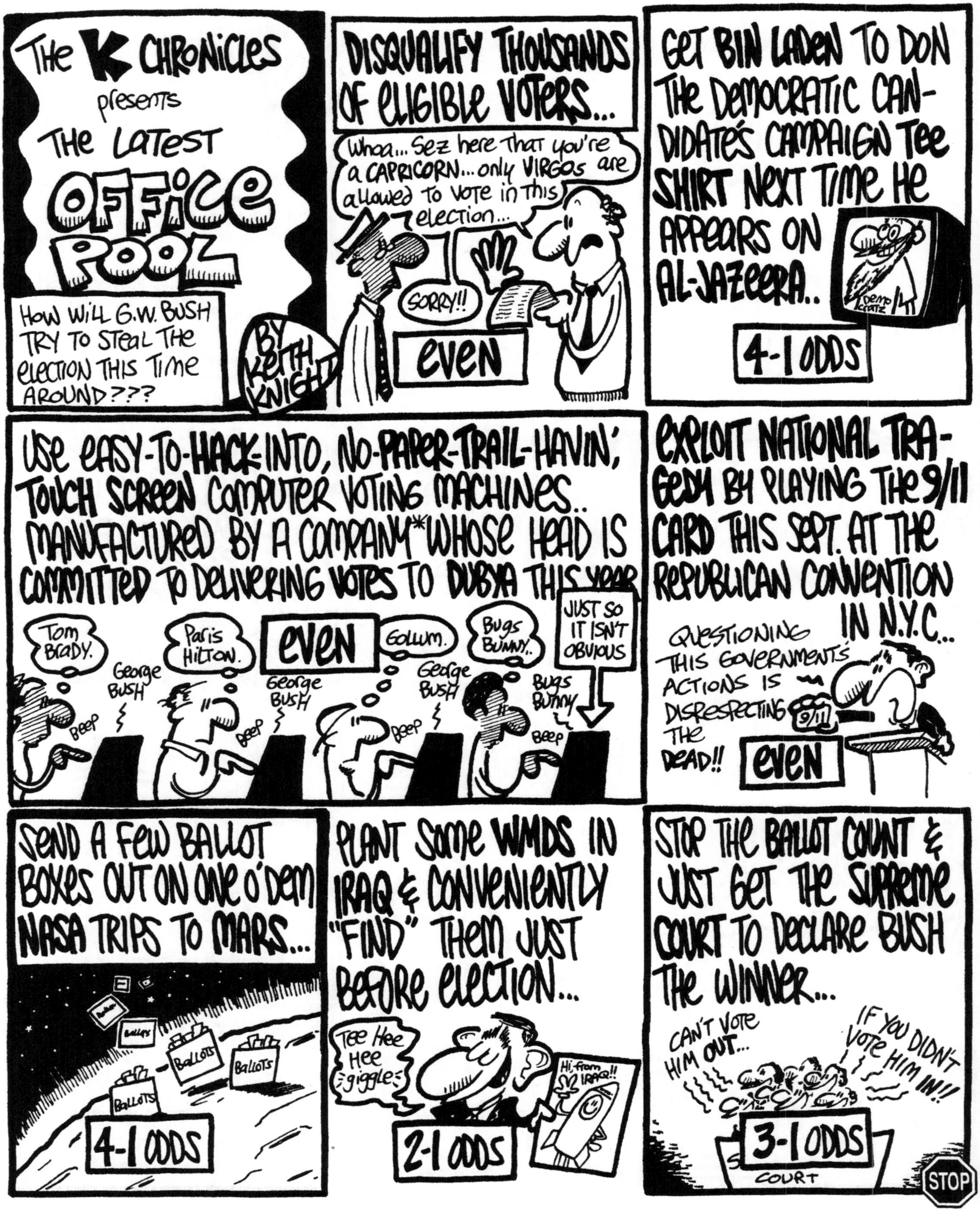
THE K CHRONICLES
presents
THE LATEST
OFFICE POOL
HOW WILL G.W. BUSH TRY TO STEAL THE ELECTION THIS TIME AROUND???
BY KEITH KNIGHT
DISQUALIFY THOUSANDS OF ELIGIBLE VOTERS...
Whoa... Sez here that you're a CAPRICORN... only VIRGOS are allowed to vote in this election...
SORRY!!
EVEN
GET BIN LADEN TO DON THE DEMOCRATIC CANDIDATE'S CAMPAIGN TEE SHIRT NEXT TIME HE APPEARS ON AL-JAZEERA..
DEMOCRATZ
4-1 ODDS
USE EASY-TO-HACK-INTO, NO-PAPER-TRAIL-HAVIN', TOUCH SCREEN COMPUTER VOTING MACHINES.. MANUFACTURED BY A COMPANY* WHOSE HEAD IS COMMITTED TO DELIVERING VOTES TO DUBYA THIS YEAR
Tom Brady.
George Bush
BEEP
Paris Hilton.
George Bush
BEEP
EVEN
Golum.
George Bush
BEEP
Bugs Bunny..
JUST SO IT ISN'T OBVIOUS
Bugs Bunny
BEEP
EXPLOIT NATIONAL TRAGEDY BY PLAYING THE 9/11 CARD THIS SEPT. AT THE REPUBLICAN CONVENTION IN N.Y.C...
QUESTIONING THIS GOVERNMENT'S ACTIONS IS DISRESPECTING THE DEAD!!
9/11
EVEN
SEND A FEW BALLOT BOXES OUT ON ONE O' DEM NASA TRIPS TO MARS...
BALLOTS
BALLOTS
BALLOTS
BALLOTS
4-1 ODDS
PLANT SOME WMDS IN IRAQ & CONVENIENTLY "FIND" THEM JUST BEFORE ELECTION...
Tee Hee Hee giggle
Hi, from IRAQ!!
2-1 ODDS
STOP THE BALLOT COUNT & JUST GET THE SUPREME COURT TO DECLARE BUSH THE WINNER...
CAN'T VOTE HIM OUT...
IF YOU DIDN'T VOTE HIM IN!!
3-1 ODDS
COURT
STOP

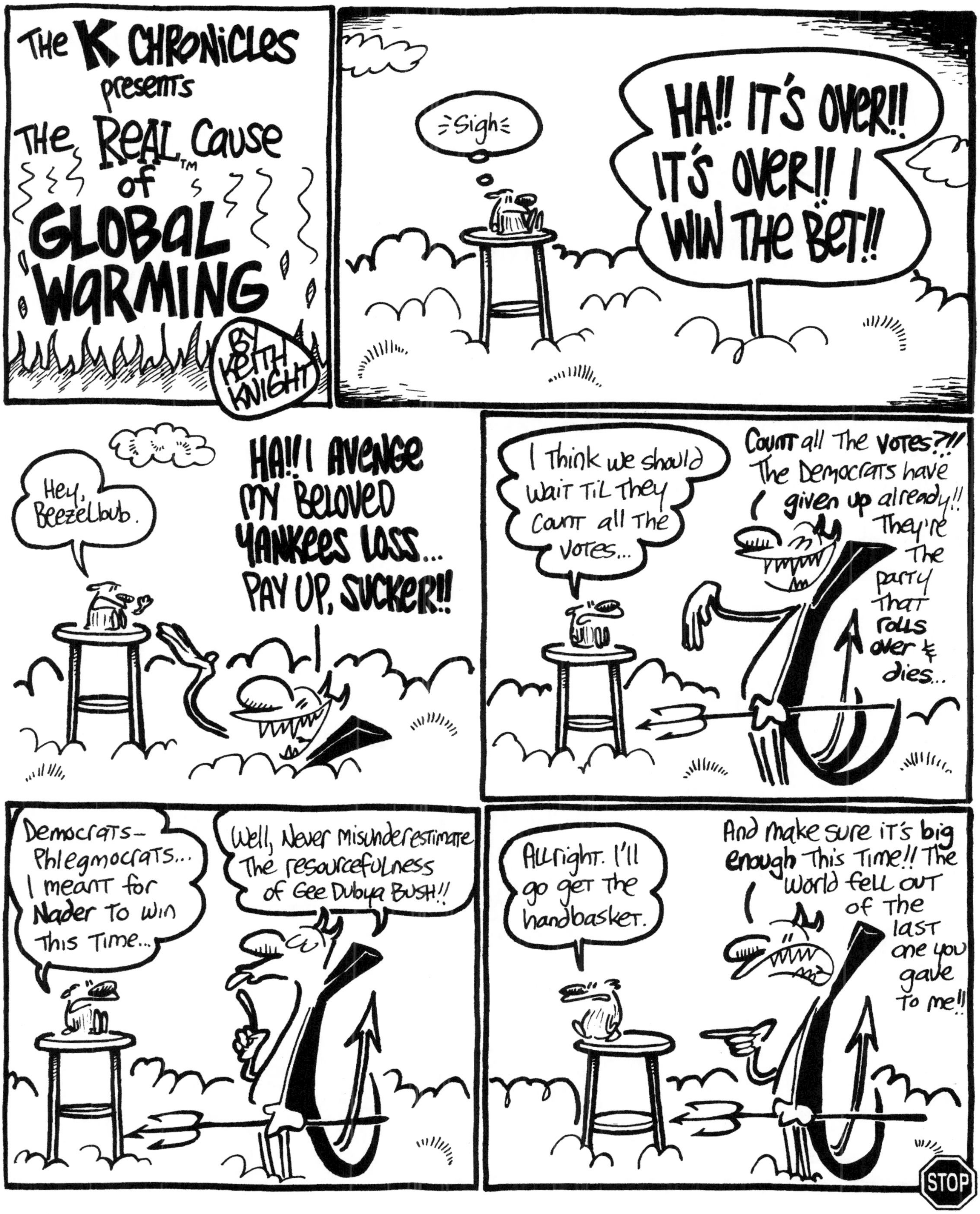
THE K CHRONICLES presents THE REAL™ CAUSE of GLOBAL WARMING
BY KEITH KNIGHT
Sigh
HA!! IT'S OVER!! IT'S OVER!! I WIN THE BET!!
Hey, Beezelbub.
HA!! I AVENGE MY BELOVED YANKEES LOSS... PAY UP, SUCKER!!
I think we should wait til they count all the votes...
Count all the votes?!! The Democrats have given up already!! They're the party that rolls over & dies...
Democrats— Phlegmocrats... I meant for Nader to win this time...
Well, never misunderestimate the resourcefulness of Gee Dubya Bush!!
Allright. I'll go get the handbasket.
And make sure it's big enough this time!! The world fell out of the last one you gave to me!!
STOP

Life's Little Victories

THE K CHRONICLES

BY KEITH KNIGHT

#1107: AT THE PARK, A RUNAWAY FRISBEE™ LANDS AT YOUR FEET...

!!!

CLOMP!!

..YOU PICK IT UP & THROW IT BACK TO THE OWNER, PERFECTLY!!

YES!!

#1108: SUCCESSFULLY PLUGGING IN ELECTRONIC GEAR... YES!!

...WITHOUT LOOKING AT THE MANUAL!!

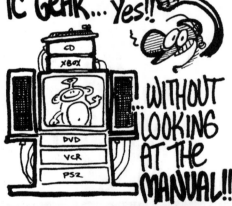

#1109: RECEIVING AN EMAIL JOKE...

SNORT! MILK

HA!! ..THAT ACTUALLY MAKES YOU LAUGH OUT LOUD!!*

* (THIS NEVER HAPPENS)

#1110: TAKING A MULTI-HOTEL SHUTTLE FROM THE AIRPORT...

FIRST STOP: MOTEL SLEEZ...
YES!!

SHUTTLE

...& IT DROPS YOU OFF FIRST!!

#1111: STUMBLING ACROSS THE ONLY GOOD SCENE OF A CRAPPY MOVIE WHILST CHANNEL SURFING...

WELL..I'M JUST GOING TO TAKE ALL MY CLOTHES OFF, RIGHT HERE!!

YES!!

#1112: YOU'RE UPSET, HURT & FRIGHTENED BY THE RECENT ELECTION RESULTS...

!!!

DAILY BLAB
FOUR MORE YEARS OF GEE DUBYA

...BUT THEN YOU REMEMBER:

I LIVE IN CANADA!! YES!!

STOP

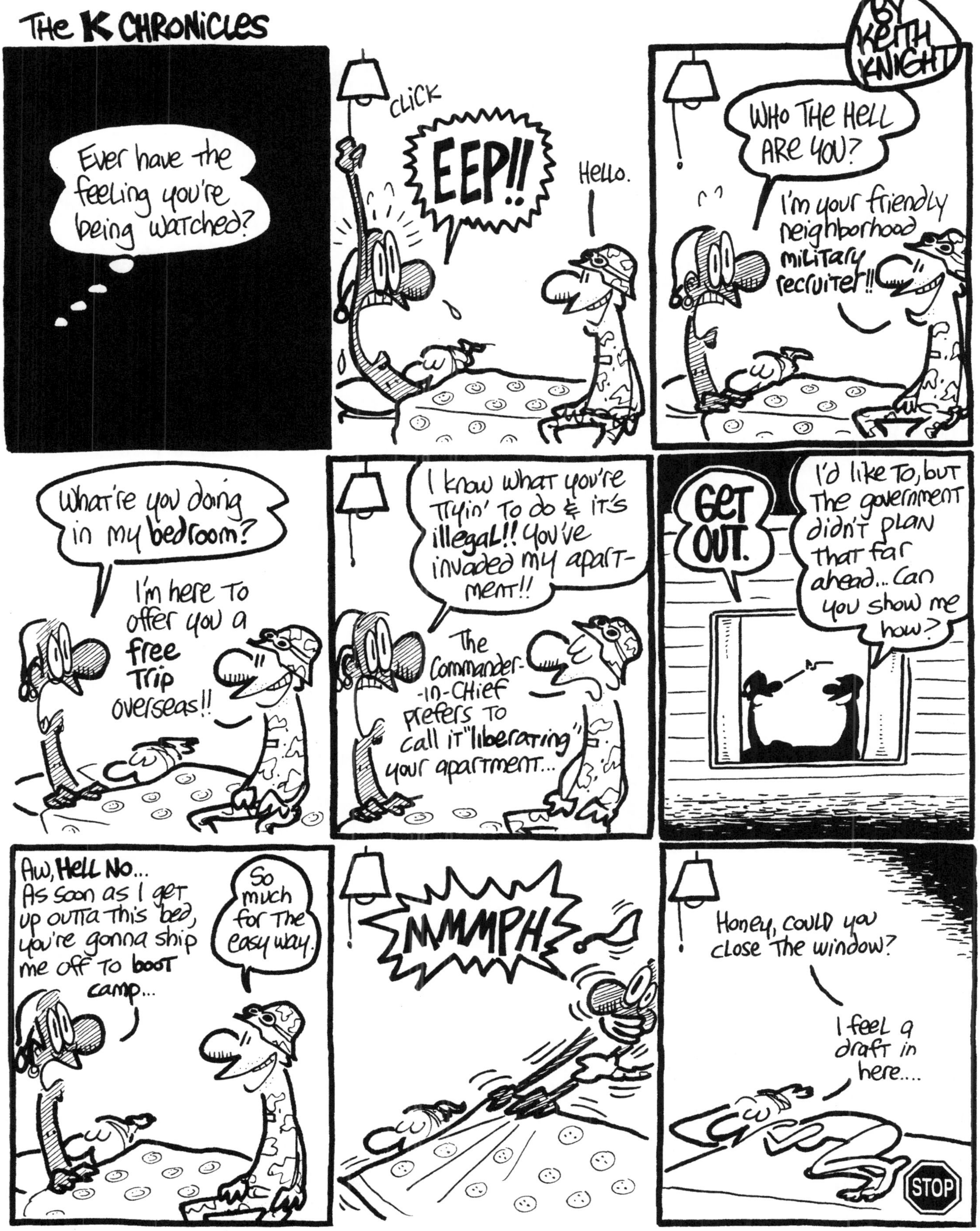
THE K CHRONICLES
BY KEITH KNIGHT
Ever have the feeling you're being watched?
CLICK
EEP!!
Hello.
WHO THE HELL ARE YOU?
I'm your friendly neighborhood military recruiter!!
What're you doing in my bedroom?
I'm here to offer you a free trip overseas!!
I know what you're tryin' to do & it's illegal!! You've invaded my apartment!!
The Commander-in-Chief prefers to call it "liberating" your apartment...
GET OUT.
I'd like to, but the government didn't plan that far ahead... Can you show me how?
Aw, Hell No... As soon as I get up outta this bed, you're gonna ship me off to boot camp...
So much for the easy way.
MMMPH
Honey, could you close the window?
I feel a draft in here....
STOP

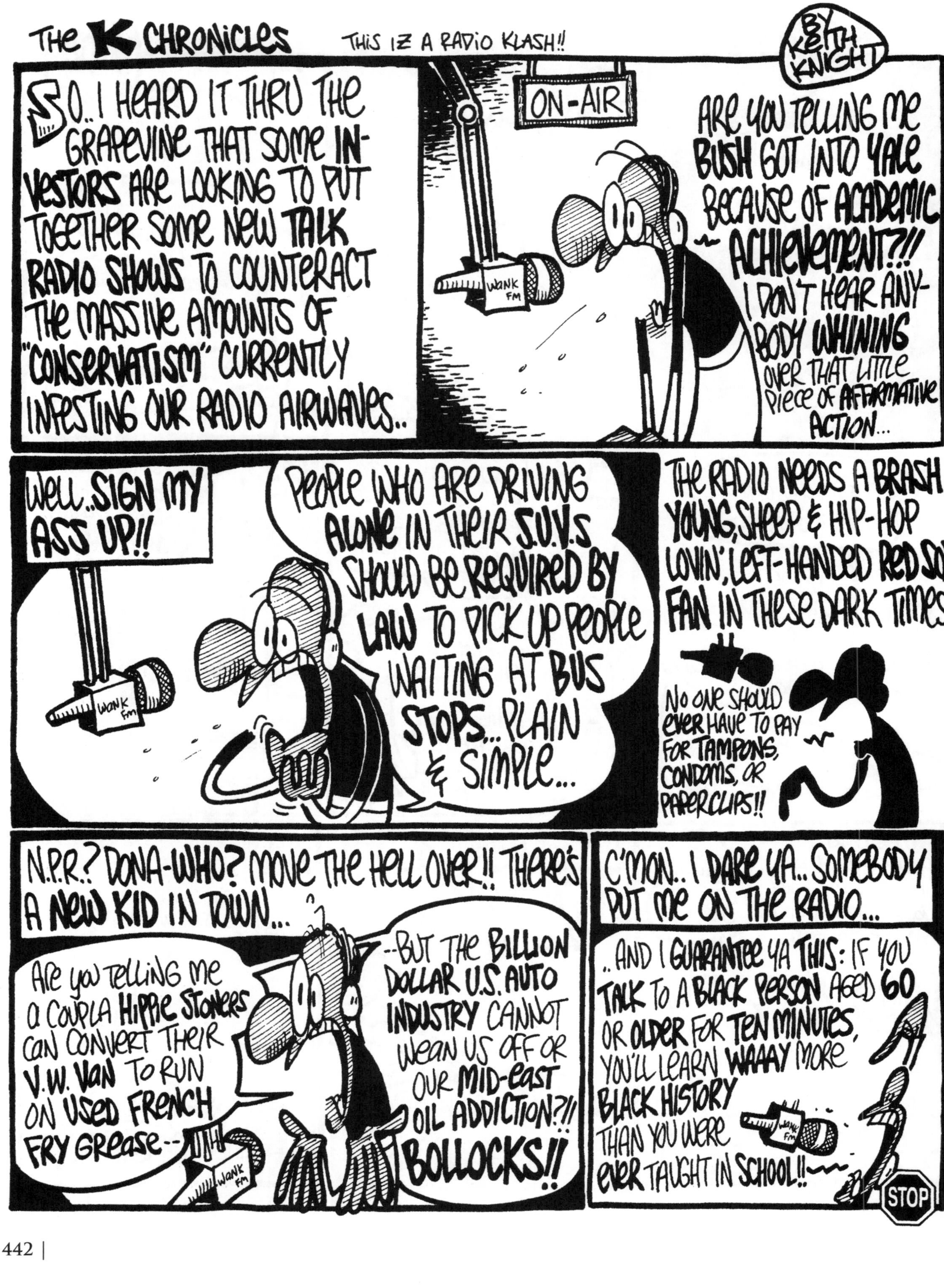
THE K CHRONICLES
THIS IZ A RADIO KLASH!!
BY KEITH KNIGHT
SO.. I HEARD IT THRU THE GRAPEVINE THAT SOME INVESTORS ARE LOOKING TO PUT TOGETHER SOME NEW TALK RADIO SHOWS TO COUNTERACT THE MASSIVE AMOUNTS OF "CONSERVATISM" CURRENTLY INFESTING OUR RADIO AIRWAVES..
ON-AIR
WANK FM
ARE YOU TELLING ME BUSH GOT INTO YALE BECAUSE OF ACADEMIC ACHIEVEMENT?!! I DON'T HEAR ANYBODY WHINING OVER THAT LITTLE PIECE OF AFFIRMATIVE ACTION...
WELL..SIGN MY ASS UP!!
PEOPLE WHO ARE DRIVING ALONE IN THEIR S.U.V.S SHOULD BE REQUIRED BY LAW TO PICK UP PEOPLE WAITING AT BUS STOPS... PLAIN & SIMPLE...
THE RADIO NEEDS A BRASH, YOUNG, SHEEP & HIP-HOP LOVIN', LEFT-HANDED RED SOX FAN IN THESE DARK TIMES..
NO ONE SHOULD EVER HAVE TO PAY FOR TAMPONS, CONDOMS, OR PAPERCLIPS!!
N.P.R.? DONA-WHO? MOVE THE HELL OVER!! THERE'S A NEW KID IN TOWN...
ARE YOU TELLING ME A COUPLA HIPPIE STONERS CAN CONVERT THEIR V.W. VAN TO RUN ON USED FRENCH FRY GREASE--
--BUT THE BILLION DOLLAR U.S. AUTO INDUSTRY CANNOT WEAN US OFF OF OUR MID-EAST OIL ADDICTION?!! BOLLOCKS!!
C'MON.. I DARE YA.. SOMEBODY PUT ME ON THE RADIO...
..AND I GUARANTEE YA THIS: IF YOU TALK TO A BLACK PERSON AGED 60 OR OLDER FOR TEN MINUTES, YOU'LL LEARN WAAAY MORE BLACK HISTORY THAN YOU WERE EVER TAUGHT IN SCHOOL!!
STOP

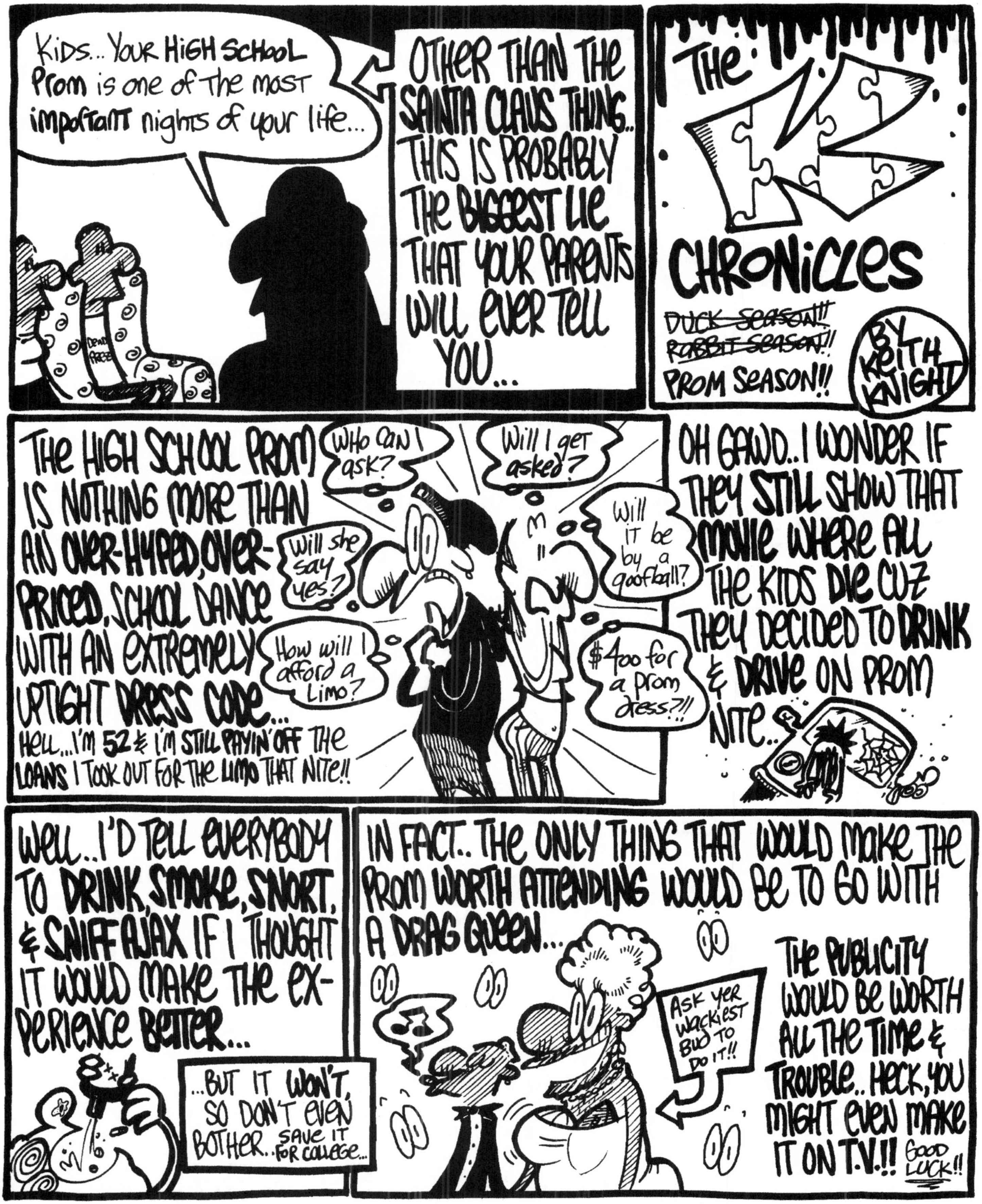
KIDS... YOUR HIGH SCHOOL Prom is one of the most important nights of your life...
OTHER THAN THE SANTA CLAUS THING... THIS IS PROBABLY THE BIGGEST LIE THAT YOUR PARENTS WILL EVER TELL YOU...
THE K CHRONICLES
DUCK SEASON!!
RABBIT SEASON!!
PROM SEASON!!
BY KEITH KNIGHT
THE HIGH SCHOOL PROM IS NOTHING MORE THAN AN OVER-HYPED, OVER-PRICED, SCHOOL DANCE WITH AN EXTREMELY UPTIGHT DRESS CODE...
HELL...I'M 52 & I'M STILL PAYIN' OFF THE LOANS I TOOK OUT FOR THE LIMO THAT NITE!!
Who can I ask?
Will I get asked?
Will she say yes?
Will it be by a goofball?
How will I afford a Limo?
$400 for a prom dress?!!
OH GAWD..I WONDER IF THEY STILL SHOW THAT MOVIE WHERE ALL THE KIDS DIE CUZ THEY DECIDED TO DRINK & DRIVE ON PROM NITE..
WELL..I'D TELL EVERYBODY TO DRINK, SMOKE, SNORT, & SNIFF AJAX IF I THOUGHT IT WOULD MAKE THE EX-PERIENCE BETTER...
...BUT IT WON'T, SO DON'T EVEN BOTHER.. SAVE IT FOR COLLEGE...
IN FACT.. THE ONLY THING THAT WOULD MAKE THE PROM WORTH ATTENDING WOULD BE TO GO WITH A DRAG QUEEN...
ASK YER WACKIEST BUD TO DO IT!!
THE PUBLICITY WOULD BE WORTH ALL THE TIME & TROUBLE.. HECK, YOU MIGHT EVEN MAKE IT ON T.V.!! GOOD LUCK!!

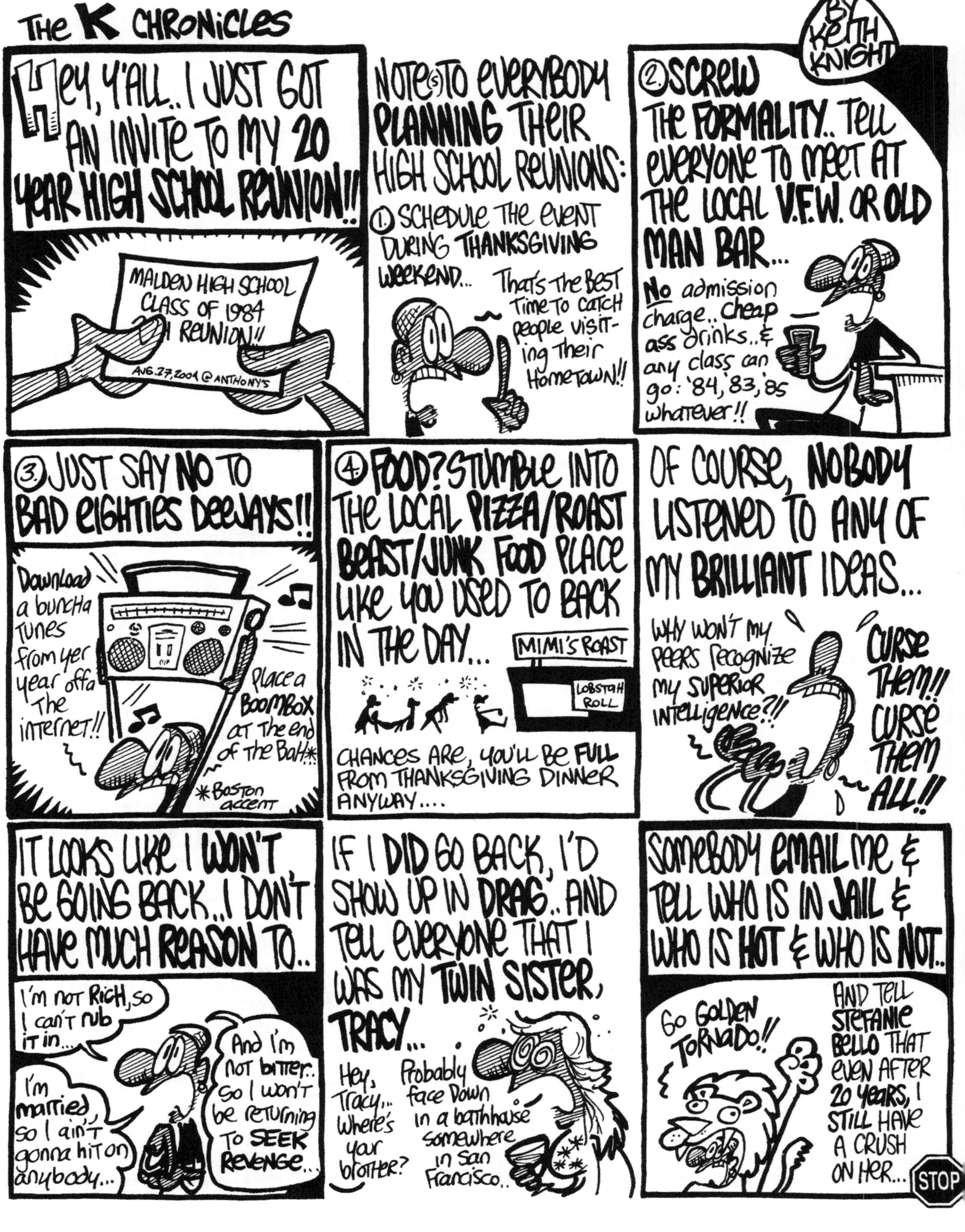
The K Chronicles
By Keith Knight
Hey, y'all.. I just got an invite to my 20 year high school reunion!!..
Malden High School Class of 1984 20th Reunion!!
Aug. 27, 2004 @ Anthony's
Note(s) to everybody planning their high school reunions:
1. Schedule the event during Thanksgiving weekend...
That's the best time to catch people visiting their hometown!!
2. Screw the formality.. Tell everyone to meet at the local V.F.W. or old man bar...
No admission charge.. cheap ass drinks.. & any class can go: '84, '83, '85 whatever!!
3. Just say no to bad eighties deejays!!
Download a buncha tunes from yer year offa the internet!!
Place a boombox at the end of the bah!*
*Boston accent
4. Food? Stumble into the local pizza/roast beast/junk food place like you used to back in the day...
Mimi's Roast
Lobstah Roll
Chances are, you'll be full from Thanksgiving dinner anyway....
Of course, nobody listened to any of my brilliant ideas...
Why won't my peers recognize my superior intelligence?!!
Curse them!! Curse them all!!
It looks like I won't be going back.. I don't have much reason to..
I'm not rich, so I can't rub it in...
I'm married, so I ain't gonna hit on anybody...
And I'm not bitter.. so I won't be returning to seek revenge...
If I did go back, I'd show up in drag.. and tell everyone that I was my twin sister, Tracy...
Hey, Tracy... where's your brother?
Probably face down in a bathhouse somewhere in San Francisco..
Somebody email me & tell who is in jail & who is hot & who is not..
Go Golden Tornado!!
And tell Stefanie Bello that even after 20 years, I still have a crush on her...
STOP

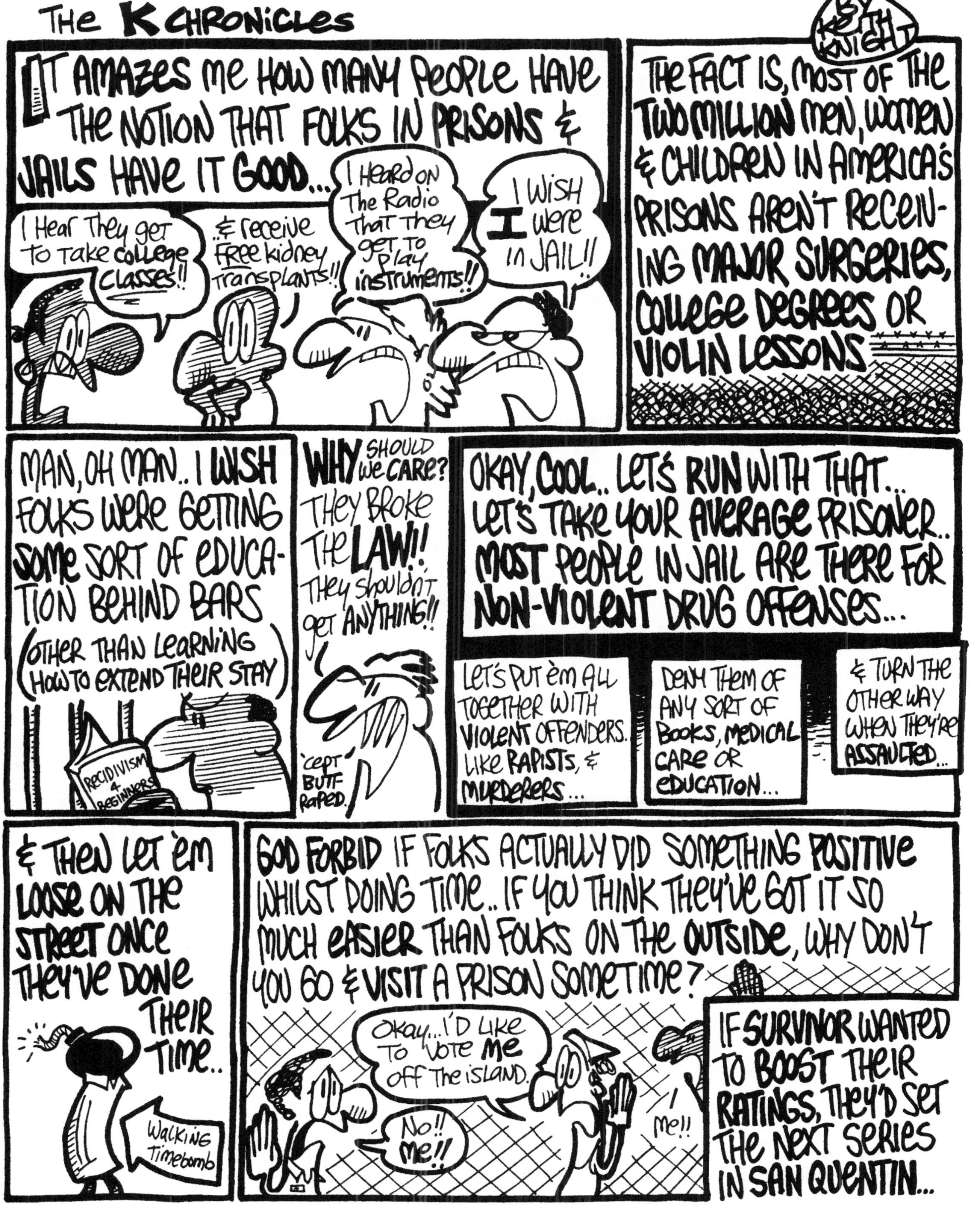
THE K CHRONICLES
BY KEITH KNIGHT
IT AMAZES ME HOW MANY PEOPLE HAVE THE NOTION THAT FOLKS IN PRISONS & JAILS HAVE IT GOOD...
I HEAR THEY GET TO TAKE COLLEGE CLASSES!!
...& RECEIVE FREE KIDNEY TRANSPLANTS!!
I HEARD ON THE RADIO THAT THEY GET TO PLAY INSTRUMENTS!!
I WISH I WERE IN JAIL!!
THE FACT IS, MOST OF THE TWO MILLION MEN, WOMEN & CHILDREN IN AMERICA'S PRISONS AREN'T RECEIVING MAJOR SURGERIES, COLLEGE DEGREES OR VIOLIN LESSONS
MAN, OH MAN.. I WISH FOLKS WERE GETTING SOME SORT OF EDUCATION BEHIND BARS
(OTHER THAN LEARNING HOW TO EXTEND THEIR STAY)
RECIDIVISM 4 BEGINNERS
WHY SHOULD WE CARE? THEY BROKE THE LAW!! THEY SHOULDN'T GET ANYTHING!!
'CEPT BUTT RAPED.
OKAY, COOL.. LET'S RUN WITH THAT.... LET'S TAKE YOUR AVERAGE PRISONER.. MOST PEOPLE IN JAIL ARE THERE FOR NON-VIOLENT DRUG OFFENSES...
LET'S PUT 'EM ALL TOGETHER WITH VIOLENT OFFENDERS. LIKE RAPISTS, & MURDERERS...
DENY THEM OF ANY SORT OF BOOKS, MEDICAL CARE OR EDUCATION...
& TURN THE OTHER WAY WHEN THEY'RE ASSAULTED...
& THEN LET 'EM LOOSE ON THE STREET ONCE THEY'VE DONE THEIR TIME...
WALKING TIMEBOMB
GOD FORBID IF FOLKS ACTUALLY DID SOMETHING POSITIVE WHILST DOING TIME.. IF YOU THINK THEY'VE GOT IT SO MUCH EASIER THAN FOLKS ON THE OUTSIDE, WHY DON'T YOU GO & VISIT A PRISON SOMETIME?
OKAY...I'D LIKE TO VOTE ME OFF THE ISLAND.
NO!! ME!!
ME!!
IF SURVIVOR WANTED TO BOOST THEIR RATINGS, THEY'D SET THE NEXT SERIES IN SAN QUENTIN...

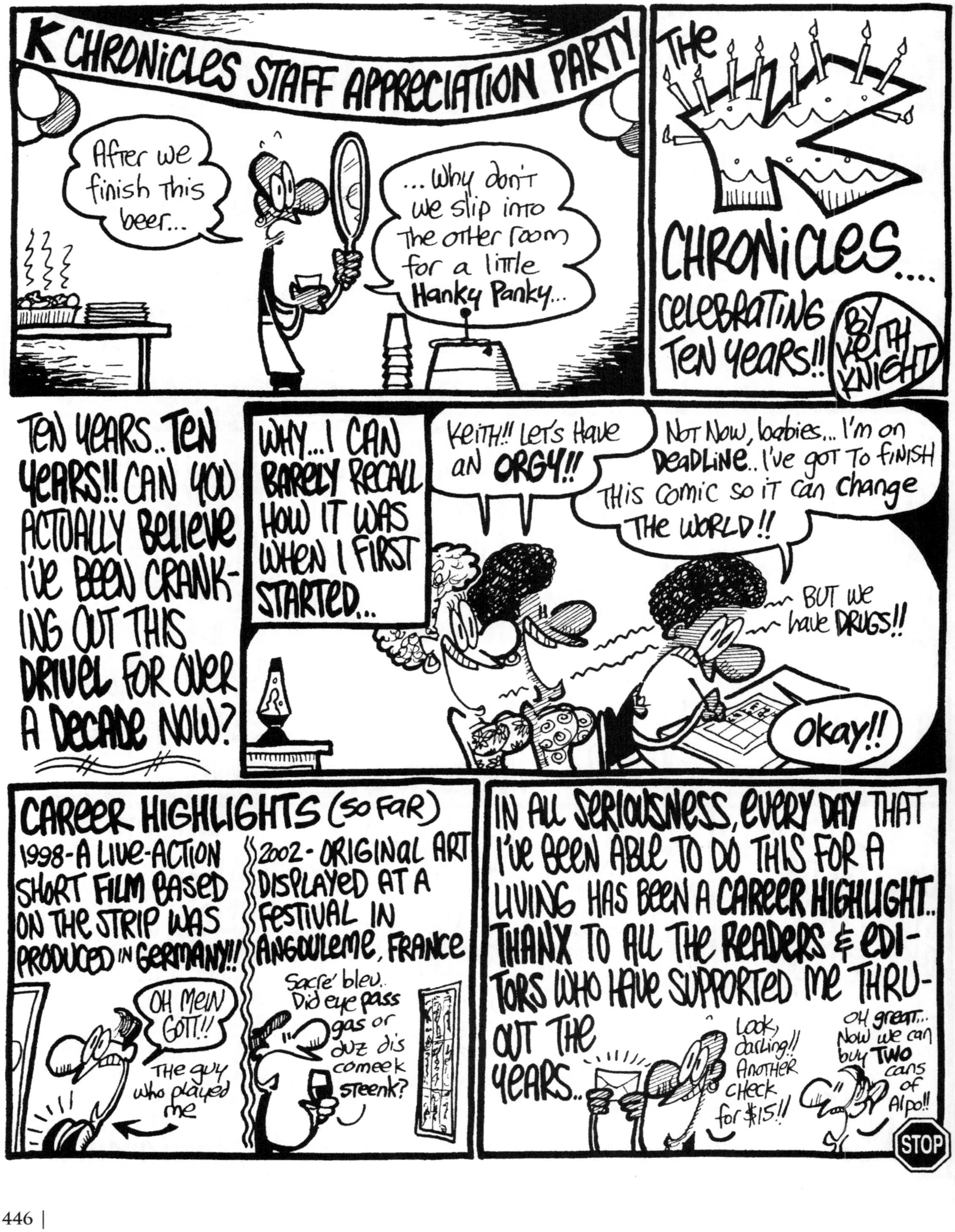
K CHRONICLES STAFF APPRECIATION PARTY
After we finish this beer...
...Why don't we slip into the other room for a little Hanky Panky...
THE K CHRONICLES.... CELEBRATING TEN YEARS!!
BY KEITH KNIGHT
TEN YEARS.. TEN YEARS!! CAN YOU ACTUALLY BELIEVE I'VE BEEN CRANK-ING OUT THIS DRIVEL FOR OVER A DECADE NOW?
WHY...I CAN BARELY RECALL HOW IT WAS WHEN I FIRST STARTED...
KEITH!! LET'S HAVE AN ORGY!!
NOT NOW, babies... I'm on DEADLINE.. I've got to finish THIS comic so it can change THE WORLD!!
BUT WE have DRUGS!!
Okay!!
CAREER HIGHLIGHTS (SO FAR)
1998-A LIVE-ACTION SHORT FILM BASED ON THE STRIP WAS PRODUCED IN GERMANY!!
OH MEIN GOTT!!
THE guy who played me
2002-ORIGINAL ART DISPLAYED AT A FESTIVAL IN ANGOULEME, FRANCE
Sacre' bleu.. Did eye pass gas or duz dis comeek steenk?
IN ALL SERIOUSNESS, EVERY DAY THAT I'VE BEEN ABLE TO DO THIS FOR A LIVING HAS BEEN A CAREER HIGHLIGHT.. THANX TO ALL THE READERS & EDI-TORS WHO HAVE SUPPORTED ME THRU-OUT THE YEARS..
Look, darling!! Another check for $15!!
OH great... Now we can buy TWO cans of Alpo!!
STOP

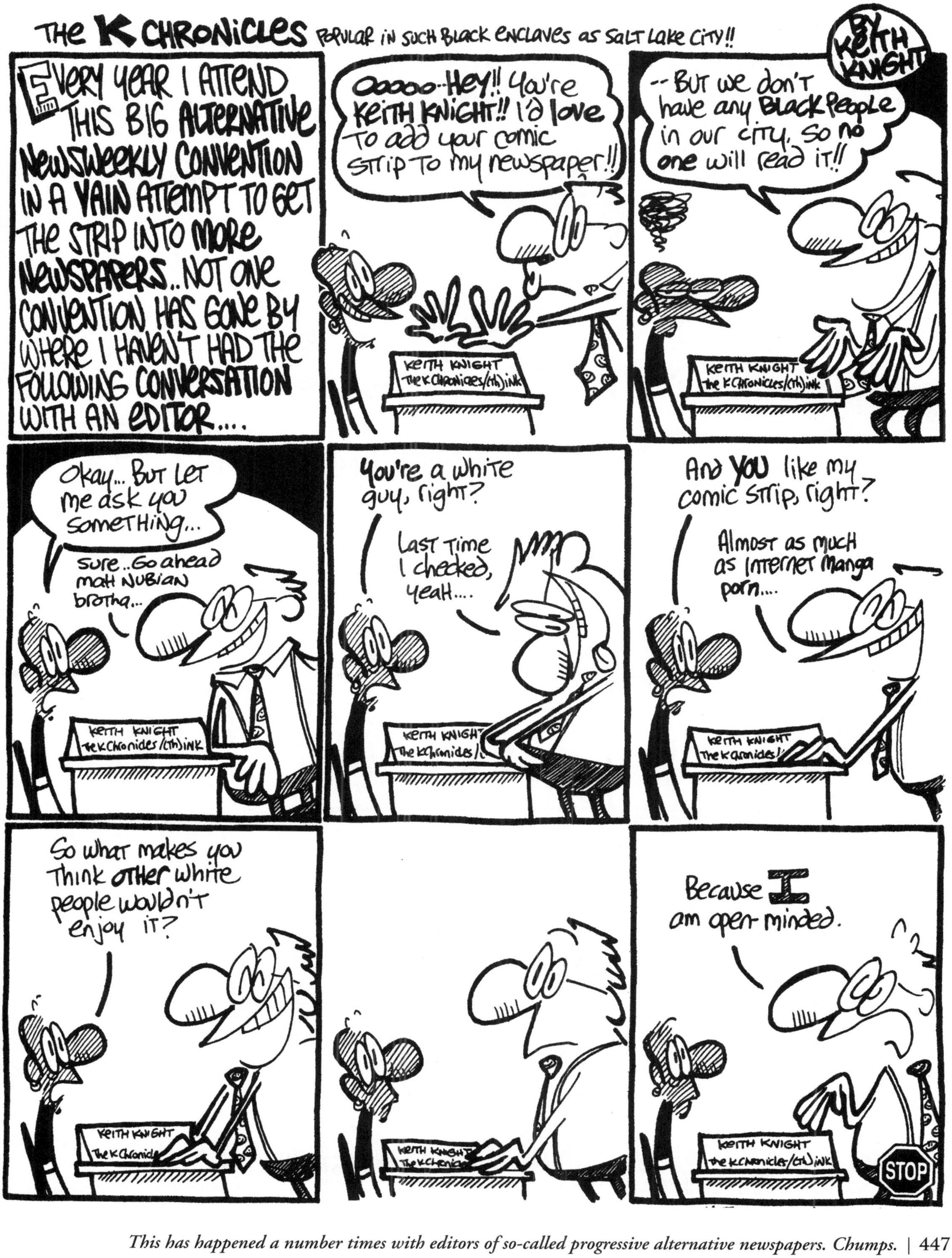
THE K CHRONICLES
POPULAR IN SUCH BLACK ENCLAVES AS SALT LAKE CITY!!
BY KEITH KNIGHT
EVERY YEAR I ATTEND THIS BIG ALTERNATIVE NEWSWEEKLY CONVENTION IN A VAIN ATTEMPT TO GET THE STRIP INTO MORE NEWSPAPERS.. NOT ONE CONVENTION HAS GONE BY WHERE I HAVEN'T HAD THE FOLLOWING CONVERSATION WITH AN EDITOR....
Ooooo-Hey!! You're Keith Knight!! I'd love to add your comic strip to my newspaper!!
KEITH KNIGHT The K Chronicles/(th)ink
-- But we don't have any Black People in our city, so no one will read it!!
Okay... But let me ask you something...
Sure.. Go ahead mah Nubian brotha...
You're a white guy, right?
Last time I checked, yeah....
And YOU like my comic strip, right?
Almost as much as Internet Manga porn....
So what makes you think OTHER white people wouldn't enjoy it?
Because I am open-minded.
STOP

This has happened a number times with editors of so-called progressive alternative newspapers. Chumps.

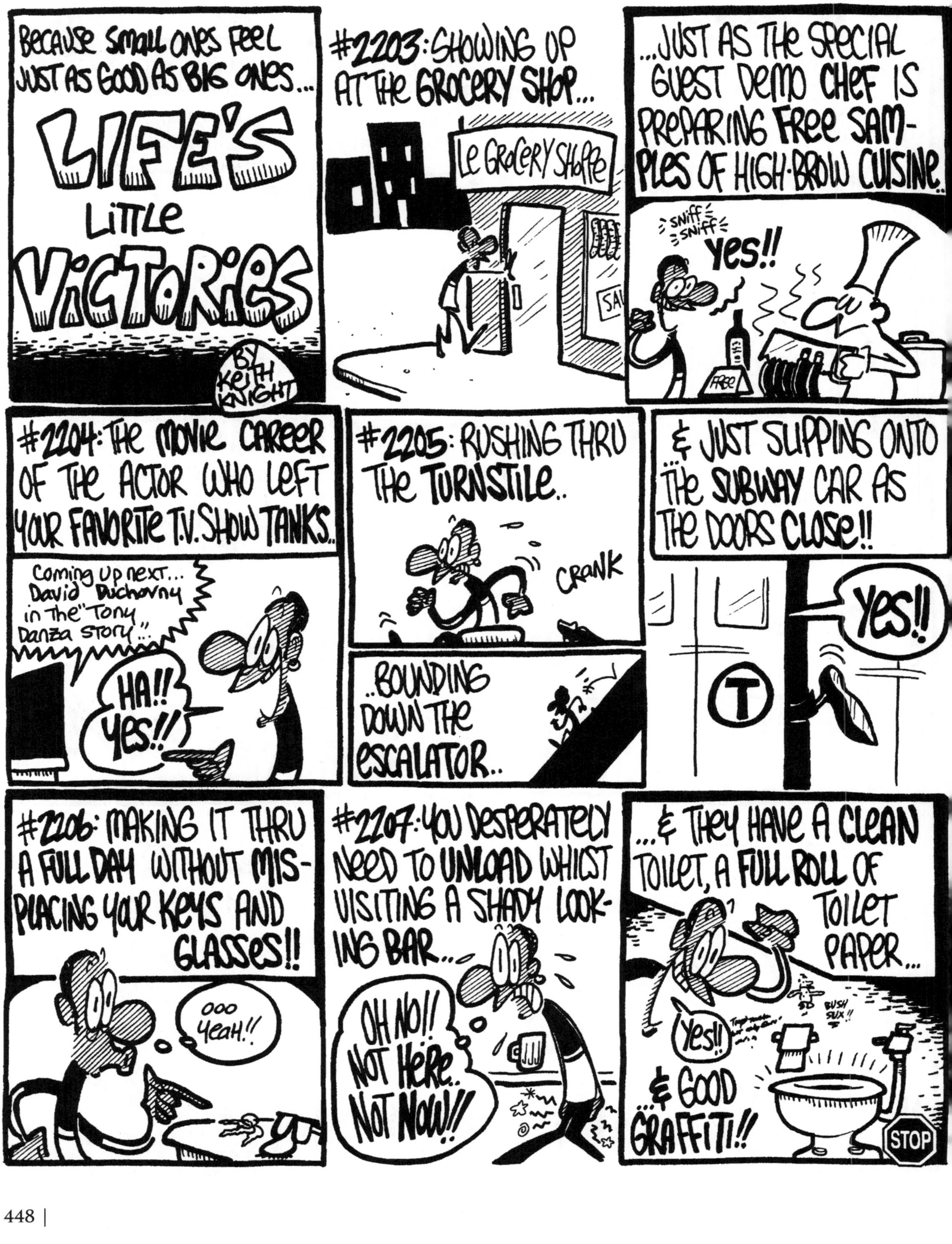
BECAUSE SMALL ONES FEEL JUST AS GOOD AS BIG ONES...
LIFE'S LITTLE VICTORIES
BY KEITH KNIGHT
#2203: SHOWING UP AT THE GROCERY SHOP...
LE GROCERY SHOPPE
SA
...JUST AS THE SPECIAL GUEST DEMO CHEF IS PREPARING FREE SAMPLES OF HIGH-BROW CUISINE..
SNIFF SNIFF
YES!!
FREE
#2204: THE MOVIE CAREER OF THE ACTOR WHO LEFT YOUR FAVORITE T.V. SHOW TANKS..
COMING UP NEXT... DAVID DUCHOVNY IN THE "TONY DANZA STORY"!!...
HA!! YES!!
#2205: RUSHING THRU THE TURNSTILE..
CRANK
..BOUNDING DOWN THE ESCALATOR..
...& JUST SLIPPING ONTO THE SUBWAY CAR AS THE DOORS CLOSE!!
T
YES!!
#2206: MAKING IT THRU A FULL DAY WITHOUT MISPLACING YOUR KEYS AND GLASSES!!
OOO YEAH!!
#2207: YOU DESPERATELY NEED TO UNLOAD WHILST VISITING A SHADY LOOKING BAR...
OH NO!! NOT HERE.. NOT NOW!!
...& THEY HAVE A CLEAN TOILET, A FULL ROLL OF TOILET PAPER...
BUSH SUX!!
YES!!
...& GOOD GRAFFITI!!
STOP

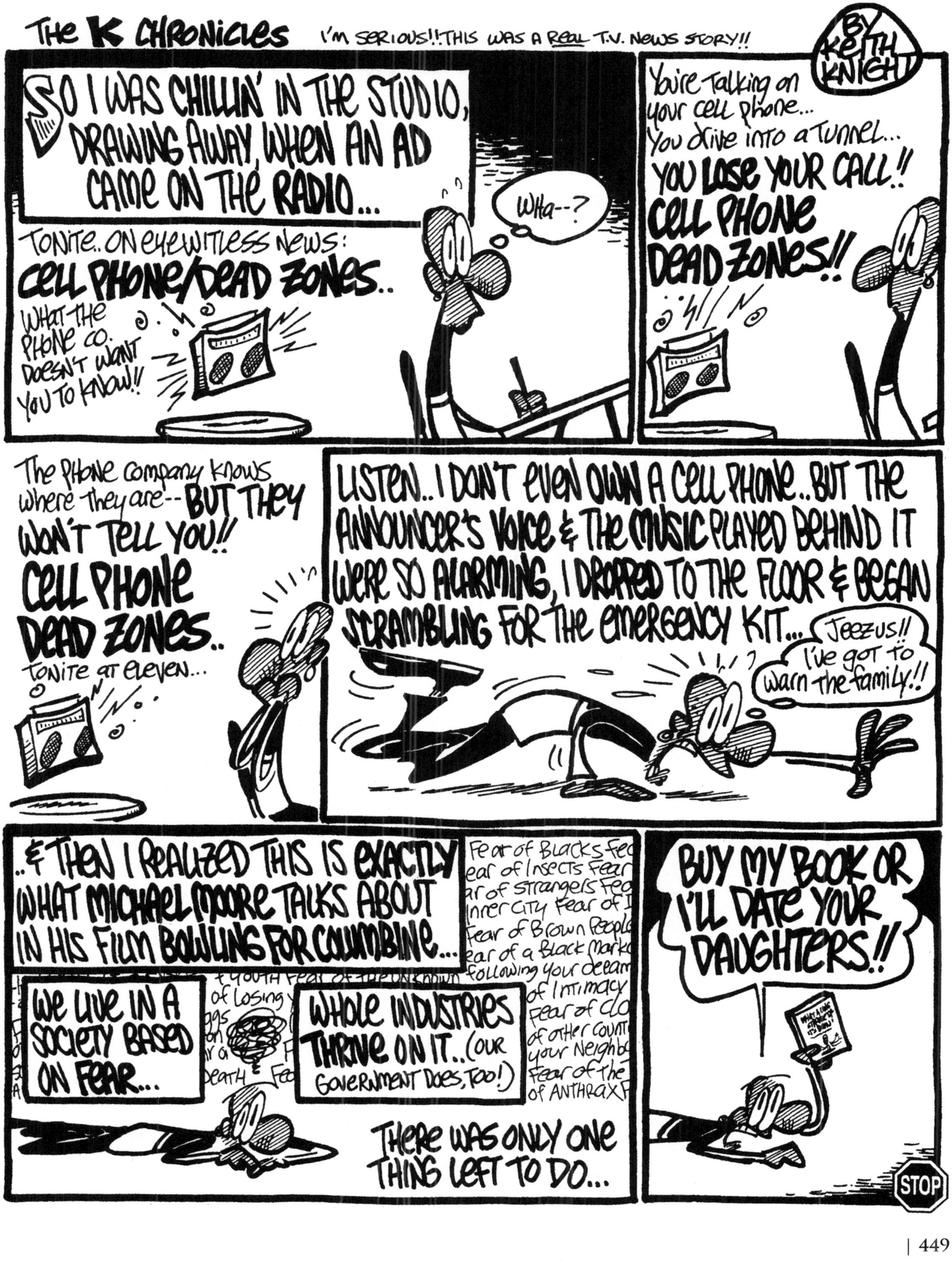
The K Chronicles
I'm serious!! This was a real T.V. news story!!
By Keith Knight
So I was chillin' in the studio, drawing away, when an ad came on the radio...
Tonite.. on eyewitless news:
Cell phone/dead zones..
What the phone co. doesn't want you to know!!
Wha--?
You're talking on your cell phone... You drive into a tunnel... You lose your call!! Cell phone dead zones!!
The phone company knows where they are-- but they won't tell you!! Cell phone dead zones.. Tonite at eleven...
Listen.. I don't even own a cell phone.. but the announcer's voice & the music played behind it were so alarming, I dropped to the floor & began scrambling for the emergency kit...
Jeezus!! I've got to warn the family!!
..& then I realized this is exactly what Michael Moore talks about in his film Bowling for Columbine...
We live in a society based on fear...
Whole industries thrive on it.. (our government does, too!)
There was only one thing left to do...
Buy my book or I'll date your daughters!!
STOP

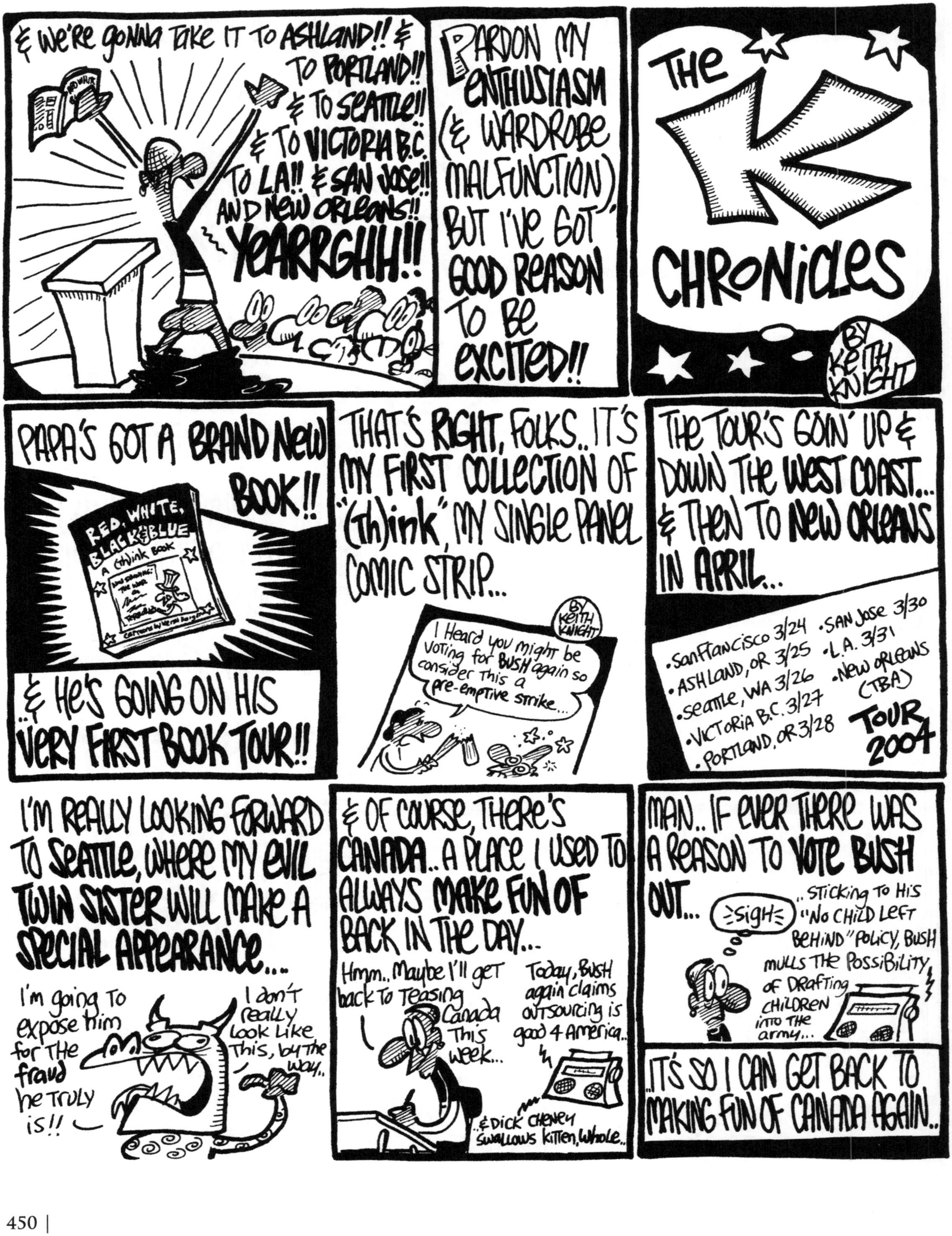

& We're gonna take it to ASHLAND!! & to PORTLAND!! & to SEATTLE!! & to VICTORIA B.C. to L.A!! & SAN JOSE!! AND NEW ORLEANS!!
YEARRGHH!!
PARDON MY ENTHUSIASM (& WARDROBE MALFUNCTION), BUT I'VE GOT GOOD REASON TO BE EXCITED!!
THE K CHRONICLES
BY KEITH KNIGHT
PAPA'S GOT A BRAND NEW BOOK!!
RED, WHITE, BLACK & BLUE
A (th)ink BOOK
..& HE'S GOING ON HIS VERY FIRST BOOK TOUR!!
THAT'S RIGHT, FOLKS.. IT'S MY FIRST COLLECTION OF "(th)ink", MY SINGLE PANEL COMIC STRIP...
BY KEITH KNIGHT
I Heard you might be voting for BUSH again so consider this a pre-emptive strike...
THE TOUR'S GOIN' UP & DOWN THE WEST COAST... & THEN TO NEW ORLEANS IN APRIL...
•San Francisco 3/24
•ASHLAND, OR 3/25
•Seattle, WA 3/26
•Victoria B.C. 3/27
•Portland, OR 3/28
•San Jose 3/30
•L.A. 3/31
•New Orleans (TBA)
TOUR 2004
I'M REALLY LOOKING FORWARD TO SEATTLE, WHERE MY EVIL TWIN SISTER WILL MAKE A SPECIAL APPEARANCE...
I'm going to expose him for the fraud he truly is!!
I don't really look like this, by the way..
& OF COURSE, THERE'S CANADA.. A PLACE I USED TO ALWAYS MAKE FUN OF BACK IN THE DAY...
Hmm.. Maybe I'll get back to teasing Canada this week...
Today, BUSH again claims outsourcing is good 4 America..
..& DICK CHENEY swallows kitten, whole..
MAN.. IF EVER THERE WAS A REASON TO VOTE BUSH OUT...
sigh
..Sticking to his "No Child Left Behind" policy, BUSH mulls the possibility of drafting children into the army...
..IT'S SO I CAN GET BACK TO MAKING FUN OF CANADA AGAIN..

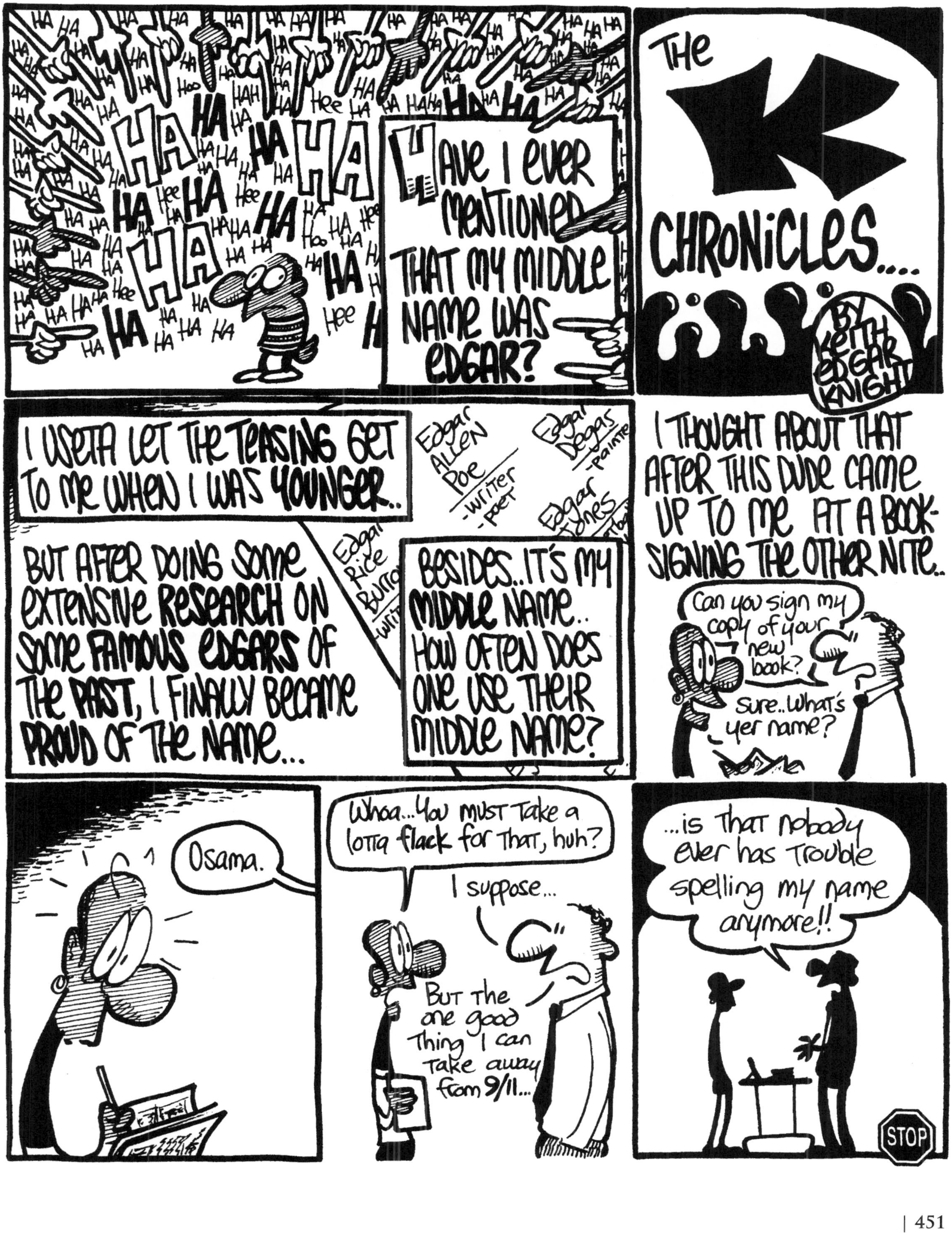
HA HA HA HA Hee Hoo HAH
Have I ever mentioned that my middle name was Edgar?
The K Chronicles....
By Keith Edgar Knight
I usetA let the teasing get to me when I was younger..
But after doing some extensive research on some famous Edgars of the past, I finally became proud of the name...
Edgar Allen Poe -writer -poet
Edgar Degas -painter
Edgar Jones
Edgar Rice Burro
Besides..it's my middle name.. How often does one use their middle name?
I thought about that after this dude came up to me at a book-signing the other nite..
Can you sign my copy of your new book?
Sure.. What's yer name?
Osama.
Whoa...You must take a lotta flack for that, huh?
I suppose...
But the one good thing I can take away from 9/11...
...is that nobody ever has trouble spelling my name anymore!!
STOP

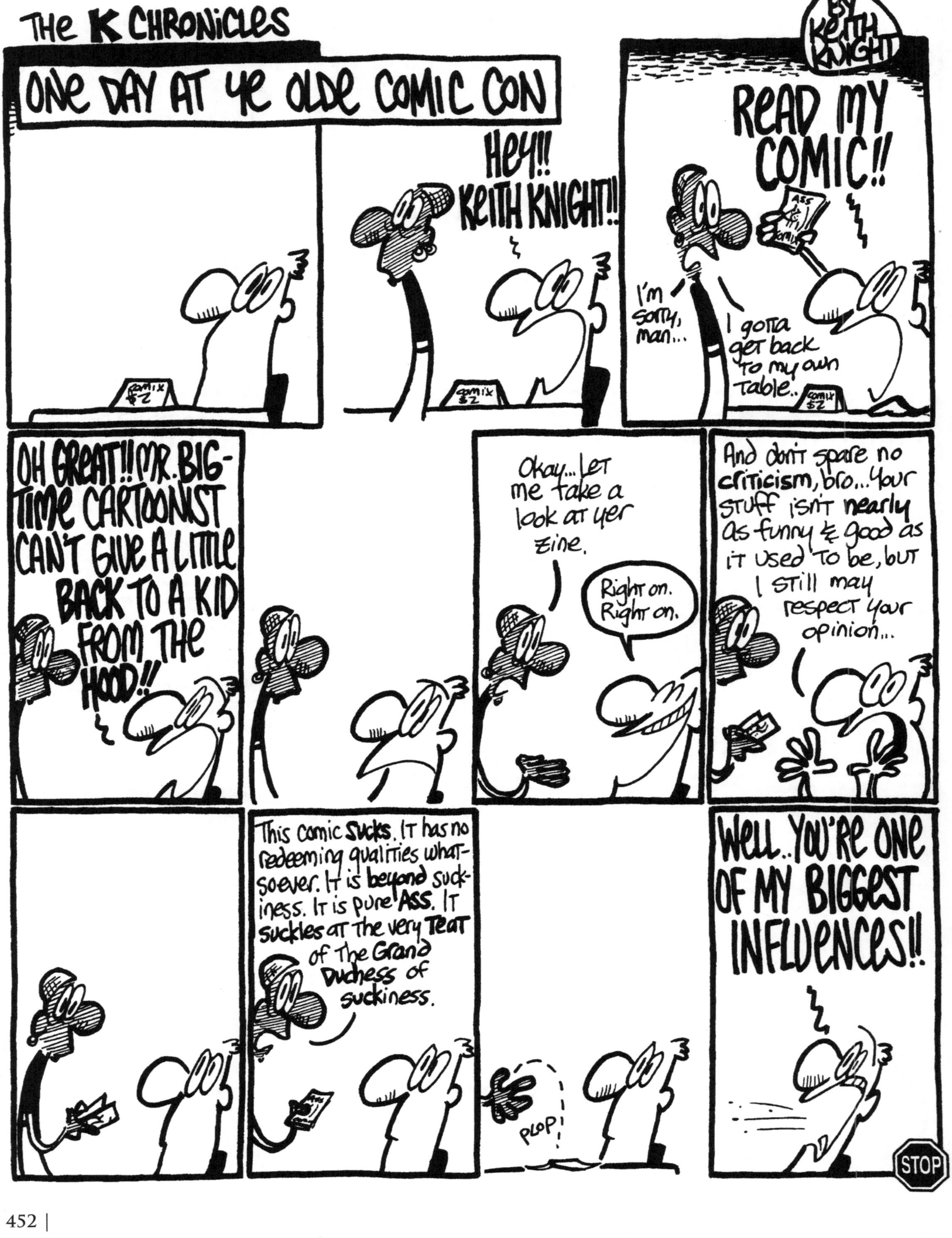
THE K CHRONICLES
BY KEITH KNIGHT
ONE DAY AT YE OLDE COMIC CON
comix $2
HEY!! KEITH KNIGHT!!
READ MY COMIC!!
ASS comix
I'm sorry, man...
I gotta get back to my own table..
OH GREAT!! MR. BIG-TIME CARTOONIST CAN'T GIVE A LITTLE BACK TO A KID FROM THE HOOD!!
Okay... Let me take a look at yer zine.
Right on. Right on.
And don't spare no criticism, bro... Your stuff isn't nearly as funny & good as it used to be, but I still may respect your opinion...
This comic sucks. It has no redeeming qualities what-soever. It is beyond suck-iness. It is pure ASS. It suckles at the very TEAT of the Grand Duchess of suckiness.
PLOP!
WELL.. YOU'RE ONE OF MY BIGGEST INFLUENCES!!
STOP

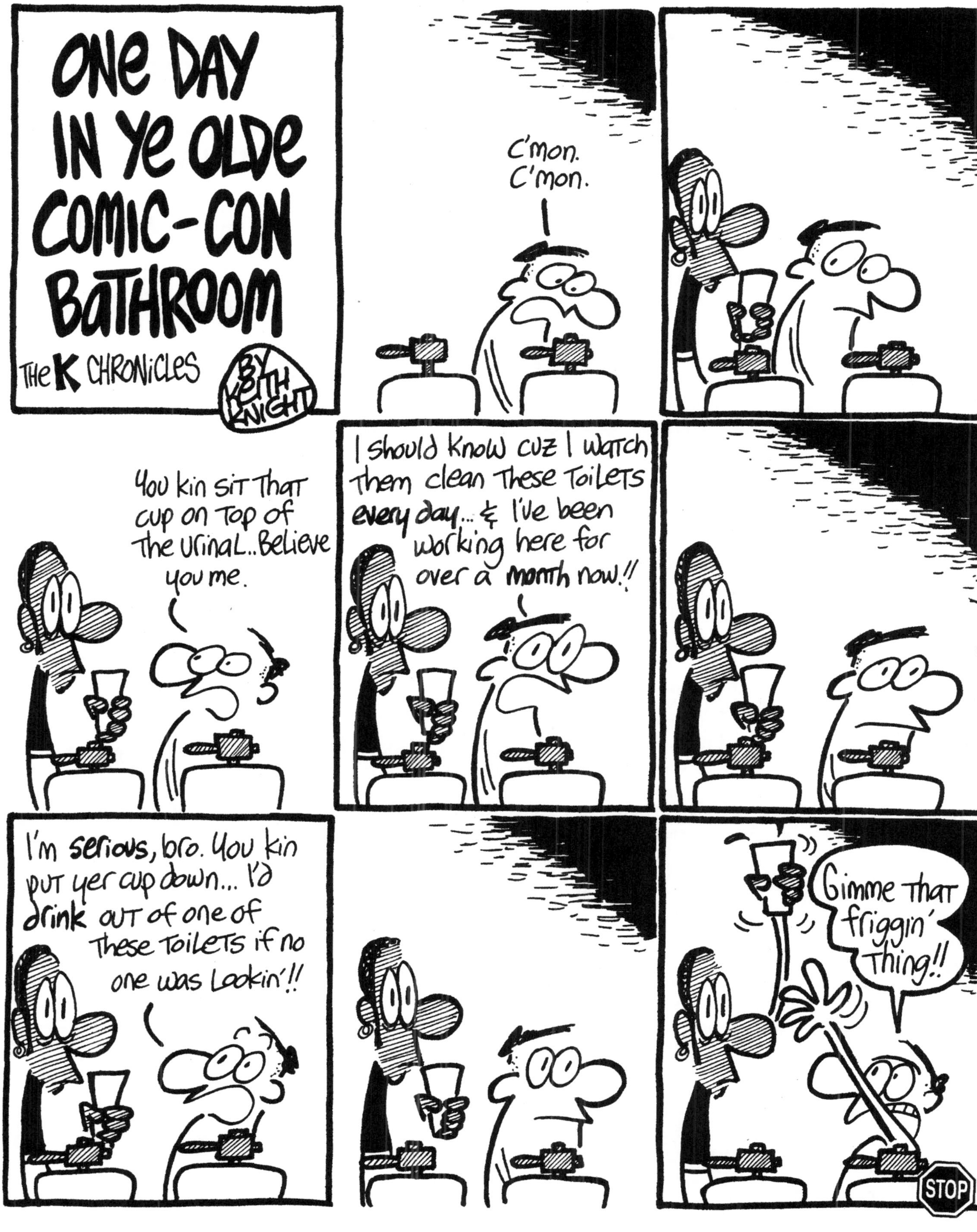
ONE DAY IN YE OLDE COMIC-CON BATHROOM
THE K CHRONICLES
BY KEITH KNIGHT
C'mon. C'mon.
You kin sit that cup on top of the urinal...Believe you me.
I should know cuz I watch them clean these toilets every day... & I've been working here for over a month now!!
I'm serious, bro. You kin put yer cup down... I'd drink out of one of these toilets if no one was lookin'!!
Gimme that friggin' thing!!
STOP

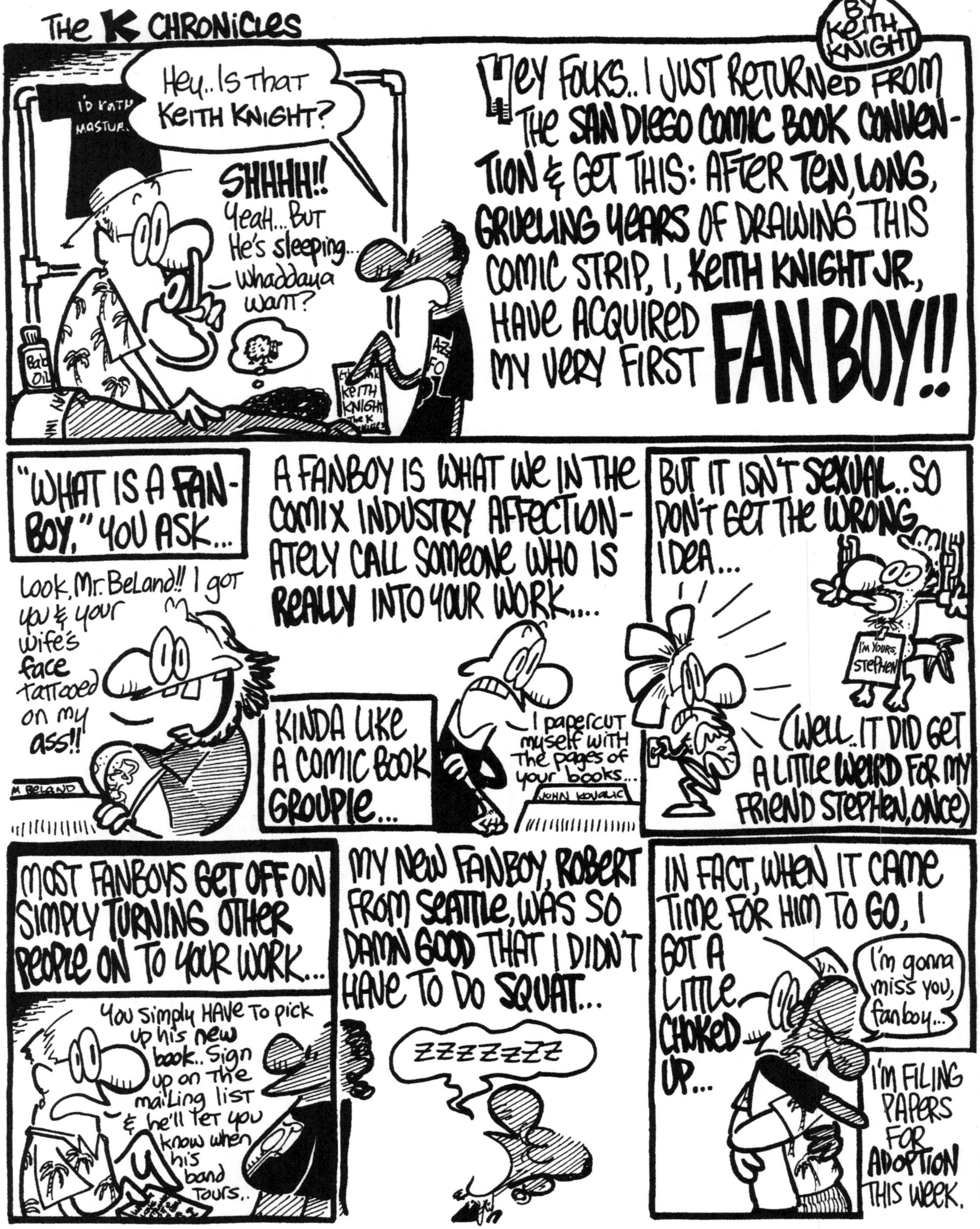
THE K CHRONICLES
BY KEITH KNIGHT
Hey.. Is that Keith Knight?
SHHHH!! Yeah... But He's sleeping... Whaddaya want?
HEY FOLKS.. I JUST RETURNED FROM THE SAN DIEGO COMIC BOOK CONVENTION & GET THIS: AFTER TEN, LONG, GRUELING YEARS OF DRAWING THIS COMIC STRIP, I, KEITH KNIGHT JR., HAVE ACQUIRED MY VERY FIRST FANBOY!!
"WHAT IS A FANBOY," YOU ASK...
Look, Mr. Beland!! I got you & your wife's face tattooed on my ass!!
M BELAND
A FANBOY IS WHAT WE IN THE COMIX INDUSTRY AFFECTIONATELY CALL SOMEONE WHO IS REALLY INTO YOUR WORK....
KINDA LIKE A COMIC BOOK GROUPIE...
I papercut myself with the pages of your books...
JOHN KOVALIC
BUT IT ISN'T SEXUAL.. SO DON'T GET THE WRONG IDEA...
I'M YOURS, STEPHEN
(WELL.. IT DID GET A LITTLE WEIRD FOR MY FRIEND STEPHEN, ONCE)
MOST FANBOYS GET OFF ON SIMPLY TURNING OTHER PEOPLE ON TO YOUR WORK...
You simply HAVE to pick up his new book.. Sign up on the mailing list & he'll let you know when his band tours..
MY NEW FANBOY, ROBERT FROM SEATTLE, WAS SO DAMN GOOD THAT I DIDN'T HAVE TO DO SQUAT...
ZZZZZZZ
IN FACT, WHEN IT CAME TIME FOR HIM TO GO, I GOT A LITTLE CHOKED UP...
I'm gonna miss you, fanboy...
I'M FILING PAPERS FOR ADOPTION THIS WEEK.

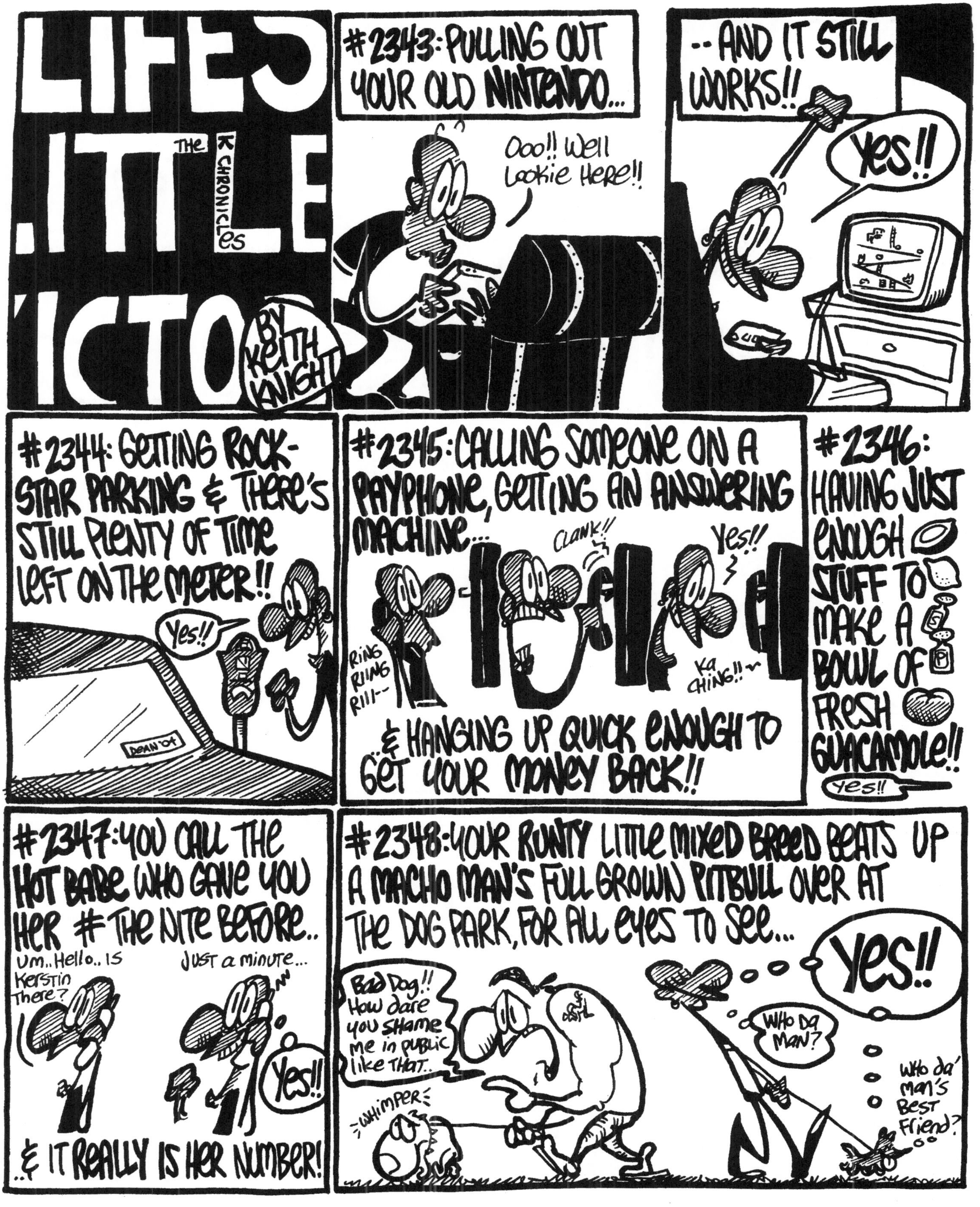
THE K CHRONICLES
BY KEITH KNIGHT
#2343: PULLING OUT YOUR OLD NINTENDO...
Ooo!! Well Lookie Here!!
-- AND IT STILL WORKS!!
Yes!!
#2344: GETTING ROCK-STAR PARKING & THERE'S STILL PLENTY OF TIME LEFT ON THE METER!!
Yes!!
DEAN '04
#2345: CALLING SOMEONE ON A PAYPHONE, GETTING AN ANSWERING MACHINE...
RING RIING RIIII--
CLANK!!
Yes!!
KA CHING!!
..& HANGING UP QUICK ENOUGH TO GET YOUR MONEY BACK!!
#2346: HAVING JUST ENOUGH STUFF TO MAKE A BOWL OF FRESH GUACAMOLE!!
Yes!!
#2347: YOU CALL THE HOT BABE WHO GAVE YOU HER # THE NITE BEFORE..
Um.. Hello.. Is Kerstin there?
JUST a minute...
Yes!!
..& IT REALLY IS HER NUMBER!
#2348: YOUR RUNTY LITTLE MIXED BREED BEATS UP A MACHO MAN'S FULL GROWN PITBULL OVER AT THE DOG PARK, FOR ALL EYES TO SEE...
Bad Dog!! How dare you shame me in public like that..
WHIMPER
YES!!
Who Da Man?
Who da' man's Best Friend?

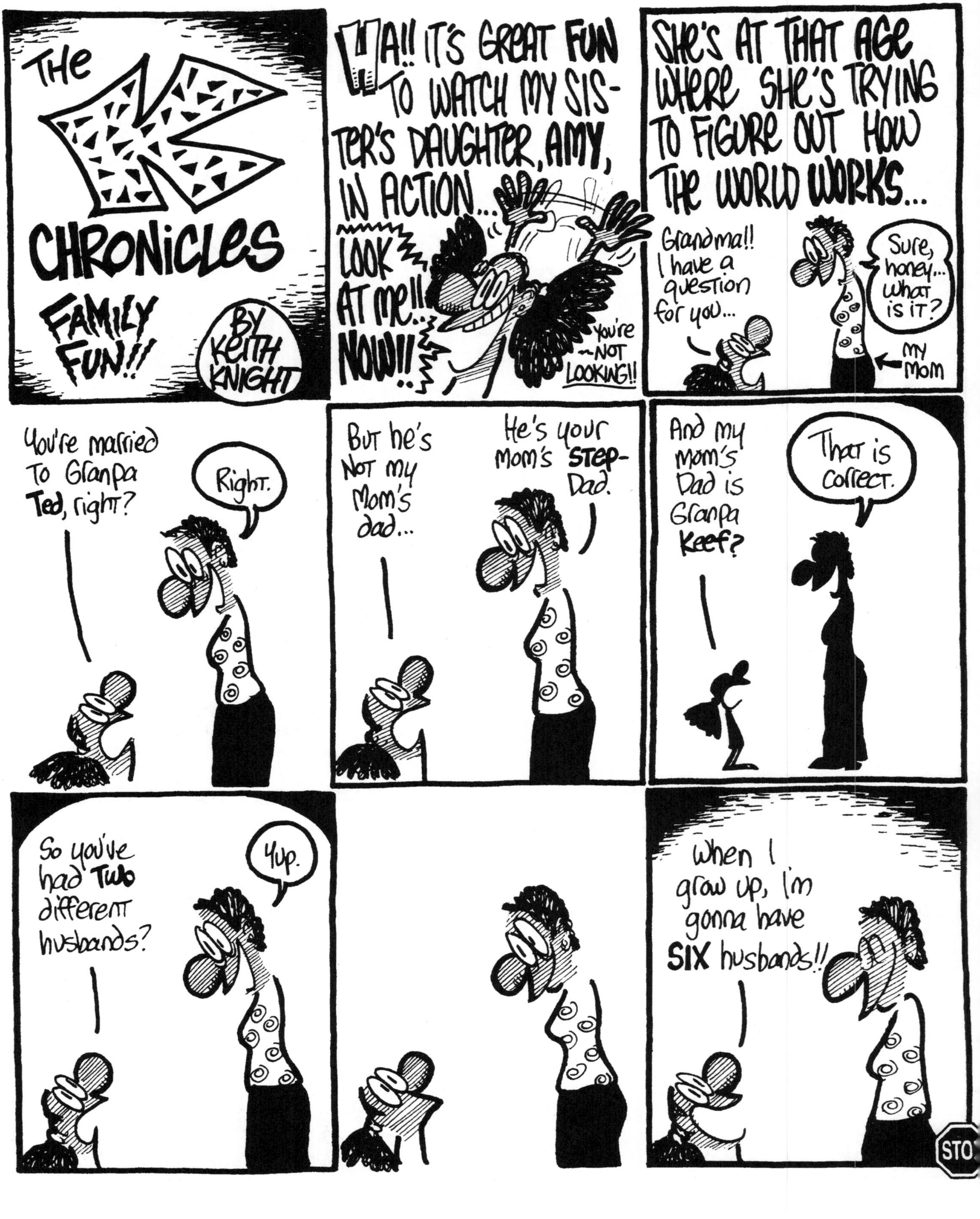
THE K CHRONICLES
FAMILY FUN!!
BY KEITH KNIGHT
HA!! IT'S GREAT FUN TO WATCH MY SIS-TER'S DAUGHTER, AMY, IN ACTION...
LOOK AT ME!!.. NOW!!
You're NOT LOOKING!!
SHE'S AT THAT AGE WHERE SHE'S TRYING TO FIGURE OUT HOW THE WORLD WORKS...
Grandma!! I have a question for you...
Sure, honey... What is it?
MY MOM
You're married to Granpa Ted, right?
Right.
But he's NOT my Mom's dad...
He's your Mom's STEP-Dad.
And my Mom's Dad is Granpa Keef?
That is correct.
So you've had TWO different husbands?
Yup.
When I grow up, I'm gonna have SIX husbands!!
STOP

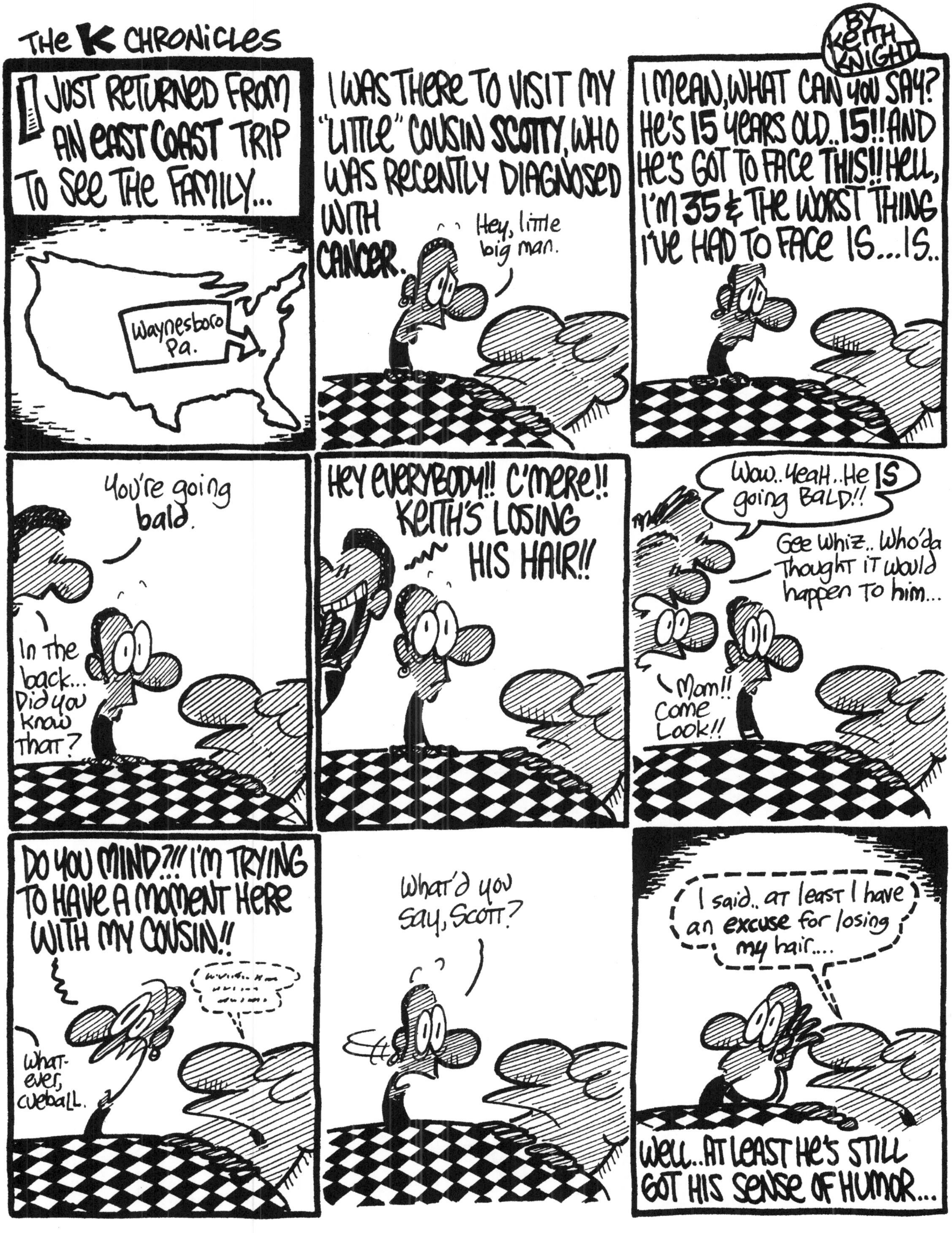
THE K CHRONICLES
BY KEITH KNIGHT
I JUST RETURNED FROM AN EAST COAST TRIP TO SEE THE FAMILY...
Waynesboro Pa.
I WAS THERE TO VISIT MY "LITTLE" COUSIN SCOTTY, WHO WAS RECENTLY DIAGNOSED WITH CANCER.
Hey, little big man.
I MEAN, WHAT CAN YOU SAY? HE'S 15 YEARS OLD..15!! AND HE'S GOT TO FACE THIS!! HELL, I'M 35 & THE WORST THING I'VE HAD TO FACE IS...IS..
You're going bald.
In the back... Did you know that?
HEY EVERYBODY!! C'MERE!! KEITH'S LOSING HIS HAIR!!
Wow.. Yeah.. He IS going BALD!!
Gee whiz.. Who'da thought it would happen to him...
Mom!! Come Look!!
DO YOU MIND?!! I'M TRYING TO HAVE A MOMENT HERE WITH MY COUSIN!!
What-ever, cueball.
What'd you say, Scott?
I said.. at least I have an excuse for losing my hair....
WELL...AT LEAST HE'S STILL GOT HIS SENSE OF HUMOR...

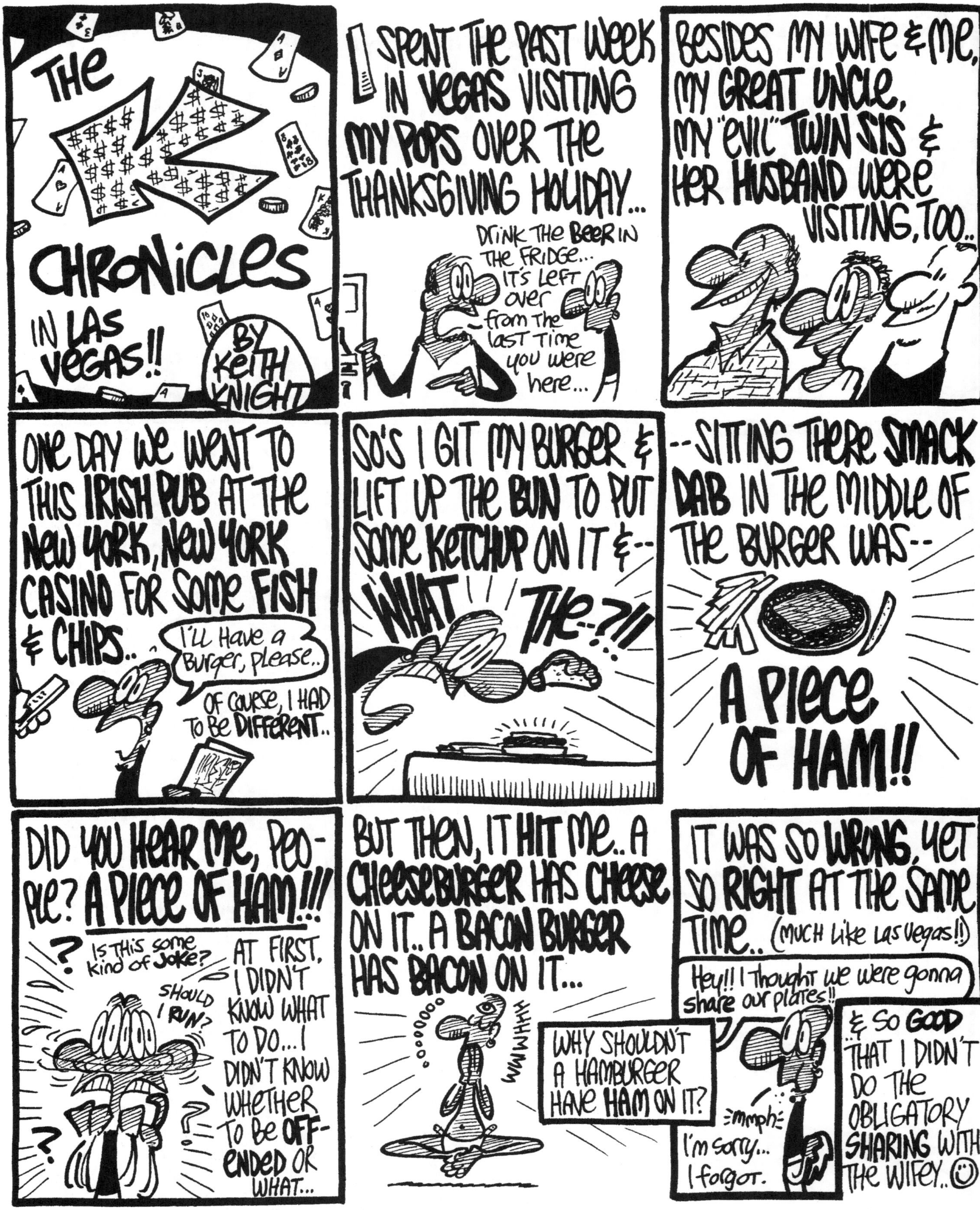
THE K CHRONICLES IN LAS VEGAS!!
BY KEITH KNIGHT
I SPENT THE PAST WEEK IN VEGAS VISITING MY POPS OVER THE THANKSGIVING HOLIDAY...
DRINK THE BEER IN THE FRIDGE... IT'S LEFT OVER FROM THE LAST TIME YOU WERE HERE...
BESIDES MY WIFE & ME, MY GREAT UNCLE, MY "EVIL" TWIN SIS & HER HUSBAND WERE VISITING, TOO..
ONE DAY WE WENT TO THIS IRISH PUB AT THE NEW YORK, NEW YORK CASINO FOR SOME FISH & CHIPS..
I'LL HAVE A BURGER, PLEASE..
OF COURSE, I HAD TO BE DIFFERENT..
SO'S I GIT MY BURGER & LIFT UP THE BUN TO PUT SOME KETCHUP ON IT &--
WHAT THE..?!!
--SITTING THERE SMACK DAB IN THE MIDDLE OF THE BURGER WAS--
A PIECE OF HAM!!
DID YOU HEAR ME, PEO-PLE? A PIECE OF HAM!!!
IS THIS SOME KIND OF JOKE?
SHOULD I RUN?
AT FIRST, I DIDN'T KNOW WHAT TO DO... I DIDN'T KNOW WHETHER TO BE OFF-ENDED OR WHAT...
BUT THEN, IT HIT ME.. A CHEESEBURGER HAS CHEESE ON IT.. A BACON BURGER HAS BACON ON IT...
HHHMMMM
WHY SHOULDN'T A HAMBURGER HAVE HAM ON IT?
IT WAS SO WRONG, YET SO RIGHT AT THE SAME TIME.. (MUCH LIKE LAS VEGAS!!)
HEY!! I THOUGHT WE WERE GONNA SHARE OUR PLATES!!
MMPH
I'M SORRY... I FORGOT.
& SO GOOD THAT I DIDN'T DO THE OBLIGATORY SHARING WITH THE WIFEY..

BY KEITH KNIGHT

OKAY..SO MY FAMILY NAME IS KNIGHT... SO IT'D MAKE SENSE THAT MY FAMILY WOULD BE FULL OF NIGHT PEOPLE...NO?

..ESPECIALLY SINCE MY DAD LIVES IN LAS VEGAS.... BUT ALAS, MY FRIENDS, THIS NOTION IS **NOT** TO BE **TRUE**...

DURING MY LATEST VISIT TO THE CITY OF SIN, MY DAD & UNCLE HAVE BEEN INSISTING THAT I GET UP AT THE **CRACK OF DAWN** FOR AN EARLY MORNING STROLL..

THE CRACK OF DAWN

!!!

GOOD GAWD, I HATE THE MORNING...

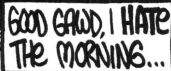

Aww..CHEEZ -n-CRACKERZ...

EVERYTHING'S ALL BRIGHT & CLEAN...

YOU SEE PEOPLE WITH **JOBS**...

OLDER FOLKS & CHILDREN..

THE DAY RESONATES WITH **HOPE** & **POSSIBILITY**...

≡BLEAH≡ AND THEN THERE'S THAT **STUPID** SUN..

YO..I'M LIKE GEORGE BENSON.. JUST GIMME THE **NIGHT**...

Wanna date?

HEAVE

HOOKERS & DEVIANTS... HOBOS & VAMPIRES...

THESE ARE MY TYPE O' FOLKS... GAWD BLESS 'EM...

LAST NIGHT, I WENT TO BED AT 11PM!! THESE EARLY MORNING STROLLS HAVE TAKEN THE WIND OUT OF MY **SAILS**... BUT, THANKFULLY, NOT OUT OF MY BOTTOM... FOR REVENGE, I DECIDED TO WAKE MY DAD UP WITH THE **CRACK OF KEEF**..

BRAPP

STOP

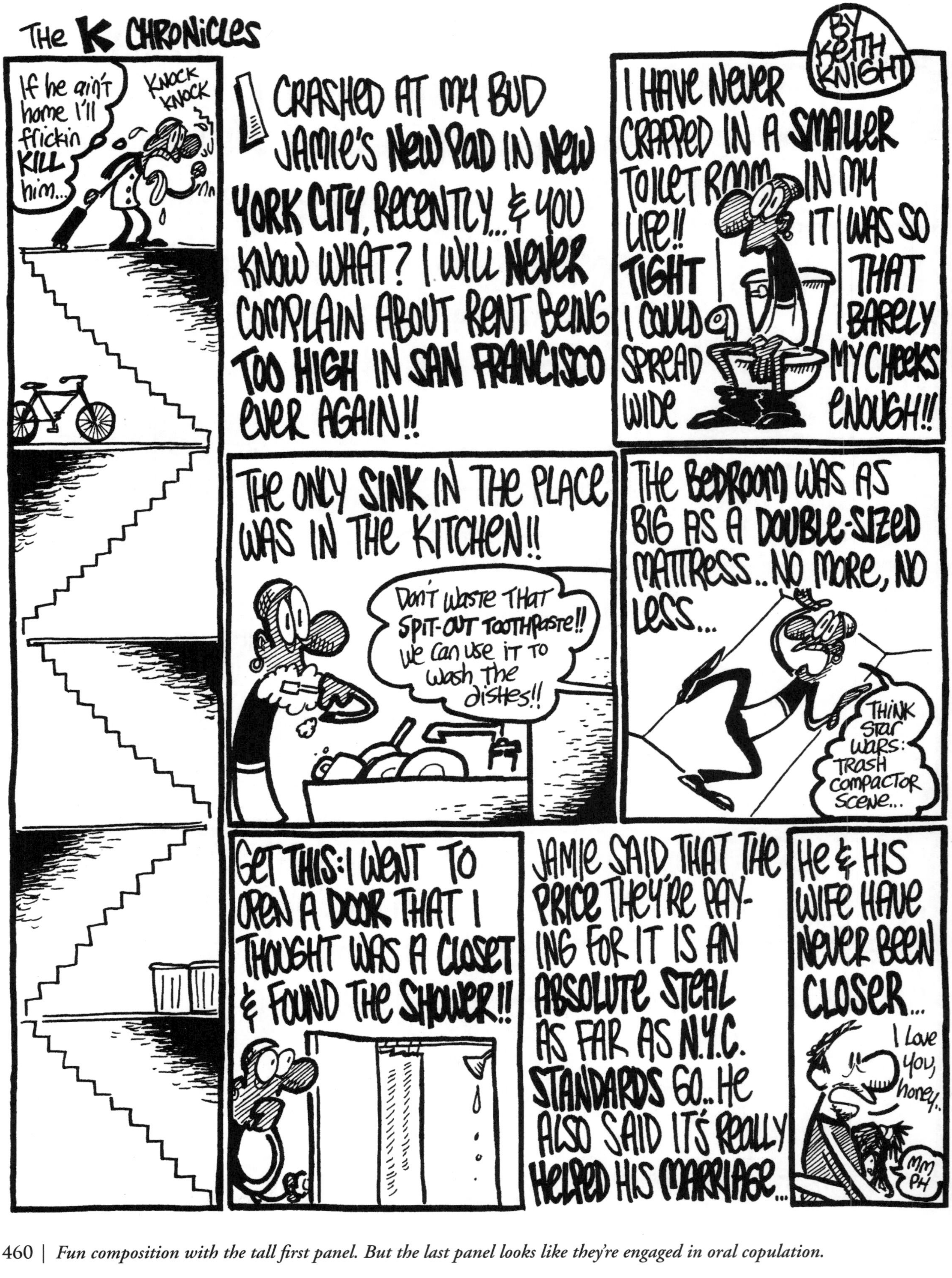
THE K CHRONICLES
BY KEITH KNIGHT
If he ain't home I'll frickin KILL him...
KNOCK KNOCK
I CRASHED AT MY BUD JAMIE'S NEW PAD IN NEW YORK CITY, RECENTLY... & YOU KNOW WHAT? I WILL NEVER COMPLAIN ABOUT RENT BEING TOO HIGH IN SAN FRANCISCO EVER AGAIN!!
I HAVE NEVER CRAPPED IN A SMALLER TOILET ROOM IN MY LIFE!! IT WAS SO TIGHT THAT I COULD BARELY SPREAD MY CHEEKS WIDE ENOUGH!!
THE ONLY SINK IN THE PLACE WAS IN THE KITCHEN!!
Don't waste that SPIT-OUT TOOTHPASTE!! We can use it to wash the dishes!!
THE BEDROOM WAS AS BIG AS A DOUBLE-SIZED MATTRESS.. NO MORE, NO LESS...
THINK STAR WARS: TRASH COMPACTOR SCENE...
GET THIS: I WENT TO OPEN A DOOR THAT I THOUGHT WAS A CLOSET & FOUND THE SHOWER!!
JAMIE SAID THAT THE PRICE THEY'RE PAYING FOR IT IS AN ABSOLUTE STEAL AS FAR AS N.Y.C. STANDARDS GO.. HE ALSO SAID IT'S REALLY HELPED HIS MARRIAGE...
HE & HIS WIFE HAVE NEVER BEEN CLOSER...
I Love you, honey..
MM PH

 Fun composition with the tall first panel. But the last panel looks like they're engaged in oral copulation.

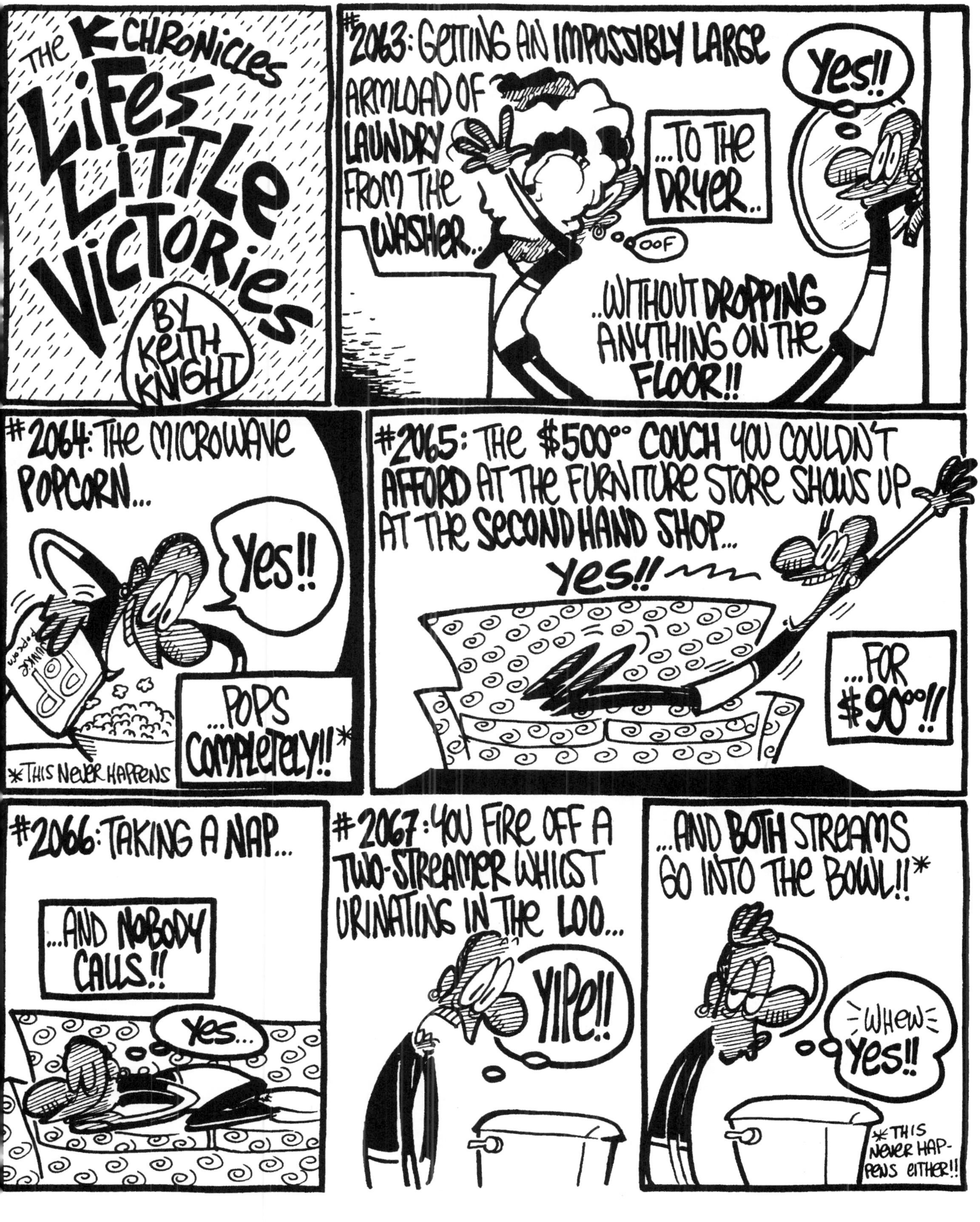
THE K CHRONICLES
LIFES LITTLE VICTORIES
BY KEITH KNIGHT
#2063: GETTING AN IMPOSSIBLY LARGE ARMLOAD OF LAUNDRY FROM THE WASHER...
...TO THE DRYER...
OOF
...WITHOUT DROPPING ANYTHING ON THE FLOOR!!
YES!!
#2064: THE MICROWAVE POPCORN...
YES!!
...POPS COMPLETELY!!*
*THIS NEVER HAPPENS
#2065: THE $500.00 COUCH YOU COULDN'T AFFORD AT THE FURNITURE STORE SHOWS UP AT THE SECOND HAND SHOP...
YES!!
...FOR $90.00!!
#2066: TAKING A NAP...
...AND NOBODY CALLS!!
YES...
#2067: YOU FIRE OFF A TWO-STREAMER WHILST URINATING IN THE LOO...
YIPE!!
...AND BOTH STREAMS GO INTO THE BOWL!!*
WHEW
YES!!
*THIS NEVER HAPPENS EITHER!!

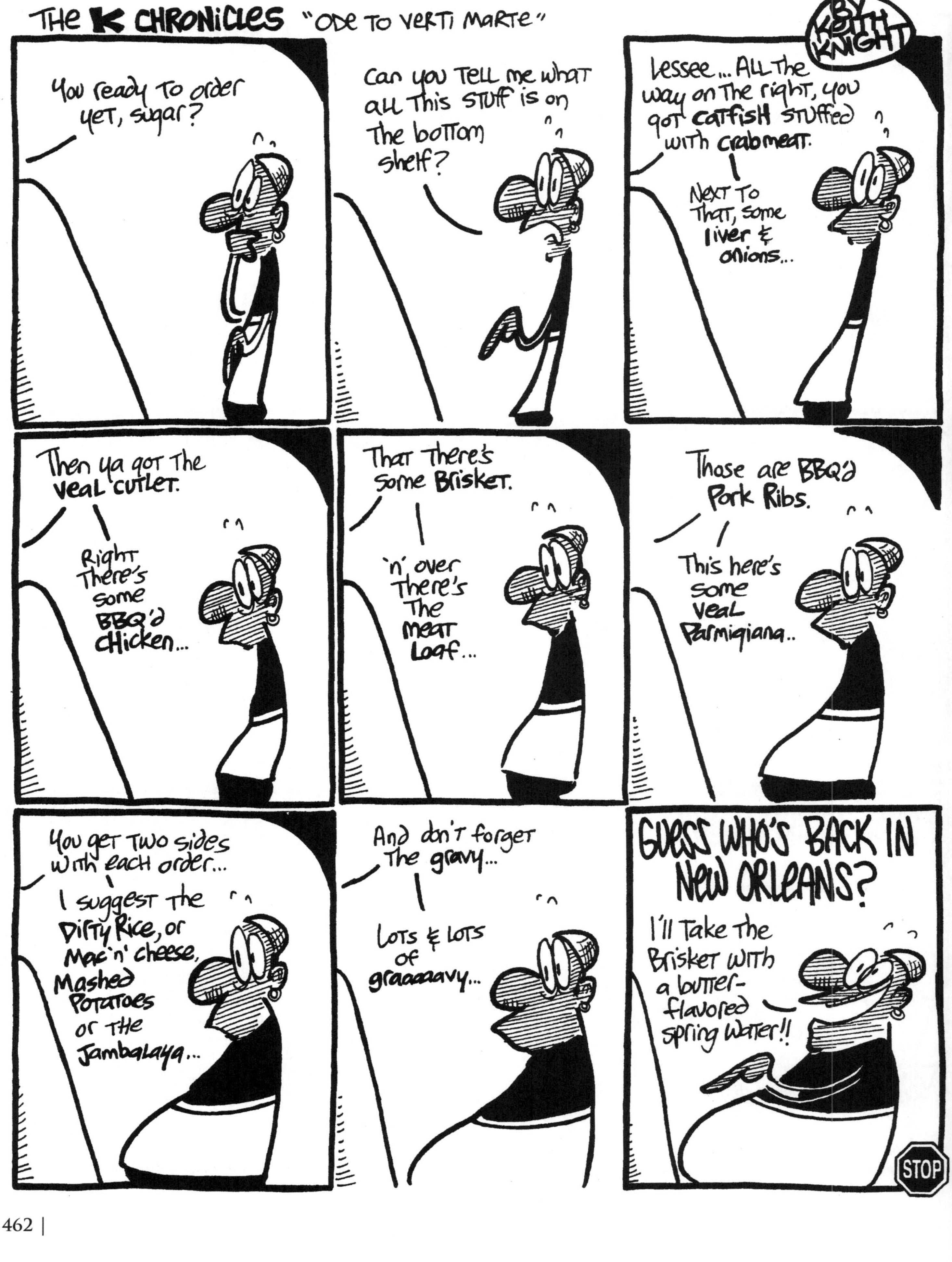
THE K CHRONICLES "ODE TO VERTI MARTE"
BY KEITH KNIGHT
You ready to order yet, sugar?
Can you tell me what all this stuff is on the bottom shelf?
Lessee... All the way on the right, you got catfish stuffed with crabmeat.
Next to that, some liver & onions...
Then ya got the veal cutlet.
Right there's some BBQ'd chicken...
That there's some brisket.
'n' over there's the meat loaf...
Those are BBQ'd Pork Ribs.
This here's some veal Parmigiana..
You get two sides with each order...
I suggest the Dirty Rice, or Mac 'n' cheese, Mashed Potatoes or the Jambalaya...
And don't forget the gravy...
Lots & lots of graaaaavy...
GUESS WHO'S BACK IN NEW ORLEANS?
I'll take the Brisket with a butter-flavored spring water!!
STOP

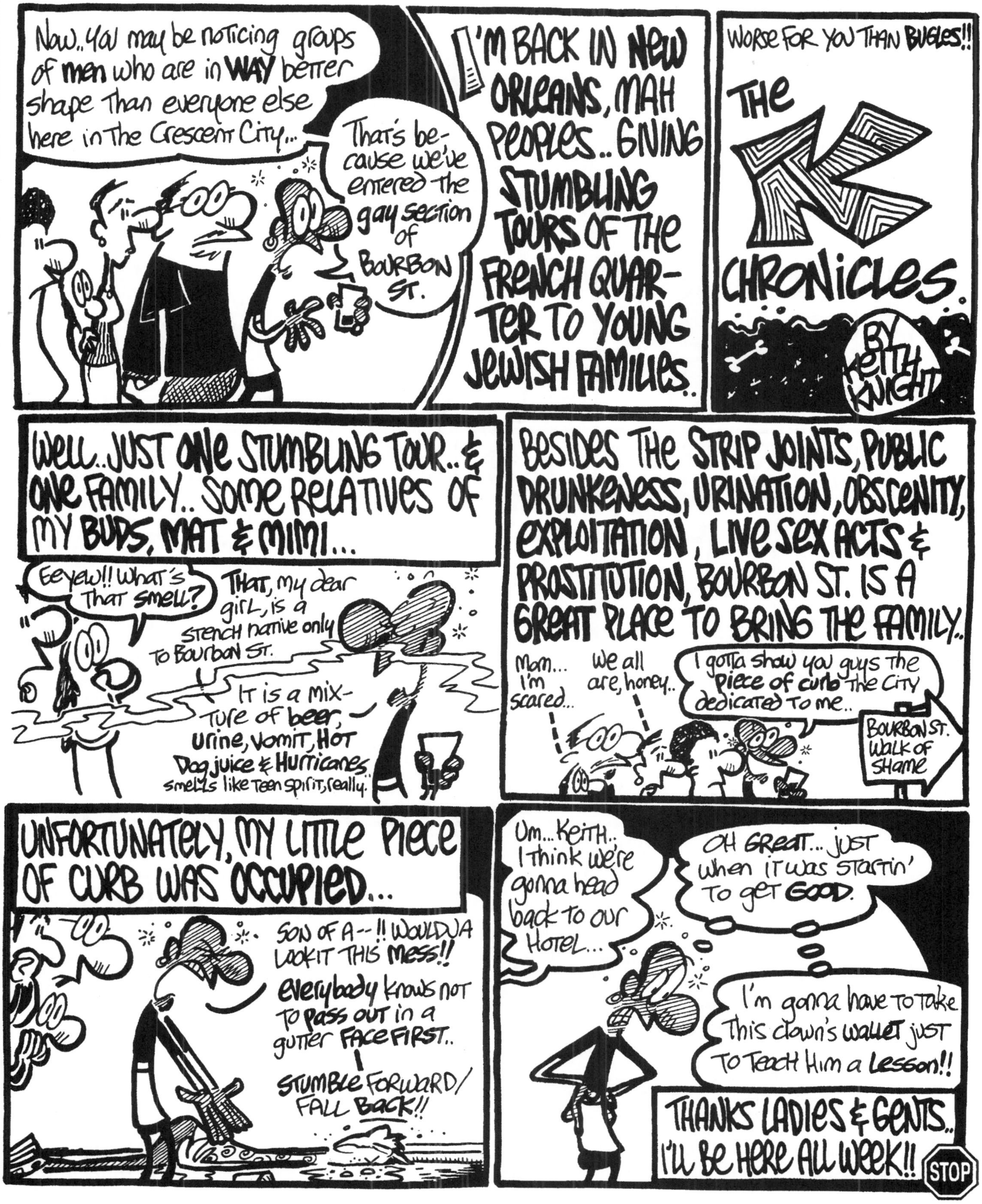
Now.. You may be noticing groups of men who are in WAY better shape than everyone else here in the Crescent City...
That's because we've entered the gay section of Bourbon St.
I'M BACK IN NEW ORLEANS, MAH PEOPLES.. GIVING STUMBLING TOURS OF THE FRENCH QUARTER TO YOUNG JEWISH FAMILIES..
WORSE FOR YOU THAN BUGLES!!
THE K CHRONICLES
BY KEITH KNIGHT
WELL.. JUST ONE STUMBLING TOUR.. & ONE FAMILY.. SOME RELATIVES OF MY BUDS, MAT & MIMI...
Eeyew!! What's that smell?
THAT, my dear girl, is a stench native only to Bourbon St.
It is a mixture of beer, urine, vomit, Hot Dog juice & Hurricanes.
smells like Teen spirit, really.
BESIDES THE STRIP JOINTS, PUBLIC DRUNKENESS, URINATION, OBSCENITY, EXPLOITATION, LIVE SEX ACTS & PROSTITUTION, BOURBON ST. IS A GREAT PLACE TO BRING THE FAMILY..
Mom... I'm scared...
We all are, honey..
I gotta show you guys the piece of curb the city dedicated to me..
BOURBON ST. WALK OF SHAME
UNFORTUNATELY, MY LITTLE PIECE OF CURB WAS OCCUPIED...
SON OF A--!! WOULDJA LOOKIT THIS MESS!!
everybody knows not to pass out in a gutter FACE FIRST..
STUMBLE FORWARD/ FALL BACK!!
Um... Keith.. I think we're gonna head back to our Hotel...
OH GREAT... JUST when it was startin' to get GOOD.
I'm gonna have to take this clown's wallet just to teach him a lesson!!
THANKS LADIES & GENTS.. I'LL BE HERE ALL WEEK!!
STOP

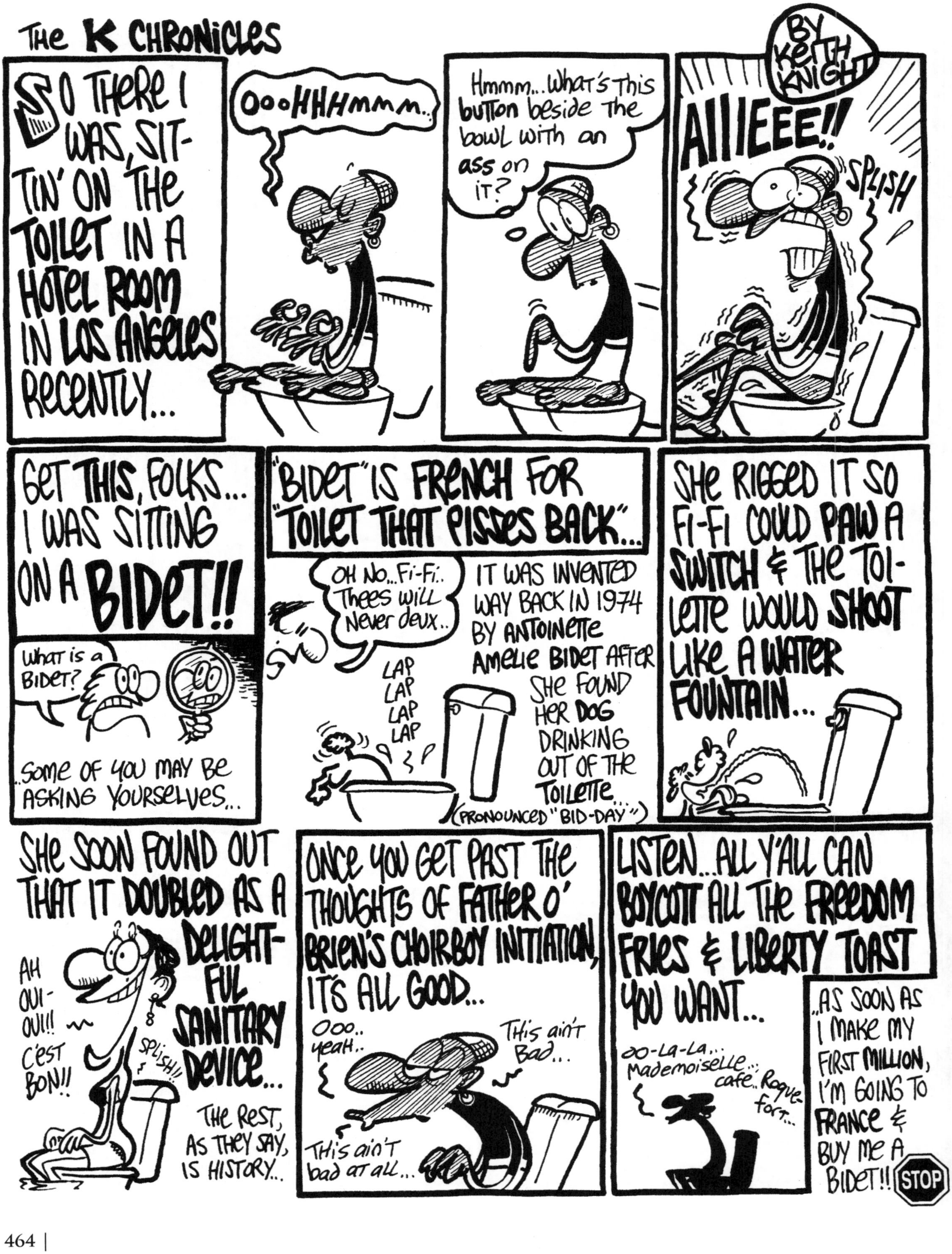

THE K CHRONICLES
BY KEITH KNIGHT
SO THERE I WAS, SITTIN' ON THE TOILET IN A HOTEL ROOM IN LOS ANGELES RECENTLY...
OooHHHmmm..
Hmmm... What's this button beside the bowl with an ass on it?
AIIIEEE!!
SPLISH
GET THIS, FOLKS... I WAS SITTING ON A BIDET!!
What is a BIDET?
..SOME OF YOU MAY BE ASKING YOURSELVES...
"BIDET" IS FRENCH FOR "TOILET THAT PISSES BACK"...
OH No...Fi-Fi.. Thees will Never deux..
IT WAS INVENTED WAY BACK IN 1974 BY ANTOINETTE AMELIE BIDET AFTER SHE FOUND HER DOG DRINKING OUT OF THE TOILETTE...
LAP LAP LAP LAP
(PRONOUNCED "BID-DAY")
SHE RIGGED IT SO FI-FI COULD PAW A SWITCH & THE TOILETTE WOULD SHOOT LIKE A WATER FOUNTAIN...
SHE SOON FOUND OUT THAT IT DOUBLED AS A DELIGHTFUL SANITARY DEVICE...
AH OUI-OUI!! C'EST BON!!
SPLISH!!
THE REST, AS THEY SAY, IS HISTORY...
ONCE YOU GET PAST THE THOUGHTS OF FATHER O'BRIEN'S CHOIRBOY INITIATION, IT'S ALL GOOD...
Ooo.. yeah..
This ain't Bad...
This ain't bad at all...
LISTEN...ALL Y'ALL CAN BOYCOTT ALL THE FREEDOM FRIES & LIBERTY TOAST YOU WANT...
oo-la-la.. Mademoiselle.. cafe.. Roquefort...
..AS SOON AS I MAKE MY FIRST MILLION, I'M GOING TO FRANCE & BUY ME A BIDET!!
STOP

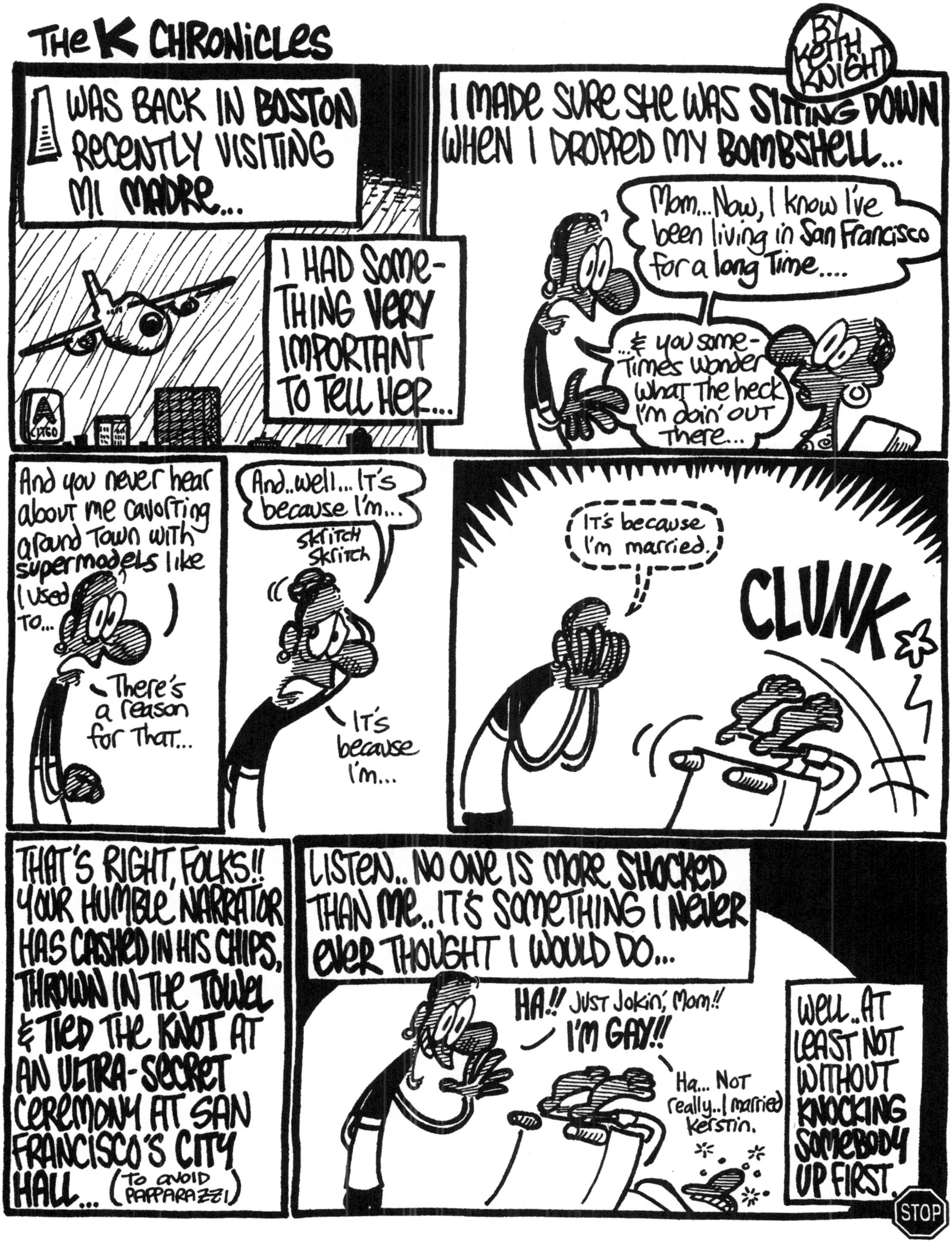

THE K CHRONICLES
BY KEITH KNIGHT
I WAS BACK IN BOSTON RECENTLY VISITING MI MADRE...
I HAD SOMETHING VERY IMPORTANT TO TELL HER...
I MADE SURE SHE WAS SITTING DOWN WHEN I DROPPED MY BOMBSHELL...
Mom... Now, I know I've been living in San Francisco for a long Time....
...& you sometimes wonder what the heck I'm doin' out there...
And you never hear about me cavorting around Town with supermodels like I used to...
There's a reason for that...
And.. well... It's because I'm...
SKRITCH SKRITCH
It's because I'm...
It's because I'm married.
CLUNK
THAT'S RIGHT, FOLKS!! YOUR HUMBLE NARRATOR HAS CASHED IN HIS CHIPS, THROWN IN THE TOWEL & TIED THE KNOT AT AN ULTRA-SECRET CEREMONY AT SAN FRANCISCO'S CITY HALL... (TO AVOID PAPPARAZZI)
LISTEN.. NO ONE IS MORE SHOCKED THAN ME.. IT'S SOMETHING I NEVER EVER THOUGHT I WOULD DO...
HA!! JUST JOKIN', MOM!! I'M GAY!!
Ha... NOT really.. I married Kerstin.
WELL.. AT LEAST NOT WITHOUT KNOCKING SOMEBODY UP FIRST.
STOP

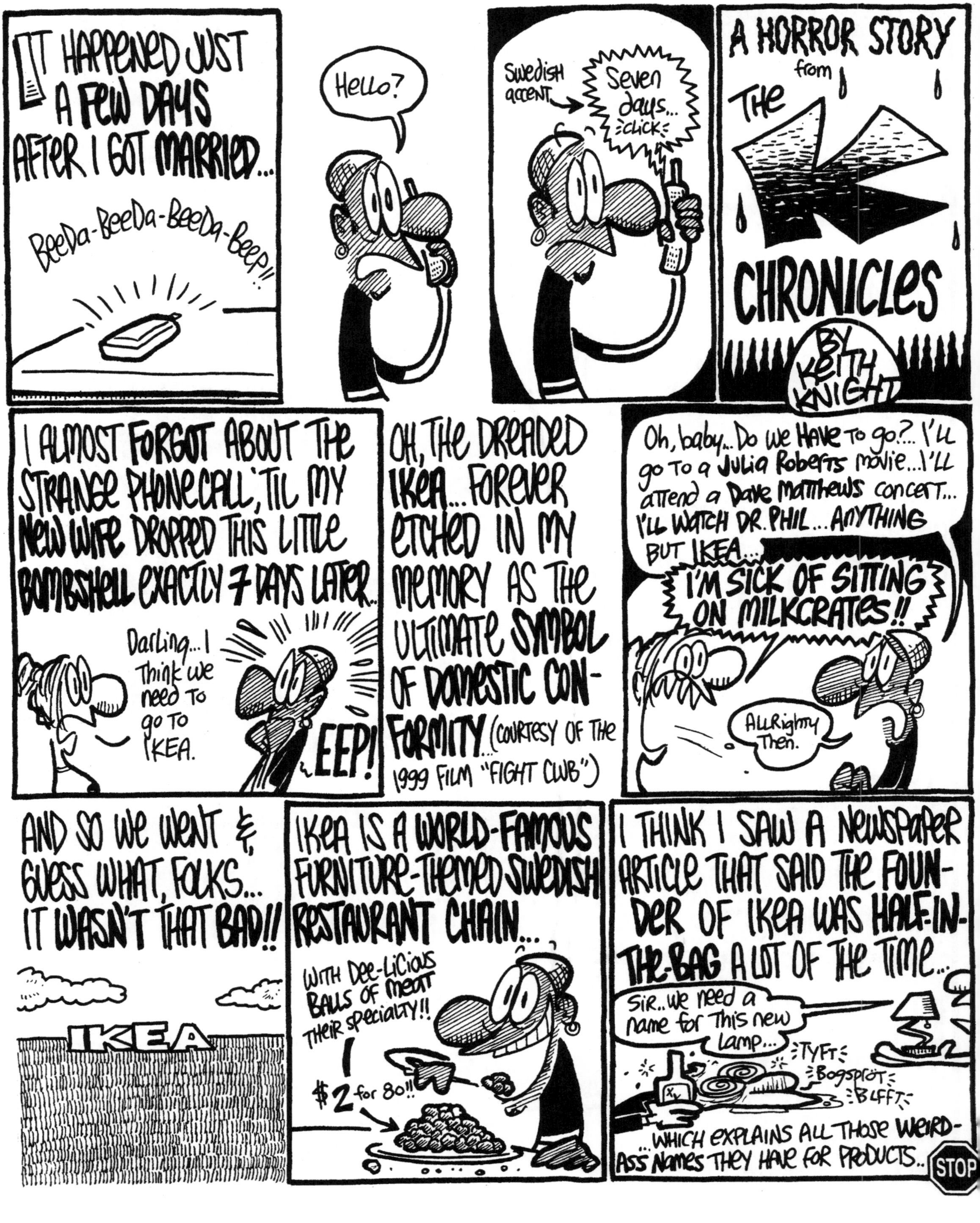
IT HAPPENED JUST A FEW DAYS AFTER I GOT MARRIED...
BeeDa-BeeDa-BeeDa-Beep!!
Hello?
Swedish accent
Seven days... click
A HORROR STORY from THE K CHRONICLES
BY KEITH KNIGHT
I ALMOST FORGOT ABOUT THE STRANGE PHONECALL, 'TIL MY NEW WIFE DROPPED THIS LITTLE BOMBSHELL EXACTLY 7 DAYS LATER...
Darling... I think we need to go to IKEA.
EEP!
OH, THE DREADED IKEA... FOREVER ETCHED IN MY MEMORY AS THE ULTIMATE SYMBOL OF DOMESTIC CONFORMITY... (COURTESY OF THE 1999 FILM "FIGHT CLUB")
Oh, baby... Do we HAVE to go?... I'll go to a Julia Roberts movie... I'll attend a Dave Matthews concert... I'll watch Dr. Phil... Anything but IKEA...
I'M SICK OF SITTING ON MILKCRATES!!
AllRighty Then.
AND SO WE WENT &, GUESS WHAT, FOLKS... IT WASN'T THAT BAD!!
IKEA
IKEA IS A WORLD-FAMOUS FURNITURE-THEMED SWEDISH RESTAURANT CHAIN...
WITH DEE-LICIOUS BALLS OF MEAT THEIR SPECIALTY!!
$2 for 80!!
I THINK I SAW A NEWSPAPER ARTICLE THAT SAID THE FOUNDER OF IKEA WAS HALF-IN-THE-BAG A LOT OF THE TIME...
Sir.. we need a name for this new lamp...
TYFT
Bogspröt
BLFFT
...WHICH EXPLAINS ALL THOSE WEIRD-ASS NAMES THEY HAVE FOR PRODUCTS..
STOP

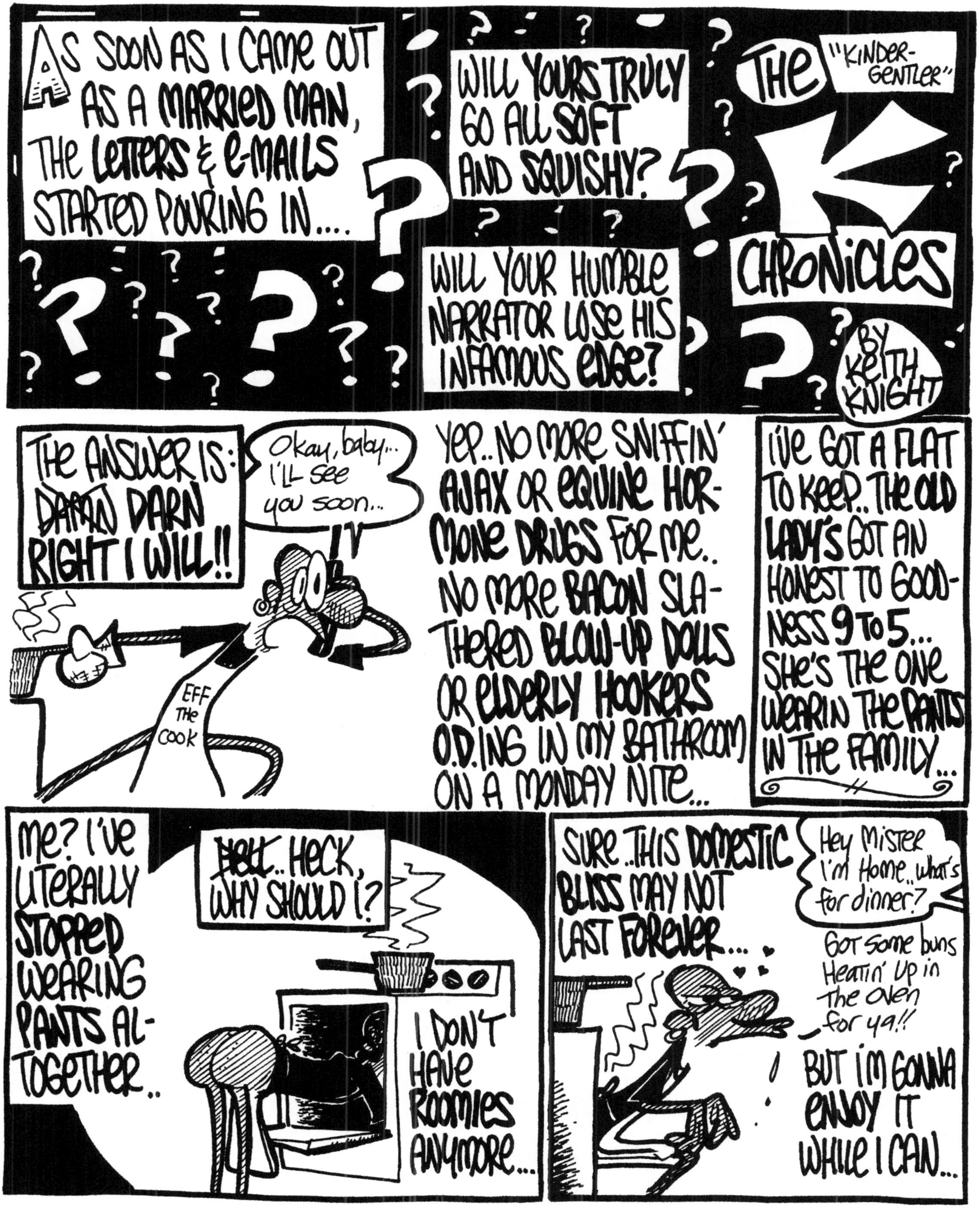

As soon as I came out as a married man, the letters & e-mails started pouring in....
Will yours truly go all soft and squishy?
Will your humble narrator lose his infamous edge?
The "Kinder-Gentler" K Chronicles
By Keith Knight
The answer is: Damn Darn right I will!!
Okay, baby... I'll see you soon...
Eff the cook
Yep.. No more sniffin' Ajax or equine hor-mone drugs for me.. No more bacon sla-thered blow-up dolls or elderly hookers O.D.ing in my bathroom on a Monday nite...
I've got a flat to keep.. The old lady's got an honest to good-ness 9 to 5... She's the one wearin the pants in the family...
Me? I've literally stopped wearing pants al-together..
Hell.. Heck, why should I?
I don't have roomies anymore...
Sure..This domestic bliss may not last forever...
Hey Mister I'm home.. what's for dinner?
Got some buns heatin' up in the oven for ya!!
But I'm gonna enjoy it while I can...

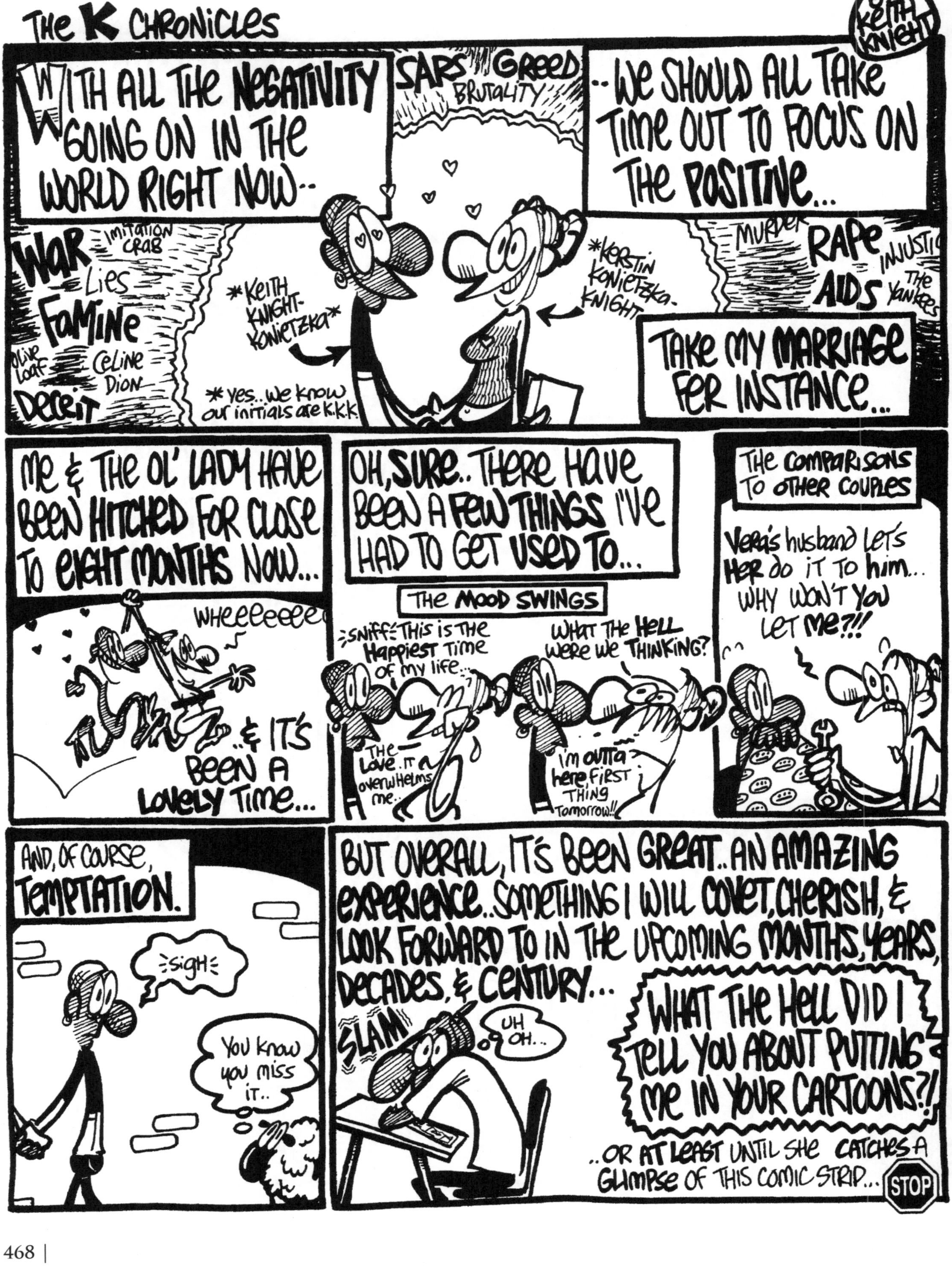
THE K CHRONICLES
BY KEITH KNIGHT
WITH ALL THE NEGATIVITY GOING ON IN THE WORLD RIGHT NOW..
SARS GREED BRUTALITY
..WE SHOULD ALL TAKE TIME OUT TO FOCUS ON THE POSITIVE...
WAR IMITATION CRAB LIES FAMINE OLIVE LOAF CELINE DION DECEIT
KEITH KNIGHT-KONIETZKA
*KERSTIN KONIETZKA-KNIGHT
*YES.. WE KNOW OUR INITIALS ARE K.K.K.
MURDER RAPE INJUSTIC AIDS THE YANKEES
TAKE MY MARRIAGE FOR INSTANCE...
ME & THE OL' LADY HAVE BEEN HITCHED FOR CLOSE TO EIGHT MONTHS NOW...
WHEEEEEEE
..& IT'S BEEN A LOVELY TIME...
OH, SURE.. THERE HAVE BEEN A FEW THINGS I'VE HAD TO GET USED TO...
THE MOOD SWINGS
SNIFF THIS IS THE HAPPIEST TIME OF MY LIFE...
THE LOVE.. IT A OVERWHELMS ME..
WHAT THE HELL WERE WE THINKING?
I'M OUTTA HERE FIRST THING TOMORROW!!
THE COMPARISONS TO OTHER COUPLES
VERA'S HUSBAND LET'S HER DO IT TO HIM... WHY WON'T YOU LET ME?!!
AND, OF COURSE, TEMPTATION.
SIGH
YOU KNOW YOU MISS IT..
BUT OVERALL, IT'S BEEN GREAT.. AN AMAZING EXPERIENCE.. SOMETHING I WILL COVET, CHERISH, & LOOK FORWARD TO IN THE UPCOMING MONTHS, YEARS, DECADES, & CENTURY...
SLAM
UH OH..
WHAT THE HELL DID I TELL YOU ABOUT PUTTING ME IN YOUR CARTOONS?!
..OR AT LEAST UNTIL SHE CATCHES A GLIMPSE OF THIS COMIC STRIP...
STOP

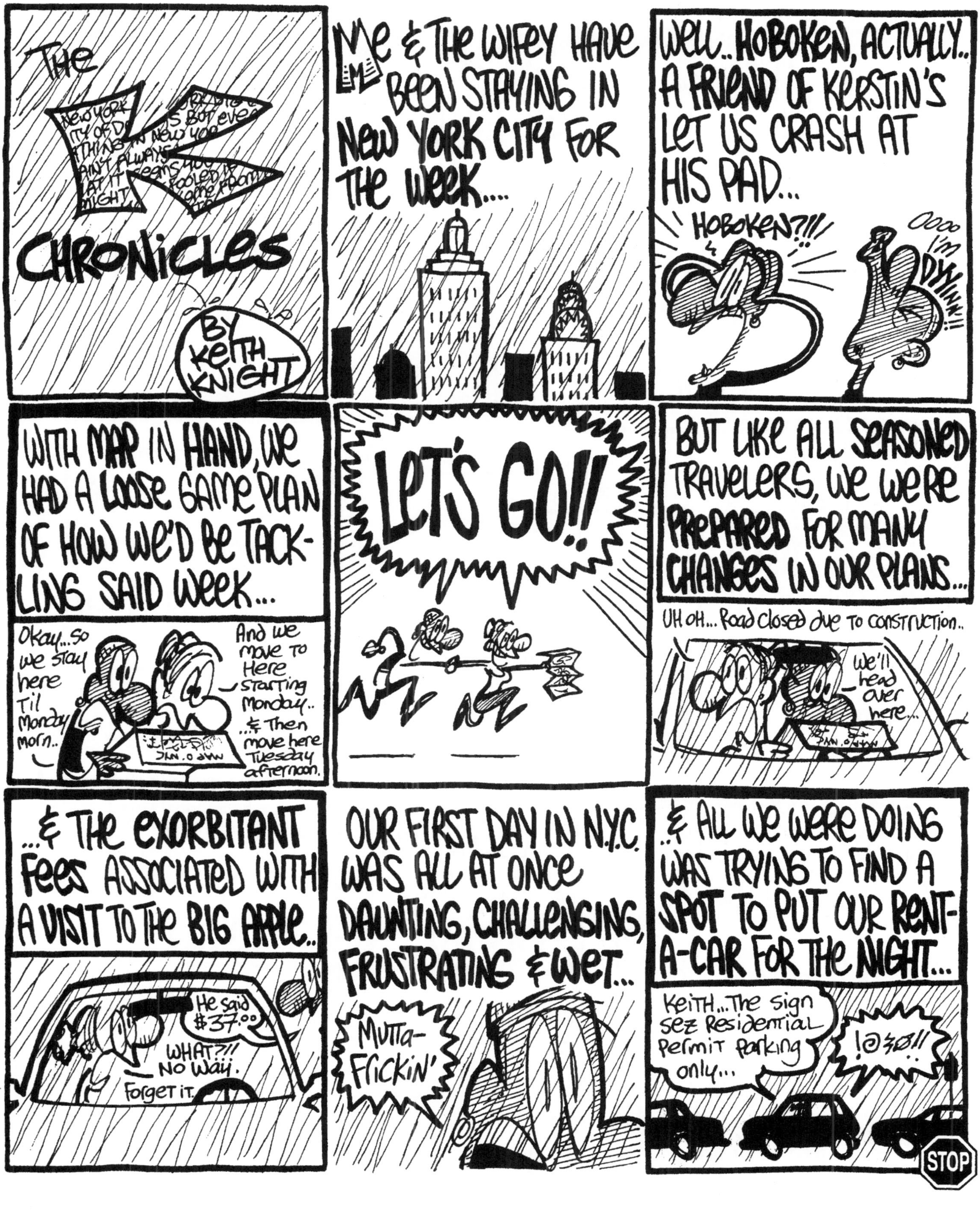
THE
CHRONICLES
BY KEITH KNIGHT
ME & THE WIFEY HAVE BEEN STAYING IN NEW YORK CITY FOR THE WEEK....
WELL.. HOBOKEN, ACTUALLY.. A FRIEND OF KERSTIN'S LET US CRASH AT HIS PAD...
HOBOKEN?!!
Oooo I'm DYIN!!
WITH MAP IN HAND, WE HAD A LOOSE GAME PLAN OF HOW WE'D BE TACKLING SAID WEEK...
Okay...so we stay here Til Monday morn..
And we move to Here starting Monday.. ...& Then move here Tuesday afternoon.
LET'S GO!!
BUT LIKE ALL SEASONED TRAVELERS, WE WERE PREPARED FOR MANY CHANGES IN OUR PLANS...
UH OH... Road closed due to construction..
We'll head over here...
...& THE EXORBITANT FEES ASSOCIATED WITH A VISIT TO THE BIG APPLE...
He said $37.00
WHAT?!! No way.
Forget it.
OUR FIRST DAY IN N.Y.C. WAS ALL AT ONCE DAUNTING, CHALLENGING, FRUSTRATING & WET...
Mutta-Frickin'
..& ALL WE WERE DOING WAS TRYING TO FIND A SPOT TO PUT OUR RENT-A-CAR FOR THE NIGHT...
KEITH...The sign sez Residential Permit Parking only...
!@#!!
STOP

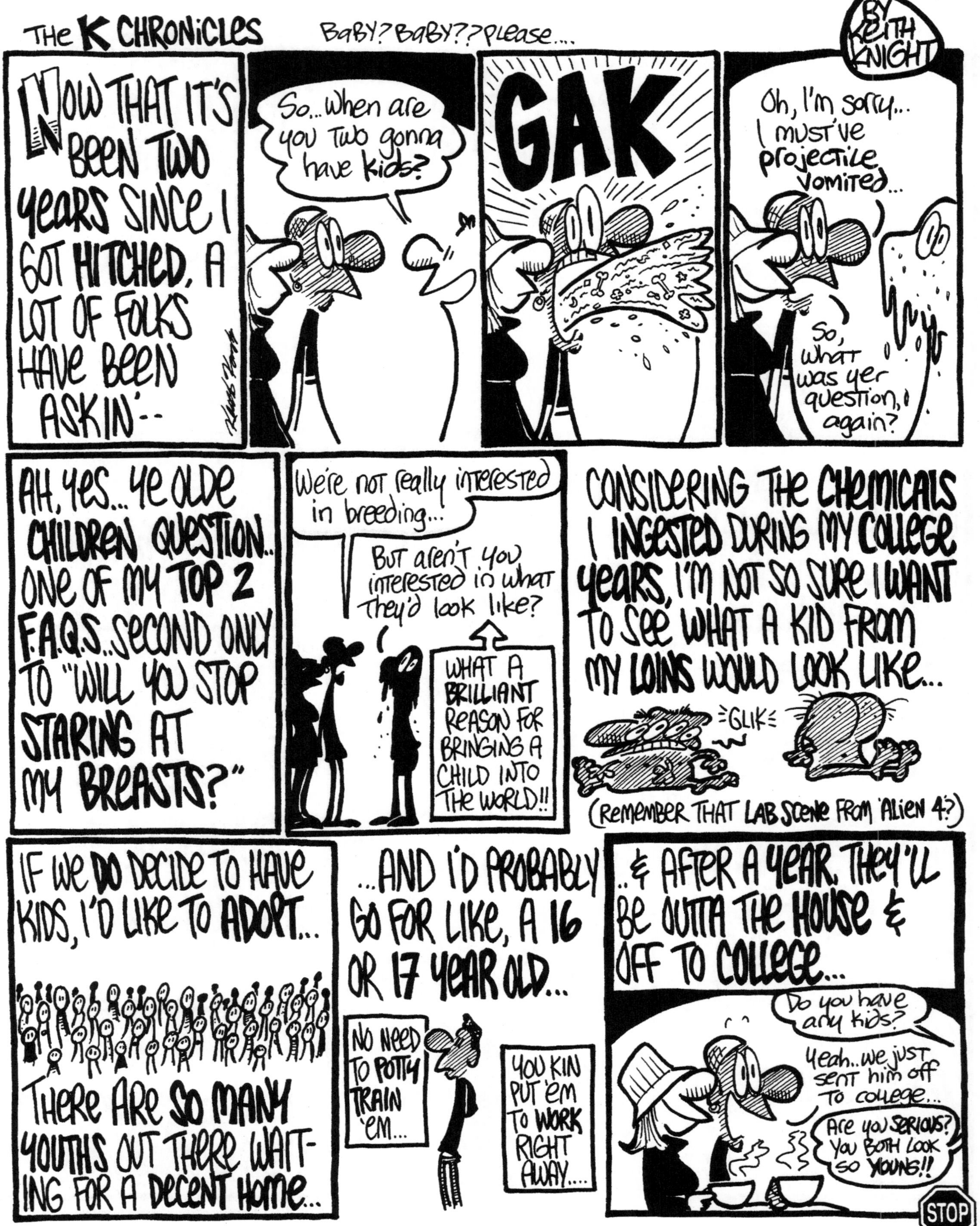
THE K CHRONICLES
BaBY? BaBY?? PLease....
BY KEITH KNIGHT
NOW THAT IT'S BEEN TWO YEARS SINCE I GOT HITCHED, A LOT OF FOLKS HAVE BEEN ASKIN'--
So...When are you two gonna have kids?
GAK
Oh, I'm sorry... I must've projectile vomited...
So, what was yer question, again?
AH, YES... YE OLDE CHILDREN QUESTION... ONE OF MY TOP 2 F.A.Q.S...SECOND ONLY TO "WILL YOU STOP STARING AT MY BREASTS?"
We're not really interested in breeding...
But aren't you interested in what they'd look like?
WHAT A BRILLIANT REASON FOR BRINGING A CHILD INTO THE WORLD!!
CONSIDERING THE CHEMICALS I INGESTED DURING MY COLLEGE YEARS, I'M NOT SO SURE I WANT TO SEE WHAT A KID FROM MY LOINS WOULD LOOK LIKE...
GLIK
(REMEMBER THAT LAB SCENE FROM 'ALIEN 4'?)
IF WE DO DECIDE TO HAVE KIDS, I'D LIKE TO ADOPT...
THERE ARE SO MANY YOUTHS OUT THERE WAITING FOR A DECENT HOME...
...AND I'D PROBABLY GO FOR LIKE, A 16 OR 17 YEAR OLD...
NO NEED TO POTTY TRAIN 'EM...
YOU KIN PUT 'EM TO WORK RIGHT AWAY....
..& AFTER A YEAR, THEY'LL BE OUTTA THE HOUSE & OFF TO COLLEGE...
Do you have any kids?
Yeah..we just sent him off to college...
Are you serious? You both look so young!!
STOP

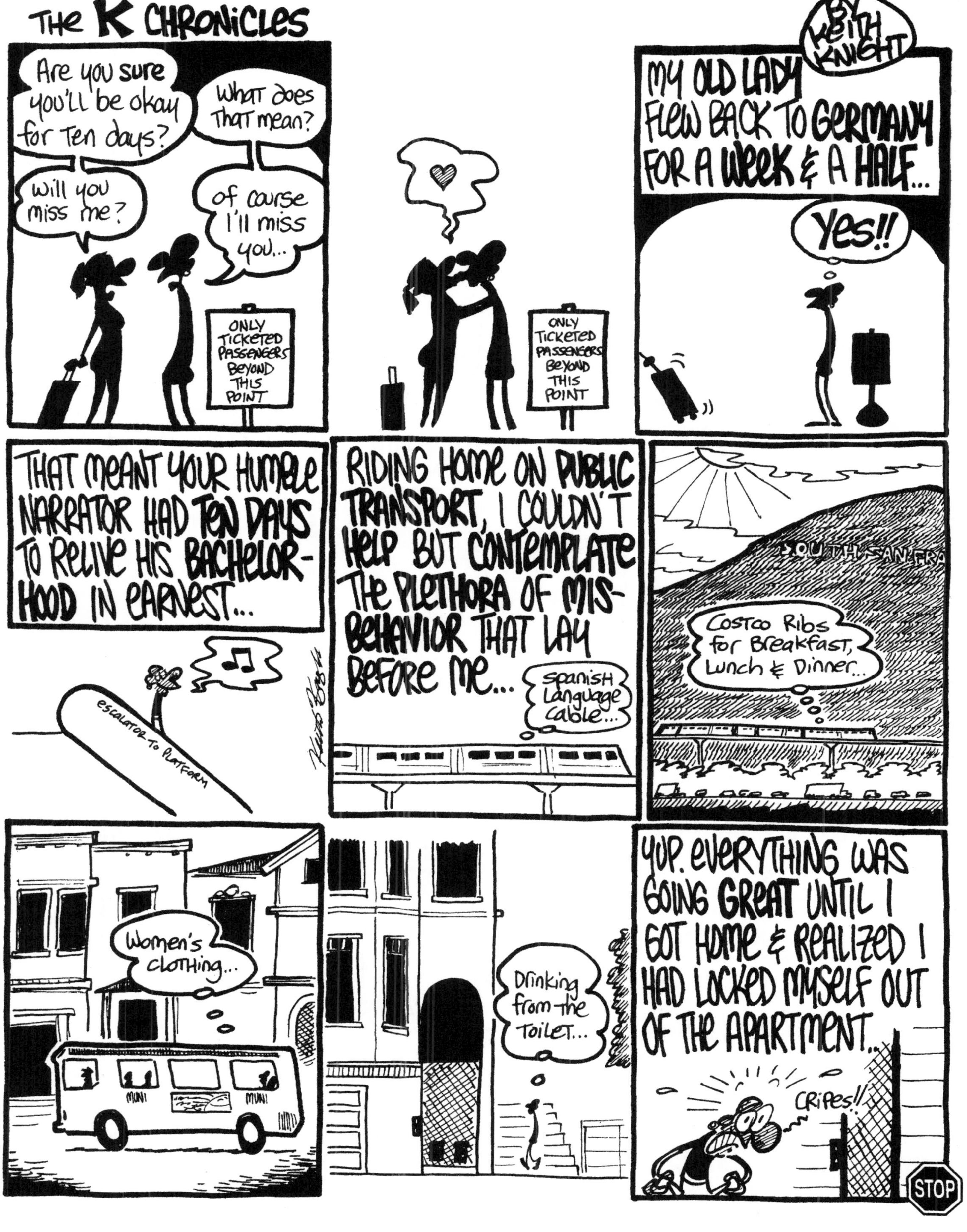
THE K CHRONICLES
BY KEITH KNIGHT
Are you sure you'll be okay for ten days?
What does that mean?
Will you miss me?
Of course I'll miss you...
ONLY TICKETED PASSENGERS BEYOND THIS POINT
ONLY TICKETED PASSENGERS BEYOND THIS POINT
MY OLD LADY FLEW BACK TO GERMANY FOR A WEEK & A HALF...
Yes!!
THAT MEANT YOUR HUMBLE NARRATOR HAD TEN DAYS TO RELIVE HIS BACHELOR-HOOD IN EARNEST...
ESCALATOR TO PLATFORM
RIDING HOME ON PUBLIC TRANSPORT, I COULDN'T HELP BUT CONTEMPLATE THE PLETHORA OF MIS-BEHAVIOR THAT LAY BEFORE ME...
Spanish Language Cable...
SOUTH SAN FRA
Costco Ribs for Breakfast, Lunch & Dinner...
Women's Clothing...
MUNI
MUNI
Drinking from the Toilet...
YUP. EVERYTHING WAS GOING GREAT UNTIL I GOT HOME & REALIZED I HAD LOCKED MYSELF OUT OF THE APARTMENT...
CRIPES!!
STOP

YOU KNOW 'EM.. YOU LOVE 'EM..

LIFE'S LITTLE VICTORIES

BY KEITH KNIGHT

#1798: YOU COME UP WITH THE **LAMEST** EXCUSE AFTER BEING STOPPED BY THE "FUZZ"...

I'm rushing home to catch The Power Puff girls!!

& THEY LET YOU GO, ANYWAY!!

Allright.. Just stay off the sidewalks... (& say 'Hi' to Blossom for me)

YES sir...

#1799: YOUR WINDSHIELD WIPERS...

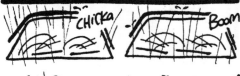

CHICKA   BOOM

CHICKA   BOOM

...KEEP THE BEAT TO YOUR FAVORITE SONG ON THE RADIO!!

#1800: YOU PASS OUT DURING A LAME MOVIE...

≈SNORE≈

& WAKE UP JUST IN TIME FOR THE ONLY GOOD PART!!

YODA!!!

≈HUH≈ WHA--? YES!!

#1801: THE CAFETERIA AT WORK/SCHOOL SERVES UP SOMETHING INTERESTING...

BLOTCH

Hey...This ain't bad.. YES!!

...& EDIBLE!!

#1802: YOU RARELY GAMBLE.. YET BET AGAINST A MAJORITY OF LOUD-MOUTHED FAMILY & FRIENDS...

~TYSON!!
~TYSON!!
~TYSON!!

You are all so very wrong...

...AND WIN!!

Lewis!! Lewis!! Lewis!!

YES!! SUCKERS!!

STOP

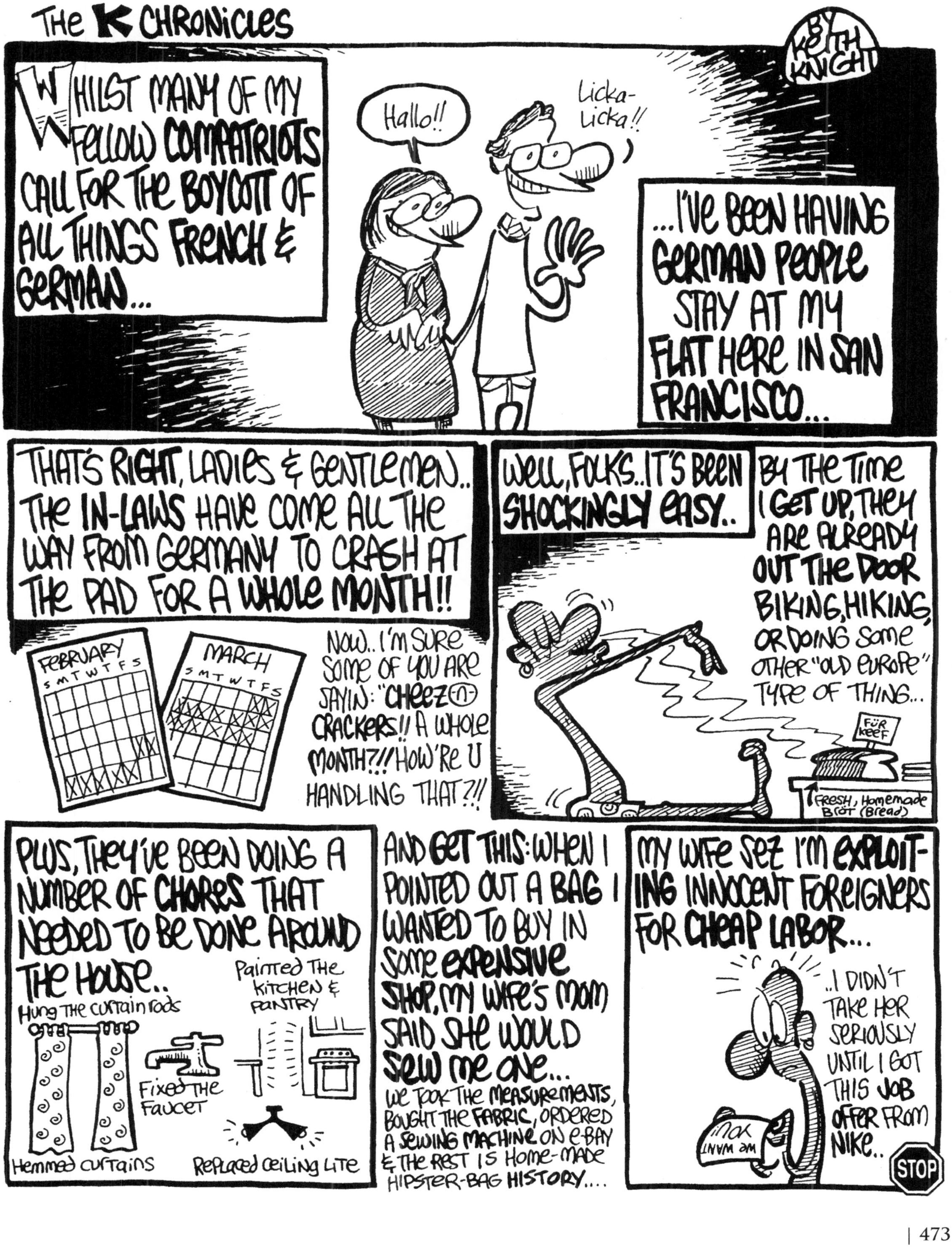
THE K CHRONICLES
BY KEITH KNIGHT
WHILST MANY OF MY FELLOW COMPATRIOTS CALL FOR THE BOYCOTT OF ALL THINGS FRENCH & GERMAN...
Hallo!!
Licka-Licka!!
...I'VE BEEN HAVING GERMAN PEOPLE STAY AT MY FLAT HERE IN SAN FRANCISCO...
THAT'S RIGHT, LADIES & GENTLEMEN.. THE IN-LAWS HAVE COME ALL THE WAY FROM GERMANY TO CRASH AT THE PAD FOR A WHOLE MONTH!!
FEBRUARY
S M T W T F S
MARCH
S M T W T F S
NOW.. I'M SURE SOME OF YOU ARE SAYIN: "CHEEZ-N-CRACKERS!! A WHOLE MONTH?!! HOW'RE U HANDLING THAT?!!
WELL, FOLKS..IT'S BEEN SHOCKINGLY EASY..
BY THE TIME I GET UP, THEY ARE ALREADY OUT THE DOOR BIKING, HIKING, OR DOING SOME OTHER "OLD EUROPE" TYPE OF THING...
FÜR KEEF
FRESH, Homemade BRÖT (Bread)
PLUS, THEY'VE BEEN DOING A NUMBER OF CHORES THAT NEEDED TO BE DONE AROUND THE HOUSE..
Hung the curtain rods
Painted the kitchen & pantry
Fixed the faucet
Hemmed curtains
Replaced ceiling lite
AND GET THIS: WHEN I POINTED OUT A BAG I WANTED TO BUY IN SOME EXPENSIVE SHOP, MY WIFE'S MOM SAID SHE WOULD SEW ME ONE...
WE TOOK THE MEASUREMENTS, BOUGHT THE FABRIC, ORDERED A SEWING MACHINE ON E-BAY & THE REST IS HOME-MADE HIPSTER-BAG HISTORY....
MY WIFE SEZ I'M EXPLOITING INNOCENT FOREIGNERS FOR CHEAP LABOR...
..I DIDN'T TAKE HER SERIOUSLY UNTIL I GOT THIS JOB OFFER FROM NIKE..
STOP

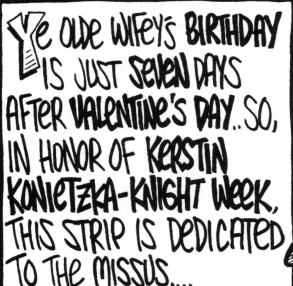

THE K CHRONICLES
SO I LOVE THE K.K.K... SO WHAT?
BY KEITH KNIGHT
YE OLDE WIFEY'S BIRTHDAY IS JUST SEVEN DAYS AFTER VALENTINE'S DAY.. SO, IN HONOR OF KERSTIN KONIETZKA-KNIGHT WEEK, THIS STRIP IS DEDICATED TO THE MISSUS....
How do I love my baby?
Here is only an Ink-Ling...
I LOVE THE WAY SHE ENTHUSIASTICALLY PLAYS BADMINTON..
I LOVE IT WHEN SHE MAKES HER OLD-SCHOOL GERMAN BAKED BREAD...
I LOVE THE WAY HER EYES SPARKLE WHEN SHE'S HAPPY...
I LOVE IT WHEN SHE GETS ALL WORKED UP AFTER WATCHING BUSH SPEAK...
GRRRRRRR..
WHOA..! TAKE IT easy, HONEY...
I LOVE TO HEAR HER LAUGH WHEN I'M DRAWING IN MY STUDIO...
Hee Hee Hee Hee Hee Hee
I LOVE IT WHEN SHE USES THE "WRONG" WORD..
THAT MOVIE WASN'T WORTH THE NINE bugs...
EXIT
& MOST OF ALL, I LOVE IT WHEN SHE GIVES ME "THE LOOK"...
WHAT? WHAT'D I do?
JUST AS LONG AS IT DOESN'T HAPPEN TOO OFTEN...

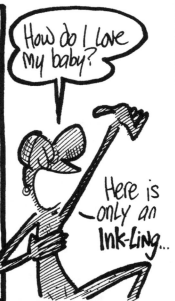

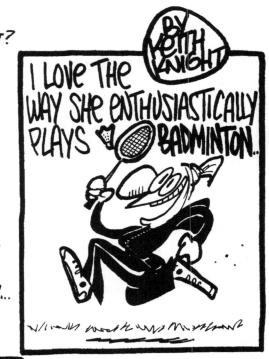

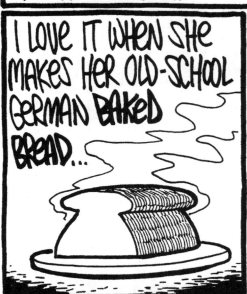

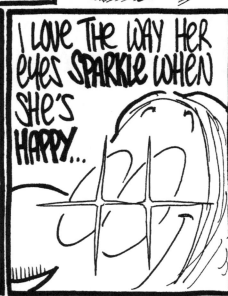

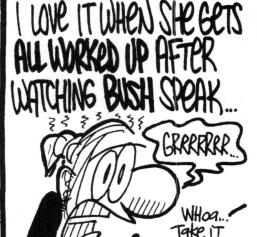

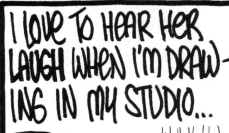

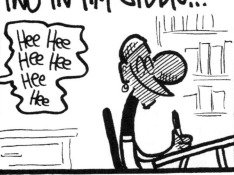

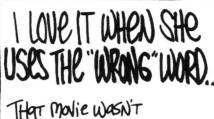

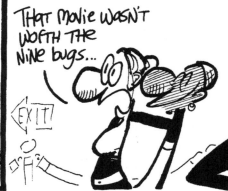

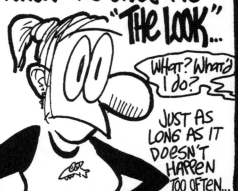

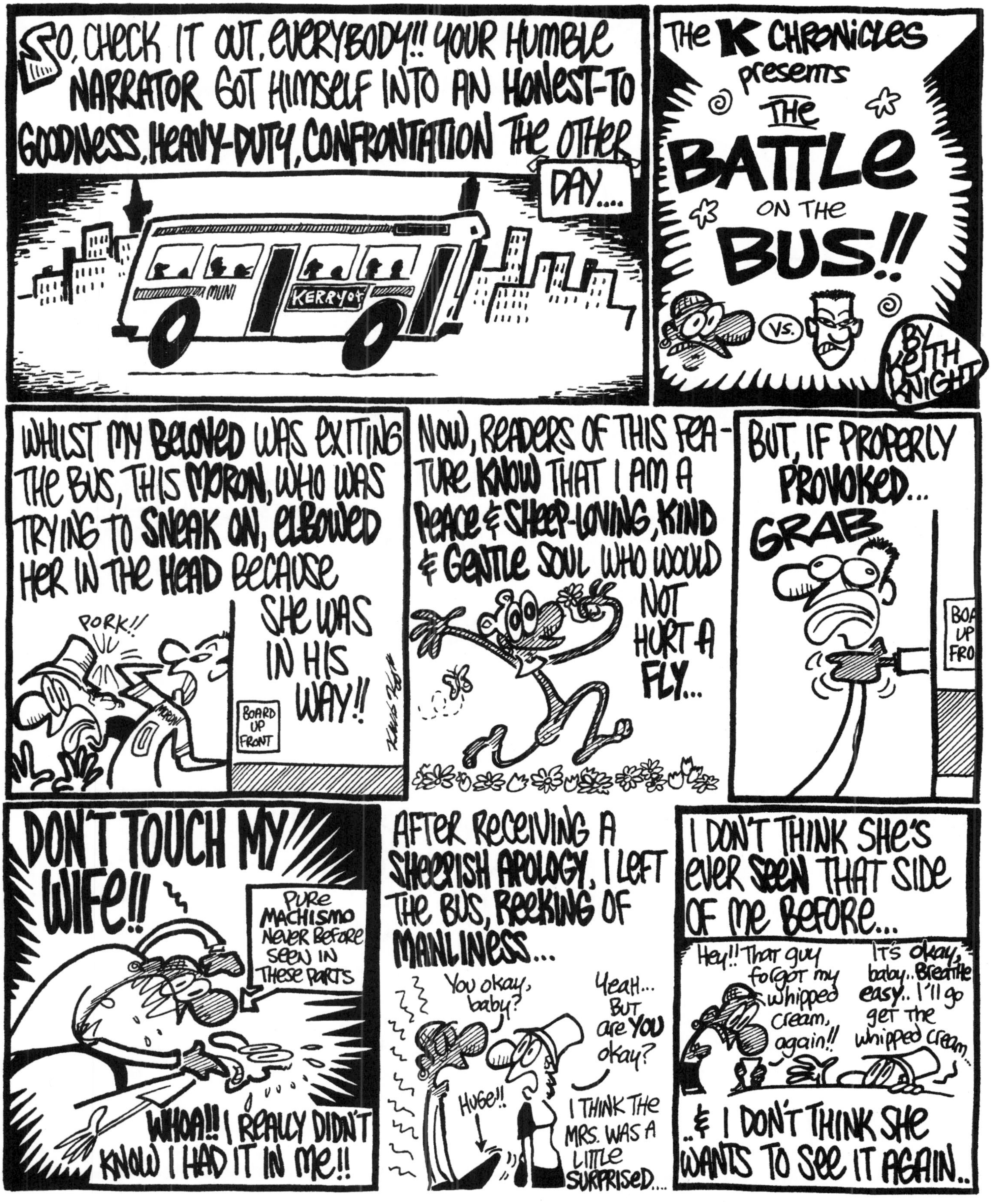

SO, CHECK IT OUT, EVERYBODY!! YOUR HUMBLE NARRATOR GOT HIMSELF INTO AN HONEST-TO GOODNESS, HEAVY-DUTY, CONFRONTATION THE OTHER
DAY....
MUNI
KERRY04
THE K CHRONICLES presents THE BATTLE ON THE BUS!!
VS.
BY KEITH KNIGHT
WHILST MY BELOVED WAS EXITING THE BUS, THIS MORON, WHO WAS TRYING TO SNEAK ON, ELBOWED HER IN THE HEAD BECAUSE
PORK!!
MORON
BOARD UP FRONT
SHE WAS IN HIS WAY!!
NOW, READERS OF THIS FEATURE KNOW THAT I AM A PEACE & SHEEP-LOVING, KIND & GENTLE SOUL WHO WOULD
NOT HURT A FLY...
BUT, IF PROPERLY PROVOKED...
GRAB
DON'T TOUCH MY WIFE!!
PURE MACHISMO NEVER BEFORE SEEN IN THESE PARTS
WHOA!! I REALLY DIDN'T KNOW I HAD IT IN ME!!
AFTER RECEIVING A SHEEPISH APOLOGY, I LEFT THE BUS, REEKING OF MANLINESS...
You okay, baby?
Yeah... But are YOU okay?
HUGE!!
I THINK THE MRS. WAS A LITTLE SURPRISED....
I DON'T THINK SHE'S EVER SEEN THAT SIDE OF ME BEFORE...
Hey!! That guy forgot my whipped cream, again!!
It's okay, baby.. Breathe easy.. I'll go get the whipped cream...
..& I DON'T THINK SHE WANTS TO SEE IT AGAIN..

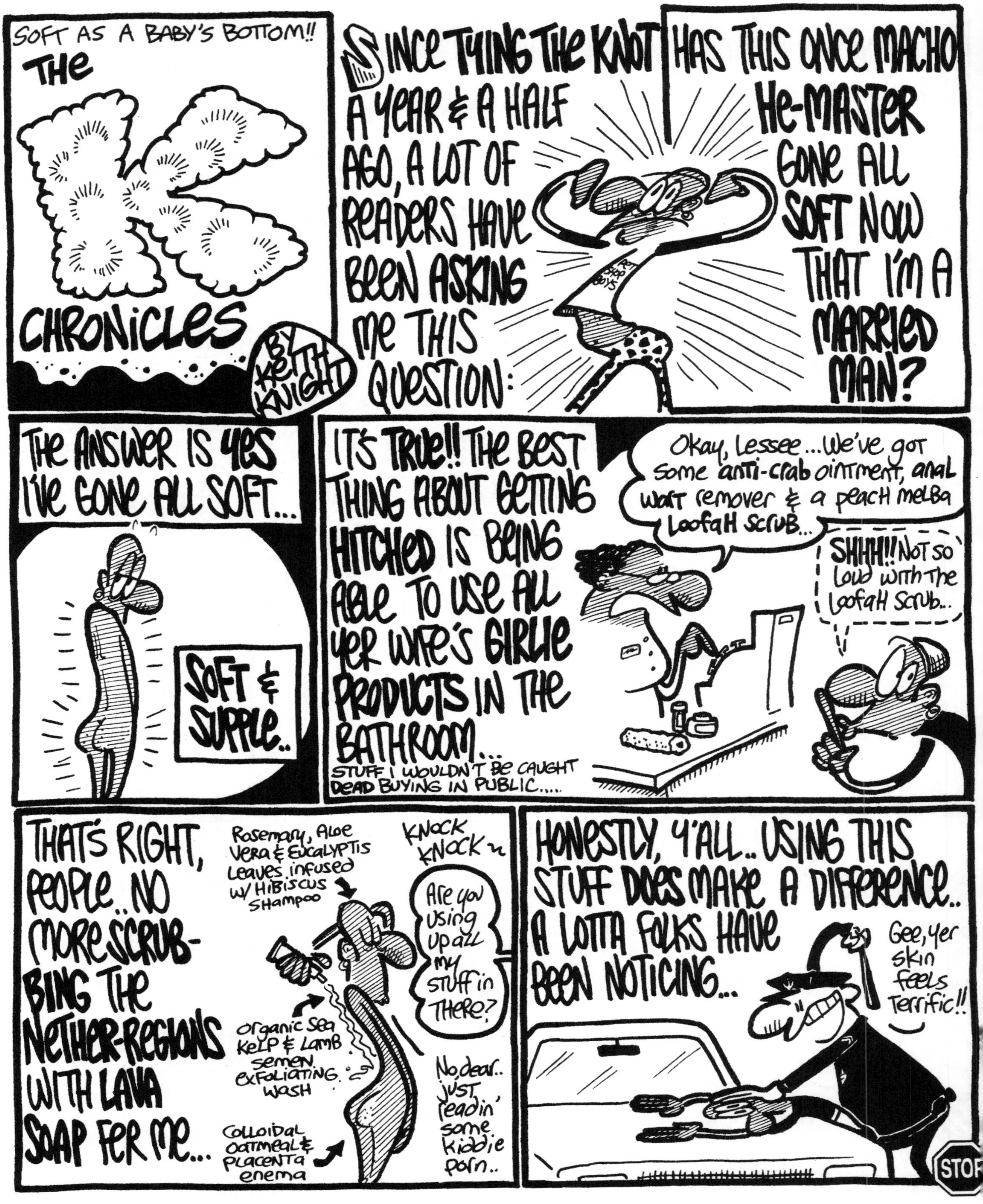
SOFT AS A BABY'S BOTTOM!!
THE K CHRONICLES
BY KEITH KNIGHT
SINCE TYING THE KNOT A YEAR & A HALF AGO, A LOT OF READERS HAVE BEEN ASKING ME THIS QUESTION:
PET SHOP BOYS
HAS THIS ONCE MACHO HE-MASTER GONE ALL SOFT NOW THAT I'M A MARRIED MAN?
THE ANSWER IS YES I'VE GONE ALL SOFT...
SOFT & SUPPLE..
IT'S TRUE!! THE BEST THING ABOUT GETTING HITCHED IS BEING ABLE TO USE ALL YER WIFE'S GIRLIE PRODUCTS IN THE BATHROOM...
STUFF I WOULDN'T BE CAUGHT DEAD BUYING IN PUBLIC....
Okay, Lessee...We've got some anti-crab ointment, anal wart remover & a peach melba Loofah scrub...
SHHH!! Not so loud with the loofah scrub...
THAT'S RIGHT, PEOPLE.. NO MORE SCRUBBING THE NETHER-REGIONS WITH LAVA SOAP FER ME...
Rosemary, Aloe Vera & Eucalyptis Leaves infused w/ HIBISCUS SHampoo
Organic Sea Kelp & Lamb semen exfoliating wash
Colloidal oatmeal & placenta enema
KNOCK KNOCK
Are you using up all my stuff in there?
No, dear.. just readin' some kiddie porn..
HONESTLY, Y'ALL.. USING THIS STUFF DOES MAKE A DIFFERENCE.. A LOTTA FOLKS HAVE BEEN NOTICING...
Gee, yer skin feels terrific!!
STOP

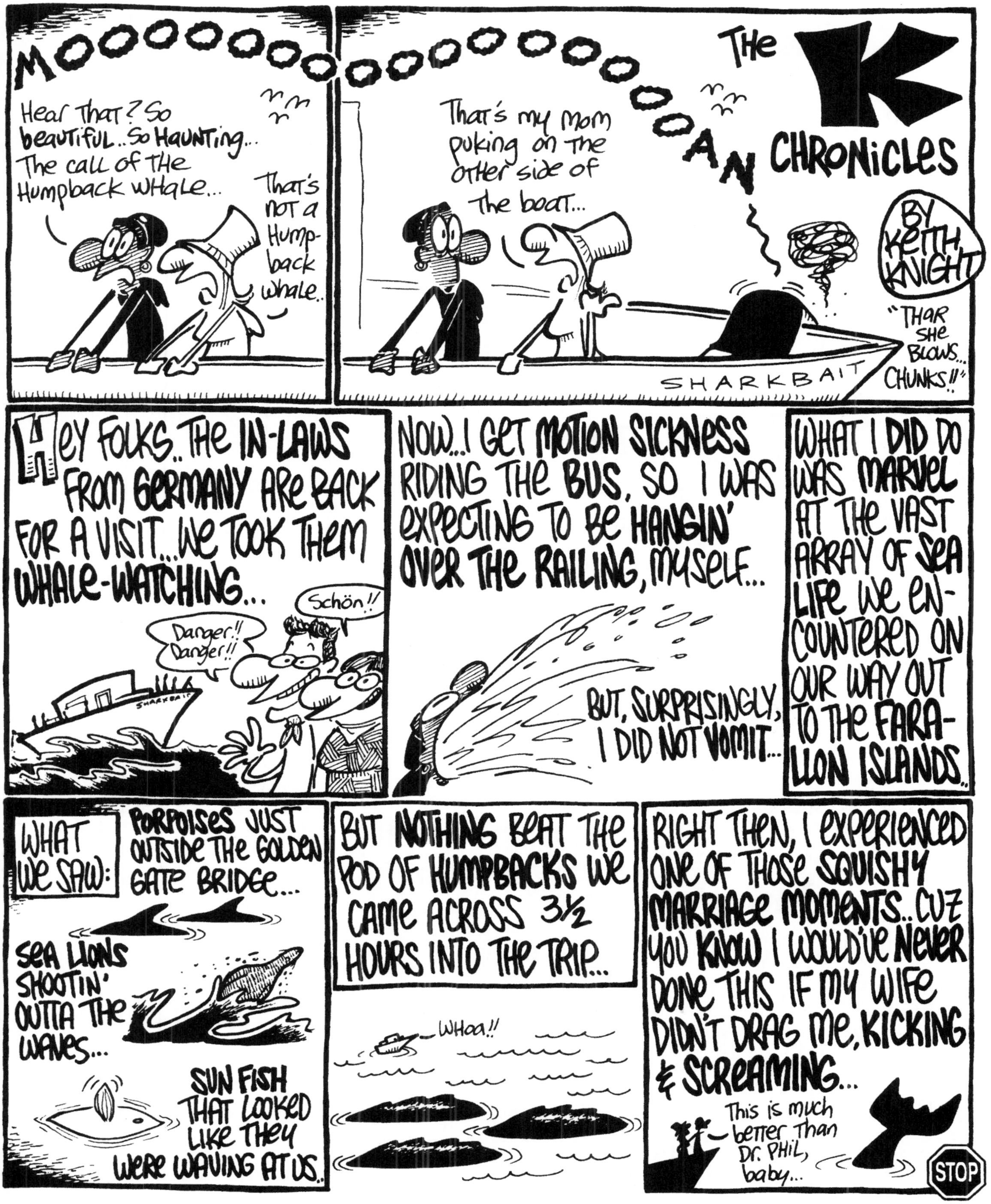
MOOOOOOOOOOOOOOOOOOOAN
Hear That? So beautiful.. So Haunting... The call of The Humpback whale...
That's not a Humpback whale..
That's my mom puking on the other side of the boat...
The K CHRONICLES
BY KEITH KNIGHT
"THAR SHE BLOWS... CHUNKS!!"
SHARKBAIT
Hey folks.. The IN-LAWS from GERMANY are back for a visit... we took them WHALE-WATCHING...
Danger!! Danger!!
Schön!!
SHARKBAIT
NOW... I GET MOTION SICKNESS RIDING THE BUS, SO I WAS EXPECTING TO BE HANGIN' OVER THE RAILING, MYSELF...
BUT, SURPRISINGLY, I DID NOT VOMIT...
WHAT I DID DO WAS MARVEL AT THE VAST ARRAY OF SEA LIFE WE EN-COUNTERED ON OUR WAY OUT TO THE FARALLON ISLANDS..
WHAT WE SAW:
PORPOISES JUST OUTSIDE THE GOLDEN GATE BRIDGE...
SEA LIONS SHOOTIN' OUTTA THE WAVES...
SUN FISH THAT LOOKED LIKE THEY WERE WAVING AT US..
BUT NOTHING BEAT THE POD OF HUMPBACKS WE CAME ACROSS 3½ HOURS INTO THE TRIP...
WHOA!!
RIGHT THEN, I EXPERIENCED ONE OF THOSE SQUISHY MARRIAGE MOMENTS.. CUZ YOU KNOW I WOULD'VE NEVER DONE THIS IF MY WIFE DIDN'T DRAG ME, KICKING & SCREAMING...
This is much better Than Dr. PHIL, baby...
STOP

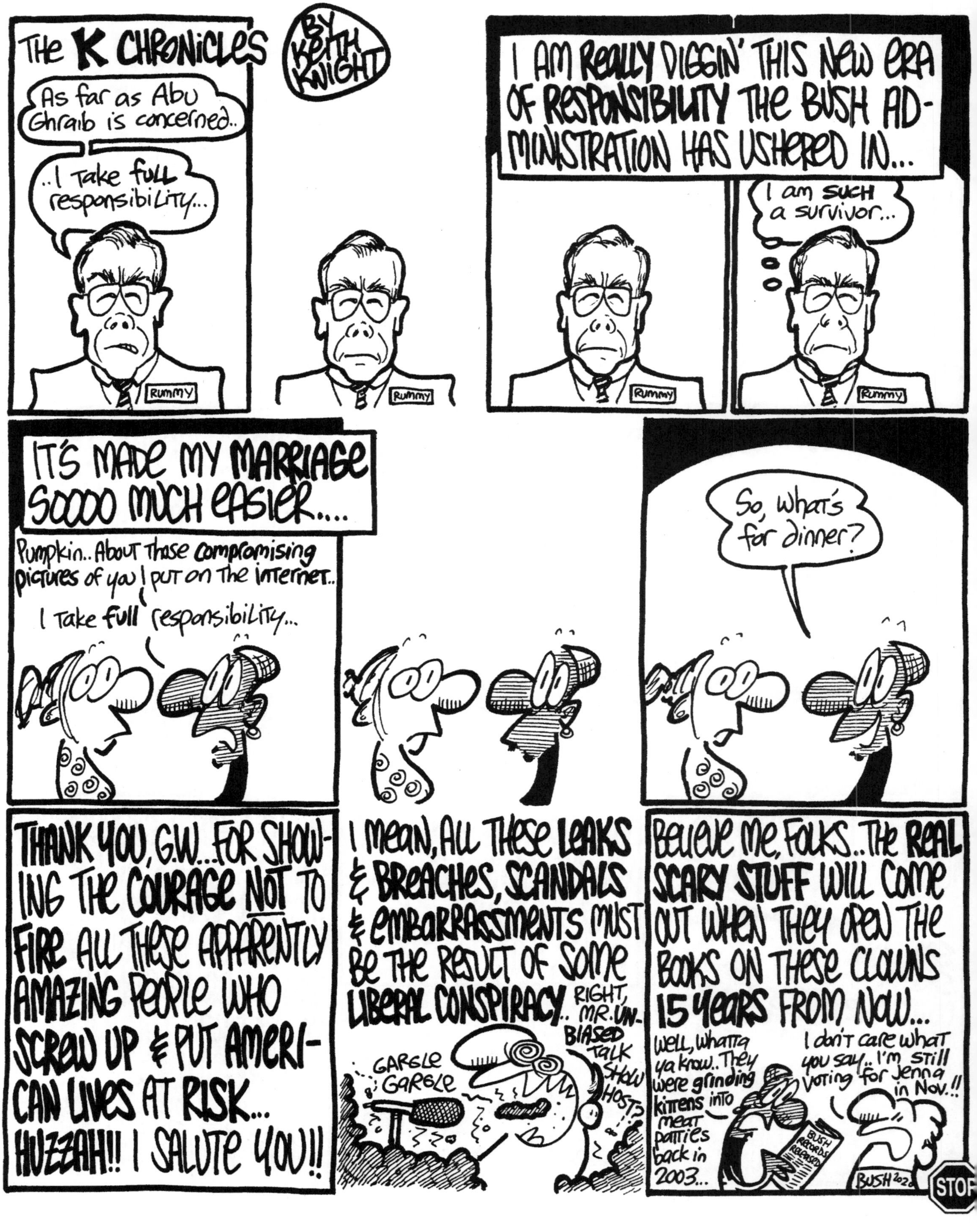

The K Chronicles
By Keith Knight
As far as Abu Ghraib is concerned..
..I take full responsibility...
RUMMY
RUMMY
I AM REALLY DIGGIN' THIS NEW ERA OF RESPONSIBILITY THE BUSH ADMINISTRATION HAS USHERED IN...
RUMMY
I am SUCH a survivor...
RUMMY
IT'S MADE MY MARRIAGE SOOOO MUCH EASIER....
Pumpkin.. About those compromising pictures of you I put on the internet..
I take full responsibility...
So, what's for dinner?
THANK YOU, G.W...FOR SHOWING THE COURAGE NOT TO FIRE ALL THESE APPARENTLY AMAZING PEOPLE WHO SCREW UP & PUT AMERICAN LIVES AT RISK... HUZZAH!! I SALUTE YOU!!
I MEAN, ALL THESE LEAKS & BREACHES, SCANDALS & EMBARRASSMENTS MUST BE THE RESULT OF SOME LIBERAL CONSPIRACY..
RIGHT, MR. UNBIASED TALK SHOW HOST?
GARGLE GARGLE
BELIEVE ME, FOLKS...THE REAL SCARY STUFF WILL COME OUT WHEN THEY OPEN THE BOOKS ON THESE CLOWNS 15 YEARS FROM NOW...
Well, whatta ya know.. They were grinding kittens into meat patties back in 2003...
BUSH RECORDS RELEASED
I don't care what you say.. I'm still voting for Jenna in Nov.!!
BUSH 2020
STOP

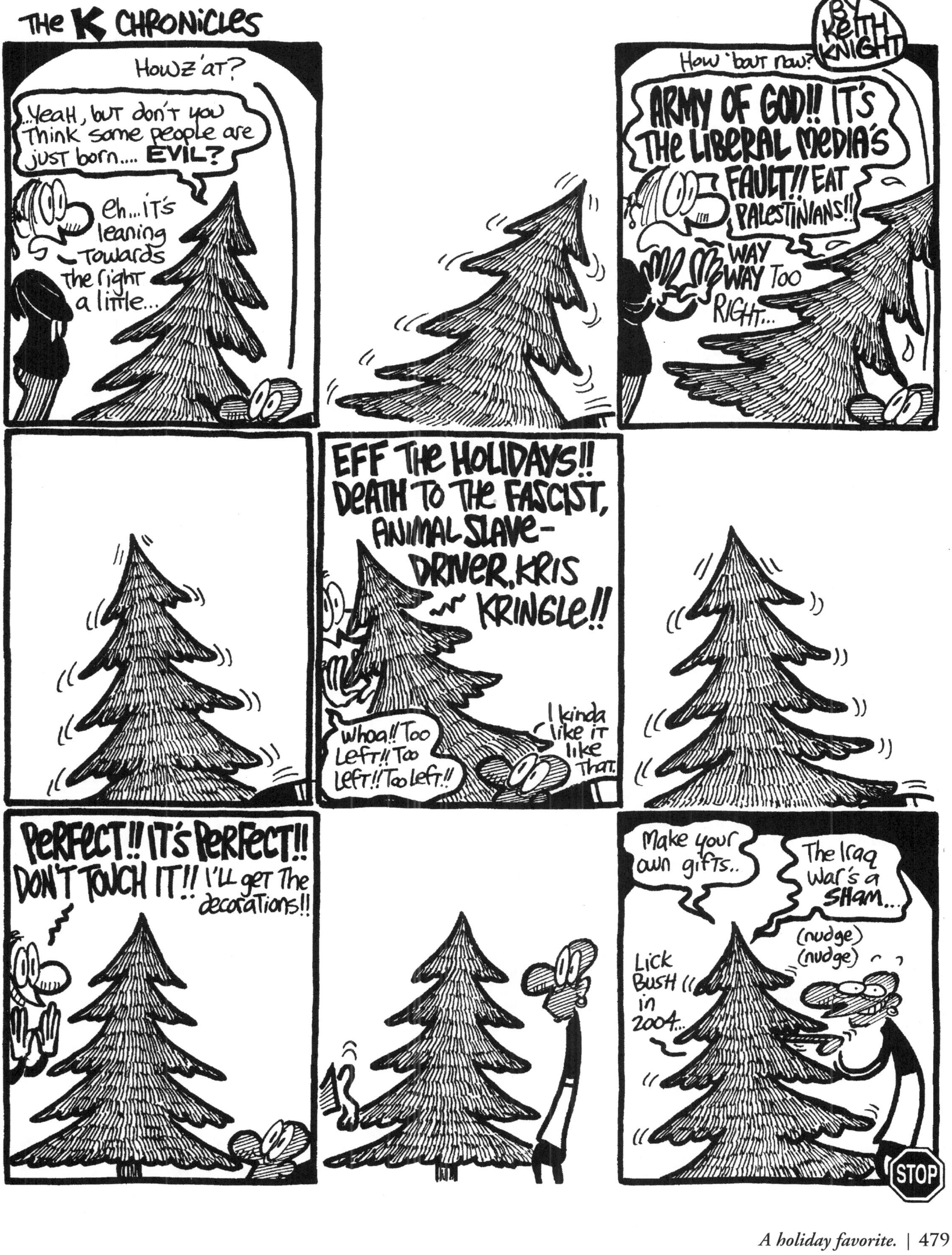
THE K CHRONICLES
BY KEITH KNIGHT
HOWZ'AT?
...YeaH, but don't you Think some people are just born.... EVIL?
eh...IT's leaning Towards the right a little...
How 'bout now?
ARMY OF GOD!! IT'S THE LIBERAL MEDIA'S FAULT!! EAT PALESTINIANS!!
WAY WAY TOO RIGHT...
EFF THE HOLIDAYS!! DEATH TO THE FASCIST, ANIMAL SLAVE-DRIVER, KRIS KRINGLE!!
Whoa!! Too Left!! Too Left!! Too Left!!
I kinda like it like That.
PERFECT!! IT'S PERFECT!! DON'T TOUCH IT!!
I'LL get The decorations!!
Make your own gifts..
The Iraq War's a SHAM...
(nudge) (nudge)
Lick BUSH in 2004...
STOP

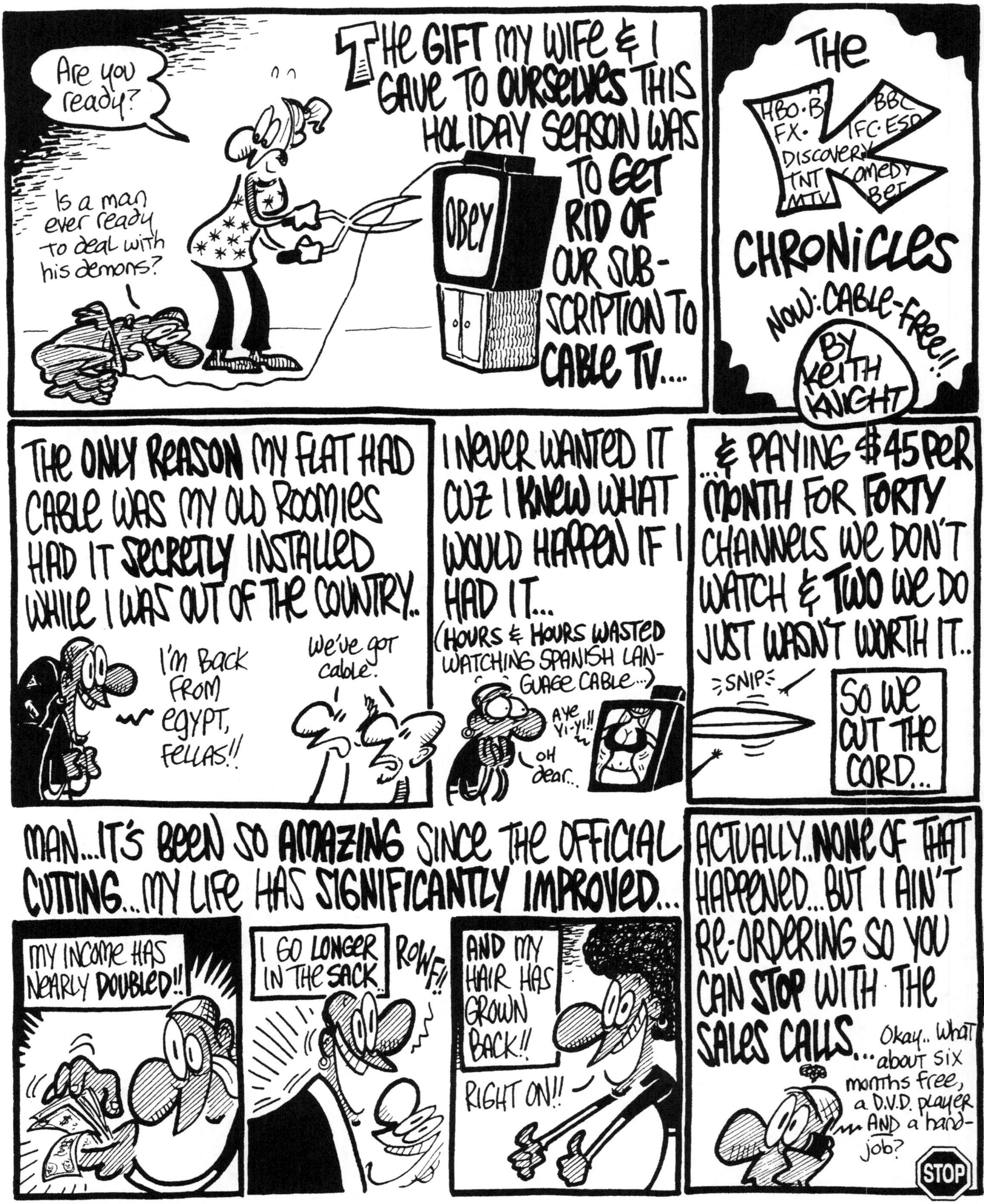

THE GIFT MY WIFE & I GAVE TO OURSELVES THIS HOLIDAY SEASON WAS TO GET RID OF OUR SUB-SCRIPTION TO CABLE TV....
Are you ready?
Is a man ever ready to deal with his demons?
OBEY
THE K CHRONICLES
HBO • FX • DISCOVERY TNT MTV BBC IFC • COMEDY BET
NOW: CABLE-FREE!!
BY KEITH KNIGHT
THE ONLY REASON MY FLAT HAD CABLE WAS MY OLD ROOMIES HAD IT SECRETLY INSTALLED WHILE I WAS OUT OF THE COUNTRY..
I'm Back From egypt, fellas!!
We've got cable.
I NEVER WANTED IT CUZ I KNEW WHAT WOULD HAPPEN IF I HAD IT...
(HOURS & HOURS WASTED WATCHING SPANISH LAN-GUAGE CABLE...)
Aye yi-yi!!
Oh dear...
...& PAYING $45 PER MONTH FOR FORTY CHANNELS WE DON'T WATCH & TWO WE DO JUST WASN'T WORTH IT...
SNIP
SO WE CUT THE CORD...
MAN...IT'S BEEN SO AMAZING SINCE THE OFFICIAL CUTTING...MY LIFE HAS SIGNIFICANTLY IMPROVED...
MY INCOME HAS NEARLY DOUBLED!!
I GO LONGER IN THE SACK
ROWF!!
AND MY HAIR HAS GROWN BACK!!
RIGHT ON!!
ACTUALLY..NONE OF THAT HAPPENED...BUT I AIN'T RE-ORDERING SO YOU CAN STOP WITH THE SALES CALLS...
Okay.. What about six months free, a D.V.D. player AND a hand-job?
STOP

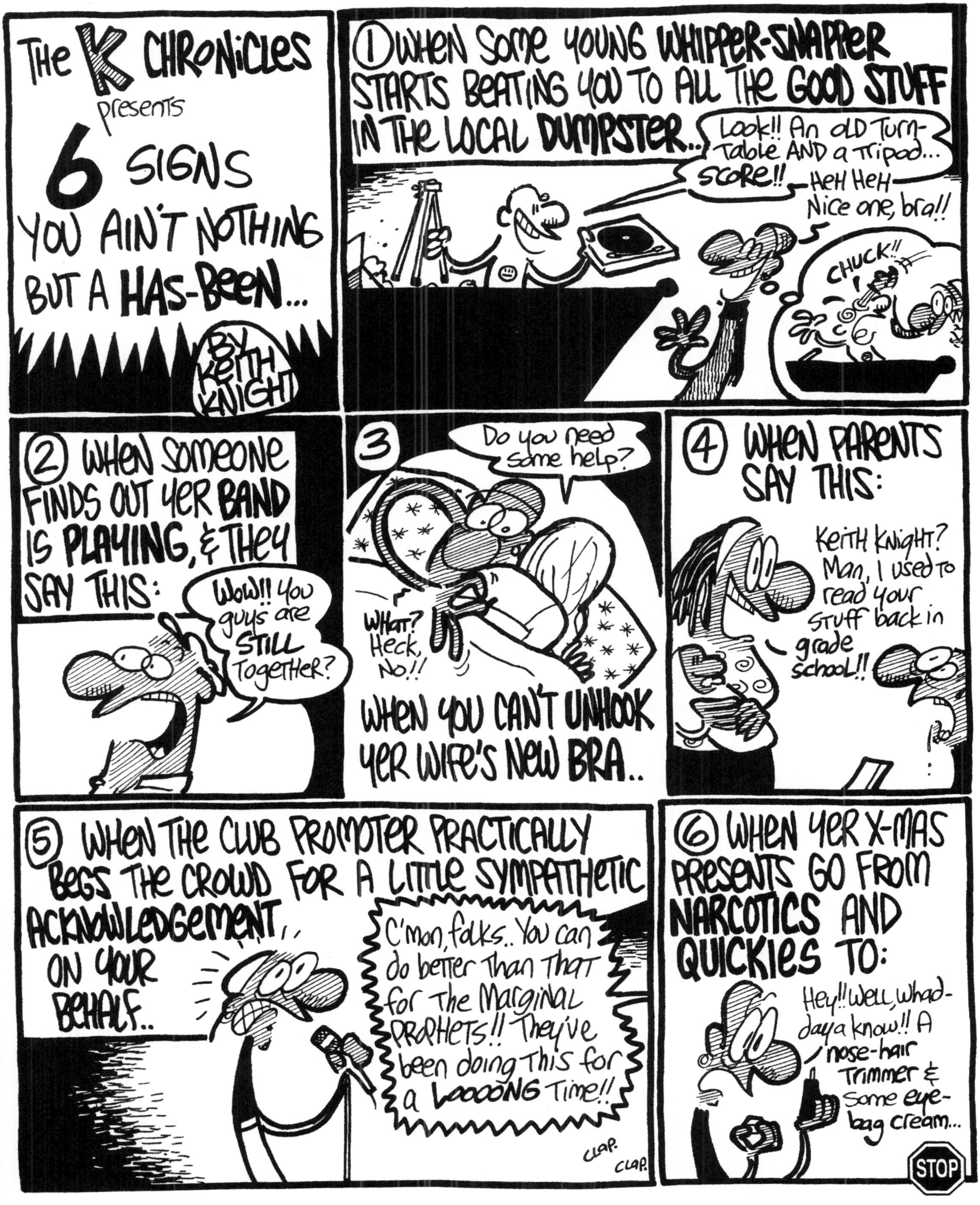

THE K CHRONICLES presents
6 SIGNS YOU AIN'T NOTHING BUT A HAS-BEEN...
BY KEITH KNIGHT
① WHEN SOME YOUNG WHIPPER-SNAPPER STARTS BEATING YOU TO ALL THE GOOD STUFF IN THE LOCAL DUMPSTER...
Look!! An old Turn-Table AND a Tripod... SCORE!!
Heh Heh Nice one, bra!!
CHUCK!!
② WHEN SOMEONE FINDS OUT YER BAND IS PLAYING, & THEY SAY THIS:
WOW!! You guys are STILL Together?
③
Do you need some help?
WHAT? Heck, No!!
WHEN YOU CAN'T UNHOOK YER WIFE'S NEW BRA..
④ WHEN PARENTS SAY THIS:
Keith Knight? Man, I used to read your stuff back in grade school!!
⑤ WHEN THE CLUB PROMOTER PRACTICALLY BEGS THE CROWD FOR A LITTLE SYMPATHETIC ACKNOWLEDGEMENT, ON YOUR BEHALF..
C'mon, folks.. You can do better than that for the Marginal Prophets!! They've been doing this for a LOOOONG Time!!
CLAP. CLAP.
⑥ WHEN YER X-MAS PRESENTS GO FROM NARCOTICS AND QUICKIES TO:
Hey!! Well, whadaya know!! A nose-hair Trimmer & Some eye-bag cream...
STOP

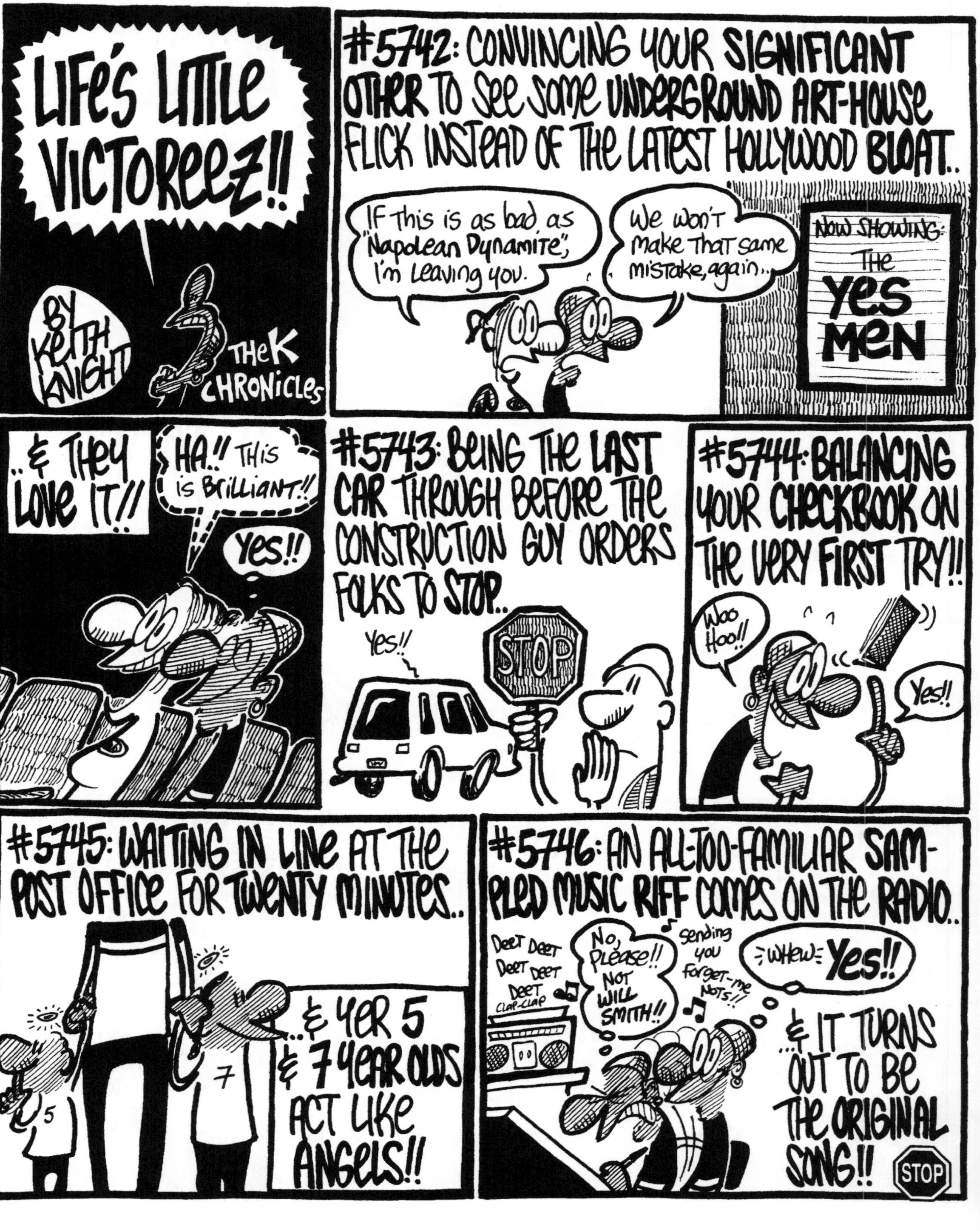
LIFE'S LITTLE VICTOREEZ!!
BY KEITH KNIGHT
THE K CHRONICLES
#5742: CONVINCING YOUR SIGNIFICANT OTHER TO SEE SOME UNDERGROUND ART-HOUSE FLICK INSTEAD OF THE LATEST HOLLYWOOD BLOAT..
If this is as bad as "Napolean Dynamite", I'm leaving you.
We won't make that same mistake, again...
NOW SHOWING: THE YES MEN
..& THEY LOVE IT!!
HA..!! THIS is BRILLIANT!!
Yes!!
#5743: BEING THE LAST CAR THROUGH BEFORE THE CONSTRUCTION GUY ORDERS FOLKS TO STOP..
Yes!!
STOP
#5744: BALANCING YOUR CHECKBOOK ON THE VERY FIRST TRY!!
Woo Hoo!!
Yes!!
#5745: WAITING IN LINE AT THE POST OFFICE FOR TWENTY MINUTES..
5
7
..& YER 5 & 7 YEAR OLDS ACT LIKE ANGELS!!
#5746: AN ALL-TOO-FAMILIAR SAMPLED MUSIC RIFF COMES ON THE RADIO..
DEET DEET DEET DEET DEET CLAP-CLAP
No, PLEASE!! NOT WILL SMITH!!
sending you forget-me nots!!
WHEW Yes!!
...& IT TURNS OUT TO BE THE ORIGINAL SONG!!
STOP

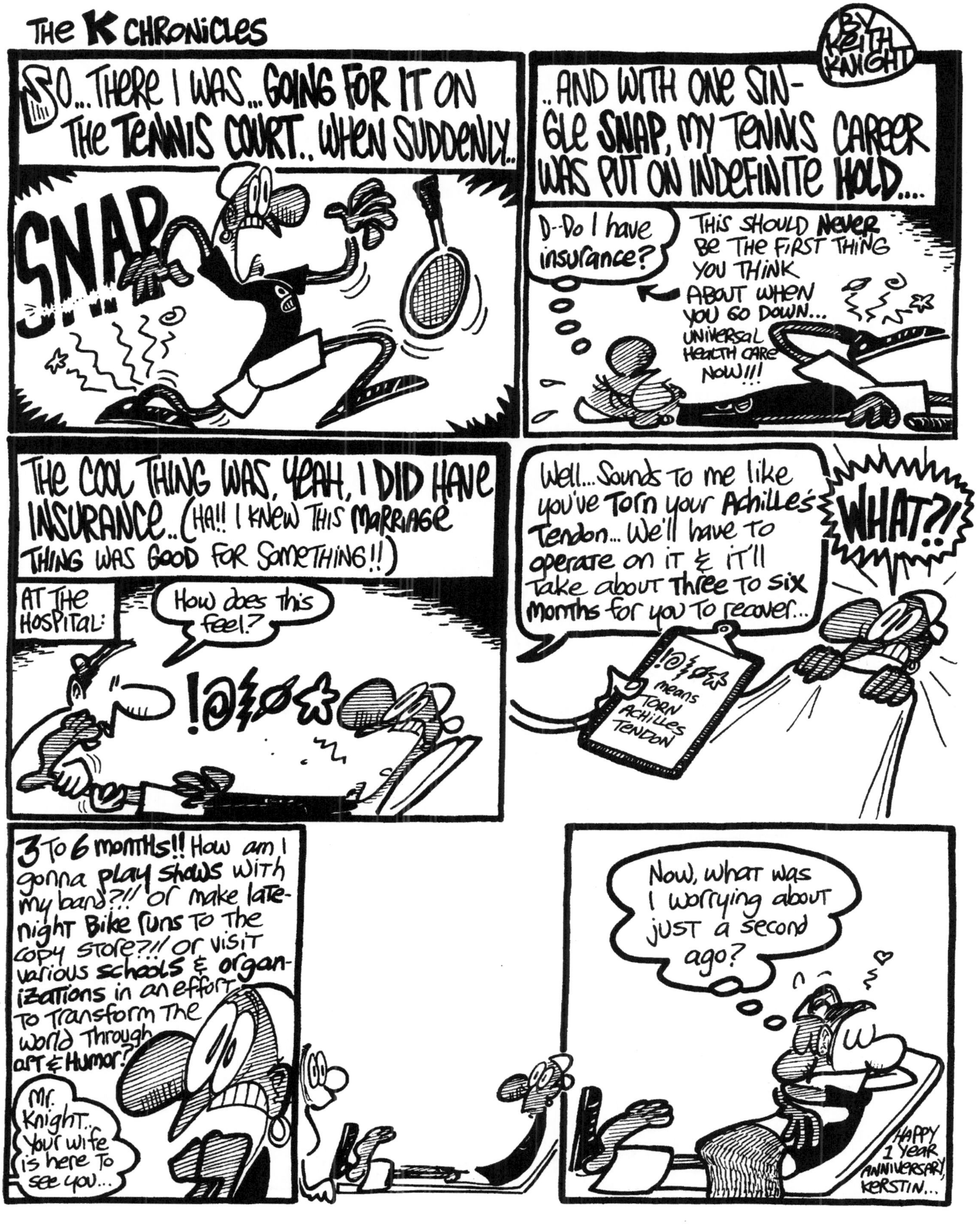
THE K CHRONICLES
BY KEITH KNIGHT
SO... THERE I WAS... GOING FOR IT ON THE TENNIS COURT.. WHEN SUDDENLY..
SNAP
..AND WITH ONE SINGLE SNAP, MY TENNIS CAREER WAS PUT ON INDEFINITE HOLD....
D-Do I have insurance?
THIS SHOULD NEVER BE THE FIRST THING YOU THINK ABOUT WHEN YOU GO DOWN... UNIVERSAL HEALTH CARE NOW!!!
THE COOL THING WAS, YEAH, I DID HAVE INSURANCE.. (HA!! I KNEW THIS MARRIAGE THING WAS GOOD FOR SOMETHING!!)
AT THE HOSPITAL:
How does this feel?
Well... Sounds to me like you've Torn your Achilles's Tendon... We'll have to operate on it & it'll take about three to six months for you to recover...
WHAT?!
means TORN ACHILLES TENDON
3 TO 6 MONTHS!! How am I gonna play shows with my band?!! or make late-night Bike runs to the copy store?!! or visit various schools & organizations in an effort to transform the world through art & humor?
Mr. Knight.. Your wife is here to see you...
Now, what was I worrying about just a second ago?
HAPPY 1 YEAR ANNIVERSARY, KERSTIN...

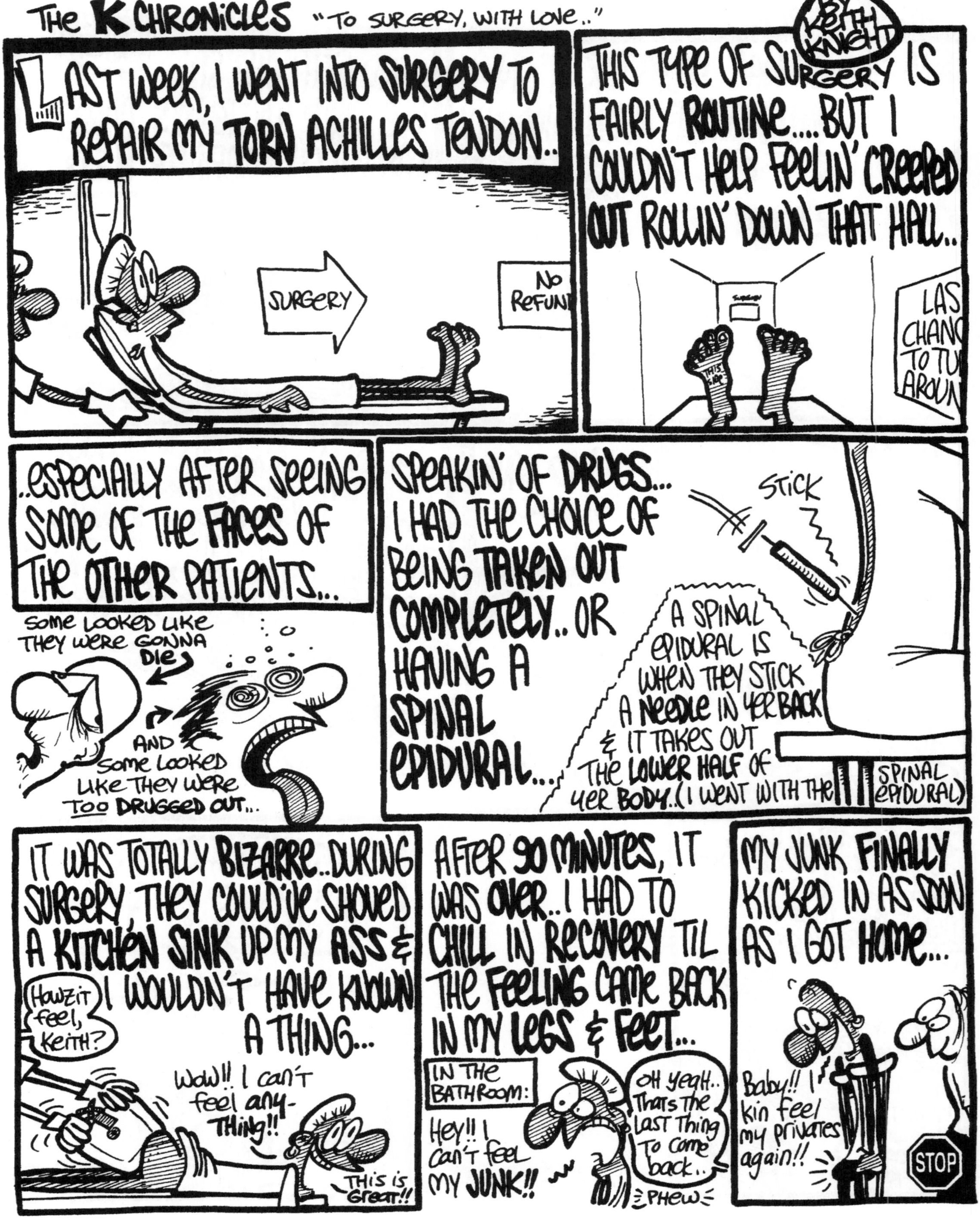
THE K CHRONICLES "TO SURGERY, WITH LOVE.."
BY KEITH KNIGHT
LAST WEEK, I WENT INTO SURGERY TO REPAIR MY TORN ACHILLES TENDON..
SURGERY
NO REFUN
THIS TYPE OF SURGERY IS FAIRLY ROUTINE.... BUT I COULDN'T HELP FEELIN' CREEPED OUT ROLLIN' DOWN THAT HALL..
LAS CHANC TO TU AROUN
..ESPECIALLY AFTER SEEING SOME OF THE FACES OF THE OTHER PATIENTS...
SOME LOOKED LIKE THEY WERE GONNA DIE
AND SOME LOOKED LIKE THEY WERE TOO DRUGGED OUT...
SPEAKIN' OF DRUGS... I HAD THE CHOICE OF BEING TAKEN OUT COMPLETELY.. OR HAVING A SPINAL EPIDURAL...
STICK
A SPINAL EPIDURAL IS WHEN THEY STICK A NEEDLE IN YER BACK & IT TAKES OUT THE LOWER HALF OF YER BODY..(I WENT WITH THE SPINAL EPIDURAL)
IT WAS TOTALLY BIZARRE..DURING SURGERY, THEY COULD'VE SHOVED A KITCHEN SINK UP MY ASS & I WOULDN'T HAVE KNOWN A THING...
HOWZIT FEEL, KEITH?
WOW!! I CAN'T FEEL ANY-THING!!
THIS IS GREAT!!
AFTER 90 MINUTES, IT WAS OVER.. I HAD TO CHILL IN RECOVERY TIL THE FEELING CAME BACK IN MY LEGS & FEET...
IN THE BATHROOM:
HEY!! I CAN'T FEEL MY JUNK!!
OH YEAH.. THAT'S THE LAST THING TO COME BACK..
PHEW
MY JUNK FINALLY KICKED IN AS SOON AS I GOT HOME...
BABY!! I KIN FEEL MY PRIVATES AGAIN!!
STOP

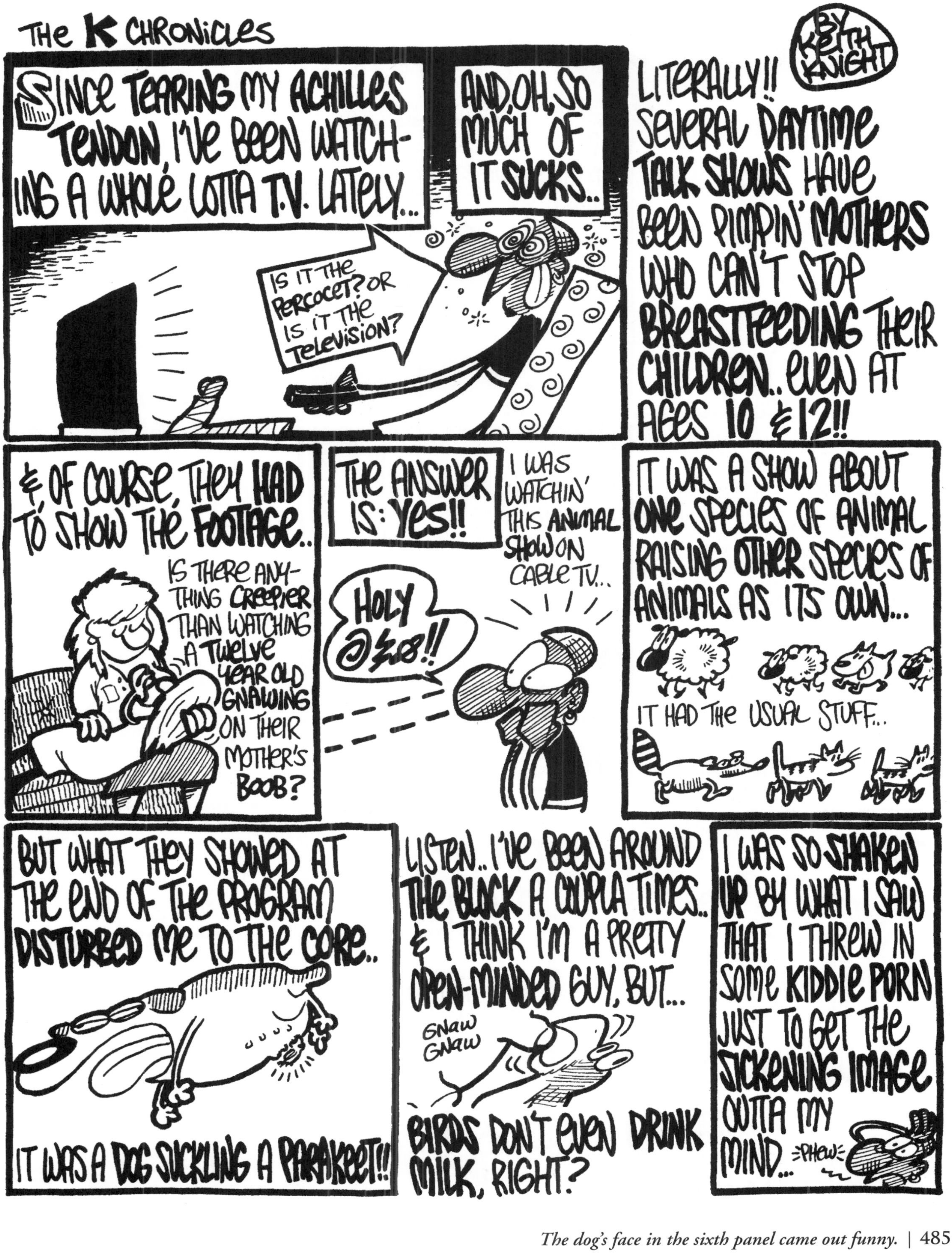

THE K CHRONICLES
BY KEITH KNIGHT
SINCE TEARING MY ACHILLES TENDON, I'VE BEEN WATCHING A WHOLE LOTTA T.V. LATELY...
AND, OH, SO MUCH OF IT SUCKS..
IS IT THE PERCOCET? OR IS IT THE TELEVISION?
LITERALLY!! SEVERAL DAYTIME TALK SHOWS HAVE BEEN PIMPIN' MOTHERS WHO CAN'T STOP BREASTFEEDING THEIR CHILDREN.. EVEN AT AGES 10 & 12!!
& OF COURSE, THEY HAD TO SHOW THE FOOTAGE..
IS THERE ANYTHING CREEPIER THAN WATCHING A TWELVE YEAR OLD GNAWING ON THEIR MOTHER'S BOOB?
THE ANSWER IS: YES!!
I WAS WATCHIN' THIS ANIMAL SHOW ON CABLE TV...
HOLY @$&!!
IT WAS A SHOW ABOUT ONE SPECIES OF ANIMAL RAISING OTHER SPECIES OF ANIMALS AS ITS OWN...
IT HAD THE USUAL STUFF...
BUT WHAT THEY SHOWED AT THE END OF THE PROGRAM DISTURBED ME TO THE CORE..
IT WAS A DOG SUCKLING A PARAKEET!!
LISTEN.. I'VE BEEN AROUND THE BLOCK A COUPLA TIMES.. & I THINK I'M A PRETTY OPEN-MINDED GUY, BUT...
GNAW GNAW
BIRDS DON'T EVEN DRINK MILK, RIGHT?
I WAS SO SHAKEN UP BY WHAT I SAW THAT I THREW IN SOME KIDDIE PORN JUST TO GET THE SICKENING IMAGE OUTTA MY MIND...
PHEW

The dog's face in the sixth panel came out funny.

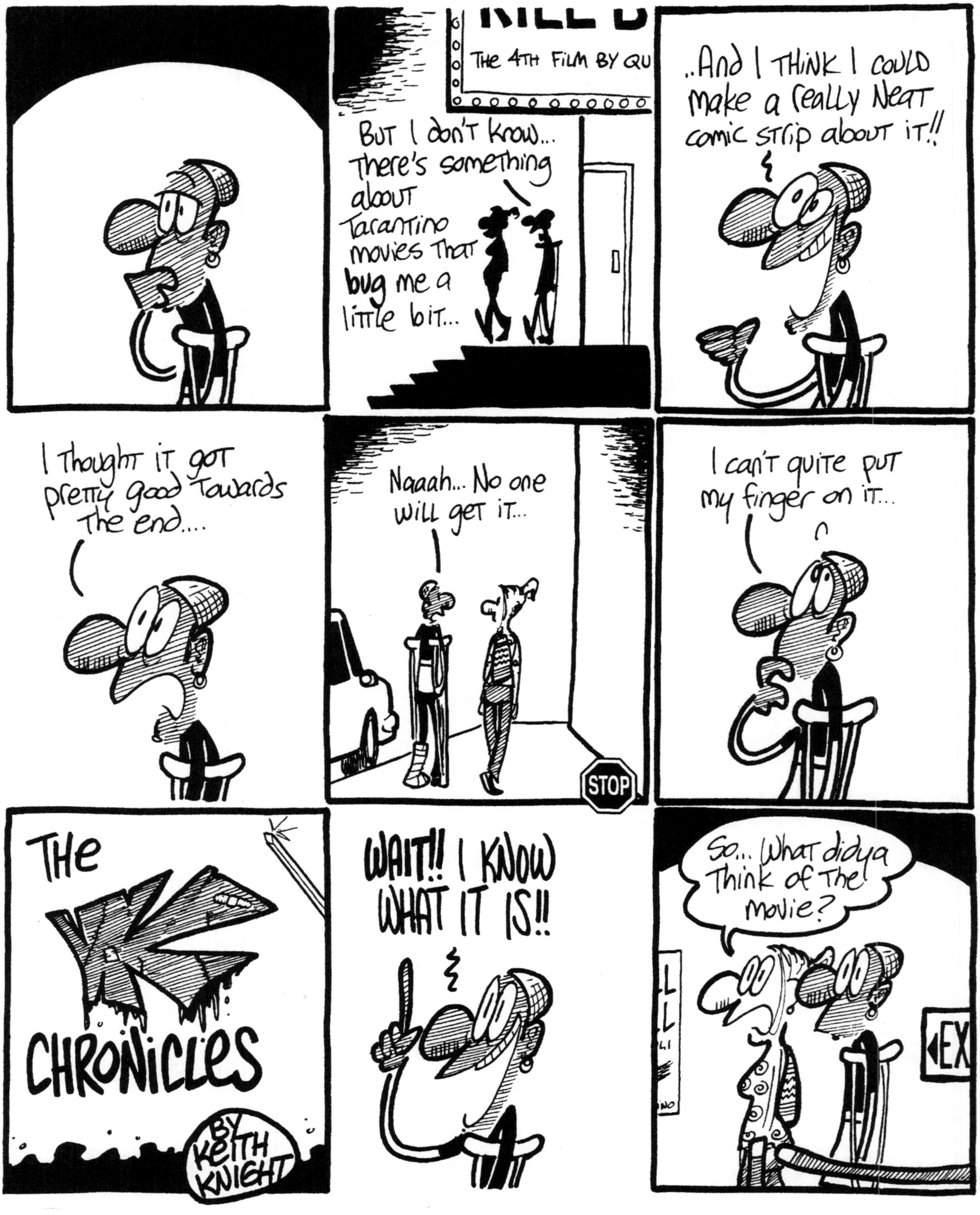
THE
CHRONICLES
BY KEITH KNIGHT
So... What didya Think of The movie?
I Thought it got pretty good Towards The end....
THE 4TH FILM BY QU
But I don't know... There's something about Tarantino movies That bug me a little bit...
I can't quite put my finger on it...
WAIT!! I KNOW WHAT IT IS!!
..And I think I could make a really Neat comic strip about it!!
Naaah... No one will get it...
STOP

 | *Proper order of the panels: 7, 9, 4, 2, 6, 8, 3, 1, 5*

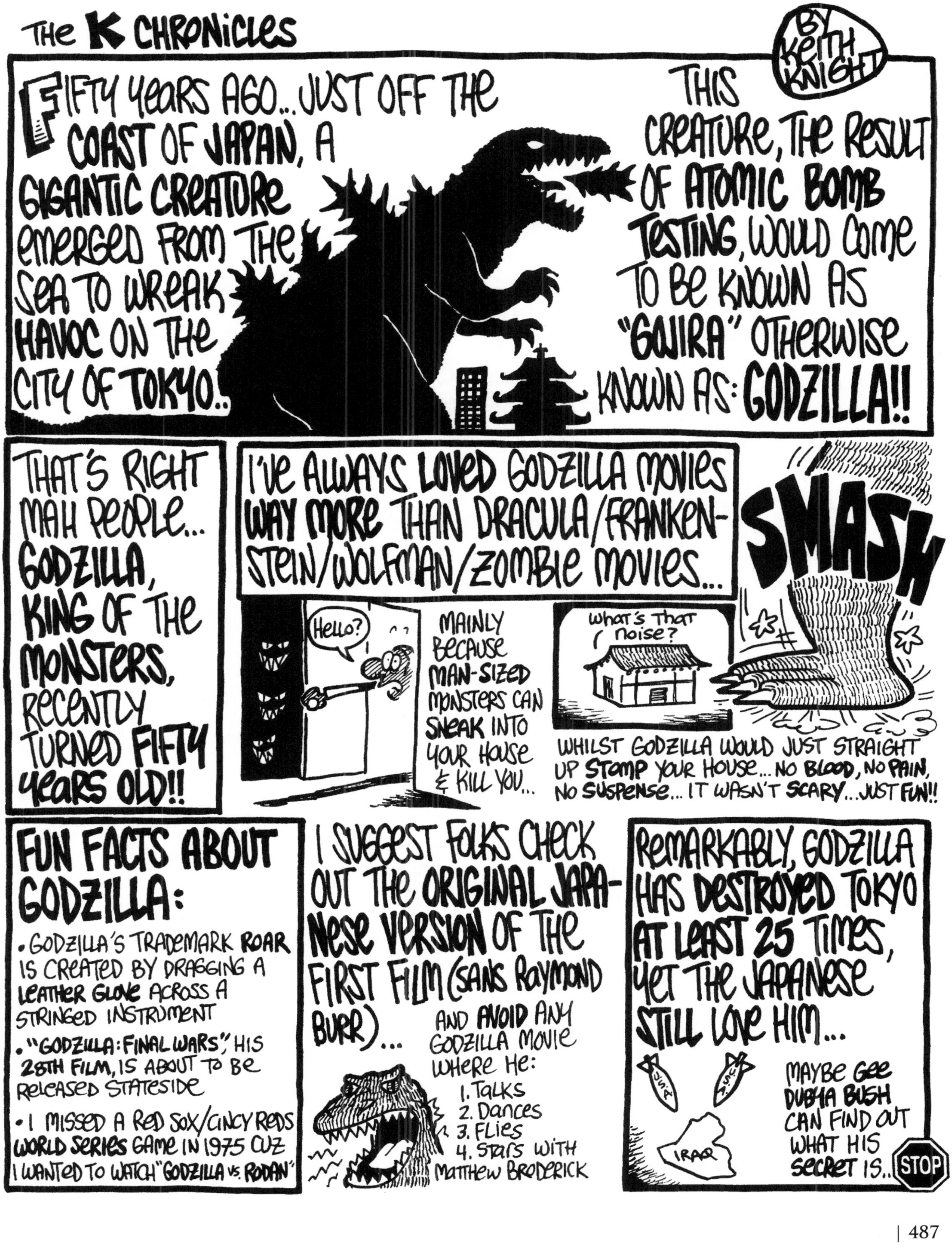
THE K CHRONICLES
BY KEITH KNIGHT
FIFTY YEARS AGO... JUST OFF THE COAST OF JAPAN, A GIGANTIC CREATURE EMERGED FROM THE SEA TO WREAK HAVOC ON THE CITY OF TOKYO..
THIS CREATURE, THE RESULT OF ATOMIC BOMB TESTING, WOULD COME TO BE KNOWN AS "GOJIRA" OTHERWISE KNOWN AS: GODZILLA!!
THAT'S RIGHT MAH PEOPLE... GODZILLA, KING OF THE MONSTERS, RECENTLY TURNED FIFTY YEARS OLD!!
I'VE ALWAYS LOVED GODZILLA MOVIES WAY MORE THAN DRACULA/FRANKENSTEIN/WOLFMAN/ZOMBIE MOVIES...
Hello?
MAINLY BECAUSE MAN-SIZED MONSTERS CAN SNEAK INTO YOUR HOUSE & KILL YOU...
What's that noise?
SMASH
WHILST GODZILLA WOULD JUST STRAIGHT UP STOMP YOUR HOUSE... NO BLOOD, NO PAIN, NO SUSPENSE... IT WASN'T SCARY... JUST FUN!!
FUN FACTS ABOUT GODZILLA:
• GODZILLA'S TRADEMARK ROAR IS CREATED BY DRAGGING A LEATHER GLOVE ACROSS A STRINGED INSTRUMENT
• "GODZILLA: FINAL WARS", HIS 28TH FILM, IS ABOUT TO BE RELEASED STATESIDE
• I MISSED A RED SOX/CINCY REDS WORLD SERIES GAME IN 1975 CUZ I WANTED TO WATCH "GODZILLA VS. RODAN"
I SUGGEST FOLKS CHECK OUT THE ORIGINAL JAPANESE VERSION OF THE FIRST FILM (SANS RAYMOND BURR)...
AND AVOID ANY GODZILLA MOVIE WHERE HE:
1. TALKS
2. DANCES
3. FLIES
4. STARS WITH MATTHEW BRODERICK
REMARKABLY, GODZILLA HAS DESTROYED TOKYO AT LEAST 25 TIMES, YET THE JAPANESE STILL LOVE HIM...
U.S.A.
U.S.A.
IRAQ
MAYBE GEE DUBYA BUSH CAN FIND OUT WHAT HIS SECRET IS..
STOP

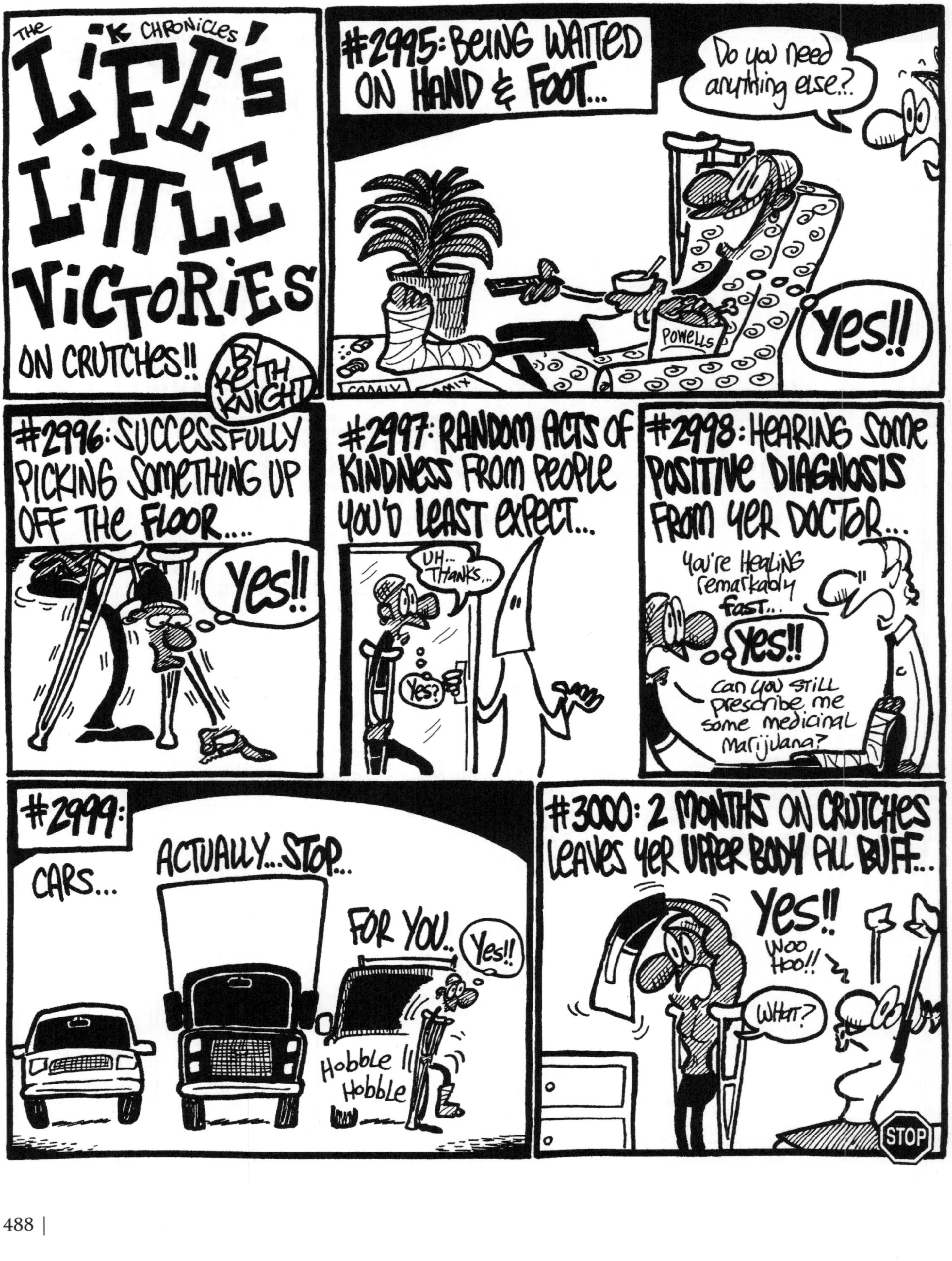

THE 'K CHRONICLES' LIFE'S LITTLE VICTORIES
ON CRUTCHES!!
BY KEITH KNIGHT
#2995: BEING WAITED ON HAND & FOOT...
Do you need anything else?..
POWELLS
Yes!!
#2996: SUCCESSFULLY PICKING SOMETHING UP OFF THE FLOOR....
Yes!!
#2997: RANDOM ACTS OF KINDNESS FROM PEOPLE YOU'D LEAST EXPECT...
UH... THANKS...
Yes?
#2998: HEARING SOME POSITIVE DIAGNOSIS FROM YER DOCTOR...
You're Healing remarkably fast...
Yes!!
Can you still prescribe me some medicinal Marijuana?
#2999:
CARS...
ACTUALLY...STOP...
FOR YOU..
Yes!!
Hobble Hobble
#3000: 2 MONTHS ON CRUTCHES LEAVES YER UPPER BODY ALL BUFF...
Yes!!
WOO HOO!!
WHAT?
STOP

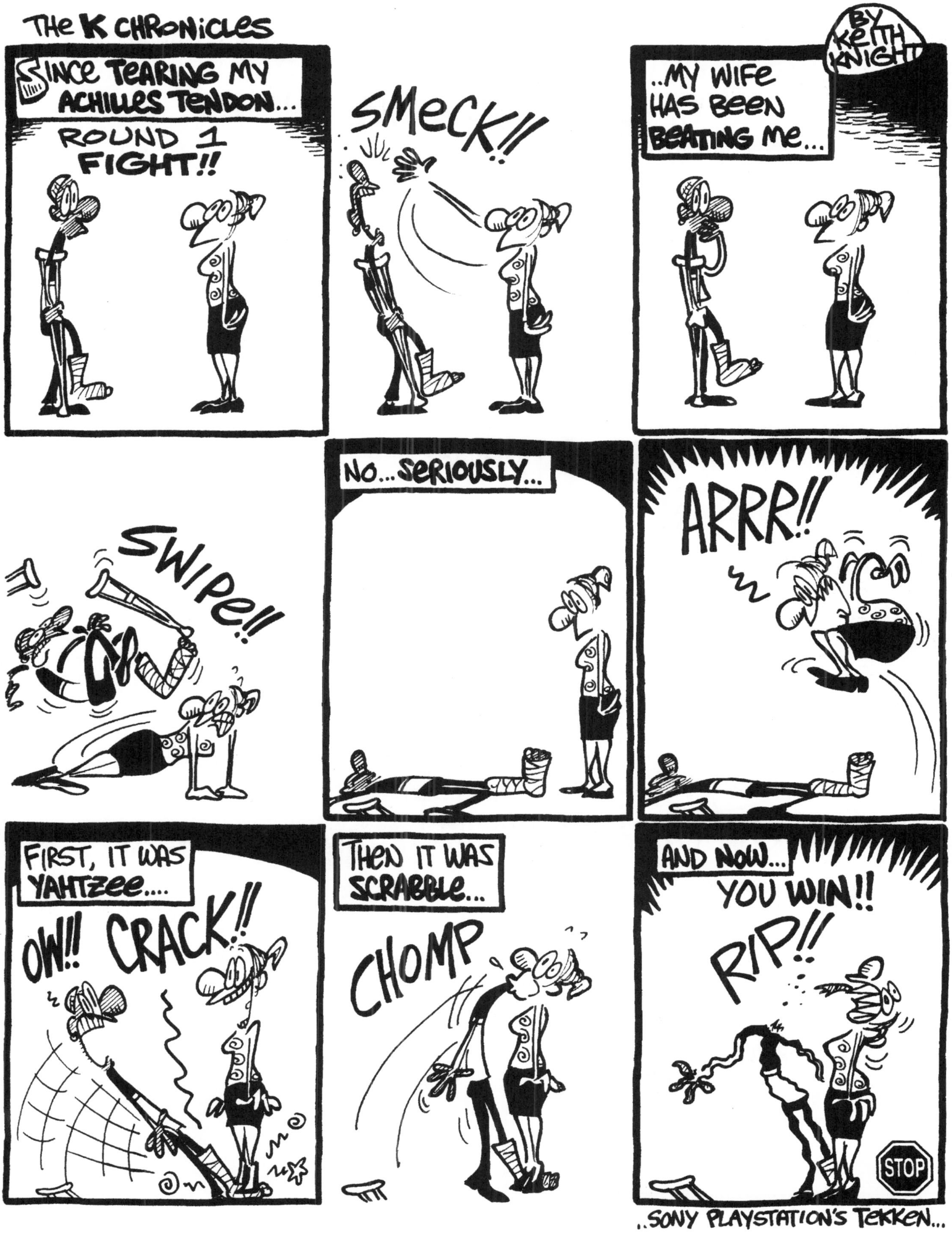

THE K CHRONICLES
BY KEITH KNIGHT
SINCE TEARING MY ACHILLES TENDON...
ROUND 1 FIGHT!!
SMECK!!
..MY WIFE HAS BEEN BEATING ME...
SWIPE!!
NO...SERIOUSLY...
ARRR!!
FIRST, IT WAS YAHTZEE....
OW!! CRACK!!
THEN IT WAS SCRABBLE...
CHOMP
AND NOW...
YOU WIN!!
RIP!!
STOP
..SONY PLAYSTATION'S TEKKEN...

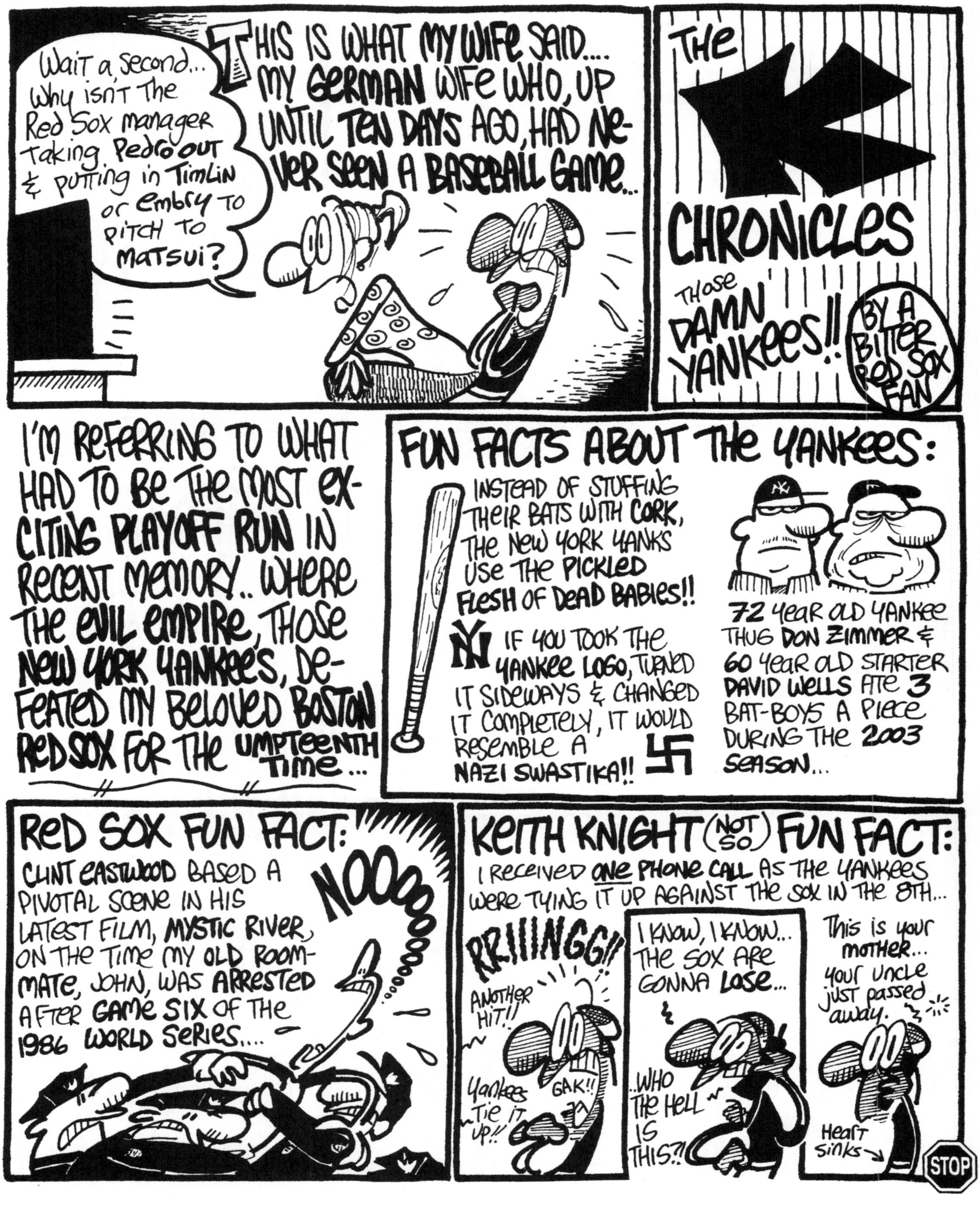

THIS IS WHAT MY WIFE SAID.... MY GERMAN WIFE WHO, UP UNTIL TEN DAYS AGO, HAD NEVER SEEN A BASEBALL GAME...
Wait a second... Why isn't the Red Sox manager taking Pedro out & putting in Timlin or Embry to pitch to Matsui?
THE K CHRONICLES
THOSE DAMN YANKEES!!..
BY A BITTER RED SOX FAN
I'M REFERRING TO WHAT HAD TO BE THE MOST EXCITING PLAYOFF RUN IN RECENT MEMORY.. WHERE THE EVIL EMPIRE, THOSE NEW YORK YANKEE'S, DEFEATED MY BELOVED BOSTON RED SOX FOR THE UMPTEENTH TIME...
FUN FACTS ABOUT THE YANKEES:
INSTEAD OF STUFFING THEIR BATS WITH CORK, THE NEW YORK YANKS USE THE PICKLED FLESH OF DEAD BABIES!!
IF YOU TOOK THE YANKEE LOGO, TURNED IT SIDEWAYS & CHANGED IT COMPLETELY, IT WOULD RESEMBLE A NAZI SWASTIKA!!
72 YEAR OLD YANKEE THUG DON ZIMMER & 60 YEAR OLD STARTER DAVID WELLS ATE 3 BAT-BOYS A PIECE DURING THE 2003 SEASON...
RED SOX FUN FACT:
CLINT EASTWOOD BASED A PIVOTAL SCENE IN HIS LATEST FILM, MYSTIC RIVER, ON THE TIME MY OLD ROOMMATE, JOHN, WAS ARRESTED AFTER GAME SIX OF THE 1986 WORLD SERIES....
NOOOoooooo
KEITH KNIGHT (NOT SO) FUN FACT:
I RECEIVED ONE PHONE CALL AS THE YANKEES WERE TYING IT UP AGAINST THE SOX IN THE 8TH...
RRIIINGG!!
ANOTHER HIT!!
Yankees tie it up!!
GAK!!
I KNOW, I KNOW... THE SOX ARE GONNA LOSE...
..WHO THE HELL IS THIS?!
This is your mother... your uncle just passed away.
Heart sinks
STOP

 The first Red Sox win in 86 years helped me cope with the second Bush "win".

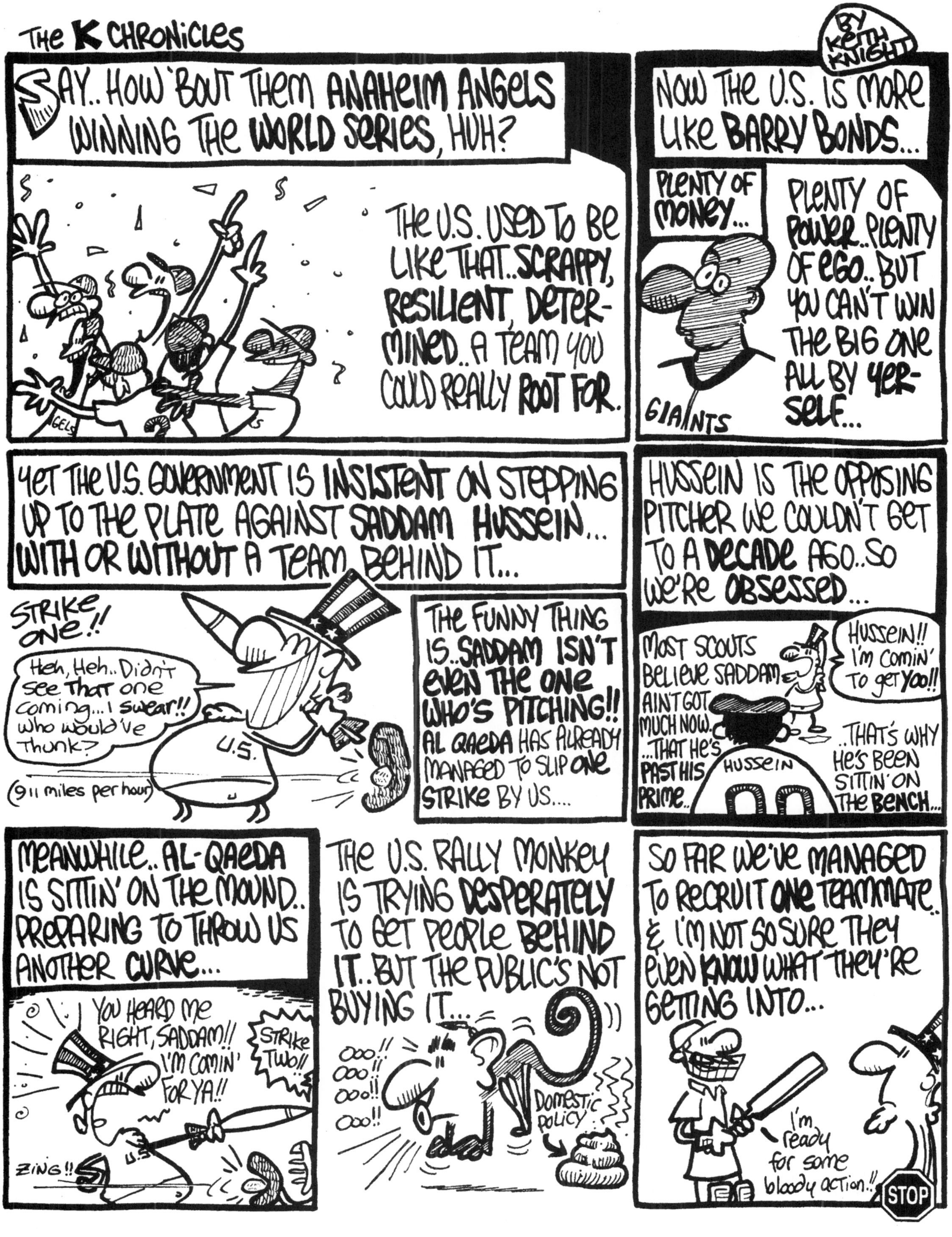
THE K CHRONICLES
BY KEITH KNIGHT
SAY.. HOW 'BOUT THEM ANAHEIM ANGELS WINNING THE WORLD SERIES, HUH?
THE U.S. USED TO BE LIKE THAT.. SCRAPPY, RESILIENT, DETERMINED.. A TEAM YOU COULD REALLY ROOT FOR.
ANGELS
NOW THE U.S. IS MORE LIKE BARRY BONDS...
PLENTY OF MONEY...
PLENTY OF POWER.. PLENTY OF EGO.. BUT YOU CAN'T WIN THE BIG ONE ALL BY YERSELF...
GIANTS
YET THE U.S. GOVERNMENT IS INSISTENT ON STEPPING UP TO THE PLATE AGAINST SADDAM HUSSEIN... WITH OR WITHOUT A TEAM BEHIND IT...
STRIKE ONE!!
Heh, Heh.. Didn't see that one coming... I swear!! who would've thunk?
U.S.
(911 miles per hour)
THE FUNNY THING IS.. SADDAM ISN'T EVEN THE ONE WHO'S PITCHING!! AL QAEDA HAS ALREADY MANAGED TO SLIP ONE STRIKE BY US....
HUSSEIN IS THE OPPOSING PITCHER WE COULDN'T GET TO A DECADE AGO.. SO WE'RE OBSESSED...
MOST SCOUTS BELIEVE SADDAM AIN'T GOT MUCH NOW. ...THAT HE'S PAST HIS PRIME..
HUSSEIN!! I'M COMIN' TO GET YOO!!
HUSSEIN
..THAT'S WHY HE'S BEEN SITTIN' ON THE BENCH...
MEANWHILE.. AL-QAEDA IS SITTIN' ON THE MOUND.. PREPARING TO THROW US ANOTHER CURVE...
YOU HEARD ME RIGHT, SADDAM!! I'M COMIN' FOR YA!!
STRIKE TWO!!
ZING!!
THE U.S. RALLY MONKEY IS TRYING DESPERATELY TO GET PEOPLE BEHIND IT.. BUT THE PUBLIC'S NOT BUYING IT...
OOO!! OOO!! OOO!! OOO!!
DOMESTIC POLICY
SO FAR WE'VE MANAGED TO RECRUIT ONE TEAMMATE.. & I'M NOT SO SURE THEY EVEN KNOW WHAT THEY'RE GETTING INTO...
I'm ready for some bloody action!!
STOP

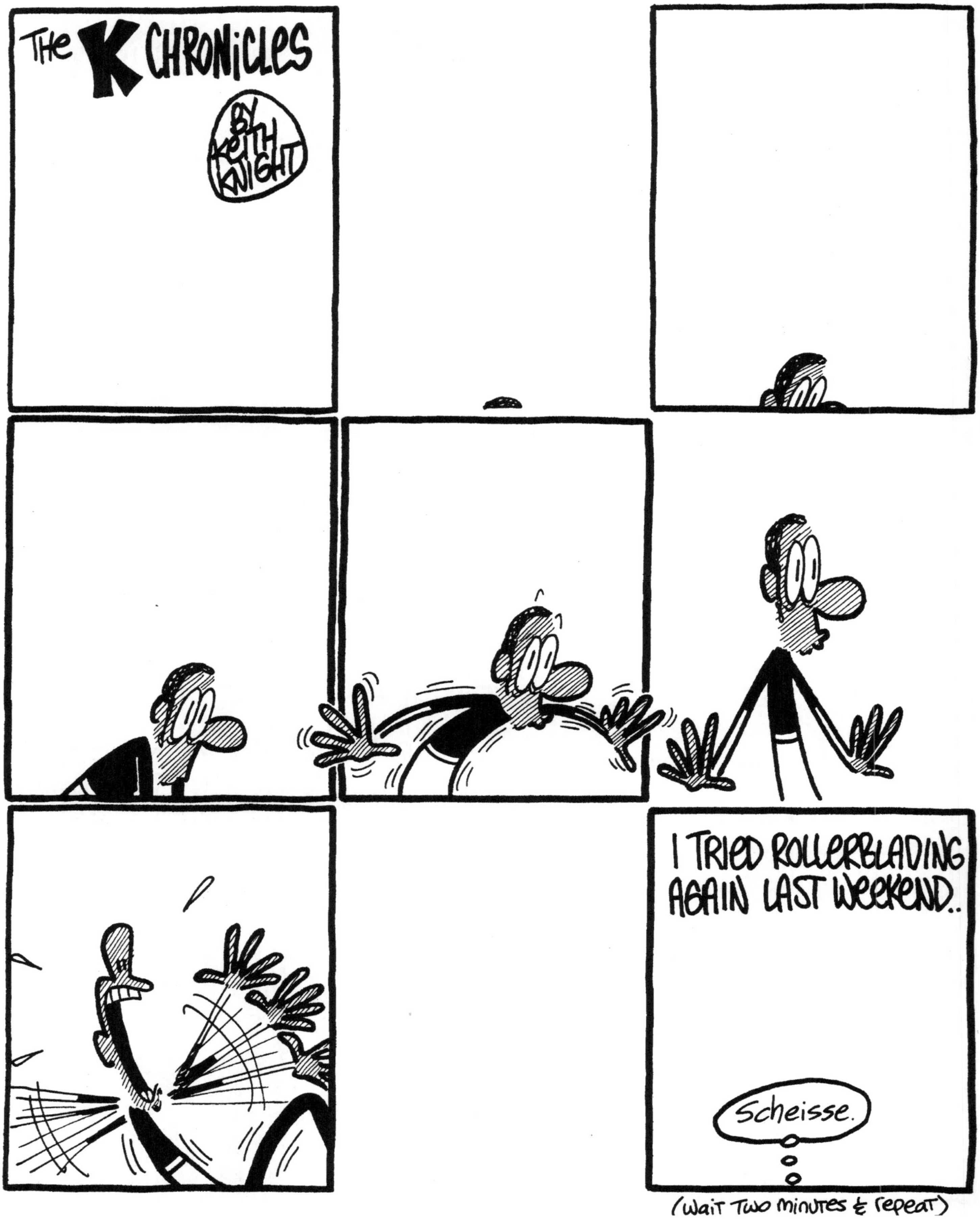
THE K CHRONICLES
BY KEITH KNIGHT
I TRIED ROLLERBLADING AGAIN LAST WEEKEND..
Scheisse.
(WAIT TWO MINUTES & REPEAT)

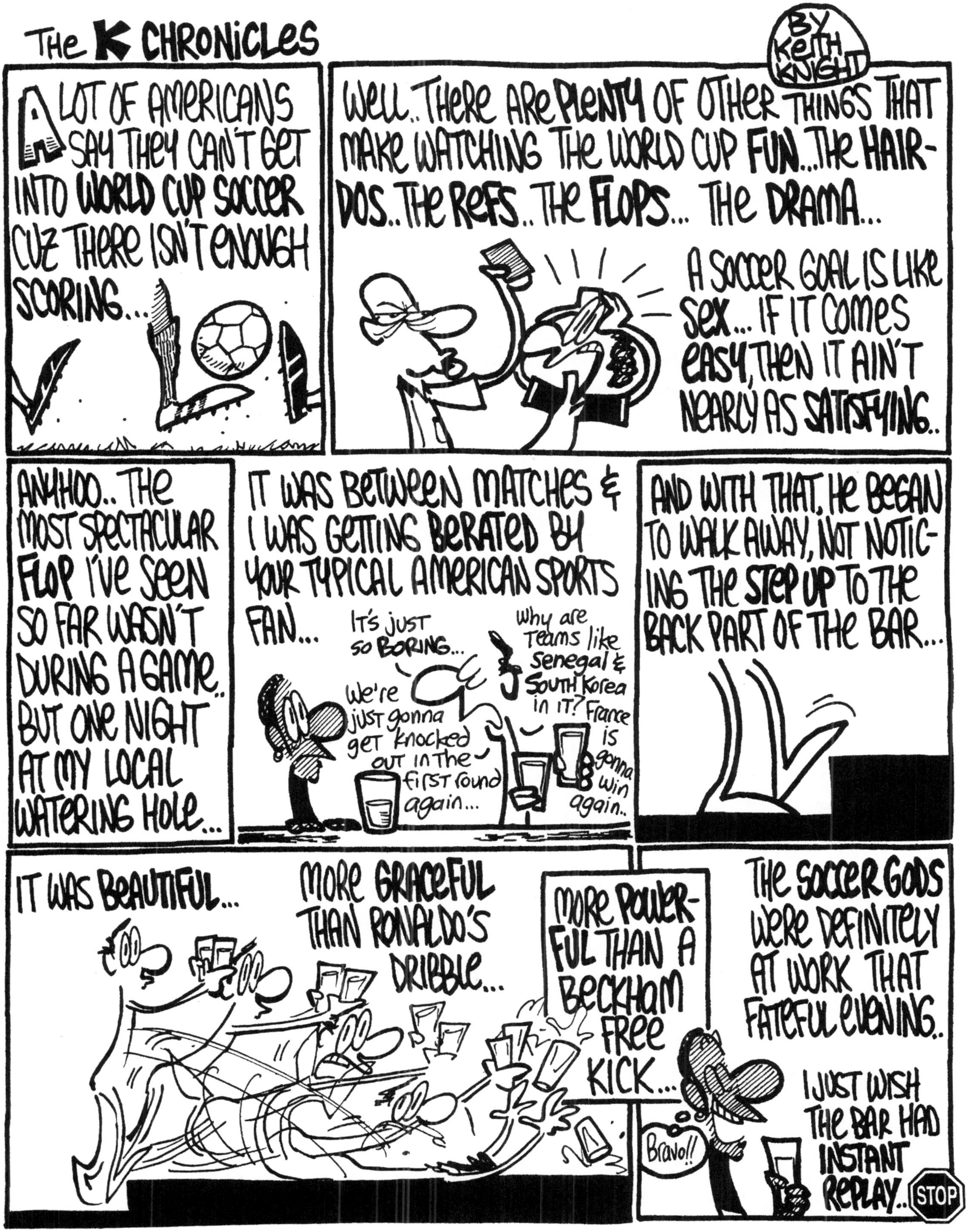
The K Chronicles
By Keith Knight
A lot of Americans say they can't get into World Cup soccer cuz there isn't enough scoring...
Well.. There are plenty of other things that make watching the World Cup fun... The hair-dos.. The refs.. The flops... The drama...
A soccer goal is like sex... If it comes easy, then it ain't nearly as satisfying..
Anyhoo.. The most spectacular flop I've seen so far wasn't during a game.. But one night at my local watering hole...
It was between matches & I was getting berated by your typical American sports fan...
It's just so boring...
We're just gonna get knocked out in the first round again...
Why are teams like Senegal & South Korea in it?
France is gonna win again..
And with that, he began to walk away, not noticing the step up to the back part of the bar...
It was beautiful...
More graceful than Ronaldo's dribble...
More powerful than a Beckham free kick...
The soccer gods were definitely at work that fateful evening..
Bravo!!
I just wish the bar had instant replay..
STOP

The K Chronicles
By Keith Knight
Baseball may be America's favorite pastime (do we have another pastime?), but football is America's favorite sport...
59-67 -38-47 Jabba the Hutt, Hutt!!
There is no greater joy to the red-blooded American male than waking up on game day..
...It's like Christmas..
Gasp
..Halloween...
How do I look?
...& St. Pattie's day all rolled into one...
You finishin' that?
The profound impact that football has on America's economy & well being is nothing short of stunning.
July Aug Sept Oct Nov
Buffalo wing sales
Beer sales
Antacid sales
But what many folks don't realize is that football has transformed the adult diaper industry into a multi-million dollar bonanza...
Grampers
Folks fed up with restroom lines have taken to wearing diapers on game day to avoid those inconvenient trips to the john..
It's saves time, energy.. plus, you never have to miss a play...
And nothing sez freedom like goin' in yer pants any time you damn well please...
Touchdown!!
Gawd bless America!!
Dump
Stop

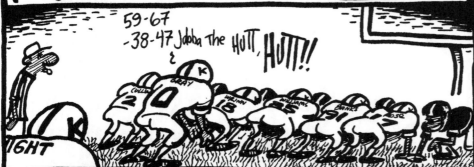

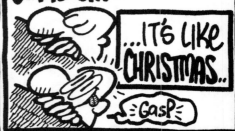

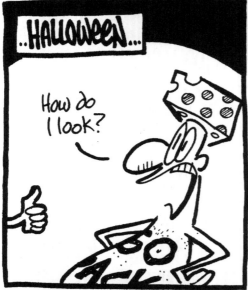

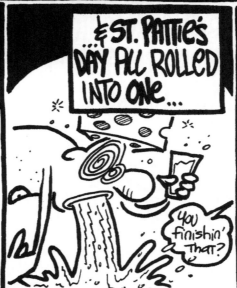

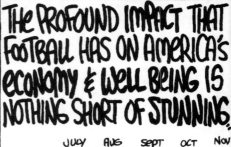

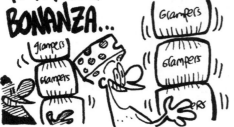

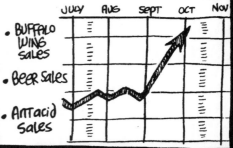

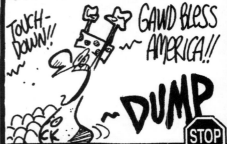

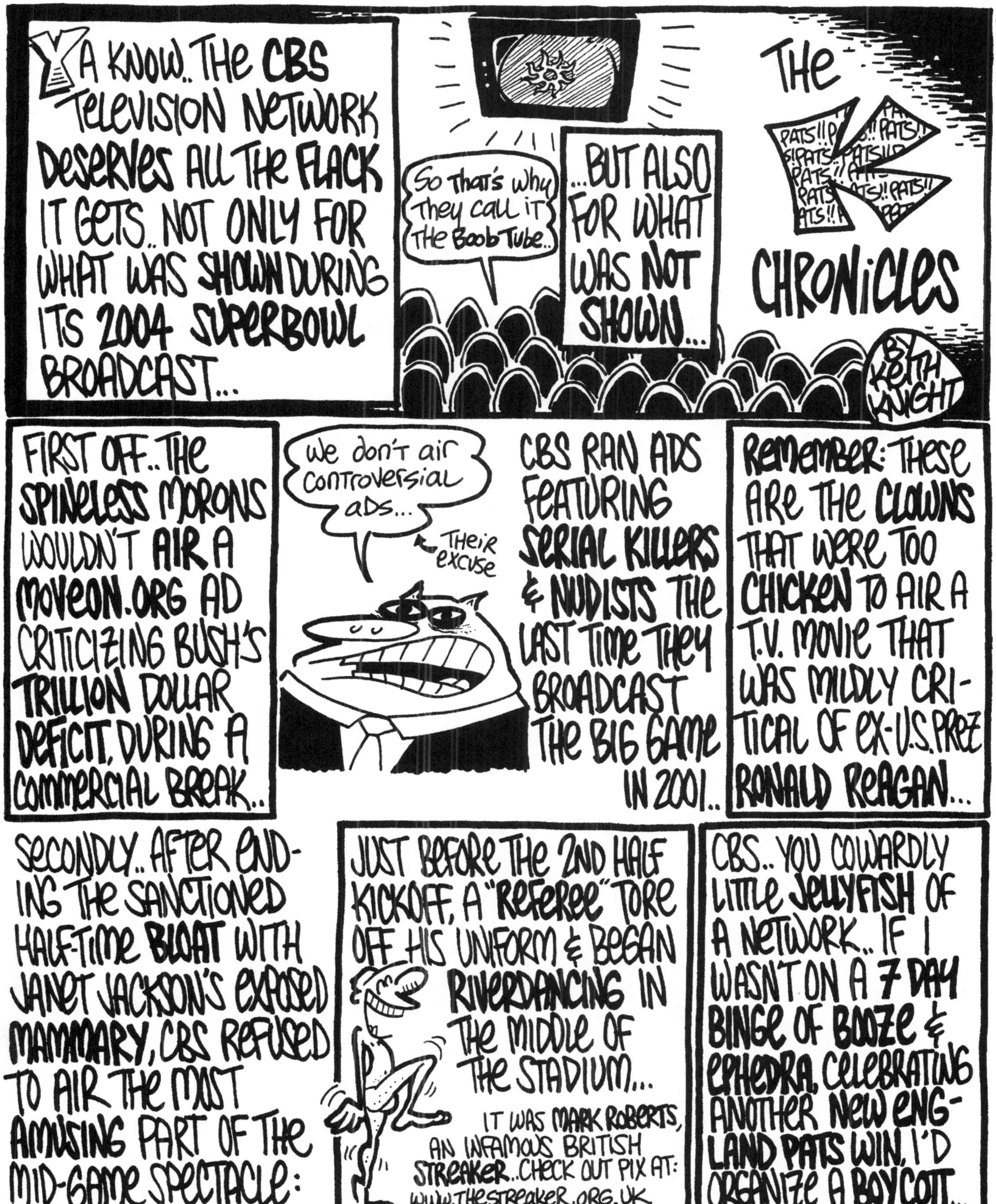

YA KNOW.. THE CBS TELEVISION NETWORK DESERVES ALL THE FLACK IT GETS.. NOT ONLY FOR WHAT WAS SHOWN DURING ITS 2004 SUPERBOWL BROADCAST...
So that's why they call it the Boob Tube..
...BUT ALSO FOR WHAT WAS NOT SHOWN...
THE K CHRONICLES
PATS!! PATS!! PATS!!
BY KEITH KNIGHT
FIRST OFF.. THE SPINELESS MORONS WOULDN'T AIR A MOVEON.ORG AD CRITICIZING BUSH'S TRILLION DOLLAR DEFICIT, DURING A COMMERCIAL BREAK..
We don't air controversial ads...
THEIR EXCUSE
CBS RAN ADS FEATURING SERIAL KILLERS & NUDISTS THE LAST TIME THEY BROADCAST THE BIG GAME IN 2001..
REMEMBER: THESE ARE THE CLOWNS THAT WERE TOO CHICKEN TO AIR A T.V. MOVIE THAT WAS MILDLY CRITICAL OF EX-U.S. PREZ RONALD REAGAN...
SECONDLY.. AFTER ENDING THE SANCTIONED HALF-TIME BLOAT WITH JANET JACKSON'S EXPOSED MAMMARY, CBS REFUSED TO AIR THE MOST AMUSING PART OF THE MID-GAME SPECTACLE:
JUST BEFORE THE 2ND HALF KICKOFF, A "REFEREE" TORE OFF HIS UNIFORM & BEGAN RIVERDANCING IN THE MIDDLE OF THE STADIUM...
IT WAS MARK ROBERTS, AN INFAMOUS BRITISH STREAKER.. CHECK OUT PIX AT: WWW.THESTREAKER.ORG.UK
CBS.. YOU COWARDLY LITTLE JELLYFISH OF A NETWORK.. IF I WASN'T ON A 7 DAY BINGE OF BOOZE & EPHEDRA, CELEBRATING ANOTHER NEW ENGLAND PATS WIN, I'D ORGANIZE A BOYCOTT...

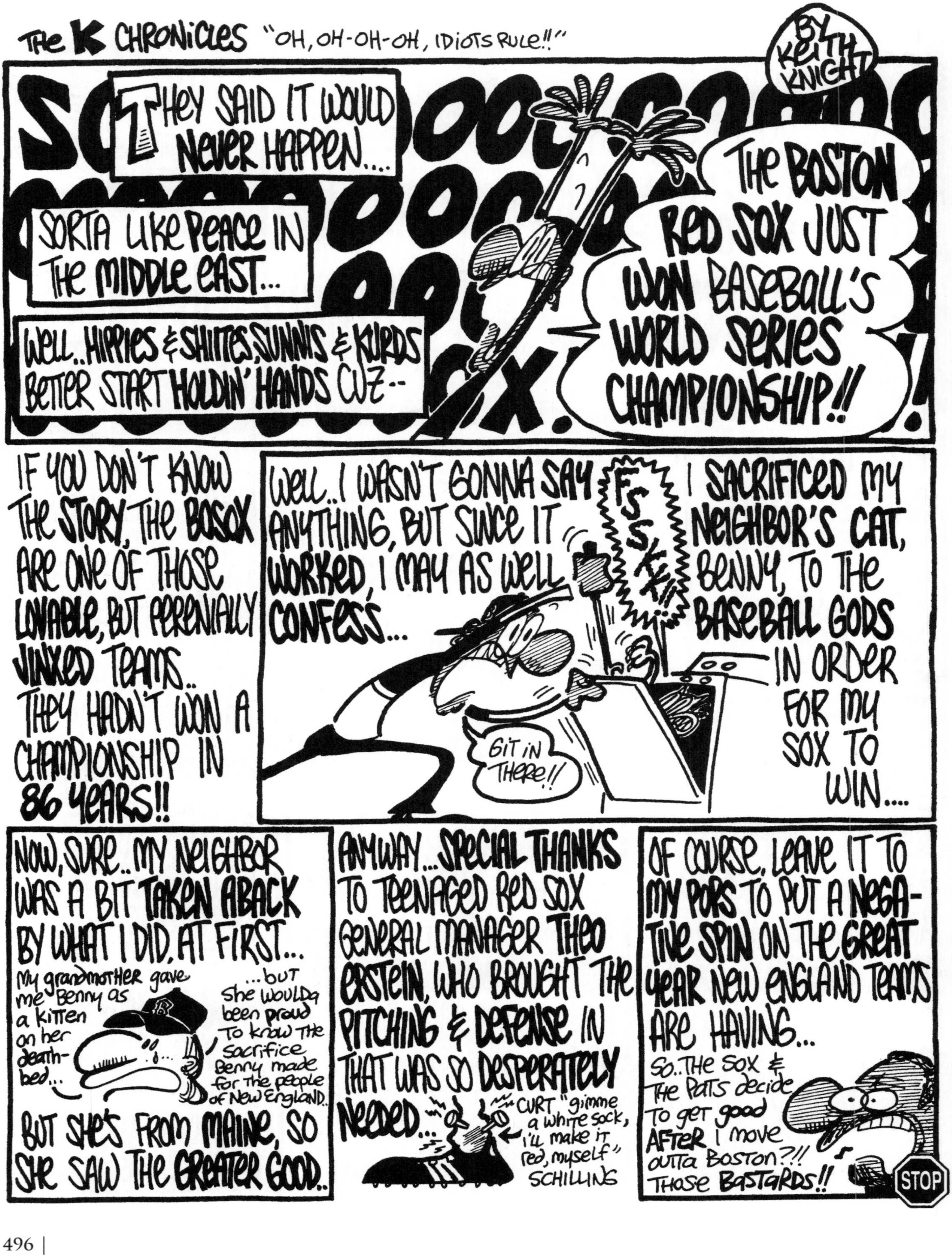
THE K CHRONICLES "OH, OH-OH-OH, IDIOTS RULE!!"
BY KEITH KNIGHT
THEY SAID IT WOULD NEVER HAPPEN....
SORTA LIKE PEACE IN THE MIDDLE EAST...
WELL.. HIPPIES & SHIITES, SUNNIS & KURDS BETTER START HOLDIN' HANDS CUZ--
SOOOOOOOOOOOOOOOOOOOOOX.!!
THE BOSTON RED SOX JUST WON BASEBALL'S WORLD SERIES CHAMPIONSHIP!!
IF YOU DON'T KNOW THE STORY, THE BOSOX ARE ONE OF THOSE LOVABLE, BUT PERENIALLY JINXED TEAMS.. THEY HADN'T WON A CHAMPIONSHIP IN 86 YEARS!!
WELL.. I WASN'T GONNA SAY ANYTHING, BUT SINCE IT WORKED, I MAY AS WELL CONFESS...
FSSKK!!
I SACRIFICED MY NEIGHBOR'S CAT, BENNY, TO THE BASEBALL GODS IN ORDER FOR MY SOX TO WIN....
GIT IN THERE!!
NOW, SURE.. MY NEIGHBOR WAS A BIT TAKEN ABACK BY WHAT I DID, AT FIRST...
My grandmother gave me Benny as a kitten on her death-bed...
...but she woulda been proud to know the sacrifice Benny made for the people of New England..
BUT SHE'S FROM MAINE, SO SHE SAW THE GREATER GOOD..
ANYWAY... SPECIAL THANKS TO TEENAGED RED SOX GENERAL MANAGER THEO EPSTEIN, WHO BROUGHT THE PITCHING & DEFENSE IN THAT WAS SO DESPERATELY NEEDED...
CURT "gimme a white sock, i'll make it red, myself" SCHILLING
OF COURSE, LEAVE IT TO MY POPS TO PUT A NEGATIVE SPIN ON THE GREAT YEAR NEW ENGLAND TEAMS ARE HAVING...
So.. The Sox & The Pats decide to get good AFTER I move outta Boston?!! Those BASTARDS!!
STOP

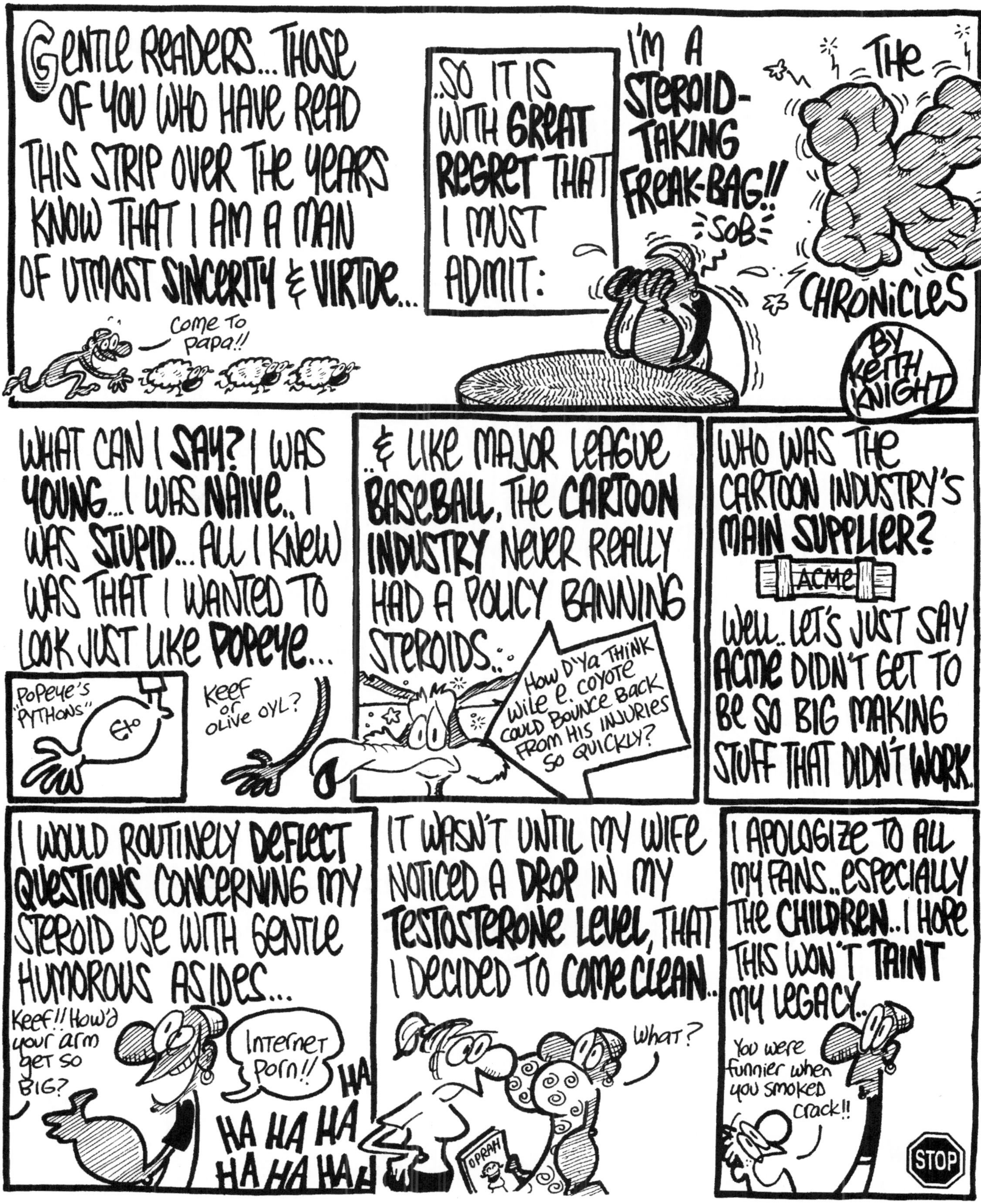
Gentle readers... those of you who have read this strip over the years know that I am a man of utmost sincerity & virtue...
Come to papa!!
..So it is with great regret that I must admit:
I'm a steroid-taking freak-bag!!
SOB
The K Chronicles
By Keith Knight
What can I say? I was young...I was naive.. I was stupid... All I knew was that I wanted to look just like Popeye...
Popeye's "pythons"
Keef or Olive Oyl?
..& like major league baseball, the cartoon industry never really had a policy banning steroids..
How d'ya think Wile E. Coyote could bounce back from his injuries so quickly?
Who was the cartoon industry's main supplier?
ACME
Well.. let's just say Acme didn't get to be so big making stuff that didn't work.
I would routinely deflect questions concerning my steroid use with gentle humorous asides...
Keef!! How'd your arm get so big?
Internet porn!!
HA HA HA HA HA HA HA HA
It wasn't until my wife noticed a drop in my testosterone level, that I decided to come clean..
What?
Oprah
I apologize to all my fans.. especially the children.. I hope this won't taint my legacy..
You were funnier when you smoked crack!!
STOP

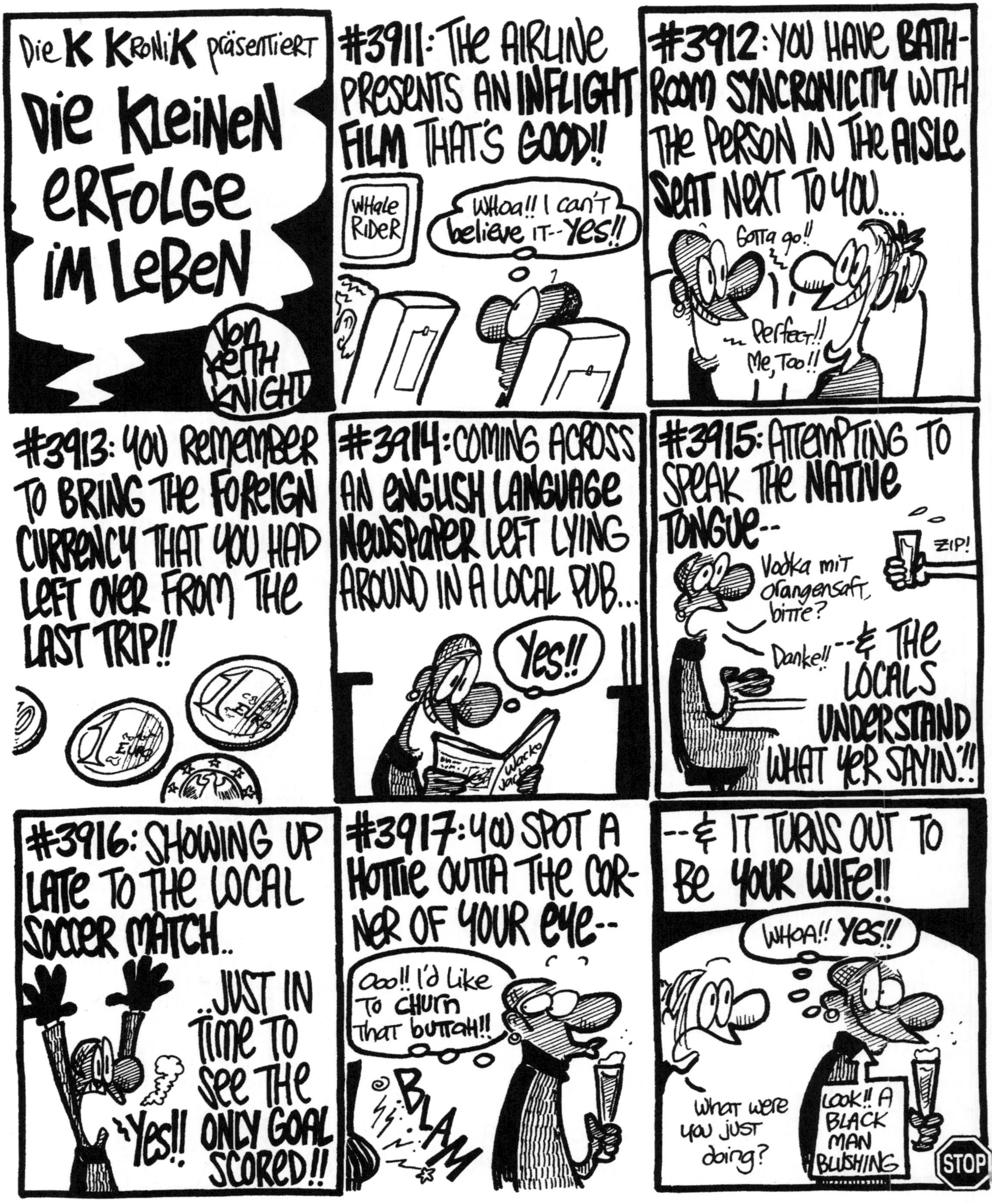

Die K Kronik präsentiert
Die Kleinen Erfolge im Leben
Von Keith Knight
#3911: The airline presents an inflight film that's good!!
Whale Rider
Whoa!! I can't believe it--Yes!!
#3912: You have bathroom syncronicity with the person in the aisle seat next to you....
Gotta go!!
...Perfect!! Me, Too!!
#3913: You remember to bring the foreign currency that you had left over from the last trip!!
1 Euro
1 Euro
#3914: Coming across an English language newspaper left lying around in a local pub...
Yes!!
Wacko Jacko
#3915: Attempting to speak the native tongue--
Vodka mit Orangensaft, bitte?
Zip!
Danke!!
--& the locals understand what yer sayin'!!
#3916: Showing up late to the local soccer match..
..Just in time to see the only goal scored!!
Yes!!
#3917: You spot a hottie outta the corner of your eye--
Ooo!! I'd like to churn that buttah!!
BLAM
--& it turns out to be your wife!!
Whoa!! Yes!!
What were you just doing?
Look!! A black man blushing
STOP

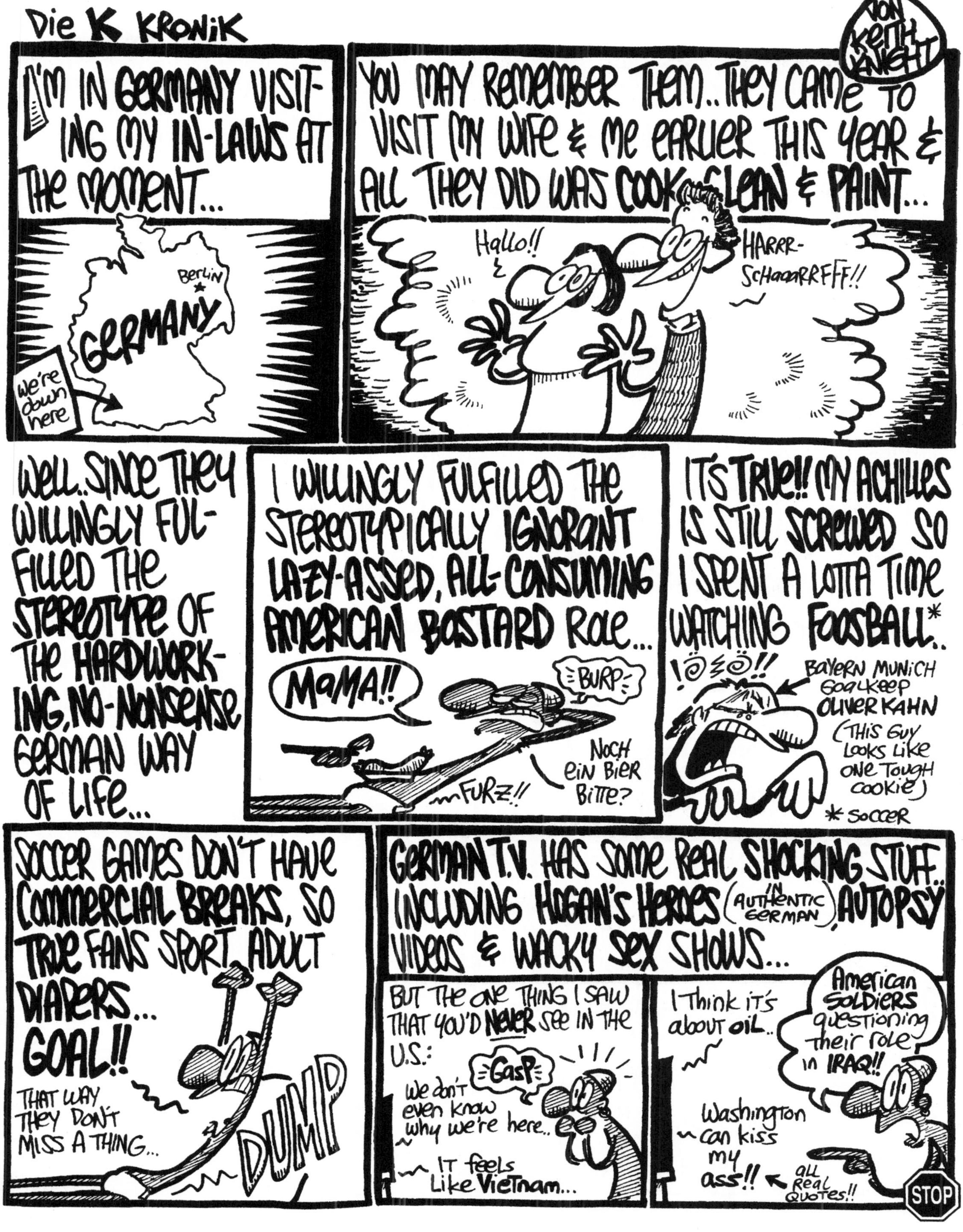

Die K Kronik
Von Keith Knight
I'M IN GERMANY VISITING MY IN-LAWS AT THE MOMENT...
Berlin
GERMANY
We're down here
YOU MAY REMEMBER THEM.. THEY CAME TO VISIT MY WIFE & ME EARLIER THIS YEAR & ALL THEY DID WAS COOK, CLEAN & PAINT...
Hallo!!
HARRR-SCHaaaRRFFF!!
WELL.. SINCE THEY WILLINGLY FULFILLED THE STEREOTYPE OF THE HARDWORKING, NO-NONSENSE GERMAN WAY OF LIFE...
I WILLINGLY FULFILLED THE STEREOTYPICALLY IGNORANT LAZY-ASSED, ALL-CONSUMING AMERICAN BASTARD ROLE...
MaMA!!
BURP
FURZ!!
NOCH EIN BIER BITTE?
IT'S TRUE!! MY ACHILLES IS STILL SCREWED SO I SPENT A LOTTA TIME WATCHING FOOSBALL*..
BAYERN MUNICH GOALKEEP OLIVER KAHN
(THIS GUY LOOKS LIKE ONE TOUGH COOKIE)
* SOCCER
SOCCER GAMES DON'T HAVE COMMERCIAL BREAKS, SO TRUE FANS SPORT ADULT DIAPERS...
GOAL!!
THAT WAY THEY DON'T MISS A THING...
DUMP
GERMAN T.V. HAS SOME REAL SHOCKING STUFF.. INCLUDING HOGAN'S HEROES (IN AUTHENTIC GERMAN), AUTOPSY VIDEOS & WACKY SEX SHOWS...
BUT THE ONE THING I SAW THAT YOU'D NEVER SEE IN THE U.S.:
GASP
We don't even know why we're here..
IT feels Like VIETNAM...
American SOLDIERS questioning their role in IRAQ!!
I Think it's about OIL..
Washington can kiss my ass!!
ALL REAL QUOTES!!
STOP

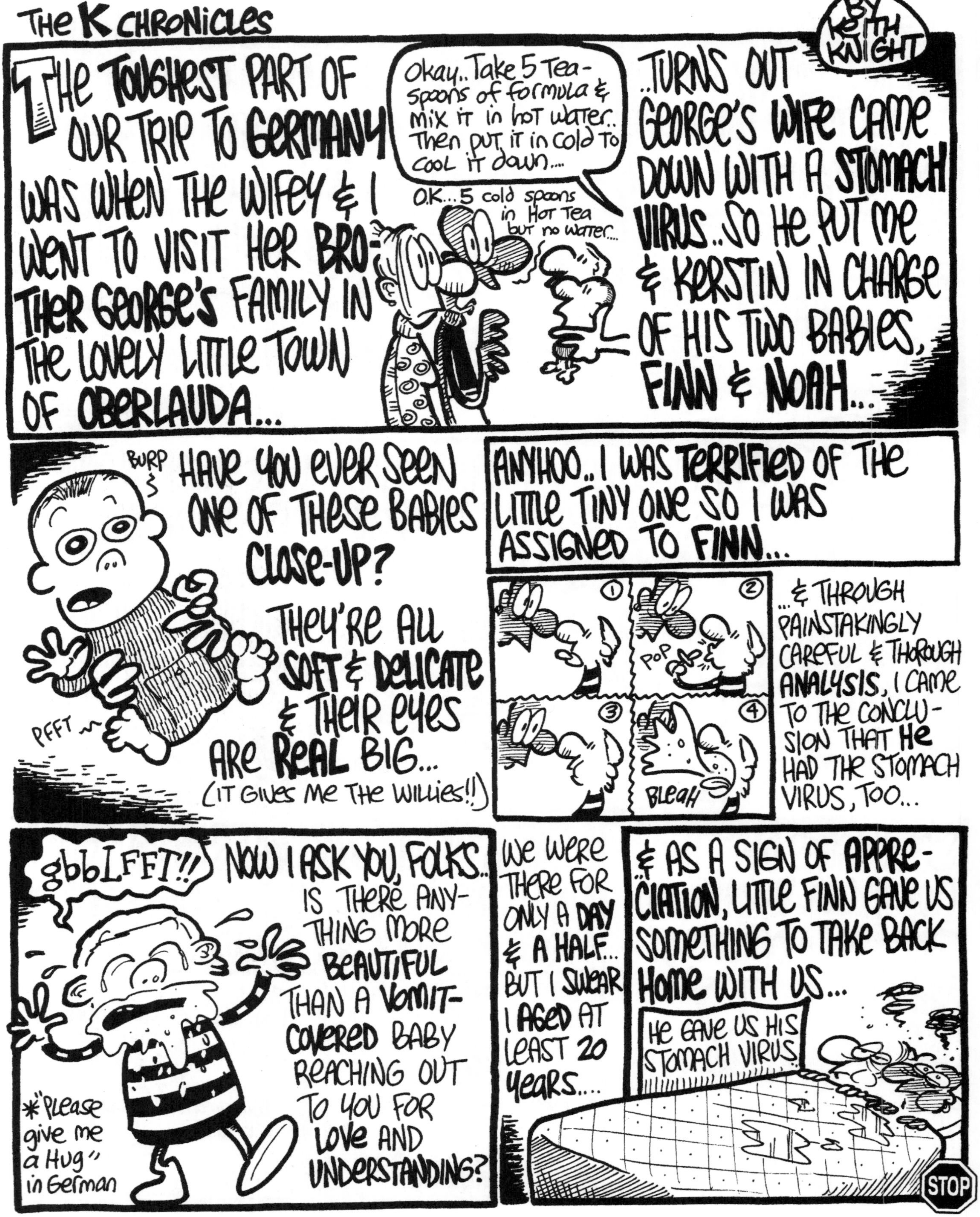

THE K CHRONICLES
BY KEITH KNIGHT
THE TOUGHEST PART OF OUR TRIP TO GERMANY WAS WHEN THE WIFEY & I WENT TO VISIT HER BROTHER GEORGE'S FAMILY IN THE LOVELY LITTLE TOWN OF OBERLAUDA...
Okay.. Take 5 Teaspoons of formula & mix it in hot water.. Then put it in cold to cool it down....
O.K...5 cold spoons in Hot Tea but no water...
..TURNS OUT GEORGE'S WIFE CAME DOWN WITH A STOMACH VIRUS.. SO HE PUT ME & KERSTIN IN CHARGE OF HIS TWO BABIES, FINN & NOAH...
BURP
HAVE YOU EVER SEEN ONE OF THESE BABIES CLOSE-UP?
THEY'RE ALL SOFT & DELICATE & THEIR EYES ARE REAL BIG...
(IT GIVES ME THE WILLIES!!)
PFFT
ANYHOO.. I WAS TERRIFIED OF THE LITTLE TINY ONE SO I WAS ASSIGNED TO FINN...
1
2
POP
3
4
BLEAH
...& THROUGH PAINSTAKINGLY CAREFUL & THOROUGH ANALYSIS, I CAME TO THE CONCLUSION THAT HE HAD THE STOMACH VIRUS, TOO...
gbbLFFT!!*
NOW I ASK YOU, FOLKS... IS THERE ANYTHING MORE BEAUTIFUL THAN A VOMIT-COVERED BABY REACHING OUT TO YOU FOR LOVE AND UNDERSTANDING?
*"Please give me a Hug" in German
WE WERE THERE FOR ONLY A DAY & A HALF... BUT I SWEAR I AGED AT LEAST 20 YEARS....
& AS A SIGN OF APPRECIATION, LITTLE FINN GAVE US SOMETHING TO TAKE BACK HOME WITH US...
HE GAVE US HIS STOMACH VIRUS.
STOP

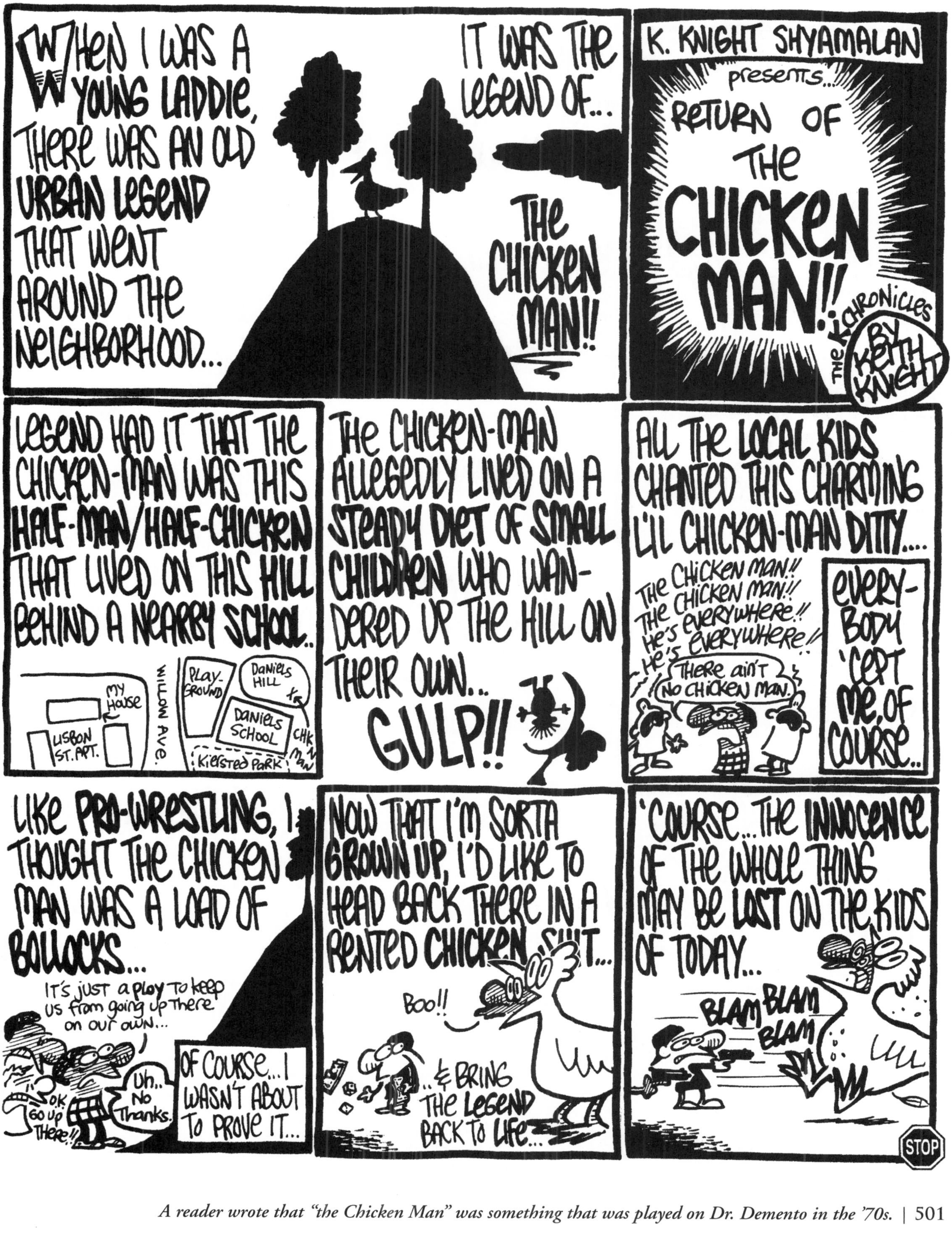
When I was a young laddie, there was an old urban legend that went around the neighborhood...
It was the legend of...
The Chicken Man!!
K. Knight Shyamalan
presents...
Return of the Chicken Man!!
The K Chronicles
By Keith Knight
Legend had it that the Chicken-Man was this half-man/half-chicken that lived on this hill behind a nearby school...
My house
Lisbon St. Apt.
Willow Ave.
Playground
Daniels Hill
X
Daniels School
Chk 'n Man
Kiersted Park
The Chicken-Man allegedly lived on a steady diet of small children who wandered up the hill on their own...
GULP!!
All the local kids chanted this charming li'l Chicken-Man ditty....
The Chicken Man!! The Chicken Man!! He's everywhere!! He's everywhere!!
There ain't no Chicken Man.
Every-body 'cept me, of course...
Like pro-wrestling, I thought the Chicken Man was a load of bollocks...
It's just a ploy to keep us from going up there on our own...
OK Go up there!!
Uh.. No Thanks.
Of course... I wasn't about to prove it...
Now that I'm sorta grown up, I'd like to head back there in a rented chicken suit...
Boo!!
...& bring the legend back to life...
'Course... the innocence of the whole thing may be lost on the kids of today...
BLAM BLAM BLAM BLAM
STOP

A reader wrote that "the Chicken Man" was something that was played on Dr. Demento in the '70s.

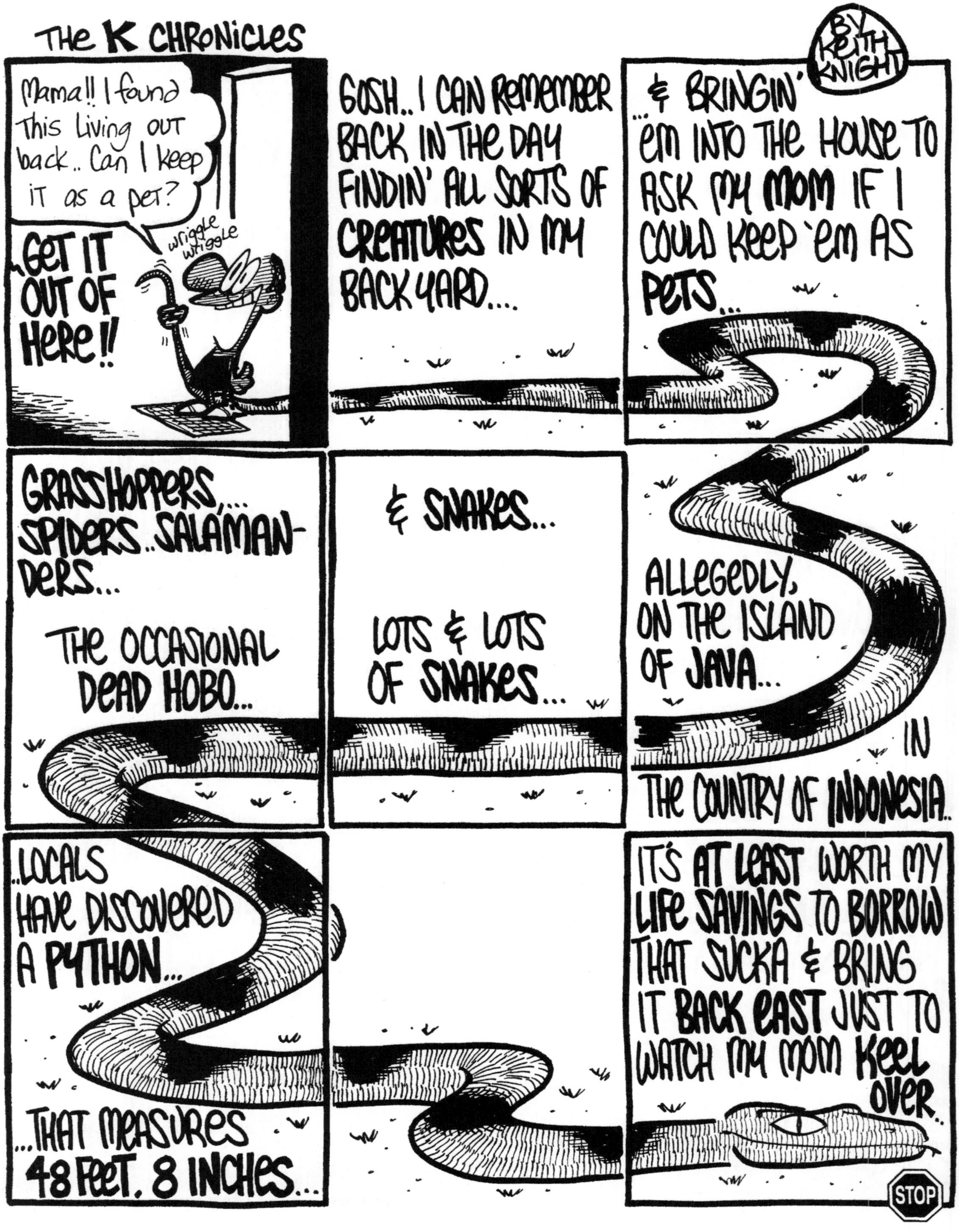

THE K CHRONICLES
BY KEITH KNIGHT
Mama!! I found This Living out back.. Can I keep it as a pet?
wriggle wriggle
..GET IT OUT OF HERE!!
GOSH.. I CAN REMEMBER BACK IN THE DAY FINDIN' ALL SORTS OF CREATURES IN MY BACKYARD....
...& BRINGIN' 'EM INTO THE HOUSE TO ASK MY MOM IF I COULD KEEP 'EM AS PETS...
GRASSHOPPERS,... SPIDERS..SALAMANDERS...
THE OCCASIONAL DEAD HOBO...
& SNAKES...
LOTS & LOTS OF SNAKES...
ALLEGEDLY, ON THE ISLAND OF JAVA...
IN THE COUNTRY OF INDONESIA..
..LOCALS HAVE DISCOVERED A PYTHON...
...THAT MEASURES 48 FEET, 8 INCHES...
IT'S AT LEAST WORTH MY LIFE SAVINGS TO BORROW THAT SUCKA & BRING IT BACK EAST JUST TO WATCH MY MOM KEEL OVER..
STOP

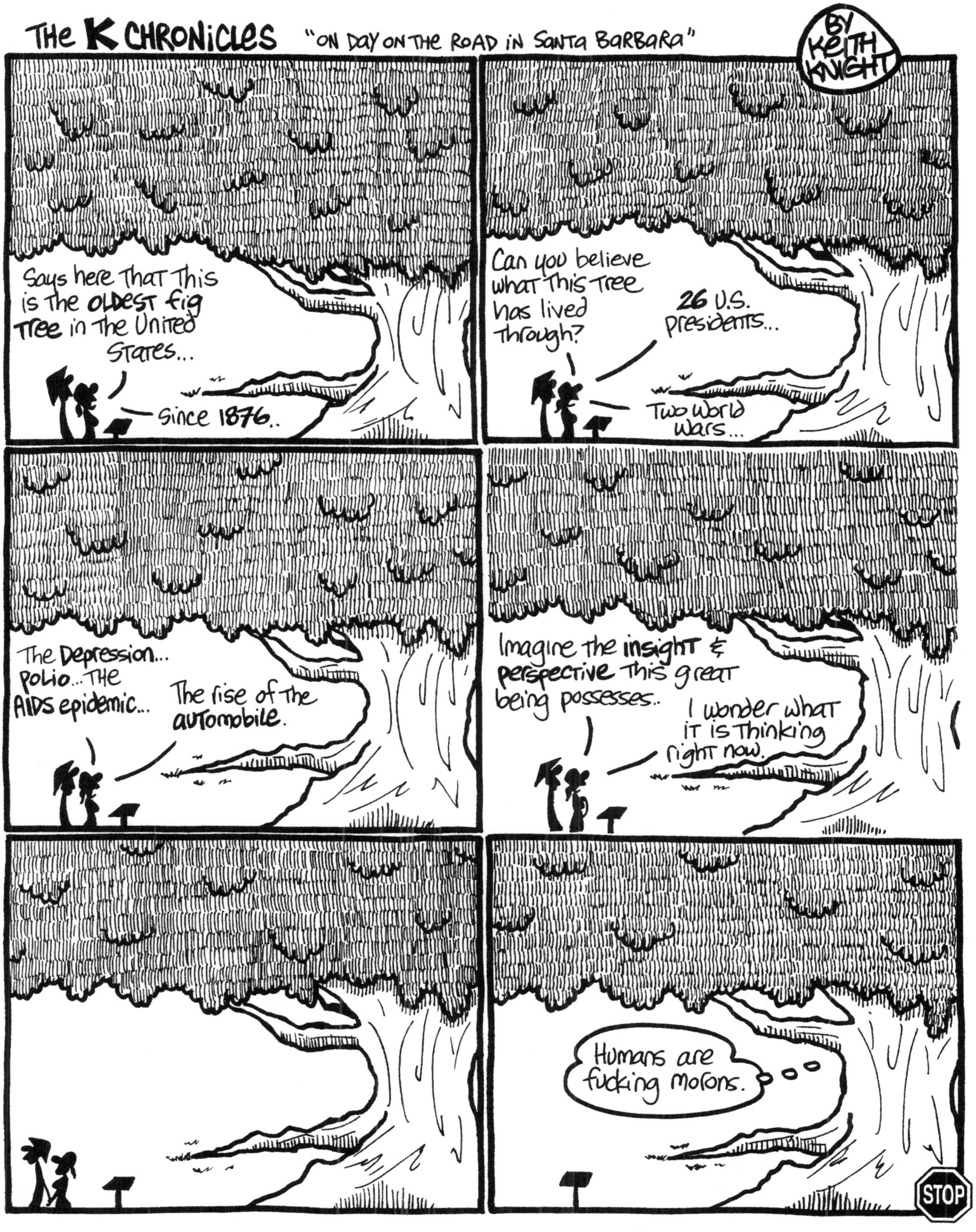
THE K CHRONICLES
"ON DAY ON THE ROAD IN SANTA BARBARA"
BY KEITH KNIGHT
Says here that this is the OLDEST fig TREE in the United States...
Since 1876..
Can you believe what this tree has lived through?
26 U.S. presidents...
Two World Wars...
The Depression... POLIO... THE AIDS epidemic...
The rise of the automobile.
Imagine the insight & perspective this great being possesses..
I wonder what it is thinking right now.
Humans are fucking morons.
STOP

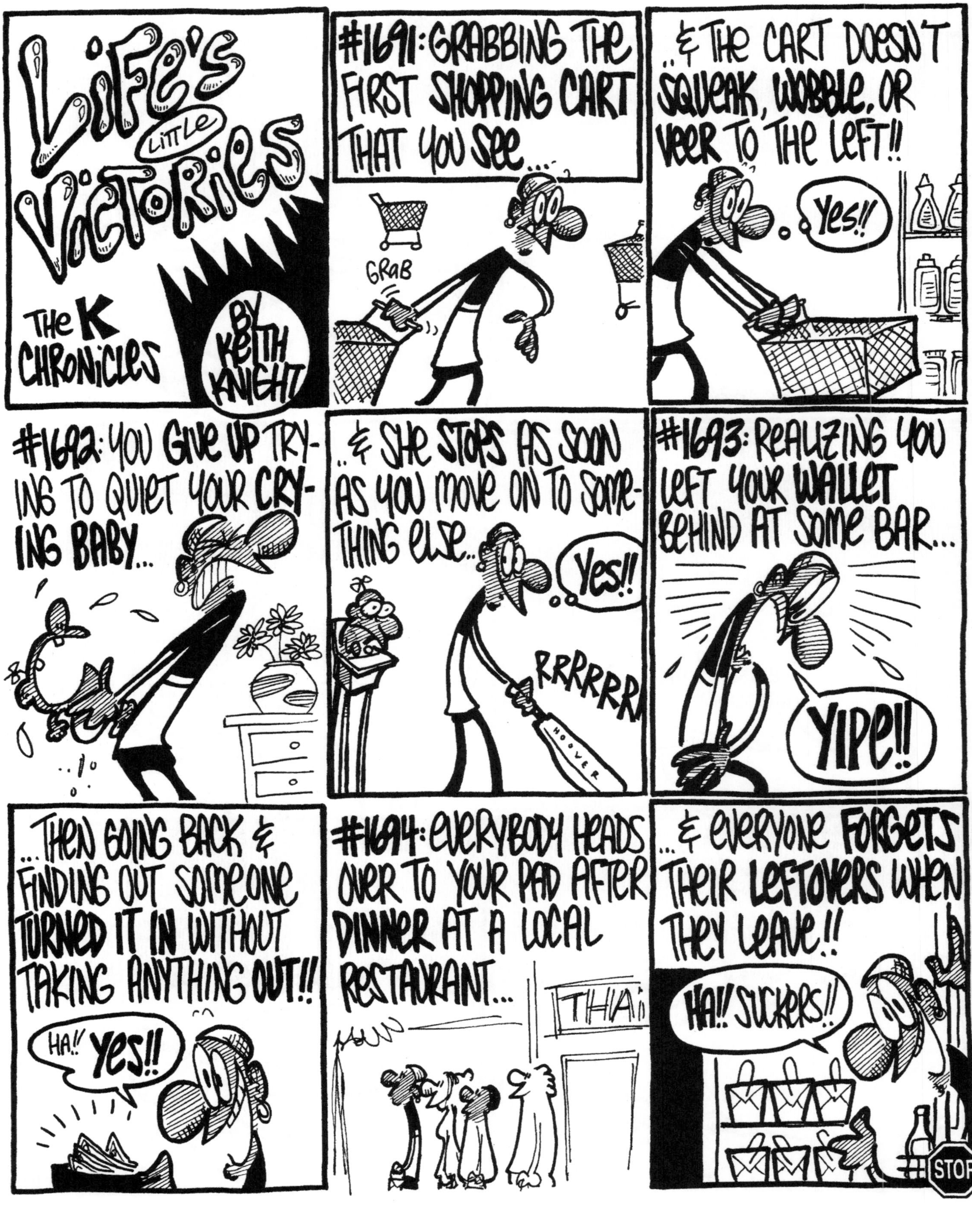
LIFE'S LITTLE VICTORIES
THE K CHRONICLES
BY KEITH KNIGHT
#1691: GRABBING THE FIRST SHOPPING CART THAT YOU SEE...
GRAB
...& THE CART DOESN'T SQUEAK, WOBBLE, OR VEER TO THE LEFT!!
YES!!
#1692: YOU GIVE UP TRYING TO QUIET YOUR CRYING BABY...
...& SHE STOPS AS SOON AS YOU MOVE ON TO SOMETHING ELSE...
YES!!
RRRRRRR
HOOVER
#1693: REALIZING YOU LEFT YOUR WALLET BEHIND AT SOME BAR...
YIPE!!
...THEN GOING BACK & FINDING OUT SOMEONE TURNED IT IN WITHOUT TAKING ANYTHING OUT!!
HA!! YES!!
#1694: EVERYBODY HEADS OVER TO YOUR PAD AFTER DINNER AT A LOCAL RESTAURANT...
THAI
...& EVERYONE FORGETS THEIR LEFTOVERS WHEN THEY LEAVE!!
HA!! SUCKERS!!
STOP

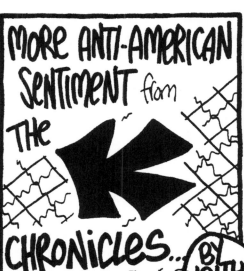

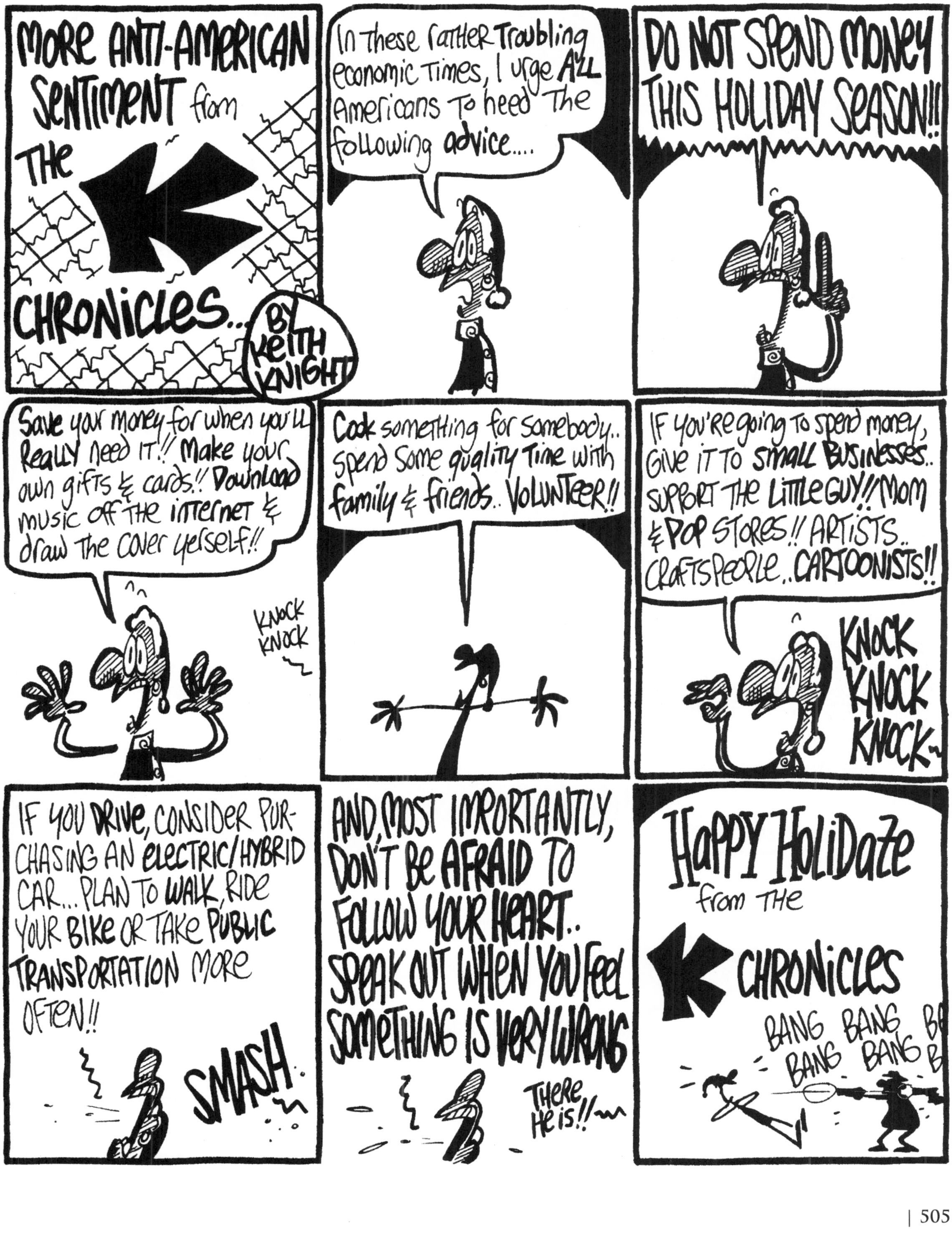

MORE ANTI-AMERICAN SENTIMENT from THE ◀ CHRONICLES.. BY KEITH KNIGHT

In these rather troubling economic times, I urge ALL Americans to heed the following advice....

DO NOT SPEND MONEY THIS HOLIDAY SEASON!!

Save your money for when you'll REALLY need it!! Make your own gifts & cards!! Download music off the internet & draw the cover yerself!!

KNOCK KNOCK

Cook something for somebody.. spend some quality time with family & friends.. VOLUNTEER!!

IF you're going to spend money, GIVE IT TO SMALL BUSINESSES.. SUPPORT THE LITTLE GUY!! MOM & POP STORES!! ARTISTS.. CRAFTSPEOPLE..CARTOONISTS!!

KNOCK KNOCK KNOCK~

IF YOU DRIVE, CONSIDER PURCHASING AN ELECTRIC/HYBRID CAR... PLAN TO WALK, RIDE YOUR BIKE OR TAKE PUBLIC TRANSPORTATION MORE OFTEN!!

SMASH!

AND, MOST IMPORTANTLY, DON'T BE AFRAID TO FOLLOW YOUR HEART.. SPEAK OUT WHEN YOU FEEL SOMETHING IS VERY WRONG

THERE HE IS!!~

Happy Holidaze from the ◀ CHRONICLES

BANG BANG BANG BANG BANG B

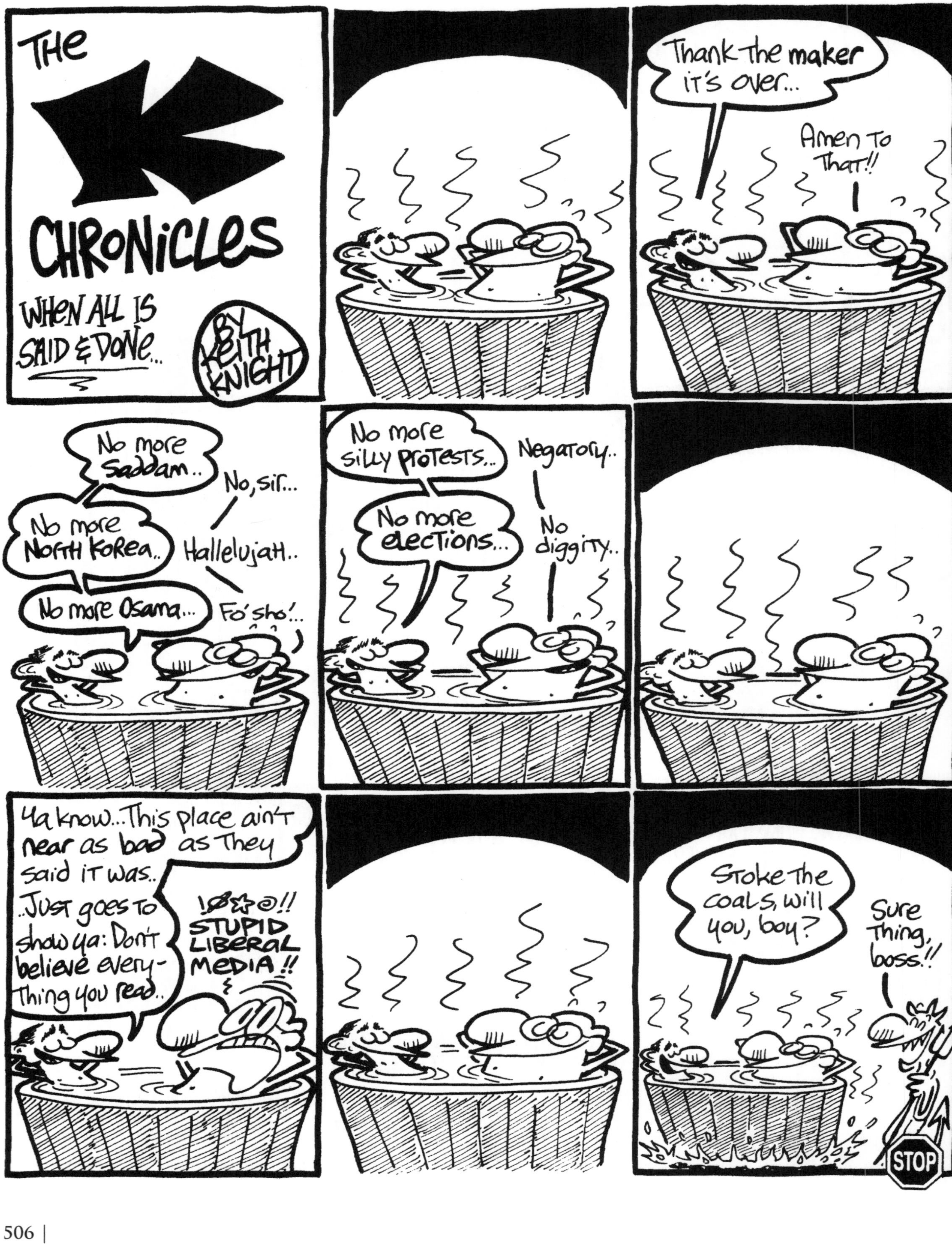
THE K CHRONICLES
WHEN ALL IS SAID & DONE...
BY KEITH KNIGHT
Thank the maker it's over...
Amen To That!!
No more Saddam..
No, sir...
No more North Korea..
Hallelujah..
No more Osama...
Fo' sho'!..
No more silly protests...
Negatory..
No more elections...
No diggity..
Ya know...This place ain't near as bad as They said it was..
..Just goes to show ya: Don't believe every-Thing you read..
!Ø✩◎!! STUPID LIBERAL MEDIA!!
Stoke the coals, will you, boy?
Sure Thing, boss!!
STOP

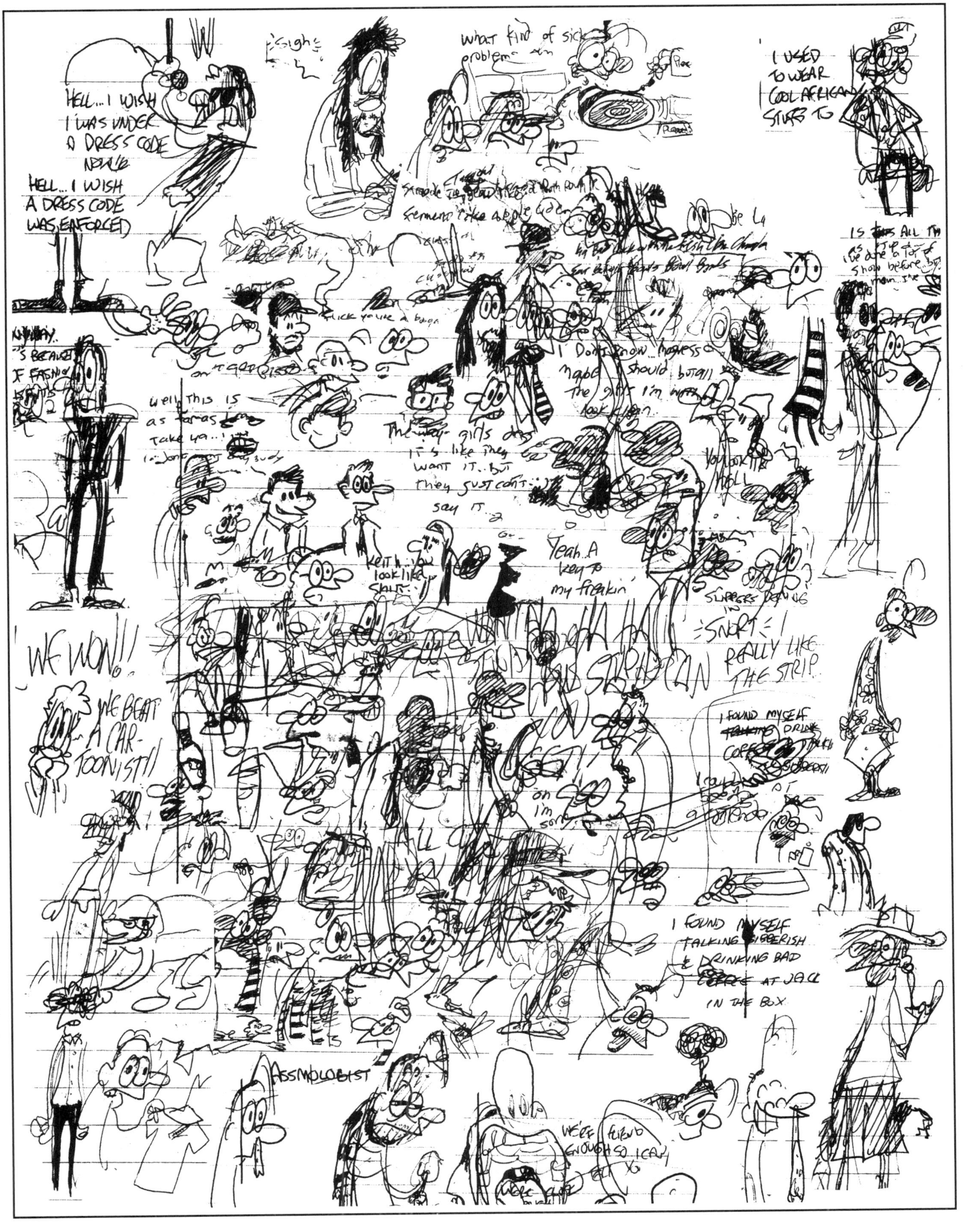
HELL... I WISH I WAS UNDER A DRESS CODE NOW
HELL... I WISH A DRESS CODE WAS ENFORCED
sigh
I USED TO WEAR COOL AFRICAN STUFF TO
well this is as far as I can take ya...!
I Don't know... maybe I should just...
It's like they WANT IT.. BUT they JUST CAN'T... say IT..
You look like Hell
Yeah. A key to my freakin'
Keith... you look like SHIT
WE WON!!
WE BEAT A CAR-TOONIST!!
REALLY LIKE THE STRIP
I FOUND MYSELF TALKING GIBBERISH & DRINKING BAD COFFEE AT JACK IN THE BOX
oh I'm sorry
ASSMOLOGIST
WE'RE FRIENDS ENOUGH SO I CAN

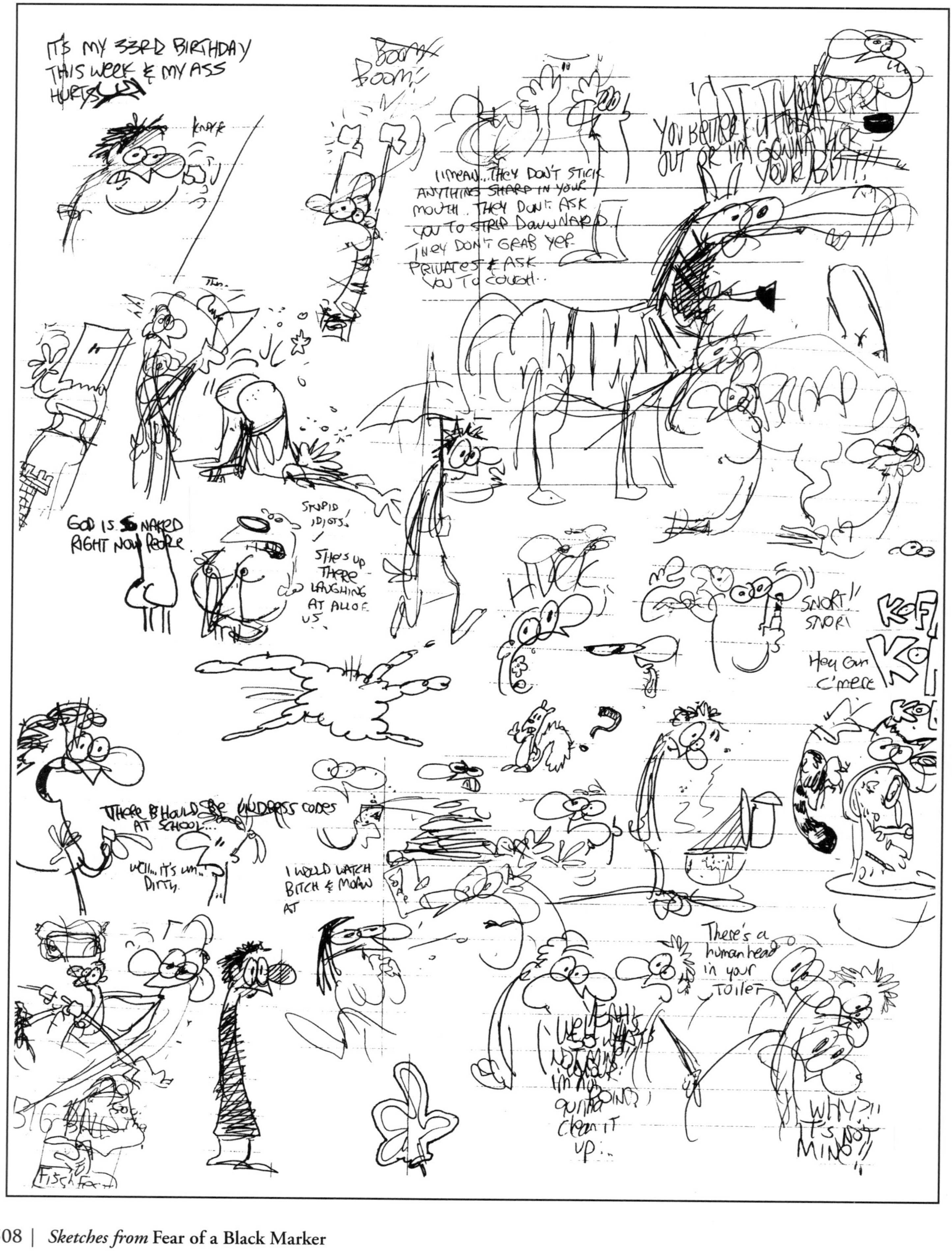

IT'S MY 33RD BIRTHDAY THIS WEEK & MY ASS HURTS
Boom!
I mean... THEY DON'T STICK ANYTHING SHARP IN YOUR MOUTH. THEY DON'T ASK YOU TO STRIP DOWNWARD. THEY DON'T GRAB YER PRIVATES & ASK YOU TO COUGH...
YOU BETTER
YOUR BUTT!!
GOD IS NAKED RIGHT NOW PEOPLE
STUPID IDIOTS!
SHE'S UP THERE LAUGHING AT ALL OF US.
SNORT!
C'mere
THERE SHOULD BE UNDRESS CODES AT SCHOOL...
Well... it's um... Dirty.
I WOULD WATCH BITCH & MOAN AT
There's a human head in your toilet
clean it up...
WHY?!! IT'S NOT MINE!!

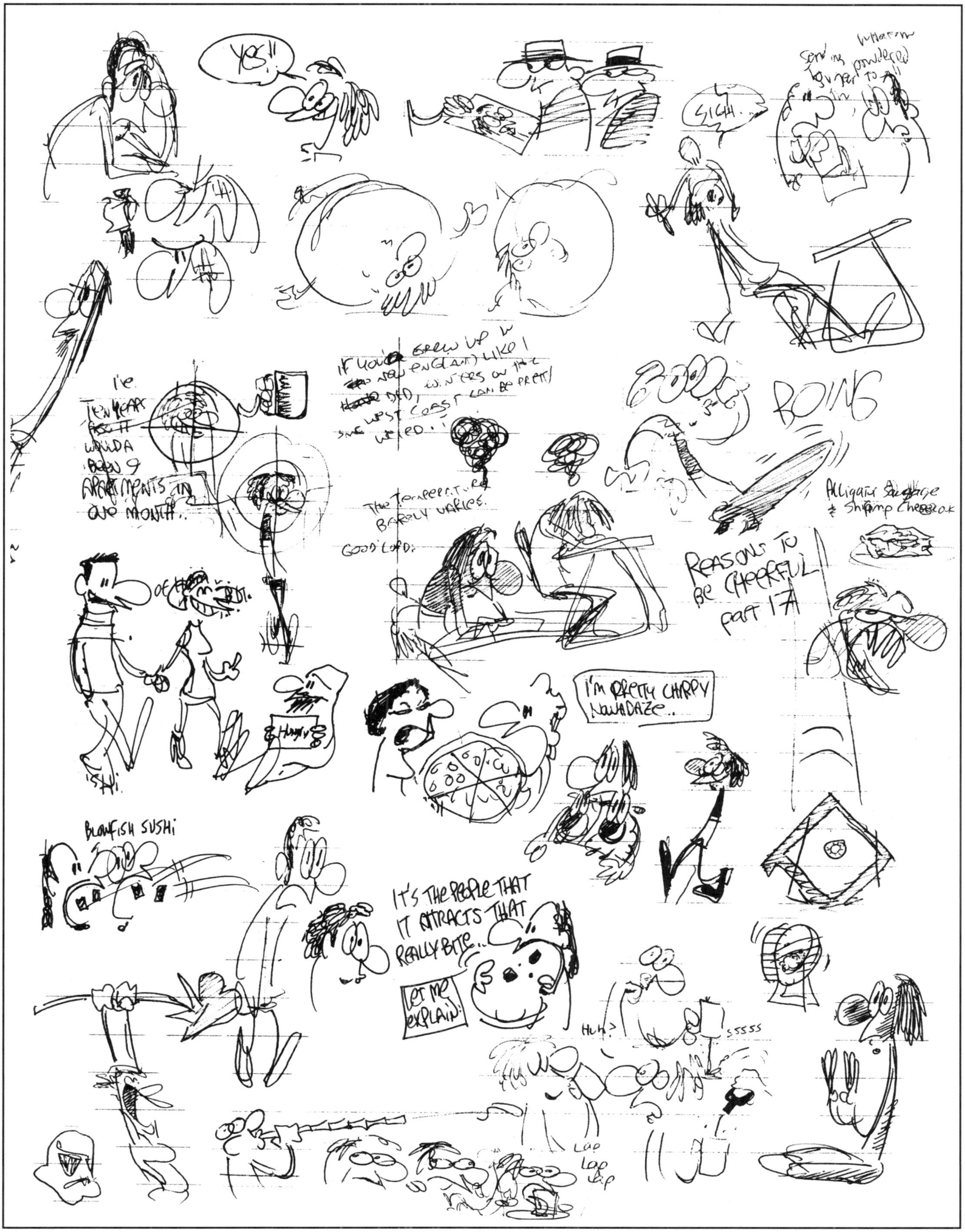

YES!!
SIGH..
IF YOU GREW UP IN NEW ENGLAND LIKE I DID, WINTERS ON THE WEST COAST CAN BE PRETTY WEIRD.
BOING
Alligator Sausage & Shrimp Cheesecake
The Temperature Barely Varies.
GOOD LORD.
REASONS TO BE CHEERFUL PART 17
I'M PRETTY CHIRPY NOWADAZE..
BLOWFISH SUSHI
IT'S THE PEOPLE THAT IT ATTRACTS THAT REALLY BITE..
LET ME EXPLAIN!
HUH?
SSSSS
Lap
Lap
Lap

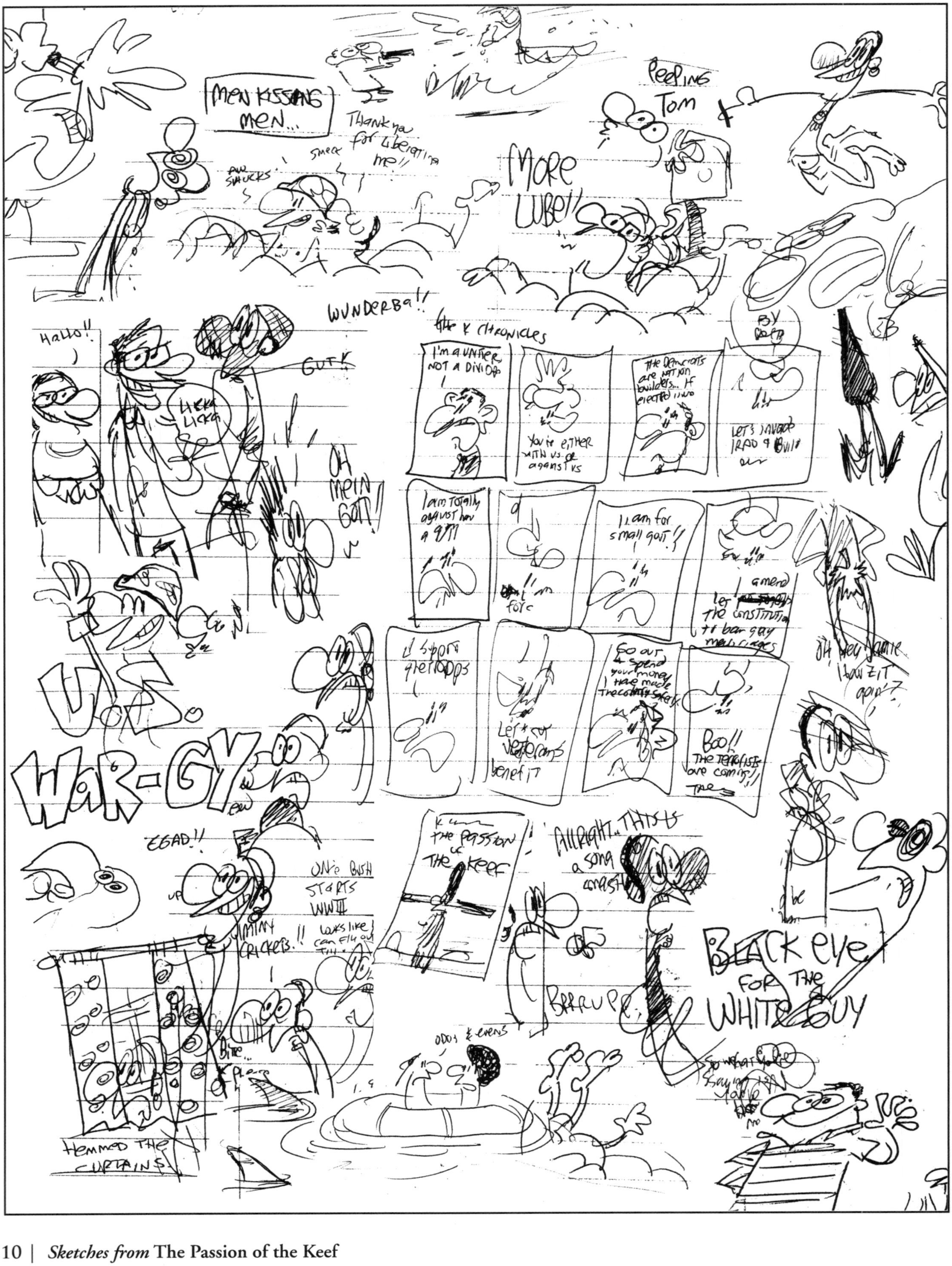
MEN KISSING MEN...
Thank you for liberating me!!
AW SHUCKS
PEEPING TOM
MORE LUBE!!
WUNDERBA!!
HALLO!!
LICKA LICKA
OH MEIN GOT!
The K Chronicles
I'm a uniter, NOT A DIVIDER
You're either with us or against us
Let's invade Iraq & build
I am for small govt!!
I amend the constitution to ban gay marriages
I support the troops
Let's cut veterans benefit
Boo!! The terrorists are coming!!
Oh, hey Jamie how's it goin'?
WAR-GY
EGAD!!
Once Bush starts WWIII
JIMINY CRICKETS!!
The Passion of The Keef
BLACK EYE FOR THE WHITE GUY
BRRRUP
odds & evens
Hemmed the curtains!

ALSO FROM DARK HORSE BOOKS!

THE TRIAL OF
COLONEL SWEETO
AND OTHER STORIES
A COLLECTION OF THE COMIC STRIPS OF THE PERRY BIBLE FELLOWSHIP

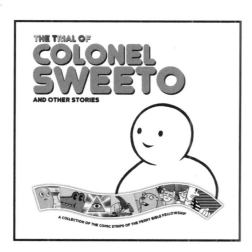

THE PERRY BIBLE FELLOWSHIP:
THE TRIAL OF COLONEL SWEETO AND OTHER STORIES
Nicholas Gurewitch

The award-winning *Perry Bible Fellowship* has achieved a worldwide cult following. Now, for the first time, the hilarious cartoons of Nicholas Gurewitch have been collected in this handsome hardcover edition. "*PBF* is hilarious and f$#@ed-up in a very sublime way." —Scott McCloud (*Understanding Comics*)

ISBN 978-1-59307-844-7
$14.95

From the creator of the acclaimed, nationally syndicated comic strip, Maakies, comes a delightful tale of adventure, imagination, ant farms, and shrunken heads!
The Adventures of
TONY MILLIONAIRE'S
SOCK MONKEY
Introduction by John Flansburgh of They Might Be Giants

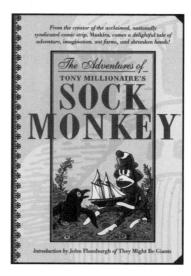

THE ADVENTURES OF TONY MILLIONAIRE'S SOCK MONKEY
Tony Millionaire

Dark Horse Maverick is proud to present Tony Millionaire's *Sock Monkey* collected in trade paperback for the first time ever! A mischievous sock monkey named Uncle Gabby and a bumbling crow named Drinky Crow are the heroes in this funny, unsettling, and oddly endearing collection, written and drawn by Tony Millionaire.

ISBN 978-1-56971-490-4
$9.95

Birds ARE Weird
PENNY ARCADE
4
Jerry Holkins & Mike Krahulik

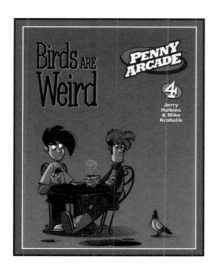

PENNY ARCADE VOLUME 4: BIRDS ARE WEIRD
Jerry Holkins and Mike Krahulik

Get your *geek* on! *Penny Arcade*, the comic strip for gamers, by gamers is now available in comic shops and bookstores everywhere. Not familiar with *Penny Arcade*? What? It's only the most popular comic strip on the web. It's just the funniest, most twisted comic that ever lampooned gamer culture.

ISBN 978-1-59307-773-0
$12.95

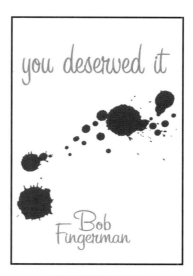

you deserved it
Bob Fingerman

YOU DESERVED IT
Bob Fingerman

Is Bob Fingerman a cynical misanthrope or a disappointed humanitarian? Dare we suggest maybe both? *You Deserved It* serves up enough yarns to make one hilariously misanthropic sweater, all in living-and-dying-color!

ISBN 978-1-59307-390-9
$9.95

AVAILABLE AT YOUR LOCAL COMICS SHOP OR BOOKSTORE! • To find a comics shop in your area, call 1-888-266-4226. For more information or to order direct visit darkhorse.com or call 1-800-862-0052 Mon.–Fri. 9 AM to 5 PM Pacific Time *Prices and availability subject to change without notice

DARK HORSE BOOKS®
darkhorse.com

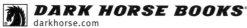

What do you get when you cross a chicken with a hare?

The funniest, most exciting all-ages graphic novel of ALL TIME!

Night is falling on the frozen landscape as Chickenhare and his turtle friend Abe find themselves on their way to be sold to Klaus—an insane taxidermist with a penchant for unique animals and enough emotional baggage to go on a very long vacation!

With the help of two mysterious new companions (not to mention a very friendly, very dead goat!), Chickenhare and Abe might be able to escape, but . . . where? Right into the lair of the deadly cave-dwelling critters known as the Shromph! . . . er, Shromps? Shromphses? Never mind! Just get ready for some fun!

Chickenhare: The House of Klaus
ISBN 978-1-59307-574-3
$9.95

darkhorse.com

AVAILABLE AT YOUR LOCAL COMICS SHOP OR BOOKSTORE
TO FIND A COMICS SHOP IN YOUR AREA, CALL 1-888-266-4226. For more information or to order direct: • On the web: darkhorse.com • Email: mailorder@darkhorse.com • Phone: 1-800-862-0052 Mon.–Fri. 9 A.M. to 5 P.M. Pacific Time. Text and illustrations of Chickenhare™ © 2006 Chris Grine. Dark Horse Books® and the Dark Horse logo are registered trademarks of Dark Horse Comics, Inc. (BL5046)